WILEY

Practitioner's Guide to
GAAS 2013

Covering all SASs, SSAEs, SSARSs, and Interpretations

BECOME A SUBSCRIBER!
Did you purchase this product from a bookstore?

If you did, it's important for you to become a subscriber. John Wiley & Sons, Inc. may publish, on a periodic basis, supplements and new editions to reflect the latest changes in the subject matter that you ***need to know*** in order stay competitive in this ever-changing industry. By contacting the Wiley office nearest you, you'll receive any current update at no additional charge. In addition, you'll receive future updates and revised or related volumes on a thirty-day examination review.

If you purchased this product directly from John Wiley & Sons, Inc., we have already recorded your subscription for this update service.

To become a subscriber, please call **1-877-762-2974** or send your name, company name (if applicable), address, and the title of the product to

mailing address: **Supplement Department**
John Wiley & Sons, Inc.
One Wiley Drive
Somerset, NJ 08875

e-mail: subscriber@wiley.com
fax: 1-732-302-2300
online: www.wiley.com

For customers outside the United States, please contact the Wiley office nearest you:

Professional & Reference Division
John Wiley & Sons Canada, Ltd.
22 Worcester Road
Etobicoke, Ontario M9W 1L1
CANADA
416-236-4433
Phone: 1-800-567-4797
Fax: 416-236-4447
Email: canada@jwiley.com

John Wiley & Sons Australia, Ltd.
33 Park Road
P.O. Box 1226
Milton, Queensland 4064
AUSTRALIA
Phone: 61-7-3859-9755
Fax: 61-7-3859-9715
Email: brisbane@johnwiley.com.au

John Wiley & Sons, Ltd.
The Atrium
Southern Gate, Chichester
West Sussex, PO19 8SQ
ENGLAND
Phone: 44-1243-779777
Fax: 44-1243-775878
Email: customer@wiley.co.uk

John Wiley & Sons (Asia) Pte. Ltd.
2 Clementi Loop #02-01
SINGAPORE 129809
Phone: 65-64632400
Fax: 65-64634604/5/6
Customer Service: 65-64604280
Email: enquiry@wiley.com.sg

WILEY

Practitioner's Guide to
GAAS 2013

Covering all SASs, SSAEs, SSARSs, and Interpretations

Joanne M. Flood

JOHN WILEY & SONS, INC.

Copyright © 1992 through 2012 by the American Institute of Certified Public Accountants, Inc. Reprinted with permission.

The book contains numerous excerpts taken from the Statements on Auditing Standards, the Statements on Standards for Attestation Engagements, and the Statements on Standards for Accounting and Review Services, and interpretations of these statements. These are noted by reference to the specific standard or AICPA Codification section, except for definitions which appear under a separate heading at the beginning of each section. These standards are copyrighted by the American Institute of Certified Public Accountants, Inc. and reprinted with permission of the AICPA.

This book contains definitions taken from Statements of Financial Accounting Standards. FAS 5, *Accounting for Contingencies*; FAS 57, *Related Party Disclosures*; FAS 133, *Accounting for Derivative Instruments and Hedging Activities*; Statement of Financial Accounting Concepts 2, *Qualitative Characteristics of Accounting Information*; and Statement of Financial Accounting Concepts 7, *Using Cash Flow Information and Present Value in Accounting Measurements*, are copyrighted by the Financial Accounting Standards Board, 401 Merritt 7, PO Box 5116, Norwalk, Connecticut 06856-5116, USA. Portions are reprinted with permission. Complete copies of these documents are available from the FASB.

This book is printed on acid-free paper. ∞

Copyright © 2013 by John Wiley & Sons, Inc. All rights reserved.

Published by John Wiley & Sons, Inc., Hoboken, New Jersey.

Published simultaneously in Canada.

No part of this publication may be reproduced, stored in a retrieval system, or transmitted in any form or by any means, electronic, mechanical, photocopying, recording, scanning, or otherwise, except as permitted under Section 107 or 108 of the 1976 United States Copyright Act, without either the prior written permission of the Publisher, or authorization through payment of the appropriate per-copy fee to the Copyright Clearance Center, 222 Rosewood Drive, Danvers, MA 01923, 978-750-8400, fax 978-646-8600, or on the Web at www.copyright.com. Requests to the Publisher for permission should be addressed to the Permissions Department, John Wiley & Sons, Inc., 111 River Street, Hoboken, NJ 07030, 201-748-6011, fax 201-748-6008, or online at http:/www.wiley.com/go/permissions.

Limit of Liability/Disclaimer of Warranty: While the publisher and author have used their best efforts in preparing this book, they make no representations or warranties with respect to the accuracy or completeness of the contents of this book and specifically disclaim any implied warranties of merchantability or fitness for a particular purpose. No warranty may be created or extended by sales representatives or written sales materials. The advice and strategies contained herein may not be suitable for your situation. You should consult with a professional where appropriate. Neither the publisher nor author shall be liable for any loss of profit or any other commercial damages, including but not limited to special, incidental, consequential, or other damages.

For general information on our other products and services please contact our Customer Care Department within the US at 800-762-2974, outside the US at 317-572-3993, or fax 317-572-4002.

Wiley also publishes its books in a variety of electronic formats. Some content that appears in print may not be available in electronic books. For more information about Wiley products, visit our website at www.wiley.com.

ISBN: 978-1-118-27726-3 (paperback); 978-1-118-41955-7 (ebk); 978-1-118-42145-1 (ebk); 978-1-118-57299-3 (ebk)

Printed in the United States of America

10 9 8 7 6 5 4 3 2 1

Contents

	Preface	xi
	About the Author	xv
	Organization and Key Changes	xvii
AU 100-230	The Auditor's Responsibilities and Functions, Introduction to GAAS, and the General Standards (Including the Quality Control Standards)	1
	AU-C 200 Overall Objectives of the Independent Auditor and the Conduct of an Audit in Accordance with Generally Accepted Auditing Standards	
	AU-C 220 Quality Control for an Engagement Conducted in Accordance with Generally Accepted Auditing Standards	
AU 311	Planning and Supervision	17
	AU-C 300 Planning an Audit	
	AU-C 210 Terms of Engagement	
AU 312	Audit Risk and Materiality in Conducting an Audit	33
	AU-C 320 Materiality in Planning and Performing an Audit	
	AU-C 450 Evaluation of Misstatements Identified during the Audit	
AU 314	Understanding the Entity and Its Environment and Assessing the Risks of Material Misstatement	49
	AU-C-315 Understanding the Entity and Its Environment and Assessing the Risks of Material Misstatement	
AU 315	Communications Between Predecessor and Successor Auditors	79
	AU-C 510 Opening Balances—Initial Audit Engagements, Including Reaudit Engagements	
	AU-C 210 Terms of Engagement	
AU 316	Consideration of Fraud in a Financial Statement Audit	93
	AU-C 240 Consideration of Fraud in a Financial Statement Audit	
AU 317	Illegal Acts by Clients	123
	AU-C 250 Consideration of Laws and Regulations in an Audit of Financial Statements	
AU 318	Performing Audit Procedures in Response to Assessed Risks and Evaluating the Audit Evidence Obtained	131
	AU-C 330 Performing Audit Procedures in Response to Assessed Risks and Evaluating the Audit Evidence Obtained	
AU 322	The Auditor's Consideration of the Internal Audit Function in an Audit of Financial Statements	161
AU 324	Service Organizations	173
	AU-C 402 Audit Considerations Relating to an Entity Using a Service Organization	
AU 325	Communicating Internal Control Related Matters Identified in an Audit	193
	AU-C 265 Communicating Internal Control Related Matters Identified in an Audit	

AU 326	Audit Evidence	205
	AU-C 500 Audit Evidence	
AU 328	Auditing Fair Value Measurements and Disclosures	211
	AU-C 540 Auditing Accounting Estimates, including Fair Value Accounting Estimates and Related Disclosures	
AU 329	Analytical Procedures	221
	AU-C 520 Analytical Procedures	
AU 330	The Confirmation Process	237
	AU-C 505 External Confirmations	
AU 331	Inventories	255
	AU-C 501 Audit Evidence—Specific Considerations for Selected Items	
AU 332	Auditing Derivative Instruments, Hedging Activities, and Investments in Securities	269
	AU-C 501 Audit Evidence—Specific Considerations for Selected Items	
AU 333	Management Representations	287
	AU-C 580 Written Representations	
AU 334	Related Parties	311
	AU-C 550 Related Parties	
AU 336	Using the Work of a Specialist	325
	AU-C 620 Using the Work of an Auditor's Specialist	
AU 337	Inquiry of Client's Lawyer Concerning Litigation, Claims, and Assessments	337
	AU-C 501 Audit Evidence—Specific Considerations for Selected Items	
AU 339	Audit Documentation	355
	AU-C 230 Audit Documentation	
AU 341	The Auditor's Consideration of an Entity's Ability to Continue as a Going Concern	369
	AU-C 570 The Auditor's Consideration of an Entity's Ability to Continue as a Going Concern	
AU 342	Auditing Accounting Estimates	385
	AU-C 540 Auditing Accounting Estimates, including Fair Value Accounting Estimates and Related Disclosures	
AU 350	Audit Sampling	393
	AU-C 530 Audit Sampling	
AU 380	The Auditor's Communication with Those Charged with Governance	419
	AU-C 260 The Auditor's Communication with Those Charged with Governance	
AU 390	Consideration of Omitted Procedures after the Report Date	429
	AU-C 585 Consideration of Omitted Procedures after the Report Release Date	
AU 410	Adherence to GAAP	437
	AU-C 700 Forming an Opinion and Reporting on Financial Statements	

AU 420	Consistency of Application of Generally Accepted Accounting Principles	**443**
	AU-C 708 Consistency of Financial Statements	
AU 431	Adequacy of Disclosure in Financial Statements	**451**
	AU-C 705 Modifications to the Opinion in the Independent Auditor's Report	
AU 504	Association with Financial Statements	**455**
AU 508	Reports on Audited Financial Statements	**463**
	AU-C 700 Forming an Opinion and Reporting on Financial Statements	
	AU-C 705 Modifications to the Opinion in the Independent Auditor's Report	
	AU-C 706 Emphasis-of-Matter Paragraphs and Other-Matter Paragraphs in the Independent Auditor's Report	
	AU-C 600 Special Considerations—Audits of Group Financial Statements (Including the Work of Component Auditors)	
	AU-C 708 Consistency of Financial Statements	
	AU-C 805 Special Considerations—Audits of Single Financial Statements and Specific Elements, Accounts, or Items of a Financial Statement	
	AU-C 560 Subsequent Events and Subsequently Discovered Facts	
AU 530	Dating of the Independent Auditor's Report	**525**
	AU-C 700 Forming an Opinion and Reporting on Financial Statements	
	AU-C 560 Subsequent Events and Subsequently Discovered Facts	
AU 532	Restricting the Use of an Auditor's Report	**531**
	AU-C 905 Alert That Restricts the Use of the Auditor's Written Communication	
AU 534	Reporting on Financial Statements Prepared for Use in Other Countries	**539**
	AU-C 910 Financial Statements Prepared in Accordance with a Financial Reporting Framework Generally Accepted in Another Country	
AU 543	Part of Audit Performed by Other Independent Auditors	**549**
	AU-C 600 Special Considerations—Audits of Group Financial Statements (Including the Work of Component Auditors)	
AU-C 600	Special Considerations—Audits of Group Financial Statements (Including the Work of Component Auditors)	**561**
AU 544	Lack of Conformity with Generally Accepted Accounting Principles	**575**
	AU-C 800 Special Considerations—Audits of Financial Statements Prepared in Accordance with Special Purpose Frameworks	
AU 550	Other Information in Documents Containing Audited Financial Statements	**579**
	AU-C 720 Other Information in Documents Containing Audited Financial Statements	
AU 551	Supplementary Information in Relation to the Financial Statements as a Whole	**583**
	AU-C 725 Supplementary Information in Relation to Financial Statements as a Whole	
AU 552	Reporting on Condensed Financial Statements and Selected Financial Data	**593**
	AU-C 810 Engagements to Report on Summary Financial Statements	
AU 558	Required Supplementary Information	**607**
	AU-C 730 Required Supplementary Information	

AU 560	Subsequent Events	619
	AU-C 560 Subsequent Events and Subsequently Discovered Facts	
AU 561	Subsequent Discovery of Facts Existing at the Date of the Auditor's Report	631
	AU-C 560 Subsequent Events and Subsequently Discovered Facts	
AU 623	Special Reports	637
	AU-C 806 Reporting on Compliance with Aspects of Contractual Agreements or Regulatory Requirements in Connection with Audited Financial Statements	
	AU-C 800 Special Considerations—Audits of Financial Statements Prepared in Accordance with Special-Purpose Frameworks	
	AU-C 805 Special Considerations—Audits of Single Financial Statements and Specific Elements, Accounts, or Items of a Financial Statement	
AU 625	Reports on the Application of Accounting Principles	671
	AU-C 915 Reports on Application of Requirements of an Applicable Financial Reporting Framework	
AU 634	Letters for Underwriters and Certain Other Requesting Parties	679
	AU-C 920 Letters for Underwriters and Certain Other Requesting Parties	
AU 711	Filings Under Federal Securities Statutes	749
	AU-C 925 Filings with the US Securities and Exchange Commission under the Securities Act of 1933	
AU 722	Interim Financial Information	759
	AU-C 930 Interim Financial Information	
AU 801	Compliance Audits	795
	AU-C 935 Compliance Audits	
AU 901	Public Warehouses: Controls and Auditing Procedures for Goods Held	807
	AU-C 501 Audit Evidence—Specific Considerations for Selected Items	
AT 101	Attest Engagements	815
AT 201	Agreed-Upon Procedures Engagements	841
AT 301	Financial Forecasts and Projections	853
AT 401	Reporting on Pro Forma Financial Information	881
AT 501	An Examination of an Entity's Internal Control Over Financial Reporting That Is Integrated with an Audit of Its Financial Statements	893
AT 601	Compliance Attestation	917
AT 701	Management's Discussion and Analysis (MD&A)—A Summary	931
AT 801	Reporting on Controls at a Service Organization	939
AR 60–90	Compilation and Review of Financial Statements	961
AR 110	Compilation of Specified Elements, Accounts, or Items of a Financial Statement	1017
AR 120	Compilation of Pro Forma Financial Information	1023
AR 200	Reporting on Comparative Financial Statements	1029

AR 300	Compilation Reports on Financial Statements Included in Certain Prescribed Forms	**1043**
AR 400	Communications between Predecessor and Successor Accountants	**1047**
AR 600	Reporting on Personal Financial Statements Included in Written Personal Financial Plans	**1051**
PCAOB 1	References in Auditor's Reports to the Standards of the Public Company Accounting Oversight Board	**1055**
PCAOB 3	Audit Documentation	**1059**
PCAOB 4	Reporting on Whether a Previously Reported Material Weakness Continues to Exist	**1065**
PCAOB 5	An Audit of Internal Control Over Financial Reporting That Is Integrated with an Audit of Financial Statements	**1079**
PCAOB 6	Evaluating Consistency of Financial Statements	**1099**
PCAOB 7	Engagement Quality Review	**1103**
PCAOB 8	Audit Risk	**1107**
PCAOB 9	Audit Planning	**1109**
PCAOB 10	Supervision of the Audit Engagement	**1113**
PCAOB 11	Consideration of Materiality in Planning and Performing an Audit	**1115**
PCAOB 12	Identifying and Assessing Risks of Material Misstatement	**1119**
PCAOB 13	The Auditor's Responses to the Risks of Material Misstatement	**1133**
PCAOB 14	Evaluating Audit Results	**1141**
PCAOB 15	Audit Evidence	**1147**
Appendix A:	**ASB Clarity Project: Extant AU Sections Mapped to the Clarified AU-C Sections**	**1151**
Appendix B:	**Cross-References to SASs, SSAEs, and SSARSs**	**1159**
Appendix C:	**List of AICPA Audit and Accounting Guides**	**1165**
Appendix D:	**Other Auditing Publications in the GAAS Hierarchy**	**1167**
Index		**1169**

PREFACE

The AICPA's Clarity Project

Background

Following the creation of the Public Company Accounting Oversight Board (PCAOB), the AICPA's Auditing Standards Board (ASB) reassessed its mission. The ASB developed a plan to converge US generally accepted auditing standards (GAAS) with the International Standards on Auditing (ISAs) issued by the International Auditing and Assurance Standards Board (IAASB). Thus, the ASB's Clarity Project began work to:

- Redraft the auditing standards for clarity—to make the standards easier to read, understand, and apply
- Converge US standards with the ISAs

The ASB is close to completing its project, and the new clarified standards are generally effective for audits of financial statements with periods ending on or after December 15, 2012. For legal and practice inspection purposes, the ASB decided early adoption was not appropriate. However, auditors may implement aspects of the new standards as long as they also comply with the current standards.

While clarity and convergence, not change, were the goals of the Clarity Project, the Project did create some changes that will require auditors to make changes in practice. This book arranges information according to the sections of the AICPA's auditing standards codification. In this edition of *Wiley GAAS*, because some readers will use it for audits that fall under the extant standards, we will use a dual guidance approach. The extant standards and the extant codification arrangement remain. However, each section of the book provides cross references to the new codification section, and where the clarified standards have resulted in changes, those changes are highlighted.

Wiley GAAS provides additional tools to guide you in this transitional year:

- A map of existing codification sections to the clarified codification sections
- Summary of changes to practice included at the beginning of each section

Format of the Clarified Standards

To align with the IAS format and to provide clarity for auditors, each of the clarity standards presents requirements in this format:

- *Introduction*—explains the purpose and scope of the standard
- *Objectives*—defines the context in which the requirements are set
- *Definitions*—explains, where relevant, specific terms
- *Requirements*—what the auditor must do to meet the objectives of the standard
- *Application and Other Explanatory Matters*—provide further guidance for carrying out the requirements of the standard

Where relevant, the standards may include guidance relevant to audits of smaller, less complex entities and governmental entities.

Clarified Standards Issued to Date

Statement on Auditing Standards (SAS) No. 122 contains the vast majority of the clarified guidance. SAS Nos. 117–121 were issued in advance of SAS No. 122 due to pressing practice needs. Others were delayed for varying reasons. The ASB has issued the following clarified standards:

- SAS No. 117, *Compliance Audits,* is effective for compliance audits for periods ending on or after December 15, 2010.

- SAS No. 118, *Other Information in Documents Containing Audited Financial Statements,* is effective for audits of financial statements for periods beginning on or after December 15, 2010.
- SAS No. 119, *Supplementary Information in Relation to the Financial Statements as a Whole,* is effective for audits of financial statements for periods beginning on or after December 15, 2010.
- SAS No. 120, *Required Supplementary Information,* is effective for audits of financial information for periods beginning on or after December 15, 2010.
- SAS No. 121, *Revised Applicability of Statement on Auditing Standards No. 100, Interim Financial Information.*
- SAS No. 122, *Codification of Auditing Standards and Procedures.* When the AICPA recodified auditing standards in 1972, it reissued all standards as SAS No. 1. This did not happen with the Clarity Project.
- SAS No. 123, *Omnibus Statement on Auditing Standards—2011,* is effective for audits of financial statements for periods ending on or after December 15, 2012. This statement conformed SAS Nos. 117–118 to the clarity standards and made other changes necessitated by the clarity project.
- SAS No. 124, *Financial Statements Prepared in Accordance with a Financial Reporting Framework Generally Accepted in Another Country,* effective for audits of financial statements for periods ending on or after December 15, 2012.
- SAS No. 125, *Alert That Restricts the Use of the Auditor's Written Communication.*
- SAS No. 126, *The Auditor's Consideration of an Entity's Ability to Continue as a Going Concern,* is effective for audits of financial statements for periods ending on or after December 15, 2012. The ASB delayed issuance of clarified going concern guidance because of the Financial Accounting Standards Board (FASB) going concern project. Recently, however, FASB divided the project into two separate and distinct phases. As a result, FASB projects to issue an Exposure Draft that addresses Phase 1, "The Liquidation Basis of Accounting," in the second quarter of 2012, and to reissue an Exposure Draft that addresses Phase II, "Going Concern," in the fourth quarter of 2012. Therefore, the ASB went ahead and released a clarified version of SAS No. 59.
- Open project—as of August 2012, the ASB has one topic remaining to be clarified: AU Section 322, The Auditor's Consideration of the Internal Audit Function in an Audit of Financial Statements.

The AICPA has categorized the clarified standards into four groups based on the type of change:

- *Substantive Changes*—expected to affect audit methodology and engagements
- *Primarily Clarifying Changes*—intended to explicitly state what may have been implicit in the extant standards, which over time resulted in diversity in practice. These changes may affect timing and responsibilities of the auditor.
- *Primarily Formatting Changes*—changes that do not expand the extant sections in any significant way and may not require adjustments to current practice
- *Standards Not Yet Issued in the Clarity Project*—as mentioned previously, there is only one standard not yet issued

Areas Substantially Unchanged by the Clarity Standards

The broad areas that have not been changed substantially by the clarified standards are:

- Audit documentation
- Auditor's communication with those charged with governance
- Risk assessment standards
- External confirmations
- Analytical procedures
- Audit sampling
- Auditing accounting estimates

- Written representations
- Subsequent events
- Consideration of omitted procedures after the report release date

Areas Substantially Changed by the Clarity Standards

Substantive changes are likely to change audit methodology and engagements. The areas that have been changed substantially by the clarified standards are:

- Illegal acts by clients
- Communicating internal control related matters identified in an audit
- Related parties
- Adherence to generally accepted accounting principles (GAAP)
- The auditor's report
- Dating of an independent auditor's report
- Part of an audit performed by other independent auditors (group audits)

Organization

The extant codification is arranged by the ten general, fieldwork, and reporting standards. These standards are superseded in the clarified standards. In their place, each clarified standard has objectives. These objectives provide a link to the overall objective of the auditor. If the auditor fulfills the objectives and the ethical requirements, then the auditor will have fulfilled the requirements stated in the ten standards.

The codification based on the clarified standards generally follows the ISA categories. These are the broad categories of the clarified codification:

AU-C 200–299	General Principles and Responsibilities
AU-C 300–499	Risk Assessment and Response to Assessed Risk
AU-C 500–599	Audit Evidence
AU-C 600–699	Using the Work of Others
AU-C 700–799	Audit Conclusions and Reporting
AU-C 800–899	Special Considerations
AU-C 900–999	Special Considerations in the United States

Resources

Wiley GAAS contains robust tools to help auditors prepare for and implement the clarified standards. Each chapter begins with the status of the code section and a summary of the changes in the clarified standards. The clarified objectives, definitions, exhibits and illustrations are integrated in the chapter and clearly identified. Extant standard references are preceded by "AU" and clarified standard references are preceded by "AU-C."

The AICPA mapping of the extant standards to the clarified standards, *ASB Clarity Project: Extant AU Sections Mapped to the Clarified AU-C Sections,* is included as Appendix A.

The AICPA has dedicated a page on its site with links to additional resources that may be helpful in implementing the changes:

http://www.aicpa.org/InterestAreas/FRC/AuditAttest/Pages/ImprovingClarityASBStandards.aspx

ABOUT THE AUTHOR

Joanne M. Flood, MBA, CPA, is an author and independent consultant on accounting and auditing technical topics and e-learning. She has experience as an auditor in both an international firm and a local firm and has worked as a senior manager in the American Institute of Certified Public Accountants (AICPA) Professional Development group. She received her MBA summa cum laude in accounting from Adelphi University and her Bachelor's degree in English from Molloy College. While in public accounting, she worked on major clients in retail, manufacturing, and finance and on small business clients in construction, manufacturing, and professional services. At the AICPA, Joanne developed and wrote e-learning, text, and instructor-led training courses on US and International Standards. She also produced training materials in a wide variety of media, including print, video, and audio, and pioneered the AICPA's e-learning product line. Joanne resides in Rockville Centre, New York, with her daughter, Elizabeth.

Joanne is the author of the following:

Financial Disclosure Checklist
Wiley GAAP
Wiley GAAS

ORGANIZATION AND KEY CHANGES

This book reduces the official language of Statements on Auditing Standards (SASs), Statements on Standards for Attestation Engagements (SSAEs), Statements on Standards for Accounting and Review Services (SSARSs), Public Company Accounting Oversight Board (PCAOB) Auditing Standards, and the interpretations of those standards into easy-to-read and understandable advice. It is designed to help CPAs in the application of, and compliance with, authoritative standards. Because this year marks the transition to the clarified standards resulting from the AICPA's Clarity Project, references to the extant standards include "AU," while references to the clarified standards include "AU-C." It is important to refer to the Preface for additional information.

This book follows the sequence of sections of the AICPA *Codification of Statements on Auditing Standards*, the *Codification of Statements on Standards for Attestation Engagements*, and the *Codification of Statements on Standards for Accounting and Review Services*. Sections are divided into the following easy-to-understand parts:

Effective Date and Applicability. A handy, brief identification of the original standard for the section, its effective date, and the circumstances that require the application of the section.

Definitions of Terms. A glossary of official definitions that gathers in one place explanations of terms that are ordinarily scattered throughout a standard.

Objectives of Section. A behind-the-scenes explanation of the reasons for the pronouncement and a capsule explanation of the most basic ideas of the section.

Fundamental Requirements. Concise listing and descriptions of those things specifically mandated by the section.

Interpretations. A brief summary of each interpretation.

Techniques for Application. Helpful techniques for complying with the fundamental requirements of the section.

Illustrations. Examples of the application of the fundamental requirements of the section.

Selected AICPA Practice Alerts and Audit Issues Task Force Advisories have also been summarized in certain sections.

As with all accounting and auditing publications, this book is merely a guide. It is not a substitute for professional judgment. It can, however, be a valuable reference tool.

The 2013 edition of this book is current through SAS 126, *The Auditor's Consideration of an Entity's Ability to Continue as a Going Concern;* SSAE 17, *Reporting on Compiled Prospective Financial Statements When the Practitioner's Independence is Impaired;* and SSARS 20, *Revised Applicability of Statements on Standards for Accounting and Review Services;* as well as the most recent PCAOB Auditing Standard 15, *Audit Evidence.*

Joanne M. Flood
August 2012

AU 100–230 The Auditor's Responsibilities and Functions, Introduction to GAAS, and the General Standards (Including the Quality Control Standards)

AU-C 200 Overall Objectives of the Independent Auditor and the Conduct of an Audit in Accordance with Generally Accepted Auditing Standards

AU-C 220 Quality Control for an Engagement Conducted in Accordance with Generally Accepted Auditing Standards

AU EFFECTIVE DATE AND APPLICABILITY

Original Pronouncements	Statements on Auditing Standards (SASs) 1, 5, 25, 41, 43, 78, 82, 95, 98, 99, 102, 104, 105, and 113.
Effective Date	All standards currently are effective.

Applicability All audits in accordance with generally accepted auditing standards (GAAS) and other services covered by SASs.

> NOTE: *All sections apply whether the financial statements are presented in conformity with generally accepted accounting principles (GAAP) or other comprehensive basis of accounting (OCBOA) unless otherwise noted.*

AU-C EFFECTIVE DATE AND SUMMARY OF CHANGES

SAS No. 122, *Codification of Auditing Standards and Procedures,* is effective for audits of financial statements with periods ending on or after December 15, 2012.

AU-C 200 supersedes AU sections 110, 201, 210, 220, and 330. What is required of the auditor is not substantially changed. However, the structure is changed by the clarified SAS, and new terminology is used.

SAS No. 95 (AU Section 150), which contains the general, field work, and reporting standards, is superseded. In its place, each clarified standard has objectives. These objectives provide a link to the overall objective of the auditor. If the auditor fulfills the objectives and the ethical requirements, then the auditor will have fulfilled the requirements stated in the ten standards.

AU-C 220 supersedes AU Section 161. AU-C 220 addresses specific responsibilities of the auditor regarding quality control standards for an audit of financial statements. Quality control is the responsibility of the audit firm. Because quality control procedures are required by Statements on Quality Control Standards (SQCS) No. 7, *A Firm's System of Quality Control,* the clarified standards should not change current practice but strengthen existing standards by making it easier to understand and apply those standards. Note that SQCS No. 8, *A Firm's System of Quality Control* (redrafted), is effective as of January 1, 2012. However, no substantive differences existed between the two quality control standards. Firms who reference SQCS No. 7 will have to update paragraph references.

AU-C 220 also addresses AU-311.28–.32, *Supervision of an Audit Requirement*.

AU DEFINITIONS OF TERMS

Auditing procedures. Acts to be performed by the auditor during the course of an audit to comply with auditing standards.

Auditing standards. Measures of audit quality and the objectives to be achieved in an audit.

Practitioner-in-charge. An individual responsible for supervising an audit engagement or signing the report on such an engagement.

Professional skepticism. An attitude that includes a questioning mind and a critical assessment of audit evidence.

Reasonable assurance. A high, but not absolute, level of assurance.

AU-C 200 DEFINITIONS OF TERMS

Source: AU-C 200.14

Applicable financial reporting framework. The financial reporting framework adopted by management and, when appropriate, those charged with governance in the preparation and fair presentation of the financial statements, that is acceptable in view of the nature of the entity and the objective of the financial statements, or that is required by law or regulation.

Audit evidence. Information used by the auditor in arriving at the conclusions on which the auditor's opinion is based. Audit evidence includes both information contained in the accounting records underlying the financial statements and other information. *Sufficiency of audit evidence* is the measure of the quantity of audit evidence. The quantity of the audit evidence needed is affected by the auditor's assessment of the risks of material misstatement and also by the quality of such audit evidence. *Appropriateness of audit evidence* is the measure of the quality of audit evidence; that is, its relevance and its reliability in providing support for the conclusions on which the auditor's opinion is based.

Audit risk. The risk that the auditor expresses an inappropriate audit opinion when the financial statements are materially misstated. Audit risk is a function of the risks of material misstatement and detection risk.

Auditor. The term used to refer to the person or persons conducting the audit, usually the engagement partner or other members of the engagement team, or, as applicable, the firm. When an AU-C section expressly intends that a requirement or responsibility be fulfilled by the engagement partner, the term *engagement partner* rather than *auditor* is used. *Engagement partner* and *firm* are to be read as referring to their governmental equivalents when relevant.

Detection risk. The risk that the procedures performed by the auditor to reduce audit risk to an acceptably low level will not detect a misstatement that exists and that could be material, either individually or when aggregated with other misstatements.

Financial reporting framework. A set of criteria used to determine measurement, recognition, presentation, and disclosure of all material items appearing in the financial statements; for example, U.S. generally accepted accounting principles, International Financial Reporting Standards (IFRSs) promulgated by the International Accounting Standards Board (IASB), or a special purpose framework.

The term *fair presentation framework* is used to refer to a financial reporting framework that requires compliance with the requirements of the framework and

1. Acknowledges explicitly or implicitly that, to achieve fair presentation of the financial statements, it may be necessary for management to provide disclosures beyond those specifically required by the framework; or
2. Acknowledges explicitly that it may be necessary for management to depart from a requirement of the framework to achieve fair presentation of the financial statements. Such departures are expected to be necessary only in extremely rare circumstances.

A financial reporting framework that requires compliance with the requirements of the framework but does not contain the acknowledgments in 1 or 2 is not a fair presentation framework.

Financial statements. A structured representation of historical financial information, including related notes, intended to communicate an entity's economic resources and obligations at a point in time or the changes therein for a period of time in accordance with a financial reporting framework. The related notes ordinarily comprise a summary of significant accounting policies and other explanatory information. The term *financial statements* ordinarily refers to a complete set of financial statements as determined by the requirements of the applicable financial reporting framework, but can also refer to a single financial statement.

Historical financial information. Information expressed in financial terms regarding a particular entity, derived primarily from that entity's accounting system, about economic events occurring in past time periods or about economic conditions or circumstances at points in time in the past.

Interpretive publications. Auditing interpretations of generally accepted accounting standards (GAAS), exhibits to GAAS, auditing guidance included in the American Institute of Certified Public Accountants (AICPA) Audit and Accounting Guides, and the AICPA Auditing Statements of Position (SOPs).

Management. The person(s) with executive responsibility for the conduct of the entity's operations. For some entities, management includes some or all of those charged with governance; for example, executive members of a governance board or an owner-manager.

Misstatement. A difference between the amount, classification, presentation, or disclosure of a reported financial statement item and the amount, classification, presentation, or disclosure that is required for the item to be presented fairly in accordance with the applicable financial reporting framework. Misstatements can arise from fraud or error.

Other auditing publications. Publications other than interpretive publications; these include AICPA auditing publications not defined as interpretive publications; auditing articles in the *Journal of Accountancy* and other professional journals; continuing professional education programs and other instruction materials, textbooks, guide books, audit programs, and checklists; and other auditing publications from state certified public accountant (CPA) societies, other organizations, and individuals.

Premise, relating to the responsibilities of management and, when appropriate, those charged with governance, on which an audit is conducted (the premise). Management and, when appropriate, those charged with governance have acknowledged and understand that they have the following responsibilities that are fundamental to the conduct of an audit in accordance with GAAS; that is, responsibility

1. For the preparation and fair presentation of the financial statements in accordance with the applicable financial reporting framework;
2. For the design, implementation, and maintenance of internal control relevant to the preparation and fair presentation of financial statements that are free from material misstatement, whether due to fraud or error; and
3. To provide the auditor with

    a. Access to all information of which management and, when appropriate, those charged with governance are aware that is relevant to the preparation and fair presentation of the financial statements, such as records, documentation, and other matters;
    b. Additional information that the auditor may request from management and, when appropriate, those charged with governance for the purpose of the audit; and
    c. Unrestricted access to persons within the entity from whom the auditor determines it necessary to obtain audit evidence.

The premise, relating to the responsibilities of management and, when appropriate, those charged with governance, on which an audit is conducted may also be referred to as the premise.

Professional judgment. The application of relevant training, knowledge, and experience within the context provided by auditing, accounting, and ethical standards, in making informed decisions about the courses of action that are appropriate in the circumstances of the audit engagement.

Professional skepticism. An attitude that includes a questioning mind, being alert to conditions that may indicate possible misstatement due to fraud or error, and a critical assessment of audit evidence.

Reasonable assurance. In the context of an audit of financial statements, a high, but not absolute, level of assurance.

Risk of material misstatement. The risk that the financial statements are materially misstated prior to the audit. This consists of two components, described as follows at the assertion level:

- **Inherent risk.** The susceptibility of an assertion about a class of transaction, account balance, or disclosure to a misstatement that could be material, either individually or when aggregated with other misstatements, before consideration of any related controls.
- **Control risk.** The risk that a misstatement that could occur in an assertion about a class of transaction, account balance, or disclosure and that could be material, either individually or when aggregated with other misstatements, will not be prevented, or detected and corrected, on a timely basis by the entity's internal control.

Those charged with governance. The person(s) or organization(s) (for example, a corporate trustee) with responsibility for overseeing the strategic direction of the entity and the obligations related to the accountability of the entity. This includes overseeing the financial reporting process. Those charged with governance may include management personnel; for example, executive members of a governance board or an owner-manager.

AU-C 220 DEFINITIONS OF TERMS

Source: AU-C 220.09

Engagement partner. The partner or other person in the firm who is responsible for the audit engagement and its performance and for the auditor's report issued on behalf of the firm and who, when required, has the appropriate authority from a professional, legal, or regulatory body.

Engagement quality control review. A process designed to provide an objective evaluation, before the report is released, of the significant judgments the engagement team made and the conclusions it reached in formulating the auditor's report. The engagement quality control review process is only for those audit engagements, if any, for which the firm has determined that an engagement quality control review is required, in accordance with its policies and procedures.

Engagement quality control reviewer. A partner, other person in the firm, suitably qualified external person, or team made up of such individuals, none of whom is part of the engagement team, with sufficient and appropriate experience and authority to objectively evaluate the significant judgments that the engagement team made and the conclusions it reached in formulating the auditor's report.

Engagement team. All partners and staff performing the engagement and any individuals engaged by the firm or a network firm who perform audit procedures on the engagement. This excludes an auditor's external specialist engaged by the firm or a network firm.

Firm. A form of organization permitted by law or regulation whose characteristics conform to resolutions of the Council of the AICPA and which is engaged in the practice of public accounting.

Monitoring. A process comprising an ongoing consideration and evaluation of the firm's system of quality control, including inspection or a periodic review of engagement documentation, reports, and clients' financial statements for a selection of completed engagements, designed to provide the firm with reasonable assurance that its system of quality control is designed appropriately and operating effectively.

Network. An association of entities, as defined in ET Section 92, *Definitions*.

Network firm. A firm or other entity that belongs to a network, as defined in ET Section 92.

Partner. Any individual with authority to bind the firm with respect to the performance of a professional services engagement. For purposes of this definition, *partner* may include an employee with this authority who has not assumed the risks and benefits of ownership. Firms may use different titles to refer to individuals with this authority.

Personnel. Partners and staff.

Professional standards. Standards promulgated by the AICPA Auditing Standards Board or the AICPA Accounting and Review Services Committee under Rule 201, *General Standards* (ET sec. 201 par. .01), or Rule 202, *Compliance with Standards* (ET sec. 202 par. .01), of the AICPA Code of Professional Conduct, or other standards-setting bodies that set auditing and attest standards applicable to the engagement being performed and relevant ethical requirements.

Relevant ethical requirements. Ethical requirements to which the engagement team and engagement quality control reviewer are subject, which consist of the AICPA Code of Professional Conduct together with rules of applicable state boards of accountancy and applicable regulatory agencies that are more restrictive.

Staff. Professionals, other than partners, including any specialists that the firm employs.

Suitably qualified external person. An individual outside the firm with the competence and capabilities to act as an engagement partner (for example, a partner of another firm).

OBJECTIVES OF AU SECTIONS 100–230

Sections 100 through 230 clarify the difference between the responsibilities of the auditor and management, the nature of auditing standards, and their relationship to quality control standards. The Sections also provide guidelines for the training, independence, and proficiency of the independent auditor, as well as the level of professional care (including the use of professional skepticism and reasonable assurance) required in the performance of audit work.

OBJECTIVES OF AU-C SECTION 200

AU-C Section 200.12 states that:

> . . . *The overall objectives of the auditor, in conducting an audit of financial statements, are to*
>
> a. *obtain reasonable assurance about whether the financial statements as a whole are free from material misstatement, whether due to fraud or error, thereby enabling the auditor to*

  express an opinion on whether the financial statements are presented fairly, in all material respects, in accordance with an applicable financial reporting framework; and
 b. *report on the financial statements, and communicate as required by GAAS, in accordance with the auditor's findings.*

OBJECTIVES OF AU-C SECTION 220

AU-C Section 220.08 states that:

> *. . . the objective of the auditor is to implement quality control procedures at the engagement level that provide the auditor with reasonable assurance that*
>
> a. *the audit complies with professional standards and applicable legal and regulatory requirements and*
> b. *the auditor's report issued is appropriate in the circumstances.*

FUNDAMENTAL REQUIREMENTS

OBJECTIVE OF ORDINARY AUDIT

To express an opinion on the fairness, in all material respects, with which the financial statements present financial position, results of operations, and cash flows in conformity with GAAP.

AUDITOR RESPONSIBILITIES

In every audit, the auditor has to obtain reasonable assurance about whether the financial statements are free of material misstatement. Material misstatement includes:

1. Material error (See Section 312)
2. Material fraud (See Section 316)
3. Illegal acts by clients (See Section 317)

MANAGEMENT RESPONSIBILITIES

The fairness of the representations made through financial statements is an implicit and integral part of management's responsibility. Management is responsible for:

1. Adopting sound accounting policies
2. Establishing and maintaining internal control that will, among other things, record, process, and report financial data that are consistent with management's assertions embodied in the financial statements

The auditor's participation in preparing financial statements does not change the character of the statements as representations of management. In brief, management is responsible for the financial statements; the auditor is responsible for expressing an opinion on those financial statements.

DEFINING PROFESSIONAL REQUIREMENTS IN STATEMENTS ON AUDITING STANDARDS

AU Section 120 clarifies that the SASs use two categories of professional requirements to describe the degree of responsibility the standards impose on auditors.

- *Unconditional requirements.* The auditor is required to comply with an unconditional requirement in all cases in which the circumstances exist to which the unconditional requirement applies. SASs use the words *must* or *is required* to indicate an unconditional requirement.
- *Presumptively mandatory requirements.* The auditor is also required to comply with a presumptively mandatory requirement in all cases in which the circumstances exist to which the presumptively mandatory requirement applies; however, in rare circumstances, the auditor may depart from a presumptively mandatory requirement provided the auditor documents his or her justification for the departure and how the alternative procedures performed in the circumstances were sufficient to achieve the objectives of the presumptively mandatory requirement. SASs use the word *should* to indicate a presumptively mandatory requirement.

The term "should consider" means that the consideration of the procedure or action is presumptively required, whereas carrying out the procedure or action is not.

AU Section 120 also clarifies that explanatory material, is intended to explain the objective of the professional requirements, rather than imposing a professional requirement for the auditor to perform.

GAAS AND THE GAAS HIERARCHY

The auditor is responsible for planning, conducting, and reporting the results of an audit according to GAAS. The hierarchy of GAAS consists of the following three tiers:

Tier 1:   Auditing Standards (which include the Statements on Auditing Standards)[1]
Tier 2:   Interpretive publications
Tier 3:   Other auditing publications

Tier 1: Auditing Standards[1]

Tier 1 consists of (1) the ten general, fieldwork, and reporting standards, and (2) the SASs. As stated in AU 150.02 the GAAS approved by the AICPA membership are:

A. General Standards

1. *Training and proficiency.* The audit must be performed by a person or persons having adequate technical training and proficiency as an auditor.
2. *Independence.* In all matters relating to the assignment, an independence in mental attitude is to be maintained by the auditor or auditors.
3. *Due care.* Due professional care is to be exercised in the planning and performance of the audit and the preparation of the report.

---

[1] AICPA has designated the Public Company Accounting Oversight Board (PCAOB) as a body to promulgate auditing and related professional practice standards relating to the preparation and issuance of audit reports of issuers.

B. **Fieldwork Standards**
   4. *Planning and supervising.* The auditor must adequately plan the work and must supervise any assistants.
   5. *The entity and its environment, including its internal control.* The auditor must obtain a sufficient understanding of the entity and its environment, including its internal control, to assess the risks of material misstatement of the financial statements due to error or fraud and to design the nature, timing, and extent of further audit procedures.
   6. *Evidential matter.* The auditor must obtain sufficient appropriate audit evidence by performing audit procedures to afford a reasonable basis for an opinion regarding the financial statements under audit.

C. **Reporting Standards**
   7. *GAAP.* The report shall state whether the financial statements are presented in accordance with GAAP.
   8. *Consistency.* The report shall identify those circumstances in which such principles have not been consistently observed in the current period in relation to the preceding period.
   9. *Disclosure.* Informative disclosures in the financial statements are to be regarded as reasonably adequate unless otherwise stated in the report.
   10. *Reporting obligation.* The report shall contain either an expression of opinion regarding the financial statements taken as a whole or an assertion to the effect that an opinion cannot be expressed. When an overall opinion cannot be expressed, the reasons should be stated. In all cases where an auditor's name is associated with financial statements, the report should contain:

      a. A clear-cut indication of the character of the auditor's work, if any
      b. The degree of responsibility the auditor is taking

NOTE: Materiality and audit risk underlie the application of the ten standards and the SASs (see Section 312).

The preceding ten formal standards apply to all other services covered by SASs unless they are clearly not relevant or the SAS specifies that they do not apply.

These ten general, fieldwork, and reporting standards provide the framework for the SASs promulgated by the Auditing Standards Board (ASB). Auditors are required under Rule 202, *Compliance with Standards,* of the AICPA Code of Professional Conduct to comply with these standards. Auditors should have sufficient knowledge of the SASs to determine when they apply and should be prepared to justify departures from the SASs.

Tier 2: Interpretive Publications

Interpretive publications are recommendations, issued under the authority of the ASB, on how to apply the SASs in specific circumstances, including engagements for entities in specialized industries. Interpretive publications are not auditing standards. They consist of the following:

- Auditing Interpretations of SASs
- Auditing guidance in AICPA Audit and Accounting Guides
- Auditing Statements of Positions
- Appendices to the SASs

> NOTE: SAS 95 notes that certain "previously issued appendices to original pronouncements" that modified other SASs are Tier 1 publications, not interpretative publications.

Auditors should be aware of and consider interpretive publications that apply to their audits. Auditors who do not follow the guidance in an applicable interpretive publication should be prepared to explain how they complied with the relevant SAS requirements addressed by such guidance.

Tier 3: Other Auditing Publications

Other auditing publications are not authoritative but may help auditors to understand and apply SASs. Such publications include all AICPA auditing publications not included under Tier 1 or Tier 2 and other auditing publications, including

- Auditing articles in professional journals, such as the *Journal of Accountancy*
- Continuing professional education programs and other instructional materials
- Textbooks and guidebooks
- Audit programs and checklists
- Other auditing publications from state CPA societies, other organizations, and individuals

An auditor should evaluate such guidance to determine whether it is both (1) *relevant* for a particular engagement and (2) *appropriate* for the particular situation. When evaluating whether the guidance is appropriate, the auditor should consider whether the publication is recognized as helpful in understanding and applying SASs, and whether the author is recognized as an auditing authority. (AICPA auditing publications that have been reviewed by the AICPA Audit and Attest Standards staff are presumed to be appropriate.)

QUALITY CONTROL STANDARDS

An audit firm should establish a quality control system to provide it with reasonable assurance that its staff meets the requirements of GAAS in its audit engagements. The nature of this system depends on such factors as an audit firm's size, the nature of its practice, its organizational structure, the degree of autonomy allowed its personnel and office, and cost-benefit considerations.

TRAINING AND PROFICIENCY OF THE INDEPENDENT AUDITOR

The auditor holds out himself or herself as being proficient in accounting and auditing. Attaining proficiency begins with formal education and continues through later experience. The auditor must be aware of and understand new authoritative pronouncements on accounting and auditing.

INDEPENDENCE[2]

To *be* independent, the auditor must be intellectually honest; to be *recognized* as independent, he or she must be free from any obligation to or interest in the client, its management, or its owners. For specific guidance, the auditor should look to AICPA and the state society rules of conduct and, if relevant, the requirements of the Securities and Exchange Commission (SEC).

DUE PROFESSIONAL CARE IN THE PERFORMANCE OF WORK

The auditor should observe the standards of fieldwork and reporting, possess the degree of skill commonly possessed by other auditors, and should exercise that skill with reasonable care and diligence. The auditor should also exercise *professional skepticism*, that is, an attitude that includes a questioning mind and a critical assessment of audit evidence. However, the auditor is not an insurer, and the audit report does not constitute a guarantee because it is based on *reasonable assurance*. Thus, an audit conducted in accordance with GAAS may not detect a material misstatement. The auditor should be alert to the possibility of collusion when performing the audit and how management may override controls in a way that would make the fraud particularly difficult to detect.

INTERPRETATIONS

There are no interpretations for this section.

TECHNIQUES FOR APPLICATION

MANAGEMENT'S RESPONSIBILITIES

Many times, clients do not understand their responsibilities for the audited financial statements. These financial statements are *management's*. They contain management's representations. The form and content of the financial statements are management's responsibility, even though the auditor may have prepared them or participated in their preparation. The SEC has stated:

> *The fundamental and primary responsibility for the accuracy of information filed with the Commission and disseminated among the investors rests upon management.* **Management does not discharge its obligations in this respect by the employment of independent accountants, however reputable** *(Accounting Series Release No. 62; emphasis added).*

Management also is responsible for implementing and maintaining an effective system of internal control.

---

[2] Section 201 of the Sarbanes-Oxley Act of 2002 and the related SEC implementing rules created significant new independence requirements for auditors of public companies. For example, the SEC prohibits certain nonaudit services such as bookkeeping, internal audit outsourcing, and valuation services. All audit and nonaudit services performed by the auditor, including tax services, must be preapproved by the company's audit committee. In March 2003, the SEC issued final rules implementing Section 201 of the Act. The rules, Strengthening the Commission's Requirements Regarding Auditor Independence, *can be found at www.sec.gov/rules/final/33-8183.htm.*

Management Representation Letter

GAAS require the auditor to obtain a management representation letter (see Section 333). In the letter, management acknowledges its responsibility for the financial statements and states its belief that the financial statements are fairly presented in conformity with GAAP. Sometimes, the client objects to this acknowledgment because of the auditor's role in the preparation of the financial statements. To avoid this misunderstanding, the auditor's engagement letter may include a paragraph such as the following:

> Generally accepted auditing standards require that we obtain from you a representation letter about the financial statements and the underlying accounting records and an acknowledgment that the financial statements are management's responsibility, and that they are presented in accordance with generally accepted accounting principles.

The annual reports of many public companies contain statements acknowledging management's responsibility for the financial statements and the underlying accounting records.

AUDITOR'S RESPONSIBILITIES

The auditor's responsibility for the financial statements he or she audits is confined to the expression of an opinion on those statements. In performing the audit, the auditor is responsible for compliance with GAAS, including the SASs.

Under the GAAS hierarchy, the auditor has a responsibility to consider SASs and interpretive publications in all audits. If such guidance is not followed, an auditor must be prepared:

- For Tier 1 SASs, to justify a departure from SASs
- For Tier 2 interpretive publications, to explain that an alternative approach achieved the objectives of GAAS

In other words, the first two categories of GAAS are "must know." When applying the Tier 3 level of GAAS, other auditing publications, the auditor should determine whether such guidance is relevant and appropriate.

To provide reasonable assurance that it is conforming with generally accepted auditing standards in its audit engagements, an accounting firm should establish quality control policies and procedures. These policies and procedures should apply not only to audit engagements but also to attest and accounting and review services for which professional standards have been established.

ESTABLISHMENT OF QUALITY CONTROL POLICIES AND PROCEDURES

The nature and extent of a firm's quality control policies and procedures depend on the following:

1. Firm size and the number of its offices
2. The degree of autonomy of personnel and practice offices
3. The knowledge and experience of its personnel
4. The nature and complexity of the firm's practice
5. The cost of developing and implementing quality control policies and procedures in relation to the benefits provided

When a firm establishes quality control policies and procedures, it also should do the following:

1. Assign responsibilities to qualified personnel to implement quality control policies and procedures.
2. Communicate quality control policies and procedures to personnel (see below).
3. Monitor the effectiveness of the quality control system. The purpose is to determine that policies and procedures and the methods of implementing and communicating them are still appropriate.

NOTE: Flaws in, or a violation of, a firm's quality control do not necessarily indicate that an audit was not performed in accordance with GAAS.

ELEMENTS OF QUALITY CONTROL

When a firm establishes its quality control policies and procedures, it should follow the five elements of quality control (see SQCS 2, *System of Quality Control for a CPA Firm's Accounting and Auditing Practice,* as amended by SQCS 4, *Amendment to System of Quality Control for a CPA Firm's Accounting and Auditing Practice*).

NOTE: CPA firms or individuals that are enrolled in an AICPA-approved practice-monitoring program are obligated to adhere to quality control standards. In addition, the Principles of Professional Conduct indicate that members should practice in firms that have in place quality control procedures to provide reasonable assurance that services are competently delivered and adequately supervised. The Statements on Quality Control apply to a CPA firm's accounting, auditing, and attest practice.

Personnel Management

Policies and procedures should provide reasonable assurance that personnel:

1. Have the characteristics to enable competent performance
2. Have the technical training and proficiency needed
3. Participate in continuing education to enable them to fulfill responsibilities and satisfy appropriate educational requirements of the AICPA and regulatory agencies
4. Selected for advancement have the necessary qualifications

SQCS 5, *The Personnel Management Element of a Firm's System of Quality Control—Competencies Required by a Practitioner-in-Charge of an Attest Engagement*, clarifies that a partner-in-charge of accounting, auditing, and attestation engagements should ordinarily:

1. Understand the role of a system of quality control and the Code of Professional Conduct
2. Understand the service to be performed
3. Be technically proficient
4. Be familiar with the industry
5. Exercise good professional judgment
6. Understand the organization's information technology systems

Firm policies and procedures should address other competencies necessary in the circumstances.

Acceptance and Continuance of Clients and Engagements

Policies and procedures should provide reasonable assurance that the firm will not be associated with clients whose management lacks integrity. A firm should:

1. Undertake only engagements that can be completed with professional competence
2. Consider the risks associated with the engagement

Moreover, a firm should obtain an understanding with the client regarding the engagement.

Engagement Performance

Policies and procedures should provide reasonable assurance that personnel meet:

1. Professional standards
2. Regulatory requirements
3. The firm's standards
4. Concurring partner review requirements applicable to SEC engagements

Policies and procedures should also provide reasonable assurance that personnel refer to authoritative literature and consult, on a timely basis, with appropriate individuals when dealing with complex, unusual, or unfamiliar issues.

Monitoring

Policies and procedures should provide reasonable assurance that the above elements of quality control are suitably designed and effectively applied. Monitoring involves:

1. Relevant and adequate policies and procedures that are complied with by members of the firm
2. Appropriate guidance and practice aids
3. Effective professional development activities

NOTE: A firm's monitoring procedures may include inspection procedures and preissuance or postissuance reviews of selected engagements by a qualified person not directly associated with performance of the engagement (which may be a partner with final responsibility for the engagement in a small firm) (see SQCS 3, Monitoring a CPA Firm's Accounting and Auditing Practice*).*

Independence, Integrity, and Objectivity

Policies and procedures should provide reasonable assurance that personnel maintain independence when required and perform all responsibilities with integrity and objectivity.

1. Independence is an impartiality that recognizes an obligation for fairness.
2. Integrity pertains to being honest and candid, and requires that service and public trust not be subordinated to personal gain.
3. Objectivity is a state of mind that imposes an obligation to be impartial, intellectually honest, and free of conflicts of interest.

ADMINISTRATION OF A QUALITY CONTROL SYSTEM

A partner or partners, depending on the size of the firm, should be responsible for monitoring the effectiveness of the firm's quality control system. The objective is to determine on a timely basis that the firm's quality control policies and procedures, assignment of responsibilities, and communication of policies and procedures continue to be appropriate.

AU ILLUSTRATIONS

The following chart illustrates the GAAS hierarchy.

ILLUSTRATION 1. GAAS HIERARCHY

Level	Elements	Authority
Tier 1 Auditing Standards	• 10 Formal Standards listed in *Fundamental Requirements* • SASs	Auditors must be familiar with all guidance in this category. Any departures must be justified.
Tier 2 Interpretive Publications	• Auditing Interpretations of SASs • Auditing guidance in AICPA Audit and Accounting Guides • Auditing Statements of Position • Appendices to SASs	Auditors must be familiar with all guidance in this category. Any departures must be justified.
Tier 3 Other Auditing Publications	• AICPA auditing publications not referred to under Tier 1 or Tier 2, such as Professional Issues Task Force (PITF) Practice Alerts • Auditing articles in professional journals • Continuing professional education programs and other instructional materials • Textbooks and guidebooks • Audit programs and checklists • Other auditing publications from state CPA societies, other organizations, and individuals	Guidance in this category is not authoritative. Auditors must determine whether guidance is appropriate and relevant in particular circumstances.

AU 311 Planning and Supervision[1]

AU-C 300 Planning an Audit

AU-C 210 Terms of Engagement

AU EFFECTIVE DATE AND APPLICABILITY

Original Pronouncements	Statements on Accounting Standards (SASs) 108 and 114.
Effective Date	The standard is currently effective.
Applicability	Audits of financial statements in accordance with generally accepted auditing standards (GAAS) (also relevant for engagements involving special reports on specified elements, accounts, and items of financial statements).

AU-C EFFECTIVE DATE AND SUMMARY OF CHANGES

SAS No. 122, *Codification of Auditing Standards and Procedures,* is effective for audits of financial statements with periods ending on or after December 15, 2012. AU-C 300 does not change extant requirements in any significant respect.

The requirements of AU 311 are clarified in AU-C 300, except for:

- AU 311.08–.10 on the early appointment of the independent auditor and establishing the terms of the engagement, which are included in AU-C 210, and
- Requirements on supervision, which are included in AU-C 220

AU DEFINITIONS OF TERMS

Assistants. Firm personnel other than the auditor with final responsibility for the audit.

---

[1] *This section is affected by the Public Company Accounting Oversight Board's (PCAOB) Standard,* Conforming Amendments to PCAOB Interim Standards Resulting from the Adoption of PCAOB Auditing Standard No. 5, An Audit of Internal Control over Financial Reporting That Is Integrated with an Audit of Financial Statements.

Auditor. Either the auditor with final responsibility for the audit or the auditor's assistants.

Audit planning. Developing an overall strategy for the expected conduct and scope of the audit.

Audit program. A reasonably detailed listing of audit procedures the auditor believes are necessary to accomplish the objectives of the audit. (It aids in instructing assistants in the work to be done.)

Supervision. Directing the efforts of assistants who are involved in accomplishing the objectives of the audit and determining whether those objectives were accomplished. It includes:

1. Instructing assistants
2. Keeping informed of significant problems in conducting audits
3. Reviewing assistants' work
4. Dealing with differences of opinion among firm personnel

OBJECTIVES OF AU SECTION 311

Section 311 provides an outline of the planning for and supervision of an audit. This includes the development of an overall audit strategy, an understanding of many aspects of the entity to be audited, and consideration of the skills and level of supervision needed to conduct the audit. Documentation includes how to establish an understanding with the client about the terms of the engagement, and the contents of the audit program. It also addresses how to handle any disagreements by assistants with audit conclusions.

OBJECTIVES OF AU-C SECTION 300

AU-C 300.04 states that "the objective of the auditor is to plan the audit so that it will be performed in an effective manner."

FUNDAMENTAL REQUIREMENTS

PLANNING

Appointment of the Independent Auditor

Early appointment of the independent auditor is preferable. Before accepting an engagement near or after the close of the fiscal year, the auditor should

1. Determine whether circumstances of the engagement are likely to allow for an adequate audit and expression of an unqualified opinion.
2. If they will not, discuss with the client the possible need for a qualified opinion or disclaimer of opinion.

NOTE: This requirement applies specifically to appointment near or after year-end. However, any time the possible necessity of a qualified opinion or disclaimer of opinion becomes apparent, it is prudent for the auditor to discuss the matter with the client.

Establishing an Understanding with the Client

The auditor should establish an understanding with the client about the services to be performed for each audit, review of a public company's financial statements, or agreed-upon procedures engagement. The understanding should include:

1. The engagement's objectives
2. Management's responsibilities
3. Auditor's responsibilities
4. The engagement's limitations

The auditor should document the understanding, preferably through a written communication with the client. If the auditor fails to establish an understanding, the auditor should decline the engagement.

NOTE: This does not require an engagement letter, but the best way to meet the requirement is to always use an engagement letter.

The understanding with the client generally includes the following matters:

1. The objective of the audit is the expression of an opinion.
2. Management is responsible for:

    a. The financial statements and the selection and application of the accounting policies
    b. Establishing and maintaining effective internal control over financial reporting
    c. Designing and implementing programs and controls to prevent and detect fraud
    d. Compliance with laws and regulations
    e. Providing all financial records and related information to the auditor
    f. Providing a written representation letter to the auditor at the end of the engagement
    g. Adjusting the financial statements to correct material misstatements
    h. Affirming in the management representation letter that any uncorrected misstatements are immaterial

3. The auditor is responsible for

    a. Conducting the audit in accordance with GAAS (including a summary of the limitations of an audit).
    b. Obtaining an understanding of internal control sufficient to plan the audit.

    NOTE: All these matters are generally included, but the auditor is not required to include them.

Other matters may be included in the understanding, such as arrangements about:

- The conduct of the engagement (for example, timing, client assistance)
- Specialists or internal auditors
- A predecessor auditor
- Fees and billing
- Indemnification arrangements if the client knowingly provides false information to the auditor

> NOTE: The AICPA's Code of Professional Conduct permits indemnification arrangements limited to knowing misrepresentations made by the client, but regulators, such as the Securities and Exchange Commission (SEC), may prohibit or restrict these agreements.

- Conditions for access to the auditor's audit documentation
- Additional services

Preliminary Engagement Activities

The auditor should perform the following activities at the beginning of the current audit engagement:

- Perform procedures regarding the continuance of the client relationship and the specific audit engagement.
- Evaluate the auditor's compliance with ethical requirements, including independence.

The purpose of performing these preliminary engagement activities is to consider any events or circumstances that may either adversely affect the auditor's ability to plan and perform the audit or may pose an unacceptable level of risk to the auditor.

The Overall Audit Strategy

You should establish and document the overall audit strategy for the audit. The overall audit strategy involves the determination of:

- The characteristics of the audit that define its scope
- The reporting objectives of the engagement related to the timing of the audit and the required communications
- Important factors that determine the focus of the audit team's efforts

The audit strategy helps the auditor determine the resources necessary to perform the engagement.

The Audit Plan

The audit plan is a more detailed, tactical plan that addresses the various audit matters identified in the audit strategy. You must develop and document an audit plan for every audit.

The audit plan should include a description of:

- The nature, timing, and extent of planned risk assessment procedures
- The nature, timing, and extent of planned further audit procedures at the relevant assertion level for each material class of transactions, account balance, and disclosure
- Other audit procedures to be carried out to comply with GAAS

Determining the Extent of Involvement of Professionals Possessing Specialized Skills

The auditor should consider whether specialized skills are needed in performing the audit. For example, the auditor may need to involve the use of an information technology (IT) specialist to:

- Determine the effect of IT on the audit
- Understand the IT controls
- Design and perform tests of IT controls or substantive procedures

In determining whether an IT professional is needed, the auditor should consider factors such as the following:

- The complexity of the entity's systems and IT controls and the manner in which they are used in conducting the entity's business
- The significance of changes made to existing systems, or the implementation of new systems
- The extent to which data is shared among systems
- The extent of the entity's participation in electronic commerce
- The entity's use of emerging technologies
- The significance of audit evidence that is available only in electronic form

Communications with Those Charged with Governance and Management

The auditor may discuss elements of planning with those charged with governance and the entity's management.

Additional Considerations in Initial Audit Engagements

Before starting an initial audit, the auditor should:

- Perform procedures regarding the acceptance of the client relationship and the specific audit engagement (see Statement on Quality Control Standards [SQCS] 2, *System of Quality Control for a CPA Firm's Accounting and Auditing Practice*, as amended).
- Communicate with the previous auditor, where there has been a change of auditors (see Section 315).

When developing the overall audit strategy and audit plan, the auditor should consider:

- Arrangements to be made with the previous auditor, for example, to review the previous auditor's audit documentation
- Any major issues (including the application of accounting principles or of auditing and reporting standards) discussed with management in connection with the initial selection as auditors, the communication of these matters to those charged with governance, and how these matters affect the overall audit strategy and audit plan
- The planned audit procedures to obtain sufficient appropriate audit evidence regarding opening balances
- The assignment of firm personnel with appropriate levels of capabilities and competence to respond to anticipated significant risks
- Other procedures required by the firm's system of quality control for initial audit engagements (for example, the firm's system of quality control may require the involvement of another partner or senior individual to review the overall audit strategy prior to commencing significant audit procedures or to review reports prior to their issuance)

SUPERVISION

Instructing Assistants

The auditor with final responsibility for the audit should inform assistants about:

1. Their responsibilities
2. The objectives of the procedures they are to perform

3. Matters that may affect the scope of the procedures they are to perform, such as:
   a. Aspects of the entity's business relevant to their assignment
   b. Possible accounting and auditing problems
4. The need to bring to his or her attention significant accounting and auditing questions raised during the audit

Extent

The extent of supervision necessary depends on such factors as:

1. Complexity of the subject matter
2. Qualifications of the assistants

Reviewing Work

The auditor should review the work of each assistant to:

1. Determine whether it was adequately performed
2. Evaluate whether the results support the conclusions to be expressed in the auditor's report

Disagreements

If differences of opinion arise among firm personnel about accounting or auditing issues in an audit, there should be:

1. Consultation to attempt resolution
2. Documentation of an assistant's disagreement, if he or she wants to be disassociated from the final resolution
3. Documentation of the basis for the final resolution

INTERPRETATIONS

COMMUNICATIONS BETWEEN THE AUDITOR AND FIRM PERSONNEL RESPONSIBLE FOR NONAUDIT SERVICES (FEBRUARY 1980 AND MARCH 2006)

The auditor should:

1. Consider the nature of nonaudit services that have been performed.
2. Assess whether the services affect the financial statements or performance of the audit.
3. Discuss the nonaudit services with personnel who performed such services, if they have implications for the audit. It may be useful to review the nonaudit engagement workpapers to help determine possible audit implications.

TECHNIQUES FOR APPLICATION

APPOINTMENT OF THE AUDITOR

A significant factor in planning fieldwork and timing auditing procedures is the timing of the auditor's appointment.

Early Appointment

Early appointment of the auditor is ideal. It allows him or her to plan the work so that it may be done effectively. An early appointment is helpful in planning the following:

1. Observation of the taking of the physical inventories
2. Confirmation of cash, receivables, and other balances
3. Count of cash and securities

Early appointment also is helpful because it allows the auditor to perform some procedures before the end of the period (interim work) such as obtaining and documenting knowledge of internal control and testing of details of transactions.

By doing interim work, the auditor can complete the audit at an early date after year-end. Early appointment also allows early consideration of difficult accounting and reporting problems and reduction of pressures to meet filing deadlines, such as those of the SEC.

Appointment Near or After Year-End

Appointment near or after the client's year-end date presents planning and timing problems for the auditor; however, these problems may be resolved. Ordinarily, the problems concern inventory observation, cash and securities counts, and confirmation requests.

Because of the late appointment, the auditor may not be able to observe the physical count of the inventory and the cash and securities at year-end. In this circumstance, the auditor should consider the client's accounting records. If the client maintains perpetual inventory records, the auditor can observe the physical count on a date after the client's year-end date and adjust that count back to year-end by using information in the perpetual inventory records. If the client maintains adequate and up-to-date securities records, the auditor can observe the count on a date after the client's year-end and adjust that count back to year-end by using information in the securities subsidiary ledger. Whenever the auditor observes a count on a date after the client's year-end date and adjusts that count back to year-end, he or she should examine, on a test basis, relevant transactions that occurred between year-end and the date of the count.

If the appointment is not too late after year-end, the auditor may be able to obtain necessary year-end confirmations, such as cash, receivables, prepayments, deposits, payables, and so on. If, however, the appointment is a month or two after year-end, the auditor may have to confirm account balances as of a date other than year-end and adjust the confirmed balances back to year-end. This procedure requires the examination on a test basis of relevant transactions that occurred between year-end and the confirmation date.

MATTERS COVERED IN ENGAGEMENT LETTER

The understanding with the client is specifically required to include

1. The engagement's objectives,
2. Responsibilities of management,
3. Responsibilities of the auditor, and
4. The engagement's limitations.

These four subject areas must be covered in the understanding. The manner and precise wording of that coverage is flexible.

Matters that are generally included in the understanding with the client are covered in *Planning and Supervision* (Section 311), under the section "Establishing an Understanding with the Client." For example, some auditors, in explaining responsibilities, describe responsibilities for detection of error, fraud, and reportable conditions of internal control, including a statement that matters of that nature that come to the auditor's attention will be communicated to management and the audit committee. These promises to communicate have sometimes been held to be separate undertakings in litigation that expand the auditor's legal duty. The auditor may wish to omit them or seek advice of legal counsel before including them.

FORMING AN AUDIT STRATEGY AND PLAN

Developing an audit strategy and an audit plan is intended to be an iterative process. As information becomes available to you over the course of your audit, you should reconsider your audit strategy and audit plan to determine whether they remain relevant. All changes to your audit strategy and plan should be documented.

Establishing an audit strategy varies according to the size of the entity and the complexity of the audit.

In audits of small entities, a very small audit team may conduct the entire audit. With a smaller team, coordination and communication between team members are easier. Consequently, establishing the overall audit strategy need not be a complex or time-consuming exercise.

MATTERS TO CONSIDER IN DEVELOPING AN AUDIT STRATEGY

Appendix to AU 311

Scope of the Audit Engagement

- The basis of reporting on which the financial information to be audited has been prepared, including any need for reconciliations to another basis of reporting
- Industry-specific reporting requirements, such as reports mandated by industry regulators
- The expected audit coverage, including the number and locations to be included
- The nature of the control relationships between a parent and its subsidiaries that determine how the group is to be consolidated
- The extent to which locations are audited by other auditors
- The nature of the subsidiaries or divisions to be audited, including the need for specialized knowledge
- The reporting currency to be used, including any need for currency translation for the financial information audited
- The need for statutory or regulatory audit requirements, for example, the Office of Management and Budget (OMB) Circular A-133, *Audits of States, Local Governments, and Non-Profit Organizations*
- The availability of the work of internal auditors and the extent of the auditor's potential reliance on such work
- The entity's use of service organizations and how the auditor may obtain evidence concerning the design or operation of controls performed by them
- The expected use of audit evidence obtained in prior audits, for example, audit evidence related to risk assessment procedures and tests of controls
- The effect of information technology on the audit procedures, including the availability of data and the expected use of computer-assisted audit techniques

- The coordination of the expected coverage and timing of the audit work with any reviews of interim financial information and the effect on the audit of the information obtained during such reviews
- The discussion of matters that may affect the audit with firm personnel responsible for performing other services to the entity
- The availability of client personnel and data

Reporting Objectives, Timing of the Audit, and Communications Required

- The entity's timetable for reporting, including interim periods
- The organization of meetings with management and those charged with governance to discuss the nature, extent, and timing of the audit work
- The discussion with management and those charged with governance regarding the expected type and timing of reports to be issued and other communications, both written and oral, including the auditor's report, management letters, and communications to those charged with governance
- The discussion with management regarding the expected communications on the status of audit work throughout the engagement and the expected deliverables resulting from the audit procedures
- Communication with auditors of other locations regarding the expected types and timing of reports to be issued and other communications in connection with the audit of other locations
- The expected nature and timing of communications among audit team members, including the nature and timing of team meetings and timing of the review of work performed
- Whether there are any other expected communications with third parties, including any statutory or contractual reporting responsibilities arising from the audit

Scope of the Audit

- With respect to materiality:
  - Setting materiality for planning purposes
  - Setting and communicating materiality for auditors of other locations
  - Reconsidering materiality as audit procedures are performed during the course of the audit
  - Identifying the material locations and account balances
- Audit areas where there is a higher risk of material misstatement
- The effect of the assessed risk of material misstatement at the overall financial statement level on scope, supervision, and review
- The selection of the audit team (including, where necessary, the engagement quality control reviewer) and the assignment of the audit work to the team members, including the assignment of appropriately experienced team members to areas where there may be higher risks of material misstatement
- Engagement budgeting, including considering the appropriate amount of time to set aside for areas where there may be higher risks of material misstatement
- The manner in which the auditor emphasizes to audit team members the need to maintain a questioning mind and to exercise professional skepticism in gathering and evaluating audit evidence

- Results of previous audits that involved evaluating the operating effectiveness of internal control, including the nature of identified weaknesses and action taken to address them
- Management's commitment to the design and operation of internal control
- Volume of transactions, which may be a factor in determining whether it is more effective for the auditor to rely on internal control
- Importance attached to internal control throughout the entity to the successful operation of the business
- Significant business developments affecting the entity, including changes in information technology, and business processes; changes in key management; and acquisitions, mergers, and divestments
- Significant industry developments, such as changes in industry regulations and new reporting requirements
- Significant accounting changes, such as changes in GAAP
- Other significant relevant developments, such as changes in the legal environment affecting the entity

AU-C 300.A25 *Appendix—Considerations in Establishing the Overall Audit*

The appendix to AU-C 300 provides examples of matters the auditor may consider in establishing the overall audit strategy, and many of these matters also will influence the detailed audit plan. The examples provided cover a broad range of matters applicable to many engagements. Although some of the following matters may be required by other AU-C sections, not all matters are relevant to every audit engagement, and the list is not necessarily complete.

Characteristics of the Engagement

The following are some examples of characteristics of the engagement:

- The financial reporting framework on which the financial information to be audited has been prepared, including any need for reconciliations to another financial reporting framework
- Industry-specific reporting requirements, such as reports mandated by industry regulators
- The expected audit coverage, including the number and locations of components to be included
- The nature of the control relationships between a parent and its components that determine how the group is to be consolidated
- The extent to which components are audited by other auditors
- The nature of the business divisions to be audited, including the need for specialized knowledge
- The reporting currency to be used, including any need for currency translation for the audited financial information
- The need for statutory or regulatory audit requirements (for example, the OMB Circular A-133, *Audits of States, Local Governments, and Nonprofit Organizations*)
- The availability of the work of internal auditors and the extent of the auditor's potential use of such work
- The entity's use of service organizations and how the auditor may obtain evidence concerning the design or operation of controls performed by them

- The expected use of audit evidence obtained in previous audits (for example, audit evidence related to risk assessment procedures and tests of controls)
- The effect of IT on the audit procedures, including the availability of data and the expected use of computer-assisted audit techniques
- The coordination of the expected coverage and timing of the audit work with any reviews of interim financial information, and the effect on the audit of the information obtained during such reviews
- The availability of client personnel and data

Reporting Objectives, Timing of the Audit, and Nature of Communications

The following examples illustrate reporting objectives, timing of the audit, and nature of communications:

- The entity's timetable for reporting, including interim periods
- The organization of meetings with management and those charged with governance to discuss the nature, timing, and extent of the audit work
- The discussion with management and those charged with governance regarding the expected type and timing of reports to be issued and other communications, both written and oral, including the auditor's report, management letters, and communications to those charged with governance
- The discussion with management regarding the expected communications on the status of audit work throughout the engagement
- Communication with auditors of components regarding the expected types and timing of reports to be issued and other communications in connection with the audit of components
- The expected nature and timing of communications among engagement team members, including the nature and timing of team meetings and timing of the review of work performed
- Whether there are any other expected communications with third parties, including any statutory or contractual reporting responsibilities arising from the audit

Significant Factors, Preliminary Engagement Activities, and Knowledge Gained on Other Engagements

The following examples illustrate significant factors, preliminary engagement activities, and knowledge gained on other engagements:

- The determination of materiality, in accordance with AU-C Section 320, *Materiality in Planning and Performing an Audit*, and, when applicable, the following:
  - The determination of materiality for components and communication thereof to component auditors in accordance with AU-C Section 600, *Special Considerations—Audits of Group Financial Statements (Including the Work of Component Auditors)*
  - The preliminary identification of significant components and material classes of transactions, account balances, and disclosures
- Preliminary identification of areas in which there may be a higher risk of material misstatement
- The effect of the assessed risk of material misstatement at the overall financial statement level on direction, supervision, and review

- The manner in which the auditor emphasizes to engagement team members the need to maintain a questioning mind and exercise professional skepticism in gathering and evaluating audit evidence
- Results of previous audits that involved evaluating the operating effectiveness of internal control, including the nature of identified deficiencies and action taken to address them
- The discussion of matters that may affect the audit with firm personnel responsible for performing other services to the entity
- Evidence of management's commitment to the design, implementation, and maintenance of sound internal control, including evidence of appropriate documentation of such internal control
- Volume of transactions, which may determine whether it is more efficient for the auditor to rely on internal control
- Importance attached to internal control throughout the entity to the successful operation of the business
- Significant business developments affecting the entity, including changes in IT and business processes; changes in key management; and acquisitions, mergers, and divestments
- Significant industry developments, such as changes in industry regulations and new reporting requirements
- Significant changes in the financial reporting framework, such as changes in accounting standards
- Other significant relevant developments, such as changes in the legal environment affecting the entity

Nature, Timing, and Extent of Resources

The following examples illustrate the nature, timing, and extent of resources:

- The selection of the engagement team (including, when necessary, the engagement quality control reviewer [see AU-C Section 220, *Quality Control for an Engagement Conducted in Accordance with Generally Accepted Auditing Standards*]) and the assignment of audit work to the team members, including the assignment of appropriately experienced team members to areas in which there may be higher risks of material misstatement
- Engagement budgeting, including considering the appropriate amount of time to set aside for areas in which there may be higher risks of material misstatement

AU ILLUSTRATION

ILLUSTRATION 1. ILLUSTRATIVE ENGAGEMENT LETTER

Auditor's Letterhead	Smith and Jones Certified Public Accountants October 7, 2011
Addressed to Client	Brock Warner Plainsmen, Inc. 2320 Tiger Blvd. Lancaster, Pennsylvania 19701
	To the Board of Directors and Shareholders (and to the Audit Committee if applicable):[2]
	This letter will confirm our understanding of the arrangements covering our audit of the financial statements of Plainsmen, Inc. for the period ending December 31, 2011.
Scope of Engagement	We will audit the company's balance sheet as of December 31, 2011, and the related statements of income, retained earnings, and cash flows for the year then ended. Our audit will be made in accordance with auditing standards generally accepted in the United States of America[3] and will include obtaining an understanding of your internal controls over financial reporting sufficient to plan the audit and making such tests of the accounting records and such other auditing procedures as we consider necessary in the circumstances. Our audit is not designed to provide any assurance on internal control. The objective of our audit is to express an unqualified opinion on the financial statements, although it is possible that facts or circumstances encountered may require us to express a less than unqualified opinion. If for any reason, we are not able to complete the audit, we will not issue a report.
Objective of Engagement and Form of Report	
Client's Representations	Our procedures will include tests of documentary evidence supporting the transactions recorded in the accounts, tests of the physical existence of inventories, and direct confirmation of receivables and certain other assets and liabilities by correspondence with selected customers, creditors, legal counsel, and banks. At the conclusion of our audit, we will require a letter from management that confirms certain representations made about the financial statements and related matters during the audit.
Client's Responsibilities	The fair presentation of financial position and results of operations in conformity with accounting principles generally accepted in the United States of America is management's responsibility. Management is responsible for the development, implementation, and maintenance of an adequate internal control system, compliance with laws and regulations, and for the accuracy of the financial statements. Management is also responsible for making all financial records and related information available to us. Although we may advise you about appropriate accounting principles and their application, the selection and method of application are responsibilities solely of management.

---

[2] For a public entity that is listed on a stock exchange, the Sarbanes–Oxley Act requires the audit committee to be directly responsible for the appointment, compensation, and oversight of the external auditor.

[3] Public companies subject to the standards of the PCAOB should state that the audit will be made in accordance with the standards of the PCAOB. See the discussion of PCAOB Standard 1, References in Auditors' Report to the Standards of the Public Company Accounting Oversight Board.

Audit Adjustments	Management is responsible for adjusting the financial statements to correct material misstatements and for confirming to us in the representation letter that the effects of any uncorrected misstatements are immaterial, both individually and in the aggregate, to the financial statements.
Limitations of the Audit	We plan and perform our audit to obtain reasonable assurance about whether the financial statements are free of material misstatements. Because of the concept of reasonable assurance and because we do not perform a detailed examination of all transactions, there is a risk that material errors, fraud, or other illegal acts may exist and not be detected by us. However, we will inform you of any material errors that come to our attention and any fraud that comes to our attention. We will also inform you of any other illegal acts that come to our attention, unless clearly inconsequential.
Communications about Internal Control	During the course of our audit we may observe opportunities for economy in, or improved controls over, your operations. We will bring such matters to the attention of the appropriate level of management either orally or in writing. However, our audit is not designed and cannot be relied on to detect significant deficiencies in the design or operation of internal controls.
Fees	Fees for our services are based on our regular per diem rates plus travel and other out-of-pocket expenses. Invoices will be rendered every two weeks and are payable upon presentation. We estimate that our fee for this audit will be between $25,000 and $30,000. Should any situation arise that would materially increase this estimate we will, of course, advise you.
Use of Client Personnel	Whenever possible, we will attempt to use your company's personnel. This effort could substantially reduce our time requirements and help you hold down audit fees.
Other Work	We will also prepare federal and state tax returns for the year ended December 31, 2011. The fee for tax return preparation should be approximately $5,000.
Acknowledgement	Please indicate your agreement to these arrangements by signing the attached copy of this letter and returning it to us.
	We appreciate your confidence in retaining us as your certified public accountants and look forward to working with you and your staff.
	Sincerely,
	Smith and Jones
Signed by CPA	Smith and Jones
Signed by Client and Returned to CPA	Approved

By	*Brock Warner*
Title	*President*
	Plainsmen, Inc.
Date	*10/7/11*

AU-C 210 ILLUSTRATION

> **ILLUSTRATION 1. ILLUSTRATIVE ENGAGEMENT LETTER —EXAMPLE OF AN AUDIT ENGAGEMENT LETTER (FROM AU-C 210.A42)**

The following is an example of an audit engagement letter for an audit of general purpose financial statements prepared in accordance with accounting principles generally accepted in the United States of America, as promulgated by the Financial Accounting Standards Board (FASB). This letter is not authoritative but is intended only to be a guide that may be used in conjunction with the considerations outlined in this SAS. The letter will vary according to individual requirements and circumstances and is drafted to refer to the audit of financial statements for a single reporting period. The auditor may seek legal advice about whether a proposed letter is suitable.

To the appropriate representative of those charged with governance of ABC Company:

[*The objective and scope of the audit*]

You have requested that we audit the financial statements of ABC Company, which comprise the balance sheet as of December 31, 20XX, and the related statements of income, changes in stockholders' equity, and cash flows for the year then ended, and the related notes to the financial statements. We are pleased to confirm our acceptance and our understanding of this audit engagement by means of this letter. Our audit will be conducted with the objective of our expressing an opinion on the financial statements.

[*The responsibilities of the auditor*]

We will conduct our audit in accordance with auditing standards generally accepted in the United States of America (GAAS). Those standards require that we plan and perform the audit to obtain reasonable assurance about whether the financial statements are free from material misstatement. An audit involves performing procedures to obtain audit evidence about the amounts and disclosures in the financial statements. The procedures selected depend on the auditor's judgment, including the assessment of the risks of material misstatement of the financial statements, whether due to fraud or error. An audit also includes evaluating the appropriateness of accounting policies used and the reasonableness of significant accounting estimates made by management, as well as evaluating the overall presentation of the financial statements.

Because of the inherent limitations of an audit, together with the inherent limitations of internal control, an unavoidable risk exists that some material misstatements may not be detected, even though the audit is properly planned and performed in accordance with GAAS.

In making our risk assessments, we consider internal control relevant to the entity's preparation and fair presentation of the financial statements in order to design audit procedures that are appropriate in the circumstances but not for the purpose of expressing an opinion on the effectiveness of the entity's internal control. However, we will communicate to you in writing concerning any significant deficiencies or material weaknesses in internal control relevant to the audit of the financial statements that we have identified during the audit.

[*The responsibilities of management and identification of the applicable financial reporting framework*]

Our audit will be conducted on the basis that [*management and, when appropriate, those charged with governance*] acknowledge and understand that they have responsibility:

1. For the preparation and fair presentation of the financial statements in accordance with accounting principles generally accepted in the United States of America;

2. For the design, implementation, and maintenance of internal control relevant to the preparation and fair presentation of financial statements that are free from material misstatement, whether due to fraud or error; and
3. To provide us with:

    a. Access to all information of which [*management*] is aware that is relevant to the preparation and fair presentation of the financial statements such as records, documentation, and other matters;
    b. Additional information that we may request from [*management*] for the purpose of the audit; and
    c. Unrestricted access to persons within the entity from whom we determine it necessary to obtain audit evidence.

As part of our audit process, we will request from [*management and, when appropriate, those charged with governance*], written confirmation concerning representations made to us in connection with the audit.

[*Other relevant information*]

[*Insert other information, such as fee arrangements, billings, and other specific terms, as appropriate.*]

[Reporting]

[*Insert appropriate reference to the expected form and content of the auditor's report. Example follows:*]

We will issue a written report upon completion of our audit of ABC Company's financial statements. Our report will be addressed to the board of directors of ABC Company. We cannot provide assurance that an unmodified opinion will be expressed. Circumstances may arise in which it is necessary for us to modify our opinion, add an emphasis-of-matter or other-matter paragraph(s), or withdraw from the engagement.

We also will issue a written report on [*insert appropriate reference to other auditor's reports expected to be issued*] upon completion of our audit.

Please sign and return the attached copy of this letter to indicate your acknowledgment of, and agreement with, the arrangements for our audit of the financial statements including our respective responsibilities.

XYZ & Co.

Acknowledged and agreed on behalf of ABC Company by

_____

[*Signed*]

[*Name and Title*]

[*Date*]

AU 312 Audit Risk and Materiality in Conducting an Audit[1]

AU-C 320 Materiality in Planning and Performing an Audit

AU-C 450 Evaluation of Misstatements Identified During the Audit

AU EFFECTIVE DATE AND APPLICABILITY

Original Pronouncement	Statement on Accounting Standards (SAS) 107.
Effective Date	The standard is currently effective.
Applicability	Audits of financial statements in accordance with generally accepted auditing standards (GAAS). (Specific requirements apply to planning audit tests and evaluating the results of audit tests.)

AU-C EFFECTIVE DATE AND SUMMARY OF CHANGES

SAS No. 122, *Codification of Auditing Standards and Procedures,* is effective for audits of financial statements with periods ending on or after December 15, 2012.

AU-C 320 does not change extant requirements in any significant respect. To bring the requirements more into conformity with International Standards on Auditing (ISA) 320, *Materiality in Planning and Performing an Audit,* and ISA 450, *Evaluation of Misstatements Identified During the Audit,* the extant standard AU-312 was divided into two standards, codified as AU-C 320 and AU-C 450. Other changes are:

- The inclusion of the definition of audit risk and its components in AU-C 200 and
- The inclusion of the auditor's responsibilities to evaluate the overall effect of audit findings on the auditor's report.

---

[1] *The section is affected by the Public Company Accounting Oversight Board's (PCAOB) Standard,* Conforming Amendments to PCAOB Interim Standards Resulting from the Adoption of PCAOB Auditing Standard No. 5, An Audit of Internal Control Over Financial Reporting That Is Integrated with an Audit of Financial Statements.

AU DEFINITIONS OF TERMS

Audit risk. The risk that the auditor may unknowingly fail to appropriately modify his or her opinion on financial statements that are materially misstated. At the account balance or class of transactions level, it consists of the risk of material misstatement, and detection risk. (It does not include business risk, inappropriate audit reporting decisions unrelated to detection and evaluation of misstatements, or erroneously concluding that the statements are materially misstated.)

Business risk. The risk of loss or injury to an auditor's professional practice from litigation, adverse publicity, or other event arising in connection with financial statements examined or reported on. (Not included in audit risk. Low business risk does not permit performance of less extensive procedures than would otherwise be appropriate under GAAS.)

Control risk. The risk that a material misstatement that could occur in an assertion will not be prevented or detected on a timely basis by the entity's internal controls. Control risk is one of two components of the risk of material misstatement.

Error. Unintentional misstatements of amounts or disclosures in financial statements.

Fraud. An intentional act by individuals among management, those charged with governance, employees, or third parties that involves the use of deception to obtain an unjust or illegal advantage.

Detection risk. The risk that the auditor will not detect a material misstatement that exists in an assertion. (Inherent risk and control risk exist independently of the audit of financial statements. Detection risk relates to the auditor's procedures and can be changed at the auditor's discretion. Detection risk should be varied by the auditor inversely in relation to the assessment of inherent risk and control risk.)

Inherent risk. The susceptibility of an assertion to a material misstatement, assuming that there are no internal controls. (Consists of the relative risk of misstatements of some assertions [for example, cash is more likely to be stolen than an inventory of coal] and to external factors such as technological developments or a declining industry characterized by many business failures.) Inherent risk is one of two components of the risk of material misstatement.

Known misstatement. The amount of misstatements specifically identified by the auditor.

Likely misstatement. The auditor's best estimate of the total misstatements in the account balances or classes of transactions examined.

Materiality. This key term is not explicitly defined in the section, but, as explained in the next section, the FASB's definition is quoted. Also, the following observations are made about materiality:

1. Financial statements are materially misstated when they contain misstatements whose effect, individually or in the aggregate, is important enough to cause them not to be presented fairly in accordance with generally accepted accounting principles (GAAP).
2. When reaching a conclusion as to whether the effect of misstatements, individually or in the aggregate, is material, an auditor ordinarily should consider their nature and amount in relation to the nature and amount of other items in the financial statements under audit.

These observations may be combined to specify that an item is material when its nature and amount in relation to the nature and amount of other items in the financial statements are important enough to affect the fair presentation of the financial statements in conformity with GAAP or an other comprehensive basis of accounting (OCBOA).

> NOTE: The auditor may want to consider the guidance provided in Staff Accounting Bulletin (SAB) 99, Materiality. This SAB addresses the application of materiality thresholds to the preparation and audit of financial statements filed with the SEC and provides guidance on qualitative factors to consider when evaluating materiality.

Misstatement. All errors and fraud, including certain illegal acts.

Risk of material misstatement. The risk that the relevant assertions related to account balances, classes of transactions, or disclosures are misstated. The risk of material misstatement consists of inherent and control risk, which are the entity's risks, existing independently of the audit of the financial statements.

AU-C DEFINITIONS OF TERMS

Source: AU-C Section 320.09

Performance materiality. The amount or amounts set by the auditor at less than materiality for the financial statements as a whole to reduce to an appropriately low level the probability that the aggregate of uncorrected and undetected misstatements exceeds materiality for the financial statements as a whole. If applicable, *performance materiality* also refers to the amount or amounts set by the auditor at less than the materiality level or levels for particular classes of transactions, account balances, or disclosures. Performance materiality is to be distinguished from tolerable misstatement.

Source: AU-C Section 450.04

Misstatement. A difference between the amount, classification, presentation, or disclosure of a reported financial statement item and the amount, classification, presentation, or disclosure required for the item to be presented fairly in accordance with the applicable financial reporting framework. Misstatements can arise from fraud or error.

Misstatements also include those adjustments of amounts, classifications, presentations, or disclosures that, in the auditor's professional judgment, are necessary for the financial statements to be presented fairly, in all material respects.

Uncorrected misstatements. Misstatements that the auditor has accumulated during the audit and that have not been corrected.

OBJECTIVES OF AU SECTION 312

Section 312 provides a framework for considering audit risk and materiality in planning audit procedures and evaluating the results of those procedures. It establishes how consideration of materiality and audit risk should affect planning audit procedures and evaluating audit findings.

It also includes explicit consideration of the risk of fraud within the audit risk model and to incorporate guidance on errors.

Section 312 also includes the requirement that an auditor document the nature and effect of aggregated misstatements, as well as his or her conclusion as to whether the aggregated misstatements cause the financial statements to be materially misstated.

OBJECTIVE OF AU-C SECTION 320

AU-C Section 320 states that the objective of the auditor is to apply the concept of materiality appropriately in planning and performing the audit.

OBJECTIVES OF AU-C SECTION 450

AU-C Section 450 states that the objective of the auditor is to evaluate the effect of:

1. Identified misstatements on the audit and
2. Uncorrected misstatements, if any, on the financial statements

THE NATURE OF AUDIT RISK AND MATERIALITY

Audit risk is the risk that the financial statements are materially misstated and the auditor fails to detect such a misstatement. The auditor must perform the audit to reduce audit risk to a low level. Audit risk is a function of two components:

1. *Risk of material misstatement,* which is the risk the risk that an account or disclosure item contains a material misstatement, and
2. *Detection risk,* which is the risk that the auditor will not detect such misstatements

To reduce audit risk to a low level requires the auditor to:

1. Assess the risk of material misstatement and, based on that assessment,
2. Design and perform further audit procedures to reduce overall audit risk to an appropriately low level

The concept of materiality recognizes that some matters are more important for the fair presentation of the financial statements than others. In performing your audit, you are concerned with matters that, individually or in the aggregate, could be material to the financial statements. Your responsibility is to plan and perform the audit to obtain reasonable assurance that you detect all material misstatements, whether caused by error or fraud.

The accounting standards define materiality as "the magnitude of an omission or misstatement of accounting information that, in light of surrounding circumstances, makes it probable that the judgment of a reasonable person relying on the information would have been changed by the omission or misstatement." Thus, materiality is influenced by your perception of the needs of financial statement users who will rely on the financial statements to make judgments about your client.

THE NATURE AND CAUSES OF MISSTATEMENTS

A misstatement may consist of:

- An inaccuracy in gathering or processing data from which financial statements are prepared
- A difference between the amount, classification, or presentation in the financial statements and the amount, classification, or presentation under GAAP
- An omission of a financial statement element, account, or item, or information required to be disclosed under GAAP
- Financial statement disclosures that are not in accordance with GAAP
- The omission of information required to be disclosed in conformity with GAAP

- An incorrect accounting estimate arising, for example, from an oversight or misinterpretation of facts; and
- Differences between management's and the auditor's judgments concerning accounting estimates, or the selection and application of accounting policies that the auditor considers inappropriate (for example, a departure from GAAP)

FUNDAMENTAL REQUIREMENTS

GENERAL

Key provisions of Section 312 include the following:

- The auditor must consider audit risk and must determine a materiality level for the financial statements taken as a whole for the purpose of:
    1. Determining the extent and nature of risk assessment procedures
    2. Identifying and assessing the risk of material misstatement
    3. Determining the nature, timing, and extent of further audit procedures
    4. Evaluating whether the financial statements taken as a whole are presented fairly, in conformity with generally accepted accounting principles
- Combined assessment of inherent and control risks is termed the risk of material misstatement.
- The auditor should assess the risk of material misstatement as a basis for further audit procedures. Although that risk assessment is a judgment rather than a precise measurement of risk, the auditor should have an appropriate basis for that assessment. Effectively, this means that the auditor cannot assess control risk "at the maximum" without having a basis for that assessment.
- Assessed risks and the basis for those assessments should be documented.
- The auditor must accumulate all known and likely misstatements identified during the audit, other than those that the auditor believes are trivial, and communicate them to the appropriate level of management.
- The auditor should request management to respond appropriately when misstatements (known or likely) are identified during the audit.

AUDIT RISK AND MATERIALITY CONSIDERATIONS—FINANCIAL STATEMENT LEVEL

The auditor should determine a materiality level for the financial statements taken as a whole for the purpose of:

- Determining the extent and nature of risk assessment procedures
- Identifying and assessing the risks of a material misstatement
- Determining the nature, timing, and extent of further audit procedures
- Evaluating whether the financial statements taken as a whole are presented fairly, in all material respects, in conformity with GAAP

In considering audit risk at the overall financial statement level, the auditor should consider risks of material misstatement that relate pervasively to the financial statements taken as a whole and often potentially relate to the many assertions. Risks of this nature often relate to the control environment and require an overall audit response, such as selecting engagement team members with an appropriate level of experience.

The auditor should consider the extent of procedures to be performed at selected locations. Factors that could influence selection include:

1. What are the types and amounts of assets at the location or component?
2. What are the types and amount of transactions executed at the location or component?
3. How centralized are the records?
4. How effective is the internal control?
5. What is the frequency, timing, and scope of management's monitoring activities?
6. What is materiality for the location or component?
7. What risks are associated with the geographic location?

In planning auditing procedures, the auditor should consider the nature, cause (if known), and amount of misstatements of which the auditor is aware from the audit of the prior period's financial statements.

Audit Risk and Materiality Considerations—Account Level

In determining the nature, timing, and extent of audit procedures to be applied to a specific account balance, class of transactions, or disclosure, the auditor should:

- Design audit procedures to obtain reasonable assurance of detecting misstatements that could be material, either individually, or in the aggregate
- Seek to reduce audit risk in such a way that will enable the auditor to express an opinion on the financial statements as a whole at an appropriately low level of audit risk
- Assess the risk of material misstatement at the relevant assertion level as a basis for further audit procedures

The model AR = Risk of material misstatement (RMM) × Detection risk (DR) expresses the general relationship of audit risk and the risks associated with the auditor's assessment risk of material misstatement (inherent control risks) and detection risk.

Planning Materiality

The auditor should determine a materiality level for the financial statements taken as a whole when establishing the overall audit strategy. This planning materiality helps guide the auditor's judgments in:

- Identifying and assessing the risks of material misstatement, and
- Planning the nature, timing, and extent of further audit procedures

Determining planning materiality is a matter of professional judgment. Typically, auditors apply a percentage to an appropriate basis (e.g., total revenues, total assets, etc.) as a starting point for determining materiality. When identifying an appropriate benchmark, the auditor may consider

- How the users use the entity's financial statements to make decisions
- The nature of the entity and the industry in which it operates
- The size of the entity, nature of its ownership and the way it is financed

If a preliminary judgment about materiality is made before the financial statements to be audited are prepared, or if significant accounting adjustments can reasonably be expected, it is helpful for the auditor to make the preliminary judgment based on:

- Annualized interim financial statements
- Financial statements of one or more prior annual periods, after considering major changes in the entity's circumstances, its industry, or the economy

Tolerable Misstatement

Tolerable misstatement is the maximum error in a population that the auditor is willing to accept. The auditor should determine one or more levels of tolerable misstatement in order to allow for the possibility that some misstatements of lesser amounts than materiality for the financial statements taken as a whole could, in the aggregate, result in a material misstatement.

Considerations as the Audit Progresses

The auditor should not assume that a misstatement is an isolated occurrence. If the nature of the identified misstatements and the circumstances of their occurrence indicate that other misstatements may exist that could be material, the auditor should consider whether the overall audit strategy and audit plan need to be revised.

Communication of Misstatements to Management

The auditor must accumulate all known and likely misstatements (except those that are "trivial") and communicate them to the appropriate level of management on a timely basis.

Known misstatements. The auditor should request management to record the adjustments needed to correct all known misstatements.

Likely misstatements. The auditor should request management to examine the class of transactions, account balance, or disclosure in order to identify and correct misstatements therein. If the likely misstatement involves difference in an estimate, the auditor should request management to review the assumptions and methods used in developing the estimate. After management has responded to the auditor's request, the auditor should reevaluate the amount of likely misstatement and, if necessary perform further audit procedures.

EVALUATING AUDIT FINDINGS

The auditor should consider the effects, both individually and in the aggregate, of uncorrected misstatements.

1. The aggregation should include likely misstatement as well as known misstatement. The aggregation consists of:

   a. Projected misstatement from substantive audit samples and known misstatement in nonsampling applications
   b. Differences between any estimated amounts in the financial statements that the auditor considers unreasonable and the *closest reasonable* estimates
   c. Uncorrected prior period misstatements that affect the current period's financial statements

   Misstatements should be aggregated in a way that enables the auditor to consider whether, in relation to individual amounts, subtotals, or totals in the financial statements, they materially misstate the financial statements.

2. Qualitative as well as quantitative considerations should be included in evaluating materiality.

3. It is ordinarily not feasible when planning an audit to anticipate all of the circumstances that may ultimately influence judgment about materiality levels in evaluating audit findings at the completion of the audit. Thus, the preliminary judgment about materiality levels will ordinarily differ from the judgment about materiality levels used in evaluating audit findings.

Closest reasonable estimate. When determining the amount of the likely misstatements to be aggregated, the auditor evaluates the *closest reasonable estimate*. This estimate can be either a range of acceptable amounts or a point estimate. If the auditor uses a range and management's recorded estimate is not in that range, the amount of the likely misstatement would be the difference between the recorded amount and the amount at the closest end of the range. If the auditor uses a point estimate, the likely misstatement would be the difference between the point estimate and the amount recorded by the client.

The auditor should be alert to the possibility that a cluster of management's recorded estimates at either end of the auditor's range of acceptable amounts may indicate a bias on the part of management. In this case, the auditor should reconsider whether other estimates reflect a similar bias and perform additional audit procedures as necessary. The auditor should also be alert to the possibility that recorded estimates may be clustered at one end of the acceptable range in a preceding year, and the other end of the range in the current year. This may indicate that management is using swings in accounting estimates to manage earnings, in which case the auditor should consider whether this needs to be communicated to the audit committee.

The qualitative characteristics of misstatements. The auditor should also consider qualitative factors when evaluating misstatements, since misstatements of relatively small amounts may have a material effect on the financial statement. This interpretation lists a number of qualitative factors that the auditor may want to consider, including:

- What are the possible effects of the misstatement on profitability or other trends, or compliance with loan covenants, other contractual agreements, and regulatory provisions?
- Does the misstatement change a loss into income (or vice versa) or increase management's compensation?
- What is the effect of the misstatement on segment information or the effect of a misclassification (e.g., a misclassification between operating and nonoperating income)?
- Are there statutory or regulatory requirements that affect materiality thresholds?
- How sensitive are the circumstances of the misstatements (e.g., a misstatement that involves a fraud or illegal act)?
- How significant is the financial statement element impacted by the misstatement (e.g., a misstatement that affects recurring earnings versus a nonrecurring charge or credit) or the significance of the misstatement or disclosures as they relate to the needs of users (e.g., the effect of misstatements on earnings contrasted with expectations)?
- What is the character of the misstatement (e.g., an error in an objectively determinable amount versus an error in an estimate, which by its nature involves a degree of subjectivity)?
- What is management's motivation?
- Do individually significant but different misstatements have offsetting effects?
- What is the likelihood that a currently immaterial misstatement may become material?

- What is the cost of correcting the misstatement?
- How great is the risk that there are possible additional undetected misstatements that might impact the auditor's evaluation?

EVALUATING WHETHER THE FINANCIAL STATEMENTS AS A WHOLE ARE FREE OF MATERIAL MISSTATEMENT

If the auditor determines that the effect of likely misstatements, individually or aggregated, causes the financial statements to be materially misstated, the auditor ordinarily should ask management to eliminate the misstatement. If the material misstatement is not eliminated, the auditor should issue a qualified or adverse opinion.

If the auditor concludes that the effects of likely misstatement, individually or aggregated, do not cause the financial statements to be materially misstated, the auditor should recognize that they could still be materially misstated due to further undetected misstatement.

1. The risk that the financial statements may be materially misstated increases as aggregated likely misstatement increases.
2. If the auditor believes that the risk of further misstatement is unacceptably high, the auditor should perform additional auditing procedures or obtain satisfaction that the entity has adjusted the financial statements to reduce the risk of material misstatement to an acceptable level.

DOCUMENTATION REQUIREMENTS

The auditor should document the following:

- The level of materiality for the financial statements as a whole and tolerable misstatement, any changes to these levels, and the basis on which those levels were determined
- A summary of uncorrected misstatements, other than those that are trivial, related to known and likely misstatements; this summary should be documented in a way that allows the auditor to:
  - Separately consider the effects of known and likely misstatements
  - Consider the aggregate effect of misstatements on the financial statements, and
  - Consider the qualitative factors that are relevant to your consideration of whether the misstatements are material
- The auditor's conclusion as to whether uncorrected misstatements, individually or in the aggregate, do or do not cause the financial statements to be materially misstated and the basis of your conclusion
- All known and likely misstatements identified by the auditor during the audit, other than those that are trivial, that have been corrected by management

INTERPRETATIONS

There are no interpretations for this section.

PROFESSIONAL ISSUES TASK FORCE PRACTICE ALERTS

94-1 DEALING WITH AUDIT DIFFERENCES

This practice alert advises auditors to consider the following issues when evaluating audit differences and deciding whether to communicate them to audit committees:

- Are audit differences material when evaluated in light of factors such as debt covenants?
- Will an agreement with management to waive "hard" audit differences and errors because "soft" credit differences offset them be appropriate if these "soft" differences never materialize?
- Do many of the audit differences trend in the same direction, indicating the possibility of management trying to achieve an earnings forecast, or even the possibility of fraud?
- Are accumulated unrecorded audit differences that are not material now likely to become more significant if the entity's leadership changes or other conditions change?

The auditor should remember that audit committees and outsiders who find out about waived audit differences may ask why those differences were not recorded. The practice alert advises auditors to encourage management to record material and immaterial audit differences because it sends a clear message about management's responsibilities. If the client still does not record audit differences, the auditor should try to agree on a plan for recording differences in the following year.

TECHNIQUES FOR APPLICATION

In applying Section 312, the auditor is faced with the following questions:

1. How to make a preliminary judgment about materiality for the financial statements taken as a whole
2. How to relate the preliminary judgment about materiality to individual account balances and classes of transactions in planning auditing procedures
3. How to consider audit risk at the financial statement level and account balance or class of transactions level and to relate the assessment of inherent risk and control risk to planning auditing procedures
4. How to relate the required assessment of the risk of material misstatement due to fraud to inherent and control risk
5. How to evaluate whether the financial statements are materially misstated based on audit findings

MAKING A PRELIMINARY JUDGMENT ABOUT MATERIALITY

To make a preliminary judgment about the amount to be considered material to the financial statements, the auditor should first recognize the nature of this amount. It is an allowance or "cushion" for undetected or uncorrected misstatement remaining in the financial statements after all audit procedures have been applied. The auditor's goal is to plan audit procedures so that if misstatements exceed this amount, there is a relatively low risk of failing to detect them.

Section 312 does not require quantification of the preliminary judgment about materiality. However, it is usually more efficient and effective to estimate a single dollar amount to be used in planning the audit. Since the amount is to be used as an aid in planning the scope of auditing procedures, use of a general rule of thumb is both practical and acceptable. For example, many auditors use 5 to 10% of before-tax income or .5 to 1% of the larger of total assets or total revenue. Adoption of a rule of thumb requires consideration of the appropriate base and the percentage of that base to be used to make the calculation.

Determining the Base

If the current financial statements are available, amounts from these statements may be used, or interim financial statements may be annualized. However, if significant audit adjustments are expected, an average from prior financial statements may be used. When historical data is used, the auditor should adjust the data for unusual items that affected prior years and for any known changes that can be expected to affect the current period.

Usually a single base is necessary because the auditor expresses an opinion on the financial statements taken as a whole rather than on individual financial statements. The most common bases for materiality judgments are:

1. Income before tax
2. Total revenue
3. Total assets

Some common approaches to using these bases include, but are not limited to the following:

1. Select from among the bases recognizing differences in client and industry circumstances. For example:

    a. If income fluctuates significantly or approaches breakeven, use total revenue.
    b. If the entity is in an industry that is asset intensive, such as a financial institution, use total assets; if the entity is a nonprofit organization, use total revenue.
    c. Otherwise, use income before taxes.

2. Use a single base that is likely to be valid across most client circumstances or industries. For example, always use the larger of total assets or total revenue.
3. Consider using appropriate percentages applied to different bases as the outside limits on a range, and select an amount within the range based on judgment. For example, select an amount between X% of income before taxes and Y% of total revenue.

The choice of approach is influenced by judgments about the importance of stability of the base versus flexibility in using judgment in the circumstances.

Nature of a Materiality Rule of Thumb

Several matters should be recognized in using a rule of thumb to estimate an amount to be used for planning materiality. First, the amount expresses the auditor's judgment about the total acceptable amount of undetected misstatement and detected but uncorrected misstatement. Thus, this amount in some circumstances may be larger than some auditors have considered to be material.

Second, because the amount includes an allowance for *undetected* misstatements and includes the *combined* effect of misstatements, it is not suitable as a threshold for evaluating the materiality of individual misstatements. Also, in evaluation the auditor should consider qualitative matters and additional information obtained during the audit.

Finally, although this approach is called a rule of thumb, it is in no sense a rule. It is simply a guide to making a planning decision. If the rule of thumb produces an amount that an auditor believes is unreasonable, the auditor's considered judgment should prevail over arbitrary adherence to the rule of thumb.

USING THE PRELIMINARY JUDGMENT IN PLANNING PROCEDURES

The auditor needs to plan audit procedures for a specific account balance or class of transactions so that misstatements in that balance or class when combined with misstatement in other balances or classes will not exceed the preliminary judgment about materiality. This may be done explicitly or judgmentally. A quantitative allocation of the preliminary judgment is not required.

Necessary Reduction of Preliminary Judgment

The first step in relating the preliminary judgment to individual balances and classes is to reduce the preliminary judgment for the amount of misstatement that is expected to be uncorrected when the audit report is issued. Naturally, known uncorrected misstatement reduces the allowance or cushion for undetected misstatement. In the following discussion, for convenience, uncorrected misstatements are assumed to be negligible, and the amount estimated in making the preliminary judgment is used in planning procedures.

Nonsampling Applications

In the application of audit procedures that do not involve audit sampling (see Section 350), the relation of the preliminary judgment to balances or classes depends on the approach to examining the account.

Some accounts are examined 100% because the account is affected by very few transactions and all of them are expected to be material. For example, stockholders' equity and long-term debt usually fall in this category, and property and equipment may be in this category. For these accounts, no relation to the preliminary judgment is relevant. The preliminary judgment is an allowance for undetected misstatement, and the normal audit approach would detect all misstatements.

For some accounts, no substantive tests are applied. The total of these accounts should be clearly immaterial. A common rule of thumb is that the total amount of these accounts should not exceed 1/3 of the preliminary judgment.

Some accounts are examined by selecting all items above a specified "material" amount. A common rule of thumb is that this amount should be between 1/6 and 1/3 of the preliminary judgment. All items larger than 1/3 of the preliminary judgment would be examined if little or no misstatement was expected or if the procedure applied to the items was one of several directed toward the same audit objective. All items larger than 1/6 of the preliminary judgment would be examined if many misstatements were expected or if the procedure applied to the items was extremely important to the auditor's conclusion. An amount between 1/3 and 1/6 could be used for circumstances between these extremes.

CONSIDERATION OF AUDIT RISK (INCLUDING FRAUD RISK)

The auditor's goal is to plan the audit to restrict audit risk to a relatively low level. Audit risk cannot be objectively measured for the financial statements taken as a whole, and the requirements of Section 312 are easier to understand and apply if one focuses on relationships at the account balance and class of transactions level. At that level, audit risk has the following three components:

1. Inherent risk
2. Control risk
3. Detection risk

The basic idea is that the auditor assesses the existing inherent risk and existing control risk and then plans audit procedures with a suitably low detection risk to reduce the overall risk (audit risk) to an acceptably low level. Inherent risk and control risk exist independently, and all the auditor can do is assess them. Detection risk is a function of the effectiveness of audit procedures; the more effective the audit procedures, the lower the detection risk. At the balance or class level, audit risk is the risk that the auditor will fail to detect an amount of misstatement that would be material when combined with misstatement in other balances or classes.

Risk of Material Misstatement Due to Fraud

The auditor is obligated to assess the risk of misstatement due to fraud even if inherent or control risk is assessed at the maximum. Furthermore, as discussed in Section 316, as long as the auditor assesses the two types of fraud risk (misstatements arising from fraudulent financial reporting and misstatements arising from misappropriation of assets) and the various categories of risk factors under each, he or she may combine the fraud risk, inherent risk, and control risk assessments.

Inherent Risk

This risk is the susceptibility of an account balance or class of transactions to misstatement that could be material. Inherent risk is influenced by the nature of the account balance or class of transactions and by other factors that may affect several or all of the balances or classes.

Assessment of inherent risk is usually based on the auditor's knowledge of the nature of the client's business, its organization, and its operating characteristics. The need for the auditor to obtain knowledge of such matters and the factors that affect them are explained in Section 311. Some auditors have formalized the approach to obtaining this knowledge through the use of questionnaires or checklists. (See Section 318 for an illustration of such a questionnaire.) Other auditors gather this information less formally but nevertheless explicitly consider it in planning procedures for specific balances or classes.

Section 312 gives the following examples of how the nature of an account balance could influence inherent risk:

- Complex calculations are more likely to be misstated than simple calculations.
- Cash is more susceptible to theft than an inventory of coal.
- Accounts consisting of amounts derived from accounting estimates pose greater risks than do accounts consisting of relatively routine factual data.

This aspect of inherent risk has been recognized in the auditing literature for several decades under the term *relative risk*.

Section 312 gives the following examples of other factors that influence inherent risk:

- Technological developments might make a particular product obsolete, thereby causing inventory to be more susceptible to overstatement.

- A declining industry characterized by a large number of business failures or a lack of sufficient working capital to continue operations might predispose management to misstate financial statements.

The relation of inherent risk assessment to planning is considered further in the following discussions of control risk and detection risk.

Control Risk

This is the risk that material misstatement may occur in an assertion and not be prevented or detected on a timely basis by the entity's internal controls. Section 312 states that the auditor may make a separate assessment of control risk or a combined assessment of inherent and control risk. However, some auditors believe that at the balance or class level, the assessment is necessarily combined from either a theoretical or practical perspective.

These auditors point out that a conceptually logical approach to evaluation of accounting control is the direct focus on the purpose of preventing or detecting **material** errors or fraud in financial statements by applying the following steps:

1. Consider the types of errors and fraud that could occur; that is, answer the question "What could go wrong?" (This is basically an assessment of inherent risk.)
2. Determine the controls that should prevent or detect such errors and fraud.
3. Determine whether the necessary procedures are prescribed and are being followed satisfactorily. (This is the assessment of control risk.)
4. Determine the effect of control weaknesses (control risk) on the nature, timing, or extent of auditing procedures. (This is the consideration of acceptable detection risk based on the assessment of inherent risk and control risk.)

The first two steps are usually performed through the development of generalized materials such as checklists and questionnaires. The third step is accomplished by analysis of the information obtained through the use of generalized materials and tests of controls.

Other auditors believe that a separate assessment of inherent risk may be made by considering factors such as the relative complexity of transaction processing, the susceptibility of the item to misstatement without regard to controls, the relative size of individual items, and the relative stability of operations. The important aspect of the assessment is that it must be made independently of control procedures. For example, the likelihood of understatement errors in payroll may be considered low no matter what control procedures exist, but overstatement caused by errors or fraud may be influenced significantly by controls.

Detection Risk—Nonsampling Considerations

The assessment of inherent risk created by factors that affect several or all balances or classes is often responded to in a general way rather than by specific modification of auditing procedures. For example, the auditor may assign more experienced personnel to the engagement, increase the level and extent of supervision, and generally conduct the audit with a heightened degree of professional skepticism. In this area, the auditor's focus is really on whether the risk level is above the ordinary for the entire audit.

At the account balance or class of transactions level, some of the factors that affect all balances or classes may influence the planned auditing procedures for a specific balance or class. Substantive tests may be applied at year-end rather than at interim dates, and unusual rather than normal procedures may be selected. Some auditors have formalized the assessment of inherent risk at the balance or class level by requiring documentation of an explicit qualitative judgment of whether the risk of material misstatement is high, moderate, or low when the audit program is prepared. Although Section 312 states that the auditor must have an "appropriate basis" whenever inherent risk is assessed at less than the maximum, Section 312 stops short of requiring this degree of formalization in audit program planning.

Detection Risk—Sampling Considerations

The assessment of inherent risk and control risk and the resultant effect on detection risk can have a dramatic effect on the sample sizes necessary to hold audit risk to an acceptably low level. The way the detection risk is considered is determined by whether the planned audit sample is statistical or nonstatistical and whether the nonstatistical plan is a formal plan (usually a PPS approximation) or an informal one.

If the sampling plan is an informal, nonstatistical one, there is no point in quantifying the assessment of inherent or control risk. As inherent and control risk increase, sample sizes should increase because the auditor must achieve a low detection risk to reduce audit risk to an acceptable level. However, about the only generalization that can be made is this relationship between risk level and sample size.

In a formal nonstatistical plan, the auditor usually has to identify one of three or four qualitative levels of assessment of inherent and control risk, and one of three or four levels of reliance on audit procedures other than the one applied using sampling (an assessment of detection risk for all relevant nonsampling procedures). For example, the auditor will select from among *maximum*, *moderate*, and *low* assessment of control risk and inherent risk, and this selection will have a predetermined effect on the sample size required. The following relationships may be used:

Control risk	Effect on sample size	Implicit detection risk in sample
Low	1	20%
Moderate	1.33	10%
Maximum	2	5%

This means that assuming that the only audit procedure applied to achieve a particular audit objective uses sampling, a qualitative assessment of control risk of "low" results in a sample size that is one half the sample size required with an assessment at the maximum level.

If a statistical plan is used, it is necessary to assess inherent risk, control risk, and detection risk applicable to nonsampling procedures, such as analytical procedures, as specific percentages and to use these percentages in a formula to determine the acceptable detection risk for the sample. The formula is explained in the appendix to Section 350. The only time it is necessary to reduce the risk assessment to specific percentages is when a statistical sampling plan is used. In all other cases, use of specific percentages and the Section 350 formula are unnecessary. The Section 350 formula assumes that inherent risk is at the maximum and no separate assessment is made.

EVALUATION OF FINANCIAL STATEMENTS

Usually the only practical way to consider whether financial statements are materially misstated at the conclusion of the audit is to use a worksheet that determines the combined effect of uncorrected misstatement on important totals or subtotals in the financial statements, for example, current assets, current liabilities, income before taxes, income taxes, net income, total assets, total liabilities, and stockholders' equity. Use of such worksheets is fairly common in auditing practice. However, it is important to recognize that the auditor may use a different amount in evaluating whether the financial statements are materially misstated than was used in planning the audit. Qualitative considerations may cause the auditor to consider smaller detected misstatements to be material. Also, for misstatements that have an effect only on the balance sheet or that affect only classification within a financial statement, an amount may have to be larger to be considered material.

In explaining the misstatements that should be combined to consider whether the financial statements are materially misstated, Section 312 refers to *known* misstatement and *likely* misstatement. Known misstatement is the amount of misstatement actually detected in applying audit procedures. Likely misstatement is essentially the same as projected misstatement in sampling applications. (See Section 350 and, in particular, "Substantive Tests" under *Techniques for Application*.) In addition to considering the combined effect of uncorrected known and likely misstatement, the auditor should consider the risk of further misstatement remaining undetected. For example, the amount estimated for planning materiality usually includes an allowance for undetected misstatement.

PRIOR PERIOD MISSTATEMENTS

Section 312 requires that prior period misstatements be considered, but permits either the *rollover* or *iron curtain* approach. Under the iron curtain approach, the effects of all cumulative uncorrected misstatements are deemed to affect the current period's income statement as well as the balance sheet. Under the rollover approach, the cumulative uncorrected misstatements, net of the uncorrected misstatements carried over from the prior year, are deemed to affect the current period's income statement. If, for example, warranties payable were understated by $150 in the prior period and $200 in the current period, the rollover approach would compare only $50 to the current income to evaluate quantitative materiality while the iron curtain approach would compare the full $200. The auditor should be alert to the fact that neither the iron curtain nor the rollover approach can be applied mechanically. The two approaches are clear alternatives only in complex situations in which a misstatement accumulates in the balance sheet. In fact, the mechanical application of the iron curtain approach in a more complex situation may have the opposite of the intended effects. For example, if warranties payable were *overstated* in the prior period by $300 and *understated* in the current period by $200, the aggregate effect on the current period income statement would be a $500 overstatement of income before tax. The uncorrected prior period misstatement would have a $300 carryover effect in the current period income statement. Therefore, careful consideration of the impact of prior period adjustments is needed, and individual facts and circumstances must be considered.

AU 314 Understanding the Entity and Its Environment and Assessing the Risks of Material Misstatement[1,2]

AU-C-315 Understanding the Entity and Its Environment and Assessing the Risks of Material Misstatement

AU EFFECTIVE DATE AND APPLICABILITY

Original Pronouncement	Statement on Auditing Standards (SAS) 109
Effective Date	This statement currently is effective.
Applicability	Audits of financial statements in accordance with generally accepted auditing standards.

---

[1] Section 404, "Management Assessment of Internal Controls" of the Sarbanes–Oxley Act of 2002, and the related Securities and Exchange Commission (SEC) implementing rules require that all public company annual reports on Form 10-K include a report containing a statement of management's responsibility to establish and maintain internal control over financial reporting, and an assessment, as of the end of the company's most recent fiscal year, of the effectiveness of those controls. The company's registered public accounting firm must attest to and report on management's assessment of the effectiveness of internal control.

[2] This section is affected by the Public Company Accounting Oversight Board's (PCAOB's) Standard, Conforming Amendments to PCAOB Interim Standards Resulting from the Adoption of PCAOB Auditing Standard No. 5, An Audit of Internal Control over Financial Reporting That Is Integrated with an Audit of Financial Statements.

AU-C EFFECTIVE DATE AND SUMMARY OF CHANGES

SAS No. 122, *Codification of Auditing Standards and Procedures,* is effective for audits of financial statements with periods ending on or after December 15, 2012. AU-C 315 does not change extant requirements in any significant respect.

The requirements of AU 314 are clarified in AU-C 315, except for the requirement:

- For the auditor to perform the audit with professional skepticism, which is included in AU-C 200
- To consider whether the entity has disclosed a particular matter appropriately, which is included in AU-C 700

AU DEFINITIONS OF TERMS

Internal control. A process affected by an entity's board of directors, management, and other personnel that is designed to provide reasonable assurance about the achievement of the entity's objectives in the following categories:

1. Reliability of financial reporting
2. Effectiveness and efficiency of operations
3. Compliance with applicable laws and regulations

Components of internal control. The five interrelated components of internal control are:

1. *Control environment.* The tone of an entity that influences the control consciousness of its people. It is the foundation for all other components of internal control, providing discipline and structure.
2. *Risk assessment.* From a financial reporting perspective, an entity's risk assessment is its identification, analysis, and management of risks relevant to the preparation of financial statements.
3. *Control activities.* The policies and procedures that help ensure that management directives are carried out.
4. *Information and communication systems support.* The information system which includes the accounting system that consists of the methods and records that the entity has to record, process, summarize, and report entity transactions, events, and conditions, and to maintain accountability for the related assets, liabilities, and equity.
5. *Monitoring.* A process to assess whether controls are operating as intended and whether they are modified as appropriate for changes in conditions.

Application controls. Control activities that apply to the processing of individual applications (e.g., edit checks of input data, sequence checks, manual follow-up of exception reports).

Assessed level of control risk. The conclusion reached as a result of assessing control risk. Control risk may be assessed at the maximum level or at some level below the maximum if supported by appropriate tests of controls.

Control risk. The risk that a material misstatement that could occur in an assertion will not be prevented or detected on a timely basis by the entity's internal control.

Controls placed in operation. An internal control procedure that is actually being used by the entity.

Detection risk. The risk that the auditor will not detect a material misstatement that exists in an assertion.

Evaluation of the effectiveness of control design. A determination of whether an internal control procedure is suitably designed to prevent or detect material misstatements in specific financial statement assertions.

Further audit procedures. Audit procedures performed after performing risk assessment procedures. Further audit procedures consist of tests of controls and substantive tests (i.e., tests of details and substantive analytical procedures).

General controls. Control activities that relate to many applications and that support application controls (e.g., controls over data center and network operations, access security, and systems and software acquisitions and maintenance).

Information technology (IT). IT encompasses automated means of originating, processing, storing, and communicating information and includes recording devices, communication systems, computer systems (including hardware and software components and data), and other electronic devices. (The auditor is primarily interested in the entity's use of IT to initiate, record, process, and report transactions or other financial data.)

Inherent risk. The susceptibility of an assertion to a material misstatement assuming there are no related internal controls.

Risk assessment procedures. Procedures used to gather information and obtain an understanding of an entity and its environment, including internal control. Risk assessment procedures are inquiry, observation, inspection of documents, analytical procedures, and reperformance of control procedures.

Risk of material misstatement in financial statement assertions. The product of inherent risk and control risk.

Test of controls. Procedures concerned with how an internal control procedure was applied, the consistency with which it was applied during the audit period, and by whom it was applied. Tests of controls used for generating evidence about operating effectiveness include inquires, inspection, observation, and reperformance of the application of the control.

AU-C DEFINITIONS OF TERMS

Source: AU-C 315.04

Assertions. Representations by management, explicit or otherwise, that are embodied in the financial statements as used by the auditor to consider the different types of potential misstatements that may occur.

Business risk. A risk resulting from significant conditions, events, circumstances, actions, or inactions that could adversely affect an entity's ability to achieve its objectives and execute its strategies or from the setting of inappropriate objectives and strategies.

Internal control. A process effected by those charged with governance, management, and other personnel that is designed to provide reasonable assurance about the achievement of the entity's objectives with regard to the reliability of financial reporting, effectiveness and efficiency of operations, and compliance with applicable laws and regulations. Internal control over safeguarding of assets against unauthorized acquisition, use, or disposition may include controls relating to financial reporting and operations objectives.

Relevant assertion. A financial statement assertion that has a reasonable possibility of containing a misstatement or misstatements that would cause the financial statements to be materially misstated. The determination of whether an assertion is a relevant assertion is made without regard to the effect of internal controls.

Risk assessment procedures. The audit procedures performed to obtain an understanding of the entity and its environment (including the entity's internal control) to identify and assess the risks of material misstatement, whether due to fraud or error, at the financial statement and relevant assertion levels.

Significant risk. An identified and assessed risk of material misstatement that, in the auditor's professional judgment, requires special audit consideration.

OBJECTIVES OF AU SECTION 314

Sections 314 and 327 are the centerpiece of the risk assessment standards. Together, these two sections provide detailed guidance on how to apply the audit risk model described in Section 312. That model describes audit risk as:

$$AR = RMM \times DR$$

where AR is audit risk, RMM is the risk of material misstatement, and DR is detection risk. The risk of material misstatement is a combination of inherent and control risk. Although the standard describes a combined risk assessment, the auditor may perform separate assessments of inherent and control risks.

NOTE: Previous auditing standards directed the auditor to gain an understanding of the entity and its business and its internal control. However, this guidance was related to audit planning. Section 314 also directs the auditor to obtain an understanding of the entity, its environment, and its internal control, but this understanding is now audit evidence to support the auditor's assessment of the risk of material misstatement and, ultimately, the opinion on the financial statements.

This shifting of the auditor's understanding of internal control within the audit process is a subtle but important distinction. By definition, "planning" is done before the commencement of fieldwork. In contrast, the gathering of audit evidence is done throughout fieldwork. Currently, there is a tendency among auditors to consider internal control only once, during planning, and then to not consider it again. As a result, internal control may be seen as separate from the "real" audit. The new standards emphasize that internal control is part of the "real" audit, providing audit evidence that ultimately supports the opinion on the financial statements.

Section 314 also describes how the auditor should identify and assess the risk of material misstatement, which provides a basis for designing further audit procedures. These further audit procedures (which consist of tests of controls and substantive tests) must be clearly linked and responsive to assessed risks.

Section 314 also introduced the concept of *significant risks*, which are risks that require special audit consideration. One or more significant risks arise on all audits.

The following is an overview of how the process is described in Section 314:

NOTE: This process for assessing risk is consistent with the process for assessing the risk of material misstatement due to fraud. Essentially it is an information gathering, assessment, and response process, in which the auditor gathers information about the entity, assimilates and synthesizes that information to make an assessment of risk, and then designs audit procedures that are responsive to those risks.

1. Perform risk assessment procedures to gather information and gain an understanding of the entity and its environment, including internal control.
2. Based on this understanding, identify risks of material misstatement, which may exist at either the financial statement or relevant assertion level.
3. Assess the risk of material misstatement, which requires the auditor to:

   - Identify the risk of material misstatement
   - Describe the identified risks in terms of what can go wrong in specific assertions
   - Consider the significance and likelihood of material misstatement for each identified risk

The assessment of the risk of material misstatement enables the auditor to design appropriate further audit procedures, which are clearly linked and responsive to the assessed risks.

NOTE: Section 314 describes risks as existing at one of two levels: the financial statement level or the relevant assertion level. This distinction is important because the nature of the auditor's response differs depending on whether the risk is a financial statement–level or assertion-level risk.

- *The risk of material misstatement at the financial statement level has a pervasive effect on the financial statements and affects many assertions. The control environment is an example of a financial statement level risk. In addition to developing assertion-specific responses, financial statement–level risks may require the auditor to develop an overall response, such as assigning more experienced team members.*
- *Assertion-level risks pertain to a single assertion or related group of assertions. Assertion-level risks will require the auditor to design and perform specific further audit procedures such as tests of controls and/or substantive procedures that are directly responsive to the assessed risk.*

Section 327 provides guidance on the design and performance of further audit procedures.

OBJECTIVES OF AU-C SECTION 315

AU-C Section 315 states that:

. . . the objective of the auditor is to identify and assess the risks of material misstatement, whether due to fraud or error, at the financial statement and relevant assertion levels through understanding the entity and its environment, including the entity's internal control, thereby providing a basis for designing and implementing responses to the assessed risks of material misstatement. (AU-C 315.03)

FUNDAMENTAL REQUIREMENTS

BASIC REQUIREMENT

In all audits, the auditor must obtain a sufficient understanding of the entity and its environment, including its internal control, to assess the risk of material misstatement of the financial statements whether due to error or fraud, and to design the nature, timing, and extent of further audit procedures.

This assessment of the risk of material misstatement becomes the basis for the proper design of further audit procedures.

NOTE: Obtaining an understanding of the entity and its environment also allows the auditor to make judgments about other audit matters, such as:

- *Materiality*
- *Whether the entity's selection and application of accounting policies are appropriate and financial statement disclosures are adequate*
- *Areas where special audit consideration may be necessary, for example, related-party transactions*
- *The expectation of recorded amounts used for performing analytical procedures*
- *The evaluation of audit evidence*

Even if the auditor plans a purely substantive audit, he or she still is required to obtain an understanding of internal control. Such an understanding is necessary to:

- Identify missing or ineffective controls
- Evaluate identified control deficiencies
- Confirm that substantive procedures alone are sufficient to design and perform an appropriate audit strategy and provide sufficient appropriate audit evidence to support the audit opinion

RISK ASSESSMENT PROCEDURES

The auditor should perform risk assessment procedures to obtain an understanding of the entity and its environment, including its internal control. Risk assessment procedures include:

1. Inquiries of management and others at the client
2. Analytical procedures
3. Observation and inspection

The auditor's risk assessment procedures provide the audit evidence necessary to support your risk assessments, which in turn support your determination of the nature, timing, and extent of further audit procedures. Thus, the results of your risk assessment procedures are an integral part of the audit evidence you obtain to support your opinion on the financial statements.

NOTE: Under the previous auditing standards, it was common for auditors to declare control risk to be maximum simply for audit efficiency, without any basis for making that assessment. Section 314 eliminates that practice by requiring auditors to document their rationale for assessing control risk. This rationale should be based on the information gathered from the performance of risk assessment procedures. The elimination of the auditor's ability to default to maximum control risk without justification is a significant change from previous practice.

A Mix of Procedures

Except for internal control, the auditor is not required to perform all the procedures for each of the five aspects of the client and its environment discussed previously. However, in the course of gathering information about the client, the auditor should perform all the risk assessment procedures.

With regard to obtaining an understanding about the design of internal controls and determining whether they have been implemented, inquiry alone is not sufficient. Thus, for these purposes, the auditor should supplement inquiries with other risk assessment procedures.

Other procedures may provide relevant information about the entity. For example:
- Some of the procedures the auditor performs to assess the risks of material misstatement due to fraud also may help gather information about the entity and its environment, particularly its internal control.

> NOTE: Because of the close connection between the assessment of the risk of material misstatement and the procedures performed to assess fraud risk, the auditor will want to:
> - Coordinate the procedures he/she performs to assess the risk of material misstatement due to fraud with his/her other risk assessment procedures
> - Consider the results of his/her assessment of fraud risk when identifying the risk of material misstatement

- When relevant to the audit, the auditor also should consider other information, which may include:
  - Information obtained from the client acceptance or continuance process
  - Experience gained on other engagements performed for the entity

> NOTE: Previous standards did not describe the procedures the auditor should perform to gain an understanding of internal control. Section 314 states that the auditor should perform "risk assessment procedures" to gather information about internal control. These risk procedures are:
> - Inquiry
> - Observation
> - Inspection of documentation
> - Analytical procedures
>
> In addition to these risk assessment procedures, auditors also may choose to perform walkthroughs of significant transactions to gain an understanding of information processing and related controls.
>
> Section 314 goes on to state that in order to gain the requisite understanding of internal control, inquiry alone is not sufficient. Auditors who historically have relied solely on inquiry to obtain an understanding of internal control will have to revise their audit process.

Updating Information from Prior Periods

If certain conditions are met, the auditor may use information obtained in prior periods as audit evidence in the current period audit. However, when the auditor intends to use information from prior periods in the current period audit, you should determine whether changes have occurred that may affect the relevance of the information for the current audit. To make this determination, the auditor should make inquiries and perform other appropriate audit procedures, such as walkthroughs of systems.

Discussion among the audit team. The members of the audit team should discuss the susceptibility of the client's financial statements to material misstatement. This discussion will allow team members to exchange information and create a shared understanding of the client and its environment, which in turn will enable each team member to:

- Gain a better understanding of the potential for material misstatement resulting from fraud or error in the assertions that are relevant to the areas assigned to them
- Understand how the results of the audit procedures that they perform may affect other aspects of the audit

This discussion among the audit team could be held at the same time as the discussion among the team related to fraud, which is required by Section 316.

UNDERSTANDING THE ENTITY AND ITS ENVIRONMENT

The auditor should obtain an understanding of the following elements of the entity and its environment:

- *External factors*, including:
  - Industry factors, such as the competitive environment, supplier and customer relationships, and technological developments
  - The regulatory environment, which includes relevant accounting pronouncements, the legal and political environment, and environmental requirements that affect the industry
  - Other matters, such as general economic conditions
- *Nature of the client,* which includes its operations, its ownership, governance, the types of investments it makes and plans to make, how it is financed, and how it is structured.
- *Objectives and strategies and related business risks,* which may result in material misstatement of the financial statements taken as a whole or as individual assertions.
- *Measurement and review of the client's financial performance,* which tells the auditor which aspects of the client's performance management considers to be important.
- *Internal control,* which consists of five components: the control environment, risk assessment, information and communication, control activities, and monitoring. These components may operate at the entity level or the individual transaction level. Obtaining an appropriate understanding of internal control will require the auditor to understand and evaluate the design of all five components of internal control and to determine whether the controls are in use by the client.

NOTE: The purpose of understanding the entity and its environment is to help identify and assess risk. For example:

- *Information about the client's industry may allow the auditor to identify characteristics of the industry that could give rise to specific misstatements.*
- *Information about the ownership of the client, how it is structured, and other elements of its nature will help identify related-party transactions that, if not properly accounted for and adequately disclosed, could lead to a material misstatement.*
- *The auditor's identification and understanding of the business risks facing the entity increase the chance of identifying financial reporting risks.*
- *Information about the performance measures used by the entity may lead the auditor to identify pressures or incentives that could motivate entity personnel to misstate the financial statements.*
- *Information about the design and implementation of internal control may identify deficiencies in control design, which increase the risk of material misstatement.*

OBTAINING AN UNDERSTANDING OF INTERNAL CONTROL

The auditor should obtain an understanding of all five components of internal control even in those instances where the auditor plans a purely substantive audit or is auditing a smaller entity with less formal controls.

Control Environment

The auditor should obtain a sufficient knowledge of the control environment to understand management's and the board of directors' attitude, awareness, and actions concerning the environment. Control environment factors include:

1. Integrity and ethical values
2. Commitment to competence
3. Board of directors or audit committee participation
4. Management's philosophy and operating style
5. Organizational structure
6. Assignment of authority and responsibility
7. Human resource policies and practices

NOTE: *The auditor should concentrate on the substance of controls (established and acted upon), not their form.*

Risk Assessment

The auditor should obtain sufficient knowledge of the entity's risk assessment process to understand how management considers and addresses risks relevant to financial reporting. Risks can occur because of the following:

1. Changes in operating environment
2. New personnel
3. New or revamped information systems
4. Rapid growth
5. New technology
6. New business models, products, or activities
7. Corporate restructurings
8. Expanded foreign operations
9. New accounting pronouncements

NOTE: *The auditor's assessment of inherent and control risks is a separate consideration and not part of the entity's risk assessment.*

Control Activities

The auditor should obtain an understanding of those control activities that are relevant to the audit. Control activities are relevant to the audit if they are related to *significant risks,* as discussed later in this section. Examples of specific control activities include:

1. Authorization
2. Asset accountability
3. Safeguarding
4. Segregation of duties (e.g., assigning different people the responsibility for authorizing transactions, recording transactions, and maintaining custody of assets)

The auditor should also obtain an understanding of the process of reconciling detail to the general ledger for significant accounts.

Information and Communication

The auditor should obtain sufficient knowledge of the accounting information system to understand:

1. The classes of transactions that are significant to the financial statements
2. The procedures, both automated and manual, by which those transactions are initiated, recorded, processed, and reported from their occurrence to inclusion in the financial statements
3. The related accounting records, whether electronic or manual, supporting information, and specific accounts involved in initiating, recording, processing and reporting transactions
4. How the information system captures other events and conditions that are significant to the financial statements
5. The financial reporting process

The auditor should understand the automated and manual procedures used to prepare financial statements and related disclosures, and how misstatements may occur. Such procedures include:

1. The procedures used to enter transaction totals into the general ledger

    NOTE: The auditor should be aware that when IT is used to automatically transfer information from transaction processing systems to general ledger or financial reporting systems, there may be little or no visible evidence of intervention in the information systems (e.g., an individual may inappropriately override automated processes by changing the amounts being automatically passed to the general ledger or financial reporting system).

2. The procedures used to initiate, record, and process standard (e.g., monthly sales and purchase transactions) and nonstandard (e.g., business combinations or disposals, or a nonrecurring accounting estimate) journal entries in the general ledger

    NOTE: Auditors should be aware that

    - *When IT is used to maintain the general ledger and prepare financial statements, such nonstandard entries may exist only in electronic form and may be more difficult to identify through physical inspection of printed documents.*
    - *Financial statement misstatements are often perpetrated by using nonstandard entries to record fictitious transactions or other events and circumstances, particularly near the end of the reporting period.*

3. Other procedures used to record recurring and nonrecurring adjustments (e.g., consolidating adjustments and reclassifications that are not made by formal journal entries)

The auditor should also obtain sufficient knowledge of the means the entity uses to communicate financial reporting roles and responsibilities and significant matters about financial reporting.

Monitoring

The auditor should obtain sufficient knowledge of the major types of activities that the entity uses to monitor internal control over financial reporting, including internal auditors (Section 322).

NOTE: Under previous standards, the auditor was required to understand the design of controls and to determine whether they have been implemented, that is, whether the entity is using them. Section 314 does not change that overall requirement; however, it does require the auditor to gain an understanding of some controls that previously did not have to be addressed. These controls include the following:

- *How the incorrect processing of significant transactions is resolved*
- *The process of reconciling detail to the general ledger for significant accounts*
- *Control activities related to "significant risks," as defined in the standard*

EVALUATING THE DESIGN OF INTERNAL CONTROL

On every audit, the auditor should obtain an understanding of internal control that is of sufficient depth to enable the auditor to:

1. Assess the risks of material misstatement of the financial statements, whether due to error or fraud
2. Design the nature, timing, and extent of further audit procedures

To meet this, the auditor should:

1. Evaluate the design of controls that are relevant to the audit and determine whether the control—either individually or in combination—is capable of effectively preventing or detecting and correcting material misstatements
2. Determine that the control has been implemented; that is, that the control exists and that the entity is using it

The auditor's evaluation of internal control design and the determination of whether controls have been implemented are critical to the assessment of the risks of material misstatement. Even if the auditor's overall audit strategy contemplates performing only substantive procedures for all relevant assertions related to material transactions, account balances, and disclosures, the auditor still needs to evaluate the design of the client's internal control.

NOTE: In evaluating control design, it is helpful to consider:

- *Whether control objectives that are specific to the unique circumstances of the client have been considered for all relevant assertions for all significant accounts and disclosures.*
- *Whether the control or combination of controls would—if operated as designed—meet the control objective.*
- *Whether all controls necessary to meet the control objective are in place.*

Distinguishing between Evaluation of Design and Tests of Controls

Obtaining an understanding of the design and implementation of internal control is different from testing its operating effectiveness.

- *Understanding the design and implementation* is required on every audit as part of the process of assessing the risks of material misstatement.
- *Testing the operating effectiveness* is necessary only when the auditor will rely on the operating effectiveness of controls to modify the nature, timing, and extent of substantive procedures or when substantive procedures alone do not provide you with sufficient audit evidence at the assertion level.

The procedures necessary to understand the design and implementation of controls do provide some limited evidence regarding the operation of the control. However, the procedures necessary to understand the design and implementation of controls generally are not sufficient to serve as a test of their operating effectiveness for the purpose of placing significant reliance on their operation.

Examples of situations where the procedures the auditor performs to understand the design and implementation of controls may provide sufficient audit evidence about their operating effectiveness include:

- Controls that are automated to the degree that they can be performed consistently provided that IT general controls over those automated controls operated effectively during the period.
- Controls that operate only at a point in time rather than continuously throughout the period. For example, if the client performs an annual physical inventory count, the auditor's observation of that count and other procedures to evaluate its design and implementation provide audit evidence that may affect the design of your substantive procedures.

Assessing the Risk of Material Misstatement

The auditor's understanding of the entity and its environment—which includes an evaluation of the design and implementation of internal control—is used to assess the risk of material misstatement. To assess the risk of material misstatement, the auditor should:

1. Identify risks throughout the process of obtaining an understanding of the entity, its internal control, and its environment.
2. Relate the identified risks to what can go wrong at the relevant assertion level.
3. Consider whether the risks could result in a material misstatement to the financial statements.
4. Consider the likelihood that the risks could result in a material misstatement of the financial statements.

Financial statement–level and assertion-level risks. The auditor should identify and assess the risks of material misstatement at both the financial statement level and the relevant assertion level.

1. *Financial statement–level risks.* Some risks of material misstatement relate pervasively to the financial statements taken as a whole and potentially affect many relevant assertions. These risks at the financial statement level may be identifiable with specific assertions at the class of transaction, account balance, or disclosure level.
2. *Relevant assertion-level risks.* Other risks of material misstatement relate to specific classes of transactions, account balances, and disclosures at the assertion level. The auditor's assessment of risks at the assertion level provide a basis for considering the appropriate audit approach for designing and performing further audit procedures.

Risks that exist at the financial statement level—for example, those that pertain to a weak control environment or to management's process for making significant accounting estimates—should be related to specific assertions. In other instances, it may not be possible to relate financial statement–level risks to a particular assertion or group of assertions. Financial statement–level assertions that cannot be related to specific assertions will require an overall response, such as the way in which the audit is staffed or supervised. Section 327 provides additional guidance on the auditor's overall responses to financial statement–level risks.

How to consider internal control when assessing risks. When making risk assessments, the auditor should identify the controls that are likely to either prevent or detect and correct material misstatements in specific assertions.

Individual controls often do not address a risk completely in themselves. Often, only multiple control activities, together with other components of internal control (for example, the control environment, risk assessment, information and communication, or monitoring), will be sufficient to address a risk. For this reason, when determining whether identified controls are likely to prevent or detect and correct material misstatements, the auditor generally considers controls in relation to significant transactions and accounting processes (for example, sales, cash receipts, or payroll), rather than ledger accounts.

Identification of significant risks. As part of assessing the risks of material misstatement, the auditor should identify significant risks, which are defined as those risks that require special audit consideration. For example, if the entity is named as a defendant in a patent infringement lawsuit that may threaten the viability of its principal product, the auditor could consider significant the risks that the lawsuit (1) would not be appropriately recorded or disclosed in accordance with GAAP or (2) may affect the entity's ability to continue as a going concern.

Significant risks arise on most audits. When the auditor determines that a risk is a significant risk, the audit procedures should include (but not be limited to):

- Obtaining an understanding of internal control, including relevant control activities, related specifically to those significant risks
- If the auditor plans to rely on the operating effectiveness of controls related to significant risks, testing the operating effectiveness of those controls in the current period; that is, using evidence about operating effectiveness that was obtained in prior periods is not appropriate
- Substantive procedures specifically designed to address the significant risk

Significant risks should be determined without regard to internal controls, that is, by considering inherent risk only.

Significant risks frequently arise from unusual, nonroutine transactions and from judgmental matters such as estimates. In addition, significant risks may relate to matters such as the following:

- *External circumstances.* External circumstances giving rise to business risks influence the determination of whether the risk requires special audit attention. For example, technological developments might make a particular product obsolete, thereby causing inventory to be more susceptible to overstatement. Recent significant economic, accounting, or other developments also may require special attention.
- *Factors in the client and its environment.* Factors in the client and its environment that relate to several or all of the classes of transactions, account balances, or disclosures may influence the relative significance of the risk. For example, a lack of suf-

ficient working capital to continue operations or a declining industry characterized by a large number of business failures may have a pervasive effect on risk for several account balances, classes of transactions, or disclosures.
- *Recent developments.* Recent significant economic, accounting, or other developments can affect the relative significance of a risk.
- *Complex calculations.* Complex calculations are more likely to be misstated that simple calculations.
- *Risk of fraud or theft.* Revenue recognition is presumed to be a financial reporting fraud risk; cash is more susceptible to misappropriation than an inventory of coal.
- *Estimates.* Accounts consisting of amounts derived from accounting estimates that are subject to significant measurement uncertainty pose greater risks than do accounts consisting of relatively routine, factual data.
- *Related-party transactions.* Related-party transactions may create business risks that can result in a material misstatement of the financial statements.

Risks for which substantive procedures alone do not provide sufficient appropriate audit evidence. For some risks it is not possible or practicable to reduce detection risk to an acceptably low level with audit evidence obtained only from substantive procedures. Examples of such situations include:

- An entity that conducts its business using IT to initiate orders for the purchase and delivery of goods based on predetermined rules of what to order and in what quantities and to pay the related accounts payable based on system-generated decisions initiated upon the confirmed receipt of goods and terms of payment
- An entity that provides services to customers via electronic media and uses IT to create a log of the services provided to its customers, to initiate and process its billings for the services, and to automatically record such amounts in the accounting records

Documentation

The auditor should document the following:

1. The discussion among the audit team regarding the susceptibility of the entity's financial statements to material misstatement due to error or fraud, including how and when the discussion occurred, the subject matter discussed, the audit team members who participated, and significant decisions reached concerning planned responses at the financial statement and relevant assertion levels.
2. Key elements of the understanding obtained regarding each of the aspects of the entity and its environment, including each of the five components of internal control, to assess the risks of material misstatement of the financial statements; the sources of information from which the understanding was obtained; and the risk assessment procedures.
3. The assessment of the risks of material misstatement both at the financial statement level and at the relevant assertion level and the basis for the assessment.
4. The risks identified as significant risks.

NOTE: Current audit practice for many auditors is to simply document the auditor's understanding of internal control. The new auditing standards require the auditor to document (in addition to the auditor's understanding of internal control) the procedures performed, the results of those procedures, and the information sources used to gain that understanding of internal control. This requirement may result in a significant change from current audit practice. For example, it is common for the documentation of the auditor's understanding of the control environment to consist solely of a checklist indicating which elements of control environment (as defined by the Committee of Sponsoring Organizations of the Treadway Commission, or COSO) are present at the client. Under the new standards, that checklist by itself would not satisfy the documentation requirements, which stipulate that the documentation include a detailed description of the procedures performed to obtain the understanding of how those elements of the control environment are designed and that they are in use at the entity.

INTERPRETATIONS

There are no interpretations for this section.

TECHNIQUES FOR APPLICATION

UNDERSTANDING THE ENTITY AND ITS ENVIRONMENT

The extent of the auditor's planning depends on the nature of the client and the experience of the auditor with that client. For example, planning for the audit of a new client is more extensive than planning for the audit of an existing client. When planning an audit, the auditor should consider the following:

1. The economy
2. The client's industry
3. The client's business
4. Firm requirements

These factors are discussed below. All factors are not appropriate for every audit. The size and complexity of the client determine which factors are relevant.

THE ECONOMY

There are certain economic conditions that significantly influence the industry and the business of the client. The auditor should be aware of these conditions and should consider them when planning the audit. Some economic factors that might affect client operations and, therefore, should be considered in planning an audit include:

1. Interest rates
2. Unemployment rates
3. Money supply
4. Foreign currency exchange rates
5. International trade agreements
6. Government regulations and legislation
7. Overall business conditions—depression, recession, inflation

THE CLIENT'S INDUSTRY

When planning the audit, the auditor should be aware of conditions in the client's industry. Factors to consider include the following:

1. Growth and financial results of the industry; possible sources of this information are the following:
    a. Industry trade association literature
    b. Publications issued by agencies such as Moody's, Standard & Poor's, and Robert Morris Associates (see Section 329)

c. Government publications issued by the Government Printing Office, Washington, D.C.

2. Cyclical and seasonal nature of the industry
3. Is the industry labor intensive or capital intensive?
4. Industry labor conditions:

   a. Is the industry unionized?
   b. Has the industry recently experienced a strike?

5. Industry accounting practices; this information may be obtained from firm members with clients in the same industry and the American Institute of Certified Public Accountants (AICPA) Industry Audit and Accounting Guides.
6. Industry price patterns and consumer reactions to price changes
7. State of industry technology
8. Competitiveness of industry:

   a. Number of bankruptcies during the past year
   b. Number of new companies organized during the current year

In addition to the information the auditor obtains about the client's industry from industry-related publications, he or she may obtain industry information from bankers, client management, auditors with clients in the same industry, and general business publications, such as the *Wall Street Journal, Businessweek, Forbes,* and *Fortune.*

THE CLIENT'S BUSINESS: NEW CLIENT

When planning the audit, the auditor should have a knowledge of the client's operations. For a new client, the primary sources of information are discussions with the predecessor auditor and inquiries of client management.

For a new client, the auditor should learn about the client and plan the audit by doing the following:

1. Communicate with predecessor auditor (see Section 315)
2. Visit client's administrative office and major facilities
3. Review year-end financial statements of prior year and interim financial statements of current and prior year
4. Review auditor's report on prior year's financial statements:

   a. Was there a scope limitation?
   b. Were certain matters emphasized?
   c. Did the auditor disclaim an opinion or issue an adverse opinion?
   d. Were there other modifications of the auditor's standard report?

5. Review prior year's income tax returns
6. Obtain the results of the most recent income tax examination
7. Review reports issued to agencies, such as the following:

   a. SEC
   b. Federal Housing Administration, Small Business Administration, and Department of Labor
   c. Credit agencies and banks

Visit to Administrative Office

During his or her visit to the client's administrative office, the auditor should do the following:

1. Meet with financial and administrative officers and obtain or determine the following:

    a. The functions of each executive
    b. The executive responsible for the audit
    c. Organization charts
    d. Locations and relative importance of all offices, showrooms, warehouses, and factories
    e. Corporate manuals or memoranda that provide information about the following:

       (1) Nature and description of the entity's products
       (2) Production and distribution methods
       (3) Internal control
       (4) General ledger chart of accounts

    f. Methods of financing the entity's operations
    g. Schedule of long-term debt
    h. Names of banks and account executive at each bank; for each bank, determine the following:

       (1) Outstanding indebtedness and terms of payment
       (2) Lines of credit
       (3) Other banking services

    i. For nonpublic companies, a schedule of stockholders with the following information:

       (1) Names
       (2) Addresses
       (3) Certificate numbers
       (4) Number of shares held
       (5) Shareholder function in the business

    j. Purchase terms:

       (1) Terms of payment
       (2) Are letters of credit used for foreign purchases?

    k. Sales terms:

       (1) Terms of payment
       (2) Are letters of credit used for foreign sales?

    l. The existence of related-party transactions such as the following:

       (1) Purchases and sales
       (2) Loans
       (3) Receiving or providing services, such as management, legal, and administrative

m. Schedule of all affiliates and nonconsolidated subsidiaries
n. Customers and suppliers on whom the entity is economically dependent
o. Most recent trial balance
p. General ledger and books of original entry:

   (1) Are accounting records up-to-date?
   (2) What is the quality of accounting records?

q. Extent of client responsibility for preparation of the following:

   (1) Trial balance
   (2) Schedules
   (3) Adjustments and accruals
   (4) Confirmations
   (5) Inventory instructions
   (6) Financial statements
   (7) Income tax returns

r. Tentative audit schedule; agree to dates for the following:

   (1) Physical inventory
   (2) Cash and securities count
   (3) Mailing and confirmations
   (4) Start of fieldwork

2. Obtain the entity's forms and documents, such as the following:

   a. Purchase requisitions
   b. Purchase orders
   c. Sales authorizations
   d. Sales orders
   e. Sales invoices
   f. Production orders
   g. Production requisitions
   h. Receipts
   i. Checks
   j. Payroll cards
   k. Sales returns and credits
   l. Purchase returns and credits

3. Examine work area that will be allocated to the auditor
4. Walk through the accounting area:

   a. Observe work conditions
   b. Meet employees
   c. Determine employee functions

Visit to Facility

During the visit to the client's facility, the auditor should do the following:

1. Meet with management
2. Walk through a production cycle and note the following:

a. Initiation of order
   b. Requisition of materials
   c. Movement of production
   d. Completion of production
   e. Storage of completed product
   f. Shipment to customer
3. Document flow of production
4. Note conditions of facility and equipment
5. Visit materials stockroom, observe condition of the inventory, and review the following:
   a. Inventory records
   b. Receiving reports
   c. Inventory reports

THE CLIENT'S BUSINESS: CONTINUING CLIENT

For a continuing client, information about the business is obtained from the following:

1. Client permanent file
2. Prior year's audit documentation
3. Prior year's audit team
4. Client's current year budgets
5. Client's current year interim financial statements
6. Members who had professional assignments with the client during the year; these assignments include the following:
   a. Review of interim financial statements
   b. Income tax planning
   c. Systems and other consulting services
7. Discussions with client management

Discussions with Client Management

The in-charge auditor and the staff member who will supervise the audit should visit the client before beginning the audit to determine the following:

1. Change in product line
2. Addition or deletion of factories, offices, warehouses, or showrooms
3. Addition of new administrative departments
4. Acquisition of subsidiaries
5. Existence of new or continuing related parties
6. Changes in production or distribution methods
7. Changes in sources of financing
8. Changes in internal control
9. Acquisition of new office equipment, such as a computer
10. Changes in key personnel
11. New long-term commitments, such as:
    a. Leases
    b. Employment contracts
12. Adoption of employee compensation and benefit plans

USING A RISK-BASED, TOP-DOWN APPROACH TO EVALUATE INTERNAL CONTROL

Section 314 does not provide any definitive guidance on how auditors can most effectively and efficiently comply with the requirement to evaluate control design on every engagement. However, auditors of nonpublic companies would be well served to apply the lessons learned by auditors of public companies who have been required to audit their client's internal controls ever since the Sarbanes–Oxley Act became effective.

Lessons from SOX 404

In the years immediately following the effective dates of Section 404 of the Sarbanes–Oxley Act (SOX 404), many auditors adopted an evaluation approach that started by identifying all (or nearly all) of the company's controls and then documenting and testing each of these to determine whether internal control as a whole was effective. As you can imagine, this approach was extremely time-consuming and costly. Moreover, this "bottom-up" approach was unnecessary to achieve the overall objective of management's evaluation.

In 2007, the SEC revised its rules and described a "risk-based, top-down" approach to understanding internal control. Auditors of nonpublic companies are not required to use this approach. However, applying its basic principles will provide an effective and efficient approach to meeting the requirements of Section 314.

In general, the key steps in this approach include the following:

1. Ask "what can go wrong?" in the preparation of the financial statements. Use your knowledge of the client, external events, and circumstances and the application of GAAP to identify risks that the entity's financial statements could be misstated. Once they are identified, you should assess the relative magnitude of these risks.
2. Identify controls that address the "what can go wrongs." The entity should have controls in place to mitigate those misstatement risks that are of some significance. You will focus your attention on those controls whose failure is most likely to result in a material misstatement. To make this determination, you will consider both:

    a. The likelihood that the control will fail, and
    b. If it did fail, the significance of the misstatement that would result

    For example, an entity may have controls over its bank balances (e.g., month-end bank reconciliations) and its petty cash on hand. Auditors will focus on the controls over the company's bank balances, because the risks related to the control failure of the reconciliation are greater than the risks related to the petty cash. That is, if the bank reconciliations fail, the misstatement of the financial statements could be material; if petty cash was misstated, the misstatement would not be material.
3. Obtain an understanding of relevant controls from the "top" down. This process of identifying controls should begin at the "top," with the broadest, most pervasive controls, and then proceed "downward" to more direct, specific controls.

A Top-Down Approach to Evaluating Controls

The consideration of the risk of material misstatement is crucial when planning and performing an evaluation of internal control. It is this consideration that helps direct the auditor's focus to the most critical areas of the company's internal control system. In a similar fashion, beginning at "the top" of the system and working "down" will help drive efficiency and direct the focus of the evaluation of internal control design.

But where is the "top" of an internal control system? And once you are there, what direction is "down?" To answer these questions requires an understanding of three key principles of internal control design:

1. Within any organization, controls operate at two distinct levels: the broad, general *entity level* and the more focused and specific *activity level*.
2. Controls are designed to mitigate risks. Some controls address risks *directly*, other controls address the same risks *indirectly*.
3. At the activity level, controls can be designed to either:

   a. Prevent errors from entering the financial information system, or
   b. Detect and correct errors that have already entered the system.

Entity-level controls sit at the "top" of the internal control structure. For example, these controls might include the company's hiring and training policies and the firewall protecting its network. There are relatively few entity-level controls. This is because, by their nature, entity-level controls have a broad (though indirect) effect on the company's financial reporting risks (as indicated by the relative size of the sphere). For example, a firewall might cover the company's inventory system, billing and receivables, and general ledger system all at once.

Entity-level controls have a very indirect effect on the financial statements. For example, the quality of the company's training can improve job performance and reduce the risk of misstatement, but training alone is not sufficient to prevent or detect an error.

At the lowest level of the pyramid are the company's most specific, narrowly focused activity-level controls. For example, an edit check to ensure that a date is formatted mm/dd/yyyy is an activity-level control. This control is specifically directed to one field on a single data entry form. The control is designed to *prevent* an error from entering the information, and it is typical for controls at this level of the pyramid to be preventive controls, designed to be performed on every transaction.

In a typical control system there are many, many activity-level controls. There are two reasons for this relative abundance of preventive activity-level controls:

1. Activity-level controls address very specific risks and have a very narrow (but direct) effect on financial reporting risks. Entities enter into many different types of transactions. In our example, paying suppliers is just one of dozens of different types of financial activities, and an organization will have activity-level controls for each of these activities. Additionally, for each transaction type, the company may face many different kinds of risk, each requiring a different kind of activity-level control. For example, not only will companies want to make sure that they pay only approved suppliers, they also will want to make sure they pay the correct amount.
2. Many internal control systems include redundant controls—multiple controls that achieve the same objective. For example, the company may use a purchase order system to make sure that its buyers are approved to enter into transactions. In addition, a manager may periodically compare actual purchases to budget to make sure that company buyers are staying within their approved limits.

Between the entity-level controls and preventive activity-level controls are the broad-based activity-level controls. A bank reconciliation is a good example of such a control. A bank reconciliation does not prevent the bookkeeper from entering an incorrect amount as a cash disbursement, but if such an error were made, a properly performed bank reconciliation should detect and correct it. Many broad-based activity-level controls are detective in nature and usually performed periodically, rather than on every transaction.

A top-down approach to internal control evaluation means that you start with entity-level controls, which have the broadest span but the most *indirect* effect on reducing financial statement misstatements. Once you have evaluated entity-level controls, you then proceed "down" to the more specific activity-level controls. At the activity level, you again begin "at the top," with those controls that are furthest along in the information processing stream. Usually, these are *detective* controls.

After evaluating detective controls, you may then proceed back down the information processing stream, back to the inception of the transaction, evaluating controls along the way.

The key to applying the top-down approach is to ask—at each step of the evaluation—"Are the controls I have evaluated so far capable of appropriately addressing the related risk of material misstatement?" If the answer is "yes," then there is no need to evaluate more controls. If the answer is "no," then you should continue to evaluate more controls further down in the structure until you reach a point where you have evaluated enough controls to evaluate the risk.

EFFECT OF IT ON INTERNAL CONTROL

IT affects the way in which transactions are initiated, recorded, processed, and reported. IT controls consist of automated controls (e.g., controls embedded in computer programs) and manual controls. Manual controls may be independent of IT, may use information produced by IT, or may be limited (1) to monitoring the effective function of IT and of automated controls and (2) to handling exceptions. An entity's mix of controls varies with the nature and complexity of its use of IT. IT enables an entity to:

1. Consistently apply predefined business rules and perform complex calculations in processing large volumes of transactions or data
2. Enhance the timeliness, availability, and accuracy of information
3. Facilitate the additional analysis of information
4. Enhance the ability to monitor the performance of activities and its policies and procedures
5. Reduce the risk that controls will be circumvented
6. Enhance the ability to achieve effective segregation of duties by implementing security controls

IT also poses specific risks to an entity's internal control, including:

1. Reliance on systems or programs that are inaccurately processing data, processing inaccurate data, or both
2. Unauthorized access to data that may result in destruction of data or improper changes to data, including the recording of unauthorized or nonexistent transactions or inaccurate recording of transactions
3. Unauthorized changes to data in master files
4. Unauthorized changes to systems or programs
5. Failure to make necessary changes to systems or programs
6. Inappropriate manual intervention
7. Potential loss of data

IT General Controls

IT general controls are entity-wide controls that apply to many if not all application systems and help ensure their continued, proper operation. For example, the effectiveness of an entity's controls relating to the access of its database will determine whether it will be successful in maintaining the integrity of that data, which may be used in a number of different applications.

If there are inadequate general controls, controls at the application level may not function properly and the information produced by the system may be largely unreliable. For that reason, IT general controls typically are included within the evaluation of internal control effectiveness.

But which IT general controls?

To answer this question, it is helpful to think of IT general controls as operating within three different domains, or stacks:

1. Database
2. Operating system
3. Network

There are three control objectives within each of these domains:

1. Systems are appropriately tested and validated prior to being placed into production.
2. Data are protected from unauthorized change.
3. Any problems or incidents in operations are properly responded to, recorded, investigated, and resolved.

To determine which IT general controls should be used for your evaluation, apply the risk-based, top-down approach. IT general controls will vary in how directly they affect the financial reporting process and therefore in the risk that their failure could result in a material misstatement of the financial statements.

IT General Controls That Are Unlikely to Affect the Financial Statements

Some IT control frameworks include controls that have only an indirect effect on IT systems. For example, the IT strategic plan and the overall IT organization and infrastructure may contribute indirectly to the effective functioning of IT systems and could be an area of interest for an IT auditor. However, these controls are so far removed from the financial reporting process that, in most situations, they will have only a negligible effect on the financial statements. The risk that a failure in one of these controls could result in a financial statement misstatement likewise is negligible. Thus, typically, these controls would not be included in an evaluation of controls over financial reporting.

IT General Controls That May Affect the Financial Reporting Process

Some IT systems process information that is not reflected in the financial statements. For example, an organization may have a sales and marketing system that tracks lead generation, customer contact information, and purchase history. IT general controls that affect the functioning of this system may or may not be included within the scope of an evaluation of financial reporting controls, depending on how management uses the information generated by the system.

For example, management and the sales team may use the information only to manage the sales process, in which case the sales system is not important to the financial reporting process. Or management may use the information generated from the sales system to monitor financial results, generate financial information, or perform some other control procedure.

For example, information in the sales system could be used to:

- Calculate bonuses to salespeople, an amount that is reported in the financial statements
- Generate a key performance indicator, which management uses to identify anomalies in the accounting records or financial statements
- Generate nonfinancial information, which management uses in its monitoring process

General controls related to nonfinancial systems may be included in management's evaluation if the risk of failure of the control is significant. If the risk is small, then the system can be excluded from the scope of the evaluation.

General Controls Directly Related to Financial Information

Other IT systems at an organization are directly related to the processing of financial information; these systems include the accounting system, the sales system, or the inventory management system. To the extent that these systems process significant financial information where a material misstatement could occur, they will be included within the scope of your evaluation.

IT systems that have a more direct effect on the financial reporting process typically are included within the scope of management's evaluation. Relevant IT general control objectives usually relate to:

- Logical access to programs and data
- Physical access to computer hardware and the physical environment within which the hardware operates
- System development and change

AU ILLUSTRATIONS

The following questionnaire will help the auditor assess risk. The existence of a condition covered by the questionnaire does not mean errors or fraud have occurred; it is a warning sign indicating increased risk in the audit areas affected. The questionnaire should be modified in accordance with the size and complexity of the entity.

| ILLUSTRATION 1. RISK ASSESSMENT QUESTIONNAIRE |

[Client]

[Audit Date]

[Prepared by / Date]   [Reviewed by / Date]

Instructions

This questionnaire should be completed before the start of fieldwork. Its purpose is to document and assess audit risk.

The information required to complete this questionnaire comes from the following sources:

1. Client responses to our inquiries
2. Our knowledge of general and industry economic conditions
3. Our knowledge of the client

This questionnaire is divided into two major sections: external and internal factors. It is designed so that every "Yes" answer adversely affects risk exposure.

For every "Yes" answer, the item should be referenced to the appropriate audit documentation. The audit documentation should state our assessment of the effect of the condition on the risk of material errors or fraud.

EXTERNAL FACTORS

	Yes	No	Working paper reference
General Economic and Financial Conditions			
1. Are there trade or other barriers to the client's international business?			
2. Have the client's domestic markets suffered from high unemployment?			
3. Have the client's domestic markets suffered from high inflation?			
4. Has legislation passed that adversely affects the client?			
5. Are interest rates high in relation to the client's capital needs?			
6. Has the client's business been adversely affected by changes in the following:			
a. Interest rates?			
b. Unemployment rates?			
c. Money supply?			
d. Foreign currency exchange rates?			
e. Overall business conditions (depression, recession, inflation)?			
Industry Economic and Financial Conditions			
1. Are the products of this industry subject to rapid obsolescence?			
2. Is the industry highly competitive?			
3. Have there been an unusual number of bankruptcies in this industry?			
4. Does the estimated income for the year deviate significantly from the industry?			
5. Did the industry experience a strike or other labor unrest?			
Uses and Users of Financial Statements			
1. Will the financial statements be filed with the SEC?			
2. Will the financial statements be submitted to the client's bank?			
3. Will the financial statements be submitted to credit agencies?			
4. Will the financial statements be submitted to stockholders?			
5. Will the financial statements be submitted to employees with reference to:			
a. Profit-sharing plans?			
b. Pension plans?			
c. Bonus arrangements?			
d. Other compensation arrangements?			
6. Will the financial statements be used in connection with negotiations relating to an acquisition or a disposal of a business or a segment of a business?			

	Yes	No	*Working paper reference*

7. Will the financial statements be used in connection with negotiations for

    a. A loan?
    b. Performance bond?
    c. Private sale of stock?

8. Are there other uses or users of these financial statements which may affect our risk? If so, list.

INTERNAL FACTORS

Management's Integrity

1. Are there any indications that management may lack integrity?
2. Does management desire favorable earnings because of the following:

    a. Need to meet forecasts?
    b. Need to support price of the entity's stock?
    c. Existence of management profit-sharing agreements?

3. Does management desire low earnings to reduce income taxes?
4. Is management dominated by one or a few individuals?
5. Does management have a poor reputation in the industry?
6. Does management have a reputation for taking unusual or unnecessary risks?
7. Has there been considerable turnover in senior management positions?
8. Are there other characteristics of management personnel that may affect our risk? If so, list.

Entity Organization

1. Does the entity lack an audit committee?
2. Does the entity fail to document its accounting system?
3. Does the entity fail to use internal auditors?
4. Do internal auditors, if any, not report to the audit committee or some other high organizational level of the entity?
5. Is the organization owner- or manager-dominated?
6. Does the entity fail to document job requirements?
7. Does management lack an understanding of accounting and administrative controls?
8. Does management fail to implement accounting and administrative controls?
9. Has management failed to correct material weaknesses in internal accounting control that can be corrected?
10. Are the entity's records generated to a significant degree by an EDP system?
11. Does the entity fail to maintain perpetual records of:

    a. Inventories?
    b. Long-lived assets?
    c. Investments?

12. If the entity maintains perpetual records, does it periodically compare them with physical counts?
13. Does management fail to communicate to other personnel a commitment to control?

	Yes	No	Working paper reference

14. Does the entity fail to maintain policy and procedures manuals?
15. Is there a high turnover of accounting and finance personnel?
16. Has the client recently changed auditors or attorneys?
17. Does a hostile relationship exist between our staff and management?
18. Has the client recently organized or acquired a subsidiary?

Financial Condition of Entity

1. Does the entity have insufficient working capital?
2. Does the entity have sufficient lines of credit?
3. Does the entity depend on relatively few customers?
4. Does the entity depend on relatively few suppliers?
5. Are there violations of debt covenants?
6. Has the entity recently experienced a significant period of losses?
7. Is the entity using short-term obligations to finance long-term projects?
8. Does the entity have excess productive capacity?
9. Does the entity have high fixed costs?
10. Has the entity experienced rapid expansion?
11. Does the entity have a significantly long operating cycle?
12. Does the entity have significant contingent liabilities?
13. Is the entity the defendant in any significant litigation?
14. Do major valuation problems exist, such as:
    a. Allowance for doubtful accounts?
    b. Inventories?
    c. Investment?
    d. Long-term construction contracts?
15. Has the client experienced severe losses from investments or joint ventures?

Nature of Transactions

1. Does the entity engage in a significant number of consignment purchases or sales?
2. Does the entity engage in significant cash transactions?
3. Does the entity engage in significant related-party transactions?
4. Has the entity engaged in significant unusual transactions during the year or near the end of the year?
5. Are there any questions on the timing of revenue recognition?

ILLUSTRATION 2. EXAMPLE CONTROL OBJECTIVES

Business Objective	*Example Control Objectives*
Corporate Culture	
Establish a culture and a tone at the top that fosters integrity, shared values, and teamwork in pursuit of the entity's objectives.	• Articulate and communicate codes of conduct and other policies regarding acceptable business practice, conflicts of interest, and expected standards of ethical and moral behavior. • Reduce incentives and temptations that can motivate employees to act in a manner that is unethical, opposed to the entity's objectives, or both. • Reinforce written policies about ethical behavior through action and leadership by example.
Personnel Policies	
The entity's personnel have been provided with the information, resources, and support necessary to effectively carry out their responsibilities.	• Identify, articulate, and communicate to entity personnel the information and skills needed to perform their jobs effectively. • Provide entity personnel with the resources needed to perform their jobs effectively. • Supervise and monitor individuals with internal control responsibilities. • Delegate authority and responsibility to appropriate individuals within the organization.
IT General Controls	

The entity's general IT policies enable the effective functioning of computer applications related to the financial reporting process.	• Logical access control protects the following, which are used in the financial reporting process:
	  • Systems
	  • Data
	  • Application, utility, and other programs
	  • Spreadsheets
	• Installation of suitable computer operating environment and controls over the physical access to hardware.
	• Proper functioning of new, upgraded, and modified systems and applications, including plans for migration, conversion, testing, and acceptance.

Risk Identification	
Implement a process that effectively identifies and responds to conditions that can significantly affect the entity's ability to achieve its financial reporting objectives.	• Identify what can go wrong in the preparation of the financial statements at a sufficient level of detail that allows management to design and implement controls to mitigate risk effectively. • Continuously identify and assess risk to account for changes in external and internal conditions.

Business Objective	*Example Control Objectives*
Antifraud Programs and Controls	
Reduce the incidence of fraud.	• Create a culture of honesty and high ethics. • Evaluate antifraud processes and controls. • Develop an effective antifraud oversight process.
Period-End Financial Reporting Processes	

Nonroutine, nonsystematic financial reporting adjustments are appropriately identified and approved.	• Management is aware of and understands the need for certain financial reporting adjustments.
	• Information required for decision-making purposes is:
	  • Identified, gathered, and communicated
	  • Relevant and reliable
	• Management analyzes the information and responds appropriately.
	• Management's response is reviewed and approved.

Selection and application of accounting principles result in financial statements that are "fairly presented."	• Management identifies events and transactions for which accounting policy choices should be made or existing policies reconsidered. • The accounting policies chosen by management have general acceptance and result in a fair presentation of financial statement information. • Information processing and internal control policies and procedures are designed to apply the accounting principles selected appropriately.
Monitoring	

Identify material weaknesses and changes in internal control that require disclosure.	• Monitoring controls operate at a level of precision that would allow management to identify a material misstatement of the financial statements. This objective applies both to:
	  • Controls that monitor other controls
	  • Controls that monitor financial information

Business Objective	Example Control Objectives

Activity-Level Control Objectives

Adequately control the initiation, processing, and disclosure of transactions.	• Identify, analyze, and manage risks that may cause material misstatements of the financial statements. • Design and implement an information system to record, process, summarize, and report transactions accurately. • Design and implement control activities, including policies and procedures applied in the processing of transactions that flow through the accounting system, in order to prevent or promptly detect material misstatements. • Monitor the design and operating effectiveness of activity-level internal controls to determine if they are operating as intended and, if not, to take corrective action.

AU 315 Communications Between Predecessor and Successor Auditors

AU-C 510 Opening Balances—Initial Audit Engagements, Including Reaudit Engagements

AU-C 210 Terms of Engagement

AU EFFECTIVE DATE AND APPLICABILITY

Original Pronouncement Statements on Auditing Standards (SASs) 84 and 93

Effective Date All standards currently are effective.

Applicability Because of some complexities in applicability, additional explanation is provided below.

AU-C EFFECTIVE DATE AND SUMMARY OF CHANGES

SAS No. 122, *Codification of Auditing Standards and Procedures,* is effective for audits of financial statements with periods ending on or after December 15, 2012.

AU-C Section 210 supersedes AU Section 315 paragraphs .03, .05–.10, and .14. The changes are primarily clarifying changes.

AU-C Section 510 .01–.02, .04, .11–.13, and .15–.23. AU-C Section 315:

- Makes clear that reviewing a predecessor auditor's audit documentation cannot be the only procedure performed to obtain sufficient appropriate audit evidence regarding opening balances
- Clarifies that initial audit engagements include reaudits

- Includes an appendix: *Illustrative Report with Disclaimer of Opinion*, and
- Requires the auditor to obtain sufficient appropriate audit evidence about whether:
  - Opening balances contain misstatements that materially affect the current period's financial statements, and
  - Accounting policies reflected in the opening balances have been consistently applied in the current period's financial statements; and changes in the accounting policies have been properly accounted for, adequately presented, and disclosed in accordance with the applicable financial reporting framework

APPLICABILITY

This section applies when a change of auditors has occurred or is in process for an audit of financial statements in accordance with generally accepted auditing standards (GAAS). This section applies to both predecessor and successor auditors. It also provides guidance when a successor becomes aware of possible misstatements in financial statements reported on by a predecessor auditor.

The section applies whenever an auditor is considering accepting an engagement to audit or reaudit financial statements, and after such auditor has been appointed to perform such an engagement. The provisions are not required if the most recent audited financial statements are more than two years prior to the beginning of the earliest period to be audited by the successor auditor.

The section also applies to engagements when a successor auditor is replaced before completing an audit engagement and issuing a report. In such situations, there are two predecessor auditors: the auditor who reported on the most recent audited financial statements and the auditor who was engaged to perform but did not complete the engagement.

This section does not discuss quality control policies pertaining to client acceptance. One of the procedures for client acceptance required by Statement on Quality Control Standards (SQCS) 2, however, is communication with the predecessor auditor.

AU DEFINITIONS OF TERMS

Predecessor auditor. An auditor who (1) has reported on the most recent audited financial statements or was engaged to perform, but did not complete, an audit of the financial statements, and (2) has resigned, declined to stand for reappointment, or been notified that his or her services have been, or may be, terminated.

Successor auditor. An auditor who is considering accepting an engagement to audit financial statements but has not yet communicated with the predecessor auditor, and an auditor who has accepted such an engagement.

AU-C SECTION 510 DEFINITIONS OF TERMS

Source: AU-C Section 510.05

Initial audit engagement. An engagement in which either (1) the financial statements for the prior period were not audited, or (2) the financial statements for the prior period were audited by a predecessor auditor.

Opening balances. Those account balances that exist at the beginning of the period. Opening balances are based upon the closing balances of the prior period and reflect the effects of transactions and events of prior periods and accounting policies applied in the prior period. Opening balances also include matters requiring disclosure that existed at the beginning of the period, such as contingencies and commitments.

Predecessor auditor. The auditor from a different audit firm who has reported on the most recent audited financial statements or was engaged to perform but did not complete an audit of the financial statements.

Reaudit. An initial audit engagement to audit financial statements that have been previously audited by a predecessor auditor.

OBJECTIVES OF AU SECTION 315

The key topics addressed in SAS 84 are that it:

- Revises the definitions of predecessor and successor auditors to reflect the existing proposal environment.
- Expands the required communications with the predecessor auditor before the successor auditor accepts an engagement to include inquiries about communications made by the predecessor auditor to audit committees or others with equivalent authority and responsibility as described in Section 316, *Consideration of Fraud in a Financial Statement Audit*, Section 317, *Illegal Acts by Clients*, and Section 325, *Communicating Internal Control Related Matters Identified in an Audit*.
- Clarifies the successor auditor's responsibility for obtaining evidence used in analyzing opening balances for the current-year financial statements and consistency of accounting principles.
- Expands the audit documentation ordinarily made available to the successor auditor by the predecessor auditor, to include documentation of planning, internal control, audit results, and other matters of continuing audit significance.
- Introduces an illustrative client consent and acknowledgment letter and an illustrative successor auditor acknowledgment letter (see *Illustrations*). A predecessor auditor may conclude that obtaining written communications from both the former client and the successor auditor will enable greater communication between both parties and greater access to the audit documentation than would be the case in the absence of such communications. The Auditing Standards Board (ASB) believes that it is in the public interest for successor auditors to have greater access to the audit documentation and, accordingly, for all auditors to have access to these letters and to use them in their practice. However, these letters are presented for illustrative purposes only and not required.

Any auditor who is engaged to perform an audit, but does not complete the audit, is considered a predecessor auditor.

OBJECTIVES OF AU-C SECTION 510

AU-C Section 510 states that:

. . . the objective of the auditor, in conducting an initial audit engagement, including a reaudit engagement, is to obtain sufficient appropriate audit evidence regarding opening balances about whether

> a. *opening balances contain misstatements that materially affect the current period's financial statements and*
> b. *appropriate accounting policies reflected in the opening balances have been consistently applied in the current period's financial statements or changes thereto are appropriately accounted for and adequately presented and disclosed in accordance with the applicable financial reporting framework.*

FUNDAMENTAL REQUIREMENTS

CHANGE OF AUDITORS

An auditor should not accept an engagement until the communications described in "Communications Before Acceptance" below have been evaluated. However, an auditor may make a proposal for an audit engagement before communicating with the predecessor auditor.

Other communications, described in "Other Communications" below, are advisable to assist in the planning of the engagement. However, the decision whether to make these other communications and the timing of them is more flexible (i.e., they may be initiated prior to engagement acceptance or subsequent thereto).

When more than one auditor is considering accepting an engagement, the predecessor auditor should not be expected to be available to respond to inquiries until a successor auditor has accepted the engagement subject to the evaluation of the "Communications Before Acceptance."

Initiative for Communicating

The successor auditor should initiate the communication. The communication may be either written or oral. Both the predecessor and successor auditors should treat any information obtained from each other as confidential information.

Communications before Acceptance

Inquiry of the predecessor auditor is required because the predecessor may provide information that will assist the successor auditor in deciding whether to accept the engagement.

The successor auditor should request permission from the prospective client to make an inquiry of the predecessor *prior to final acceptance of the engagement*. The successor auditor should ask the prospective client to authorize the predecessor to respond fully to the successor auditor's inquiries. If a prospective client refuses to permit the predecessor auditor to respond or limits the response, the successor auditor should inquire as to the reasons and consider the implications of that refusal in deciding whether to accept the engagement.

The successor auditor should make specific and reasonable inquiries of the predecessor about:

1. Information about management's integrity
2. Disagreements with management about accounting principles, auditing procedures, or other similarly significant matters
3. Communications to audit committees or others with equivalent authority and responsibility regarding fraud (Section 316), illegal acts by clients (Section 317), and internal control–related matters (Section 325)
4. The predecessor auditor's understanding concerning the reasons for the change of auditors

The predecessor auditor should respond promptly, fully, and factually. However, if the predecessor decides, due to unusual circumstances such as impending, threatened, or potential litigation; disciplinary proceedings; or other unusual circumstances, not to respond fully, he or she should indicate that the response is limited.

If the successor auditor receives a limited response, that auditor should consider the implications of the limited response in deciding whether to accept the engagement.

Other Communications

The successor auditor should ask that the client authorize the predecessor to allow a review of the predecessor auditor's audit documentation. (*Illustrations* contains a client consent and acknowledgment letter that may be used by the predecessor auditor.) Before permitting access to the audit documentation, the predecessor auditor may obtain a written communication from the successor auditor about the use of the audit documentation. (*Illustrations* contains a successor auditor acknowledgment letter.)

The predecessor auditor should:

1. Determine the audit documentation to be made available for review and whether the documentation may be copied
2. Ordinarily allow the successor auditor to review audit documentation, including documentation of planning, internal control, audit results, and other matters of continuing accounting and auditing significance, such as the documented analysis of balance sheet accounts, and documentation relating to contingencies
3. Reach an understanding with the successor auditor about the use of the audit documentation (the extent, if any, to which a predecessor auditor allows access to the audit documentation is a matter of professional judgment)

SUCCESSOR AUDITOR'S USE OF COMMUNICATIONS

The successor auditor should obtain sufficient competent evidence to afford a basis for expressing an opinion. For the successor auditor, the communication with his or her predecessor will provide evidence about:

- The impact of the opening balances on the current year financial statements
- The consistency of accounting principles
- The risk of material misstatement (that is, the communication may be considered a risk assessment procedure.)

Determining the relevance and reliability of this evidence is a matter of professional judgment. Audit evidence may include:

1. The most recent audited financial statements
2. The predecessor auditor's report
3. The results of inquiries of the predecessor auditor

4. The results of the successor auditor's review of the predecessor's audit documentation for to the most recently completed audit
5. Audit procedures performed on the current period's transactions

The successor auditor may wish to make inquiries about the professional reputation and standing of the predecessor auditor (Section 543, *Part of Audit Performed by Other Independent Auditors*).

In reporting on the audit, the successor auditor should not refer to the report or work of the predecessor auditor in his or her audit report to support the successor auditor's opinion.

AUDITS OF FINANCIAL STATEMENTS THAT HAVE BEEN PREVIOUSLY AUDITED

If an auditor is asked to audit financial statements that have been previously audited (i.e., a reaudit), the auditor considering whether to accept the reaudit engagement is also a successor auditor, and the auditor who previously reported is also a predecessor auditor.

In addition to the communications described in "Communications before Acceptance" above, the auditor should state that the purpose of the inquiries is to obtain information about whether to accept an engagement to reaudit the financial statements. If the successor auditor accepts the reaudit engagement, he or she may consider the information obtained from inquiries of the predecessor auditor and review of the predecessor auditor's report and audit documentation for the purpose of planning the reaudit. However, the information obtained from those inquiries and any review of the predecessor auditor's report and audit documentation is not a sufficient basis for issuing an opinion.

The successor auditor should plan and perform the reaudit in accordance with GAAS, but should not assume responsibility for the predecessor auditor's work or issue a report that reflects divided responsibility. The predecessor auditor is not considered a specialist (Section 336) or an internal auditor (Section 322).

If, in a reaudit engagement, the successor auditor cannot obtain sufficient competent evidential matter to express an opinion on the financial statements, the successor auditor's opinion should be qualified or the successor should disclaim an opinion because of the inability to perform necessary procedures.

The successor auditor should ask for audit documentation for the period or periods under reaudit and the period prior to the reaudit period. However, the extent of access to the audit documentation is a matter of the predecessor auditor's judgment.

When performing the reaudit, the successor auditor should, when inventory is material, observe or perform some physical counts of inventory at a date after the reaudit period, in connection with a current audit or otherwise, and apply appropriate tests of intervening transactions.

DISCOVERY OF POSSIBLE MISSTATEMENTS IN FINANCIAL STATEMENTS REPORTED ON BY A PREDECESSOR

During the audit or reaudit, the successor auditor may become aware of information that may indicate that financial statements reported on by the predecessor auditor require revision. In this situation, the successor auditor should ask that the client inform the predecessor auditor and arrange for the three parties to discuss this information and try to resolve the matter.

The successor auditor should communicate to the predecessor auditor any information discussed in Section 561, *Subsequent Discovery of Facts Existing at the Date of the Auditor's Report*, that the predecessor may need to consider.

If the client will not inform the predecessor auditor or if the successor auditor is not satisfied with the way that the matter is resolved, the successor auditor should consider (1) any potential implications on the current engagement, (2) whether to resign from the engagement, and (3) whether consultation with legal counsel about further action is appropriate.

INTERPRETATIONS

There are no interpretations for this section.

PROFESSIONAL ISSUES TASK FORCE PRACTICE ALERTS

97-3 CHANGES IN AUDITORS AND RELATED TOPICS

This Practice Alert provides guidance to successor auditors when there has been a change of auditors. The alert clarifies the successor auditor's responsibility for:

- Requesting that the client authorize a review of the predecessor auditor's audit documentation.
- Analyzing opening balances on the current year financial statements and for evaluating the consistency of accounting principles.

If the successor auditor is not allowed access to the predecessor auditor's audit documentation, the successor auditor should use professional judgment in determining the nature, timing, and extent of procedures to be performed on opening balances, including determining the need to audit the previous financial statements.

The practice alert also gives guidance on requests to reissue reports. Guidance on reissuing reports is discussed in Section 508.

TECHNIQUES FOR APPLICATION

REVISIONS OF FINANCIAL STATEMENTS REPORTED ON BY THE PREDECESSOR AUDITOR

It is possible that during the audit the successor auditor will become aware of information that leads him or her to believe that financial statements reported on by the predecessor may require revision. The successor should prepare a worksheet with appropriate supporting documentation and should request the client to arrange a meeting between the predecessor, the successor, and the client.

NOTE: *If the client refuses, or if the successor is not satisfied with the results of the conference, the successor should consult his or her attorney.*

At the meeting, the predecessor auditor is advised to do the following:

1. Review the worksheet and supporting documentation of the successor auditor
2. Determine whether the report should be revised

If the predecessor auditor determines that the report should be revised, the guidance provided in Section 561, *Subsequent Discovery of Facts Existing at the Date of the Auditor's Report*, may be pertinent.

REISSUANCE OF PREDECESSOR'S REPORT

Generally, business enterprises present their financial statements for the current and preceding years. For example, the SEC requires presentation of the two most recent annual balance sheets and the three most recent statements of income and cash flows. In these situations, the successor auditor may do the following:

1. Refer to the predecessor's previously issued report in his or her report, but only as it relates to the financial statements of the prior year on which the predecessor reported
2. Request that the client ask the predecessor auditor to reissue the previously issued report

Guidance and illustrations on reference to, and reissuance of, the predecessor's previously issued report are provided in Section 508.

AU ILLUSTRATIONS

Following are illustrations of (1) client consent and acknowledgment, and (2) a successor auditor acknowledgment letter. (The equivalent AU-C 510 illustrations and the illustrative Report with Disclaimer of Opinion follow these two AU 315 illustrations.)

ILLUSTRATION 1. ILLUSTRATIVE CLIENT CONSENT AND ACKNOWLEDGMENT LETTER

The predecessor auditor may request a consent and acknowledgment letter from the client to reduce misunderstandings about the scope of the communications being authorized. The following letter is presented for illustrative purposes only and is not required by professional standards.

June 30, 20X6

Widget Enterprises
Anytown, NY

You have given your consent to allow Smith & Jones, LLP, as successor independent auditors for Widget Enterprises (Widget), access to our audit documentation for our audit of the December 31, 20X5 financial statements of Widget. You also have given your consent to us to respond fully to Smith & Jones, LLP inquiries. You understand and agree that the review of our audit documentation is undertaken solely for the purpose of obtaining an understanding about Widget and certain information about our audit to assist Smith & Jones, LLP in planning the audit of the December 31, 20X6 financial statements of Widget.

Please confirm your agreement with the foregoing by signing and dating a copy of this letter and returning it to us.

Attached is the form of the letter we will furnish Smith & Jones, LLP regarding the use of the audit documentation.

Very truly yours,

Hemingway & Masterson, LLC
By: _____

Accepted:

Widget Enterprises
By: _____   Date: _____

ILLUSTRATION 2. ILLUSTRATIVE SUCCESSOR AUDITOR ACKNOWLEDGMENT LETTER

The following letter is presented for illustrative purposes only and is not required by professional standards.

August 30, 20X6

Smith & Jones, LLP
Anytown, NY

We have previously audited, in accordance with auditing standards generally accepted in the United States of America, the December 31, 20X5 financial statements of Widget Enterprises (Widget). We rendered a report on those financial statements and have not performed any audit procedures subsequent to the audit report date. In connection with your audit of Widget's 20X6 financial statements, you have requested access to our audit documentation prepared in connection with that audit. Widget has authorized our firm to allow you to review that audit documentation.

Our audit, and the audit documentation prepared in connection therewith, of Widget's financial statements was not planned or conducted in contemplation of your review. Therefore, items of possible interest to you may not have been specifically addressed. Our use of professional judgment and the assessment of audit risk and materiality for the purpose of our audit means that matters may have existed that would have been assessed differently by you. We make no representation as to the sufficiency or appropriateness of the information in our audit documentation for your purposes.

We understand that the purpose of your review is to obtain information about Widget and our 20X5 audit results to assist you in planning your 20X6 audit of Widget. For that purpose only, we will provide you access to our audit documentation that relates to that objective.

Upon request, we will provide copies of that audit documentation that provide factual information about Widget. You agree to subject any such copies or information otherwise derived from our audit documentation to your normal policy for retention of audit documentation and protection of confidential client information. Furthermore, in the event of a third-party request for access to our audit documentation prepared in connection with your audits of Widget, you agree to obtain our permission before voluntarily allowing any such access to our audit documentation or information otherwise derived from our audit documentation, and to obtain on our behalf any releases that you obtain from such third party. You agree to advise us promptly and provide us a copy of any subpoena, summons, or other court order for access to your audit documentation that include copies of our audit documentation or information otherwise derived therefrom.

Because your review of our audit documentation is undertaken solely for the purpose described above and may not entail a review of all our audit documentation, you agree that (1) the information obtained from the review will not be used by you for any other purpose, (2) you will not comment, orally or in writing, to anyone as a result of that review as to whether our audit was performed in accordance with auditing standards generally accepted in the United States of America, (3) you will not provide expert testimony or litigation services or otherwise accept an engagement to comment on issues relating to the quality of our audits, and (4) you will not use the audit procedures or results thereof documented in our audit documentation as evidential matter in rendering your opinion on the 20X6 financial statements of Widget, except as contemplated in Statement on Auditing Standards 84.

Please confirm your agreement with the foregoing by signing and dating a copy of this letter and returning it to us.

Very truly yours,

Hemingway and Masterson, LLC
By: _____

Accepted:

Smith & Jones, LLP
By: _____ Date: _____

AU-C 510 ILLUSTRATIONS

> **ILLUSTRATION 1. REPORT WITH DISCLAIMER OF OPINION ON RESULTS OF OPERATIONS AND CASH FLOWS AND UNMODIFIED OPINION ON FINANCIAL POSITION**

Circumstances include the following:

- The auditor did not observe the counting of the physical inventory at the beginning of the current period and was unable to obtain sufficient appropriate audit evidence regarding the opening balances of inventory.
- The possible effects of the inability to obtain sufficient appropriate audit evidence regarding opening balances of inventory are deemed to be material and pervasive to the entity's results of operations and cash flows.
- The financial position at year-end is fairly presented.
- A disclaimer of opinion regarding the results of operations and cash flows and an unmodified opinion regarding financial position are considered appropriate in the circumstances.

Independent Auditor's Report

[*Appropriate Addressee*]

Report on the Financial Statements

We have audited the accompanying balance sheet of ABC Company as of December 31, 20X1, and were engaged to audit the related statements of income, changes in stockholders' equity, and cash flows for the year then ended, and the related notes to the financial statements.

Management's Responsibility for the Financial Statements

Management is responsible for the preparation and fair presentation of these financial statements in accordance with accounting principles generally accepted in the United States of America; this includes the design, implementation, and maintenance of internal control relevant to the preparation and fair presentation of financial statements that are free from material misstatement, whether due to fraud or error.

Auditor's Responsibility

Our responsibility is to express an opinion on these financial statements based on conducting the audit in accordance with auditing standards generally accepted in the United States of America. Because of the matters described in the Basis for Disclaimer of Opinion paragraph, however, we were not able to obtain sufficient appropriate audit evidence to provide a basis for an audit opinion on the income statement and the cash flow statement.

We conducted our audit of the balance sheet in accordance with auditing standards generally accepted in the United States of America. Those standards require that we plan and perform the audit to obtain reasonable assurance about whether the balance sheet is free from material misstatement.

An audit involves performing procedures to obtain audit evidence about the amounts and disclosures in the financial statements. The procedures selected depend on the auditor's judgment, including the assessment of the risks of material misstatement of the financial statements, whether due to fraud or error. In making those risk assessments, the auditor considers internal control relevant to the entity's preparation and fair presentation of the financial statements in order to design audit procedures that are appropriate in the circumstances, but not for the purpose of expressing an opinion on the effectiveness of the entity's internal control. Accordingly, we express no such opinion. An audit also includes evaluating the appropriateness of accounting policies used and the reasonableness of significant accounting estimates made by management, as well as evaluating the overall presentation of the financial statements.

We believe that the audit evidence we have obtained is sufficient and appropriate to provide a basis for our unmodified opinion on the financial position.

Basis for Disclaimer of Opinion on the Results of Operations and Cash Flows

We were not engaged as auditors of the Company until after December 31, 20X0, and, therefore, did not observe the counting of physical inventories at the beginning of the year. We were unable to satisfy ourselves by performing other auditing procedures concerning the inventory held at December 31, 20X0. Since opening inventories enter into the determination of net income and cash flows, we were unable to determine whether any adjustments might have been necessary in respect of the profit for the year reported in the income statement and the net cash flows from operating activities reported in the cash flow statement.

Disclaimer of Opinion on the Results of Operations and Cash Flows

Because of the significance of the matter described in the Basis for Disclaimer of Opinion paragraph, we have not been able to obtain sufficient appropriate audit evidence to provide a basis for an audit opinion on the results of operations and cash flows for the year ended December 31, 20X1. Accordingly, we do not express an opinion on the results of operations and cash flows for the year ended December 31, 20X1.

Opinion on the Financial Position

In our opinion, the balance sheet presents fairly, in all material respects, the financial position of ABC Company as of December 31, 20X1, in accordance with accounting principles generally accepted in the United States of America.

Report on Other Legal and Regulatory Requirements

[*Form and content of this section of the auditor's report will vary depending on the nature of the auditor's other reporting responsibilities.*]

[*Auditor's signature*]

[*Auditor's city and state*]

[*Date of the auditor's report*]

ILLUSTRATION 2. ENTITY CONSENT AND ACKNOWLEDGMENT LETTER

Paragraph .07 requires that the auditor request management to authorize the predecessor auditor to allow a review of the predecessor auditor's audit documentation and for the predecessor auditor to respond fully to inquiries by the auditor, thereby providing the auditor with information to assist in planning and performing the engagement. Paragraph .A4 states that the predecessor auditor may request a consent and acknowledgment letter from the entity to document this authorization in an effort to reduce misunderstandings about the scope of the communications being authorized. The following letter is presented for illustrative purposes only and is not required by professional standards.

[*Date*]

ABC Enterprises

[*Address*]

You have given your consent to allow [*name of successor CPA firm*], as independent auditors for ABC Enterprises (ABC), access to our audit documentation for our audit of the December 31, 20X1 financial statements of ABC. You also have given your consent to us to respond fully to [*name of successor CPA firm*] inquiries. You understand and agree that the review of our audit documentation is undertaken solely for the purpose of obtaining an understanding about ABC and certain information about our audit to assist [*name of successor CPA firm*] in planning and performing the audit of the December 31, 20X2 financial statements of ABC.

Please confirm your agreement with the foregoing by signing and dating a copy of this letter and returning it to us.

Attached is the form of the letter we will furnish [*name of successor CPA firm*] regarding the use of the audit documentation.

Very truly yours,

[*Predecessor Auditor*]

By: _____

Accepted:

ABC Enterprises

By: _____

Date: _____

ILLUSTRATION 3. ILLUSTRATIVE SUCCESSOR AUDITOR ACKNOWLEDGMENT LETTER

Paragraph .A6 states that the predecessor auditor may request that the auditor confirm in writing his or her agreement regarding the use of the predecessor auditor's audit documentation before permitting access to it. The following letter is presented for illustrative purposes only and is not required by professional standards.

[*Date*]

[*Successor Auditor*]

[*Address*]

We have previously audited, in accordance with auditing standards generally accepted in the United States of America, the December 31, 20X1 financial statements of ABC Enterprises (ABC). We rendered a report on those financial statements and have not performed any audit procedures subsequent to the audit report date. In connection with your audit of ABC's 20X2 financial statements, you have requested access to our audit documentation prepared in connection with that audit. ABC has authorized our firm to allow you to review that audit documentation.

Our audit, and the audit documentation prepared in connection therewith, of ABC's financial statements were not planned or conducted in contemplation of your review. Therefore, items of possible interest to you may not have been specifically addressed. Our use of professional judgment and the assessment of audit risk and materiality for the purpose of our audit mean that matters may have existed that would have been assessed differently by you. We make no representation about the sufficiency or appropriateness of the information in our audit documentation for your purposes.

We understand that the purpose of your review is to obtain information about ABC and our 20X1 audit results to assist you in planning and performing your 20X2 audit of ABC. For that purpose only, we will provide you access to our audit documentation that relates to that objective.

Upon request, we will provide copies of audit documentation that provides factual information about ABC. You agree to subject any such copies or information otherwise derived from our audit documentation to your normal policy for retention of audit documentation and protection of confidential entity information. Furthermore, in the event of a third-party request for access to your audit documentation prepared in connection with your audits of ABC, you agree to obtain our permission before voluntarily allowing any such access to our audit documentation or information otherwise derived from our audit documentation, and to obtain on our behalf any releases that you obtain from such third party. You agree to advise us promptly and provide us a copy of any subpoena, summons, or other court order for access to your audit documentation that include copies of our audit documentation or information otherwise derived therefrom.

Please confirm your agreement with the foregoing by signing and dating a copy of this letter and returning it to us.

Very truly yours,

[*Predecessor Auditor*]

By: _____

Accepted:

[*Successor Auditor*]

By: _____

Date: _____

Even with management's consent, access to the predecessor auditor's audit documentation may still be limited. Experience has shown that the predecessor auditor may be willing to grant broader access if given additional assurance concerning the use of the audit documentation. Accordingly, the auditor might consider agreeing to the following additional limitations on the review of the predecessor auditor's audit documentation in order to obtain broader access:

- The auditor will not comment, orally or in writing, to anyone as a result of the review about whether the predecessor auditor's engagement was performed in accordance with generally accepted auditing standards.
- The auditor will not provide expert testimony or litigation support services or otherwise accept an engagement to comment on issues relating to the quality of the predecessor auditor's audit.
- The auditor accepts sole responsibility for the nature, timing, and extent of audit work performed and the conclusions reached in expressing an opinion on the 20X2 financial statements of ABC.

The following paragraph illustrates the previous text:

Because your review of our audit documentation is undertaken solely for the purpose described previously and may not entail a review of all our audit documentation, you agree that (1) the information obtained from the review will not be used by you for any other purpose, (2) you will not comment, orally or in writing, to anyone as a result of that review about whether our audit was performed in accordance with generally accepted auditing standards, (3) you will not provide expert testimony or litigation support services or otherwise accept an engagement to comment on issues relating to the quality of our audit, and (4) you accept sole responsibility for the nature, timing and extent of audit work performed and the conclusions reached in expressing your opinion on the 20X2 financial statements of ABC.

AU 316 Consideration of Fraud in a Financial Statement Audit[1]

AU-C 240 Consideration of Fraud in a Financial Statement Audit

AU EFFECTIVE DATE AND APPLICABILITY

Original Pronouncement	Statement on Auditing Standards (SAS) 99
Effective Date	This standard currently is effective.
Applicability	Audits of financial statements in accordance with generally accepted auditing standards (GAAS).

AU-C EFFECTIVE DATE

SAS No. 122, *Codification of Auditing Standards and Procedures,* is effective for audits of financial statements with periods ending on or after December 15, 2012.

AU-C 230 does not change extant requirements in any significant respect. The definition of fraud was changed to conform to ISA 240.

AU DEFINITIONS OF TERMS

Fraud. An intentional act that results in a material misstatement in financial statements that are the subject of an audit. The primary distinction between fraud and error is whether the underlying action that causes the misstatement of the financial statements is intentional or unintentional.

Fraud risk factors. Events or conditions that indicate incentives/pressures to perpetrate fraud, opportunities to carry out the fraud, or attitudes/rationalizations to justify a fraudulent action. These conditions may alert the auditor to a possibility that fraud may exist.

---

[1] The section is affected by the Public Company Accounting Oversight Board's (PCAOB) Standard, Conforming Amendments to PCAOB Interim Standards Resulting from the Adoption of PCAOB Auditing Standard No. 5, An Audit of Internal Control Over Financial Reporting Performed in Conjunction with an Audit of Financial Statements.

Misstatements arising from fraudulent financial reporting. Intentional misstatements or omissions of amounts or disclosures in financial statements designed to deceive financial statement users when the effect causes the financial statements not to be presented, in all material respects, in conformity with generally accepted accounting principles (GAAP).

Misstatements arising from misappropriation of assets. The theft of an entity's assets where the effect of the theft causes the financial statements not to be presented in conformity with GAAP (sometimes referred to as defalcation).

AU-C DEFINITIONS OF TERMS

Source: 240.11

Fraud. An intentional act by one or more individuals among management, those charged with governance, employees, or third parties, involving the use of deception that results in a misstatement in financial statements that are the subject of an audit.

Fraud risk factors. Events or conditions that indicate an incentive or pressure to perpetrate fraud, provide an opportunity to commit fraud, or indicate attitudes or rationalizations to justify a fraudulent action.

OBJECTIVES OF AU SECTION 316

The accounting profession has always had trouble explaining to critics why an audit conducted in accordance with professional standards might fail to detect a material misstatement of financial statements caused by fraud.

Over the years, there have been several pronouncements issued to attempt to explain the auditor's responsibility for fraud detection. This section is the latest attempt.

In its March 1993 report *In the Public Interest*, the Public Oversight Board (POB) of the American Institute of Certified Public Accountants (AICPA) Securities and Exchange Commission (SEC) Practice section noted: "Attacks on the accounting profession from a variety of sources suggested a significant public concern over the profession's performance. Of particular moment is the widespread belief that auditors have a responsibility for detecting management fraud which they are not now meeting." The POB, in its report, made two recommendations addressing fraud. They were:

1. Accounting firms should ensure that auditors more consistently implement, and be more sensitive to the need to exercise, the professional skepticism required by SAS 53.
2. The ASB, the SEC Practice section, or some other appropriate body should develop guidelines to assist auditors in assessing the likelihood that fraud which may affect financial information may be occurring, and to specify additional auditing procedures when there is a heightened likelihood of management fraud.

In 1993, AICPA's Board of Directors issued a report, *Meeting the Financial Reporting Needs of the Future: A Public Commitment from the Public Accounting Profession.* In this report, AICPA's Board of Directors supported recommendations and initiatives of others to assist auditors in the detection of material misstatements in financial statements resulting from fraud, and encouraged every participant in the financial reporting process—management, their advisors, regulators, and independent auditors—to share in this responsibility.

The Auditing Standards Board (ASB) decided to undertake a project on fraud in large measure because of the Expectation Gap Roundtable findings and the reports of the POB and the AICPA's Board of Directors. In keeping with its commitment to serve the public interest by improving the detection of material fraud in financial statements, the ASB issued SAS 82, *Consideration of Fraud in a Financial Statement Audit*, in 1997. SAS 82 provided expanded operational guidance on the consideration of fraud in conducting a financial statement audit. It also strengthened the auditor's ability to fulfill his or her responsibility to plan and perform the audit to obtain reasonable assurance about whether financial statements are free of material misstatements, whether caused by error or fraud.

After SAS 82 was issued, several developments occurred.

- The ASB formed the Fraud Research Steering Task Force, which sponsored five academic research projects to reexamine fraud.
- The POB's Panel on Audit Effectiveness, in its "Report and Recommendations" in 2000, included a number of recommendations concerning earnings management and fraud.
- The International Auditing Practices Committee of the International Federation of Accountants issued International Standard on Auditing (ISA) 240, *The Auditor's Responsibility to Consider Fraud and Error in an Audit of Financial Statements*. The ISA incorporated many of the concepts in SAS 82, but also provided guidance beyond that included in SAS 82.

In response to these developments, the ASB formed a new Fraud Task Force in 2000 to revise SAS 82. In 2002, the Auditing Standards Boards issued SAS 99, *Consideration of Fraud in a Financial Statement Audit*. The new SAS does not change the auditor's responsibility to plan and perform the audit to obtain reasonable assurance about whether the financial statements are free of material misstatement, whether caused by error or fraud. However, SAS 99 does establish specific new performance requirements and provides guidance to auditors in fulfilling that responsibility, as it relates to fraud.

OBJECTIVES OF AU-C SECTION 240

The objectives of the auditor are to:

1. Identify and assess the risks of material misstatement of the financial statements due to fraud;
2. Obtain sufficient appropriate audit evidence regarding the assessed risks of material misstatement due to fraud, through designing and implementing appropriate responses; and
3. Respond appropriately to fraud or suspected fraud identified during the audit.

FUNDAMENTAL REQUIREMENTS

BASIC REQUIREMENT

In every audit, the auditor is obligated to plan and perform the audit to obtain reasonable assurance about whether the financial statements are free of material misstatement, whether caused by error or fraud.

Professional Skepticism

As defined in Section 100-230, professional skepticism is an attitude that includes a questioning mind and critical assessment of audit evidence. The auditor should conduct the entire engagement with an attitude of professional skepticism, recognizing that fraud could be present, regardless of past experience with the entity or beliefs about management's integrity. The auditor should not let his or her beliefs about management's integrity allow the auditor to be satisfied with any audit evidence that is less than persuasive. Finally, the auditor should continuously question whether information and evidence obtained suggest that material misstatement caused by fraud has occurred.

Engagement Team Discussion about Fraud ("Brainstorming")

When planning the audit, members of the audit team should discuss where and how the financial statements may be susceptible to material misstatement caused by fraud. This discussion should include the following:

- Exchange ideas and brainstorm about where the financial statements are susceptible to fraud, how assets could be stolen, and how management might engage in fraudulent financial reporting.
- Emphasize the need to maintain the proper mindset throughout the audit regarding the potential for fraud. As previously discussed, the auditor should continually exercise professional skepticism and have a questioning mind when performing the audit and evaluating audit evidence. Engagement team members should thoroughly probe issues, acquire additional evidence when necessary, and consult with other team members and firm experts as needed.
- Consider known external and internal factors affecting the entity that might create incentives and opportunities to commit fraud, and indicate an environment that enables rationalizations for committing fraud.
- Consider the risk that management might override controls.
- Consider how to respond to the susceptibility of the financial statements to material misstatement caused by fraud.
- For the purposes of this discussion, set aside any of the audit team's prior beliefs about management's honesty and integrity.

The discussion would normally include key audit team members. Other factors that should be considered when planning the discussion include:

- Whether to have multiple discussions if the audit involves more than one location
- Whether to include specialists assigned to the audit

Audit team members should continue to communicate throughout the audit about the risks of material misstatement due to fraud.

Obtaining Information Needed to Identify Fraud Risks

In addition to performing procedures required under Section 311, *Planning and Supervision*, the auditor should obtain information needed to identify the risks of material misstatement due to fraud by:

- Asking management and others within the entity about their views on the risk of fraud and how such risks are addressed.

- Considering unusual or unexpected relationships identified by analytical procedures performed while planning the audit.
- Considering whether any fraud risk factors exist.
- Considering other information that may be helpful in identifying fraud risk.

Inquiries of Management

The auditor should make the following inquiries of management:

- Does management know about actual or suspected fraud?
- Have there been any allegations of actual or suspected fraud from employees, former employees, analysts, regulators, short sellers, and others?
- Does management understand the entity's fraud risk, including any identified risk factors or account balances or classes of transactions for which a fraud risk is likely to exist?
- What programs and controls does the entity have to help prevent, deter, and detect fraud? How does management monitor such programs?
- When there are multiple locations, how are operating locations or business segments monitored? Is fraud more likely to exist at any one of the locations or business segments?
- Does management communicate its views on business practices and ethical behavior to employees, and if so, how?
- Has management reported to the audit committee or equivalent body how the entity's internal control prevents, deters, and detects fraud?

When evaluating management's responses to these inquiries, auditors should remember that management is often in the best position to commit fraud. Therefore, the auditor should determine when it is necessary to corroborate those responses with other information. When responses are inconsistent, the auditor should obtain additional audit evidence.

Inquiries of the Audit Committee

The auditor should make the following inquiries of the audit committee:

- What are the audit committee's (or at least the chair's) views of the risk of fraud?
- Does the audit committee know about actual or suspected fraud in the entity?

The auditor should also understand how the audit committee oversees the entity's assessment of fraud risks and the mitigating programs and controls.

Inquiries of Internal Auditors

The auditor should make the following inquiries of internal auditors:

- What are the internal auditors' views on the risk of fraud?
- Have the internal auditors performed procedures to identify or detect fraud during the year?
- Has management satisfactorily responded to any finding from procedures performed to identify or detect fraud?
- Are the internal auditors aware of any actual or suspected fraud?

Inquiries of Others within the Organization

The auditor should also ask others within the entity whether they are aware of actual or suspected fraud, using professional judgment to determine to whom these inquiries are made and how extensive the inquiries should be. The following are examples of people that may provide helpful information and, therefore, that the auditor may wish to consider directing inquiries to:

1. Anyone at varying levels of authority whom the auditor deals with during the audit, such as when the auditor is obtaining an understanding of the entity's internal controls, observing inventory, performing cutoff procedures, or getting explanations for fluctuations noted during analytical procedures
2. Operating staff not directly involved in financial reporting
3. Employees involved in initiating, recording, or processing complex or unusual transactions
4. In-house legal counsel

Considering the Results of Analytical Procedures

When performing the required analytical procedures in planning the audit as discussed in Section 329, *Analytical Procedures*, the auditor may find unusual or unexpected relationships as a result of comparing the auditor's expectations with recorded amounts or ratios developed from such amounts. The auditor should consider those results in identifying the risk of material misstatement due to fraud.

The auditor should also perform analytical procedures *relating to revenue* with the objective of identifying unusual or unexpected relationships involving revenue accounts that may indicate a material misstatement due to fraudulent financial reporting. Examples of such procedures include:

- Comparing sales volume with production capacity (sales volume greater than production capacity might indicate fraudulent sales)
- Trend analysis of revenues by month and sales return by month shortly before and after the reporting period (the analysis may point to undisclosed side agreements with customers to return goods)

Although analytical procedures performed during audit planning may be helpful in identifying the risk of material misstatement due to fraud, they may only provide a broad indication, since such procedures use data aggregated at a high level. Therefore, the results of such procedures should be considered along with other information obtained by the auditor in identifying fraud risk.

Considering Fraud Risk Factors

Using professional judgment, the auditor should consider whether information obtained about the entity and its environment indicates that fraud risk factors are present, and, if so, whether it should be considered when identifying and assessing the risk of material misstatement due to fraud.

Examples of fraud risk factors are presented in Illustrations 1 and 2. These risk factors are classified based on the three conditions usually present when fraud exists:

1. Incentive/pressure
2. Opportunity
3. Attitude/rationalization

Considering Other Information

The auditor should evaluate other information that may be helpful in identifying fraud risk. The auditor should consider:

- Any information from procedures performed when deciding to accept or continue with a client
- Results of review of interim financial statements
- Identified inherent risks
- Information from the discussion among engagement team members

IDENTIFYING FRAUD RISKS

Attributes

The auditor should use professional judgment and information obtained when identifying the risks of material misstatement due to fraud. The auditor should consider the following attributes of the risk when identifying risks:

- *Type* (Does the risk involve fraudulent financial reporting or misappropriation of assets?)
- *Significance* (Could the risk lead to a material misstatement of the financial statements?)
- *Likelihood* (How likely is it that the risk would lead to a material misstatement of the financial statements?)
- *Pervasiveness* (Does the risk impact the financial statements as a whole, or does it relate to an assertion, account, or class of transactions?)

The auditor should evaluate whether identified fraud risks can be related to certain account balances or classes of transactions and related assertions, or whether they relate to the financial statements as a whole. Examples of accounts or classes of transactions that might be more susceptible to fraud risk include:

- Liabilities from a restructuring because of the subjectivity in estimating them
- Revenues for a software developer, because of their complexity

NOTE: *The auditor should document the identified fraud risks.*

Presumption about Improper Revenue Recognition as a Fraud Risk

Since fraudulent financial reporting often involves improper revenue recognition, the auditor should ordinarily presume that there is a risk of material misstatement due to fraudulent revenue recognition.

NOTE: *The auditor should document the reasons supporting his or her conclusion when improper revenue recognition is not identified as a fraud risk.*

Consideration of the Risk of Management Override of Controls

The auditor should also recognize that, even when other specific risks of material misstatement are not identified, there is a risk that management can override controls. The auditor should address this risk as discussed in the section below on "Addressing the Risk of Management Override."

ASSESSING IDENTIFIED RISKS

As part of the understanding of internal control required by Section 319, the auditor should

1. Evaluate whether the entity's programs and controls that address identified risks have been appropriately designed and placed in operation. Programs and controls may involve specific controls, such as those designed to prevent theft, or broad programs, such as one that promotes ethical behavior.
2. Consider whether programs and controls mitigate identified risks of material misstatement due to fraud or whether control deficiencies exacerbate risks.
3. Assess identified risks, taking into account the evaluation of programs and controls.
4. Consider this assessment when responding to the identified risks of material misstatement due to fraud.

RESPONDING TO THE RESULTS OF THE ASSESSMENT

The auditor responds to assessment of risk of material misstatement due to fraud by:

- Exercising professional skepticism
- Evaluating audit evidence
- Considering programs and controls to address those risks

Examples of the use of professional skepticism would include:

- Designing additional or different audit procedures to obtain more reliable evidence
- Obtaining additional corroboration of management's responses or representations

The auditor should respond to the risk of material misstatement in the following ways:

1. Evaluate the overall conduct of the audit.
2. Adjust the nature, timing, and extent of audit procedures performed in response to identified risks.
3. Perform certain procedures to address the risk that management will override controls.

NOTE: The auditor should document a description of the auditor's response to identified fraud risks.

If the auditor concludes that it is not practical to design audit procedures to sufficiently address the risks of material misstatement due to fraud, the auditor should consider withdrawing from the engagement and communicating the reason to the audit committee.

Overall Response to Risk

Judgments about the risk of material misstatements due to fraud may affect the audit in the following ways:

1. *Assignment of personnel and supervision.* The personnel assigned to the engagement should have the knowledge, skill, and experience necessary to address the auditor's assessment of the level of risk of the engagement. The extent of supervision should also reflect the level of risk.
2. *Accounting principles.* The auditor should evaluate management's selection and application of significant accounting principles, particularly those relating to subjec-

tive measurements and complex transactions. The auditor should also consider whether the collective application of the principles indicates a bias that may create a material misstatement.
3. *Predictability of audit procedures.* The auditor should vary procedures from year to year to create an element of unpredictability. For example, the auditor may perform unannounced procedures or use a different sampling method.

Adjusting Audit Procedures

The auditor may respond to identified risks by adjusting the nature, timing, and extent of audit procedures performed. Specifically

- The *nature* of procedures may need to be modified to provide more reliable and persuasive evidence, or to corroborate management's representations. For example, the auditor may need to rely more on independent sources, physical observation of assets, or computer-assisted audit techniques.
- The *timing* of procedures may need to be changed. For example, the auditor may decide to perform more procedures at year-end, rather than relying on tests from an interim date.
- The *extent* of procedures applied should reflect the assessment of fraud risk and may need to be adjusted. For example, the auditor may increase sample sizes, perform more detailed analytical procedures, or perform more computer-assisted audit techniques.

Additional examples of ways to modify the nature, timing, and extent of tests to respond to the fraud risk assessment, examples of responses to identified risks arising from fraudulent financial reporting, and examples of responses to risks from misstatements arising from the misappropriation of assets can be found in "Techniques for Application."

NOTE: *Audit procedures may involve both substantive tests and tests of controls. However, since management may be able to override controls, it is unlikely that audit risk can be reduced to an appropriate level by performing only tests of controls.*

Addressing the Risk of Management Override

The auditor should perform the following procedures to specifically address the risk for management's override of controls.

Examine journal entries and other adjustments for evidence of possible material misstatement due to fraud, and test the appropriateness and authorization of such entries. The following procedures should help the auditor in addressing possible recording of inappropriate or unauthorized journal entries or making financial statement adjustments, such as consolidating adjustments, report combinations, or reclassifications not reflected in formal journal entries. The auditor should specifically:

1. Understand the financial reporting process, understand the design of controls over journal entries and other adjustments, and determine that such controls are suitably designed and placed in operation
2. Identify and select journal entries and other adjustments for testing, while considering the following:

- What is our assessment of the risk of material misstatement due to fraud? (The auditor may identify a specific class of journal entries to examine after considering a specific fraud risk factor.)
- How effective are controls over journal entries and other adjustments? (Even if controls are implemented and operating effectively, the auditor should identify and test specific items.)
- Based on our understanding of the entity's financial reporting process, what is the nature of evidence that can be examined? (Regardless of whether journal entries are automated or processed manually, the auditor should select journal entries to be tested from the general ledger, and examine support for those items. In addition, if journal entries and adjustments are in electronic form only, the auditor may require that an information technology [IT] specialist extract the data.)

NOTE: Computer Assisted Audit Techniques (CAATs) such as data extraction applications, frequently are the most effective and efficient means for identifying and selecting journal entries and adjustments for testing.

- What are the characteristics of fraudulent entries or adjustments, or the nature and complexity of accounts? Illustration 3 provides a worksheet to use in identifying characteristics of fraudulent journal entries or adjustments, or accounts that may be more likely to contain inappropriate journal entries or adjustments. (When audits involve multiple locations, the auditor should consider whether to select journal entries from various locations.)
- Are there any journal entries or other adjustments processed outside the normal course of business, (i.e., nonstandard or nonrecurring entries)? The auditor should consider placing additional emphasis in identifying and testing items processed outside the normal course of business, because such items may not be subject to the same level of internal control as other entries.

3. Determine the timing of testing. Fraud may occur throughout a period, and so the auditor should consider the need to test journal entries throughout the period under audit. However, the auditor should also consider that fraudulent journal entries are often made at the end of the reporting period, and should focus on entries made during that time.
4. Ask individuals in the financial reporting process about inappropriate or unusual activity relating to journal entries and adjustments.

NOTE: The auditor should document the results of procedures performed to address the possibility that management might override controls.

Reviewing accounting estimates for biases that could result in fraud. The auditor should consider whether differences between amounts supported by audit evidence and the estimates included in the financial statements, even if individually reasonable, indicate a possible bias on the part of entity's management. If so, the auditor should reconsider the estimates taken as a whole.

The auditor should retrospectively review significant accounting estimates in prior year's financial statements to determine whether there is a possible bias on the part of management. (Significant accounting estimates are those based on highly sensitive assumptions or significantly affected by management's judgment.) The review should provide information to the auditor about a possible management bias that can be helpful in evaluating the current year's estimates. If a management bias is identified, the auditor should evaluate whether the bias represents a risk for material misstatement due to fraud.

Evaluating whether the rationale for significant unusual transactions is appropriate. Personnel at the entity engaged in trying to hide a theft or commit fraudulent financial reporting might use unusual or nonstandard transactions to conceal the fraud. The auditor should understand the business rationale for such transactions and whether the rationale suggests that the transactions are fraudulent. When evaluating the transactions, the auditor should consider:

- Is the transaction overly complex?
- Has management discussed the nature and accounting for the transaction with the audit committee or board of directors?
- Is management focusing more on achieving a particular accounting treatment than the underlying economics?
- Have any transactions involving special purpose entities or other unconsolidated related parties been approved by the audit committee or board of directors?
- Do transactions involve previously unidentified related parties?
- Do transactions involve parties that cannot support the transaction without the help of the audited entity?

EVALUATING AUDIT EVIDENCE

The auditor should:

1. Assess the risk of material misstatement due to fraud throughout the audit
2. Evaluate whether analytical procedures performed as substantive tests or in the overall review indicate a previously unidentified fraud risk
3. Evaluate the risk of material misstatement due to fraud at or near the completion of fieldwork
4. Respond to misstatements that may result from fraud
5. Consider whether identified misstatements may be indicative of fraud, and if so, evaluate their implications

Assessing the Risk of Material Misstatements Due to Fraud

The auditor should continuously assess the risk of material misstatement due to fraud throughout the audit. The auditor should be alert for conditions that may change or support a judgment regarding the risk assessment. These conditions are listed in Illustration 4.

Evaluating Analytical Procedures

The auditor should consider whether analytical procedures performed as substantive tests or in the overall review stage of the audit indicate a risk of material misstatement due to fraud. The auditor should perform analytical procedures relating to revenue through the end of the reporting period, either as part of the overall review of the audit or separately. If not included during the overall review stage of the audit, the auditor should perform analytical procedures specifically related to potentially fraudulent revenue recognition.

The auditor should be alert to responses to inquiries about analytical relationships that are:

- Vague or implausible
- Inconsistent with other audit evidence

NOTE: *The auditor should document other conditions or analytical relationships that result in additional procedures, and any other responses the auditor feels are necessary.*

Evaluating Fraud Risk at or Near the Completion of Fieldwork

The auditor should, at or near the end of fieldwork, evaluate whether the results of auditing procedures and observations affect the earlier assessment of the risk of material misstatement due to fraud. When making this evaluation, the auditor with final responsibility for the audit should confirm that all audit team members have been communicating information about fraud risks to each other throughout the audit.

Responding to misstatements that may result from fraud. When misstatements are identified, the auditor should consider whether they are indicative of fraud. The auditor may need to consider the impact on materiality and other related responses.

If the auditor believes that the misstatements are or may result from fraud, but the effect is not material to the financial statements, the auditor should evaluate the implications for the rest of the audit. If the auditor determines that there are implications, such as implications about management's integrity, the auditor would reevaluate the assessment of the risk of material misstatement due to fraud and its impact on the nature, timing, and extent of substantive tests and the assessment of control risk if control risk were assessed below the maximum.

If the auditor believes that the misstatements are fraudulent, or may result from fraud, and the effect is material (or if the auditor cannot evaluate the materiality of the effect) the auditor should:

1. Try to obtain additional evidence to determine whether fraud occurred and what its effect would be
2. Consider how it affects the rest of the audit
3. Discuss the matter and a plan for further investigation with a level of management at least one level above those involved, as well as senior management and the audit committee (if senior management is involved, it may be appropriate for the auditor to hold the discussion with the audit committee)
4. Consider suggesting that the client consult legal counsel

After evaluating the risk of material misstatement, the auditor may determine that he or she should withdraw from the engagement and communicate the reason to the audit committee. The auditor may wish to consult legal counsel when considering withdrawing from the engagement.

NOTE: *Because of the wide variety of circumstances involved, it is not possible to definitively point out when the auditor should withdraw. However, the auditor may want to consider the implications of the fraud for management's integrity and the cooperation and effectiveness of management and/or board of directors when considering whether to withdraw.*

COMMUNICATION ABOUT POSSIBLE FRAUD TO MANAGEMENT, THE AUDIT COMMITTEE, AND OTHERS

The auditor should communicate any evidence that fraud may exist, even if such fraud is inconsequential, to the appropriate level of management.

The auditor should directly inform the audit committee about:

- Fraud involving senior management
- Fraud that causes a material misstatement of the financial statements

The auditor should reach an understanding with the audit committee about the nature and extent of communications that need to be made to the committee about misappropriations committed by lower-level employees.

The auditor should consider whether the following are reportable conditions that should be communicated to senior management and the audit committee:

- Identified risks of material misstatement due to fraud that have continuing control implications (whether or not transactions or adjustments that could result from fraud have been detected)
- A lack of, or deficiencies in, programs and controls to mitigate the risk of fraud

The auditor may also want to communicate other identified risks of fraud to the audit committee, either in the overall communication of business and financial statement risks affecting the entity or in the communication about the quality of the entity's accounting principles (see Section 380).

Ordinarily, the auditor is not required to disclose possible fraud to anyone other than the client's senior management and audit committee, and in fact would be prevented by the duty of confidentiality from doing so. However, a duty to disclose to others outside the entity may exist when:

1. Complying with certain legal and regulatory requirements
2. Responding to a successor auditor's inquiries
3. Responding to a subpoena
4. Complying with requirements of a funding agency or other specified agency for audits that receive governmental financial assistance

The auditor may wish to consult legal counsel before discussing these matters outside the client to evaluate the auditor's ethical and legal obligations for client confidentiality.

NOTE: The auditor should document these communications to management, the audit committee, and others.

DOCUMENTATION

The auditor should document:

- The engagement team's discussion, when planning the audit, about the entity's susceptibility to fraud; the documentation should include how and when the discussion occurred, audit team members participating, and the subject matter covered
- Procedures performed to obtain the information for identifying and assessing the risks of material misstatements due to fraud
- Specific risks of material misstatement due to fraud identified by the auditor, and a description of the auditor's response to those risks
- If improper revenue recognition has not been identified as a risk factor, the reasons supporting such conclusion
- The results of procedures performed that addressed the risk that management would override controls
- Other conditions and analytical relationships that caused the auditor to believe that additional procedures or responses were required, and any other further responses to address risks or other conditions
- The nature of communications about fraud to management, the audit committee, and others

INTERPRETATIONS

There are no interpretations for this section.

PROFESSIONAL ISSUES TASK FORCE PRACTICE ALERTS

98-2 PROFESSIONAL SKEPTICISM AND RELATED TOPICS

This Practice Alert was written after SAS 82 was issued and highlighting two areas that warrant professional skepticism and attention to audit evidence.

1. A review of nonstandard journal entries, highlighting the importance of attention to nonstandard entries.
2. Review of original and final source documents. The Practice Alert reemphasized the need to consider obtaining original documents, rather than photocopies. The alert also emphasized the importance of certain precautions with facsimile responses, such as confirming information with sender via telephone and asking the sender to send an original directly to the auditor.

98-3 RESPONDING TO THE RISK OF IMPROPER REVENUE RECOGNITION

This Practice Alert notes that much of the litigation against accounting firms and a number of SEC Accounting and Auditing Enforcement Releases involve revenue recognition issues. This Practice Alert:

- Reminds auditors of certain factors or conditions that can indicate improper, aggressive, or unusual revenue recognition practices
- Suggests ways that auditors may reduce the risk of failing to detect such practices
- Reminds auditors that one should ordinarily presume that improper revenue recognition is a fraud risk factor for all audits
- Reminds auditors of their responsibilities to communicate with the board of directors and audit committees

03-02 JOURNAL ENTRIES AND OTHER ADJUSTMENTS

This Practice Alert assists auditors in designing and performing audit procedures regarding journal entries and other adjustments. Highlights of the alert include guidance on:

- How to understand the entity's financial reporting process and its controls over journal entries and other adjustments.
- How to assess the risk of material misstatement from journal entries and other adjustments, including when such entries exist only in electronic form. The alert also suggest that auditors discuss, in their brainstorming session, the ways in which management could originate and post inappropriate entries or adjustments, the kinds of unusual combinations of debits and credits to watch for, and the types of entries and adjustments that could result in a material misstatement that might not be detected by standard audit procedures.
- Making inquiries about fraud of those involved in the financial reporting process. The alert recommends that where practical, and regardless of the fraud risk assessment, the auditor should ask (1) accounting and data entry personnel about whether

those individual were asked to make unusual entries, and (2) selected programmers and IT staff about any unusual and/or unsupported entries.
- Evaluating the completeness of journal entry and other sources of adjustments. Since journal entries and other adjustment may be made outside the general ledger, the auditor should completely understand how the various general ledgers are combined and the accounts grouped to create the consolidated financial statements.
- Identifying and selecting entries and adjustments for testing. The alert points out that the auditor may need to employ CAATs to identify entries and adjustments to test. These techniques are often designed to detect entries made at unusual times of day, by unusual users, or electronic entries not documented in the general ledger.
- Testing other adjustments, including comparing the adjustments to underlying supporting information, and considering the rationale underlying the adjustment and the reason it was not in a formal journal entry.
- Documenting the results of procedures related to journal entries and other adjustments.

TECHNIQUES FOR APPLICATION

MANAGEMENT'S RESPONSIBILITIES

Management is responsible for designing and implementing programs to prevent, deter, and detect fraud. When management and others, such as the audit committee and board of directors, set the proper tone of proper ethical conduct, the opportunities for fraud are significantly reduced.

DESCRIPTION AND CHARACTERISTICS OF FRAUD

Although fraud is a broad legal concept, the auditor's interest specifically relates to fraudulent acts that cause a material misstatement of financial statements. Two types of misstatements are relevant to the auditor's consideration in a financial statement audit.

1. Misstatements arising from fraudulent financial reporting

> *NOTE: Fraudulent financial reporting does not need to involve a grand plan or conspiracy. Management may rationalize that a misstatement is appropriate because it is an aggressive interpretation of accounting rules, or that it is a temporary misstatement that will be corrected later.*

2. Misstatements arising from misappropriation of assets

Fraudulent financial reporting and misappropriation of assets differ in that fraudulent financial reporting is committed, usually by management, to deceive financial statement users while misappropriation of assets is committed against an entity, most often by employees.

Fraud generally involves the following three conditions:

1. A pressure or an incentive to commit fraud
2. A perceived opportunity to do so
3. Rationalization of the fraud by the individual(s) committing it

However, not all three conditions must be observed to conclude that there is an identified risk. It is particularly difficult to observe that the correct environment for rationalizing fraud is present.

The auditor should be aware that the presence of each of the three conditions may vary, and is influenced by factors such as the size, complexity, and ownership of the entity. These three conditions usually are present for both types of fraud.

The auditor should also be alert to the fact that fraudulent financial reporting often involves the override of controls, and that management's override of controls can occur in unpredictable ways. Also, fraud may be concealed through collusion, making it particularly difficult to detect.

Although fraud usually is concealed, the presence of risk factors or other conditions may alert the auditor to its possible existence.

FRAUD RISK FACTORS

Fraud risk factors may come to the auditor's attention while performing procedures relating to acceptance or continuance of clients, during engagement planning or obtaining an understanding of an entity's internal control, or while conducting fieldwork. Accordingly, the assessment of the risk of material misstatement due to fraud is a cumulative process that includes a consideration of risk factors individually and in combination. As noted earlier, assessment of fraud risk factors is not a simple matter of counting the factors present and converting to a level of fraud risk. A few risk factors or even a single risk factor may heighten significantly the risk of fraud.

IDENTIFYING FRAUD RISKS

When identifying fraud risks, the auditor may find it helpful to consider information obtained along with the three conditions—incentives/pressures, opportunities, and attitudes/rationalizations—that are usually present when fraud exists. However, as stated above, the auditor should not assume that all three conditions must be present or observed. In addition, the extent to which any condition is present may vary.

The size, complexity, and ownership of the entity may also affect the identification of fraud risks.

Modifying the Nature, Timing, and Extent of Audit Procedures to Address Risk

According to AU 316.53, the following are examples of ways to modify the nature, timing, and extent of tests in response to identified risks of material misstatement due to fraud:

- Perform unannounced or surprise procedures at locations
- Ask that inventories be counted as close as possible to the end of the reporting period
- Orally confirm with major customers and suppliers in addition to sending written confirmations
- Send confirm requests to a specific party in an organization
- Perform substantive analytical procedures using disaggregated data, such as comparing gross profit or operating margins by location, line of business, or month to auditor-developed expectations
- Interview personnel involved in areas where a fraud risk has been identified to get their views about the risk and how controls address the risk

- Discuss with other independent auditors auditing other subsidiaries, divisions, or branches the extent of work that should be performed to address the risk of fraud resulting from transactions and activities among those components

Examples of Responses to Identified Risks of Misstatements from Fraudulent Financial Reporting

The following examples are from AU 316.54:

Revenue recognition. The auditor may consider:

- Performing substantive analytical procedures relating to revenue using disaggregated data, such as comparing revenue reported by month or by product line or business segment during the current reporting period with comparable prior periods
- Confirming with customers certain relevant contract terms and the absence of side agreements, because the appropriate accounting often is influenced by such terms or agreements (for example, acceptance criteria, delivery and payment terms, the absence of future or continuing vendor obligations, the right to return the product, guaranteed resale amounts, and cancellation or refund provisions often are relevant in such circumstances)
- Inquiring of the entity's sales and marketing personnel or in-house legal counsel regarding sales or shipments near the end of the period and their knowledge of any unusual terms or conditions associated with these transactions
- Being physically present at one or more locations at period-end to observe goods being shipped or being readied for shipment (or returns processing) and performing other appropriate cutoff procedures
- For those situations for which revenue transactions are electronically initiated, processed, and recorded, testing controls to determine whether they provide assurance that recorded revenue transactions occurred and are properly recorded

Inventory quantities. The auditor may consider:

- Examining the entity's inventory records to identify locations or items that require specific attention during or after the physical inventory count
- Performing additional procedures during the count, such as rigorously examining the contents of boxes, checking the manner in which goods are stacked for hollow squares, or examining the quality of liquid substances for purity, grade, or concentration
- Performing additional testing of count sheets, tags, or other records to reduce the possibility of subsequent alteration or inappropriate compilation
- Performing additional procedures to test the reasonableness of quantities counted, such as comparing quantities for the current period with prior periods by class or category of inventory or location
- Using CAATs

Management estimates. The auditor may want to supplement the audit evidence obtained. The auditor may

- Engage a specialist
- Develop an independent estimate for comparison
- Evaluate information gathered about the entity and its environment

- Retrospectively review similar management judgments and assumptions from prior periods

Examples of Responses to Identified Risks of Misstatements Arising from Misappropriation of Assets

The auditor will usually direct a response to identified risks of misstatements arising from misappropriation of assets to certain account balances. The scope of the work should be linked to the specific information about the identified misappropriation risk. The auditor may consider some of the procedures listed in "Examples of Responses to Identified Risks of Misstatements Arising from Fraudulent Financial Reporting." However, in some cases, the auditor may:

- Obtain an understanding of the controls related to preventing or detecting the misappropriation and testing of such controls
- Physically inspect assets near the end of the period
- Apply substantive analytical procedures, such as the development by the auditor of an expected dollar amount at a high level of precision to be compared with a recorded amount

EVALUATING ANALYTICAL PROCEDURES AS PART OF AUDIT EVIDENCE

As part of the auditor's evaluation of analytical procedures performed as substantive tests or in the overall review stage of the audit, and those analytical procedures that relate to revenue through the end of the reporting period, the auditor may find it helpful to consider the following issues:

1. Are there any unusual relationships involving revenues and income at year-end, such as an unexpectedly large amount of revenue reported at the very end of the reporting period from nonstandard transactions, or income that is not consistent with cash flow trends from operations?
2. Are there other unusual or unexpected analytical relationships that should be evaluated? AU 316.72 provides the following examples:

    - An unusual relationship between net income and cash flows from operations may occur if management recorded fictitious revenues and receivables but was unable to manipulate cash.
    - Inconsistent changes in inventory, accounts payable, sales or cost of sales between the prior period and the current period may indicate a possible employee theft of inventory, because the employee was unable to manipulate all of the related accounts.
    - Comparing the entity's profitability to industry trends, which management cannot manipulate, may indicate trends or differences for further consideration.
    - Unexplained relationships between bad debt write-offs and comparable industry data, which employees cannot manipulate, may indicate a possible theft of cash receipts.
    - Unusual relationships between sales volume taken from the accounting records and production statistics maintained by operating personnel—which may be more difficult for management to manipulate—may indicate a possible misstatement of sales.

In planning the audit, the auditor will most likely use a list of fraud risk factors to serve as a "memory jogger." This list may be taken from the examples listed in the next section ("AU Illustrations"), or the examples provided may be tailored to the client. The documentation of this list of fraud risk factors considered is *not* required, but represents good practice.

During the planning and performance of the audit, the auditor may identify some of the fraud risk factors from the list as being present at the client. Of those risk factors present, some will be addressed sufficiently by the planned audit procedures; others may require the auditor to extend audit procedures.

REQUIRED ACTIONS/COMMUNICATION REQUIRED FOR DISCOVERED FRAUD

When the auditor discovers or suspects fraud, the actions and communications required are somewhat complex, especially when an SEC client is involved. The actions/communications required by Title III of the Private Securities Litigation Reform Act of 1995, by the SEC Practice section (SECPS) for its members, and by the SEC in Form 8-K add to the complexity.

The best approach is to decide which of the following three situations governs and follow the guidance presented below for the applicable situation.

Situation 1.

Section 316 Actions/Communications Requirements for Material Fraud + Any Fraud Involving Senior Management for Non-SEC Clients
Auditor should:

1. Consider implications for other aspects of audit
2. Reevaluate the assessment of the risk of fraud
3. Discuss matter and the approach to further investigation with appropriate level of management[2]
4. Obtain additional evidential matter, including suggesting that client consult with legal counsel
5. Consider whether any risk factors identified represent reportable conditions (Section 325)
6. Consider withdrawing from the engagement and communicating reasons to the audit committee (or board of directors, etc.)
7. Report the fraud to the audit committee or, in a small business, to the owner-manager

> *NOTE: If perpetrator controls audit committee or board of directors, go directly to client's legal counsel. If perpetrator is a general partner acting against interest of limited partners, obtain legal advice and consider communicating to limited partners. If perpetrator is owner-manager of a small business, auditor has little choice but to communicate with perpetrator and has no obvious course of action but to withdraw. However, first the auditor should consult with his or her legal counsel.*

8. Insist that the financial statements be revised and, if they are not, express a qualified or adverse opinion (if precluded from obtaining needed evidence, disclaim an opinion or withdraw)

---

[2] *Fraud that involves senior management or fraud that causes a material misstatement of the financial statements should be reported directly to the audit committee.*

Situation 2.

Section 316 Actions/Communications Requirements for Material Fraud + Any Fraud Involving Senior Management for SEC Clients
Auditor should:

1. Follow steps in the Situation 1 checklist + additional items 2–4 below.
2. Consider Section 10A(b) of the Securities Exchange Act of 1934 (Title III, Private Securities Litigation Reform Act of 1995):
   a. Matter is reported to board of directors and it does not take appropriate action.
   b. Auditor concludes that failure to take remedial action is expected to cause departure from standard audit report or cause withdrawal.
   c. Auditor should report conclusion in item b of this list to board of directors (e.g., on Monday).
   d. Client is required to notify SEC (within one business day) of auditor's conclusion described in item b (e.g., by Tuesday).
   e. Client is required to furnish report to SEC in item d to auditor within one business day (e.g., by Tuesday).
   f. If auditor doesn't receive report in item e, auditor notifies SEC within one business day following failure to receive (e.g., on Wednesday).
3. If auditor withdraws or resigns from engagement, auditor must send copy of resignation to the SEC within five business days.
4. Follow SEC requirements for reporting on Form 8-K.
   a. Upon auditor's withdrawal, client must disclose within four business days the following information on a Form 8-K, filed with the SEC, with a copy to the auditor on the same day:
      - Auditor's resignation
      - Auditor's conclusion that the information coming to his/her attention *has a material impact* on the fairness or reliability of the client's financial statements or audit report and that this matter was not resolved to the auditor's satisfaction before resignation
   b. Auditor must prepare a letter stating agreement or disagreement with client's statements after reading Form 8-K. If auditor disagrees, he/she must disclose differences of opinion in a letter to client as promptly as possible. Client must then file the letter with the SEC within ten business days after filing the Form 8-K. Notwithstanding the ten-business-day requirement, client has two business days from the date of receipt to file the letter with the SEC.

Situation 3.

Section 316 Actions/Communication Requirements for Immaterial Fraud + Not Involving Senior Management for All Clients (Public and Nonpublic)
Auditor should:

1. Evaluate implications for other aspects of audit, especially organizational position of persons involved
2. Bring to attention of, and discuss with, appropriate level of management (even if inconsequential)

3. Communicate matter to audit committee unless matter is clearly below communication threshold previously agreed to by auditor and the audit committee
4. Consider whether any risk factors identified represent reportable conditions (Section 325)

ANTIFRAUD PROGRAMS AND CONTROLS

The Committee of Sponsoring Organizations of the Treadway Commission (COSO) framework does not include a discussion related to the prevention and detection of fraud. An established set of criteria for evaluating the effectiveness of fraud-related controls does not exist. However, the SEC guidance does suggest that management may find helpful information in the document "Management Anti-Fraud Programs and Controls," which was published as an exhibit to Section 316, *Consideration of Fraud in a Financial Statement Audit*.

The guidance in that document is based on the presumption that entity management has both the responsibility and the means to take action to reduce the occurrence of fraud at the entity. To fulfill this responsibility, management should:

- Create and maintain a culture of honesty and high ethics
- Evaluate the risks of fraud and implement the processes, procedures, and controls needed to mitigate the risks and reduce the opportunities for fraud
- Develop an appropriate oversight process

In many ways, the guidance offered in "Management Anti-Fraud Programs and Controls" echoes the concepts and detailed guidance contained in the COSO report. The primary difference is that the antifraud document reminds management that it must be aware of and design the entity's internal control to specifically address material misstatements caused by fraud and not limit efforts to the detection and prevention of unintentional errors.

Culture of Honesty and Ethics

A culture of honesty and ethics includes these elements:

- A value system founded on integrity.
- A positive workplace environment where employees have positive feelings about the entity.
- Human resource policies that minimize the chance of hiring or promoting individuals with low levels of honesty, especially for positions of trust.
- Training—both at the time of hire and on an ongoing basis—about the entity's values and its code of conduct.
- Confirmation from employees that they understand and have complied with the entity's code of conduct and that they are not aware of any violations of the code.
- Appropriate investigation and response to incidents of alleged or suspected fraud.

Evaluating Antifraud Programs and Controls

The entity's risk assessment process (as described in the separate chapter on AU 311) should include the consideration of fraud risk. With an aim toward reducing fraud opportunities, the entity should take steps to:

- Identify and measure fraud risk
- Mitigate fraud risk by making changes to the entity's activities and procedures
- Implement and monitor an appropriate system of internal control

Develop an Appropriate Oversight Process

The entity's audit committee or board of directors should take an active role in evaluating management's:

- Creation of an appropriate culture
- Identification of fraud risks
- Implementation of antifraud measures

To fulfill its oversight responsibilities, audit committee members should be financially literate, and each committee should have at least one financial expert. Additionally, the committee should consider establishing an open line of communication with members of management one or two levels below senior management to assist in identifying fraud at the highest levels of the organization or investigating any fraudulent activity that might occur.

AU ILLUSTRATIONS

ILLUSTRATION 1. RISK FACTORS—FRAUDULENT FINANCIAL REPORTING

The following are examples of risk factors, reproduced with permission from AU Section 316, relating to misstatements arising from fraudulent financial reporting:

Incentives/Pressures

a. Financial stability or profitability is threatened by economic, industry, or entity operating conditions, such as (or indicated by):

   - High degree of competition or market saturation, accompanied by declining margins.
   - High vulnerability to rapid changes, such as changes in technology, product obsolescence, or interest rates.
   - Significant declines in customer demand and increasing business failures in either the industry or overall economy.
   - Operating losses making the threat of bankruptcy, foreclosure, or hostile takeover imminent.
   - Recurring negative cash flows from operations or an inability to generate cash flows from operations while reporting earnings and earnings growth.
   - Rapid growth or unusual profitability, especially compared to that of other companies in the same industry.
   - New accounting, statutory, or regulatory requirements.

b. Excessive pressure exists for management to meet the requirements or expectations of third parties due to the following:

   - Profitability or trend level expectations of investment analysts, institutional investors, significant creditors, or other external parties (particularly expectations that are unduly aggressive or unrealistic), including expectations created by management in, for example, overly optimistic press releases or annual report messages.
   - Need to obtain additional debt or equity financing to stay competitive—including financing of major research and development or capital expenditures.
   - Marginal ability to meet exchange listing requirements or debt repayment or other debt covenant requirements.
   - Perceived or real adverse effects of reporting poor financial results on significant pending transactions, such as business combinations or contract awards.

c. Information available indicates that management or the board of directors' personal financial situation is threatened by the entity's financial performance arising from the following:

- Significant financial interests in the entity.
- Significant portions of their compensation (for example, bonuses, stock options, and earn-out arrangements) being contingent upon achieving aggressive targets for stock price, operating results, financial position, or cash flow.[3]
- Personal guarantees of debts of the entity.

d. There is excessive pressure on management or operating personnel to meet financial targets set up by the board of directors or management, including sales or profitability incentive goals.

Opportunities

a. The nature of the industry or the entity's operations provides opportunities to engage in fraudulent financial reporting that can arise from the following:

- Significant related-party transactions not in the ordinary course of business or with related entities not audited or audited by another firm.
- A strong financial presence or ability to dominate a certain industry sector that allows the entity to dictate terms or conditions to suppliers or customers that may result in inappropriate or non-arm's-length transactions.
- Assets, liabilities, revenues, or expenses based on significant estimates that involve subjective judgments or uncertainties that are difficult to corroborate.
- Significant, unusual, or highly complex transactions, especially those close to period end that post difficult "substance over form" questions.
- Significant operations located or conducted across international borders in jurisdictions where differing business environments and cultures exist.
- Significant bank accounts or subsidiary or branch operations in tax-haven jurisdictions for which there appears to be no clear business justification.

b. There is ineffective monitoring of management as a result of the following:

- Domination of management by a single person or small group (in a nonowner-managed business) without compensating controls.
- Ineffective board of directors or audit committee oversight over the financial reporting process and internal control.

c. There is a complex or unstable organizational structure, as evidenced by the following:

- Difficulty in determining the organization or individuals that have controlling interest in the entity.
- Overly complex organizational structure involving unusual legal entities or managerial lines of authority.
- High turnover of senior management, counsel, or board members.

d. Internal control components are deficient as a result of the following:

- Inadequate monitoring of controls, including automated controls and controls over interim financial reporting (where external reporting is required).
- High turnover rates or employment of ineffective accounting, internal audit, or information technology staff.

---

[3] Management incentive plans may be contingent upon achieving targets relating only to certain accounts or selected activities of the entity, even though the related accounts or activities may not be material to the entity as a whole.

– Ineffective accounting and information systems, including situations involving reportable conditions.

Attitudes/Rationalizations

Risk factors reflective of attitudes/rationalizations by board members, management, or employees, that allow them to engage in and/or justify fraudulent financial reporting, may not be susceptible to observation by the auditor. Nevertheless, the auditor who becomes aware of the existence of such information should consider it in identifying the risks of material misstatement arising from fraudulent financial reporting. For example, auditors may become aware of the following information that may indicate a risk factor:

- Ineffective communication, implementation, support, or enforcement of the entity's values or ethical standards by management or the communication of inappropriate values or ethical standards.
- Nonfinancial management's excessive participation in or preoccupation with the selection of accounting principles or the determination of significant estimates.
- Known history of violations of securities laws or other laws and regulations, or claims against the entity, its senior management, or board members alleging fraud or violations of laws and regulations.
- Excessive interest by management in maintaining or increasing the entity's stock price or earnings trend.
- A practice by management of committing analysts, creditors, and other third parties to achieve aggressive or unrealistic forecasts.
- Management failing to correct known reportable conditions on a timely basis.
- An interest by management in employing inappropriate means to minimize reported earnings for tax-motivated reasons.
- Recurring attempts by management to justify marginal or inappropriate accounting on the basis of materiality.
- The relationship between management and the current or predecessor auditor is strained, as exhibited by the following:
    – Frequent disputes with the current or predecessor auditor on accounting, auditing, or reporting matters.
    – Unreasonable demands on the auditor, such as unreasonable time constraints regarding the completion of the audit or the issuance of the auditor's report.
    – Formal or informal restrictions on the auditor that inappropriately limit access to people or information or the ability to communicate effectively with the board of directors or audit committee.
    – Domineering management behavior in dealing with the auditor involving attempts to influence the scope of the auditor's work or the selection or continuance of personnel assigned to or consulted on the audit engagement.

ILLUSTRATION 2. RISK FACTORS—MISAPPROPRIATION OF ASSETS

The following are examples of risk factors, reproduced with permission from AU Section 316, relating to misstatements arising from misappropriation of assets:

Incentives/Pressures

a. Personal financial obligations may create pressure on management or employees with access to cash or other assets susceptible to theft to misappropriate those assets.
b. Adverse relationships between the entity and employees with access to cash or other assets susceptible to theft may motivate those employees to misappropriate those assets. For example, adverse relationships may be created by the following:

- Known or anticipated future employee layoffs.
- Recent or anticipated changes to employee compensation or benefit plans.
- Promotions, compensation, or other rewards inconsistent with expectations.

Opportunities

a. Certain characteristics or circumstances may increase the susceptibility of assets to misappropriation. For example, opportunities to misappropriate assets increase when there are the following:

   - Large amounts of cash on hand or processed.
   - Inventory items that are small in size, of high value, or in high demand.
   - Easily convertible assets, such as bearer bonds, diamonds, or computer chips.
   - Fixed assets that are small in size, marketable, or lacking observable identification of ownership.

b. Inadequate internal control over assets may increase the susceptibility of misappropriation of those assets. For example, the misappropriation of assets may occur because there is the following:

   - Inadequate segregation of duties or independent checks.
   - Inadequate management oversight of employees responsible for assets, for example, inadequate supervision or monitoring of remote locations.
   - Inadequate job applicant screening of employees with access to assets.
   - Inadequate recordkeeping with respect to assets.
   - Inadequate system of authorization and approval of transactions (for example, in purchasing)
   - Inadequate physical safeguards over cash, investments, inventory, or fixed assets.
   - Lack of complete and timely reconciliations of assets.
   - Lack of timely and appropriate documentation of transactions, for example, credits for merchandise returns.
   - Lack of mandatory vacations for employees performing key control functions.
   - Inadequate management understanding of information technology, which enables information technology employees to perpetrate a misappropriation.
   - Inadequate access controls over automated records, including controls over and review of computer systems events logs.

Attitudes/Rationalizations

Risk factors reflective of employee attitudes/rationalizations that allow them to justify misappropriation of assets, are generally not susceptible to observation by the auditor. Nevertheless, the auditor who becomes aware of the existence of such information should consider it in identifying the risks of material misstatement arising from misappropriation of assets. For example, auditors may become aware of the following attitudes or behavior of employees who have access to assets susceptible to misappropriation:

- Disregard for the need for monitoring or reducing risks related to misappropriation of assets.
- Disregard for internal control over misappropriation of assets by overriding existing controls or by failing to correct known internal control deficiencies.
- Behavior indicating displeasure or dissatisfaction with the company or its treatment of the employee.
- Changes in behavior or lifestyle that may indicate assets have been misappropriated.

ILLUSTRATION 3. WORKSHEET TO IDENTIFY FRAUDULENT ENTRIES OR ADJUSTMENTS (ADAPTED FROM AU 316.61)

Inappropriate journal entries and other adjustments often have certain unique characteristics. The auditor should use the following questions to help identify characteristics of inappropriate journal entries and other adjustments:

- Is the entry made to an unrelated, unusual, or seldom-used account?
- Is the entry made by an individual who typically does not make journal entries?
- Is the entry made at closing of the period or postclosing with little or no explanation or description?
- Do entries made during the preparation of financial statements lack account numbers?
- Does the entry contain round numbers or a consistent ending number?

The auditor should use the following questions to identify journal entries and adjustments made to accounts that have the following characteristics:

- Does the account consist of transactions that are complex or unusual in nature?
- Does the account contain significant estimates and period-end adjustments?
- Has the account been prone to errors in the past?
- Has the account not been regularly reconciled on a timely basis?
- Does the account contain unreconciled differences?
- Does the account contain intercompany transactions?
- Is the account otherwise associated with an identified risk of material misstatement due to fraud?

ILLUSTRATION 4. LIST OF CONDITIONS THAT MAY CHANGE OR SUPPORT THE FRAUD RISK ASSESSMENT (FROM AU 316.68)

Conditions may be identified during fieldwork that change or support a judgment regarding the assessment of the risks, such as the following:

- Discrepancies in the accounting records, including

    - Transactions that are not recorded in a complete or timely manner or are improperly recorded as to amount, accounting period, classification, or entity policy.
    - Unsupported or unauthorized balances or transactions.
    - Last-minute adjustments that significantly affect financial results.
    - Evidence of employees' access to systems and records inconsistent with that necessary to perform their authorized duties.
    - Tips or complaints to the auditor about alleged fraud.

- Conflicting or missing evidential matter, including

    - Missing documents.
    - Documents that appear to have been altered.
    - Unavailability of other than photocopies or electronically transmitted documents when documents in original form are expected to exist.
    - Significant unexplained items on reconciliations.
    - Inconsistent, vague, or implausible responses from management or employees arising from inquiries procedures.
    - Unusual discrepancies between the entity's records and confirmation replies.
    - Missing inventory or physical assets of significant magnitude.
    - Unavailable or missing electronic evidence, inconsistent with the entity's record retention practices or policies.

- Inability to produce evidence of key systems development and program change testing and implementation activities for current year system changes and deployments.

• Problematic or unusual relationships between the auditor and management, including

- Denial of access to records, facilities, certain employees, customers, vendors, or others from whom audit evidence might be sought.
- Undue time pressures imposed by management to resolve complex or contentious issues.
- Complaints by management about the conduct of the audit or management intimidation of audit team members, particularly in connection with the auditor's critical assessment of audit evidence or in the resolution of potential disagreements with management.
- Unusual delays by the entity in providing requested information.
- Unwillingness to facilitate auditor access to key electronic files for testing through the use of computer-assisted audit techniques.
- Denial of access to key IT operations staff and facilities, including security, operations, and systems development personnel.
- An unwillingness to add or revise disclosures in the financial statements to make them more complete and transparent.

ILLUSTRATION 5. EXAMPLE PROGRAM FOR MANAGEMENT OVERRIDE OF INTERNAL CONTROL

Audit Program for Management Override of Internal Control

Page _____ of _____

Company: Balance Sheet Date:

Audit Objective	Audit Procedure for Consideration	N/A Performed By	Workpaper Index
	AUDIT OBJECTIVES A. To identify risk of material misstatement due to fraud caused by inappropriate or unauthorized journal entries B. To determine whether management is not unduly biased in the preparation of significant accounting estimates C. To determine whether significant unusual transactions have not been entered into to engage in fraudulent financial reporting or conceal a misappropriation of assets		
A.	**Review of Journal Entries** 1. Obtain an understanding of the company's financial reporting process and the controls over nonstandard journal entries. Document the following: a. The sources of entries posted to the general ledger (for example, subledgers, cash receipts journal, etc.)		

Audit Objective	Audit Procedure for Consideration	N/A Performed By	Workpaper Index
	b. How the journal entries are recorded and whether physical documentation exists c. The individuals responsible for: (a) initiating, (b) reviewing, and (c) approving the journal entries d. The controls in place to prevent and detect unauthorized entries		
A.	2. Obtain an understanding of the adjustments posted by the entity to prepare its financial statements (for example, reclassification or consolidating entries). Document the following:		
	a. The nature of the adjustments posted to the financial statements that are not posted to the general ledger b. How the adjustments are posted to the financial statements c. The individuals responsible for: (a) initiating, (b) reviewing, and (c) approving the adjustments d. The controls in place to prevent and detect unauthorized adjustments		
A.	3. Identify and select significant nonstandard journal entries and other significant adjustments for testing. In making this selection, consider the following:		

	a. The effectiveness of the company's controls over journal entries and adjustments
	b. The characteristics of fraudulent entries or adjustments, such as
	  • Made to unrelated, unusual, or seldom-used accounts
	  • Made by individuals who typically do not make journal entries
	  • Recorded at the end of the reporting period or as postclosing entries
	  • Entries that have little or no explanation or account numbers
	  • Containing round numbers or a consistent ending number
	c. The nature and complexity of the accounts. Examples include accounts that
	  • Contain transactions that are complex or unusual in nature
	  • Contain significant estimates or period-end adjustments
	  • Have been prone to errors in the past
	  • Cannot be reconciled on a timely basis or that contain significant unreconciled differences
	  • Contain intercompany transactions		

Audit Objective	Audit Procedure for Consideration	N/A Performed By	Workpaper Index
	• Are otherwise associated with an identified risk of material misstatement due to fraud		
	d. Journal entries or other adjustments processed outside the normal course of business		
A.	4. Ask individuals involved in the financial reporting process, including IT personnel (if appropriate), about the presence or observations of inappropriate or unusual activity relating to the processing of journal entries or other adjustments.		
A.	5. Document the following: a. The journal entries and adjustments selected for testing b. The nature and purpose of the journal entry or adjustment c. Whether the journal entries and adjustments were properly approved d. A conclusion regarding the propriety of the journal entries and adjustments tested		
	Retrospective Review of Estimates		
B.	6. Identify and document a. Accounting estimates that are significant to the financial statements b. For each significant estimate, the key underlying assumptions made by management		
B.	7. For the prior reporting period, compare the key assumptions made by management at the time the financial statements were prepared to actual events, management actions, or results obtained subsequent to that time.		
B.	8. Determine whether the results of your procedures indicate a bias on the part of management that may affect the financial statements. If no bias is detected, document this conclusion.		
	Significant Unusual Transactions		
C.	9. Identify and document significant unusual transactions entered into during the reporting period. Consider documenting • The counterparty(ies) to the transaction • How the transaction was accounted, presented and disclosed in the financial statements • The process followed by the entity to approve the transaction and its accounting treatment • Management's stated business rationale for the transaction		

Audit Objective	Audit Procedure for Consideration	N/A Performed By	Workpaper Index
C.	10. Determine and document whether the management's rationale for the transaction (or lack thereof) suggests that the transaction may have been entered into to engage in fraudulent financial reporting or conceal a misappropriation of assets. In making your determination, consider whether: • The form of such transactions is overly complex • Management has discussed the nature of an accounting for such transactions with ABC Co., the audit committee, or board of directors • Management is placing more emphasis on the need for a particular accounting treatment than on the underlying economics of the transaction • Transactions that involve unconsolidated related parties have been properly reviewed and approved by the audit committee or board of directors • The transactions involve previously unidentifiable related parties or parties that do not have the substance or the financial strength to support the transaction without assistance from the entity under the audit **CONCLUSION** We have performed procedures sufficient to achieve the stated audit objective, and the results of these procedures are adequately presented in the accompanying workpapers. (If you are unable to conclude on the objective, prepare a memo documenting your reason.) _____ _____ _____		

AU 317 Illegal Acts by Clients

AU-C 250 Consideration of Laws and Regulations in an Audit of Financial Statements

AU EFFECTIVE DATE AND APPLICABILITY

Original Pronouncement	Statement on Auditing Standards (SAS) 54.
Effective Date	This statement currently is effective.
Applicability	Audits of financial statements in accordance with generally accepted auditing standards.

AU-C EFFECTIVE DATE AND SUMMARY OF CHANGES

SAS No. 122, *Codification of Auditing Standards and Procedures,* is effective for audits of financial statements with periods ending on or after December 15, 2012.

AU-C Section 250 supersedes AU Section 317 and contains some substantive changes to requirements. It requires the performance of procedures to identify instances of noncompliance with those laws and regulations that may have a material effect on the financial statements. The auditor is specifically required to inspect correspondence with the relevant licensing or regulatory authorities. This is a new requirement and is expected to affect current practice.

There are also several changes that make explicit requirements that are implicit in AU Section 317. These are not expected to change practice:

- Obtain an understanding of the legal and regulatory framework.
- Obtain an understanding of how the entity is complying with that framework.
- Determine whether the auditor has a responsibility to report suspected noncompliance to parties outside the entity
- Document identified or suspected noncompliance, including the results of any discussions about such items.

In addition, there is a difference in the AU Section 317 concept of "no assurance" and AU-C Section 250 concept of "inherent limitations of an audit." AU-C Section 250 states that because of the inherent limitations of an audit, some material misstatements in the financial statements may not be detected even when the audit is properly planned and performed in accordance with GAAS. The extant standard states, in relation to illegal acts, that an audit performed in accordance with GAAS provides no assurance that noncompliance with laws and regulations will be detected or that any contingent liabilities that may result will be disclosed. These differing descriptions are not expected to affect current practice.

The requirement in AU Section 317 to obtain a written representation from management concerning the absence of noncompliance with laws or regulations is included in AU-C 580, *Written Representations*.

AU DEFINITIONS OF TERMS

Illegal acts. Violations of laws or governmental regulations. For purposes of this section, a distinction is made between the following types of illegal acts:

- Illegal acts with a direct and material effect on determination of financial statement amounts.
- Other illegal acts.

AU-C 250 DEFINITIONS OF TERMS

Source: AU-C 250.11

Noncompliance. Acts of omission or commission by the entity, either intentional or unintentional, which are contrary to the prevailing laws or regulations. Such acts include transactions entered into by, or in the name of, the entity or on its behalf by those charged with governance, management, or employees. Noncompliance does not include personal misconduct (unrelated to the business activities of the entity) by those charged with governance, management, or employees of the entity.

OBJECTIVES OF AU SECTION 317

Illegal acts are so diverse that articulating the auditor's responsibility for their detection and reporting has proven to be very complex. Some laws and regulations, such as the Internal Revenue Code regulations concerning income tax expense, clearly fall within the auditor's expertise, and the audit of financial statements normally includes testing compliance with such laws and regulations. Other laws and regulations, such as those on occupational safety and health or food and drug administration, are clearly outside the auditor's expertise and are not susceptible to testing by customary auditing procedures. Some laws and regulations fall in between these extremes.

Simple criteria for distinguishing those laws and regulations that should be of greater concern to the auditor have not been found. The materiality of the consequences of violation is not suitable. Many laws and regulations outside the auditor's expertise and not susceptible to audit testing could have consequences very material to the financial statements if violated. Even the relation to financial matters is not conclusive. For example, laws concerning securities trading are financially related, but involve complex legal concepts.

This section takes the approach of dividing illegal acts into two broad categories or types. The auditor's responsibility for detection of illegal acts differs depending on the type of illegal act. The auditor's responsibility to detect misstatements resulting from illegal acts having a direct and material effect on the determination of financial statement amounts (except disclosure of contingencies) is the same as that for errors (see Section 312) and fraud (see Section 316). For other illegal acts, the auditor should be aware of the possibility that such illegal acts may have occurred. If specific information comes to the auditor's attention that such acts may have occurred, the auditor should apply audit procedures specifically directed toward ascertaining whether an illegal act has occurred. However, an audit in accordance with generally accepted auditing standards (GAAS) provides no assurance that illegal acts will be detected or that any contingent liabilities that may result will be disclosed.

In this section, the requirements are directed primarily toward what the auditor should do when a possible illegal act comes to his or her attention and there is no general obligation to apply any audit procedures specifically designed to detect illegal acts.

OBJECTIVES OF AU-C SECTION 250

AU-C 250 states that:

. . . the objectives of the auditor are to

   a. *obtain sufficient appropriate audit evidence regarding material amounts and disclosures in the financial statements that are determined by the provisions of those laws and regulations generally recognized to have a direct effect on their determination (see paragraph .06a),*
   b. *perform specified audit procedures that may identify instances of noncompliance with other laws and regulations that may have a material effect on the financial statements (see paragraph .06b), and*
   c. *respond appropriately to noncompliance or suspected noncompliance with laws and regulations identified during the audit.*

FUNDAMENTAL REQUIREMENTS[1]

AUDIT PROCEDURES ABSENT EVIDENCE OF POSSIBLE ILLEGAL ACTS

An audit does not normally include audit procedures specifically designed to detect illegal acts. However, audit procedures may bring possible illegal acts to the auditor's attention. The auditor should be aware of the possibility that illegal acts may have occurred. If information indicates that illegal acts may have occurred, the auditor should apply audit procedures to address the matter.

The auditor should ask management about the client's compliance with laws and regulations. Where applicable, the auditor should also ask management about:

1. Policies relating to prevention of illegal acts
2. Use of directives issued by the client
3. Periodic representations obtained by the client from management at appropriate levels of authority concerning compliance with laws and regulations

---

[1] *The requirements apply to those illegal acts with an indirect and contingent effect. Those illegal acts with a direct and material effect are treated the same as errors (see Section 312) or fraud (see Section 316).*

The auditor also ordinarily obtains written management representations about the absence of violations or possible violations of laws or regulations whose effects should be considered for disclosure in the financial statements or as a basis for recording a loss contingency (see Section 333). The auditor does not need to perform any further procedures in this area absent specific information concerning possible illegal acts.

EVIDENCE OF POSSIBLE ILLEGAL ACTS

According to AU 317.09, the auditor should be aware that specific information such as the following may raise a question concerning possible illegal acts:

1. Violations of laws or regulations cited in reports of examinations by regulatory agencies that have been made available to the auditor
2. Unusually large payments in cash
3. Large payments for unspecified services to consultants, affiliates, or employees
4. Failure to file tax returns or pay government duties or similar fees that are common to the entity's industry or the nature of its business

RESPONSE TO POSSIBLE ILLEGAL ACTS

When the auditor becomes aware of information about a possible illegal act, the auditor should obtain an understanding of (1) the nature of the possible illegal act, (2) the circumstances in which the act occurred, and (3) sufficient other information to allow the auditor to consider the effect on the financial statements.

The auditor should inquire of management at a level above those involved, if possible. If management does not provide satisfactory information that there has been no illegal act, the auditor should respond by:

1. Consulting with the client's legal counsel (with the client's permission) or other specialists about applying relevant laws and regulations to the circumstances and the possible effects on the financial statements
2. Applying additional procedures, if necessary, to further understand the nature of the acts; the additional procedures might include:

    a. Examining supporting documents, such as invoices
    b. Confirming significant information with other parties to the transaction
    c. Determining if the transaction was properly authorized
    d. Considering whether other similar transactions may have occurred
    e. Applying procedures to identify other similar transactions

EVALUATION OF DETECTED OR EXPECTED ILLEGAL ACTS

The auditor should consider the quantitative and qualitative aspects of the illegal act. Loss contingencies resulting from illegal acts that may be required to be disclosed should be evaluated similar to other loss contingencies.

The auditor should consider the implications of an illegal act for the rest of the audit, particularly whether the auditor can rely on client representations. Factors to consider include the relationship of the perpetration and concealment, if any, of the illegal act to specific control procedures and the level of management or employees involved.

EFFECT ON THE AUDIT REPORT

If the auditor concludes that an illegal act that has a material effect on the financial statements has not been properly accounted for or disclosed, the auditor should issue a qualified or an adverse opinion.

If the client prevents the auditor from obtaining sufficient competent evidential matter to evaluate whether an illegal act that could be material to the financial statements has occurred, or is likely to have occurred, the auditor generally should disclaim an opinion.

CONSIDERATION OF WITHDRAWAL

If the client refuses to accept the auditor's report as modified because of an illegal act, the auditor should withdraw from the engagement and communicate, in writing, the reasons for withdrawal to the audit committee or to the board of directors.

Even when the illegal act is not material to the financial statements, the auditor may decide to withdraw from the engagement when the client does not take the remedial action the auditor considers necessary in the circumstances.

INTERNAL COMMUNICATIONS

The auditor should be sure that the audit committee or others with equivalent authority and responsibility are adequately informed about illegal acts that come to the auditor's attention. (The auditor should communicate directly with the audit committee or equivalent body if senior management is involved in the illegal act.) Since clearly inconsequential matters need not be communicated to the audit committee, the auditor may agree in advance with the audit committee on the nature of matters to be communicated.

Any communication should:

1. Describe the illegal act
2. Describe the circumstances of its occurrence
3. Describe the financial statement effect
4. Be oral or written, but if the communication is oral, be documented in the audit workpapers

EXTERNAL COMMUNICATIONS

The auditor is not ordinarily responsible for disclosing an illegal act outside the client's organization and such disclosure would be precluded by the auditor's ethical or legal obligation of confidentiality, unless the matter affects his opinion on the financial statements. The auditor should recognize, however, that in the following circumstances, a duty to notify parties outside the client may exist:

1. To the SEC when the client reports an auditor change on Form 8-K (or to comply with other legal and regulatory requirements, such as Section 10A of the 1934 Act)
2. To a successor auditor under Section 315
3. To a court in response to a subpoena
4. To a funding agency or other specified agency in audits of entities that receive financial assistance from a government agency

INTERPRETATIONS

There are no interpretations for this section.

TECHNIQUES FOR APPLICATION

DISTINCTION BETWEEN RESPONSIBILITY FOR DETECTION OF ILLEGAL ACTS AND FRAUD

The auditor should plan and perform the audit to provide reasonable assurance that material fraud will be detected. The same responsibility applies to material, direct-effect illegal acts. An intentional material misstatement or omission in financial information filed with the SEC is a violation of federal securities laws and should be regarded as a material illegal act. However, the appropriate guidance for the audit approach to these matters is Section 316. For indirect-effect illegal acts, the auditor should be aware of the possibility that such illegal acts may have occurred. If a possible indirect-effect illegal act having a material effect on the financial statements is detected, the auditor should apply specific procedures to determine if an illegal act has occurred. Examples of customary audit procedures that might bring possible illegal acts to the auditor's attention include:

1. Reading minutes
2. Making inquiries of management and legal counsel concerning litigation, claims, and assessments
3. Performing substantive tests of sensitive transactions
4. Making inquiries of management concerning compliance with laws and regulations
5. Obtaining a representation letter that includes comments concerning the absence of violations of laws and regulations

REQUIRED PROCEDURES

In spite of the fact that this section states that the auditor does not apply procedures specifically directed to the detection of illegal acts, there are some required procedures. The required procedures are:

1. Inquire of management concerning the client's compliance with laws and regulations.
2. If applicable, inquire of management concerning:
   a. Policies on prevention of illegal acts, and
   b. Use of directives and periodic representations obtained from management at appropriate levels of authority concerning compliance with laws and regulations

In addition, written representations concerning the absence of illegal acts are usually included in the management representation letter.

A question that often arises in practice is whether obtaining a management representation letter meets the separately stated requirement to inquire of management concerning the client's compliance with laws and regulations. Practice differs on this point. Some auditors obtain the typical written representations from management and make no separate oral inquiries on illegal acts.

Other auditors believe it is prudent to make separate inquiries near the conclusion of the audit. As part of the closing conference with the client, they obtain additional oral assurances from the client on the absence of violations of laws and regulations. This oral communication is intended to evoke candor and stress the importance the auditor attaches to being fully informed on such matters. Because Section 316 does require the auditor to inquire about fraud, in practice the inquiries about fraud and illegal acts are typically combined. These inquiries are a separate audit step and are normally documented in the audit program or other working papers.

The inquiries concerning policies on illegal acts and use of directives and obtaining written representations from management personnel are required only when applicable. For example, if management personnel are required to complete a questionnaire on compliance with a code of conduct, it would be prudent for the auditor to become familiar with the process and review returned questionnaires. However, if an entity does not have a code of conduct or does not require management personnel to make representations on compliance, the entity's policies and procedures are not necessarily deficient.

AU 318 Performing Audit Procedures in Response to Assessed Risks and Evaluating the Audit Evidence Obtained

AU-C 330 Performing Audit Procedures in Response to Assessed Risks and Evaluating the Audit Evidence Obtained

AU EFFECTIVE DATE AND APPLICABILITY

Original Pronouncement	Statement on Auditing Standards (SAS) 110.
Effective Date	This statement currently is effective.
Applicability	Audits of financial statements in accordance with generally accepted auditing standards (GAAS).

AU-C EFFECTIVE DATE AND SUMMARY OF CHANGES

SAS No. 122, *Codification of Auditing Standards and Procedures,* is effective for audits of financial statements with periods ending on or after December 15, 2012.
AU-C 330 does not change extant requirements in any significant respect.

AU DEFINITIONS OF TERMS

Further audit procedures. Audit procedures performed after performing risk assessment procedures. Further audit procedures consist of tests of controls and substantive tests (i.e., tests of details and substantive analytical procedures).
Substantive procedures. Procedures performed to detect material misstatements at the assertion level. Includes substantive analytical procedures and tests of detail.

Tests of controls. Procedures concerned with how an internal control procedures was applied, the consistency with which it was applied during the audit period, and by whom it was applied. Tests of controls used for generating evidence about operating effectiveness include inquiries, inspection, observation, and reperformance of the application of the control.

AU-C 330 DEFINITIONS OF TERMS

Substantive procedure. An audit procedure designed to detect material misstatements at the assertion level. Substantive procedures comprise:

1. Tests of details (classes of transactions, account balances, and disclosures) and
2. Substantive analytical procedures

Test of controls. An audit procedure designed to evaluate the operating effectiveness of controls in preventing, or detecting and correcting, material misstatements at the assertion level.

OBJECTIVES OF AU SECTION 318

Sections 318 and 314 are the centerpiece of the risk assessment standards. Together, these two sections provide detailed guidance on how to apply the audit risk model described in Section 312. That model describes audit risk as:

$$AR = RMM \times DR$$

where AR is audit risk, RMM is the risk of material misstatement, and DR is detection risk. The RMM is a combination of inherent and control risk. Although the standard describes a combined risk assessment, the auditor may perform separate assessments of inherent and control risks.

Section 318 provides guidance on the design and performance of further audit procedures, which consist of tests of controls (an element of RMM), and substantive procedures, which are related to detection risk. It provides a significant amount of new guidance that previously did not exist in the auditing literature.

The assessment of the risk of material misstatement serves as the basis for the design of further audit procedures. Further audit procedures should be clearly linked and responsive to the assessed risks.

NOTE: SAS 107 describes risks as existing at one of two levels: the financial statement level or the relevant assertion level. This distinction is important because the nature of the auditor's response differs depending on whether the risk is a financial statement–level or an assertion-level risk.

- *The risk of material misstatement at the financial statement level has a pervasive effect on the financial statements and affects many assertions. The control environment is an example of a financial statement–level risk. In addition to developing assertion-specific responses, financial statement–level risks may require the auditor to develop an overall response, such as assigning more experienced audit team members.*
- *Assertion-level risks pertain to a single assertion or related group of assertions. Assertion-level risks will require the auditor to design and perform specific further audit procedures, such as tests of controls and/or substantive procedures that are directly responsive to the assessed risk.*

OBJECTIVE OF AU-C SECTION 330

AU-C Section 330 states that "the objective of the auditor is to obtain sufficient appropriate audit evidence regarding the assessed risks of material misstatement through designing and implementing appropriate responses to those risks."

FUNDAMENTAL REQUIREMENTS

BASIC REQUIREMENT

To reduce audit risk to an acceptably low level, the auditor should:

- Determine overall responses to address the assessed risks of material misstatement at the financial statement level, and
- Design and perform further audit procedures whose nature, timing, and extent are responsive to the assessed risks of material misstatement at the relevant assertion level.

NOTE: *Further audit procedures consist of either tests of controls or substantive tests. Often, a combined approach using both tests of controls and substantive procedures is an effective approach.*

Audit procedures performed in previous audits and example procedures provided by illustrative audit programs may help the auditor understand the types of further audit procedures that are possible to perform. However, prior year procedures and example audit programs do not provide a sufficient basis for determining the nature, timing, and extent of audit procedures to perform in the current audit. The assessment of the risk of material misstatement in the current period is the primary basis for designing further audit procedures in the current period.

OVERALL RESPONSES

The auditor should determine overall responses to financial statement–level risks of material misstatement. Those overall responses may include:

- Emphasizing to the audit team the need to maintain professional skepticism in gathering and evaluating audit evidence
- Assigning more experienced staff or those with specialized skills
- Using specialists
- Providing more supervision
- Incorporating additional elements of unpredictability in the selection of further audit procedures
- Making general changes to the nature, timing, or extent of further audit procedures, such as performing substantive procedures at period end instead of at an interim date

DESIGNING THE NATURE, TIMING, AND EXTENT OF FURTHER AUDIT PROCEDURES

The auditor should design and perform further audit procedures whose nature, timing, and extent are responsive to and clearly linked with the assessment of the risk of material misstatement. In designing further audit procedures, the auditor should consider matters such as:

- The significance of the risk

- The likelihood that a material misstatement will occur
- The characteristics of the class of transactions, account balance, or disclosure involved
- The nature of the specific controls used by the entity, in particular, whether they are manual or automated
- Whether the auditor expects to obtain audit evidence to determine if the entity's controls are effective in preventing or detecting material misstatements

Regardless of the audit approach selected, the auditor should design and perform substantive procedures for all relevant assertions related to each material class of transactions, account balance, and disclosure.

Nature

The nature of audit procedures refers to their type. Selecting the type of audit procedure to perform is of most importance in designing tests that are responsive to assessed risks.

The higher the auditor's assessment of risk, the more reliable and relevant is the audit evidence sought by the auditor from substantive procedures. Section 326 provides guidance on the relative reliability of various types of audit evidence.

In some instances, the auditor may use information produced by the entity's information system in performing audit procedures. For example, the auditor may use the entity's aging of accounts receivable to test the adequacy of their allowance for doubtful accounts. When the auditor uses information from the entity's system in this manner, the auditor should obtain audit evidence about the accuracy and completeness of the information. This audit evidence may come from tests of controls, substantive procedures, or both.

Timing

Timing refers to when audit procedures are performed or the period or date to which the audit evidence applies. Tests of controls may be performed either at an interim date or at period end. In considering when to perform audit procedures, the auditor should consider matters such as:

- The control environment
- When relevant information is available (for example, electronic files may subsequently be overwritten, or procedures to be observed may occur only at certain times)
- The nature of the risk (for example, if there is a risk of inflated revenues to meet earnings expectations by subsequent creation of false sales agreements, the auditor may examine contracts available on the date of the period end)
- The period or date to which the audit evidence relates

When further audit procedures are performed at an interim date, the auditor should consider the additional evidence that is necessary for the remaining period.

Extent

Extent refers to the quantity of a specific audit procedure to be performed—for example, a sample size. The auditor determines the extent of an audit procedure after considering:

- Tolerable misstatement
- The assessed risk of material misstatement
- The degree of assurance the auditor plans to obtain

As the risk of material misstatement increases, the extent of audit procedures also should increase.

NOTE: Increasing the extent of audit procedures is effective only if the nature of the procedures is responsive to the risk of material misstatement. For example, the confirmation of accounts receivable is a test primarily directed to the existence assertion. If the auditor is concerned about the completeness assertion, increasing the number of confirmations sent to customers will not be effective.

TESTS OF CONTROLS

The auditor should test controls when

- The auditor will rely on the operating effectiveness of controls to modify the nature, timing and extent of substantive procedures, or
- Substantive procedures alone will not be sufficient. Section 319 provides guidance on determining when substantive procedures alone will not be sufficient.

NOTE: When determining whether to rely on the operating effectiveness of controls to modify the nature, timing, and extent of substantive procedures, the auditor may consider matters such as the following:

- *The incremental cost of testing controls, which includes the cost of testing not just the controls that have a direct effect on the assertion, but also those controls upon which the direct controls depend. When considering incremental testing costs, consider that the costs of evaluating control design already have been incurred (because the auditor must evaluate control design on every audit) and that the incremental cost of obtaining audit evidence about the effective operation of controls may not be substantial.*
- *In many circumstances, audit evidence obtained from tests of controls may be relevant for a three-year period. That is, the costs of testing controls may provide benefit for three audit periods.*
- *The benefits to be derived from testing controls. In many cases, testing controls may have benefits that extend beyond the relevant assertion to be addressed by the substantive procedures. For example, testing controls may provide audit evidence about the reliability of the entity's IT system, which can allow the auditor to rely on other information produced by the system to perform substantive tests. For example, information obtained from a reliable IT system can contribute to more reliable analytical procedures.*

The auditor will perform risk assessment procedures to evaluate the design of the entity's internal control, and these procedures may provide some limited audit evidence about the operating effectiveness of internal control. But risk assessment procedures by themselves generally will not provide sufficient appropriate audit evidence to support relying on controls to modify the nature, timing, and extent of substantive procedures.

Nature

As the planned level of assurance increases, the auditor should seek more reliable or more extensive audit evidence about the operating effectiveness of controls. For example, if the auditor has determined that, for a particular assertion, substantive procedures alone will not be sufficient, then the auditor would want to select tests of controls that will provide more reliable audit evidence.

When designing tests of controls, the auditor should consider the need to obtain audit evidence supporting the effective operation of controls directly related to the relevant assertion as well as other indirect controls on which those controls depend. For example, if the auditor tests an IT application control, he or she should consider the need to test the IT general controls upon which the effective operation of the application control depends.

Timing

When determining the timing of tests of controls, the auditor should consider whether audit evidence is needed about how the control operated as of a point in time or how it operated throughout the audit period. This determination will depend on the auditor's overall objective. For example, to test the controls over the entity's physical inventory count, the auditor's objective would be related to how the control operated at the point in time the physical inventory count was taken. On the other hand, to modify the nature, timing, and extent of, say, revenue transactions or accounts payable, the auditor would want to test the operation of controls throughout the audit period.

If certain conditions are met, the auditor may use audit evidence about the operating effectiveness of controls obtained in prior audits. These conditions include the following:

- The auditor should obtain audit evidence about whether changes to the controls have occurred since the prior audit. If the controls have changed since they were last tested, the auditor should test the controls in the current period, to the extent they affect the relevance of the audit evidence from the prior period.
- The auditor should test the operating effectiveness of controls at least once every third year in an annual audit. When there are a number of controls for which the auditor determines that it is appropriate to use audit evidence in prior audits, the auditor should test the operating effectiveness of some controls each year.

NOTE: When considering whether it is appropriate to use audit evidence about the operating effectiveness of controls obtained in prior audits, the auditor should consider matters such as:

- *The effectiveness of other elements of internal control, including the control environment, the entity's monitoring of controls, and the entity's risk assessment process*
- *The risks arising from the characteristics of the control, including whether controls are manual or automated*
- *The effectiveness of IT general controls*
- *The effectiveness of the control and its application by the entity, including the nature and extent of deviations in the application of the control from tests of operating effectiveness in prior audits*
- *Whether the lack of a change in a particular control poses a risk due to changing circumstances*
- *The risk of material misstatement and the extent of reliance on the control*

In general, the higher the risk of material misstatement, or the greater the auditor's reliance on controls, the shorter the time period that should elapse between testing the controls.

Extent

In general, the greater the auditor's planned reliance on the operating effectiveness of controls, the greater the extent of testing. Other factors that the auditor should consider when determining the extent of tests of controls include the following:

- The frequency of the performance of the control by the entity during the period
- The length of time during the audit period that the auditor is relying on the operating effectiveness of the control

- The relevance and reliability of the audit evidence to be obtained in supporting that the control prevents, or detects and corrects, material misstatements at the relevant assertion level
- The extent to which audit evidence is obtained from tests of other controls related to the relevant assertion
- The expected deviation from the control

Generally, IT processing is inherently consistent. Therefore, the auditor may be able to limit the testing to one or a few instances of the control operations, providing that IT general controls operate effectively.

SUBSTANTIVE PROCEDURES

The auditor's substantive procedures should include:

- Performing tests directed to the relevant assertions related to each material class of transactions, account balance, and disclosures
- Agreeing the financial statements, including their accompanying notes to the underlying accounting records, and
- Examining material journal entries and other adjustments made during the course of preparing the financial statements

Section 318 describes *significant risks* and how the auditor identifies significant risks. With regard to performing procedures related to significant risks, the auditor should perform tests of details or a combination of tests of details and substantive analytical procedures. That is, the auditor is precluded from performing only substantive tests of details in response to significant risks.

Nature

The auditor should design tests of details responsive to the assessed risk with the objective of obtaining sufficient appropriate audit evidence to achieve the planned level of assurance at the relevant assertion level. In designing substantive analytical procedures, the auditor should consider matters such as:

- The suitability of using substantive analytical procedures, given the assertions
- The reliability of the data, whether internal or external, from which the expectation of recorded amounts or ratios is developed
- Whether the expectation is sufficiently precise to identify the possibility of a material misstatement at the desired level of assurance
- The amount of any difference in recorded amounts from expected values that is acceptable

Timing

In some circumstances, the auditor may perform substantive procedures as of an interim date, which increases the risk that misstatements that exist at the period end will not be detected by the auditor. As such, when substantive tests are performed at an interim date, the auditor should perform further substantive procedures or substantive procedures combined with tests of controls to cover the period between the interim tests and period end.

When considering whether to perform substantive procedures at an interim date, the auditor should consider factors such as:

- The control environment and other relevant controls
- The availability of information at a later date that is necessary for the auditor's procedures
- The objective of the substantive procedure
- The assessed risk of material misstatement
- The nature of the class of transactions or account balance and relevant assertions
- The ability of the auditor to reduce the risk that misstatements that exist at the period end are not detected by performing appropriate substantive procedures or substantive procedures combined with tests of controls to cover the remaining period

If the auditor detects misstatements at an interim date, the auditor should consider modifying the planned nature, timing, or extent of the substantive procedures covering the remaining period.

Extent

The greater the risk of material misstatement, the greater the extent of substantive procedures. In designing tests of details, the auditor normally thinks of the extent of testing in terms of the sample size, which is affected by the planned level of detection risk, tolerable misstatement, expected misstatement, and the nature of the population. However, the auditor also should consider other matters, such as selecting large or unusual items from a population rather than sampling items from the population.

EVALUATING THE SUFFICIENCY AND APPROPRIATENESS OF THE AUDIT EVIDENCE OBTAINED

The auditor should conclude whether sufficient appropriate audit evidence has been obtained to reduce to an appropriate low level the risk of material misstatements in the financial statements. The auditor's judgment as to what constitutes sufficient appropriate audit evidence is influenced by factors such as the following:

- Significance of the potential misstatement in the relevant assertion and the likelihood of its having a material effect, individually or aggregated with other potential misstatements, on the financial statements
- Effectiveness of management's responses and controls to address the risks
- Experience gained during previous audits with respect to similar potential misstatements
- Results of audit procedures performed, including whether such audit procedures identified specific instances of fraud or error
- Source and reliability of available information
- Persuasiveness of the audit evidence
- Understanding of the entity and its environment, including its internal control

DOCUMENTATION

The auditor should document the following:

1. The overall responses to address the assessed risks of misstatement at the financial statement level
2. The nature, timing, and extent of the further audit procedures
3. The linkage of those procedures with the assessed risks at the relevant assertion level
4. The results of the audit procedures

5. The conclusions reached with regard to the use in the current audit of audit evidence about the operating effectiveness of controls that was obtained in a prior audit

INTERPRETATIONS

There are no interpretations for this section.

TECHNIQUES FOR APPLICATION

TESTING AT INTERIM DATES

Convenience-Timed Tests

Some audit tests can be applied at any convenient selected date before the balance sheet date and completed as part of year-end procedures. Examples are:

1. Tests of details of the additions to, and reduction of, accounts such as property, investments, debt, and equity
2. Tests of details of transactions affecting income and expense accounts
3. Tests of accounts that are not generally audited by testing the details of items composing the balance, such as warranty reserves and certain deferred charges
4. Analytical procedures applied to income or expense accounts

The common denominator in these tests is that the nature and extent of procedures applied are not necessarily influenced by doing a portion of the testing before the balance sheet date. For example, the auditor may decide to vouch all property additions and retirements over a specified dollar amount. The nature and extent of the test are not influenced by whether the testing is done all at year-end or one portion is done at an interim date and the remainder at year-end.

Misstatements Detected at Interim Dates

Section 318 does not address the issue of misstatements detected at an interim date. For example, if the auditor confirms accounts receivable as of October 31 and discovers an error in the receivables balance, how should that misstatement be handled, given that the opinion is on the balance sheet as of December 31, not October 31?

As a practical matter, the auditor should evaluate the results of interim testing to assess the possibility of misstatement at the balance sheet date. This evaluation is influenced by:

1. The potential implications of the nature and cause of the misstatements detected at the interim date
2. The possible relationship to other phases of the audit; for example, do the misstatements detected indicate a need to reconsider the assessment of control risk?
3. Corrections that the entity subsequently records
4. The results of auditing procedures that cover the remaining period

This assessment may cause the auditor to reperform principal substantive tests at year-end or to otherwise expand the scope of substantive tests at year-end.

NOTE: Even if the misstatement detected at an interim date is corrected prior to year-end, there may be implications for evaluation of misstatements at year-end. Unless the auditor has applied procedures sufficient to provide reasonable assurance that similar misstatements have not occurred, the auditor may need to project a misstatement from interim to year-end.

Considering Control Risk When Testing at an Interim Date

When performing principal substantive tests at an interim date, the primary control focus is on asset safeguarding and controls that address the completeness assertion. If the design of these controls in not effective, then the substantive tests related to existence and completeness assertions should be applied at year-end.

Keep in mind that this consideration is tied to specific assertions, not to the overall account. For example, confirmation of receivables does not address the completeness assertion, which means that receivables could be confirmed at an interim date even if controls to address completeness were not effectively designed. However, the auditor would still need to consider the nature, timing, and extent of further audit procedures related to the completeness assertion.

Length of Remaining Period

How long can the remaining period be? Section 318 offers only the general observation that the potential for increased audit risk tends to become greater as the remaining period becomes longer.

In practice, many auditors believe the remaining period should not exceed three months (i.e., for a December 31 audit, testing certain balances as of September 30). Another rule of thumb is to consider a remaining period of one month as creating a relatively low increase in audit risk. Ordinarily, if the remaining period is one month, substantive tests to cover the remaining period can be restricted to test such as

- Comparison of the account balance at year-end with the balance at the interim date to identify unusual amounts or relationships.
- Investigation of unusual amounts or relationships.
- Application of other analytical procedures to the year-end balance.

Naturally, as with any rule of thumb, the auditor should be aware that in specific circumstances, factors may increase audit risk, and the principal substantive tests will have to be applied at year-end.

DESIGNING AUDIT PROCEDURES

There is an almost infinite variety of approaches that an auditor can use in practice to achieve the objectives of Section 318. The following illustration shows some examples of further audit procedures that may be performed to meet certain audit objectives.

Illustrative assertions about account balances	*Examples of substantive procedures*
Existence or Occurrence	
Inventories included in the balance sheet physically exist.	Observing physical inventory counts. Obtaining confirmation of inventories at locations outside the entity. Testing of inventory transactions between a preliminary physical inventory date and the balance sheet date.

Illustrative assertions about account balances	Examples of substantive procedures

Existence or Occurrence

Inventories represent items held for sale or use in the normal course of business.	Reviewing perpetual inventory records, production records, and purchasing records for indication of current activity. Comparing inventories with a current sales catalog and subsequent sales and delivery reports. Using the work of specialists to corroborate the nature of specialized products.

Completeness

Inventory quantities include all products, materials, and supplies on hand.	Observing physical inventory counts. Analytically comparing the relationship of inventory balances to recent purchasing, production, and sales activities. Testing shipping and receiving cutoff procedures.
Inventory quantities include all products, materials, and supplies owned by the entity that are in transit or stored at outside locations.	Obtaining confirmation of inventories at locations outside the entity. Analytically comparing the relationship of inventory balances to recent purchasing, production, and sales activities. Testing shipping and receiving cutoff procedures.
Inventory listings are accurately compiled and the totals are properly included in the inventory accounts.	Tracing test counts recorded during the physical inventory observation to the inventory listing. Accounting for all inventory tags and count sheets used in recording the physical inventory counts. Testing the clerical accuracy of inventory listing. Reconciling physical counts with perpetual records and general ledger balances and investigating significant fluctuations.

Rights and Obligations

The entity has legal title or similar rights of ownership to the inventories.	Observing physical inventory counts. Obtaining confirmation of inventories at locations outside the entity. Examining paid vendors' invoices, consignment agreements, and contracts.
Inventories exclude items billed to customers or owned by others.	Examining paid vendor's invoices, consignment agreements, and contracts. Testing shipping and receiving cutoff procedures.

Valuation or Allocation

Inventories are properly stated at cost (except when market is lower).	Examining paid vendors' invoices. Reviewing direct labor rates. Testing the computation of standard overhead rates. Examining analyses of purchasing and manufacturing standard cost variances.

Illustrative assertions about account balances	Examples of substantive procedures
Existence or Occurrence	
Slow-moving, excess, defective, and obsolete items included in inventories are properly identified.	Examining an analysis of inventory turnover. Reviewing industry experience and trends. Analytically comparing the relationship of inventory balances to anticipated sales volume. Touring the plant. Inquiring of production and sales personnel concerning possible excess of obsolete inventory items.
Inventories are reduced, when appropriate, to replacement cost or net realizable value.	Obtaining current market value quotations. Reviewing current production costs. Examining sales after year-end and open purchase order commitments.
Presentation and Disclosure	
Inventories are properly classified in the balance sheet as current assets.	Reviewing drafts of the financial statements.
The major categories of inventories and their bases of valuation are adequately disclosed in the financial statements.	Reviewing the drafts of the financial statements. Comparing the disclosures made in the financial statements to the requirements of generally accepted accounting principles.
The pledge or assignment of any inventories is appropriately disclosed.	Obtaining confirmation of inventories pledged under loan agreements.

This approach can be time-consuming and result in a substantial amount of repetition. For example, developing specific audit objectives for the existence of each asset normally results in the repetitive statement that the particular asset does, in fact, exist and is available for its intended use. There is more variation for specific audit objectives related to presentation and disclosure, but disclosure checklists are available for that assertion and related specific objectives.

TESTS OF INTERNAL CONTROL OPERATING EFFECTIVENESS

Test Design Considerations

Your tests of operating effectiveness should be designed to determine:

- How the control procedure was performed
- The consistency with which it was applied
- By whom it was applied

Risk-Based Approach to Designing Tests

The reliability of a test is influenced by three factors:

1. *Nature*. The type of the test you perform is referred to as its "nature."

    There are four types of tests:

    - *Inquiry*. Think of inquiry as providing circumstantial evidence about the performance of a control. For example, if you ask the accounting clerk "Did you perform the month-end reconciliation?" the reply "yes" does not provide you with as

much evidence as you would get from reviewing the actual reconciliation. For controls related to higher risks of misstatement, you will want to supplement your inquiries with other tests.
- *Observation*. You may observe the performance of a control procedure. For example, the annual count of inventory or an edit check built in to a computer application are controls whose performance you might observe. The observation of a control is a reliable test, but it applies only to the point in time you observed the control. If the control is performed only once during the period (e.g., the inventory count), that one observation may be sufficient. But if the control is performed throughout a period (e.g., the edit check), you will need to perform other tests if you want evidence that the control was performed consistently.
- *Documentation*. You may inspect the documentation of the performance of the control. For example, if cash disbursements over a certain dollar amount require dual signatures, then you could inspect a number of checks over that amount to determine that they contain two signatures.

In many instances, particularly for controls associated with higher risks, you will perform a combination of procedures. A walk-through is an example of a combination of inquiry, observation, and inspection of documentation.

2. *Timing*. You are required to determine whether controls are operating effectively as of the company's fiscal year-end. The closer your tests are to year-end, the more reliable; the farther away from year-end, the less reliable. Ideally, you would perform all your tests as of the balance sheet date, but practically, this is not possible. Some test will be performed in advance of year-end. For example, you may decide to test the controls relating to payroll as of October 31.

The bigger the difference between the "as of" date of the tests and year-end, the less reliable the tests. In our example, if payroll controls are tested as of October 31, there is a chance that the operating effectiveness of those controls changed during the two months from October 31 to December 31.

Plan on testing controls related to low risks of material misstatement in advance of year-end. Controls related to higher risks should be performed as close to year-end as possible.

3. *Extent*. The extent of your procedures refers to the number of tests you perform. In the previous example of certain cash disbursements requiring dual signatures, the question is "How many checks should I examine?" The greater the extent of your tests—in this case, the more checks you examine—the more reliable your conclusion. Controls related to higher risk of misstatement will require more extensive testing than those related to lower risk.

When you do test controls in advance of year-end, you will want to consider the need to perform additional tests to establish the effectiveness of the control procedure from the time the tests were performed until year-end.

For example, if you tested the effectiveness of bank reconciliations as of June 30 and the reporting date was December 31, you should consider performing tests to cover the period from July 1 through December 31. These tests may *not* require you to repeat the detailed tests performed at June 30 for the subsequent six-month period. If you establish the effectiveness of the control procedure at June 30, you may be able to support a conclusion about the effectiveness of the control at the reporting date indirectly through the consideration of entity-level controls and other procedures, such as:

- *The effectiveness of personnel-related controls, such as the training and supervision of personnel who perform control procedures.* For example, are the people performing the bank reconciliations adequately supervised, and was their work reviewed during the second half of the year?
- *The effectiveness of risk identification and management controls, including change management.* For example, would management be able to identify changes in the entity's business or its circumstances that would affect the continued effectiveness of bank reconciliations as a control procedure?
- *The effectiveness of the monitoring component of the entity's internal control.*
- *Inquiries of personnel to determine what changes, if any, occurred during the period that would affect the performance of controls.*
- *Repeating the procedures performed earlier in the year, focusing primarily on elements of the control procedure that have changed during the period.* For example, if the entity added new bank accounts or new personnel performing certain bank reconciliations, you would focus your tests on those accounts and individuals.

Information Technology Application Controls

Again, the types of procedures you perform for the period between June 30 and December 31 will depend on the risk related to the control. Application controls are the structure, policies, and procedures that apply to separate, individual business process application systems. They include both the automated control procedures (i.e., those routines contained within the computer program) and the policies and procedures associated with user activities, such as the manual follow-up required to investigate potential errors identified during processing.

As with all other control procedures, information technology (IT) application controls should be designed to achieve specified control objectives, which in turn are driven by the risks to achieving certain business objectives. In general, the objectives of a computer application are to ensure that:

- Data remain complete, accurate, and valid during their input, update, and storage.
- Output files and reports are distributed and made available only to authorized users.

Specific application-level controls should address the risks to achieving these objectives. The way in which IT control objectives are met will depend on the types of technologies used by the entity. For example, the specific control procedures used to control access to an online, real-time database will be different from those procedures related to access of a "flat file" stored on a disk.

An IT controls specialist most likely will be needed to understand the risks involved in various technologies and the related activity-level controls.

Shared Activities

Some activities in a company are performed centrally and affect several different financial account balances. For example, cash disbursements affect not only cash balances but also accounts payable and payroll. The most common types of shared activities include:

- Cash receipts
- Cash disbursements
- Payroll
- Data processing

When designing your activity-level tests, you should be sure to coordinate your tests of shared activities with your tests of individual processing streams. For example, you should plan on testing cash disbursements only once, not several times for each different processing stream that includes cash disbursements.

Sample Sizes and Extent of Tests

Whenever you test activity-level controls, you will have to determine the extent of your tests. If you are testing the reconciliation of significant general ledger accounts to the underlying detailed trial balance, how many reconciliations should you look at? If the control is something that is performed on every transaction—for example, the authorization of payments to vendors—how many should you test?

The extent of your tests should be sufficient to support your conclusion on whether the control is operating effectively at a given point in time. Determining the sufficiency of the extent of your tests is a matter of judgment that is affected by a number of factors. Exhibit 1 lists these factors and indicates how they will affect the extent of your tests.

Exhibit 1. Determining the Extent of Tests

	Effect on the Extent of Tests	
Factor to consider	**Increase number of tests**	**Decrease number of tests**
How frequently the control procedure is performed	Procedure performed often (e.g., daily)	Procedure performed occasionally (e.g., once a month)
Importance of control	Important control (e.g., control of addresses multiple assertions or it is a period-end detective control)	Less important control
Degree of judgment required to perform the control	High degree of judgment	Low degree of judgment
Complexity of control procedure	Relatively complex control procedure	Relatively simple control procedure
Level of competence of the person performing the control procedure	Highly competent	Less competent

When determining the extent of tests, you also should consider whether the control is manual or automated. When a control is performed manually, the consistency with which that control is performed can vary greatly. In contrast, once a control becomes automated, it is performed the same way each and every time. For that reason, you should plan on performing more extensive tests of manual controls than you will for automated controls.

In some circumstances, testing a single operation of an automated control may be sufficient to obtain a high level of assurance that the control operated effectively, *provided that* IT general controls operated effectively throughout the period.

Sample Sizes for Tests of Transactions

You do not have to test every performance of a control to draw a valid conclusion about the operating effectiveness of the control. For example, suppose that one of the controls a manufacturing company performs in its revenue cycle is to match the shipping report to the customer's invoice to make sure that the customer was billed for the right number of items and the revenue was recorded in the proper period. Over the course of a year, the company has thousands of shipments. How many of those should be tested to draw a conclusion?

Statistical Sampling Principles

You do not have to perform a statistical sample to determine your sample size, but it does help to apply the basic principles of statistical sampling theory. In a nutshell, the size of your sample is driven by three variables:

1. *Confidence level.* This variable has to do with how confident you are in your conclusion. If you want to be very confident that you reached the correct conclusion (say, 95% confident), then your sample size will be larger than if you want a lower confidence level (say, 60%).
2. *Tolerable rate of error.* This variable addresses the issue of how many deviations in the performance of the control would be acceptable for you still to conclude that the control is operating effectively. If you can accept a high rate of error (the procedure is performed incorrectly 20% of the time), then your sample size will be smaller than if you can accept only a slight rate of error (the procedure is performed incorrectly only 2% of the time).
3. *Expected error rate of the population.* This variable has to do with your expectation of the true error rate in the population. Do you think that the control procedure was performed correctly every single time it was performed (0% deviation rate), or do you think that a few errors might have been made? The lower the expected error rate, the lower the sample size.

Note that the size of the population does not affect the sample size (unless it is very small, e.g., when a control procedure is performed only once a month, in which case the population consists of only 12 items).

In practice, most companies have chosen sample sizes for tests of transactions that range from 20 items to 60 items. It is common for independent auditors to offer some guidance on sample sizes.

Be careful in simply accepting sample sizes without questioning the underlying assumptions for the three variables just listed. In reviewing these assumptions, you should ask:

- Am I comfortable with the assumed confidence level? Given the importance of the control and other considerations, do I need a higher level of confidence (which would result in testing more items), or is the assumed level sufficient?
- Is the tolerable rate of error acceptable? Can I accept that percentage of errors in the application of the control procedure and still conclude that the control is operating "effectively"?
- Is the expected population deviation rate greater than 0%? Some sample sizes are determined using the assumption that the expected population deviation rate is 0%. Although this assumption reduces the initial sample size, if a deviation is discovered, the sample size must be increased to reach the same conclusion about control effectiveness. Unless you have a strong basis for assuming a population deviation rate of 0%, you should assume that the population contains some errors. That assumption will increase your initial sample size, but it usually is more efficient to start with a slightly higher sample size rather than increasing sample sizes subsequently, as deviations are discovered.

Sample Sizes for Tests of Other Controls

You also will need to determine sample sizes for controls that are performed less frequently than every transaction or every day. Because the population sizes for these types of controls are so small, traditional sampling methodologies need to be adjusted. Exhibit 2 lists the sample sizes that have evolved in practice for tests of smaller populations.

Exhibit 2. Sample Sizes for Small Populations

Frequency of Control Performance	Typical Sample Sizes
Annually	1
Quarterly	2 or 3
Monthly	2 to 6
Weekly	5 to 15

TYPES OF TESTS

Inquiry and Focus Groups

Formal inquiries of entity personnel—either individually or as part of a focus group—can be a reliable source of evidence about the operating effectiveness of application-level controls. Inquiries can serve two main purposes:

1. To confirm your understanding of the design of the control (what should happen).
2. To identify exceptions to the entity's stated control procedures (what *really* happens).

Confirming control design. Typically, this process consists primarily of a review of documentation (such as policies and procedures manuals) and limited inquiries of high-level individuals or those in the accounting department. To confirm this understanding of the processing stream and control procedures, you should expand your inquiries to include operating personnel and those responsible for performing the control.

When conducting your inquiries, consider:

- Focus first on what should happen and whether the employees' understanding of the control procedure is consistent with your understanding. This strategy accomplishes two important objectives:

  1. It provides you with a baseline understanding of the procedure that everyone can agree on. It helps to start with everyone on the same page. You can then discuss exceptions to the norm later.
  2. If the employees' understanding of what should happen varies significantly from what is documented, that may indicate a weakness in entity-level controls. For example, you may determine that a weakness in the entity's hiring or training policies is the cause of the lack of understanding of what should happen. This weakness may have implications for the operating effectiveness of other application-level controls.

  Differences between the documentation and the employees' understanding of the procedures also may indicate that the implementation or use of the entity's automated documentation tool was poorly planned or executed. For example, documentation of a new control may have been created without informing operating personnel of the change.
- *Ask open-ended questions.* Open-ended questions get people talking and allow them to *volunteer information.* The results of your inquiries are more reliable when individuals volunteer information that is consistent with your own understanding rather than simply confirming that understanding with a direct statement.

- *Focus on how the procedure is applied and documented.* As described earlier, operating effectiveness is determined by how the procedure was applied, the consistency with which it was applied, and by whom (e.g., whether the person performing the control has other, conflicting duties). The last two elements will be the subject of your inquiries to identify exceptions to the stated policy. Questions about what somebody does or how he or she documents control performance (e.g., by initialing a source document) typically are less threatening than questions related to consistency ("Under what circumstances do you *not* follow the required procedure?") or possible incompatible functions.
- *Interviewers should share their findings and observations with each other.* Research indicates that the effectiveness of inquiries as an evidence-gathering technique improves when engagement team members debrief the results.
- *Ask "What could go wrong?"* Interviewees will easily understand a line of questioning that starts with:

    "Tell me what could go wrong in processing this information."

    Followed by:

    "What do you do to make sure those errors don't occur?"

    Toward that end, consider using the financial statement assertions model to frame your questions. As described previously, one way to organize your understanding of activity-level controls is to link them to financial statement assertions. You can use these assertions to formulate questions. For example, the question "What procedures do you perform to make sure that you capture all the transactions?" is related to the completeness assertion.
- *Consider the difference between processes and controls.* A process changes or manipulates the information in the stream. Processes introduce the possibility of error. Controls detect errors or prevent them from occurring during the processing of information. Your inquiries should confirm your understanding of *both* the steps involved in processing the information and the related controls.

    The duties of an individual employee may include the processing of information (e.g., the manual input of data into the computer system or the preparation of source documents), control procedures (e.g., the performance of a reconciliation or the follow-up on items identified in an exception report), or both. In making your inquiries, you should remain cognizant of the distinction between processes and controls and the responsibilities of the individual being interviewed.

Identify exceptions. In every entity, there will be differences between the company's stated procedures and what individuals actually do in the course of everyday work. The existence of differences is normal. In testing the effectiveness of application-level controls, you should anticipate that these differences will exist, and you should plan your procedures to identify them and assess how they affect the effectiveness of activity-level controls. Differences between what *should* happen and what *really* happens can arise from:

- The existence of transactions that were not contemplated in the design of the system.
- Different application of the procedure according to division, location, or differences between people.
- Changes in personnel or in their assigned responsibilities during the period under review.

- Practical, field-level workarounds, a way to satisfy other objectives, such as bypassing a control to better respond to customer needs.

Once you and the interviewee reach a common understanding of the company's stated procedures, you should be prepared to discuss the circumstances that result in a variation from these procedures. When making these inquiries:

- *Don't make value judgments.* In any organization, the information that flows through a processing stream will follow the path of least resistance. Controls that are seen as barriers to the processing of legitimate transactions that meet the company's overall objectives may be bypassed. The employee may not be at fault. More important, if you adopt a judgmental attitude toward the interviewee, he or she will be less inclined to participate productively in the information-gathering process, and your interview will lose effectiveness.
- *Separate information gathering from evaluation.* Remember that this phase of your inquiries is a two-step process: (1) identify the exceptions to the stated policy, and (2) assess the effect that these have on operating effectiveness. Keep these two objectives separate. Be careful that you don't perform your evaluation prematurely, before you gather all the necessary information. When performing your inquiries, remember that your only objective is to gather information; you will perform your evaluation once you have completed your inquiries.
- *Use hypothetical or indirect questions to probe sensitive areas.* Many interviewees will feel uncomfortable describing to you how they circumvent company policies or how they have incompatible duties that could leave the company vulnerable to fraud. To gather this type of information, use indirect questioning techniques that do not confront employees directly or otherwise put them on the defensive. For example, you might preface your questions with qualifying statements, such as:

  - "If a situation arose in which…"
  - "Suppose that…"
  - "If someone wanted to…"

- Ask them directly about their opinion of control effectiveness. The overall objective of your inquiry is to gather information to assess the effectiveness of controls. The opinions of those who perform the control procedures on a daily basis are important. Ask them to share those opinions. Do they think the controls are effective? Why or why not?

Qualifications of employees. Assessing the operating effectiveness of control activities requires you to consider who performs such activities. Your inquiries should determine whether the interviewee is qualified to perform the required procedures. To be "qualified," the individual should have the necessary skills, training, and experience and should have no incompatible functions.

Focus groups. As a supplement to, or perhaps instead of, interviewing people individually, you may wish to facilitate a group discussion about the entity's activity-level control activities and their effectiveness. The purpose of the group discussion would be the same as a discussion with individuals: to confirm your understanding of control design and to gather information about operating effectiveness. However, group discussions are advantageous in that they

- *Enable you to see the whole process.* You may be able to convene a group of individuals who represent every step in the processing stream, from the initiation of the transaction through to its posting in the general ledger. A group discussion that includes these members will help you to understand more quickly how the entire process fits together.
- *Foster communication and understanding.* In conducting your group discussion, you will bring together people in the company who may not interact on a regular basis, and you will engage them in a discussion about operating procedures and controls. By participating in this process, employees will gain a greater understanding of their responsibilities and how these fit into the larger picture. This improved understanding among employees will allow your project to provide value to the company that goes beyond mere compliance.

To conduct a group discussion, follow these five steps:

1. *Review the documentation of the processing stream and determine who should be invited to participate.* Groups of 5 to 10 people usually work the best—everyone can make a meaningful contribution to the conversation without things getting out of hand. Try to make sure that someone is present who has experience with every process, control, document, or electronic file described in your documentation of the processing stream.
2. *Prepare a flowchart of the process on a large sheet of paper.* Use sticky notes to document processes and control points. Your group discussion will be highly interactive, and the participants will have the opportunity to change your original flowchart to provide a more accurate description of what really happens in the process. Therefore, you should prepare your flowchart in a way that allows the group to work with it easily. Low-tech, high-touch works the best.
3. *Assemble the group and explain:*

    - The *purpose of the discussion,* as described previously.
    - The *process*, in which you will facilitate a discussion of how the process really works and the participants will be free to describe what happens by modifying the flowchart.
    - *How long the discussion will take.* Usually, one to two hours is the longest that group discussion of this nature can remain productive. If you need more time, it is better to have more sessions rather than have longer sessions.

4. *Post the flowchart on the wall and walk the participants through your understanding of the process.*
5. *Facilitate a discussion among the participants.* Be sure to:

    a. Reach an understanding about what should happen.
    b. Identify those instances in which exceptions exist (what really happens).

    Throughout the discussion, encourage the participants to change the flowchart as necessary so that it reflects what they have said.

Tests of Transactions

Some control procedures allow you to select a sample of transactions that were recorded during the period and:

- Examine the documentation indicating that the control procedure was performed.
- Reperform the procedure to determine that the control was performed properly. For example, the process for recording inventory purchases may require physically matching a paper-based warehouse receiving report with an approved purchase order.
- Determine that the purchase order was properly approved, as indicated by a signature.
- Determine that the vendor is an approved vendor.
- Observe evidence (e.g., checkmarks, initials) that warehouse personnel counted the goods received.

To test the effectiveness of this control procedure, you could:

- Examine documentation that the control was performed, including:

  - Documents were matched.
  - Purchase order was signed.
  - Receiving report was marked.

- Determine that the control was performed properly, including:

  - Purchase order and receiving report are for the same transaction.
  - Vendor is an approved vendor.
  - Signer of the purchase order has the authority to approve the transaction.

Computer application controls also may lend themselves to similar testing techniques. For example, suppose that purchased goods are accompanied by a bar code that identifies the goods received and their quantities. The bar code is scanned, and the information is matched electronically to purchase order files and approved vendor master files. Unmatched transactions are placed in a suspense file for subsequent follow-up. (As indicated previously, the computer application control consists of both the programmed elements of the control and the manual follow-up of identified errors.) To test the effectiveness of this control, you could:

- Prepare a file of test transactions and run through the system to determine that all errors are identified.
- Review the resolution of the suspense account items performed throughout the period to determine that they were resolved properly.

When performing tests of transactions, you will have to address issues related to the extent of testing: how many items to test. Suggestions for considering the extent of tests were provided earlier in this chapter.

Before performing your tests of transactions, you also should define what you will consider a control procedure error. In instances in which the evidence of performing the procedure is documented (e.g., an initial or signature), the lack of documentation (a missing signature) should be considered an error in the operation of the control. That is, in order for a documented control to be considered properly performed, *both* of these points must be true:

- The documentation indicates that the control procedure was performed.
- Your reperformance of the procedure indicates it was performed properly.

Reconciliations

Reconciliations are a common control procedure; examples are bank reconciliations or the reconciliation of the general ledger account total to a subsidiary ledger. In some instances, a well-designed reconciliation can provide an effective control over most of a processing stream. Testing the effectiveness of a reconciliation is similar to tests of transactions.

- Review documentation that the test was performed on a timely basis throughout the period.
- Reperform the test to determine that all reconciling items were identified properly.
- Investigate the resolution of significant reconciling items.

Observation

You may be able to observe the application of some control procedures, such as computer input controls like edit checks. A physical inventory count also lends itself to observation as a means of assessing effectiveness. For a control performed only occasionally, such as a physical count, it may be possible to observe the control each time it is performed. For controls that are performed continuously for large volumes of transactions, you will need to supplement your observations with other tests, such as:

- Inquiry
- Test of entity-level controls

Evaluating Test Results

The results of your tests of activity-level controls should support your conclusion about their operating effectiveness. If your tests revealed no deviations or exceptions in the performance of control procedures, then you should be able to conclude that the control is operating effectively (assuming that the scope of your test work, as discussed earlier in this chapter, was sufficient).

When your tests of operating effectiveness uncover exceptions to the company's prescribed control procedures, you should determine whether additional tests are required to assess operating effectiveness. A control testing exception is not necessarily a control deficiency. You may determine that the exception was an isolated instance of noncompliance with the established control procedure. However, if you do conclude that a testing exception is not a control deficiency, then you should perform and document additional test work to support your conclusion. In most instances, control testing exceptions usually are not considered to be isolated instances of noncompliance.

For example, when your test work reveals deficiencies in either the design or the operating effectiveness of a control procedure, you will need to exercise your judgment in order to reach a conclusion about control effectiveness.

Ultimately, you should consider that you are making a conclusion about the effectiveness of internal control *as a whole*. When you evaluate activity-level controls, you should consider the effectiveness of the entire information-processing stream, not individual control procedures in isolation.

EXAMPLES OF EVIDENTIAL MATTER THAT MAY SUPPORT THE SPECIFIC ASSERTIONS EMBODIED IN FINANCIAL STATEMENTS

Another approach is a source list of procedures or evidential matter to be used as a resource in developing audit programs. The following chart indicates what this approach might look like for some common financial statement components. Usually such source lists present either evidential matter or procedures but, to avoid repetition, not both. For example, if the evidential matter is minutes of board meetings, the procedure is to read the minutes. Or if the procedure is to inspect a broker's advice, the evidential matter is the broker's advice.

Another approach is to use standardized audit programs developed for common components of financial statements. This approach is not illustrated here. Many auditors prefer source lists to packaged programs because of a concern that standardized programs promote routine application and do not encourage exercise of judgment.

SOURCE LIST OF PROCEDURES OR EVIDENTIAL MATTER

Elements of financial statements	Existence or occurrence	Completeness	Rights and obligations	Valuation or allocation	Presentation and disclosure
Cash	Bank confirmations	Bank reconciliations	Bank confirmations	Foreign currency exchange rates from newspapers, and so on	Confirmation of restrictions on bank balances
	Cash counts	Interbank transfer schedules			Contractual agreements relating to escrow funds, compensating balances, sinking funds, and so on
	Certificates of deposit and savings account books	Subsequent "cutoff" bank statements			
		Review of controls over cash receipts and disbursements			
Marketable securities	Security counts	Analyses of general ledger account activity	Certificate of ownership	Broker's advices and documents supporting purchases of securities	Representation and other information regarding management's intention to retain securities
	Security confirmations	Confirmations of security positions with brokers and dealers	Security confirmations	Market value quotations	Minutes of board or committee meetings
	Custodian's reports	Custodian's reports		Appraised values of infrequently traded securities	Contractual terms of debt securities and preferred stocks
		Review of subsequent transactions		Foreign currency exchange rates from newspapers, and so on	Confirmation of securities pledged under loan agreements, and so on
		Review of controls over security of investments and transactions			
Receivables	Confirmation of account balances	Tests of year-end sales and shipping cutoff procedures	Confirmation of account balances	Aging of open balances	Confirmation of terms with debtors
	Underlying customer orders and agreements, invoices, and shipping documents	Reconciliation of trial balances and general control accounts	Subsequent collections	Credit experience and terms	Sales agreement and contract terms

Elements of financial statements	Existence or occurrence	Completeness	Rights and obligations	Valuation or allocation	Presentation and disclosure
Receivables (continued)	Subsequent collections	Analytical relationship of balances to recent sales volume	Sales records	Credit reports on customers	Terms of notes receivable and collateral held
	Customer correspondence	Analyses of general ledger account activity	Customer correspondence	Correspondence on collection follow-up	Confirmation of receivables sold with recourse, discounted, pledged, and so on
	Sales records	Review of controls over billings and cash receipts	Promissory notes	History of sales returns and allowances	
				Industry experience and trends	
				Subsequent collections, credits, and write-offs	
				Discussion with credit and collection personnel	
				Review of controls over credit extension and collection	
				Foreign currency exchange rate from newspapers, and so on	
Inventory	Physical counts	Tests of year-end shipping and receiving cutoff procedures	Physical counts and confirmations	Purchasing and manufacturing cost records	Confirmation of inventories pledged under loan agreements, and so on
	Confirmation of inventories not on hand	Reconciliations of physical counts with perpetual records and general ledger balances	Paid vendors' invoices	Vendors' invoices	
	Perpetual inventory records	Analytical relationship of balances to recent purchasing, production, and sales activity	Consignment agreements	Review of labor rates	
	Underlying purchasing records, including purchase orders, vendors' invoices, and receiving reports	Analyses of general ledger account activity	Purchase agreements and contracts	Analyses of purchasing and manufacturing standard cost variances	

Elements of financial statements	Existence or occurrence	Completeness	Rights and obligations	Valuation or allocation	Presentation and disclosure
Inventory (continued)	Underlying production records	Review of controls over accounting for receiving, production, and shipping activities	Physical observations and confirmations	Open purchase commitments	
	Subsequent sales and delivery reports	Review of controls over inventory records		Current market value quotations and replacement cost information	
				Plant tour for possible excess and obsolescence	
				Discussion with production and sales personnel	
				Inventory turnover schedules	
				Industry experience and trends	
				Analytical relationship of balances to anticipated sales volume	
Prepaid assets and deferred charges	Invoices, contracts, agreements, and other documents supporting additions to balances	Analyses of general ledger account activity	Documents supporting additions to balances	Documents supporting additions to balances	Terms of insurance policies, tax bills, and so on (current vs. non-current)
		Review of controls over accounts payable and cash disbursements		Recalculation of amortization	
		Review of subsequent transactions		Recomputation of ending account balances	
				Analytical relationship of balances to estimated future utilization of assets	
				Discussion of realizability of deferred charges with appropriate personnel	
				Industry experience and trends	

Elements of financial statements	Existence or occurrence	Completeness	Rights and obligations	Valuation or allocation	Presentation and disclosure
Fixed assets	Physical observations	Plant tour	Documents supporting confirmations	Documents supporting acquisitions	Minutes, representations, and other information regarding management's intention to abandon or dispose of fixed assets
	Documents supporting acquisitions, including authorizations in minutes, construction contracts, purchase orders, invoices, work orders, and so on	Analyses of general ledger activity	Lease agreements	Lease agreement terms	Confirmation of fixed assets pledged under loan agreements, and so on
	Confirmation of equipment maintained at outside locations	Reconciliation of account activity to subsidiary property records		Appraisal reports, replacement cost quotations, and so on	Terms of lease agreements
		Analytical relationship of fixed asset dispositions to replacements		Recalculation of depreciation and amortization	
		Confirmation of construction contracts payable		Analytical relationship of current year's depreciation and amortization to fixed asset costs	
		Vouching of repair and maintenance expense accounts		Industry experience and trends	
		Review of controls over accounts payable and cash disbursements			
		Review of controls over construction work in progress			

Elements of financial statements	Existence or occurrence	Completeness	Rights and obligations	Valuation or allocation	Presentation and disclosure
Intangible assets	Documents supporting acquisitions, including authorizations in minutes, purchase agreements, contracts, and so on	Review of controls over accounts payable and cash disbursements	Documents supporting acquisition	Documents supporting acquisitions	Terms of contracts and purchase agreement
				Appraisal reports	Minutes of board or committee meetings
				Recalculation of amortization Representations and other information regarding use and realizability of assets Industry experience and trends Verification of foreign currency exchange rates	
Accounts payable	Confirmation of selected accounts	Circularization of vendors	Confirmation of selected balances	Foreign currency exchange rate from newspapers, and so on	Confirmation of terms with creditors
	Supporting documents including purchase orders, invoices, receiving reports, check requests, and so on	Tests of year-end purchasing and receiving cutoff procedures	Purchase contracts and vendor statements		Purchase agreement and contract terms
	Vendor statements	Reconciliation of trial balances and general ledger control accounts Review of subsequent payments Review of unmatched vendor invoices and receiving reports Review of controls over purchasing, receiving, and cash disbursements			

Elements of financial statements	Existence or occurrence	Completeness	Rights and obligations	Valuation or allocation	Presentation and disclosure
Accrued taxes and other expenses	Tax bills, invoices, and other documents supporting charges for services	Analysis of general ledger account activity	Tax bills, invoices, and other documents supporting charges for services	Documents relating to items accrued	Terms of tax bills, and so on
	Subsequent payments	Comparison of account balances between years	Subsequent payments	Recalculation of amortization	Internal Revenue Service agents' reports
	Industry experience	Review of controls over recording of cash disbursements		Recomputation of ending account balance	
				Discussion of estimated future costs with entity personnel	
Debt	Confirmation with lenders	Bank confirmations	Notes and loan agreements	Current interest rate quotations	Confirmation of terms with lenders
	Note and loan agreements	Representations from management	Lease agreements	Foreign currency exchange rate from newspapers, and so on	Terms of note and loan agreements
	Lease agreements	Reference in minutes to commitments, obligations, acquisitions, and so on			Terms of lease
	Authorization in minutes of board meetings	Correspondence from legal counsel			Current bank prime rate schedules
Revenue	Documents in support of selected revenue transactions including customer orders, contracts, shipping documents, and sales invoices	Tests of year-end sales and shipping cutoff procedures	Not applicable	Discussions with engineers regarding percentage of completion of long-term projects	Terms of documents supporting revenue transactions, including long-term contracts
	Review of controls over shipping and billing activities	Review of subsequent transactions		Recalculations of percentage of completion computations	
	Documents in support of selected expense transactions including purchase orders, contracts, check requests, and so on	Review of controls over shipping and billing activities		History of sales returns and allowances	

Elements of financial statements	Existence or occurrence	Completeness	Rights and obligations	Valuation or allocation	Presentation and disclosure
Revenue (continued)	Review of controls over recording long-term contract activity		Industry experience and trends	Subsequent credit memos	

NOTE: Revenue recognition continues to pose significant audit risk to auditors. Therefore, auditors should be aware that the AICPA's Audit and Accounting Guide, **Auditing Revenue in Certain Industries**, summarizes key accounting guidance regarding whether and when revenue should be recognized in accordance with GAAP, identifies circumstances and transactions that may signal improper revenue recognition, and provides guidance on auditing revenue transactions in selected industries not covered by existing AICPA Audit and Accounting Guides. In addition, the SEC has issued Staff Accounting Bulletin 104, **Revenue Recognition**, which summarized certain of the SEC staff's views in applying GAAP to revenue recognition in financial statements. These two publications may be useful to auditors in evaluating revenue recognition issues.

Elements of financial statements	Existence or occurrence	Completeness	Rights and obligations	Valuation or allocation	Presentation and disclosure
Expense	Documents in support of selected expense transactions including purchase order contracts, check requests, and so on	Test of year-end purchasing cutoff procedures	Not applicable	Recomputation of depreciation and amortization	Terms of documents supporting selected expense transactions, including large and unusual purchases
	Confirmation of large and unusual purchases with suppliers	Review of subsequent transactions		Recomputation of amortization of prepaid and accrued expense and deferred charges	
	Review of controls over accounts payable and cash disbursements	Comparison of account balances between years		Analytical relationship of balances to total revenue	
		Review of control over accounts payable and cash disbursements			

AU 322 The Auditor's Consideration of the Internal Audit Function in an Audit of Financial Statements[1]

AU EFFECTIVE DATE AND APPLICABILITY

Original Pronouncement	Statement on Auditing Standards (SAS) 65.
Effective Date	This statement currently is effective.
Applicability	Audits of financial statements in accordance with generally accepted auditing standards (GAAS).

AU-C STATUS

The Auditing Standards Board has completed work on the Clarity Project, except for AU Section 322. The delay is caused by the desire of the ASB to align this topic with the International Auditing and Assurance Standards Board's (IAASB's) related draft standard. The clarified standard is expected to be issued in 2013.

DEFINITIONS OF TERMS

Internal audit function. Consists of one or more individuals who perform internal auditing activities. It is an independent appraisal function and part of the control environment that requires internal auditors to be independent of the activity they audit. An important responsibility of the internal audit function is to monitor the performance of an entity's controls.

Internal auditors. Client personnel responsible for providing (1) analyses, (2) evaluations, (3) assurances, (4) recommendations, and (5) other information to management and the board of directors or to others with equivalent authority and responsibility.

---

[1] *This section is affected by the Public Company Accounting Oversight Board's (PCAOB's) Standard,* Conforming Amendments to PCAOB Interim Standards Resulting from the Adoption of PCAOB Auditing Standard No. 5, An Audit of Internal Control over Financial Reporting That Is Integrated with an Audit of Financial Statements.

OBJECTIVES OF AU SECTION 322

Section 322 does not require the independent auditor to use the work of internal auditors. However, Section 319, *Consideration of Internal Control in a Financial Statement Audit*, requires the auditor to obtain a sufficient understanding of internal control to plan the audit. The internal audit function is part of internal control; it is part of the control environment. Section 322 provides sources of information and appropriate inquiries for the auditor to make to obtain the required understanding.

The major points of Section 322 are as follows:

1. If the entity has an internal audit function that acts as a higher level of control over the operation of control procedures, it will usually influence the independent auditor's assessment of control risk and, as a result, may influence the scope of the audit procedures. The independent auditor should determine what work of the internal auditors is relevant to a financial statement audit and whether it is efficient to use that work.
2. Internal auditors may be used to provide direct assistance to the independent auditor by performing substantive tests or tests of controls.
3. For either use (item 1 or 2), the independent auditor should review the competence and objectivity of internal auditors and evaluate their work.
4. The only limitation on the use of internal auditors for either purpose, assuming that the independent auditor is satisfied with competence, objectivity, and work performance, is that significant audit judgments should be made by the independent auditor.
5. The work of internal auditors may affect the independent auditor's procedures; however, the independent auditor should perform enough of his or her own procedures to obtain sufficient, competent evidential matter to support the auditor's report. In making judgments about the extent of the effect of the internal auditors' work on the independent auditor's procedures, the independent auditor considers the following about the financial statement amounts worked on by internal auditors:

    a. The materiality of financial statement amounts; that is, account balances or classes of transactions.
    b. The risk, inherent risk and control risk, of material misstatement of the assertions (see Section 326, *Evidential Matter*) related to these financial statement amounts.
    c. The degree of subjectivity involved in the evaluation of the audit evidence gathered in support of the assertions.

As the materiality of the financial statement amounts increases and either the risk of material misstatement or the degree of subjectivity increases, the need for the auditor to perform his or her own tests of the assertions increases. As these factors decrease, the need for the independent auditor to perform his or her own tests of the assertions decreases.

As a practical matter, the section permits the independent auditor to use the work of internal auditors to reduce audit costs. In effect, the section officially sanctions the use of internal auditors—it is permissible—but the section does not provide a mandate on minimum use.

Another important point to recognize is that the section is concerned with the internal audit *function* and not client personnel who simply have the title of internal auditor. For example, personnel who reconcile bank accounts or recompute the amount of invoices might be called auditors, but the independent auditor would not view their work any differently than that of other personnel who perform those specific procedures. The section is concerned with internal auditors who act as a higher level of control—an additional layer of control to ensure that routine control procedures are operating.

FUNDAMENTAL REQUIREMENTS

BASIC REQUIREMENT

When the independent auditor obtains an understanding of internal control, he or she should obtain an understanding of the internal audit function that is sufficient to identify internal audit activities that are relevant to planning the audit.

To obtain an understanding of the internal audit function, the independent auditor ordinarily should make inquiries, listed in AU 322.05, of appropriate management and internal audit personnel about the internal auditors':

- Organizational status within the entity
- Audit plan, including the nature, timing, and extent of audit work
- Access to records and whether there are limitations on the scope of their activities
- Application of professional internal audit standards

> NOTE: Standards for the professional practice of internal auditing have been developed by the Institute of Internal Auditors and the General Accounting Office.

COMPETENCE AND OBJECTIVITY

If the independent auditor decides to consider how the internal auditors' work might affect the scope of the audit, he or she should assess the competence and objectivity of the internal auditors.

> NOTE: After obtaining the required understanding of internal auditing, the auditor may decide that the internal auditors' work is not relevant to the audit or that it is not efficient to use their work.

Assessing Competence

According to AU 322.09, when the independent auditor assesses the internal auditors' competence, he or she should obtain or update information from prior years about factors such as the following:

- Educational level and professional experience of internal auditors
- Professional certification and continuing education
- Audit policies, programs, and procedures
- Practices regarding assignment of internal auditors
- Supervision and review of internal auditors' activities
- Quality of audit documentation, reports, and recommendations
- Evaluation of internal auditors' performance

Assessing Objectivity

When the independent auditor assesses the internal auditors' objectivity, he or she should obtain or update information from prior years about factors such as (1) the organizational status of the person responsible for the internal audit function, and (2) policies to maintain the internal auditors' objectivity about the areas audited.

PROCEDURES

When the internal auditors' work is expected to affect the audit, the independent auditor should (1) consider the extent of the effect, (2) coordinate work with internal auditors, and (3) evaluate and test the effectiveness of the internal auditors' work.

Evaluating the Effectiveness of Internal Auditors' Work

The independent auditor should perform procedures to evaluate the quality and effectiveness of the internal auditors' work that significantly affects the nature, timing, and extent of the auditors' procedures. According to AU 322.25, in developing evaluation procedures, the auditor should consider whether the internal auditors':

- Scope of work is appropriate to meet the objectives
- Audit programs are adequate
- Work performed, including evidence of supervision and review, is adequately documented
- Conclusions are appropriate in the circumstances
- Reports are consistent with the results of the work performed

Testing the Effectiveness of Internal Auditors' Work

The independent auditor should test some of the internal auditors' work related to significant financial statement assertions. These tests may be made by (1) reperforming some of the work done by internal auditors or by (2) examining similar controls, transactions, or balances. Afterwards, the auditor should compare the results of his or her work to the results of the internal auditors' work.

SUFFICIENCY OF EVIDENCE

Even though the internal auditors' work may impact the auditor's procedures, the auditor is responsible for gathering sufficient competent evidential matter to support his or her audit report.

DIRECT ASSISTANCE TO THE INDEPENDENT AUDITOR

When internal auditors provide direct assistance to the independent auditor, the independent auditor should:

- Evaluate the internal auditors' competence and objectivity
- Supervise, review, evaluate, and test the internal auditors work
- Inform the internal auditors of their responsibilities, the objectives of the procedures they are to perform, and matters that may affect the scope of the audit procedures
- Inform the internal auditors that all significant accounting and auditing issues identified during the audit should be brought to the independent auditors' attention

INTERPRETATIONS

There are no interpretations for this section.

TECHNIQUES FOR APPLICATION

EFFECT OF USE OF INTERNAL AUDITORS' WORK ON THE AUDIT

The use of the internal auditors' work affects the scope of the audit, especially when the independent auditor performs:

1. Procedures to obtain an understanding of the entity's internal control
2. Procedures to assess risk
3. Substantive procedures

Obtaining an Understanding of Internal Control

The independent auditor's understanding of the entity's internal control should include knowledge about the design of relevant policies, procedures, and records and whether they have been placed in operation (see Section 318). The independent auditor, when obtaining an understanding of the internal audit function (see below), may review flowcharts prepared by the internal auditors to obtain information about the design of policies and procedures.

To obtain information about whether the controls have been placed in operation, the independent auditor may consider the results of procedures performed by the internal auditors on the controls.

Risk Assessment

If the independent auditor plans to assess control risk below the maximum, he or she should test controls (see Section 318). The results of the internal auditors' tests of controls may provide information about the effectiveness of the entity's internal control and change the nature, timing, and extent of testing the auditor would otherwise need to perform.

Monitoring

The company's internal audit function also plays a role in the monitoring component of internal control. The auditor's understanding of internal audit will therefore provide evidence about the design and possibly operating effectiveness of management's monitoring of internal control.

Substantive Procedures

Internal auditors may perform substantive tests, such as the confirmation of receivables and the observation of inventories. The independent auditor, therefore, may be able to change the timing of the confirmation procedures, the number of receivables to be confirmed, or the number of locations of inventories to be observed.

OBTAINING AN UNDERSTANDING OF THE INTERNAL AUDIT FUNCTION

As part of the independent auditor's obtaining an understanding of internal control, he or she should obtain an understanding of the internal audit function.

To obtain an understanding of the internal audit function, the independent auditor might do the following:

1. Read the entity's manuals
2. Review the entity's policies and management directives concerning the internal audit function

3. Make inquiries of management and internal audit personnel about the internal audit function, as described in "Fundamental Requirements"
4. Review internal auditors' audit documentation
5. Consider the entity's organization chart and organization chart of the internal audit department

Inquiries

As described in "Fundamental Requirements," the independent auditor should make inquiries of appropriate management and internal audit personnel about the internal auditors' work. The inquiries should answer the following questions:

1. What are the primary responsibilities of internal auditors?
2. What do internal auditors do when:
    a. They believe misstatements have occurred?
    b. They believe the entity's policies are not being properly executed?
    c. They believe weaknesses exist in internal control?
3. What importance does management attach to the internal audit function?
4. What does management do with recommendations and reports of internal auditors?

To determine how the internal audit department functions, the independent auditor should seek answers to the following questions:

1. How are scopes of examinations determined?
2. How are audit procedures determined?
3. How are reports prepared?
4. Who receives the reports?
5. What are the follow-up procedures?

Review of Audit Documentation

Section 318 requires the independent auditor to obtain an understanding of internal control and to determine whether relevant policies, procedures, and records have been placed in operation. A review of the internal auditors' audit documentation, schedules, flowcharts, questionnaires, checklists, etc. will help the independent auditor determine if the relevant policies, procedures, and records have been placed in operation. It also will help the independent auditor obtain an understanding of the internal audit function.

Organization Charts

To determine the position of the internal audit department in the organization, the independent auditor might obtain an organization chart of the entity. The independent auditor would then determine the following:

1. To whom do internal auditors report?
2. To what extent do internal auditors have access to top management and to the audit committee or the full board of directors?

Ready access to top management and to the audit committee indicates that the internal audit department could act independently.

To determine the size of the internal audit department and the responsibilities of each member, the independent auditor might obtain an organization chart of the department. The responsibilities of the members indicate whether the department performs an internal audit function or an accounting control function.

ASSESSING RELEVANCE AND EFFICIENCY

Relevance

When the independent auditor reviews the internal auditors' audit documentation (see above, "Obtaining an Understanding of the Internal Audit Function"), he or she can determine which of the internal auditors' work is relevant to a financial statement audit. Other procedures that may be used by the independent auditor to determine the relevancy of the internal auditors' work include the following:

1. Consider knowledge from prior audits
2. Review how the internal auditors allocate their resources to financial or operating areas of the entity
3. Read internal audit reports to obtain a detailed understanding about the scope of internal audit activities

Efficiency

Determining whether it is efficient to use the internal auditors' work requires the professional judgment of the independent auditor. The independent auditor should answer the question: Is it less time-consuming and cheaper, and as effective, to use the internal auditors' work than to do original work himself or herself?

ASSESSING COMPETENCE AND OBJECTIVITY OF INTERNAL AUDITORS

In assessing competence and objectivity, the auditor will consider information obtained from the following sources:

1. Previous experience with internal auditors
2. Discussions with management
3. Results of any recent external quality review of the internal audit function

When assessing competence and objectivity, the independent auditor should consider using the guidance provided in professional internal auditing standards, such as those promulgated by the Institute of Internal Auditors and the General Accounting Office.

Competence

Information that the independent auditor should obtain about the competence of internal auditors is specified in "Fundamental Requirements." The independent auditor should apply the following procedures to obtain that information:

1. Determine personnel policies relative to hiring, training, job assignment, promotion, supervision, and review
2. Review personnel files
3. Determine entity policy on training programs
4. Scan audit documentation of internal auditors
5. Consider adequacy of audit documentation review by supervisors in internal audit department

Objectivity

The independent auditor should obtain or update information from prior years about the organizational status of the internal auditor responsible for the internal audit function and policies to maintain internal auditors' objectivity about the areas audited.

According to AU 322.10, the information about the organizational status of the internal auditor responsible for the internal audit function should include the following:

1. Whether the internal auditor reports to an officer of sufficient status to ensure broad audit coverage and adequate consideration of, and action on, the findings and recommendations of the internal auditors
2. Whether the internal auditor has direct access and reports regularly to the board of directors, the audit committee, or the owner-manager
3. Whether the board of directors, the audit committee, or the owner-manager oversees employment decisions related to the internal auditor

Policies to maintain auditors' objectivity about the areas audited should include the following:

1. Policies prohibiting internal auditors from auditing areas where relatives are employed in important or audit-sensitive positions
2. Policies prohibiting internal auditors from auditing areas where they were recently assigned or are scheduled to be assigned on completion of responsibilities in the internal audit function

The independent auditor also should determine the scopes of examinations of the internal auditors. He or she should ascertain that the scopes were not restricted and that they were established solely by the internal audit department.

EXTENT OF THE EFFECT OF THE INTERNAL AUDITORS' WORK

Factors affecting the extent of the effect of the internal auditors' work on the scope of the audit were described in "Objectives of Section." These factors are (1) materiality, (2) risk, and (3) subjectivity.

The independent auditor may decide to use the internal auditors' work for assertions related to material financial statement amounts where the risk of material misstatement or the degree of subjectivity involved is high. In these circumstances, the internal auditors' work cannot alone reduce audit risk to a level that would eliminate the need for the independent auditor to apply any procedures to those assertions. Examples of those assertions are: (1) valuation of assets and liabilities involving significant accounting estimates (for example, accounts receivable; property, plant, and equipment; product warranties), (2) existence and disclosure of related-party transactions, (3) contingencies, (4) uncertainties, and (5) subsequent events. The independent auditor should apply some audit procedures to these assertions, in addition to considering the internal auditors' work.

The independent auditor may decide to use the internal auditors' work for assertions related to less material financial statement amounts where the risk of material misstatement or the degree of subjectivity involved is low. In these circumstances, the internal auditors' work may reduce audit risk to an acceptable level so that the independent auditor does not have to apply any further procedures to those assertions. Examples of those assertions are the existence of cash, prepaid assets, and fixed-asset additions.

COORDINATION OF WORK

According to AU 322.23, if the internal auditors' work will have an effect on the independent auditor's procedures, it would be efficient for them to coordinate their work by doing the following:

1. Holding periodic meetings
2. Scheduling audit work
3. Providing access to internal auditors' audit documentation
4. Reviewing audit reports
5. Discussing possible accounting and auditing issues

EVALUATING AND TESTING EFFECTIVENESS OF INTERNAL AUDITORS' WORK

Evaluating

Procedures to evaluate the work of internal auditors include a review of the following:

1. Scope of work
2. Instructions to internal audit staff
3. Audit documentation

Scope of work. The independent auditor should review the scope of the internal auditors' work to determine that it was established by them and was in no way restricted.

Instructions to staff. To determine that the internal auditors were properly instructed, the independent auditor should read all written instructions. The independent auditor also should review audit programs to determine that they were adequate.

Review of audit documentation. To determine the quality of internal auditors' work, the independent auditor should review their audit documentation to determine that:

1. Audit documentation adequately records work performed, including evidence of supervision and review
2. There is evidence of follow-up and disposition of questions and errors
3. Conclusions are appropriate in the circumstances
4. Reports are consistent with the results of work performed

Testing

To determine the effectiveness of the internal auditors' work, the independent auditor should test their work by examining documentary evidence of work performed. He or she should either (1) examine some of the controls, transactions, or balances examined by the internal auditors or (2) examine similar controls, transactions, or balances not actually examined by the internal auditors. In either case, the independent auditor should compare the results of his or her tests with the results of the internal auditors' work.

USING INTERNAL AUDITORS TO PROVIDE DIRECT ASSISTANCE TO THE INDEPENDENT AUDITOR

When the independent auditor uses internal auditors to provide him or her with direct assistance, he or she should apply the procedures described above (see *Fundamental Requirements*). In addition, the independent auditor should review and evaluate the internal auditors' audit documentation to the same extent he or she would review and evaluate the audit documentation of the independent auditors' staff.

AU ILLUSTRATIONS

This section contains (1) a checklist that may be used by the independent auditor when he or she uses the work of internal auditors and (2) a copy of the flowchart from AU 322 that describes its requirements.

ILLUSTRATION 1. CHECKLIST FOR USING WORK OF INTERNAL AUDITORS

_____
[*Client*]

_____
[*Audit date*]

This checklist should be used on all engagements where the firm intends to use the work of internal auditors.

The work of internal auditors should be evaluated in two situations, as follows:

1. Internal audit as a separate, higher level of control.
2. Use of internal auditors to assist firm in testing controls, gaining an understanding of controls, and substantive testing.

	Performed by	*Date*

Acquire an Understanding of Internal Audit Function
1. Review internal audit department and note the following:
   a. Hiring policies
   b. Total number of employees
   c. Number of employees by title; for example, supervisor, senior, and so on
   d. Department's place in organization structure
   e. To whom department reports
2. Review current year's reports and note the following:
   a. Number and nature of audits
   b. Scope of audits
   c. Recommendations
   d. To whom issued
   e. Action on recommendations
Relevancy and Efficiency
1. Determine what work of the internal auditors is relevant to a financial statement audit.
2. Determine whether it is efficient to use the internal auditors' work as part of our audit.
Competence of Internal Auditors
1. Determine if entity conducts training programs for internal auditors.
2. If entity does not conduct training programs, determine if internal auditors attend outside seminars.
3. Review personnel files and compare with hiring policies.
4. Review department library.
5. Review, on a test basis, current year's audit documentation and note the following:		

	Performed by	Date

    a. Quality of work
    b. Adequacy of documentation
    c. Adequacy of supervision

Objectivity of Internal Audits

1. Review, on a test basis, scope of audits.
2. Determine how scope was established.
3. Determine work performed by internal auditors and ascertain that work was independent of accounting functions.
4. Review, on a test basis, reports of internal audit department:

    a. Recommendations
    b. To whom issued
    c. Action on recommendations

Evaluating Work of Internal Auditors

1. Select, on a test basis, audits performed by the department during the year and do the following:

    a. Determine if scope is appropriate for job.
    b. Review audit programs.
    c. Review preaudit instructions.
    d. Review audit documentation for

        (1) Completeness of documentation
        (2) Follow-up and disposition of questions and errors

2. Determine if audit reports and conclusions are consistent with findings noted in audit documentation.
3. Test work of internal auditors:

    a. Examine the same transactions and account balances.
    b. Examine similar transactions and account balances.
    c. Compare results to findings of internal auditors.

Direct Assistance of Internal Auditors

1. Meet with internal auditors:

    a. Discuss areas of work.
    b. Review program.
    c. Review procedures.

2. Review completed audit documentation of internal auditors.
3. Consider the need to test the work performed by internal auditors.

ILLUSTRATION 2. THE AUDITOR'S CONSIDERATION OF THE INTERNAL AUDIT FUNCTION IN AN AUDIT OF FINANCIAL STATEMENTS

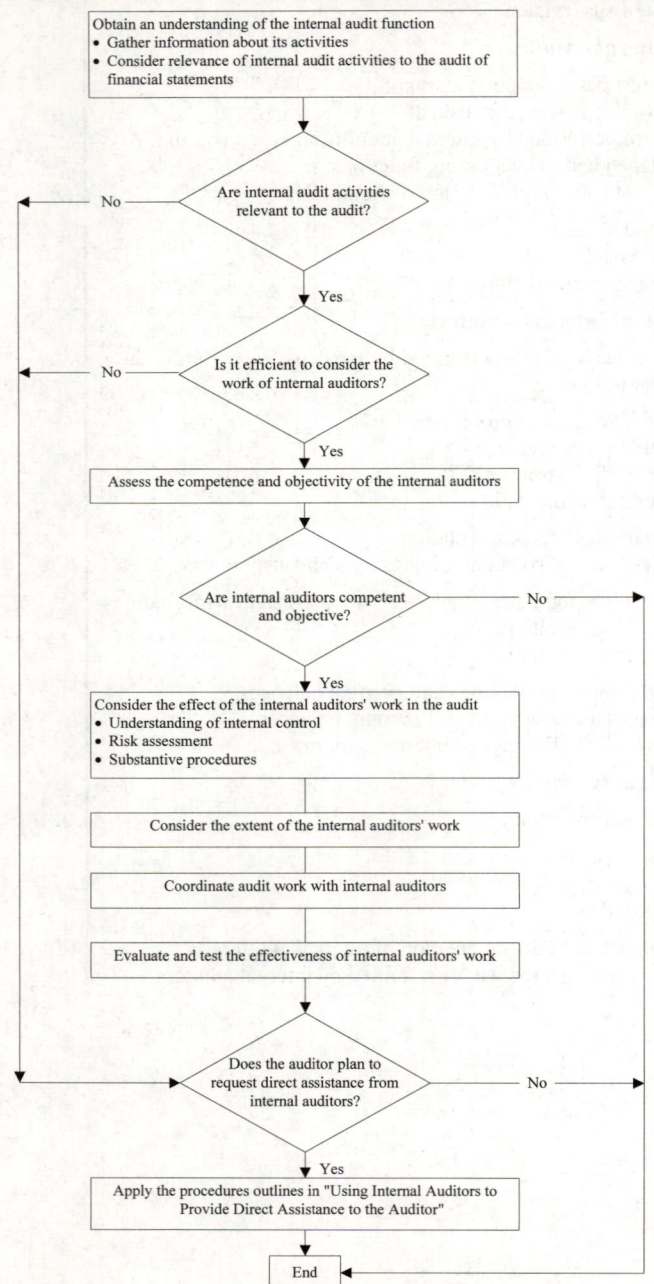

Copyright © 2004 by the American Institute of Certified Public Accountants, Inc. Reprinted with permission.

AU 324 Service Organizations[1]

AU-C 402 Audit Considerations Relating to an Entity Using a Service Organization

AU EFFECTIVE DATE AND APPLICABILITY

Original Pronouncement	Statements on Auditing Standards (SAS) 70, 78, 88, and 98.
Effective Date	These statements currently are effective.
Applicability	Practitioners auditing financial statements of an entity that uses a service organization, such as a data processing service center, a bank trust department, or a mortgage banker servicing mortgages for others. Practitioners issuing service auditor reports.

AU-C EFFECTIVE DATE AND SUMMARY OF CHANGES

SAS No. 122, *Codification of Auditing Standards and Procedures,* is effective for audits of financial statements with periods ending on or after December 15, 2012.

Statements on Standards for Attestation Engagements (SSAE) No. 16, *Reporting on Controls at a Service Organization,* supersedes the guidance for service auditors in this AU section for service auditors' reports for periods ending on or after June 15, 2011. Earlier implementation of SSAE No. 16 is permitted. The guidance for user auditors in this section remains in effect until the clarified SAS *Audit Considerations Relating to an Entity Using a Service Organization* (AUC-402) becomes effective and supersedes the guidance for user auditors in this AU section.

AU-C 402 contains guidance only for *user* auditors. Guidance for *service* auditors is contained in SSAE No. 16 (AT Section 901).

---

[1] This section is affected by the Public Company Accounting Oversight Board's (PCAOB's) Standard, Conforming Amendments to PCAOB Interim Standards Resulting from the Adoption of PCAOB Auditing Standard No. 5, An Audit of Internal Control over Financial Reporting That Is Integrated with an Audit of Financial Statements.

AU-C 402:

- Makes changes in the auditor's report
- Adds new requirements for the auditor to conduct communications with client management about the service organization, and
- Requires the auditor to evaluate the impact of certain matters to audit procedures

AU-C 402 makes the following changes to AU 324:

- A user organization is now referred to as a user entity

To explain a modification of the user auditor's opinion, a user auditor may make reference to the work of a service auditor in the user auditor's report. In that case, the user auditor's report must indicate that such reference does not diminish the user auditor's responsibility for that opinion.

The user auditor must inquire of management of the entity about whether the service organization has reported to the user entity any fraud, noncompliance with laws and regulations, or unconnected misstatements. If so, it requires the user auditor to evaluate how such matters affect the nature, timing, and extent of the user auditor's further audit procedures

When evaluating the sufficiency and appropriateness of the audit evidence provided by a service auditor's report, the user auditor should be satisfied regarding the adequacy of the standards under which the service auditor's report was issued.

AU DEFINITIONS OF TERMS

Reports on controls placed in operation and tests of operating effectiveness. A service auditor's report on a service organization's description of controls that covers (1) suitability of control design, (2) controls placed in operation, and (3) whether controls tested were sufficiently effective to provide reasonable assurance that control objectives were achieved during the period specified.

Reports on controls placed in operation. A service auditor's report on a service organization's description of controls addressing (1) whether controls were suitably designed to achieve specified control objectives, and (2) whether controls had been placed in operation at a specific date.

Service auditor. The auditor who reports on the processing of transactions by the service organization.

Service organization. The entity (or segment of an entity) that provides services to the user organization.

Subsequent events. Changes in a service organization's controls that could affect user organizations' information systems that occur subsequent to the period covered by the service auditor's report but before the date of the service auditor's report.

User auditor. The auditor who reports on the financial statements of the user organization.

User organization. The entity that has engaged a service organization and whose financial statements are being audited.

AU-C DEFINITIONS OF TERMS

Source: AU-C 402.08

Complementary user entity controls. Controls that management of the service organization, in the design of its service, assumes will be implemented by user entities and which, if necessary to achieve the control objectives stated in management's description of the service organization's system, are identified as such in that description.

Report on management's description of a service organization's system and the suitability of the design of controls (referred to in this section as a *type 1 report*). A report that comprises the following:

1. Management's description of the service organization's system
2. A written assertion by management of the service organization about whether, in all material respects, and based on suitable criteria:
   a. Management's description of the service organization's system fairly presents the service organization's system that was designed and implemented as of a specified date
   b. The controls related to the control objectives stated in management's description of the service organization's system were suitably designed to achieve those control objectives as of the specified date
3. A service auditor's report that expresses an opinion on the matters in 2(a–b)

Report on management's description of a service organization's system and the suitability of the design and operating effectiveness of controls (referred to in this section as *type 2 report*). A report that comprises the following:

1. Management's description of the service organization's system
2. A written assertion by management of the service organization about whether in all material respects and, based on suitable criteria
   a. Management's description of the service organization's system fairly presents the service organization's system that was designed and implemented throughout the specified period
   b. The controls related to the control objectives stated in management's description of the service organization's system were suitably designed throughout the specified period to achieve those control objectives
   c. The controls related to the control objectives stated in management's description of the service organization's system operated effectively throughout the specified period to achieve those control objectives
3. A service auditor's report that
   a. Expresses an opinion on the matters in 2(a–c)
   b. Includes a description of the service auditor's tests of controls and the results thereof

Service auditor. A practitioner who reports on controls at a service organization.

Service organization. An organization or segment of an organization that provides user entities with services that are relevant to those user entities' internal control over financial reporting.

Service organization's system. The policies and procedures designed, implemented, and documented by management of the service organization to provide user entities with the services covered by the service auditor's report. Management's description of the service organization's system identifies the services covered, the period to which the description relates (or in the case of a type 1 report, the date to which the description relates), the control objectives specified by management or an outside party, the party specifying the control objectives (if not specified by management), and the related controls.

Subservice organization. A service organization used by another service organization to perform some of the services provided to user entities that are relevant to those user entities' internal control over financial reporting.

User auditor. An auditor who audits and reports on the financial statements of a user entity.

User entity. An entity that uses a service organization and whose financial statements are being audited.

OBJECTIVES OF AU SECTION 324

The Statement provides guidance to auditors of financial statements of an entity that uses a service organization to process transactions. The Statement applies when an entity obtains services from another entity that are part of its information system. A service organization's services are part of an entity's information system if they affect any of the following:

1. Transaction initiation
2. Accounting records and supplemental detail
3. Processing of accounting information
4. Financial reporting process

Bank trust departments are service organizations because they invest and service assets for others. An example of a user organization for a bank trust department is an employee benefit plan. Data processing service centers are service organizations because they process transactions and related data for others. Similarly, mortgage bankers that service mortgages for other entities are service organizations.

A bank that processes checking account transactions or a broker who executes securities transactions is not included under the Statement's definition of *service organizations*. When services are limited to executing transactions specifically authorized by the client, the Statement is not applicable. The Statement also is not applicable to the audit of transactions arising from financial interest in partnerships, corporations, and joint ventures (see Section 332 for guidance on financial instruments).

More and more entities are outsourcing activities to service organizations. There is often a belief by the user organization that the service organization can be totally relied upon and that the user organization needs only to have limited, if any, controls. Section 324 is intended to help auditors determine what additional information they might need when auditing an entity that uses a service organization. It also makes it clear that the guidance applies if an entity obtains services from another organization that are part of the entity's information system. Also, it clarifies the factors that an auditor should use in determining the significance of service organization's controls to the user organization's control. In other words, the audit procedures that are appropriate when a service organization's procedures are significant to the audited entity are not optional. The auditor has to evaluate the interaction between the audited entity and all service organizations used by that entity.

OBJECTIVES OF AU-C SECTION 402

AU-C Section 402 states that

... the objectives of the user auditor, when the user entity uses the services of a service organization, are to

    a. *obtain an understanding of the nature and significance of the services provided by the service organization and their effect on the user entity's internal control relevant to the audit, sufficient to identify and assess the risks of material misstatement.*

    b. *design and perform audit procedures responsive to those risks.*

FUNDAMENTAL REQUIREMENTS: USER AUDITORS

When an entity uses a service organization, part of the processing that the auditor usually finds in the client's internal control is physically and operationally separate from that entity (the user organization). In some circumstances, the user organization may be able to implement effective internal controls. This occurs when the user organization authorizes all transactions and maintains accountability that would detect unauthorized transactions or activity.

In other circumstances, the service organization's procedures relevant to the user organization need to be included when the user auditor is obtaining an understanding of internal control. One source of additional information to obtain this understanding is a service auditor's report.

The key factors for a user auditor to consider in deciding whether additional information such as a service auditor's report is needed are:

1. Degree of interaction between the activity at the service organization and that of the user organization
2. Nature of the transactions processed
3. Materiality of the transaction processed

The auditor's understanding of internal control should be sufficient to "plan the audit." Additional information from the service center or a service auditor's report may not be needed if the auditor obtains at the user organization a sufficient understanding of the controls placed in operation by the service organizations whose services are part of the entity's information system to identify types of potential misstatements, to consider factors that affect the risk of material misstatement, and to design substantive tests.

Information about a service organization's controls may be obtained from various sources, including:

1. User and technical manuals
2. System overviews
3. The contract between the user organization and the service organization

4. Reports by service auditors, internal auditors, or regulatory authorities on the service organization's controls
5. The user auditor's prior experience with the service organization (if the services and the service organization's controls are highly standardized)

If the user auditor cannot obtain sufficient evidence to achieve the audit objectives, the user auditor should issue a qualified opinion or disclaim an opinion because of a scope limitation.

AU 324.24 defines two types of service auditor's reports.

1. Report on controls placed in operation

NOTE: This type of report can help in obtaining an understanding of internal control to plan the audit, but it is not usually an adequate basis for reducing the assessed level of control risk below maximum.

2. Report on controls placed in operation and tests of operating effectiveness

Both types of service auditor's reports provide an opinion on whether:

1. The accompanying description presents fairly, in all material respects, the aspects of the service organization's controls that may be relevant to a user organization's internal control, and
2. The controls have been placed in operation as of a date, and
3. The controls are suitably designed to provide reasonable assurance that the specified control objectives would be achieved.

The second type of service auditor's report adds a list of tests of controls performed by the service auditor and an opinion on whether the controls tested were operating with sufficient effectiveness to provide reasonable, but not absolute, assurance that the related control objectives were achieved during the period specified.

Before using a service auditor's report, the user auditor should make inquiries about the service auditor's professional reputation (see Section 543). Also, the user auditor should consider:

1. Discussing the audit procedures and their results with the service auditor
2. Reviewing the service auditor's audit program
3. Reviewing the service auditor's audit documentation

FUNDAMENTAL REQUIREMENTS: SERVICE AUDITORS

According to AU 324.22, the service auditor is responsible for the representations in his or her report and for exercising due care in the application of procedures that support those representations.

The service auditor should perform the engagement in accordance with the general standards and the relevant fieldwork and reporting standards. The service auditor should be independent from the service organization, but need not be independent from each user organization.

If the service auditor becomes aware of illegal acts, fraud, or uncorrected errors attributable to the service organization, the service auditor should discuss the matter with an appropriate level of management of the service organization to determine whether this information has been communicated to the affected user organizations. If management is unwilling to make the communication, the service auditor should inform the service organization's audit committee or its equivalent, and if the audit committee fails to respond appropriately, consult with an attorney and consider resigning from the engagement.

The service auditor should obtain written representations from the service organization's management. See the "AU Illustrations" section for an example of such a representation letter.

If the service auditor is asked to apply substantive procedures to user transactions or assets at the service organization, the auditor may make specific reference in his or her report to having carried out the designated procedures and include a sufficient description of the procedures to allow user auditors to decide whether to use the results as evidence to support their opinions.

RESPONSIBILITY FOR SUBSEQUENT EVENTS

A service auditor should consider the following types of subsequent events that come to his or her attention:

1. *Events that provide additional information about conditions that existed during the period covered by the service auditor's report.* The service auditor should use this information to determine whether controls at the service organization that could affect user organizations' information systems were placed in operation, suitably designed, and operating effectively during the engagement period.
2. *Events that provide information about conditions that arose subsequent to the period covered by the service auditor's report that require disclosure to prevent users from being misled.* This type of information usually will not affect the service auditor's report if the information is appropriately disclosed by the service organization's management. The service auditor should determine whether management has disclosed such information in the section of the service auditor's report titled "Other Information Provided by the Service Organization." If the information is not disclosed, the service auditor should consider disclosing it.

A service auditor is not responsible for detecting subsequent events. However, a service auditor should ask management whether it is aware of any subsequent events through the date of the service auditor's report that would have a significant effect on user organizations and should obtain a management representation regarding subsequent events.

AU INTERPRETATIONS

DESCRIBING TESTS OF OPERATING EFFECTIVENESS AND THE RESULTS OF SUCH TESTS (APRIL 1995)

Paragraph .44f of Section 324 requires that a service auditor's report that includes tests of operating effectiveness describe "tests applied" and the "results of the tests."

In describing "tests applied," the service auditor should indicate whether sampling was used or all of the items in a population were tested.

In describing the "results of the tests," the service auditor should include exceptions and other information (whether or not control objective has been achieved) that in his or her judgment could be relevant to user auditors. The following should be included:

1. Sample size
2. Number of exceptions
3. Nature of exceptions

If no exceptions are noted, that should be indicated.

SERVICE ORGANIZATIONS THAT USE THE SERVICES OF OTHER SERVICE ORGANIZATIONS (SUBSERVICE ORGANIZATIONS) (ISSUED APRIL 1995, REVISED FEBRUARY 1997, REVISED APRIL 2002)

When a service organization uses a subservice organization, the user auditor should determine whether the subserver's processing significantly affects assertions in the user organization's financial statements. To obtain the required understanding of control, the user auditor may need to consider control at both the service and subservice organizations.

A service auditor also may need to consider functions performed at both organizations and the effect of controls at the subserver on the service organization.

The service organization's description of control should include a description of the processing performed by the subservice organization (identity of subserver is not required).

There are two alternative methods of presenting the description of controls by the subserver and reporting on those controls by the service auditor:

1. Carve-out method (control objectives and controls of subserver are excluded)
2. Inclusive method (control objectives and controls of subserver are included)

Both methods require the description of processing discussed above. If that description is omitted or the service organization does not disclose the existence of a subserver, the auditor may need to issue a qualified or adverse opinion as to the fairness of the presentation.

The interpretation provides illustrative service auditor reports using the carve-out and the inclusive methods.

RESPONSIBILITIES OF SERVICE ORGANIZATIONS AND SERVICE AUDITORS WITH RESPECT TO FORWARD-LOOKING INFORMATION IN A SERVICE ORGANIZATION'S DESCRIPTION OF CONTROLS (FEBRUARY 2002, REVISED MARCH 2006, DECEMBER 2010)

This interpretation clarifies that Section 324 does not apply to design deficiencies that potentially could affect processing of user organizations' transactions in *future periods*. A service auditor would *not* be required to identify, in his or her report, design deficiencies that do not affect processing during the period covered by the service auditor's examination but that may represent potential problems in future periods, such as a lack of contingency planning or provisions for disaster recovery. However, if a service auditor becomes aware of such design deficiencies, the service auditor may choose to communicate this to the service organization's management. The service auditor may advise management to disclose this information and its plans for correcting the design deficiencies in a section of the service auditor's document titled "Other Information Provided by the Service Organization." In this case, the service auditor should read the information, consider applying analogous guidance in Section 550, and include a paragraph in his or her report such as the following that disclaims an opinion on the information provided by the service organization:

> The information in Section 7 describing ABC Bank Trust's plans to modify its disaster recovery plan is presented by ABC Bank Trust to provide additional information and is not a part of

ABC Bank Trust's description of controls that may be relevant to a user organization's internal control. Such information has not been subjected to the procedures applied in the examination of the description of the controls applicable to the processing of transactions for user organizations and, accordingly, we express no opinion or provide no assurance on it.

A service auditor also may decide to communicate information about the design deficiencies in the section of the service auditor's document titled "Other Information Provided by the Service Auditor."

STATEMENTS ABOUT THE RISK OF PROJECTING EVALUATIONS OF THE EFFECTIVENESS OF CONTROLS TO FUTURE PERIODS (FEBRUARY 2002)

This interpretation clarifies that sample service auditor's reports in Section 324 may be expanded to describe the risk of projecting to the future conclusions about the effectiveness of controls. The sentence in the sample report in Illustrations 1 and 4 could be expanded, as illustrated below, to describe the risk of projecting an evaluation of the controls to future periods because of changes to the system or controls, or the failure to make needed changes to the system or controls (new language is in italics).

> Furthermore, the projection of any conclusions, based on our findings, to future periods is subject to the risk that changes *made to the system or controls, or the failure to make needed changes to the system or controls,* may alter the validity of such conclusions.

PROFESSIONAL ISSUES TASK FORCE PRACTICE ALERT

99-2 HOW THE USE OF A SERVICE ORGANIZATION AFFECTS INTERNAL CONTROL CONSIDERATIONS

More and more entities are outsourcing activities to service organizations. This alert states that in these situations, it is critical for the user auditor to consider the guidance in Section 324 and the implications the service organization may have to the audit. Therefore, the alert clarifies and highlights factors that an auditor should consider in those audits. Some of the key points covered in the alert are:

- User auditors should apply the guidance in Section 324 whenever a service organization's services are part of the user organization's information system.
- The nature and materiality of the transactions processed for the user organization and the degree of interaction between internal controls at the user organization and the service organization are key factors in determining the significance of the service organization's controls.
- After obtaining a service auditor's report, the user auditor should consider whether the service auditor's report is satisfactory for his or her purposes. This may include making inquiries concerning the service auditor's professional reputation (see Section 543), reading the report to determine whether the service auditor demonstrates an understanding of the subject matter, and if necessary, contacting the service organization to perform additional testing.
- If a service auditor's report on controls placed in operation is dated before the beginning of the period under audit, the user auditor should consider updating the information to determine whether there have been any relevant changes in the service organization's controls, and if so, what the effect of those changes are on his/her audit.

TECHNIQUES FOR APPLICATION: USER AUDITORS

REPORTS ON CONTROLS PLACED IN OPERATION

This report has two elements:

1. The service auditor's report on whether the service organization's description of its controls presents fairly the controls placed in operation as of a specific date, and
2. The service auditor's opinion that the controls have been suitably designed to provide reasonable assurance that the stated control objectives would be achieved if the controls were complied with satisfactorily.

This type of report generally helps in obtaining an understanding of the entity's internal control sufficient to plan the audit. It does not allow the user auditor to reduce the assessed level of control risk below the maximum.

REPORT ON CONTROLS PLACED IN OPERATION AND TESTS OF OPERATING EFFECTIVENESS

This report includes both elements of a "placed in operation" report and adds a third; it refers to a list of tests performed by the service auditor of specific controls. The test period covered is described and is a minimum of six months. The user auditor decides what evidential matter is needed to reduce the assessed level of control risk. In some cases, the tests of operating effectiveness performed by the service auditor may provide such evidence. (Other potential sources of this evidence are tests of the user organization's controls over the activities of the service organization, or tests of controls performed by the user auditor at the service organization.)

The user auditor selects the audit approach:

1. Is it more efficient to obtain evidential matter about the operating effectiveness to permit assessing control risk below the maximum, or
2. Is the more efficient approach to assess control risk at the maximum and plan other audit procedures suitable for that level of risk of material misstatement?

CONSIDERATIONS IN USING A SERVICE AUDITOR'S REPORT

A service auditor's report with a "clean opinion" does not mean the service organization controls are effective for the user organization. It means that the control objectives listed and their related controls are described accurately. For example:

1. The report may not address all of the control objectives that the user auditor would find helpful. Key control objectives relating to transactions processed by service organizations are often defined in the description as responsibilities of the user organization, not of the service organization.
2. The description may state that the system was designed with the assumption that certain internal controls would be implemented by the user organization. In this case, the service auditor's report includes "and user organizations applied the internal controls contemplated in the design of the service organization's controls" in the scope and opinion paragraphs.
3. One criterion used by service auditors to determine whether a *significant deficiency* exists is whether user organizations would "generally be expected to have controls in

place to mitigate such design deficiencies." The user auditor needs to consider whether his or her client has these expected controls in place.

Obtaining a service auditor's report is the starting point for careful reading of the description to obtain an understanding of internal control and how it is integrated between the service organization and the user organization.

The user auditor should make inquiries concerning the service auditor's professional reputation. (See Section 543.)

The user auditor should consider the scope and results of the service auditor's work to decide whether the report provides the needed information and evidential matter that the user auditor needs to achieve the audit objectives. In some cases, the user auditor may clarify his or her understanding of the service auditor's procedures and conclusions by discussing the scope and results of the work with the service auditor and reviewing the service auditor's audit program and workpapers.

The user auditor's audit report on the financial statements should **not** refer to the report of the service auditor. The service auditor is not responsible for examining any portion of the financial statements.

When the user auditor wishes to reduce the assessed level of control risk and is using a service auditor's report that reports the results of tests of controls over a specified time period, the user auditor should consider the appropriateness of the time period covered in evaluating the tests performed and results to assess the level of control risk for the user organization.

TECHNIQUES FOR APPLICATION: SERVICE AUDITORS

REPORTS ON CONTROLS PLACED IN OPERATION

To evaluate the description of the service organization's controls, the service auditor:

1. Obtains information on the controls through:

    a. Discussions with service organization personnel
    b. Reference to documentation, such as system flowcharts and narratives

2. Considers whether the information needed by the user auditors is included:

    a. Controls that affect user organization's internal control are included. The linkage of the controls to the stated control objectives should be considered.
    b. Sufficient information is presented for user auditors to obtain an understanding of those controls.
    c. Specific control objectives of the service organization relevant to user organizations are presented. The control objectives should be "reasonable in the circumstances" and consistent with the service organization's contractual obligations.

3. Obtains evidence of whether controls have been placed in operation by:

    a. Previous experience with the service organization
    b. Inquiry of service organization personnel
    c. Inspection of service organization documents and records
    d. Observation of service organization activities and operations

4. Evaluates whether significant deficiencies exist that either:

a. Preclude reasonable assurance that specified control objectives would be achieved, or
b. Could adversely affect the ability to record, process, summarize, or report financial data to user organizations without error when user organizations would not generally be expected to have controls to mitigate such design deficiencies. (Such deficiencies should be included in the report even if they do not relate to the specified control objectives.)

5. Considers whether changes in controls made within twelve months before the date being reported on would be considered significant to user organizations and their auditors. If so, the description should communicate the changes. If management does not include the changes that the service auditor considers significant, the changes should be described in the service auditor's report.
6. Considers whether the system was designed with the assumption that certain controls would be implemented by the user organization. If so, such presumed user organization controls should be included in the description. The service auditor's report will then have an added phrase referring to the user organization controls. (See "Illustrations.")

REPORTS ON CONTROLS PLACED IN OPERATION AND TESTS OF OPERATING EFFECTIVENESS

The service auditor performs the procedures described above under "Reports on Controls Placed in Operation." In addition, the service auditor performs tests of controls to determine whether specified controls are operating with sufficient effectiveness to achieve specified control objectives.

NOTE: Section 350, Audit Sampling, *provides guidance on the application and evaluation of audit sampling in performing tests of controls.*

Management of the service organizations specifies whether all or selected applications and control objectives will be addressed by the tests. The service auditor determines, in his or her judgment:

1. Which controls are necessary to achieve the control objectives to be addressed
2. The nature, timing, and extent of tests of controls needed to evaluate operating effectiveness

The tests should be applied to controls throughout the period covered by the report.

MODIFICATION OF THE SERVICE AUDITOR'S REPORT

Incomplete or Inaccurate Description

If the service auditor concludes that the service organization's description is inaccurate or incomplete, the service auditor's report should be modified to state the conclusion and provide a description sufficient to provide user auditors with an understanding. For this situation, the service auditor adds an explanatory paragraph before the opinion paragraph, and the first sentence of the opinion includes the phrase "except for the matter . . ." (see "AU Illustrations").

Significant Deficiencies

If the service auditor concludes that significant deficiencies in the design or operation exist, the deficiencies are included in an explanatory paragraph before the opinion paragraph, and the *second* sentence of the opinion includes the phrase "except for the deficiency . . . ." (see "AU Illustrations").

The Statement provides an example of a significant deficiency in the *design* of the policies and procedures. However, it does not specifically illustrate the situation wherein the results of the service auditor's tests of controls indicate a deficiency in the operation that precludes the service auditor from expressing the opinion that the controls tested were operating with sufficient effectiveness to provide reasonable assurance that the control objectives were achieved during the period.

AU ILLUSTRATIONS

Following are illustrative service auditor reports adapted from Section 324 on:

1. Controls placed in operation—no exceptions
2. Controls placed in operation—inaccurate or incomplete description
3. Controls placed in operation—significant deficiencies in the design or operation
4. Controls placed in operation and tests of operating effectiveness—no exceptions

All service auditor reports should be accompanied by a description of the service organization's controls. Illustration 5 presents a service organization management representation letter, which is required.

> **ILLUSTRATION 1. SERVICE AUDITOR'S REPORT ON CONTROLS PLACED IN OPERATION—NO EXCEPTIONS NOTED**

To Basic Service Organization:

We have examined the accompanying description of controls related to the payroll processing system of Basic Service Organization. Our examination included procedures to obtain reasonable assurance about whether (1) the accompanying description presents fairly, in all material respects, the aspects of Basic Service Organization's controls that may be relevant to a user organization's internal control as it relates to an audit of financial statements, (2) the controls included in the description were suitably designed to achieve the control objectives specified in the description, if those controls were complied with satisfactorily [and user organizations applied the controls contemplated in the design of Basic Service Organization's controls], and (3) such controls had been placed in operation as of December 31, 20X6. The control objectives were specified by XYZ Company. Our examination was performed in accordance with standards established by the American Institute of Certified Public Accountants and included those procedures we considered necessary in the circumstances to obtain a reasonable basis for rendering our opinion.

We did not perform procedures to determine the operating effectiveness of controls for any period. Accordingly, we express no opinion on the operating effectiveness of any aspects of Basic Service Organization's controls, individually or in the aggregate.

In our opinion, the accompanying description of the aforementioned application presents fairly, in all material respects, the relevant aspects of Basic Service Organization's controls that had been placed in operation as of December 31, 20X6. Also, in our opinion, the controls, as described above, are suitably designed to provide reasonable assurance that the specified control objectives would be achieved if the described controls were complied with satisfactorily (and user organizations applied the internal controls contemplated in the design of Basic Service Organization's controls).

The description of controls at Basic Service Organization is as of December 31, 20X6, and any projection of such information to the future is subject to the risk that, because of change, the description may no longer portray the controls in existence. The potential effectiveness of specific controls at the Service Organization is subject to inherent limitations and, accordingly, errors or fraud may occur and not be detected. Furthermore, the projection of any conclusions, based on our findings, to future periods is subject to the risk that changes may alter the validity of such conclusions.

This report is intended solely for use by the management of Basic Service Organization, its customers, and the independent auditors of its customers.

> **ILLUSTRATION 2. SERVICE AUDITOR'S REPORT ON CONTROLS PLACED IN OPERATION—INACCURATE OR INCOMPLETE DESCRIPTION**

To Basic Service Organization:

We have examined the accompanying description of controls related to the payroll processing system of Basic Service Organization. Our examination included procedures to obtain reasonable assurance about whether (1) the accompanying description presents fairly, in all material respects, the aspects of Basic Service Organization's controls that may be relevant to a user organization's internal control as it relates to an audit of financial statements, (2) the controls included in the description were suitably designed to achieve the control objectives specified in the description, if those controls were complied with satisfactorily [and user organizations applied the controls contemplated in the design of Basic Service Organization's controls], and (3) such controls had been placed in operation as of December 31, 20X6. The control objectives were specified by XYZ Company. Our examination was performed in accordance with standards established by the American Institute of Certified Public Accountants and included those procedures we considered necessary in the circumstances to obtain a reasonable basis for rendering our opinion.

We did not perform procedures to determine the operating effectiveness of controls for any period. Accordingly, we express no opinion on the operating effectiveness of any aspects of Basic Service Organization's controls, individually or in the aggregate.

The accompanying description states that Basic Service Organization uses operator identification numbers and passwords to prevent unauthorized access to the system. Based on inquiries of staff personnel and inspection of activities, we determined that such procedures are employed in Applications A and B, but are not required to access the system in Applications C and D.

In our opinion, except for the matter referred to in the preceding paragraph, the accompanying description of the aforementioned applications presents fairly, in all material respects, the relevant aspects of Basic Service Organizations controls that had been placed in operation as of December 31, 20X6. Also, in our opinion, the controls as described are suitably designed to provide reasonable assurance that the specified control objectives would be achieved if the described controls were complied with satisfactorily (and user organizations applied the controls contemplated in the design of Basic Service Organization's controls).

The description of controls at Basic Service Organization is as of December 31, 20X6 and any projection of such information to the future is subject to the risk that, because of change, the description may no longer portray the controls in existence. The potential effectiveness of specific controls at the Service Organization is subject to inherent limitations and, accordingly, errors or fraud may occur and not be detected. Furthermore, the projection of any conclusions, based on our findings, to future periods is subject to the risk that changes may alter the validity of such conclusions.

This report is intended solely for use by the management of Basic Service Organization, its customers, and the independent auditors of its customers.

ILLUSTRATION 3. SERVICE AUDITOR'S REPORT ON CONTROLS PLACED IN OPERATION—SIGNIFICANT DEFICIENCIES IN THE DESIGN OR OPERATION

To Basic Service Organization:

We have examined the accompanying description of controls related to the payroll processing system of Basic Service Organization. Our examination included procedures to obtain reasonable assurance about whether (1) the accompanying description presents fairly, in all material respects, the aspects of Basic Service Organization's controls that may be relevant to a user organization's internal control as it relates to an audit of financial statements, (2) the controls included in the description were suitably designed to achieve the control objectives specified in the description, if those controls were complied with satisfactorily (and user organizations applied the controls contemplated in the design of Basic Service Organization's controls), and (3) such controls had been placed in operation as of December 31, 20X6. The control objectives were specified by XYZ Company. Our examination was performed in accordance with standards established by the American Institute of Certified Public Accountants and included those procedures we considered necessary in the circumstances to obtain a reasonable basis for rendering our opinion.

We did not perform procedures to determine the operating effectiveness of controls for any period. Accordingly, we express no opinion on the operating effectiveness of any aspects of Basic Service Organization's controls, individually or in the aggregate.

As discussed in the accompanying description, from time to time the Service Organization makes changes in application programs to correct deficiencies or to enhance capabilities. The procedures followed in determining whether to make changes, in designing the changes, and in implementing them do not include review and approval by authorized individuals who are independent from those involved in making the changes. There are also no specified requirements to test such changes or provide test results to an authorized reviewer prior to implementing the changes.

In our opinion, the accompanying description of the aforementioned application presents fairly, in all material respects, the relevant aspects of Basic Service Organization's controls that had been placed in operation as of December 31, 20X6. Also, in our opinion, except for the deficiency referred to in the preceding paragraph, the controls as described are suitably designed to provide reasonable assurance that the specified control objectives would be achieved if the described controls were complied with satisfactorily (and user organizations applied the controls contemplated in the design of Basic Service Organization's controls).

The description of controls at Basic Service Organization is as of December 31, 20X6 and any projection of such information to the future is subject to the risk that, because of change, the description may no longer portray the controls in existence. The potential effectiveness of specific controls at the Service Organization is subject to inherent limitations and, accordingly, errors or fraud may occur and not be detected. Furthermore, the projection of any conclusions, based on our findings, to future periods is subject to the risk that changes may alter the validity of such conclusions.

This report is intended solely for use by the management of Basic Service Organization, its customers, and the independent auditors of its customers.

ILLUSTRATION 4. SERVICE AUDITOR'S REPORT ON CONTROLS PLACED IN OPERATION AND TESTS OF OPERATING EFFECTIVENESS—NO EXCEPTIONS NOTED

To Basic Service Organization:

We have examined the accompanying description of controls related to the payroll processing system of Basic Service Organization. Our examination included procedures to obtain reasonable assurance about whether (1) the accompanying description presents fairly, in all material respects, the aspects of Basic Service Organization's controls that may be relevant to a user organization's internal control as it relates to an audit of financial statements, (2) the controls included in the description were suitably designed to achieve the control objectives specified in the description, if those controls were complied with satisfactorily [and user organizations applied the controls contemplated in the design of Basic Service Organization's controls], and (3) such controls had been placed in operation as of December 31, 20X6. The control objectives were specified by XYZ Company. Our examination was performed in accordance with standards established by the American Institute of Certified Public Accountants and included those procedures we considered necessary in the circumstances to obtain a reasonable basis for rendering our opinion.

In our opinion, the accompanying description of the aforementioned applications presents fairly, in all material respects the relevant aspects of Basic Service Organization's controls that had been placed in operation as of December 31, 20X6. Also, in our opinion, the controls as described are suitably designed to provide reasonable assurance that the specified control objectives would be achieved if the described controls were complied with satisfactorily [and user organizations applied the controls contemplated in the design of Basic Service Organization's controls].

In addition to the procedures we considered necessary to render our opinion as expressed in the previous paragraph, we applied tests to specific controls, listed in Schedule 1, to obtain evidence about their effectiveness in meeting control objectives, described in Schedule 1, during the period from July 1, 20X6 to December 31, 20X6. The specific controls and the nature, timing, and extent, and results of the tests are listed in Schedule 1. This information has been provided to user organizations of Basic Service Organization and to their auditors to be taken into consideration, along with information about control at user organizations, when making assessments of control risk for user organizations. In our opinion the controls that were tested, as described in Schedule 1, were operating with sufficient effectiveness to provide reasonable, but not absolute, assurance that the control objectives specified in Schedule 1 were achieved during the period from July 1, 20X6 to December 31, 20X6. [However, the scope of our engagement did not include tests to determine whether control objectives not listed in Schedule 1 were achieved; accordingly we express no opinion on the achievement of control objectives not included in Schedule 1.]

The relative effectiveness and significance of specific controls at Basic Service Organization and their effect on assessments of control risk at user organizations are dependent on their interaction with the controls and other factors present at individual user organizations. We have performed no procedures to evaluate the effectiveness of controls at individual user organizations.

The description of controls at Basic Service Organization is as of December 31, 20X6 and information about tests of the operating effectiveness of specific controls covers the period from December 31, 20X6 to July 1, 20X6. Any projection of such information to the future is subject to the risk that, because of change, the description may no longer portray the system in existence. The potential effectiveness of specific controls at the Service Organization is subject to inherent limitations and, accordingly, errors or fraud may occur and not be detected. Furthermore, the projection of any conclusions, based on our findings, to future periods is subject to the risk that changes may alter the validity of such conclusions.

This report is intended solely for use by the management of Basic Service Organization, its customers, and the independent auditors of its customers.

ILLUSTRATION 5. SERVICE ORGANIZATION MANAGEMENT REPRESENTATION LETTER (APPLIES TO BOTH TYPES OF REPORTS)

[*Client Letterhead*]

February 15, 20X6
Smith & Jones
1 Oldtown Road
Anywhere, USA

We have engaged you to examine the description of controls related to the payroll processing system of Basic Service Organization as of December 31, 20X6 for the purpose of expressing an opinion as to whether the description presents fairly, in all material respects, the relevant aspects of Basic Service Organization's controls that had been placed in operation as of December 31, 20X6, and as to whether the controls, as described, are suitably designed to provide reasonable assurance that the specified control objective would be achieved if the described controls were complied with satisfactorily. In connection with this examination, we confirm, to the best of our knowledge and belief, the following representations made to you during your examination.

1. We are responsible for establishing and maintaining appropriate controls relating to the processing of transactions for user organizations.
2. We believe the control objectives we have specified in the description are appropriate. They are both reasonable in the circumstances and consistent with our contractual obligations.
3. The description of controls presents fairly, in all material respects, the aspects of Basic Service Organization's controls that may be relevant to a user organization's internal control.
4. The controls, as described, had been placed in operation as of December 31, 20X6.
5. We believe the controls were suitably designed to achieve the specified control objectives.
6. We have disclosed to you all significant changes in controls that have occurred since Basic Service Organization's last examination.
7. There are no (We have disclosed to you all) illegal acts, fraud, or uncorrected errors attributable to Basic Service Organization's management or employees that may affect one or more user organizations.
8. There are no (We have disclosed to you all) design deficiencies in controls of which we are aware, including those for which we believe the cost of corrective action may exceed the benefits.
9. There are no (We have disclosed to you all) subsequent events that would have a significant effect on user organizations.
10. We have disclosed to you all instances, of which we are aware, when controls have not operated with sufficient effectiveness to achieve the specified control objective during the period July 1, 20X6 to December 31, 20X6.

Very truly yours,

NOTE: Representation 10 above should be included in the report when the scope of work includes tests of operating effectiveness. It is also beneficial to include in the report on controls placed in operation.

ILLUSTRATION 6. AUDIT PROGRAM FOR AN AUDITOR'S REVIEW OF A SERVICE AUDITOR'S REPORT

Page _____ of _____

**Audit Program for
Consideration of Section 324 Reports**

Company: _____ Balance Sheet Date: _____

Audit Objective	Audit Procedure for Consideration	N/A Performed By	Workpaper Index
	AUDIT OBJECTIVES		
	A. Determine whether a Section 324 report is required to:		
	• Obtain an understanding of the design of internal controls and whether they have been placed in operation (all audits) • Assess control risk below the maximum for certain financial statement assertions (if applicable)		
	B. Read and understand the Section 324 report to determine how service organization's controls affect the:		
	• Types of potential misstatements to the entity's financial statements • Factors that affect the risk of material misstatement • Design of substantive audit tests • Assessment of control risk for individual assertions		
	Planning		
A.	1. Identify transactions that are processed by a service organization.		
A.	2. Link the transactions identified in step 1 to the entity's financial statements and relevant assertions.		
A.	3. Determine whether a Section 324 report is needed for each of the transactions identified in step 1.		
	a. If a Section 324 report is not needed or is unavailable, then either		
	i. Perform alternative procedures to obtain the information necessary to plan the audit, or ii. Modify the auditor's report for a scope limitation.		
A.	4. Obtain the necessary Section 324 report(s), either from the client or directly from the service organization.		

Audit Objective	Audit Procedure for Consideration	N/A Performed By	Workpaper Index
	Read and Assess the Implication of the Section 324 Report		
B.	5. Read the service auditor's report and assess its implications for the audit of the entity's financial statements, including:		
	a. Whether the service auditor prepare a Type I or Type II report		
	b. The nature of the opinions rendered and whether these included any modifications to the standard reporting language.		
	c. The timing of the engagement, that is,		
	i. The date "as of" which the description of controls applies.		
	ii. The period of time covered by the tests of operating effectiveness of controls, if control risk is to be assessed below the maximum.		
B.	6. Read the description of the service organization's controls and evaluate the effect of the following on the audit of the entity's financial statements:		
	a. Whether the description includes all significant transactions, processes, computer applications, or business units that affect the audit of the entity's financial statements		
	b. Whether the description includes all five components of internal control		
	c. Whether the description is sufficiently detailed to understand how the service organization's processing affects the entity's financial statements		
	d. Changes to service organization controls		
	e. Instances of noncompliance with service organization controls		
	f. Whether the description of controls is adequate to provide an understanding of those elements of the entity's accounting information system maintained by the service organization		
B.	7. List all complementary user organization controls identified in the Section 324 report that the service auditor assumed were maintained by the entity.		
	Cross-reference this list to the audit work performed to:		
	a. Understand the design of these complementary user controls and whether they have been placed in operation, and		
	b. If applicable, tests of operating effectiveness of these controls.		

Audit Objective	Audit Procedure for Consideration	N/A	Performed By	Workpaper Index
	Tests of Operating Effectiveness (if applicable)			
B.	8. Review the service auditor's description of the tests of controls and assess their adequacy for your purposes. Consider:			
	a. The link between the financial statement assertion and the control objective.			
	b. The link between the control objective and the controls tested.			
	c. The nature, timing, and extent of the tests performed.			
B.	9. Evaluate the results of the tests of controls and determine whether they support assessing control risk below the maximum.			

AU 325 Communicating Internal Control Related Matters Identified in an Audit[1]

AU-C 265 Communicating Internal Control Related Matters Identified in an Audit

AU EFFECTIVE DATE AND APPLICABILITY

Original Pronouncements	Statement on Auditing Standards (SAS) 112, superseded by SAS 115.
Effective Date	Audits of financial statements for periods ending on or after December 15, 2009.
Applicability	Audits of financial statements in accordance with generally accepted auditing standards (GAAS).

AU-C EFFECTIVE DATE

SAS No. 122, *Codification of Auditing Standards and Procedures,* is effective for audits of financial statements with periods ending on or after December 15, 2012.

The clarified SAS makes explicit requirements that were implicit in the extant standard and adds two new requirements.

AU-C Section 265 makes explicit the following requirements:

- To determine whether, on the basis of the audit work performed, the auditor has identified one or more deficiencies in internal control.

---

[1] *Auditors of issuers of financial statements should be aware that this section is superseded for an integrated audit by the Public Company Accounting Oversight Board (PCAOB) 5. However, new guidance for situations when an audit of internal control over financial statements is not required for an issuer (financial statement audit only) is provided by the PCAOB's Standard,* Conforming Amendments to PCAOB Interim Standards Resulting from the Adoption of PCAOB Auditing Standard No. 5, An Audit of Internal Control over Financial Reporting That Is Integrated with an Audit of Financial Statements.

- To include specific matters in a written communication stating that no material weaknesses were identified during the audit that are similar to those in the written communication of significant deficiencies and material weaknesses.

AU-C 265 adds the following requirements:

- The requirement to communicate, in writing or orally, only to management, other deficiencies in internal control identified during the audit that have not been communicated to management by other parties and that, in the auditor's professional judgment, are of sufficient importance to merit management's attention.
- The requirement to include in the written communication an explanation of the potential effects of the significant deficiencies and material weaknesses identified. Management and those charged with governance need this information to enable them to take appropriate remedial action. The clarified SAS includes guidance addressing that the potential effects need not be quantified.

AU DEFINITIONS OF TERMS

Control deficiency. A *control deficiency* exists when the design or operation of a control does not allow management or employees, in the normal course of performing their assigned functions, to prevent or detect and correct misstatements on a timely basis.

Control deficiency—design. A deficiency in *design* exists when (1) control necessary to meet the control objective is missing or (2) an existing control is not properly designed so that even if the control operates as designed, the control objective would not be met.

Control deficiency—operation. A deficiency in *operation* exists when a properly designed control does not operate as designed or when the person performing the control does not possess the necessary authority or competence to perform the control effectively.

Material weakness. A significant deficiency or combination of significant deficiencies, resulting in a reasonable possibility that a material financial statements misstatement will not be prevented, or detected and corrected on a timely basis.

Significant deficiency. A *significant deficiency* is a control deficiency, or combination of control deficiencies, that is less severe than a material weakness, and yet is important enough to merit attention by those charged with governance.

NOTE: A misstatement is "inconsequential" if a reasonable person would conclude, after considering the possibility of further undetected misstatements, that the misstatement, whether individually or when aggregated with other misstatements, clearly would be immaterial to the financial statements. If a reasonable person would not reach such a conclusion regarding a particular misstatement, that misstatement is more than inconsequential.

AU-C DEFINITIONS OF TERMS

Source: AU-C Section 265.07

Deficiency in internal control. A deficiency in internal control exists when the design or operation of a control does not allow management or employees, in the normal course of performing their assigned functions, to prevent, or detect and correct, misstatements on a timely basis. A deficiency in *design* exists when (1) a control necessary to meet the control objective is missing, or (2) an existing control is not properly designed so that, even if the control operates as designed, the control objective would not be met. A deficiency in *operation* exists when a properly designed control does not operate as designed or when the person performing the control does not possess the necessary authority or competence to perform the control effectively.

Material weakness. A deficiency or a combination of deficiencies in internal control, such that there is a reasonable possibility that a material misstatement of the entity's financial statements will not be prevented, or detected and corrected, on a timely basis.

Significant deficiency. A deficiency, or a combination of deficiencies, in internal control that is less severe than a material weakness yet important enough to merit attention by those charged with governance.

OBJECTIVES OF AU SECTION 325

This section:

- Defines the terms *control deficiency*, *significant deficiency*, and *material weakness*
- Provides guidance on evaluating the severity of control deficiencies
- Requires the auditor to communicate, in writing, to management and those charged with governance (e.g., the audit committee or its equivalent), significant deficiencies and material weaknesses identified in an audit

The section provides guidance in identifying and reporting conditions that relate to an entity's internal control observed during an audit of financial statements. It does not apply to the reporting of material weaknesses noted in an attest engagement to report on entity's internal control.

The section also provides for establishing, between the auditor and client, agreed-upon criteria for identifying and reporting on matters in addition to those required to be reported on by this section.

OBJECTIVES OF AU-C SECTION 265

AU-C Section 265 states that "the objective of the auditor is to appropriately communicate to those charged with governance and management deficiencies in internal control that the auditor has identified during the audit and that, in the auditor's professional judgment, are of sufficient importance to merit their respective attentions."

FUNDAMENTAL REQUIREMENTS

GENERAL

The auditor must evaluate the severity of the control deficiencies identified during the audit to determine whether those deficiencies, individually or in combination, are significant deficiencies or material weaknesses.

NOTE: The auditor is not *required to search out or have procedures in place to identify control deficiencies. In other words, when an auditor "trips across" an internal control deficiency in the course of an audit, the auditor must then evaluate the deficiency.*

Significant deficiencies and material weaknesses must be communicated in writing to management and those charged with governance as a part of each audit.

The auditor may communicate matters that he or she does not consider to be reportable conditions but which nonetheless may be of benefit to the entity.

DETERMINATION OF DEFICIENCY SEVERITY

Determining the severity of a deficiency depends on (1) the magnitude of a misstatement resulting from the deficiency, and (2) whether there is a reasonable possibility that the entity's controls will fail to prevent, or detect and correct, a misstatement. A key point is that the determination of severity of a deficiency *does not* depend on whether the misstatement actually occurred.

The magnitude of a misstatement can be impacted by such factors as the amounts or transaction volumes comprising the financial statements that are exposed to the deficiency. When evaluating the magnitude of a potential misstatement, the recorded amount is considered the maximum amount by which an account balance can be overstated.

One can evaluate whether a deficiency presents a reasonable possibility of misstatement without quantifying a specific range for the probability of occurrence. It is quite possible that the probability of a small misstatement will exceed the probability of a large misstatement.

If there are multiple deficiencies that impact the same account, disclosure, or assertion, this increases the likelihood of a material misstatement, which may constitute a significant deficiency or a material weakness.

If the auditor becomes aware of compensating controls that may limit the severity of a deficiency, the auditor may consider their effects, provided that the auditor has tested these controls for operating effectiveness. Compensating controls can only limit the severity of a deficiency, not eliminate it.

INDICATORS OF MATERIAL WEAKNESS

The following are indicators of material weaknesses in internal controls:

- Fraud by senior management, even if immaterial.
- Correction of a material misstatement due to error or fraud.
- Identification of a material misstatement that would not have been detected by the entity's internal controls.
- Ineffective oversight of financial reporting and internal controls.

RISK FACTORS

The reasonable possibility that one or more deficiencies will result in a financial statement misstatement is affected by risk factors. Risk factors include the following:

- The nature of the financial statement accounts, transaction types, disclosures, and assertions
- The susceptibility of assets or liabilities to loss or fraud
- The extent of judgment required to determine amounts, as well as the level of subjectivity and complexity in these decisions
- The interaction of controls with each other
- The interaction of deficiencies with each other
- The future consequences of the deficiency

COMMUNICATION OF INTERNAL CONTROL RELATED MATTERS

Significant deficiencies or material weaknesses identified during an audit should be communicated in writing to both management and those responsible for the entity's controls. This communication should include reference to prior communications regarding significant deficiencies and material weaknesses that were not remediated following previous audits. While management may have made a conscious decision to accept the risk of a control deficiency, the auditor must still communicate the issue regardless of management's decision.

The auditor should not issue a written communication that no significant deficiencies were identified during the audit.

Timing

This communication should be made by the report release date and no later than 60 days following the report release date. For significant issues in need of immediate correction, the auditor may choose to communicate some issues during the audit, and can do so other than in writing; however, even if remediated, these issues should still be included in a written communication at the end of the audit.

Content

The written communication should include the following items:

- A statement that the auditor is expressing an opinion on the financial statements, not on the effectiveness of internal controls
- A statement that the auditor is not expressing an opinion on the effectiveness of internal control
- A statement that the auditor's consideration of internal control may not identify all significant deficiencies or material control weaknesses
- Definitions of material weakness and significant deficiency
- Identification of significant deficiencies and material weaknesses
- A statement indicating that the communication is intended solely for the information and use of management and those responsible for controls, and should not be used by anyone other than the specified parties

The content of the communication can contain additional topics, such as recommendations for improvement in such areas as administrative or operational efficiency, as well as less than significant deficiencies or immaterial weaknesses. Any verbal communications should be documented. The auditor may also note the general inherent limitations of internal control, including the possibility of management override of those controls. It may also be acceptable to specifically describe the extent of the auditor's consideration of internal control.

The auditor may be asked to issue a communication indicating that no material weaknesses were identified, which then would be submitted to governmental authorities. The "Illustrations" section contains a sample communication that may be used.

Management Response

Management may prepare a written response to the auditor's communication. Such responses typically describe corrective actions taken, plans to issue new controls, or a statement that management believes the cost of new controls exceeds their benefit. If this response is included in a document that also contains the auditor's controls communication, the auditor may include a disclaimer paragraph, such as:

> ABC Company's written response to the significant deficiencies [and material weaknesses] identified in our audit was not subjected to the auditing procedures applied in the audit of the financial statements and, accordingly, we express no opinion on it.

INTERPRETATIONS

COMMUNICATING DEFICIENCIES IN INTERNAL CONTROL OVER COMPLIANCE IN AN OFFICE OF MANAGEMENT AND BUDGET CIRCULAR A-133 AUDIT (ISSUED MARCH 2010)

Circular A-133 contains guidelines for reporting significant deficiencies and material weaknesses. A *deficiency in internal control* over compliance arises when the design or operation of a control does not allow management or employees to prevent or detect and correct noncompliance. A *material weakness in internal control* over compliance is a deficiency in internal control over compliance where there is a reasonable possibility that material noncompliance with a type of compliance requirement of a federal program will not be prevented or detected and corrected in a timely manner. A *significant deficiency in internal control* over compliance is a deficiency in internal control over compliance with a type of compliance requirement of a federal program that is less severe than a material weakness in internal control over compliance, but which is important enough to merit attention by those charged with governance.

COMMUNICATION OF SIGNIFICANT DEFICIENCIES AND MATERIAL WEAKNESSES PRIOR TO THE COMPLETION OF THE COMPLIANCE AUDIT FOR PARTICIPANTS IN OFFICE OF MANAGEMENT AND BUDGET SINGLE AUDIT PILOT PROJECT (ISSUED MARCH 2010, REVISED: JANUARY 2012, EFFECTIVE FOR AUDITS OF FINANCIAL STATEMENTS FOR PERIODS ENDING ON OR AFTER DECEMBER 15, 2012)

Section 325 permits an auditor to communicate deficiencies and material weaknesses in writing to management before completing a financial statement audit, and this also applies to a compliance audit.

COMMUNICATION OF SIGNIFICANT DEFICIENCIES AND MATERIAL WEAKNESSES PRIOR TO THE COMPLETION OF THE COMPLIANCE AUDIT FOR AUDITORS THAT ARE NOT PARTICIPANTS IN OFFICE OF MANAGEMENT AND BUDGET PILOT PROJECT (ISSUED MARCH 2010)

If the auditor decides to communicate with management regarding any significant deficiencies or material weaknesses in internal control, he or she may do so using the guidelines in Section 325, *Communicating Internal Control Related Matters Identified in an Audit*.

APPROPRIATENESS OF IDENTIFYING NO SIGNIFICANT DEFICIENCIES OR NO MATERIAL WEAKNESSES IN AN INTERIM COMMUNICATION (ISSUED MARCH 2010, REVISED: JANUARY 2012, EFFECTIVE FOR AUDITS OF FINANCIAL STATEMENTS FOR PERIODS ENDING ON OR AFTER DECEMBER 15, 2012)

In the preceding scenarios, the auditor should not issue a written communication stating that no significant deficiencies were identified during an audit as of an interim date, only at the end of an audit.

TECHNIQUES FOR APPLICATION

Evaluation of Control Deficiencies

The auditor must evaluate identified control deficiencies to determine whether they are—individually or in the aggregate—significant deficiencies or material weaknesses. When evaluating control deficiencies, the auditor should consider both the likelihood and the magnitude of the misstatement that could result from the deficiency.

Likelihood of the misstatement. The likelihood of a misstatement is a continuous spectrum that ranges from "remote" to "reasonably possible" to "probable," as these terms are defined in Accounting Standards Codification (ASC) 450, *Contingencies*. The following diagram illustrates this range, with "probable" as somewhat less than 100% certainty and "remote" as greater than 0% chance.

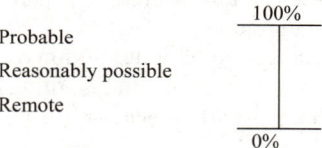

Magnitude of the misstatement. The magnitude of a misstatement also is a continuous spectrum with two key thresholds, "inconsequential" to "material," as illustrated in the following diagram.

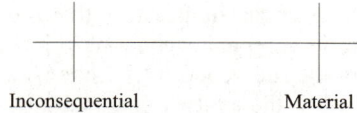

The combination of likelihood and magnitude. The evaluation of control deficiencies requires the auditor to consider both the likelihood and magnitude of the misstatement. Combining the previous two diagrams illustrates this concept.

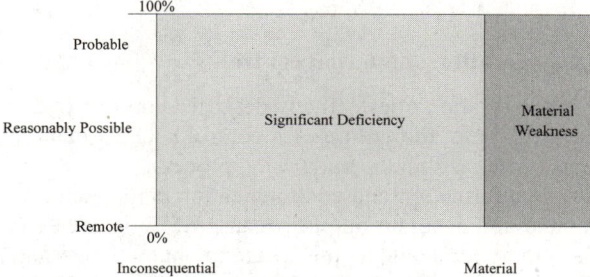

When a control deficiency exists, there is a chance that the internal control system will fail to either prevent or detect a misstatement. This diagram illustrates that if the likelihood of the misstatement being included in the financial statements is greater than remote and the magnitude of the misstatement is greater than inconsequential, then the deficiency is at least a significant deficiency. If the magnitude of the potential misstatement is greater than material, then a material weakness exists.

Examples of Circumstances That May Be Control Deficiencies, Significant Deficiencies, or Material Weaknesses

The appendix to Section 325 lists the following as examples of circumstances that may be control deficiencies in the design of controls, or failures in the operation of internal control. As such, auditors should consider these matters when designing and performing risk assessment procedures to gain an understanding of the design and implementation of internal control and when performing and evaluating the results of further audit procedures.

Deficiencies in internal control design.

- Inadequate design of internal control over the preparation of the financial statements being audited
- Inadequate design of internal control over a significant account or process
- Inadequate documentation of the components of internal control
- Insufficient control consciousness within the organization—for example, the tone at the top and the control environment
- Absent or inadequate segregation of duties within a significant account or process
- Absent or inadequate controls over the safeguarding of assets (this applies to controls that the auditor determines would be necessary for effective internal control over financial reporting)
- Inadequate design of information technology (IT) general and application controls that prevents the information system from providing complete and accurate information consistent with financial reporting objectives and current needs
- Employees or management who lack the qualifications and training to fulfill their assigned functions (for example, in an entity that prepares financial statements in accordance with generally accepted accounting principles (GAAP), the person responsible for the accounting and reporting function lacks the skills and knowledge to apply GAAP in recording the entity's financial transactions or preparing its financial statements)
- Inadequate design of monitoring controls used to assess the design and operating effectiveness of the entity's internal control over time
- The absence of any internal process to report deficiencies in internal control to management on a timely basis

Failures in the operation of internal control.

- Failure in the operation of effectively designed controls over a significant account or process; for example, the failure of a control such as dual authorization for significant disbursements within the purchasing process.
- Failure of the information and communication component of internal control to provide complete and accurate output because of deficiencies in timeliness, completeness, or accuracy; for example, the failure to obtain timely and accurate consolidating information from remote locations that is needed to prepare the financial statements.
- Failure of controls designed to safeguard assets from loss, damage, or misappropriation. This circumstance may need careful consideration before it is evaluated as a significant deficiency or material weakness. For example, assume that a company uses security devices to safeguard inventory (preventive controls) and also performs periodic physical inventory counts (detective control) timely in relation to its financial reporting. Although the physical inventory count does not safeguard the inven-

tory from theft or loss, it prevents a material misstatement of the financial statements if performed effectively and timely. Therefore, given that the definitions of material weakness and significant deficiency relate to likelihood of misstatement of financial statements, the failure of a preventive control such as inventory tags will not result in a significant deficiency or material weakness if the detective control (physical inventory) prevents a misstatement of the financial statements. Material weaknesses relating to controls over the safeguarding of assets would only exist if the company does not have effective controls (considering both safeguarding and other controls) to prevent or detect and correct a material misstatement of the financial statements.

- Failure to perform reconciliations of significant accounts. For example, accounts receivable subsidiary ledgers are not reconciled to the general ledger account in a timely or accurate manner.
- Undue bias or lack of objectivity by those responsible for accounting decisions; for example, consistent understatement of expenses or overstate of allowances at the direction of management.
- Misrepresentation by client personnel to the auditor (an indicator of fraud).
- Management override of controls.
- Failure of an application control caused by a deficiency in the design or operation of an IT general control.
- An observed deviation rate that exceeds the number of deviations expected by the auditor in a test of the operating effectiveness of a control. For example, if the auditor designs a test in which he or she selects a sample and expects no deviations, the finding of one deviation is a nonnegligible deviation rate because, based on the results of the auditor's test of the sample, the desired level of confidence was not obtained.

AU ILLUSTRATIONS

The following illustrations are adapted from Section 325:

1. Communication of significant deficiencies and material weaknesses
2. Communication indicating that no material weaknesses were identified

ILLUSTRATION 1. COMMUNICATION REGARDING SIGNIFICANT DEFICIENCES AND MATERIAL WEAKNESSES

In planning and performing our audit of the financial statements of ABC Company as of and for the year ended December 31, 20XX, in accordance with auditing standards generally accepted in the United States of America, we consider ABC Company's internal control over financial reporting (internal control) as a basis for designing our auditing procedures for the purpose of expressing our opinion on the financial statements, but not for the purpose of expressing an opinion on the effectiveness of the Company's internal control. Accordingly, we do not express an opinion on the effectiveness of the Company's internal control.

Our consideration of internal control was for the limited purpose described in the preceding paragraph and would not necessarily identify all deficiencies in internal control that might be significant deficiencies or material weaknesses and therefore, there can be no assurance that all deficiencies, significant deficiencies, or material weaknesses have been identified. However, as discussed below, we identified certain deficiencies in internal control that we consider to be significant deficiencies [*and other deficiencies that we consider to be material weaknesses*].

A deficiency in internal control exists when the design or operation of a control does not allow management or employees, in the normal course of performing their assigned functions, to prevent or detect and correct misstatements on a timely basis. A material weakness is a deficiency or combination of deficiencies in internal control, such that there is a reasonable possibility that a material misstatement of the entity's financial statements will not be prevented, or detected and corrected, on a timely basis. We consider the following deficiencies in the Company's internal control to be material weaknesses:

[*Describe the material weaknesses that were identified.*]

[*A significant deficiency is a deficiency, or a combination of deficiencies, in internal control that is less severe than a material weakness, yet important enough to merit attention by those charged with governance. We consider the following deficiencies in the Company's internal control to be significant deficiencies:*]

[*Describe the significant deficiencies that were identified.*]

This communication is intended solely for the information and use of management, [*identify the body or individuals charged with governance*], others within the organization, and [*identify any specified governmental authorities*] and is not intended to be and should not be used by anyone other than these specified parties.

ILLUSTRATION 2. COMMUNICATION INDICATING THAT NO MATERIAL WEAKNESSES WERE IDENTIFIED

In planning and performing our audit of the financial statements of ABC Company as of and for the year ended December 31, 20XX, in accordance with auditing standards generally accepted in the United States of America, we consider the Company's internal control over financial reporting (internal control) as a basis for designing our auditing procedures for the purpose of expressing our opinion on the financial statements, but not for the purpose of expressing an opinion on the effectiveness of the Company's internal control. Accordingly, we do not express an opinion on the effectiveness of the Company's internal control.

A deficiency in internal controls exists when the design or operation of a control does not allow management or employees, in the normal course of performing their assigned functions, to prevent, or detect and correct misstatements on a timely basis. A material weakness is a deficiency or combination of deficiencies in internal control such that there is a reasonable possibility that a material misstatement of the entity's financial statements will not be prevented, or detected and corrected, on a timely basis.

Our consideration of internal control was for the limited purpose described in the first paragraph and was not designed to identify all deficiencies in internal control that might be deficiencies, significant deficiencies, or material weaknesses. We did not identify any deficiencies in internal control that we consider to be material weaknesses, as defined above.

This communication is intended solely for the information and use of management, [*identify the body or individuals charged with governance*], others within the organization, and [*identify any specified governmental authorities*] and is not intended to be and should not be used by anyone other than these specified parties.

[*If one or more significant deficiencies have been identified, the auditor may add the following sentence to the third paragraph of the communication:*

However, we identified certain deficiencies in internal control that we consider to be significant deficiencies, and communicated them in writing to management and those charged with governance on (date). A significant deficiency is a deficiency, or a combination of deficiencies, in internal control that is less severe than a material weakness, yet important enough to merit attention by those charged with governance.]

AU-C 265 ILLUSTRATIONS

ILLUSTRATION 1. COMMUNICATION REGARDING SIGNIFICANT DEFICIENCIES AND MATERIAL WEAKNESSES

To Management and [*identify the body or individuals charged with governance, such as the entity's Board of Directors*] of ABC Company

In planning and performing our audit of the financial statements of ABC Company (the "Company") as of and for the year ended December 31, 20XX, in accordance with auditing standards generally accepted in the United States of America, we considered the Company's internal control over financial reporting (internal control) as a basis for designing audit procedures that are appropriate in the circumstances for the purpose of expressing our opinion on the financial statements, but not for the purpose of expressing an opinion on the effectiveness of the Company's internal control. Accordingly, we do not express an opinion on the effectiveness of the Company's internal control.

Our consideration of internal control was for the limited purpose described in the preceding paragraph and was not designed to identify all deficiencies in internal control that might be [*material weaknesses* or *material weaknesses or significant deficiencies*] and therefore, [*material weaknesses* or *material weaknesses or significant deficiencies*] may exist that were not identified. However, as discussed below, we identified certain deficiencies in internal control that we consider to be [*material weaknesses or significant deficiencies or material weaknesses and significant deficiencies*].

A deficiency in internal control exists when the design or operation of a control does not allow management or employees, in the normal course of performing their assigned functions, to prevent, or detect and correct, misstatements on a timely basis. A material weakness is a deficiency, or a combination of deficiencies, in internal control, such that there is a reasonable possibility that a material misstatement of the entity's financial statements will not be prevented, or detected and corrected, on a timely basis. [*We consider the following deficiencies in the Company's internal control to be material weaknesses:*]

[*Describe the material weaknesses that were identified and an explanation of their potential effects.*]

[*A significant deficiency is a deficiency, or a combination of deficiencies, in internal control that is less severe than a material weakness, yet important enough to merit attention by those charged with governance. We consider the following deficiencies in the Company's internal control to be significant deficiencies:*]

[*Describe the significant deficiencies that were identified and an explanation of their potential effects.*]

[*If the auditor is communicating significant deficiencies and did not identify any material weaknesses, the auditor may state that none of the identified significant deficiencies are considered to be material weaknesses.*]

This communication is intended solely for the information and use of management, [*identify the body or individuals charged with governance*], others within the organization, and [*identify any governmental authorities to which the auditor is required to report*] and is not intended to be, and should not be, used by anyone other than these specified parties.

[*Auditor's signature*]
[*Auditor's city and state*]
[*Date*]

[Amended, December 2011, to reflect conforming changes necessary due to the issuance of SAS No. 125.]

> **ILLUSTRATION 2. COMMUNICATION INDICATING THAT NO MATERIAL WEAKNESSES WERE IDENTIFIED**
>
> To Management and [*identify the body or individuals charged with governance, such as the entity's Board of Directors*] of NPO Organization:
>
> In planning and performing our audit of the financial statements of NPO Organization (the "Organization") as of and for the year ended December 31, 20XX, in accordance with auditing standards generally accepted in the United States of America, we considered the Organization's internal control over financial reporting (internal control) as a basis for designing audit procedures that are appropriate in the circumstances for the purpose of expressing our opinion on the financial statements, but not for the purpose of expressing an opinion on the effectiveness of the Organization's internal control. Accordingly, we do not express an opinion on the effectiveness of the Organization's internal control.
>
> A deficiency in internal control exists when the design or operation of a control does not allow management or employees, in the normal course of performing their assigned functions, to prevent, or detect and correct, misstatements on a timely basis. A material weakness is a deficiency, or a combination of deficiencies, in internal control, such that there is a reasonable possibility that a material misstatement of the entity's financial statements will not be prevented, or detected and corrected, on a timely basis.
>
> Our consideration of internal control was for the limited purpose described in the first paragraph and was not designed to identify all deficiencies in internal control that might be material weaknesses. Given these limitations, during our audit we did not identify any deficiencies in internal control that we consider to be material weaknesses. However, material weaknesses may exist that have not been identified.
>
> [*If one or more significant deficiencies have been identified, the auditor may add the following: Our audit was also not designed to identify deficiencies in internal control that might be significant deficiencies. A significant deficiency is a deficiency, or a combination of deficiencies, in internal control that is less severe than a material weakness, yet important enough to merit attention by those charged with governance. We communicated the significant deficiencies identified during our audit in a separate communication dated [date].*]
>
> This communication is intended solely for the information and use of management, [*identify the body or individuals charged with governance*], others within the organization, and [*identify any governmental authorities to which the auditor is required to report*], and is not intended to be, and should not be, used by anyone other than these specified parties.
>
> [*Auditor's signature*]
> [*Auditor's city and state*]
> [*Date*]
>
> [*Amended, December 2011, to reflect conforming changes necessary due to the issuance of SAS No. 125.*]

AU 326 Audit Evidence[1]

AU-C 500 Audit Evidence

AU EFFECTIVE DATE AND APPLICABILITY

Original Pronouncements	Statement on Accounting Standards (SAS) 106.
Effective Date	This statement currently is effective.
Applicability	Audits of financial statements in accordance with generally accepted auditing standards (GAAS); also applies to special reports on financial statements prepared in conformity with a comprehensive basis of accounting other than generally accepted accounting procedures (GAAP) and on specified elements, accounts, or items expressing an opinion.

AU-C EFFECTIVE DATE AND SUMMARY OF CHANGES

SAS No. 122, *Codification of Auditing Standards and Procedures,* is effective for audits of financial statements with periods ending on or after December 15, 2012.

AU-C 500 does not change extant requirements in any significant respect, except that the requirements in AU 326 addressing the auditor's use of assertions in obtaining audit evidence are included in AU-C 315, *Understanding the Entity and Its Environment and Assessing the Risks of Material Misstatement.*

AU DEFINITIONS OF TERMS

Appropriateness. A quality of evidential matter that relates to its *reliability* and *relevance*.

Assertions. Representations by management that are embodied in financial statement components. They are classified in these broad categories.

Assertions about *classes of transactions and events for the period* under audit:

1. *Occurrence.* Transactions and events that have been recorded have occurred and pertain to the entity.

---

[1] This section is affected by the Public Company Accounting Oversight Board's (PCAOB's) Standard, Conforming Amendments to PCAOB Interim Standards Resulting from the Adoption of PCAOB Auditing Standard No. 5, An Audit of Internal Control Over Financial Reporting That Is Integrated with an Audit of Financial Statements.

2. *Completeness.* All transactions and events that should have been recorded have been recorded.
3. *Accuracy.* Amounts and other data relating to recorded transactions and events have been recorded appropriately.
4. *Cutoff.* Transactions and events have been recorded in the correct accounting period.
5. *Classification.* Transactions and events have been recorded in the proper accounts.

Assertions about *account balances at the period end*:

1. *Existence.* Assets, liabilities, and equity interests exist.
2. *Rights and obligations.* The entity holds or controls the rights to assets, and liabilities are the obligations of the entity.
3. *Completeness.* All assets, liabilities, and equity interests that should have been recorded have been recorded.
4. *Valuation and allocation.* Assets, liabilities, and equity interests are included in the financial statements at appropriate amounts, and any resulting valuation or allocation adjustments are appropriately recorded.

Assertions about *presentation and disclosure*:

1. *Occurrence and rights and obligations.* Disclosed events and transactions have occurred and pertain to the entity.
2. *Completeness.* All disclosures that should have been included in the financial statements have been included.
3. *Classification and understandability.* Financial information is appropriately presented and described, and disclosures are clearly expressed.
4. *Accuracy and valuation.* Financial and other information are disclosed fairly and at appropriate amounts.

Audit evidence. All the information used by the auditor in arriving at the conclusion on which the audit opinion is based.

Audit objectives. Specific objectives to be achieved by applying audit procedures, developed from assertions, to enable the auditor to obtain evidential matter sufficient to form conclusions on the validity of the assertions.

Corroborating information. Documentary material (such as checks, invoices, contracts, and minutes of meetings), confirmations and other written representations, as well as any other information obtained by the auditor from inquiry, observation, inspection, physical examination, or valid reasoning.

Sufficiency. A quality of evidential matter that relates to the *amount* necessary to support an informed opinion on the financial statements.

Underlying accounting data. Books of original entry, general and subsidiary ledgers, related accounting manuals, as well as informal and memorandum records (such as worksheets, computations, and reconciliations) supporting the financial statements.

AU-C DEFINITIONS OF TERMS

Source: AU-C 500.05

Accounting records. The records of initial accounting entries and supporting records, such as checks and records of electronic fund transfers; invoices; contracts; the general and subsidiary ledgers; journal entries and other adjustments to the financial statements that are not reflected in journal entries; and records, such as worksheets and spreadsheets, supporting cost allocations, computations, reconciliations, and disclosures.

Appropriateness (of audit evidence). The measure of the quality of audit evidence (that is, its relevance and reliability in providing support for the conclusions on which the auditor's opinion is based).

Audit evidence. Information used by the auditor in arriving at the conclusions on which the auditor's opinion is based. Audit evidence includes both information contained in the accounting records underlying the financial statements and other information.

Management's specialist. An individual or organization possessing expertise in a field other than accounting or auditing, whose work in that field is used by the entity to assist the entity in preparing the financial statements.

Sufficiency (of audit evidence). The measure of the quantity of audit evidence. The quantity of the audit evidence needed is affected by the auditor's assessment of the risks of material misstatement and also by the quality of such audit evidence.

OBJECTIVES OF AU SECTION 326

Audit evidence is all the information used by the auditor to support the audit opinion. It includes the information contained in the accounting records and other information. Audit evidence is cumulative in nature and includes information obtained from a variety of procedures and sources.

The auditor should obtain audit evidence by testing the accounting records, for example, through analysis and review or reconciling related information. However, the accounting records do not provide sufficient appropriate audit evidence on which to base an audit opinion, so the auditor should obtain other evidence.

OBJECTIVE OF AU-C SECTION 500

AU-C Section 500 states that "the objective of the auditor is to design and perform audit procedures that enable the auditor to obtain sufficient appropriate audit evidence to be able to draw reasonable conclusions on which to base the auditor's opinion." AU-C 500.04

GENERAL GUIDES TO APPROPRIATENESS OF EVIDENCE

Appropriateness of evidence depends on the circumstances, so there are important exceptions to the following presumptions. They are, however, useful general guides.

1. Evidential matter from independent sources outside an entity is more reliable than that secured solely within the entity.
2. Accounting data are more reliable when developed under effective internal control.
3. Direct personal knowledge obtained from the auditor's own physical examination, inspection, observation, or computation is more reliable than information obtained indirectly.
4. Audit evidence is more reliable when it exists in documentary form.
5. Audit evidence provided by original documents is more reliable that audit evidence provided by photocopies or facsimiles.

When information produced by the entity is used by the auditor to perform further audit procedures (for example, analytical procedures), the auditor should obtain audit evidence about the accuracy and completeness of the information.

GENERAL GUIDES TO SUFFICIENCY OF EVIDENCE

The amount of competent evidential matter necessary to provide a reasonable basis for an opinion depends largely on the exercise of professional judgment.

1. Usually the auditor must rely on evidence that is persuasive rather than convincing; an auditor is seldom convinced beyond all doubt about all aspects of the statements being audited.
2. There should be a rational relationship between the cost and usefulness of evidence, but the difficulty and expense of a test is not a valid reason for omitting it.

FUNDAMENTAL REQUIREMENTS

Use of Assertions

The auditor should use relevant assertions for classes of transactions, accounts balances, and presentation and disclosures in sufficient detail:

1. To form a basis for the assessment of risks of material misstatement
2. To consider the different types of potential misstatements that may occur
3. Designing further audit procedures that are responsive to the assessed risks

For example:

Financial statement component	Payables
Assertion	Completeness
Types of potential misstatements	Entity may fail to record valid payables
Procedure	Perform a search for unrecorded liabilities

Relevant assertions are assertions that have a meaningful bearing on whether the account is stated fairly. For each significant class of transactions, account balance, and presentation and disclosure, the auditor should determine the relevance of each of the financial statement assertions. To identify relevant assertions, the auditor should determine the source of likely potential misstatements, for example, by evaluating:

- The nature of the assertion
- The volume of transactions or data related to the assertion
- The nature and complexity of the systems

Audit Procedures for Obtaining Audit Evidence

The auditor should obtain audit evidence to draw reasonable conclusions on which to base the audit opinion by performing audit procedures to:

1. Obtain an understanding of the entity and its environment, including its internal control, to assess the risks of material misstatement. These procedures are referred to as "risk assessment procedures" and are described in more detail in SAS 109 (Section 319).

2. When necessary, or when the auditor has determined to do so, test the operating effectiveness of controls. Section 327 provides guidance on the nature, timing, and extent of tests of controls.
3. Detect material misstatements by performing substantive procedures, which are substantive analytical procedures, tests of details, or a combination of both.

Risk assessment procedures (described in more detail in Section 319) must be performed in order to provide a basis for the assessment of risk.

NOTE: Previous standards did not require auditors to perform risk assessment procedures, per se. Some of the procedures now considered risk assessment procedures were considered to be part of audit planning and not necessarily designed to provide audit evidence. By requiring auditors to perform risk assessment procedures to support risk assessments, Section 326 essentially eliminates the ability of auditors to "default" to assessing risk at the maximum without having a basis for that assessment.

The auditor should use one or more types of the following audit procedures:

1. Inspection of records or documents such as checks, invoices, contracts, and minutes of meetings.
2. Inspection of tangible assets, such as inventory.
3. Observation of a process or procedure being performed by entity personnel.
4. Inquiry of knowledgeable persons inside or outside the entity.
5. Obtaining confirmation and other written representation from knowledgeable people within and outside the entity.
6. Recalculation by checking the mathematical accuracy of documents or records.
7. Reperformance of the entity's procedures or controls.
8. Analytical procedures, as described in Section 329.

INTERPRETATIONS

AUDIT EVIDENCE FOR AN AUDIT OF INTERIM FINANCIAL STATEMENTS (ISSUED FEBRUARY 1974; MODIFIED OCTOBER 1980; REVISED MARCH 2006; REVISED JUNE 2009)

1. The third standard of fieldwork on evidential matter applies to all engagements leading to an expression of opinion on financial information.
2. Audit evidence obtained for an audit of annual financial statements may also be used in an audit of interim financial statements, and vice versa.
3. Because additional estimates are used in measuring certain times for interim financial information, the evidence that is needed to test those estimates may differ from evidence required for the audit of annual financial information.

THE EFFECT OF AN INABILITY TO OBTAIN EVIDENTIAL MATTER RELATING TO INCOME TAX ACCRUALS (ISSUED MARCH 1981; REVISED APRIL 2003; REVISED DECEMBER 2005; REVISED MARCH 2006; REVISED MARCH 2008; REVISED JUNE 2009)

1. Occasionally, the client may not (a) prepare or maintain appropriate documentation of the calculation or contents of the income tax accrual, or (b) permit the auditor ac-

cess to the documentation or necessary information, or to entity personnel with information about the income tax accrual.
2. In these circumstances, the client has imposed a scope limitation on the audit, and the auditor should determine the effect of the limitation on his or her ability to express an opinion on the financial statements. The auditor may express an unqualified opinion, a qualified opinion, or disclaim an opinion (see Section 508).
3. The auditor should document all relevant information that he or she obtains about the income tax accrual. The documentation should include results of auditing procedures and should include significant elements of the client's analysis of the tax contingencies or reserves. The documentation should be sufficient for an experienced auditor to understand the extent and results of auditing procedures performed. It should include the client's analysis of tax contingencies and reserves, support for related disclosures, and for assessing deferred tax assets.
4. The opinion of the client's legal counsel about the appropriateness of the income tax accrual is **not** sufficient competent evidential matter for the accrual.
5. If a client is basing its position on a material tax accrual on an outside advisor's opinion, the auditor should obtain the opinion, or the client's summarization of that opinion.
6. Similarly, an auditor cannot rely solely on the conclusions of a third-party tax adviser without careful consideration by the auditor. The auditor should have access to the tax adviser's opinions and supporting evidence. If the auditor cannot obtain sufficient competent evidence, the auditor has a scope limitation.

The Auditor's Consideration of the Completeness Assertion (April 1986; Revised March 2006)

1. Management's written representations about the completeness assertions and the auditor's assessment of control risk, by themselves, do not constitute sufficient competent evidential matter as to the completeness assertion.
2. The auditor should obtain other evidence by performing substantive tests, such as analytical procedures and tests of details of accounts related to the account that may not include all transactions.
3. The auditor should consider that for some transactions (e.g., revenues in cash at a casino or a charitable organization) it may be necessary to perform tests of controls and assess control risk below the maximum.

AU 328 Auditing Fair Value Measurements and Disclosures

AU-C 540 Auditing Accounting Estimates, Including Fair Value Accounting Estimates and Related Disclosures

AU EFFECTIVE DATE AND APPLICABILITY

Original Pronouncement	Statement on Accounting Standards (SAS) 101.
Effective Date	This standard currently is effective.
Applicability	Audits of financial statements in accordance with generally accepted auditing standards (GAAS).
	NOTE: The section does not address specific types of assets, liabilities, components of equity, transactions, or industry-specific practices. Such guidance can be found in other SASs, such as Section 332, "Auditing Derivative Instruments, Hedging Activities, and Investments in Securities."

AU-C EFFECTIVE DATE AND SUMMARY OF CHANGES

SAS No. 122, *Codification of Auditing Standards and Procedures,* is effective for audits of financial statements with periods ending on or after December 15, 2012.

AU-C 540 does not change extant requirements in any significant respect. AU-C 540 supersedes AU-C 328, *Auditing Fair Value Measurements and Disclosures,* and AU 342, *Auditing Accounting Estimates.*

AU DEFINITIONS OF TERMS

Fair value. According to the Financial Accounting Standards Board (FASB) Statement of Financial Accounting Concepts 7, *Using Cash Flow Information and Present Value in*

Accounting Measurements, the fair value of an asset or liability is the amount at which that asset (liability) could be bought (incurred) or sold (settled) in a current transaction between willing parties, that is, other than in a forced or liquidation sale.

Significant assumptions. Generally, significant assumptions cover matters that materially affect the fair value measurement and may include those that are:

1. Sensitive to variation or uncertainty in amount or nature of the item—for example, assumptions about short-term interest rates may be less susceptible to variation compared to assumptions about long-term interest rates
2. Susceptible to misapplication or bias

AU-C DEFINITIONS OF TERMS

Source: AU-C 540.07

Accounting estimate. An approximation of a monetary amount in the absence of a precise means of measurement. This term is used for an amount measured at fair value when there is estimation uncertainty, as well as for other amounts that require estimation. When this section addresses only accounting estimates involving measurement at fair value, the term *fair value accounting estimates* is used.

Auditor's point estimate or auditor's range. The amount or range of amounts, respectively, derived from audit evidence for use in evaluating the recorded or disclosed amount(s).

Estimation uncertainty. The susceptibility of an accounting estimate and related disclosures to an inherent lack of precision in its measurement.

Management bias. A lack of neutrality by management in the preparation and fair presentation of information.

Management's point estimate. The amount selected by management for recognition or disclosure in the financial statements as an accounting estimate.

Outcome of an accounting estimate. The actual monetary amount that results from the resolution of the underlying transaction(s), event(s), or condition(s) addressed by the accounting estimate.

OBJECTIVES OF AU SECTION 328

More and more generally accepted accounting principles (GAAP) pronouncements require the use of fair value measurements when presenting and disclosing certain assets, liabilities, and components of equity in the financial statements. Such measurements have become both increasingly complex and yet important for financial statement users. The ASB decided that practitioners needed overall guidance when auditing fair value measurements and disclosures.

Since assumptions used in measuring fair value are similar to those used in developing other accounting estimates, this section addresses issues similar to those in Section 342, "Auditing Accounting Estimates," along with guidance that is specific to fair value estimates.

Section 328 provides the standards and guidance for auditing fair value measurements in financial statements and the related disclosures.

OBJECTIVE OF AU-C SECTION 540

The objective of the auditor is to obtain sufficient appropriate audit evidence about whether, in the context of the applicable financial reporting framework

1. Accounting estimates, including fair value accounting estimates, in the financial statements, whether recognized or disclosed, are reasonable and
2. Related disclosures in the financial statements are adequate.

FUNDAMENTAL REQUIREMENTS

According to AU 328.03, the auditor should obtain sufficient competent audit evidence to provide reasonable assurance that fair value measurements and disclosures conform with GAAP.

UNDERSTANDING HOW FAIR VALUE IS DETERMINED AND ASSESSING RISK

The auditor should understand the entity's process for determining fair value measurements and disclosures and the relevant controls sufficient to develop an effective audit approach. The auditor uses this understanding when assessing the risk of material misstatement and then determining the nature, timing, and extent of audit procedures to perform. The auditor should be aware that, as the accounting and financial reporting requirements for fair value measurements become more complex, the risk of material misstatement may increase.

NOTE: The section notes that since fair value measurements often involve subjective judgments, this may affect the nature of controls, the possibility of management override of controls, and the inherent limitations of internal control.

EVALUATING CONFORMITY OF FAIR VALUE MEASUREMENTS AND DISCLOSURES WITH GAAP

The auditor is required to evaluate whether the fair value measurements and disclosures in the financial statements conform with GAAP. The auditor uses the understanding of GAAP requirements, knowledge of the entity's business and industry, and the results of audit procedures to evaluate the accounting for and disclosure of fair values. The auditor's understanding of the business is particularly important in certain cases, such as the following:

1. When the asset or liability or the valuation method is highly complex, such as when valuing complex derivatives
2. When valuing items that may be affected by the entity's circumstances and operations, such as the valuation of intangible assets acquired in a business combination
3. When assessing the need to recognize an impairment loss under GAAP. The results of audit procedures should also be considered when making this assessment

The auditor should also evaluate the intent and ability of management to carry out specific courses of action where intent is relevant to the use of fair value measurements, the related presentation and disclosure requirements, and how changes in fair value are reported in the financial statements. The auditor's procedures ordinarily include reviewing budgets, minutes, written plans and other documentation and making inquires of management, corroborating management's responses as necessary, to:

1. Evaluate management's history of carrying out its stated intentions regarding assets or liabilities
2. Evaluate management's reasons for choosing a particular course of action and its ability to carry out the action in light of economic circumstances and contractual commitments

When the entity uses a valuation method, the auditor should evaluate whether the entity's measurement method is appropriate in the circumstances. The evaluation requires the use of professional judgment along with an understanding of management's rationale for selecting a particular method, obtained by discussing the reasons for selecting the valuation method with management. The auditor also considers the following:

1. Has management sufficiently evaluated and applied required GAAP criteria, if any, to support the selected method?
2. Is the valuation method appropriate in light of the nature of the item valued and the entity's business, industry, and operating environment?
3. If different valuation methods result in significantly different fair value measurements, how has the entity investigated the reasons for these differences in establishing its fair value measurements?

The auditor should evaluate whether the entity's method for determining fair value measurements is applied consistently, and if so, whether such consistency is appropriate in light of any changes in the entity's circumstances, environment, or changes in accounting principles.

If management changes the method for determining fair value, the auditor considers whether management can adequately demonstrate that the new method is more appropriate.

NOTE: Section 328 notes that an example of an appropriate change might be discontinuing an old valuation method when an active market for an equity security is created.

ENGAGING A SPECIALIST

The auditor should consider whether to engage and use the work of a specialist as evidential matter in performing substantive tests of material financial statement assertions. This consideration usually is part of forming an overall audit strategy. If the auditor decides to use a specialist, he or she considers whether the specialist's understanding of fair value and the method to be used by the specialist are consistent with those of management and with GAAP. The auditor may discuss such matters with the specialist or read the specialist's report. The auditor should also apply the guidance in Section 336, *Using the Work of a Specialist*.

TESTING THE ENTITY'S FAIR VALUE MEASUREMENTS AND DISCLOSURES

Based on the auditor's assessment of the risk of material misstatement, the auditor should test the entity's fair value measurements and disclosures. The nature, timing, and extent of audit procedures may vary widely because of differences in the complexity of fair value measurements and levels of the risk of material misstatement. Such substantive tests may involve:

1. Testing management's significant assumptions, the valuation model, and the underlying data
2. Developing corroborating independent fair value estimates, or
3. Reviewing subsequent events and transactions

Testing Significant Assumptions, the Valuation Model, and the Underlying Data

The auditor evaluates the following when testing the entity's fair value measurements and disclosures:

1. Are management's assumptions reasonable and consistent with market information?
2. Was the fair value determined using an appropriate model?
3. Did management use relevant and reasonably available information?

The auditor should evaluate whether management's significant assumptions, taken individually and as a whole, provide a reasonable basis for the entity's fair value measurements and disclosures. The auditor pays particular attention to significant assumptions that support complex valuation methods and consider whether they are reasonable and consistent with market information. The auditor should keep in mind, however, that he or she is not required to obtain evidence to provide an opinion on the assumptions, but rather evaluate whether such assumptions provide a reasonable basis for the fair value measurements in the context of the audit.

The auditor should test the data used in preparing the fair value measurements and disclosures and evaluate whether the fair value measurements have been properly determined from the data and assumptions. The auditor evaluates whether the data is accurate, complete, and relevant. The auditor also evaluates whether the data and management's assumptions support the measurements. Such tests of data may include:

- Verification of the data's source
- Mathematical recomputation of inputs
- Review of the consistency of information, including consistency with management's intent and ability to carry out planned actions

Developing Corroborating Independent Fair Value Estimates

If the auditor decides to develop an independent fair value estimate to corroborate management's estimate, the auditor evaluates management's assumptions. The auditor may decide to develop his or her own assumptions to make a comparison with management's fair value measurements. However, the auditor should still understand and evaluate management's assumptions. This understanding will help to ensure that the auditor's independent estimate considers all significant variables, and will help in evaluating significant differences in the auditor's estimate and management's estimate. The auditor should also test the data that management uses to develop the fair values, as discussed previously.

Reviewing Subsequent Events and Transactions

Subsequent events and transactions that reflect circumstances existing at the balance sheet date may substantiate fair value measurements and reduce the need to apply other audit procedures to substantiate the measurements. However, if subsequent events or transactions reflect changes in circumstances occurring after the balance sheet date, then such events are not competent evidence of the fair value measurement at the balance sheet date.

NOTE: *For example, a change in the price of an equity security with an active market change reflects a change in circumstances and would not provide competent evidence of the fair value measurement of the security at the balance sheet date. The section notes that this consideration of subsequent events is a substantive test and differs from the review of subsequent events in Section 560,* Subsequent Events.

Fair Value Disclosures

The auditor should evaluate whether the entity's fair value disclosures are adequate and are in conformity with GAAP. The auditor would use essentially the same procedures to audit the fair value disclosures as used in auditing fair value measurements in the financial statements. The auditor obtains sufficient competent audit evidence that the valuation principles are appropriate and consistently applied, and that the valuation method and significant assumptions used are properly disclosed as required by GAAP.

When evaluating the adequacy of disclosure, the auditor considers whether disclosures of items with a high degree of measurement uncertainty sufficiently inform users of this uncertainty.

When fair value information required under GAAP is not included because it is not practicable to reliably determine fair value, the auditor evaluates whether the disclosures in these circumstances are adequate or whether the lack of disclosure causes the financial statements to be materially misstated.

Evaluating the Results of Audit Procedures

The auditor should evaluate the sufficiency and competence of audit evidence obtained for fair value measurements and disclosures and whether the evidence is consistent with other audit evidence. The auditor's evaluation of whether the fair value measurements and disclosures are in conformity with GAAP is done in the context of the financial statements as a whole. (See Section 312.)

Written Management Representations

The auditor should obtain written management representations about whether significant assumptions are reasonable and whether they appropriately reflect management's intent and ability to carry out specific courses of action relevant to the use of fair value measurements and disclosures.

The auditor may also obtain written representations concerning whether:

- The measurement methods and related assumptions are appropriate and the methods are consistently applied
- Fair value disclosures are complete and adequate
- Subsequent events would require that fair value measurements and disclosures be adjusted

Communication with Audit Committees

Section 380, *The Auditor's Communication with Those Charged with Governance*, requires that certain significant accounting estimates be communicated to audit committees. The auditor should determine that the audit committee is informed about management's process for formulating sensitive accounting estimates, including fair value estimates, and the basis for the auditor's conclusions about those estimates. The auditor may consider communicating:

- The nature of significant assumptions underlying fair value measurements
- The subjectivity of the assumptions
- The materiality of the measurements to the financial statements as a whole

INTERPRETATIONS

AUDITING INTEREST IN TRUSTS HELD BY A THIRD-PARTY TRUSTEE AND REPORTED AT FAIR VALUE (JUNE 2005; REVISED APRIL 2007; JUNE 2009)

When a not-for-profit organization has an interest in another entity, it must report the fair value of a trust. When testing the existence and measurement of this interest, it is not sufficient to receive a confirmation from the trustee of the other entity for the purposes of auditing the fair value of the interest. A confirmation on an investment-by-investment basis does constitute adequate audit evidence with respect to the existence assertion. If the auditor cannot audit the existence or measurement of interests in trusts, this is a scope limitation.

TECHNIQUES FOR APPLICATION

GENERAL

Fair value of an asset, liability, or component of equity may be measured when the item is initially recorded or at a later date when the value of the item changes. GAAP requires that certain items be recorded at fair value, but may provide for different treatments of changes in fair value that occur over time. For example, certain changes in fair value are reflected in net income, while others may be shown as an element of other comprehensive income.

The Nature of Fair Value Measurements

Fair value measurements, other than those with observable market prices, are inherently imprecise because such measurements involve uncertainty and are based on assumptions that may change over time. The auditor is responsible for considering information available to the auditor at the time of the audit and is not responsible for predicting future conditions, transactions, or events that, had they been known at the time of the audit, might affect actions and assumptions underlying fair value measurements and disclosures.

Measuring fair value may be relatively simple for certain assets or liabilities, such as actively traded securities. For other items, fair value measurement may be much more complex and require the use of a valuation method.

Relation to Other Audit Procedures

Other audit procedures may also provide evidence about fair value measurements and disclosures. For example, examining an asset to verify its existence may also provide evidence about the physical condition that would affect its valuation.

MANAGEMENT'S RESPONSIBILITIES

Management is responsible for determining the fair value measurements and disclosures in the financial statements, including:

1. Establishing the process for determining fair values and disclosures
2. Selecting appropriate valuation methods
3. Identifying and supporting significant assumptions
4. Performing the valuation
5. Determining that the presentation and disclosure of the fair value measurements are in conformity with GAAP

Understanding How Fair Value Is Determined and Assessing Risk

The auditor should consider the following when obtaining an understanding of the entity's process for determining fair values and disclosures:

1. General considerations, including:

    a. The role of information technology in the fair value process
    b. The types of accounts or transactions requiring fair value (e.g., do the accounts consist of routine recurring transactions or unusual transactions?)
    c. Whether the entity uses a service organization

2. Information about management's assumptions, including:

    a. Significant assumptions used to determine fair value
    b. The process for developing and applying assumptions and monitoring changes in them, and
    c. The documentation supporting the assumptions

    > NOTE: The auditor should consider whether management used available market information in developing assumptions.

3. Information about controls over:

    a. The process for determining fair values, including data controls and whether duties are segregated between personnel responsible for committing the entity to the underlying transactions and those responsible for making the valuation
    b. The ability to change controls and security procedures for valuation models and the associated information systems
    c. Consistency, timeliness, and reliability of the data for valuation models

4. Information about the personnel involved, including:

    a. The expertise and experience of the personnel making the fair value measurements
    b. Whether a specialist is used

Testing the Entity's Fair Value Measurements and Disclosures

Complex fair value measurements normally tend to be more uncertain, resulting from:

- A longer forecast period
- More significant and complex assumptions
- Greater subjectivity in the assumptions and factors used in the process
- Greater uncertainty as to future events underlying the assumptions used
- Less or no objective data when highly subjective factors are used

Examples of considerations when developing auditing procedures include:

- Fair value measurements may be made at a date other than the required financial statement reporting date. When this happens, the auditor obtains evidence that management has accounted for any changes affecting the measurements that occur between the measurement and reporting dates.
- If collateral is a factor when measuring fair value, the auditor obtains sufficient competent audit evidence regarding the existence, value, rights, and access to or

transferability of the collateral. The auditor should consider whether all appropriate liens have been filed and whether the collateral has been appropriately disclosed.
- The auditor considers whether additional procedures are needed to obtain sufficient competent audit evidence about the appropriateness of a fair value measurement, such as physically inspecting an asset to verify the current physical condition and the effect on fair value.

Tests of Significant Assumptions

When evaluating significant assumptions used by management, the auditor considers the following:

- Assumptions will vary depending upon the characteristics of the item valued and the valuation method used.
- Assumptions will be supported by different types of internal and external evidence, and the auditor evaluates the source and reliability of such evidence.
- Because assumptions are often interdependent, assumptions should be evaluated individually and as a whole. Auditors should be alert to the fact that an assumption can appear reasonable when considered individually but not when considered along with other assumptions.
- The valuation may be sensitive to changes in significant assumptions, such as market conditions. If necessary, the auditor encourages management to use sensitivity analysis or other techniques to identify sensitive assumptions. If management does not do so, the auditor should consider whether to employ such techniques.
- If assumptions are based on historical information, whether that basis is justified.

Assumptions should be realistic and consistent with:

- The overall economic climate, the economic climate of the industry, the entity's own economic circumstances, and market information
- The entity's plans
- Prior period assumptions, if still appropriate, and any applicable past experience
- Risk related to cash flows, including possible variations in the amount and timing of cash flows and the effect on the discount rate, if applicable
- The extent to which management relies on historical financial information and whether such reliance is appropriate
- Any other financial statement matters, such as assumptions used for other types of accounting estimates

The auditor may also compare fair value measurements from prior periods to help evaluate the reliability of the entity's process for making such measurements. If variances from prior period measurements exist, the auditor considers whether they result from changes in market or economic circumstances.

Testing the Valuation Model

The auditor does not function as an appraiser and does not substitute his or her judgment for management's when evaluating valuation models. Instead, the auditor should review the model and determine whether:

- The assumptions are reasonable.
- The model is appropriate for that entity.

NOTE: Section 328 notes that an example of where a method might not be appropriate is the use of discounted cash flows by a start-up entity for valuing an equity investment if there is no current revenue stream on which to base future forecasts of earnings or cash flows.

AU 329 Analytical Procedures[1]

AU-C 520 Analytical Procedures

AU EFFECTIVE DATE AND APPLICABILITY

Original Pronouncement	Statements on Auditing Standards (SASs) 56 and 96.
Effective Date	These standards currently are effective.
Applicability	Audits of financial statements in accordance with generally accepted auditing standards (GAAS).

NOTE: Some of the guidance provided in this Statement might be useful in other engagements in which analytical procedures are normally applied, such as reviews of interim information or examinations of prospective financial information, even though it is not required to be applied in those engagements.

AU-C EFFECTIVE DATE

SAS No. 122, *Codification of Auditing Standards and Procedures,* is effective for audits of financial statements with periods ending on or after December 15, 2012. AU-C 520 does not change extant requirements in any significant respect.

AU DEFINITIONS OF TERMS

Analytical procedures. Analytical procedures consist of evaluations of financial information made by an auditor of *plausible and expected* relationships among both financial and nonfinancial data. They range from simple comparisons (the current year with the preceding year) to the use of complex models involving many relationships and elements of data (regression analysis).

A basic premise underlying the application of analytical procedures is that plausible relationships among data may reasonably be expected to exist and continue except as particular conditions (specific unusual transactions or events, accounting changes, business changes, random fluctuations, or misstatements) cause changes.

---

[1] This section is affected by the Public Company Accounting Oversight Board's (PCAOB's) Standard, Conforming Amendments to PCAOB Interim Standards Resulting from the Adoption of PCAOB Auditing Standard No. 5, An Audit of Internal Control over Financial Reporting Performed That Is Integrated with an Audit of Financial Statements.

AU-C DEFINITION OF TERM

Source: AU-C 520.05

Analytical procedures. Evaluations of financial information through analysis of plausible relationships among both financial and nonfinancial data. Analytical procedures also encompass such investigation as is necessary of identified fluctuations or relationships that are inconsistent with other relevant information or that differ from expected values by a significant amount.

OBJECTIVES OF AU SECTION 329

INTRODUCTION

The term "analytical review procedures" was introduced in the official auditing literature in 1972. Such procedures were used in practice well before then and were commonly referred to as ratio and trend analysis and comparisons. The auditor's reliance on substantive tests may be derived from:

1. Tests of details of transactions and balances
2. Analytical review procedures
3. Any combination of those two types of substantive tests

Analytical procedures are now *required* in the planning and final review stages of an audit. The primary motivation for the requirement is that analytical procedures are effective in identifying misstatements and alerting the auditor to the possibility of certain types of material fraud.

OBJECTIVES OF AU-C SECTION 520

AU-C Section 520.03 states that

the objectives of the auditor are to

a. obtain relevant and reliable audit evidence when using substantive analytical procedures and
b. design and perform analytical procedures near the end of the audit that assist the auditor when forming an overall conclusion about whether the financial statements are consistent with the auditor's understanding of the entity.

PLANNING THE AUDIT

The objective of using analytical procedures in planning the audit is to increase the auditor's understanding of the client and identify specific audit risks by considering unusual or unexpected balances or relationships in aggregate data. Specifically, the objective is to identify the existence of unusual transactions and events, and amounts, ratios, and trends, that might identify matters that have audit planning ramifications.

OVERALL REVIEW

The objective of using analytical procedures in the overall review of the audited financial statements near the completion of the audit is to help the auditor in assessing the validity of the conclusions reached during the audit, including the opinion on the financial statements.

SUBSTANTIVE TESTS

The section does not require the auditor to use analytical procedures as a substantive test (see "Fundamental Requirements"). The auditor may, however, use these procedures as a substantive test. When used as a substantive test, the objective of analytical procedures is to accumulate evidence supporting the validity of a specific account balance assertion. For example, the results of applying an average interest rate to average debt outstanding would provide evidence supporting the amount of interest expense.

FUNDAMENTAL REQUIREMENTS

PLANNING THE AUDIT

The auditor is *required* to use analytical procedures in planning the audit. The purpose of analytical procedures at this stage of the audit is to assist the auditor in planning the nature, timing, and extent of the auditing procedures that will be used to obtain evidence in support of specific account balances or classes of transactions.

NOTE: Analytical procedures are a risk assessment procedure that may be used to gain an understanding of the entity and its environment and provide a basis for assessing the risk of material misstatement.

OVERALL REVIEW

The auditor is *required* to use analytical procedures in the overall review of the audited financial statements. The results of this review may indicate that additional audit evidence may be needed.

SUBSTANTIVE TESTS

The auditor *may* use analytical procedures to obtain evidential matter about particular assertions related to account balances or classes of transactions. When used for this purpose, analytical procedures are substantive tests.

1. When using analytical procedures for substantive testing, the auditor should assess the reliability of the data by considering:
   - Was the data obtained from independent sources outside the entity?
   - Are the data sources in the entity independent of those who are responsible for the data being audited?
   - Was the data developed under a reliable system with adequate controls?
   - Was the data subject to audit testing in the current or prior year?
   - Were the expectations developed from data using various sources?
2. The auditor should consider the amount of difference from his or her expectation that can be accepted without additional investigation.
3. The auditor should evaluate significant unexpected differences.
4. Management explanations should ordinarily be corroborated with other evidence.
5. If an explanation for a difference cannot be obtained, the auditor should perform other audit procedures if a likely misstatement has occurred.

6. The auditor should consider that an unexplained difference might increase the risk of material misstatement.

NOTE: To be used as a substantive test, an analytical procedure has to provide persuasive evidence. Audit objectives cannot be achieved by the application of analytical procedures that only provide overall comfort—the evidence has to be persuasive.

The auditor should document all of the following when an analytical procedure is used as the principal substantive test for an assertion:

- The expectation and factors considered in its development, when the expectation is not readily determinable from the existing documentation.
- Results of comparing the expectation to the recorded amounts or ratios developed from the recorded amounts.
- Any additional auditing procedures performed (and the results of such procedures) to respond to significant unexpected differences arising from the analytical procedure.

INTERPRETATIONS

There are no interpretations for this section.

PROFESSIONAL ISSUES TASK FORCE PRACTICE ALERTS

98-1 THE AUDITOR'S USE OF ANALYTICAL PROCEDURES

This Practice Alert provides guidance to practitioners on:

1. *Applying substantive analytical procedures.* Analytical procedures are based on expectations, which are the auditor's prediction of what a recorded account balance or ratio should be. In forming an expectation, the auditor should determine that a relationship is plausible, or, in other words, expected to exist based on the auditor's understanding of the client and the client's industry.

    The auditor might consider the following items included in the Practice Alert:

    - Forces external to the client's industry
    - The client's position in the industry
    - The client's processes for achieving its objectives
    - The prior years' audits and results
    - The client's budgeted and actual amounts
    - Discussions held with client personnel responsible for preparing recorded account balances or ratios and financial and nonfinancial results of similar entities operating in the industry

    An expectation is usually developed using:

    - Prior year data adjusted for anticipated change
    - Current period data
    - Budgets or forecasts
    - Nonfinancial data from inside the entity

The account balance being tested can be estimated using external data, such as data from an industry regulator or trade association.

The alert also provides guidance of factors that limit or preclude using external information, and identifies factors that the auditor should consider when evaluating the relationship between data used and the account balance being tested.

2. *Identifying difficulties noted in the performance of analytical procedures and ways to avoid them.* The Practice Alert highlights difficulties such as:

- Avoiding the use of an unaudited balance as a starting point for analysis.
- Being careful to watch for a pattern of unusual fluctuations
- Avoiding overreliance on management's explanations
- Developing expectations using data at the appropriate level of disaggregation

3. *How analytical procedures can assist in evaluating fraud risk.* The Alert provides guidance on how analytical procedures can assist the auditor in evaluating the risk of fraud. Although the results of analytical procedures do not provide the auditor with evidence to determine whether fraud has resulted in a material misstatement to the financial statements, such procedures do help the auditor to determine if account balances have an increased chance of being subjected to fraud.

Finally, the Practice Alert also covers various bases for developing expectations, such as trend analysis, ratio analysis, reasonableness testing, and regression analysis, as well as consideration of the precision of the expectation. These topics are covered in the *Techniques for Application* section.

TECHNIQUES FOR APPLICATION

INTRODUCTION

Analytical procedures include (1) comparisons, (2) ratio analysis, (3) trend analysis, (4) variance analysis, (5) preparation of common-size financial statements, and (6) regression analysis. The specific procedures used are determined by the nature of the client's business and its industry, availability of data, degree of precision required, and auditor judgment.

When applying analytical procedures, the auditor may use data from outside the accounting system or financial statements, such as:

1. Units produced or sold
2. Number of employees
3. Hours worked by nonsalaried employees
4. Square feet of selling space
5. Budget information; if, however, the budget is primarily a motivational tool (goals instead of expectations) its usefulness for analytical procedures is limited

The remainder of this section contains a general discussion of various techniques for the application of analytical procedures, followed by an explanation of how these procedures could be applied to the specific phases of the audit—planning, accumulation of audit evidence (substantive tests), and overall review.

ANALYTICAL PROCEDURES: GENERAL

When the auditor applies analytical procedures, he or she usually *computes, compares,* and *analyzes ratios, trends,* and *variances.* Generally, ratio analysis, trend analysis, and variance analysis are used together. In addition to these analyses, some auditors use regression analysis in applying analytical procedures.

Ratio analysis involves the following:

1. The computation of significant financial relationships, such as current assets to current liabilities
2. The comparison of current period ratios with one or more of the following:
   a. Similar ratios of a prior period or periods
   b. Similar ratios of the industry
   c. Similar ratios generally viewed as acceptable by bankers or other credit grantors
3. The analysis of unexpected deviations between current period ratios and those with which they are compared

Trend analysis involves the following:

1. The selection of a base period
2. The computation of subsequent periods' financial data, such as sales as a percentage of base period data
3. The comparison of current period's percentages with those of prior periods
4. The analysis of unexpected changes in percentages between the current period and prior periods

Variance analysis involves the following:

1. The determination of acceptable levels for the financial data being analyzed
2. The comparison of current period financial data with the acceptable levels
3. The analysis of unexpected deviations between current period financial data and the acceptable level for such data

COMPARISONS WITH INDUSTRY

In applying analytical procedures, the auditor may wish to compare the financial data of the client with those of the client's industry. For a diversified entity, however, comparisons may not be effective unless the auditor compares client segment data with appropriate industry data.

COMPARISONS WITH NATIONAL ECONOMIC DATA

The auditor may wish to compare the client's financial data with national economic data such as the following:

1. Economic indicators—leading, lagging, coincident
2. Gross domestic product
3. Disposable income
4. Consumer price index
5. Wholesale price index
6. Unemployment rate

The data are issued monthly, the first five by the US Department of Commerce and the sixth by the US Department of Labor. All of the data and other national economic data are reported in The *Wall Street Journal*.

RATIO ANALYSIS

The most common analytical procedure is ratio analysis. Ratios may be classified based on their sources as follows:

1. Balance sheet ratios
2. Income statement ratios
3. Mixed ratios (these ratios contain numbers from more than one financial statement)

Some of the more common ratios, their classification, method of computation, and the attribute measured are shown in the following list:

Ratio	Formula	Purpose
Liquidity ratios—Measure the entity's ability to meet its short-term obligations, and provide an indication of the entity's solvency.		
Current ratio	= $\dfrac{\text{Current assets}}{\text{Current liabilities}}$	Indicates whether claims of short-term creditors can be met with current assets.
Quick ratio or acid test	= $\dfrac{\text{Current assets} - \text{Inventory}}{\text{Current liabilities}}$	Measures the entity's ability to pay off short-term creditors without relying on the sale of inventories.
Leverage ratios—Measure the extent to which the entity is financed by debt and provide a measure of the risk of the entity borne by the creditors.		
Debt ratio	= $\dfrac{\text{Total debt}}{\text{Total assets}}$	Indicates percentage of total funds provided by creditors; high ratios when economy is in downturn indicate more risk for creditors.
Times interest earned	= $\dfrac{\text{Earnings before interest and taxes}}{\text{Interest charges}}$	Measures extent to which earnings can decline and still provide entity with ability to meet annual interest costs; failure to meet this obligation may result in legal action by creditors, possibly resulting in bankruptcy.
Long-term debt to equity	= $\dfrac{\text{Long-term debt}}{\text{Stockholders' equity}}$	Indicates the proportion of the entity financed through long-term debt vs. owners' equity.
Activity ratios—Measure how effectively an entity employs its resources.		
Inventory turnover	= $\dfrac{\text{Cost of goods sold}}{\text{Average inventory}}$	Estimates how many times a year inventory is sold.
Age of inventory	= $\dfrac{\text{360 days}}{\text{Inventory turnover}}$	Indicates number of days of inventory on hand at year-end.
Accounts receivable turnover	= $\dfrac{\text{Net credit sales}}{\text{Average accounts receivable}}$	Estimates how many times a year accounts receivable are collected.

Ratio	Formula	Purpose
Age of accounts receivable	= 360 days / Accounts receivable turnover	Indicates the age of accounts receivable or number of days sales not collected.
Total asset turnover	= Net sales / Total assets	Estimates volume of sales based on total assets

Profitability ratios—Measure how effectively the entity is being managed.

Ratio	Formula	Purpose
Sales to total assets	= Net sales / Total assets	Indicates the ability of an entity to use its assets to generate sales.
Gross margin	= Gross margin / Net sales	Provide a percentage relationship based on sales.
Profit margin on sales	= Net income / Net sales	Indicates the return an entity receives on sales.
Net operating margin	= Operating income / Net sales	Indicates management's effectiveness at using entity's assets to generate operating income.
Return on total assets	= (Net income + Interest expense) / Total assets	Indicates the return an entity receives for its assets.
Return on common stockholders' equity	= (Net income − Preferred dividends) / Average stockholders' equity	Indicates return on investment to common stockholders.

These ratios are some, but not all, of the ratios that may be used in applying analytical procedures. The auditor should use his or her knowledge of the client and its industry to develop relevant and meaningful ratios.

Ratio analysis has limitations in that it concentrates on the past and deals in aggregates. However, ratios serve as warning signs and indicators that are helpful in discovering existing or potential trouble spots when applied in trend analysis and variance analysis.

TREND ANALYSIS

Trend analysis indicates the relevant changes in data from period to period. For example, assume the following sales in successive income statements:

Year	20X1	20X2	20X3	20X4	20X5
Sales	$200	$300	$350	$450	$500

If 20X1 is selected as the base year, sales for that year are 100% and sales for 20X2 are 150% (300 ÷ 200). Sales in a trend statement are as follows:

Year	20X1	20X2	20X3	20X4	20X5
Sales	100%	150%	175%	225%	250%

Any year may be the base year, and the auditor may select a moving base year. At the end of 20X6, he or she may decide to develop a new five-year trend statement by eliminating 20X1 and making 20X2 the base year or 100%.

Trend statements may be developed from any data. For example, assume the following gross profit percentages:

Year	20X1	20X2	20X3	20X4	20X5
Profit	42%	43%	45%	45%	40%

If 20X1 is selected as the base year, its gross profit percentage would be 100.0%, and 20X2 would be 102.4% (43% ÷ 42%). Gross profit percentages in a trend statement are as follows:

Year	20X1	20X2	20X3	20X4	20X5
Profit	100.0%	102.4%	107.1%	107.1%	95.2%

The unusual decline in the trend from 20X4 to 20X5 alerts the auditor to an area (sales and cost of goods sold) requiring special attention and, perhaps, additional audit procedures.

Maintaining trend statements for significant numbers, sales, cost of goods sold, repairs and maintenance, selling expenses, and so on, and for significant ratios aids the auditor in detecting unusual deviations from prior periods.

VARIANCE ANALYSIS

An auditor may wish to compare current data with predetermined acceptable levels (the norms). Deviations from these levels require investigation. This process is known as variance analysis.

When applying variance analysis, the auditor may use data for his or her norms from the following sources:

1. Entity budgets
2. Entity forecasts
3. Industry data
4. Prior period data

When using industry data in analytical procedures, the auditor may convert the client's financial statements to common-size financial statements.

COMMON-SIZE FINANCIAL STATEMENTS

A common-size financial statement is one in which the numbers are converted to percentages. The dollars of cash, receivables, inventory, and other assets in the balance sheet are converted to percentages based on the relationship of each asset to total assets.

Common-size financial statements aid the auditor in comparing financial data of businesses of different sizes because not numbers but proportions are being compared. Further, most industry data such as those issued by Dun & Bradstreet are common size.

The following balance sheet is presented in amounts and in common size.

	Amount	Common size
Cash	$ 200	6.7%
Accounts receivable	500	16.7
Inventories	700	23.3
Property, plant and equipment, net	1,500	50.0
Other assets	100	3.3
Total	$3,000	100.0%
Accounts payable	$ 300	10.0%
Other current liabilities	100	3.3
Long-term debt	900	30.0
Stockholders' equity	1,700	56.7
Total	$3,000	100.0%

Common-size income statements also may be prepared based on sales as the 100% figure.

REGRESSION ANALYSIS

Regression analysis is the means by which a relation between variables is used to make inferences about such variables. The relationships are expressed in terms of a dependent variable and one or more independent variables.

Regression is used in auditing to make inferences as to what account balances *should be* for comparison with what account balances *are*. Ordinarily, a linear regression model is used when the auditor applies regression analysis.

Linear Regression

The linear regression model defines the relationship between the dependent variable and the independent variable or variables in terms of a straight line. To determine meaningful relationships, the auditor should identify those independent variables that affect the dependent variable. Although these relationships will never be exact and will differ at various times, useful inferences are possible as long as the relationships indicate that a relatively stable pattern exists between the dependent variable and the independent variable or variables.

Defining the Variables

To develop the regression model, the auditor should define the variables. In defining the variables, the auditor will use his or her knowledge of the client and previously audited historical data. In developing regression models, the auditor also may use external independent variables, such as gross national product, disposable net income, unemployment rate, and so on.

The Linear Regression Formula

The linear regression formula is as follows:

$$Y = a + bX$$

In this formula, a is the value of Y when X is equal to 0. The slope of the regression line is b, which indicates the change in Y for each unit of change in X. For example, assume the auditor wishes to make inferences about the amount of recorded selling expenses. Based on his or her knowledge of the client, the auditor determines the following:

1. Fixed selling expenses amount to $10,000. In the regression formula, this amount is a.
2. Selling expenses (Y) increase as sales (X) increase.
3. From prior data, the auditor determines that for each dollar of sales, selling expenses increase by $.05. In the regression formula, this amount is b.

In the regression formula, the preceding information is expressed as follows:

$$\text{Selling expense } (Y) = \$10{,}000 \ (a) + [.05 \ (b) \times \text{Sales } (X)]$$

Therefore, if sales were $10 million, the auditor would expect selling expenses to be $510,000, determined as follows:

$$Y = \$10{,}000 + .05 \times \$10{,}000{,}000$$
$$Y = \$510{,}000$$

Applying Regression Analysis

After defining the variables and determining the values for a and b, the auditor should perform other steps before making inferences. These steps are as follows:

1. Calculate the correlation coefficient
2. Calculate point estimates
3. Determine the standard deviation
4. Determine the standard error
5. Calculate the precision interval
6. Calculate the confidence interval

PERMANENT FILE FOR ANALYTICAL PROCEDURES

Because analytical procedures are based in part on industry data and client prior period data, this data may be maintained in the client permanent file for subsequent use. The data to be maintained depend on the nature of the analytical procedures.

When the auditor compares current period results with prior periods, the comparisons may include the following:

1. Quarter to quarter during the current year
2. Month to month during the current year
3. Season to season during the current year
4. Current year's quarter, month, or season with the similar period of prior years

The auditor may maintain in the client permanent file all periodic data used in the analysis.

The auditor also may include in the permanent file, when applicable, the following:

1. The percentages used in trend analysis
2. The percentages used in common-size financial statements
3. The ratios used in ratio analysis
4. The industry data used and the source of the data

There is no specified period of time for which permanent file data should be retained; however, it is advisable to retain these data for at least five years.

PLANNING THE AUDIT

Analytical procedures used in planning the audit are directed to (1) improving the auditor's understanding of the client's business and the transactions and events that have occurred since the last audit, and (2) identifying areas that may represent risks relevant to the current audit. For example, a lower than usual accounts receivable turnover ratio indicates possible collectibility problems. The auditor, therefore, should prepare an audit program for accounts receivable that emphasizes testing for the adequacy of the allowance for doubtful accounts.

Recommended Procedures

The Statement does not require the auditor to apply specific procedures. The sophistication, extent, and timing of the procedures are based on the auditor's judgment and may vary widely, depending on the size and complexity of the client.

Analytical procedures used in planning the audit might include the following:

1. *Account balance comparison.* Compare unadjusted trial balance amounts of the current period to adjusted trial balance amounts of the prior period.

2. *Computation of significant ratios.* Compute ratios, such as gross margin, inventory turnover, and receivables turnover, and compare them to prior year ratios or industry ratios.
3. *Other ratios.* Compute ratios using nonfinancial and financial data; for example, sales per square foot of sales space.

For a large, complex entity, analytical procedures might include regression analysis to estimate the amount of certain account balances and extensive analysis of quarterly financial information.

The results of analytical procedures used in planning the audit combined with the auditor's knowledge of the client's business and industry serve as a basis for inquiries and the effective planning of substantive tests.

OVERALL REVIEW

The application of analytical procedures in the overall review stage of the audit is one of the last tests of the audit. Analytical procedures at this stage of the audit assist the auditor in assessing the conclusions reached concerning certain account balances and in evaluating the overall financial statement presentation.

Recommended Procedures

The overall review generally includes reading the financial statements and accompanying notes and considering the following:

1. The adequacy of evidence accumulated for account balances considered unusual or unexpected in the planning stage or during the audit
2. Unusual or unexpected balances or relationships that were not previously identified
3. The overall reasonableness of the financial statements and the adequacy of the financial statement disclosures

In addition to reading the financial statements and accompanying notes, the auditor may consider using other analytical procedures, such as the following:

1. Comparison to similar financial data for the prior year or the client's industry
2. Ratio analysis
3. Trend analysis
4. Development of common-size financial statements

Results of Overall Review

The results of the overall review may indicate that additional audit evidence is needed. Because of this possibility, the auditor should try to complete the overall review before the end of fieldwork.

SUBSTANTIVE TESTS

The extent to which the auditor uses analytical procedures as a substantive test depends on the level of assurance he or she wants in achieving a particular audit objective. The higher the level of assurance desired, the more predictable the relationship should be. As a general rule, relationships involving income statement accounts are more predictable than relationships involving only balance sheet accounts.

It may be difficult or impossible to achieve certain substantive audit objectives without relying to some extent on analytical procedures (e.g., this is often the case in testing for unrecorded transactions).

Some audit objectives may be difficult or impossible to achieve by relying solely on analytical procedures (e.g., testing an account balance that is not expected to show a predictable relationship with other operating or financial data).

Analytical procedures may be more effective and efficient than tests of details for assertions in which potential misstatements would not be apparent from an examination of the detailed evidence or in which detailed evidence is not readily available (e.g., comparison of aggregate purchases with quantities received may indicate duplication payments that may not be apparent from testing individual transactions).

Differences from expected relationships would often be good indicators of potential omissions, whereas evidence that an individual transaction should have been recorded may not be readily available.

The expected effectiveness and efficiency of an analytical procedure in detecting errors or fraud depends on, among other things:

- The nature of the assertion
- The plausibility of the relationship
- The reliability of the data used to develop the expectation
- The precision of the expectation

Availability and Reliability of Data

The auditor obtains assurance from analytical procedures based upon the consistency of the recorded amounts with the expectations developed from data derived from other sources. Other sources for data include industry trade associations; data service organizations, such as Dun & Bradstreet and Standard & Poor's Corp. industry trade journals; and the client's prior year's audited financial statements. In circumstances where the auditor specializes in a specific industry, the auditor may use clients' data to develop plausible expectations (for example, gross margin percentage, other income statement ratios, and receivable and inventory turnover ratios).

The reliability of the data used to develop the expectations should be appropriate for the desired level of assurance from the analytical procedures.

In general, the following factors influence the reliability of data used for analytical procedures:

- Whether the data was obtained from independent sources outside the entity or from sources within the entity.
- Whether sources within the entity were independent of those who are responsible for the amount being audited.
- Whether the data was developed under a reliable system with effectively designed controls.
- Whether the data was subjected to audit testing in the current or prior year.
- Whether the expectations were developed using data from a variety of sources.

Precision of the Expectation

The expectation of the relationship that exists should be precise enough to provide the desired level of assurance that differences that may be potential material misstatements would be identified for the auditor to investigate. Expectations developed at a detailed level ordinarily have a greater chance of detecting misstatements of a given amount than do broad comparisons. For example, expectations developed at a division level will have a greater chance of detecting misstatement than expectations developed at an entity level.

DOCUMENTATION

As with any other auditing procedure, the auditor should document the application of analytical procedures. Section 329 requires certain documentation when an analytical procedure is used as the principal substantive test for an assertion. In addition, the following are recommended:

1. Procedures to be applied should be listed in the audit program.
2. Audit documentation should record the results of the procedures applied.
3. Auditor conclusions should appear in the audit documentation.
    a. What effect did the results have in planning the audit?
    b. If procedures applied in the overall review indicated that additional procedures were required, reference should be made in the audit documentation to those sections that document the additional procedures.
    c. If procedures applied as substantive tests indicated unexpected fluctuations, an explanation of these fluctuations should appear in the audit documentation. The auditor's explanation should include audit evidence supporting that explanation.

AU ILLUSTRATIONS

The following illustrations give examples of the application of analytical procedures and suggested follow-up audit procedures.

ILLUSTRATION 1

Facts

A company had sales (all credit) for the year of $120,000. Its accounts receivable at year-end amounted to $20,000. Its day's sales in accounts receivable is computed as follows:

1. Sales $120,000
2. Accounts receivable 20,000
3. Average daily sales (Sales $120,000 ÷ 360 days) 333
4. Day's sales in accounts receivable [Accounts receivable ÷ Average daily sales ($20,000 ÷ $333)] 60

In the previous year, the day's sales in accounts receivable was forty-five.

Analysis

The company is not collecting its receivables as rapidly as it did in the previous year. This increase in the day's sales in accounts receivable indicates a possible problem in the collectibility of the receivables.

Auditing Procedures

The auditor may consider doing some or all of the following:

1. Review cash receipts and remittance advices for the subsequent period.
2. Obtain credit reports on significant past due accounts.
3. Analyze year-end sales to determine any unusually large sales. Determine the nature of these sales and ascertain that they were recorded in the proper accounting period.

Illustration 2

Facts

A company has cost of sales for the year of $108,000. Its inventory amounted to $20,000 at the beginning of the year and $16,000 at the end of the year. Its inventory turnover is determined as follows:

1. Average inventory
   Beginning balance $20,000
   Ending balance 16,000
   Total $36,000
   Total divided by 2 .... $18,000

   NOTE: A better indication of the average inventory may be obtained by using month-end inventories, if available.

2. Cost of goods sold $108,000
3. Cost of goods sold ÷ Average inventory = Inventory turnover 6

In the previous year, the inventory turnover was four.

Analysis

An increase in the inventory turnover ratio may occur because of improved purchasing, production, and pricing policies. It may also be caused by one of the following:

1. Poor credit rating of client. If the client has a poor credit rating, it may not be getting all of the inventory it requires. This will cause inventory levels to decline, and if sales do not decline as rapidly, the inventory turnover ratio will increase.
2. Unrecorded purchases.
3. Unusual inventory shrinkage.
4. Overly conservative inventory valuation.
5. Error in computing the inventory.

Auditing Procedures

There are no specific auditing procedures when the high turnover is caused by insufficient inventory because of a poor credit rating. In that situation, however, the auditor might want to obtain a credit report on the client and should approach the audit with more skepticism than usual.

If the auditor believes the high turnover is caused by other than a poor credit rating, he or she may do the following:

1. Review debit balances in the accounts payable schedule. A debit balance might indicate a payment without the accompanying entry for a purchase.
2. Review inventory controls to determine the possibility of theft. Also, if the company is a manufacturer, review production records to determine spoilage and waste.
3. Compare inventory costs with inventory values.
4. Review inventory computations.

ILLUSTRATION 3

Facts

Following is a trend statement of selected income and expense items:

Year	20X1	20X2	20X3	20X4	20X5
Sales	100	116	133	151	168
Selling expenses	100	115	132	150	175

Analysis

Sales have increased at a steady rate over the five-year period, and selling expenses matched this increase for the first four years. In the fifth year, however, the increase in selling expenses was disproportionate to previous years' increases and to the current year's increase in sales. The increase may have been caused by one of the following:

1. Misclassification of expenses
2. Classification of prepayments as expenses
3. Recording of nonbusiness expenses

Auditing Procedures

If a trend statement indicates a disproportionate increase in an expense, the auditor should apply additional substantive tests to this expense. To determine the reason for the disproportionate increase in selling expenses in the preceding example, the auditor may review invoices for major expense items in order to answer the following:

1. Were administrative or nonselling expenses classified as selling expenses?
2. At year-end, did the entity make advance payments for the subsequent year's selling program and classify these payments as an expense rather than as a prepayment?
3. Are expenses of executives that are personal in nature being charged to the entity?

AU 330 The Confirmation Process

AU-C 505 External Confirmations

AU EFFECTIVE DATE AND APPLICABILITY

Original Pronouncement Statement on Auditing Standards (SAS) 67.

Effective Date This statement currently is effective.

Applicability Audits of financial statements or other financial information made in accordance with generally accepted auditing standards (GAAS).

AU-C EFFECTIVE DATE AND SUMMARY OF CHANGES

SAS No. 122, *Codification of Auditing Standards and Procedures,* is effective for audits of financial statements with periods ending on or after December 15, 2012.

AU-C Section 505 supersedes AU Section 330.

The requirement to confirm accounts receivable has been moved from AU Section 330 to AU-C 330 because it is considered part of the process of determining the procedures to perform. AU-C 505 presumes that the auditor has already determined an external confirmation is the appropriate audit procedure.

AU-C 505.08 address the responsibilities of the auditor when management refuses to allow the auditor to send a confirmation request. If management refuses to allow the auditor to perform external confirmation procedures, the auditor should:

1. Inquire about management's reasons for the refusal and seek audit evidence about their validity and reasonableness;
2. Evaluate the implications of management's refusal on the auditor's assessment of the relevant risks of material misstatement, including the risk of fraud, and on the nature, timing, and extent of other audit procedures; and
3. Perform alternative audit procedures designed to obtain relevant and reliable audit evidence.

This is a new requirement.

The ASB has added application material regarding the use of oral responses to confirmation requests as audit evidence. AU-C 505 clarifies that the receipt of an oral response to a confirmation request does not meet the definition of an external confirmation. When the auditor concludes that an oral or other confirmation response is unreliable, the auditor may need to revise the assessment of the risks of material misstatement at the assertion level and modify planned audit procedures.

AU-C 505.A24 offers examples of alternative procedures:

- For accounts receivable balances, examining specific subsequent cash receipts (including matching such receipts with the actual items being paid), shipping documentation, or other client documentation providing evidence for the existence assertion
- For accounts payable balances, examining subsequent cash disbursements or correspondence from third parties and other records, such as receiving reports and statements that the client receives from vendors providing evidence for the completeness assertion

In AU-C Section 505, the term external confirmation includes audit evidence obtained by electronic or other medium. AU-C Section 505 clarifies that:

- Access to the information must come from the third party
- Access provided by management to the auditor does not meet the definition of an external confirmation
- Even when audit evidence is received from external sources, the auditor must consider the risk that the electronic confirmation process is not secure or is improperly controlled

AU DEFINITIONS OF TERMS

Accounts receivable. An entity's claims against customers that have arisen from the sale of goods or services in the normal course of business, and a financial institution's loans.

Blank form of confirmation request. A blank form—a type of positive confirmation request—does not state amounts or other information on the confirmation request. The recipient is asked to provide the amount or furnish other information.

The confirmation process. The process of obtaining and evaluating a direct communication from a third party in response to a request for information about a particular item affecting financial statement assertions. The process includes:

1. Selecting items for confirmation
2. Designing the confirmation request
3. Communicating the confirmation request to the appropriate third party
4. Obtaining the response from the third party
5. Evaluating the information, or lack thereof, provided by the third party about the audit objectives, including the reliability of that information

Negative form of confirmation request. Recipient is asked to respond only if he or she disagrees with the information given. Negative requests may be used to reduce audit risk to an acceptable level when *all* of the following exist:

1. The combined assessed level of inherent risk and control risk is low.
2. A large number of small balances is involved.
3. The auditor has no reason to believe that the recipients of the requests are unlikely to give them consideration.

Positive form of confirmation request. Recipient is asked to respond whether he or she agrees or disagrees with the information stated on the request. Positive forms provide audit evidence only when responses are received from the recipients.

AU-C DEFINITIONS OF TERMS

Source: AU-C 505.06

Exception. A response that indicates a difference between information requested to be confirmed or contained in the entity's records, and information provided by the confirming party.

External confirmation. Audit evidence obtained as a direct written response to the auditor from a third party (the confirming party), either in paper form or by electronic or other medium (for example, through the auditor's direct access to information held by a third party).

Negative confirmation request. A request that the confirming party respond directly to the auditor only if the confirming party disagrees with the information provided in the request.

Nonresponse. A failure of the confirming party to respond, or fully respond, to a positive confirmation request or a confirmation request returned undelivered.

Positive confirmation request. A request that the confirming party respond directly to the auditor by providing the requested information or indicating whether the confirming party agrees or disagrees with the information in the request.

OBJECTIVES OF AU SECTION 330

The auditor uses the confirmation process to obtain sufficient competent evidential matter. Confirmation is performed to obtain evidence from third parties about financial statement assertions made by management.

In general, it is presumed that "evidential matter . . . obtained from independent sources outside an entity . . . provide greater assurance of reliability for the purposes of an independent audit than that secured solely within the entity." Confirmation requests do not, however, address all assertions equally well. For example, accounts receivable confirmations are likely to be more effective for the existence and the rights-and-obligations assertions (see Section 326 for the five categories of assertions) than for the valuation assertion.

Section 330 addresses *all* types of confirmations including, but not limited to, accounts receivable confirmations. It relates the confirmation process to inherent and control risk. The greater the combined assessed level of inherent and control risk, the greater the assurance that the auditor needs from substantive tests. As this combined level of risk increases, the auditor designs substantive tests to obtain more or different evidence about a financial statement assertion. In those circumstances, the auditor should consider using confirmation procedures instead of, or in conjunction with, tests directed toward documents or parties within the entity. In circumstances where the combined assessed level of inherent and control risk is low, it may be appropriate for the auditor to consider not using confirmations. For example, if the combined assessed level of inherent and control risk over the existence of cash is low, the auditor might limit substantive procedures to inspecting client-provided bank statements rather than confirming cash balances.

Another factor that influences the use of confirmations is the nature of transactions. Confirmation of the terms of a transaction would be appropriate if that transaction was unusual or complex and the combined assessed level of inherent and control risk was high.

OBJECTIVE OF AU-C SECTION 505

AU-C 505 states that "The objective of the auditor, when using external confirmation procedures, is to design and perform such procedures to obtain relevant and reliable audit evidence."

FUNDAMENTAL REQUIREMENTS

GENERAL

The auditor should consider the use of confirmations for situations where the combined assessed level of inherent risk and control risk is high.

The auditor should consider confirming the terms of unusual or complex transactions when the combined assessed level of inherent risk and control risk is high.

The auditor should consider the materiality of an account balance and his or her assessment of inherent risk and control risk when deciding whether the evidence provided by confirmations reduces audit risk for the related assertions to an acceptably low level.

The auditor should perform additional procedures when he or she concludes that evidence provided by confirmations alone is not sufficient to reduce audit risk to an acceptably low level. For example, the auditor may perform sales cutoff tests in addition to confirming accounts receivable to obtain sufficient evidence concerning the completeness and existence assertions for accounts receivable.

The auditor should exercise an appropriate level of professional skepticism throughout the confirmation process.

DESIGNING THE CONFIRMATION REQUEST

The auditor should design the confirmation request to satisfy the specific audit objective. Factors the auditor should consider include the following:

1. Assertions addressed (see Section 326, *Audit Evidence*)
2. Conditions likely to affect the reliability of the confirmations
3. Form of the confirmation request
4. Prior experience on the audit or similar engagements
5. Nature of information being confirmed
6. Intended respondent

When using negative confirmations, the auditor should:

1. Perform other substantive procedures to supplement the use of the negative confirmations
2. Investigate relevant information provided on returned negative confirmations
3. Reconsider the combined assessed level of inherent and control risk and consider the effect on planned audit procedures when his or her investigation of responses indicates a pattern of misstatements
4. Be aware that unreturned negative confirmation requests rarely provide significant evidence concerning financial statement assertions
5. Be aware that negative confirmation requests are more likely to generate responses indicating misstatements if a larger number of requests are sent

The auditor should consider the type of information respondents will be readily able to confirm when designing confirmation requests. For example, respondents, because of the nature of their accounting system, may not be able to confirm account balances but may be able to confirm transactions, terms of loans, and other information.

The auditor should obtain an understanding of the substance of the client's arrangements and transactions with third parties to determine the appropriate information to include on the confirmation request. For example:

1. The auditor should consider confirming the *terms* of unusual transactions or sales, such as bill and hold sales, in addition to amounts.
2. If the auditor believes there is at least a moderate degree of risk that there may be significant oral modifications to agreements (for example, unusual payment terms or liberal rights of return), he or she should inquire about those modifications. A method of doing this is to confirm both the terms of the agreement and whether oral modifications exist.

THE RESPONDENT

The confirmation request should be addressed to a person whom the auditor believes is knowledgeable about the information to be confirmed.

If a question arises about the respondent's competence, knowledge, motivation, ability, objectivity, or willingness to respond, the auditor should consider the effect in designing the confirmation request and evaluating the response. In those circumstances, the auditor should also determine whether other procedures are necessary.

If there are unusual circumstances where the auditor should exercise a heightened degree of professional skepticism concerning the respondent's competence, knowledge, motivation, ability, objectivity, or willingness to respond, the auditor should consider whether there is sufficient basis for concluding that the confirmation request is being sent to a respondent whom the auditor believes will provide meaningful and competent evidence. Examples of such circumstances are significant unusual year-end transactions that have a material effect on the financial statements and when the respondent is the custodian of a material amount of the audited entity's assets.

CONTROL OF CONFIRMATIONS

The auditor should maintain control of the confirmation requests and responses. There should be no client intervention from the mailing of the requests to the receipt of the responses.

Because of the risks associated with facsimile responses (difficulty of ascertaining the sources of the responses), the auditor should consider performing the following in order to treat the confirmation as valid audit evidence:

1. Verifying the source and contents of the response through a telephone call to the purported sender
2. Asking the purported sender to mail the original confirmation directly to the auditor

Oral confirmations should be documented in the workpapers. If the information is significant, the auditor should ask the parties involved to submit written confirmation of that information directly to the auditor.

NONRESPONSES

If the recipients do not respond to the confirmation request, other than a negative confirmation request, the auditor should generally follow up with a second and sometimes a third request to those who did not respond.

If the auditor does not receive replies to positive confirmation requests, he or she should apply alternative procedures to the nonresponse to obtain the necessary evidence (see "Techniques for Application"). The auditor does not have to apply alternative procedures if:

1. He or she has not identified unusual qualitative factors or systematic characteristics related to the nonresponses (for example, all nonresponses pertain to year-end transactions).
2. He or she is testing for overstatement and the nonresponses in the aggregate, when projected as 100% misstatements to the population and added to the total of all other unadjusted differences, would not affect the auditor's decision about whether the financial statements are materially misstated.

EVALUATING THE RESULTS

According to AU 330.33, the auditor should evaluate the combined evidence provided by the confirmations and the alternative procedures to determine whether sufficient evidence has been obtained. In performing the evaluation, the auditor should consider the following:

1. The reliability of the evidence
2. The nature of any exceptions, including quantitative and qualitative implications of those exceptions
3. The evidence provided by other procedures
4. Whether additional evidence is necessary

If additional evidence is needed, the auditor should request additional confirmations or extend other tests, such as tests of details or analytical procedures.

CONFIRMATION OF ACCOUNTS RECEIVABLE

Confirmation of accounts receivable, including a financial institution's loans, is a generally accepted auditing procedure (GAAP). It is therefore presumed that the auditor will request the confirmation of accounts receivable during an audit.

The presumption that the auditor will confirm accounts receivable may be overcome if one of the following exists:

1. Accounts receivable are not material to the financial statements.
2. The use of confirmations would be ineffective (for example, based on experience, the auditor concludes that response rates will be inadequate or that responses will be unreliable).
3. In some circumstances, the auditor's combined assessed level of inherent and control risk may be low, and that level, in conjunction with evidence expected to be provided by substantive tests, is sufficient to reduce audit risk to an acceptably low level for the applicable financial statement assertions.

NOTE: If confirmations are not used because experience with the entity indicates the procedure would not be effective, the auditor needs to design suitable alternative procedures to achieve audit objectives.

If the auditor does not confirm accounts receivable, he or she should document the reasons for not doing so.

INTERPRETATIONS

THE CONFIRMATION PROCESS (APRIL 2007; NOVEMBER 2008)

Properly controlled electronic communications may be considered reliable audit evidence, but the confirmation process must minimize the possibility that the results will be compromised. Validation of the sender of electronic information can include encryption, electronic digital signatures, and procedures to verify Web site authenticity. An assurance trust services report or another auditor's report may assist the auditor in assessing the design and operating effectiveness of the electronic and manual controls with respect to the electronic confirmation process. The auditor should also verify the e-mail addresses to which confirmations are sent and may contact the purported sender by telephone to verify that electronic communications sent to the auditor corresponds to the information transmitted by the sender.

PROFESSIONAL ISSUES TASK FORCE PRACTICE ALERT

03-01 AUDIT CONFIRMATIONS

This Practice Alert provides additional guidance to auditors on using confirmations. To improve the confirmation response rate, the alert suggests that auditors request information that the recipient is likely and able to confirm. Confirmations should also include relevant information required for the recipient's response.

The alert suggests that the auditor consider the following techniques to improve the confirmation response rate:

- Is the wording clear?
- Has the confirmation been sent to a specified individual?
- Does the confirmation identify the organization being audited?
- Has the client manually signed the request?
- Does the confirmation indicate a clear deadline for responding?

The auditor should also consider calling the respondent to obtain oral confirmation and request that the written confirmation be returned. Sending out second and third requests may also be helpful.

The alert also provides guidance on negative versus positive confirmation requests, non-responses to positive confirmations, verifying fax confirmations, the use of alternative procedures, and using client personnel. Among other things, the alert notes that:

- The auditor should thoroughly investigate all exceptions to positive confirmation requests.
- The auditor should carefully consider any requests by management not to confirm certain balances or other information. The auditor should challenge those reasons, and seek corroborating evidence.

If the auditor receives an electronic confirmation, he must consider the risk that the confirmation is not from the proper source, that the sender may not be authorized to respond, and that the integrity of the transmission may have been compromised.

If management requests that certain balances not be confirmed (as may occur when there is a dispute with the confirmation recipient), the auditor must consider the reason for the request and its impact on audit risk, and apply alternative procedures as needed.

Finally, the Alert provides guidance on the confirmation of specific areas, including accounts receivable, related-party transactions, accounts payable, and the terms of unusual or complex agreements or transactions.

TECHNIQUES FOR APPLICATION

TIMING OF CONFIRMATION REQUEST

For both positive and negative confirmation requests, the debtor is provided with the balance as of a specified date. The date may be as follows:

1. Year-end date
2. Date prior to year-end (this date generally is one or two months prior to year-end)

It is recommended that confirmation requests be sent to debtors approximately a week before the date specified in the request. If the debtor is in a foreign country, the request should be mailed earlier.

Confirming Prior to Year-End

The auditor may decide to request that the debtor confirm the balance as of a date before year-end. If the auditor follows this procedure, however, he or she should perform the following procedures during the year-end procedures:

1. Perform selective other substantive tests of transactions from the confirmation date to the balance sheet date. These tests would include the following:
    a. Review subsequent sales invoices and related bills of lading.
    b. Review subsequent customer cash receipts and related remittance advices.
2. If balances change significantly from confirmation date to year-end, it is recommended that the auditor reconfirm.

USE OF NEGATIVE FORM OF CONFIRMATION REQUEST

If the negative form of confirmation request is used, the auditor should normally do one of the following:

1. Send out more requests than if the positive form is used.
2. Apply other auditing procedures to a greater extent than if the positive form is used. Other auditing procedures include examination of the following:
    a. Subsequent cash receipts.
    b. Subsequent cash remittance advices.
    c. Sales and shipping documents.

STEPS IN CONFIRMATION PROCESS

The steps in the process of confirming receivables follow:

1. Obtain aged schedule of accounts receivable.
2. Select accounts for confirmation.
3. Prepare and mail confirmation requests.
4. Process responses to confirmation requests.
5. Summarize confirmation results.

Obtain Aged Schedule of Accounts Receivable

The auditor should obtain an aged schedule of accounts receivable as of the confirmation date. He or she should apply the following procedures to this schedule:

1. Determine that totals are correct.
2. Compare all or a selected sample of account balances with the account balances in the accounts receivable subsidiary ledger.
3. Investigate credit balances.

Select Accounts for Confirmation

Auditors have used, and some continue to use, judgment in selecting accounts for confirmation. Statistical sampling methods, however, are ideal for the selection process. Whatever method of selection is used, the auditor generally considers the following accounts:

1. All accounts with a balance over a predetermined amount; the predetermined amount is based on the auditor's assessment of materiality
2. Some or all accounts with zero balances
3. Accounts with old unpaid items, especially when subsequent sales have been paid
4. Accounts written off during the year under review
5. Accounts with entities related to the client but not audited by the auditor
6. Certain accounts that appeared on the prior year's accounts receivable schedule but not on the current year's
7. Accounts with credit balances:
    a. Occasionally, the client will not want confirmation requests sent to these accounts. If the amounts are material, it might result in a scope limitation; however, this is generally not the case.
    b. If accounts with credit balances are not confirmed, alternative auditing procedures should be applied.
8. Of the remaining accounts, a representative portion both in dollar amount and number of accounts should be selected.

Prepare and Mail Confirmation Requests

The auditor should observe the following procedures in preparing and mailing confirmation requests:

1. Prepare schedule of accounts to be confirmed (see the section "AU Illustrations"):
    a. Organize the accounts alphabetically.
    b. Include the address.
    c. Include the amount.
    d. Assign each account a number. This number also should be placed on the confirmation request.
    e. Total the dollar amount of receivables selected for confirmation and compute as a percentage of the total dollar amount of the receivables.

 f. Determine the number of confirmation requests and compute as a percentage of the total number of accounts.
 g. Leave sufficient blank columns after the customer's name to insert the following information when the confirmation reply is received:

  (1) Date reply received
  (2) Amount confirmed
  (3) Explanation of difference between amount customer confirmed and client amount

 h. Leave a blank column for insertion of the date the second request was mailed.
 i. Indicate at bottom the date the first requests were mailed.

2. Request that client address confirmation forms and prepare customer statements:

 a. If auditor desires that client not know which accounts are to be confirmed, he or she should have his or her staff address confirmations.
 b. If auditor desires that client not know which accounts are to be confirmed but wants client to address confirmations, he or she should request client to address confirmation to all accounts and then eliminate the accounts not selected for confirmation.

3. When the auditor receives the addressed confirmation with the account balance and the customer statement, he or she should compare that balance with the balance on the schedule.
4. Independently, some customer addresses should be checked. These tests can be made by comparing the address on confirmation with the address in the telephone book.
5. After confirmations have been reviewed and numbered, the auditor should insert them and the customer statement in his or her firm's envelopes, that is, envelopes with the firm's return address.
6. In addition to inserting the confirmation request in the envelope, insert a postage-paid return envelope bearing the auditor's address.
7. When the requests have been stamped, the auditor should mail them.

From the time the auditor receives the addressed confirmation requests containing the account balances, he or she should never lose control. The confirmation requests always should remain in the auditor's custody or under his or her supervision until mailed.

Process Responses to Confirmation Requests

 When confirmation replies are received, the auditor should do the following:

1. Enter for each account the following:

 a. Date received
 b. Amount confirmed

2. If the amount confirmed differs from the account balance, the following should be done:

 a. Photocopy confirmation reply.
 b. Give photocopy to client and request that the difference be reconciled and provide documentation for reconciling items.
 c. Review documentation for reconciling items.

d. If documentation is satisfactory, enter reasons for difference in receivable confirmation schedule.

3. If the amount confirmed differs from the account balance, and the client cannot satisfactorily reconcile the difference, the auditor should do the following:

   a. If the difference is small, the auditor may ignore it. If there are a significant number of small differences, however, the auditor should analyze them. If the analysis of the significant number of small differences indicates a deficiency in the receivable controls, the auditor may have to apply additional auditing procedures to satisfy himself or herself of the accounts receivable balance.
   b. If the difference is significant, request the client to correspond with the debtor. Make certain the correspondence states that the debtor response should be sent directly to the auditor.

A CPA firm needs to establish a mechanism for ensuring that responses mailed to the CPA firm are obtained and considered by the audit team in the field on a timely basis. Also, a firm needs to ensure that responses that relate to transaction terms and other complex matters (such as compliance with laws and regulations for a governmental entity) are considered by appropriately experienced audit team members.

Summarize Confirmation Results

Near the conclusion of the engagement, the auditor should prepare a worksheet summarizing confirmation results. The worksheet should contain the following:

1. Number and dollar amount of confirmations sent and the percentage of these to the total receivables
2. Number and dollar amount of confirmations received with no exceptions indicated and the percentage of these to the total confirmations requests
3. Number and dollar amount of confirmations received with exceptions that were satisfactorily reconciled by the client; compute the percentage of these to the total confirmations requested
4. Number and dollar amount of confirmations received with exceptions that were not satisfactorily reconciled by the client:

   a. Determine total dollar amount of differences between client records and confirmation responses.
   b. Determine reasons for differences and materiality of differences.
   c. Compute the percentage of these to the total confirmations requested.

5. Review of statistics with a determination of whether the results of the confirmation procedures provided sufficient competent evidential matter as to the existence of the receivables; if the auditor is not satisfied with the results of the confirmation procedures, he or she should perform other procedures such as the following:

   a. Review subsequent cash receipts and accompanying remittance advices.
   b. Review individual sales invoices and related shipping documents.

A confirmation worksheet is presented in "AU Illustrations."

NONRESPONSE TO CONFIRMATION REQUESTS

If a response to a confirmation request is not received within a reasonable period of time—two to three weeks—a second request should be sent. The auditor should note in the receivable confirmation worksheet the date the second request was mailed.

Telephone Call to Debtor

If the nonresponse pertains to an account with a significant balance, the auditor should consider making a telephone call to the customer. If the auditor confirms by telephone, he or she should do the following:

1. Obtain the name and title of the person providing the information.
2. Request that the information provided be confirmed in writing.

Other Auditing Procedures

If the nonresponse pertains to an account with a significant balance, the auditor should consider reviewing the customer file to determine the following:

1. Cash receipts subsequent to year-end
2. Items paid for subsequent to year-end; this is done by reviewing customer remittance advices

NONDELIVERY OF CONFIRMATION REQUEST

If a confirmation request is returned to the auditor because it was not delivered, the auditor should do the following:

1. Determine customer's new address and mail confirmation request.
2. If customer went out of business, ascertain that client has established appropriate allowance.

CONFIRMATION RESPONSES NOT EXPECTED

Sometimes the auditor does not expect a response to a confirmation request based on past experience with the entity or with customers similar to those of the entity.

When the auditor does not expect a response to a traditional confirmation request, he or she should do the following:

1. Request confirmation of specific items included in the account balance.
2. Review subsequent customer remittances. Where these amounts are significant, it is recommended that for a period of time subsequent to the balance sheet date, the auditor be present whenever the client receives mail. The auditor should open all mail from customers unable to confirm balances and compare remittance advices to ledger balances.
3. Undertake other procedures to validate the existence of the customer and sales to the customer. (For example, the customer could be looked up in a phone directory and called.)

When fraud risk factors are present and confirmation of receivables is not possible, the auditor should employ unusual procedures if necessary to validate the existence of the customer and the sales to that customer.

CONFIRMATION CHECKLIST

To make certain all procedures have been applied in the confirmation of receivables, the auditor should design a confirmation checklist. One is presented in "AU Illustrations."

AU ILLUSTRATIONS

This section contains illustrations of the following for accounts receivable:

1. Confirmation checklist
2. Positive confirmation with statement
3. Positive confirmation without statement
4. Negative confirmation
5. Subsequent payments confirmation
6. Confirmation of selected transactions
7. Description of confirmation worksheet

ILLUSTRATION 1. ACCOUNTS RECEIVABLE CONFIRMATION CHECKLIST

[*Client*]

[*Audit date*]

Instructions. This checklist is divided into two sections, as follows:

1. General information
2. Procedures

If a procedure listed is not applicable, insert "N/A" in the column "Performed by" and explain why in the "Explanation" column.

General Information

1. Date confirmation sent.

	Positive confirmation	*Negative confirmation*
First request		
Second request		N/A
Third request		N/A

2. For positive confirmation, list the following:

	Number of receivables	*Amount of receivables*
a. Accounts receivable		
b. Confirmations sent		
c. Percentage		
d. Responses		
e. Percentage of confirmations sent		
f. Percentage of total receivables		

3. For negative confirmation, list the following:

	Number of receivables	Amount of receivables
a. Accounts receivable		
b. Confirmations sent		
c. Percentage		
d. Responses		
e. Percentage of confirmations sent		
f. Percentage of total receivables		

Procedure	Performed by	Date	Explanation
1. Obtain from client aged schedule of accounts receivable.			
2. Determine that all accounts listed in the accounts receivable schedule are customer accounts.			
3. Check that total in accounts receivable is correct and compare total with balance for accounts receivable in general ledger.			
4. Compare all or a selected sample of account balances in the schedule with account balances in the accounts receivable subsidiary ledger.			
5. Select accounts for positive confirmations.			
6. Select accounts for negative confirmations.			

7. Prepare schedule of accounts to be confirmed, listing the following:
  a. Confirmation number
  b. Name of account
  c. Address of account
  d. Receivable balance
  e. Balance confirmed
  f. Difference
  g. Explanation of difference			

8. On a test basis, check account addresses to source independent of accounts receivable department, such as:
  a. Customer file
  b. Telephone book			

9. Mail confirmation requests in envelope with firm return address. Include the following:
  a. Customer statement
  b. Letter requesting confirmation
  c. Firm postage-paid envelope			

10. For confirmation responses, do the following:
  a. Enter balance confirmed.
  b. Require client to reconcile any differences.
  c. Review documentation for reconciling items.			

11. Send second requests.			
12. Send third requests.			

13. For nonresponses of significant balances, do the following:
  a. Review subsequent cash receipts.
  b. Review customer remittance advices.			

Procedure	Performed by	Date	Explanation
14. If customer indicates it cannot confirm balance owed, request confirmation of			
a. Specified invoices			
b. Specified cash receipts			
15. Nondelivery of request. Mail to new address.			
16. Facsimile response.			
a. Photocopy response.			
b. Verify source and contents of response by telephone call to sender.			
c. Request sender to mail original confirmation request.			

ILLUSTRATION 2. ACCOUNTS RECEIVABLE: POSITIVE CONFIRMATION WITH STATEMENT

[Control number]

[Client letterhead]

[Date]

[Name and address of customer]

Gentlemen:

    Our auditors, [name and address], are conducting an audit of our financial statements. Please examine the accompanying statement and either confirm its correctness or report any differences to our auditors.

    Your prompt attention to this request will be appreciated. An envelope is enclosed for your reply.

Very truly yours,

_____

[Client signature and title]

Confirmation

    The balance receivable from us of [amount] as of [date] is correct except as noted below:

_____

[Debtor name]

Date _____ By _____

NOTE: This confirmation also may be used as a second request by stamping or printing in a prominent location "SECOND REQUEST" and mailing with a copy of the statement.

ILLUSTRATION 3. ACCOUNTS RECEIVABLE: POSITIVE CONFIRMATION WITHOUT STATEMENT

[Client letterhead]

[Control number]

[Date]

[*Name and address of customer*]

Gentlemen:

Our auditors, [*name and address*], are conducting an audit of our financial statements. Please confirm to them our receivable from you of [*amount*] as of [*date*].

Your prompt attention to this request will be appreciated. An envelope is enclosed for your reply.

Very truly yours,

_____
[*Client signature and title*]

Confirmation

The balance receivable from us of [*amount*] as of [*date*] is correct except as noted below:

_____
[*Debtor name*]

Date _____   By _____

NOTE: This confirmation also may be used as a second request by stamping or printing in a prominent location "SECOND REQUEST."

ILLUSTRATION 4. ACCOUNTS RECEIVABLE: NEGATIVE CONFIRMATION WITH STATEMENT, GUMMED STICKER, OR RUBBER STAMP

Auditor's Confirmation Request

Please examine this statement. If it does not agree with your records, please report any exceptions directly to our auditors

[*Auditor's name*]
[*Auditor's address*]

who are conducting an audit of our financial statements. An envelope is enclosed for your reply.

NOTE: This format may be used as a gummed sticker attached to a statement or as a rubber stamp imprinted on a statement.

ILLUSTRATION 5. ACCOUNTS RECEIVABLE: SUBSEQUENT PAYMENTS CONFIRMATION

[Client letterhead]

[Control number]

[Date]

[*Name and address of customer*]

Gentlemen:

Our records indicate that between [*date*] and [*date*], you made payments to us of [*amount*].

In connection with an audit of our financial statements, please confirm the payments and their allocation listed below or report any differences to our auditors, [*name and address*].

Check or voucher				Applicable to invoices dated	
Date	Number	Amount	Deductions	Before	After

Your prompt attention to this request will be appreciated. An envelope is enclosed for your reply.

Very truly yours,

_____
[*Client signature and title*]

Confirmation

The payments and their allocation listed above agree with our records except as noted below:

_____
[*Debtor name*]

Date _____ By _____

ILLUSTRATION 6. ACCOUNTS RECEIVABLE: CONFIRMATION OF SELECTED TRANSACTIONS, OPEN INVOICE SYSTEM

[*Control number*]

[*Client letterhead*]

[*Date*]

[*Name and address of customer*]

Gentlemen:

We understand that you do not maintain an accounts payable ledger showing balances due each vendor. However, we would appreciate your assistance in providing limited confirmation of specific transactions to permit the completion of our annual audit.

Please confirm to our auditors, [*name and address*], that the invoices listed below were proper and were unpaid as of [*date*].

Invoice		Customer			
No.	Date	P.O. No.	Location	Amount	

Your prompt response will be appreciated. An envelope is enclosed for your reply.

Very truly yours,

_____
[*Client signature and title*]

Confirmation

The invoices listed above were properly charged to our account and were unpaid as of [*date*] except as noted below.

_____
[*Debtor name*]

Date _____ By _____

ILLUSTRATION 7. ACCOUNTS RECEIVABLE: DESCRIPTION OF CONFIRMATION WORKSHEET

Description. An accounts receivable confirmation worksheet ordinarily should include the following columns:

1. Customer name
2. Control number
3. Indication of second request
4. Balance per client
5. Amount confirmed
6. Differences
7. Explanation of differences:

    a. Receipts in transit

    (1) Date deposited
    (2) Amount

    b. Credits issued

    (1) Date
    (2) Amount

    c. Shipments in transit

    (1) Date shipped
    (2) Amount

    d. Other

AU 331 Inventories

AU-C 501 Audit Evidence—Specific Considerations for Selected Items

AU EFFECTIVE DATE AND APPLICABILITY

Original Pronouncements Statements on Auditing Statements (SASs) 1, 43, and 67.

Effective Date These statements are now effective.

Applicability Audits of financial statements in accordance with generally accepted auditing standards (GAAS) and special reports involving inventories.

AU-C EFFECTIVE DATE AND SUMMARY OF CHANGES

SAS No. 122, *Codification of Auditing Standards and Procedures,* is effective for audits of financial statements with periods ending on or after December 15, 2012.

AU-C Section 501 combines the requirements and guidance from extant AU Section 331, *Inventories;* 332, *Auditing Derivative Instruments, Hedging Activities and Investments in Securities*; and 337, *Inquiry of a Client's Lawyer concerning Litigation, Claims, and Assessments.*

AU-C Section 501 does not change the extant requirements of AU 331 in any significant manner.

AU DEFINITIONS OF TERMS

Observing inventories. Being present when the inventory is counted and, by observation, tests, and inquiries, becoming satisfied about the following:

1. The effectiveness of the methods of counting the inventory
2. The extent of reliance that may be placed on the client's representations about the quantities and physical condition of the inventories

AU-C DEFINITIONS OF TERMS

AU-C Section 501 does not include definitions.

OBJECTIVES OF AU SECTION 331

Observation of inventories has been a "generally accepted auditing procedure" (GAAP) since 1939. The first auditing statement, SAP 1, was issued as a result of a study of the McKesson & Robbins fraud. The statement dealt with the procedures of confirming receivables and observing inventories. It was revised or amended three times before this section was originally issued in 1970 as SAP 43. The significant changes made in SAP 43 follow:

1. No modification of the audit report is required if it is impractical or impossible to observe inventories. The auditor should satisfy himself or herself, however, by alternative procedures.
2. There are no alternative procedures for *ending* inventories. The auditor *always* should make or observe some physical counts.

OBJECTIVES OF AU-C SECTION 501

AU-C Section 501 states that:

. . . the objective of the auditor is to obtain sufficient appropriate audit evidence regarding the
   a. valuation of investments in securities and derivative instruments;
   b. existence and condition of inventory;
   c. completeness of litigation, claims, and assessments involving the entity; and
   d. presentation and disclosure of segment information, in accordance with the applicable financial reporting framework.

FUNDAMENTAL REQUIREMENTS: OBSERVATION

QUANTITIES DETERMINED SOLELY BY PHYSICAL COUNT

When quantities are determined solely by physical count and all counts are made as of the balance sheet date or within a reasonable time before or after the balance sheet date, the auditor should ordinarily be present when inventory is counted.

PERPETUAL INVENTORY RECORDS

If these records are well kept and checked by the client periodically by comparisons with physical counts, the auditor may observe inventory either during or after the end of the period under audit.

CLIENT USE OF STATISTICAL SAMPLING METHODS

When used in determining inventory quantities, an annual physical count of each item of inventory may not be necessary. In these circumstances the auditor should

1. Be satisfied that the sampling plan is statistically valid, that it has been properly applied, and that the results are reasonable.
2. Be present to observe some physical counts to satisfy himself or herself of the effectiveness of the counting procedures used.

NOTE: Sampling to determine financial statement amount generally must be more rigorous and precise than might be appropriate for audit sampling.

NECESSITY TO OBSERVE PHYSICAL COUNT

The auditor should make, or observe, some physical counts of the ending inventory. Tests of the accounting records alone are not sufficient for the auditor to become satisfied about inventory quantities at the balance sheet date.

BEGINNING INVENTORIES

Sometimes the auditor may not have observed the beginning inventory of a period he or she is being asked to report on. Ordinarily, this occurs in new engagements. *If the auditor is satisfied about the current year-end inventory,* he or she may be able to satisfy himself or herself of prior period inventories by the following procedures:

1. Tests of prior transactions
2. Reviews of records of prior counts
3. Tests of gross profit

INVENTORIES HELD IN PUBLIC WAREHOUSES

Ordinarily the auditor should obtain direct confirmation, in writing, from the custodian. If these inventories represent a significant proportion of current or total assets, however, the auditor should also apply one or more of the following procedures:

1. Review and test client's procedures for investigating the warehouseman and evaluating his or her performance.
2. Observe physical counts of goods, if practicable.
3. If warehouse receipts have been pledged as collateral, confirm details of pledged receipts with lenders.
4. Do one of the following:

   a. Obtain an independent auditor's report on the warehouseman's control procedures affecting the custody of goods and pledging of receipts.
   b. Perform alternative procedures at the warehouse to gain reasonable assurance that the warehouseman's information is reliable.

FUNDAMENTAL REQUIREMENTS: REPORTING

SCOPE LIMITATION IMPOSED BY CLIENT

Section 508, *Reports on Audited Financial Statements*, deals with scope limitations. Generally, if the client restricts the scope of the audit as to observation of inventories, the auditor should disclaim an opinion on the financial statements.

Scope Limitation Imposed by Circumstances

Circumstances may make it impracticable or impossible for the auditor to observe inventories. If the auditor is able to satisfy himself or herself of these assets by applying alternative procedures, there is no significant scope limitation. In these circumstances, the auditor's report should not refer to the omission of procedures or the use of alternative procedures.

NOTE: *There are no alternative procedures for inventory observation. The auditor should make or observe some inventory counts for ending inventory.*

INTERPRETATIONS

There are no interpretations for this section. (However, see Section 508 on a report of an outside inventory-taking firm as an alternative procedure and the discussion on the same topic in "Techniques for Application," "Outside Inventory-Taking Firm," in this section.)

PROFESSIONAL ISSUES TASK FORCE PRACTICE ALERT

Practice Alert 94-2 Consideration of Fraud in Audit Procedures Related to Inventory Observation

This practice alert, which focuses on the physical existence of inventories, discusses some ways in which inventory frauds have been perpetrated and presents information that might help prevent such frauds from going undetected. The main message of the alert is that the auditor should always maintain professional skepticism when performing the audit and not rely too much on the client's representations.

Other topics covered in this alert include:

- *Inventories held for or by others*. The auditor should make sure that consigned goods are properly identified and excluded from inventory. The auditor should also follow the guidance in *Fundamental Requirements* of this section.
- *Use of a specialist*. The auditor may need to use a specialist to determine quantities or value special-purpose inventory and would therefore follow the guidance in Section 336, *Using the Work of a Specialist*.
- *Postobservation matters*. The auditor should consider performing additional procedures focusing on inventory quantities.

TECHNIQUES FOR APPLICATION

Timing and Extent of Inventory Observation

The timing and extent of inventory observation are determined by the client's inventory system and the effectiveness of its inventory controls. If the client maintains perpetual inventory records and the inventory controls are effective, the auditor may limit the extent of his or her observation and may observe the physical count at various times during the year.

Periodic Inventory System

If the client has a periodic inventory system, a physical inventory should be taken at least once during the year. No matter how many times during the year the client takes a physical inventory, the auditor should observe the count that occurs at or near year-end.

For purposes of this section, it is assumed that the client has a periodic inventory system. However, the same procedures, with minor modifications, may be used when observing inventory accounted for under a perpetual system.

INVENTORY IN A PUBLIC WAREHOUSE

A client may have a significant amount of inventory in a public warehouse. Auditing procedures in these circumstances are described in "Fundamental Requirements."

INVENTORY HELD BY CUSTODIAN OTHER THAN A PUBLIC WAREHOUSE

Occasionally, the client's inventory is held by a consignee or a subcontractor.

Procedures

When the amount held by the custodian is significant, the auditor should observe the count of the inventory, if it is practicable. If observation is not practicable, the auditor should do the following:

1. Review all documents underlying the transaction.
2. Determine the reliability of the custodian by doing the following:
    a. Obtain credit report, if available.
    b. If custodian is a public company, obtain last annual and most recent quarterly reports.
    c. Make inquiries of client, bankers, and industry.
3. Confirm with custodian as to quantities of inventory held.

STEPS IN THE OBSERVATION OF INVENTORY

The two major steps in the observation of a physical inventory are as follows:

1. Planning the physical inventory
2. Taking the physical inventory

Planning the Physical Inventory

Planning the physical inventory is essential. The auditor should review or prepare the client instructions and should work closely with the client in the planning stage. The inventory should be taken at a time when operations are suspended or minimal.

The client has primary responsibility for planning and conducting the physical inventory. Because of the auditor's important role in the taking of the inventory, however, he or she should participate in the planning stage.

Before taking the inventory, the client should submit a plan containing the following:

1. Date and time inventory is to be taken
2. Locations of inventory
3. Method of counting and recording
4. Instructions to employees
5. Provisions for the following:

a. Receipts and shipments of inventory during the counts
b. Segregation of inventory not owned by client
c. Physical arrangement of inventory

Date and time of inventory. If the client has a periodic inventory system, the physical inventory should be taken at or near year-end. The inventory should be taken at a time when operations have ceased or are at a reduced level. Ideally, the physical inventory should be taken when the client is not operating, such as weekends or after hours.

Locations of inventory. The client's plan should indicate the location of all inventory. Inventory usually is located at the following:

1. Client's premises; client should indicate where on its premises inventory is located
2. Plants at locations other than the client's major premises
3. In transit
4. On consignment
5. In a public warehouse
6. At nonrelated factories for processing

The client's plan should indicate how inventory will be taken at the various locations.

Method of counting and recording. When a physical inventory is taken, it ordinarily requires two people; one to call the count and the other to record it, or one to count the inventory and the other to check the count. Ordinarily, it is recorded in duplicate on one of the following:

1. Prenumbered inventory sheets
2. Prenumbered inventory tags

When the count is completed, the auditor keeps one copy of the sheets or tags.

Instructions to employees. Before the client counts the inventory, the auditor should review the instructions to the employees. Instructions should include the following:

1. Method of counting and recording:

   a. Will one person count and record and then have another check?
   b. Will one person call the count to a second person, who will record it?

2. Method of arranging inventory before physical count:

   a. Will inventory be segregated by style number, serial number, or in some other way?
   b. Will inventory be moved to a specific area?

3. Method of description (how inventory will be described when recorded):

   a. Style number
   b. Serial number
   c. Part number
   d. Other

4. Method of controlling inventory tags or inventory sheets:

   a. Who will have custody?
   b. How will they be distributed to employees taking the physical inventory?

5. How and when inventory tags or sheets should be gathered
6. Custody of inventory tags or sheets when the count is completed

If the client is a manufacturer, the instructions to the employees also should indicate how the stage of completion is determined for work in process.

Other considerations. The plan for the physical inventory also should provide for the following:

1. Receipts and shipments of inventory during the count:

    a. Whenever possible, no merchandise should be shipped until after the physical count. If this is not feasible, merchandise that will be shipped should be segregated.
    b. A designated area on the client's premises should be used for merchandise received during the count.

2. Segregation of inventory not owned by the client, such as the following:

    a. Inventory on consignment
    b. Bill-and-hold merchandise (merchandise invoiced to a customer but not yet shipped)
    c. Customer merchandise being repaired by the client

3. The physical arrangement of the inventory

Preplanning for Inventory Observation

Before the client counts the inventory, the auditor should prepare his or her program for the observation. Before preparing this program, the auditor should do the following:

1. Review last year's inventory observation audit documentation to ascertain the following:

    a. Nature of inventory
    b. Materiality of specific items
    c. Components of inventory
    d. Nature of any problems

2. Review and discuss with client its physical inventory plan.
3. Visit all locations where significant amounts of inventory are held. Determine if the location is conducive to the physical count.
4. Consider the need for using the services of an outside specialist to assist in identification and valuation problems of certain inventory items.
5. Prepare personnel assignments for inventory observation.

TAKING THE PHYSICAL INVENTORY

Audit Program for Inventory Observation

After preliminary reviews, the auditor should prepare his or her observation program (see the "AU Illustrations" section). The program should include the following:

1. Obtain cutoff numbers (i.e., last receiving number and last shipping number prior to physical count).
2. Inform staff of client inventory procedures.
3. Assign sufficient staff to observe that client procedures are properly executed.
4. Determine the extent to which client counts will be test counted.
5. Randomly select cartons of inventory and have them opened to ascertain that inventory does, in fact, exist.

6. Randomly select inventory items and, as appropriate, do the following:

   a. Have client measure them.
   b. Have client weigh them.

7. When client counts are test counted, compare count with what appears on inventory tag, sheet, or card. Also, compare inventory serial number, style number, and description with what appears on the inventory tag, sheet, or card. List numbers where these procedures were applied.
8. Obtain the range of numbers for the inventory tags, sheets, or cards used to record the inventory:

   a. At conclusion of count, ascertain that all numbers distributed for the count are accounted for.
   b. Be sure to specifically identify for later reference the numbers of all unused inventory tags, sheets, or cards.

9. Make a note of all tags, sheets, or cards that represent obsolete, defective, excess, or slow-moving inventory.
10. For work in process, review with knowledgeable employees the following:

    a. Estimated cost to complete per production records.
    b. Estimated costs to date. Review, on a test basis, documentation such as:

    (1) Material invoices
    (2) Labor costs

11. After the inventory has been completed, tour area with supervisor and ascertain that all items have been tagged.
12. Account for all numbers distributed.
13. Supervise the collection of all tags, sheets, or cards, being careful to note that none of the inventory is moved.
14. Make certain that inventory not owned by the client is not included in the count.
15. If specialists are used, observe their procedures.
16. For finished goods inventory, do, on a test basis, the following:

    a. Inspect them to ascertain that they are complete.
    b. If feasible, have some units disassembled to ascertain that all components have been included.

17. After all tags, sheets, or cards have been collected, review numbers to ascertain that all numbers are accounted for (see 8a and b).
18. Separate the original and the copy of the tags, sheets, or cards, leaving the original with the client and taking the copy for audit files.

At completion of the physical inventory, the auditor should prepare an inventory observation memorandum that includes the following:

1. Receiving and shipping cutoff numbers
2. Entity personnel who supervised the count
3. Number range for inventory tags, sheets, or cards

OUTSIDE INVENTORY-TAKING FIRM

Clients may retain outside firms of nonaccountants to take their physical inventories. This does not relieve the auditor, however, of the responsibility to observe physical inventories.

Auditor's Procedures

If a client retains an outside inventory firm to count its inventories, the auditor's primary concern is the effectiveness of the outside firm's procedures. To evaluate the procedures of the outside firm, the auditor should do the following:

1. Examine the firm's inventory observation program
2. Observe the firm's procedures and controls
3. Observe some physical counts of inventory
4. Recompute calculations of the submitted inventory on a test basis

If the auditor is satisfied with the procedures of the outside firm, he or she may reduce, *not eliminate*, his or her work on the physical count of the inventory.

Restrictions on Auditor

Any restrictions on the auditor's judgment concerning the extent of his or her contact with the inventory counted by an outside firm is a scope limitation.

INVENTORY OBSERVATION CHECKLIST

To make certain all procedures have been applied in the observation of inventories, the auditor should design an inventory observation checklist. One is presented in "AU Illustrations."

AU ILLUSTRATIONS

This section contains illustrations of the following:

1. Inventory observation checklist
2. Confirmation of inventories on consignment
3. Confirmation of inventories in public warehouses

ILLUSTRATION 1. INVENTORY OBSERVATION CHECKLIST

[*Client*]

[*Audit Date*]

[*Date of Physical Inventory*]

Instructions

This checklist is divided into four sections.

1. General information
2. Procedures performed prior to date of physical inventory
3. Procedures performed at date of physical inventory
4. Procedures performed after date of physical inventory

If a procedure is not applicable, insert N/A in the column "Performed by" and explain why in the "Explanation" column.

GENERAL

1. List inventory locations.

    a. _____
    b. _____
    c. _____
    d. _____

2. List staff members assigned to observe the inventory count.

    a. _____
    b. _____
    c. _____
    d. _____
    e. _____
    f. _____

3. List client personnel supervising the inventory count.

    a. _____
    b. _____
    c. _____
    d. _____

4. If inventory was ticketed—inventory tags, etc.—indicate range of ticket numbers.

    a. From _____
    b. To _____

5. If inventory was not ticketed, explain briefly how inventory was counted.
6. Nature of inventory.

    a. Finished goods _____
    b. Work in process _____
    c. Raw materials _____

7. Describe client's physical inventory procedures. Instead of this description, attach copy of client's instructions.
8. Indicate the following:

    a. Last receiving number prior to physical count _____
    b. Last sales number prior to physical count.

        (1) Bill of lading number _____
        (2) Sales invoice number _____

9. Indicate the following:

    a. Inventory tickets.

        (1) Number used _____
        (2) Number checked _____

    b. Inventory value.

        (1) Total $_____
        (2) Amount checked $_____

Procedure	Performed by	Date	Explanation

Prior to Date of Physical Inventory

1. Visit inventory locations. Note critical areas.

    a. Receiving
    b. Shipping
    c. Production
    d. Stock
    e. _____

2. Review inventory instructions.

    a. Date and time
    b. Locations
    c. Method of counting and recording
    d. Segregation of inventory

      (1) By style number
      (2) By serial number
      (3) By part number
      (4) _____

3. Discuss with client the following:

    a. Physical arrangement of inventory
    b. Segregation of inventory not owned
    c. Receipts and shipments of inventory during count
    d. Production during count

4. Ascertain other locations of inventory.

    a. In transit
    b. On consignment
    c. In public warehouse
    d. At contractor
    e. Bill and hold
    f. Merchandise for repair

5. Review prior year's observation audit documentation for

    a. Nature of inventory
    b. Materiality of specific items
    c. Components of inventory
    d. Nature of any problems

6. Consider need for using the services of outside specialist.
7. Discuss inventory observation with staff.

At Date of Physical Inventory

1. Obtain cutoff numbers for shipments and receipts.
2. Obtain first and last inventory ticket numbers.
3. Ascertain that inventory was arranged and segregated as required by inventory instructions.

Procedure	Performed by	Date	Explanation

4. Ascertain that operations were halted during the count.

   a. Receiving
   b. Shipping
   c. Production

5. If operations were not halted during the counts, prepare memo indicating how control was maintained.

6. Ascertain when counting and tagging was completed.

   a. Before your arrival
   b. After your arrival

7. If inventory is counted and tagged after your arrival, observe if method of counting and tagging conforms with instructions.
8. Determine that all inventory was tagged.
9. Count the inventory on a test basis and compare with quantity entered on inventory tag.
10. Prepare schedule indicating your count and client's count for tags checked.
11. If test count indicates significant difference, increase number of tags tested.
12. Have client correct tags with errors.
13. Where inventory is in sealed containers:

    a. Have client open them on a test basis and count inventory.
    b. Compare count with that indicated on tag.

14. For finished goods, ascertain on a test basis that they are in fact completed.

    a. Lift some of them.
    b. Have some of them disassembled, if feasible.

15. For work in process, note on a test basis, the following:

    a. Amount of material
    b. Amount of labor

16. Review inventory for old and obsolete items.

    a. Discussion with client
    b. Amount of labor

17. Tour inventory area and ascertain that all inventory has been tagged or otherwise counted.
18. Observe the pulling of the inventory tickets and obtain your copies immediately. Make certain that none of the tickets are altered.
19. Account for all inventory ticket numbers.

Procedure	Performed by	Date	Explanation
After Date of Physical Inventory			

1. Compare client's inventory sheets with your copies of inventory tickets for the following:
   a. All ticket numbers have been accounted for
   b. Description and quantity on tickets agrees with inventory sheets			

2. If client maintains perpetual inventory records, test check inventory tickets against those records.			

ILLUSTRATION 2. INVENTORIES: CONFIRMATION OF INVENTORIES ON CONSIGNMENT

[*Client letterhead*]

[*Control number*]

[*Date*]

[*Name and address of consignee*]

Gentlemen:

    Our auditors, [*name and address*], are conducting an audit of our financial statements. Please confirm to them our merchandise consigned to you as of [*date*], as described below:

                        Description   Quantity

    Your prompt attention to this request will be appreciated. An envelope is enclosed for your reply.

                                                                  Very truly yours,

                                                                 [*Client signature and title*]

Confirmation:

    The consigned merchandise listed above is all that is held by us as of [*date*] except as noted below:

                                                                  [*Consignee name*]

Date _____   By_____

> **ILLUSTRATION 3. INVENTORIES: CONFIRMATION OF INVENTORIES IN PUBLIC WAREHOUSES**

[Client letterhead]

[Control number]

[Date]

[Name and address of warehouse]

Gentlemen:

Our auditors, [name and address], are conducting an audit of our financial statements. Please furnish them with a list of our inventory at your warehouse as of [date] and a statement that this merchandise was stored on your premises for our account at that date.

Your prompt attention to this request will be appreciated. An envelope is enclosed for your reply.

Very truly yours,

_____
[Client signature and title]

Confirmation:

The attached list, prepared by us, represents all merchandise stored on our premises as of [date] for the account of [Client name].

_____
[Warehouse name]

Date _____ By _____

AU 332 Auditing Derivative Instruments, Hedging Activities, and Investments in Securities[1]

AU-C 501 Audit Evidence—Specific Considerations for Selected Items

AU EFFECTIVE DATE AND APPLICABILITY

Original Pronouncement	Statement on Auditing Standards (SAS) 92.
Effective Date	This statement is now effective.
Applicability	Derivative instruments, including certain derivative instruments embedded in contracts; debt and equity securities; and hedging activities in which the entity designates a derivative or a nonderivative financial instrument as a hedge for which generally accepted accounting principles (GAAP) permit hedge accounting.

AU-C EFFECTIVE DATE

SAS No. 122, *Codification of Auditing Standards and Procedures,* is effective for audits of financial statements with periods ending on or after December 15, 2012.

AU-C 501 supersedes AU Section 332. AU-C 501 combines the requirements and guidance from extant AU Section 331, *Inventories*; 332, *Auditing Derivative Instruments, Hedging Activities and Investments in Securities*; and 337, *Inquiry of a Client's Lawyer Concerning Litigation, Claims, and Assessments.*

The ASB found that many of the requirements of AU Section 332 are essentially the same as Section 540, *Auditing Accounting Estimates, Including Fair Value Accounting Estimates, and Related Disclosures* The ASB decided that the application of those requirements in the other clarified standards to the subject matter addressed by AU Section 332 is most

---

[1] This section is affected by the Public Company Accounting Oversight Board's (PCAOB's) Standard, Conforming Amendments to PCAOB Interim Standards Resulting from the Adoption of PCAOB Auditing Standard No. 5, An Audit of Internal Control Over Financial Reporting That Is Integrated with an Audit of Financial Statements.

appropriately addressed as interpretative guidance in the AICPA Audit Guide *Auditing Derivative Instruments, Hedging Activities, and Investments in Securities*. Consideration of these requirements and related application guidance will be a specific focus in the audit guide.

AU-C Section 501 excludes requirements and guidance addressing auditing investments accounted for using the equity method because the auditing of equity investees is addressed more broadly by AU-C Section 600, *Special Considerations—Audits of Group Financial Statements (Including the Work of Component Auditors)*.

AU-C 501.4–10, and the related application material address those requirements (primarily auditing the valuation assertion) that have been retained from AU Section 332.

AU DEFINITIONS OF TERMS

DERIVATIVE INSTRUMENTS AND HEDGING ACTIVITIES

This section uses the definitions of derivatives and hedging activities in Financial Accounting Standards Board (FASB) Accounting Standards Codification (ASC) 815, *Accounting for Derivative Instruments and Hedging Activities*, as amended under the codification, this is ASC 815. Hereinafter, we will refer to it as FASB ASC 815. FASB ASC 815 addresses the accounting for derivatives that are either freestanding or embedded in contracts or agreements. For purposes of applying the guidance in this SAS, a derivative is a financial instrument or other contract with all three of the characteristics listed in FASB ASC 815; that is:

1. It has
   a. One or more underlyings (a specified interest rate, security price, commodity price, foreign exchange rate, or other variable) and
   b. One or more notional amounts or payment provisions or both.

   Those terms determine the amount of the settlement or settlements, and, in some cases, whether settlement is required.
2. It requires no initial net investment or an initial net investment that is smaller than would be required for other types of contracts that would be expected to have a similar response to changes in market factors.
3. Its terms require or permit net settlement, it can readily be settled net by a means outside the contract, or it provides for delivery of an asset that puts the recipient in a position not substantially different from net settlement.

An entity may enter into a derivative for investment purposes or to designate it as a hedge of exposure to changes in fair value (referred to as a fair value hedge), exposure to variability in cash flows (referred to as a cash flow hedge), or foreign currency exposure. The guidance in this section applies to hedging activities in which the entity designates a derivative or a nonderivative financial instrument as a hedge of exposure for which FASB ASC 815 permits hedge accounting.

AU-C 501 DEFINITIONS OF TERMS

AU-C 501 contains no definitions.

OBJECTIVES OF AU SECTION 332

As the accounting standards for investing and related activities have become more complex and detailed, the related auditing guidance has followed suit. Section 332 applies to investments in all securities as well as to derivative instruments and hedging activities.

There are two types of securities—debt securities and equity securities. This section uses the definitions of debt security and equity security that are in the FASB Master Glossary.

Section 332 contains the basic notion that an investee's unaudited financial statements generally do not provide sufficient evidential matter. However, it adds a cautionary note that even audited financial statements might not be sufficient because of factors such as significant differences in fiscal year-ends or accounting principles between the investor and investee or changes in ownership or conditions.

Section 332 includes substantial guidance on the effect on audit approach and procedures of complexities and risks related to derivatives, involvement of service organizations, and accounting requirements applicable to hedging activities.

The AICPA issued an Audit Guide entitled *Auditing Derivative Instruments, Hedging Activities, and Investments in Securities* (Guide). The guide contains many illustrative examples of both the accounting for and auditing of the most common types of derivatives, particularly those that are prevalent at small business entities. The Committee of Sponsoring Organizations of the Treadway Commission (COSO) issued *Internal Control Issues in Derivatives Usage: An Information Tool for Considering the COSO "Internal Control—Integrated Framework" in Derivatives Applications* in 1996. Although the COSO document precedes FASB ASC 815, its guidance may be useful to entities in developing controls over derivatives transactions and to auditors in assessing control risk for assertions about those transactions.

The Auditing Standards Board issued Statement of Position (SOP) 01-3, *Performing Agreed-Upon Procedures Engagements That Address Internal Control over Derivative Transactions as Required by the New York State Insurance Law,* which provides guidance to practitioners on performing an agreed-upon procedures engagement that enables insurance companies to meet the requirements of the New York Derivative Law (the Law) that amends Article 14 of the New York Insurance Law. The Law requires insurers who enter into derivative transactions to file with the State of New York Insurance Department (Department) a statement describing an independent CPA's assessment of the insurance company's internal control over derivative transactions. This assessment is considered part of the evaluation of internal control prescribed by Section 307(b) of the New York State Insurance Law. An assessment is required regardless of whether the derivative transactions are material to the insurer's financial statements.

The Independence Standards Board[2] issued Interpretation 99-1 on assisting clients in implementing FASB ASC 815. It includes guidance on the effect of assistance on accounting application of FASB ASC 815 and derivative valuation consulting on the auditor's independence.

OBJECTIVES OF AU-C SECTION 501

The objective of the auditor is to obtain sufficient appropriate audit evidence regarding the:

---

[2] The ISB was dissolved on July 31, 2001.

1. Valuation of investments in securities and derivative instruments;
2. Existence and condition of inventory;
3. Completeness of litigation, claims, and assessments involving the entity; and
4. Presentation and disclosure of segment information, in accordance with the applicable financial reporting framework.

FUNDAMENTAL REQUIREMENTS

REQUIRED RISK ASSESSMENT IN PLANNING

The auditor should consider the inherent risk and control risk for assertions about derivatives and securities when designing audit procedures.

CONTROL RISK ASSESSMENT

The auditor should assess control risk for the related assertions after obtaining an understanding of internal control over derivatives and securities transactions.

For assertions for which the auditor plans to assess control risk below the maximum, the auditor should:

- Identify specific controls relevant to the assertions that are likely to prevent or detect material misstatements that have been placed in operation by either the entity or a service organization.
- Gather evidential matter about whether controls are operating effectively.

NOTE: Gathering evidential matter about the operating effectiveness of controls is often referred to simply as testing controls.

Confirmations of balances or transactions from a service organization do not provide evidence about its controls.

NOTE: "Internal Controls Issues in Derivatives Usage," published by COSO, is a helpful tool for understanding and evaluating controls related to derivatives.

DESIGNING AUDITING PROCEDURES

In designing auditing procedures for assertions about derivatives and securities, the auditor should consider the following about the entity:

- Its size
- Its organizational structure
- The nature of the entity's operations
- The types, frequency, and complexity of its derivatives and securities transactions
- Its controls over those transactions

IMPORTANCE OF IDENTIFYING AND TESTING CONTROLS

In some circumstances, the auditor will need to identify controls placed in operation by the entity or service organization and gather evidence about the operating effectiveness of the controls to reduce audit risk to an acceptable level.

For example, the auditor likely would be unable to reduce audit risk to an acceptable level without identifying and testing controls for assertions about the occurrence of earnings if the entity has a large number of derivatives or securities transactions. Relevant controls include those over the authorization, recording, custody, and segregation of duties.

DESIGNING SUBSTANTIVE PROCEDURES BASED ON RISK ASSESSMENT

When determining the nature, timing, and extent of substantive procedures to be performed to detect material misstatements of the financial statement assertions, the auditor should use the assessed levels of inherent risk and control risk for assertions about derivatives and securities.

The auditor should consider whether the results of other audit procedures conflict with management's assertions about derivatives and securities, and, if so, consider the impact on the sufficiency of evidential matter.

COMPLETENESS ASSERTION FOR DERIVATIVES

In designing tests of the completeness assertion for derivatives, the auditor should not focus exclusively on evidence relating to cash receipts and disbursements. Derivatives may involve only a commitment to perform under a contract and not an initial exchange of tangible considerations.

The auditor should consider the following procedures:

1. Make inquiries, including inquiries about operating activities that might present risks hedged by derivatives.
2. Inspect agreements.
3. Read minutes of meetings of the board of directors or the finance, investment, or other committees.
4. Read any other relevant information.

TESTS OF VALUATION ASSERTIONS

The auditor should design tests of valuation assertions according to the valuation method used for measurement or disclosure in accordance with GAAP.

GAAP may:

1. Require that a derivative or security be valued based on cost, the investee's financial results, or fair value
2. Require disclosures about the value of a derivative or security and specify that impairment losses should be recognized in earnings prior to realization
3. Vary depending on the type of security, the nature of the transaction, management's objectives related to the security, and the type of entity

VALUATION BASED ON COST

If GAAP requires that the derivative or security be valued based on cost, the auditor should evaluate management's conclusion about recognizing an impairment loss for an other-than-temporary decline in a security's fair value below its cost.

VALUATION BASED ON AN INVESTEE'S FINANCIAL RESULTS

If GAAP required that the derivative or security be valued based on the investee's financial results, the auditor should obtain sufficient evidence to support those financial results, including but not limited to the equity method of accounting (see APB Opinion 18). The investor's auditor should:

- Read financial statements and the audited report of the investee, if available. Audited financial statements of the investee and an audit report satisfactory for the investor auditor's purpose may constitute sufficient evidential matter.
- Ask that the investor arrange with the investee to have another auditor apply appropriate auditing procedures if the investee's financial statements are not audited or the investee's audit report is not satisfactory.
- Obtain sufficient evidence to support the carrying amount of the security if this amount reflects factors not recognized in the investee's financial statements or if the asset's fair values are materially different from the carrying amounts.
- Add an explanatory paragraph to the auditor's report because of the change in reporting period if a change in time lag occurs that materially affects the investor's financial statements.

NOTE: *A time lag in reporting between the date of the financial statements of the investor and the investee should be consistent from period to period. The effect may be material when, for example, the time lag is not consistent with the prior period in comparative statements or if a significant transaction occurred during the time lag. In this case, the auditor should determine if management has properly considered the lack of comparability.*

- Evaluate management's conclusion about recognizing an impairment loss for an other-than-temporary decline in a security's fair value below its cost.
- Obtain evidence about (1) whether unrealized profits and losses on transactions between the entity and the investee are properly eliminated when the equity method of accounting is used to account for an investment under GAAP and (2) the disclosures of material related-party transactions are adequate.
- Read the investee's interim financial statements and make inquiries of the investor to identify subsequent events (those occurring after the date of the investee's financial statements but before the date of the investor auditor's report) that are material to the investor's financial statements. Subsequent events discussed in Section 560, "Subsequent Events," should be disclosed in the notes to the investor's financial statements and labeled "unaudited."

NOTE: *The events or transactions discussed in Section 560,* Subsequent Events, *should be recognized when recording the investor's share of the investee's results of operations.*

VALUATION BASED ON FAIR VALUE

If GAAP requires that the derivative or security be valued based on fair value, the auditor should obtain evidence supporting management's assertions about the fair value of derivatives and securities measured or disclosed at fair value. The auditor should:

- Determine whether GAAP specifies the method to be used for calculating the fair value of the derivatives and securities, and evaluate whether the fair value calculations are consistent with that valuation method.
- Consider the guidance in Section 342, *Auditing Accounting Estimates,* if appropriate, and the guidance in Section 312, *Audit Risk and Materiality in Conducting an Audit,* guidance on considering a difference between an estimated amount best supported by the audit evidence and the estimated amount in the financial statements.

SOURCES OF FAIR VALUE INFORMATION

If derivatives or securities are listed on national exchanges or over-the-counter markets, quoted market prices are available in financial publications, the exchange, the National Association of Securities Dealers Automated Quotations Systems (NASDAQ), pricing services, and other sources.

Quoted market prices for certain other derivatives and securities can be obtained from broker-dealers who are market makers or through the National Quotation Bureau. However, special knowledge may be necessary for understanding the way in which the quote was developed. For example, National Quotation Bureau quotes may not be based on recent trades and may only indicate interest and not an actual price for the underlying derivative or security.

If quoted market prices for derivatives or securities are not available, broker-dealers or other third-party sources can often develop fair value estimates using internally or externally developed valuation models. The auditor should understand the method used in developing the estimate. The auditor may also decide to obtain estimates from more than one pricing source. This may be appropriate if either:

- There is a relationship between the pricing source and the entity that might impair objectivity, such as an affiliate or a counterparty involved in selling or structuring the product.
- The valuation is based on highly subjective or particularly sensitive assumptions.

NOTE: When fair value estimates are obtained from broker-dealers and other third-party sources, the auditor should consider whether guidance in Section 336, Using the Work of a Specialist, *applies. The guidance in Section 350,* Audit Sampling, *may be applicable if the third-party source derives the fair value of the derivative or security by using modeling or similar techniques. If the entity uses a pricing service to obtain prices of securities and derivatives, the guidance in Section 324,* Service Organizations, *may be appropriate.*

FAIR VALUE DETERMINED USING A MODEL

The entity may use a valuation model, such as the present value of expected future cash flows, option-pricing models, matrix pricing, option-adjusted spread models, and fundamental analysis, to value a derivative or security.

NOTE: Section 332 notes that when the entity uses a valuation model, the auditor should not assume the role of an appraiser and is not expected to substitute his or her judgment for that of management. When GAAP requires that quoted market prices be used to determine fair value, a valuation model should not *be used.*

The auditor should perform procedures such as the following to obtain evidence about management's assertions about fair value as determined by the model:

- Assess whether the model is reasonable and appropriate. (For example, estimates of future cash flows should be based on reasonable and supportable assumptions.) Since evaluating appropriateness may require knowledge of valuation techniques and other factors, the auditor may need to involve a specialist to assess the model.
- Calculate the value using the auditor's model or a model developed by the auditor's specialist to corroborate the reasonableness of the entity's value.
- Compare the fair value with subsequent or recent transactions.

USE OF COLLATERAL IN EVALUATING FAIR VALUE

If collateral is important in evaluating the security, the auditor should obtain evidence regarding the:

- Existence
- Fair value
- Transferability
- Investor's rights to the collateral

NOTE: Negotiable securities, real estate, chattels, or other property is often assigned as collateral for debt securities.

IMPAIRMENT LOSSES

The auditor should evaluate management's conclusion about whether it is necessary to recognize in earnings an impairment loss for a decline in fair value that is other than temporary. In doing so, the auditor should evaluate (1) whether management has considered relevant information about whether a decline is other than temporary and (2) management's conclusions about recognizing an impairment loss. The auditor is required to obtain evidence about such factors that tend to corroborate or conflict with management's conclusions. When an impairment loss is recognized, the auditor should obtain evidence supporting the recorded amount of the impairment adjustment and determine whether the entity has appropriately followed GAAP.

UNREALIZED APPRECIATION OR DEPRECIATION IN FAIR VALUE OF A DERIVATIVE

The auditor should obtain evidence to support the amount of unrealized appreciation or depreciation in the fair value of a derivative that is recognized in earnings or other comprehensive income or that is disclosed because of the ineffectiveness of a hedge.

NOTE: GAAP may specify how to account for unrealized appreciation and depreciation of the fair value of the entity's derivatives and securities. GAAP requires the entity to report a change in the unrealized appreciation or depreciation in the fair value of a derivative designated as:

- *A fair value hedge in earnings, with the ineffective portion of the hedge disclosed*
- *A cash flow hedge in two components, with the ineffective portion reported in earnings and the effective portion reported in other comprehensive income*

GAAP also requires reporting of a change in the unrealized appreciation or depreciation in fair value of:

- *A derivative that was previously designated as a hedge but is no longer highly effective, or a derivative that is not designated as hedge, in earnings*
- *An available-for-sale security in other comprehensive income*

GAAP may also require reclassification of amounts from accumulated other comprehensive income to earnings. For example, such reclassifications may be required because a hedged transaction is determined to no longer be probable of occurring.

ASSERTIONS ABOUT PRESENTATION AND DISCLOSURE

The auditor should evaluate whether the derivatives and securities are presented and disclosed in conformity with GAAP.

ADDITIONAL CONSIDERATIONS RELATED TO GATHERING EVIDENTIAL MATTER ABOUT HEDGING ACTIVITIES

The auditor should gather evidential matter to:

- Determine whether management complied with hedge accounting requirements, including designation and documentation requirements
- Support management's expectation at the inception of the hedge that the relationship will be highly effective and periodically assess ongoing effectiveness
- Support the recorded change in the hedged item's fair value attributable to the hedged risk
- Determine whether management has properly applied GAAP to the hedged item
- Evaluate whether a forecasted transaction that is hedged is probable of occurring

NOTE: *The likelihood that a forecasted transaction will take place cannot be based solely on management intent.*

ASSERTIONS RELATED TO MANAGEMENT'S ABILITY AND INTENT

If GAAP requires that management's intent and ability be considered in valuing securities, in evaluating management's intent and ability the auditor should:

- Understand management's process for classifying securities as trading, available-for-sale, or held-to-maturity
- For equity method investments, ask management if the entity has the ability to exercise significant influence over the operating and financial policies of the investee and evaluate the attendant circumstances that serve as a basis for management's conclusions
- If the investment is accounted for contrary to the presumption established by GAAP for use of the equity method, obtain sufficient competent evidential matter about whether that presumption has been overcome and whether the reasons for not accounting for the investment in keeping with that presumption are appropriately disclosed.
- Consider whether management's activities support or conflict with its stated intent. For example, the auditor should evaluate management's assertion that it intends to hold debt securities to their maturity by examining evidence such as documentation of management's strategies and sales and other historical activities with respect to those securities and similar securities.
- Determine whether management is required by GAAP to document its intentions and specify the content and timeliness of that documentation. The auditor should inspect the documentation and obtain evidence about its timeliness. Evidential matter supporting the classification of debt and equity securities may be more informal than the documentation required for hedging activities.
- Determine whether management's activities, contractual agreements, or the entity's financial condition support its ability. For example:
  - Evidence about an entity's ability to hold debt securities to their maturity may be provided by the entity's financial position, working capital needs, operating results, debt agreements, guarantees, alternate sources of liquidity, and other relevant contractual obligations, as well as laws and regulations

- Management's cash flow projections may not support the entity's ability to hold debt securities to their maturity
- If management cannot obtain information from an investee, it may suggest that it does not have the ability to significantly influence the investee
- If the entity asserts that it maintains effective control over securities transferred under a repurchase agreement, the contractual agreement may indicate that the entity actually surrendered control over the securities and therefore should appropriately account for the transfer as a sale instead of a secured borrowing.

MANAGEMENT REPRESENTATIONS

The auditor ordinarily should obtain written management representations confirming management's intent and ability concerning assertions about derivatives and securities, and consider obtaining representations about other aspects of derivatives and securities transactions that affect assertions about them.

NOTE: Examples of such representations might include management's intent and ability to hold a debt security to maturity or to enter into a forecasted transaction to which hedge accounting is applied.

INTERPRETATIONS

AUDITING DERIVATIVE INSTRUMENTS, HEDGING ACTIVITIES, AND INVESTMENTS IN SECURITIES (JULY 2005; REVISED APRIL 2007)

When testing the existence and measurement of an investment in securities, it is not sufficient to receive a confirmation with respect to the valuation assertion. However, a confirmation on an investment-by-investment basis does constitute adequate audit evidence with respect to the existence assertion. If the auditor cannot audit the existence or measurement of interests in investments in securities, this may be a scope limitation.

TECHNIQUES FOR APPLICATION

SPECIAL SKILL OR KNOWLEDGE MIGHT BE NEEDED TO PLAN OR PERFORM AUDITING PROCEDURES RELATED TO DERIVATIVES OR SECURITIES

Examples of situations that might require special skill or knowledge to plan or perform auditing procedures related to derivatives or securities are when the auditor:

- Obtains an understanding of an entity's information system for derivatives and securities, including services provided by a service organization. The auditor may need to have special skills or knowledge about computer applications when significant information about derivatives and securities is transmitted, processed, maintained, or accessed electronically.
- Identifies controls placed in operation by a service organization that provides services to an entity that are part of the entity's information system for derivatives and securities. The auditor may need to have an understanding of the operating characteristics of entities in a certain industry.

- Gains an understanding of GAAP for assertions about derivatives. The auditor may need special knowledge because of the complexity of those principles. In addition, a complex derivative may require the auditor to have special knowledge to evaluate the measurement and disclosure of the derivative in conformity with GAAP.
- Gains an understanding of how fair values of derivatives and securities are determined, including the appropriateness of various types of valuation models and the reasonableness of key factors and assumptions. The auditor may need to know about valuation concepts.
- Assesses inherent risk and control risk for assertions about derivatives used in hedging activities. The auditor may need an understanding of general risk management concepts and typical asset/liability management strategies.

If the auditor seeks assistance from employees of the auditor's firm, or others outside the firm, with the necessary skill or knowledge, the auditor should consider the guidance in Section 311, *Planning and Supervision*. If the auditor plans to use the work of a specialist, the auditor should consider the guidance in Section 336, *Using the Work of a Specialist*.

ASSESSING INHERENT RISK FOR AN ASSERTION ABOUT A DERIVATIVE OR SECURITY

The primary inherent risk is the susceptibility of an assertion about a derivative or security to a material misstatement, assuming there are no related controls. According to AU 332.08, examples of considerations that might affect the auditor's assessment of inherent risk are as follows:

- *Management's objectives*. The complexity of accounting requirements based on management's objectives may increase the inherent risk for certain assertions.
- *The complexity of the features of the derivative or security*. The complexity of the features of the derivative or security may increase the complexity of measurement and disclosure considerations required by GAAP.
- *Whether the transaction that gave rise to the derivative or security involved the exchange of cash*. Derivatives that do not involve an initial exchange of cash are subject to an increased risk that they will not be identified for valuation and disclosure considerations.
- *The entity's experience with the derivative or security*. An entity's inexperience with a derivative or security increases the inherent risk for assertions about it.
- *Whether a derivative is freestanding or an embedded feature of an agreement*. Embedded derivatives are less likely to be identified by management, which increases the inherent risk for certain assertions.
- *Whether external factors affect the assertion*. Assertions about derivatives and securities may be affected by a variety of risks related to external factors, such as

  - *Credit risk*, which exposes the entity to the risk of loss as a result of the issuer of a debt security or the counterparty to a derivative failing to meet its obligation.
  - *Market risk*, which exposes the entity to the risk of loss from adverse changes in market factors that affect the fair value of a derivative or security, such as interest rates, foreign exchange rates, and market indexes for equity securities.
  - *Basis risk*, which exposes the entity to the risk of loss from ineffective hedging activities. Basis risk is the difference between the fair value (or cash flows) of the hedged item and the fair value (or cash flows) of the hedging derivative. The en-

tity is subject to the risk that fair values (or cash flows) will change so that the hedge will no longer be effective.
- *Legal risk*, which exposes the entity to the risk of loss from a legal or regulatory action that invalidates or otherwise precludes performance by one or both parties to the derivative or security.

Changes in external factors can also affect assertions about derivatives and securities. The following are examples:

- The increase in credit risk associated with amounts due under debt securities issued by entities that operate in declining industries increases the inherent risk for valuation assertions about those securities.
- Significant changes in, and the volatility of, general interest rates increase the inherent risk for the valuation of derivatives whose value is significantly affected by interest rates.
- Significant changes in default rates and prepayments increase the inherent risk for the valuation of retained interests in a securitization.
- The fair value of a foreign currency forward contract will be affected by changes in the exchange rate, and the fair value of a put option for an available-for-sale security will be affected by changes in the fair value of the underlying security.

- *The evolving nature of derivatives and the applicable GAAP.* As new forms of derivatives are developed, interpretive accounting guidance for them may not be issued until after the derivatives are broadly used in the marketplace. In addition, GAAP for derivatives may be subject to frequent interpretation by various standard-setting bodies. Evolving interpretative guidance and its applicability increase the inherent risk for valuation and other assertions about existing forms of derivatives.
- *Significant reliance on outside parties.* An entity that relies on external expertise may be unable to appropriately challenge the specialist's methodology or assumptions. This may occur, for example, when a valuation specialist values a derivative.
- *GAAP may require developing assumptions about future conditions.* As the number and subjectivity of those assumptions increase, the inherent risk of material misstatement increases for certain assertions. For example, inherent risk for valuation assertions based on assumptions about debt securities whose value fluctuates with changes in prepayments (for example, interest-only strips) increases as the expected holding period lengthens. Similarly, the inherent risk for assertions about cash flow hedges fluctuates with the subjectivity of the assumptions and probability, timing, and amounts of future cash flows.

ASSESSING CONTROL RISK FOR ASSERTIONS ABOUT DERIVATIVES OR SECURITIES

To achieve its objectives, management of an entity with extensive derivatives transactions should consider the following:

- Are derivative transactions monitored by a control staff that is fully independent of derivatives activities?
- Do derivatives personnel obtain at least oral approval from senior management independent of derivatives activities prior to exceeding limits?
- Does senior management properly address limit excesses and divergences from approved derivatives strategies?

- Are derivatives positions accurately transmitted to the risk measurement systems?
- Are appropriate reconciliations performed to ensure data integrity across the full range of derivatives, including any new or existing derivatives that may be monitored apart from the main processing networks?
- Do derivatives traders, risk managers, and senior management define constraints on derivatives activities and justify identified excesses?
- Does senior management, an independent group, or an individual that management designates perform a regular review of the identified controls and financial results of the derivatives activities to determine whether controls are being effectively implemented and the entity's business objectives and strategies are being achieved?
- Are limits reviewed in the context of changes in strategy, risk tolerance of the entity, and market conditions?

The required extent of the auditor's understanding of internal control over derivatives and securities depends on how much information the auditor needs to identify the types of potential misstatements, consider factors that affect the risk of material misstatement, design tests of controls where appropriate, and design substantive tests. The understanding could include controls over derivatives and securities transactions from initiation to inclusion in the financial statements and might encompass controls placed in operation by the entity and by service organizations whose services are part of the entity's information system.

THE EFFECT OF A SERVICE ORGANIZATION ON AUDIT APPROACH AND PROCEDURES

AU 332 provides guidance on how service organizations apply to audits of derivatives and securities.

1. *Determining applicability of Section 324,* Service Organizations. A service organization's services are part of an entity's information system for derivatives and securities if they affect any of the following:

   - The initiation of the entity's derivatives and securities transactions
   - The accounting records, supporting information, and specific accounts involved in processing and reporting derivatives and securities transactions
   - The processing of accounting transactions from their initiation to their inclusion in the financial statements, including electronic means (such as computers and electronic data interchange) used to transmit, process, maintain, and access information
   - The entity's process for reporting information about derivatives and securities transactions in its financial statements, including significant accounting estimates and disclosures

2. *Examples where Section 324, applies.* A service organization's services that would be part of an entity's information system include, for example:

   - Initiating the purchase or sale of equity securities by a service organization acting as investment advisor or manager.
   - Services that are ancillary to holding an entity's securities, such as:
     - The collection of dividend and interest income and the distribution of that income to the entity
     - Receipt of notice of corporate actions

- Receipt of security purchase and sale transactions
- Receipt of payments from purchasers and disbursing proceeds to sellers for security purchase and sale transactions
- Recording securities transactions for the entity

- Maintaining custody of securities; either in physical or electronic form, is referred to as *holding* securities; performing ancillary services is referred to as *servicing* securities.
- A pricing service providing fair values of derivatives and securities through paper documents or electronic downloads that the entity uses to value its derivatives and securities for financial statement reporting.

A service organization's services that would not be part of an entity's information system include, for example:

- Executing trades by a securities broker that are initiated by either the entity or its investment advisor
- Holding an entity's securities

3. *Obtaining information.* Information about the nature of a service organization's services that are part of an entity's information system for derivative and securities transactions, or its controls over those services, may be gathered from various sources, such as:

- User manuals
- System overviews
- Technical manuals
- The contract between the entity and the service organization
- Reports by auditors, internal auditors, or regulatory authorities on the information system and other controls placed in operation by a service organization
- Asking or observing personnel at the entity or at the service organization
- Prior experience with the service organization if the services and the service organization's controls over those services are highly standardized

4. *Effect on audit procedures.* Providing services that are part of an entity's information system may affect the nature, timing, and extent of the auditor's substantive procedures for assertions about derivatives and securities in a variety of ways. The following are examples:

- Supporting documentation, such as derivative contracts and securities purchases and sales advices, may need to be inspected at the service organization's facilities.
- Service organizations may electronically transmit, process, maintain, or access significant information about an entity's securities. To reduce audit risk to an acceptable level, the auditor may be required to identify controls placed in operation by the service organization or the entity and gather evidential matter about the operating effectiveness of those controls.
- Service organizations may initiate securities transactions, and hold and service securities for an entity. In determining the level of detection risk for substantive tests, the auditor should consider whether duties are segregated and other controls for the services provided. For example:

- One service organization initiates transactions as an investment advisor and another service organization holds and services those securities. In this case, the auditor may corroborate the information provided by the two organizations by confirming holdings with the holder of the securities and applying other substantive tests to transactions reported by the entity based on information provided by the investment advisor. In certain situations, the auditor also may confirm transaction or holdings with the investment advisor and review the reconciliation of differences.
- If one service organization both initiates transactions as an investment advisor and holds and services the securities, the auditor may be unable to sufficiently limit audit risk without obtaining evidential matter about the operating effectiveness of one or more of the service organization's controls, since all of the information that the auditor has is based on the service organization's information. An example of such controls is when independent departments are established that provide the investment advisory services and the holding and servicing of securities, then reconciling the information about the securities that is provided by each department.

AU ILLUSTRATIONS

ILLUSTRATION 1. EXAMPLES OF SUBSTANTIVE PROCEDURES FOR EXISTENCE OR OCCURRENCE ASSERTIONS[3] (FROM AU 332.21)

Examples of substantive procedures for existence or occurrence assertions about derivatives and securities are:

- Confirmation with the issuer of the security.
- Confirmation with the holder of the security, including securities in electronic form, or with the counterparty to the derivative.
- Confirmation of settled transactions with the broker-dealer or counterparty.
- Confirmation of unsettled transactions with the broker-dealer or counterparty.
- Physical inspection of the security or derivative contract.
- Reading executed partnership or similar agreements.
- Inspecting underlying agreements and other forms of supporting documentation, in paper or electronic form, for:
  - Amounts reported
  - Evidence that would preclude the sales treatment of a transfer
  - Unrecorded repurchase agreements
- Inspecting supporting documentation for subsequent realization or settlement after the end of the reporting period.
- Performing analytical procedures. For example, the absence of a material difference from an expectation that interest income will be a fixed percentage of a debt security based on

---

[3] Existence assertions relate to whether the derivatives and securities reported in the financial statements through recognition or disclosure exist at the date of the statement of financial position. Occurrence assertions relate to whether derivatives and securities transactions reported in the financial statements, as a part of earnings, other comprehensive income, or cash flows or through disclosure, occurred.

the effective interest rate determined when the entity purchased the security provides evidence about existence of the security.

> **ILLUSTRATION 2. EXAMPLES OF SUBSTANTIVE PROCEDURES FOR COMPLETENESS ASSERTIONS[4] (FROM AU 332.22)**

Examples of substantive procedures for completeness assertions about derivatives and securities are:

- Requesting the counterparty to a derivative or the holder of a security to provide information about it, such as whether there are any side agreements or agreements to repurchase securities sold.
- Requesting counterparties or holders who are frequently used, but with whom the accounting records indicate there are presently no derivatives or securities, to state whether they are counterparties to derivatives with the entity or holders of its securities.
- Inspecting financial instruments and other agreements to identify embedded derivatives.
- Inspecting documentation in paper or electronic form for activity subsequent to the end of the reporting period.
- Performing analytical procedures. For example, a difference from an expectation that interest expense is a fixed percentage of a note based on the interest provisions of the underlying agreement may indicate the existence of an interest rate swap agreement.
- Comparing previous and current account detail to identify assets that have been removed from the accounts and testing those items further to determine that the criteria for sales treatment have been met.
- Reading other information, such as minutes of meetings of the board of directors or finance, asset/liability, investment, or other committees.

Derivatives may involve only a commitment to perform under a contract and not an initial exchange of tangible consideration. Thus, auditors designing tests related to the completeness assertion should not focus exclusively on evidence relating to cash receipts and disbursements. When testing for completeness, auditors should consider making inquiries, inspecting agreements, and reading other information, such as minutes of meetings of the board of directors or finance, asset/liability, investment, or other committees. Auditors should also consider making inquiries about aspects of operating activities that might present risks hedged using derivatives. For example, if the entity conducts business with foreign entities, the auditor should inquire about any arrangements the entity has made for purchasing foreign currency. Or, if an entity is in an industry in which commodity contracts are common, the auditor should inquire about any commodity contracts with fixed prices that run for unusual durations or involve unusually large quantities. The auditor also should consider inquiring as to whether the entity has converted interest-bearing debt from fixed to variable, or vice versa, using derivatives.

If one or more service organizations provide services that are part of the entity's information system for derivatives, the auditor may be unable to sufficiently limit audit risk for assertions about the completeness of derivatives without obtaining evidential matter about the operating effectiveness of controls at one or more of the service organizations. Testing reconciliations of in-

---

[4] *Completeness assertions relate to whether all the entity's derivatives and securities are reported in the financial statements through recognition or disclosure. They also relate to whether all derivatives and securities transactions are reported in the financial statements as a part of earnings, other comprehensive income, or cash flows, or through disclosure. The extent of substantive procedures for completeness may vary in relation to the assessed level of control risk. The auditor should consider that derivatives may not involve an initial exchange of tangible consideration, and thus it may be difficult to limit audit risk for assertions about the completeness of derivatives to an acceptable level with an assessed level of control risk at the maximum.*

formation provided by two or more of the service organizations may not sufficiently limit audit risk for assertions about the completeness of derivatives.

ILLUSTRATION 3. EXAMPLES OF SUBSTANTIVE PROCEDURES FOR RIGHTS AND OBLIGATIONS ASSERTIONS[5] (FROM AU 332.25)

Examples of substantive procedures for assertions about rights and obligations associated with derivatives and securities are:

- Confirming significant terms with the counterparty to a derivative or the holder of a security, including the absence of any side agreements.
- Inspecting underlying agreements and other forms of supporting documentation, in paper or electronic form.
- Considering whether the findings or other auditing procedures, such as reviewing minutes of meetings of the board of directors and reading contracts and other agreements, provide evidence about rights and obligations, such as pledging of securities as collateral or selling securities with a commitment to repurchase them.

---

[5] *Assertions about rights and obligations relate to whether the entity has the rights and obligations associated with derivatives and securities, including pledging arrangements, reported in the financial statements.*

AU 333 Management Representations[1]

AU-C 580 Written Representations

AU EFFECTIVE DATE AND APPLICABILITY

Original Pronouncement	Statements on Auditing Standards (SASs) 85, 89, and 99.
Effective Date	These statements are now effective.
Applicability	Audits of financial statements in accordance with generally accepted auditing standards (GAAS).

AU-C EFFECTIVE DATE

SAS No. 122, *Codification of Auditing Standards and Procedures,* is effective for audits of financial statements with periods ending on or after December 15, 2012.

AU-C 580 does not change extant requirements in any significant respect.

AU DEFINITIONS OF TERMS

Representation letter. Written representations obtained from management to confirm oral representations explicitly or implicitly given to the auditor, to indicate and document the continuing appropriateness of such representations, and to reduce the possibility of misunderstanding concerning the matters that are the subject of the representations. It has the following characteristics:

1. Presented in writing and covers all periods addressed in audit report.
2. Addressed to the auditor.
3. Dated no earlier than the date of the auditor's report.
4. Signed by management on client letterhead.

---

[1] The guidance in this section, including the sample engagement letter included in Illustration 1, is designed for nonissuers (as defined in the Summary of Key Changes provided immediately before Section 100-230). Auditors of issuers should consider changes that would need to be made for the standards of the Public Company Accounting Oversight Board (PCAOB) and other Securities and Exchange Commission (SEC) requirements for public companies, including the changes in the PCAOB's *Auditing Standard,* Conforming Amendments to PCAOB Interim Standards Resulting from Adoption of PCAOB Auditing Standard No. 5, An Audit of Internal Control over Financial Reporting That Is Integrated with an Audit of Financial Statements.

5. Acknowledges management's responsibility for the financial statements and management's belief that the financial statements are presented in accordance with generally accepted accounting principles (GAAP).
6. Confirms management's oral and written representations to the auditor during the course of the audit.
7. Tailored to the entity's circumstances.

AU-C DEFINITIONS OF TERMS

Source: AU-C 580.07

Written representation. A written statement by management provided to the auditor to confirm certain matters or to support other audit evidence. Written representations in this context do not include financial statements, the assertions therein, or supporting books and records.

OBJECTIVES OF AU SECTION 333

SAS 19, *Client Representations*, was issued in June 1977 and needed updating to reflect changes in accounting standards and auditing practice. As a result, SAS 85, *Management Representations*, superseded SAS 19. SAS 85 accomplishes a number of objectives. The significant changes are as follows:

1. Clarifies the requirement for an auditor to obtain written representations for all periods covered by the audit report.
2. Adds a required representation in which management states its belief that the financial statements are fairly presented in accordance with generally accepted accounting principles or other comprehensive basis of accounting (footnote 3 of SAS 85 requires that a representation letter be obtained for other comprehensive basis of accounting [OCBOA] financial statements).
3. Expands the list of specific representations to be obtained that are consistent with practice and that reflect new standards (e.g., Statement of Position [SOP] 94-6, *Disclosure of Certain Significant Risks and Uncertainties*).
4. States that the representation letter should be tailored to cover representations unique to entity's business and industry (see the "Illustrations" section for additional representations that may be needed).
5. Requires that auditor investigate and consider the reliability of representations that are contradicted by other evidence.
6. Includes guidance about explicit materiality levels that may be included in the representation letter (see the illustrative representation letter in "Illustrations" that includes a materiality discussion).
7. Requires that a predecessor auditor obtain an updated representation letter from the client when requested by a former client to reissue the audit report on prior period financial statements (see "AU Illustrations" for an illustrative updating management representation letter).

SAS 89, *Audit Adjustments*, was issued in 1999 to require management to acknowledge its responsibility for any uncorrected misstatements that management deems to be immaterial.

The representation letter is valid corroborative evidence. It is competent evidence; however, it is *not* sufficient evidence. It complements other auditing procedures, but it is *not* a substitute for these procedures.

In 2002, SAS 99, *Consideration of Fraud in a Financial Statement Audit*, amended this section to require that the auditor obtain management representations concerning fraud and the risk of fraud.

OBJECTIVES OF AU-C SECTION 580

AU-C section 580.06 states that:

. . . the objectives of the auditor are to

    a. *obtain written representations from management and, when appropriate, those charged with governance that they believe that they have fulfilled their responsibility for the preparation and fair presentation of the financial statements and for the completeness of the information provided to the auditor;*
    b. *support other audit evidence relevant to the financial statements or specific assertions in the financial statements by means of written representations if determined necessary by the auditor or required by other AU-C sections; and*
    c. *respond appropriately to written representations provided by management and, when appropriate, those charged with governance or if management or, when appropriate, those charged with governance do not provide the written representations requested by the auditor.*

FUNDAMENTAL REQUIREMENTS

RELIANCE ON MANAGEMENT REPRESENTATIONS

Management representation letters represent evidential matter and they serve to:

1. Establish and remind management that they are primarily responsible for the financial statements
2. Document representations explicitly or implicitly given to the auditor
3. Reduce the possibility of misunderstanding

Representation letters complement other auditing procedures and are not a substitute for those auditing procedures needed to support an opinion on the financial statements.

According to AU 333.04, if a representation made by management is contradicted by other audit evidence, the auditor should investigate the circumstances and consider the reliability of the representations made. In this situation, the auditor should consider whether reliance on other representations made by management is appropriate and justified.

OBTAINING WRITTEN REPRESENTATIONS

The auditor should obtain written representations from management should be obtained for all financial statements and periods covered by his or her report. If comparative financial statements are reported on, the representation letter should address all periods reported on.

NOTE: *If the auditor is reporting on consolidated financial statements, the representation letter should relate to those statements. If the auditor is reporting on the separate financial statements of a component of a consolidated group, including the parent company, the representation letter should also relate to the separate statements.*

According to AU 333.06, specific representations in a representation letter for financial statements presented in accordance with GAAP should cover the following (see "Illustrations" for an illustrative management representation letter):

Financial Statements

1. Management's acknowledgement of its responsibility for the fair presentation in the financial statements of financial position, results of operations, and cash flows in conformity with GAAP
2. Management's belief that the financial statements are fairly presented in conformity with GAAP

Completeness of Information

3. Availability of all financial records and related data
4. Completeness and availability of all minutes of meetings of stockholders, directors, and committees of directors
5. Communications from regulatory agencies concerning noncompliance with, or deficiencies in, financial reporting practices
6. Absence of unrecorded transactions

Recognition, Measurement, and Disclosure

7. Management's belief that any uncorrected misstatements (a summary of which is included in or attached to the letter) are immaterial, both individually and in the aggregate
8. Management's acknowledgement of its responsibility for designing and implementing programs and controls to prevent and detect fraud
9. Knowledge of actual or suspected fraud involving (1) management, (2) employees who have significant roles in internal control, or (3) others where the fraud could have a material effect on the financial statements
10. Knowledge of any allegations of actual or suspected fraud made by current or former employees, analysts, regulators, short sellers, or others
11. Plans or intentions that may affect the carrying value or classification of assets or liabilities
12. Information concerning related-party transactions and amounts receivable from, or payable to, related parties
13. Guarantees, whether written or oral, under which the entity is contingently liable
14. Significant estimates and material concentrations known to management that are required to be disclosed in accordance with the American Institute of Certified Public Accountants (AICPA) Statement of Position 94-6, *Disclosure of Certain Significant Risks and Uncertainties*
15. Violations or possible violations of laws and regulations whose effects should be considered for disclosure in the financial statements or as a basis for recording a loss contingency
16. Unasserted claims or assessments that the entity's lawyer has advised are probable of assertion and must be disclosed in accordance with the Financial Accounting Standards Board (FASB) Statement 5, *Accounting for Contingencies*

17. Other liabilities or loss contingencies that are required to be accrued or disclosed by FASB Statement 5
18. Satisfactory title to assets, liens or encumbrances on assets, and assets pledged as collateral
19. Compliance with aspects of contractual agreements that may affect the financial statements

Subsequent Events

20. Information concerning subsequent events

TAILORING THE REPRESENTATION LETTER

Ordinarily, the representation letter should also be modified to include additional representations from management covering matters specific to the entity's business or industry.

NOTE: Consult relevant AICPA industry audit and accounting guides for additional representations that are unique to a particular industry.

MATERIALITY CONSIDERATIONS

Management's representations may be limited to material matters, provided management and the auditor have reached an understanding on materiality. Materiality may be different for different representations. Materiality may be addressed explicitly in the representation letter, in either qualitative or quantitative terms. Materiality considerations do not apply to items that are not directly related to amounts included in the financial statements—for example, items 1, 3, 4, and 5 under "Obtaining Written Representations." Likewise, materiality does not apply to item 9 for management and employees who have significant roles in internal control.

ADDRESSING AND DATING THE LETTER

The representation letter should be addressed to the auditor and should be dated no earlier than the date of the auditor's report. If the report is dual dated, the auditor should consider whether to obtain additional representations for subsequent events.

SIGNING THE LETTER

The management representation letter should be signed by those in management with overall financial and operating responsibility whom the auditor believes are responsible for, and knowledgeable about, directly or through others in the organization, the matters covered by the representations. Normally this includes the chief executive officer and chief financial officer or others with equivalent positions in the entity.

The auditor should obtain a representation letter from current management for all periods covered by the auditor's report, even if current management was not present during all such periods.

The auditor may also want to have other individuals provide written representations. For example, the auditor could obtain from the person responsible for keeping minutes of stockholders, directors, and committees of directors, a written representation stating that such minutes are complete.

UPDATING LETTERS

As discussed in Section 508, *Reports on Audited Financial Statements*, a predecessor auditor in certain circumstances is required to obtain an updating representation letter. Also, auditors should obtain updated written representations from management when performing subsequent events procedures in connection with Securities Act of 1933 filings. The updated letter should state whether previous representations should be modified or whether subsequent events necessitate adjustment or disclosures in the financial statements.

SCOPE LIMITATIONS

If management refuses to furnish a representation letter, the auditor should ordinarily issue a disclaimer of opinion because of the limitation on audit scope or withdraw from the engagement. If the auditor concludes that a qualified opinion is appropriate, he or she should consider the effects of the refusal in relying on other management representations.

If the auditor is precluded from performing necessary procedures on a matter that is material to the financial statements, even though management has given representations on the matter, the auditor should qualify the opinion or disclaim an opinion because of the scope limitation.

INTERPRETATIONS

MANAGEMENT REPRESENTATIONS ON VIOLATIONS AND POSSIBLE VIOLATIONS OF LAWS AND REGULATIONS (MARCH 1979; REVISED JUNE 2009)

One of the required representations in a management letter is "violations or possible violations of laws or regulations whose effects should be considered for disclosure in the financial statements or as a basis for recording a loss contingency." The reference to "possible violations" does not change or go beyond the guidance in FASB ASC 450, *Accounting for Contingencies*, or Section 317, *Illegal Acts by Clients*.

TECHNIQUES FOR APPLICATION

AUDITOR'S RELATIONSHIP WITH A SMALL NONPUBLIC CLIENT

The *independent* auditor's relationship with a small or nonpublic client usually is closer than the relationship with a large or publicly held client. In these circumstances, the independent auditor may significantly influence *client* decisions, such as the following:

1. Depreciation methods
2. Accounting for start-up and similar costs
3. Accounting for revenues
4. Accounting for leases
5. Inventory valuation methods

Even though the auditor's influence may be significant, it is management's responsibility to decide whether to accept the auditor's recommendations. The client representation letter is management's acknowledgment of this responsibility.

To avoid problems at the date of completion of fieldwork, when the auditor asks management to sign the client representation letter, he or she should consider some or all of the following approaches:

1. Describe management's responsibilities in the engagement letter.
2. Discuss accounting policies and choices with management during the year and at the end of the year.
3. Define technical terms that appear in the representation letter.

Engagement Letter

The engagement letter is a written agreement signed by both the client and the auditor. It establishes the nature and terms of the engagement.

Because the engagement letter formalizes the terms of retention, it is suggested that a paragraph such as the following be added to the letter:

> We may prepare or help prepare the financial statements of XYZ Corp., but these financial statements are solely the representations of management. We may advise as to which accounting principles should be applied to the financial statements and the method of application, but the selection and the method of application are determinations made solely by management.

When the engagement letter is signed, it is advisable to tell the client what the paragraph means and that at the end of the fieldwork management must sign a representation letter in which it acknowledges its responsibility.

Although it is important to agree about management responsibility at the beginning of the engagement, it is equally important to remind management of its responsibility during the year.

Procedures during the Year

For the audit of a nonpublic client, the auditor usually is involved throughout the year. Decisions about accounting principles and methods are made during the year. For example, depreciation methods are determined, decisions are made to capitalize start-up costs and similar expenditures, and the method of accounting for various revenue streams may be established. In these circumstances, it is recommended that the auditor do the following:

1. Review the decision with management
2. Explain financial statements effect of the decision to management
3. Document the decision

NOTE: Include name of person who made the decision.

Procedures at End of Year

At the end of the year, the auditor should review with management the accounting principles applied during the year. The auditor should prepare a list of the accounting principles and explain their financial statement effect.

Before asking management to sign the representation letter, the auditor should review with them the draft of the financial statements, including the notes and the auditor's report. If the auditor has not prepared the notes and the report, he or she should tell management about their content.

DATE OF REPRESENTATION LETTER

The auditor is concerned with material events and transactions that occur to the date of completion of fieldwork. This is the date of the auditor's report and the date to which he or she wants information from client lawyers and management. For this reason, the subsequent events review extends to this date. *Also, the management representation letter should be signed as of the date the fieldwork is completed.* (For more information about dating representation letters and reports, see Section 560, *Subsequent Events*.)

EXPLICITLY ADDRESSING MATERIALITY IN THE REPRESENTATION LETTER

The auditor is permitted to reach an understanding with management on materiality and then management representations may be limited to material matters, except for certain items. Materiality may be addressed in quantitative or qualitative terms. An example of a quantitative expression would be 3% of before-tax income. A qualitative expression would be, for example, a significant change in the trend of earnings or revenue. The FASB's definition of materiality from Concepts Statement 2 is applicable to both quantitative and qualitative aspects of materiality. The conceptual description used alone, if read literally, would permit management to omit items larger than would be quantitatively material based on qualitative considerations. The authors do not recommend using it for that reason. The authors recommend that a quantitative expression of materiality, well below the planning materiality amount, be used, in conjunction with the FASB's conceptual definition. A common rule of thumb is one-sixth of planning materiality for the quantitative expression.

AU ILLUSTRATIONS[2]

The following items presented in this section are from Section 333, *Management Representations*.

1. Illustrative Management Representation Letter for GAAP Financial Statements
2. Additional Illustrative Representations
3. Illustrative Updating Management Representation Letter

ILLUSTRATION 1. ILLUSTRATIVE MANAGEMENT REPRESENTATION LETTER FOR GAAP FINANCIAL STATEMENTS (FROM AU 333.16)

The following representation letter, which is based on GAAP financial statements, is presented for illustrative purposes only.

> If matters exist that should be disclosed to the auditor, they should be indicated by modifying the related representation. For example, if an event subsequent to the date of the balance sheet has been disclosed in the financial statements, the final paragraph could be modified as follows: "To the best of our knowledge and belief, except as discussed in Note X to the financial statements, no events have occurred . . ." In appropriate circumstances, item 9 could be modified as follows: "The company has no plans or intentions that may materially affect the carrying value or classification of assets and liabilities, except for its plans to dispose of segment A, as disclosed in Note X to the financial statements, which are discussed in the minutes of the December 7, 20X6, meetings of the board of directors." Similarly, if management has received a communication regarding an

---

[2] *Illustrations 1, 2, and 3, are designed for nonissuers (as defined in the Summary of Key Changes provided immediately before Section 100-230). Auditors of issuers should consider the standards of the PCAOB (see Appendix A) and other SEC requirements for public companies.*

allegation of fraud or suspected fraud, item 8 could be modified as follows: "Except for the allegation discussed in the minutes of the December 7, 20X6, meeting of the board of directors (or disclosed to you at our meeting on October 15, 20X6), we have no knowledge of any allegations of fraud or suspected fraud affecting the company received in communications from employees, former employees, analysts, regulators, short sellers, or others."

Certain terms used in the illustrative letter are described elsewhere in authoritative literature. Examples are fraud (SAS 99, *Consideration of Fraud in a Financial Statement Audit)*, and related parties, (SAS 45, *Omnibus Statement on Auditing Standards)*. The auditor may wish to furnish those definitions to management or request that the definitions be included in the written representations.

[*Client Letterhead*]

[*Date*]

To [*Independent Auditor*]

We are providing this letter in connection with your audit(s) of the [*identification of financial statements*] of [*name of entity*] as of [*dates*] and for the [*periods*] for the purpose of expressing an opinion as to whether the [*consolidated*] financial statements present fairly, in all material respects, the financial position, results of operations, and cash flows of [*name of entity*] in conformity with accounting principles generally accepted in the United States of America. We confirm that we are responsible for the fair presentation in the [*consolidated*] financial statements of financial position, results of operations, and cash flows in conformity with accounting principles generally accepted in the United States of America.

Certain representations in this letter are described as being limited to matters that are material. Items are considered material if they exceed [*insert dollar amount*] or if they, regardless of size, involve an omission or misstatement of accounting information that, in the light of surrounding circumstance, makes it probable that the judgment of a reasonable person relying on the information would be changed or influenced by the omission or misstatements.

We confirm, to the best of our knowledge and belief [*as of (date of auditor's report)*], the following representations made to you during your audit(s).

1. The financial statements referred to above are fairly presented in conformity with accounting principles generally accepted in the United States of America.
2. We have made available to you all:
    a. Financial records and related data.
    b. Minutes of the meetings of stockholders, directors, and committees of directors, or summaries of actions of recent meetings for which minutes have not yet been prepared.
3. There have been no communications from regulatory agencies concerning noncompliance with, or deficiencies in, financial reporting practices.
4. There are no material transactions that have not been properly recorded in the accounting records underlying the financial statements.
5. We believe that the uncorrected financial statement misstatements summarized in the accompanying schedule[3] are immaterial, both individually and in the aggregate.
6. We acknowledge our responsibility for the design and implementation of programs and controls to prevent and detect fraud.
7. We have no knowledge of any fraud or suspected fraud affecting the entity involving:
    a. Management, or
    b. Employees who have significant roles in internal control, or
    c. Others where the fraud could have a material effect on the financial statements

---

[3] *Schedule not included in this illustration.*

8. We have no knowledge of any allegations of fraud or suspected fraud affecting the entity received in communications from employees, former employees, analysts, regulators, short sellers, or others.
9. The entity has no plans or intentions that may materially affect the carrying value or classification of assets and liabilities.
10. The following have been properly recorded or disclosed in the financial statements:
    a. Related-party transactions, including sales, purchases, loans, transfers, leasing arrangements, and guarantees, and amounts receivable from or payable to related parties.
    b. Guarantees, whether written or oral, under which the entity is contingently liable.
    c. Significant estimates and material concentrations known to management that are required to be disclosed in accordance with the AICPA's Statement of Position 94-6, *Disclosures of Certain Significant Risks and Uncertainties*. (Significant estimates are estimates at the balance sheet date that could change materially within the next year. Concentrations refer to volumes of business, revenues, available sources of supply, or markets or geographic areas for which events could occur that would significantly disrupt normal finances within the next year.)
11. There are no:
    a. Violations or possible violations of laws or regulations whose effects should be considered for disclosure in the financial statements or as a basis for recording a loss contingency.
    b. Unasserted claims or assessments that our lawyer has advised us are probable of assertion and must be disclosed in accordance with Financial Accounting Standards Board (FASB) Statement 5, *Accounting for Contingencies*.
12. The entity has satisfactory title to all owned assets, and there are no liens or encumbrances on such assets nor has any asset been pledged as collateral.
13. The entity has complied with all aspects of contractual agreements that would have a material effect on the financial statements in the event of noncompliance.

[Add additional representations that are unique to the entity's business or industry. See Illustration 2.]

To the best of our knowledge and belief, no events have occurred subsequent to the balance sheet date and through the date of this letter that would require adjustment to or disclosure in the aforementioned financial statements.

_____
[*Name of Chief Executive Officer and Title*]

_____
[*Name of Chief Financial Officer and Title*]

ILLUSTRATION 2. ADDITIONAL ILLUSTRATIVE REPRESENTATIONS (FROM AU 333.17)

Representation letters ordinarily should be tailored to include additional appropriate representations from management relating to matters specific to the entity's business or industry. The auditor also should be aware that certain AICPA Audit Guides recommend that the auditor obtain written representations concerning matters that are unique to a particular industry. The following is a list of additional representations that may be appropriate in certain situations. This list is not intended to be all-inclusive.

General

Condition	Illustrative Example
Unaudited interim information accompanies the financial statements.	The unaudited interim financial information accompanying [*presented in Note X to*] the financial statements for the [*identify all related periods*] has been prepared and presented in conformity with generally accepted accounting principles applicable to interim financial information [*and with Item 302(a) of Regulation S-K*]. The accounting principles used to prepare the unaudited interim financial information are consistent with those used to prepare the audited financial statements.
The impact of a new accounting principle is not known.	We have not completed the process of evaluating the impact that will result from adopting Financial Accounting Standards Board (FASB) Statement [*XXX, Name*], as discussed in Note [*X*]. The company is therefore unable to disclose the impact that adopting FASB Statement [*XXX*] will have on its financial position and the results of operations when such Statement is adopted.
There is justification for a change in accounting principles.	We believe that [*describe the newly adopted accounting principle*] is preferable to [*describe the former accounting principle*] because [*describe management's justification for the change in accounting principles*].
Financial circumstances are strained, with disclosure of management's intentions and the entity's ability to continue as a going concern.	Note [*X*] to the financial statements discloses all of the matters of which we are aware that are relevant to the company's ability to continue as a going concern, including significant conditions and events, and management's plans.
The possibility exists that the value of specific significant long-lived assets or certain identifiable intangibles may be impaired.	We have reviewed long-lived assets and certain identifiable intangibles to be held and used for impairment whenever events or changes in circumstances have indicated that the carrying amount of its assets might not be recoverable and have appropriately recorded the adjustment.
The entity engages in transactions with variable interest entities	We have evaluated all transactions involving variable interest entities to determine that the accounting for such transactions is in accordance with generally accepted accounting principles.

General

Condition	Illustrative Example
	Specifically [*indicate appropriate accounting principles*]
	• FASB Interpretation 46(R) *Consolidation of Variable Interest Entities* (revised December, 2003)
	• Conditions pursuant to paragraph 35 of FASB Statement 140, *Accounting for Transfers and Servicing of Financial Assets and Extinguishment of Liabilities.*
	• EITF Issue No. 96-16, *Investor's Accounting for an Investee When the Investor Has a Majority of the Voting Interest but the Minority Shareholder or Shareholders Have Certain Approval or Veto Rights.*
	• EITF Issue 96-21, *Implementation in Accounting for Leasing Transactions Involving Special-Purpose Entities.*
The work of a specialist has been used by the entity.	We agree with the finding of specialists in evaluating the [*describe assertion*] and have adequately considered the qualifications of the specialist in determining the amounts and disclosures used in the financial statements and underlying accounting records. We did not give or cause any instructions to be given to specialists with respect to the values or amounts derived in an attempt to bias their work, and we are not otherwise aware of any matters that have had an impact on the independence or objectivity of the specialists.

Assets

Condition	Illustrative Example
Cash	
Disclosure is required of compensating balances or other arrangements involving restrictions on cash balances, line of credit, or similar arrangements.	Arrangements with financial institutions involving compensating balances or other arrangements involving restrictions on cash balances, line of credit, or similar arrangements have been properly disclosed.
Financial Instruments	
Management intends to, and has the ability to, hold to maturity debt securities classified as held-to-maturity.	Debt securities that have been classified as held-to-maturity have been so classified due to the company's intent to hold such securities to maturity and the company's ability to do so. All other debt securities have been classified as available-for-sale or trading.
Management considers the decline in value of debt or equity securities to be temporary.	We consider the decline in value of debt or equity securities classified as either available-for-sale or held-to-maturity to be temporary.

Assets

Condition	Illustrative Example
Management has determined the fair value of significant financial instruments that do not have readily determinable market values.	The methods and significant assumptions used to determine fair values of financial instruments are as follows: [*describe methods and significant assumptions used to determine fair values of financial instruments*]. The methods and significant assumptions used result in a measure of fair value appropriate for financial statement measurement and disclosure purposes.
There are financial instruments with off-balance-sheet risk and financial instruments with concentrations of credit risk.	The following information about financial instruments with off-balance-sheet risk and financial instruments with concentrations of credit risk has been properly disclosed in the financial statements: 1. The extent, nature, and terms of financial instruments with off-balance-sheet risk. 2. The amount of credit risk of financial instruments with off-balance-sheet risk and information about the collateral supporting such financial instruments. 3. Significant concentrations of credit risk arising from all financial instruments and information about the collateral supporting such financial instruments.

Receivables

Receivables have been recorded in the financial statements.	Receivables recorded in the financial statements represent valid claims against debtors for sales or other charges arising on or before the balance sheet date and have been appropriately reduced to their estimated net realizable value.

Inventories

Excess or obsolete inventories exist.	Provision has been made to reduce excess or obsolete inventories to their estimated net realizable value.

Investments

There are unusual considerations involved in determining the application of equity accounting.	[*For investments in common stock that are either nonmarketable or of which the entity has a 20% or greater ownership interest, select the appropriate representation from the following:*]

Assets

Condition	Illustrative Example
	• The equity method is used to account for the company's investment in the common stock of [*investee*] because the company has the ability to exercise significant influence over the investee's operating and financial policies. • The cost method is used to account for the company's investment in the common stock of [*investee*] because the company does not have the ability to exercise significant influence over the investee's operating and financial policies.
Deferred Charges	
Material expenditures have been deferred.	We believe that all material expenditures that have been deferred to future periods will be recoverable.
Deferred Tax Assets	
A deferred tax asset exists at the balance sheet date.	The valuation allowance has been determined pursuant to the provisions of FASB Statement 109, *Accounting for Income Taxes*, including the company's estimation of future taxable income, if necessary, and is adequate to reduce the total deferred tax asset to an amount that will more likely than not be realized. [*Complete with appropriate wording detailing how the entity determined the valuation allowance against the deferred tax asset.*] or A valuation allowance against deferred tax assets at the balance sheet date is not considered necessary because it is more likely than not the deferred tax asset will be fully realized.

Liabilities

Condition	Illustrative Example
Debt	
Short-term debt could be refinanced on a long-term basis and management intends to do so.	The company has excluded short-term obligations totaling $[*amount*] from current liabilities because it intends to refinance the obligations on a long-term basis. [*Complete with appropriate wording detailing how amounts will be refinanced as follows:*]

Condition	Liabilities Illustrative Example
	• The company has issued a long-term obligation [*debt security*] after the date of the balance sheet but prior to the issuance of the financial statements for the purpose of refinancing the short-term obligations on a long-term basis. • The company has the ability to consummate the refinancing, by using the financing agreement referred to in Note [*X*] to the financial statements.
Tax-exempt bonds have been issued.	Tax-exempt bonds issued have retained their tax-exempt status.

Taxes

Management intends to reinvest undistributed earnings of a foreign subsidiary.	We intend to reinvest the undistributed earnings of [*name of foreign subsidiary*].

Contingencies

Estimates and disclosures have been made of environmental remediation liabilities and related loss contingencies.	Provision has been made for any material loss that is probable from environmental remediation liabilities associated with [*name of site*]. We believe that such estimate is reasonable based on available information and that the liabilities and related loss contingencies and the expected outcome of uncertainties have been adequately described in the company's financial statements.
Agreements may exist to repurchase assets previously sold.	Agreements to repurchase assets previously sold have been properly disclosed.

Pension and Postretirement Benefits

An actuary has been used to measure pension liabilities and costs.	We believe that the actuarial assumptions and methods used to measure pension liabilities and cost for financial accounting purposes are appropriate in the circumstances.
There is involvement with a multiemployer plan.	We are unable to determine the possibility of a withdrawal liability in a multiemployer benefit plan. or We have determined that there is the possibility of a withdrawal liability in a multiemployer plan in the amount of $[*XX*].
Postretirement benefits have been eliminated.	We do not intend to compensate for the elimination of postretirement benefits by granting an increase in pension benefits. or

Liabilities

Condition	Illustrative Example
	We plan to compensate for the elimination of postretirement benefits by granting an increase in pension benefits in the amount of $[XX].
Employee layoffs that would otherwise lead to a curtailment of a benefit plan are intended to be temporary.	Current employee layoffs are intended to be temporary.
Management intends to either continue to make or not make frequent amendments to its pension or other postretirement benefit plans, which may affect the amortization period of prior service cost, or has expressed a substantive commitment to increase benefit obligations.	We plan to continue to make frequent amendments to its pension or other postretirement benefit plans, which may affect the amortization period of prior service cost. or We do not plan to make frequent amendments to its pension or other postretirement benefit plans.

Equity

Condition	Illustrative Example
There are capital stock repurchase options or agreements or capital stock reserved for options, warrants, conversions, or other requirements.	Capital stock repurchase options or agreements or capital stock reserved for options, warrants, conversions, or other requirements have been properly disclosed.

Income Statement

Condition	Illustrative Example
There may be a loss from sales commitments.	Provisions have been made for losses to be sustained in the fulfillment of, or from inability to fulfill, any sales commitments.
There may be losses from purchase commitments.	Provisions have been made for losses to be sustained as a result of purchase commitment for inventory quantities in excess of normal requirements or at prices in excess of prevailing market prices.
Nature of the product or industry indicates the possibility of undisclosed sales terms.	We have fully disclosed to you all sales terms, including all rights of return or price adjustments and all warranty provisions.

ILLUSTRATION 3. ILLUSTRATIVE UPDATING MANAGEMENT REPRESENTATION LETTER (FROM AU 333.18)

[Client Letterhead]

[Date]

To [Auditor]

In connection with your audit(s) of the [identification of financial statements] of [name of entity] as of [dates] and for the [periods] for the purpose of expressing an opinion as to whether the [*consolidated*] financial statements present fairly, in all material respects, the financial position, results of operations, and cash flows of [*name of entity*] in conformity with accounting principles generally accepted in the United States of America, you were previously provided with a representation letter under the date of [*date of previous representation letter*]. No information has come to our attention that would cause us to believe that any of those previous representations should be modified.

To the best of our knowledge and belief, no events have occurred subsequent to [*date of latest balance sheet reported on by auditor*] and through the date of this letter that would require adjustment to or disclosure in the aforementioned financial statements.

_____
[*Name of Chief Executive Officer and Title*]

_____
[*Name of Chief Financial Officer and Title*]

AU-C 580 ILLUSTRATIONS

ILLUSTRATION 1. ILLUSTRATIVE REPRESENTATION LETTER (FROM AU-C 580.A35)

The following illustrative letter includes written representations that are required by this and other AU-C sections in effect for audits of financial statements for periods ending on or after December 15, 2012. It is assumed in this illustration that the applicable financial reporting framework is accounting principles generally accepted in the United States, that the requirement in Section 570, *The Auditor's Consideration of an Entity's Ability to Continue as a Going Concern*, to obtain a written representation is not relevant, and that no exceptions exist to the requested written representations. If there were exceptions, the representations would need to be modified to reflect the exceptions.

[*Entity Letterhead*]

[*To Auditor*]

[*Date*]

This representation letter is provided in connection with your audit of the financial statements of ABC Company, which comprise the balance sheet as of December 31, 20XX, and the related statements of income, changes in stockholders' equity, and cash flows for the year then ended, and the related notes to the financial statements, for the purpose of expressing an opinion on whether the financial statements are presented fairly, in all material respects, in accordance with accounting principles generally accepted in the United States (US GAAP).

Certain representations in this letter are described as being limited to matters that are material. Items are considered material, regardless of size, if they involve an omission or misstatement of accounting information that, in the light of surrounding circumstances, makes it probable that the judgment of a reasonable person relying on the information would be changed or influenced by the omission or misstatement.

Except where otherwise stated below, immaterial matters less than $[*insert amount*] collectively are not considered to be exceptions that require disclosure for the purpose of the following representations. This amount is not necessarily indicative of amounts that would require adjustment to or disclosure in the financial statements.

We confirm that, [*to the best of our knowledge and belief, having made such inquiries as we considered necessary for the purpose of appropriately informing ourselves*] [*as of (date of auditor's report),*]:

Financial Statements

- We have fulfilled our responsibilities, as set out in the terms of the audit engagement dated [*insert date*], for the preparation and fair presentation of the financial statements in accordance with US GAAP.
- We acknowledge our responsibility for the design, implementation, and maintenance of internal control relevant to the preparation and fair presentation of financial statements that are free from material misstatement, whether due to fraud or error.
- We acknowledge our responsibility for the design, implementation, and maintenance of internal control to prevent and detect fraud.
- Significant assumptions used by us in making accounting estimates, including those measured at fair value, are reasonable.
- Related-party relationships and transactions have been appropriately accounted for and disclosed in accordance with the requirements of US GAAP.
- All events subsequent to the date of the financial statements and for which US GAAP requires adjustment or disclosure have been adjusted or disclosed.
- The effects of uncorrected misstatements are immaterial, both individually and in the aggregate, to the financial statements as a whole. A list of the uncorrected misstatements is attached to the representation letter.
- The effects of all known actual or possible litigation and claims have been accounted for and disclosed in accordance with US GAAP.

[*Any other matters that the auditor may consider appropriate.*]

Information Provided

- We have provided you with:
  - Access to all information of which we are aware that is relevant to the preparation and fair presentation of the financial statements such as records, documentation, and other matters
  - Additional information that you have requested from us for the purpose of the audit; and
  - Unrestricted access to persons within the entity from whom you determined it necessary to obtain audit evidence
- All transactions have been recorded in the accounting records and are reflected in the financial statements.
- We have disclosed to you the results of our assessment of the risk that the financial statements may be materially misstated as a result of fraud.
- We have [*no knowledge of any*] [*disclosed to you all information that we are aware of regarding*] fraud or suspected fraud that affects the entity and involves:
  - Management
  - Employees who have significant roles in internal control; or
  - Others when the fraud could have a material effect on the financial statements
- We have [*no knowledge of any*] [*disclosed to you all information that we are aware of regarding*] allegations of fraud, or suspected fraud, affecting the entity's financial statements communicated by employees, former employees, analysts, regulators or others.
- We have disclosed to you all known instances of noncompliance or suspected noncompliance with laws and regulations whose effects should be considered when preparing financial statements.
- We [*have disclosed to you all known actual or possible*] [*are not aware of any pending or threatened*] litigation, claims, and assessments whose effects should be considered when preparing the financial statements [*and we have not consulted legal counsel concerning litigation, claims, or assessments*].

- We have disclosed to you the identity of the entity's related parties and all the related-party relationships and transactions of which we are aware.

[*Any other matters that the auditor may consider necessary.*]

_____
[*Name of Chief Executive Officer and Title*]

_____
[*Name of Chief Financial Officer and Title*]

[*Revised March 2012 to reflect conforming changes necessary due to the issuance of SAS No. 122.*]

ILLUSTRATION 2. ILLUSTRATIVE SPECIFIC WRITTEN REPRESENTATIONS (FROM AU-C 580.A36)

Condition	Illustrative Specific Written Representation
General	
Unaudited interim information accompanies the financial statements.	The unaudited interim financial information accompanying [*presented in Note X to*] the financial statements for the [*identify all related periods*] has been prepared and fairly presented in conformity with generally accepted accounting principles (GAAP) applicable to interim financial information. The accounting principles used to prepare the unaudited interim financial information are consistent with those used to prepare the audited financial statements.
The effect of a new accounting principle is not known.	We have not completed the process of evaluating the effect that will result from adopting the guidance in Financial Accounting Standards Board (FASB) Accounting Standards Update 20YY-XX, as discussed in Note [*X*]. The company is therefore unable to disclose the effect that adopting the guidance in FASB Accounting Standards Update 20YY-XX will have on its financial position and the results of operations when such guidance is adopted.
Financial circumstances are strained, with disclosure of management's intentions and the entity's ability to continue as a going concern.	Note [*X*] to the financial statements discloses all of the matters of which we are aware that are relevant to the company's ability to continue as a going concern, including significant conditions and events and management's plans.
The possibility exists that the value of specific significant long-lived assets or certain identifiable intangibles may be impaired.	We have reviewed long-lived assets and certain identifiable intangibles to be held and used for impairment whenever events or changes in circumstances have indicated that the carrying amount of the assets might not be recoverable and have appropriately recorded the adjustment.

Condition	Illustrative Specific Written Representation
The entity has a variable interest in another entity.	Variable interest entities (VIEs) and potential VIEs and transactions with VIEs and potential VIEs have been properly recorded and disclosed in the financial statements in accordance with GAAP.
	We have considered both implicit and explicit variable interests in (1) determining whether potential VIEs should be considered VIEs, (2) calculating expected losses and residual returns, and (3) determining which party, if any, is the primary beneficiary.
	We have provided you with lists of all identified variable interests in (1) VIEs, (2) potential VIEs that we considered but judged not to be VIEs, and (3) entities that were afforded the scope exceptions of Financial Accounting Standards Board (FASB) *Accounting Standards Codification*™ (ASC) 810, *Consolidation*.
	We have advised you of all transactions with identified VIEs, potential VIEs, or entities afforded the scope exceptions of FASB ASC 810.
	We have made available all relevant information about financial interests and contractual arrangements with related parties, de facto agents, and other entities, including but not limited to their governing documents, equity and debt instruments, contracts, leases, guarantee arrangements, and other financial contracts and arrangements.
	The information we provided about financial interests and contractual arrangements with related parties, de facto agents and other entities includes information about all transactions, unwritten understandings, agreement modifications, and written and oral side agreements.
	Our computations of expected losses and expected residual returns of entities that are VIEs and potential VIEs are based on the best information available and include all reasonably possible outcomes.
	Regarding entities in which the company has variable interests (implicit and explicit), we have provided all information about events and changes in circumstances that could potentially cause reconsideration about whether the entities are VIEs or whether the company is the primary beneficiary or has a significant variable interest in the entity.
	We have made and continue to make exhaustive efforts to obtain information about entities in which the company has an implicit or explicit interest but that were excluded from complete analysis under FASB ASC 810 due to lack of essential information to determine one or more of the following: whether the entity is a VIE, whether the company is the primary beneficiary, or the accounting required to consolidate the entity.

Condition	Illustrative Specific Written Representation
The work of a specialist has been used by the entity.	We agree with the findings of specialists in evaluating the [*describe assertion*] and have adequately considered the qualifications of the specialist in determining the amounts and disclosures used in the financial statements and underlying accounting records. We did not give or cause any instructions to be given to specialists with respect to the values or amounts derived in an attempt to bias their work, and we are not otherwise aware of any matters that have had an effect on the independence or objectivity of the specialists.
Assets	
Cash Disclosure is required of compensating balances or other arrangements involving restrictions on cash balances, lines of credit, or similar arrangements.	Arrangements with financial institutions involving compensating balances or other arrangements involving restrictions on cash balances, line of credit, or similar arrangements have been properly disclosed.
Financial Instruments Management intends to and has the ability to hold to maturity debt securities classified as held-to-maturity.	Debt securities that have been classified as held-to-maturity have been so classified due to the company's intent to hold such securities to maturity and the company's ability to do so. All other debt securities have been classified as available-for-sale or trading.
Management considers the decline in value of debt or equity securities to be temporary.	We consider the decline in value of debt or equity securities classified as either available-for-sale or held-to-maturity to be temporary.
Management has determined the fair value of significant financial instruments that do not have readily determinable market values.	The methods and significant assumptions used to determine fair values of financial instruments are as follows: [*describe methods and significant assumptions used to determine fair values of financial instruments*]. The methods and significant assumptions used result in a measure of fair value appropriate for financial statement measurement and disclosure purposes.
Financial instruments with off-balance-sheet risk and financial instruments with concentrations of credit risk exist.	The following information about financial instruments with off-balance-sheet risk and financial instruments with concentrations of credit risk has been properly disclosed in the financial statements: 1. The extent, nature, and terms of financial instruments with off-balance-sheet risk 2. The amount of credit risk of financial instruments with off-balance-sheet risk and information about the collateral supporting such financial instruments 3. Significant concentrations of credit risk arising from all financial instruments and information about the collateral supporting such financial instruments

Condition	Illustrative Specific Written Representation
Investments Unusual considerations are involved in determining the application of equity accounting.	[*For investments in common stock that are either nonmarketable or of which the entity has a 20% or greater ownership interest, select the appropriate representation from the following:*] The equity method is used to account for the company's investment in the common stock of [*investee*] because the company has the ability to exercise significant influence over the investee's operating and financial policies. The cost method is used to account for the company's investment in the common stock of [*investee*] because the company does not have the ability to exercise significant influence over the investee's operating and financial policies.
The entity had loans to executive officers, nonaccrued loans or zero interest rate loans.	Loans to executive officers have been properly accounted for and disclosed.
Liabilities	
Debt Short-term debt could be refinanced on a long-term basis and management intends to do so.	The company has excluded short-term obligations totaling $[*amount*] from current liabilities because it intends to refinance the obligations on a long-term basis. [*Complete with appropriate wording detailing how amounts will be refinanced as follows:*] The company has issued a long-term obligation [*debt security*] after the date of the balance sheet but prior to the issuance of the financial statements for the purpose of refinancing the short-term obligations on a long-term basis. The company has the ability to consummate the refinancing, by using the financing agreement referred to in Note [*X*] to the financial statements.
Tax-exempt bonds have been issued.	Tax-exempt bonds issued have retained their tax-exempt status.
Taxes Management intends to reinvest undistributed earnings of a foreign subsidiary.	We intend to reinvest the undistributed earnings of [*name of foreign subsidiary*].
Pension and Postretirement Benefits An actuary has been used to measure pension liabilities and costs.	We believe that the actuarial assumptions and methods used to measure pension liabilities and costs for financial accounting purposes are appropriate in the circumstances.
Involvement with a multiemployer plan exists.	We are unable to determine the possibility of a withdrawal liability in a multiemployer benefit plan. *or* We have determined that there is the possibility of a withdrawal liability in a multiemployer plan in the amount of $[*XX*].

Condition	Illustrative Specific Written Representation
Postretirement benefits have been eliminated.	We do not intend to compensate for the elimination of postretirement benefits by granting an increase in pension benefits. *or* We plan to compensate for the elimination of postretirement benefits by granting an increase in pension benefits in the amount of $[*XX*].
Employee layoffs that would otherwise lead to a curtailment of a benefit plan are intended to be temporary.	Current employee layoffs are intended to be temporary.
Management intends to either continue to make or not make frequent amendments to its pension or other postretirement benefit plans, which may affect the amortization period of prior service cost, or has expressed a substantive commitment to increase benefit obligations.	We plan to continue to make frequent amendments to the pension or other postretirement benefit plans, which may affect the amortization period of prior service cost. *or* We do not plan to make frequent amendments to the pension or other postretirement benefit plans.
Equity	
Capital stock repurchase options or agreements or capital stock reserved for options, warrants, conversions, or other requirements exist.	Capital stock repurchase options or agreements or capital stock reserved for options, warrants, conversions, or other requirements have been properly disclosed.

ILLUSTRATION 3. ILLUSTRATIVE UPDATING MANAGEMENT REPRESENTATION LETTER (FROM AU-C 580)

The following letter is presented for illustrative purposes only. It may be used in the circumstances described in paragraph .A17 of this section. Management need not repeat all of the representations made in the previous representation letter.

If matters to be disclosed to the auditor exist, they may be listed following the representation. For example, if an event subsequent to the date of the balance sheet has been disclosed in the financial statements, the final paragraph could be modified as follows: "To the best of our knowledge and belief, except as discussed in Note X to the financial statements, no events have occurred. . . ."

[*Date*]

To [*Auditor*]

In connection with your audit(s) of the [*identification of financial statements*] of [*name of entity*] as of [*dates*] and for the [*periods*] for the purpose of expressing an opinion as to whether the [*consolidated*] financial statements present fairly, in all material respects, the financial position, results of operations, and cash flows of [*name of entity*] in accordance with accounting principles generally accepted in the United States of America, you were previously provided with a representation letter under date of [*date of previous representation letter*]. No information has come to our attention that would cause us to believe that any of those previous representations should be modified.

To the best of our knowledge and belief, no events have occurred subsequent to [*date of latest balance sheet reported on by the auditor*] and through the date of this letter that would require adjustment to or disclosure in the aforementioned financial statements.

_____
[*Name of Chief Executive Officer and Title*]

_____
[*Name of Chief Financial Officer and Title*]

[*Paragraph added, March 2012, to reflect conforming changes necessary due to the issuance of SAS No. 122.*]

AU 334 Related Parties

AU-C 550 Related Parties

AU EFFECTIVE DATE AND APPLICABILITY

Original Pronouncement Statement on Accounting Standards (SAS) 45.

Effective Date This statement is now effective.

Applicability Audits of financial statements in conformity with generally accepted auditing standards (GAAS).

AU-C EFFECTIVE DATE AND SUMMARY OF CHANGES

SAS No. 122, *Codification of Auditing Standards and Procedures,* is effective for audits of financial statements with periods ending on or after December 15, 2012.

AU-C 550 supersedes: AU Section 334. It also makes a substantive change. AU Section 334 is focused on auditing the amounts and disclosures pursuant to U.S. generally accepted accounting principles (GAAP), and is centered on the provisions of Financial Accounting Standards Board (FASB) Statement No. 57. AU-C 550 is framework-neutral. It encompasses financial reporting frameworks in addition to US GAAP, such as International Financial Reporting Standards. as well as special-purpose frameworks described in AU-C Section 800, *Special Considerations—Audits of Financial Statements Prepared in Accordance with Special-Purpose Frameworks*

AU DEFINITIONS OF TERMS

The section itself has no general definitions, but it uses terms defined in paragraph 1 and the glossary of Financial Accounting Standards (FAS) Accounting Standards Codification (ASC) 850, *Related-Party Disclosures*.

Affiliate. A party that, directly or indirectly though one or more intermediaries, controls, is controlled by, or is under common control with an enterprise.

Control. The possession, direct or indirect, of the power to direct or cause the direction of the management and policies of an enterprise through ownership, by contract, or otherwise.

Immediate family. Family members whom a principal owner or a member of management might control or influence, or by whom they might be controlled or influenced because of the family relationship.

Management. Persons who are responsible for achieving the objectives of the enterprise and who have the authority to establish policies and make decisions by which those objectives are to be pursued. Management normally includes members of the board of directors, the chief executive officer, chief operating officer, vice presidents in charge of principal business functions (such as sales, administration, or finance), and other persons who perform similar policymaking functions. Persons without formal titles also may be members of management.

Principal owners. Owners of record or known beneficial owners of more than 10% of the voting interests of the enterprise.

Related parties.

- Affiliates of the enterprise
- Entities for which investments are accounted for by the equity method
- Trusts for the benefit of employees, such as pension and profit-sharing trusts that are managed by or under the trusteeship of management
- Principal owners
- Management
- Members of the immediate families of principal owners and management
- Other parties, if one party controls or can significantly influence the management or operating policies of the other to an extent that one of the parties might be prevented from pursuing its own separate interest
- Another party that can significantly influence the management or operating policies of the transacting parties or that has an ownership interest in one of the transacting parties and can significantly influence the other to an extent that one or more of the transacting parties might be prevented from pursuing its own separate interests

AU-C DEFINITIONS OF TERMS

Arm's-length transaction. A transaction conducted on such terms and conditions between a willing buyer and a willing seller who are unrelated and are acting independently of each other and pursuing their own best interests.

Related party. A party defined as a related party in GAAP.

OBJECTIVES OF AU SECTION 334

Special attention to related parties has a long history in auditing. From the auditor's perspective, related-party transactions have two distinct, but not mutually exclusive, aspects: adequate disclosure and fraud detection.

The disclosure aspect is emphasized in FAS ASC 850. Some related-party transactions may be the direct result of the relationship. Without that relationship, the transaction might not have occurred at all or might have had substantially different terms. Thus, disclosure of the nature and amount of transactions with related parties is necessary for a proper understanding of the financial statements.

Inadequate disclosure of related-party transactions may result in misleading financial statements, so the auditor should be concerned with identifying such transactions in the audit and evaluating the adequacy of their disclosure. The auditor should also be concerned, however, with the possibility that an undisclosed relationship with a party to a material transaction has been used to fabricate transactions. That is, the transactions may be fraudulent or without substance. Section 334 clearly acknowledges the possibility that a related-party relationship may be a tool for fraud by management.

SAS 6 was issued in 1975 primarily in response to some spectacular fraud cases in which management's involvement in material transactions was obscured either by inadequate disclosure or outright concealment. The SAS was more disclosure-oriented than fraud-oriented, however, because fraud is the exception rather than the norm. Nevertheless, the auditor should be aware of the possibility of fraud. The SAS observed:

> In the absence of evidence to the contrary, transactions with related parties should not be assumed to be outside the ordinary course of business.
>
> The auditor should view related-party transactions within the framework of existing pronouncements, placing primary emphasis on the adequacy of disclosure. In addition, the auditor should be aware that the substance of a particular transaction could be significantly different from its form.

OBJECTIVES OF AU-C SECTION 550

AU-C 550 states that:

. . . the objectives of the auditor are to

a. *obtain an understanding of related-party relationships and transactions sufficient to be able to*

   i. *recognize fraud risk factors, if any, arising from related-party relationships and transactions that are relevant to the identification and assessment of the risks of material misstatement due to fraud.*

   ii. *conclude, based on the audit evidence obtained, whether the financial statements, insofar as they are affected by those relationships and transactions, achieve fair presentation.*

b. *obtain sufficient appropriate audit evidence about whether related-party relationships and transactions have been appropriately identified, accounted for, and disclosed in the financial statements.*

FUNDAMENTAL REQUIREMENTS

ACCOUNTING CONSIDERATIONS

FAS ASC 850, *Related-Party Disclosures*, provides that:

1. Material related-party transactions other than compensation arrangements, expense allowances, and other similar items in the ordinary course of business should be disclosed. (Disclosure of transactions eliminated in consolidated or combined statements is not required in those statements.)
2. The disclosures shall include:
   a. The nature of the relationship(s).
   b. A description of the transactions for each of the periods for which income statements are presented and such other information necessary to understand the effects of the transactions on the financial statements (including transactions to which no amounts or nominal amounts were ascribed).

c. The dollar amounts of transactions for each period for which an income statement is presented. (The effects of any change in the method of establishing the terms from the prior period should also be disclosed.)
d. Amounts due from or to related parties as of each balance sheet date presented and the terms and manner of settlement.

AUDIT PROCEDURES

An audit cannot be expected to provide assurance that all related-party transactions will be discovered. Nevertheless, the auditor should be aware of:

1. The possibility that material related-party transactions exist that could affect the financial statements
2. Common ownership or management control relationships that are required by FAS ASC 850 to be disclosed even though there are no transactions

In determining the scope of work to be performed, the auditor should obtain an understanding of management responsibilities and the relationship of each of the entity's component to the total entity. The auditor should consider controls over management activities and the business purpose served by the various components.

NOTE: Business structure and operating style are occasionally deliberately designed to obscure related-party transactions.

The auditor should recognize that the following transactions may indicate related parties:

1. Transactions to borrow or lend at no interest or at rates significantly different from market rates
2. The sale of real estate at a price significantly different from its appraised value
3. A nonmonetary exchange of property for similar property
4. Loans made with no scheduled terms for the time or method of repayment

The following are factors that the auditor should be aware of that may motivate transactions with related parties:

1. Is there a lack of sufficient working capital or credit to continue the business?
2. Does management have an urgent desire for a continued favorable earnings record to support the price of the entity's stock?
3. Is the earnings forecast overly optimistic?
4. Does the entity depend on one or a few products, customers, or transactions for continued success?
5. Is the entity in a declining industry with many business failures?
6. Does the entity have excess capacity?
7. Is the entity involved in significant litigation, especially between stockholders and management?
8. Are there significant dangers of obsolescence because the entity is in a high-technology industry?

NOTE: These are fraud "warning signs" or risk factors. The presence of one or more factors is not proof of fraud, but the auditor should increase his or her awareness of the possibility of fraud. If the risk is high, the auditor might increase the scope of substantive tests designed to identify undisclosed relationships or use some of the expanded procedures enumerated in Section 334. (See also Section 316, Consideration of Fraud in a Financial Statement Audit*.)*

Basic Approach

To identify material related-party transactions the auditor should:

1. Identify related parties (through inquiry and review of relevant information to determine the identity of related parties so that material transactions with these parties known to be related can be examined).

> NOTE: According to Section 334, the auditor should place emphasis on testing identified material related-party transactions.

2. Identify material transactions (consider whether there are indications of previously undisclosed relationships for material transactions).
3. Examine identified material related-party transactions.

> NOTE: In Section 334, the procedures are grouped essentially in the preceding categories. In the following discussion, a different grouping is used to emphasize distinctions between specific procedures for related parties and general procedures.

Specific Procedures

Section 334 includes some procedures performed solely for the purpose of identifying related parties or related-party transactions.

1. Inquire of management:

    a. Names of all related parties
    b. Whether there were any transactions with these parties during the period
    c. Whether the entity has procedures for identifying and properly accounting for related-party transactions; if so, evaluate these procedures

    > NOTE: This is covered in the management representation letter. It is helpful to give management the technical definition of related parties at the time of initial inquiry and in the letter.

2. Obtain the names of all pension and other trusts established for the benefit of employees and the names of officers and trustees of the trusts.
3. Review stockholder listings of closely held entities and identify principal stockholders.
4. Provide audit staff with the names of known related parties so that they can identify transactions with such parties.
5. For indications of undisclosed relationships, review the nature and extent of business transacted with major:

    a. Customers
    b. Suppliers
    c. Borrowers
    d. Lenders

6. Consider whether transactions are occurring but not being given accounting recognition, such as the client receiving or providing accounting, management, or other services at no charge, or a major stockholder absorbing corporate expenses.

General Procedures

The procedures in Section 334 for identifying related parties and for identifying transactions with related parties include several procedures that are usually performed in an audit. These are normal procedures performed for several purposes that may also identify related parties.

General procedure	Relevance to related parties
Review prior years' audit documentation.	Identify names of known related parties.
Review minutes of meetings of board of directors and executive or operating committees.	Obtain information on material transactions authorized or discussed.
Review confirmations of compensating balance arrangements.	Identify whether balances are or were maintained for or by related parties.
Review invoices from law firms for regular or special services.	Identify indications of related parties or related-party transactions.
Review confirmations of loans receivable and payable.	Identify whether there are guarantees and the nature of relationship to guarantor.
Review material investment transactions.	Determine whether investment created related party.
Review accounting records for large, unusual, or nonrecurring transactions or balances, particularly at or near end of reporting period.	Consider whether transactions are with related parties.
Inquire of predecessor, principal, or other auditors of related entities (this inquiry should be made at an early stage of the audit).	Obtain their knowledge of related parties or related-party transactions.

Procedures: Public Companies

Some procedures in Section 334 are relevant only for public companies:

1. Review filings with the SEC and other regulatory agencies for the names of related parties and for other businesses in which officers and directors occupy directorships or other management positions.
2. Review proxy and other material filed with the SEC and comparable data filed with other regulatory agencies for information on material transactions with related parties.
3. Review "conflict-of-interest" statements obtained by the entity from its management.

Procedures for Identified Transactions

After a related-party transaction is identified, the auditor should apply substantive tests to that transaction. Inquiry of management is not sufficient. According to AU 334.09, procedures that should be considered are:

1. Obtaining an understanding of the transaction's business purpose.

    NOTE: Until the auditor understands the business sense of the transaction, he or she cannot complete the audit.

2. Examining invoices, executed copies of agreements, contracts, and other pertinent documents, such as receiving reports and shipping documents.
3. Determining whether the transaction has been approved by the board of directors or other appropriate officials.

4. Testing for reasonableness the compilation of amounts to be disclosed or considered for disclosure.
5. Inspecting or confirming and obtaining satisfaction that collateral is transferable and appropriately valued.
6. For intercompany account balances:
    a. Arranging for examination at concurrent dates, even if fiscal years differ
    b. Arranging for examination of specified, important, and representative related-party transactions by auditors for each of the parties with an exchange of relevant information

NOTE: A principal auditor–other auditor relationship may exist, and the component not audited by the principal auditor may have conducted related-party transactions that are complex or unusual. In these circumstances, the principal auditor should request access to the other auditor's audit documentation concerning this matter.

Expanded Procedures

If the auditor concludes that it is necessary to fully understand a related-party transaction, he or she should consider the following procedures that might otherwise be unnecessary:

1. Confirm the amount and terms of the transaction, including guarantees and other significant data, with the other party.
2. Inspect evidence in the other party's possession.
3. Confirm or discuss significant information with intermediaries (banks, guarantors, agents, or attorneys).
4. If there is reason to believe that material transactions with unfamiliar customers, suppliers, or others may lack substance, refer to financial publications, trade journals, credit agencies, and other information sources.
5. Obtain information on the financial capability of the other party for material uncollected balances, guarantees, or other obligations.

Equivalence Representations

No representations need be made in the financial statements that related-party transactions were consummated on terms equivalent to those that prevail in arm's-length transactions. If representations are made that state or imply that, FAS 57 requires that the entity be able to substantiate them. Thus, the auditor should consider whether there is sufficient support for such a representation, if made, and appropriately qualify his or her opinion if there is not such support.

NOTE: Lack of substantiation of representations made on equivalence of material related-party transactions should result in a qualified or adverse opinion because of a departure from GAAP.

AU INTERPRETATIONS

EXCHANGE OF INFORMATION BETWEEN THE PRINCIPAL AND OTHER AUDITOR ON RELATED PARTIES (APRIL 1979)

The principal auditor and the other auditor should, at an early stage in the audit, obtain from each other the names of known related parties.

Examination of Identified Related-Party Transactions with a Component (April 1979)

Audit procedures may have to be applied to a component audited by another auditor. When unusual or complex related-party transactions exist, the principal auditor may need access to the relevant portions of the other auditor's workpapers. Access ordinarily should be provided.

The Nature and Extent of Auditing Procedures for Examining Related-Party Transactions (May 1986)

The higher the auditor's assessment of risk regarding related-party transactions, the more extensive or effective the audit tests should be. To understand the business purpose or to obtain sufficient evidence about the transaction, the auditor may:

1. Refer to audited or unaudited financial statements of the related party
2. Apply procedures at the related party
3. Audit the financial statements of the related party

The auditor should consider obtaining representations from senior management and its board of directors about whether they or other related parties engaged in any transactions with the entity during the period.

Management's and Auditor's Responsibilities for Related-Party Disclosures Prefaced by Terminology Such as "Management Believes That" (May 2000; June 2009)

As discussed above under "Equivalence Representations," if management makes an assertion in financial statements about equivalency that is prefaced by "management believes that" or "it is the company's belief that," the auditor's responsibility is not changed. That is, the auditor must obtain evidence relating to the equivalency assertion, and management must still substantiate the asserted equivalence. If the auditor believes that the representation is unsubstantiated, depending on the materiality of the related-party transaction, the auditor should express either a qualified or adverse opinion because of a GAAP departure.

TECHNIQUES FOR APPLICATION

Preliminary Evaluation of Risk

A preliminary evaluation concerning the likelihood of related-party transactions is usually made during the planning of the audit when the risk assessment questionnaire is completed (see Section 311, *Planning and Supervision*). This evaluation includes:

1. Obtaining an understanding of the structure of the entity and management responsibilities.
2. Considering the business purpose of the various components of the entity.
3. Considering the control consciousness within the entity and controls over management activities.

Purpose of Auditing Procedures Designed Specifically for Related-Party Transactions

The purpose of auditing procedures designed specifically for related-party transactions is to determine the *existence* of related parties and to *identify* significant related-party transactions, including those not recognized in the accounting records.

If the auditor identifies significant related-party transactions, he or she should *examine* these transactions and *evaluate the adequacy* of their disclosure.

The auditor also is concerned with the adequacy of disclosure of economic dependence (see below).

Determining the Existence of Related Parties

The existence of some related parties, such as parent–subsidiary, investor–investee, and affiliates, is obvious. To determine the existence of other related parties, specific audit procedures are necessary. These procedures were described in "Fundamental Requirements" and are listed in the related-party checklist in the "AU Illustrations" section.

Identifying Related-Party Transactions

Related-party transactions and similar transactions that require disclosure may be classified as follows:

1. Those recognized in the accounting records
2. No-charge transactions
3. Those that create economic dependence

Related-Party Transactions Recognized in the Accounting Records

To identify these transactions, specific audit procedures are necessary. These procedures were described in "Fundamental Requirements" and are listed in the related-party checklist in "AU Illustrations."

No-Charge Transactions

Sometimes a related party provides services that are not given accounting recognition. Examples of these services are the following:

1. Accounting and managerial
2. Credit and collection
3. Professional

To identify no-charge transactions, the auditor should compare expenses with sales and

1. Investigate deviations from industry standards
2. Investigate deviations from prior year

These are essentially analytical procedures (see Section 329, *Analytical Procedures*).

Transactions That Create Economic Dependence

FAS ASC 850 does not address the issue of economic dependence. Related parties do not exist solely because one party is economically dependent on another. If one party exercises significant influence over the other, however, a related-party situation does exist and should be disclosed. In situations where economic dependence does not create related parties, disclosure may still be necessary to keep the financial statements from being misleading.

EXAMINING RELATED-PARTY TRANSACTIONS

When the auditor identifies related-party transactions, he or she should analyze them to determine the following:

1. The purpose of the transactions
2. The nature of the transactions
3. The extent of the transactions
4. The effect of the transactions on the financial statements

To determine the preceding, the auditor applies normal auditing procedures and also may have to apply extended auditing procedures.

MANAGEMENT REPRESENTATION LETTER

Much of the information about related parties is obtained through inquiry of management. The responses to these inquiries should be formalized in the management representation letter (see Section 333, *Management Representations*).

If no related-party transactions occurred, a statement to that effect should appear in the management representation letter. If related-party transactions occurred, the following should be noted:

1. Identification of the related parties
2. Identification of the transactions
3. The nature of the transactions
4. The amount of the transactions

The auditor should also consider obtaining written representations from the client's senior management and its board of directors about whether they or other related parties engaged in any transactions with the entity.

AU ILLUSTRATIONS

This section contains the following illustrations:

1. Paragraph in auditor's report calling attention to the existence of related parties
2. Notes to financial statements disclosing the existence of related parties
3. Related-party checklist

ILLUSTRATION 1. AUDITOR'S REPORT PARAGRAPH CALLING ATTENTION TO THE EXISTENCE OF RELATED PARTIES

This section does not require the auditor to note the existence of related-party transactions in the report. If the auditor decides to call the user's attention to related-party transactions, however, he or she may include a separate explanatory paragraph in the report. Following is a separate paragraph from an auditor's report on the audit of the combined financial statements of the leasing and financing subsidiaries of Pullman Incorporated:

> The leasing and financing subsidiaries engage in significant transactions with Pullman Incorporated as described in Note 2 of the notes to combined financial statements.

ILLUSTRATION 2. DISCLOSURE IN NOTES TO FINANCIAL STATEMENTS

Following are illustrations of the disclosure of related-party transactions in the notes to financial statements:

Related-Party Transactions

A Director of the Company is a principal in two companies that are distributors of the Company's products. Total sales to these related companies aggregated $86,000 in 20X2 and $91,000 in 20X1. At August 31, 20X2, these companies owed the company $35,983, of which $25,525 was owed beyond the Company's normal credit terms.

Related-Party Transactions

The Company occupies premises leased from two officer-shareholders for which $74,000 was paid in 20X2 and $27,000 was paid in 20X1. The lease agreement calls for minimum future payments of $86,000 in 20X3, $94,000 in 20X4, $101,000 in 20X5 and $114,000 in 20X6. The Company loaned $102,000 to these officer-shareholders to provide the down payment for their purchase of the property in 20X0. This loan was repaid during 20X1.

ILLUSTRATION 3. RELATED-PARTY CHECKLIST

Checklist
_____

Related Parties
_____

_____

[Client]

_____ _____ _____ _____
[Audit date]   [Date completed]   [Reviewed by]   [Date]

Instructions. This checklist is designed to assist the auditor in complying with the requirement that material related-party transactions be identified and evaluated for disclosure. If this checklist is not used, the audit program should include appropriate procedures for related-party transactions. This checklist does not apply to transactions that are eliminated in consolidation.

Many procedures performed for related-party transactions are normal auditing procedures executed during other phases of the audit. These procedures are indicated in this checklist by an asterisk (*).

Procedures for auditing related-party transactions involve the following:

1. Gaining an understanding of management's responsibilities, internal accounting controls related to management's activities, and the relationship of each component of the entity to the total business
2. Obtaining knowledge of related parties and planning and executing the audit so that material transactions—individually or in the aggregate—with related parties are identified and evaluated for disclosure

Part 1 of this checklist is concerned with the existence and identification of related parties and related-party transactions. Part 2 is concerned with the examination and evaluation of identified related-party transactions and the adequacy of disclosure of these transactions in the client's financial statements. Part 2 should *not* be done if Part 1 has been completed and it is concluded that no related-party transactions exist.

The "Inquiry of, W/P reference" column should provide the name and position of the client personnel queried and, where applicable, reference to the supporting audit documentation, including client permanent files. If a procedure is not applicable "N/A" should be placed in the "Inquiry of, W/P reference" column.

PART 1: EXISTENCE AND IDENTIFICATION

Procedure	Performed by	Inquiry of, W/P reference
*1. Review prior year's audit documentation for names of known related parties and related-party transactions.		
2. Evaluate client procedures for identifying, accounting for, and disclosing related-party transactions, including procedures established to monitor or avoid conflicts of interest in purchasing, contracting, or similar business activities.		
3. Review conflict-of-interest statements obtained by the entity from its management.		
4. For nonpublic entities, review stock certificate book or schedule of stockholders to identify principal stockholders.		
*5. Review material filed with the SEC, taxing authorities, and other regulatory bodies.		
6. Inquire about the names of related parties and whether there were transactions with them.		
7. Inquire about whether the client is under common ownership or management control with another entity.		
8. Obtain the names of all pension and profit-sharing trusts established for the benefit of employees, and the names of the officers and trustees and their trusts. (If the trusts are managed by or under the trusteeship of management, they are related parties.)		
*9. Inquire of predecessor auditor and principal auditor or other auditors of related entities about their knowledge of existing related parties and the extent of management involvement in material transactions.		
*10. Review the extent and nature of business transacted with major customers, suppliers, borrowers, and lenders for indications of previously undisclosed relationships.		
11. Inquire about transactions occurring but not being given accounting recognition, such as receiving or providing accounting, management, or other services at no charge, or a major stockholder absorbing corporate expenses.		
*12. Review confirmations or compensating balance arrangements for indications that balances are maintained for or by related parties.		
*13. Review confirmations of loans receivable and payable for indications of guarantees. If guarantees are indicated, determine their nature and the relationship of the guarantors to the client.		
*14. Review material investment transactions to determine if the nature and extent of the investments created related parties.		
*15. Review minutes of meetings of board of directors and executive committees or operations for discussions or authorization of material or unusual transactions.		
*16. Review large, unusual, or nonrecurring transactions, especially those recognized at or near the end of the period under audit. If appropriate, inquire whether the transactions involved a related party.		

AU Illustrations

Procedure	Performed by	Inquiry of, W/P reference
*17. Review invoices from law firms and other specialists for indications of related parties or related-party transactions.		
18. Prepare or update a carryforward schedule of related parties and information on known continuing related-party transactions. Provide copy of schedule to audit personnel and other auditors of related entities.		

PART 2: EXAMINATION AND EVALUATION

(To be filled out only if Part 1 indicates the existence of related-party transactions.)

Procedure	Performed by	Inquiry of, W/P reference
1. Obtain an understanding of the business purpose of the transactions. If necessary, consult with attorney or other specialist.		
2. Examine invoices, agreements, contracts, and other relevant documents, such as receiving reports and shipping documents.		
3. Determine that the transactions have been authorized by the appropriate party.		
4. Arrange for audits of intercompany account balances at the same date.		
5. Arrange for the examination of specific related-party transactions by auditors for each of the parties and for the exchange of relevant information.		
6. Inspect or confirm collateral received in connection with related-party transactions and obtain satisfaction regarding the value and transferability of the collateral.		
7. To understand fully a specific related-party transaction, consider doing the following:		
a. Confirm transaction amounts and terms, including guarantees and other significant data, with other parties to the transaction.		
b. Inspect evidence in the possession of other parties to the transaction.		
c. Confirm or discuss significant information with intermediaries, such as banks, guarantors, agents, or lawyers.		
d. Refer to financial publications, trade journals, credit agencies, and other sources if there is reason to believe that unfamiliar customers, suppliers, or other business enterprises with which material amounts of business have been transacted may lack substance.		
e. For material uncollected balances, guarantees, and other obligations, obtain information about the financial capability of other parties to the transaction.		
8. Recompute the compilation of amounts to be disclosed.		
9. Determine that the financial statements adequately disclose related-party transactions.		

AU 336 Using the Work of a Specialist

AU-C 620 Using the Work of an Auditor's Specialist

AU EFFECTIVE DATE AND APPLICABILITY

Original Pronouncement	Statement on Auditing Standards (SAS) 73.
Effective Date	This statement is now effective.
Applicability	Audits of financial statements in accordance with generally accepted auditing standards (GAAS).
	Applies to all audit engagements and to engagements performed under Section 623, *Special Reports*.
	Guidance in this section is applicable when

1. Management engages or employs a specialist and the auditor uses that specialist's work as evidential matter in performing substantive tests to evaluate material financial statement assertions.
2. Management engages a specialist employed by the auditor's firm to provide advisory services, and the auditor uses that specialist's work as evidential matter in performing substantive tests to evaluate material financial statement assertions.
3. The auditor engages a specialist, and uses that specialist's work as evidential matter in performing substantive tests to evaluate material financial statement assertions.

NOTE: *If a specialist employed by the auditor's firm participates in the audit, the specialist should be properly supervised in the same manner as others on the audit team. In this situation Section 311,* Planning and Supervision, *applies.*

AU-C EFFECTIVE DATE AND SUMMARY OF CHANGES

SAS No. 122, *Codification of Auditing Standards and Procedures,* is effective for audits of financial statements with periods ending on or after December 15, 2012.

AU-C 620 supersedes AU Section 336 and makes the following changes.

Because audit evidence produced by management's experts (internal or external) needs to be evaluated by the auditor for relevance and reliability like any other audit evidence, AU-C Section 500, *Audit Evidence,* now includes the requirements and guidance addressing the use of management's specialist. This does not change extant requirements.

AU Section 336 specifically scopes out from the standard use of specialists employed by the firm who participate in the audit. However, the clarified SAS *encompasses* in-firm specialists. This change in the scope of the standard will affect current practice, because it will create incremental documentation requirements.

AU DEFINITIONS OF TERMS

Specialist. A person (or firm) possessing special skill or knowledge in a particular field other than accounting or auditing. Specialists include, but are not limited to actuaries, appraisers, engineers, environmental consultants, and geologists.

AU-C DEFINITIONS OF TERMS

Source: AU-C 620.06

Auditor's specialist. An individual or organization possessing expertise in a field other than accounting or auditing, whose work in that field is used by the auditor to assist the auditor in obtaining sufficient appropriate audit evidence. An auditor's specialist may be either an auditor's internal specialist (who is a partner or staff, including temporary staff, of the auditor's firm or a network firm) or an auditor's external specialist.

Expertise. Skills, knowledge, and experience in a particular field.

Management's specialist. An individual or organization possessing expertise in a field other than accounting or auditing, whose work in that field is used by the entity to assist the entity in preparing the financial statements.

OBJECTIVES OF AU SECTION 336

This section provides a basis for more detailed guidance to be provided in industry audit guides on the use of particular types of specialists in various specialized industries. For example, audit guides related to insurance companies provide guidance on the use of the work of actuaries who determine loss reserves.

Section 336 takes the position that the auditor should obtain an understanding of the specialist's methods and assumptions but would ordinarily be able to use the work of the specialist unless the auditor believes the specialist's findings are unreasonable. In other words, the auditor does not have to substantiate the reasonableness of the specialist's findings but is expected to have done enough to recognize clearly unreasonable findings. It also prohibits reference to the specialist in the auditor's report unless the auditor is qualifying the opinion based at least in part on the specialist's findings.

This section clarifies the circumstances when the guidance concerning use of the work of a specialist would have to be applied. Essentially, the guidance applies when an auditor uses a specialist's work as evidential matter in performing substantive tests to evaluate material financial statement assertions. The applicability of the guidance is not influenced by who engaged the specialist. The section notes that an auditor may encounter complex or subjective matters potentially material to the financial statements that may require special skill or knowledge, and that in the auditor's judgment require using the work of a specialist to obtain competent evidential matter. In those cases, such as insurance loss reserves, in which a material financial statement amount or disclosure is developed by a specialist, use of the work of a specialist would be essential unless the audit team includes an auditor with the knowledge, training, and experience of such a specialist.

OBJECTIVES OF AU-C SECTION 620

AU-C 620 states that:

. . . the objectives of the auditor are

    a. to determine whether to use the work of an auditor's specialist and
    b. if using the work of an auditor's specialist, to determine whether that work is adequate for the auditor's purposes.

FUNDAMENTAL REQUIREMENTS

NOTE: Typically, the auditor will consider the need to use a specialist as part of forming an overall audit strategy.

QUALIFICATIONS OF A SPECIALIST

The auditor should consider the following to evaluate whether the specialist has the necessary qualifications:

1. Professional certification, license, or other recognition of competence
2. Reputation and standing in the view of peers and other knowledgeable parties
3. Experience in the kind of work under consideration

NOTE: For example, an actuary determining property and casualty loss reserves should have experience in the property and casualty insurance field.

WORK OF A SPECIALIST

The auditor should obtain an understanding of the nature of the specialist's work that covers the following:

1. Objectives and scope
2. Relationship to client
3. Methods or assumptions used
4. Comparison of item 3 with methods or assumptions used in preceding period
5. Appropriateness for intended purpose
6. Form and content of specialist's findings

NOTE: Sometimes it may be necessary to contact the specialist to ensure the specialist is aware of the auditor's intended use of the work.

RELATIONSHIP TO CLIENT

The auditor should evaluate whether the specialist's relationship to the client, if any, might impair the specialist's objectivity; if so, the auditor should perform additional procedures to determine whether the specialist's assumptions, methods, or findings are not unreasonable, or engage another specialist for that purpose.

USING FINDINGS

The auditor should perform procedures to:

1. Obtain an understanding of the methods and assumptions used
2. Test data (accounting and other data) provided to the specialist and, in considering the extent of testing, assess the control risk relevant to the data
3. Evaluate whether the findings support the related financial statement assertions
4. In the circumstance in which the auditor believes the findings are unreasonable, apply additional procedures

> NOTE: Additional procedures might include obtaining the opinion of another specialist.

EFFECT ON AUDIT REPORT

If there is a material difference between the specialist's findings and the assertions in the financial statements, the auditor should do the following:

1. If the matter cannot be resolved by applying additional audit procedures, obtain the opinion of another specialist, unless it appears that the matter cannot be resolved.
2. If the matter has not been resolved, qualify the opinion or disclaim an opinion because of the inability to obtain sufficient competent evidence.
3. If the auditor concludes the difference indicates the assertions are not in conformity with generally accepted accounting principles (GAAP), qualify the opinion or express an adverse opinion.

REPORT REFERENCE TO SPECIALIST

The auditor should not refer to the work or findings of, or identify the specialist in the audit report, unless the findings of the specialist cause the auditor to depart from an unqualified opinion or add explanatory language to the standard report.

> NOTE: If the auditor concludes there is a scope limitation or GAAP departure, the auditor would qualify the audit opinion. An explanatory paragraph should not be added for an uncertainty that is adequately presented and disclosed in accordance with GAAP.

AU INTERPRETATIONS

THE USE OF LEGAL INTERPRETATIONS AS EVIDENTIAL MATTER TO SUPPORT MANAGEMENT'S ASSERTION THAT A TRANSFER OF FINANCIAL ASSETS HAS MET THE ISOLATION CRITERION IN PARAGRAPH 9(A) OF FINANCIAL ACCOUNTING STANDARDS BOARD STATEMENT 140 (DECEMBER 2001); REVISED MARCH 2006, JUNE 2009, OCTOBER 2011; EFFECTIVE FOR AUDITS OF FINANCIAL STATEMENTS FOR PERIODS ENDING ON OR AFTER DECEMBER 15, 2012

Financial Accounting Standards Board (FASB) Accounting Standards Codification (ASC) 860, *Transfers and Servicing*, requires that a transferor of financial assets must surrender control over the financial assets to account for the transfer as a sale. Paragraph 9(a) states several conditions that must be met to provide evidence of surrender of control. One of these conditions is that the transferred assets must have been isolated from the transferor and its creditors. The determination of whether this isolation criterion has been met depends on facts and circumstances and should be assessed primarily from a legal perspective.

Decision to Use a Specialist

The auditor should first consider whether to use the work of a legal specialist to support management's assertion that the isolation criterion has been met. The specialist can be the client's internal or external attorney who is knowledgeable about applicable law. While the use of a legal specialist will not be necessary for routine transfers of assets, a legal specialist is necessary for transfers involving complex legal structures, continuing involvement by the transferor, or other legal issues.

If the auditor uses a legal opinion to support the accounting conclusion, the auditor may need, in certain circumstances, to obtain updates of the opinion to confirm that there have been no subsequent changes in relevant law or applicable regulations or in the pertinent facts of the transaction that would change the previous opinion. Updates may be necessary when:

- The legal opinion relates to multiple transfers under a single structure, and such transfers occur over an extended period of time under that structure.
- Management asserts that a new transaction has a structure that is the same as a prior structure for which a legal opinion that complies with this interpretation was used as evidence to support an assertion that the transfer of assets met the isolation criterion.

The auditor should also consider whether management needs to obtain period updates to confirm that there have been no subsequent changes in relevant law or applicable regulations that may affect the conclusions in the previous opinion in the case of other transfers.

Assessing the Adequacy of the Legal Opinion

In assessing the adequacy of the legal opinion, the auditor should:

- Consider whether the legal specialist has experience with relevant matters, including knowledge of the U.S. Bankruptcy Code and other federal, state, and foreign law.
- Consider whether the legal specialist has knowledge of the transaction on which management's assertion is based.
- For transactions that may be affected by provisions of the Federal Deposit Insurance Act, consider whether the legal specialist has experience with the rights and powers of receivers, conservators, and liquidating agents under that Act.
- Obtain an understanding of the assumptions used by the legal specialist and make appropriate tests of information.
- Consider the form and content of the document provided by the legal specialist.
- Evaluate whether the legal specialist's findings support management's assertions about the isolation criterion.

A legal opinion that includes any of the following would not be persuasive evidence that a transfer of assets has met the isolation criterion:

- An inadequate opinion, inappropriate opinion, or a disclaimer of opinion
- A limit on the scope of the opinion to facts and circumstances that are not applicable to the transaction
- Language that does not provide persuasive evidence, such as the following examples provided in the interpretation:
  - "We are unable to express an opinion . . ."
  - "It is our opinion, based upon limited facts . . ."

- "We are of the view . . ." or "it appears . . ."
- "There is a reasonable basis to conclude that . . ."
- "In our opinion, the transfer would be *either* a sale *or* a grant of a perfected security interest . . ."
- "In our opinion, there is a reasonable possibility . . ."
- "In our opinion, the transfer *should* be considered a sale . . ."
- "It is our opinion that the entity will be able to assert meritorious arguments . . ."
- "In our opinion, it is more likely than not . . ."
- "In our opinion, the transfer would *presumptively* be . . ."
- "In our opinion, it is probable that . . ."

- Conclusions about hypothetical transactions if they are not relevant to management's assertions or do not contemplate all the facts and circumstances of the transaction

If a legal specialist's response does not provide persuasive evidence that a transfer of assets has met the isolation criterion, and no other relevant evidential matter exists, derecognition of the transferred assets is not in conformity with GAAP, and the auditor should consider expressing a qualified or adverse opinion (see Section 508, *Reports on Audited Financial Statements*).

Restricted Use Legal Opinions

Legal opinions that restrict the use of the opinion to the client, or to third parties other than the auditor, would *not* be acceptable audit evidence. In this case, the auditor should ask the client to obtain the legal specialist's written permission for the auditor to use the opinion for the purpose of evaluating management's assertion that the isolation criterion has been met.

If the legal specialist does not grant permission for the auditor to use a legal opinion that is restricted to the client or to third parties other than the auditor, a scope limitation exists, and the auditor should consider qualifying or disclaiming an opinion (see Section 508).

The following example from the interpretation illustrates a letter from a legal specialist to a client that adequately communicates permission for the auditor to use the legal specialist's opinion for the purpose of evaluating management's assertion that a transfer of financial assets meets the isolation criterion of FAS ASC 860:

> Notwithstanding any language to the contrary in our opinions of even date with respect to certain bankruptcy issues relating to the above-referenced transaction, you are authorized to make available to your auditors such opinions solely as evidential matter in support of their evaluation of management's assertion that the transfer of the receivables meets the isolation criterion of ASC 860, provided a copy of this letter is furnished to them in connection therewith. In authorizing you to make copies of such opinions available to your auditors for such purpose, we are not undertaking or assuming any duty or obligation to your auditors or establishing any lawyer-client relationship with them. Further, we do not undertake or assume any responsibility with respect to financial statements of you or your affiliates.

The following would *not* adequately communicate permission for the auditor to use:

- "Use but not rely on" language in which a letter from a legal specialist authorizes the client to make copies available to the auditor but states that the auditor is not authorized to rely thereon
- Other language that similarly restricts the auditor's use of the legal specialist's opinion

The auditor may wish to consult with his or her legal counsel in circumstances where it is not clear that the auditor may use the legal specialist's opinion.

Finally, the interpretation provides:

- Two examples of the conclusions in a legal opinion for an entity that is subject to receivership or conservatorship under provisions of the Federal Deposit Insurance Act. The conclusions in the examples provide persuasive evidence, in the absence of contradictory evidence, to support management's assertion that the transferred financial assets have been put presumptively beyond the reach of the entity and its creditors, even in conservatorship or receivership.
- Examples of additional paragraphs addressing substantive consolidation that applies when the entity to which the assets are sold or transferred is an affiliate of the selling entity. These paragraphs may also apply in other situations as noted by the legal specialist.

TECHNIQUES FOR APPLICATION

EXAMPLES OF USE OF A SPECIALIST

The following are examples of common uses of specialists:

1. Determination of postemployment and postretirement benefit-related amounts by an actuary
2. Determination of environmental cleanup obligations by an environmental consultant
3. Determination of oil and gas reserves by a petroleum engineer
4. Determination of the valuation of a financial institution's real estate investments or real estate collateral by an appraiser
5. Determination of loss reserves of an insurance company by an actuary

The auditor is not required to use a specialist automatically whenever the client has engaged a specialist. The distinction between the circumstances that require use and other circumstances involving use of real estate appraisers discussed by the Auditing Standards Board provides an instructive example. The key is the relation of the specialist's work to the financial statement assertions. A financial institution normally obtains a real estate appraisal for loans collateralized by real estate as part of the loan origination process. In testing controls over the loan origination process, the auditor normally would inspect the appraisal to see that it conformed with the institution's policies and procedures. This is not use of a specialist's work that requires application of the guidance in Section 336. This is a test of controls, not a substantive test, and the specialist's work is not being used to evaluate a material financial statement assertion.

In contrast, in the evaluation of the need for a reserve on a problem loan, the auditor might inspect an appraisal to consider whether the collateral value is below the loan amount. This is a substantive test involving the valuation assertion, and loss reserves are usually material to a financial institution's financial statements. Application of the guidance in Section 336 is required.

USE OF A LAWYER AS A SPECIALIST

Section 336 applies to attorneys engaged as specialists in situations other than to provide services to a client concerning litigation, claims, or assessments. Section 337, *Inquiry of a Client's Lawyer Concerning Litigation, Claims, and Assessments*, applies to an attorney's response to audit inquiries concerning litigation, claims, and assessments. Section 336 applies to other use of an attorney's work, such as interpreting the provisions of a contractual agreement.

An auditor, however, cannot use an attorney's work to evaluate material assertions related to income tax matters. Generally, the auditor's education, training, and experience enable him or her to be competent to assess the presentation of income tax matters in financial statements.

DOCUMENTATION OF THE UNDERSTANDING OF THE WORK TO BE PERFORMED BY THE SPECIALIST

Section 336 indicates that in *some* cases, the auditor may decide it is necessary to contact the specialist to determine that the specialist is aware that his or her work will be used for evaluating the assertions in the financial statements.

Frequently, the nature and purpose of the specialist's work is clearly understood within the industry, such as the use of a petroleum engineer to determine oil and gas reserves by an oil and gas producer. In some cases, such as for a real estate appraiser, the specialist's report routinely documents the specialist's qualifications and purpose of the engagement.

Thus, the auditor has considerable discretion in deciding whether it is necessary to contact the specialist and in documenting the understanding with the specialist.

For those circumstances in which documentation is appropriate, the "AU Illustrations" section provides an engagement letter form.

SPECIALIST RELATED TO CLIENT

Section 336 clearly indicates that the purpose of considering the specialist's relationship is to evaluate whether there are circumstances that might impair the specialist's objectivity. If the client has the ability to directly or indirectly control or significantly influence the specialist, objectivity might be impaired. The influence might arise from employment, ownership, contractual right, family relationship, or otherwise.

A specialist without a relationship to the client is more likely to be objective, and that specialist's work will provide the auditor with greater assurance of reliability.

If the specialist has a relationship with the client, the auditor should assess the risk that the specialist's objectivity might be impaired. If the auditor believes the relationship might impair the specialist's objectivity, the auditor should perform additional procedures.

The additional procedures involve heightened scrutiny of the specialist's assumptions, methods, or findings to determine that the findings are not unreasonable. The auditor might decide another specialist should be engaged for this purpose.

The "Illustrations" section contains a form that can be used to document information concerning the relationship of the specialist to the client.

SPECIALIST EMPLOYED BY CPA FIRM

Some CPA firms have employed specialists to provide consulting services to clients. For example, some CPA firms employ actuaries, real estate appraisers, or environmental specialists.

If the client has engaged a specialist employed by the CPA firm to determine an amount or disclosure that is material to the financial statements, the guidance in Section 336 applies to the auditor's use of that specialist's work. This means the auditor has to apply the same procedures that Section 336 would require to be applied to the work of a specialist unrelated to the CPA firm. For example, the auditor would have to obtain an understanding of the methods and assumptions used by the specialist and evaluate whether the specialist's findings support the related assertions in the financial statements.

In some cases, the auditor might decide to engage a specialist. For example, a specialist might be engaged by the auditor to apply additional procedures when the client uses a related specialist. In these circumstances, a specialist employed by the CPA firm might be used. In this case, the specialist is functioning as a member of the audit team. The auditor would need to provide proper supervision of that specialist in the same manner as any other member of the audit team. On the other hand, if the auditor engages a specialist not employed by the CPA firm, then the guidance in Section 336 applies. When the CPA firm uses a firm specialist as a member of the audit team, the specialist is an assistant on the audit with all that such status implies. The specialist has to adhere to GAAS and be properly supervised. Extra supervision is required when the specialist is not knowledgeable about GAAP, GAAS, and the Code of Professional Conduct.

TESTS OF DATA USED BY THE SPECIALIST

In many cases, the client has to provide data to the specialist. For example, the management of an insurance company would provide data on insurance in force to an actuary engaged to determine loss reserves, and a financial institution might provide a real estate appraiser with income statements of a project that collateralizes a loan.

Section 336 indicates that the auditor should make appropriate tests of data provided to the specialist. In other words, the data to be tested is not limited to accounting data.

In deciding the extent of testing of data that is necessary, the auditor should consider the control risk associated with production of the data. Section 336 does not mention inherent risk. Thus, the implication is that the auditor would need to substantiate data provided to the specialist unless the data is produced by a system with a relatively low control risk. Also, the extent of testing considered necessary would depend on the nature and materiality of the related financial statement assertion.

NEED TO REFER TO AUDIT GUIDES OR STATEMENTS OF POSITION (SOPs)

If there is more specific guidance on the use of a specialist in an audit guide or Statement of Position (SOP), the auditor should refer to the more detailed guidance. An audit guide or SOP cannot reduce the procedures needed when a specialist's work is used. However, the guidance might specify additional procedures or limit the auditor's discretion in determining the scope of procedures. For example, SOP 92-4, *Auditing Insurance Entities' Loss Reserves*, provides that an outside loss reserve specialist—that is, one who is not an officer or employee of the insurance company—should be used. When the auditor has the necessary knowledge and experience, the auditor may serve as the loss reserve specialist.

An AICPA audit guide or SOP might also provide informative guidance on the methods and assumptions of a specialist that is useful in evaluating whether a specialist's findings support financial statement assertions. For example, there is an AICPA guide on real estate appraisals that describes the various methods used by an appraiser. Some methods might produce a value that is not suitable for supporting financial statement assertions in certain circumstances. For example, the market value determined by an appraiser based on stabilized net operating income might not be appropriate when the real estate's fair value is the appropriate measure.

AU ILLUSTRATIONS

The following are illustrations of:

1. An engagement letter from a client to a specialist
2. An independence letter for a specialist

ILLUSTRATION 1. ENGAGEMENT LETTER FROM CLIENT TO SPECIALIST

[*Client's letterhead*]

[*Addressed to specialist's firm*]

This letter confirms our understanding for the services you provide as an independent specialist in connection with the audit of the financial statements of [name of client] for the year ended [date]. If you agree to this understanding, please sign one copy of this letter and return it to us.

Our understanding is as follows:

1. You understand that the results of your work will be used by our auditors, [*name of auditors*], as corroborating evidence in connection with their audit of the aforementioned financial statements for the purpose of expressing an opinion on whether the statements are presented fairly in all material respects in conformity with accounting principles generally accepted in the United States of America.
2. The objectives of your work are as follows:

    [*List objectives, such as determining fair market value of inventory, fair value of stock in a closely held corporation, pension expense, and pension liability, etc.*]

3. The scope of your work is as follows:

    [*List procedures that it is anticipated the specialist will apply. In this list, indicate that scope is in no way restricted.*]

4. The methods and assumptions you will use will cover the following areas:

    [*List methods and assumptions such as the following: estimated rate of return and estimated life expectancy of employees for pension expense and pension liability, estimated rate of return and estimated cash flows for valuation of stock in a closely held corporation, etc.*]

5. Your report will be submitted directly to us with a copy to our auditors no later than [*date*]. Your report will include the following:

    a. Scope of work
    b. Methods used and statement of consistency of the methods used with those used in the prior year
    c. Assumptions used
    d. Results, in detail, of your work
    e. Your opinion on the information that will appear in our financial statements and accompanying notes

6. You are independent with respect to us and our management. Principals, officers, owners of your firm and members of their immediate families, and members of your staff in the office working on this engagement are not in any way—nor have you been in any way—associated with us and our management except in your capacity as an outside specialist.

[*This paragraph would be modified if there is a relationship between the specialist and the client.*]

7. Fees for your services will be at your usual per diem rate of [*amount*].

Very truly yours,

_____
[*Client's name*]

_____
[*Signature and title*]

Agreed to:

_____
[*Name and title of specialist*]   [*Date*]

ILLUSTRATION 2. STATEMENT OF SPECIALIST'S INDEPENDENCE

[*Client's letterhead*]

[*Addressed to specialist firm*]

In connection with their audit of our financial statements for the year ended [date], please describe directly to our auditors, [name of firm], the nature and extent of any relationship noted below that you have with the Entity, exclusive of your engagement as [type of work, i.e., actuary, appraiser, etc.]. A stamped, self-addressed envelope is enclosed for your convenience.

Very truly yours,

_____
[*Client's name*]

By _____

_____
[*Title*]

Specialist Representation:

Except as noted below, the principals, officers, owners of our firm and members of their immediate families, and members of our staff in the office doing the work described above are not associated with [name of client], as follows:

1. By direct or indirect financial interest
2. As an officer, employee, or member of the board of directors
3. In any capacity, other than our normal business relationship, where we have a vested interest in the success of the Entity

Exceptions: _____
_____
_____
_____

_____   _____   _____   _____
[*Date*]   [*Firm*]   [*Signature*]   [*Title*]

AU 337 Inquiry of a Client's Lawyer Concerning Litigation, Claims, and Assessments

AU-C 501 Audit Evidence—Specific Considerations for Selected Items

AU EFFECTIVE DATE AND APPLICABILITY

Original Pronouncement	Statement on Auditing Standards (SAS) 12.
Effective Date	This standard is now effective.
Applicability	Audits of financial statements in accordance with generally accepted auditing standards (GAAS).

AU-C EFFECTIVE DATE AND SUMMARY OF CHANGES

SAS No. 122, *Codification of Auditing Standards and Procedures,* is effective for audits of financial statements with periods ending on or after December 15, 2012.

AU-C 501 combines the requirements and guidance from extant AU Section 331, *Inventories;* 332, *Auditing Derivative Instruments, Hedging Activities and Investments in Securities*; and 337, *Inquiry of a Client's Lawyer Concerning Litigation, Claims, and Assessments.*

AU 337.06 states, in part, "the auditor should request the client's management to send a letter of inquiry to those lawyers with whom management consulted concerning litigation, claims, and assessments." AU-C 501 takes a more principle-based approach. AU-C 501.18 requires the auditor to seek direct communication with the entity's external legal counsel (through a letter of inquiry) if the auditor assesses a risk of material misstatement regarding litigation or claims, or when audit procedures performed indicate that material litigation or claims may exist.

AU-C Section 501 supersedes *Appendix—Illustrative Inquiry Letter to Legal Counsel* and *Exhibit II—American Bar Association Statement of Policy Regarding Lawyers' Responses to Auditors' Request for Information* and rescinds *Exhibit I—Excerpts from Financial Accounting Standards Board Accounting Standards Codification 450, Contingencies.*

AU DEFINITIONS OF TERMS

The section itself has no general definitions, but it uses terms that have been defined by the Financial Accounting Standards Board (FASB) and the American Bar Association (ABA). SFAS 5, *Accounting for Contingencies*, paragraphs 1 and 3 define the following terms used in the section.

Loss contingency. An existing condition, situation, or set of circumstances involving uncertainty as to possible loss to an enterprise that will ultimately be resolved when one or more future events occur or fail to occur. (The likelihood that the future event will confirm the loss or impairment of an asset or the incurrence of a liability can range from probable to remote.)

Probable. The future event is *likely* to occur.

Reasonably possible. The chance of the future event occurring is more than remote but less than likely.

Remote. The chance of the future event occurring is slight.

The ABA has defined the following terms used in the section:

Threatened litigation. A potential claimant has manifested to the client an awareness of, and present intention to assert, a possible claim or assessment.

Unasserted claim or assessment. No claimant has manifested an awareness or intention to assert a claim or assessment, but it is probable a claim will be asserted, and there is a reasonable possibility the outcome will be unfavorable.

AU-C DEFINITIONS OF TERMS

AU-C 501 has no definitions of terms.

OBJECTIVES OF AU SECTION 337

Before Section 337 was issued, auditors generally viewed lawyers as the primary source of evidence on litigation, claims, and assessments. For many years, auditors thought they were able to obtain all the information they needed. About two years before the section was issued (1976), however, there was a growing movement among lawyers that threatened to halt the flow of information from lawyers to auditors. Also, preliminary discussions between the ABA and the AICPA indicated that lawyers' responses to inquiries from auditors were far more limited than they appeared on the surface.

Section 337 and the ABA Statement of Policy provide for an exchange of information within a framework that should be understandable and acceptable to lawyers and auditors. Nevertheless, care is necessary in phrasing audit inquiry letters and evaluating responses to ensure that sufficient information is obtained. Suggestions for achieving that are made in "Techniques for Application."

Section 337 is the result of a cooperative effort between the AICPA and the ABA to prescribe procedures to be followed by auditors and lawyers in discharging their separate professional responsibilities. The procedures developed for pending or threatened litigation differ from those applicable to unasserted claims. A lawyer will, with the client's consent, confirm the completeness of a list of pending or threatened litigation and furnish information on that litigation.

For unasserted claims, the procedures are more complex and less conclusive. Essentially, a lawyer will confirm that he or she has advised the client of unasserted claims that have come to his or her attention that the client should consider disclosing. The auditor then informs the lawyer of unasserted claims the client has brought to the auditor's attention. Presumably, if this exchange makes the lawyer aware that the client is concealing information from the auditor, the lawyer will persuade the client to furnish the information and, failing that, resign from the engagement. The lawyer will not explicitly confirm the completeness of the list of unasserted claims, however, or furnish information on them directly to the auditor. This complex process was agreed to by the AICPA and the ABA to preserve the attorney–client privilege and yet make it possible for the auditor to assess the adequacy of disclosure in financial statements.

Lawyers also agreed to evaluate the chance of an unfavorable outcome and to provide an estimate, if one can be made, of the amount or range of potential loss. The ABA Statement of Policy imposes significant constraints, however, on the circumstances when an evaluation or estimate is appropriate.

OBJECTIVES OF AU-C SECTION 501

AU-C Section 501 states that:

the objective of the auditor is to obtain sufficient appropriate audit evidence regarding the

a. *valuation of investments in securities and derivative instruments;*
b. *existence and condition of inventory;*
c. *completeness of litigation, claims, and assessments involving the entity; and*
d. *presentation and disclosure of segment information, in accordance with the applicable financial reporting framework.*

FUNDAMENTAL REQUIREMENTS

This section establishes requirements in four areas:

1. Accounting considerations
2. Audit procedures other than inquiry of lawyers
3. Inquiry of the client's lawyer and related considerations
4. Evaluation of the lawyer's response

ACCOUNTING CONSIDERATIONS

The relevant accounting standards are found in FASB Accounting Standards Codification (ASC) 450, *Contingencies*.

1. Accrual of a loss is required if:

   a. The amount can be reasonably estimated, and
   b. At the date of the financial statements, it is *probable* that an asset has been impaired or a liability incurred. (That is, it is probable that a future event will occur confirming the loss.)

2. Disclosure of a loss contingency is required if:

   a. No accrual is made because either the amount cannot be estimated or it was not probable that an asset was impaired or a liability incurred at the financial statement date or there is exposure to loss in excess of an accrual.

b. There is at least a reasonable possibility that a loss or an additional loss may have been incurred.
3. Disclosure should be made of:
   a. The nature of the contingency
   b. The possible loss or range of loss or a statement that an estimate cannot be made
4. Disclosure of the nature of an accrual, and sometimes the amount accrued, should be made if it is necessary for the financial statements not to be misleading.
5. Disclosure of an unasserted claim or assessment is required if:
   a. It is probable that a claim will be asserted
   b. There is at least a reasonable possibility that the outcome will be unfavorable
6. In evaluating whether accrual or disclosure is required of pending or threatened litigation or possible claims or assessments, the following factors must be considered:
   a. The period in which the cause for legal action occurred (the date of the underlying cause of action rather than the date of a lawsuit or claim affects whether accrual is appropriate)
   b. The likelihood of an unfavorable outcome
   c. The ability to estimate the loss

   NOTE: *These same factors are the focus of the auditor's procedures.*

7. In evaluating the likelihood of an unfavorable outcome, the following factors must be considered:
   a. The nature of the litigation, claim, or assessment
   b. The progress of the case up to the date the financial statements are issued
   c. The opinions of legal counsel and other advisers
   d. The experience of the entity or other entities in similar cases
   e. Any decision of management on how the entity intends to respond

   NOTE: *The same factors are the focus of the auditor's inquiry of the client's lawyer.*

AUDIT PROCEDURES OTHER THAN INQUIRY OF LAWYERS

Several customary audit procedures other than inquiry of the client's lawyer are required:

1. Inquire of, and discuss with, the client's management its procedures for identifying, evaluating, and accounting for litigation, claims, and assessments.
2. Examine documents held by the client, such as correspondence and invoices from lawyers.

   NOTE: *This does not include documents subject to the lawyer–client privilege.*

3. Read minutes of meetings of stockholders, board of directors, and related client committees.
4. Read contracts, loan agreements, leases, and correspondence from taxing or other government agencies.

5. Obtain information from banks concerning loan agreements.
6. Inspect other documents for possible guarantees made by the client.

INQUIRY OF CLIENT'S LAWYER

The primary audit procedures for litigation, claims, and assessments are a combination of inquiries of the client's management and lawyers. The auditor should:

1. Ask the client's management to send letters of inquiry to those lawyers consulted on litigation, claims, and assessments.
2. Obtain written assurances from management that:
   a. It has disclosed all matters required to be disclosed by FASB ASC 450.
   b. It has disclosed all unasserted claims that the lawyer has advised are probable of assertion and must be disclosed under ASC 450.

   NOTE: These two assurances obviously overlap, but the separate assurance is required for unasserted claims because of the different treatment accorded them to preserve the lawyer-client privilege. These assurances may be included in the management representation letter (see Section 333, Management Representations*).*

3. Inform the lawyer, with the client's permission, that the client has given the assurance concerning unasserted claims.

   NOTE: Usually this is covered in the inquiry letter.

Content of Inquiry to Lawyer

According to AU 337.09, the inquiry letter to the lawyer should cover the following matters:

1. Identification of the client, the financial statements under audit, and the date of the audit.
2. A list that describes and evaluates pending or threatened litigation, claims, and assessments. For each matter on the list, the lawyer should be asked to furnish:
   a. A description of the nature of the matter
   b. The progress of the case to date
   c. The action the entity intends to take
   d. An evaluation of the likelihood of an unfavorable outcome and an estimate, if possible, of the amount or range of possible loss
   e. An identification of any omissions or a statement that the list of matters is complete

   NOTE: The list may be prepared by management or by the lawyer. Under either approach, management normally consults with the lawyer on the response to the auditor.

3. A list that describes and evaluates unasserted claims (that are probable of assertion and reasonably possible of having an unfavorable outcome) prepared by management.
4. A statement on the client's understanding of the lawyer's professional responsibility concerning unasserted claims.
5. A request that the lawyer confirm the understanding stated in item 4.

6. A request that the lawyer specifically identify the nature of and reasons for any limitation on his or her response.
7. The date by which the lawyer's response should be sent to the auditor.
8. A request that the lawyer specify the latest date covered by his or her review (the effective date).

Oral Response

In special circumstances, representations may be made orally by the lawyer. For example, evaluation of the effect of legal advice on unsettled points of law might be covered in a conference among auditor, client, and lawyer. The auditor should document significant conclusions reached on accounting matters in such a conference in the audit workpapers.

Client Changes Lawyer or Lawyer Resigns

Because the special treatment accorded unasserted claims rests on the lawyer's professional responsibility, the auditor should consider the need to make inquiries concerning why the lawyer is no longer associated with the client.

EVALUATION OF LAWYER'S RESPONSE

In evaluating the lawyer's response, the auditor needs to be aware that some limitations on responses may affect his or her opinion. Others have no effect.

Limitations with No Effect

A lawyer may appropriately limit his or her response in the following ways:

1. To matters to which he or she has given substantive attention in the form of legal consultation or representation

    NOTE: This means essentially that the lawyer does not do a legal audit. He or she does not undertake to evaluate all legal exposures or reconsider earlier conclusions.

2. To matters that are considered individually or collectively material, provided the lawyer and auditor have agreed on the amounts to be used

Limitations with Effect

A limitation such as the following may preclude an unqualified opinion:

1. *Scope.* If a lawyer refuses to furnish information requested in the ordinary inquiry letter, it is a limitation on the scope of the audit that results in a qualified or disclaimed opinion.
2. *Uncertainty.* If a lawyer is unable to evaluate the likelihood of an unfavorable outcome or estimate the amount or range of potential loss, it is an uncertainty. The guidance in Section 508, *Reports on Audited Financial Statements*, should be followed, which may result in the auditor qualifying or disclaiming an opinion because of the scope limitation.

INTERPRETATIONS

SPECIFYING RELEVANT DATE IN AN AUDIT INQUIRY LETTER (MARCH 1977)

The audit inquiry letter should specify the effective date of the lawyer's response and the latest date that the response should be mailed. Ordinarily, a two-week period should be allowed between the effective date and the mail date. If the lawyer's response does not specify an effective date, the auditor can assume that the date of the response is the effective date.

RELATIONSHIP BETWEEN DATE OF LAWYER'S RESPONSE AND AUDITOR'S REPORT (MARCH 1977; REVISED DECEMBER 2005)

The effective date of the lawyer's response should be specified to reasonably approximate the expected date of the auditor's report as is practicable in the circumstances.

FORM OF AUDIT INQUIRY LETTER WHEN CLIENT REPRESENTS THAT NO UNASSERTED CLAIMS AND ASSESSMENTS EXIST (MARCH 1977; REVISED JUNE 2009)

When clients have stated that no unasserted claims exist, that portion of the inquiry letter may be worded as follows:

> Unasserted Claims and Assessments—we have represented to our auditors that there are no unasserted possible claims that you have advised us are probable of assertion and must be disclosed, in accordance with FASB ASC 450, *Contingencies*.

DOCUMENTS SUBJECT TO LAWYER–CLIENT PRIVILEGE (MARCH 1977)

An inability to review documents or correspondence that are subject to lawyer–client privilege is not a scope limitation. The auditor may want to confirm with the lawyer that such information is subject to privilege and was considered by the lawyer in his or her response to the inquiry letter.

ALTERNATIVE WORDING OF THE ILLUSTRATIVE AUDIT INQUIRY LETTER TO A CLIENT'S LAWYER (JUNE 1983; REVISED JUNE 2009)

This interpretation recognizes the acceptability of the alternative inquiry letter that is presented in the "AU Illustrations" section. The letter presented in "Illustrations" has been adapted from the interpretation.

CLIENT HAS NOT CONSULTED A LAWYER (JUNE 1983; REVISED MARCH 2006; REVISED JUNE 2009)

If the client has not consulted a lawyer, the auditor normally relies on a review of internally available evidence and management representations regarding litigation, claims, and assessments. "AU Illustrations" contains a suitable management representation in this situation.

If the auditor becomes aware of potentially material litigation, claims, and assessments, the auditor should discuss with the client its need for legal counsel in order to determine loss contingencies; refusal by the client to do so may result in a scope limitation.

Assessment of a Lawyer's Evaluation of the Outcome of Litigation (Issued June 1983; Revised February 1997; Revised June 2009)

Written responses from lawyers may contain wording that is vague or ambiguous and may be of limited use to auditors. Lawyers are not required to use terms such as "probable" or "remote" in their evaluations. Other wording may be acceptable if the response can be classified according to the three probability classifications in FASB ASC 450, *Contingencies* (probable, reasonably possible, and remote).

Some examples of acceptable language, even through "remote" is not used, are as follows:

- "We are of the opinion that this action will not result in any liability to the company."
- "It is our opinion that the possible liability to the company in this proceeding is nominal in amount."
- "We believe the company will be able to defend this action successfully."
- "We believe that the plaintiff's case against the company is without merit."
- "Based on the facts known to us, after a full investigation, it is our opinion that no liability will be established against the company in these suits."

The following are examples of unacceptable lawyers' evaluations since they are unclear as to the likelihood of an unfavorable outcome.

- "This action involves unique characteristics wherein authoritative legal precedents do not seem to exist. We believe that the plaintiff will have serious problems establishing the company's liability under the act; nevertheless, if the plaintiff is successful, the award may be substantial."
- "It is our opinion that the company will be able to assert meritorious defenses to this action." (The term "meritorious defenses" indicates that the company's defenses will not be summarily dismissed by the court; it does not necessarily indicate counsel's opinion that the company will prevail.)
- "We believe the action can be settled for less than the damages claimed."
- "We are unable to express an opinion as to the merits of the litigation at this time. The company believes there is absolutely no merit to the litigation." (If client's counsel, with the benefit of all relevant information, is unable to conclude that the likelihood of an unfavorable outcome is "remote," it is unlikely that management would be able to form a judgment to that effect.)
- "In our opinion, the company has a substantial chance of prevailing in this action." (A "substantial chance," a "reasonable opportunity," and similar terms indicate more uncertainty than an opinion that the company will prevail.)

If the auditor is uncertain about the lawyer's evaluation, he or she should clarify the communication via a follow-up letter or conference.

Use of the Client's Inside Counsel in the Evaluation of Litigation, Claims, and Assessments (June 1983; Revised March 2006)

Audit inquiry letters should be sent to those lawyers who have the primary responsibility for, and knowledge about, particular litigation, claims, and assessments. Such lawyers may be inside counsel or outside lawyers. If inside counsel has the primary responsibility, their response ordinarily would be considered adequate. However, there may be circumstances when outside lawyers have significant involvement in the matter. In these situations, the opinion of inside counsel should be confirmed by the outside lawyers. If differences exist, the auditor should discuss the matter with the parties involved to resolve the conflict in views. Failure to reach agreement between the lawyers may require the auditor to consider appropriate modification of the audit report. (See "Reliance on House or Inside Counsel" in "Techniques for Application.")

USE OF EXPLANATORY LANGUAGE ABOUT THE ATTORNEY–CLIENT PRIVILEGE OR THE ATTORNEY WORK–PRODUCT PRIVILEGE (FEBRUARY 1990)

In some cases, to emphasize the attorney–client privilege or the attorney work–product privilege, some clients and attorneys in the audit inquiry letter and in the attorney's response letter include explanatory language indicating that the privileges are not waived. This explanatory language does not result in a limitation of the scope of the audit. Such explanatory language simply makes explicit what has been implicit; therefore, inclusion or noninclusion of the language does not change the attorney–client or work–product privileges.

USE OF EXPLANATORY LANGUAGE CONCERNING UNASSERTED POSSIBLE CLAIMS OR ASSESSMENTS IN LAWYER'S RESPONSES TO AUDIT INQUIRY LETTERS (JANUARY 1997; REVISED JUNE 2009)

To emphasize the preservation of attorney–client privilege for unasserted claims, some lawyers include additional comments in their response letters stating that it would be inappropriate to respond to a general inquiry about unasserted claims. The explanation continues to state that they cannot comment on the adequacy of the entity's listing of unasserted claims, if any. The inclusion of this kind of explanatory information is not a limitation on the scope of the audit.

TECHNIQUES FOR APPLICATION

Until litigation, claims, and assessments are finally settled, they might not enter the flow of data to the client's accounting records. Therefore, they might be difficult to identify.

This section provides the auditor with guidance on procedures he or she should consider for identifying litigation, claims, and assessments when performing an audit in accordance with generally accepted auditing standards. In practice, questions often arise about applying this section in the following areas:

1. Ensuring adequate description of case
2. Client without a lawyer
3. Effective date of lawyer's response
4. Evaluating lawyer's opinion
5. Lawyers on board of directors
6. Litigation not investigated by lawyers
7. Litigation with insurance companies
8. Reliance on house or inside counsel
9. Refusal of attorney to respond
10. Resignation of attorney
11. Review of interim financial information
12. Alternative form letter of inquiry

ENSURING ADEQUATE DESCRIPTION OF CASE

There are two types of lawyer's letters, either of which the client may send.

1. The form illustrated in Section 337 in which the client lists the pending and threatened litigation.
2. An alternative or short form in which the client requests the lawyer to list the pending and threatened litigation.

Both types of letters are included in "AU Illustrations."

When the client sends the short-form letter to its lawyer, the lawyer may not provide a sufficiently detailed description of the pending or threatened litigation in his or her response. To avoid this type of inadequate response, the client should request the lawyer to list for each pending or threatened litigation the following:

1. The nature of the litigation
2. Identification of the proceedings
3. Description of the asserted claim
4. The amount of monetary or other damages sought
5. Statement as to whether the potential damages are covered by insurance and the extent to which they are covered
6. The progress of the case
7. Entity's response or intended response to the litigation

CLIENT WITHOUT A LAWYER

As discussed in "Interpretations," a client not having a lawyer should not present unusual audit problems. Inquiry of a client's lawyer is a procedure applied by the auditor to identify pending or threatened litigation. Other procedures described in this section are the following:

1. Inquires of management
2. Discussions with management
3. Examination of relevant documents

These procedures were described earlier in "Fundamental Requirements." The auditor may conclude that the client has no litigation, claims, or assessments that require disclosure or these procedures may identify such matters.

Client Assertions

When the client does not retain an attorney, it ordinarily will state that there are no asserted or unasserted litigation, claims, and assessments. In these circumstances, the client should include these assertions on absence of litigation and lack of an attorney in the client representation letter (see "AU Illustrations").

Auditor Discovery of Claims

In the application of other procedures, the auditor may discover the following:

1. A material asserted claim
2. A situation in which a material unasserted claim exists

In these circumstances, the auditor should recommend that the client seek legal advice. If the client does not accept this recommendation, the auditor should consider it a scope limitation and may need to modify his or her report.

EFFECTIVE DATE OF LAWYER'S RESPONSE

If the effective date of the lawyer's response is the balance sheet date or a date not close enough to the date the fieldwork is completed, the auditor will have to initiate a second inquiry to the lawyer. This second inquiry may be either another letter to the lawyer or a telephone call from the auditor to the lawyer. Responses to a telephone call should be documented.

EVALUATING LAWYER'S OPINION

The auditor does not have the expertise of a lawyer. Therefore, he or she requires the opinion of a lawyer on legal matters relating to the client. It is the lawyer's opinion on litigation, claims, and assessments that helps the auditor reach a conclusion on the appropriateness of accounting for, and disclosure of, litigation and other contingent liabilities. However, the lawyer's opinion on a legal matter might not be clear and, thus, not acceptable for the auditor's purposes. Examples of such responses are presented in "Interpretations."

Unacceptable Attorney Response

If the auditor receives a response from a client attorney that is not helpful in evaluating the litigation for accounting purposes, he or she should review the matter with the attorney and the client. The purpose of this review is to obtain a more complete and acceptable response from the attorney.

The auditor may not be able to obtain a satisfactory response from the client's attorney and may not be able to obtain sufficient other corroborating evidence to support management's evaluation of the litigation. In these circumstances, the auditor has a scope limitation that may require a qualified or disclaimed opinion.

Avoidance of Unacceptable Attorney Response

To avoid unacceptable attorney responses, the letter of inquiry should specifically request that the evaluation of the litigation reflect the attorney's opinion. Also, the attorney should be requested to specify litigation for which he or she can express no opinion on a probable outcome or a range of potential loss. The attorney should be requested to state reasons for this type of response.

LAWYERS ON BOARD OF DIRECTORS

In response to the client's letter of inquiry, the lawyer is not required to include information he or she received as a director or officer of the client unless he or she also received the information in the capacity of attorney for the client.

A reply that excludes information the attorney obtained solely as a member of the board of directors or as an officer of the client is acceptable. The letter of inquiry should request that the attorney indicate if he or she is excluding such information. If the attorney indicates that he or she is excluding this information, the auditor may wish to obtain specific written representations from the attorney concerning the information.

LITIGATION NOT INVESTIGATED BY THE LAWYER

A lawyer's response is limited to those matters to which he or she has given substantive attention. If a lawyer is not able to investigate a matter adequately and render a satisfactory opinion regarding material litigation, the auditor generally should attempt to arrange a meeting with the client's management and the lawyer. The purpose of this meeting is to determine what can be done to enable the lawyer to respond satisfactorily.

Delay Issuance of Financial Statements

If a lawyer cannot render a satisfactory opinion concerning material litigation because he or she has not given the matter substantive attention, the problem may be resolved if the client is able to and agrees to delay the issuance of its financial statements. The delay will give the lawyer time to study the matter and formulate a satisfactory opinion.

Audit Scope Limitation

A lawyer's *inability* to evaluate material litigation is not a limitation on the scope of an audit. If the lawyer cannot evaluate the litigation, and if the auditor cannot obtain sufficient other evidence to corroborate the information about the matter, however, the matter is a limitation on the scope of the audit.

LITIGATION WITH INSURANCE COMPANY

In some cases, litigation, claims, and assessments are defended by the client's insurance company. In these circumstances, the client's attorney may decline to provide an opinion. The attorney may be knowledgeable, however, about the litigation and its probable outcome, especially those matters in which there is a reasonable prospect that the liability will exceed the insurance coverage. In these circumstances, the client should request that the lawyer provide the auditor with an opinion on the probable outcome of the litigation.

If the client's lawyer cannot render an opinion on litigation handled by the client's insurance company, the auditor should ask the client to send a letter of inquiry to the insurance company or the insurance company's counsel.

RELIANCE ON HOUSE OR INSIDE COUNSEL

The letter to the client's lawyer is the auditor's primary means of obtaining corroboration of the information furnished by management concerning litigation, claims, and assessments. In certain circumstances the corroboration may come from evidential matter provided by the client's legal department or inside general counsel.

Many entities employ inside counsel or house counsel. Some entities maintain legal departments. Attorneys employed by the client are bound by the American Bar Association's Code of Professional Ethics. Therefore, the auditor may accept as corroborative evidence responses from house counsel. In these circumstances, the usual distinction between internal evidence and external independent evidence does not apply.

A response from house counsel is generally acceptable; however, it cannot be substituted for a response from outside counsel when outside counsel refuses to respond to a valid inquiry or when outside counsel is clearly more knowledgeable about litigation.

House counsel and outside counsel may have devoted substantive attention to a matter, and their opinions may differ on the possible outcome. In this situation, the auditor should attempt to resolve the difference by discussion with the parties involved.

Although inside counsel and outside counsel are both subject to the same ethical responsibilities, the auditor has to be aware that house counsel is a member of management and operates within the client's control environment. Thus, the auditor has to consider the presence of fraud risk indicators and the nature of the representations in evaluating a response from house counsel.

REFUSAL OF ATTORNEY TO RESPOND

An auditor may encounter a situation in which the attorney refuses to respond to the client's letter of inquiry. In these situations, the auditor is faced with a scope limitation sufficient to preclude an unqualified opinion.

If the attorney refuses to respond, the auditor should attempt to have a meeting with the attorney and the client to resolve the problem. If the attorney continues to refuse to respond to the letter of inquiry, the auditor should decide whether to issue an "except for" opinion or to disclaim an opinion (see Section 508, *Reports on Audited Financial Statements*).

RESIGNATION OF ATTORNEY

The auditor always should be concerned when a client's attorney is replaced or has resigned. If the auditor has reason to believe an attorney has been replaced or has resigned, he or she should ask management about the reasons for the resignation or replacement. If an attorney has resigned, the auditor, with the client's consent, should discuss the matter with the attorney.

REVIEW OF INTERIM FINANCIAL INFORMATION

When an accountant reviews interim financial information under Section 772, *Interim Financial Information*, it is not necessary to send an inquiry letter to the client's lawyer concerning litigation, claims, and assessments. The accountant would be prudent, however, to communicate, at least orally, with the attorney regarding updated information on the previous audit inquiry responses concerning litigation, claims, and assessments.

Securities Act of 1933

When an accountant's report on audited financial statements is included in a filing under the Securities Act of 1933, regardless of whether unaudited interim information is included, he or she should inquire of the client's legal counsel concerning litigation, claims, and assessments. In this situation, the lawyer should be requested to update his or her previous audit inquiry response to the estimated effective date of the registration statement.

Ordinarily, a request to the lawyer to update a previous audit inquiry response is limited to the following:

1. Changes from the lawyer's previous evaluation of litigation, claims, and assessments
2. Any new matters arising since the previous response

ALTERNATIVE FORM LETTER OF INQUIRY

Section 337 provides an example of a letter of inquiry in which the client lists all pending and threatened litigation, claims, and assessments. This illustration assumes either that the client had house counsel prepare the list or that the client management consulted with the attorney.

Section 337 indicates that the client may request that the attorney prepare the list of pending and threatened litigation, claims, and assessments. A letter of inquiry of this nature is referred to as the alternative form letter.

AU ILLUSTRATIONS

The following are illustrated below.

1. Standard form letter of inquiry (from AU 337A.01)
2. Alternative form letter of inquiry (from AU 337.11)
3. Management representation when entity has no attorney

> **ILLUSTRATION 1. INQUIRY OF A CLIENT'S LAWYER CONCERNING LITIGATION, CLAIMS, AND ASSESSMENTS: STANDARD FORM LETTER OF INQUIRY (FROM AU 337A.01)**

[Client letterhead]

[Date]

[Name and address
of lawyer and salutation]

In connection with an audit of our financial statements at [balance sheet date] and for the [period] then ended, management of the Company has prepared and furnished to our auditors, [name and address of auditors], a description and evaluation of certain contingencies, including those set forth below [or attached] involving matters with respect to which you have devoted substantive attention on behalf of the Company in the form of legal consultation or representation. These contingencies are regarded by management of the Company as material for this purpose [or for the purpose of your response to this letter, we believe that as to each contingency an amount in excess of $\_\_\_\_$ would be material, and in total, $\$_____$]. Your response should include matters that existed at [balance sheet date] and during the period from that date to the date of completion of their audit, which is anticipated to be on or about [date].

Pending or Threatened Litigation, Claims, and Assessments (Excluding Unasserted Claims and Assessments)

[Ordinarily, management of the Company would provide for each matter the following information: (1) the name of the case, (2) the nature of the litigation, (3) description of the asserted claim, (4) the amount of monetary or other damages sought, (5) how management is responding or intends to respond to the litigation, (6) statement of whether potential damages are covered by insurance and, if covered, to what extent, and (7) management's evaluation of the likelihood of an unfavorable outcome and an estimate, if one can be made, of the amount or range or potential loss. After all matters have been listed, the following paragraph appears.]

Please furnish to our auditors such explanation, if any, that you consider necessary to supplement the foregoing information, including an explanation of those matters on which your views may differ from those stated and an identification of the omission of any pending or threatened litigation, claims, and assessments or a statement that the list of these matters is complete.

Unasserted Claims and Assessments Considered by Management to Be Probable of Assertion and That, If Asserted, Would Have at Least a Reasonable Possibility of an Unfavorable Outcome

[Ordinarily, management of the company would state that it had represented to the auditor that there were no unasserted claims that required accrual or disclosure or, if such matters had been identified, provide for each matter the following information: (1) the nature of the matter, (2) how management intends to respond if the claim is asserted, and (3) management's evaluation of the likelihood of an unfavorable outcome and an estimate, if one can be made, of the amount or range of potential loss. After all matters have been listed, the following paragraph appears.]

Please furnish to our auditors such explanation, if any, that you consider necessary to supplement the foregoing information, including an explanation of those matters on which your views may differ from those stated.

We understand that in the course of performing legal service for us with respect to a matter recognized to involve an unasserted possible claim or assessment that may call for financial statement disclosure, if you have formed a professional conclusion that we should disclose or consider disclosure concerning such possible claim or assessment, as a matter of professional responsibility to us, you will so advise us and will consult with us concerning the question of such disclosure and the applicable requirements of Statement of Financial Accounting Standards 5. Please specifically confirm to our auditors that our understanding is correct.

Other Matters

Please specifically identify the nature of and reasons for any limitations on your response.

Please indicate the amount owed to you for services and expenses, billed and unbilled, at [*balance sheet date*].

Very truly yours,

_____
[*Client signature and title*]

ILLUSTRATION 2. INQUIRY OF A CLIENT'S LAWYER CONCERNING LITIGATION, CLAIMS, AND ASSESSMENTS: ALTERNATIVE FORM LETTER OF INQUIRY (FROM AU 337.11)

[*Client letterhead*]

[*Date*]

[*Name and address
of lawyer and salutation*]

In connection with an audit of our financial statements at [*balance sheet date*] and for the [*period*] then ended, please furnish our auditors, [*name and address of auditors*], with the information requested below concerning certain contingencies involving matters with respect to which you have devoted substantive attention on behalf of the Company in the form of legal consultation or representation. [*If a materiality limit has been agreed to by management and the auditor, the following sentence should be added.*] For the purpose of your response to this letter, we believe that for each contingency an amount in excess of $_____ would be material, and in total, $_____. Your response should include matters that existed at [*balance sheet date*] and during the period from that date to the date of completion of their audit, which is anticipated to be on or about [*date*].

Pending or Threatened Litigation, Claims and Assessments (Excluding Unasserted Claims and Assessments)

Please prepare a description of all litigation, claims, and assessments. The description of each case should include, but not be limited to, the following:

1. The nature of the litigation, including the following:
   a. Identification of the proceedings
   b. The claims asserted
   c. The amount of monetary or other damages sought
   d. Whether potential damages are covered by insurance and if so, to what extent
   e. Objectives of plaintiff other than monetary or other damages
2. The progress of the case to date
3. How management is responding, or intends to respond, to the litigation
4. Your evaluation of the likelihood of an unfavorable outcome
5. An estimate of the amount or range of potential loss

Unasserted Claims and Assessments

We understand that in the course of performing legal service for us with respect to a matter recognized to involve an unasserted possible claim or assessment that may call for financial statement disclosure, if you have formed a professional conclusion that we should disclose or consider disclosure concerning such possible claim or assessment, you will so advise us and will consult with us concerning the question of such disclosure and the applicable requirements of Statement of Financial Accounting Standards 5, as a matter of professional responsibility to us. Please specifically confirm to our auditors that our understanding is correct.

We have represented to our auditors that you have not advised us of any unasserted claims or assessments that are probable of assertion and must be disclosed in accordance with Statement of Financial Accounting Standards 5.

Other Matters

Please specifically identify the nature of, and reasons for, any limitation on your response.

Please indicate the amount owed to you for services and expenses [*billed and unbilled*] at [*balance sheet date*].

Very truly yours,

_____

[*Client signature and title*]

ILLUSTRATION 3. MANAGEMENT REPRESENTATION WHEN ENTITY HAS NO ATTORNEY

[*Client letterhead*]

[*Date*]

[*Name and address
of CPA firm and salutation*]

We are not aware of any pending or threatened litigation, claims, or assessments or unasserted claims or assessments that are required to be accrued or disclosed in the financial statements in accordance with Statement of Financial Accounting Standards 5, and we have not consulted a lawyer concerning litigation, claims, or assessments.

Very truly yours,

_____

[*Client signature and title*]

Appendix—Illustrative Audit Inquiry Letter to Legal Counsel

In connection with an audit of our financial statements at [*balance sheet date*] and for the [*period*] then ended, management of the Company has prepared and furnished to our auditors, [*name and address of auditors*], a description and evaluation of certain contingencies, including those set forth below involving matters with respect to which you have been engaged and to which you have devoted substantive attention on behalf of the Company in the form of legal consultation or representation. These contingencies are regarded by management of the Company as material for this purpose (management may indicate a materiality limit if an understanding has been reached with the auditor). Your response should include matters that existed at [*balance sheet date*] and during the period from that date to the date of your response.

[*Alternative wording when management requests the lawyer to prepare the list that describes and evaluates pending or threatened litigation, claims, and assessments is as follows*:]

In connection with an audit of our financial statements as of [*balance sheet date*] and for the [*period*] then ended, please furnish our auditors, [*name and address of auditors*], with the information requested below concerning certain contingencies involving matters with respect to which you have devoted substantive attention on behalf of the Company in the form of legal consultation or representation. [*When a materiality limit has been established based on an understanding between management and the auditor, the following sentence should be added: This request is limited to contingencies amounting to (amount) individually or items involving lesser amounts that exceed (amount) in the aggregate.*]

Pending or Threatened Litigation (Excluding Unasserted Claims)

[*Ordinarily the information would include the following: (1) the nature of the litigation, (2) the progress of the case to date, (3) how management is responding or intends to respond to the litigation (for example, to contest the case vigorously or to seek an out-of-court settlement), and (4) an evaluation of the likelihood of an unfavorable outcome and an estimate, if one can be made, of the amount or range of potential loss.*] This letter will serve as our consent for you to furnish to our auditor all the information requested herein. Accordingly, please furnish to our auditors such explanation, if any, that you consider necessary to supplement the foregoing information, including an explanation of those matters for which your views may differ from those stated and an identification of the omission of any pending or threatened litigation, claims, and assessments, or a statement that the list of such matters is complete.

[*Alternative wording when management requests the lawyer to prepare the list that describes and evaluates pending or threatened litigation, claims, and assessments is as follows*]:

Regarding pending or threatened litigation, claims, and assessments, please include in your response: (1) the nature of each matter, (2) the progress of each matter to date, (3) how the Company is responding or intends to respond (for example, to contest the case vigorously or seek an out-of-court settlement), and (4) an evaluation of the likelihood of an unfavorable outcome and an estimate, if one can be made, of the amount or range of potential loss.

Unasserted Claims and Assessments (Considered by Management to be Probable of Assertion and That, if Asserted, Would Have at Least a Reasonable Possibility of an Unfavorable Outcome)

[*Ordinarily management's information would include the following: (1) the nature of the matter, (2) how management intends to respond if the claim is asserted, and (3) an evaluation of the likelihood of an unfavorable outcome and an estimate, if one can be made, of the amount or range of potential loss.*] Please furnish to our auditors such explanation, if any, that you consider necessary to supplement the foregoing information, including an explanation of those matters for which your views may differ from those stated.

We understand that whenever, in the course of performing legal services for us with respect to a matter recognized to involve an unasserted possible claim or assessment that may call for financial statement disclosure, if you have formed a professional conclusion that we should disclose or consider disclosure concerning such possible claim or assessment, as a matter of professional responsibility to us, you will so advise us and will consult with us concerning the question of such disclosure and the applicable requirements of Financial Accounting Standards Board (FASB) Accounting Standards Codification (ASC) 450, *Contingencies*. Please specifically confirm to our auditors that our understanding is correct.

[*Alternative wording when management requests the lawyer to prepare the list that describes and evaluates pending or threatened litigation, claims, and assessments is as follows*]:

We have represented to our auditors that there are no unasserted possible claims or assessments that you have advised us are probable of assertion and must be disclosed in accordance with FASB ASC 450. We understand that whenever, in the course of performing legal services for us with respect to a matter recognized to involve an unasserted possible claim or assessment that may call for financial statement disclosure, you have formed a professional conclusion that we should disclose or consider disclosure concerning such possible claim or assessment, as a matter of professional responsibility to us, you will so advise us and will consult with us concerning the question of such disclosure and the applicable requirements of FASB ASC 450. Please specifically confirm to our auditors that our understanding is correct.

Please specifically identify the nature of and reasons for any limitation on your response.

[*The auditor may request the client to inquire about additional matters, for example, unpaid or unbilled charges or specified information on certain contractually assumed obligations of the Company, such as guarantees of indebtedness of others.*]

[*Alternative wording when management requests the lawyer to prepare the list that describes and evaluates pending or threatened litigation, claims, and assessments is as follows:*]

Your response should include matters that existed as of (balance-sheet date) and during the period from that date to the effective date of your response. Please specifically identify the nature of and reasons for any limitations on your response. Our auditors expect to have the audit completed about [*expected completion date*]. They would appreciate receiving your reply by that date with a specified effective date no earlier than [*ordinarily two weeks before expected completion date*].

[*Wording that could be used in an audit inquiry letter, instead of the heading and first paragraph, when the client believes that there are no unasserted claims or assessments (to be specified to the lawyer for comment) that are probable of assertion and that, if asserted, would have a reasonable possibility of an unfavorable outcome as specified by FASB ASC 450,* Contingencies, *is as follows*:]

Unasserted claims and assessments—We have represented to our auditors that there are no unasserted possible claims that you have advised us are probable of assertion and must be disclosed, in accordance with Financial Accounting Standards Board (FASB) Accounting Standards Codification (ASC) 450, *Contingencies*. [*The second paragraph in the section relating to unasserted claims and assessments would not be altered.*]

AU 339 Audit Documentation

AU-C 230 Audit Documentation

IMPORTANT NOTE: The guidance in this section applies to audits of nonissuers. Auditors of issuers and public entities subject to SEC rules should refer to the guidance in Public Company Accounting Oversight Board (PCAOB) 3, Audit Documentation.

AU EFFECTIVE DATE AND APPLICABILITY

Original Pronouncement Statement on Auditing Standards (SAS) 103.

Effective Date This standard currently is effective.

Applicability Audits of financial statements in accordance with generally accepted auditing standards (GAAS).

AU-C EFFECTIVE DATE AND SUMMARY OF CHANGES

SAS No. 122, *Codification of Auditing Standards and Procedures,* is effective for audits of financial statements with periods ending on or after December 15, 2012. AU-C 230 does not change extant requirements in any significant respect. Requirements related to the following aspects of audit documentation are included in Statements on Quality Control Standards (SQCS) No. 8:

- Retention
- Confidentiality
- Integrity
- Accessibility
- Retrievability

AU-C DEFINITIONS OF TERMS

Source: AU-C 230.06

Audit documentation. The record of audit procedures performed, relevant audit evidence obtained, and conclusions the auditor reached (terms such as *working papers* or *workpapers* are also sometimes used).

Audit file. One or more folders or other storage media, in physical or electronic form, containing the records that constitute the audit documentation for a specific engagement.

Documentation completion date. The date, no later than 60 days following the report release date, on which the auditor has assembled for retention a complete and final set of documentation in an audit file.

Experienced auditor. An individual (whether internal or external to the firm) who has practical audit experience and a reasonable understanding of:

1. Audit processes;
2. GAAS and applicable legal and regulatory requirements;
3. The business environment in which the entity operates; and
4. Auditing and financial reporting issues relevant to the entity's industry.

Report release date. The date the auditor grants the entity permission to use the auditor's report in connection with the financial statements.

OBJECTIVES OF AU SECTION 339

This section establishes standards and provides guidance on audit documentation. Other sections contain specific documentation requirements (see Appendix B).

Audit documentation serves the following functions:

1. Provides principal support for the auditor's report
2. Provides principal support for the auditor's representation that the audit was made in accordance with GAAS, especially the standard of fieldwork
3. Aids the auditor in conducting and supervising the audit

The following are examples of audit documentation:

1. Audit program
2. Analyses
3. Memoranda
4. Letters of confirmation
5. Representation letters
6. Abstracts or photocopies of documents
7. Schedules or commentaries

Audit documentation is an essential element of audit quality. Although documentation alone does not guarantee audit quality, the process of preparing sufficient and appropriate documentation contributes to the quality of an audit.

The precise form and content of working papers are matters the auditor decides based on several factors listed in the section (see "Fundamental Requirements").

OBJECTIVES OF AU-C SECTION 230

AU-C Section 230.05 states that

> ... the objective of the auditor is to prepare documentation that provides
>
> a. a sufficient and appropriate record of the basis for the auditor's report; and
> b. evidence that the audit was planned and performed in accordance with GAAS and applicable legal and regulatory requirements.

FUNDAMENTAL REQUIREMENTS

REQUIREMENT FOR AUDIT DOCUMENTATION

The auditor must prepare audit documentation in connection with each engagement in sufficient detail to provide a clear understanding of:

- The work performed, including the nature, timing, extent, and results of audit procedures performed
- The evidence obtained and its source, and the conclusions reached

The form and content of the audit documentation should be designed for the specific engagement.

FORM, CONTENT, AND EXTENT OF AUDIT DOCUMENTATION

The quantity, type, and content of the audit documentation are based on the auditor's professional judgment and vary with the engagement. Factors to consider in determining the content of audit documentation are discussed in the following paragraphs. Additional factors to consider in designing audit documentation are explained in "Techniques for Application."

The Audience

The auditor should prepare audit documentation that would allow an experienced auditor having no previous connection with the audit to understand:

- The nature, timing, and extent of auditing procedures performed to comply with SASs and applicable legal and regulatory requirements,
- The results of the audit procedures performed and the audit evidence obtained,
- The conclusions reached on significant matters, and
- That the accounting records agree or reconcile with the audited financial statements or other audited information.

"Experienced auditor" means someone who possesses the competencies and skills that would have enabled him or her to perform the audit. An experienced auditor is one who would have "an understanding of audit processes and of auditing and reporting issues relevant to the industry in which the entity operates."

Oral Explanations

Oral explanations on their own do not represent sufficient support for the work the auditor performed or conclusions the auditor reached but may be used by the auditor to clarify or explain information contained in the audit documentation.

NOTE: *For example, if the auditing standards state that you should obtain an understanding of the entity's control environment, but there is no evidence that the auditor obtained such an understanding, then the auditor can not make a plausible claim that the understanding was obtained but just not documented.*

Sufficiency of Audit Documentation

Audit documentation should include:

- Who reviewed specific audit work and the date the work was completed
- Who performed the audit documentation and the date of such review

- Show the agreement or reconciliation of accounting records with financial statements or other information being reported

Audit documentation should also include:

- An identification of the items tested in tests of operating effectiveness of controls and substantive tests of details that involve document inspection or confirmation. This can be accomplished by indicating the source of the items selected and the specific selection criteria.

NOTE: The following indicate ways in which the identification of selected items can be accomplished.

- *Identifying characteristics, such as specific invoice numbers of the items included in the sample, when a haphazard or random sample is selected.*
- *When all items over a specified dollar amount are selected, describe the scope and identification of the listing, (for example, all payables over $10,000 from the December accounts payable journal).*
- *When a systematic sample is selected from a population of documents, identify the source of the documents and indicate the starting point and the sampling interval.*

Auditors can determine whether the identification is accomplished by asking themselves whether another auditor unconnected to the engagement would be able to identify the particular items selected for testing by reviewing the audit program and related documentation.

Factors to Consider in Determining the Nature and Extent of Audit Documentation

The auditor should consider the following factors in determining the nature and extent of the documentation for an audit area or auditing procedure:

- What is the risk of material misstatement associated with the assertion, or account or class of transactions?
- What is the extent of judgment involved in performing the work and evaluating results?
- What is the nature of the auditing procedure?
- What is the significance of evidence obtained to the tested assertion?
- What is the nature and extent of identified exceptions?
- Is there a need to document a conclusion or basis for a conclusion not readily determinable from the documentation of the work performed?

Documentation of Significant Findings

The auditor should document significant audit findings or issues, actions taken to address them (including additional evidence obtained) and the basis of the conclusions reached. Significant audit findings or issues include

- Matters that are both significant and involve the appropriate selection, application, and consistency of accounting principles with regard to the financial statements, including related disclosures. Such matters often relate to (1) accounting for complex or unusual transactions, or (2) estimates and uncertainties, and the related management assumptions, if applicable.
- Results of auditing procedures that indicate that the financial statements or disclosures could be materially misstated or that the auditing procedures need to be significantly modified.

- Circumstances that cause significant difficulty in applying necessary auditing procedures.
- Other findings that could result in a modified auditor's report.

Revisions to Documentation

The auditor should complete the assembly of the final audit file on a timely basis, but within 60 days following the report release date. After this date, the auditor must not delete or discard existing audit documentation. If changes are made to the audit documentation after this date, the auditor should document the change, when and by whom the changes were made, the specific reasons for the change, and the effect of the changes, if any, on the auditor's previous conclusions.

OWNERSHIP AND CONFIDENTIALITY

The auditor owns the audit documentation, but his or her ownership rights are limited by ethical and legal rules on confidential relationships with clients. The auditor should adopt reasonable procedures to protect the confidentiality of client information. The auditor should also adopt reasonable procedures to prevent unauthorized access to the audit documentation. The auditor should retain the audit documentation for a period sufficient to meet the needs of the auditor's practice and to satisfy pertinent legal requirements of records retention. Record-retention procedures should allow the auditor to access electronic audit documentation throughout the retention period.

NOTE: Rules of the Securities and Exchange Commission (SEC) and other federal and local governmental agencies may be pertinent.

Sometimes audit documentation may serve as a source of reference for the client, but it should not be considered as a part of, or a substitute for, the client's accounting records.

DOCUMENTATION REQUIREMENTS IN OTHER SECTIONS

Certain other sections require documentation of specific matters. These requirements are presented in Illustration 1. In addition, other standards, such as government auditing standards, laws, or regulations, may also contain specific documentation requirements.

INTERPRETATIONS

PROVIDING ACCESS TO OR COPIES OF AUDIT DOCUMENTATION TO A REGULATOR (ISSUED JULY 1994; REVISED JUNE 1996; REVISED OCTOBER 2000; REVISED JANUARY 2002; REVISED DECEMBER 2005)

A regulator may request access to an auditor's audit documentation to fulfill a quality review requirement or to assist in establishing the scope of a regulatory examination. In making the request, the regulator may ask to make photocopies and may also make such copies available to others. When regulators make a request for access, the auditor should:

1. Consider advising the client about the request and indicating that he or she intends to comply. In some cases the auditor may wish or be required to confirm in writing the requirements to provide access (see Illustration 1).
2. Make arrangement with the regulator for the review.
3. Maintain control over the original audit documentation.

4. Consider submitting a letter to the regulator (see Illustration 2).
5. Obtain the client's consent to provide access when not required to provide access (see Illustration 3).

TECHNIQUES FOR APPLICATION

STANDARDIZATION OF AUDIT DOCUMENTATION

Audit documentation should be designed for the specific engagement; however, audit documentation supporting certain accounting records may be standardized.

The auditor should analyze the nature of his or her clients and the complexity of their accounting systems. This analysis will indicate accounts for which audit documentation may be standardized. An auditor ordinarily may be able to standardize audit documentation for a small business client as follows:

1. Cash, including cash on hand
2. Short-term investments
3. Trade accounts receivable
4. Notes receivable
5. Other receivables
6. Prepaid expenses
7. Property, plant, and equipment
8. Long-term investments
9. Intangible assets
10. Deposits
11. Accrued expenses
12. Taxes payable
13. Long-term debt
14. Stockholders' equity accounts

PREPARATION OF AUDIT DOCUMENTATION

All audit documentation should have certain basic information, such as the following:

1. Heading

   a. Name of client.
   b. Description of audit documentation, such as

      (1) Proof of cash—Fishkill Bank & Trust Company.
      (2) Accounts receivable—confirmation statistics.

   c. Period covered by engagement.

      (1) For the year ended . . .

2. An index number

   a. All audit documentation should be numbered for easy reference. Audit documentation is identified using various systems, such as the following:

      (1) Alphabetic
      (2) Numbers
      (3) Roman numerals

(4) General ledger account numbers
(5) A combination of the preceding

3. Preparer and reviewer identification

   a. Identification of person who prepared audit documentation and date of preparation

   (1) If client prepared the audit documentation, this should be noted. Person who checked papers also should be identified.

   b. Identification of person who reviewed the audit documentation and date of review

4. Explanation of symbols

   a. Symbols used in the audit documentation should be explained. Symbols indicate matters such as the following:

   (1) Columns were footed
   (2) Columns were cross-footed
   (3) Data were traced to original sources

5. Source of information

   a. The audit documentation should indicate source of information:

   (1) Client records
   (2) Client personnel

Related Accounts

One page of audit documentation may provide documentation for more than one account. Many balance sheet accounts are related to income statement accounts. In these circumstances, the audit work on the accounts should be documented in one page of audit documentation. Examples of related accounts are the following:

1. Notes receivable and interest income
2. Depreciable assets, depreciation expense, and accumulated depreciation
3. Prepaid expenses and the related income statement expenses, such as insurance, interest, and supplies
4. Long-term debt and interest expense
5. Deferred income taxes and income tax expense

Client Preparation of Audit Documentation

It is advisable to have the client's employees prepare as much as possible of the auditor's audit documentation. This increases the efficiency of the audit. The auditor should identify the audit documentation as "Prepared by the Client" (PBC) and note the auditor who reviewed the client-prepared audit documentation. The preparation of audit documentation by the client does not impair the auditor's independence. However, the auditor should test the information in client-prepared audit documentation.

QUALITY OF AUDIT DOCUMENTATION

Audit documentation aids the execution and supervision of the current year's engagement. Also, such documentation helps the auditor in planning and executing the following year's audit. Audit documentation also serves as the auditor's reference for answering questions from the client. For example, a bank or a credit agency may want information that the auditor can provide to the client for submission to the third party from the audit documentation.

In case of litigation against the client, the auditor's audit documentation may be subpoenaed. In litigation against the auditor, the audit documentation will be used as evidence. Therefore audit documentation should be accurate, complete, and understandable. After audit documentation is reviewed, additional work, if any, is done, and modifications are made to the audit documentation, all review notes and all to-do points should be discarded because the issues they addressed have been appropriately responded to in the audit documentation.

Likewise, miscellaneous notes, memoranda, e-mails, and other communications among members of the audit engagement team created during the audit should be included or summarized in the audit documentation when needed to identify issues or support audit conclusions; otherwise, they should be discarded. Any information added after completion of fieldwork should be dated at the date added.

AUDIT DOCUMENTATION DEFICIENCIES

Some of the more common audit documentation deficiencies are failure to:

1. Express a conclusion on the account being analyzed
2. Explain exceptions noted
3. Obtain sufficient information for note disclosure
4. Reference information
5. Update and revise permanent file
6. Post adjusting and reclassification journal entries to appropriate audit documentation
7. Indicate source of information
8. Promptly review audit documentation prepared by assistants
9. Sign or date audit documentation
10. Foot client-prepared schedules
11. Explain tick marks

AU ILLUSTRATIONS

Illustrations 1, 2, and 3 are adapted from AICPA Interpretations of AU 339.

1. An auditor's written communication to client when not required to provide access
2. An auditor's letter to a regulator
3. A confirmation that the auditor may be required to provide access when required by law or regulation

Illustration 4, which lists audit documentation requirements in other sections, is adapted from the appendix to AU 339.

ILLUSTRATION 1. AUDITOR'S WRITTEN COMMUNICATION TO CLIENT WHEN NOT REQUIRED TO PROVIDE ACCESS (ADAPTED FROM AN INTERPRETATION OF AU 339)

The audit documentation for this engagement is the property of Guy & Co. and constitutes confidential information. However, we have been requested to make certain audit documentation available to [*name of regulator*] for [*describe the regulator's basis for its request*]. Furthermore, upon request, we may provide photocopies of selected audit documentation to [*name of regulator*].

You have authorized Guy & Co. to allow [*name of regulator*] access to the audit documentation in the manner discussed above. Please confirm your agreement to the above by signing below and returning it [*name of auditor, address*].

Firm signature
_____

Agreed and acknowledged:
_____

[*Name and title*]
_____

[*Date*]

ILLUSTRATION 2. AUDITOR'S LETTER TO REGULATOR (FROM AN INTERPRETATION OF AU 339)

[*Date*]

[*Name and Address of Regulatory Agency*]

Your representatives have requested access to our audit documentation in connection with our audit of December 31, 20X1 financial statements of Widget Company. It is our understanding that the purpose of your request is [*state purpose: for example, "to facilitate your regulatory examination"*].

Our audit of Widget Company December 31, 20X1 financial statements was conducted in accordance with auditing standards generally accepted in the United States of America, the objective of which is to form an opinion as to whether the financial statements, which are the responsibility and representations of management, present fairly, in all material respects, the financial position, results of operations and cash flows in conformity with generally accepted accounting principles. Under generally accepted auditing standards, we have the responsibility, within the inherent limitations of the auditing process, to design our audit to provide reasonable assurance that errors and fraud that have a material effect on the financial statements will be detected, and to exercise due care in the conduct of our audit. The concept of selective testing of the data being audited, which involves judgment both as to the number of transactions to be audited and as to the areas to be tested, has been generally accepted as a valid and sufficient basis for any auditor to express an opinion on financial statements. Thus, our audit, based on the concept of selective testing, is subject to the inherent risk that material errors or fraud, if they exist, would not be detected. In addition, an audit does not address the possibility that material errors or fraud may occur in the future. Also, our use of professional judgment and the assessment of materiality for the purpose of our audit means that matters may have existed that would have been assessed differently by you.

The audit documentation was prepared for the purpose of providing principal support for our report on Widget Company December 31, 20X1 financial statements and to aid in the conduct and supervision of our audit. The audit documentation is the principal record of the auditing procedures performed, the evidence obtained, and the conclusions reached in the engagement. The auditing procedures that we performed were limited to those we considered necessary under generally accepted auditing standards to enable us to formulate and express an opinion on the financial statements taken as a whole. Accordingly, we make no representation as to the sufficiency or appropriateness, for your purposes, of either the information continued in our audit documentation or our audit procedures. In addition, any notations, comments, and individual conclusions appearing on any of the audit documentation do not stand alone, and should not be read as an opinion on any individual amounts, accounts, balances, or transactions.

Our audit of Widget Company December 31, 20X1 financial statements was performed for the purpose stated above and has not been planned or conducted in contemplation of your [*state purpose: for example, "regulatory examination"*] or for the purpose of assessing Widget Company compliance with laws and regulations. Therefore, items of possible interest to you may not have been specifically addressed. Accordingly, our audit and the audit documentation prepared in connection therewith, should not supplant other inquiries and procedures that should be undertaken by the [*name of regulatory agency*] for the purpose of monitoring and regulating statements of Widget Company. In addition, we have not audited any financial statements of Widget Company since [*date of audited balance sheet referred to in the first paragraph above*] nor have we performed any audit procedures since [*date*], the date of our auditor's report, and significant events or circumstances may have occurred since that date.

The audit documentation constitutes and reflects work performed or evidence obtained by [*name of auditor*] in its capacity as independent auditor for Widget Company. The documents contain trade secrets and confidential commercial and financial information of our firms and Widget Company that is privileged and confidential, and we expressly reserve all rights with respect to disclosures to third parties. Accordingly, we request confidential treatment under the Freedom of Information Act or similar laws and regulations when requests are made for the audit documentation or information contained therein or any documents created by the [*name of regulatory agency*] containing information derived therefrom. We further request that written notice be given to our firm before distribution of the information in the audit documentation [or photocopies thereof] to others, including other governmental agencies, except when such distribution is required by law or regulation.

[*If it is expected that photocopies will be requested, add:*]

Any photocopies of our audit documentation we agree to provide you will be identified as "Confidential Treatment Requested by (*name of auditor, address, telephone number*)."]

Firm signature
_____

ILLUSTRATION 3. CONFIRMATION THAT AUDITOR MAY BE REQUIRED TO PROVIDE ACCESS WHEN REQUIRED BY LAW OR REGULATION (FROM AN INTERPRETATION OF AU 339)

The audit documentation for this engagement is the property of [*name of auditor*] and constitutes confidential information. However, we may be requested to make certain audit documentation available to [*name of regulator*] for [*describe the regulator's basis for its request*]. Access to such audit documentation will be provided under the supervision of [*name of auditor*] personnel. Furthermore, upon request, we may provide photocopies of selected audit documentation to [*name of regulator*].

You have authorized [*name of auditor*] to allow [*name of regulator*] access to the audit documentation in the manner discussed above. Please confirm your agreement to the above by signing below and returning to [*name of auditor, address*].

Firm signature
_____

Agreed and acknowledged:
_____
[*Name and title*]
_____
[*Date*]

ILLUSTRATION 4. AUDIT DOCUMENTATION REQUIREMENTS IN OTHER STATEMENTS ON AUDITING STANDARDS (ADAPTED FROM AU 339)

Reference	Documentation requirement(s)
Section 311: *Planning and Supervision* Section 312: *Audit Risk and Materiality in Conducting an Audit*	An overall audit strategy and audit plan and any changes to them. 1. The levels of materiality, as discussed in paragraph 27, and tolerable misstatement, including any changes thereto, used in the audit and the basis on which those levels were determined. 2. A summary of uncorrected misstatements, other than those that are trivial, related to known and likely misstatements. 3. The auditor's conclusion as to whether uncorrected misstatements, individually or in aggregate, do or do not cause the financial statements to be materially misstated, and the basis for that conclusion. 4. All known and likely misstatements identified by the auditor during the audit, other than those that are trivial, that have been corrected by management. Uncorrected misstatements should be documented in a manner that allows the auditor to: 5. Separately consider the effects of known and likely misstatements, including uncorrected misstatements identified in prior periods; 6. Consider the aggregate effect of misstatements on the financial statements; and 7. Consider the qualitative factors that are relevant to the auditor's consideration whether misstatements are material (see paragraph 60).
Section 314: *Understanding the Entity and Its Environment and Assessing the Risks of Material Misstatement*	1. The discussion among the audit team regarding the susceptibility of the entity's financial statements to material misstatement due to error or fraud. 2. Key elements of the understanding obtained regarding each entity aspect that assess the risks of material misstatement of the financial statements. 3. Assessment of the risks of material misstatement. 4. The risks identified and related controls evaluated.
Section 316: *Consideration of Fraud in a Financial Statement Audit* [1]	1. The discussion among engagement personnel in planning the audit regarding the susceptibility of the entity's financial statements to material misstatement due to fraud, including how and when the discussion occurred, the audit team members who participated, and the subject matter discussed. 2. The procedures performed to obtain information necessary to identify and assess the risks of material misstatement due to fraud.

[1] *This section reflects generally accepted auditing standards modified by the AICPA after April 16, 2003. Therefore this section is not part of the standards adopted or established by the PCAOB.*

Reference	Documentation requirement(s)
Section 316: *Consideration of Fraud in a Financial Statement Audit*	3. Specific risk of material misstatement due to fraud that were identified and a description of the auditor's response to those risks. 4. If the auditor has not identified in a particular circumstance, improper revenue recognition as a risk of material misstatement due to fraud, the reasons supporting the auditor's conclusion. 5. The results of the procedures performed to further address the risk of management override controls. 6. Other conditions and analytical relationships that caused the auditor to believe that additional auditing procedures or other responses were required and any further responses the auditor concluded were appropriate, to address such risks or other conditions. 7. The nature of communications about fraud made to management, the audit committee and others.
Section 317: *Illegal Acts by Clients*	Oral communications to the audit committee or others with equivalent authority and responsibility regarding illegal acts that come to the auditor's attention.
Section 318: *Understanding the Entity and Its Environment and Assessing the Risks of Material Misstatement*	1. The discussion among the audit team regarding the susceptibility of the entity's financial statements to material misstatement due to error or fraud, including how and when the discussion occurred, the subject matter discussed, the audit team member who participated, and significant decisions reached concerning planned responses at the financial statement and relevant assertion levels. 2. Key elements of the understanding obtained regarding each of the aspects of the entity and its environment, including each of the components of internal control, to assess the risks of material misstatement of the financial statements; the sources of information from which the understanding was obtained; and the risk assessment procedures. 3. The assessment of the risks of material misstatement both at the financial statement level and at the relevant assertion level and the basis for the assessment. 4. Significant risks and related controls.
Section 329: *Analytical Procedures*	When an analytical procedure is used as the principal substantive test of an assertion, 1. The expectation and factors considered in its development (where that expectation is not otherwise readily determinable from the documentation of the work performed). 2. Results of the comparison of the expectation to the recorded amounts or ratios developed from recorded amounts. 3. Any additional auditing procedures performed in response to significant unexpected differences arising from the analytical procedure and the results of such additional procedures.

Reference	Documentation requirement(s)
Section 330: *The Confirmation Process*	Oral confirmations. Also, when the auditor has not requested confirmations in the examination of accounts receivable, document how the auditor overcame this presumption.
Section 333: *Management Representations*	Written representations from management.
Section 341: *The Auditor's Consideration of an Entity's Ability to Continue as a Going Concern*	1. The conditions or events that led the auditor to believe that there is substantial doubt about the entity's ability to continue as a going concern, 2. The work performed in connection with the auditor's evaluation of management's plans, 3. The auditor's conclusion as to whether substantial doubt about the entity's ability to continue as a going concern for a reasonable period of time remains or is alleviated, and 4. The consideration and effect of that conclusion on the financial statements, disclosures, and the audit report.
Section 380: *Communications with Audit Committees*	Any oral communications with the audit committee regarding the scope and results of the audit.
Section 508: *Reports on Audited Financial Statements*	Predecessor auditor: representation letters from management of the former client and from the successor auditor before reissuing (or consenting to the reissue of) a report previously issued on the financial statements of a prior period.
Section 534: *Reporting on Financial Statements Prepared for Use in Other Countries*	Written representations from management regarding the purpose and uses of financial statements prepared in conformity with the accounting principles of another country.
Section 722: *Interim Financial Information*	Document preparation related to the review of interim financial information.
Section 801: *Compliance Auditing Considerations in Audits of Governmental Entities and Recipients of Governmental Financial Assistance*	Oral communications to management and the audit committee or others with equivalent authority and responsibility when the auditor becomes aware during a GAAS audit that the entity is subject to an audit requirement that may not be encompassed in the terms of the engagement.

AU-C ILLUSTRATION

> **ILLUSTRATION 1. AUDIT DOCUMENTATION REQUIREMENTS IN OTHER AU-C SECTIONS (FROM AU-C 230.A30)**

The following lists the main paragraphs in other AU-C sections that contain specific documentation requirements.

a.	Paragraphs .10, .13, and .16 of Section 210, *Terms of Engagement*
b.	Paragraphs .25–.26 of Section 220, *Quality Control for an Engagement Conducted in Accordance with Generally Accepted Auditing Standards*
c.	Paragraphs .43–.46 of Section 240, *Consideration of Fraud in a Financial Statement Audit*
d.	Paragraph .28 of Section 250, *Consideration of Laws and Regulations in an Audit of Financial Statements*
e.	Paragraph .20 of Section 260, *The Auditor's Communication with Those Charged with Governance*
f.	Paragraph .12 of Section 265, *Communicating Internal Control Related Matters Identified in an Audit*
g.	Paragraph .14 of Section 300, *Planning an Audit*
h.	Paragraph .33 of Section 315, *Understanding the Entity and Its Environment and Assessing the Risks of Material Misstatement*
i.	Paragraph .14 of Section 320, *Materiality in Planning and Performing an Audit*
j.	Paragraphs .30–.33 of Section 330, *Performing Audit Procedures in Response to Assessed Risks and Evaluating the Audit Evidence Obtained*
k.	Paragraph .12 of Section 450, *Evaluation of Misstatements Identified during the Audit*
l.	Paragraph .20 of Section 501, *Audit Evidence—Specific Considerations for Selected Items*
m.	Paragraph .08 of Section 520, *Analytical Procedures*
n.	Paragraph .22 of Section 540, *Auditing Accounting Estimates, Including Fair Value Accounting Estimates, and Related Disclosures*
o.	Paragraph .28 of Section 550, *Related Parties*
p.	Paragraph .18 of Section 570, *The Auditor's Consideration of an Entity's Ability to Continue as a Going Concern*
q.	Paragraphs .49 and .64 of Section 600, *Special Considerations—Audits of Group Financial Statements (Including the Work of Component Auditors)*
r.	Paragraph .13 of Section 915, *Reports on Application of Requirements of an Applicable Financial Reporting Framework*
s.	Paragraphs .42–.43 of Section 930, *Interim Financial Information*
t.	Paragraphs .39–.42 of Section 935, *Compliance Audits*

AU 341 The Auditor's Consideration of an Entity's Ability to Continue as a Going Concern

AU-C 570 The Auditor's Consideration of an Entity's Ability to Continue as a Going Concern

AU EFFECTIVE DATE AND APPLICABILITY

Original Pronouncements	Statements on Auditing Standards (SASs) 59, 64, 77, and 96.
Effective Date	These statements are now effective.
Applicability	Audits of financial statements in accordance with generally accepted auditing standards (GAAS).
	NOTE: The Statement applies in the audit of any type of entity. It is applicable to both profit-making and not-for-profit organizations. Thus, it would apply, for example, in the audit of a municipality. Also, the Statement applies to both GAAP (generally accepted accounting principles)–basis financial statements and OCBOA (Other Comprehensive Bases of Accounting)–basis financial statements, (e.g., cash or modified cash basis, tax basis, or regulatory basis). However, it does not apply to liquidation-basis financial statements.

AU-C EFFECTIVE DATE

SAS No. 126, *The Auditor's Consideration of an Entity's Ability to Continue as a Going Concern,* is effective for audits of financial statements for periods ending on or after December 15, 2012.

SAS No. 126 does not change or expand SAS No. 59, as amended, in any significant respect. The Auditing Standards Board (ASB) has moved forward with the clarity redraft of SAS No. 59, as amended, so that it is consistent with the format of the other clarified SASs that were recently issued. However, the ASB decided to delay convergence with International Standard on Auditing 570, *Going Concern*, pending the Financial Accounting Standards Board's (FASB's) anticipated development of accounting guidance addressing going concern.

AU-C DEFINITION OF TERM

Source : AU-C 570.07

Reasonable period of time. A period of time not to exceed one year beyond the date of the financial statements being audited.

OBJECTIVES OF AU SECTION 341

The "going concern" concept has long been a tenet of financial accounting. It has been called an assumption, a concept, a basic fixture, and a postulate, and has usually been stated somewhat as follows:

Continuation of entity operations is usually assumed in financial accounting in the absence of evidence to the contrary.

The auditor has an obligation to make an assessment of a client's ability to continue as a going concern.

Note that the section does not mandate any procedures especially and solely directed to searching for conditions or events that would indicate a going concern problem. The obligation is to assess the information obtained from procedures used for other purposes.

Report modification may result solely from substantial doubt about continued existence regardless of whether there is any uncertainty associated with the recoverability and classification of recorded amounts. Under this section, continued existence has a separate status. There could be substantial doubt about continued existence even when there is no question about recoverability and classification.

When the audit report is modified for a material uncertainty, the opinion is unqualified, but disclosure of the going concern uncertainty is made in an explanatory paragraph that follows the opinion paragraph. This type of uncertainty is the only one that requires a report modification.

The section states that "a reasonable period of time" is a period not to exceed one year beyond the balance sheet date.

OBJECTIVES OF AU-C SECTION 570

AU-C Section 570 states that:

. . . the objectives of the auditor are to

    a. *evaluate and conclude, based on the audit evidence obtained, whether there is substantial doubt about the entity's ability to continue as a going concern for a reasonable period of time;*
    b. *assess the possible financial statement effects, including the adequacy of disclosure regarding uncertainties about the entity's ability to continue as a going concern for a reasonable period of time; and*
    c. *determine the implications for the auditor's report.*

FUNDAMENTAL REQUIREMENTS

AUDITOR'S RESPONSIBILITY

The auditor should evaluate whether there is substantial doubt about the entity's ability to continue as a going concern for a reasonable period of time, not to exceed one year beyond the date of the financial statements being audited (i.e., the balance sheet date). However, the auditor is *not* required to design audit procedures specifically to identify conditions and events that indicate a "going concern" problem.

PROCEDURES REQUIRED

The auditor should consider whether the results of his or her usual audit procedures indicate that there could be substantial doubt.

ADDITIONAL PROCEDURES

If the auditor has substantial doubt about the entity's ability to continue as a going concern for a reasonable period of time, he or she should:

1. Obtain information about management's plans to mitigate the problem
2. Assess the likelihood of effective implementation of the plans
3. Identify those elements that are especially significant to mitigating the going concern problem and plan and perform auditing procedures to obtain evidential matter about those elements

PROSPECTIVE FINANCIAL INFORMATION

If prospective financial information is significant to management's plans, the auditor should obtain that information and should consider the adequacy of support for the significant assumptions. The auditor should pay special attention to those assumptions that are:

1. Material to the prospective financial information
2. Particularly sensitive or susceptible to change
3. Not consistent with historical trends

AUDITOR CONCLUSIONS—SUBSTANTIAL DOUBT EXISTS

If the auditor concludes that there is substantial doubt about the entity's ability to continue as a going concern for a reasonable period of time, he or she should (1) consider whether the condition is adequately disclosed and (2) modify the auditor's standard report by including an explanatory paragraph (following the opinion paragraph) or disclaim an opinion. The auditor's conclusion should be expressed in the report using the terms "substantial doubt" and "going concern."

AUDITOR CONCLUSIONS—SUBSTANTIAL DOUBT DOES NOT EXIST

If the auditor concludes that substantial doubt does not exist about the entity's ability to continue as a going concern for a reasonable period of time, he or she should consider whether the matter needs to be disclosed.

NOTE: *The absence of reference to substantial doubt in the auditor's report does not mean that the auditor is providing assurance about an entity's ability to continue as a going concern.*

INADEQUATE DISCLOSURE

If the auditor concludes that the entity's disclosures about its ability to continue as a going concern for a reasonable period of time are inadequate, the auditor's report should be qualified or adverse because of a departure from GAAP.

NOTE: The need to consider the adequacy of disclosure of going concern problems is independent of the auditor's decision to modify the audit report; that is, disclosure may be necessary even when the report is not modified.

DOCUMENTATION REQUIREMENTS

If, after considering the aggregate of events and conditions identified during the audit, the auditor believes that there is substantial doubt about the ability of the entity to continue as a going concern for a reasonable period of time, the auditor should document all of the following:

1. The conditions or events that led to the auditor's belief that there is substantial doubt about the entity's ability to continue as a going concern.
2. Those parts of management's plans that are particularly significant to overcoming the adverse effects of conditions or events.
3. The auditing procedures performed and evidence obtained to evaluate management's plans.
4. The auditor's conclusions about whether substantial doubt about the going concern issue remains.
   - If substantial doubt exists, document the possible effects of the conditions or events on the financial statements and the adequacy of the related disclosures.
   - If substantial doubt is alleviated, document the conclusion about whether disclosure of the principal conditions and events that led the auditor to believe there was substantial doubt is needed.
5. The auditor's conclusion about whether to include an explanatory paragraph in the audit report to reflect the conclusion that substantial doubt remains. If going concern disclosures are inadequate, the auditor should document the conclusion about whether to express a qualified or adverse opinion to reflect the GAAP departure.

INTERPRETATIONS

ELIMINATING A GOING CONCERN EXPLANATORY PARAGRAPH FROM A REISSUED REPORT (AUGUST 1995)

An auditor may be asked by the client to reissue the audit report and eliminate the going concern paragraph. Such requests usually occur after the going concern matter has been resolved. The auditor has no obligation to reissue the audit report. However, if the auditor decides to reissue the report, he or she should

1. Audit the event or transaction that prompted the request to reissue.
2. Perform the procedures in Section 560.
3. Consider at the date of reissue the conditions and events that related to negative trends, internal matters, external matters, and other indications of financial difficulty.

Also consider at the date of reissue management plans, including prospective financial information, the financial statement effects, and the effects on the audit report.
4. Perform any audit procedures considered necessary.
5. Reassess the going concern status of the entity.

TECHNIQUES FOR APPLICATION

PROCEDURES

The auditor's evaluation of whether there is a substantial doubt about the entity's ability to continue as a going concern for a reasonable period of time (not to exceed one year beyond the balance sheet date) is based on his or her knowledge of relevant *conditions* and *events* that exist at, or occurred before, completion of fieldwork. It is not necessary for the auditor to design audit procedures specifically to identify conditions and events that indicate a going concern problem. *Regular auditing procedures are sufficient.*

Regular auditing procedures that may identify conditions and events that indicate a going concern problem include the following:

1. *Analytical procedures.* Analytical procedures used as a substantive test or used in the planning and overall review stages of the audit may indicate:

    a. Negative trends
    b. Slow-moving inventory
    c. Receivable collectibility problems
    d. Liquidity and solvency problems

2. *Review of subsequent events.* Subsequent events, such as the bankruptcy of a major customer, confirm adverse conditions that existed at the balance sheet date. Other subsequent events that indicate a possible going concern problem include:

    a. Collapse of the market price of the entity's inventory
    b. Withdrawal of line of credit by bank
    c. Expropriation of entity's assets

3. *Review of compliance with the terms of debt and loan agreements.* Violation of debt covenants results in debt default.
4. *Reading of minutes.* Minutes of meetings of stockholders, board of directors, and board committees may indicate:

    a. Potentially expensive litigation
    b. Loss of lines of credit
    c. Loss of a major supplier
    d. Changes in the operation of the business that could result in significant losses

5. *Inquiry of legal counsel.* Responses to inquiries of the entity's legal counsel about litigation, claims, and assessments could indicate possible significant losses because of product liability claims, copyright or patent infringement, contract violations, and illegal acts.
6. *Confirmations concerning financial support.* Confirmation with related parties and third parties of the details of arrangements to provide or maintain financial support may indicate loss of bank lines of credit or loss of third-party guarantees of entity indebtedness.

INDICATIONS OF GOING CONCERN PROBLEMS

Regular audit procedures such as those described above may reveal conditions and events that indicate there could be substantial doubt about the entity's ability to continue as a going concern for a reasonable period of time. Examples of these conditions and events (going concern warning signs or red flags) are as follows:

1. Negative trends:

    a. Declining sales
    b. Increasing costs
    c. Recurring operating losses
    d. Working capital deficiencies
    e. Negative cash flows from operations
    f. Adverse key financial ratios

2. Internal matters:

    a. Chaotic and inefficient accounting system
    b. Loss of key management or operations personnel
    c. Work stoppages or other labor difficulties
    d. Substantial dependence on the success of a particular project
    e. Uneconomic long-term commitments
    f. Need to significantly revise operations

3. External events that have occurred:

    a. Legal proceedings
    b. Legislation or similar matters that might jeopardize operating ability
    c. Loss of a key franchise, license, or patent
    d. Loss of a principal customer or supplier
    e. Uninsured catastrophes such as drought, earthquake, or flood

4. Other indications of possible financial difficulties:

    a. Default on loan or similar agreements
    b. Arrearages in dividends
    c. Denial of usual trade credit from suppliers
    d. Noncompliance with statutory capital requirements
    e. Seeking new sources or methods of financing

CONSIDERATION OF MANAGEMENT'S PLANS

If, after considering the conditions and events described above, the auditor believes there is substantial doubt about the entity's ability to continue as a going concern for a reasonable period of time, he or she should consider management's plans for addressing these conditions and events.

Management's plans may be classified as follows:

1. Plans to dispose of assets
2. Plans to borrow money or restructure debt
3. Plans to reduce or delay expenditures
4. Plans to increase ownership equity

PLANS TO DISPOSE OF ASSETS

If management plans to dispose of assets, the auditor should consider the following:

1. How marketable are the assets that management plans to sell?
2. Are there any restrictions on the disposal of assets?
3. What are the possible effects of disposal?

Marketability of Assets

The auditor should do the following:

1. If the assets are securities, review market quotations to determine price and volume.

   a. If the securities are unlisted, review management documentation and correspondence with prospective buyer.

2. If the assets are intangible assets—patents, franchises, copyrights—review the following:

   a. Cash generated by the asset over the previous years
   b. Management's documentation of estimated sales price
   c. Correspondence with prospective buyer

3. If the assets are long-lived assets—property, plant, and equipment—review the following:

   a. Current market for the assets and current market value
   b. Management's documentation of estimated sales price
   c. Correspondence with prospective buyer

4. If management contemplates sales of receivables to a financial institution, review the following:

   a. Allowances for doubtful accounts, and sales returns and allowances
   b. Management's documentation of estimated sales price
   c. Correspondence with financial institution

5. If the assets are a complete segment of the entity, review the following:

   a. Segment operations over the previous years
   b. Management's documentation of estimated sales price
   c. Correspondence with prospective buyer

Restrictions on Disposal of Assets

Under certain circumstances, the entity may be prohibited from disposing of assets. If management contemplates disposal, the auditor should do the following:

1. Review all loan agreements
2. Review mortgages, financing arrangements, and other asset encumbrances

Effects of Disposal

The auditor should consider possible adverse effects of the proposed disposal of assets. He or she should do the following:

1. Discuss with management the estimated effect of the disposal on the continuing operations of the entity.

2. Prepare pro forma financial statements of the entity, after excluding the assets that will be disposed of.
3. Analyze the pro forma financial statements to determine the effect of the disposal on operations and cash flows.

PLANS TO BORROW MONEY OR RESTRUCTURE DEBT

If management plans to borrow money or restructure debt, the auditor should consider the following:

1. How available is debt financing?
2. Is collateral available and sufficient?
3. Are there restrictions on additional borrowing?
4. Are there existing or committed arrangements to restructure or subordinate debt or to obtain guarantees of loans to the entity?

Availability of Debt Financing

The auditor should do the following:

1. Review management's plan.
2. Determine if there are existing or committed arrangements, such as lines of credit.
3. Determine feasibility of factoring receivables. Consider the impact on operations of factor's fees and interest charges.
4. Ascertain the availability of assets for sale-leaseback arrangements.

Availability and Sufficiency of Collateral

If there is a question about an entity's continued existence, it is probable that it will not be able to borrow funds without collateral. The auditor should consider the availability and sufficiency of assets as collateral. Assets to be considered are the following:

1. Marketable securities
2. Receivables
3. Inventories
4. Property, plant, and equipment

Restrictions on Additional Borrowing

Existing loan agreements may prohibit the entity from borrowing additional funds. To determine this, the auditor should do the following:

1. Review mortgage agreements.
2. Review bond indentures.
3. Review bank loan agreements.

Existing or Committed Arrangements

If there are existing plans or commitments to modify existing loans or to guarantee existing or new loans, the auditor should do the following:

1. Review management's plans for:
    a. Debt restructuring
    b. Subordination of existing debt
    c. Obtaining loan guarantees

2. Review correspondence and documents pertaining to the arrangements.
3. Confirm the arrangement with the other party, for example, the bank.

PLANS TO REDUCE OR DELAY EXPENDITURES

When a question arises about the continued existence of an entity, it is not uncommon for the entity to reduce or delay expenditures, such as the following:

1. Repairs and maintenance
2. Advertising
3. Research and development
4. Additions to property, plant, and equipment

If management plans to reduce or delay these expenditures, the auditor should do the following:

1. Review management's plans.
2. Discuss with management the plan's effects on operations.

PLANS TO INCREASE OWNERSHIP EQUITY

When a question arises about the continued existence, it is not uncommon for the entity to offer equity capital to an investor. Also, it is not uncommon for investors to search for entities in need of additional capital.

Ordinarily, in these circumstances, the entity will sell its stock to the investor at a discount from market value. In certain circumstances, the investor may have plans to bring profitable businesses into the troubled entity to use the troubled entity's net operating loss carryforward. In these situations, the auditor should do the following:

1. Review the plan.
2. Determine the tax consequences of the plan.
3. Determine the plan's impact on existing shareholders.
4. Discuss with management the adequacy of the investment.

The auditor's concern is that the funds will be sufficient to ease the liquidity problem and to provide sufficient working capital.

CONSIDERATION OF MANAGEMENT FORECASTS

The auditor is not required to examine management forecasts; however, he or she should read these forecasts and apply his or her knowledge of the client. The auditor should pay special attention to cash flows and the implementation of management plans. The auditor is interested in whether the forecasts provide a reasonable basis for the belief that the entity will be in business a year from the current balance sheet date.

Obtain Management Assumptions

The auditor should ask management for its assumptions, especially assumptions about the following:

1. General economic conditions
2. Industry economic conditions
3. Sales
4. Cost of sales
5. Cost of labor
6. Expenditures for plant and equipment

7. Selling, general, and administrative expenses
8. Borrowings, interest expense, and extension of lines of credit
9. Income taxes, if any

Sources of Management Assumptions

The auditor should ask management for sources for its assumptions in developing the prospective data, especially the following:

1. Assumptions material to the forecasts or projections
2. Assumptions that are unusually uncertain or sensitive to variation
3. Assumptions that deviate from historical trends

Possible sources for assumptions are the following:

1. Government publications
2. Industry publications
3. Economic forecasts
4. Entity budgets
5. Labor agreements
6. Sales backlog
7. Debt agreements

When the auditor reads management's assumptions, he or she may want to consider the following:

1. Historical trends of the entity
2. Historical trends of the industry
3. Comparison of prior year's forecasts with actual results

Internal Consistency of Assumptions

Management assumptions should be internally consistent. Examples of this internal consistency are the following:

1. There should be a logical relationship between net cash flow and the following:

    a. Sales
    b. Expenses
    c. Expenditures
    d. Receivables
    e. Payables

2. There should be a logical relationship between sales and the following:

    a. Cost of sales
    b. Labor
    c. Rent
    d. Advertising

3. There should be a logical relationship between income statement items and balance sheet items such as the following:

    a. Sales to receivables
    b. Cost of sales to inventories
    c. Sales to working capital

FINANCIAL STATEMENT EFFECTS

Substantial Doubt Exists

If the auditor concludes, after considering management's plans, that there is substantial doubt about the entity's ability to continue as a going concern for a reasonable period of time, he or she should consider possible effects on the financial statements and the adequacy of the related disclosure. Disclosure might include the following:

1. Conditions and events creating the doubt, such as recurring operating losses, negative cash flows, working capital deficiency, and violation of debt covenants
2. Possible effect of conditions and events, such as a cutback in operations, a layoff of employees, or a bankruptcy filing
3. Management's evaluation of the significance of the conditions and events and any mitigating factors
4. Whether operations may need to be discontinued
5. Management's plans, including relevant prospective financial information

> NOTE: It is not intended that the prospective financial information should meet the minimum presentation guidelines of Statement on Standards for Accountants' Services on Prospective Financial Information, Financial Forecasts and Projections. Also, the inclusion of prospective financial information does not require procedures beyond those required by generally accepted auditing standards (see above, "Consideration of Management Forecasts").

6. Information about recoverability or classification of recorded asset amounts or the amounts or classification of liabilities

Substantial Doubt Does Not Exist

After considering management's plans, the auditor may conclude that substantial doubt about the entity's ability to continue as a going concern for a reasonable period of time does not exist. In these circumstances, the auditor should nonetheless consider the need to disclose the conditions and events responsible for the initial doubt and any mitigating factors, including management's plans.

EFFECTS ON THE AUDITOR'S REPORT

If the auditor concludes that substantial doubt exists about the entity's ability to continue as a going concern for a reasonable period of time, the auditor's standard report should include an explanatory paragraph, *following the opinion paragraph*, to reflect that conclusion. In these circumstances, the auditor ordinarily expresses an unqualified opinion (see the next section, "Disclaimer of Opinion"). The auditor may no longer express a "subject to" opinion for any uncertainty (see Section 508, *Reports on Audited Financial Statements*). The auditor's conclusion should be expressed using a phrase such as "substantial doubt about its (the entity's) ability to continue as a going concern." The report wording must include the terms "substantial doubt" and "going concern" and should be stated unconditionally.

The following (from AU 341.13) is an example of an explanatory paragraph:

> The accompanying financial statements have been prepared assuming that the Company will continue as a going concern. As discussed in Note X to the financial statements, the Company has suffered recurring losses from operations and has a net capital deficiency that raise substantial doubt about its ability to continue as a going concern. Management's plans in regard to these matters are also described in Note X. The financial statements do not include any adjustments that might result from the outcome of this uncertainty.

Disclaimer of Opinion

Instead of issuing an unqualified opinion with an explanatory paragraph following the opinion paragraph, the auditor may disclaim an opinion if he or she concludes that there is substantial doubt about the entity's ability to continue as a going concern for a reasonable period of time. A disclaimer of opinion is permitted at the auditor's discretion, but never required.

Inadequate Disclosure

If the auditor concludes that the entity's disclosures about its ability to continue as a going concern for a reasonable period of time are not adequate, the auditor's report should be modified for a departure from generally accepted accounting principles. This may result in either a qualified (except for) or adverse opinion (see Section 508).

Prior Period Audit Report

The fact that the auditor is issuing a "going concern" report on the current period financial statements does not imply that a going concern problem existed in the prior period. Therefore, the auditor's report on prior period financial statements presented for comparative purposes with the current period financial statements need not be changed.

Subsequent Period Audit Report

The auditor may have issued a "going concern" report on the prior period financial statements that are presented for comparative purposes with the current period financial statements. If the going concern problem has been resolved during the current period, the explanatory paragraph included in the auditor's report on those prior period financial statements should *not* be repeated.

AU ILLUSTRATION

The following checklist may be used by the auditor to assess his or her doubt about a client's ability to continue as a going concern and to evaluate management's plans for addressing the issue.

ILLUSTRATION 1. GOING CONCERN CHECKLIST

_____
[*Client*]

_____
[*Audit Date*]

Instructions

This checklist should be used in every audit of financial statements to assess whether there is significant doubt about the "going concern" assumption. It is divided into two parts. Part I should always be completed. Part II should be completed only when, as a result of completing Part I, the auditor concludes that significant doubt may exist.

If an item is not applicable, insert "N/A" in the Yes/No column.

Part I

		Yes/No	Date	Comment
1.	Have audit procedures identified any of the following conditions or events that may raise a question about the client's continued existence?			
	a. Recurring operating losses			
	b. Working capital deficiencies			
	c. Negative cash flows from operations			
	d. Adverse key financial ratios, such as the current ratio and the quick asset ratio			
	e. Default on loan or similar agreements			
	f. Dividend arrearages			
	g. Denial of usual trade credit from suppliers			
	h. Noncompliance with statutory capital requirements			
	i. Necessity of seeking new sources or methods of financing			
	j. Loss of key management or operations personnel			
	k. Work stoppages or other labor difficulties			
	l. Substantial dependence on the success of a particular project			
	m. Uneconomic long-term commitments			
	n. Legal proceedings, legislation, or similar matters that might jeopardize entity's ability to operate			
	o. Loss of key franchise, license, or patent			
	p. Loss of a principal customer or supplier			
	q. Uninsured catastrophe			
	r. Other factors that create an uncertainty about going-concern status			
2.	Analyze the conditions or events identified in question 1 and conclude whether they raise a question about ability to continue as a going concern. (If the conclusion is "Yes," complete the procedures described in Part II.)			

Part II

		Performed by	Date	Explanation or conclusion
Consideration of Management Plans				
1.	Discuss situation with management and determine plans for correcting conditions. Is management planning to:			
	a. Dispose of assets?			
	b. Borrow money or restructure debt?			
	c. Reduce or delay expenditures?			
	d. Increase ownership equity?			
2.	Fill out appropriate section or sections below.			

	Performed by	Date	Explanation or conclusion

Liquidate assets

3. Inquire about marketability of assets.
4. Inquire about restrictions on the disposal of assets.
5. Inquire about effects on operations of disposal.

Borrow money or restructure debt

6. Inquire about the availability of new debt.
7. Inquire about the availability of collateral to support new debt.
8. Inquire about restrictions on additional debt.
9. Read management's plans for:

   a. Debt restructuring
   b. Subordination of existing debt
   c. Obtaining loan guarantees

Reduce or delay expenditures

10. Read management's plans for reducing or delaying expenditures for the following:

    a. Repairs and maintenance
    b. Advertising
    c. Research and development
    d. Property, plant, and equipment
    e. Other

11. Discuss with management the effect on operations of the reduction or delay.
12. Read management's plan to sell equity securities.
13. Discuss tax consequences of plan with our tax department.
14. Inquire about plan's impact on existing shareholders.
15. Discuss with management the adequacy of the investment.

Management Forecasts

1. Read management's assumptions about the following:

   a. General economic conditions
   b. Industry economic conditions
   c. Sales
   d. Cost of sales
   e. Cost of labor
   f. Capital expenditures
   g. Selling, general, and administrative expenses
   h. Interest expenses
   i. New borrowings
   j. Income taxes

2. Recompute mathematical calculations.
3. Consider the internal consistency of the forecasts.

	Performed by	Date	Explanation or conclusion
Adequacy of Disclosure and Auditor's Report			
1. Consider the need to disclose the following:			
a. Conditions and events that created the doubt about continued existence			
b. Possible effects of significant conditions and events			
c. Management's evaluation of conditions and events			
d. Possible disposal of a component of an entity			
e. Management's plans, including relevant prospective financial information			
f. Information about recoverability or classification of recorded asset amounts or the amounts or classification of liabilities			
2. Consider need to modify report.			
a. Add explanatory paragraph.			
b. Disclaim an opinion (discretionary).			

AU 342 Auditing Accounting Estimates[1]

AU-C 540 Auditing Accounting Estimates, Including Fair Value Accounting Estimates and Related Disclosures

AU EFFECTIVE DATE AND APPLICABILITY

Original Pronouncement	Statement on Auditing Standards (SAS) 57.
Effective Date	This standard is now effective.
Applicability	Audits of financial statements in accordance with generally accepted auditing standards (GAAS).

AU-C EFFECTIVE DATE AND SUMMARY OF CHANGES

SAS No. 122, *Codification of Auditing Standards and Procedures,* is effective for audits of financial statements with periods ending on or after December 15, 2012.

AU-C 540 does not change the extant requirements of AU 342 in any significant respect. AU-C 540 supersedes AU-C 328, *Auditing Fair Value Measurements and Disclosures,* and AU 342, *Auditing Accounting Estimates.*

AU DEFINITIONS OF TERMS

Accounting estimate. An accounting estimate is an approximation of a financial statement element, item, or account. Accounting estimates are included in historical financial statements because (1) the measurement of some amounts or the valuation of some accounts is uncertain, pending the outcome of future events, or (2) relevant data concerning events that have already occurred cannot be accumulated on a timely cost-effective basis.

Accounting estimates in historical financial statements measure the effects of past business transactions or events, or the present status of an asset or liability. Examples of ac-

---

[1] This section is affected by the Public Company Accounting Oversight Board's (PCAOB's) Standard, Conforming Amendments to PCAOB Interim Standards Resulting from the Adoption of PCAOB Auditing Standard No. 5, An Audit of Internal Control Over Financial Reporting That Is Integrated with an Audit of Financial Statements.

counting estimates include (1) net realizable values of inventory and accounts receivable, (2) property and casualty insurance loss reserves, (3) revenue from contracts accounted for by the percentage-of-completion method, and (4) pension and warranty expenses. (The "Illustration" section contain a list of typical accounting estimates. The examples are taken from Section 342.)

Key factors. The Statement does not define this term; however, it states that the auditor normally concentrates on key factors in evaluating the reasonableness of accounting estimates. The term is defined in Section AT 301, *Financial Forecasts and Projections*, as follows:

> *Key factors encompass matters that affect items such as sales, production, service, and financing activities. They are the foundation for prospective financial statements and are the bases for assumptions.*

AU-C DEFINITIONS OF TERMS

Source: AU-C 540.07

Accounting estimate. An approximation of a monetary amount in the absence of a precise means of measurement. This term is used for an amount measured at fair value when there is estimation uncertainty, as well as for other amounts that require estimation. When this section addresses only accounting estimates involving measurement at fair value, the term *fair value accounting estimates* is used.

Auditor's point estimate or auditor's range. The amount or range of amounts, respectively, derived from audit evidence for use in evaluating the recorded or disclosed amount(s).

Estimation uncertainty. The susceptibility of an accounting estimate and related disclosures to an inherent lack of precision in its measurement.

Management bias. A lack of neutrality by management in the preparation and fair presentation of information.

Management's point estimate. The amount selected by management for recognition or disclosure in the financial statements as an accounting estimate.

Outcome of an accounting estimate. The actual monetary amount that results from the resolution of the underlying transaction(s), event(s), or condition(s) addressed by the accounting estimate.

OBJECTIVES OF AU SECTION 342

Estimation is essential in the preparation of financial statements. Exact measurement of some amounts or the valuation of some accounts is uncertain until (1) the outcome of future events is known, or (2) all relevant data concerning events that have already occurred are accumulated.

Because they involve uncertainty and subjectivity, and because controls over them are more difficult to establish than controls over factual information, accounting estimates ordinarily are more susceptible to material misstatements than factual data. It is, therefore, necessary for the auditor to devote adequate audit resources to accounting estimates in light of the degree of uncertainty and subjectivity, quality of controls, and other relevant circumstances.

Section 342 provides guidance to auditors (1) on identifying circumstances that require accounting estimates, and (2) on obtaining and evaluating sufficient competent evidential matter to support accounting estimates in an audit of financial statements in accordance with GAAS.

OBJECTIVE OF AU-C SECTION 540

AU-C 540 states:

the objective of the auditor is to obtain sufficient appropriate audit evidence about whether, in the context of the applicable financial reporting framework

    a. *accounting estimates, including fair value accounting estimates, in the financial statements, whether recognized or disclosed, are reasonable and*
    b. *related disclosures in the financial statements are adequate.*

(AU-C 540.06)

FUNDAMENTAL REQUIREMENTS

AUDITOR'S RESPONSIBILITY

The auditor is responsible for evaluating the reasonableness of accounting estimates made by management. The auditor should consider, with an attitude of professional skepticism, both the subjective and objective factors on which accounting estimates are based in planning and performing procedures to evaluate those estimates.

AUDITOR'S OBJECTIVE

The auditor should evaluate accounting estimates to obtain reasonable assurance that:

1. All accounting estimates that could be material have been developed by management.
2. Those estimates are reasonable.
3. The estimates are presented and disclosed in conformity with generally accepted accounting principles (GAAP).

IDENTIFYING CIRCUMSTANCES THAT REQUIRE MATERIAL ACCOUNTING ESTIMATES

When evaluating whether management has identified all material accounting estimates, the auditor should consider performing the following procedures:

1. Consider assertions embodied in the financial statements to determine what accounting estimates are needed (see "Illustration" for examples of accounting estimates included in financial statements).
2. Consider information obtained when performing other auditing procedures (see the "Techniques for Application" section).
3. Ask management about whether circumstances exist that may indicate the need to make an accounting estimate.

In addition to the guidance provided by Section 342:

- Section 316, *Consideration of Fraud in a Financial Statement Audit*, states that the auditor should perform a retrospective review of estimates to respond to the risk of management override.

- Section 318, *Performing Audit Procedures in Response to Assessed Risks and Evaluating the Audit Evidence Obtained*, alerts the auditor that accounting estimates often are the source of significant risks.

NOTE: In evaluating whether all material estimates have been identified, the auditor considers the circumstances of the industry, the entity's method of conducting business, new accounting pronouncements, and other relevant internal or external factors.

EVALUATING REASONABLENESS

In evaluating reasonableness of accounting estimates, the auditor should do the following:

1. As a general rule, consider the historical experience of the entity in making past estimates and the auditor's experience in the industry.
2. Understand how management developed the estimate.
3. Based on the understanding obtained in item 2, the auditor should do one or a combination of the following:
   a. Review and test management's process for developing the estimate.
   b. Develop an independent expectation of the estimate to corroborate whether management's estimate is reasonable.
   c. Review subsequent events or transactions occurring before the completion of fieldwork.

NOTE: In evaluating reasonableness, the auditor should concentrate on key factors and assumptions that are

1. *Significant*
2. *Sensitive to variations*
3. *Deviations from historical patterns*
4. *Subjective and susceptible to misstatement and bias*

AU INTERPRETATION

PERFORMANCE AND REPORTING GUIDANCE RELATED TO FAIR VALUE DISCLOSURES (FEBRUARY 1993; REVISED OCTOBER 2000; REVISED MARCH 2006; REVISED JUNE 2009)

The auditor should determine if the fair value disclosures presented represent only those required by Financial Accounting Standards Board (FASB) Accounting Standards Codification (ASC) 825, *Financial Instruments*, or whether additional voluntary disclosures are also presented.

For both required and voluntary disclosures, the auditor should reasonably assure that:

1. The valuation of principles are acceptable, consistently applied, and supported by underlying documentation.
2. The methods of estimation and significant assumptions used are properly disclosed.

Only Required Information Presented

If no other report modifications are needed, the auditor may issue a standard audit report. The auditor may elect to add an emphasis-of-matter paragraph calling attention to the nature and possible range of fair values. If required information is not presented, the auditor should consider whether a qualified or adverse opinion is required because of the departure from GAAP.

Both Required and Voluntary Information Presented

The auditor may audit the voluntary information only if:

1. The measurement and disclosure criteria used are reasonable.
2. Competent persons using the measurement and disclosure criteria would ordinarily obtain similar results.

Voluntary fair values may be presented as a complete balance sheet presentation or a less-than-complete balance sheet. When a complete balance sheet is presented, the following paragraph from AU 9342.06 should be added to the audit report:

> We have also audited in accordance with auditing standards generally accepted in the United States of America the supplemental fair value balance sheet of ABC Company as of December 31, 20X1. As described in Note X, the supplemental fair value balance sheet has been prepared by management to present relevant financial information that is not provided by the historical-cost balance sheets and is not intended to be a presentation in conformity with generally accepted accounting principles. In addition, the supplemental fair value balance sheet does not purport to present the net realizable, liquidation, or market value of ABC Company as a whole. Furthermore, amounts ultimately realized by ABC Company from the disposal of assets may vary significantly from the fair values presented. In our opinion, the supplemental fair value balance sheet referred to above presents fairly, in all material respects, the information set forth therein as described in Note X.

When the required and voluntary fair values do not constitute a complete balance sheet and are located on the face of the financial statements or in footnotes, the standard audit report may be presented. However, if the partial disclosures are included in a separate schedule or exhibit in an auditor-submitted document, the auditor should add an additional paragraph to the audit report (see Section 551, *Reporting on Information Accompanying the Basic Financial Statements in the Auditor-Submitted Documents*) indicating that the fair value information is presented for additional analysis purposes and is not a required part of the basic financial statements. In situations when the auditor is not engaged to audit the voluntary fair value information or is unable to audit it, and the information is presented in an auditor-submitted document (on the face of the financial statements or in notes thereto or in a supplemental format), the voluntary information should be labeled "unaudited" and the auditor should disclaim an opinion on it (see Section 551). Finally, when the audited disclosures are presented on the face of the financial statements, in footnotes, or as supplements in a client-prepared document, the information should simply be labeled "unaudited."

TECHNIQUES FOR APPLICATION

CLIENT'S RESPONSIBILITIES

In applying procedures to identify circumstances that require accounting estimates and evaluate the reasonableness of the estimates, the auditor should be aware of the entity's responsibilities in the development of accounting estimates.

Developing Accounting Estimates

Management should establish the process for preparing accounting estimates. The process may not be documented or formally applied; however, it usually consists of:

1. Determining when accounting estimates are required
2. Determining the factors that influence the accounting estimate
3. Assembling data on which to base the estimate
4. Developing appropriate assumptions
5. Estimating the amount
6. Determining that the estimate is presented in the financial statements in conformity with appropriate accounting principles and that disclosure is adequate

If management's process for developing accounting estimates is documented, generally the auditor should review the documentation. If the process is not documented, the auditor should make inquiries of management to determine how management developed its accounting estimates.

Internal Control

An entity's internal control may reduce the likelihood that accounting estimates may be materially misstated. Aspects of control related to accounting estimates include the following:

1. Does management communicate the need for proper accounting estimates?
2. Are appropriate data on which to base the estimate accumulated?
3. Are estimates prepared by qualified personnel?
4. Are accounting estimates and supporting data adequately reviewed and approved?
5. Are past accounting estimates compared with actual results?
6. Has management considered whether the accounting estimate is consistent with its plans?

When the auditor documents his or her understanding of the entity's internal control, he or she should document those aspects related to accounting estimates.

IDENTIFYING CIRCUMSTANCES THAT REQUIRE ACCOUNTING ESTIMATES

1. *Read the financial statements.* The auditor should read the financial statements, including the notes, to determine if any elements, accounts, or items require an accounting estimate. The auditor's knowledge of the client's operations and industry help the auditor determine those components of the financial statements that require accounting estimates.
2. *Obtain information by performing other procedures.* By performing customary auditing procedures—reading minutes, inquiries, substantive tests of account balances—the auditor may obtain information that might indicate the need for an accounting estimate. The auditor should evaluate this information which includes the following:
    a. Information about changes made or to be made in the entity's business that may indicate that an account estimate is needed (see Section 311, *Planning and Supervision*). For example, estimates must be made if the entity has disposed of, or plans to dispose of, a segment of the business.

b. Changes in the process for accumulating financial information. Documenting the auditor's understanding of the entity's internal control would provide this information.
c. Information about identified litigation, claims, and assessments, and other contingencies. Inquiring of client's lawyer and analysis of client's legal expenses would provide this information (see Section 337, *Inquiry of a Client's Lawyer Concerning Litigation, Claims and Assessments*).
d. Information from reading available minutes of meetings of stockholders, directors, and appropriate committees.
e. Information included in regulatory or examination reports, supervisory correspondence, and similar materials from regulatory agencies.

In addition, other auditing procedures, such as confirmation of receivables and observation of inventories might provide information about the need to reconsider the estimate for allowance for doubtful accounts or provide an estimate for inventory obsolescence.

3. *Make inquiries of management.* Throughout the audit the auditor makes inquiries of management. An inquiry should be made concerning the need for an accounting estimate.

EVALUATING THE REASONABLENESS OF ACCOUNTING ESTIMATES

Review and Test Management's Process

In evaluating the reasonableness of accounting estimates, the auditor may consider performing the following procedures:

1. Consider the understanding that has been obtained of the process established by management to develop accounting estimates and whether the process is appropriate in the circumstances.
2. Identify controls over the process and the supporting data.
3. Identify the sources of information that management used in forming the assumptions, and consider whether the information is reliable and sufficient for the purpose based on information gathered in other audit tests.
4. Consider whether there are other key factors or alternative assumptions about the factors.
5. Evaluate whether the assumptions are consistent with one another, the supporting data, and relevant historical data.
6. Analyze historical data used in developing the assumptions to assess its comparability and consistency with data of the period under audit, and determine whether it is sufficiently reliable for the purpose.
7. Consider whether changes in the business or industry may cause other factors to significantly affect the assumptions.
8. Review available documentation of the assumptions used to develop the accounting estimates, and inquire about any of the entity's other plans, goals, and objectives, as well as considering their relationship to the assumptions.
9. Test the calculations used to translate the assumptions and key factors into the accounting estimate.
10. Consider whether there are more appropriate ways to translate assumptions into estimates.
11. Consider obtaining the opinion of a specialist regarding certain assumptions (see Section 336, *Using the Work of a Specialist*).

Develop an Expectation

Based on his or her understanding of the facts and circumstances and knowledge of the client and its industry, the auditor may develop an independent expectation of the estimate by using factors and assumptions not used by the entity and compare that to the client's estimate. Analytical procedures are a common method used in this approach (see Section 329, *Analytical Procedures*).

Review Subsequent Events

In evaluating the reasonableness of an accounting estimate, the auditor may review subsequent events to confirm the estimate or the appropriateness of the factors and assumptions used to develop the estimate or to obtain additional relevant information. For example, a loan that was 60 days past due at year-end might be 180 days past due near the completion of the audit.

AU ILLUSTRATION

The following list is taken from the Section 342 Appendix. It is not all-inclusive.

ILLUSTRATION 1. EXAMPLES OF ACCOUNTING ESTIMATES

Receivables:
  Uncollectible receivables
  Allowance for loan losses
  Uncollectible pledges

Inventories:
  Obsolete inventory
  Net realizable value of inventories where future selling prices and future costs are involved
  Losses on purchase commitments

Financial instruments:
  Valuation of securities
  Trading vs. investment security classification
  Probability of high correlation of a hedge
  Sales of securities with puts and calls

Productive facilities, natural resources and intangibles:
  Useful lives and residual values
  Depreciation and amortization methods
  Recoverability of costs
  Recoverable reserves

Accruals:
  Property and casualty insurance company loss reserves
  Compensation in stock option plans and deferred plans
  Warranty claims
  Taxes on real and personal property
  Renegotiation refunds
  Actuarial assumptions in pension costs

Revenues:
  Airline passenger revenue
  Subscription income
  Freight and cargo revenue
  Dues income
  Losses on sales contracts

Contracts:
  Revenue to be earned
  Costs to be incurred
  Percent of completion

Leases:
  Initial direct costs
  Executory costs
  Residual values

Litigation:
  Probability of loss
  Amount of loss

Rates:
  Annual effective tax rate in interim reporting
  Imputed interest rates on receivables and payables
  Gross profit rates under program method of accounting

Other:
  Losses and net realizable value on disposal of segment or restructuring of a business
  Fair values in nonmonetary exchanges
  Interim period costs in interim reporting
  Current values in personal financial statements

AU 350 Audit Sampling

AU-C 530 Audit Sampling

AU EFFECTIVE DATE AND APPLICABILITY

Original Pronouncements Statements on Auditing Standards (SASs) 39, 43, 45, and 111.

Effective Date These standards are now effective.

Applicability Audits of financial statements in accordance with generally accepted auditing standards (GAAS). The section applies to *audit sampling*, whether the sampling is statistical or nonstatistical (see *Definitions* and *Objectives of Section*).

AU-C EFFECTIVE DATE

SAS No. 122, *Codification of Auditing Standards and Procedures,* is effective for audits of financial statements with periods ending on or after December 15, 2012. AU-C 530 does not change extant requirements in any significant respect.

AU DEFINITIONS OF TERMS

Audit sampling. The application of an audit procedure to less than 100% of the items within an account balance or class of transactions for the purpose of evaluating some characteristics of the balance or class.

Audit risk. The uncertainty inherent in applying audit procedures.

Dual-purpose sample. A sample designed (1) to assess control risk, and (2) to test whether the recorded monetary amount of transactions is correct.

Nonsampling risk. All aspects of audit risk that are not due to sampling (for example, selecting auditing procedures that do not achieve a specific objective, or failing to recognize misstatements).

Population. The items comprising the account balance or class of transactions.

Risk of incorrect acceptance. The risk that the sample supports the conclusion that the recorded account balance is not materially misstated when it is materially misstated (aspect of sampling risk for substantive test).

Risk of incorrect rejection. The risk that the sample supports the conclusion that the recorded account balance is materially misstated when it is not materially misstated (aspect of sampling risk for substantive test).

Risk of assessing control risk too low. The risk that the assessed level of control risk based on the sample is less than the true operating effectiveness of the control (aspect of sampling risk for tests of controls).

Risk of assessing control risk too high. The risk that the assessed level of control risk based on the sample is greater than the true operating effectiveness of the control (aspect of sampling risk for tests of controls).

Sampling risk. The risk that the auditor's conclusions may be different from the conclusions he or she would reach if the (audit) test were applied in the same way to all items in the account balance or class of transactions (varies inversely with sample size).

Substantive test. An audit procedure designed to obtain evidence about the validity and propriety of the accounting treatment of transactions and balances or to detect misstatements.

Tolerable misstatement. The maximum monetary misstatement for an account balance or class of transactions that may exist without causing the financial statements to be materially misstated. (A planning concept—tolerable misstatement combined for the entire audit plan should not exceed preliminary estimates of materiality levels.)

Tolerable rate. The maximum rate of deviations from a prescribed internal control that the auditor would be willing to accept without altering his or her assessment of the level of control risk.

Unexamined items. Selected sample items that cannot be examined because they are missing (for example, supporting documentation for a selected sample item cannot be located).

AU-C DEFINITIONS OF TERMS

Source: AU-C 530.04

Audit sampling (sampling). The selection and evaluation of less than 100% of the population of audit relevance such that the auditor expects the items selected (the sample) to be representative of the population and, thus, likely to provide a reasonable basis for conclusions about the population. In this context, *representative* means that evaluation of the sample will result in conclusions that, subject to the limitations of sampling risk, are similar to those that would be drawn if the same procedures were applied to the entire population.

Nonsampling risk. The risk that the auditor reaches an erroneous conclusion for any reason not related to sampling risk.

Population. The entire set of data from which a sample is selected and about which the auditor wishes to draw conclusions.

Sampling risk. The risk that the auditor's conclusion based on a sample may be different from the conclusion if the entire population were subjected to the same audit procedure. Sampling risk can lead to two types of erroneous conclusions:

1. In the case of a test of controls, that controls are more effective than they actually are, or in the case of a test of details, that a material misstatement does not exist when, in fact, it does. The auditor is primarily concerned with this type of erroneous conclusion because it affects audit effectiveness and is more likely to lead to an inappropriate audit opinion.
2. In the case of a test of controls, that controls are less effective than they actually are, or in the case of a test of details, that a material misstatement exists when, in fact, it

does not. This type of erroneous conclusion affects audit efficiency because it would usually lead to additional work to establish that initial conclusions were incorrect.

Sampling unit. The individual items constituting a population.

Statistical sampling. An approach to sampling that has the following characteristics:

1. Random selection of the sample items
2. The use of an appropriate statistical technique to evaluate sample results, including measurement of sampling risk

A sampling approach that does not have these two characteristics is considered nonstatistical sampling.

Stratification. The process of dividing a population into subpopulations, each of which is a group of sampling units that have similar characteristics.

Tolerable misstatement. A monetary amount set by the auditor, in respect of which the auditor seeks to obtain an appropriate level of assurance that the monetary amount set by the auditor is not exceeded by the actual misstatement in the population.

Tolerable rate of deviation. A rate of deviation set by the auditor, in respect of which the auditor seeks to obtain an appropriate level of assurance that the rate of deviation set by the auditor is not exceeded by the actual rate of deviation in the population.

OBJECTIVES OF AU SECTION 350

The section is not just for statistical samplers. It applies equally to nonstatistical and statistical sampling. Either approach to audit sampling, *when properly applied*, can provide sufficient evidential matter. And it establishes specific requirements essential for proper application.

Because the section establishes requirements that apply whenever audit sampling is used, the definition of audit sampling becomes very important. Audit sampling is defined as "the application of an audit procedure to less than 100% of the items within an account balance or class of transactions for the purpose of evaluating some characteristic of the balance or class." Thus, whenever the auditor intends to reach a conclusion about whether an account balance or class of transactions is misstated based on an examination of less than all the items in the balance or class, he or she should adhere to its requirements.

One effect of the section on practice should be to place a premium on the auditor's decision to sample. If the auditor is sampling, he or she should adhere to the section. If the auditor has some other audit objective, the section does not apply. Thus, the auditor can no longer simply decide that a procedure will be applied on a test basis. Careful consideration should go into a decision that the best approach to an audit test involves use of audit sampling (see "Techniques for Application").

SAS 39 marks an important milestone in the development of statistical sampling in the auditing literature.

1. In 1963, Statement on Auditing Procedure (SAP) 33 acknowledged that the use of statistical sampling in an audit was in accordance with GAAS. This meant that statistical sampling was permissible under professional standards.
2. In 1972, SAP 54 was issued with an appendix on the use of statistical sampling in audit tests. The appendix explained the relationship of statistical terms to established

auditing concepts, such as materiality and risk, and provided guidance on the incorporation of statistical sampling in planning and applying audit procedures.
3. In 1981, SAS 39 moved statistical sampling from the subordinate status of an appendix to the body of the statement and equated statistical and nonstatistical sampling in a common approach. Basically, the SAS says that there is an underlying rationale for sampling in auditing that is applicable whether the sampling is statistical or nonstatistical. Whether that parity is a boon or a burden for nonstatistical audit sampling will depend on distinguishing the specific requirements of the SAS from its other aspects (see "Techniques for Application").

If the auditor is sampling, the selection of sample items should not be judgmental. It must be expected to be representative. All audit sampling has to be either statistical or nonstatistical.

OBJECTIVES OF AU-C SECTION 530

AU-C states that "the objective of the auditor, when using audit sampling, is to provide a reasonable basis for the auditor to draw conclusions about the population from which the sample is selected" (AU-C 530.04).

FUNDAMENTAL REQUIREMENTS

In planning a particular sample, the auditor should:

1. Determine the specific audit objective to be achieved.
2. Determine that the audit procedure, or combination of procedures, to be applied will achieve that objective.
3. Determine that the population from which he or she draws the sample is appropriate for the specific audit objective.

NOTE: The following requirements apply equally to nonstatistical and statistical audit samples.

EXAMINED 100%

Some items exist for which, in the auditor's judgment, acceptance of some sampling risk is not justified. All of these items should be examined. (Items examined 100% are not part of the items subject to sampling.)

NOTE: Some items may individually be so significant or may have such a high likelihood of being misstated that they should not be sampled.

SAMPLE SELECTION

According to AU 350.24, sample items should be selected in such a way that the sample can be expected to be representative of the population. That is, the auditor should select a sample he or she believes is representative of the items comprising the pertinent account balance or class of transactions.

STRATIFICATION

The auditor may be able to decrease required sample size by separating items subject to sampling into relatively homogeneous groups on the basis of some characteristic related to the specific audit objective.

UNEXAMINED SAMPLE ITEMS

The treatment of unexamined selected sample items depends on their effect on the auditor's evaluation of the sample. In a substantive test, if considering the unexamined items to be misstated would not alter the auditor's evaluation of sample results, the items may be ignored. If the evaluation would be changed, the auditor should apply alternative procedures for those items and consider the implications of the reasons for his or her inability to examine the items. In a test of controls, selected items that cannot be examined should be treated as deviations.

NOTE: Before ignoring or simply considering unexamined or missing items as misstated or deviations, the auditor should consider whether the unexamined items might be indicative of fraud.

SAMPLE SIZE: SUBSTANTIVE TEST

To determine the number of items to be selected in a sample for a particular substantive test of details, the auditor should consider:

1. Tolerable misstatement
2. Allowable risk of incorrect acceptance
3. Characteristics of the population

NOTE: For a statistical audit sample, these factors should be reduced to specific amounts for use in a formula or table to calculate sample size. For a nonstatistical sample, specific amounts are often neither required nor possible, and the auditor considers qualitative relationships. For example, as tolerable misstatement increases, sample size decreases.

SAMPLE SIZE: TEST OF CONTROLS

To determine the number of items to be selected for a particular sample for a test of controls, the auditor should consider:

1. Tolerable rate of deviation from controls being tested, based on the planned assessed level of control risk
2. Expected or likely rate of deviation
3. Allowable risk of assessing control risk too low

PROJECTION OF MISSTATEMENTS

The auditor should project the misstatement results of the sample to the account balance or class of transactions from which the sample was selected.

AGGREGATION OF MISSTATEMENTS

The auditor should aggregate projected misstatements for all audit sampling applications and all known misstatements from nonsampling applications when he or she evaluates whether the financial statements taken as a whole may be materially misstated.

QUALITATIVE ASPECTS

In addition to evaluating quantitative sample results (frequency of deviations or frequency and amount of monetary misstatements), the auditor should consider the qualitative aspects of sample results, such as the nature and cause of deviations or monetary misstatements.

NOTE: The qualitative evaluation includes consideration of whether sample results might be indicative of fraud.

RELATING BALANCE SHEET AND INCOME STATEMENT SAMPLING

Accounts in the balance sheet and income statement are often related. In obtaining assurance from balance sheet accounts, an auditor can frequently also obtain some assurance regarding related income statement accounts and vice versa. Thus, the extent of tests performed on balance sheet accounts may be considered when determining whether additional audit evidence regarding one or more assertions needs to be obtained from direct tests of income statement accounts.

INTERPRETATIONS

APPLICABILITY (JANUARY 1985; REVISED MARCH 2006)

The auditor's examination of less than 100% of the items comprising an account balance or class of transactions is not an audit sampling application under Section 350 in the following circumstances:

1. It is not the auditor's intent to extend the conclusions reached from the sample to the remaining items in the account balance or class of transactions.
2. The auditor examines 100% of the items in a given population (or breaks an account balance or class of transactions down into two populations and examines 100% of the subpopulation while considering the second subpopulation immaterial).
3. The auditor is testing controls that do not leave a documentary trail (for example, the auditor's observation of a client's physical inventory).
4. The auditor is not performing a test of details for a given substantive test.

TECHNIQUES FOR APPLICATION: NONSAMPLING

DISTINGUISHING SAMPLING FROM OTHER AUDIT TESTS

Because Section 350 applies equally to nonstatistical sampling (often called judgment sampling) and statistical sampling, whether a procedure involves audit sampling becomes a critical decision. Some audit procedures obviously do not involve sampling, such as:

- Analytical procedures
- Inquiries and observation used in tests of controls that do not result in documentary evidence of performance and in audit planning
- Examination of 100% of the items in an account balance or class of transactions

In general, an audit procedure involves sampling whenever evidence relating to individual items is used as a basis for a conclusion about the population from which the items were selected. However, there are two types of audit tests that do not involve audit sampling that should be carefully distinguished because they are commonly thought of as being done on a test basis:

1. Key-item tests
2. Flow-of-transaction tests (walk-throughs)

Key-Item Tests

These tests are substantive tests of details of all the items in a population that individually or in total could contain monetary misstatements that approximate tolerable misstatement. This approach does not test those items that in total are not material. The results of this kind of test cannot be projected to the balance or class as a whole. The evidence obtained only supports evaluation of the items tested.

This kind of test can be used primarily when most of the dollar amount of an account balance is concentrated in a comparatively few key items such that the remainder of the items in the balance could be entirely misstated without having a material effect on the financial statements.

Flow-of-Transactions Tests

If the auditor's objective is to obtain a better understanding of the flow of a particular class of transactions through the accounting system, sampling is not involved. In this kind of test the auditor traces one or a few of the different types of transactions through the related documents and records. It is often called a walk-through. This test does not involve sampling if the auditor is trying to confirm his or her understanding of how the accounting system works.

TECHNIQUES FOR APPLICATION: NONSTATISTICAL AUDIT SAMPLING[1]

INTRODUCTION

The auditor performs two separate groups of procedures in audit sampling:

1. Sample selection and evaluation of the sample results
2. Audit procedures in examining the sample items

---

[1] The American Institute of Certified Public Accountants (AICPA) published a revised edition of its Audit Sampling Guide *in 2008*. This new guide includes significant new case studies and an in-depth look at nonstatistical audit sampling. The appendices include sampling tables, testing considerations, and a comparison of the key provisions of the risk assessment standards.

This new guide also includes expanded guidance related to the risk assessment standards and the documentation and communication of internal-control matters under SAS 112. Expanded guidance includes the application of sampling to tests of controls and details, determining the sample size, and evaluating sample results.

The audit procedures performed on the sample items do not depend on the method of sample selection. Items selected by either nonstatistical or statistical sampling methods are subject to the same audit procedures.

A properly designed nonstatistical sampling plan can provide results that are as effective as results from a properly designed statistical sampling plan. The significant difference between nonstatistical and statistical sampling is that statistical sampling measures the sampling risk associated with sampling procedures. Sampling risk arises from the possibility that when a test of controls or substantive test is applied to a sample, the auditor's conclusions might be different from those that would have been made if the tests were applied in the same way to all items in the population. That is, the sample selected from the population might not be representative of that population. For tests of controls, sampling risk is the risk of assessing control risk too low or too high. For substantive testing, sampling risk is the risk of incorrect acceptance or incorrect rejection of the amount tested.

METHODS OF SAMPLE SELECTION

Sample items should be selected in a way so that the sample can be expected to be representative of the population; therefore, all items in the population should have a chance of being selected. Common methods of selecting samples are:

- Block sampling
- Haphazard sampling
- Random number sampling
- Systematic sampling

Block sampling does not meet the requirements for a representative sample. The other three do. Ordinarily, only the last two methods are used in statistical sampling.

Block Sampling

A block sample is obtained by selecting several items in sequence. Once the first item in the block is selected, the remainder of the block is chosen automatically. For example, the sample may consist of all vouchers processed during a two-week period or all vouchers processed on specific days. Block samples could theoretically be representative samples but are rarely used because they are inefficient. The time and expense to select sufficient blocks so that the sample could be considered representative of the total population is prohibitive.

Haphazard Sampling

A haphazard sample is obtained by selecting, without any conscious bias, items regardless of their size, source, or other distinguishing characteristics. It is not the selection of sample units in a careless manner; the units are selected in a manner so that the sample can be expected to be representative of the population. For example, the sample may consist of vouchers pulled from all vouchers processed for the year. Excluding items from the sample on the basis of judgment invalidates the requirement for a representative sample.

Random Number Sampling

A random sample is obtained by selecting numbers from a random number table or by generating numbers randomly by computer and matching them with document numbers, such as check numbers and invoice numbers.

Systematic Sampling

A systematic sample is obtained by selecting items at uniform intervals. The interval is determined by dividing the number of physical units in the population by the sample size. A starting point is selected at random in the first interval, and one item is selected from the population at each of the uniform intervals from the random starting point. For example, in a population of 20,000 units and a desired sample of 100 units, every 200th item will be selected from the starting point. Neither the size nor the unusualness of an item should be allowed to influence selection. The auditor can select large and unusual items in addition to items sampled, however.

TESTS OF CONTROLS

After the auditor obtains and documents his or her understanding of internal control, he or she may wish to assess control risk at below the maximum for certain assertions. For these assertions, the auditor should perform tests of controls (see Section 319). When testing controls, the auditor may use attribute sampling.

Attribute Sampling

An attribute is a characteristic of interest. For example, some attributes of a sale that are of interest to the auditor may be the following:

1. Authorization by the sales order department
2. Approval by the credit department
3. Comparison of merchandise shipped and merchandise listed on the sales invoice for agreement

In testing for attributes, the auditor is concerned with how many times a prescribed internal control failed to operate; every deviation from a prescribed control is given equal weight in the sample evaluation, regardless of the dollar amount of the transaction. Based on the occurrence rate in the sample, the auditor decides if he or she can assess control risk at below the maximum.

For nonstatistical attribute sampling, the auditor does the following:

1. Judgmentally determines sample size
2. Selects the sample
3. Applies audit procedures to the sample units
4. Evaluates the results of the application of audit procedures to the sample

Determination of sample size. The auditor determines sample size and evaluates sample results using subjective judgment to apply the criteria specified in SAS 39 and his or her own experience with the client. The auditor may, but is not required to, use statistical tables to determine sample size for nonstatistical compliance tests. (See "References" at the end of this section.) Sample sizes, according to SAS 39, should be based on the tolerable rate of deviation from the control procedures being tested, the expected rate of deviations, and the allowable risk of assessing control risk too low.

The auditor is not required to select a number of items comparable to a statistical sample size. If his or her past experience with a continuing client has been good, the auditor might continue to use sample sizes that have proven effective.

Selection of sample units. The auditor may use one of the methods described earlier for selecting the sample. In selecting the sample, the auditor may encounter the following:

1. Voided documents
2. Unused or inapplicable documents
3. Inability to examine selected items

Voided documents. If the auditor selects a voided document—for example, a voided sales invoice—he or she should replace it with another. The auditor should obtain reasonable assurance, however, that the document was properly voided and was not a deviation from prescribed internal control.

Unused or inapplicable documents. If the auditor selects an unused or inapplicable document, he or she should treat it the same as a voided document.

Inability to examine selected items. If for any reason—for example, the document cannot be located—he or she cannot examine a selected item, the auditor should consider this a deviation from prescribed policies or procedures. Also, the auditor should consider reasons for this deviation and the effect it has on his or her understanding and assessed level of control risk of particular control procedures.

Evaluating sample results. After he or she has completed the examination of the sample units and noted the deviation from prescribed policies or procedures, the auditor:

1. Calculates the deviation rate
2. Considers sampling risk
3. Considers qualitative aspects of deviations
4. Extends the sample when control deviations are found
5. Assesses the potential magnitude of a control deficiency
6. Reaches a conclusion

Calculation of deviation rate. The deviation rate is the number of observed deviations divided by the sample size. This is the auditor's best estimate of the deviation rate for the population from which the sample was selected. In statistics, it is called a point estimate.

Consideration of sampling risk. When he or she evaluates a sample for a test of controls, the auditor should consider sampling risk (see "Definitions of Terms"). For a nonstatistical sample, sampling risk cannot be quantified. Generally, however, sample results do not support assessed risk below the maximum if the actual deviation rate exceeds or is close to the expected population deviation rate used in designing the sample.

Qualitative aspects of deviations. The qualitative aspects of the observed deviations should be considered by the auditor. Each deviation from a prescribed policy procedure should be analyzed to determine its nature and cause. Deviations that occurred when the person responsible for performing the task was on vacation are not as serious as intentional failure to perform prescribed policies or procedures or misunderstood instructions of prescribed policies or procedures. The nature and cause of deviations may influence the auditor's decision to assess control risk below the maximum or perform additional audit procedures.

Reaching a conclusion. Based on the sample results and on his or her experience and judgment, the auditor reaches a conclusion about the level of control risk. If the auditor concludes that he or she cannot assess control risk below the maximum, he or she may:

- Test additional items with the hope of reducing sampling risk
- Modify planned substantive tests

Documentation of Sampling Procedures

This section does not require specific documentation of audit sampling applications; however, the auditor might consider including the following in the audit documentation:

1. A description of the control tested
2. Objectives of the sampling application, including its relationship to planned substantive testing
3. Definitions of the population and the sampling unit
4. Definition of a deviation
5. Assessments of:

   a. Risk of assessing control risk too low
   b. Tolerable deviation rate
   c. Expected population deviation rate

6. Method of determining sample size
7. Method of selecting sample
8. Description of how sampling procedure was performed and a list of sample deviations
9. Evaluation of sample and summary of conclusions, including:

   a. Number of sample deviations
   b. Explanation of how sampling risk was considered
   c. Determination of whether sample results supported planned assessed level of control risk
   d. Qualitative aspects of deviations
   e. Effects of evaluation of results on planned substantive tests

SUBSTANTIVE TESTS

In using nonstatistical sampling for substantive tests, the auditor should do the following:

1. Identify individually significant items
2. Define the population
3. Define the sample unit
4. Determine the sample size
5. Select the sample
6. Evaluate the sample results (quantitatively and qualitatively)
7. Consider sampling risk
8. Document the sampling procedures

Identify Individually Significant Items

In using sampling for substantive tests, the auditor may decide that for certain items, accepting some sampling risk is not justified. For example, the auditor may decide to examine *all* items over a specified dollar amount. Items tested 100% are not part of the sample. Dividing a population into relatively homogeneous units is known as stratification. Excluding individually significant items provides an initial stratification. The auditor may further subdivide the remaining population, however, into subgroups of items with similar values.

Define the Population

The population consists of the class of transactions or the account balance to be tested. Because the auditor will project the results of the sample to the population, he or she must specify the population so that the sample units come from that population. For example, accounts receivable has four different populations:

1. All accounts
2. Accounts with zero balances
3. Accounts with debit balances
4. Accounts with credit balances

The audit objective determines which population is appropriate.

Define the Period Covered by the Test

When testing during interim work, the auditor should consider what additional evidence needs to be obtained for the remaining period. If the testing is not extended to all transactions occurring in the remaining period, the population only consists of transactions for the interim period and the results of the test can only be projected to that period. In this case, the auditor obtains other evidence to conclude on the operating effectiveness of those controls during the period not covered by the tests.

When the auditor requires assurance regarding the effectiveness of controls as of a specific date, the transactions on or close to that date constitute the population from which a sample is selected. If it is impractical to perform these tests in that period, it may be appropriate to conduct tests for an earlier period instead.

Define the Sample Unit

A sampling unit is any item in the population. For example, a sampling unit may be a customer account or an individual transaction.

Determine Sample Size

For nonstatistical sampling, sample size can be subjectively determined. Factors 1 to 4 should be considered and 5 might be considered:

1. Amounts of the individual items in the population
2. Variability and size of the population
3. Risk of incorrect acceptance
4. Tolerable misstatement and expected misstatement
5. Statistical table or formula

Amounts of individual items. Accounting populations usually include a few very large amounts, a number of moderately large amounts, and a large number of small amounts. In these circumstances, if the population is not stratified, much larger sample sizes are necessary.

Variability and size of the population. Populations are characterized by some variability; that is, not every item in the population is the same amount. Statistically, this variation is measured by the standard deviation. The larger the variability of the population, the larger the standard deviation. For nonstatistical sampling, the standard deviation is not quantified; it is estimated in qualitative terms, such as small variability or large variability. *The larger the estimated variability of the population, the larger the sample size required.* To estimate variability, the auditor may use:

- His or her judgment
- Prior year results
- A pilot sample

The number of items in the population generally has little effect on the sample size for substantive tests; therefore, it is generally not efficient to determine sample size as a fixed percentage of the population.

Risk of incorrect acceptance. In determining sample size, the auditor should consider the risk of incorrect acceptance (an aspect of sampling risk). As the level of risk of incorrect acceptance increases, the sample size for the substantive test decreases. For example, a 10% level of risk of incorrect acceptance requires a smaller sample to achieve the same results than does a 5% level of risk. If he or she assessed control risk at lower than the maximum for a given assertion, the auditor can accept a larger risk of incorrect acceptance for the substantive test related to the assertion.

Risk of incorrect rejection. The auditor should also consider the risk of incorrect rejection when determining the sample size. To limit the risk of incorrect rejection, one can increase the sample size. An alternative solution is to perform additional procedures when testing finds a higher amount of misstatement than expected.

Tolerable misstatement and expected misstatement. For an account balance or a class of transactions, the sample size, given the risk of incorrect acceptance, increases as the tolerable misstatement for that balance or class of transactions decreases. As the size or frequency of expected misstatements decreases, the sample size also decreases.

Statistical table or formula. After he or she determines sample size for nonstatistical sampling, the auditor may wish to, but is not required to, compare it with the sample size from a statistical table or formula. The auditor may also use a statistical table or formula to determine sample size for a nonstatistical sample. The distinguishing feature of statistical sampling is mathematical evaluation of sample results using the laws of probability. Use of statistical methods for sample size determination and selection of sample items do not by themselves make the audit sample a statistical sample.

Select the Sample

The auditor should select the sample units by using any method that can be expected to result in a representative sample. For substantive tests of account balances, the auditor ordinarily stratifies the population before selecting the sample.

Evaluate Sample Results

The section requires the auditor to project the misstatement results of the sample to the population from which the sample was selected.

One method of projecting the misstatement is to divide the dollar amount of the misstatement in the sample by the percentage of the sample dollars to the total dollars in the population. For example, if the sample amounted to 5% of the population (in dollars), and if $1,000 of misstatement was observed in the sample, the misstatement projected to the population is $20,000 ($1,000 ÷ 5%). This is the best estimate of the misstatement in the population.

Another method of projecting the misstatement is to multiply the average unit misstatement in the sample by the number of units in the population. For example, if there were 200 units in the sample and $600 in misstatements was observed, the average misstatement in the sample is $3 ($600 ÷ 200). If there are 30,000 units in the population, the misstatement projected to the population is $90,000 (30,000 × $3).

Projected misstatement is the best estimate of the misstatement in the population. In statistics, it is called the point estimate.

Consider Sampling Risk

For nonstatistical sampling, the auditor uses his or her experience with the client and professional judgment when considering sampling risk. If the projected misstatement does not exceed expected misstatement, the auditor may reasonably conclude that there is an acceptably low risk that the true misstatement exceeds the tolerable misstatement. However, if the projected misstatement exceeds or approximates expected misstatement, the auditor may reasonably conclude that there is an unacceptably high risk that the true misstatement exceeds the tolerable misstatement.

If he or she believes the recorded amount may be misstated, the auditor ordinarily suggests that the entity investigate the misstatements and, if appropriate, adjust the recorded amount.

Document Sampling Procedures

This section does not require specific documentation of audit sampling applications; however, the auditor might consider including the following in the audit documentation:

1. Objectives of the test and a description of other procedures, if any, directed to these same objectives
2. Definitions of the population and the sampling unit
3. Definition of a misstatement
4. Assessment of:
    a. Risk of incorrect acceptance
    b. Risk of incorrect rejection (solely a matter of *efficiency*)
    c. Tolerable misstatement
    d. Expected population misstatement
5. Sampling technique used
6. Method of selecting sample
7. Description of how sampling procedure was performed and a list of sample errors
8. Evaluation of sample and summary of conclusions, including:
    a. Projection of misstatements
    b. Consideration of sampling risk
    c. Qualitative aspects of the misstatements

TECHNIQUES FOR APPLICATION: STATISTICAL AUDIT SAMPLING

INTRODUCTION

There are many valid ways of applying statistical sampling. The method described in this section is a highly efficient application.

Statistical samples can be designed to satisfy either or both of the following objectives:

1. *The detection objective.* The detection of a misstatement or deviation if it exists in the population at a specified rate or amount.
2. *The estimation objective.* The estimation of the extent of detected misstatements or deviations.

Random sampling enables the auditor to project sample results mathematically and to state, with measurable precision and confidence, the estimated rate of deviation in the population under audit (attribute sampling), or the estimated dollar amount of misstatement in the population (dollar value,[2] or variables, sampling).

CALCULATING SAMPLE SIZE

Given that the auditor is willing to accept some sampling risk, the most important risk to consider in the planning of a test procedure is the risk of incorrect acceptance (or risk of assessing control risk too low). In the simplified approach to be presented below, this risk, whether for substantive tests or tests of control, will be referred to as the detection risk. Detection risk is the chance that an audit sample will fail to disclose misstatement if the misstatement in the population exceeds the tolerable misstatement (or tolerable rate of deviation). The complement of the detection risk is the detection confidence. The sample size approach that controls the detection risk is known as a discovery sample size.

Discovery Sampling

A discovery sample is the smallest sample size capable of providing a specified chance (confidence) of detecting misstatement when the misstatement in the population exceeds tolerable misstatement. If a discovery sample is selected and discloses no misstatement, then the auditor can assert, with specified confidence, that the population misstatement does not exceed tolerable misstatement.

Discovery sampling is an efficient, yet powerful, approach in determining the extent of testing required to satisfy an audit test objective and is especially useful for testing populations that are nearly free of misstatement. If misstatements exist, they are likely to be detected. If misstatements are detected, the sample results can then be used to project the detected misstatements to the population from which the sample was selected.

Discovery sample sizes are easily calculated. For tests of controls, the sample size (n) is obtained by dividing the confidence factors (CF) by the tolerable deviation rate (TDR), or:

$$n = CF/TDR$$

Confidence factors for discovery sample size follow.

Confidence level (%)	80.0	90.0	95.0	97.5	99.0	99.5
RISK (%) (1 – confidence level)	20.0	10.0	5.0	2.5	1.0	.5
Confidence factor (CF)	1.61	2.31	3.00	3.69	4.61	5.30

For substantive tests, the confidence factor is multiplied by the population book value (B) and divided by the tolerable misstatement amount (TMA), or:

$$n = (B \times CF)/TMA$$

For example, assume that a population has a book value of $3,530,000. The auditor wishes to have an 80% chance of detecting misstatement in the sample if the amount of misstatement in the population exceeds $70,000. The discovery sample size is:

$$n = (3,530,000 \times 1.61)/70,000$$
$$= 82 \text{ items (rounded up)}$$

Note that when the foregoing method is applied to samples selected with equal chance, it is assumed that misstatements tend to be randomly distributed throughout the population. If

---

[2] *Dollar value sampling is also referred to as probability-proportional-to-size sampling.*

this is not likely to be the case, the auditor should consider stratifying the population so as to segregate those portions of the population that, in his or her judgment, are more likely to be prone to misstatement.

Sample Sizes When Deviations or Misstatements Are Expected

If a population is not expected to be nearly free of deviation or misstatement, a discovery sample size will often be too small to enable the auditor to conclude that the population deviation or misstatement is less than tolerable deviation or misstatement. In addition to the aforementioned factors, the auditor considers the expected deviation rate (EDR) when planning a test of controls or the expected misstatement amount (EMA) when planning a substantive test. For a test of controls, the sample size formula is:

$$n = \left(\frac{CF}{TDR - EDR}\right)\left[1 + \left(\frac{EDR}{TDR - EDR}\right)\right]$$

For a substantive test using dollar unit sampling, or when sampling with equal chance for randomly distributed errors or overstatement:

$$n = \left[\frac{(B)(CF)}{TMA - EMA}\right]\left[1 + \left(\frac{EMA}{TMA - EMA}\right)\right]$$

The confidence factor is determined from the list of confidence factors given earlier. There is a tendency to understate somewhat the sample size for confidence levels of 97.5% or higher. This can be corrected by using the following factors:

Confidence level	Confidence factor
97.5	3.84
99.0	5.43
99.5	6.63

Suppose, in the previous example, the auditor expects as much as $20,000 of misstatement in the population, based on his or her previous experience. The sample size is:

$$n = \left[\frac{(3{,}530{,}000)(1.61)}{70{,}000 - 20{,}000}\right]\left[1 + \left(\frac{20{,}000}{70{,}000 - 20{,}000}\right)\right]$$

$$= 160 \text{ items (rounded up)}$$

Note that the foregoing formula applies only when EDR is less than TDR (or EMA is less than TMA). As a practical matter, the auditor should consider applying this formula only if EDR or EMA is no more than TDR/2 or TMA/2, respectively.

As the expected deviation or misstatement approaches or exceeds one-half the tolerable deviation or misstatement, it becomes increasingly difficult to establish, with a reasonable sample size, that the population deviation or misstatement does not exceed the specified tolerable level. Tests of controls may not be appropriate when numerous deviations are expected—the auditor may choose not to assess control risk lower than the maximum. Accordingly, the auditor may modify his or her substantive testing objective to obtaining an estimate of the dollar amount of misstatement in the population.

In this case, the auditor specifies the desired precision (P) for the estimate to be obtained. This is usually an amount between TMA/2 and TMA. The sample size formula is:

$$n = \left(\frac{(B)(CF)}{P}\right)\left(1 + \frac{EMA}{P}\right)$$

For example, the expected misstatement in a $9,450,000 population may be as high as $600,000. The auditor wishes to obtain an estimate of the maximum amount of overstatement that could exist. The auditor's desired precision is $400,000. The confidence level is 97.5%. The sample size is:

$$n = \left[\frac{(9,450,000)(3.84)}{400,000}\right]\left[1 + \left(\frac{600,000}{400,000}\right)\right]$$

$$= 227 \text{ items (rounded up)}$$

Small Populations

Some important controls do not operate frequently, but still require testing. For example, controls over the year-end close only occur once a year, while controls over a bi-monthly payroll only occur 24 times per year. The following table provides a sample size guidance for these smaller populations:

Control frequency and population size	Sample size
Quarterly (4)	2
Monthly (12)	2-4
Semimonthly (24)	3-8
Weekly (52)	5-9

Other Methods for Calculating Sample Size

The preceding parts of this section describe the simplest methods for calculating sample sizes. The methods are well suited to testing controls and substantive tests for overstatement (such as tests of existence, collectibility, or lower of cost or market). Numerous other methods exist, particularly for substantive tests. (See the "References" section at the end of this chapter.)

RISK AND CONFIDENCE IN SUBSTANTIVE TESTS OF DETAILS

The *detection risk* (SAS 39 refers to it as the risk of incorrect acceptance) is the chance that the statistical sampling results will lead the auditor to conclude incorrectly that the misstatement in the population does not exceed the tolerable misstatement.

The complement of the detection risk is a one-sided confidence level that may be expressed in either of two ways: (1) the confidence that the magnitude of misstatement in the population is greater than zero; or (2) the confidence that the magnitude of misstatement in the population is less than the tolerable misstatement.

The audit test risk is associated with the detection objective. When planning a test it is specified by the auditor.

The *estimation risk* (SAS 39 refers to it as the risk of incorrect rejection) is the chance that the calculated confidence interval does not include the true value of the population. This confidence interval is two-sided because it makes simultaneous use of two confidence limits, an upper misstatement limit and a lower misstatement limit.

The simultaneous use of two confidence limits is associated with the estimation objective. When planning to achieve the estimation objective, the auditor specifies a two-sided confidence level that will achieve the auditor-specified precision. When evaluating the results of a sample, the auditor calculates the precision (and confidence limits) associated with the specified confidence level.

The following table gives the relationship between a one-sided confidence level and a two-sided confidence level:

One-sided confidence level (%)	Two-sided confidence level (%)
99.5	99.0
99.0	98.0
97.5	95.0
95.0	90.0
90.0	80.0
80.0	60.0
75.0	50.0

STATISTICAL EVALUATION OF A SAMPLE IN SUBSTANTIVE TESTS OF DETAILS

The auditor can evaluate a statistical sample by calculating a *point estimate* and a *confidence interval* around the point estimate at the specified *confidence level*. The point estimate is the projection of the detected misstatements to the population from which the sample was selected. The confidence interval and the confidence level are related measurements. The confidence level is the chance that a confidence interval that is calculated as a result of a random sample will include the actual misstatement within its limits. The width of this interval indicates the amount of precision that the auditor has achieved with the estimate. The two end points of the confidence interval are called the upper and lower confidence limits (UCL and LCL, respectively).

The confidence interval for a specified confidence level can be expressed in three ways:

1. The population misstatement is not more than the UCL (a one-sided confidence limit).
2. The population misstatement is not less than the LCL (a one-sided confidence limit).
3. The population misstatement is included between the LCL and the UCL (two-sided confidence limits).

For example, suppose the evaluation is as follows:

Two-sided confidence: 90%

$LCL = $ 5,000 of overstatement error
$UCL = $15,000 of overstatement error

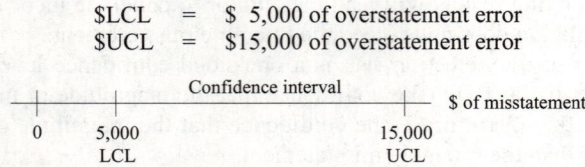

The auditor could conclude, with 90% confidence (two-sided), that the misstatement in the population is $5,000 – $15,000 of overstatement. The auditor could, alternatively, conclude, with 95% confidence, that the misstatement was no less than $5,000 of overstatement, or that the misstatement was no more than $15,000 of overstatement. If the tolerable misstatement is $10,000, the auditor concludes that the population is overstated (because the lower confidence limit is greater than $0) and that the misstatement may exceed the tolerable misstatement (because the upper confidence limit is greater than the tolerable misstatement). Only if the upper confidence limit were less than $10,000 would the auditor be able to conclude that any existing misstatement was not likely to exceed the tolerable misstatement.

The complement of confidence is risk. In statistical sampling there are two aspects of risk: detection risk, which is associated with the detection objective; and estimation risk, which is associated with the estimation objective. Both aspects and their related confidence levels are discussed in the following sections.

CALCULATING CONFIDENCE LIMITS

The calculations for a point estimate and confidence limits depend on the method by which the sample was selected and on certain data assumptions—for example, the assumption that an item cannot be overstated by more than its recorded value. A variety of evaluation methods are given in Arkin's *Handbook*.

Three basic methods for evaluating statistical samples are presented. The methods presented do not cover all situations, but they provide the auditor with the means to evaluate samples on an attributes basis for tests of controls and on a dollar-value basis for substantive tests for overstatement.

EQUAL-PROBABILITY SAMPLING: ATTRIBUTES EVALUATION

Point Estimate

The point estimate of the rate of deviation in the population (D) is obtained by dividing the number of deviations (m) that occurred in the sample by the sample size (n). The formula is:

$$D\% = (100)(m/n)$$

For example, if three deviations are disclosed in a sample of 150 items, the point estimate is:

$$D\% = (100)(3/150)$$
$$= 2.0\%$$

Confidence Limits

The upper confidence limit (UCL%) of the rate of deviation in the population is obtained by dividing the upper confidence limit factor (ULF) in Table 1 by the sample size (n). The formula is:

$$UCL\% = (100)(ULF/n)$$

The appropriate row in Table 1 is determined by the number of deviations in the sample. The appropriate column is determined by the auditor's specified confidence level, which, in Table 1, is given as a one-sided confidence level.

A lower confidence limit is obtained in the same manner, except that Table 2 is used to obtain the lower limit factor (LLF). The formula is:

$$LCL\% = (100)(LLF/n)$$

For example, to obtain an upper 95% confidence limit for a sample of 150 that disclosed three deviations, first obtain the upper limit factor from Table 1 (ULF = 7.76). The upper limit is:

$$UCL\% = (100)(7.76/150)$$
$$= 5.17\%$$

Thus, the auditor can be 95% confident that the population deviation rate does not exceed 5.17%.

To obtain a lower 95% confidence limit for the same sample outcome, obtain the lower limit factor from Table 2 (LLF = 0.81). The lower limit is:

$$LCL\% = (100)(.81/150)$$
$$= .54\%$$

Thus, the auditor can also be 95% confident that the population deviation rate is at least .54%.

If the auditor wishes to express the sample results on a two-sided basis, he or she would be 90% confident that the population deviation rate is between .54% and 5.17%. (See the list given earlier for the relationship between one-sided and two-sided confidence levels.)

DOLLAR VALUE EVALUATION

The following procedures are applicable to the most common type of substantive tests of details—the test for overstatement in an account balance or class of transactions. They may be used (1) for tests of the existence assertion, such as in the confirmation of receivables, (2) for tests of the valuation assertion, such as collectibility, lower of cost or market, or obsolescence, or (3) for tests of the classification assertion. The following conditions should apply to the population:

1. The population does not consist of commingled debit-balance, or credit-balance, and zero-balance items. For example, if the auditor is testing an asset account, the population should consist only of debit-balance items.
2. The maximum amount by which an item may be overstated is its recorded value.

It should be noted that these data conditions are not unduly restrictive and are appropriate for testing the aforementioned financial statement assertions.

EQUAL-PROBABILITY SAMPLING: VARIABLES EVALUATION

Point Estimate

The point estimate of the amount of misstatement in the population ($M_\$$) is determined by (1) calculating the ratio (R) of the total overstatement misstatement in the sample (Σm) to the total book value of the sample (Σb), and (2) multiplying the ratio by the total book value (B) of the population from which the sample was selected. The formula is:

$$M_\$ = (B)(R)$$
$$= (B)(\Sigma m/\Sigma b)$$

For example, 3 misstatements are disclosed in a sample of 150 items. The total misstatement in the 3 items is $225. The total book value of the 150 items is $15,300. The total book value of the population is $1,492,000. The misstatement ratio R is:

$$R = 225/15,300$$
$$= .0147$$

The point estimate of the total misstatement in the population is:

$$M_\$ = 1,492,000 \times .0147$$
$$= \$21,932$$

Confidence Limits

The upper confidence limit ($UCL_\$$) of the amount of overstatement misstatement in the population is obtained by dividing the upper confidence limit factor (ULF) in Table 1 by the sample size (n) and multiplying the result by the population book value (B). The formula is:

$$UCL_\$ = (B)(ULF/n)$$

The appropriate row in Table 1 depends on the sample total equivalent misstatement (m'), which is obtained by multiplying the misstatement ratio (R) by the sample size (n). The formula is:

$$m' = (n)(R)$$

In the example the total equivalent misstatement is:

$$m' = (150)(.0147) = 2.21$$

Locate the upper limit factor in the column of Table 1 that is headed by the desired one-sided confidence level. Note that it may be necessary to interpolate between two successive values of TEM. In the example, the 95% confidence ULF is 6.30 for m equal to 2. The ULF is 7.76 for m equal to 3. Thus, the appropriate ULF, obtained by linear interpolation, is 6.61. The calculation is:

$$\text{ULF} = 6.30 + (.21)(7.76 - 6.30)$$
$$= 6.61 \text{ (rounded off)}$$

The upper 95% confidence limit of the amount of misstatement in the population is:

$$\text{UCL}_\$ = (1{,}492{,}000)(6.61/150)$$
$$= \$65{,}700 \text{ (rounded off)}$$

The lower confidence limit is calculated using the sample procedure, except that the lower confidence limit factor is obtained from Table 2. The formula is:

$$\text{LCL}_\$ = (B)(\text{LLF}/n)$$

In the example, the 95% confidence LLF, obtained by interpolation, is .45. Thus, the lower confidence limit is:

$$\text{LCL}_\$ = (1{,}492{,}000)(.45/150)$$
$$\$4{,}500 \text{ (rounded off)}$$

Thus, the auditor can be 95% confident that the total misstatement in the population is no more than $65,700. The auditor can also be 95% confident that the total misstatement is at least $4,500. Furthermore, the auditor can be 90% confident that the total misstatement is between $4,500 and $65,700. (See the earlier list for the relationship between one-sided and two-sided confidence levels.)

It should be noted that to apply the foregoing procedure, the total book value of the population (B) must be known to be accurately footed, because both the estimate and the confidence limits are obtained directly from this number.

Table 1. Upper Limit Factors, m Deviations or Misstatements in Sample (m' Equivalent Deviations of Misstatements)

Deviations or Misstatements in Sample (m)	Confidence (One-sided)						
	99.5	99.0	97.5	95.0	90.0	80.0	75.0
0	5.30	4.61	3.69	3.00	2.31	1.61	1.39
1	7.43	6.64	5.58	4.75	3.89	3.00	2.70
2	9.28	8.41	7.23	6.30	5.33	4.28	3.93
3	10.98	10.05	8.77	7.76	6.69	5.52	5.11
4	12.60	11.61	10.25	9.16	8.00	6.73	6.28
5	14.15	13.11	11.67	10.52	9.28	7.91	7.43
6	15.66	14.58	13.06	11.85	10.54	9.08	8.56
7	17.14	16.00	14.43	13.15	11.78	10.24	9.69
8	18.58	17.41	15.77	14.44	13.00	11.38	10.81
9	20.00	18.79	17.09	15.71	14.21	12.52	11.92
10	21.40	20.15	18.40	16.97	15.41	13.66	13.02

Deviations or Misstatements in Sample (m)	Confidence (One-sided)						
	99.5	99.0	97.5	95.0	90.0	80.0	75.0
11	22.78	21.50	19.69	18.21	16.60	14.78	14.13
12	24.15	22.83	20.97	19.45	17.79	15.90	15.22
13	25.50	24.14	22.24	20.67	18.96	17.02	16.32
14	26.84	25.45	23.49	21.89	20.13	18.13	17.40
15	28.17	26.75	24.75	23.10	21.30	19.24	18.49
16	29.49	28.04	25.99	24.31	22.46	20.34	19.58
17	30.80	29.31	27.22	25.50	23.61	21.44	20.66
18	32.10	30.59	28.45	26.70	24.76	22.54	21.74
19	33.39	31.85	29.68	27.88	25.91	23.64	22.81
20	34.67	33.11	30.89	29.07	27.05	24.73	23.89
21	35.95	34.36	32.11	30.25	28.19	25.82	24.96
22	37.22	35.61	33.31	31.42	29.33	26.91	26.03
23	38.49	36.85	34.52	32.59	30.46	28.00	27.10
24	39.75	38.08	35.72	33.76	31.59	29.09	28.17
25	41.01	39.31	36.91	34.92	32.72	30.17	29.24
26	42.26	40.54	38.10	36.08	33.84	31.25	30.31
27	43.50	41.76	39.29	37.24	34.96	32.33	31.37
28	44.74	42.98	40.47	38.39	36.08	33.41	32.43
29	45.98	44.19	41.65	39.55	37.20	34.49	33.50
30	47.21	45.41	42.83	40.70	38.32	35.57	34.56
31	48.44	46.61	44.01	41.84	39.43	36.64	35.62
32	49.67	47.82	45.18	42.99	40.55	37.72	36.68
33	50.89	49.02	46.35	44.13	41.66	38.79	37.74
34	52.11	50.22	47.52	45.27	42.77	39.86	38.79
35	53.33	51.41	48.68	46.41	43.88	40.93	39.85
36	54.54	52.61	49.84	47.55	44.98	42.00	40.91
37	55.75	53.80	51.00	48.68	46.09	43.07	41.96
38	56.96	54.98	52.16	49.81	47.19	44.14	43.02
39	58.17	56.17	53.32	50.94	48.29	45.21	44.07
40	59.37	57.35	54.47	52.07	49.39	46.27	45.12
41	60.57	58.53	55.63	53.20	50.49	47.34	46.18
42	61.77	59.71	56.78	54.33	51.59	48.40	47.23
43	62.96	60.89	57.93	55.45	52.69	49.47	48.28
44	64.15	62.06	59.07	56.58	53.79	50.53	49.33
45	65.35	63.24	60.22	57.70	54.88	51.59	50.38
46	66.53	64.41	61.36	58.82	55.98	52.66	51.43
47	67.72	65.58	62.51	59.94	57.07	53.72	52.48
48	68.91	66.74	63.65	61.08	58.16	54.78	53.53
49	70.09	67.91	64.79	62.18	59.25	55.84	54.58
50	71.27	69.07	65.92	63.29	60.34	56.90	55.62

Table 2. Lower Limit Factors, m Deviations or Misstatements in Sample (m' Equivalent Deviations of Misstatements)

Deviations or Misstatements in Sample (m)	Confidence (One-sided)						
	99.5	99.0	97.5	95.0	90.0	80.0	75.0
0	0.	0.	0.	0.	0.	0.	0.
1	.01	.01	.03	.05	.11	.22	.29
2	.10	.14	.24	.35	.53	.82	.96
3	.33	.43	.61	.81	1.10	1.53	1.72
4	.67	.82	1.08	1.36	1.74	2.29	2.53
5	1.07	1.27	1.62	1.97	2.43	3.08	3.36
6	1.53	1.78	2.20	2.61	3.15	3.90	4.21
7	2.03	2.33	2.81	3.28	3.89	4.73	5.08
8	2.57	2.90	3.45	3.98	4.65	5.57	5.95
9	3.13	3.50	4.11	4.69	5.43	6.42	6.83
10	3.71	4.13	4.79	5.42	6.22	7.28	7.72
11	4.32	4.77	5.49	6.16	7.02	8.15	8.61
12	4.94	5.42	6.20	6.92	7.82	9.03	9.51
13	5.58	6.09	6.92	7.68	8.64	9.91	10.42

Deviations or Misstatements in Sample (m)	Confidence (One-sided)						
	99.5	99.0	97.5	95.0	90.0	80.0	75.0
14	6.23	6.78	7.65	8.46	9.46	10.79	11.32
15	6.89	7.47	8.39	9.24	10.29	11.68	12.23
16	7.56	8.18	9.14	10.03	11.13	12.57	13.15
17	8.25	8.89	9.90	10.83	11.97	13.46	14.06
18	8.94	9.61	10.66	11.63	12.82	14.36	14.98
19	9.64	10.34	11.43	12.44	13.67	15.26	15.90
20	10.35	11.08	12.21	13.25	14.52	16.17	16.83
21	11.06	11.82	12.99	14.07	15.38	17.07	17.75
22	11.79	12.57	13.78	14.89	16.24	17.98	18.68
23	12.52	13.32	14.58	15.71	17.10	18.89	19.60
24	13.25	14.08	15.37	16.54	17.97	19.81	20.53
25	13.99	14.85	16.17	17.38	18.84	20.72	21.47
26	14.74	15.62	16.98	18.21	19.71	21.64	22.40
27	15.49	16.39	17.79	19.05	20.59	22.55	23.33
28	16.24	17.17	18.60	19.90	21.46	23.47	24.27
29	17.00	17.95	19.42	20.74	22.34	24.39	25.20
30	17.76	18.74	20.24	21.59	23.22	25.32	26.14
31	18.53	19.53	21.06	22.44	24.11	26.24	27.08
32	19.30	20.32	21.88	23.29	24.99	27.16	28.02
33	20.07	21.12	22.71	24.15	25.88	28.09	28.96
34	20.85	21.91	23.54	25.01	26.77	29.02	29.90
35	21.63	22.72	24.37	25.86	27.66	29.94	30.84
36	22.42	23.52	25.21	26.73	28.55	30.87	31.79
37	23.20	24.33	26.05	27.59	29.44	31.80	32.73
38	23.99	25.14	26.89	28.45	30.34	32.73	33.68
39	24.79	25.95	27.73	29.32	31.24	33.67	34.62
40	25.58	26.77	28.57	30.19	32.13	34.60	35.57
41	26.38	27.58	29.42	31.06	33.03	35.53	36.51
42	27.18	28.40	30.26	31.93	33.93	36.47	37.46
43	27.98	29.22	31.11	32.81	34.83	37.40	38.41
44	28.79	30.05	31.97	33.68	35.74	38.34	39.36
45	29.59	30.87	32.82	34.56	36.64	39.27	40.31
46	30.40	31.70	33.87	35.44	37.55	40.21	41.28
47	31.21	32.53	34.53	36.31	38.45	41.15	42.21
48	32.03	33.38	35.39	37.20	39.36	42.09	43.16
49	32.84	34.19	36.25	38.08	40.27	43.03	44.11
50	33.86	35.03	37.11	38.96	41.17	43.97	45.06

Point Estimate

The point estimate of the amount ($M_\$$) of overstatement misstatement in the population is obtained by multiplying the population book value (B) by the average item misstatement ratio (r). The misstatement ratio (r) for a sample item is obtained by dividing the amount of misstatement (m) in the item by the item's book value (b). Thus,

$$r = m/b$$

for each item in the sample. Note that r will be zero for most of the sample items in a typical audit application. This greatly simplifies the calculation of the average ratio r. The formula for the average misstatement ratio is:

$$r = (\Sigma r)/n$$

or the total equivalent misstatement (m), which is the sum of the item ratios divided by the sample size. The formula for the point estimate of the population misstatement amount is:

$$M_\$ = (B)(r)$$

Suppose the data of the previous example were obtained for a sample that was selected with probability proportional to size (that is, dollar unit sampling), instead of equal-probability sampling. The sample data follow:

Population book value (B): $1,492,000
Sample size: 150 items

Item	Book value (b)	Misstatement amount (m)	Misstatement ratio (r)	
1	183	37	.20	
2	452	185	.41	
3	3	3	1.00	
4	95	0	.00	
--	--	--	--	
--	--	--	--	
--	--	--	--	
$n =$ 150	214	0	0.00	
	$15,300	$225	1.61	$= m'$

The average misstatement ratio is

$$r = 1.61/150 = .011$$

The point estimate of population misstatement is

$$M_\$ = 1,492,000 \times .011 = \$16,412$$

Confidence Limits

The upper confidence limit ($UCL_\$$) of the amount of overstatement misstatement in the population is obtained by dividing the upper confidence limit factor (ULF) in Table 1 by the sample size (n), and multiplying the result by the population book value (B). The formula is:

$$UCL_\$ = (B)(ULF/n)$$

For any specified confidence level the ULF is determined by the total equivalent misstatement (m'), which, in dollar unit sampling, is the sum of the sample item misstatement ratios (Σr). The formula is:

$$m' = \Sigma r$$

If the calculated m' is between two successive values of m in Table 1, the auditor can determine the ULF by interpolation. In the example, m' is calculated to be 1.61 equivalent misstatements. The 95% confidence factors for 1 and 2 misstatements are 4.75 and 6.30, respectively. Thus, the interpolated confidence factor for $m' = 1.61$ is:

$$ULF = 4.75 + (.61)(6.30 - 4.75) = 5.70 \text{ (rounded off)}$$

Thus, the upper 95% confidence limit is:

$$UCL_\$ = (1,492,000)(5.70/150) = \$56,700 \text{ (rounded off)}$$

The lower confidence limit is calculated in the same manner, except that the lower limit factor is obtained by interpolating between successive values of LLF in Table 2. Thus,

$$\text{LCL}_\$ = (B)(\text{LLF}/n)$$

In the example, the lower 95% confidence factor is:

$$\begin{aligned}\text{LLF} &= .05 + (.61)(.35 - .05) \\ &= .23 \text{ (rounded off)}\end{aligned}$$

The lower confidence limit is:

$$\begin{aligned}\text{LCL}_\$ &= (1{,}492{,}000)(.23/150) \\ &= \$2{,}300 \text{ (rounded off)}\end{aligned}$$

The auditor can state, with 95% confidence, that the population overstatement does not exceed $56,700. The auditor can also state, with 95% confidence, that the misstatement is at least $2,300. Moreover, the auditor can be 90% confident that the actual population overstatement misstatement is between $2,300 and $56,700. (See the earlier list for the relationship between one-sided and two-sided confidence levels.)

REFERENCES

An auditor who uses statistical sampling is well-advised to refer to *Audit Sampling: An Introduction,* (New York, NY: John Wiley & Sons, 2001) by Dan M. Guy, D. R. Carmichael, and R. Whittington.

AU 380 The Auditor's Communication with Those Charged with Governance[1]

AU-C 260 The Auditor's Communication with Those Charged with Governance

AU EFFECTIVE DATE AND APPLICABILITY

Original Pronouncement	Statement on Auditing Standards (SAS) 114.
Effective Date	This statement currently is effective.
Applicability	Audits of financial statements in accordance with generally accepted auditing standards (GAAS) of entities who have an audit committee (or other committee formally designated with oversight for financial reporting) and all public entities (i.e., Securities and Exchange Commission [SEC] engagements—see "Definitions of Terms").

AU-C EFFECTIVE DATE AND SUMMARY OF CHANGES

SAS No. 122, *Codification of Auditing Standards and Procedures,* is effective for audits of financial statements with periods ending on or after December 15, 2012.

---

[1] Section 204, Auditor Reports to Audit Committees, *and the related SEC implementing rule 33-8138, "Strengthening the Commission's Requirements Regarding Auditor Independence," require that the auditor communicate:*

1. All critical accounting policies and practices
2. All alternative accounting and disclosure treatments of material financial information that has been discussed with management, including the ramifications of the use of such alternative treatments and disclosures and the treatment preferred by the auditor

The SEC's Financial Reporting Release 60, Cautionary Advice Regarding Disclosure about Critical Accounting Policies, *defines "critical accounting policies" as those policies that are both most important to the company in portraying the company's financial position and results, and that require management's most difficult, subjective, or complex judgments, often as a result of the need to make estimates about highly uncertain matters.*

AU-C 260 does not change extant requirements in any significant respect. It does include a requirement to communicate matters related to other information included in documents containing audited financial statements.

AU DEFINITIONS OF TERMS

Management. The person(s) responsible for achieving the objectives of the entity and who have the authority to establish policies and make decisions by which those objectives are to be pursued. Management is responsible for the financial statements, including designing, implementing and maintaining effective internal control over financial reporting.

Those charged with governance. The person(s) with responsibility for overseeing the strategic direction of the entity and obligations related to the accountability of the entity. This includes overseeing the financial reporting process. In some cases, those charged with governance are responsible for approving the entity's financial statements (in other cases management has this responsibility). For entities with a board of directors, this term encompasses the term "board of directors" or "audit committee" used elsewhere in GAAS.

AU-C DEFINITIONS OF TERMS

Management. The person(s) with executive responsibility for the conduct of the entity's operations. For some entities, management includes some or all of those charged with governance; for example, executive members of a governance board or an owner-manager.

Those charged with governance. The person(s) or organization(s) (for example, a corporate trustee) with responsibility for overseeing the strategic direction of the entity and the obligations related to the accountability of the entity. This includes overseeing the financial reporting process. Those charged with governance may include management personnel; for example, executive members of a governance board or an owner-manager.

OBJECTIVES OF AU SECTION 380

Effective communication between an auditor and his or her client plays in important role in achieving audit objectives. Section 380 is built on the premise that those charged with governance at the entity have a responsibility to oversee the financial reporting progress, and the standard requires the auditor to communicate to those individuals matters significant and relevant to that oversight responsibility.

The principal purposes of this required communications are to:

1. Communicate clearly with those charged with governance both the responsibilities of the auditor in relation to the financial statement audit and an overview of the scope and timing of the audit.
2. Obtain from those charged with governance information relevant to the audit.
3. Provide those charged with governance with timely observations arising from the audit that are relevant to their responsibilities in overseeing the financial reporting process.

The standard also provides a framework for the auditor's communication that includes matters such as the form and timing of the communication.

OBJECTIVES OF AU-C SECTION 260

The objectives of the auditor are to:

a. *communicate clearly with those charged with governance the responsibilities of the auditor regarding the financial statement audit and an overview of the planned scope and timing of the audit.*
b. *obtain from those charged with governance information relevant to the audit.*
c. *provide those charged with governance with timely observations arising from the audit that are significant and relevant to their responsibility to oversee the financial reporting process.*
d. *promote effective two-way communication between the auditor and those charged with governance.*

(AU-C 260.05)

FUNDAMENTAL REQUIREMENTS

GENERAL RESPONSIBILITY

The auditor *must* communicate with those charged with governance matters related to the financial statement audit that are, in the auditor's professional judgment, significant and relevant to the responsibilities of those charged with governance in overseeing the financial reporting process. Certain matters *should* be communicated in each audit (as described below; however the auditor is not required to perform procedures specifically to identify these matters.

THOSE CHARGED WITH GOVERNANCE

The auditor *should* determine "those charged with governance" (see the two sections on "Definitions of Terms"). Governance structures vary by entity; however in most entities, governance is the collective responsibility of a governing body, such as a board of directors, a supervisory board, partners, proprietors, a committee of management, trustees, or equivalent. In some entities, one person, such as the owner-manager, may be the sole person charged with governance of the entity.

When "those charged with governance" are not clearly identifiable, the auditor and the engaging party should agree on the person(s) with whom the auditor will communicate.

In those situations where the entity's governance structure includes subgroups (e.g., an audit committee), the auditor also should evaluate whether communication with a subgroup is sufficient.

COMMUNICATION PROCESS

The auditor should communicate with those charged with governance regarding the timing and expected general content of communications. The auditor may also communicate matters such as:

- The purpose of communications. When the purpose is clear, the auditor and those charged with governance are in a better position to have a mutual understanding of relevant issues and the expected actions arising from the communication process.
- The person(s) on the audit team and among those charged with governance who will communicate regarding particular matters.

- The auditor's expectation that communication will be two way, and that those charged with governance will communicate with the auditor matters they consider relevant to the audit. Such matters might include strategic decisions that may significantly affect the nature, timing, and the extent of audit procedures; the suspicion or the detection of fraud; or concerns about the integrity or competence of senior management.
- The process for taking action and reporting back on matters communicated by the auditor.
- The process for taking action and reporting back on matters communicated by those charged with governance.

The auditor should evaluate whether the two-way communication between the auditor and those charged with governance has been adequate for the purpose of the audit.

Form of Communication

The auditor should communicate in writing significant findings from the audit (see "Matters to be Communicated"). All other communications may be oral or in writing. When matters are to be communicated orally, the auditor should document them.

Timing of Communication

The auditor should communicate with those charged with governance on a sufficiently timely basis to enable those charged with governance to take appropriate action.

MATTERS TO BE COMMUNICATED

The auditor should communicate with those charged with governance

1. The auditor's responsibilities under generally accepted auditing standards.
2. An overview of the planned scope and timing of the audit.
3. Significant findings from the audit.

The Auditor's Responsibilities

The auditor *should* communicate the following:

- The auditor is responsible for forming and expressing an opinion about whether the financial statements are presented fairly.
- The audit does not relieve management or those charged with governance of their responsibilities.

The auditor *may* communicate other matters such as

- The auditor is responsible for performing the audit in accordance with GAAS.
- An audit is designed to obtain reasonable, not absolute, assurance.
- An audit includes consideration of internal control as a basis for designing audit procedures, but not for expressing an opinion on the effectiveness of internal control over financial reporting.
- The auditor is responsible for communicating significant matters related to the audit that are relevant to the responsibilities of those charged with governance.
- When applicable, the auditor is also responsible for communicating particular matters required by laws or regulations, by agreement with the entity, or by additional requirements applicable to the engagement.

Overview of the Planned Scope and Timing of the Audit

The auditor *should* communicate an overview of the planned scope and timing of the audit.

To meet that general requirement, the auditor *may* communicate matters such as the following:

- How the auditor proposes to address the significant risks of material misstatement
- The auditor's approach to internal control
- The concept of materiality in planning and executing the audit
- Where the entity has an internal audit function, the extent to which the auditor will use the work of internal audit
- The views of those charged with governance about:

  - The appropriate person(s) in the entity's governance structure with whom to communicate
  - The allocation of responsibilities between those charged with governance and management
  - The entity's objectives and strategies, and the related business risks that may result in material misstatements
  - Matters those charged with governance consider warrant particular attention during the audit, and any areas where they request additional procedures to be undertaken
  - Significant communications with regulators
  - Other matters those charged with governance believe are relevant to the audit of the financial statements

- The attitudes, awareness, and actions of those charged with governance concerning (1) the entity's internal control and its importance in the entity and (2) the detection or the possibility of fraud.
- The actions of those charged with governance in response to developments in financial reporting, laws, accounting standards, corporate governance practices, and other related matters.
- The actions of those charged with governance in response to previous communications with the auditor.

Significant Findings

The auditor *should* communicate the following matters:

- The auditor's views about qualitative aspects of the entity's significant accounting practices, including accounting policies, accounting estimates, and financial statement disclosures
- Significant difficulties, if any, encountered during the audit; these may include:

  - Significant delays in management providing required information
  - An unnecessarily brief time within which to complete the audit
  - Extensive unexpected effort required to obtain sufficient appropriate audit evidence
  - The unavailability of expected information
  - Restrictions imposed on the auditors by management

- Management's unwillingness to provide information about management's plans for dealing with the adverse effects of the conditions or events that lead the auditor to believe there is substantial doubt about the entity's ability to continue as a going concern
- Uncorrected misstatements, other than those the auditor believes are trivial, if any
- Disagreements with management, if any
- Other findings or issues, if any, arising from the audit that are significant and relevant to those charged with governance

Unless all of those charged with governance are involved in managing the entity, the auditor also should communicate:

- Material, corrected misstatements that were brought to the attention of management as a result of audit procedures
- Representations the auditor is requesting from management
- Management's consultations with other accountants
- Significant issues, if any, that were discussed, or the subject of correspondence, with management

AUDITOR'S JUDGMENTS ABOUT THE QUALITY OF THE ENTITY'S ACCOUNTING PRINCIPLES

The auditor *should discuss* his or her judgments about the quality, not just the acceptability, of the company's accounting principles with the audit committees of SEC clients. Such discussion should include management as a participant and should include:

- Matters such as the consistency of application of the entity's accounting policies and the clarity and completeness of the entity's financial statements and related disclosures
- Certain items that have a significant impact on the representational faithfulness,[2] verifiability,[3] neutrality,[4] and consistency of the accounting information included in the financial statements, such as:
  - New or changed accounting policies
  - Estimates, judgments, and uncertainties
  - Unusual transactions

INTERPRETATIONS

There are no interpretations for this section.

---

[2] *Representational faithfulness means that the amounts and disclosures in the company's financial statements represent what really happened. It includes the concept of substance over form.*

[3] *Verifiability means that accountants using the same measurement method would obtain similar results.*

[4] *Neutrality means that information in financial statements cannot be selected to favor one set of financial statement users over another.*

PROFESSIONAL ISSUES TASK FORCE PRACTICE ALERTS

99-1 GUIDANCE FOR INDEPENDENCE DISCUSSIONS WITH AUDIT COMMITTEES

Independence Standard 1, *Independence Discussions with Audit Committees* (the Standard),[5] requires annual written and oral communications between the auditor and the audit committee (or board of directors if there is no audit committee) of a public company client regarding relationships that, in the auditor's professional judgment, may reasonably be thought to bear on the independence. The standard also requires written confirmation that the auditor is independent of the company within the meaning of the Securities Acts administered by the SEC.

This practice alert is designed to address implementation issues relative to the Standard and is designed to assist firms in:

- Reviewing and improving policies and procedures for identifying and communicating with audit committees those matters that may affect the auditor's independence, which should in turn assist audit committees/board of directors in fulfilling certain of their corporate governance responsibilities
- Helping auditors to fulfill their responsibilities to serve the public interest and strengthen the public's confidence in audited financial information

Although the guidance in the alert focuses on communications between the auditor and the audit committee/board of directors, the auditor is also encouraged to have similar communications with senior management.

The alert provides the following guidance:

- Firms should have policies and procedures for independence communications with audit committees. The alert provides examples of relationships that may impact the auditor's independence, along with relevant safeguards. The alert also suggests that the auditor not conclude that a relationship need not be disclosed because independence is not impaired, especially when information about the relationship may help the audit committee understand auditor independence for this entity's specific circumstances.
- The auditor should consider engaging the audit committee chair in discussions concerning the chair's views on relationships that may reasonably be thought to bear on independence and what should be disclosed. The alert provides a sample letter to the audit committee chair that could be used to initiate these discussions.
- Auditors should periodically discuss new or revised independence standards, emerging independence issues, and common threats to auditor objectivity to help audit committees expand their knowledge of independence matters. The alert provides a summary of common threats to auditor objectivity and related safeguards that mitigate these threats.
- The ISB Standard requires written communications that summarize relationships that may reasonably be thought to bear on independence and confirm that, in the auditor's professional judgment, the auditor is independent of the company within the meaning of the Securities Acts.

---

[5] The Independence Standards Board, which adopted this statement, was dissolved on July 31, 2001. However, ISB 1 will continue in effect.

The alert also emphasizes that disclosure of relationships that may reasonably be thought to bear on independence should not be construed to imply that the auditor's independence has been impaired, but rather as a tool to foster discussion between the auditor and the audit committee regarding the nature of the relationship.

The auditor should meet with the audit committee to discuss all applicable actual and proposed relationships between the company and the auditor. The ISB intentionally left timing flexible as long as the communication is done annually.

The alert provides a sample letter relating to annual independence discussions with audit committees and confirmation that the auditor is independent of the company within the meaning of the Securities Acts.

Finally, the alert also provides guidance on initial public offerings, the initial year of application, prospective clients, and failure to comply with the standard. The alert was updated in 2000 to provide guidance on ISB Interpretation 00-1 that relates to the applicability of ISB Statement 1 to secondary auditors.

00-2 GUIDANCE FOR COMMUNICATION WITH AUDIT COMMITTEES REGARDING ALTERNATIVE TREATMENTS OF FINANCIAL INFORMATION WITHIN GENERALLY ACCEPTED ACCOUNTING PRINCIPLES (REVISED)

In 1999, the Auditing Standards Board issued SAS 90, which requires that the independent auditor of an SEC client discuss with a client's audit committee the quality, not just acceptability, of the entity's accounting principles. (See "Auditor's Judgments About the Quality of the Entity's Accounting Principles" under "Fundamental Requirements.") In addition, the Sarbanes–Oxley Act requires that auditors report to, and be overseen by, the entity's audit committee.

This Practice Alert is intended to assist auditors in identifying relevant matters to discuss with an entity's audit committee the quality of accounting principles used in the preparation of entity's financial statements. To meet the objectives of SAS 90, the Alert recommends that:

- Communications should be tailored to and understandable by all members of the audit committee.
- Audit committee members are advised of independence issues on a timely basis.

Topics that management and the auditor should consider discussing with the audit committee would include, but not be limited to

1. What accounting principles does the entity use for which acceptable alternatives are available?
2. What are judgments and estimates that affect the financial statements?
3. What are factors that affect asset and liability carrying values?
4. Does the entity use special structures or timing of actions that affect financial statements?
5. What are continuing issues and choices that affect financial reporting?
6. How frequent and significant are transactions with related parties, particularly those not in the ordinary course of business?
7. Are there any unusual arrangements such as bill-and-hold transactions?
8. How clear and transparent are the financial statements and disclosures?
9. What audit adjustments were identified in the audit?
10. What are materiality thresholds and cost/benefit judgments?

The practice alert also provides guidance if the auditor or the audit committee wants to address the degree of aggressiveness or conservatism of the accounting principles applied in the financial statements.

TECHNIQUES FOR APPLICATION

QUALITATIVE ASPECTS OF ACCOUNTING PRACTICES

Auditors should seek to have an open and constructive communication with those charged with governance about the qualitative aspects of the entity's significant accounting practices. This communication may include comment on the acceptability of significant accounting practices.

When making this communication, the auditor should explain why he or she consider the practice not to be appropriate. When necessary, the auditor should request changes. If requested changes are not made, the auditor should inform those charged with governance that the auditor will consider the effect of this on the financial statements of the current and future years, and on the auditor's report.

Matters that may be communicated include the following:

Accounting Policies

- The appropriateness of the accounting policies to the particular circumstances of the entity, considering the need to balance the cost of providing information with the likely benefit to users of the entity's financial statements. Where acceptable alternative accounting policies exist, the communication may include identification of the financial statement items that are affected by the choice of significant policies as well as information on accounting policies used by similar entities.
- The initial selection of, and changes in, significant accounting policies, including the application of new accounting pronouncements. The communication may include the effect of the timing and method of adoption of a change in accounting policy on the current and future earnings of the entity; and the timing of a change in accounting policies in relation to expected new accounting pronouncements.
- The effect of significant accounting policies in controversial or emerging areas (or those unique to an industry, particularly when there is a lack of authoritative guidance or consensus).
- The effect of the timing of transactions in relation to the period in which they are recorded.

Accounting Estimates

For items for which estimates are significant, issues discussed in SAS No. 57, *Auditing Accounting Estimates*, and SAS No. 101, *Auditing Fair Value Measurements and Disclosures* include, for example:

- Management's identification of accounting estimates
- Management's process for making accounting estimates
- Risks of material misstatement
- Indicators of possible management bias

Financial Statement Disclosures

- The issues involved, and related judgments made, in formulating particularly sensitive financial statement disclosures (for example, disclosures related to revenue recognition, going concern, subsequent events, and contingency issues)
- The overall neutrality, consistency, and clarity of the disclosures in the financial statements

Related Matters

- The potential effect on the financial statements of significant risks and exposures, and uncertainties, such as pending litigation, that are disclosed in the financial statements.
- The extent to which the financial statements are affected by unusual transactions, including nonrecurring amounts recognized during the period, and the extent to which such transactions are separately disclosed in the financial statements.
- The factors affecting asset and liability carrying values, including the entity's bases for determining useful lives assigned to tangible and intangible assets. The communication may explain how factors affecting carrying values were selected and how alternative selections would have affected the financial statements.
- The selective correction of misstatements, for example, correcting misstatements with the effect of increasing reported earning, but not those that have the effect of decreasing reported earnings.

AU 390 Consideration of Omitted Procedures After the Report Date

AU-C 585 Consideration of Omitted Procedures After the Report Release Date

AU EFFECTIVE DATE AND APPLICABILITY

Original Pronouncement	Statement on Auditing Standards (SAS) 46.
Effective Date	This standard is now effective.
Applicability	Circumstances when:

- Subsequent to the date of the auditor's report on audited financial statements, the auditor concludes that one or more auditing procedures considered necessary at the time of the audit in the circumstances then existing were omitted from the audit, but
- There is no indication that the financial statements are not fairly presented in conformity with generally accepted accounting principles (GAAP) or, if applicable, another comprehensive basis of accounting.

NOTE: This section does not apply in the following circumstances:

1. *An engagement in which an auditor's work is at issue in a threatened or pending legal proceeding (see "Definitions of Terms" sections) or regulatory investigation.*
2. *An engagement in which an auditor subsequent to the date of his or her report on audited financial statements becomes aware that facts regarding those financial statements may have existed at that date and might have affected the financial statements or the audit report had he or she then been aware of them (see Section 561,* Subsequent Discovery of Facts Existing at the Date of the Auditor's Report*).*

AU-C EFFECTIVE DATE AND SUMMARY OF CHANGES

SAS No. 122, *Codification of Auditing Standards and Procedures,* is effective for audits of financial statements with periods ending on or after December 15, 2012.

AU-C 585 does not change extant requirements in any significant respect.

AU DEFINITIONS OF TERMS

Omitted procedure. An auditing procedure that was not applied in the audit of financial statements and that subsequent to the date of the auditor's report on those financial statements was considered to be necessary at the time of the audit in the circumstances then existing.

Present ability to support previously expressed opinion. The professional judgment of the auditor that (1) based on auditing procedures applied in a previous audit of financial statements and the facts and circumstances existing at the time of that audit, or (2) based on additional information or analysis since that audit, the auditor's report on those financial statements still is appropriate.

Threatened legal proceeding. Circumstances in which a potential claimant has indicated to the auditor an awareness of, and present intention to assert, a possible claim.

AU-C DEFINITIONS OF TERMS

Source: AU-C 585.05

Omitted procedure. An auditing procedure that the auditor considered necessary in the circumstances existing at the time of the audit of the financial statements but which was not performed.

OBJECTIVES OF AU SECTION 390

GENERAL

The issuance of Section 390 is an indirect result of the development of peer review and quality control standards (see Statement on Quality Control Standards [SQCS] 2, *System of Quality Control for a CPA Firm's Accounting and Auditing Practice*). An auditor is not required to carry out retrospective review of his or her work once a report has been issued on audited financial statements. Audit documentation is reviewed, however, in connection with peer reviews and in-house inspections. These reviews may reveal the omission of necessary auditing procedures. This section provides guidance to the auditor on considerations and procedures to be applied when omitted auditing procedures are discovered after the audit report has been issued.

BACKGROUND

The initial stimulus for the section resulted from peer reviews of members of the American Institute of Certified Public Accountants (AICPA) Division for Firms and the oversight program on peer reviews of the Public Oversight Board (POB). In 1980, the POB informed the AICPA of its concern when reviewers concluded that an audit had not been conducted in accordance with generally accepted auditing standards (GAAS). At the time, auditors had no guidance on appropriate procedures in these circumstances. The POB recommended that the proper standard-setting body issue guidance on procedures a firm should apply when it becomes aware of an audit that may not have been made in accordance with GAAS. This section is the response to the POB recommendation.

PROFESSIONAL DISAGREEMENTS

This section does not apply to professional disagreements about whether an auditing procedure is necessary in a specific engagement under circumstances existing at the time of the audit. For example, a peer reviewer may suggest that an auditing procedure was necessary (e.g., confirming additional receivables), and the auditor may disagree.

The alleged omitted auditing procedure might be one that professionals could reasonably disagree about (e.g., judgments about materiality). In these circumstances, every effort should be made to convince the reviewer that the auditor's judgment was appropriate.

NO SUBSTITUTE FOR OMITTED PROCEDURES

The omitted procedure may be one for which there is no alternative (e.g., making or observing some inventory counts), or the omission may be the failure to apply any auditing procedures to obtain evidential matter for a significant audit objective (e.g., accepting management representations and not testing percentage of completion on a material construction contract). In these circumstances, the auditor cannot maintain that these are matters about which reasonable professionals might disagree.

DISTINCTION FROM SECTION 561

Section 561, *Subsequent Discovery of Facts Existing at the Date of the Auditor's Report*, provides guidance when the auditor becomes aware, subsequent to the date of the report on the audited financial statements, that facts may have existed at that date which might have affected the financial statements or the audit report had the auditor been aware of those facts. The "facts" usually relate to the financial statements and whether those financial statements are presented fairly in all material respects in conformity with generally accepted accounting principles.

Section 561 applies to facts that indicate possible misstatement of financial statements. On the other hand, Section 390 applies to the possible omission of auditing procedures. The application of Section 561 is initiated by a possible GAAP failure; the application of Section 390 is initiated by a possible GAAS failure. However, when omitted auditing procedures are applied, the auditor may become aware that facts may have existed at the date of the auditor's report and might have affected the report had the auditor been aware of those facts (see "Fundamental Requirements"). In that situation, Section 561 is applicable.

OBJECTIVES OF AU-C SECTION 585

AU-C Section 585 states that:

> ... *the objectives of the auditor are to*

a. assess the effect of omitted procedures of which the auditor becomes aware on the auditor's present ability to support the previously expressed opinion on the financial statements, and
b. respond appropriately.

(AU-C 585.04)

FUNDAMENTAL REQUIREMENTS

IMPORTANCE OF OMITTED PROCEDURES

If the auditor decides that a situation involving an omitted procedure exists, he or she should determine if the omitted procedure currently affects his or her ability to support the previously expressed opinion (see "Techniques for Application").

NOTE: In these circumstances, the auditor would be well advised to consult with his or her attorney.

APPLYING OMITTED PROCEDURES

The auditor should promptly attempt to apply the omitted procedure or alternative procedures that would provide a satisfactory basis for the original opinion on the financial statements if he or she:

1. Decides that the omitted procedure impairs his or her present ability to support the previously expressed opinion, and
2. Believes that there are persons relying currently, or likely to rely, on the financial statements and the related auditor's report.

INABILITY TO APPLY OMITTED PROCEDURES

If the auditor is not able to apply the omitted procedure or appropriate alternative procedures, the auditor should consult his or her attorney to determine the proper action concerning the auditor's responsibilities to:

1. The client
2. Regulatory authorities having jurisdiction over the client
3. Persons relying, or likely to rely, on the auditor's report

NOTE: This section does not require the auditor to notify the client of the omitted auditing procedures.

SUBSEQUENT DISCOVERY OF FACTS EXISTING AT DATE OF AUDITOR'S REPORT

When the auditor subsequently applies the omitted procedure or alternative procedures, he or she may become aware of facts regarding the financial statements that existed at the date of the auditor's report and would have affected the report had the auditor been aware of them. In these circumstances, the auditor should:

1. Advise the client to disclose the newly discovered facts and their impact on the financial statements to persons who are known to be relying currently, or who are likely to rely, on the financial statements and the related auditor's report
2. Take whatever steps he or she believes necessary to be satisfied that the client has made the specified disclosures

The auditor also would be well advised to consult with his or her attorney.

If the client refuses to make the disclosures requested, the auditor should follow the guidance in Section 561 under "Fundamental Requirements."

INTERPRETATIONS

There are no interpretations for this section.

TECHNIQUES FOR APPLICATION

GENERAL

The objective of the auditor's assessment of the importance of the omitted procedure is to determine if it is:

1. Necessary to apply the omitted procedure
2. Necessary to apply alternative procedures
3. Appropriate not to apply either the omitted procedure or alternative procedures

URGENCY OF RESOLUTION

Whenever the auditor becomes aware of an omitted procedure, he or she should act promptly. In these circumstances, a client has issued what it represented to be audited financial statements that may not have been audited properly. The client may be able to wait a short period of time (to be determined by the client, the auditor, and their lawyers) for the matter to be resolved; however, it cannot wait too long before notifying interested parties. The urgency of resolution may differ for public versus nonpublic companies.

Public Companies

Public companies file audited financial statements with the SEC. If the auditor becomes aware of an omitted procedure concerning these financial statements, he or she should consider the client's possible obligation for timely disclosure of significant events. Form 8-K must be filed within four business days after occurrence of most significant events.

Nonpublic Companies

Nonpublic companies may submit audited financial statements to banks, bonding companies, credit agencies, and others. If these financial statements were not audited properly *and* are misleading, the client should notify immediately anyone relying on them. Although there is no specified time period within which to notify interested parties, the client probably will consider its reputation and its exposure to lawsuits in determining when to notify them. It would therefore be prudent for the auditor to complete all procedures before a significant period of time has elapsed.

DETERMINING IMPORTANCE OF OMITTED PROCEDURES

To determine the importance of the omitted procedure to the auditor's present ability to support the previously expressed opinion, he or she should:

1. Review documentation of the audit
2. Discuss circumstances with audit personnel and others

3. Review documentation of the subsequent audit

Review Audit Documentation

The auditor should review relevant audit documentation to determine if:

1. Other procedures were applied that compensated for the one omitted or made the one omitted less important. For example, the review of subsequent cash collected and the related customer remittance advices might compensate for inadequate confirmation of receivables or make the failure to obtain enough receivable confirmations less important than usual.
2. A lower level of control risk was justified so that the omitted procedure was not necessary. The auditor should review audit documentations on:
    a. The documentation of the understanding of internal control
    b. Tests of controls

Discussions with Audit Personnel

The auditor should discuss the audit with audit personnel to determine if:

1. The omitted procedure or a related procedure was discussed
2. The omitted procedure was performed but not documented
3. The omitted procedure affected an item considered not material

The auditor should determine if the alleged omitted procedure was performed, and if not, why not.

Review Subsequent Period Audit Documentation

The auditor should review audit documentation for the subsequent period to determine if procedures applied provide audit evidence to support the previously expressed opinion. For example:

1. Costing of subsequent period sales may provide audit evidence about existence of prior period inventory.
2. A review of subsequent period changes in receivables may provide audit evidence about existence of prior period receivables.
3. A review of subsequent period liabilities may provide evidence that a contingency did not exist at the end of the prior period.

AU ILLUSTRATION

ILLUSTRATION 1. APPLYING THE OMITTED PROCEDURE

If the auditor concludes that the omitted procedure should be performed, he or she should apply it promptly. In these circumstances, the auditor would have to discuss the matter with the client. Following are possible omitted procedures and suggested methods of correcting the omission.

Possible Omitted Procedure	Remedy
1. Failure to obtain management representation letter.	Obtain letter retroactive to date of auditor's report.
2. Failure to obtain a sufficient number of confirmations of receivables.	Confirm retroactive to balance sheet date. If control risk is assessed at less than the maximum, confirm currently, and work back to balance sheet date.
3. Failure to observe a sufficient quantity of inventory.	If control risk is assessed at less than the maximum, observe count of specific styles or components, and work back to year-end. If control risk is assessed at the maximum, the entire inventory may have to be taken currently before the auditor can work back to year-end.
4. Failure to make inquiry of client's lawyer.	Make inquiry retroactive to date of auditor's report.
5. Failure to obtain sufficient evidence about the value of investments in nonpublic investees.	Review recent audited financial statements, if available. If recent audited financial statements are not available, review recent unaudited financial statements, and apply selected audit procedures. Consult with investee's accountant.
6. Failure to apply procedures for identifying related-party transactions.	Apply procedures for current and prior period (see Section 334, *Related Parties*).

AU 410 Adherence to GAAP

AU-C 700 Forming an Opinion and Reporting on Financial Statements

EFFECTIVE DATE AND APPLICABILITY

Original Pronouncements	Section 410: Statements on Auditing Standards (SASs) 1 and 62.
Effective Date	These statements currently are effective.
Applicability	Audits of generally accepted accounting principles (GAAP) financial statements in accordance with generally accepted auditing standards (GAAS).

EFFECTIVE DATE AND SUMMARY OF CHANGES

SAS No. 122, *Codification of Auditing Standards and Procedures,* is effective for audits of financial statements with periods ending on or after December 15, 2012.

AU-C Sections 700, 705, and 706 include auditor report changes and include close integration with AU-C Sections 210, *Terms of Engagement,* and 580.

AU-C Sections 700, 705, and 706 supersede:

- AU Section 410,
- AU Section 530, *Dating of the Independent Auditor's Report*, (as amended) paragraphs .01–.02,
- AU Section 508, *Reports on Audited Financial Statements,* supersedes paragraphs .01–.11, .14–.15, .19–.32, .35–.52, .58–.70, and .74–.76

Paragraph .08 of AU Section 508 requires a statement in the auditor's report that the financial statements are the responsibility of the company's management. Paragraph 25 of the clarified SAS proposes a requirement to describe management's responsibility for the preparation and fair presentation of the financial statements in more detail than what was required in AU Section 508. The description includes an explanation that management is responsible for the preparation and fair presentation of the financial statements in accordance with the applicable financial reporting framework, and that this responsibility includes the design, implementation, and maintenance of internal control relevant to the preparation and fair presentation of financial statements that are free from material misstatement, whether due to fraud or error.

The clarified SAS proposes the use of headings throughout the auditor's report to clearly distinguish each section of the report.

This chapter includes information on AU-C 700. Consult the chapters on AU 508 and AU 530 for additional information on the auditor's reports.

AU DEFINITIONS OF TERMS

Generally accepted accounting principles (GAAP). A technical accounting term that encompasses all the conventions, rules, and procedures necessary to define accepted accounting practice at a particular time. (As used in the reporting standards, GAAP includes accounting principles and practices as well as the methods of applying them.)

GAAP recognizes the importance of reporting transactions and events in accordance with their substance.

AU-C DEFINITIONS OF TERMS

Source: AU-C 700.11

Comparative financial statements. A complete set of financial statements for one or more prior periods included for comparison with the financial statements of the current period.

Comparative information. Prior period information presented for purposes of comparison with current period amounts or disclosures that is not in the form of a complete set of financial statements. Comparative information includes prior period information presented as condensed financial statements or summarized financial information.

Condensed financial statements. Historical financial information that is presented in less detail than a complete set of financial statements, in accordance with an appropriate financial reporting framework. Condensed financial statements may be separately presented as unaudited financial information or may be presented as comparative information.

General purpose financial statements. Financial statements prepared in accordance with a general purpose framework.

General purpose framework. A financial reporting framework designed to meet the common financial information needs of a wide range of users.

Unmodified opinion. The opinion expressed by the auditor when the auditor concludes that the financial statements are presented fairly, in all material respects, in accordance with the applicable financial reporting framework.

OBJECTIVES OF AU SECTION 410

To express an opinion on the "fairness" of financial statements, the independent auditor requires a standard to determine whether those financial statements are, in fact, presented fairly. That standard or framework is GAAP. Without that framework, the auditor would have no uniform standard for judging the presentation of financial position, results of operations, and cash flows in financial statements.

OBJECTIVES OF AU-C SECTION 700

AU-C 700 states that:

the objectives of the auditor are to

a. *form an opinion on the financial statements based on an evaluation of the audit evidence obtained, including evidence obtained about comparative financial statements or comparative financial information, and*
b. *express clearly that opinion on the financial statements through a written report that also describes the basis for that opinion.*

FUNDAMENTAL REQUIREMENTS

FRAMEWORK FOR OPINION

The independent auditor's judgment about whether the financial statements are fairly presented should be applied within the framework of GAAP. The auditor should evaluate whether the substance of a transaction or event differs materially from its form.

REPORTING STANDARD

The first standard of reporting is: "The report shall state whether the financial statements are presented in accordance with generally accepted accounting principles." AU 410.02 states that this standard is construed not to require a statement of fact by the auditor but an opinion.

BASIS FOR AUDITOR'S OPINION

AU 410.02 states that "the term *generally accepted accounting principles* as used in reporting standards is construed to include not only accounting principles and practices but also the methods of applying them."

RULE 203 PRONOUNCEMENTS

An auditor should *not* express an unqualified opinion on financial statements that contain a material departure from a pronouncement covered by Rule 203 of the American Institute of Certified Public Accountants (AICPA) Code of Professional Conduct (category 1 under both the nongovernmental and the governmental hierarchies).

Rule 203 pronouncements: Exception. An auditor should express an unqualified opinion on financial statements that contain a material departure from a pronouncement covered by Rule 203 of the AICPA Code of Professional Conduct in those unusual circumstances where literal application of that pronouncement might result in misleading financial statements. In those unusual circumstances, the auditor should:

1. Add a separate paragraph to the report that describes the departure, its approximate effects, if practicable, and the reasons why the departure is necessary to prevent the financial statements from being misleading
2. Express an unqualified opinion on conformity with GAAP

NOTE: Circumstances that would cause adherence to a Rule 203 pronouncement to result in misleading financial statements are likely to be exceedingly rare in practice. According to an interpretation of Rule 203, examples of circumstances that may justify a departure from GAAP are new legislation or the evolution of a new form of business transaction. An unusual degree of materiality or the existence of conflicting industry practices are examples of circumstances that would not ordinarily be regarded as unusual in the context of Rule 203. *Only a handful of such reports have ever been issued. (See the "AU Illustrations" section. Also see Section 508,* Reports on Audited Financial Statements.*)*

SECURITIES AND EXCHANGE COMMISSION (SEC)

Rules and interpretive releases of the SEC have a level of authority equal to that of category 1 pronouncements for SEC registrants.

INTERPRETATIONS

THE IMPACT ON THE AUDITOR'S REPORT OF ACCOUNTING GUIDANCE PRIOR TO ITS EFFECTIVE DATE (ISSUED OCTOBER 1979; REVISED DECEMBER 1992, JUNE 1993, AND FEBRUARY 1997; REVISED JUNE 2009)

The auditor should not qualify his or her opinion if an entity does not adopt accounting guidance prior to its effective date as long as the accounting principles being followed are currently acceptable.

For financial statements that are prepared on the basis of accounting principles that are acceptable at the financial statement date but that will not be acceptable in the future, the auditor should consider whether disclosure of the impending change in principle and resulting restatement are essential. In cases where the estimated impact of the impending changes is unusually material, disclosure is best made by supplementing the historical financial statements with pro forma financial data that give effect to the future adjustment as if it had occurred on the date of the balance sheet. The auditor may also decide to include an explanatory paragraph that highlights the changes. If essential information is not disclosed, the auditor should express a qualified or adverse opinion.

TECHNIQUES FOR APPLICATION

AUDITOR AWARENESS

The auditor should be aware of the content of the GAAP pronouncements. The auditor may obtain this awareness by subscribing to the various services published by the FASB, GASB, and AICPA.

METHODS OF APPLICATION

The auditor should also be aware of the different methods of applying accounting principles. For example, inventory cost may be computed under the FIFO, LIFO, or average cost method.

AU ILLUSTRATION

The following is illustrated:

1. Auditor's report and explanatory note to the financial statements when adherence to an authoritative pronouncement would, in a very rare circumstance, make the financial statements misleading.

Illustration 1. Auditor's Report and Note to Financial Statements for Rule 203 Departure[1]

To the Stockholders and Board of Directors of ABC Company.

We have examined the consolidated balance sheets of ABC Company and consolidated subsidiaries as of December 31, 20X8 and 20X7, and the related consolidated statements of income, additional capital, and changes in financial position for the years then ended. Our examinations were made in accordance with generally accepted auditing standards and, accordingly, included such tests of the accounting records and such other auditing procedures as we considered necessary in the circumstances. We did not examine the financial statements of the Corporation's health spa subsidiaries for the years ended December 31, 20X8 and 20X7, which statements reflect total assets and revenues constituting 7% and 4% in 20X8 and 6% and 3% in 20X7, respectively, of the related consolidated totals. These statements were examined by other independent accountants whose reports thereon have been furnished to us and our opinion expressed herein, insofar as it relates to the amounts included for such subsidiaries, is based solely upon the reports of the other independent accountants.

As explained in Note A (9), the Corporation's health spa subsidiaries have changed their method of recording revenues from the recognition of revenue at the time of sale to the recognition of revenue over the membership term and have applied this change retroactively in their financial statements. The other independent accountants' reports, referred to previously, stated, "Accounting Principles Board (APB) Opinion Number 20, 'Accounting Changes,' provides that such a change be made by including, as an element of net earnings during the year of change, the cumulative effect of the change on prior years. Had APB Opinion Number 20 been followed literally, the cumulative effect of the accounting change would have been included as a charge in the 20X8 statement of operations. Because of the magnitude and pervasiveness of this change, we believe a literal application of APB Opinion Number 20 would result in a misleading presentation, and that this change should therefore be made on a retroactive basis." Accordingly, the accompanying consolidated financial statements for 20X7 have been restated.

In our opinion, based upon our examination and the aforementioned reports of the other independent accountants, the financial statements referred to above present fairly the consolidated financial position of ABC Company and consolidated subsidiaries at December 31, 20X8 and 20X7, and the consolidated results of their operations and changes in financial position for the years then ended, in conformity with generally accepted accounting principles applied on a consistent basis, after restatement for the change, with which the other independent accountants and we concur, in the method of revenue recognition by the health spa subsidiaries referred to in the preceding paragraph.

Ernst & Young

New York, NY

February 27, 20X9
(March 6, 20X9, as to the reports of other independent accountants)

(9) Change in Accounting for Membership Revenues

The corporation has two subsidiaries, one of which is 80% owned, which operate health spas. These *companies* sell health club memberships that have specific terms, which presently range up to thirty months. In prior years, revenue from sale of memberships, less a deferred portion, was taken into income at time of sale. The deferred portion was taken into revenue on a straight-line basis over the membership terms and was equivalent to the estimated future costs of providing facilities and services. These costs consisted of a pro rata share of estimated future operating expenses. In December 20X7, Deloitte & Touche, independent accountants for the Corporation's health spa subsidiaries, informed the Corporation that they had taken a position as a firm that, they suggested, should be effective for fiscal years ended after December 31, 20X7, to recognize membership fee revenue and associated costs over the period of membership.

The subsidiaries have concluded that, even though the change has not been required by an authoritative accounting body, there is sufficient authoritative support within similar industries and they have accepted the change suggested by their independent accountants.

Accounting Principles Board (APB) Opinion Number 20, *Accounting Changes*" provides that such a change be made by including, as an element of net earnings during the year of change, the cumulative effect of the change on prior years. Had APB Opinion Number 20 been followed literally, the cumulative effect of the accounting change would have been included as a charge, net of tax benefits, in the 20X8 consolidated statement of income and would have resulted in reporting a consolidated net loss of $3,398,000 ($.24 per common share) in 20X8 and a consolidated net income of $18,171,000 ($.44 per common share) in 20X7. Because of the magnitude and pervasiveness of this change, the Corporation believes a literal application of APB Opinion Number 20 would result in a misleading presentation, and that this change should, therefore, be made on a retroactive basis. The Corporation's and the subsidiaries' independent accountants concur in this treatment.

As a result of retroactive treatment of the change in the method of accounting for membership revenues, the consolidated financial statements for prior years have been restated. The effect of the change was to reduce consolidated net income for 20X8 by $90,000 and to increase consolidated net income previously reported for 20X7 by $5,160,000 ($.16 per share). The increase in deferred revenue at January 1, 20X7, net of related tax benefits, resulted in an adjustment to opening retained earnings of $19,037,000.

---

[1] This report example does not reflect the new report form required by SAS 58 (see Section 508). The authors are not aware of any Rule 203 exception reports that have been issued under the SAS 58 report format.

AU 420 Consistency of Application of Generally Accepted Accounting Principles

AU-C 708 Consistency of Financial Statements

AU EFFECTIVE DATE AND APPLICABILITY

Original Pronouncements	Statements on Auditing Procedures (SAPs) 53, 43, and 88.
Effective Date	These statements currently are effective.
Applicability	Audit of financial statements in accordance with generally accepted auditing standards (GAAS).

NOTE: The consistency standard does not apply in the audit of the financial statements of a new entity. It applies either to financial statements prepared in accordance with generally accepted accounting procedures (GAAP) or another comprehensive basis of accounting.

AU-C EFFECTIVE DATE AND SUMMARY OF CHANGES

SAS No. 122, *Codification of Auditing Standards and Procedures,* is effective for audits of financial statements with periods ending on or after December 15, 2012.

The clarified standard supersedes AU Section 420 (SAS No. 1, *Codification of Auditing Standards and Procedures,* Section 420, *Consistency of Application of Generally Accepted Accounting Principles*, as amended)

The clarified SAS does not change or expand existing standards in any significant respect except as follows:

- AU Section 420 states that changes and material reclassifications made in previously issued financial statements to enhance comparability with current financial statements ordinarily would not need to be referred to in the independent auditor's report. However, the clarified SAS requires the auditor to compare and evaluate a material change in financial statement classification and the related disclosure to determine whether such a change is also either a change in accounting principle or an adjust-

ment to correct a material misstatement in previously issued financial statements. If so, the requirements in the clarified SAS apply.
- The clarified SAS recognizes that the applicable financial reporting framework usually sets forth the method of accounting for accounting changes and, therefore, the references to accounting guidance included in AU Section 420 have not been included in the clarified SAS.
- To reflect a more principles-based approach to standard setting, certain requirements that are duplicative of broader requirements in AU Section 420 have been moved to application and other explanatory material. In the Auditing Standards Board's (ASB's) view, this has not changed the overall effectiveness of the clarified SAS.

AU DEFINITIONS OF TERMS

Accounting change. A change in:

1. An accounting principle
2. An accounting estimate
3. The reporting entity (a special type of change in accounting principle)

NOTE: Only a change in accounting principle (items 1 or 3 in the prior list) affects consistency.

Accounting principle. Accounting principles, practices, and the methods of applying them.

NOTE: Other definitions are presented in "Fundamental Requirements" because the definition is the substance of the requirement.

Comparability. Comparison of financial statements between years may be affected by:

1. Accounting changes
2. An error in financial statements of prior years
3. Changes in classification
4. Events or transactions that are substantially different from those of prior periods

NOTE: All these things affect comparability, but only certain accounting changes affect consistency.

AU-C DEFINITIONS OF TERMS

Source: AU-C 708.04

Current period. The most recent period upon which the auditor is reporting.

OBJECTIVES OF AU SECTION 420

Before APB Opinion 20, *Accounting Changes*, was issued, most of the accounting guidance as well as audit reporting guidance on accounting changes was covered in the auditing literature. An important feature of the auditing guidance was a distinction between changes in circumstances that caused accounting changes and other, presumably discretionary, changes. Only a discretionary change affected consistency reporting.

Opinion 20 established several new accounting requirements and codified some existing practices. Opinion 20:

1. Created a presumption that an accounting principle, once adopted, should not be changed in accounting for similar transactions or events. The presumption can be overcome only if the new accounting principle is justified as being *preferable*.
2. Specified the accounting treatment of the effect of accounting changes on the financial statements. This is essentially a cumulative-effect adjustment except for certain specified changes made by retroactive restatement.
3. Specified the disclosure requirements for various types of accounting changes.

Opinion 20 does not apply to changes made to conform to new authoritative pronouncements, but such pronouncements specify the applicable accounting treatment and disclosure.

The auditing literature was modified to mesh with Opinion 20. The old distinction between changes in circumstances and other changes disappeared. The auditing literature adopted the classification of accounting changes of Opinion 20 and specified those that affect consistency and those that do not. Once a change is put in the slot specified in Opinion 20, reference to lists of changes affecting and not affecting consistency reporting in this section determines the appropriate reporting on consistency.

Although these refinements have been made in consistency reporting, the basic objective of consistency reporting by the auditor has remained the same. It is:

1. To give assurance that the comparability of financial statements between periods has not been materially affected by changes in accounting principle.
2. If comparability has been materially affected by changes in accounting principle, to require appropriate reporting by the independent auditor on the changes

OBJECTIVES OF AU-C SECTION 708

AU-C section 708 states that:

. . . the objectives of the auditor are to

  a. evaluate the consistency of the financial statements for the periods presented and
  b. communicate appropriately in the auditor's report when the comparability of financial statements between periods has been materially affected by a change in accounting principle or by adjustments to correct a material misstatement in previously issued financial statements.

FUNDAMENTAL REQUIREMENTS

REPORTING STANDARD

According to AU 420.01, the second standard of reporting is: "The auditor must identify in the auditor's report those circumstances in which such principles have not been consistently observed in the current period in relation to the preceding period."

CONSISTENCY IMPLICATION OF AUDITOR'S STANDARD REPORT

According to AU 411.04, the auditor's standard report implies that the auditor is satisfied that the comparability of financial statements between periods has not been materially affected by changes in accounting principles and that such principles have been consistently applied between or among periods because either (1) no change in accounting principles has occurred, or (2) there has been a change in accounting principles or in the method of their application, but the effect of the change on the comparability of the financial statements is not material. In these cases, the auditor would not refer to consistency in his or her report.

A change in accounting principle that has a material effect on the comparability of financial statements requires an explanatory paragraph after the opinion paragraph in the auditor's report.

PERIODS TO WHICH CONSISTENCY STANDARD RELATES

The financial statements included in the consistency implication depend on what financial statements are covered by the auditor's report:

1. *Current period only*—the consistency of application of accounting principles in relation to the preceding period only (even if financial statements for one or more preceding periods are presented)
2. *Two or more years (no other statements presented)*—the consistency of application of accounting principles between such years
3. *Two or more years (prior year presented but not included in auditor's report)*—consistency between years included in report and also the consistency of such years with the prior year

CHANGES AFFECTING CONSISTENCY

The following changes, if they have a material effect, require the addition of an explanatory paragraph after the opinion paragraph that describes the inconsistency.

1. **Change in Accounting Principle**

    Adoption of a GAAP different from the one used in the prior period. An example is a change from the straight-line method to the declining balance method of depreciation for all newly acquired assets in a class. An investee accounted for by the equity method may change an accounting principle. If this change causes a material lack of comparability in the financial statements of the investor, the auditor should add an explanatory paragraph to the auditor's report following the opinion paragraph.

2. **Change in Reporting Entity**

    This is a special type of change in accounting principle and is limited mainly to:

    a. A presentation of consolidated or combined statements instead of statements of individual entities
    b. A change in specific subsidiaries included in the group of entities in the consolidation

    ---
    NOTE: *This means a change in consolidation policy and not the creation, cessation, purchase, or disposition of a subsidiary.*
    ---

c. A change in entities included in combined financial statements

3. **Correction of an Error in Principle**

    A change from an accounting principle that is not generally accepted to one that is, including correcting a mistake in applying a principle.

    NOTE: *APB Opinion 20 specifies that the accounting treatment of the change is the correction of an error, but the method of accounting for the change does not affect its classification as a change in accounting principle for audit reporting purposes.*

4. **Change in Principle Inseparable from Change in Estimate**

    A change in estimate that is achieved by changing an accounting principle. An example is changing from deferring and amortizing a cost to expensing it when incurred because future benefits of the cost have become doubtful.

    NOTE: *Again, although the accounting treatment is that for a change in estimate, the change in principle affects audit reporting.*

5. **Changes in Presentation of Cash Flows**

    A change in an entity's policy for determining which items are treated as cash equivalents. This type of change should be effected by restating financial statements for earlier years presented for comparative purposes. This change in the presentation of cash flows requires the addition of an explanatory paragraph after the opinion paragraph.

CHANGES NOT AFFECTING CONSISTENCY

The following changes, if they have a material effect on comparability, require disclosure in the financial statements but have no effect on the auditor's report and its implications for consistency.

1. **Change in Accounting Estimate**

    Examples of items for which estimates are made include uncollectible receivables, inventory obsolescence, warranty costs, and service lives and salvage values of depreciable assets. As new events occur or additional information is obtained, a change in such accounting estimates may be necessary.

2. **Error Correction Not Involving Principle**

    Correction of an error not involving an accounting principle includes mathematical mistakes, oversight, or misuse of facts that existed when the financial statements were originally prepared.

3. **Changes in Classification or Reclassification**

    Use of classifications within the financial statements different from classifications in prior years may be made. For example, "cash on hand" might be combined with "cash in bank" in a new classification, "cash."

    NOTE: *A change in classification that significantly affects measurement of financial position or operating results requires a consistency modification—for example, a change in types of items reported as extraordinary.*

4. **Substantially Different Transactions or Events**

   Accounting principles are adopted when events or transactions first become material. Initial adoption or modification of an accounting principle necessitated by transactions or events clearly different in substance from past transactions or events does not affect consistency.

5. **Changes Expected to Have a Material Future Effect**

   If an accounting change has no material effect on the current financial statements but is reasonably certain to have a substantial future effect, disclosure of the change should be made whenever the statements of the period of the change are presented but *need not* cause modification of the audit report.

   NOTE: *This means that the auditor does not have to modify the audit report for the inconsistency, but modification is permissible if the auditor wishes.*

FIRST YEAR AUDITS

If the independent auditor has not audited an entity's financial statements for the preceding year, he or she should apply reasonable and practicable procedures, such as reviewing underlying financial records and predecessor auditor's audit documentation, to obtain assurance as to the consistency of accounting principles employed in the current and the preceding year.

The independent auditor may not be able to obtain sufficient, competent evidential matter about the consistent application of accounting principles and the amounts of assets and liabilities at the beginning of the current year. In these circumstances, if these amounts could materially affect current operating results, in addition to modifying the auditor's report for a scope limitation as to consistency, the independent auditor would also be unable to express an opinion on the current year's results of operations and cash flows.

INTERPRETATIONS

THE EFFECT OF APB OPINION 28 ON CONSISTENCY (FEBRUARY 1974)

Auditors may be engaged to report on financial information for an annual period and a subsequent interim period. APB Opinion 28 may appear to produce changes in the methods of applying accounting principles. For example, the entity, as permitted under APB Opinion 28, may use the gross profit method to estimate the interim inventory; whereas, for the annual financial statements, a physical inventory may be taken. The modifications permitted by APB Opinion 28 constitute a difference in circumstances, not a change in accounting principle. Therefore, the auditor should not add an explanatory paragraph to the audit report because of an inconsistency.

IMPACT ON THE AUDITOR'S REPORT OF FIFO TO LIFO CHANGE IN COMPARATIVE FINANCIAL STATEMENTS (JANUARY 1975; AMENDED APRIL 1989)

For a FIFO to LIFO change made in the earlier year presented and reported on (20X2 and 20X1 comparative financial statements presented—change made in 20X1), there is no inconsistency in the application of accounting principles. Comparability between the earliest year and subsequent year(s) is not affected, since no cumulative effect is reported in the year of change. (There is no cumulative effect since the ending inventory for 20X0 is the beginning inventory for 20X1 for LIFO purposes.) The auditor should not refer to the change from FIFO to LIFO in his or her report.

THE EFFECT OF ACCOUNTING CHANGES BY AN INVESTEE ON CONSISTENCY (ISSUED JULY 1980; REVISED JUNE 1993)

As discussed in "Fundamental Requirements," a change in accounting principles by an investee accounted for by the equity method requires the auditor to add an explanatory paragraph because of an inconsistency.

CHANGE IN PRESENTATION OF ACCUMULATED BENEFIT INFORMATION IN THE FINANCIAL STATEMENTS OF A DEFINED BENEFIT PENSION PLAN (DECEMBER 1980)

A change in the format of presentation of accumulated benefit information (e.g., on the face of a financial statement or in a separate statement) or a change in the date as of which such information is presented is a reclassification, not an inconsistency.

THE EFFECT ON THE AUDITOR'S REPORT OF AN ENTITY'S ADOPTION OF A NEW ACCOUNTING STANDARD THAT DOES NOT REQUIRE THE ENTITY TO DISCLOSE THE EFFECT OF THE CHANGE IN THE YEAR OF ADOPTION (APRIL 2002)

If an entity adopts an accounting standard and the standard does not require the entity to disclose the effect of the change in the year of adoption, Section 420 does not require the auditor to independently determine the effect of that change. However, this section requires that the auditor add an explanatory paragraph to his or her report for *material* changes in accounting principles. In determining whether such a paragraph is necessary, the auditor should consider:

- The materiality of the change's cumulative effect
- The entity's voluntary disclosure about the effect of the change in accounting principle

AU 431 Adequacy of Disclosure in Financial Statements

AU-C 705 Modifications to the Opinion in the Independent Auditor's Report

AU EFFECTIVE DATE AND APPLICABILITY

Original Pronouncement	Statement on Accounting Standards (SAS) 32.
Effective Date	This statement currently is effective.
Applicability	Audits of financial statements in accordance with generally accepted auditing standards (GAAS).

AU-C EFFECTIVE DATE AND SUMMARY OF CHANGES

SAS No. 122, *Codification of Auditing Standards and Procedures,* is effective for audits of financial statements with periods ending on or after December 15, 2012.

AU-C Section 705 has no significant changes from the extant standard.

AU DEFINITIONS OF TERMS

Adequate disclosure. Material matters include the (1) form, (2) arrangement, and (3) content of the financial statements and the appended notes, including:

- Terminology used
- Amount of detail given
- Classification of items
- Bases of amounts

AU-C DEFINITIONS OF TERMS

Source: AU-C 705.06

Modified opinion. A qualified opinion, an adverse opinion, or a disclaimer of opinion.

Pervasive. A term used in the context of misstatements to describe the effects on the financial statements of misstatements or the possible effects on the financial statements of misstatements, if any, that are undetected due to an inability to obtain sufficient appropriate audit evidence. Pervasive effects on the financial statements are those that, in the auditor's professional judgment:

- Are not confined to specific elements, accounts, or items of the financial statements;
- If so confined, represent or could represent a substantial proportion of the financial statements; or
- With regard to disclosures, are fundamental to users' understanding of the financial statements.

OBJECTIVES OF AU SECTION 431

This section is a carryover from the explanation of the reporting standard on adequate disclosure issued when GAAS were originally proposed in 1947. Thus, it is more philosophical than operational.

OBJECTIVES OF AU-C SECTION 705

AU-C section 705 states that

. . . the objective of the auditor is to express clearly an appropriately modified opinion on the financial statements that is necessary when

a. the auditor concludes, based on the audit evidence obtained, that the financial statements as a whole are materially misstated or
b. the auditor is unable to obtain sufficient appropriate audit evidence to conclude that the financial statements as a whole are free from material misstatement."

FUNDAMENTAL REQUIREMENTS

REPORTING STANDARD

According to 431.01, the third standard of reporting is "Informative disclosures in the financial statements are to be regarded as reasonably adequate unless otherwise stated in the report."

BASIC REQUIREMENT

If management fails to disclose information required by generally accepted accounting principles (GAAP), the auditor should:

1. Issue a qualified or adverse opinion
2. Provide the information in the report (see below for exceptions to this requirement)

EXCEPTIONS TO NEED TO INCLUDE INFORMATION

The auditor may omit the information from the audit report if:

1. The omission is recognized as appropriate by an AU section.
2. The information is *not* reasonably obtainable from management's accounts and records.
3. Providing the information would require the auditor to assume the position of a preparer of financial information. For example, an auditor would not be expected to provide:

    a. A basic financial statement, such as a statement of cash flows
    b. Segment information

ACCOUNTING SERVICES PERMISSIBLE

An independent auditor may participate in preparing financial statements, including accompanying notes. This participation does not change the character of the statements as management's representations.

NOTE: This means that providing accounting services in conjunction with an audit is permissible and the fact that the auditor rather than management has prepared disclosure information does not create any reporting requirement. (However, for a Securities and Exchange Commission [SEC] reporting company, the auditor would lose his or her independence by performing accounting services such as bookkeeping.)

INTERPRETATIONS

There are no interpretations for this section.

TECHNIQUES FOR APPLICATION

To aid the auditor in determining that all material matters have been adequately disclosed, a disclosure checklist may be completed at the end of the audit. The auditor may prepare his or her own disclosure checklists; however, checklists may be obtained from many sources, such as the American Institute of Certified Public Accountants (AICPA).

AU 504 Association with Financial Statements

AU EFFECTIVE DATE AND APPLICABILITY

Original Pronouncements	Statements on Auditing Standards (SASs) 26, 35, and 72.
Effective Date	These statements currently are effective.
Applicability	Accountants' reports on:

1. Unaudited financial statements of public entities
2. Comparative financial statements of public or nonpublic entities when the financial statements of one period are audited
3. Financial statements of public entities when the accountant is not independent

AU-C EFFECTIVE DATE AND SUMMARY OF CHANGES

SAS No. 122, *Codification of Auditing Standards and Procedures,* is effective for audits of financial statements with periods ending on or after December 15, 2012.

These requirements will be superseded by AU-C 600. For more information, see the separate chapter on AU-C 600.

AU DEFINITIONS OF TERMS

Association. An accountant is associated with financial statements when he or she has consented to the use of his or her name in a report, document, or written communication containing the statements, or when he or she submits to the client or others financial statements that he or she has prepared or assisted in preparing.

NOTE: The accountant would be associated with the financial statements even though his or her name did not appear.

Public entity. Any entity (1) whose securities trade in a public market either on a domestic or foreign stock exchange or in the over-the-counter market, including securities quoted only locally or regionally, (2) that makes a filing with a regulatory agency in preparation for the sale of any class of its securities in a public market, or (3) a subsidiary, corporate joint venture, or other entity controlled by an entity described in (1) or (2).

OBJECTIVES OF AU SECTION 504

In 1978, the Accounting and Review Services Committee of the American Institute of Certified Public Accountants (AICPA) issued Statement on Standards for Accounting and Review Services (SSARS) 1, *Compilation and Review of Financial Statements*. SSARS 1 applies to unaudited financial statements of nonpublic entities.

The basic purpose of this section was to replace existing sections that covered all unaudited financial statements. It updated the SASs for SSARSs by removing guidance for unaudited financial statements of nonpublic entities.

This section provides guidance to the accountant when he or she is associated with a *public entity's* unaudited financial statements:

1. Prepared in conformity with generally accepted accounting principles (GAAP)
2. Prepared in accordance with comprehensive basis of accounting (OCBOA) other than GAAP (see Section 623, *Special Reports*)
3. Not in conformity with GAAP or OCBOA
4. On which the accountant provides negative assurance

The section also provides guidance to the accountant when he or she is associated with:

1. A public entity's financial statements that are unaudited because the accountant is not independent
2. A **public or a nonpublic** entity's unaudited and audited financial statements presented in comparative form

FUNDAMENTAL REQUIREMENTS

UNAUDITED FINANCIAL STATEMENTS

The basic requirements are

1. When an accountant is associated with financial statements of a public entity, but has not audited or reviewed them, the accountant should disclaim an opinion. His or her report should only identify the financial statements and state that they were not audited and that no opinion is expressed.
2. Each page of the financial statements should be marked "UNAUDITED."
3. The accountant should read the financial statements. He or she has no responsibility to apply any other procedures.
4. Procedures applied should not be described in the accountant's report.
5. For public entities that do not have annual audits, the accountant should refer to SSARSs for guidance.

Report on GAAP Financial Statements

An accountant associated with a *public* entity's unaudited GAAP financial statements should follow the preceding guidance and issue the following report illustrated in AU 504.05:

> The accompanying balance sheet of Widget Company as of December 31, 20X1, and the related statements of income and retained earnings, and cash flows for the year then ended, were not audited by us and, accordingly, we do not express an opinion on them.

[*Signature*]

[*Date*]

Report on OCBOA Financial Statements

An accountant associated with a *public* entity's unaudited OCBOA financial statements should basically follow the guidance presented earlier in "Unaudited Financial Statements," but the report language should be modified to recognize the basis of accounting. An example of such a report is illustrated in AU 504.07.

> The accompanying statement of assets and liabilities resulting from cash transactions of Widget Corporation as of December 31, 20X1, and the related statement of revenues collected and expenses paid during the year then ended were not audited by us and, accordingly, we do not express an opinion on them.

[*Signature*]

[*Date*]

A note to the financial statements should describe the basis of accounting and how it differs from GAAP; however, the monetary effect of the difference does not have to be presented.

Report Modified for Lack of Independence

An accountant who is not independent with respect to a *public* entity's financial statements should basically follow the guidance in "Unaudited Financial Statements," explained earlier in this section, but the report language should be modified to recognize the lack of independence. The accountant should disclaim an opinion on the financial statements and state that he or she is not independent. The reason the accountant is not independent, however, should not be described in the report. An example of such a report is illustrated in AU 504.10.

> We are not independent with respect to Widget Company, and the accompanying balance sheet as of December 31, 20X1, and the related statements of income and retained earnings and cash flows for the year then ended were not audited by us and, accordingly, we do not express an opinion on them.

[*Signature*]

[*Date*]

If he or she is not independent with respect to the financial statements of a nonpublic entity, the accountant should follow the guidance in Statements on Standards for Accounting and Review Services (SSARSs).

Financial Statements Not in Conformity with GAAP

An accountant associated with a public entity's unaudited financial statements that are not in conformity with GAAP (for inadequate disclosure, see below) should suggest that they be revised. If the statements are not revised, the accountant should describe the departure in his or her report. The description should refer to the nature of the departure and, if possible, state the effects on the financial statements. If the effects are not reasonably determinable, the report should state this fact. (Accountants' reports on unaudited financial statements not in conformity with GAAP are presented in the "Illustrations" section.) If management does not revise the financial statements or does not accept the accountant's report with the description of the departure, the accountant should refuse to be associated with the financial statements and, if necessary, withdraw from the engagement.

Inadequate Disclosure in Financial Statements

An accountant associated with a public entity's unaudited financial statements that do not contain adequate disclosure should describe this departure from GAAP in his or her report and, if practicable, include the necessary information for adequate disclosure. When it is not practicable to include omitted disclosures in the report, the accountant should state this fact. For example, when all, or substantially all, disclosures have been omitted, the accountant should indicate this in the report; however, he or she is not expected to include the omitted disclosures. (An accountant's report on unaudited financial statements that do not include adequate disclosure is presented in "AU Illustrations.") If the client does not revise the financial statements or does not accept the accountant's report with the description of the inadequate disclosure, the accountant should refuse to be associated with the financial statements and, if necessary, withdraw from the engagement.

NOTE: If a nonpublic entity omits all, or substantially all, disclosures from its unaudited financial statements, the accountant should follow the guidance of SSARSs in reporting on these financial statements. SSARSs prescribe specific wording for this situation. That wording may be used in a similar report on a public entity, but this section does not require use of that specific language.

AUDITED AND UNAUDITED FINANCIAL STATEMENTS IN COMPARATIVE FORM

For documents filed with the SEC, unaudited financial statements presented in comparative form with audited financial statements should be marked "UNAUDITED." The unaudited financial statements should *not* be referred to in the auditor's report.

NOTE: The reason for this different treatment is the legal significance of including a "report" in an SEC filing.

For all other documents, the unaudited financial statements should be marked "UNAUDITED," *and* the report on the prior period should be reissued or the report on the current period should include a separate paragraph describing the responsibility assumed for the prior period's financial statements.

NOTE: For information on the reissuance of auditors' reports, see Section 530, Dating of the Independent Auditor's Report; for information on the reissuance of compilation or review reports, see SSARS 2 (Section 3200).

Prior Period Audited—Current Period Unaudited

When the prior period financial statements were audited and the report on the current period will have a separate paragraph about those financial statements, the separate paragraph should contain the following:

1. The financial statements of the prior period were audited previously
2. The date of the previous period's report
3. The type of opinion previously issued

4. If the opinion of the previous period was other than unqualified, the reason
5. No auditing procedures were performed after the date of the previous period's report

An example of an appropriate separate paragraph from AU 504.16 is as follows:

> The financial statements for the year ended December 31, 20X1, were audited by us, and we expressed an unqualified opinion on them in our report dated March 1, 20X2, but we have not performed any auditing procedures since that date.

Prior Period Unaudited—Current Period Audited

When the financial statements of the prior period were not audited and the report on the current period will have a separate paragraph about those financial statements, the separate paragraph should contain the following:

1. A statement indicating the service performed in the prior period
2. The date of the previous period's report
3. A description of any material modifications noted in the previous period's report
4. A statement that the service was less in scope than an audit and that the service does not provide a basis for expressing an opinion on the financial statements taken as a whole

Public Entity Financial Statements

If the financial statements are those of a public entity, the separate paragraph should include an "unaudited" disclaimer of opinion or a description of a review, whichever is appropriate.

Nonpublic Entity Financial Statements

If the financial statements are those of a nonpublic entity and they were compiled or reviewed, the separate paragraph should describe the service performed. The separate paragraph describing a review, illustrated in AU 504.17, might be as follows:

> The 20X1 financial statements were reviewed by us, and our report thereon, dated March 1, 20X2, stated we were not aware of any material modifications that should be made to those statements for them to be in conformity with generally accepted accounting principles. However, a review is substantially less in scope than an audit and does not provide a basis for the expression of an opinion on the financial statements taken as a whole.

The separate paragraph describing a compilation, also illustrated in AU 504.17, might be as follows:

> The 20X1 financial statements were compiled by us, and our report thereon, dated March 1, 20X2, stated we did not audit or review those financial statements and, accordingly, express no opinion or other form of assurance on them.

NEGATIVE ASSURANCE

Ordinarily, when a disclaimer of opinion is issued, it should not be modified by the accountant's expression of assurance that he or she has no knowledge of departures from generally accepted accounting principles. Exceptions to this general rule follow:

1. Review reports as described in SSARS 1
2. Letters for underwriters in which the auditor reports on his or her limited procedures with respect to unaudited financial statements or other financial data necessary for a

securities offering (see Section 634, *Letters for Underwriters and Certain Other Requesting Parties*)

3. Review reports on interim financial information (see Section 722, *Interim Financial Information*)

CLIENT-PREPARED COMMUNICATION

A public entity may prepare a written communication containing financial statements that have not been audited or reviewed and name the accountant in the document. In these circumstances, the accountant should request that (1) his or her name not be included or (2) that the financial statements be marked "UNAUDITED" and a notation made that he or she does not express an opinion on them. If the client does not comply, the accountant should advise the client that the accountant has not consented to the use of his or her name and should consider other actions, such as consulting his or her lawyer.

INTERPRETATIONS

ANNUAL REPORT DISCLOSURE OF UNAUDITED FOURTH QUARTER INTERIM DATA (ISSUED NOVEMBER 1979; REVISED NOVEMBER 2002; JUNE 2009)

Unless specifically engaged to do so, the auditor does not have an obligation to audit interim data—such as disclosure of fourth quarter adjustments—presented in a note to annual audited financial statements. Disclosure of fourth quarter adjustments is a requirement, in certain circumstances, of FASB ASC 270-10-50 on interim financial information, and is not essential for fair presentation of annual financial statements in conformity with GAAP. The note would ordinarily be marked to indicate it has not been audited. Omission of the note disclosure when required should be mentioned in the audit report, but would not result in a qualified opinion because the annual financial statements reported on would conform with GAAP.

AUDITOR'S IDENTIFICATION WITH CONDENSED FINANCIAL DATA (NOVEMBER 1979)

Financial reporting services, such as Dun & Bradstreet, furnish subscribers with information that frequently includes identification of the entity's auditor, condensed financial information, and other data. The auditor and the entity do not have the ability to restrain a financial reporting service from publishing this information. In this context, the accountant has not consented to the use of his or her name, there is no "association" in the sense of Section 504, and there is no reporting obligation.

APPLICABILITY OF GUIDANCE ON REPORTING WHEN NOT INDEPENDENT (NOVEMBER 1979)

In determining whether he or she is independent and whether the reporting requirements of Section 504 therefore apply, the accountant should consider the ethical requirements of the AICPA and the relevant state society of CPAs or state board of accountancy. These ethics requirements should be considered in evaluating independence whether the financial statements are audited or unaudited.

TECHNIQUES FOR APPLICATION

REPORTING ON TAX RETURNS

SAS and SSARS requirements do not apply to *any* tax returns or other forms (such as Form 990) filed solely with taxing authorities. This means: *If it is a tax form, the accountant may sign it and not issue a report.* Financial statements that correlate with the data in the return may be attached as a supplement to the return without triggering a reporting obligation. If the client wants it or if the CPA firm adopts a policy requiring it, however, an accountant's report in conformity with the applicable SAS or SSARS is permissible.

UNAUDITED FINANCIAL STATEMENTS IN SEC FILINGS

The Securities Act of 1933 imposes a heavy legal burden on the auditor and other professionals. Section 11 of the Act allows any person who purchased securities described in the registration statement to sue the auditor. Under this section, all the purchaser must do is prove that the financial statements were misleading or materially misstated. The auditor has the burden of demonstrating as a defense that, among other things, an adequate audit was conducted in the circumstances.

Because of the burden placed on the auditor by Section 11 of the 1933 Act, he or she should not explicitly report on unaudited statements in a registration statement filed with the SEC under the 1933 Act.

AU ILLUSTRATIONS

When an accountant reads a public company's unaudited financial statements, he or she may become aware of departures from GAAP, including inadequate disclosures. Following are reports describing these departures in the following situations:

1. Inventories stated below cost—effects of departure not determined
2. Land recorded at appraised values—effects of departure determined
3. Omission of disclosure—restrictions on retained earnings

If the effects of a GAAP departure have been determined, the effects should be disclosed, but the accountant need not undertake to determine the effects.

ILLUSTRATION 1. INVENTORIES STATED BELOW COST—EFFECTS OF DEPARTURE NOT DETERMINED

The accompanying balance sheet of the XYZ Company as of December 31, 20X1, and the related statements of income and retained earnings and cash flows for the year then ended were not audited by us, and accordingly, we do not express an opinion on them.

Under generally accepted accounting principles, the components of inventory cost are material, labor, and overhead. Management has informed us that the inventory of finished goods is stated in the accompanying financial statements at material cost only. The effects of this departure from generally accepted accounting principles on the accompanying financial statements have not been determined.

ILLUSTRATION 2. LAND RECORDED AT APPRAISED VALUES—EFFECTS OF DEPARTURE DETERMINED

The accompanying balance sheet of the XYZ Company as of December 31, 20X1, and the related statements of income and retained earnings and cash flows for the year then ended were not audited by us, and accordingly, we do not express an opinion on them.

Under generally accepted accounting principles, land is ordinarily stated at cost. Management has informed us that the Company has recorded its land at appraised value and that if generally accepted accounting principles had been followed, the land account would have been decreased by $_____.

ILLUSTRATION 3. OMISSION OF DISCLOSURE—RESTRICTIONS ON RETAINED EARNINGS

The accompanying balance sheet of the XYZ Company as of December 31, 20X1, and the related statements of income and retained earnings and cash flows for the year then ended were not audited by us, and accordingly, we do not express an opinion on them.

The financial statements do not disclose that the debentures issued on July 31, 20X1, limit the payment of cash dividends to 50% of earnings for 20X1 and thereafter. Generally accepted accounting principles require disclosure of matters of this nature.

AU 508 Reports on Audited Financial Statements [1]

AU-C 700 Forming an Opinion and Reporting on Financial Statements

AU-C 705 Modifications to the Opinion in the Independent Auditor's Report

AU-C 706 Emphasis-of-Matter Paragraphs and Other-Matter Paragraphs in the Independent Auditor's Report

---

[1] *This section is affected by the Public Company Accounting Oversight Board's (PCAOB's) Standard,* Conforming Amendments to PCAOB Interim Standards Resulting from the Adoption of PCAOB Auditing Standard No. 5, An Audit of Internal Control over Financial Reporting That Is Integrated with an Audit of Financial Statements.

AU-C 600 Special Considerations—Audits of Group Financial Statements (Including the Work of Component Auditors)

AU-C 708 Consistency of Financial Statements

AU-C 805 Special Considerations—Audits of Single Financial Statements and Specific Elements, Accounts, or Items of a Financial Statement

AU-C 560 Subsequent Events and Subsequently Discovered Facts

IMPORTANT NOTE: The guidance in this section applies to audits of nonissuers. Auditors of issuers and public entities subject to Securities and Exchange Commission (SEC) rules should refer to the guidance in Public Company Accounting Oversight Board's PCAOB No. 1, References in Auditors' Reports to the Standards of the Public Company Accounting Oversight Board, *for changes made to the guidance in this section.*

AU EFFECTIVE DATE AND APPLICABILITY

Original Pronouncements	Statements on Auditing Standards (SASs) 58, 64, 79, 85, 93, and 98.
Effective Date	These statements currently are effective.
Applicability	Auditor's reports issued in connection with audits of historical financial statements that are intended to present financial position, results of operations, and cash flows in conformity with generally accepted accounting principles (GAAP).
	The Statement does not apply to unaudited financial statements as described in Section 504, *Association with Financial Statements*. It also does not apply to reports on incomplete financial information or other special presentations as described in Section 623, *Special Reports*.

AU-C EFFECTIVE DATE AND SUMMARY OF CHANGES

SAS No. 122, *Codification of Auditing Standards and Procedures,* is effective for audits of financial statements with periods ending on or after December 15, 2012.

AU-C Sections 700, 705, and 706 include auditor report changes and are closely integrated with AU-C sections 210, *Terms of Engagement,* and 580, *Written Representations.*

AU-C Sections 700, 705, and 706 supersede:

- AU Section 410, *Adherence to Generally Accepted Accounting Principles*
- AU Section 508, *Reports on Audited Financial Statements*, paragraphs .01–.11, .14–.15, .19–.32, .35–.52, .58–.70, and .74–.76
- AU Section 530, *Dating of the Independent Auditor's Report* (as amended), paragraphs .01–.02

The primary changes pertain more to appearance and presentation than substance; however, they are significant. The clarified standards include auditor report changes:

- The description of management's responsibility,
- The use of headings, and
- The introduction of two new terms—*emphasis-of-matter* and *other-matter paragraphs*—replacing the term *explanatory paragraph.*

The introduction paragraph will no longer reference either management's or the auditor's responsibility. The clarified SAS requires a new section titled "Management's Responsibility for the Financial Statements." This new section is required to describe management's responsibility for the preparation and fair presentation of the financial statements in more detail than what was required in AU Section 508. The description includes an explanation that management is responsible for the preparation and fair presentation of the financial statements in accordance with the applicable financial reporting framework, and that this responsibility includes the design, implementation, and maintenance of internal control relevant to the preparation and fair presentation of financial statements that are free from material misstatement, whether due to fraud or error.

The clarified SAS also requires a section headed "Auditor's Responsibility." This section requires a statement related to the auditor's responsibility to express an opinion on the financial statements based on an audit and another statement that the audit was conducted in accordance with US GAAP or other standards, if applicable. This section replaces the "scope" paragraph.

The opinion paragraph will have the heading "Opinion." The use of the heading clearly differentiates the opinion from the report. If the opinion is qualified, the opinion paragraph must be followed by a paragraph with the appropriate heading:

- Basis for Qualified Opinion
- Basis for Adverse Opinion
- Basis for Disclaimer of Opinion

If the auditor has other responsibilities, such as reporting on legal or regulatory requirements, additional guidance is provided.

Signature and dating of report remain essentially the same.

AU-C Section 706 introduces and describes two paragraphs in the auditor's report:

1. An *emphasis-of-matter* paragraph refers to a matter appropriately presented or disclosed in the financial statements. An emphasis-of-matter paragraph is any paragraph added to the auditor's report that relates to a matter that is appropriately presented or disclosed in the financial statements.

    Certain standards require an emphasis-of-matter paragraph, whereas other emphasis-of-matter paragraphs are added at the discretion of the auditor, consistent with current practice. However, all such paragraphs are to be considered emphasis-of-matter paragraphs, because they are intended to draw the users' attention to a particular matter.

2. An *other-matter* as a paragraph included in the auditor's report refers to a matter other than those presented or disclosed in the financial statements that, in the auditor's judgment, is relevant to the users' understanding of the audit, the auditor's responsibilities, or the auditor's report.

AU DEFINITIONS OF TERMS

Adverse opinion. An adverse opinion states that the financial statements do not present fairly the financial position, results of operations, and cash flows of the entity in conformity with GAAP. An adverse opinion is an opinion, even though negative, and cannot be expressed unless an audit in accordance with GAAS has been performed.

Audit. An audit, as referred to in the standard report, is an audit of historical financial statements performed in accordance with GAAS in effect at the time the audit is performed. GAAS includes the ten standards as well as Statements on Auditing Standards (SASs) that interpret those standards and, when relevant, the American Institute of Certified Public Accountants (AICPA) Audit and Accounting Guides.

Auditor's standard report. The auditor's standard report states that the financial statements present fairly, in all material respects, an entity's financial position, results of operations, and cash flows in conformity with GAAP. It has a title that includes the word *independent*, and *three paragraphs*—an *introductory paragraph* that identifies the financial statements audited and the division of responsibility between the auditor and management, a *scope paragraph* that describes the nature of an audit, and an *opinion paragraph* that expresses the auditor's opinion on the financial statements audited.

Continuing auditor. An auditor who has audited the financial statements of the current period and of one or more consecutive periods immediately prior to the current period.

Disclaimer of opinion. A disclaimer of opinion means that the auditor is unable to and does not express an opinion on the financial statements.

Explanatory language added to the auditor's standard report. Certain circumstances, while not affecting the auditor's unqualified opinion on the financial statements, may require that the auditor add an explanatory paragraph (or other explanatory language) to the report.

Qualified opinion. A qualified opinion states that, except for the effects of the matter(s) to which the qualification relates, the financial statements present fairly, in all material respects, the financial position, results of operations, and cash flows of the entity in conformity with GAAP.

Unqualified opinion. An unqualified opinion states that the financial statements present fairly, in all material respects, the financial position, results of operations, and cash flows of the entity in conformity with GAAP. This is the opinion expressed in the auditor's standard report.

Updated report. A report issued in conjunction with the report on current period financial statements by a continuing auditor that takes into consideration information that the auditor has become aware of during the audit of the current period financial statements.

AU-C DEFINITIONS OF TERMS

Source: AU-C 700.11

Comparative financial statements. A complete set of financial statements for one or more prior periods included for comparison with the financial statements of the current period.

Comparative information. Prior period information presented for purposes of comparison with current period amounts or disclosures that is not in the form of a complete set of financial statements. Comparative information includes prior period information presented as condensed financial statements or summarized financial information.

Condensed financial statements. Historical financial information that is presented in less detail than a complete set of financial statements, in accordance with an appropriate financial reporting framework. Condensed financial statements may be separately presented as unaudited financial information or may be presented as comparative information.

General purpose financial statements. Financial statements prepared in accordance with a general purpose framework.

General purpose framework. A financial reporting framework designed to meet the common financial information needs of a wide range of users.

Unmodified opinion. The opinion expressed by the auditor when the auditor concludes that the financial statements are presented fairly, in all material respects, in accordance with the applicable financial reporting framework.

AU-C 705 Definitions

Source: 705.07

Modified opinion. A qualified opinion, an adverse opinion, or a disclaimer of opinion.

Pervasive. A term used in the context of misstatements to describe the effects or possible effects, on the financial statements of misstatements, if any, that are undetected due to an inability to obtain sufficient appropriate audit evidence. Pervasive effects on the financial statements are those that, in the auditor's professional judgment:

- Are not confined to specific elements, accounts, or items of the financial statements;
- If so confined, represent or could represent a substantial proportion of the financial statements; or
- With regard to disclosures, are fundamental to users' understanding of the financial statements.

AU-C 706 Definitions

Source: 706.05

Emphasis-of-matter paragraph. A paragraph included in the auditor's report that is required by GAAS, or is included at the auditor's discretion, and that refers to a matter appropriately presented or disclosed in the financial statements that, in the auditor's professional judgment, is of such importance that it is fundamental to users' understanding of the financial statements.

Other-matter paragraph. A paragraph included in the auditor's report that is required by GAAS, or is included at the auditor's discretion, and that refers to a matter other than those presented or disclosed in the financial statements that, in the auditor's professional judgment, is relevant to users' understanding of the audit, the auditor's responsibilities, or the auditor's report.

OBJECTIVES OF AU SECTION 508

The primary objective of this section is to help ensure the public's understanding of the auditor's role by requiring the auditor's report to more explicitly address in nontechnical language the following matters: (1) responsibility assumed, (2) procedures performed, and (3) degree of assurance provided.

SAS 58 prescribed a new form of standard report for auditors and deleted all reference to "consistency," eliminated "subject to" qualifications, and substituted "audited" for "examined." It required all auditors' reports to have a title that includes the word *independent* (for example, Independent Auditor's Report).

In conjunction with deleting the routine reference to "consistency" in the auditor's standard report, SAS 58 revised the second standard of reporting in the ten generally accepted auditing standards, as follows:

The report shall identify those circumstances in which such principles (GAAP) have not been consistently observed in the current period in relation to the preceding period.

Thus, the auditor does not include an explicit opinion on consistency in normal circumstances, but adds an explanatory paragraph to highlight an inconsistency.

SAS 79 eliminated the reporting requirement to add an explanatory paragraph for all uncertainties, except substantial doubt about ability to continue as a going concern (see Section 341, *The Auditor's Consideration of an Entity's Ability to Continue as a Going Concern*).

The removal of the uncertainties reporting requirement culminated a long debate about the relevance of this form of reporting that was set in motion by the Financial Accounting Standards Board's (FASB) Statement 5 on loss contingencies. Under GAAP, when an uncertainty is properly disclosed, the financial statements are not deficient and no audit report modification is warranted.

SAS 93, *Omnibus Statement on Auditing Standards—2000,* amends SAS 58 to include a reference to the United States of America as the country of origin of the accounting principles used to prepare the financial statements and the auditing standards that the auditor follows in performing the audit. This change was made because financial statements in conformity with US GAAP and audited according to US GAAS are increasingly available beyond US borders.

OBJECTIVES OF AU-C SECTIONS

AU-C 700 states that:

. . . the objectives of the auditor are to

    a. *form an opinion on the financial statements based on an evaluation of the audit evidence obtained, including evidence obtained about comparative financial statements or comparative financial information, and*

    b. *express clearly that opinion on the financial statements through a written report that also describes the basis for that opinion.*

AU-C 705 states that:

. . . the objective of the auditor is to express clearly an appropriately modified opinion on the financial statements that is necessary when

    a. *the auditor concludes, based on the audit evidence obtained, that the financial statements as a whole are materially misstated or*

    b. *the auditor is unable to obtain sufficient appropriate audit evidence to conclude that the financial statements as a whole are free from material misstatement*

AU-C 706 states that:

. . . the objective of the auditor, having formed an opinion on the financial statements, is to draw users' attention, when in the auditor's judgment it is necessary to do so, by way of clear additional communication in the auditor's report, to

    a. *a matter, although appropriately presented or disclosed in the financial statements, that is of such importance that it is fundamental to users' understanding of the financial statements or*

    b. *as appropriate, any other matter that is relevant to users' understanding of the audit, the auditor's responsibilities, or the auditor's report.*

FUNDAMENTAL REQUIREMENTS: AUDITOR'S STANDARD REPORT

COMPONENTS OF AUDITOR'S STANDARD REPORT

The auditor's standard report should include the following:

1. A title that includes the word *independent* (for example, Independent Auditor's Report). A title is not required for an auditor's report if the auditor is not independent. (Section 504, *Association with Financial Statements,* provides guidance on reporting when an auditor is not independent.)
2. An introductory paragraph with statements that:

a. The financial statements explicitly identified in the report as to title and date were audited.
b. The financial statements are the responsibility of the entity's management.
c. The auditor's responsibility is to express an opinion on the financial statements based on the audit.

3. A scope paragraph with statements that:

   a. The audit was conducted in accordance with GAAS and an identification of the United States of America as the country of origin of those standards (e.g., auditing standards generally accepted in the United States of America, or US GAAS).
   b. Those standards require that the auditor plan and perform the audit to obtain reasonable assurance about whether the financial statements are free of material misstatement.
   c. An audit includes:

      (1) Examining, on a test basis, evidence supporting the amounts and disclosures in the financial statements
      (2) Assessing the accounting principles used and significant estimates made by management
      (3) Evaluating the overall financial statement presentation

   d. The auditor believes that the audit provides a reasonable basis for the opinion.

4. An opinion paragraph that presents the auditor's opinion as to whether the financial statements present fairly, in all material respects, the financial position of the entity as of the balance sheet date and the result of its operations and its cash flows for the period then ended in conformity with GAAP. The opinion should identify the United States of America as the country of origin of those accounting principles (e.g., accounting principles generally accepted in the United States of America, or US GAAP).[2]

5. The manual or printed signature of the auditing firm and the date of the audit report, which is normally the date of completion of fieldwork.

The "AU Illustrations" section at the end of this chapter contains examples of the auditor's standard report on financial statements covering a single year (Illustration 1) and on comparative financial statements (Illustration 2). The illustrations also contain examples of audit reports on comparative financial statements when the opinions differ between years (Illustrations 14 and 15).

ADDRESSEE

The auditor's report may be addressed to the entity whose financial statements are being audited, its board of directors, or its shareholders. For an unincorporated entity, the report should be addressed as circumstances dictate. For example:

---

[2] *A US auditor may also be engaged to report on a US entity's financial statements that have been prepared in conformity with accounting principles generally accepted in another country, in which case the auditor should refer to Section 534,* Reporting on Financial Statements Prepared for Use in Other Countries.

- **Unincorporated entity.** The report should be addressed to the partners, or to the general partner of a limited partnership, to joint venturers, or to the proprietor of a sole proprietorship.
- **Audit of entity not the client of the auditor.** When an auditor is retained to audit the financial statements of an entity that is not the auditor's client, the report should be addressed to the one who retained the auditor and not to the directors or shareholders of the entity whose financial statements were audited.

NOTE: Under Section 301, Public Company Audit Committees, *and the SEC's related implementing Rule No. 33-8138, "Strengthening the Commission's Requirements Regarding Auditor Independence," the audit committee is "directly responsible for the appointment, compensation, and oversight of the work of any registered public accounting firm employed by that issuer . . . for the purpose of preparing or issuing an audit report or related work, and each such registered public accounting firm shall report directly to the audit committee." Therefore, audit reports of listed companies should be addressed to the audit committee. It is acceptable to also address the report to the stockholders and boards of directors.*

FUNDAMENTAL REQUIREMENTS: EXPLANATORY LANGUAGE ADDED TO THE AUDITOR'S STANDARD REPORT

GENERAL

Circumstances may require the auditor to add an explanatory paragraph or explanatory language to the standard report, even though the circumstances do not affect the auditor's unqualified opinion. Unless specifically stated otherwise, the explanatory paragraph may either precede or follow the opinion paragraph. AU 508.11 lists the following circumstances that may require explanatory language:

1. The auditor's opinion is based in part on the report of another auditor (see *Illustrations* and Section 543, *Part of Audit Performed by Other Independent Auditors*).
2. The financial statements contain a departure from a promulgated accounting principle to prevent them from being misleading. (These situations are covered by Rule 203 of the AICPA Code of Professional Ethics. Also, see Section 410/411.)
3. There is substantial doubt about the entity's ability to continue as a going concern (see Section 341, *The Auditor's Consideration of an Entity's Ability to Continue as a Going Concern*).
4. There has been a material change between periods in accounting principles or in the method of their application.
5. Certain circumstances relating to reports on comparative financial statements exist (e.g., prior year audited by another accountant whose report is not presented).
6. Selected quarterly financial data required by SEC Regulation S-K has been omitted or has not been reviewed (see Section 722, *Review of Interim Financial Information*).
7. The following circumstances pertaining to supplementary information required by the FASB, the Governmental Accounting Standards Board (GASB), or the Federal Accounting Standards Advisory Board (FASAB) exist:

    a. The information has been omitted.
    b. The information presented departs materially from FASB, GASB, or FASAB guidelines.

c. The auditor is unable to complete prescribed procedures on the information.
d. The auditor has doubts about whether the information conforms to FASB, GASB, or FASAB guidelines.

8. Other information in a document containing audited financial statements is materially inconsistent with information appearing in the financial statements (see Section 550, *Other Information in Documents Containing Audited Financial Statements*).
9. The auditor may, but is not required to, add an explanatory paragraph when he or she wishes to emphasize a matter concerning the financial statements.

OPINION BASED IN PART ON REPORT OF ANOTHER AUDITOR

When the auditor decides to refer to another auditor's report as a basis, in part, for the opinion on the financial statements, he or she should disclose this fact in the introductory paragraph of the report and should refer to the other auditor's report in the opinion paragraph (see Illustration 4 and Section 543, *Part of Audit Performed by Other Independent Auditors*).

DEPARTURE FROM A PROMULGATED PRINCIPLE

Rule 203 of the AICPA Code of Professional Conduct states that the auditor should not express an unqualified opinion if the financial statements contain a material departure from an accounting principle promulgated by the bodies designated by Council of the AICPA to establish such principles. Rule 203, however, provides for the possibility that literal application of a principle may, in unusual circumstances, result in misleading financial statements. In those unusual circumstances, the auditor's report should include a separate paragraph or paragraphs containing the following:

1. A description of the departure
2. The approximate effects of the departure, if practicable
3. Reasons why compliance with the principle would result in misleading financial statements

The explanatory paragraph(s) may either precede or follow the opinion paragraph. In these circumstances, the auditor may express an unqualified opinion with respect to the conformity of the financial statements with GAAP. Illustration 10 presents an example of an auditor's report in these circumstances.

NOTE: *The financial statements conform with GAAP because the departure from a promulgated principle (pronouncement) is necessary to keep the financial statements from being misleading.*

LACK OF CONSISTENCY

If there has been a change in accounting principles or in the method of their application that has a material effect on the comparability of financial statements, the auditor should add an explanatory paragraph *following* the opinion paragraph which (1) notes the change, (2) identifies the nature of the change, and (3) refers to the note in the financial statements that discusses the change.

The auditor does not indicate concurrence with the change. If he or she does not concur, the opinion should be qualified because of the GAAP departure or be an adverse opinion (see "Fundamental Requirements: Departures from Unqualified Opinions").

Explanatory Paragraph

The following is an example of an appropriate explanatory paragraph (following the opinion paragraph) for a change in accounting principle or the method of application:

> As discussed in Note X to the financial statements, the Company changed its method of computing depreciation in 20X2.

Reports on Financial Statements of Subsequent Years

The explanatory paragraph described above is required in the auditor's report of financial statements of subsequent years as long as the year of change is presented and reported on. An exception to this requirement occurs when a change in accounting principle that does not require a cumulative effect adjustment is made at the beginning of the earliest year presented and reported on (for example, a change from FIFO to LIFO).

If the accounting change is accounted for by retroactive restatement of the financial statements affected, the explanatory paragraph is required only in the year of change.

EMPHASIS OF A MATTER

The auditor may add an explanatory paragraph, either preceding or following the opinion paragraph, to emphasize a matter regarding the financial statements, but nonetheless express an unqualified opinion on these statements. The auditor should not refer to this type of explanatory paragraph in the opinion paragraph.

FUNDAMENTAL REQUIREMENTS: DEPARTURES FROM UNQUALIFIED OPINIONS

GENERAL

Circumstances may require that the auditor not express an unqualified opinion on the financial statements. Depending on the circumstances, the auditor should express a qualified opinion ("except for") or an adverse opinion or disclaim an opinion.

QUALIFIED OPINIONS

When the auditor expresses a qualified opinion, he or she should

1. Add one or more separate explanatory paragraph(s) *preceding* the opinion paragraph of the report that disclose(s) all of the substantive reasons for the qualified opinion.
2. Add appropriate qualifying language to the opinion paragraph, including the word *except* or *exception* in a phrase such as *except for* or *with the exception of*.
3. Add a reference in the opinion paragraph to the explanatory paragraph(s).

Qualified opinions are expressed when there is a scope limitation or a departure from GAAP, and the auditor has decided not to disclaim an opinion or express an adverse opinion, respectively.

The illustrations contain examples of auditors' reports qualified because of a scope limitation (Illustration 5) and qualified because of a departure from GAAP (Illustrations 7 and 8).

NOTE: Disclosing all the substantive reasons for an opinion means that all GAAP departures and scope limitations that are material and known to the auditor should be disclosed. For example, the *auditor should disclose a known misapplication of the lower of cost or market method in inventory evaluation, even though the opinion has been qualified for a scope limitation related to inventory.*

Scope Limitation

Restrictions on the audit's scope, whether imposed by the client or by circumstances, may require the auditor to qualify the opinion or to disclaim an opinion. *Ordinarily*, the auditor should disclaim an opinion on the financial statements when restrictions that significantly limit the scope of the audit are imposed by the client.

Uncertainties and scope limitations. If the auditor has not obtained sufficient evidential matter concerning an uncertainty, he or she should consider the need to express a qualified opinion ("except for") or to disclaim an opinion. Qualifying or disclaiming an opinion because of a scope limitation is appropriate when sufficient evidential matter does or did exist but was not available to the auditor (for example, management did not retain certain records, or management imposed a scope restriction). If it is expected that evidence concerning the resolution of the uncertainty will become available in the future, an unqualified opinion with an explanatory paragraph is appropriate.

Notes to financial statements. Notes to financial statements may contain unaudited information that should be subjected to auditing procedures. If the auditor is not able to apply necessary auditing procedures to these disclosures, he or she should qualify the opinion or disclaim an opinion because of the scope limitation. However, some disclosures, such as the pro forma effects of a business combination or a subsequent event, are not necessary to fairly present the financial statements in accordance with GAAP and, therefore, may be identified as *unaudited* or as *not covered by the auditor's report*.

Reporting on one basic financial statement. The auditor may audit and express an unqualified opinion on one of the basic financial statements if the scope of the audit is not restricted. Illustration 3 contains an example of an auditor's report on the audit of a balance sheet.

Departure from GAAP

When financial statements are materially affected by a departure from GAAP, the auditor should issue a qualified opinion or an adverse opinion.

When the auditor expresses a qualified opinion, he or she should include a separate explanatory paragraph or paragraphs before the opinion paragraph disclosing (1) all substantive reasons that led to the conclusion that there was a departure from GAAP and (2) the principal effects of the departure on the financial statements, if practicable (see Section 431, *Adequacy of Disclosure in the Financial Statements*). If the effects of the departure are not reasonably determinable, the auditor's report should state that fact.

The opinion paragraph of a report qualified because of a departure from GAAP should include appropriate qualifying language and refer to the explanatory paragraph(s).

Illustrations 7 and 8 contain an example of an auditor's report qualified because of a departure from GAAP.

NOTE: Disclosing all substantive reasons for a GAAP departure means that all known instances of violation of GAAP involved should be mentioned. For example, the auditor should not disclose that a building is stated at appraised value and fail to mention that the increase to appraised value was made to capitalize a realized loss on the sale of another asset.

Inadequate disclosure. If the financial statements, including the notes to the financial statements, do not disclose information required by GAAP, the auditor should issue a qualified or adverse opinion because of this departure from GAAP and should provide the information in the auditor's report, if practicable (see Section 431, *Adequacy of Disclosure in the Financial Statements*). Illustration 13 contains an example of an auditor's report qualified because of inadequate disclosure.

NOTE: At times, current-year financial statements are prepared on the basis of accounting principles that are acceptable at the financial statement date but will have to be restated in the following year because of the issuance of a statement of financial accounting standards whose effective date is after the date of the current year's financial statements. In those circumstances, if the auditor decides that the matter should be disclosed in the current year's financial statements and it is not, the auditor should express a qualified or adverse opinion as to conformity with GAAP.

Omission of statement of cash flows. If an entity issues a balance sheet and an income statement but fails to present a statement of cash flows, the auditor normally should qualify the opinion. The auditor is not required to prepare a basic financial statement and include it in the auditor's report if the entity's management does not present the statement.

Illustration 11 contains an example of an auditor's report qualified because of the omission of the statement of cash flows.

Uncertainties and departures from GAAP. Matters involving risks or uncertainties may cause a departure from GAAP because of the following:

1. Inadequate disclosure
2. Inappropriate accounting principles
3. Unreasonable accounting estimates

The auditor should qualify the opinion or express an adverse opinion if he or she concludes that a matter involving a risk or an uncertainty is not adequately disclosed in the financial statements (see FASB Accounting Standards Codification [ASC] 450, *Contingencies*, for the required disclosures of some uncertainties).

The auditor should qualify the opinion or express an adverse opinion if he or she concludes that the accounting principle used to report a transaction involving an uncertainty causes the financial statements to be materially misstated. An example is a sale on account where collection is uncertain that is reported under the accrual method instead of under the installment or cost recovery method as required by GAAP.

The auditor should qualify the opinion or express an adverse opinion if he or she concludes that management has made an unreasonable estimate of the future outcome of an uncertainty and that its effect is to cause the financial statements to be materially misstated (see Section 312, *Audit Risk and Materiality in Conducting an Audit* and Section 342, *Auditing Accounting Estimates*).

Accounting changes—general. The auditor should express a qualified opinion if (1) a newly adopted accounting principle is not an accounting principle that is generally accepted, (2) the method of accounting for the effect of the change is not in conformity with GAAP, or (3) management has not provided reasonable justification for the change in accounting principle. If the effects of the change are sufficiently material, the auditor should express an adverse opinion on the financial statements.

If management has not provided reasonable justification for a change in accounting principle, the auditor should, in subsequent years, continue to qualify the opinion on the financial statements of the year of change as long as those financial statements are presented and reported on. The auditor's opinion on financial statements of subsequent years need not be qualified.

Illustration 12 contains an example of an auditor's report qualified because management did not provide reasonable justification for a change in accounting principle.

Accounting changes—subsequent years. Whenever the auditor expresses a qualified or an adverse opinion on the conformity of financial statements with GAAP for the year of change, the auditor should do the following when reporting on subsequent year's financial statements:

1. Disclose the reservations with respect to the financial statements for the year of change if those financial statements are presented and reported on with the subsequent year's financial statements.
2. If an entity has adopted an accounting principle that is not generally accepted, the auditor should express a qualified or an adverse opinion on the subsequent year's financial statements, depending on the materiality of the departure of those financial statements.
3. If an entity accounts for the effects of a change in accounting principle prospectively when it should have reported the cumulative effects of the change in the year of change, the auditor should express a qualified or an adverse opinion on the subsequent year's financial statements, depending on the materiality of the effect of the departure from GAAP on those financial statements.

ADVERSE OPINIONS

An adverse opinion is expressed when the auditor believes the financial statements taken as a whole are not presented fairly in conformity with GAAP.

When the auditor expresses an adverse opinion, he or she should do the following:

1. Disclose in a separate explanatory paragraph *before* the opinion paragraph of the report all substantive reasons for the opinion.
2. State the principal effects of the subject matter that caused the adverse opinion on financial position, results of operations, and cash flows, if practicable (see Section 431, *Adequacy of Disclosure in the Financial Statements*). If the effects are not reasonably determinable, the auditor's report should state this fact.
3. Include in the opinion paragraph a direct reference to the separate explanatory paragraph.

Illustration 9 contains an example for an auditor's report expressing an adverse opinion.

NOTE: Because an adverse opinion is an opinion, it should not be expressed unless the auditor has performed an audit of sufficient scope to be able to express an opinion.

DISCLAIMER OF OPINION

The auditor disclaims an opinion when he or she has not performed an audit sufficient in scope to enable him or her to form an opinion on the financial statements. Ordinarily, the auditor should disclaim an opinion on the financial statements when significant scope restrictions are imposed by the client.

The auditor should *not* disclaim an opinion because he or she believes there are material departures from GAAP.

The auditor should do the following when disclaiming an opinion because of a scope limitation:

1. Indicate in a separate explanatory paragraph the reasons why the audit did not comply with GAAS.
2. State in the disclaimer of opinion paragraph that the scope of the audit was not sufficient to warrant the expression of opinion.
3. The auditor's report should not include a scope paragraph.

Illustration 6 contains an example of an auditor's report disclaiming an opinion because of a scope limitation.

NOTE: Even though the auditor disclaims an opinion, the auditor should disclose any known GAAP departures.

FUNDAMENTAL REQUIREMENTS: REPORTS ON COMPARATIVE FINANCIAL STATEMENTS

GENERAL

A continuing auditor should update his or her report on the prior period financial statements presented on a comparative basis with the current period financial statements. When updating his or her report, the auditor should consider the effects of circumstances or events coming to his or her attention during the audit of the current period financial statements that may affect the prior period financial statements (see below, "Change of Opinion").

The auditor's report on comparative financial statements should be dated as of the date of completion of fieldwork for the most recent audit.

CHANGE OF OPINION

In an updated report, if the auditor expresses an opinion different from the one previously expressed on prior period financial statements, he or she should do the following:

1. Disclose all substantive reasons for the different opinion in a separate explanatory paragraph *before* the opinion paragraph of the report.
2. The explanatory paragraph should disclose the following:

    a. The date of the auditor's previous report
    b. The kind of opinion previously expressed
    c. The circumstances or events that caused the auditor to express a different opinion
    d. The updated opinion on the prior period financial statements is different from the opinion previously expressed on those financial statements

Illustration 16 contains an example of an auditor's report with an opinion different from the one previously expressed on prior period financial statements.

REISSUANCE OF PREDECESSOR AUDITOR'S REPORT

Predecessor's Procedures

Before reissuing or consenting to the reuse of a report previously issued on financial statements of a prior period, when those financial statements are to be presented on a comparative basis with audited financial statements of a subsequent period, a predecessor auditor should consider whether the previous report on those statements is still appropriate. The predecessor should do the following:

1. Read the current period financial statements.
2. Compare the prior period financial statements that the predecessor reported on with the financial statements to be presented on a comparative basis.
3. Obtain letters of representation from:

   a. The successor auditor, stating whether the successor's audit revealed matters that might have a material effect on, or require disclosure in, the financial statements reported on by the predecessor auditor, and
   b. Management of the former client, stating:

   (1) Whether any information has come to management's attention that would cause them to believe that any previous representations should be modified, and
   (2) Whether any events have occurred subsequent to the balance sheet date of the latest prior period financial statements reported on by the predecessor auditor that would require adjustment to, or disclosure in, those financial statements. (Illustration 17D contains an example of a letter of representation from a successor auditor and from management.)

Based on the above procedures, if the predecessor auditor believes the previously issued report must be revised, he or she should make inquiries about the matter and perform other procedures considered necessary.

Revision of Previously Issued Report

If the predecessor auditor concludes that the previously issued report should be revised, the updated report should disclose all substantive reasons for the different opinion in a separate explanatory paragraph *preceding* the opinion paragraph of the report. The explanatory paragraph should disclose the following:

1. The auditor's previous report date
2. The kind of opinion previously expressed
3. The circumstances or events that caused the auditor to express a different opinion
4. The updated opinion on the prior period financial statements is different from the opinion previously expressed on those financial statements

Dating of Reissued Report

When reissuing the auditor's report on prior period financial statements, the predecessor auditor should use the date of the previous report.

If the predecessor revises the report or the previously reported-on financial statements are restated, the predecessor auditor should dual date the report.

PREDECESSOR AUDITOR'S REPORT NOT PRESENTED

General

When the predecessor auditor's report on prior period financial statements is not presented, the successor auditor should disclose in the introductory paragraph of his or her report the following:

1. The prior period financial statements were audited by another auditor
2. The predecessor auditor's report date
3. The type of report issued by the predecessor auditor
4. The substantive reasons for a report other than the standard report

Illustration 17 contains examples of successor auditor reports when the predecessor auditor's report is not presented.

Prior Period Financial Statements Restated

When the prior period financial statements have been restated, the introductory paragraph of the successor auditor's report should state that a predecessor auditor reported on the prior period financial statements before restatement. If the successor auditor is able to satisfy himself or herself as to the appropriateness of the restatement, he or she may also include the following paragraph from AU 508.74 in the report:

> We also audited the adjustments described in Note X that were applied to restate the 20X1 financial statements. In our opinion, such adjustments are appropriate and have been properly applied.

INTERPRETATIONS

REPORT OF AN OUTSIDE INVENTORY-TAKING FIRM AS AN ALTERNATIVE PROCEDURE FOR OBSERVING INVENTORIES (ISSUED JULY 1975; REVISED OCTOBER 2000: REVISED MARCH 2006)

Some companies, such as retail stores or automobile dealers, use outside specialists in the taking of physical inventories to count, list, price, and subsequently compute the dollar amount of inventory on hand. The fact that inventory is counted by outside specialists is not by itself a satisfactory substitute for the auditor's own observation or taking of some physical counts.

The auditor would ordinarily apply the following procedures:

1. Examine the outside specialist's work program.
2. Observe its counting procedures.
3. Make or observe some physical counts.
4. Recompute calculations of submitted inventory on a test basis.
5. If appropriate, apply tests to intervening transactions.

The independent auditor might, as a matter of professional judgment, decide to reduce the extent of work because of the work of outside specialists, but any restrictions imposed by management or others would be a scope limitation. If the inventory is counted by an outside firm of nonaccountants, this is not a satisfactory substitute for the auditor's own observation.

REPORTING ON FINANCIAL STATEMENTS PREPARED ON A LIQUIDATION BASIS OF ACCOUNTING (ISSUED DECEMBER 1984; REVISED JUNE 1993 AND FEBRUARY 1997; REVISED OCTOBER 2000; REVISED JUNE 2009; REVISED OCTOBER 2011 EFFECTIVE FOR AUDITS OF FINANCIAL STATEMENTS FOR PERIODS ENDING ON OR AFTER DECEMBER 15, 2012)

An entity is not viewed as a going concern if liquidation is imminent. In these circumstances, the liquidation basis of accounting is GAAP. If the liquidation basis has been properly applied and adequate disclosures are made, the auditor should issue an unqualified opinion.

If financial statements on the liquidation basis are presented in comparative form with a prior period's going-concern basis financial statements, the auditor's report should include an explanatory paragraph that describes the change in basis of accounting. (Illustrations 19 and 20 present examples of auditor's reports on financial statements on the liquidation basis of accounting.)

(The above terminology has been revised to reflect the clarified standards and is effective for audits of financial statements for periods ending on or after December 15, 2012:

> Typically, the financial statements of entities that adopt a liquidation basis of accounting are presented along with financial statements of a period prior to adoption of a liquidation basis that were prepared on the basis of GAAP for going concerns. Section 706, *Emphasis-of Matter Paragraphs and Other-Matter Paragraphs in the Independent Auditor's Report*, requires the auditor to include an emphasis-of-matter paragraph when a matter that is appropriately presented or disclosed in the financial statements is of such importance, in the auditor's professional judgment, that it is fundamental to users' understanding of the financial statements. In such circumstances, the emphasis-of-matter paragraph would state that the entity has changed the basis of accounting used to determine the amounts at which assets and liabilities are carried from the going concern basis to a liquidation basis.)

REFERENCE IN AUDITOR'S STANDARD REPORT TO MANAGEMENT'S REPORT (JANUARY 1989)

The auditor's standard report on financial statements should not refer to a separate report by management, if management chooses to present one, that describes management's financial reporting responsibilities. The standard auditor's report should still state that management is responsible for the financial statements, but a cross-reference to a report by management might be misinterpreted by users.

REPORTING ON AUDITS CONDUCTED IN ACCORDANCE WITH AUDITING STANDARDS GENERALLY ACCEPTED IN THE UNITED STATES OF AMERICA AND IN ACCORDANCE WITH INTERNATIONAL STANDARDS ON AUDITING (MARCH 2002; REVISED MAY 2008)

As discussed in this section, the auditor is required to (1) indicate in his or her report that the audit was conducted in accordance with GAAS and (2) identify the United States of America as the country of origin of those standards. However, nothing in this section prohibits an auditor from stating that the audit was conducted in accordance with another set of auditing standards. If the audit was also conducted in accordance with International Standards on Auditing in their entirety, the auditor may indicate this in his or her report.

When reporting on an audit performed in accordance with US GAAS and International Standards on Auditing, the auditor should comply with US reporting standards.

The following is an example from the interpretation (AU 9508.59) of a paragraph in a report for an audit performed in accordance with US GAAS and International Standards on Auditing:

> We conducted our audit in accordance with auditing standards generally accepted in the United States of America and in accordance with International Standards on Auditing. Those standards require that we plan and perform the audit to obtain reasonable assurance about whether the financial statements are free of material misstatement. An audit includes examining, on a test basis, evidence supporting the amounts and disclosures in the financial statements. An audit also

includes assessing the accounting principles used and significant estimates made by management, as well as evaluating the overall financial statement presentation. We believe that our audit provides a reasonable basis for our opinion.

REPORTING AS SUCCESSOR AUDITOR WHEN PRIOR-PERIOD AUDITED FINANCIAL STATEMENTS WERE AUDITED BY A PREDECESSOR AUDITOR WHO HAS CEASED OPERATIONS (NOVEMBER 2002; REVISED JUNE 2009)

If prior period financial statements were audited by a predecessor auditor who has ceased operations, and such statements are presented for comparative purposes with the current financial statements, the successor auditor should indicate in the introductory paragraph of his or her report that the financial statements of the prior period were audited by another auditor and should indicate the date and type of report. (If the report was not unqualified, the auditor should also indicate the substantive reasons for the report qualifications.) The successor auditor also should state that the other auditor has ceased operations, but should not name the other auditor.

The interpretation presents the following example of such a report (AU 9508.61):

> The financial statements of ABC Company as of December 31, 20X1, and for the year then ended were audited by other auditors who have ceased operations. Those auditors expressed an unqualified opinion on those financial statements in their report dated March 31, 20X2.

For SEC engagements, the SEC staff has stated that in annual reports, the predecessor's latest prior period report should be reprinted with a legend indicating that the report is a copy of the previously issued report and that the report has not been reissued.

If the prior period financial statements are subsequently restated, the successor auditor cannot report on the restated adjustments until the audit of the current period financial statements is complete. If the successor auditor is asked to report on the restated financial statements without also reporting on the current period audited financial statements, the successor auditor would need to reaudit the prior period statements.

EFFECT ON AUDITOR'S REPORT OF OMISSION OF SCHEDULE OF INVESTMENTS BY INVESTMENT PARTNERSHIPS THAT ARE EXEMPT FROM SECURITIES AND EXCHANGE COMMISSION REGISTRATION UNDER THE INVESTMENT COMPANY ACT OF 1940 (APRIL 2003; REVISED JUNE 2009)

When an auditor is reporting on financial statements of an investment partnership that is exempt from SEC registration and that does not include required Schedule of Investments information, the auditor is required to include the missing information in a qualified or an adverse report, if practicable. The auditor should not describe "the nature of the omitted disclosures" in the qualified or adverse report.

CLARIFICATION IN THE AUDIT REPORT OF THE EXTENT OF TESTING OF INTERNAL CONTROL OVER FINANCIAL REPORTING IN ACCORDANCE WITH GAAS (JUNE 2004; REVISED MARCH 2006)

Nonissuers, as defined in the Summary of Key Changes that immediately precedes Section 100-230, are required to perform audits under GAAS as established by the Auditing Standards Board of the AICPA. An auditor of a nonissuer may want to clarify that an audit performed under GAAS does not require the same level of testing and reporting on internal control over financial reporting as required for an audit by Section 404(b) of the Sarbanes–

Oxley Act for entities subject to the rules of the SEC. (See the summary of PCAOB Standard No. 5, *An Audit of Internal Control Over Financial Reporting That Is Integrated with an Audit of Financial Statements*, presented later in this publication.) The interpretation suggests that the following language can be inserted as the third sentence in the scope paragraph:

> An audit includes consideration of internal control over financial reporting as a basis for designing audit procedures that are appropriate in the circumstances, but not for the purpose of expressing an opinion on the effectiveness of the Company's internal control over financial reporting. Accordingly, we express no such opinion.

The interpretation notes that this additional language should not be used when a nonissuer voluntarily engages its auditor to audit and report on the effectiveness of internal control over financial reporting, or does so to comply with regulatory requirements.

REFERENCE TO PCAOB STANDARDS IN AN AUDIT REPORT ON A NONISSUER (JUNE 2004)

PCAOB Standard No. 1, *Reference in Auditors' Reports to the Standards of the Public Company Accounting Oversight Board*, requires that audit reports for engagements performed in accordance with PCAOB standards include a statement that the engagement was conducted in accordance with the standards of the PCAOB. A company that is not subject to the rules of PCAOB standards (a nonissuer) is not precluded from conducting the audit in accordance with the standards of the PCAOB and including a statement about this in the audit report. (Issuers and nonissuers are defined in the Summary of Key Changes immediately preceding Section 100-230.) Therefore, if an auditor is engaged to perform an audit of a nonissuer under PCAOB standards, the auditor would state in the report that the audit was conducted in accordance with both US GAAS (as required by Section 508, *Reports on Audited Financial Statements*) and with PCAOB standards. The scope paragraph would state that "We conducted our audit in accordance with generally accepted auditing standards as established by the Auditing Standards Board (United States) and in accordance with the auditing standards of the Public Company Accounting Oversight Board (United States)." (The auditor may use the reference to the Auditing Standards Board to clarify the source of GAAS in this type of reporting situation.)

NOTE: The PCAOB has issued a series of staff questions and answers titled *Audits of Financial Statements of Nonissuers Performed Pursuant to the Standards of the Public Company Accounting Oversight Board. Among other things, these questions clarify that a firm does not need to be registered with the PCAOB in order to audit a nonissuer under PCAOB standards. The PCAOB also clarifies what standards apply when the report refers to the standards of the PCAOB. The authors strongly recommend that auditors read these questions and answers if they are considering performing an audit of a nonissuer under PCAOB standards. The questions and answers can be found on the PCAOB's website at www.pcaobus.org.*

This interpretation notes that an audit report of a subsidiary, investee, or other type of affiliate of an issuer that is not itself an issuer should refer to the audit as having been performed according to GAAS if the report will not be filed with the SEC. For example, an issuer's subsidiary may be subject to certain regulations that require an audit performed according to *Government Auditing Standards* (the "Yellow Book"). In this case the audit report on the subsidiary would refer to GAAS and generally accepted government auditing standards.

Finally, the interpretation suggests in AU 9508.92 that the following language be used to clarify that the purpose and extent of the auditor's testing of internal control over financial reporting was to determine the auditor's procedures and was not sufficient to express an opinion on the effectiveness of internal control. This language is suggested because an audit of a nonissuer performed under PCAOB auditing standards does not require an audit of internal control as required by PCAOB Auditing Standard 5, *An Audit of Internal Control over Financial Reporting That Is Integrated with an Audit of Financial Statements*, unless otherwise required by a regulator with jurisdiction over the nonissuer. The language can be inserted as the third sentence in the scope paragraph.

> *The Company is not required to have, nor were we engaged to perform, an audit of its internal control over financial reporting. Our audit included consideration of internal control over financial reporting as a basis for designing audit procedures that are appropriate in the circumstances, but not for the purpose of expressing an opinion on the effectiveness of the Company's internal control over financial reporting. Accordingly we express no such opinion.*

This additional language should not be used when a nonissuer voluntarily engages its auditor to audit and report on the effectiveness of internal control over financial reporting, or does so to comply with regulatory requirements.

> NOTE: Practitioners should be aware that the AICPA's Center for Public Audit Firms, which replaced the SEC Practice Section, has notified its member firms of certain requirements that apply to employee stock purchase, savings, and similar plans that are required to file Form 11-K pursuant to Section 15(d) of the Securities Exchange Act of 1934. Such plans are considered issuers and must submit an audit report to the SEC in accordance with PCAOB standards. However, these 11-K plans also may be subject to the Employee Retirement Income Security Act (ERISA) and, therefore, may be required to submit an audit to the US Department of Labor in accordance with GAAS. Because PCAOB Auditing Standard 1 does not allow reference to GAAS, and because the Center believes that the Department of Labor will not accept audit reports not referencing GAAS, firms need to conduct audits of these 11-K plans according to two sets of standards. They also must prepare two separate audit reports to meet these requirements.

FINANCIAL STATEMENTS PREPARED IN CONFORMITY WITH INTERNATIONAL FINANCIAL REPORTING STANDARDS AS ISSUED BY THE INTERNATIONAL ACCOUNTING STANDARDS BOARD (MAY 2008)

When an auditor reports on financial statements prepared in conformity with International Financial Reporting Standards (IFRS), the auditor would refer, in the auditor's report, to IFRS rather than to US GAAP. A sample opinion paragraph is:

> *In our opinion, the financial statements referred to above present fairly, in all material respects, the financial position of ABC Company as of December 31, 20X2 and 20X1, and the results of its operations, comprehensive income, changes in equity, and its cash flows for the years then ended, in conformity with International Financial Reporting Standards as issued by the International Accounting Standards Board.*

PROFESSIONAL ISSUES TASK FORCE PRACTICE ALERTS

97-3 CHANGES IN AUDITORS AND RELATED TOPICS

This practice alert discusses appropriate procedures for successor auditors, such as:

- Requesting that the client authorize the predecessor auditor to permit a review of the predecessor audit documentation after the successor auditor has accepted the engagement
- Remembering that, since the client and successor auditor are responsible for the opening balances on the current year financial statements and consistency of accounting principles, the successor must obtain sufficient competent evidential matter to provide a reasonable basis for expressing an opinion.

In addition, predecessor auditors must consider relevant matters when asked by a former client to reissue their audit reports. Matters include deciding whether to reestablish a client relationship and evaluating the former client's intended use of the predecessor auditor's report.

This practice alert states that before consenting to include his or her report on previously audited financial statements, a predecessor auditor should perform procedures similar to its client acceptance and continuation procedures as required by Statement on Quality Control Standards (SQCS) 2, *System of Quality Control for a CPA Firm's Accounting and Auditing Practice*, and may wish to consider the guidance in Practice Alert 2003-3, *Acceptance and Continuance of Clients and Engagements*.

The auditor typically would evaluate whether specific events have occurred, such as a major change in:

- Management
- Directors
- Ownership
- Legal counsel
- Financial condition
- Litigation status
- Nature of the entity's business
- Scope of the engagement

Consideration of:

- Whether the client has selected an underwriter that has been the subject of adverse publicity
- The professional reputation and experience of both the successor auditor and legal counsel associated with subsequent years' financial statements

After consideration of these factors, the predecessor auditor should then consider whether his or her report is still appropriate under the circumstances, using guidance provided in this section under "Fundamental Requirements: Reports on Comparative Financial Statements." If, after performing the appropriate procedures, a predecessor becomes aware of subsequent events or transactions that require adjustment, additional disclosure or reclassification, the predecessor auditor should make inquiries and perform any other necessary procedures.

An auditor may decide not to consent to the use of his or her previously issued report and is not required to subsequently sign a consent for inclusion of that report in a registration statement or for any other reason. The auditor does not need to disclose or communicate the reasons for not issuing the report to either the entity or its audit committee. If the predecessor does not reissue his or her report, the successor may be engaged to audit the financial statements previously reported on and should follow the guidance in "Fundamental Requirements" of Section 315, *Communications between Predecessor and Successor Auditors*.

Finally, the alert discusses the use of indemnification clauses when reissuing reports. SEC independence rules prohibit indemnification agreements between auditors and current publicly held clients. However, the SEC staff has agreed not to question a predecessor auditor's independence with respect to a former client for indemnification agreements, provided that:

1. The indemnification letter would be void and any advanced funds would be returned to a client if a former auditor is found liable for malpractice, and
2. The indemnification provision is entered into after a successor auditor has issued an audit report on the former client's most recent financial statements included in the client's registration statement.

TECHNIQUES FOR APPLICATION

The following table lists the circumstances requiring modification of the auditor's standard report and the effect of the modification on the auditor's standard report.

Circumstances	Types of Opinion			
	Unqualified	Qualified	Adverse	Disclaimer
1. Opinion based in part on report of another auditor	x			
2. Rule 203 opinion	x			
3. Lack of consistency	x			
4. Required quarterly data omitted or not reviewed	x			
5. Required supplementary information omitted or not reviewed	x			
6. Other information in a document containing audited financial statements is materially inconsistent with financial statement information	x			
7. Emphasis of matter	x			
8. Scope limitation		x		x
9. Report on one financial statement only	x			
10. Departure from GAAP		x	x	
11. Inadequate disclosure		x	x	
12. Change in accounting principle:				
a. Newly adopted principle not generally accepted		x	x	
b. Incorrect method of accounting for the effect of the change		x	x	
c. Reasonable justification for change not provided		x	x	

SCOPE LIMITATION

General

The decision to qualify the opinion or to disclaim an opinion depends on the auditor's assessment of the importance of the omitted procedure to his or her ability to form an opinion on the financial statements being audited. The auditor's assessment is affected by the following:

1. Nature and magnitude of the potential effects
2. Significance to financial statements of item to scope limitation
3. Pervasiveness of the item

Pervasiveness generally relates to the number of items in the financial statement; that is, is the matter isolated to a few items or does it affect many? For example, ending inventory affects many items—current assets, current ratio, gross profit, income taxes, and net income—whereas an investment accounted for by the equity method affects few line items in the financial statements.

Common Restrictions on Scope

Common restrictions on the scope of the audit involve (1) observation of physical inventories, (2) confirmation of accounts receivable, and (3) long-term investments accounted for by the equity method when the auditor is unable to obtain audited financial statements of the investee.

If the auditor did not observe the ending inventory because of circumstances such as appointment after year-end, he or she should apply alternative procedures. Alternative procedures may include observing all or part of the physical inventory after year-end and rolling it back to year-end by adjusting for additions and sales between year-end and the date the physical inventory was observed. Whatever alternative procedures are used, the auditor should always make, or observe, some physical counts of the inventory and apply appropriate tests to the transactions between year-end and the date of the observation. (See Section 331, *Inventories*.)

If the auditor did not confirm accounts receivable at year-end because of circumstances such as appointment after year-end, he or she might do either of the following at the time of appointment:

1. Try to confirm year-end balances or individual sales and cash receipts.
2. Confirm balances at a date subsequent to year-end and apply appropriate tests to transactions between year-end and the confirmation date.

Some debtors are unable to confirm balances at any time. In these circumstances, the auditor should consider examining subsequent cash receipts or specific sales invoices. In all instances in which accounts receivable are not substantiated by confirmation, the auditor has to document how the presumption that receivables will be confirmed was overcome (see Section 330, *The Confirmation Process*).

If the auditor is unable to obtain audited financial statements of the investee for investments accounted for by the equity method, he or she should examine other types of financial statements (compiled, reviewed, internal) and, depending on the materiality of the investment, apply appropriate auditing procedures to these statements.

If there is a scope limitation and the auditor satisfies himself or herself as to the account balance by applying alternate procedures, the auditor's report should not make reference to these circumstances.

Restrictions Imposed by Client

As noted under "Fundamental Requirements," when scope limitations are imposed by the client, the auditor should ordinarily disclaim an opinion on the financial statements. The rationale for a disclaimer in these circumstances is that the client is in a position to avoid the limitation and the auditor cannot know what would be found by release of the restriction.

Departure from GAAP

The decision to express a qualified or an adverse opinion because of a departure from GAAP depends on the degree of materiality of the departure. Criteria for determining the degree of materiality of a departure from GAAP are:

1. Dollar magnitude of the effects
2. Significance of the item to the entity (for example, inventories to a manufacturing company)
3. Pervasiveness of the misstatements
4. Impact of the misstatement on the financial statements taken as a whole

In practice, auditors also consider the likely purpose of management in departing from GAAP. A judgment that management intended to mislead users would ordinarily cause the auditor to express an adverse opinion.

Litigation Services

A practitioner engaged to provide expert consulting or witness services is not subject to the requirements of GAAS, including the reporting standards. However, an expert engaged by plaintiffs or defendants in an auditor malpractice matter may testify about the application of GAAS to the circumstances.

AU ILLUSTRATIONS

The following are illustrations of auditors' reports, explanatory paragraphs, a letter from successor auditor to predecessor auditor, and a letter from management to the predecessor auditor.

1. Auditor's Standard Report: Financial Statements Covering a Single Year (Adapted from AU 508.08)
2. Auditor's Standard Report on Comparative Financial Statements (Adapted from AU 508.08)
3. Auditor's Report on One Basic Financial Statement (Adapted from AU 508.34)
4. Auditor's Report: Opinion Based in Part on Report of Another Auditor (Adapted from AU 508.13)
5. Auditor's Report: Qualified Opinion—Scope Limitation (Adapted from AU 508.26)
6. Auditor's Report: Disclaimer of Opinion—Scope Limitation (Adapted from AU 508.63)
7. Auditor's Report: Qualified Opinion—Departure from GAAP Explained in Report (Adapted from AU 508.39)
8. Auditor's Report: Qualified Opinion—Departure from GAAP Explained in a Note (Adapted from AU 508.40)
9. Auditor's Report: Adverse Opinion—Departure from GAAP (Adapted from AU 508.60)
10. Auditor's Report: Rule 203 Opinion
11. Auditor's Report: Omission of Statement of Cash Flows (Adapted from AU 508.44)
12. Auditor's Report: Management Has Not Provided Reasonable Justification for Change in Accounting Principle (Adapted from AU 508.17)
13. Auditor's Report: Inadequate Disclosure (Adapted from AU 508.42)

14. Auditor's Standard Report on the Prior Year Financial Statements and a Qualified Opinion on the Current Year Financial Statements (Adapted from AU 508.67)
15. Auditor's Standard Report on the Current Year Financial Statements with a Disclaimer of Opinion on the Prior Year Statements of Income, Retained Earnings, and Cash Flows (Adapted from AU 508.67)
16. Auditor's Report: Opinion Different from Opinion Previously Expressed (Adapted from AU 508.69)
17. Auditor's Report: Predecessor Auditor's Report Not Presented (Adapted from AU 508.74)
18. Illustrative Updating Management Representation Letter (Adapted from AU 333.18)
19. Auditor's Report on Single-Year Financial Statements in Year of Adoption of Liquidation Basis (Adapted from AU 9508.36)
20. Auditor's Report on Comparative Financial Statements in Year of Adoption of Liquidation Basis (Adapted from AU 9508.36)

ILLUSTRATION 1. AUDITOR'S STANDARD REPORT: FINANCIAL STATEMENTS COVERING A SINGLE YEAR (ADAPTED FROM AU 508.08)

To the Board of Directors
Widget Company
Main City, USA

Independent Auditor's Report

We have audited the accompanying balance sheet of Widget Company as of December 31, 20X6, and the related statements of income, retained earnings, and cash flows for the year then ended. These financial statements are the responsibility of the Company's management. Our responsibility is to express an opinion on these financial statements based on our audit.

We conducted our audit in accordance with auditing standards generally accepted in the United States of America. Those standards require that we plan and perform the audit to obtain reasonable assurance about whether the financial statements are free of material misstatement. An audit includes examining, on a test basis, evidence supporting the amounts and disclosures in the financial statements. An audit also includes assessing the accounting principles used and significant estimates made by management, as well as evaluating the overall financial statement presentation. We believe that our audit provides a reasonable basis for our opinion.

In our opinion, the financial statements referred to above present fairly, in all material respects, the financial position of Widget Company as of [*at*] December 31, 20X6, and the results of its operations and its cash flows for the year then ended in conformity with accounting principles generally accepted in the United States of America.

Smith and Jones
February 15, 20X7

ILLUSTRATION 2. AUDITOR'S STANDARD REPORT ON COMPARATIVE FINANCIAL STATEMENTS (ADAPTED FROM AU 508.08)

To the Board of Directors
Widget Company
Main City, USA

Independent Auditor's Report

We have audited the accompanying balance sheets of Widget Company as of December 31, 20X6 and 20X5, and the related statements of income, retained earnings, and cash flows for the years then ended. These financial statements are the responsibility of the Company's management. Our responsibility is to express an opinion on these financial statements based on our audit.

We conducted our audits in accordance with auditing standards generally accepted in the United States of America. Those standards require that we plan and perform the audit to obtain reasonable assurance about whether the financial statements are free of material misstatement. An audit includes examining, on a test basis, evidence supporting the amounts and disclosures in the financial statements. An audit also includes assessing the accounting principles used and significant estimates made by management, as well as evaluating the overall financial statement presentation. We believe that our audits provide a reasonable basis for our opinion.

In our opinion, the financial statements referred to above present fairly, in all material respects, the financial position of Widget Company as of [*at*] December 31, 20X6 and 20X5, and the results of its operations and its cash flows for the years then ended in conformity with accounting principles generally accepted in the United States of America.

Smith and Jones
February 15, 20X7

ILLUSTRATION 3. AUDITOR'S REPORT ON ONE BASIC FINANCIAL STATEMENT (ADAPTED FROM AU 508.34)

To the Board of Directors
Widget Company
Main City, USA

Independent Auditor's Report

We have audited the accompanying balance sheet of Widget Company as of December 31, 20X6. This financial statement is the responsibility of the Company's management. Our responsibility is to express an opinion on this financial statement based on our audit.

We conducted our audit in accordance with auditing standards generally accepted in the United States of America. Those standards require that we plan and perform the audit to obtain reasonable assurance about whether the financial statements are free of material misstatement. An audit includes examining, on a test basis, evidence supporting the amounts and disclosures in the financial statements. An audit also includes assessing the accounting principles used and significant estimates made by management, as well as evaluating the overall financial statement presentation. We believe that our audit provides a reasonable basis for our opinion.

In our opinion, the balance sheet referred to above presents fairly, in all material respects, the financial position of Widget Company as of December 31, 20X6, in conformity with accounting principles generally accepted in the United States of America.

Smith and Jones
February 15, 20X7

ILLUSTRATION 4. AUDITOR'S REPORT: OPINION BASED IN PART ON REPORT OF ANOTHER AUDITOR (ADAPTED FROM AU 508.13)

To the Board of Directors
Widget Company
Main City, USA

Independent Auditor's Report

    We have audited the consolidated balance sheets of Widget Company and subsidiaries as of December 31, 20X6 and 20X5, and the related consolidated statements of income, retained earnings, and cash flows for the years then ended. These financial statements are the responsibility of the Company's management. Our responsibility is to express an opinion on these financial statements based on our audits. We did not audit the financial statements of B Company, a wholly owned subsidiary, which statements reflect total assets of $_____ and $_____ as of December 31, 20X6 and 20X5, respectively, and total revenues of $_____ and $_____ for the years then ended. Those statements were audited by other auditors whose report has been furnished to us, and our opinion, insofar as it relates to the amounts included for B Company, is based solely on the report of the other auditors.

    We conducted our audits in accordance with auditing standards generally accepted in the United States of America. Those standards require that we plan and perform the audit to obtain reasonable assurance about whether the financial statements are free of material misstatement. An audit includes examining, on a test basis, evidence supporting the amounts and disclosures in the financial statements. An audit also includes assessing the accounting principles used and significant estimates made by management, as well as evaluating the overall financial statement presentation. We believe that our audits and the report of other auditors provide a reasonable basis for our opinion.

    In our opinion, based on our audits and the report of other auditors, the consolidated financial statements referred to above present fairly, in all material respects, the financial position of Widget Company as of December 31, 20X6 and 20X5, and the results of its operations and its cash flows for the years then ended in conformity with accounting principles generally accepted in the United States of America.

Smith and Jones
February 15, 20X7

ILLUSTRATION 5. AUDITOR'S REPORT: QUALIFIED OPINION—SCOPE LIMITATION (ADAPTED FROM AU 508.26)

To the Board of Directors
Widget Company
Main City, USA

Independent Auditor's Report

[*Same first paragraph as the standard report*]

    Except as discussed in the following paragraph, we conducted our audits in accordance with auditing standards generally accepted in the United States of America. Those standards require that we plan and perform the audit to obtain reasonable assurance about whether the financial statements are free of material misstatement. An audit includes examining, on a test basis, evidence supporting the amounts and disclosures in the financial statements. An audit also includes assessing the accounting principles used and significant estimates made by management, as well as evaluating the overall financial statement presentation. We believe that our audits provide a reasonable basis for our opinion.

We were unable to obtain audited financial statements supporting the Company's investment in a foreign affiliate stated at $_____ and $_____ at December 31, 20X6 and 20X5, respectively, or its equity in earnings of the affiliate of $_____ and $_____, which is included in net income for the years then ended as described in Note X to the financial statements; nor were we able to satisfy ourselves as to the carrying value of the investment in the foreign affiliate or the equity in its earnings by other auditing procedures.

In our opinion, except for the effects of such adjustment, if any, as might have been determined to be necessary had we been able to examine evidence regarding the foreign affiliate investment and earnings, the financial statements referred to in the first paragraph above present fairly, in all material respects, the financial position of Widget Company as of December 31, 20X6 and 20X5, and the results of its operations and its cash flows for the years then ended in conformity with accounting principles generally accepted in the United States of America.

Smith and Jones
February 15, 20X7

ILLUSTRATION 6. AUDITOR'S REPORT: DISCLAIMER OF OPINION—SCOPE LIMITATION (ADAPTED FROM AU 508.63)

To the Board of Directors
Widget Company
Main City, USA

Independent Auditor's Report

We were engaged to audit the accompanying balance sheets of Widget Company as of December 31, 20X6 and 20X5, and the related statements of income, retained earnings, and cash flows for the years then ended. These financial statements are the responsibility of the Company's management.

[*Second paragraph of standard report should be omitted*]

The Company did not make a count of its physical inventory in 20X6 or 20X5, stated in the accompanying financial statements at $_____ as of December 31, 20X6, and at $_____ as of December 31, 20X5. Further, evidence supporting the cost of property and equipment acquired prior to December 31, 20X5, is no longer available. The Company's records and circumstances do not permit the application of other auditing procedures to inventories or property and equipment.

Since the Company did not take physical inventories, and we were not able to apply other auditing procedures to satisfy ourselves as to inventory quantities and the cost of property and equipment, the scope of our work was not sufficient to enable us to express, and we do not express, an opinion on these financial statements.

Smith and Jones
February 15, 20X7

ILLUSTRATION 7. AUDITOR'S REPORT: QUALIFIED OPINION—DEPARTURE FROM GAAP EXPLAINED IN REPORT (ADAPTED FROM AU 508.39)

To the Board of Directors
Widget Company
Main City, USA

Independent Auditor's Report

[*Same first and second paragraphs as the standard report*]

The Company has excluded, from property and debt in the accompanying balance sheets, certain lease obligations that, in our opinion, should be capitalized in order to conform with accounting principles generally accepted in the United States of America. If these lease obligations were capitalized, property would be increased by $_____ and $_____, long-term debt by $_____ and $_____, and retained earnings by $_____ and $_____ as of December 31, 20X6 and 20X5, respectively. Additionally, net income would be increased (decreased) by $_____ and $_____ and earnings per share would be increased (decreased) by $_____ and $_____, respectively, for the years then ended.

In our opinion, except for the effects of not capitalizing certain lease obligations as discussed in the preceding paragraph, the financial statements referred to above present fairly, in all material respects, the financial position of Widget Company as of December 31, 20X6 and 20X5, and the results of its operations and its cash flows for the years then ended in conformity with accounting principles generally accepted in the United States of America.

Smith and Jones
February 15, 20X7

ILLUSTRATION 8. AUDITOR'S REPORT: QUALIFIED OPINION—DEPARTURE FROM GAAP EXPLAINED IN A NOTE (ADAPTED FROM AU 508.40)

To the Board of Directors
Widget Company
Main City, USA

Independent Auditor's Report

[*Same first and second paragraphs as the standard report*]

As more fully described in Note X to the financial statements, the Company has excluded certain lease obligations from property and debt in the accompanying balance sheets. In our opinion, accounting principles generally accepted in the United States of America require that such obligations be included in the balance sheets.

In our opinion, except for the effects of not capitalizing certain lease obligations as discussed in the preceding paragraph, the financial statements referred to above present fairly, in all material respects, the financial position of Widget Company as of December 31, 20X6 and 20X5, and the results of its operations and its cash flows for the years then ended in conformity with accounting principles generally accepted in the United States of America.

Smith and Jones
February 15, 20X7

ILLUSTRATION 9. AUDITOR'S REPORT: ADVERSE OPINION—DEPARTURE FROM GAAP (ADAPTED FROM AU 508.60)

To the Board of Directors
Widget Company
Main City, USA

Independent Auditor's Report

[*Same first and second paragraphs as the standard report*]

As discussed in Note X to the financial statements, the Company carries its property, plant, and equipment accounts at appraisal values, and provides depreciation on the basis of such values. Further, the Company does not provide for income taxes for differences between financial income and taxable income arising because of the use, for income tax purposes, of the installment method of reporting gross profit from certain types of sales. Accounting principles generally accepted in the United States of America require that property, plant, and equipment be stated at an amount not in excess of cost, reduced by depreciation based on such amount, and that deferred income taxes be provided.

Because of the departures from accounting principles generally accepted in the United States of America identified above, as of December 31, 20X6 and 20X5, inventories have been increased $_____ and $_____ by inclusion in manufacturing overhead of depreciation in excess of that based on cost; property, plant, and equipment, less accumulated depreciation, is carried at $_____ and $_____ in excess of an amount based on the cost to the Company; deferred income taxes of $_____ and $_____ have not been recorded; resulting in an increase of $_____ and $_____ in retained earnings and in appraisal surplus of $_____ and $_____, respectively. For the years ended December 31, 20X6 and 20X5, cost of goods sold has been increased $_____ and $_____, respectively, because of the effects of the depreciation accounting referred to above and deferred income taxes of $_____ and $_____ have not been provided, resulting in an increase in net income of $_____ and $_____, respectively.

In our opinion, because of the effects of the matters discussed in the preceding paragraphs, the financial statements referred to above do not present fairly, in conformity with accounting principles generally accepted in the United States of America, the financial position of Widget Company as of December 31, 20X6 and 20X5, or the results of its operations or its cash flows for the years then ended.

Smith and Jones
February 15, 20X7

ILLUSTRATION 10. AUDITOR'S REPORT: RULE 203 OPINION

To the Board of Directors
Widget Company
Main City, USA

Independent Auditor's Report

[*Same first and second paragraphs as the standard report*]

As explained in Note X to the financial statements, the Company has changed its method of recording revenues from the recognition of revenue at the time of sale to the recognition of revenue over the membership term and has applied this change retroactively in its financial statements. Accounting Principles Board (APB) Opinion 20, *Accounting Changes*, provides that such a change be made by including, as an element of net earnings during the year of change, the cumulative effect of the change on prior years. Had APB Opinion 20 been followed literally, the cumulative effect of the accounting change would have been included as a change in the 20X6 income statement. Because of the magnitude and pervasiveness of this change, we believe a literal application of APB Opinion 20 would result in a misleading presentation, and that the change should therefore be made on a retroactive basis. Accordingly, the accompanying consolidated financial statements for 20X5 have been restated.

In our opinion, the financial statements referred to above present fairly, in all material respects, the consolidated financial position of Widget Corporation and consolidated subsidiaries as of December 31, 20X6 and 20X5, and the consolidated results of their operations and their cash flows for the years then ended in conformity with accounting principles generally accepted in the United States of America.

Smith and Jones
February 15, 20X7

ILLUSTRATION 11. AUDITOR'S REPORT: OMISSION OF STATEMENT OF CASH FLOWS (ADAPTED FROM AU 508.44)

To the Board of Directors
Widget Company
Main City, USA

Independent Auditor's Report

We have audited the accompanying balance sheets of Widget Company as of December 31, 20X6 and 20X5, and the related statements of income and retained earnings for the years then ended. These financial statements are the responsibility of the Company's management. Our responsibility is to express an opinion on these financial statements based on our audit.

[*Same second paragraph as the standard report*]

The Company declined to present a statement of cash flows for the years ended December 31, 20X6 and 20X5. Presentation of such statement summarizing the Company's operating, investing, and financing activities is required by accounting principles generally accepted in the United States of America.

In our opinion, except that the omission of a statement of cash flows results in an incomplete presentation as explained in the preceding paragraph, the financial statements referred to above present fairly, in all material respects, the financial position of Widget Company as of December 31, 20X6 and 20X5, and the results of its operations for the years then ended in conformity with accounting principles generally accepted in the United States of America.

Smith and Jones
February 15, 20X7

ILLUSTRATION 12. AUDITOR'S REPORT: MANAGEMENT HAS NOT PROVIDED REASONABLE JUSTIFICATION FOR CHANGE IN ACCOUNTING PRINCIPLE (ADAPTED FROM AU 508.17)

To the Board of Directors
Widget Company
Main City, USA

Independent Auditor's Report

[*Same first and second paragraphs as the standard report*]

As disclosed in Note X to the financial statements, the Company adopted, in 20X6, the first-in, first-out method of accounting for its inventories, whereas it previously used the last-in, first-out method. Although use of the first-in, first-out method is in conformity with accounting principles generally accepted in the United States of America, in our opinion the Company has not provided reasonable justification for making this change as required by those principles.

In our opinion, except for the change in accounting principle discussed in the preceding paragraph, the financial statements referred to above present fairly, in all material respects, the financial position of Widget Company as of December 31, 20X6 and 20X5, and the results of its operations and its cash flows for the years then ended in conformity with accounting principles generally accepted in the United States of America.

Smith and Jones
February 15, 20X7

ILLUSTRATION 13. AUDITOR'S REPORT: INADEQUATE DISCLOSURE (ADAPTED FROM AU 508.42)

To the Board of Directors
Widget Company
Main City, USA

Independent Auditor's Report

[Same first and second paragraphs as the standard report]

The Company's financial statements do not disclose [describe the nature of the omitted disclosures]. In our opinion, disclosure of this information is required by accounting principles generally accepted in the United States of America.

In our opinion, except for the omission of the information discussed in the preceding paragraph, the financial statements referred to above present fairly, in all material respects, the financial position of Widget Company as of December 31, 20X6 and 20X5, and the results of its operations and its cash flows for the years then ended in conformity with accounting principles generally accepted in the United States of America.

Smith and Jones
February 15, 20X7

ILLUSTRATION 14. AUDITOR'S STANDARD REPORT ON THE PRIOR YEAR FINANCIAL STATEMENTS AND A QUALIFIED OPINION ON THE CURRENT YEAR FINANCIAL STATEMENTS (ADAPTED FROM AU 508.67)

To the Board of Directors
Widget Company
Main City, USA

Independent Auditor's Report

[Same first and second paragraphs as the standard report]

The Company has excluded, from property and debt in the accompanying 20X6 balance sheet, certain lease obligations that were entered into in 20X6 which, in our opinion, should be capitalized in order to conform with accounting principles generally accepted in the United States of America. If these lease obligations were capitalized, property would be increased by $_____, long-term debt by $_____, and retained earnings by $_____, as of December 31, 20X6, and net income and earnings per share would be increased (decreased) by $_____ and $_____, for the year then ended.

In our opinion, except for the effects on the 20X6 financial statements of not capitalizing certain lease obligations as described in the preceding paragraph, the financial statements referred to above present fairly, in all material respects, the financial position of Widget Company as of December 31, 20X6 and 20X5, and the results of its operations and its cash flows for the years then ended in conformity with accounting principles generally accepted in the United States of America.

Smith and Jones
February 15, 20X7

> **ILLUSTRATION 15. AUDITOR'S STANDARD REPORT ON THE CURRENT YEAR FINANCIAL STATEMENTS WITH A DISCLAIMER OF OPINION ON THE PRIOR YEAR STATEMENTS OF INCOME, RETAINED EARNINGS, AND CASH FLOWS (ADAPTED FROM AU 508.67)**

To the Board of Directors
Widget Company
Main City, USA

Independent Auditor's Report

[*Same first paragraph as the standard report*]

Except as explained in the following paragraph, we conducted our audits in accordance with auditing standards generally accepted in the United States of America. Those standards require that we plan and perform our audit to obtain reasonable assurance about whether the financial statements are free of material misstatement. An audit includes examining, on a test basis, evidence supporting the amounts and disclosures in the financial statements. An audit also includes assessing the accounting principles used and significant estimates made by management, as well as evaluating the overall financial statements presentation. We believe that our audits provide a reasonable basis for our opinion.

We did not observe the taking of physical inventory as of December 31, 20X4, because that date was prior to our appointment as auditors for the Company, and we were unable to satisfy ourselves regarding inventory quantities by means of other auditing procedures. Inventory amounts as of December 31, 20X4, enter into the determination of net income and cash flows for the year ended December 31, 20X5.

Because of the matter discussed in the preceding paragraph, the scope of our work was not sufficient to enable us to express, and we do not express, an opinion on the results of operations and cash flows for the year ended December 31, 20X5.

In our opinion, the balance sheets of Widget Company as of December 31, 20X6 and 20X5, and the related statements of income, retained earnings, and cash flows for the year ended December 31, 20X6, present fairly, in all material respects, the financial position of Widget Company as of December 31, 20X6 and 20X5, and the results of its operations and its cash flows for the year ended December 31, 20X6, in conformity with accounting principles generally accepted in the United States of America.

Smith and Jones
February 15, 20X7

> **ILLUSTRATION 16. AUDITOR'S REPORT: OPINION DIFFERENT FROM OPINION PREVIOUSLY EXPRESSED (ADAPTED FROM AU 508.69)**

To the Board of Directors
Widget Company
Main City, USA

Independent Auditor's Report

[*Same first and second paragraphs as the standard report*]

In our report dated March 1, 20X6, we expressed an opinion that the 20X5 financial statements did not fairly present financial position, results of operations, and cash flows in conformity with accounting principles generally accepted in the United States of America because of two departures from such principles: (1) the Company carried its property, plant, and equipment at appraisal values, and provided for depreciation on the basis of such values and (2) the Company did not provide for deferred income taxes with respect to differences between income for financial reporting purposes and taxable income. As described in Note X, the Company has changed its method of accounting for these items and restated its 20X5 financial statements to conform with accounting principles generally accepted in the United States of America. Accordingly, our present opinion on the 20X5 financial statements, as presented herein, is different from that expressed in our previous reports.

In our opinion, the financial statements referred to above present fairly, in all material respects, the financial position of Widget Company as of December 31, 20X6 and 20X5, and the results of its operations and its cash flows for the years then ended in conformity with accounting principles generally accepted in the United States of America.

Smith and Jones
February 15, 20X7

ILLUSTRATION 17. AUDITOR'S REPORT: PREDECESSOR AUDITOR'S REPORT NOT PRESENTED (ADAPTED FROM AU 508.74)

A. Independent Auditor's Report—Financial Statements Not Restated

We have audited the balance sheet of Widget Company as of December 31, 20X6, and the related statements of income, retained earnings, and cash flows for the year then ended. These financial statements are the responsibility of the Company's management. Our responsibility is to express an opinion on these financial statements based on our audit. The financial statements of Widget Company as of December 31, 20X5, were audited by other auditors whose report dated March 31, 20X6, expressed an unqualified opinion on those statements.

[*Same second paragraph as the standard report*]

In our opinion, the 20X6 financial statements referred to above present fairly, in all material respects, the financial position of Widget Company as of December 31, 20X6, and the results of its operations and its cash flows for the year then ended in conformity with accounting principles generally accepted in the United States of America.

Smith and Jones
February 15, 20X7

B. Modification of First Paragraph

[*If the predecessor auditor's report was other than the standard report, the wording that may be included in the successor's report would be as follows:*]

. . .were audited by other auditors whose report dated March 1, 20X6, on those statements included an explanatory paragraph that described the change in accounting principle discussed in Note X to the financial statements.

C. Independent Auditor's Report—Predecessor Auditor's Report Not Presented—Financial Statements Restated

We have audited the balance sheet of Widget Company as of December 31, 20X6, and the related statements of income, retained earnings, and cash flows for the year then ended. These financial statements are the responsibility of the Company's management. Our responsibility is to express an opinion on these financial statements based on our audit. The financial statements of Widget Company as of December 31, 20X5, were audited by other auditors whose report dated March 31, 20X6, expressed an unqualified opinion on those statements before restatement. We also audited the adjustments described in Note X that were applied to restate the 20X5 financial statements. In our opinion, such adjustments are appropriate and have been properly applied.

[*Same second paragraph as the standard report*]

In our opinion, the 20X6 financial statements referred to above present fairly, in all material respects, the financial position of Widget Company as of December 31, 20X6, and the results of its operations and its cash flows for the year ended in conformity with accounting principles generally accepted in the United States of America.

Smith and Jones
February 15, 20X7

NOTE: This illustration assumes that the successor auditor was engaged to audit and applied sufficient procedures to be satisfied as to the appropriateness of the restatement adjustments.

D. Letter of Representation from Successor Auditor to Predecessor Auditor

[*Date*]

Name of Predecessor Auditor
Address

Dear Sir:

In connection with the reissuance of your report on the consolidated financial statements of Widget Company and subsidiaries for the years ended December 31, 20X2 and 20X1, we wish to advise you that we have audited the consolidated financial statements of Widget Company and subsidiaries as of December 31, 20X3. As set forth in our report dated March 10, 20X4, our audit was made in accordance with auditing standards generally accepted in the United States of America.

Our audit of the consolidated financial statements of Widget Company and subsidiaries as of December 31, 20X3, disclosed no events or transactions to March 10, 20X4, that, in our opinion, would require modification of the financial statements of Widget Company and subsidiaries for the years ended December 31, 20X2, and 20X1.

This letter is solely for your information in connection with your previously mentioned reports.

Very truly yours,

ILLUSTRATION 18. ILLUSTRATIVE UPDATING MANAGEMENT REPRESENTATION LETTER (ADAPTED FROM AU 333.18)

[*Date*]

To [*Auditor*]

In connection with your audit(s) of the [*identification of financial statements*] of [*name of entity*] as of [*dates*] and for the [*periods*] for the purpose of expressing an opinion as to whether the [*consolidated*] financial statements present fairly, in all material respects, the financial position, results of operations, and cash flows of [*name of entity*] in conformity with accounting principles generally accepted in the United States of America, you were previously provided with a representation letter under the date of [*date of previous representation letter*]. No information has come to our attention that would cause us to believe that any of those previous representations should be modified.

To the best of our knowledge and belief, no events have occurred subsequent to [*date of latest balance sheet reported on by the auditor*] and through the date of this letter that would require adjustment to or disclosure in the aforementioned financial statements.

[*Name of Chief Executive Officer and Title*]

[*Name of Chief Financial Officer and Title*]

NOTE: *If matters exist that should be disclosed to the auditor, they should be indicated by listing them. For example, if an event subsequent to the date of the balance sheet has been disclosed in the financial statements, the final paragraph could be modified as follows: "To the best of our knowledge and belief, except as discussed in Note X to the financial statements, no events have occurred...."*

ILLUSTRATION 19. AUDITOR'S REPORT ON SINGLE-YEAR FINANCIAL STATEMENTS IN YEAR OF ADOPTION OF LIQUIDATION BASIS (ADAPTED FROM AU 9508.36)

Independent Auditor's Report

We have audited the statement of net assets in liquidation of Widget Company as of December 31, 20X6, and the related statement of changes in net assets in liquidation for the period from April 26, 20X6, to December 31, 20X6. In addition, we have audited the statements of income, retained earnings, and cash flows for the period from January 1, 20X6, to April 25, 20X6. These financial statements are the responsibility of the Company's management. Our responsibility is to express an opinion on these financial statements based on our audit.

We conducted our audit in accordance with auditing standards generally accepted in the United States of America. These standards require that we plan and perform the audit to obtain reasonable assurance about whether the financial statements are free of material misstatement. An audit includes examining, on a test basis, evidence supporting the amounts and disclosures in the financial statements. An audit also includes assessing the accounting principles used and significant estimated made by management, as well as evaluating the overall financial statement presentation. We believe that our audit provides a reasonable basis for our opinion.

As described in Note X to the financial statements, the stockholders of Widget Company approved a plan of liquidation on April 25, 20X6, and the company commenced liquidation shortly thereafter. As a result, the company has changed its basis of accounting for periods subsequent to April 25, 20X6, from the going-concern basis to a liquidation basis.

In our opinion, the financial statements referred to above present fairly, in all material respects, the net assets in liquidation of Widget Company as of December 31, 20X6, the changes in its net assets in liquidation for the period from April 26, 20X6 to December 31, 20X6, and the results of its operations and its cash flows for the period from January 1, 20X6, to April 25, 20X6, in conformity with accounting principles generally accepted in the United States of America applied on the bases described in the preceding paragraph.

Smith and Jones
February 15, 20X7

ILLUSTRATION 20. AUDITOR'S REPORT ON COMPARATIVE FINANCIAL STATEMENTS IN YEAR OF ADOPTION OF LIQUIDATION BASIS (ADAPTED FROM AU 9508.36)

Independent Auditor's Report

We have audited the balance sheet of Widget Company as of December 31, 20X5, and the related statements of income, retained earnings, and cash flows for the year then ended, and the statements of income, retained earnings, and cash flows for the period from January 1, 20X6, to April 25, 20X6. In addition, we have audited the statement of net assets in liquidation as of December 31, 20X6, and the related statement of changes in net assets in liquidation for the period from April 25, 20X6, to December 31, 20X6. These financial statements are the responsibility of the Company's management. Our responsibility is to express an opinion on these financial statements based on our audits.

We conducted our audits in accordance with auditing standards generally accepted in the United States of America. Those standards require that we plan and perform the audit to obtain reasonable assurance about whether the financial statements are free of material misstatements. An audit includes examining, on a test basis, evidence supporting the amounts and disclosures in the financial statements. An audit also includes assessing the accounting principles used and significant estimates made by management, as well as evaluating the overall financial statement presentation. We believe that our audits provide a reasonable basis for our opinion.

As described in Note X to the financial statements, the stockholders of Widget Company approved a plan of liquidation on April 25, 20X6, and the company commenced liquidation shortly thereafter. As a result, the company has changed its basis of accounting for periods subsequent to April 25, 20X6, from the going-concern basis to a liquidation basis.

In our opinion, the financial statements referred to above present fairly, in all material respects, the financial position of Widget Company as of December 31, 20X5, the results of its operations and its cash flows for the year then ended and for the period from January 1, 20X6, to April 25, 20X6, its net assets in liquidation as of December 31, 20X6, and the changes in its net assets in liquidation for the period from April 26, 20X6, to December 31, 20X6, in conformity with accounting principles generally accepted in the United States of America applied on the bases described in the preceding paragraph.

Smith and Jones
May 20, 20X7

AU-C 700 ILLUSTRATIONS

1. An Auditor's Report on Consolidated Comparative Financial Statements Prepared in Accordance with Accounting Principles Generally Accepted in the United States of America
2. An Auditor's Report on a Single Year Prepared in Accordance with Accounting Principles Generally Accepted in the United States of America
3. An Auditor's Report on Consolidated Comparative Financial Statements Prepared in Accordance with Accounting Principles Generally Accepted in the United States of America When the Audit Has Been Conducted in Accordance with Both Auditing Standards Generally Accepted in the United States of America and International Standards on Auditing
4. An Auditor's Report on a Single Year Prepared in Accordance with Accounting Principles Generally Accepted in the United States of America When Comparative Summarized Financial Information Derived from Audited Financial Statements for the Prior Year Is Presented
5. An Auditor's Report on a Single Year Prepared in Accordance with Accounting Principles Generally Accepted in the United States of America When Comparative Summarized Financial Information Derived from Unaudited Financial Statements for the Prior Year Is Presented

> **ILLUSTRATION 1. AN AUDITOR'S REPORT ON CONSOLIDATED COMPARATIVE FINANCIAL STATEMENTS PREPARED IN ACCORDANCE WITH ACCOUNTING PRINCIPLES GENERALLY ACCEPTED IN THE UNITED STATES OF AMERICA**

Circumstances include the following:

- Audit of a complete set of general purpose consolidated financial statements (comparative).

- The financial statements are prepared in accordance with accounting principles generally accepted in the United States of America.

Independent Auditor's Report

[*Appropriate Addressee*]

Report on the Financial Statements

We have audited the accompanying consolidated financial statements of ABC Company and its subsidiaries, which comprise the consolidated balance sheets as of December 31, 20X1 and 20X0, and the related consolidated statements of income, changes in stockholders' equity, and cash flows for the years then ended, and the related notes to the financial statements.

Management's Responsibility for the Financial Statements

Management is responsible for the preparation and fair presentation of these consolidated financial statements in accordance with accounting principles generally accepted in the United States of America; this includes the design, implementation, and maintenance of internal control relevant to the preparation and fair presentation of consolidated financial statements that are free from material misstatement, whether due to fraud or error.

Auditor's Responsibility

Our responsibility is to express an opinion on these consolidated financial statements based on our audits. We conducted our audits in accordance with auditing standards generally accepted in the United States of America. Those standards require that we plan and perform the audit to obtain reasonable assurance about whether the consolidated financial statements are free from material misstatement.

An audit involves performing procedures to obtain audit evidence about the amounts and disclosures in the consolidated financial statements. The procedures selected depend on the auditor's judgment, including the assessment of the risks of material misstatement of the consolidated financial statements, whether due to fraud or error. In making those risk assessments, the auditor considers internal control relevant to the entity's preparation and fair presentation of the consolidated financial statements in order to design audit procedures that are appropriate in the circumstances, but not for the purpose of expressing an opinion on the effectiveness of the entity's internal control. Accordingly, we express no such opinion.

An audit also includes evaluating the appropriateness of accounting policies used and the reasonableness of significant accounting estimates made by management, as well as evaluating the overall presentation of the consolidated financial statements.

We believe that the audit evidence we have obtained is sufficient and appropriate to provide a basis for our audit opinion.

Opinion

In our opinion, the consolidated financial statements referred to above present fairly, in all material respects, the financial position of ABC Company and its subsidiaries as of December 31, 20X1 and 20X0, and the results of their operations and their cash flows for the years then ended in accordance with accounting principles generally accepted in the United States of America.

Report on Other Legal and Regulatory Requirements

[*Form and content of this section of the auditor's report will vary depending on the nature of the auditor's other reporting responsibilities.*]

[*Auditor's signature*]

[*Auditor's city and state*]

[*Date of the auditor's report*]

> **ILLUSTRATION 2. AN AUDITOR'S REPORT ON A SINGLE YEAR PREPARED IN ACCORDANCE WITH ACCOUNTING PRINCIPLES GENERALLY ACCEPTED IN THE UNITED STATES OF AMERICA**

Circumstances include the following:

- Audit of a complete set of general purpose financial statements (single year).
- The financial statements are prepared in accordance with accounting principles generally accepted in the United States of America.

Independent Auditor's Report

[*Appropriate* Addressee]

Report on the Financial Statements

We have audited the accompanying financial statements of ABC Company, which comprise the balance sheet as of December 31, 20X1, and the related statements of income, changes in stockholders' equity, and cash flows for the year then ended, and the related notes to the financial statements.

Management's Responsibility for the Financial Statements

Management is responsible for the preparation and fair presentation of these financial statements in accordance with accounting principles generally accepted in the United States of America; this includes the design, implementation, and maintenance of internal control relevant to the preparation and fair presentation of financial statements that are free from material misstatement, whether due to fraud or error.

Auditor's Responsibility

Our responsibility is to express an opinion on these financial statements based on our audit. We conducted our audit in accordance with auditing standards generally accepted in the United States of America. Those standards require that we plan and perform the audit to obtain reasonable assurance about whether the financial statements are free from material misstatement.

An audit involves performing procedures to obtain audit evidence about the amounts and disclosures in the financial statements. The procedures selected depend on the auditor's judgment, including the assessment of the risks of material misstatement of the financial statements, whether due to fraud or error. In making those risk assessments, the auditor considers internal control relevant to the entity's preparation and fair presentation of the financial statements in order to design audit procedures that are appropriate in the circumstances, but not for the purpose of expressing an opinion on the effectiveness of the entity's internal control. Accordingly, we express no such opinion. An audit also includes evaluating the appropriateness of accounting policies used and the reasonableness of significant accounting estimates made by management, as well as evaluating the overall presentation of the financial statements.

We believe that the audit evidence we have obtained is sufficient and appropriate to provide a basis for our audit opinion.

Opinion

In our opinion, the financial statements referred to above present fairly, in all material respects, the financial position of ABC Company as of December 31, 20X1, and the results of its operations and its cash flows for the year then ended in accordance with accounting principles generally accepted in the United States of America.

Report on Other Legal and Regulatory Requirements

[*Form and content of this section of the auditor's report will vary depending on the nature of the auditor's other reporting responsibilities.*]

[*Auditor's signature*]

[*Auditor's city and state*]

[*Date of the auditor's report*]

> **ILLUSTRATION 3. AN AUDITOR'S REPORT ON CONSOLIDATED COMPARATIVE FINANCIAL STATEMENTS PREPARED IN ACCORDANCE WITH ACCOUNTING PRINCIPLES GENERALLY ACCEPTED IN THE UNITED STATES OF AMERICA WHEN THE AUDIT HAS BEEN CONDUCTED IN ACCORDANCE WITH BOTH AUDITING STANDARDS GENERALLY ACCEPTED IN THE UNITED STATES OF AMERICA AND INTERNATIONAL STANDARDS ON AUDITING**

Circumstances include the following:

- Audit of a complete set of general purpose financial statements (comparative).
- The financial statements are prepared in accordance with accounting principles generally accepted in the United States of America.
- The financial statements are audited in accordance with auditing standards generally accepted in the United States of America and International Standards on Auditing.

Independent Auditor's Report

[*Appropriate Addressee*]

Report on the Financial Statements

We have audited the accompanying financial statements of ABC Company, which comprise the balance sheets as of December 31, 20X1 and 20X0, and the related statements of income, changes in stockholders' equity, and cash flows for the years then ended, and the related notes to the financial statements.

Management's Responsibility for the Financial Statements

Management is responsible for the preparation and fair presentation of these financial statements in accordance with accounting principles generally accepted in the United States of America; this includes the design, implementation, and maintenance of internal control relevant to the preparation and fair presentation of financial statements that are free from material misstatement, whether due to fraud or error.

Auditor's Responsibility

Our responsibility is to express an opinion on these financial statements based on our audits. We conducted our audits in accordance with auditing standards generally accepted in the United States of America and in accordance with International Standards on Auditing. Those standards require that we plan and perform the audit to obtain reasonable assurance about whether the financial statements are free from material misstatement.

An audit involves performing procedures to obtain audit evidence about the amounts and disclosures in the financial statements. The procedures selected depend on the auditor's judgment, including the assessment of the risks of material misstatement of the financial statements, whether due to fraud or error. In making those risk assessments, the auditor considers internal control relevant to the entity's preparation and fair presentation of the financial statements in order to design audit procedures that are appropriate in the circumstances, but not for the purpose of expressing an opinion on the effectiveness of the entity's internal control. Accordingly, we express no such opinion. An audit also includes evaluating the appropriateness of accounting policies used and the reasonableness of significant accounting estimates made by management, as well as evaluating the overall presentation of the financial statements.

We believe that the audit evidence we have obtained is sufficient and appropriate to provide a basis for our audit opinion.

Opinion

In our opinion, the financial statements referred to above present fairly, in all material respects, the financial position of ABC Company as of December 31, 20X1 and 20X0, and the results of its operations and its cash flows for the years then ended in accordance with accounting principles generally accepted in the United States of America.

Report on Other Legal and Regulatory Requirements

[*Form and content of this section of the auditor's report will vary depending on the nature of the auditor's other reporting responsibilities.*]

[*Auditor's signature*]

[*Auditor's city and state*]

[*Date of the auditor's report*]

ILLUSTRATION 4. AN AUDITOR'S REPORT ON A SINGLE YEAR PREPARED IN ACCORDANCE WITH ACCOUNTING PRINCIPLES GENERALLY ACCEPTED IN THE UNITED STATES OF AMERICA WHEN COMPARATIVE SUMMARIZED FINANCIAL INFORMATION DERIVED FROM AUDITED FINANCIAL STATEMENTS FOR THE PRIOR YEAR IS PRESENTED

Circumstances include the following:

- Audit of a complete set of general purpose financial statements (single year).
- Prior year summarized comparative financial information derived from audited financial statements is presented.
- The financial statements are prepared in accordance with accounting principles generally accepted in the United States of America.

Independent Auditor's Report

[*Appropriate Addressee*]

Report on the Financial Statements

We have audited the accompanying financial statements of XYZ Not-for-Profit Organization, which comprise the statement of financial position as of September 30, 20X1, and the related statements of activities and cash flows for the year then ended, and the related notes to the financial statements.

Management's Responsibility for the Financial Statements

Management is responsible for the preparation and fair presentation of these financial statements in accordance with accounting principles generally accepted in the United States of America; this includes the design, implementation, and maintenance of internal control relevant to the preparation and fair presentation of financial statements that are free from material misstatement, whether due to fraud or error.

Auditor's Responsibility

Our responsibility is to express an opinion on these financial statements based on our audit. We conducted our audit in accordance with auditing standards generally accepted in the United States of America. Those standards require that we plan and perform the audit to obtain reasonable assurance about whether the financial statements are free from material misstatement.

An audit involves performing procedures to obtain audit evidence about the amounts and disclosures in the financial statements. The procedures selected depend on the auditor's judgment, including the assessment of the risks of material misstatement of the financial statements, whether due to fraud or error. In making those risk assessments, the auditor considers internal control relevant to the organization's preparation and fair presentation of the financial statements in order to design audit procedures that are appropriate in the circumstances, but not for the purpose of expressing an opinion on the effectiveness of the organization's internal control. Accordingly, we express no such opinion. An audit also includes evaluating the appropriateness of accounting policies used and the reasonableness of significant accounting estimates made by management, as well as evaluating the overall presentation of the financial statements.

We believe that the audit evidence we have obtained is sufficient and appropriate to provide a basis for our audit opinion.

Opinion

In our opinion, the financial statements referred to above present fairly, in all material respects, the financial position of XYZ Not-for-Profit Organization as of September 30, 20X1, and the changes in its net assets and its cash flows for the year then ended in accordance with accounting principles generally accepted in the United States of America.

Report on Summarized Comparative Information

We have previously audited the XYZ Not-for-Profit Organization's 20X0 financial statements, and we expressed an unmodified audit opinion on those audited financial statements in our report dated December 15, 20X0. In our opinion, the summarized comparative information presented herein as of and for the year ended September 30, 20X0 is consistent, in all material respects, with the audited financial statements from which it has been derived.

Report on Other Legal and Regulatory Requirements

[*Form and content of this section of the auditor's report will vary depending on the nature of the auditor's other reporting responsibilities.*]

[*Auditor's signature*]

[*Auditor's city and state*]

[*Date of the auditor's report*]

> **ILLUSTRATION 5. AN AUDITOR'S REPORT ON A SINGLE YEAR PREPARED IN ACCORDANCE WITH ACCOUNTING PRINCIPLES GENERALLY ACCEPTED IN THE UNITED STATES OF AMERICA WHEN COMPARATIVE SUMMARIZED FINANCIAL INFORMATION DERIVED FROM UNAUDITED FINANCIAL STATEMENTS FOR THE PRIOR YEAR IS PRESENTED**

Circumstances include the following:

- Audit of a complete set of general purpose financial statements (single year).
- Prior year summarized comparative financial information derived from unaudited financial statements is presented.

- The financial statements are prepared in accordance with accounting principles generally accepted in the United States of America.

Independent Auditor's Report

[*Appropriate Addressee*]

Report on the Financial Statements

We have audited the accompanying financial statements of XYZ Not-for-Profit Organization, which comprise the statement of financial position as of September 30, 20X1, and the related statements of activities and cash flows for the year then ended, and the related notes to the financial statements.

Management's Responsibility for the Financial Statements

Management is responsible for the preparation and fair presentation of these financial statements in accordance with accounting principles generally accepted in the United States of America; this includes the design, implementation, and maintenance of internal control relevant to the preparation and fair presentation of financial statements that are free from material misstatement, whether due to fraud or error.

Auditor's Responsibility

Our responsibility is to express an opinion on these financial statements based on our audit. We conducted our audit in accordance with auditing standards generally accepted in the United States of America. Those standards require that we plan and perform the audit to obtain reasonable assurance about whether the financial statements are free from material misstatement.

An audit involves performing procedures to obtain audit evidence about the amounts and disclosures in the financial statements. The procedures selected depend on the auditor's judgment, including the assessment of the risks of material misstatement of the financial statements, whether due to fraud or error. In making those risk assessments, the auditor considers internal control relevant to the organization's preparation and fair presentation of the financial statements in order to design audit procedures that are appropriate in the circumstances, but not for the purpose of expressing an opinion on the effectiveness of the organization's internal control. Accordingly, we express no such opinion. An audit also includes evaluating the appropriateness of accounting policies used and the reasonableness of significant accounting estimates made by management, as well as evaluating the overall presentation of the financial statements.

We believe that the audit evidence we have obtained is sufficient and appropriate to provide a basis for our audit opinion.

Opinion

In our opinion, the financial statements referred to above present fairly, in all material respects, the financial position of XYZ Not-for-Profit Organization as of September 30, 20X1, and the changes in its net assets and its cash flows for the year then ended in accordance with accounting principles generally accepted in the United States of America.

Report on Summarized Comparative Information

The summarized comparative information presented herein as of and for the year ended September 30, 20X0, derived from those unaudited financial statements, has not been audited, reviewed, or compiled and, accordingly, we express no opinion on it.

Report on Other Legal and Regulatory Requirements

[*Form and content of this section of the auditor's report will vary depending on the nature of the auditor's other reporting responsibilities.*]

[*Auditor's signature*]

[*Auditor's city and state*]

[*Date of the auditor's report*]

AU-C 705 ILLUSTRATIONS

The following auditor's reports with modifications to the opinion are illustrated:

1. An Auditor's Report Containing a Qualified Opinion Due to a Material Misstatement of the Financial Statements
2. An Auditor's Report Containing a Qualified Opinion for Inadequate Disclosure
3. An Auditor's Report Containing an Adverse Opinion Due to a Material Misstatement of the Financial Statements
4. An Auditor's Report Containing a Qualified Opinion Due to the Auditor's Inability to Obtain Sufficient Appropriate Audit Evidence
5. An Auditor's Report Containing a Disclaimer of Opinion Due to the Auditor's Inability to Obtain Sufficient Appropriate Audit Evidence about a Single Element of the Financial Statements
6. An Auditor's Report Containing a Disclaimer of Opinion Due to the Auditor's Inability to Obtain Sufficient Appropriate Audit Evidence about Multiple Elements of the Financial Statements
7. An Auditor's Report in Which the Auditor Is Expressing an Unmodified Opinion in the Prior Year and a Modified Opinion (Qualified Opinion) in the Current Year
8. An Auditor's Report in Which the Auditor Is Expressing an Unmodified Opinion in the Current Year and a Disclaimer of Opinion on the Prior-Year Statements of Income, Changes in Stockholders' Equity, and Cash Flows

ILLUSTRATION 1. AN AUDITOR'S REPORT CONTAINING A QUALIFIED OPINION DUE TO A MATERIAL MISSTATEMENT OF THE FINANCIAL STATEMENTS

Circumstances include the following:

- Audit of a complete set of general purpose financial statements (comparative) prepared in accordance with accounting principles generally accepted in the United States of America.
- Inventories are misstated. The misstatement is deemed to be material but not pervasive to the financial statements. Accordingly, the auditor's report contains a qualified opinion.

Independent Auditor's Report

[*Appropriate Addressee*]

Report on the Financial Statements

We have audited the accompanying financial statements of ABC Company, which comprise the balance sheets as of December 31, 20X1 and 20X0, and the related statements of income, changes in stockholders' equity, and cash flows for the years then ended, and the related notes to the financial statements.

Management's Responsibility for the Financial Statements

Management is responsible for the preparation and fair presentation of these financial statements in accordance with accounting principles generally accepted in the United States of America; this includes the design, implementation, and maintenance of internal control relevant to the preparation and fair presentation of financial statements that are free from material misstatement, whether due to fraud or error.

Auditor's Responsibility

Our responsibility is to express an opinion on these financial statements based on our audits. We conducted our audits in accordance with auditing standards generally accepted in the United States of America. Those standards require that we plan and perform the audit to obtain reasonable assurance about whether the financial statements are free from material misstatement.

An audit involves performing procedures to obtain audit evidence about the amounts and disclosures in the financial statements. The procedures selected depend on the auditor's judgment, including the assessment of the risks of material misstatement of the financial statements, whether due to fraud or error. In making those risk assessments, the auditor considers internal control relevant to the entity's preparation and fair presentation of the financial statements in order to design audit procedures that are appropriate in the circumstances, but not for the purpose of expressing an opinion on the effectiveness of the entity's internal control. Accordingly, we express no such opinion. An audit also includes evaluating the appropriateness of accounting policies used and the reasonableness of significant accounting estimates made by management, as well as evaluating the overall presentation of the financial statements.

We believe that the audit evidence we have obtained is sufficient and appropriate to provide a basis for our qualified audit opinion.

Basis for Qualified Opinion

The Company has stated inventories at cost in the accompanying balance sheets. Accounting principles generally accepted in the United States of America require inventories to be stated at the lower of cost or market. If the Company stated inventories at the lower of cost or market, a writedown of $XXX and $XXX would have been required as of December 31, 20X1 and 20X0, respectively. Accordingly, cost of sales would have been increased by $XXX and $XXX, and net income, income taxes, and stockholders' equity would have been reduced by $XXX, $XXX, and $XXX, and $XXX, $XXX, and $XXX, as of and for the years ended December 31, 20X1 and 20X0, respectively.

Qualified Opinion

In our opinion, except for the effects of the matter described in the Basis for Qualified Opinion paragraph, the financial statements referred to above present fairly, in all material respects, the financial position of ABC Company as of December 31, 20X1 and 20X0, and the results of its operations and its cash flows for the years then ended in accordance with accounting principles generally accepted in the United States of America.

Report on Other Legal and Regulatory Requirements

[*Form and content of this section of the auditor's report will vary depending on the nature of the auditor's other reporting responsibilities.*]

[*Auditor's signature*]

[*Auditor's city and state*]

[*Date of the auditor's report*]

ILLUSTRATION 2. AN AUDITOR'S REPORT CONTAINING A QUALIFIED OPINION FOR INADEQUATE DISCLOSURE

Circumstances include the following:

- Audit of a complete set of general purpose financial statements (comparative) prepared in accordance with accounting principles generally accepted in the United States of America.
- The financial statements have inadequate disclosures. The auditor has concluded that (1) it is not practicable to present the required information and (2) the effects are such that an adverse opinion is not appropriate. Accordingly, the auditor's report contains a qualified opinion.

Independent Auditor's Report

[*Appropriate Addressee*]

Report on the Financial Statements

We have audited the accompanying financial statements of ABC Company, which comprise the balance sheets as of December 31, 20X1 and 20X0, and the related statements of income, changes in stockholders' equity, and cash flows for the years then ended, and the related notes to the financial statements.

Management's Responsibility for the Financial Statements

Management is responsible for the preparation and fair presentation of these financial statements in accordance with accounting principles generally accepted in the United States of America; this includes the design, implementation, and maintenance of internal control relevant to the preparation and fair presentation of financial statements that are free from material misstatement, whether due to fraud or error.

Auditor's Responsibility

Our responsibility is to express an opinion on these financial statements based on our audits. We conducted our audits in accordance with auditing standards generally accepted in the United States of America. Those standards require that we plan and perform the audit to obtain reasonable assurance about whether the financial statements are free from material misstatement.

An audit involves performing procedures to obtain audit evidence about the amounts and disclosures in the financial statements. The procedures selected depend on the auditor's judgment, including the assessment of the risks of material misstatement of the financial statements, whether due to fraud or error. In making those risk assessments, the auditor considers internal control relevant to the entity's preparation and fair presentation of the financial statements in order to design audit procedures that are appropriate in the circumstances, but not for the purpose of expressing an opinion on the effectiveness of the entity's internal control. Accordingly, we express no such opinion. An audit also includes evaluating the appropriateness of accounting policies used and the reasonableness of significant accounting estimates made by management, as well as evaluating the overall presentation of the financial statements.

We believe that the audit evidence we have obtained is sufficient and appropriate to provide a basis for our qualified audit opinion.

Basis for Qualified Opinion

The Company's financial statements do not disclose [*describe the nature of the omitted information that is not practicable to present in the auditor's report*]. In our opinion, disclosure of this information is required by accounting principles generally accepted in the United States of America.

Qualified Opinion

In our opinion, except for the omission of the information described in the Basis for Qualified Opinion paragraph, the financial statements referred to above present fairly, in all material respects, the financial position of ABC Company as of December 31, 20X1 and 20X0, and the results of its operations and its cash flows for the years then ended in accordance with accounting principles generally accepted in the United States of America.

Report on Other Legal and Regulatory Requirements

[*Form and content of this section of the auditor's report will vary depending on the nature of the auditor's other reporting responsibilities.*]

[*Auditor's signature*]

[*Auditor's city and state*]

[*Date of the auditor's report*]

> **ILLUSTRATION 3. AN AUDITOR'S REPORT CONTAINING AN ADVERSE OPINION DUE TO A MATERIAL MISSTATEMENT OF THE FINANCIAL STATEMENTS**

Circumstances include the following:

- Audit of a complete set of consolidated general purpose financial statements (single year) prepared in accordance with accounting principles generally accepted in the United States of America.
- The financial statements are materially misstated due to the nonconsolidation of a subsidiary. The material misstatement is deemed to be pervasive to the financial statements. Accordingly, the auditor's report contains an adverse opinion. The effects of the misstatement on the financial statements have not been determined because it was not practicable to do so.

Independent Auditor's Report

[*Appropriate Addressee*]

Report on the Consolidated Financial Statements

We have audited the accompanying consolidated financial statements of ABC Company and its subsidiaries, which comprise the consolidated balance sheet as of December 31, 20X1, and the related consolidated statements of income, changes in stockholders' equity, and cash flows for the year then ended, and the related notes to the financial statements.

Management's Responsibility for the Financial Statements

Management is responsible for the preparation and fair presentation of these consolidated financial statements in accordance with accounting principles generally accepted in the United States of America; this includes the design, implementation, and maintenance of internal control relevant to the preparation and fair presentation of consolidated financial statements that are free from material misstatement, whether due to fraud or error.

Auditor's Responsibility

Our responsibility is to express an opinion on these consolidated financial statements based on our audit. We conducted our audit in accordance with auditing standards generally accepted in the United States of America. Those standards require that we plan and perform the audit to obtain reasonable assurance about whether the consolidated financial statements are free from material misstatement.

An audit involves performing procedures to obtain audit evidence about the amounts and disclosures in the consolidated financial statements. The procedures selected depend on the auditor's judgment, including the assessment of the risks of material misstatement of the consolidated financial statements, whether due to fraud or error. In making those risk assessments, the auditor considers internal control relevant to the entity's preparation and fair presentation of the consolidated financial statements in order to design audit procedures that are appropriate in the circumstances, but not for the purpose of expressing an opinion on the effectiveness of the entity's internal control. Accordingly, we express no such opinion. An audit also includes evaluating the appropriateness of accounting policies used and the reasonableness of significant accounting estimates made by management, as well as evaluating the overall presentation of the consolidated financial statements.

We believe that the audit evidence we have obtained is sufficient and appropriate to provide a basis for our adverse audit opinion.

Basis for Adverse Opinion

As described in Note X, the Company has not consolidated the financial statements of subsidiary XYZ Company that it acquired during 20X1 because it has not yet been able to ascertain the fair values of certain of the subsidiary's material assets and liabilities at the acquisition date. This investment is therefore accounted for on a cost basis by the Company. Under accounting principles generally accepted in the United States of America, the subsidiary should have been consolidated because it is controlled by the Company. Had XYZ Company been consolidated, many elements in the accompanying consolidated financial statements would have been materially affected. The effects on the consolidated financial statements of the failure to consolidate have not been determined.

Adverse Opinion

In our opinion, because of the significance of the matter discussed in the Basis for Adverse Opinion paragraph, the consolidated financial statements referred to above do not present fairly the financial position of ABC Company and its subsidiaries as of December 31, 20X1, or the results of their operations or their cash flows for the year then ended.

Report on Other Legal and Regulatory Requirements

[*Form and content of this section of the auditor's report will vary depending on the nature of the auditor's other reporting responsibilities.*]

[*Auditor's signature*]

[*Auditor's city and state*]

[*Date of the auditor's report*]

ILLUSTRATION 4. AN AUDITOR'S REPORT CONTAINING A QUALIFIED OPINION DUE TO THE AUDITOR'S INABILITY TO OBTAIN SUFFICIENT APPROPRIATE AUDIT EVIDENCE

Circumstances include the following:

- Audit of a complete set of general purpose financial statements (single year) prepared in accordance with accounting principles generally accepted in the United States of America.
- The auditor was unable to obtain sufficient appropriate audit evidence regarding an investment in a foreign affiliate. The possible effects of the inability to obtain suffi-

cient appropriate audit evidence are deemed to be material but not pervasive to the financial statements. Accordingly, the auditor's report contains a qualified opinion.

Independent Auditor's Report

[*Appropriate Addressee*]

Report on the Financial Statements

We have audited the accompanying financial statements of ABC Company, which comprise the balance sheet as of December 31, 20X1, and the related statements of income, changes in stockholders' equity, and cash flows for the year then ended, and the related notes to the financial statements.

Management's Responsibility for the Financial Statements

Management is responsible for the preparation and fair presentation of these financial statements in accordance with accounting principles generally accepted in the United States of America; this includes the design, implementation, and maintenance of internal control relevant to the preparation and fair presentation of financial statements that are free from material misstatement, whether due to fraud or error.

Auditor's Responsibility

Our responsibility is to express an opinion on these financial statements based on our audit. We conducted our audit in accordance with auditing standards generally accepted in the United States of America. Those standards require that we plan and perform the audit to obtain reasonable assurance about whether the financial statements are free from material misstatement.

An audit involves performing procedures to obtain audit evidence about the amounts and disclosures in the financial statements. The procedures selected depend on the auditor's judgment, including the assessment of the risks of material misstatement of the financial statements, whether due to fraud or error. In making those risk assessments, the auditor considers internal control relevant to the entity's preparation and fair presentation of the financial statements in order to design audit procedures that are appropriate in the circumstances, but not for the purpose of expressing an opinion on the effectiveness of the entity's internal control. Accordingly, we express no such opinion. An audit also includes evaluating the appropriateness of accounting policies used and the reasonableness of significant accounting estimates made by management, as well as evaluating the overall presentation of the financial statements.

We believe that the audit evidence we have obtained is sufficient and appropriate to provide a basis for our qualified audit opinion.

Basis for Qualified Opinion

ABC Company's investment in XYZ Company, a foreign affiliate acquired during the year and accounted for under the equity method, is carried at $XXX on the balance sheet at December 31, 20X1, and ABC Company's share of XYZ Company's net income of $XXX is included in ABC Company's net income for the year then ended. We were unable to obtain sufficient appropriate audit evidence about the carrying amount of ABC Company's investment in XYZ Company as of December 31, 20X1 and ABC Company's share of XYZ Company's net income for the year then ended because we were denied access to the financial information, management, and the auditors of XYZ Company. Consequently, we were unable to determine whether any adjustments to these amounts were necessary.

Qualified Opinion

In our opinion, except for the possible effects of the matter described in the Basis for Qualified Opinion paragraph, the financial statements referred to above present fairly, in all material respects, the financial position of ABC Company as of December 31, 20X1, and the results of its operations and its cash flows for the year then ended in accordance with accounting principles generally accepted in the United States of America.

Report on Other Legal and Regulatory Requirements

[*Form and content of this section of the auditor's report will vary depending on the nature of the auditor's other reporting responsibilities.*]

[*Auditor's signature*]

[*Auditor's city and state*]

[*Date of the auditor's report*]

ILLUSTRATION 5. AN AUDITOR'S REPORT CONTAINING A DISCLAIMER OF OPINION DUE TO THE AUDITOR'S INABILITY TO OBTAIN SUFFICIENT APPROPRIATE AUDIT EVIDENCE ABOUT A SINGLE ELEMENT OF THE FINANCIAL STATEMENTS

Circumstances include the following:

- Audit of a complete set of general purpose financial statements (single year) prepared in accordance with accounting principles generally accepted in the United States of America.
- The auditor was unable to obtain sufficient appropriate audit evidence about a single element of the financial statements. That is, the auditor was unable to obtain audit evidence about the financial information of a joint venture investment accounted for under the proportionate consolidation approach. The investment represents more than 90% of the Company's net assets. The possible effects of this inability to obtain sufficient appropriate audit evidence are deemed to be both material and pervasive to the financial statements. Accordingly, the auditor's report contains a disclaimer of opinion.
- The auditor concluded that it was unnecessary to include in the auditor's report specific amounts for the Company's proportional share of the assets, liabilities, income, and expenses of the joint venture investment because the investment represents more than 90% of the Company's net assets, and that fact is disclosed in the auditor's report.

Independent Auditor's Report

[*Appropriate Addressee*]

Report on the Financial Statements

We were engaged to audit the accompanying financial statements of ABC Company, which comprise the balance sheet as of December 31, 20X1, and the related statements of income, changes in stockholders' equity, and cash flows for the year then ended, and the related notes to the financial statements.

Management's Responsibility for the Financial Statements

Management is responsible for the preparation and fair presentation of these financial statements in accordance with accounting principles generally accepted in the United States of America; this includes the design, implementation, and maintenance of internal control relevant to the preparation and fair presentation of financial statements that are free from material misstatement, whether due to fraud or error.

Auditor's Responsibility

Our responsibility is to express an opinion on these financial statements based on conducting the audit in accordance with auditing standards generally accepted in the United States of America. Because of the matter described in the Basis for Disclaimer of Opinion paragraph, however, we were not able to obtain sufficient appropriate audit evidence to provide a basis for an audit opinion.

Basis for Disclaimer of Opinion

The Company's investment in XYZ Company, a joint venture, is carried at $XXX on the Company's balance sheet, which represents more than 90% of the Company's net assets as of December 31, 20X1. We were not allowed access to the management and the auditors of XYZ Company. As a result, we were unable to determine whether any adjustments were necessary relating to the Company's proportional share of XYZ Company's assets that it controls jointly, its proportional share of XYZ Company's liabilities for which it is jointly responsible, its proportional share of XYZ Company's income and expenses for the year, and the elements making up the statements of changes in stockholders' equity and cash flows.

Disclaimer of Opinion

Because of the significance of the matter described in the Basis for Disclaimer of Opinion paragraph, we have not been able to obtain sufficient appropriate audit evidence to provide a basis for an audit opinion. Accordingly, we do not express an opinion on these financial statements.

Report on Other Legal and Regulatory Requirements

[*Form and content of this section of the auditor's report will vary depending on the nature of the auditor's other reporting responsibilities.*]

[*Auditor's signature*]

[*Auditor's city and state*]

[*Date of the auditor's report*]

ILLUSTRATION 6. AN AUDITOR'S REPORT CONTAINING A DISCLAIMER OF OPINION DUE TO THE AUDITOR'S INABILITY TO OBTAIN SUFFICIENT APPROPRIATE AUDIT EVIDENCE ABOUT MULTIPLE ELEMENTS OF THE FINANCIAL STATEMENTS

Circumstances include the following:

- Audit of a complete set of general purpose financial statements (single year) prepared in accordance with accounting principles generally accepted in the United States of America.
- The auditor was unable to obtain sufficient appropriate audit evidence about multiple elements of the financial statements. That is, the auditor was unable to obtain audit evidence about the entity's inventories and accounts receivable. The possible effects of this inability to obtain sufficient appropriate audit evidence are deemed to be both material and pervasive to the financial statements. Accordingly, the auditor's opinion contains a disclaimer of opinion.

Independent Auditor's Report

[*Appropriate Addressee*]

Report on the Financial Statements

We were engaged to audit the accompanying financial statements of ABC Company, which comprise the balance sheet as of December 31, 20X1, and the related statements of income, changes in stockholders' equity, and cash flows for the year then ended, and the related notes to the financial statements.

Management's Responsibility for the Financial Statements

Management is responsible for the preparation and fair presentation of these financial statements in accordance with accounting principles generally accepted in the United States of America; this includes the design, implementation, and maintenance of internal control relevant to the preparation and fair presentation of financial statements that are free from material misstatement, whether due to fraud or error.

Auditor's Responsibility

Our responsibility is to express an opinion on these financial statements based on conducting the audit in accordance with auditing standards generally accepted in the United States of America. Because of the matters described in the Basis for Disclaimer of Opinion paragraph, however, we were not able to obtain sufficient appropriate audit evidence to provide a basis for an audit opinion.

Basis for Disclaimer of Opinion

We were not engaged as auditors of the Company until after December 31, 20X1, and, therefore, did not observe the counting of physical inventories at the beginning or end of the year. We were unable to satisfy ourselves by other auditing procedures concerning the inventory held at December 31, 20X1, which is stated in the balance sheet at $XXX. In addition, the introduction of a new computerized accounts receivable system in September 20X1 resulted in numerous misstatements in accounts receivable. As of the date of our audit report, management was still in the process of rectifying the system deficiencies and correcting the misstatements. We were unable to confirm or verify by alternative means accounts receivable included in the balance sheet at a total amount of $XXX at December 31, 20X1. As a result of these matters, we were unable to determine whether any adjustments might have been found necessary in respect of recorded or unrecorded inventories and accounts receivable, and the elements making up the statements of income, changes in stockholders' equity, and cash flows.

Disclaimer of Opinion

Because of the significance of the matters described in the Basis for Disclaimer of Opinion paragraph, we have not been able to obtain sufficient appropriate audit evidence to provide a basis for an audit opinion. Accordingly, we do not express an opinion on these financial statements.

Report on Other Legal and Regulatory Requirements

[*Form and content of this section of the auditor's report will vary depending on the nature of the auditor's other reporting responsibilities.*]

[*Auditor's signature*]

[*Auditor's city and state*]

[*Date of the auditor's report*]

> **ILLUSTRATION 7. AN AUDITOR'S REPORT IN WHICH THE AUDITOR IS EXPRESSING AN UNMODIFIED OPINION IN THE PRIOR YEAR AND A MODIFIED OPINION (QUALIFIED OPINION) IN THE CURRENT YEAR**

Circumstances include the following:

- Audit of a complete set of general purpose financial statements (comparative) prepared in accordance with accounting principles generally accepted in the United States of America.
- Certain lease obligations have been excluded from the financial statements in the current year. The effect of the exclusion is material but not pervasive. The auditor expressed an unmodified opinion in the prior year and is expressing a modified opinion (qualified opinion) in the current year.

Independent Auditor's Report

[*Appropriate Addressee*]

Report on the Financial Statements

We have audited the accompanying financial statements of ABC Company, which comprise the balance sheets as of December 31, 20X1 and 20X0, and the related statements of income, changes in stockholders' equity, and cash flows for the years then ended, and the related notes to the financial statements.

Management's Responsibility for the Financial Statements

Management is responsible for the preparation and fair presentation of these financial statements in accordance with accounting principles generally accepted in the United States of America; this includes the design, implementation, and maintenance of internal control relevant to the preparation and fair presentation of financial statements that are free from material misstatement, whether due to fraud or error.

Auditor's Responsibility

Our responsibility is to express an opinion on these financial statements based on our audits. We conducted our audits in accordance with auditing standards generally accepted in the United States of America. Those standards require that we plan and perform the audit to obtain reasonable assurance about whether the financial statements are free from material misstatement.

An audit involves performing procedures to obtain audit evidence about the amounts and disclosures in the financial statements. The procedures selected depend on the auditor's judgment, including the assessment of the risks of material misstatement of the financial statements, whether due to fraud or error. In making those risk assessments, the auditor considers internal control relevant to the entity's preparation and fair presentation of the financial statements in order to design audit procedures that are appropriate in the circumstances, but not for the purpose of expressing an opinion on the effectiveness of the entity's internal control. Accordingly, we express no such opinion. An audit also includes evaluating the appropriateness of accounting policies used and the reasonableness of significant accounting estimates made by management, as well as evaluating the overall presentation of the financial statements.

We believe that the audit evidence we have obtained is sufficient and appropriate to provide a basis for our qualified audit opinion.

Basis for Qualified Opinion

The Company has excluded, from property and debt in the accompanying 20X1 balance sheet, certain lease obligations that were entered into in 20X1 which, in our opinion, should be capitalized in accordance with accounting principles generally accepted in the United States of America. If these lease obligations were capitalized, property would be increased by $XXX, long-term debt by $XXX, and retained earnings by $XXX as of December 31, 20X1, and net income and earnings per share would be increased (decreased) by $XXX and $XXX, respectively, for the year then ended.

Qualified Opinion

In our opinion, except for the effects on the 20X1 financial statements of not capitalizing certain lease obligations as described in the Basis for Qualified Opinion paragraph, the financial statements referred to above present fairly, in all material respects, the financial position of ABC Company as of December 31, 20X1 and 20X0, and the results of its operations and its cash flows for the years then ended in accordance with accounting principles generally accepted in the United States of America.

Report on Other Legal and Regulatory Requirements

[*Form and content of this section of the auditor's report will vary depending on the nature of the auditor's other reporting responsibilities.*]

[*Auditor's signature*]

[*Auditor's city and state*]

[*Date of the auditor's report*]

ILLUSTRATION 8. AN AUDITOR'S REPORT IN WHICH THE AUDITOR IS EXPRESSING AN UNMODIFIED OPINION IN THE CURRENT YEAR AND A DISCLAIMER OF OPINION ON THE PRIOR-YEAR STATEMENTS OF INCOME, CHANGES IN STOCKHOLDERS' EQUITY, AND CASH FLOWS

Circumstances include the following:

- Audit of a complete set of general purpose financial statements (comparative) prepared in accordance with accounting principles generally accepted in the United States of America.
- The auditor was unable to observe the physical inventory as at December 31, 20X0, as at that time the auditor had not been engaged. Accordingly, the auditor was unable to obtain sufficient appropriate audit evidence regarding the net income and cash flows for the year ended December 31, 20X1. The effects of the inability to obtain sufficient appropriate audit evidence are deemed material and pervasive.
- The auditor expressed an unmodified opinion on December 31, 20X1 and 20X0 balance sheets and a disclaimer of opinion on the 20X0 statements of income, changes in stockholders' equity, and cash flows.

Independent Auditor's Report

[*Appropriate Addressee*]

Report on the Financial Statements

We have audited the accompanying financial statements of ABC Company, which comprise the balance sheets as of December 31, 20X2 and 20X1, and the related statements of income, changes in stockholders' equity, and cash flows for the years then ended, and the related notes to the financial statements.

Management's Responsibility for the Financial Statements

Management is responsible for the preparation and fair presentation of these financial statements in accordance with accounting principles generally accepted in the United States of America; this includes the design, implementation, and maintenance of internal control relevant to the preparation and fair presentation of financial statements that are free from material misstatement, whether due to fraud or error.

Auditor's Responsibility

Our responsibility is to express an opinion on these financial statements based on our audits. Except as explained in the Basis for Disclaimer of Opinion paragraph, we conducted our audits in accordance with auditing standards generally accepted in the United States of America. Those standards require that we plan and perform the audit to obtain reasonable assurance about whether the financial statements are free from material misstatement.

An audit involves performing procedures to obtain audit evidence about the amounts and disclosures in the financial statements. The procedures selected depend on the auditor's judgment, including the assessment of the risks of material misstatement of the financial statements, whether due to fraud or error. In making those risk assessments, the auditor considers internal control relevant to the entity's preparation and fair presentation of the financial statements in order to design audit procedures that are appropriate in the circumstances, but not for the purpose of expressing an opinion on the effectiveness of the entity's internal control. Accordingly, we express no such opinion. An audit also includes evaluating the appropriateness of accounting policies used and the reasonableness of significant accounting estimates made by management, as well as evaluating the overall presentation of the financial statements.

We believe that the audit evidence we have obtained is sufficient and appropriate to provide a basis for our audit opinions on the balance sheets as of December 31, 20X2 and 20X1, and the statements of income, changes in stockholders' equity, and cash flows for the year ended December 31, 20X2.

Basis for Disclaimer of Opinion on 20X1 Operations and Cash Flows

We did not observe the taking of the physical inventory as of December 31, 20X0, since that date was prior to our engagement as auditors for the Company, and we were unable to satisfy ourselves regarding inventory quantities by means of other auditing procedures. Inventory amounts as of December 31, 20X0 enter into the determination of net income and cash flows for the year ended December 31, 20X1.

Disclaimer of Opinion on 20X1 Operations and Cash Flows

Because of the significance of the matter described in the Basis for Disclaimer of Opinion paragraph, we have not been able to obtain sufficient appropriate audit evidence to provide a basis for an audit opinion on the results of operations and cash flows for the year ended December 31, 20X1. Accordingly, we do not express an opinion on the results of operations and cash flows for the year ended December 31, 20X1.

Opinion

In our opinion, the balance sheets of ABC Company as of December 31, 20X2 and 20X1, and the statements of income, changes in stockholders' equity, and cash flows for the year ended December 31, 20X2, present fairly, in all material respects, the financial position of ABC Company as of December 31, 20X2 and 20X1, and the results of its operations and its cash flows for the year ended December 31, 20X2 in accordance with accounting principles generally accepted in the United States of America.

Report on Other Legal and Regulatory Requirements

[*Form and content of this section of the auditor's report will vary depending on the nature of the auditor's other reporting responsibilities.*]

[*Auditor's signature*]

[*Auditor's city and state*]

[*Date of the auditor's report*]

AU-C 706 ILLUSTRATIONS

The following auditor's reports with emphasis-of-matter or other-matter paragraphs are illustrated:

1. An Auditor's Report with an Emphasis-of-Matter Paragraph Because There Is Uncertainty Relating to a Pending Unusually Important Litigation Matter
2. An Auditor's Report with an Other-Matter Paragraph That May Be Appropriate When an Auditor Issues an Updated Report on the Financial Statements of a Prior Period That Contains an Opinion Different from the Opinion Previously Expressed
3. An Auditor's Report with a Qualified Opinion Due to a Material Misstatement of the Financial Statements and an Emphasis-of-Matter Paragraph Because There Is Uncertainty Relating to a Pending Unusually Important Litigation Matter

ILLUSTRATION 1. AN AUDITOR'S REPORT WITH AN EMPHASIS-OF-MATTER PARAGRAPH BECAUSE THERE IS UNCERTAINTY RELATING TO A PENDING UNUSUALLY IMPORTANT LITIGATION MATTER

Circumstances include the following:

- Audit of a complete set of general purpose financial statements (single year) prepared in accordance with accounting principles generally accepted in the United States of America.
- There is uncertainty relating to a pending unusually important litigation matter.
- The auditor's report includes an emphasis-of-matter paragraph.

Independent Auditor's Report

[*Appropriate Addressee*]

Report on the Financial Statements

We have audited the accompanying financial statements of ABC Company, which comprise the balance sheet as of December 31, 20X1, and the related statements of income, changes in stockholders' equity, and cash flows for the year then ended, and the related notes to the financial statements.

Management's Responsibility for the Financial Statements

Management is responsible for the preparation and fair presentation of these financial statements in accordance with accounting principles generally accepted in the United States of America; this includes the design, implementation, and maintenance of internal control relevant to the preparation and fair presentation of financial statements that are free from material misstatement, whether due to fraud or error.

Auditor's Responsibility

Our responsibility is to express an opinion on these financial statements based on our audit. We conducted our audit in accordance with auditing standards generally accepted in the United States of America. Those standards require that we plan and perform the audit to obtain reasonable assurance about whether the financial statements are free from material misstatement.

An audit involves performing procedures to obtain audit evidence about the amounts and disclosures in the financial statements. The procedures selected depend on the auditor's judgment, including the assessment of the risks of material misstatement of the financial statements, whether due to fraud or error. In making those risk assessments, the auditor considers internal control relevant to the entity's preparation and fair presentation of the financial statements in order to design audit procedures that are appropriate in the circumstances, but not for the purpose of expressing an opinion on the effectiveness of the entity's internal control. Accordingly, we express no such opinion. An audit also includes evaluating the appropriateness of accounting policies used and the reasonableness of significant accounting estimates made by management, as well as evaluating the overall presentation of the financial statements.

We believe that the audit evidence that we have obtained is sufficient and appropriate to provide a basis for our audit opinion.

Opinion

In our opinion, the financial statements referred to above present fairly, in all material respects, the financial position of ABC Company as of December 31, 20X1, and the results of its operations and its cash flows for the year then ended in accordance with accounting principles generally accepted in the United States of America.

Emphasis of Matter

As discussed in Note X to the financial statements, the Company is a defendant in a lawsuit [*briefly describe the nature of the litigation consistent with the Company's description in the note to the financial statements*]. Our opinion is not modified with respect to this matter.

Report on Other Legal and Regulatory Requirements

[*Form and content of this section of the auditor's report will vary depending on the nature of the auditor's other reporting responsibilities.*]

[*Auditor's signature*]

[*Auditor's city and state*]

[*Date of the auditor's report*]

ILLUSTRATION 2. AN AUDITOR'S REPORT WITH AN OTHER-MATTER PARAGRAPH THAT MAY BE APPROPRIATE WHEN AN AUDITOR ISSUES AN UPDATED REPORT ON THE FINANCIAL STATEMENTS OF A PRIOR PERIOD THAT CONTAINS AN OPINION DIFFERENT FROM THE OPINION PREVIOUSLY EXPRESSED

Circumstances include the following:

- Audit of a complete set of general purpose financial statements (comparative) prepared in accordance with accounting principles generally accepted in the United States of America.
- The auditor's report on the prior period financial statements expressed an adverse opinion due to identified departures from accounting principles generally accepted in the United States of America that resulted in the financial statements being materially misstated. The entity has elected to change its method of accounting for the matters

that gave rise to the adverse opinion in the prior period, and has restated the prior period financial statements. Therefore, the auditor has expressed an unmodified opinion on the comparative financial statements.
- The auditor's report includes an other-matter paragraph indicating that the updated report on the financial statements of the prior period contains an opinion different from the opinion previously expressed, as required by Section 700, *Forming an Opinion and Reporting on Financial Statements*.
- Although the entity changed its method of accounting for the matters that gave rise to the adverse opinion in the prior period, the principal objective of the communication in the other-matter paragraph is to draw users' attention to the change in the auditor's opinion on the prior period financial statements. The other-matter paragraph also refers to the change in accounting principle and the related disclosure in the financial statements. Therefore, the other-matter paragraph also meets the objective of communicating the change in accounting principle as required by Section 708, *Consistency of Financial Statements*, and a separate emphasis-of-matter paragraph is not considered necessary.

Independent Auditor's Report

[*Appropriate Addressee*]

Report on the Financial Statements

We have audited the accompanying financial statements of ABC Company, which comprise the balance sheets as of December 31, 20X1 and 20X0, and the related statements of income, changes in stockholders' equity, and cash flows for the years then ended, and the related notes to the financial statements.

Management's Responsibility for the Financial Statements

Management is responsible for the preparation and fair presentation of these financial statements in accordance with accounting principles generally accepted in the United States of America; this includes the design, implementation, and maintenance of internal control relevant to the preparation and fair presentation of financial statements that are free from material misstatement, whether due to fraud or error.

Auditor's Responsibility

Our responsibility is to express an opinion on these financial statements based on our audits. We conducted our audits in accordance with auditing standards generally accepted in the United States of America. Those standards require that we plan and perform the audit to obtain reasonable assurance about whether the financial statements are free from material misstatement.

An audit involves performing procedures to obtain audit evidence about the amounts and disclosures in the financial statements. The procedures selected depend on the auditor's judgment, including the assessment of the risks of material misstatement of the financial statements, whether due to fraud or error. In making those risk assessments, the auditor considers internal control relevant to the entity's preparation and fair presentation of the financial statements in order to design audit procedures that are appropriate in the circumstances, but not for the purpose of expressing an opinion on the effectiveness of the entity's internal control. Accordingly, we express no such opinion. An audit also includes evaluating the appropriateness of accounting policies used and the reasonableness of significant accounting estimates made by management, as well as evaluating the overall presentation of the financial statements.

We believe that the audit evidence that we have obtained is sufficient and appropriate to provide a basis for our audit opinion.

Opinion

In our opinion, the financial statements referred to above present fairly, in all material respects, the financial position of ABC Company as of December 31, 20X1 and 20X0, and the results of its operations and its cash flows for the years then ended in accordance with accounting principles generally accepted in the United States of America.

Other Matter

In our report dated March 1, 20X1, we expressed an opinion that the 20X0 financial statements did not fairly present the financial position, results of operations, and cash flows of ABC Company in accordance with accounting principles generally accepted in the United States of America because of two departures from such principles: (1) ABC Company carried its property, plant, and equipment at appraisal values, and provided for depreciation on the basis of such values, and (2) ABC Company did not provide for deferred income taxes with respect to differences between income for financial reporting purposes and taxable income. As described in Note X, the Company has changed its method of accounting for these items and restated its 20X0 financial statements to conform with accounting principles generally accepted in the United States of America. Accordingly, our present opinion on the restated 20X0 financial statements, as presented herein, is different from that expressed in our previous report.

Report on Other Legal and Regulatory Requirements

[*Form and content of this section of the auditor's report will vary depending on the nature of the auditor's other reporting responsibilities.*]

[*Auditor's signature*]

[*Auditor's city and state*]

[*Date of the auditor's report*]

ILLUSTRATION 3. AN AUDITOR'S REPORT WITH A QUALIFIED OPINION DUE TO A MATERIAL MISSTATEMENT OF THE FINANCIAL STATEMENTS AND AN EMPHASIS-OF-MATTER PARAGRAPH BECAUSE THERE IS UNCERTAINTY RELATING TO A PENDING UNUSUALLY IMPORTANT LITIGATION MATTER

Circumstances include the following:

- Audit of a complete set of general purpose financial statements (single year) prepared in accordance with accounting principles generally accepted in the United States of America.
- Inventories are misstated. The misstatement is deemed to be material but not pervasive to the financial statements.
- There is uncertainty relating to a pending unusually important litigation matter.
- The auditor's report includes a qualified opinion and also includes an emphasis-of-matter paragraph.

Independent Auditor's Report

[*Appropriate Addressee*]

Report on the Financial Statements

We have audited the accompanying financial statements of ABC Company, which comprise the balance sheet as of December 31, 20X1, and related statements of income, changes in stockholders' equity, and cash flows for the year then ended, and the related notes to the financial statements.

Management's Responsibility for the Financial Statements

Management is responsible for the preparation and fair presentation of these financial statements in accordance with accounting principles generally accepted in the United States of America; this includes the design, implementation, and maintenance of internal control relevant to the preparation and fair presentation of financial statements that are free from material misstatement, whether due to fraud or error.

Auditor's Responsibility

Our responsibility is to express an opinion on these financial statements based on our audit. We conducted our audit in accordance with auditing standards generally accepted in the United States of America. Those standards require that we plan and perform the audit to obtain reasonable assurance about whether the financial statements are free from material misstatement.

An audit involves performing procedures to obtain audit evidence about the amounts and disclosures in the financial statements. The procedures selected depend on the auditor's judgment, including the assessment of the risks of material misstatement of the financial statements, whether due to fraud or error. In making those risk assessments, the auditor considers internal control relevant to the entity's preparation and fair presentation of the financial statements in order to design audit procedures that are appropriate in the circumstances, but not for the purpose of expressing an opinion on the effectiveness of the entity's internal control. Accordingly, we express no such opinion. An audit also includes evaluating the appropriateness of accounting policies used and the reasonableness of significant accounting estimates made by management, as well as evaluating the overall presentation of the financial statements.

We believe that the audit evidence we have obtained is sufficient and appropriate to provide a basis for our qualified audit opinion.

Basis for Qualified Opinion

The Company has stated inventories at cost in the accompanying balance sheet. Accounting principles generally accepted in the United States of America require inventories to be stated at the lower of cost or market. If the Company stated inventories at the lower of cost or market, a write-down of $XXX would have been required as of December 31, 20X1. Accordingly, cost of sales would have been increased by $XXX and net income, income taxes, and stockholders' equity would have been reduced by $XXX, $XXX, and $XXX, as of and for the year ended December 31, 20X1, respectively.

Qualified Opinion

In our opinion, except for the effects of the matter described in the Basis for Qualified Opinion paragraph, the financial statements referred to above present fairly, in all material respects, the financial position of ABC Company as of December 31, 20X1, and the results of its operations and its cash flows for the year then ended in accordance with accounting principles generally accepted in the United States of America.

Emphasis of Matter

As discussed in Note X to the financial statements, the Company is a defendant in a lawsuit [*briefly describe the nature of the litigation consistent with the Company's description in the note to the financial statements*]. Our opinion is not modified with respect to this matter.

Report on Other Legal and Regulatory Requirements

[*Form and content of this section of the auditor's report will vary depending on the nature of the auditor's other reporting responsibilities.*]

[*Auditor's signature*]

[*Auditor's city and state*]

[*Date of the auditor's report*]

LIST OF AU-C SECTIONS CONTAINING REQUIREMENTS FOR EMPHASIS-OF-MATTER PARAGRAPHS

This list identifies paragraphs in other AU-C sections that require the auditor to include an emphasis-of-matter paragraph in the auditor's report in certain circumstances. The list is not a substitute for considering the requirements and related application and other explanatory material in AU-C sections.

- Paragraph .16c of Section 560, *Subsequent Events and Subsequently Discovered Facts*
- Paragraphs .12 and .16 of Section 570, *The Auditor's Consideration of an Entity's Ability to Continue as a Going Concern*
- Paragraphs .08–.09 and .11–.13 of Section 708, *Consistency of Financial Statements*
- Paragraphs .19 and .21 of Section 800, *Special Considerations—Audits of Financial Statements Prepared in Accordance with Special Purpose Frameworks*

LIST OF AU-C SECTIONS CONTAINING REQUIREMENTS FOR OTHER-MATTER PARAGRAPHS

This list identifies paragraphs in other AU-C sections that require the auditor to include an other-matter paragraph in the auditor's report in certain circumstances. The list is not a substitute for considering the requirements and related application and other explanatory material in AU-C sections.

- Paragraph .16c of Section 560, *Subsequent Events and Subsequently Discovered Facts*
- Paragraphs .53–.54 and .56–.57 of Section 700, *Forming an Opinion and Reporting on Financial Statements*
- Paragraph .12 of Section 720, *Other Information in Documents Containing Audited Financial Statements*
- Paragraph .09 of Section 725, *Supplementary Information in Relation to the Financial Statements as a Whole*
- Paragraph .07 of Section 730, *Required Supplementary Information*
- Paragraph .20 of Section 800, *Special Considerations—Audits of Financial Statements Prepared in Accordance with Special Purpose Frameworks*
- Paragraph .13 of Section 806, *Reporting on Compliance with Aspects of Contractual Agreements or Regulatory Requirements in Connection with Audited Financial Statements*
- Paragraph .07 of Section 905, *Alert That Restricts the Use of the Auditor's Written Communication*

AU 530 Dating of the Independent Auditor's Report[1]

AU-C 700 Forming an Opinion and Reporting on Financial Statements

AU-C 560 Subsequent Events and Subsequently Discovered Facts

AU EFFECTIVE DATE AND APPLICABILITY

Original Pronouncements   Statements on Auditing Standards (SASs) 1, 29, 98, and 103.

Effective Date   These statements currently are effective.

Applicability   Audits of financial statements in accordance with generally accepted auditing standards (GAAS).

AU-C EFFECTIVE DATE AND SUMMARY OF CHANGES

SAS No. 122, *Codification of Auditing Standards and Procedures,* is effective for audits of financial statements with periods ending on or after December 15, 2012.

The clarified SAS combines the requirements and guidance from extant AU Section 530, AU Section 560, AU Section 561, and paragraphs .71–.73 of AU Section 508. The clarified SAS does not change or expand these extant AU sections in any significant respect.

---

[1] This section is affected by the Public Company Accounting Oversight Board's (PCAOB's) Standard, Conforming Amendments to PCAOB Interim Standards Resulting from the Adoption of PCAOB Auditing Standard No. 5, An Audit of Internal Control over Financial Reporting That Is Integrated with an Audit of Financial Statements.

AU DEFINITIONS OF TERMS

Date of auditor's report. The date on which the auditor has obtained sufficient appropriate audit evidence to support the opinion.

NOTE: Ordinarily, this is the date that the auditor and the client agree on the form and content of the financial statements. Sometimes, the date is a matter of judgment (see the section titled "Techniques for Application"). It is the date up to which the auditor is responsible for keeping informed about events affecting the financial statements being reported on.

Dual-dated report. Auditor's report with different dates: (1) the date of completion of fieldwork, and (2) the date a specific event occurred after completion of the fieldwork but before issuance of the auditor's report.

NOTE: An auditor also may dual date a reissued audit report because of an event that occurs after issuance of the original audit report.

Reissued report. Auditor's report issued subsequent to the date the original report was issued.

NOTE: "Reissued report" is used to refer broadly to subsequent reprinting by the auditor of a prior audit report with release to the client as well as reuse by the client in conjunction with issuance of a new document of a prior report. Reuse by the client requires that certain procedures be performed before the auditor can consent (see Section 508).

Report release date. The date the auditor grants the entity permission to use the auditor's report in connection with the financial statements. Usually this date will be the date the auditor delivers the audit report to the entity.

Subsequent events. For purposes of this section, events occurring after the date of the auditor's report but before issuance of the related financial statements that require adjustment of or disclosure in the financial statements (see Section 560, *Subsequent Events*).

AU-C DEFINITIONS OF TERMS

Source: AU-C 560.07

Date of the auditor's report. The date that the auditor dates the report on the financial statements, in accordance with Section 700 (Ref: par. .A14)

Date of the financial statements. The date of the end of the latest period covered by the financial statements.

Subsequent events. Events occurring between the date of the financial statements and the date of the auditor's report.

Subsequently discovered facts. Facts that become known to the auditor after the date of the auditor's report that, had they been known to the auditor at that date, may have caused the auditor to revise the auditor's report.

OBJECTIVES OF AU SECTION 530

This section tells the auditor how to date the report in the following circumstances:

1. Under ordinary conditions
2. Subsequent events
3. Reissuance of report

SAS 29 (see Section 551, *Reporting on Financial Information Accompanying the Basic Financial Statements in Auditor-Submitted Documents*) created a difference in responsibilities for types of reissued reports. If the client is furnished with additional copies of a previously issued report, the auditor has no responsibility to perform any procedures prior to reprinting the report unless the auditor has become aware of the need to adjust or make disclosure in the financial statements. In the case of a predecessor auditor consenting to reuse a previous report, additional procedures are always required (see Section 508, *Reports on Audited Financial Statements*).

OBJECTIVES OF AU-C SECTION 560

AU-C Section 560 states that:

... *the objectives of the auditor are to*

a. *obtain sufficient appropriate audit evidence about whether events occurring between the date of the financial statements and the date of the auditor's report that require adjustment of, or disclosure in, the financial statements are appropriately reflected in those financial statements in accordance with the applicable financial reporting framework and*
b. *respond appropriately to facts that become known to the auditor after the date of the auditor's report that, had they been known to the auditor at that date, may have caused the auditor to revise the auditor's report.*

FUNDAMENTAL REQUIREMENTS

ORDINARY CONDITIONS

Under ordinary conditions, the auditor should date his or her report as of the date of completion of fieldwork. The auditor does not have to make inquiries or apply other auditing procedures after the date of his or her report under ordinary conditions. However, additional procedures might be required (see the sections titled "Reissuance of Report" and "Unusual Conditions").

Subsequent Events Requiring Adjustment of Financial Statements

Some events that require adjustment might be made without disclosure, but some events require additional disclosure to be understood.

1. *Financial statements adjusted, no disclosure.* When the adjustment is made but disclosure of the event is not necessary, the auditor's report should be dated as of the date of completion of fieldwork.
2. *Financial statements adjusted, disclosure.* When the adjustment is made with disclosure of the event, the auditor should dual date the report or date it as of the date of the event (see "Subsequent Events Review").

3. *Financial statements not adjusted.* If the financial statements are not adjusted, the auditor should qualify his or her opinion or, if appropriate, express an adverse opinion.

Subsequent Events Requiring Disclosure

Some subsequent events only require disclosure of information in the notes to the financial statements.

1. *Disclosure made.* Disclosure would be made in a note to the financial statements, but might also be referred to in the auditor's report. In either circumstance, the auditor should dual date his or her report or date it as of the event (see "Subsequent Events Review").
2. *No disclosure.* If the subsequent event is not disclosed, the auditor should qualify the opinion, or if appropriate, express an adverse opinion. In these circumstances, the auditor should either dual date the report or date it as of the date of the event (see "Subsequent Events Review").

SUBSEQUENT EVENTS REVIEW

A subsequent events review is the auditor's review of transactions and events occurring after the date of the balance sheet and up to the date of the auditor's report. Its purpose is to determine whether the financial statements being reported on require adjustment or additional disclosures (see Section 560).

If the auditor dates the report as of the date of the subsequent event rather than dual dating the report, he or she should extend the subsequent events review to that date (see Section 560).

REISSUANCE OF REPORT

When the auditor reissues the report and uses the original report date, he or she does not have to investigate or inquire about events affecting the financial statements reported on that may have occurred between the original date and the reissuance date.

NOTE: *However, see Section 508 for additional requirements that apply when there are comparative financial statements. If the auditor is a continuing auditor, the report has to be updated. If the auditor is a predecessor auditor and the client is reusing the report, additional procedures are required, including a requirement to obtain an updating representation letter from management and a representation letter from the successor auditor.*

Events Requiring Adjustment or Disclosure

The auditor may be aware of an event that occurred between the original report date and the reissuance date that affects the financial statements reported on. This event may require disclosure to prevent the financial statements from being misleading. Events occurring between the original report date and the reissuance date do not require adjustment of the financial statements unless the adjustment results in the correction of an error (see Section 560).

When the auditor reissues the report and the financial statements have been adjusted or events have been disclosed in the notes, he or she should dual date the report or date it as of the date of the event responsible for the adjustment or the disclosure.

NOTE: *The effect of the event may cause the auditor to express an opinion different from the one he or she originally expressed.*

UNAUDITED NOTE

An event that requires disclosure only may be disclosed in a note to the financial statements marked "unaudited." In these circumstances, the auditor's report would have the original date. An example of the heading to use for this type of note follows:

> Event (Unaudited) Subsequent to the Date of the Report of the Independent Auditor.

UNUSUAL CONDITIONS

Under ordinary conditions, the auditor has no responsibility to make any inquiry or carry out any procedures for the period after the date of his or her report. An exception might arise if the audit report is reissued as explained previously. An exception might also arise in either of the following circumstances.

Subsequent Discovery of Facts

If, subsequent to the date of the report, the auditor becomes aware of facts that may have existed at that date which might have affected the report, additional procedures are required (see Section 561, *Subsequent Discovery of Facts Existing at the Date of the Auditor's Report*).

Filing under the 1933 Act

If the financial statements subsequently are incorporated in a filing under the Securities Act of 1933, additional procedures are required (see Section 711, *Filings under Federal Securities Statutes*).

INTERPRETATIONS

There are no interpretations for this section.

TECHNIQUES FOR APPLICATION

DETERMINING THE DATE OF COMPLETION OF FIELDWORK

There is no authoritative pronouncement that provides guidance on how to determine the date of completion of fieldwork. The date is usually the *same* as the date of the management representation letter (see Section 333, *Management Representations*) and the date up to which lawyers are asked to respond (see Section 337, *Inquiry of a Client's Lawyer Concerning Litigation, Claims, and Assessments*) concerning litigation, claims, and assessments.

Ordinarily, the date of completion of the fieldwork is the date on which the auditor in charge of the engagement and the client's chief financial officer agree on the form and content of the financial statements. The auditor and the client may arrange for a formal closing conference to review the financial statements. The conclusion of this conference may be considered the date of completion of the fieldwork. If there is no formal closing conference, the date of completion of the fieldwork may be considered to be the date the audit staff finally leaves the client's premises, provided no significant adjustments are expected after that date.

If any procedures that are necessary to the expression of an opinion are performed after the audit staff leaves the client's premises, the substantial completion of those procedures is the completion of fieldwork. Additional advice on issues concerning dating of the audit report is presented in the "Techniques for Application" section of the chapter on Section 560, *Subsequent Events*.

PERIOD BETWEEN COMPLETION OF FIELDWORK AND ISSUANCE OF AUDITOR'S REPORT

Ordinarily, there is a lapse of two to three weeks between the date of the auditor's report (the date of completion of the fieldwork) and its issuance. During this period, the auditor might review the audit documentation a final time to make certain there are no open items, put the audit documentation in a form suitable to be filed, and prepare the final audit report and financial statements. During this period, the auditor is not required to apply any procedures unless information about subsequent events comes to the attention of the auditor (see Section 530, *Dating of the Independent Auditor's Report*).

If the period between the date of the auditor's report and the issuance of the financial statements exceeds approximately three weeks, it would be prudent for the auditor to call the client and inquire about subsequent events. If the delay is unusually long, it may be advisable to extend the subsequent events review and redate the report.

DUAL DATING REPORT

When an event that requires disclosure or adjustment of financial statements occurs between the date of the auditor's report and the issuance of the financial statements, or between the date of issuance and the date of reissuance, the auditor may dual date the report or extend the date of the report and the subsequent events review to the date of the event. Because extending the date of the report extends the auditor's responsibility, the auditor is acting prudently in always dual dating reports requiring disclosure of subsequent events.

An example of the dual dating of an auditor's report is as follows:

> February 16, 20X1, except for Note X as to which the date is February 25, 20X1.

AU 532 Restricting the Use of an Auditor's Report

AU-C 905 Alert That Restricts the Use of the Auditor's Written Communication

AU EFFECTIVE DATE AND APPLICABILITY

Original Pronouncement	Statement on Auditing Standards (SAS) 87.
Effective Date	This statement currently is effective.
Applicability	Engagements involving the issuance of reports based on:
	1. Subject matter or presentations on measurement or disclosure criteria contained in contractual agreements or regulatory provisions.
	2. A by-product of a financial statement audit.
	NOTE: *Does not apply to Section 324,* Service Organizations, *or reports issued under Section 634,* Letters for Underwriters and Certain Other Requesting Parties.

AU-C EFFECTIVE DATE AND SUMMARY OF CHANGES

SAS No. 125, *Alert That Restricts the Use of the Auditor's Written Communication,* is effective for audits of financial statements with periods ending on or after December 15, 2012.

AU-C 905 clarifies that it applies to auditor's reports and other written communications issued in connection with a GAAS engagement and requires an alert that restricts the use of the auditor's written communication when the subject matter of that communication is based on:

1. Measurement or disclosure criteria that are determined by the auditor to be suitable only for a limited number of users who can be presumed to have an adequate understanding of the criteria;

2. Measurement or disclosure criteria that are available only to the specified parties; or
3. Matters identified by the auditor during the course of the audit engagement when the identification of such matters is not the primary objective of the audit engagement (commonly referred to as a by-product report).

In the "AU Illustrations" section at the end of this chapter, you can find an appendix to AU-C 950 that lists other clarified SASs that require an alert that restricts the use of the auditor's written communication or that otherwise address the inclusion of such alerts.

AU Section 532 requires the auditor to consider informing his or her client that restricted-use reports are not intended for distribution to nonspecified parties. However, AU-C 905 makes clear that an auditor is not responsible for controlling, and cannot control, distribution of the auditor's written communication after its release. The alert is designed to avoid misunderstandings related to the use of the written communication, particularly when taken out of the context in which it is intended to be used. An auditor may consider informing the entity or other specified parties that the written communication is not intended for distribution to parties other than those specified in the written communication.

AU DEFINITIONS OF TERMS

General-use reports. Reports that are not restricted to specified parties, such as reports on financial statements prepared in conformity with generally accepted accounting principles (GAAP) or other comprehensive bases of accounting (OCBOA).

Restricted-use reports. Reports intended for specified parties. Restriction may result from the following:

- Purpose of report
- Nature of procedures applied
- Basis of assumptions used
- Extent of knowledge of procedures
- Potential for report to be misunderstood

AU-C DEFINITIONS OF TERMS

Source: AU-C 905

Specified parties. The intended users of the auditor's written communication.

OBJECTIVES OF AU SECTION 532

Section 532 was issued to identify when an auditor's (or an accountant's) report should be restricted and to specify the language in the restricted-use report paragraph. The standard serves as a conceptual document in that other sections presenting restricted-use reports were amended or conformed to the requirements herein. Section 532 replaces the terms *restricted distribution* and *general distribution* with *restricted use* and *general use* and defines the last two terms.

The standard reminds auditors that they may restrict the use of any general-use report and requires auditors to restrict combined reports that contain general-use and restricted-use reports on different subject matter.

OBJECTIVES OF AU-C SECTION 905

AU-C Section 905 states that:

the objective of the auditor is to restrict the use of the auditor's written communication by including an alert when the potential exists for the auditor's written communication to be misunderstood if taken out of the context in which the auditor's written communication is intended to be used.

FUNDAMENTAL REQUIREMENTS

REPORTS REQUIRED TO BE RESTRICTED

The auditor should restrict the use of a report when:

1. The subject matter or the presentation being reported on is based on measurement or disclosure criteria contained in contractual agreements or regulatory provisions that are not in conformity with GAAP or OCBOA.
2. The auditor's report is a by-product of a financial statement audit and the procedures applied were designed for the audit, not to provide assurance on the subject matter of the report.

IDENTIFICATION OF RESTRICTED PARTIES

The auditor should restrict reports based on contractual agreements or regulatory provisions to parties to the agreement or to the responsible regulatory agency.

The auditor should restrict by-product reports to an entity's audit committee, board of directors, management, or others within the organization, specified regulatory agencies, and parties to the contract for compliance with contractual agreements.

COMBINED REPORTS COVERING BOTH RESTRICTED-USE AND GENERAL-USE SUBJECT MATTER OR PRESENTATIONS

The auditor should restrict the use of a single combined restricted-use and general-use report to specified parties.

INCLUSION OF A SEPARATE RESTRICTED-USE REPORT AND A SEPARATE GENERAL-USE REPORT IN THE SAME DOCUMENT

A separate restricted-use report may be included in a document that contains a separate general-use report, provided the combined report is restricted.

ADDING NEW SPECIFIED PARTIES

After the engagement is completed or in the course of such an engagement, the client may ask the auditor to add other specified parties. An auditor should not agree to add other specified parties to a by-product report.

For a subject matter or presentation type report, the auditor may agree to add other specified parties after considering such factors as identity of the other parties and intended use of the report. If the auditor adds other specified parties, he or she should obtain affirmative acknowledgment, ordinarily in writing, from the other parties about their understanding of the engagement, measurement or disclosure criteria, and the report.

If other parties are added after issuance of the auditor's report, the auditor may reissue the report or provide other acknowledgment that new parties have been added. If the report is reissued, the report date should not be changed. If the auditor provides written acknowledgment of the addition, the acknowledgment should state that no subsequent or new procedures have been performed.

LIMITING REPORT DISTRIBUTION

The auditor should consider informing the client that restricted-use reports are not intended to be distributed to nonspecified parties. However, an auditor is not responsible for controlling the client's restricted-use report distribution.

REQUIRED RESTRICTED-USE REPORT LANGUAGE

The auditor should add a separate paragraph at the end of the report that:

1. States that the report is intended solely for the information and use of the specified parties
2. Identifies the parties
3. States that the report is not intended to be, and should not be, used by nonspecified parties

The "Illustration" section contains an example of a restricted-use paragraph.

INTERPRETATIONS

There are no interpretations for this section.

TECHNIQUES FOR APPLICATION

The following sections present by-product reports:

1. Section 325, *Communicating Internal Control Related Matters Identified in an Audit*
2. Section 380, *The Auditor's Communication with Those Charged with Governance*
3. Section 623, *Special Reports*, for reports on compliance with contractual agreements or regulatory requirements

The auditor should refer to the aforementioned sections for guidance that conforms to Section 532.

Note that auditors will rarely have to apply Section 532, because the amendments and conforming changes have been made in the relevant sections throughout this book.

AU ILLUSTRATION

The following example of a restricted-use paragraph is from Section 532.

This report is intended solely for the information and use of [*the specified parties*] and is not intended to be, and should not be, used by anyone other than these specified parties.

AU-C 905 ILLUSTRATIONS

ILLUSTRATION 1. LIST OF SECTIONS RELATING TO THE RESTRICTED USE OF THE AUDITOR'S WRITTEN COMMUNICATION (SOURCE AU-C 905 APPENDIX A)

Listed below are paragraphs in other sections that contain specific requirements to include an alert that restricts the use of the auditor's written communication or that otherwise address the inclusion of such alerts. The list is not a substitute for considering the requirements and related application and other explanatory material in the other sections.

- Paragraph .17 of Section 260, *The Auditor's Communication with Those Charged with Governance*
- Paragraphs .14*d*, .A32, and .A38–.A39 of Section 265, *Communicating Internal Control Related Matters Identified in an Audit*
- Paragraph .A16 of Section 725, *Supplementary Information in Relation to the Financial Statements as a Whole*
- Paragraphs .20, .A26–.A27, and .A33 of Section 800, *Special Considerations—Audits of Financial Statements Prepared in Accordance with Special-Purpose Frameworks*
- Paragraphs .12–.13 and .A6–.A8 of Section 806, *Reporting on Compliance with Aspects of Contractual Agreements or Regulatory Requirements in Connection with Audited Financial Statements*
- Paragraphs .14*f* and .A6 of Section 915, *Reports on Application of Requirements of an Applicable Financial Reporting Framework*
- Paragraphs .33 and .A34 of Section 920, *Letters for Underwriters and Certain Other Requesting Parties*
- Paragraphs .30.31*i*, and .A33 of Section 935, *Compliance Audits*

ILLUSTRATION 2. ILLUSTRATIVE *AUDITOR'S* WRITTEN COMMUNICATION

The following is an illustrative *auditor's* written communication encompassing the requirements in paragraph .14.

To Management and [*identify the body or individuals charged with governance, such as the entity's Board of Directors*] of ABC Company

In planning and performing our audit of the financial statements of ABC Company (the "Company") as of and for the year ended December 31, 20XX, in accordance with auditing standards generally accepted in the United States of America, we considered the Company's internal control over financial reporting (internal control) as a basis for designing audit procedures that are appropriate in the circumstances for the purpose of expressing our opinion on the financial statements, but not for the purpose of expressing an opinion on the effectiveness of the Company's internal control. Accordingly, we do not express an opinion on the effectiveness of the Company's internal control.

Our consideration of internal control was for the limited purpose described in the preceding paragraph and was not designed to identify all deficiencies in internal control that might be [*mate-*

rial weaknesses or *material weaknesses or significant deficiencies*] and therefore, [*material weaknesses* or *material weaknesses or significant deficiencies*] may exist that were not identified. However, as discussed below, we identified certain deficiencies in internal control that we consider to be [*material weaknesses* or *significant deficiencies* or *material weaknesses and significant deficiencies*].

A deficiency in internal control exists when the design or operation of a control does not allow management or employees, in the normal course of performing their assigned functions, to prevent, or detect and correct, misstatements on a timely basis. A material weakness is a deficiency, or a combination of deficiencies, in internal control, such that there is a reasonable possibility that a material misstatement of the entity's financial statements will not be prevented, or detected and corrected, on a timely basis. [*We consider the following deficiencies in the Company's internal control to be material weaknesses:*]

[*Describe the material weaknesses that were identified and an explanation of their potential effects.*]

[*A significant deficiency is a deficiency, or a combination of deficiencies, in internal control that is less severe than a material weakness, yet important enough to merit attention by those charged with governance. We consider the following deficiencies in the Company's internal control to be significant deficiencies:*]

[*Describe the significant deficiencies that were identified and an explanation of their potential effects.*]

[*If the auditor is communicating significant deficiencies and did not identify any material weaknesses, the auditor may state that none of the identified significant deficiencies are considered to be material weaknesses.*]

This communication is intended solely for the information and use of management, [*identify the body or individuals charged with governance*], others within the organization, and [*identify any governmental authorities to which the auditor is required to report*] and is not intended to be, and should not be, used by anyone other than these specified parties.

[*Auditor's Signature*]

[*Auditor's City and State*]

[*Date*]

ILLUSTRATION 3. ILLUSTRATIVE NO MATERIAL WEAKNESS COMMUNICATION

The following is an illustrative *auditor's* written communication indicating that no material weaknesses were identified during the audit *of a not-for-profit organization*.

To Management and [*identify the body or individuals charged with governance, such as the entity's Board of Directors*] of ABC Company [*NPO Organization*]

In planning and performing our audit of the financial statements of ABC Company (the "Company") [*NPO Organization (the Organization)*] as of and for the year ended December 31, 20XX, in accordance with auditing standards generally accepted in the United States of America, we considered the Company's [*Organization's*] internal control over financial reporting (internal control) as a basis for designing audit procedures that are appropriate in the circumstances for the purpose of expressing our opinion on the financial statements, but not for the purpose of expressing an opinion on the effectiveness of the Company's [*Organization's*] internal control. Accordingly, we do not express an opinion on the effectiveness of the Company's [*Organization's*] internal control.

A deficiency in internal control exists when the design or operation of a control does not allow management or employees, in the normal course of performing their assigned functions, to prevent, or detect and correct, misstatements on a timely basis. A material weakness is a deficiency, or a combination of deficiencies, in internal control, such that there is a reasonable possibility that a material misstatement of the entity's financial statements will not be prevented, or detected and corrected, on a timely basis.

Our consideration of internal control was for the limited purpose described in the first paragraph and was not designed to identify all deficiencies in internal control that might be material weaknesses. Given these limitations, during our audit we did not identify any deficiencies in internal control that we consider to be material weaknesses. However, material weaknesses may exist that have not been identified.

[*If one or more significant deficiencies have been identified, the auditor may add the following: Our audit was also not designed to identify deficiencies in internal control that might be significant deficiencies. A significant deficiency is a deficiency, or a combination of deficiencies, in internal control that is less severe than a material weakness, yet important enough to merit attention by those charged with governance. We communicated the significant deficiencies identified during our audit in a separate communication dated [date].*]

This communication is intended solely for the information and use of management, [*identify the body or individuals charged with governance*], others within the organization, and [*identify any governmental authorities to which the auditor is required to report*] and is not intended to be, and should not be, used by anyone other than these specified parties.

[*Auditor's Signature*]

[*Auditor's City and State*]

[*Date*]

[No amendments to paragraph A40.]

AU 534 Reporting on Financial Statements Prepared for Use in Other Countries

AU-C 910 Financial Statements Prepared in Accordance with a Financial Reporting Framework Generally Accepted in Another Country

AU EFFECTIVE DATE AND APPLICABILITY

Original Pronouncement	Statement on Auditing Standards (SAS) 51.
Effective Date	This statement currently is effective.
Applicability	Engagements to report on the financial statements of a U.S. entity that have been prepared in conformity with accounting principles generally accepted in another country for use outside the U.S.

AU-C EFFECTIVE DATE AND SUMMARY OF CHANGES

SAS No. 122, *Codification of Auditing Standards and Procedures,* is effective for audits of financial statements with periods ending on or after December 15, 2012.

AU-C 910 requires the auditor to obtain an understanding of a relevant financial reporting framework commonly accepted in another country and relevant auditing standards other than the generally accepted auditing standards (GAAS). The extant standard requires the auditor to consider consulting an expert. This is not a requirement in AU-C 910 and has been moved to the application section.

AU-C 910 eliminates the concept of limited use. If a report that is to be used in the United States is prepared in accordance with a financial reporting framework generally accepted in another country, the auditor is required to include an emphasis-of-matter paragraph highlighting the foreign reporting framework, and the auditor is permitted to express an unqualified opinion.

AU DEFINITIONS OF TERMS

Dual statements. Two sets of financial statements for the same entity—one prepared in conformity with U.S. generally accepted accounting principles (GAAP) and another prepared in conformity with accounting principles generally accepted in another country.

Limited distribution in the United States. Distribution of financial statements to parties (such as banks, institutional investors, and similar knowledgeable parties) that deal with the entity directly in a manner that permits such parties to discuss differences from US GAAP and their significance.

US entity. An entity that is either organized or domiciled in the United States.

US-style report modified. The auditor's standard report as described in Section 508, *Reports on Audited Financial Statements*, modified for use outside the United States.

AU-C DEFINITIONS OF TERMS

AU-C 910 contains no definitions.

OBJECTIVES OF AU SECTION 534

A US entity may need to prepare financial statements for use outside the United States that are prepared in conformity with accounting principles that are generally accepted in another country, but not in conformity with US GAAP. For example, this situation may arise in the following circumstances:

1. The financial statements are to be included in the consolidated financial statements of a non-US parent.
2. The financial statements are to be used by a significant group of foreign investors.
3. The financial statements are to be used to raise capital in another country.

Section 534 provides guidance on appropriate reporting in these circumstances. An SAS was necessary because of a provision of the American Institute of Certified Public Accountants (AICPA) ethics code that was in effect at the time. ET Section 92.02 of the Code indicated that in circumstances that would entitle a reader to assume US practices were followed, the auditor must adhere to Rule 202 (GAAS) and Rule 203 (GAAP).

Practice varied considerably because of uncertainty about the conditions that would entitle a reader to assume that US practices were followed. Some auditors believed that it was appropriate to follow foreign standards—both accounting and auditing. Others believed that it was necessary to adhere to US standards. The Code of Professional Conduct adopted in 1988 is applicable to *all* AICPA members including those who practice outside the United States.

Section 534 takes the position that in all circumstances it is necessary for a US auditor (whether practicing within the United States or outside the United States) to adhere to the general and fieldwork standards of US GAAS. However, it relaxes the reporting standards for financial statements prepared for foreign use with no, or limited, US distribution. In those circumstances, the auditor may issue a specially worded US-style report that expresses an unqualified opinion on conformity with foreign accounting principles or the standard report of another country.

OBJECTIVES OF AU-C SECTION 910

AU-C Section 910 states that:

... the objective of the auditor, when engaged to report on financial statements prepared in accordance with a financial reporting framework generally accepted in another country, when such audited financial statements are intended for use outside the United States, is to address appropriately the special considerations that are relevant to

   a. *the acceptance of the engagement,*
   b. *the planning and performance of the engagement, and*
   c. *forming an opinion and reporting on the financial statements.*

FUNDAMENTAL REQUIREMENTS

PURPOSE AND USE OF FINANCIAL STATEMENTS

Before reporting on financial statements prepared in conformity with accounting principles of another country, the auditor should:

1. Clearly understand their purpose and use
2. Obtain *written* management representations on such purpose and use

GENERAL AND FIELDWORK STANDARDS

In auditing financial statements prepared in conformity with accounting principles of another country, the auditor should:

1. Perform the procedures that are necessary to comply with the general and fieldwork standards of US GAAS
2. Modify such procedures as necessary for differences in financial statement assertions caused by the accounting principles of the other country

   NOTE: For example, procedures for testing deferred tax balances would not be needed if the other country's principles do not require or permit recognition of deferred taxes.

3. Obtain an understanding of accounting principles generally accepted in the other country by reading statutes or professional literature and, if necessary, by consulting with persons with appropriate expertise.

COMPLIANCE WITH FOREIGN AUDITING STANDARDS

If the auditor is asked to apply the auditing standards of another country in auditing financial statements prepared for use in the other country, the auditor should:

1. Read the statutes or professional literature that describes auditing standards generally accepted in that country

2. Consider consulting persons having expertise in the auditing standards of the other country
3. Comply with the general and fieldwork standards of both the other country and US GAAS

REPORTING STANDARDS

If financial statements are prepared for use only outside the United States or have only limited distribution within the United States, the auditor may report using either:

1. A US-style report modified to report on the accounting principles of another country; or
2. The report form of the other country

Modified US-Style Report

A US-style report modified to report on financial statements prepared in conformity with the accounting principles of another country should include the following:

1. A title containing the word independent (for example, Independent Auditor's Report).
2. An introductory paragraph with statements that:
   a. The financial statements identified in the report were audited.
   b. Refers to the note to the financial statements that describes the basis of presentation of the financial statements on which the auditor is reporting, including identification of the nationality of the accounting principles.
   c. The financial statements are the responsibility of the entity's management and that the auditor's responsibility is to express an opinion based on the audit.
3. A scope paragraph with statements that:
   a. The audit was conducted in accordance with auditing standards generally accepted in the United States of America and, if appropriate, with the auditing standards of the other country.
   b. US standards require that the auditor plan and perform the audit to obtain reasonable assurance about whether the financial statements are free of material misstatement.
   c. An audit includes:
      (1) Examining, on a test basis, evidence supporting the amounts and disclosures in the financial statements.
      (2) Assessing the accounting principles used and significant estimates made by management.
      (3) Evaluating the overall financial statement presentation.
   d. The auditor believes that the audit provides a reasonable basis for the opinion.
4. An opinion paragraph that presents the auditor's opinion as to whether the financial statements are presented fairly, in all material respects, in conformity with the basis of accounting described. If the auditor concludes that the financial statements are not fairly presented on the basis of accounting described, he or she should add an explanatory paragraph, preceding the opinion paragraph, to the auditor's report that discloses all substantive reasons for that conclusion. The opinion paragraph of the

auditor's report should be appropriately modified, and reference should be made to the explanatory paragraph.
5. An explanatory paragraph following the opinion paragraph if the auditor is auditing comparative financial statements and the described basis of accounting has not been applied in a manner consistent with that of the preceding period. The explanatory paragraph should describe the change in accounting principle and refer to the note to the financial statements that discusses the change and its effect on the financial statements.
6. The manual or printed signature of the auditing firm and the date of the report.

Foreign Report Form

The auditor may use another country's standard report if:

1. That report would be used by auditors in the other country in similar circumstances.
2. The auditor understands and can make the attestations included in such a report.
3. The other country is identified in the report when the auditor believes the report or the financial statements may otherwise be misunderstood because they resemble those prepared in conformity with US standards.

If the auditor uses the standard report of another country, the auditor should comply with that country's reporting standards and should recognize the following points:

1. Even if the report appears similar to a US-style report, it may convey a different meaning and entail different responsibilities due to custom or culture.
2. The report may also require the auditor to provide explicit or implicit assurance of statutory compliance or otherwise require understanding of local law.
3. In addition to foreign professional standards, the auditor needs to understand applicable legal responsibilities.
4. The auditor should consider consulting with persons with expertise in the audit reporting practices of the other country.

Dual Statements

If financial statements are needed for use both in another country and within the United States, the auditor may report on two sets of financial statements:

1. One set prepared in conformity with foreign accounting standards for use outside the United States; and
2. Another set prepared in conformity with US GAAP.

If dual statements are prepared, the auditor may wish to include, in one or both of the reports, a statement that another report has been issued on the entity's statements prepared in conformity with accounting principles of another country (see "AU Illustrations").

US Distribution

If financial statements prepared in conformity with accounting principles of another country will have more than limited US distribution, the auditor should use the US standard report modified (qualified or adverse) for departures from US GAAP. The auditor may also, in a separate paragraph to the report, express an opinion on whether the financial statements are presented in conformity with accounting principles generally accepted in another country.

INTERPRETATIONS

FINANCIAL STATEMENTS PREPARED IN CONFORMITY WITH INTERNATIONAL FINANCIAL REPORTING STANDARDS AS ISSUED BY THE INTERNATIONAL ACCOUNTING STANDARDS BOARD (MAY 2008)

Section 534 is not applicable to financial statements prepared in conformity with International Financial Reporting Standards (IFRS). When an auditor reports on financial statements of a US entity prepared in conformity with IFRS, the auditor would refer to Section 508, *Reports on Audited Financial Statements*.

An entity may prepare financial statements in conformity with a jurisdictional variation of IFRS; Section 534 applies to such financial statements prepared for use outside the United States.

FINANCIAL STATEMENTS AUDITED IN ACCORDANCE WITH INTERNATIONAL STANDARDS ON AUDITING (MAY 2008)

When a US auditor performs a financial audit of a US entity in accordance with International Standards on Auditing (ISA), and where the statements are for use outside the United States, the auditor should comply with the standards of US GAAS as well as any additional requirements of the ISA. When the financial statements are intended for general use only outside the United States, the auditor may use either a US-or ISA-style report. If the financial statements are intended for use in the United States, then the auditor should use the US-style report.

TECHNIQUES FOR APPLICATION

The most difficult aspect of applying Section 534 in practice is the time and effort required to obtain an adequate understanding of the following:

1. Accounting principles generally accepted in the other country
2. General and fieldwork auditing standards of the other country
3. Audit reporting practices of the other country

In all these areas, the SAS suggests that the auditor should consider consulting with persons with expertise in the area. The need for consultation is a matter of professional judgment and depends, in part, on the formality and extensiveness of promulgated standards in the particular country.

In some countries, accounting principles may not be well-developed. A broad range of practices may be acceptable and professional literature may not have sufficient authority or general acceptance. In these circumstances, the auditor should establish that the client's principles and practices are appropriate in the circumstances and are disclosed in a clear and comprehensive manner. For guidance on the appropriateness of the accounting principles used, the auditor may refer to International Accounting Standards established by the International Accounting Standards Committee.

AU ILLUSTRATIONS

The following examples of reporting are adapted from AU 534.

1. A U.S.-style report modified for use outside the United States
2. An additional paragraph for a report on dual statements

ILLUSTRATION 1. US-STYLE REPORT MODIFIED FOR USE OUTSIDE THE UNITED STATES (FROM AU 534.10)

To the Board of Directors
Worldwide Company
Anytown, USA

Independent Auditor's Report

We have audited the accompanying balance sheet of Worldwide Company as of December 31, 20X5, and the related statements of income, retained earnings, and cash flows for the year then ended which, as described in Note 5, have been prepared on the basis of accounting principles generally accepted in [name of country]. These financial statements are the responsibility of the Company's management. Our responsibility is to express an opinion on these financial statements based on our audit.

We conducted our audit in accordance with auditing standards generally accepted in the United States of America (and in [name of country]). US standards require that we plan and perform the audit to obtain reasonable assurance about whether the financial statements are free of material misstatement. An audit includes examining, on a test basis, evidence supporting the amounts and disclosures in the financial statements. An audit also includes assessing the accounting principles used and significant estimates made by management, as well as evaluating the overall financial statement presentation. We believe that our audit provides a reasonable basis for our opinion.

In our opinion, the financial statements referred to above present fairly, in all material respects, the financial position of Worldwide Company as of [at] December 31, 20X5, and the results of its operations and its cash flows for the year then ended in conformity with accounting principles generally accepted in [name of country].

Smith and Jones
February 15, 20X6

ILLUSTRATION 2. ADDITIONAL PARAGRAPH FOR REPORT ON DUAL STATEMENTS (FROM AU 534.13)

We also have reported separately on the financial statements of Worldwide Company for the same period presented in accordance with accounting principles generally accepted in [name of country]. (The significant differences between the accounting principles accepted in [name of country] and those generally accepted in the United States of America are summarized in Note 5.)

AU-C 910 ILLUSTRATIONS

The following are illustrations of auditor's reports on financial statements prepared in accordance with a financial reporting framework generally accepted in another country.

546 AU 534 Reporting on Financial Statements Prepared for Use in Other Countries

1. US Form of Independent Auditor's Report to Report on Financial Statements Prepared in Accordance with a Financial Reporting Framework Generally Accepted in Another Country That Are Intended for Use Only Outside the United States
2. US Form of Independent Auditor's Report to Report on Financial Statements Prepared in Accordance with a Financial Reporting Framework Generally Accepted in Another Country That Also Are Intended for Use in the United States

> **ILLUSTRATION 1. US FORM OF INDEPENDENT AUDITOR'S REPORT TO REPORT ON FINANCIAL STATEMENTS PREPARED IN ACCORDANCE WITH A FINANCIAL REPORTING FRAMEWORK GENERALLY ACCEPTED IN ANOTHER COUNTRY THAT ARE INTENDED FOR USE ONLY OUTSIDE THE UNITED STATES**

Independent Auditor's Report

[*Appropriate Addressee*]

We have audited the accompanying financial statements of ABC Company, which comprise the balance sheet as of December 31, 20X1, and the related statements of income, changes in stockholders' equity, and cash flows for the year then ended, and the related notes to the financial statements, which, as described in note X to the financial statements, have been prepared on the basis of [*specify the financial reporting framework generally accepted*] in [*name of country*].

Management's Responsibility for the Financial Statements

Management is responsible for the preparation and fair presentation of these financial statements in accordance with [*specify the financial reporting framework generally accepted*] in [*name of country*]; this includes the design, implementation, and maintenance of internal control relevant to the preparation and fair presentation of financial statements that are free from material misstatement, whether due to fraud or error.

Auditor's Responsibility

Our responsibility is to express an opinion on these financial statements based on our audit. We conducted our audit in accordance with auditing standards generally accepted in the United States of America (and in [*name of country*]). Those standards require that we plan and perform the audit to obtain reasonable assurance about whether the financial statements are free from material misstatement.

An audit involves performing procedures to obtain audit evidence about the amounts and disclosures in the financial statements. The procedures selected depend on the auditor's judgment, including the assessment of the risks of material misstatement of the financial statements, whether due to fraud or error. In making those risk assessments, the auditor considers internal control relevant to the entity's preparation and fair presentation of the financial statements in order to design audit procedures that are appropriate in the circumstances, but not for the purpose of expressing an opinion on the effectiveness of the entity's internal control. Accordingly, we express no such opinion. An audit also includes evaluating the appropriateness of accounting policies used and the reasonableness of significant accounting estimates made by management, as well as evaluating the overall presentation of the financial statements.

We believe that the audit evidence we have obtained is sufficient and appropriate to provide a basis for our audit opinion.

Opinion

In our opinion, the financial statements referred to above present fairly, in all material respects, the financial position of ABC Company as of December 31, 20X1, and the results of its operations and its cash flows for the year then ended in accordance with [*specify the financial reporting framework generally accepted*] in [*name of country*].

[*Auditor's signature*]

[*Auditor's city and state*]

[*Date of the auditor's report*]

> **ILLUSTRATION 2. US FORM OF INDEPENDENT AUDITOR'S REPORT TO REPORT ON FINANCIAL STATEMENTS PREPARED IN ACCORDANCE WITH A FINANCIAL REPORTING FRAMEWORK GENERALLY ACCEPTED IN ANOTHER COUNTRY THAT ALSO ARE INTENDED FOR USE IN THE UNITED STATES**

Independent Auditor's Report

[*Appropriate Addressee*]

We have audited the accompanying financial statements of ABC Company, which comprise the balance sheet as of December 31, 20X1, and the related statements of income, changes in stockholders' equity, and cash flows for the year then ended, and the related notes to the financial statements, which, as described in note X to the financial statements, have been prepared on the basis of [*specify the financial reporting framework generally accepted*] in [*name of country*].

Management's Responsibility for the Financial Statements

Management is responsible for the preparation and fair presentation of these financial statements in accordance with [*specify the financial reporting framework generally accepted*] in [*name of country*]; this includes the design, implementation, and maintenance of internal control relevant to the preparation and fair presentation of financial statements that are free from material misstatement, whether due to fraud or error.

Auditor's Responsibility

Our responsibility is to express an opinion on these financial statements based on our audit. We conducted our audit in accordance with auditing standards generally accepted in the United States of America (and [*in name of country*]). Those standards require that we plan and perform the audit to obtain reasonable assurance about whether the financial statements are free from material misstatement.

An audit involves performing procedures to obtain audit evidence about the amounts and disclosures in the financial statements. The procedures selected depend on the auditor's judgment, including the assessment of the risks of material misstatement of the financial statements, whether due to fraud or error. In making those risk assessments, the auditor considers internal control relevant to the entity's preparation and fair presentation of the financial statements in order to design audit procedures that are appropriate in the circumstances, but not for the purpose of expressing an opinion on the effectiveness of the entity's internal control. Accordingly, we express no such opinion. An audit also includes evaluating the appropriateness of accounting policies used and the reasonableness of significant accounting estimates made by management, as well as evaluating the overall presentation of the financial statements.

We believe that the audit evidence we have obtained is sufficient and appropriate to provide a basis for our audit opinion.

Opinion

In our opinion, the financial statements referred to above present fairly, in all material respects, the financial position of ABC Company as of December 31, 20X1, and the results of its operations and its cash flows for the year then ended in accordance with [*specify the financial reporting framework generally accepted*] in [*name of country*].

Emphasis of Matter

As discussed in Note X to the financial statements, the Company prepares its financial statements in accordance with [*specify the financial reporting framework generally accepted*] in [*name of country*], which differ(s) from accounting principles generally accepted in the United States of America. Our opinion is not modified with respect to this matter.

[*Auditor's signature*]

[*Auditor's city and state*]

[*Date of the auditor's report*]

AU 543 Part of Audit Performed by Other Independent Auditors[1]

AU-C 600 Special Considerations—Audits of Group Financial Statements (Including the Work of Component Auditors)

AU EFFECTIVE DATE AND APPLICABILITY

Original Pronouncements	Statement on Auditing Procedure (SAP) 45 (codified in Statement on Auditing Standards [SAS] 1) and SAS 64.
Effective Date	These statements currently are effective.
Applicability	Audits of financial statements in accordance with generally accepted auditing standards (GAAS) when the auditor uses the work and reports of other independent auditors.

AU-C EFFECTIVE DATE AND SUMMARY OF CHANGES

SAS No. 122, *Codification of Auditing Standards and Procedures,* is effective for audits of financial statements with periods ending on or after December 15, 2012.

The AU 543 requirements will be superseded by AU-C 600. See the separate chapter on AU-C 600 for additional information.

---

[1] This section is affected by the Public Company Accounting Oversight Board's (PCAOB's) *Standard, Conforming Amendments to PCAOB Interim Standards Resulting from the Adoption of PCAOB Auditing Standard No. 5, An Audit of Internal Control over Financial Reporting That Is Integrated with an Audit of Financial Statements, and by an amendment to interim auditing standards made concurrently with the issuance of PCAOB Auditing Standard 3,* Audit Documentation.

AU DEFINITIONS OF TERMS

Other independent auditor. The auditor who expresses an opinion on the financial statements of a subsidiary, division, branch, or investee that are incorporated in the financial statements of the reporting entity.

Principal auditor. The auditor who expresses an opinion on the financial statements of the reporting entity. (The financial statements may be consolidated or combined, or the reporting entity may have significant investments accounted for by the equity method.) The principal auditor performs a significant portion of the work and has sufficient knowledge of the operations of the reporting entity. There is no strict quantitative measure for determining the principal auditor (see the section on "Techniques for Application").

OBJECTIVES OF AU SECTION 543

The financial statements of a part of a reporting entity may be audited by auditors other than the principal auditor. The parts audited by other auditors may be subsidiaries, divisions, branches, or investments accounted for by the equity method.

This section provides guidance on the professional judgments the auditor makes in deciding

1. Whether he or she may serve as principal auditor and use the work and reports of other auditors.
2. The form and content of the principal auditor's report when he or she uses the work and reports of other auditors.

NOTE: A principal auditor may refer to the work of other auditors in the report (see below) to indicate the divided responsibility of the auditors. This reference is not a qualification of the principal auditor's opinion. A report that makes reference to other auditors is not inferior to a report without such reference.

The basic notion of a report that makes reference to the report of the other auditor is *divided responsibility*. The principal auditor divides responsibility with the other auditor. For this reason the report should clearly describe the portion of the financial statements audited by the other auditor.

FUNDAMENTAL REQUIREMENTS

THE PRINCIPAL AUDITOR DECISION

When more than one auditor is involved in auditing the financial statements of the reporting entity, a decision must be made on which one is the principal auditor. In making the decision, the auditor should consider:

1. Proportions of assets, revenue, and income audited
2. Materiality and significance of the components audited
3. Overall knowledge and understanding of the reporting entity

RESPONSIBILITY FOR THE WORK OF OTHER AUDITORS

The principal auditor should decide whether to assume responsibility for the work of other auditors insofar as that work relates to his or her expression of an opinion on the financial statements taken as a whole.

Decision to Assume Responsibility

If the principal auditor decides to assume responsibility for the work of other auditors, he or she should *not* make reference in the report to the work of the other auditors.

Decision Not to Assume Responsibility

If the principal auditor decides not to assume responsibility for the work of other auditors, he or she should make reference in the report to the work of the other auditors (see Illustrations 1 and 2).

NOTE: *The decision to assume or not assume responsibility has significant legal as well as professional consequences. In a report that makes reference, the principal auditor does not intend to assume any legal responsibility for the work of the other auditor.*

Principal Auditor's Report with Reference

In the introductory paragraph of the report, the principal auditor should indicate the division of responsibility for the audited financial statements by disclosing the magnitude of the portion of those statements audited by other auditors. This is done by stating either the dollar amounts or the percentages that these amounts are to total assets, total revenues, net income or other criteria. The criteria selected depend on what most clearly indicates the portion of the financial statements audited by other auditors. The scope paragraph should also refer to the other auditors. The opinion paragraph should indicate that the opinion is based in part on the report of the other auditors.

NOTE: *The other auditor may be named only if he or she gives permission and if the report is presented with that of the principal auditor.*

REQUIRED PROCEDURES

Whether the principal auditor decides to make reference to the work of other auditors or makes no reference, he or she should:

1. Make inquiries concerning the professional reputation and independence of the other auditors
2. Coordinate his or her activities with those of the other auditors

(See "Techniques for Application.")

ADDITIONAL PROCEDURES UNDER DECISION TO ASSUME RESPONSIBILITY

The extent of additional procedures is determined by the principal auditor. These procedures might include the following:

1. Visit the other auditor and discuss his or her audit procedures
2. Review the other auditor's audit program

> NOTE: The principal auditor should consider directing the other auditor as to the scope of his or her work.

3. Review the other auditor's audit documentation
4. Participate in discussions with management of the component whose financial statements are being audited by the other auditor
5. Perform supplemental tests of the accounting records of the component whose financial statements are being audited by the other auditor

MODIFICATION OF OPINION

If he or she decides neither to assume responsibility for the other auditor's work nor to accept a division of responsibility with him or her, the principal auditor should qualify his or her opinion or disclaim an opinion. The reasons should be stated, and the magnitude of the portion of the financial statements responsible for the qualification or disclaimer should be disclosed.

MODIFICATIONS IN OTHER AUDITOR'S REPORT

If the other auditor's opinion is other than a standard report, the principal auditor should decide whether to recognize the modification in his or her own report. The decision is based on the nature and significance of the modification and its materiality in relation to the financial statements of the reporting entity taken as a whole.

> NOTE: If the subject of the modification is not material and the other auditor's report is not presented, the principal auditor is not required to make reference to the matter in the report. If the other auditor's report is presented, however, the principal auditor may decide to refer to the modification even if the matter is not material to the financial statements of the reporting entity. For example, he or she may state that the matter is not material.

INTERPRETATIONS

SPECIFIC PROCEDURES PERFORMED BY THE OTHER AUDITOR AT THE PRINCIPAL AUDITOR'S REQUEST (ISSUED APRIL 1979; REVISED NOVEMBER 1996)

When the principal auditor requests that the other auditor perform procedures, the principal auditor should provide specific instructions on procedures to be performed, materiality considerations for that purpose, and other information that may be necessary in the circumstances. The other auditor should perform the requested procedures in accordance with the instructions and report the findings solely for the use of the principal auditor. These auditor-to-auditor communications do not have to meet the requirements of an agreed-upon procedures engagement.

INQUIRIES OF THE PRINCIPAL AUDITOR BY THE OTHER AUDITOR (APRIL 1979)

The other auditor should inquire of the principal auditor regarding related-party transactions. The other auditor should consider whether to make additional inquiries based on whether there are unusual or complex transactions or relationships between the component he or she is auditing and the components audited by the principal auditor. Also, the other auditor should consider whether, in the past, matters relevant to his or her own audit were known by the principal auditor.

The other auditor might provide the principal auditor with a draft of the financial statements and audit report expected to be issued to facilitate the principal auditor's response.

FORM OF INQUIRIES OF THE PRINCIPAL AUDITOR MADE BY THE OTHER AUDITOR (APRIL 1979)

See the "AU Illustrations" section for an example of the form of inquiry letter the other auditor might send the principal auditor.

If the principal auditor's response is limited because his or her audit has not progressed to a point that enables a meaningful response, the other auditor should consider whether acceptable alternative procedures can be applied, whether to delay report issuance, or whether to qualify or disclaim an opinion because of the scope limitation.

FORM OF PRINCIPAL AUDITOR'S RESPONSE TO INQUIRIES FROM OTHER AUDITORS (APRIL 1979)

The principal auditor's response may be written or oral, depending on what the other auditor has requested.

See "AU Illustrations" for an example of a principal auditor's written response. Information that may have a significant effect on the other auditor's audit should be in writing.

PROCEDURES OF THE PRINCIPAL AUDITOR (APRIL 1979)

The principal auditor's response should ordinarily be made by the auditor with final responsibility for the engagement. This auditor should take reasonable steps to be informed of matters pertinent to the other auditor's inquiry, such as inquiring of principal assistants and directing them to keep him or her informed of significant matters. Procedures directed solely toward responding to the other auditor that would not affect his or her own audit are not required. However, the principal auditor should update the response for significant matters that come to his or her attention after the original response, but before completion of the audit.

APPLICATION OF ADDITIONAL PROCEDURES CONCERNING THE AUDIT PERFORMED BY THE OTHER AUDITOR (DECEMBER 1981; REVISED MARCH 2006)

The principal auditor's judgment about the extent of additional procedures to be applied, if any, to obtain information about the adequacy of the other auditor's audit may be affected by knowledge of the other auditor's quality control policies and procedures.

Other factors that might affect the extent of additional procedures are previous experience with the other auditor, the materiality of the portion of the financial statements audited by the other auditor, the extent of control of the principal auditor over the other auditor's work, and results of the principal auditor's other procedures.

TECHNIQUES FOR APPLICATION

DETERMINATION OF PRINCIPAL AUDITOR

There are no simple rules or precise formulas for determining who is the principal auditor. The decision is based on professional judgment; however, consideration should be given to the following:

1. Proportions of assets, revenue, and income audited
2. Materiality and significance of the components audited
3. Overall knowledge and understanding of the reporting entity

Presumption of Securities and Exchange Commission

There is no rule that the principal auditor should audit a specific proportion of the financial statement amounts; however, the Securities and Exchange Commission (SEC) staff informally has taken the position that a majority coverage of total assets, revenue, or net income, whichever is appropriate, is presumed necessary.

Many auditors use the same guidelines that the SEC follows. Before serving as principal auditor, they would ordinarily need to audit at least a majority of total assets or total revenue. This guideline is used as a goal, however, rather than as an arbitrary cutoff. Some of the factors that may cause auditors not to adhere to percentages of total assets or total revenue are:

1. *Unusual years*. The financial position or operating results in a particular year may have been affected by unusual circumstances that cause the normal relationships among components to be temporarily out of line.
2. *Centralization of control*. The parent or controlling entity may exert such control over the operations and accounting of other components that the auditor of that entity has sufficient knowledge of the other components without auditing them.
3. *Unusual components*. The nature of the business of components may be such that asset size is out of proportion to the importance of such components. For example, a financial institution may be large in size but not proportionately important to a consolidated group.
4. *Equal components*. The components may be nearly equal in size so that no single component has a majority of assets or revenue, and each component may historically have had different auditors. In this case, someone has to act as principal auditor, and the principal auditor will ordinarily gain sufficient knowledge of the other components by applying some of the procedures suggested in the section for circumstances when there is a decision not to make reference.
5. *Past experience*. The auditor may have audited the financial statements of some components in prior years and, thus, have sufficient knowledge of them to act as principal auditor.
6. *Change of auditors planned*. A change in auditors may be planned so that an auditor who will audit a majority of assets or revenue in future years considers it efficient to obtain sufficient knowledge of those components in the current year.

DECISION TO ASSUME RESPONSIBILITY

Ordinarily, the principal auditor is able to assume responsibility for the work of other auditors when:

1. The other auditor is an associated or correspondent firm.
2. The other auditor was retained by the principal auditor, *and* the work was supervised by the principal auditor.
3. The principal auditor applies procedures he or she considers necessary to be satisfied about the quality of the other auditor's audit.
4. The portion of the financial statements audited by other auditors is not material to the financial statements reported on by the principal auditor.

Other factors the principal auditor should consider are:

1. The quality control policies and procedures of the other auditor and the results of past peer reviews (see discussion in "Reputation and Independence of Other Auditors")
2. Previous experience with the other auditor
3. Control that he or she will exercise over the conduct of the other auditor's audit

DECISION NOT TO ASSUME RESPONSIBILITY

The principal auditor may decide not to assume responsibility for the work of other auditors because:

1. It is impracticable to review their work or perform other procedures.
2. The financial statements of the components audited by other auditors may be extremely material in relation to the total, regardless of any other considerations.

REPUTATION AND INDEPENDENCE OF OTHER AUDITORS

To determine the reputation and independence of the other auditors, the principal auditor might apply such procedures as:

1. Communicate with the American Institute of Certified Public Accountants (AICPA), the applicable state societies of CPAs, or, in the case of a foreign auditor, the corresponding professional organization.

    a. The Professional Ethics Division will respond to inquiries about whether individuals are members of the Institute and whether complaints against members have been adjudicated.
    b. The Division for CPA Firms will:

      (1) Respond to inquiries about whether specific firms are members of either the AICPA Alliance for CPA Firms (formerly the Private Companies Practice Section) or the SEC Practice Section.
      (2) Indicate whether a firm has undergone peer review. (For a fee, copies of peer review reports will be supplied.)
      (3) Indicate whether any sanctions against a firm have been announced.

    c. The AICPA Practice Monitoring Staff or the appropriate state society can respond as to whether firms are members and indicate whether the firm had a quality review.

2. Make inquiries of bankers, credit agencies, other credit grantors, attorneys, and other professionals about the reputation of the other auditors.
3. Obtain a representation (see "AU Illustrations") from the other auditors that they are independent as required by the AICPA and, if appropriate, the SEC.

COORDINATION OF ACTIVITIES

The principal auditor may wish to have the other auditor perform certain procedures. In these circumstances, he or she should provide specific instructions on procedures to be performed, materiality considerations for this purpose, and other necessary information.

NOTE: *The other auditor should perform the requested procedures in accordance with the principal auditor's instructions.*

The principal auditor should communicate with the other auditor to determine that:

1. The auditor is aware that the financial statements he or she will audit will be included in the financial statements on which the principal auditor will report.
2. The auditor is aware that his or her report will be relied on or, if applicable, referred to by the principal auditor.
3. The auditor has knowledge of financial reporting requirements of regulatory agencies, such as the SEC, if appropriate.
4. The auditor is aware that a review will be made to determine uniformity of accounting practices and elimination of intercompany transactions and accounts.

NOTE: For foreign auditors, the principal auditor should determine that they are familiar with US generally accepted accounting principles (GAAP) and GAAS and that they will conduct their audits and report in accordance with these principles and standards.

LONG-TERM INVESTMENTS

Equity Method

For investments accounted for under the equity method, the investor's auditor is similar to a principal auditor. In these circumstances, it is prudent for the investor's auditor to refer to the work of the investee's auditor.

Cost Method

For investments accounted for under the cost method, the work and reports of other auditors may be a significant part of the evidence for these investments. In these circumstances, depending on the materiality of the investments in relation to the financial statements taken as a whole, the investor's auditor may be similar to a principal auditor.

AU ILLUSTRATIONS

The following principal auditor reports are illustrated below:

1. Reference to subsidiary's auditor
2. Reference to investee's auditor

The following also are illustrated:

3. Representation letter from the other auditor.
4. Letter of inquiry from other auditor to principal auditor.
5. Principal auditor's response to letter of inquiry from other auditor.

ILLUSTRATION 1. REFERENCE TO SUBSIDIARY'S AUDITOR (ADAPTED FROM AU 543.09)

To the Board of Directors
Widget Company
Main City, USA

Independent Auditor's Report

We have audited the accompanying balance sheet of Widget Company and subsidiaries as of December 31, 20X5, and the related consolidated statements of income and retained earnings and cash flows for the year then ended. These financial statements are the responsibility of the Company's management. Our responsibility is to express an opinion on these financial statements based on our audits. We did not audit the financial statements of Basic Company, a wholly owned subsidiary, which statements reflect total assets and revenues constituting 20% and 22%, respectively, of the related consolidated totals. Those statements were audited by other auditors whose report has been furnished to us, and our opinion, insofar as it relates to the amounts included for Basic Company, is based solely on the report of the other auditors.

We conducted our audit in accordance with auditing standards generally accepted in the United States of America. Those standards require that we plan and perform the audit to obtain reasonable assurance about whether the financial statements are free of material misstatement. An audit includes examining, on a test basis, evidence supporting the amounts and disclosures in the financial statements. An audit also includes assessing the accounting principles used and significant estimates made by management, as well as evaluating the overall financial statement presentation. We believe that our audit and the report of the other auditors provide a reasonable basis for our opinion.

In our opinion, based on our audit and the report of the other auditors, the consolidated financial statements referred to above present fairly, in all material respects, the financial position of Widget Company as of December 31, 20X5, and the results of its operations and its cash flows for the year then ended in conformity with accounting principles generally accepted in the United States of America.

Smith and Jones
February 15, 20X6

ILLUSTRATION 2. REFERENCE TO INVESTEE'S AUDITOR

To the Board of Directors
Widget Company
Main City, USA

Independent Auditor's Report

We have audited the consolidated balance sheet of Widget Company and subsidiaries as of December 31, 20X5, and the related consolidated statements of income and retained earnings and cash flows for the year then ended. These financial statements are the responsibility of the Company's management. Our responsibility is to express an opinion on these financial statements based on our audit. We did not audit the financial statements of Basic Company, an affiliated company, owned 25% in 20X5, which is accounted for in the accompanying financial statements by the equity method of accounting. The equity in net income of this affiliated company constitutes 15% of net income for the year ended December 31, 20X5. The financial statements of the affiliated company were audited by other auditors, whose report has been furnished to us, and our opinion, insofar as it relates to the amounts included for Basic Company, is based solely on the report of the other auditors.

We conducted our audit in accordance with auditing standards generally accepted in the United States of America. Those standards require that we plan and perform the audit to obtain reasonable assurance about whether the financial statements are free of material misstatement. An audit includes examining, on a test basis, evidence supporting the amounts and disclosures in the financial statements. An audit also includes assessing the accounting principles used and significant estimates made by management, as well as evaluating the overall financial statement presentation. We believe that our audit and the report of the other auditors provides a reasonable basis for our opinion.

In our opinion, based on our audit and the report of the other auditors, the consolidated financial statements referred to above present fairly, in all material respects, the financial position of Widget Company as of [at] December 31, 20X5, and the results of its operations and its cash flows for the year then ended in conformity with accounting principles generally accepted in the United States of America.

Smith and Jones
February 15, 20X6

ILLUSTRATION 3. REPRESENTATION LETTER FROM OTHER AUDITOR

[*Other auditor's letterhead*]
[*Date*]
Principal Auditor
[*Address*]

Gentlemen:

We have audited the financial statements of ABC, Inc., for the year ended December 31, 20X6. Because you will report on the consolidated financial statements of Widget Company for the year ended December 31, 20X6, which will include the financial statements of ABC, Inc., we have been requested to furnish you with the following information for the period covered by our report.

1. Our firm is independent with respect to the parent company, any subsidiary, or affiliated companies following the provisions of the AICPA Code of Professional Conduct and the independence rulings of the SEC; for example

   a. None of the partners of our firm, nor any of the staff members employed by any office doing the work on this audit, has any direct or material indirect financial interest in or indebtedness owing from the parent company, any subsidiary, or affiliated companies.
   b. None of the partners of our firm, nor any of the staff members employed by any office doing the work on this audit, is connected with the parent company, any subsidiary, or affiliated companies as a promoter, underwriter, voting trustee, director, officer, or employee.
   c. To the best of our knowledge, there are no other relationships or circumstances that would impair our independence with respect to the parent company or any subsidiary or affiliate companies.

2. In connection with our audit of ABC, Inc., nothing has come to our attention that in our judgment would have a material effect on, or require mention in, the financial statements of Widget Company.

3. The financial statements as reported on by us are suitable for consolidation with Widget Company, with adjustment only for normal consolidation and elimination entries, as follows:

   [*Itemization*]

   _____
   _____

4. We understand that in reporting on XYZ Company, you will cite your reliance on our report covering our audit of ABC, Inc.

Yours very truly,
[*Other auditor's firm signature*]

ILLUSTRATION 4. LETTER OF INQUIRY FROM OTHER AUDITOR TO PRINCIPAL AUDITOR (FROM AU 9543.09)

We are auditing the financial statements of [*name of client*] as of [*date*] and for the [*financial statement period*] for the purpose of expressing an opinion on whether the financial statements present fairly, in all material respects, the financial position, results of operations, and cash flows of [*name of client*] in conformity with accounting principles generally accepted in the United States of America.

A draft of the financial statements referred to above and a draft of our report are enclosed solely to aid you in responding to this inquiry. Please provide us [*in writing/orally*] with the following information in connection with your current audit of the consolidated financial statements of [*name of parent company*]:

1. Transactions or other matters [*including adjustments made during consolidation or contemplated at the date of your reply*] that have come to your attention that you believe require adjustment to or disclosure in the financial statements of [*name of client*] being audited by us.
2. Any limitation on the scope of your audit that is related to the financial statements of [*name of client*] being audited by us, or that limits your ability to provide us with the information requested in this inquiry.

Please make your response as of a date near [*expected date of the auditor's report*].

NOTE: The letter should be addressed to the principal auditor and signed by the other auditor.

ILLUSTRATION 5. PRINCIPAL AUDITOR'S RESPONSE TO LETTER OF INQUIRY FROM OTHER AUDITOR (FROM AU 9543.14)

This letter is furnished to you in response to your request that we provide you with certain information in connection with your audit of the financial statements of [*name of components*], and [*subsidiary, division, branch, or investment*] of Parent Company for the year ended [*date*].

We are in the process of performing an audit of the consolidated financial statements of Parent Company for the year ended [*date*] (but have not completed our work as of this date). The objective of our audit is to enable us to express an opinion on the consolidated financial statements of Parent Company and, accordingly, we have performed no procedures directed toward identifying matters that would not affect our audit or our report. However, solely for the purpose of responding to your inquiry, we have read the draft of the financial statements of [*name of component*] as of [*date*] and for the [*period of audit*] and the draft of your report on them, included with your inquiry dated [*date of inquiry*].

Based solely on the work we have performed [to date] in connection with our audit of the consolidated cash flows, which would not necessarily reveal all or any of the matters covered in your inquiry, we advise you that:

1. No transactions or other matters (including adjustments made during consolidation or contemplated at this date) have come to our attention that we believe require adjustment to, or disclosure in, the financial statements of [*name of component*] being audited by you.
2. No limitation has been placed by Parent Company on the scope of our audit that, to our knowledge, is related to the financial statements [*of name of component*] being audited by you that has limited our ability to provide you with the information requested in your inquiry.

NOTE: The letter should be addressed to the other auditor and signed by the principal auditor.

AU-C 600 SPECIAL CONSIDERATIONS—AUDITS OF GROUP FINANCIAL STATEMENTS (INCLUDING THE WORK OF COMPONENT AUDITORS)

AU-C EFFECTIVE DATE AND APPLICABILITY

Original Pronouncements	Statement on Auditing Standards (SAS) 122
Effective Date	This standard is currently effective.
Applicability	All audits in accordance with generally accepted auditing standards and other services covered by SASs.

NOTE: All sections apply whether the financial statements are presented in conformity with generally accepted accounting principles (GAAP) or other comprehensive basis of accounting (OCBOA) unless otherwise noted.

AU-C EFFECTIVE DATE AND SUMMARY OF CHANGES

SAS No. 122, *Codification of Auditing Standards and Procedures,* is effective for audits of group financial statements with periods ending on or after December 15, 2012.

The effort to converge US generally accepted accounting standards (GAAS) with international standards on auditing resulted in the introduction of the "Group Audit" standard. This standard is based on ISA 600, *The Work of Related Auditors and Other Auditors in the Audit of Group Financial Statements.* AU 543 contains only limited guidance in this area.

AU-C 600 introduces several new concepts (see also the definitions section below):

- Component—performs work on the financial auditor—no longer referred to as "other auditor"
- Group
- Group engagement—this term replaces "principal auditor"
- Group engagement team
- Group financial statements—encompasses not only consolidated or combined financial statements, but also business activities in addition to separate entities. This standard applies regardless of whether or not different auditors are involved.

AU-C 600 creates significant changes in the scoping of multilocation audits. In its risk alert, *Understanding the Responsibilities of Auditors for Audits of Group Financial State-*

ments—2012, the AICPA identifies the following items that may have the most impact on current practice:

- Acceptance and continuance considerations
- The group engagement team's process to assess risk
- The determination of materiality to be used to audit the group financial statements
- The determination of materiality to be used for procedures related to components
- The selection of components, account balances, or both; classes of transactions; or disclosures for testing
- Identification of significant component
- Communications between the group engagement team and component auditors
- Assessing the adequacy and appropriateness of audit evidence by the group engagement team in forming an opinion on the group financial statements

AU-C 600 DEFINITIONS OF TERMS

Source: AU-C 600.11

Component. An entity or business activity for which group or component management prepares financial information that is required by the applicable financial reporting framework to be included in the group financial statements.

Component auditor. An auditor who performs work on the financial information of a component that will be used as audit evidence for the group audit. A component auditor may be part of the group engagement partner's firm, a network firm of the group engagement partner's firm, or another firm.

Component management. Management responsible for preparing the financial information of a component.

Component materiality. The materiality for a component determined by the group engagement team for the purposes of the group audit.

Group. All the components whose financial information is included in the group financial statements. A group always has more than one component.

Group audit. The audit of group financial statements.

Group audit opinion. The audit opinion on the group financial statements.

Group engagement partner. The partner or other person in the firm who is responsible for the group audit engagement and its performance and for the auditor's report on the group financial statements that is issued on behalf of the firm. When joint auditors conduct the group audit, the joint engagement partners and their engagement teams collectively constitute the group engagement partner and the group engagement team. This section does not, however, address the relationship between joint auditors or the work that one joint auditor performs in relation to the work of the other joint auditor.

Group engagement team. Partners, including the group engagement partner, and staff who establish the overall group audit strategy, communicate with component auditors, perform work on the consolidation process, and evaluate the conclusions drawn from the audit evidence as the basis for forming an opinion on the group financial statements.

Group financial statements. Financial statements that include the financial information of more than one component. The term *group financial statements* also refers to combined financial statements aggregating the financial information prepared by components that are under common control.

Group management. Management responsible for the preparation and fair presentation of the group financial statements.

Group-wide controls. Controls designed, implemented, and maintained by group management over group financial reporting.

Significant component. A component identified by the group engagement team (a) that is of individual financial significance to the group, or (b) that, due to its specific nature or circumstances, is likely to include significant risks of material misstatement of the group financial statements.

OBJECTIVES OF AU-C SECTION 600

AU-C Section 600 states that:

. . . the objectives of the auditor are to determine whether to act as the auditor of the group financial statements and, if so, to

> *a. determine whether to make reference to the audit of a component auditor in the auditor's report on the group financial statements;*
> *b. communicate clearly with component auditors; and*
> *c. obtain sufficient appropriate audit evidence regarding the financial information of the components and the consolidation process to express an opinion about whether the group financial statements are prepared, in all material respects, in accordance with the applicable financial reporting framework.*

FUNDAMENTAL REQUIREMENTS

The clarified SAS articulates the degree of involvement required when reference is made to component auditors in the auditor's report. If the group engagement partner does not make reference to a component auditor in the auditor's report, all of the requirements of the clarified SAS apply. If the group engagement partner does make reference to the component auditor in auditor's report, some of the requirements do not apply.

For reference to the component auditor to be made in the auditor's report on the group financial statements, the component financial statements need to be prepared using the same financial reporting framework as the group financial statements and the component auditor has performed an audit on the financial statements of the component in accordance with GAAS or, when required by law or regulation, with auditing standards promulgated by the Public Company Accounting Oversight Board. The Accounting Standards Board (ASB) believes that this requirement makes explicit what is implicit in extant AU Section 543.

Responsibilities

The group engagement partner is responsible for:

- Direction, supervision, and performance of the group audit engagement in compliance with professional standards and regulatory and legal requirements and
- Determining whether the auditor's report that is issued is appropriate in the circumstances

The group engagement team or the firm may assist the group engagement partner in fulfilling the group audit responsibilities. The clarified SAS provides guidance on when such assistance is permitted. Reference the definitions section of this chapter for more on roles and responsibilities.

Engagement Acceptance and Continuance

Auditors must base their determination on whether or not to accept an engagement or continue with a client on whether the auditor believes they believe they will be able to obtain sufficient appropriate audit evidence over the group financial statements, including whether the group engagement team will have appropriate access to information.

Risk Assessment Standards

The extant SAS was written prior to the risk assessment standards. The clarified SAS incorporates application of the risk assessment standards into the performance of group audits and discusses specific applications.

Involvement with Component Auditors

The clarified SAS requires the group engagement team to gain an understanding of the component auditor, including:

- Professional competence
- Ethical requirements, particularly independence, and
- The extent to which the group engagement team will be able to be involved in the work of the component auditor (a new requirement)

After gaining an understanding of the component auditor, the group engagement partner may choose to either:

- Assume responsibility for, and thus be required to be involved in, the work of component auditors, insofar as that work relates to the expression of an opinion on the group financial statements, or
- Not assume responsibility for, and accordingly make reference to, the audit of a component auditor in the auditor's report on the group financial statements

Involvement in the work performed by a component auditor involves the group engagement team:

- Establishing component materiality to be used by the component auditor.
- Performing risk assessment procedures, and
- Participating in the assessment of risks of material misstatement and the planned audit response

These may be performed together with the component auditor or by the group engagement team.

Materiality

The clarified SAS requires the group engagement team to determine:

- Materiality, including performance materiality for the group as a whole,
- Component materiality—determined by the group engagement team, whether or not the group engagement partner is making reference to the audit of a component auditor, and
- Thresholds for recording passed adjustments.

Component materiality, including performance materiality, must be lower than group materiality.

Assessed Risks

The clarified SAS includes requirements and guidance relating to work to be performed on all components for which the group engagement partner is assuming responsibility for the work of the component auditor, whether that work is performed by the group engagement team or component auditors. The clarified SAS includes requirements and guidance specifying the nature, timing, and extent of group engagement team's involvement in the work of the component auditors.

The auditor must audit components that are financially significant. For components considered significant due to their likelihood of including significant risks of material misstatements, an audit or other audit procedures are performed. For components that are not significant, the group engagement team performs analytical procedures at the group level.

The clarified SAS also includes requirements and guidance related to:

- Internal controls,
- The consolidation process, and
- Subsequent events.

Communication with Others

The group engagement team is required to

- Communicate specific items to the component auditor,
- Request that the component auditor communicate with the group engagement team about certain matters, and
- Communicate specific items to group management or those charged with governance of the group, or both.

Documentation

The clarified SAS requires specific documentation, including:

- An analysis of the components indicating the significant components and the type of work performed on the components.
- Nature, timing, and extent of involvement of group team with component auditors.
- Written communications between the group team and component auditors.
- The financial statements and audit reports of those components to which the group auditor is making reference.

ILLUSTRATIONS

The following Appendices and Exhibits are from AU-C 600.

- Appendix A. Understanding the Group, Its Components, and Their Environments—Examples of Matters about Which the Group Engagement Team Obtains an Understanding
- Appendix B. Examples of Conditions or Events That May Indicate Risks of Material Misstatement of the Group Financial Statements

- Appendix C. Required and Additional Matters Included in the Group Engagement Team's Letter of Instruction
- Exhibit A. Illustrations of Auditor's Reports on Group Financial Statements
  - Illustration 1—A Report with a Qualified Opinion When the Group Engagement Team Is Not Able to Obtain Sufficient Appropriate Audit Evidence on Which to Base the Group Audit Opinion
  - Illustration 2—A Report in Which the Auditor of the Group Financial Statements Is Making Reference to the Audit of a Component Auditor
    - Illustration of Potential Component Auditor Representations in Governmental Entities and Not-for-Profit Organizations
- Exhibit B. Illustrative Component Auditor's Confirmation Letter
- Exhibit C. Sources of Information

APPENDIX A. UNDERSTANDING THE GROUP, ITS COMPONENTS, AND THEIR ENVIRONMENTS—EXAMPLES OF MATTERS ABOUT WHICH THE GROUP ENGAGEMENT TEAM OBTAINS AN UNDERSTANDING

The examples provided cover a broad range of matters; however, not all matters are relevant to every group audit engagement, and the list of examples is not necessarily complete.

Group-Wide Controls

Group-wide controls may include a combination of the following:

- Regular meetings between group and component management to discuss business developments and review performance
- Monitoring of components' operations and their financial results, including regular reporting routines, which enables group management to monitor components' performance against budgets and take appropriate action
- Group management's risk assessment process (that is, the process for identifying, analyzing, and managing business risks, including the risk of fraud, that may result in material misstatement of the group financial statements)
- Monitoring, controlling, reconciling, and eliminating intragroup account balances, transactions, and unrealized profits or losses at group level
- A process for monitoring the timeliness and assessing the accuracy and completeness of financial information received from components
- A central IT system controlled by the same general IT controls for all or part of the group
- Control activities within an IT system that are common for all or some components
- Monitoring of controls, including activities of internal audit and self-assessment programs
- Consistent policies and procedures, including a group financial reporting procedures manual
- Group-wide programs, such as codes of conduct and fraud prevention programs
- Arrangements for assigning authority and responsibility to component management

Internal audit may be regarded as part of group-wide controls, for example, when the internal audit function is centralized. *The Auditor's Consideration of the Internal Audit Function in an Audit of Financial Statements* addresses the group engagement team's evaluation of the competence and objectivity of the internal auditors when it plans to use their work.

Consolidation Process

The group engagement team's understanding of the consolidation process may include matters such as the following:

- Matters relating to the applicable financial reporting framework, such as the following:

    - The extent to which component management has an understanding of the applicable financial reporting framework
    - The process for identifying and accounting for components, in accordance with the applicable financial reporting framework
    - The process for identifying reportable segments for segment reporting, in accordance with the applicable financial reporting framework
    - The process for identifying related party relationships and related party transactions for reporting, in accordance with the applicable financial reporting framework
    - The accounting policies applied to the group financial statements, changes from those of the previous financial year, and changes resulting from new or revised standards under the applicable financial reporting framework
    - The procedures for dealing with components with financial year-ends different from the group's year-end

- Matters relating to the consolidation process, such as the following:

    - Group management's process for obtaining an understanding of the accounting policies used by components and, when applicable, ensuring that uniform accounting policies are used to prepare the financial information of the components for the group financial statements and that differences in accounting policies are identified and adjusted, when required, in terms of the applicable financial reporting framework. Uniform accounting policies are the specific principles, bases, conventions, rules, and practices adopted by the group, based on the applicable financial reporting framework, that the components use to report similar transactions consistently. These policies are ordinarily described in the financial reporting procedures manual and reporting package issued by group management.
    - Group management's process for ensuring complete, accurate, and timely financial reporting by the components for the consolidation
    - The process for translating the financial information of foreign components into the currency of the group financial statements
    - How IT is organized for the consolidation, including the manual and automated stages of the process and the manual and programmed controls in place at various stages of the consolidation process
    - Group management's process for obtaining information on subsequent events

- Matters relating to consolidation adjustments, such as the following:

    - The process for recording consolidation adjustments, including the preparation, authorization, and processing of related journal entries and the experience of personnel responsible for the consolidation

- The consolidation adjustments required by the applicable financial reporting framework
- Business rationale for the events and transactions that gave rise to the consolidation adjustments
- Frequency, nature, and size of transactions between components
- Procedures for monitoring, controlling, reconciling, and eliminating intragroup account balances, transactions, and unrealized profits or losses
- Steps taken to arrive at the fair value of acquired assets and liabilities, procedures for amortizing goodwill (when applicable), and impairment testing of goodwill, in accordance with the applicable financial reporting framework
- Arrangements with a controlling interest or noncontrolling interest regarding losses incurred by a component (for example, an obligation of the noncontrolling interest to compensate such losses)

APPENDIX B. EXAMPLES OF CONDITIONS OR EVENTS THAT MAY INDICATE RISKS OF MATERIAL MISSTATEMENT OF THE GROUP FINANCIAL STATEMENTS

The examples provided cover a broad range of conditions or events; however, not all conditions or events are relevant to every group audit engagement, and the following list of examples is not necessarily complete:

- A complex group structure, especially when there are frequent acquisitions, disposals, or reorganizations
- Poor corporate governance structures, including decision-making processes, that are not transparent
- Nonexistent or ineffective groupwide controls, including inadequate group management information on monitoring of components' operations and their results
- Components operating in foreign jurisdictions that may be exposed to factors such as unusual government intervention in areas such as trade and fiscal policy, restrictions on currency and dividend movements, and fluctuations in exchange rates
- Business activities of components that involve high risk, such as long-term contracts or trading in innovative or complex financial instruments
- Uncertainties regarding which components' financial information requires incorporation in the group financial statements, in accordance with the applicable financial reporting framework (for example, whether any special-purpose entities or nontrading entities exist and require incorporation)
- Unusual related-party relationships and transactions
- Prior occurrences of intragroup account balances that did not balance or reconcile on consolidation
- The existence of complex transactions that are accounted for in more than one component
- Components' application of accounting policies that differ from those applied to the group financial statements
- Components with different financial year-ends, which may be utilized to manipulate the timing of transactions
- Prior occurrences of unauthorized or incomplete consolidation adjustments
- Aggressive tax planning within the group or large cash transactions with entities in tax havens

- Frequent changes of auditors engaged to audit the financial statements of components

APPENDIX C. REQUIRED AND ADDITIONAL MATTERS INCLUDED IN THE GROUP ENGAGEMENT TEAM'S LETTER OF INSTRUCTION

The following matters are relevant to the planning of the work of a component auditor: [*Required matters are italicized.*]

- *A request for the component auditor, knowing the context in which the group engagement team will use the work of the component auditor, to confirm that the component auditor will cooperate with the group engagement team*
- The timetable for completing the audit
- Dates of planned visits by group management and the group engagement team and dates of planned meetings with component management and the component auditor
- A list of key contacts
- *The work to be performed by the component auditor, the use to be made of that work, and arrangements for coordinating efforts at the initial stage of and during the audit, including the group engagement team's planned involvement in the work of the component auditor*
- *The ethical requirements that are relevant to the group audit and, in particular, the independence requirements*
- In the case of an audit or review of the financial information of the component, component materiality
- *In the case of an audit or review of, or specified audit procedures performed on, the financial information of the component, the threshold above which misstatements cannot be regarded as clearly trivial to the group financial statements*
- *A list of related parties prepared by group management and any other related parties of which the group engagement team is aware and a request that the component auditor communicates on a timely basis to the group engagement team related parties not previously identified by group management or the group engagement team*
- Work to be performed on intragroup account balances, transactions, and unrealized profits or losses
- Guidance on other statutory reporting responsibilities (for example, reporting on group management's assertion on the effectiveness of internal control)
- When a time lag between completion of the work on the financial information of the components and the group engagement team's conclusion on the group financial statements is likely, specific instructions for a subsequent events review

The following matters are relevant to the conduct of the work of the component auditor:

- The findings of the group engagement team's tests of control activities of a processing system that is common for all or some components and tests of controls to be performed by the component auditor
- *Identified significant risks of material misstatement of the group financial statements, due to fraud or error, that are relevant to the work of the component auditor, and a request that the component auditor communicate on a timely basis any other significant risks of material misstatement of the group financial statements, due to fraud or error, identified in the component and the component auditor's response to such risks*

- The findings of internal audit, based on work performed on controls at or relevant to components
- A request for timely communication of audit evidence obtained from performing work on the financial information of the components that contradicts the audit evidence on which the group engagement team originally based the risk assessment performed at group level
- A request for a written representation on component management's compliance with the applicable financial reporting framework or a statement that differences between the accounting policies applied to the financial information of the component and those applied to the group financial statements have been disclosed
- Matters to be documented by the component auditor

Other information, such as the following:

- A request that the following be reported to the group engagement team on a timely basis:
  - Significant accounting, financial reporting, and auditing matters, including accounting estimates and related judgments
  - Matters relating to the going concern status of the component
  - Matters relating to litigation and claims
  - Material weaknesses in controls that have come to the attention of the component auditor during the performance of the work on the financial information of the component and information that indicates the existence of fraud
- A request that the group engagement team be notified of any significant or unusual events as early as possible
- A request that the matters listed in be communicated to the group engagement team when the work on the financial information of the component is completed

EXHIBIT A. ILLUSTRATIONS OF AUDITOR'S REPORTS ON GROUP FINANCIAL STATEMENTS

ILLUSTRATION 1. A REPORT WITH A QUALIFIED OPINION WHEN THE GROUP ENGAGEMENT TEAM IS NOT ABLE TO OBTAIN SUFFICIENT APPROPRIATE AUDIT EVIDENCE ON WHICH TO BASE THE GROUP AUDIT OPINION

In this example, the group engagement team is unable to obtain sufficient appropriate audit evidence relating to a significant component accounted for by the equity method because the group engagement team was unable to obtain the audited financial statements of the component as of December 31, 20X1 and 20X0, including the auditor's report thereon. In this example, the auditor of the group financial statements is not making reference to the report of a component auditor.

In the auditor's professional judgment, the effect on the group financial statements of this inability to obtain sufficient appropriate audit evidence is material but not pervasive.

If, in the auditor's professional judgment, the effect on the group financial statements of the inability to obtain sufficient appropriate audit evidence is material and pervasive, the auditor would disclaim an opinion, in accordance with *Modifications to the Opinion in the Independent Auditor's Report*.

Independent Auditor's Report

[*Appropriate Addressee*]

Report on the Consolidated Financial Statements

We have audited the accompanying consolidated financial statements of ABC Company and its subsidiaries, which comprise the consolidated balance sheets as of December 31, 20X1 and 20X0, and the related consolidated statements of income, changes in stockholders' equity, and cash flows for the years then ended, and the related notes to the financial statements.

Management's Responsibility for the Financial Statements

Management is responsible for the preparation and fair presentation of these consolidated financial statements in accordance with accounting principles generally accepted in the United States of America; this includes the design, implementation, and maintenance of internal control relevant to the preparation and fair presentation of consolidated financial statements that are free from material misstatement, whether due to fraud or error.

Auditor's Responsibility

Our responsibility is to express an opinion on these consolidated financial statements based on our audits. We conducted our audits in accordance with auditing standards generally accepted in the United States of America. Those standards require that we plan and perform the audit to obtain reasonable assurance whether the consolidated financial statements are free from material misstatement.

The audit involves performing procedures to obtain audit evidence about the amounts and disclosures in the consolidated financial statements. The procedures selected depend on the auditor's judgment, including the assessment of the risks of material misstatement of the consolidated financial statements, whether due to fraud or error. In making those risk assessments, the auditor considers internal control relevant to the entity's preparation and fair presentation of the consolidated financial statements in order to design audit procedures that are appropriate in the circumstances, but not for the purpose of expressing an opinion on the effectiveness of the entity's internal control. Accordingly, we express no such opinion.

An audit also includes evaluating the appropriateness of accounting policies used and the reasonableness of significant accounting estimates made by management, as well as evaluating the overall presentation of the consolidated financial statements.

We believe that the audit evidence we have obtained is sufficient and appropriate to provide a basis for our qualified audit opinion.

Basis for Qualified Opinion

We were unable to obtain audited financial statements supporting the Company's investment in a foreign affiliate stated at $_____ and $_____ at December 31, 20X1 and 20X0, respectively, or its equity in earnings of that affiliate of $_____ and $_____, which is included in net income for the years then ended as described in Note X to the consolidated financial statements; nor were we able to satisfy ourselves as to the carrying value of the investment in the foreign affiliate or the equity in its earnings by other auditing procedures.

Qualified Opinion

In our opinion, except for the possible effects of the matter described in the Basis for Qualified Opinion paragraph, the consolidated financial statements referred to above present fairly, in all material respects, the financial position of ABC Company and its subsidiaries as of December 31, 20X1 and 20X0, and the results of their operations and their cash flows for the years then ended in accordance with accounting principles generally accepted in the United States of America.

[Auditor's signature]

[Auditor's city and state]

[Date of the auditor's report]

ILLUSTRATION 2. A REPORT IN WHICH THE AUDITOR OF THE GROUP FINANCIAL STATEMENTS IS MAKING REFERENCE TO THE AUDIT OF A COMPONENT AUDITOR

In this example, the auditor of the group financial statements is making reference to the audit of a component auditor.

Independent Auditor's Report

[Appropriate Addressee]

Report on the Consolidated Financial Statements

We have audited the accompanying consolidated financial statements of ABC Company and its subsidiaries, which comprise the consolidated balance sheets as of December 31, 20X1 and 20X0, and the related consolidated statements of income, changes in stockholders' equity, and cash flows for the years then ended, and the related notes to the financial statements.

Management's Responsibility for the Financial Statements

Management is responsible for the preparation and fair presentation of these consolidated financial statements in accordance with accounting principles generally accepted in the United States of America; this includes the design, implementation, and maintenance of internal control relevant to the preparation and fair presentation of consolidated financial statements that are free from material misstatement, whether due to fraud or error.

Auditor's Responsibility

Our responsibility is to express an opinion on these consolidated financial statements based on our audits. We did not audit the financial statements of B Company, a wholly-owned subsidiary, which statements reflect total assets constituting 20% and 22%, respectively, of consolidated total assets at December 31, 20X1 and 20X0, and total revenues constituting 18% and 20%, respectively, of consolidated total revenues for the years then ended. Those statements were audited by other auditors, whose report has been furnished to us, and our opinion, insofar as it relates to the amounts included for B Company, is based solely on the report of the other auditors. We conducted our audits in accordance with auditing standards generally accepted in the United States of America. Those standards require that we plan and perform the audit to obtain reasonable assurance about whether the consolidated financial statements are free from material misstatement.

An audit involves performing procedures to obtain audit evidence about the amounts and disclosures in the consolidated financial statements. The procedures selected depend on the auditor's judgment, including the assessment of the risks of material misstatement of the consolidated financial statements, whether due to fraud or error. In making those risk assessments, the auditor considers internal control relevant to the entity's preparation and fair presentation of the consolidated financial statements in order to design audit procedures that are appropriate in the circumstances, but not for the purpose of expressing an opinion on the effectiveness of the entity's internal control. Accordingly, we express no such opinion. An audit also includes evaluating the appropriateness of accounting policies used and the reasonableness of significant accounting estimates made by management, as well as evaluating the overall presentation of the consolidated financial statements.

We believe that the audit evidence we have obtained is sufficient and appropriate to provide a basis for our audit opinion.

Opinion

In our opinion, based on our audit and the report of the other auditors, the consolidated financial statements referred to above present fairly, in all material respects, the financial position of ABC Company and its subsidiaries as of December 31, 20X1 and 20X0, and the results of their operations and their cash flows for the years then ended in accordance with accounting principles generally accepted in the United States of America.

[*Auditor's signature*]

[*Auditor's city and state*]

[*Date of the auditor's report*]

EXHIBIT B. ILLUSTRATIVE COMPONENT AUDITOR'S CONFIRMATION LETTER

The following is not intended to be a standard letter. Confirmations may vary from one component auditor to another and from one period to the next. In this example, confirmations expected only when the auditor of the group financial statements is assuming responsibility have been italicized.

Confirmations often are obtained before work on the financial information of the component commences.

[*Component Auditor Letterhead*]

[*Date*]

[*To Audit Firm*]

This letter is provided in connection with your audit of the group financial statements of [*name of parent*] as of and for the year ended [*date*] for the purpose of expressing an opinion on whether the group financial statements present fairly, in all material respects, the financial position of the group as of [*date*] and of the results of its operations and its cash flows for the year then ended in accordance with [*indicate applicable financial reporting framework*].

We acknowledge receipt of your instructions dated [*date*], requesting us to perform the specified work on the financial information of [*name of component*] as of and for the year ended [*date*].

We confirm that:

1. *We will be able to comply with the instructions. / We advise you that we will not be able to comply with the following instructions [specify instructions] for the following reasons [specify reasons].*
2. *The instructions are clear, and we understand them. / We would appreciate it if you could clarify the following instructions [specify instructions].*
3. *We will cooperate with you and provide you with access to relevant audit documentation.*

We acknowledge that:

1. The financial information of [*name of component*] will be included in the group financial statements of [*name of parent*].

2. *You may consider it necessary to be further involved in the work you have requested us to perform on the financial information of [*name of component*] as of and for the year ended [*date*].*
3. *You intend to evaluate and, if considered appropriate, use our work for the audit of the group financial statements of [*name of parent*].*

In connection with the work that we will perform on the financial information of [*name of component*], a [*describe component, e.g., wholly-owned subsidiary, subsidiary, joint venture, investee accounted for by the equity or cost methods of accounting*] of [*name of parent*], we confirm the following:

1. We have an understanding of [*indicate relevant ethical requirements*] that is sufficient to fulfill our responsibilities in the audit of the group financial statements and will comply therewith. In particular, and with respect to [*name of parent*] and the other components in the group, we are independent within the meaning of [*indicate relevant ethical requirements*] and comply with the applicable requirements of [*refer to rules*] promulgated by [*name of regulatory agency*].
2. We have an understanding of auditing standards generally accepted in the United States of America and [*indicate other auditing standards applicable to the audit of the group financial statements, such as* Government Auditing Standards] that is sufficient to fulfill our responsibilities in the audit of the group financial statements and will conduct our work on the financial information of [*name of component*] as of and for the year ended [*date*] in accordance with those standards.
3. We possess the special skills (e.g., industry specific knowledge) necessary to perform the work on the financial information of the particular component.
4. We have an understanding of [*indicate applicable financial reporting framework or group financial reporting procedures manual*] that is sufficient to fulfill our responsibilities in the audit of the group financial statements.

We will inform you of any changes in the above representations during the course of our work on the financial information of [*name of component*].

[*Auditor's signature*]

Illustration of Potential Component Auditor Representations in Governmental Entities and Not-for-Profit Organizations

5. We have an understanding of relevant laws and regulations that may have a direct and material effect on the financial statements of [*name of component*]. In particular, we have an understanding of [*indicate relevant laws and regulations*].

Exhibit C. Sources of Information

The American Institute of Certified Public Accountants (AICPA) Professional Ethics Team can respond to inquiries about whether individuals are members of the AICPA and whether complaints against members have been adjudicated by the Joint Trial Board. The team cannot respond to inquiries about public accounting firms or provide information about letters of required corrective action issued by the team or pending disciplinary proceedings or investigations. The AICPA Peer Review Program staff or the applicable state CPA society administering entity can respond to inquiries about whether specific public accounting firms are enrolled in the AICPA Peer Review Program and the date of acceptance and the period covered by the firm's most recently accepted peer review.

AU 544 Lack of Conformity with Generally Accepted Accounting Principles

AU-C 800 Special Considerations—Audits of Financial Statements Prepared in Accordance with Special Purpose Frameworks

AU EFFECTIVE DATE AND APPLICABILITY

Original Pronouncements	Statement on Auditing Procedure (SAP) 33 (codified in Statement on Auditing Standards [SAS] 1); SAS 2, 62, and 77.
Effective Date	These statements currently are effective.
Applicability	Audits of financial statements of regulated companies in accordance with generally accepted auditing standards (GAAS) when the financial statements are presented for purposes other than regulatory filings.

AU-C EFFECTIVE DATE AND SUMMARY OF CHANGES

SAS No. 122, *Codification of Auditing Standards and Procedures*, is effective for audits of financial statements with periods ending on or after December 15, 2012.

AU Section 334 is focused on auditing the amounts and disclosures pursuant to accounting principles generally accepted in the United States (US GAAP), and it is centered on the provisions of Financial Accounting Standards Board (FASB) Statement No. 57. AU-C 800 is framework neutral, encompassing financial reporting frameworks in addition to US GAAP, such as International Financial Reporting Standards as promulgated by the International Accounting Standards Board.

The objectives, requirements, and definitions in AU-C 800 are applicable irrespective of whether the applicable financial reporting framework establishes requirements for related-party disclosures.

AU DEFINITION OF TERM

Regulated companies. Companies, such as public utilities and insurance companies, whose accounting practices are prescribed by governmental regulatory authorities or commissions.

AU-C DEFINITIONS OF TERMS

Source: AU-C 800.07

Special purpose financial statements. Financial statements prepared in accordance with a special purpose framework.

Special purpose framework. A financial reporting framework other than GAAP that is one of the following bases of accounting:

1. **Cash basis.** A basis of accounting that the entity uses to record cash receipts and disbursements and modifications of the cash basis having substantial support (for example, recording depreciation on fixed assets).
2. **Tax basis.** A basis of accounting that the entity uses to file its income tax return for the period covered by the financial statements.
3. **Regulatory basis.** A basis of accounting that the entity uses to comply with the requirements or financial reporting provisions of a regulatory agency to whose jurisdiction the entity is subject (for example, a basis of accounting that insurance companies use pursuant to the accounting practices prescribed or permitted by a state insurance commission).
4. **Contractual basis.** A basis of accounting that the entity uses to comply with an agreement between the entity and one or more third parties other than the auditor.

The cash, tax, and regulatory bases of accounting are commonly referred to as *other comprehensive bases of accounting (OCBOA)*.

OBJECTIVES OF AU SECTION 544

Governmental regulatory authorities or commissions may prescribe accounting practices for regulated companies. Examples of these companies include public utilities, common carriers, insurance companies, and financial institutions. Sometimes the prescribed accounting practices are not in conformity with GAAP. This section tells the auditor the kind of report he or she should issue when a regulated company presents financial statements for purposes other than regulatory filings that follow accounting practices prescribed by regulatory authorities or commissions that are not in conformity with GAAP.

Differences between prescribed accounting practices and accounting practices applicable to nonregulated businesses that are caused by the rate-making process can be in conformity with GAAP. Guidance on accounting for regulated enterprises is contained in several FASB

Statements of Financial Accounting Standards, particularly SFAS 71, *Accounting for the Effects of Certain Types of Regulation,* SFAS 90, *Regulated Enterprises—Accounting for Abandonments and Disallowances of Plant Costs,* SFAS 92, *Regulated Enterprises—Accounting for Phase-in Plans,* and SFAS 101, *Regulated Enterprises—Accounting for the Discontinuation of Application of FASB Statement 71.*

OBJECTIVES OF AU-C SECTION 800

AU-C section 800 states that:

. . . the objective of the auditor, when applying generally accepted auditing standards (GAAS) in an audit of financial statements prepared in accordance with a special-purpose framework, is to address appropriately the special considerations that are relevant to

    a. the acceptance of the engagement,
    b. the planning and performance of that engagement, and
    c. forming an opinion and reporting on the financial statements.

FUNDAMENTAL REQUIREMENTS

DEPARTURES FROM GAAP

The auditor should express a qualified opinion or an adverse opinion when a regulated company issues financial statements to anyone other than its regulatory agency that are prepared in conformity with accounting practices prescribed by regulatory authorities or commissions that do not conform with GAAP.

FINANCIAL STATEMENTS SOLELY FOR FILING WITH REGULATORY AGENCY

The auditor may report on a regulated company's financial statements as being prepared in accordance with a comprehensive basis of accounting other than generally accepted accounting principles (see Section 623, *Special Reports*) *only* if the statements are *solely* for filing with the regulatory agency.

FINANCIAL STATEMENTS FOR OTHER THAN FILING WITH REGULATORY AGENCY

The auditor may be asked to report on the fair presentation of financial statements in conformity with a regulatory prescribed basis of accounting in presentations other than filings with the regulatory agency. In these circumstances, the auditor's standard report should be modified because of the departure from GAAP, and, in an additional paragraph, an opinion may be expressed on the conformity of the financial statements with the prescribed method.

NOTE: *The additional paragraph is added at the auditor's discretion; it is never required.*

INTERPRETATIONS

There are no interpretations for this section.

AU 550 Other Information in Documents Containing Audited Financial Statements

AU-C 720 Other Information in Documents Containing Audited Financial Statements

AU EFFECTIVE DATE AND APPLICABILITY

Original Pronouncement	Statement on Auditing Standards (SAS) 118.
Effective Date	This statement currently is effective.
Applicability	Annual reports or similar documents that are issued to owners or similar stakeholders, and annual reports of governments and organizations for charitable or philanthropic purposes that are available to the public that contain audited financial statements and the auditor's related report.

AU-C EFFECTIVE DATE AND SUMMARY OF CHANGES

To address practice issues, SAS No. 118, *Other Information in Documents Containing Audited Financial Statements*, was one of the clarified standards issued before SAS No. 122. It was issued in February 2010 and is effective for audits of financial statements for periods beginning on or after December 15, 2010.

SAS No. 118 was codified in AU 550 when issued, but was moved to AU-C 720 with the issuance of SAS No. 122. Some conforming changes were made in specific paragraphs and footnotes due to the issuance of SAS No. 122, but no substantive changes were made.

AU DEFINITIONS OF TERMS

Inconsistency. Information that conflicts with the information contained within the audited financial statements. Such an inconsistency may raise doubts about audit conclusions based on audit evidence that was previously obtained, and possibly about the basis for the auditor's opinion on the financial statements.

Other information. Both financial and nonfinancial information (not including the financial statements and related auditor's report) that is included in a document that contains audited financial statements and the auditor's related report. It does not include required supplementary information. Examples of other information are financial summaries, employment data, planned capital expenditures, financial ratios, the names of officers and directors, and selected quarterly data.

Misstatement of fact. Other information unrelated to matters appearing in the audited financial statements that is incorrectly stated or presented. If this misstatement is material, it can undermine the credibility of a document that also contains audited financial statements.

AU-C DEFINITIONS OF TERMS

Source: AU-C 720.05

Inconsistency. Other information that conflicts with information contained in the audited financial statements. A material inconsistency may raise doubt about the audit conclusions drawn from audit evidence previously obtained and, possibly, about the basis for the auditor's opinion on the financial statements.

Misstatement of fact. Other information that is unrelated to matters appearing in the audited financial statements that is incorrectly stated or presented. A material misstatement of fact may undermine the credibility of the document containing audited financial statements.

Other information. Financial and nonfinancial information (other than the financial statements and the auditor's report thereon) that is included in a document containing audited financial statements and the auditor's report thereon, excluding required supplementary information.

OBJECTIVES OF AU SECTION 550

A document containing audited financial statements and the associated auditor's report may include other information that could undermine the credibility of the financial statement and auditor's report. This section describes the steps that an auditor should follow to ascertain the presence of material inconsistencies or material misstatements of facts in this other information, and subsequent steps, required if such issues do exist.

OBJECTIVE OF AU-C SECTION 720

AU-C Section 720.04 states that:

. . . the objective of the auditor is to respond appropriately when the auditor becomes aware that documents containing audited financial statements and the auditor's report thereon in-

clude other information that could undermine the credibility of those financial statements and the auditor's report.

FUNDAMENTAL REQUIREMENTS

The auditor should take the following steps:

1. *Read other information.* Read the other information in the document, looking for any inconsistencies with the audited financial statements. The auditor should obtain this information from management or those charged with governance prior to the report release date; if the information is not available prior to the report release date, then read the information as soon as practicable thereafter.

   NOTE: *The auditor may delay the release of the auditor's report until management provides the other information to the auditor.*

2. *Procedures.* Inform those charged with governance of the auditor's responsibility regarding the other information, as well as any procedures performed on it and the results.

3. *Treatment of material inconsistencies.* If there is a material inconsistency in the other information, determine whether the audited financial statements or the other information should be revised. Use the following table to select the correct treatment, which assume that the report has not yet been released:

Situation	Auditor Action
There is a material inconsistency that requires revision of the financial statements, and management refuses to make the revision.	Modify the auditor's opinion in accordance with Section 508, *Reports on Audited Financial Statements*.
There is a material inconsistency that requires revision of the other information and management refuses to make the revision.	Communicate the issue to those charged with governance. Also, either include in the auditor's report an explanation of the material inconsistency, or withhold the auditor's report, or withdraw from the engagement.

If the report has already been released, then instead use the following table to select the correct treatment:

Situation	Auditor Action
There is a material inconsistency that requires revision of the financial statements	Apply Section 561, *Subsequent Discovery of Facts Existing at the Date of the Auditor's Report*
There is a material inconsistency that requires revision of the other information and management agrees to make the revision.	Complete those procedures necessary under the circumstances.
There is a material inconsistency that requires revision of the other information management refuses to make the revision.	Notify those charged with governance, and take further actions as appropriate.

NOTE: *When management agrees to make a revision to a document that has already been issued, the auditor may review the steps taken by management to ensure that those in receipt of the previous document version are informed of the need for a revised document.*

4. *Treatment of material misstatements.* If there is a material misstatement of fact, discuss the situation with management. Then, if there is still an apparent material misstatement of fact, ask management to consult with a qualified third party; the auditor should consider any advice received from this third party. If there is still a material misstatement of fact and management refuses to correct it, then notify those charged with governance of the situation, and take further actions as appropriate.

NOTE: *Following discussion of an apparent material misstatement of fact with management, the auditor may conclude that there are valid differences of judgment or opinion.*

INTERPRETATIONS

There are no interpretations for this section.

ILLUSTRATION

It is not necessary to reference the other information in the auditor's report on the financial statements. However, if the auditor believes that he or she could be associated with the information, this may imply a level of assurance that the auditor did not intend. Accordingly, consider using the disclaimer in Illustration 1 to disclaim an opinion on the other information.

ILLUSTRATION 1. EXPLANATORY PARAGRAPH TO DISCLAIM AN OPINION ON OTHER INFORMATION (FROM AU 550.A13 AND AU-C 720.A13).

Our audit was conducted for the purpose of forming an opinion on the basic financial statements as a whole. The [*identify the other information*] is presented for purposes of additional analysis and is not a required part of the basic financial statements. Such information has not been subjected to the auditing procedures applied in the audit of the basic financial statements, and accordingly, we do not express an opinion or provide any assurance on it.

AU 551 Supplementary Information in Relation to the Financial Statements as a Whole

AU-C 725 Supplementary Information in Relation to Financial Statements as a Whole

EFFECTIVE DATE AND APPLICABILITY

Original Pronouncements	Statement on Auditing Standards (SAS) 119.
Effective Date	This statement currently is effective.
Applicability	Audits of financial statements in accordance with generally accepted auditing standards (GAAS) if the statements and the auditor's report on them are included in a document that the auditor submits to the client or others.

EFFECTIVE DATE AND APPLICABILITY

To address practice issues, SAS No. 119, *Supplementary Information in Relation to the Financial Statements as a Whole*, was one of the clarified standards issued before SAS No. 122. It was issued in February 2010 and is effective for audits of financial statements for periods beginning on or after December 15, 2010.

SAS No. 119 was codified in AU 551 when issued, but was moved to AU-C 725 with the issuance of SAS No. 122. Some conforming changes were made in specific paragraphs and footnotes due to the issuance of SAS No. 122, but no substantive changes were made.

AU DEFINITION OF TERM

Supplementary information. Information presented outside the basic financial statements, excluding required supplementary information that is not considered necessary for the financial statements to be fairly presented in accordance with the applicable financial reporting framework. Examples of supplementary information are consolidating information, historical summaries of items extracted from the basic financial statements, and statistical data.

AU-C DEFINITION OF TERM

Source: AU-C 725.04

Supplementary information. Information presented outside the basic financial statements, excluding required supplementary information that is not considered necessary for the financial statements to be fairly presented in accordance with the applicable financial reporting framework. Such information may be presented in a document containing the audited financial statements or separate from the financial statements.

OBJECTIVES OF AU SECTION 551

An auditor may be engaged to report on whether information that is supplemental to the financial statements is fairly stated, in all material respects, in relation to the financial statements as a whole. When the auditor takes on this task, the objective is to both evaluate the presentation of the supplementary material in relation to the financial statements, and to report on whether such information is fairly stated, in all material respects, in relation to the financial statements as a whole.

OBJECTIVE OF AU-C SECTION 725

AU-C 725.03 states that:

the objective of the auditor, when engaged to report on supplementary information in relation to the financial statements as a whole, is to

  a. evaluate the presentation of the supplementary information in relation to the financial statements as a whole and
  b. report on whether the supplementary information is fairly stated, in all material respects, in relation to the financial statements as a whole.

FUNDAMENTAL REQUIREMENTS

An auditor should determine that all of the following conditions are met in order to determine whether supplementary information is fairly stated, in all material respects, in relation to the financial statements as a whole:

- *Source material*. The supplementary information was derived from the accounting records used to prepare the financial statements.
- *Period*. The supplementary information encompasses the same period as the financial statements.
- *Auditor*. The auditor was the principal auditor of the financial statements, which were audited.
- *Opinion type*. Neither an adverse opinion nor a disclaimer of opinion was issued on the financial statements.

- *Accompaniment.* The supplementary information will accompany the audited financial statements, or the entity will make the audited financial statements available.

Further, management must acknowledge that it is responsible for the following:

- *Supplementary information.* The preparation of supplementary information.
- *Representations.* The following written representations:
  - It acknowledges responsibility for presentation of the supplementary information.
  - It believes the supplementary information is fairly presented.
  - The measurement and presentation methods have not changed from those used in the prior period, or the reasons for such changes.
  - Any significant assumptions or interpretations underlying the supplementary information.
  - It will make the audited financial statements available whenever the supplementary information is not presented with those statements.
- *Audit report inclusion.* The inclusion of the auditor's report on the supplementary information in any documents containing such information.
- *Inclusion with financials.* The inclusion of the supplementary information with the audited financial statements, or to make the financial statements available.

Finally, the auditor should perform the following procedures, using the same materiality level used in his or her audit of the financial statements:

1. *Inquiries.* Inquire about the purpose of the supplementary information and the criteria used to prepare it.
2. *Form and content.* Determine whether the form and content of the supplementary information complies with any applicable criteria.
3. *Preparation methods.* Gain an understanding of the methods used to prepare the supplementary information, whether these methods have changed from those used in previous periods, and if so, why the changes were made.
4. *Reconciliation.* Reconcile the supplementary information to the accounting records used to prepare the financial statements.
5. *Assumptions.* Make inquiries about significant assumptions used in the preparation of the supplementary information.
6. *Appropriateness and completeness.* Evaluate the appropriateness and completeness of the supplementary information.

When the entity includes the supplementary information with its financial statements, the auditor reports on this additional information either in an explanatory paragraph following the opinion paragraph, or in the separate report. The explanatory paragraph or separated report should include the following items:

1. State that the audit was conducted to form an opinion on the financial statements as a whole.
2. State that the supplementary information provides additional analysis and is not a required part of the financial statements.
3. State that management is responsible for the supplementary information, and that this information was derived from the accounting records used to prepare the financial statements.
4. State that the supplementary information has been subjected to the auditing procedures used in the financial statements audit, along with additional procedures, such as

reconciling the information to the records used to prepare the financial statements, in accordance with GAAS.
5. If the opinion is unqualified and the supplementary information is fairly stated, then state that the supplementary information is fairly stated, in all material respects, in relation to the financial statements as a whole.
6. If the opinion is qualified and that qualification affects the supplementary information, state that, in the auditor's opinion, such information is fairly stated, in all material respects, in relation to the financial statements as a whole.

NOTE: If the financial statements are presented without the supplementary information, the auditor should report on the supplementary information in a separate report. When preparing this separated report, the report should include a reference to the report on the financial statements, the report's date, and report modifications, and the nature of the opinion expressed therein.

OPINION ON SUPPLEMENTARY INFORMATION

If the auditor issues an adverse opinion or a disclaimer of opinion on an entity's financial statements, and the auditor has also been engaged to deliver an opinion on the supplementary information, he or she cannot express a separate opinion on the supplementary information. When permitted by law, the auditor can withdraw from the engagement to report on the supplementary information. If the auditor cannot withdraw, then the report on the supplementary information should state that, due to the significance of the matter disclosed in the auditor's report, it is inappropriate to express an opinion on the supplementary information. If the auditor concludes that the supplementary information is misstated, then discuss the matter with management and propose appropriate revisions. If management does not revise the supplementary material accordingly, then either modify the auditor's opinion on the supplementary information to describe the misstatements, or withhold the report.

AU-C INTERPRETATIONS

Dating the Auditor's Report on Supplementary Information

The auditor's report on supplementary information should not be dated earlier than the date on which the auditor completed the procedures required by AU-C Section 725. When the auditor completes those procedures subsequent to the date of the auditor's report on the audited financial statements, the auditor is not required to obtain additional evidence with respect to the audited financial statements. When reporting on the supplementary information (either in a separate report or in an explanatory paragraph within the auditor's report on the financial statements) after the date of the auditor's report on the financial statements, an auditor may make it clear that no additional procedures were performed on the audited financial statements subsequent to the date of the auditor's report on those financial statements.

Although not required, an auditor may

1. When issuing a separate report on the supplementary information, include in such report a statement that the auditor has not performed any auditing procedures with respect to the audited financial statements subsequent to the date of the auditor's report on those audited financial statements, or
2. When reissuing a report on the audited financial statements to include an explanatory paragraph to report on the supplementary information, include two report dates to indicate that the date of reporting on the supplementary information is as of a later date.

AU ILLUSTRATIONS

The following are illustrative audit reports adapted from AU Section 551:

1. An explanatory paragraph where there is an unqualified opinion on the financial statements and the supplementary information is fairly stated.
2. An explanatory paragraph where there is a qualified opinion on the financial statements and a qualified opinion on the supplementary information.
3. An explanatory paragraph when disclaiming an opinion on the financial statements.
4. An explanatory paragraph when there is an adverse opinion on the financial statements.
5. An explanatory paragraph when reporting separately on supplementary information and there is an unqualified opinion on the financial statements and an unqualified opinion on the supplementary information.
6. An explanatory paragraph when reporting separately on supplementary information and there are qualified opinions on both the financial statements and supplementary information.
7. An explanatory paragraph when reporting separately on supplementary information and the auditor disclaims an opinion on the financial statements.
8. An explanatory paragraph when reporting separately on supplementary information and the auditor issues an adverse opinion on the financial statements.

ILLUSTRATION 1. EXPLANATORY PARAGRAPH WITH UNQUALIFIED OPINION ON FINANCIAL STATEMENTS AND SUPPLEMENTARY INFORMATION IS FAIRLY STATED

Our audit was conducted for the purpose of forming an opinion on the financial statements as a whole. The [*identify accompanying supplementary information*] is presented for purposes of additional analysis and is not a required part of the financial statements. Such information is the responsibility of management and was derived from and relates directly to the underlying accounting and other records used to prepare the financial statements. The information has been subjected to the auditing procedures applied in the audit of the financial statements and certain additional procedures, including comparing and reconciling such information directly to the underlying accounting and other records used to prepare the financial statements or to the financial statements themselves, and other additional procedures in accordance with auditing standards generally accepted in the United States of America. In our opinion, the information is fairly stated in all material respects in relation to the financial statements as a whole.

ILLUSTRATION 2. EXPLANATORY PARAGRAPH WITH A QUALIFIED OPINION ON FINANCIAL STATEMENTS AND A QUALIFIED OPINION ON SUPPLEMENTARY INFORMATION

Our audit was conducted for the purpose of forming an opinion on the financial statements taken as a whole. The [*identify accompanying supplementary information*] is presented for purposes of additional analysis and is not a required part of the financial statements. Such information is the responsibility of management and was derived from and relates directly to the underlying accounting and other records used to prepare the financial statements. The information has been subjected to the auditing procedures applied in the audit of the financial statements and certain additional procedures, including comparing and reconciling such information directly to the underlying accounting and other records used to prepare the financial statements or to the financial statements themselves, and other additional procedures in accordance with auditing standards generally accepted in the United States of America. In our opinion, except for the effect on the supplementary information of [*describe reason for qualification of the auditor's opinion on the financial statements and reference the explanatory paragraph*], the information is fairly stated in all material respects in relation to the financial statements as a whole.

> **ILLUSTRATION 3. EXPLANATORY PARAGRAPH WHEN DISCLAIMING AN OPINION ON THE FINANCIAL STATEMENTS**

We were engaged for the purpose of forming an opinion on the basic financial statements as a whole. The [*identify accompanying supplementary information*] is presented for purposes of additional analysis and is not a required part of the financial statements. Because of the significance of the matter described above [*may describe the basis for the disclaimer of opinion*], it is inappropriate to and we do not express an opinion on the supplementary information referred to above.

> **ILLUSTRATION 4. EXPLANATORY PARAGRAPH WHEN DISCLAIMING AN OPINION ON THE FINANCIAL STATEMENTS**

Our audit was conducted for the purpose of forming an opinion on the financial statements as a whole. The [*identify accompanying supplementary information*] is presented for the purposes of additional analysis and is not a required part of the financial statements. Because of the significance of the matter described above [*may describe the basis for the adverse opinion*], it is inappropriate to and we do not express an opinion on supplementary information referred to above.

> **ILLUSTRATION 5. EXPLANATORY PARAGRAPH WHEN REPORTING SEPARATELY FOR SUPPLEMENTARY INFORMATION, WITH UNQUALIFIED OPINIONS ON BOTH THE FINANCIAL STATEMENTS AND SUPPLEMENTARY INFORMATION**

We have audited the financial statements of ABC Company as of and for the year ended December 31, 20X1, and have issued our report thereon dated [*date of the auditor's report on the financial statements*], which contained an unqualified opinion on those financial statements. Our audit was performed for the purpose of forming an opinion on the financial statement as a whole. The [*identify supplementary information*] is presented for the purposes of additional analysis and is not a required part of the financial statements. Such information is the responsibility of management and was derived from and relates directly to the underlying accounting and other records used to prepare the financial statements. The information has been subjected to the auditing procedures applied in the audit of the financial statements and certain additional procedures, including comparing and reconciling such information directly to the underlying accounting and other records used to prepare the financial statements or to the financial statements themselves, and other additional procedures in accordance with auditing standards generally accepted in the United States of America. In our opinion, the information is fairly stated in all material respects in relation to the financial statements as a whole.

> **ILLUSTRATION 6. EXPLANATORY PARAGRAPH WITH QUALIFIED OPINIONS ON THE FINANCIAL STATEMENTS AND SUPPLEMENTARY INFORMATION**

We have audited the financial statements of ABC Company as of and for the year ended December 31, 20X1, and have issued our report thereon dated [*date of the auditor's report on the financial statements, the nature of the opinion expressed on the financial statements, and a description of the report modifications*], Our audit was performed for the purpose of forming an opinion on the financial statements as a whole. The [*identify supplementary information*] is presented for the purposes of additional analysis and is not a required part of the financial statements. Such information is the responsibility of management and was derived from and relates directly to the underlying accounting and other records used to prepare the financial statements. The information has been subjected to the auditing procedures applied in the audit of the financial statements and certain additional procedures, including comparing and reconciling such information directly to the underlying accounting and other records used to prepare the financial statements or to the financial statements themselves, and other additional procedures in accordance with auditing standards generally accepted in the United States of America. In our opinion, except for the effect on the accompanying information of the qualified opinion on the financial statements as described above, the information is fairly stated in all material respects in relation to the financial statements as a whole.

ILLUSTRATION 7. EXPLANATORY PARAGRAPH WITH DISCLAIMER ON THE FINANCIAL STATEMENTS

We were engaged to audit the financial statements of ABC Company as of and for the year ended December 31, 20X1, and have issued our report thereon dated [*date of the auditor's report on the financial statements*]. However, the scope of our audit of the financial statements was not sufficient to enable us to express an opinion because [*describe reasons*], and accordingly we did not express an opinion on such financial statements. The [*identify the supplementary information*] is presented for purposes of additional analysis and is not a required part of the basic financial statements. Because of the significance of the matter discussed above, it is inappropriate to and we do not express an opinion on the supplementary information referred to above.

ILLUSTRATION 8. EXPLANATORY PARAGRAPH WITH ADVERSE OPINION ON THE FINANCIAL STATEMENTS

We were engaged to audit the financial statements of ABC Company as of and for the year ended December 31, 20X1, and have issued our report thereon dated [*date of the auditor's report on the financial statements*] which stated that the financial statements are not presented fairly in accordance with [*identify the applicable financial reporting framework, such as GAAP*] because [*describe reasons*]. The [*identify the supplementary information*] is presented for purposes of additional analysis and is not a required part of the basic financial statements. Because of the significance of the matter discussed above, it is inappropriate to and we do not express an opinion on the supplementary information referred to above.

AU-C 725 ILLUSTRATIONS

The following are illustrations from AU-C 725:

1. An Other-Matter Paragraph When the Auditor Is Issuing an Unmodified Opinion on the Financial Statements and an Unmodified Opinion on the Supplementary Information
2. An Other-Matter Paragraph When the Auditor Is Issuing a Qualified Opinion on the Financial Statements and a Qualified Opinion on the Supplementary Information
3. An Other-Matter Paragraph When the Auditor Is Disclaiming an Opinion on the Financial Statements
4. An Other-Matter Paragraph When the Auditor Is Issuing an Adverse Opinion on the Financial Statements
5. A Separate Report When the Auditor Is Issuing an Unmodified Opinion on the Financial Statements and an Unmodified Opinion on the Supplementary Information
6. A Separate Report When the Auditor Is Issuing a Qualified Opinion on the Financial Statements and a Qualified Opinion on the Supplementary Information

7. A Separate Report When the Auditor Is Disclaiming an Opinion on the Financial Statements
8. A Separate Report When the Auditor Is Issuing an Adverse Opinion on the Financial Statements

ILLUSTRATION 1. AN OTHER-MATTER PARAGRAPH WHEN THE AUDITOR IS ISSUING AN UNMODIFIED OPINION ON THE FINANCIAL STATEMENTS AND AN UNMODIFIED OPINION ON THE SUPPLEMENTARY INFORMATION

Our audit was conducted for the purpose of forming an opinion on the financial statements as a whole. The [*identify accompanying supplementary information*] is presented for purposes of additional analysis and is not a required part of the financial statements. Such information is the responsibility of management and was derived from and relates directly to the underlying accounting and other records used to prepare the financial statements. The information has been subjected to the auditing procedures applied in the audit of the financial statements and certain additional procedures, including comparing and reconciling such information directly to the underlying accounting and other records used to prepare the financial statements or to the financial statements themselves, and other additional procedures in accordance with auditing standards generally accepted in the United States of America. In our opinion, the information is fairly stated in all material respects in relation to the financial statements as a whole.

ILLUSTRATION 2. AN OTHER-MATTER PARAGRAPH WHEN THE AUDITOR IS ISSUING A QUALIFIED OPINION ON THE FINANCIAL STATEMENTS AND A QUALIFIED OPINION ON THE SUPPLEMENTARY INFORMATION

Our audit was conducted for the purpose of forming an opinion on the financial statements as a whole. The [*identify accompanying supplementary information*] is presented for purposes of additional analysis and is not a required part of the financial statements. Such information is the responsibility of management and was derived from and relates directly to the underlying accounting and other records used to prepare the financial statements. The information has been subjected to the auditing procedures applied in the audit of the financial statements and certain additional procedures, including comparing and reconciling such information directly to the underlying accounting and other records used to prepare the financial statements or to the financial statements themselves, and other additional procedures in accordance with auditing standards generally accepted in the United States of America. In our opinion, except for the effect on the supplementary information of [*describe reason for qualification of the auditor's opinion on the financial statements and reference the other-matter paragraph*], the information is fairly stated in all material respects in relation to the financial statements as a whole.

ILLUSTRATION 3. AN OTHER-MATTER PARAGRAPH WHEN THE AUDITOR IS DISCLAIMING AN OPINION ON THE FINANCIAL STATEMENTS

We were engaged for the purpose of forming an opinion on the basic financial statements as a whole. The [*identify accompanying supplementary information*] is presented for the purposes of additional analysis and is not a required part of the financial statements. Because of the significance of the matter described above [*the auditor may describe the basis for the disclaimer of opinion*], it is inappropriate to and we do not express an opinion on the supplementary information referred to above.

ILLUSTRATION 4. AN OTHER-MATTER PARAGRAPH WHEN THE AUDITOR IS ISSUING AN ADVERSE OPINION ON THE FINANCIAL STATEMENTS

Our audit was conducted for the purpose of forming an opinion on the financial statements as a whole. The [*identify accompanying supplementary information*] is presented for the purposes of additional analysis and is not a required part of the financial statements. Because of the significance of the matter described above [*the auditor may describe the basis for the adverse opinion*], it is inappropriate to and we do not express an opinion on the supplementary information referred to above.

ILLUSTRATION 5. A SEPARATE REPORT WHEN THE AUDITOR IS ISSUING AN UNMODIFIED OPINION ON THE FINANCIAL STATEMENTS AND AN UNMODIFIED OPINION ON THE SUPPLEMENTARY INFORMATION

We have audited the financial statements of XYZ Entity as of and for the year ended June 30, 20X1, and have issued our report thereon dated [*date of the auditor's report on the financial statements*] which contained an unmodified opinion on those financial statements. Our audit was performed for the purpose of forming an opinion on the financial statements as a whole. The [*identify supplementary information*] is presented for the purposes of additional analysis and is not a required part of the financial statements. Such information is the responsibility of management and was derived from and relates directly to the underlying accounting and other records used to prepare the financial statements. The information has been subjected to the auditing procedures applied in the audit of the financial statements and certain additional procedures, including comparing and reconciling such information directly to the underlying accounting and other records used to prepare the financial statements or to the financial statements themselves, and other additional procedures in accordance with auditing standards generally accepted in the United States of America. In our opinion, the information is fairly stated in all material respects in relation to the financial statements as a whole.

ILLUSTRATION 6. A SEPARATE REPORT WHEN THE AUDITOR IS ISSUING A QUALIFIED OPINION ON THE FINANCIAL STATEMENTS AND A QUALIFIED OPINION ON THE SUPPLEMENTARY INFORMATION

We have audited the financial statements of XYZ Entity as of and for the year ended June 30, 20X1, and have issued our report thereon dated [*date of the auditor's report on the financial statements, the nature of the opinion expressed on the financial statements, and a description of the report modifications*]. Our audit was performed for the purpose of forming an opinion on the financial statements as a whole. The [*identify supplementary information*] is presented for the purposes of additional analysis and is not a required part of the financial statements. Such information is the responsibility of management and was derived from and relates directly to the underlying accounting and other records used to prepare the financial statements. The information has been subjected to the auditing procedures applied in the audit of the financial statements and certain additional procedures, including comparing and reconciling such information directly to the underlying accounting and other records used to prepare the financial statements or to the financial statements themselves, and other additional procedures in accordance with auditing standards generally accepted in the United States of America. In our opinion, except for the effect on the accompanying information of the qualified opinion on the financial statements as described above, the information is fairly stated in all material respects in relation to the financial statements as a whole.

ILLUSTRATION 7. A SEPARATE REPORT WHEN THE AUDITOR IS DISCLAIMING AN OPINION ON THE FINANCIAL STATEMENTS

We were engaged to audit the financial statements of XYZ Entity as of and for the year ended June 30, 20X1, and have issued our report thereon dated [*date of the auditor's report on the financial statements*]. However, the scope of our audit of the financial statements was not sufficient to enable us to express an opinion because [*describe reasons*] and accordingly we did not express an opinion on such financial statements. The [*identify the supplementary information*] is presented for purposes of additional analysis and is not a required part of the basic financial statements. Because of the significance of the matter discussed above, it is inappropriate to and we do not express an opinion on the supplementary information referred to above.

ILLUSTRATION 8. A SEPARATE REPORT WHEN THE AUDITOR IS ISSUING AN ADVERSE OPINION ON THE FINANCIAL STATEMENTS

We have audited the financial statements of XYZ Entity as of and for the year ended June 30, 20X1, and have issued our report thereon dated [*date of the auditor's report on the financial statements*] which stated that the financial statements are not presented fairly in accordance with [*identify the applicable financial reporting framework (for example, accounting principles generally accepted in the United States of America [GAAP])*] because [*describe reasons*]. The [*identify the supplementary information*] is presented for purposes of additional analysis and is not a required part of the basic financial statements. Because of the significance of the matter discussed above, it is inappropriate to and we do not express an opinion on the supplementary information referred to above.

AU 552 Reporting on Condensed Financial Statements and Selected Financial Data[1]

AU-C 810 Engagements to Report on Summary Financial Statements

AU EFFECTIVE DATE AND APPLICABILITY

Original Pronouncements	Statements on Auditing Standards (SASs) 42 and 71.
Effective Date	These statements currently are effective.
Applicability	Accountants' reports:

1. On condensed financial statements in a client-prepared document for an annual or interim period, derived from audited financial statements of a public entity that is required to file, at least annually, complete audited financial statements with a regulatory agency; or
2. On selected financial data in a client-prepared document of a public or nonpublic entity, derived from audited financial statements that are presented in a document that includes audited financial statements, or that (if a public entity) incorporates such statements by reference. (See "AU Objectives of Section 552" and "Objectives of AU-C Section 810" for additional explanation of applicability.)

AU-C EFFECTIVE DATE AND SUMMARY OF CHANGES

SAS No. 122, Codification of Auditing Standards and Procedures, is effective for audits of financial statements with periods ending on or after December 15, 2012.

---

[1] *Several of the reports in this section are filed by public companies. We assume that they would be issuers, and have conformed these reports to refer to the standards of the Public Company Accounting Oversight Board (PCAOB).*

The clarified SAS addresses the auditor's responsibilities when reporting on summary financial statements derived from financial statements audited by that same auditor. Accordingly, an auditor cannot report on summary financial statements unless the auditor has audited the financial statements from which the summary financial statements are derived. According to the American Institute of Certified Public Accountants (AICPA) document, *Summary of Differences Between Clarified SASs and Existing SASs*, the clarified SAS also:

- Eliminates reporting on selected financial data.
- Introduces the notion of criteria for preparing summary financial statements and requires the auditor to determine whether the criteria applied by management in the preparation of the summary financial statements are acceptable.
- Requires the auditor to obtain management's agreement that it acknowledges and understands its responsibilities for the summary financial statements, including its responsibility to make the audited financial statements readily available to the intended users of the summary financial statements. Being available upon request is not considered readily available.
- Stipulates specific procedures to be performed as the basis for the auditor's opinion on the summary financial statements.
- Stipulates specific elements of the auditor's report, including management's responsibility and a description of the auditor's procedures.
- Requires the auditor to request management to provide, in the form of a representation letter addressed to the auditor, written representations relating to the summary financial statements.
- Requires, when the auditor has concluded that an unmodified opinion on the summary financial statements is appropriate, the auditor's opinion to state that the summary financial statements are consistent, in all material respects, with the audited financial statements from which they have been derived, in accordance with the applied criteria. SAS No. 42 required that the auditor's opinion state whether the information set forth in the summary financial statements is fairly presented, in all material respects, in relation to the complete set of financial statements from which it has been derived.
- Requires, when the auditor's report on the audited financial statements contains an adverse opinion or a disclaimer of opinion, the auditor to withdraw from the engagement when withdrawal is possible under applicable law or regulation. Otherwise, the auditor is required to state in the report that it is inappropriate to express, and the auditor does not express, an opinion on the summary financial statements.
- Clarifies the auditor's responsibilities related to subsequent events and subsequently discovered facts when the date of the auditor's report on the summary financial statements is later than the date of the auditor's report on the audited financial statements.
- Includes specific requirements relating to comparatives, unaudited information presented with summary financial statements, and other information included in a document containing the summary financial statements and related auditor's report.
- Addresses the auditor's responsibilities as they relate to the auditor's association with summary financial statements.

AU DEFINITIONS OF TERMS

Condensed financial statements. Financial statements presented in considerably less detail than complete financial statements that are intended to present financial position, results of operations, and cash flows in conformity with generally accepted accounting principles (GAAP).

NOTE: The section has no informative explanation of the extent of condensation permissible. Because GAAP does not specify the extent of detail necessary in complete financial statements, this is understandable. Usually in condensed statements many financial statement components are combined and notes are omitted. The required form of reporting was intended to avoid forcing the accountant to evaluate the extent of condensation.

Selected financial data. Selected components of financial statements (usually of prior periods) that management has determined should be presented. Under SEC regulations, for example, management has to present the following selected data for each of the last five fiscal years:

1. Net sales or operating revenue
2. Income or loss from continuing operations in total and per common share
3. Total assets
4. Long-term obligations and redeemable preferred stock
5. Cash dividends declared per common share

NOTE: In condensed financial statements all the components of financial statements are included, but many of them are combined. In selected financial data only specific components are presented.

Selected financial data includes specific components appearing in financial statements and data calculated from such components, such as working capital. It does not include nonfinancial information, such as number of employees.

AU-C DEFINITIONS OF TERMS

Source: AU-C 810.0

Applied criteria. The criteria applied by management in the preparation of the summary financial statements.

Summary financial statements. Historical financial information that is derived from financial statements but that contains less detail than the financial statements, while still providing a structured representation consistent with that provided by the financial statements of the entity's economic resources or obligations at a point in time or the changes therein for a period of time. Summary financial statements are separately presented and are not presented as comparative information.

OBJECTIVES OF AU SECTION 552

The goal at the inception of the project that led to issuance of this section was to provide some guidance on accountants' reports in SEC filings on some new kinds of required information so that there would be reasonable uniformity in practice. The more ambitious task of providing comprehensive guidance on reporting on condensed financial information was considered too complex and hence too time-consuming. By the time the section was in place, practice could be diverse, and less desirable practice might be entrenched. Protests during exposure about the narrow applicability of the proposed guidance forced a compromise of sorts. Through footnotes and cross-references to other literature, the section identifies the reporting guidance that applies to all forms of condensed financial statements.

AUDITOR-SUBMITTED DOCUMENTS

In an auditor-submitted document (see Section 551, *Reporting on Information Accompanying the Basic Financial Statements in Auditor-Submitted Documents*), condensed financial statements and selected financial data are treated no differently from any other information that might accompany the basic financial statements. Section 551 applies, and if the information has been subjected to sufficient auditing procedures, the auditor reports on whether it is fairly stated in all material respects in relation to the basic financial statements taken as a whole. Usually the auditor will have audited the basic financial statements from which the condensed financial statements and selected financial data are derived and will be able to give this assurance.

CLIENT-PREPARED DOCUMENTS: PUBLIC ENTITIES

Here the reporting guidance differs for condensed financial statements versus selected data.

Condensed Financial Statements

The form of reporting in this section for condensed financial statements can be used only in a client-prepared document containing annual or interim condensed financial statements, derived from audited financial statements of a public entity that is required to file, at least annually, complete audited financial statements with a regulatory agency. The justification for permitting the specified assurance on condensed financial statements is the discipline of an annual filing requirement and the guaranteed public availability of information on an entity that this discipline provides. Note that the audited financial statements from which the condensed financial statements are derived do not actually have to be filed. For example, complete audited financial statements for an interim period might never be filed.

The form of reporting in the section cannot be used in client-prepared documents of all public entities (only those subject to a regulatory agency's annual filing requirements). For public entities not subject to a filing requirement, there are two options. If the client-prepared document contains complete audited financial statements, the Section 551 form of report could be used. If the client-prepared document does not contain complete audited financial statements, an adverse opinion is required (see the discussion for nonpublic entities).

Selected Data

The section provides guidance on reporting on selected financial data in all client-prepared documents of public and nonpublic entities (see "Fundamental Requirements").

CLIENT-PREPARED DOCUMENTS: NONPUBLIC ENTITIES

Selected financial data in a client-prepared document of a nonpublic entity are covered by the reporting guidance in this section. Condensed financial statements of such entities are not covered. This means the form of report described in this section cannot be issued on the condensed financial statements of a nonpublic entity. If the condensed financial statements are in a client-prepared document that contains audited financial statements, the Section 551 form of report could be used. If the condensed financial statements are in a client-prepared (or auditor-submitted) document that does not contain complete audited financial statements, there are two options:

1. An adverse opinion
2. A compilation report for statements that omit substantially all disclosures

Although the natural inclination may be to use a compilation report, the report illustrated in a footnote to the section (reproduced in the "Illustrations" section at the end of the chapter) has the following attractive features:

1. The first paragraph describes the fact that the complete financial statements from which the condensed financial statements are derived were audited.
2. The information omitted from the condensed financial statements does not need to be included in the report (an exemption from the usual requirements of an adverse opinion).
3. Although the opinion paragraph states that the condensed financial statements are not presented fairly in conformity with GAAP, this may be more acceptable to the client than the warning paragraph in a compilation report on the omission of substantially all disclosures.

OBJECTIVES OF AU-C SECTION 810

AU-C Section 810 states that:

... the objectives of the auditor are

a. to determine whether it is appropriate to accept the engagement to report on summary financial statements and,
b. if engaged to report on summary financial statements, to

i. perform the procedures necessary as the basis for the auditor's opinion on the summary financial statements;
ii. form an opinion on whether the summary financial statements are consistent, in all material respects, with the audited financial statements from which they have been derived, in accordance with the applied criteria, based on an evaluation of the conclusions drawn from the evidence obtained; and
iii. express clearly that opinion through a written report that also describes the basis for that opinion.

FUNDAMENTAL REQUIREMENTS

CONDENSED FINANCIAL STATEMENTS

Form of Report

The auditor's report on condensed financial statements that are derived from complete financial statements that he or she has audited should include:

1. A statement that the auditor has audited and expressed an opinion on the complete financial statements.
2. The date of the audit report on the complete financial statements.
3. The type of opinion issued.

4. Whether, in the auditor's opinion, the information set forth in the condensed financial statements is fairly stated in all material respects in relation to the complete financial statements from which it has been derived.

NOTE: Several things should be noted about this requirement.

1. *This form of report can be used only in a client-prepared document of a public entity subject to an annual filing requirement of a regulatory agency. Reporting is optional. The auditor may report at the client's request, but see "Client Statements in Document," which follows.*
2. *The report states that the information set forth in the condensed financial statements and not the condensed financial statements is fairly stated. This means that the report expresses no judgment on the extent of condensation.*
3. *An example of this form of report is given in "Illustrations."*

Client Statements in Document

In a client-prepared document, a client might name the auditor and state that condensed financial statements are derived from audited financial statements. By itself, this kind of client statement does not trigger a reporting requirement for the auditor *if* the document contains audited statements or incorporates them by reference to information filed with a regulatory agency. If audited complete financial statements are not in the document or incorporated by reference and the company is public and subject to an annual filing requirement, the auditor should ask the client either to:

1. Not include his or her name or
2. Include his or her report on the condensed financial statements

NOTE: Presumably, if the entity is not subject to an annual filing requirement, the only option is to ask not to be named or to express an adverse opinion on the condensed financial statements.

Comparative Presentation with Interim Information

Condensed financial statements might be presented in comparative form with interim information for a later period that has been reviewed. The auditor may append the report on the condensed financial statements to the review report. (An example combined report is presented in "Illustrations.")

Marking Condensed Statements

It is desirable that the condensed financial statements be clearly marked as condensed.

NOTE: This is not a requirement.

Dating Report

A footnote in the section observes that reference to the date of the original audit report in the report on condensed financial statements removes any implication that records, events, or transactions after that date have been audited. Nothing else is mentioned about dating.

NOTE: Presumably, the report date for a separate report on condensed financial statements should be the date of the original audit report because that is when fieldwork was completed. A combined report on both a review of interim information and on condensed financial statements could be dated as of the completion of the review or might be dual-dated.

SELECTED FINANCIAL DATA

Form of Report

The auditor's report on selected financial data should specifically identify the data being reported on and include:

1. A statement that the auditor has audited and expressed an opinion on the complete financial statements
2. The type of opinion issued
3. Whether, in the auditor's opinion, the information set forth in the selected financial data is fairly stated in all material respects in relation to the complete financial statements from which it has been derived

NOTE: Several things should be noted about this requirement.

1. *This form of report may be used only in a client-prepared document (public or nonpublic entity) that contains audited financial statements or, for a public entity, that incorporates such statements by reference to information filed with a regulatory agency. Reporting on selected financial data is optional. The auditor may report at the client's request, but there is no requirement to report. However, see "Client Statements in Document," which follows.*
2. *The report states that the information set forth in the selected financial data and not the selected financial data is fairly stated. This means that the report expresses no judgment on the appropriateness of selection. However, if a regulatory agency has specified the selected financial data that have to be presented, the auditor should take exception to omission of the specified information.*
3. *Because the report on selected financial data is normally included as a paragraph in the standard report, dating is not an issue.*
4. *An example of this form of report is given in "Illustrations."*

Client Statements in Document

A client might name the auditor and state that selected data are derived from financial statements he or she audited. If the client-prepared document contains audited financial statements or incorporates them by reference to information filed with a regulatory agency, the auditor is not required to report on the selected financial data. If the document does not contain audited financial statements or incorporate them by reference, the auditor should:

1. Ask the client not to name or refer to him or her, or
2. Disclaim an opinion on the selected financial data and ask that the disclaimer be included.

NOTE: These requirements are more stringent than those for condensed financial statements. In effect, the auditor is not permitted to be associated, even if not named, with selected financial data unless audited financial statements are included in the document or incorporated by reference; a client may not even state that the selected financial data is derived from audited financial statements.

INTERPRETATIONS

There are no interpretations for this section.

AU ILLUSTRATIONS

The following reports adapted from AU Section 552 are illustrated:

1. A separate report on condensed financial statements
2. A combined report on reviewed and condensed financial statements
3. An adverse opinion on separately presented condensed financial statements
4. A standard report with a report on selected financial data

ILLUSTRATION 1. SEPARATE REPORT ON CONDENSED FINANCIAL STATEMENTS (FROM AU 552.06)

To the Board of Directors
Widget Company
Main City, USA

Report of Independent Registered Public Accounting Firm

We have audited, in accordance with the standards of the Public Company Accounting Oversight Board (United States), the consolidated balance sheet of Widget Company and subsidiaries as of December 31, 20X5, and the related consolidated statements of income, retained earnings, and cash flows for the year then ended (not presented herein); and in our report dated February 15, 20X6, we expressed an unqualified opinion on those consolidated financial statements.

In our opinion, the information set forth in the accompanying condensed consolidated financial statements is fairly stated, in all material respects, in relation to the consolidated financial statements from which it has been derived.

Smith and Jones
March 15, 20X6

ILLUSTRATION 2. COMBINED REPORT ON REVIEWED AND CONDENSED FINANCIAL STATEMENTS (FROM AU 552.08)

To the Board of Directors
Widget Company
Main City, USA

Report of Independent Registered Public Accounting Firm

We have reviewed the condensed consolidated balance sheet of Widget Company and subsidiaries as of March 31, 20X6, and the related condensed consolidated statements of income and cash flows for the three-month periods ended March 31, 20X6 and 20X5. These financial statements are the responsibility of the company's management.

We conducted our review in accordance with the standards of the Public Company Accounting Oversight Board (United States). A review of interim financial information consists principally of applying analytical procedures to financial data, and making inquiries of persons responsible for financial and accounting matters. It is substantially less in scope than an audit in accordance with the standards of the Public Company Accounting Oversight Board (United States), the objective of which is the expression of an opinion regarding the financial statements taken as a whole. Accordingly, we do not express such an opinion.

Based on our review, we are not aware of any material modifications that should be made to the condensed consolidated financial statements referred to above for them to be in conformity with US generally accepted accounting principles.

We have previously audited, in accordance with the standards of the Public Company Accounting Oversight Board (United States), the consolidated balance sheet as of December 31,

20X5, and the related consolidated statements of income, retained earnings, and cash flows for the year then ended (not presented herein); and in our report dated February 15, 20X6, we expressed an unqualified opinion on those consolidated financial statements. In our opinion, the information set forth in the accompanying condensed consolidated balance sheet as of December 31, 20X5, is fairly stated in all material respects in relation to the consolidated balance sheet from which it has been derived.

Smith and Jones
April 15, 20X6

ILLUSTRATION 3. ADVERSE OPINION ON SEPARATELY PRESENTED CONDENSED FINANCIAL STATEMENTS (FROM AU 552.07, FOOTNOTE 6)

To the Board of Directors
Widget Company
Main City, USA

Independent Auditor's Report

We have audited the consolidated balance sheet of Widget Company and subsidiaries as of December 31, 20X5, and the related earnings, and cash flows for the year then ended (not presented herein). These financial statements are the responsibility of the Company's management. Our responsibility is to express an opinion on these financial statements based on our audit.

We conducted our audit in accordance with auditing standards generally accepted in the United States of America. Those standards require that we plan and perform the audit to obtain reasonable assurance about whether the financial statements are free of material misstatement. An audit includes examining, on a test basis, evidence supporting the amounts and disclosures in the financial statements. An audit also includes assessing the accounting principles used and significant estimates made by management, as well as evaluating the overall financial statement presentation. We believe that our audit provides a reasonable basis for our opinion.

The condensed consolidated balance sheet as of December 31, 20X5, and the related condensed statements of income, retained earnings, and cash flows for the year then ended, presented on pages xx–xx, are presented as a summary and therefore do not include all of the disclosures required by accounting principles generally accepted in the United States of America.

In our opinion, because of the significance of the omission of the information referred to in the preceding paragraphs, the condensed consolidated financial statements referred to above do not present fairly, in conformity with accounting principles generally accepted in the United States of America, the financial position of Widget Company and subsidiaries as of December 31, 20X5, or the results of its operations or its cash flows for the year then ended.

Smith and Jones
March 15, 20X6

ILLUSTRATION 4. STANDARD REPORT WITH REPORT ON SELECTED FINANCIAL DATA (FROM AU 552.10)

To the Board of Directors
Widget Company
Main City, USA

Report of Independent Registered Public Accounting Firm

We have audited the consolidated balance sheets of Widget Company and subsidiaries as of December 31, 20X5 and 20X4, and the related consolidated statements of income, retained earnings, and cash flows for each of the three years in the period ended December 31, 20X5. These financial statements are the responsibility of the Company's management. Our responsibility is to express an opinion on these financial statements based on our audit.

We conducted our audits in accordance with the standards of the Public Company Accounting Oversight Board (United States). Those standards require that we plan and perform the audit to obtain reasonable assurance about whether the financial statements are free of material misstatement. An audit includes examining, on a test basis, evidence supporting the amounts and disclosures in the financial statements. An audit also includes assessing the accounting principles used and significant estimates made by management, as well as evaluating the overall financial statement presentation. We believe that our audits provided a reasonable basis for our opinion.

In our opinion, the consolidated financial statements referred to above present fairly, in all material respects, the financial position of the Widget Company and subsidiaries as of December 31, 20X5 and 20X4, and the results of their operations and their cash flows for each of the three years in the period ended December 31, 20X5, in conformity with accounting principles generally accepted in the United States of America.

We have also previously audited, in accordance with the standards of the Public Company Accounting Oversight Board (United States), the consolidated balance sheets as of December 31, 20X3, 20X2, and 20X1, and the related statements of income, retained earnings, and cash flows for the years ended December 31, 20X2 and 20X1 (none of which are presented herein); and we expressed unqualified opinions on those consolidated financial statements.

In our opinion, the information set forth in the selected financial data for each of the five years in the period ended December 31, 20X5, appearing on page xx, is fairly stated, in all material respects, in relation to the consolidated financial statements from which it has been derived.

Smith and Jones
March 15, 20X6

AU-C 810 ILLUSTRATIONS

The following reports on summary financial statements are illustrated:

1. An Unmodified Opinion Is Expressed on the Summary Financial Statements (the Auditor's Report on the Summary Financial Statements Is Dated Later Than the Date of the Auditor's Report on the Financial Statements from Which the Summary Financial Statements Are Derived)
2. An Unmodified Opinion Is Expressed on the Summary Financial Statements and a Qualified Opinion Is Expressed on the Audited Financial Statements
3. An Adverse Opinion Is Expressed on the Audited Financial Statements (as a Result of the Adverse Opinion on the Audited Financial Statements, It Is Inappropriate to Express, and the Auditor Does Not Express, an Opinion on the Summary Financial Statements)
4. An Adverse Opinion Is Expressed on the Summary Financial Statements Because They Are Not Consistent, in All Material Respects, with the Audited Financial Statements, in Accordance with the Applied Criteria

> **ILLUSTRATION 1. AN UNMODIFIED OPINION IS EXPRESSED ON THE SUMMARY FINANCIAL STATEMENTS (THE AUDITOR'S REPORT ON THE SUMMARY FINANCIAL STATEMENTS IS DATED LATER THAN THE DATE OF THE AUDITOR'S REPORT ON THE FINANCIAL STATEMENTS FROM WHICH THE SUMMARY FINANCIAL STATEMENTS ARE DERIVED)**

Circumstances include all of the following:

- An unmodified opinion is expressed on the audited financial statements.

- Criteria are developed by management for the preparation of the summary financial statements and are adequately disclosed in Note X. The auditor has determined that the criteria are acceptable in the circumstances.
- An unmodified opinion is expressed on the summary financial statements.
- The auditor's report on the summary financial statements is dated later than the date of the auditor's report on the financial statements from which the summary financial statements are derived.

Independent Auditor's Report on Summary Financial Statements

[Appropriate Addressee]

The accompanying summary financial statements, which comprise the summary balance sheet as of December 31, 20X1, the summary income statement, summary statement of changes in stockholders' equity, and summary cash flow statement for the year then ended, and the related notes, are derived from the audited financial statements of ABC Company as of and for the year ended December 31, 20X1. We expressed an unmodified audit opinion on those audited financial statements in our report dated February 15, 20X2. The audited financial statements, and the summary financial statements derived therefrom, do not reflect the effects of events, if any, that occurred subsequent to the date of our report on the audited financial statements.

The summary financial statements do not contain all the disclosures required by *[describe financial reporting framework applied in the preparation of the financial statements of ABC Company]*. Reading the summary financial statements, therefore, is not a substitute for reading the audited financial statements of ABC Company.

Management's Responsibility for the Summary Financial Statements

Management is responsible for the preparation of the summary financial statements on the basis described in Note X.

Auditor's Responsibility

Our responsibility is to express an opinion about whether the summary financial statements are consistent, in all material respects, with the audited financial statements based on our procedures, which were conducted in accordance with auditing standards generally accepted in the United States of America. The procedures consisted principally of comparing the summary financial statements with the related information in the audited financial statements from which the summary financial statements have been derived, and evaluating whether the summary financial statements are prepared in accordance with the basis described in Note X. We did not perform any audit procedures regarding the audited financial statements after the date of our report on those financial statements.

Opinion

In our opinion, the summary financial statements of ABC Company as of and for the year ended December 31, 20X1 referred to above are consistent, in all material respects, with the audited financial statements from which they have been derived, on the basis described in Note X.

[Auditor's signature]

[Auditor's city and state]

[Date of the auditor's report]

ILLUSTRATION 2. AN UNMODIFIED OPINION IS EXPRESSED ON THE SUMMARY FINANCIAL STATEMENTS AND A QUALIFIED OPINION IS EXPRESSED ON THE AUDITED FINANCIAL STATEMENTS

Circumstances include all of the following:

- A qualified opinion is expressed on the audited financial statements.
- Criteria are developed by management for the preparation of the summary financial statements and are adequately disclosed in Note X. The auditor has determined that the criteria are acceptable in the circumstances.
- An unmodified opinion is expressed on the summary financial statements.

Independent Auditor's Report on Summary Financial Statements

[*Appropriate Addressee*]

The accompanying summary financial statements, which comprise the summary balance sheet as of December 31, 20X1, the summary income statement, summary statement of changes in stockholders' equity, and summary cash flow statement for the year then ended, and the related notes, are derived from the audited financial statements of ABC Company as of and for the year ended December 31, 20X1. We expressed a qualified audit opinion on those audited financial statements in our report dated February 15, 20X2 (see below).

The summary financial statements do not contain all the disclosures required by [*describe financial reporting framework applied in the preparation of the financial statements of ABC Company*]. Reading the summary financial statements, therefore, is not a substitute for reading the audited financial statements of ABC Company.

Management's Responsibility for the Summary Financial Statements

Management is responsible for the preparation of the summary financial statements on the basis described in Note X.

Auditor's Responsibility

Our responsibility is to express an opinion about whether the summary financial statements are consistent, in all material respects, with the audited financial statements based on our procedures, which were conducted in accordance with auditing standards generally accepted in the United States of America. The procedures consisted principally of comparing the summary financial statements with the related information in the audited financial statements from which the summary financial statements have been derived, and evaluating whether the summary financial statements are prepared in accordance with the basis described in Note X.

Opinion

In our opinion, the summary financial statements of ABC Company as of and for the year ended December 31, 20X1 referred to above are consistent, in all material respects, with the audited financial statements from which they have been derived, on the basis described in Note X.

The summary financial statements are misstated to the equivalent extent as the audited financial statements of ABC Company as of and for the year ended December 31, 20X1. The misstatement of the audited financial statements is described in our qualified audit opinion in our report dated February 15, 20X2. Our qualified audit opinion is based on the fact that the Company's inventories are carried in the balance sheet in those audited financial statements at $XXX. Management has not stated the inventories at the lower of cost or net realizable value but has stated them solely at cost, which constitutes a departure from [*describe financial reporting framework applied in the preparation of the financial statements of ABC Company*]. The Company's records indicate that, had management stated the inventories at the lower of cost or net realizable value, an amount of $XXX would have been required to write the inventories down to their net realizable value. Accordingly, cost of sales would have been increased by $XXX, and income tax, net income, and stockholders' equity would have been reduced by $XXX, $XXX, and $XXX, respectively. Our qualified audit opinion states that, except for the effects of the described matter, those financial statements present fairly, in all material respects, the financial position of ABC Company as of December 31, 20X1, and the results of its operations and its cash flows for the year then ended in accordance with [*describe financial reporting framework applied in the preparation of the financial statements of ABC Company*].

[*Auditor's signature*]

[*Auditor's city and state*]

[*Date of the auditor's report*]

> **ILLUSTRATION 3. AN ADVERSE OPINION IS EXPRESSED ON THE AUDITED FINANCIAL STATEMENTS (AS A RESULT OF THE ADVERSE OPINION ON THE AUDITED FINANCIAL STATEMENTS, IT IS INAPPROPRIATE TO EXPRESS, AND THE AUDITOR DOES NOT EXPRESS, AN OPINION ON THE SUMMARY FINANCIAL STATEMENTS)**

Circumstances include both of the following:

- An adverse opinion is expressed on the audited financial statements. As a result of the adverse opinion on the audited financial statements, it is inappropriate to express, and the auditor does not express, an opinion on the summary financial statements, as described in paragraph .16.
- Criteria are developed by management for the preparation of the summary financial statements and are adequately disclosed in Note X. The auditor has determined that the criteria are acceptable in the circumstances.

Independent Auditor's Report on Summary Financial Statements

[*Appropriate Addressee*]

Management derived the accompanying summary financial statements, which comprise the summary balance sheet as of December 31, 20X1, the summary income statement, summary statement of changes in stockholders' equity, and summary cash flow statement for the year then ended, and the related notes, from the audited financial statements of ABC Company as of and for the year ended December 31, 20X1. Management is responsible for the preparation of these summary financial statements on the basis described in Note X.

In our report dated February 15, 20X2, we expressed an adverse audit opinion on the financial statements of ABC Company as of and for the year ended December 31, 20X1. The basis for our adverse audit opinion was [*describe basis for adverse audit opinion*]. Our adverse audit opinion stated that [*describe adverse audit opinion*].

Because of the significance of the matter discussed above, it is inappropriate to express, and we do not express, an opinion on the summary financial statements of ABC Company as of and for the year ended December 31, 20X1.

[*Auditor's signature*]

[*Auditor's city and state*]

[*Date of the auditor's report*]

> **ILLUSTRATION 4. AN ADVERSE OPINION IS EXPRESSED ON THE SUMMARY FINANCIAL STATEMENTS BECAUSE THEY ARE NOT CONSISTENT, IN ALL MATERIAL RESPECTS, WITH THE AUDITED FINANCIAL STATEMENTS, IN ACCORDANCE WITH THE APPLIED CRITERIA**

Circumstances include all of the following:

- An unmodified opinion is expressed on the audited financial statements.
- Established criteria for the preparation of summary financial statements exist.
- The auditor expresses an adverse opinion on the summary financial statements because they are not consistent, in all material respects, with the audited financial statements, in accordance with the applied criteria.

Independent Auditor's Report on Summary Financial Statements

[*Appropriate Addressee*]

The accompanying summary financial statements, which comprise the summary balance sheet as of December 31, 20X1, the summary income statement, summary statement of changes in stockholders' equity, and summary cash flow statement for the year then ended, and the related notes, are derived from the audited financial statements of ABC Company as of and for the year ended December 31, 20X1. We expressed an unmodified audit opinion on those audited financial statements in our report dated February 15, 20X2.

The summary financial statements do not contain all the disclosures required by [*describe financial reporting framework applied in the preparation of the financial statements of ABC Company*]. Reading the summary financial statements, therefore, is not a substitute for reading the audited financial statements of ABC Company.

Management's Responsibility for the Summary Financial Statements

Management is responsible for the preparation of the summary financial statements on the basis described in Note X.

Auditor's Responsibility

Our responsibility is to express an opinion about whether the summary financial statements are consistent, in all material respects, with the audited financial statements based on our procedures, which were conducted in accordance with auditing standards generally accepted in the United States of America. The procedures consisted principally of comparing the summary financial statements with the related information in the audited financial statements from which the summary financial statements have been derived, and evaluating whether the summary financial statements are prepared in accordance with the basis described in Note X.

Basis for Adverse Opinion

[*Describe matter that caused the summary financial statements not to be consistent, in all material respects, with the audited financial statements, in accordance with the applied criteria.*]

Adverse Opinion

In our opinion, because of the significance of the matter discussed in the *Basis for Adverse Opinion* paragraph, the summary financial statements of ABC Company as of and for the year ended December 31, 20X1 referred to above are not consistent with the audited financial statements from which they have been derived, on the basis described in Note X.

[*Auditor's signature*]

[*Auditor's city and state*]

[*Date of the auditor's report*]

AU 558 Required Supplementary Information

AU-C 730 Required Supplementary Information

AU EFFECTIVE DATE AND APPLICABILITY

Original Pronouncement	Statement on Auditing Standards (SAS) 120.
Effective Date	These standards currently are effective.
Applicability	Audits of financial statements that are required to be accompanied by certain supplementary information.

AU-C EFFECTIVE DATE AND SUMMARY OF CHANGES

To address practice issues, SAS No. 120, *Required Supplementary Information*, was one of the clarified standards issued before SAS No. 122. It was issued in February 2010 and is effective for audits of financial statements for periods beginning on or after December 15, 2010.

SAS No. 120 was codified in AU 558 when issued, but was moved to AU-C 730 with the issuance of SAS No. 122. Some conforming changes were made in specific paragraphs and footnotes due to the issuance of SAS No. 122, but no substantive changes were made.

AU DEFINITIONS OF TERMS

Applicable financial reporting framework. The financial reporting framework that has been adopted by management for the preparation of its financial statements.

Basic financial statements. Financial statements that are presented in accordance with an applicable financial reporting framework established by a designated accounting standard setter.

Designated accounting standard setter. A body designated by the American Institute of Certified Public Accountants (AICPA) council to establish GAAS, which are the Financial Accounting Standards Board (FASB), the Governmental Accounting Standards Board (GASB), the Federal Accounting Standards Advisory Board (FASAB), and the International Accounting Standards Board (IASB).

Required supplementary information. Additional reporting required by a designated accounting standard setter that accompanies an entity's basic financial statements. The designated accounting standard setter considers this supplementary information to be essential for placing the basic financial statements in an appropriate context.

AU-C DEFINITIONS OF TERMS

Source: AU-C 730.04

Applicable financial reporting framework. The financial reporting framework adopted by management and, when appropriate, those charged with governance in the preparation and fair presentation of the financial statements that is acceptable in view of the nature of the entity and the objective of the financial statements, or that is required by law or regulation.

Basic financial statements. Financial statements presented in accordance with an applicable financial reporting framework as established by a designated accounting standards setter, excluding required supplementary information.

Designated accounting standards setter. A body designated by the Council of the AICPA to promulgate generally accepted accounting principles (GAAP) pursuant to Rule 202, *Compliance with Standards* (ET sec. 202 par. .01), and Rule 203, *Accounting Principles* (ET sec. 203 par. .01) of the AICPA Code of Professional Conduct.

Prescribed guidelines. The authoritative guidelines established by the designated accounting standards setter for the methods of measurement and presentation of the required supplementary information.

Required supplementary information. Information that a designated accounting standards setter requires to accompany an entity's basic financial statements. Required supplementary information is not part of the basic financial statements; however, a designated accounting standards setter considers the information to be an essential part of financial reporting for placing the basic financial statements in an appropriate operational, economic, or historical context. In addition, authoritative guidelines for the methods of measurement and presentation of the information have been established.

OBJECTIVES OF AU SECTION 558

An accounting standard setter may require that certain information accompany an entity's financial statements. This section addresses the auditor's responsibility to perform certain procedures in order to communicate whether some or all of the supplementary information has not been presented in accordance with the guidelines promulgated by the accounting standard setter, or when material modifications should be made to the supplementary information.

OBJECTIVES OF AU-C SECTION 730

AU-C 730.03 states that:

> . . . the objectives of the auditor when a designated accounting standards setter requires information to accompany an entity's basic financial statements are to perform specified procedures in order to

a. describe, in the auditor's report, whether required supplementary information is presented and
   b. communicate therein when some or all of the required supplementary information has not been presented in accordance with guidelines established by a designated accounting standards setter or when the auditor has identified material modifications that should be made to the required supplementary information for it to be in accordance with guidelines established by the designated accounting standards setter.

FUNDAMENTAL REQUIREMENTS

PROCEDURES

The auditor should apply these procedures to required supplementary information:

1. *Preparation methods.* Make inquiries regarding the preparation of supplementary information. This should include whether the information is being measured and presented in accordance with specific guidelines, whether these methods have changed and the reasons for doing so, and whether there were any significant assumptions underlying these methods.
2. *Consistency review.* Compare the information for consistency with the responses to the inquiries in step 1, as well as to the basic financial statements and other knowledge obtained during the basic financial statements audit.
3. *Written representations.* Obtain written representations from management that it acknowledges its responsibility for the required supplementary information, that the information is measured and presented in accordance with specific guidelines, whether these methods have changed and the reasons for doing so, and regarding any significant assumptions underlying these methods.

NOTE: *If the auditor cannot complete these procedures due to significant difficulties in dealing with management, then inform those charged with governance.*

REPORTING ON SUPPLEMENTARY INFORMATION

Include an explanatory paragraph in the auditor's report, after the opinion paragraph that refers to the supplementary information. This paragraph should explain the following items, as applicable:

1. *The required supplementary information is included, and the auditor has applied the procedures noted above.* If so, state that the applicable financial reporting framework requires that the supplementary information be presented to supplement the basic financial statements. Also, state that such information, although not a part of the basic financial statements, is required by the designated accounting standard setter, which considers it to be an essential part of financial reporting for placing the context. Further, state that the auditor has applied certain limited procedures to the required supplementary information in accordance with auditing standards generally accepted in the United States of America, which consisted of inquiries of management about the methods of preparing the information and comparing the information for consistency with management's responses to the auditor's inquiries, the basic financial statements, and other knowledge the auditor obtained during the audit of the basic financial statements. Finally, state that the auditor does not express an opinion or provide any assurance on the information, because the limited procedures do not

provide the auditor with sufficient evidence to express an opinion or provide any assurance.
2. *The required supplementary information is omitted.* If so, state that management has omitted the information that is required to be presented by the designated accounting standard setter. Also, state that such missing information, although not a part of the basic financial statements is required by the designated accounting standard setter, who considers it to be an essential part of financial reporting for placing the basic financial statements in an appropriate operational, economic, or historical context. Finally, state that the auditor's opinion on the basic financial statements is not affected by the missing information.
3. *Some required supplementary information is missing and some is presented in accordance with the guidelines.* If so, state that management has omitted information that the designated accounting standard setter requires be presented to supplement the basic financial statements. Also state that such missing information, although not a part of the basic financial statements, is required by the designated accounting standard setter, which considers it to be an essential part of financial reporting for placing the basic financial statements in an appropriate operational, economic, or historical context. Finally, state that the auditor's opinion on the basic financial statements is not affected by the missing information.
4. *There are material departures from the guidelines.* If so, state that although the auditor's opinion on the basic financial statements is not affected, there are material departures from the guidelines (and describe the material departures).
5. *The auditor was unable to complete the procedures noted above.* If so, state that the auditor was unable to apply certain limited procedures to the required supplementary information in accordance with auditing standards generally accepted in the United States, and state the reasons. Also state that the auditor does not express an opinion or provide any assurance on the information.
6. *The auditor has unresolved doubts about whether the supplementary information is presented in accordance with the guidelines.* If so, state that although the auditor's opinion on the basic financial statements is not affected, the results of the limited procedures have raised doubts about whether material modifications should be made to the required supplementary information for it to be presented in accordance with the guidelines established the designated accounting standard setter.

NOTE: *Required supplementary information is not part of the basic financial statements, so the auditor's opinion on the fairness of presentation of financial statements is not affected by the presentation of the supplementary information or the failure to present some or all of it.*

Examples of the above variations on the auditor's report regarding required supplementary information are noted below under "Illustrations."

INTERPRETATIONS

SUPPLEMENTARY OIL AND GAS INFORMATION (FEBRUARY 1989; REVISED JUNE 2009)

FASB ASC 932-235, *Extractive Activities—Oil and Gas Notes to Financial Statements*, requires that publicly traded entities with significant oil- and gas-producing activities include, with complete sets of annual financial statements, disclosures of proved oil and gas reserve quantities, changes in reserve quantities, a standardized measure of discounted future net cash flows relating to reserve quantities, and changes in the standardized measure. The SEC requires that the disclosures related to annual periods be presented for each annual period for which an income statement is required and the disclosures as of the end of an annual period be presented as of the date of each audited balance sheet required. These disclosures are supplementary information and may be presented outside the basic financial statements. In these circumstances, the auditor should consider the provisions of this section.

When making the inquiries in this section, the auditor's inquiries should be directed to management's understanding of the specific requirements for disclosure of supplementary oil and gas reserve information, including the following from AU 9558.04–.05:

1. The factors considered in determining the reported reserve quantity information, such as including in the information the following:

    a. Quantities of all domestic and foreign proved oil and gas reserves owned by the entity net of interests of others.
    b. Reserves attributable to consolidated subsidiaries.
    c. A proportionate share of reserves of investees that are proportionately consolidated.
    d. Reserves relating to royalty interests owned.

2. The separate disclosure of items such as the following:

    a. The entity's share of oil and gas produced from royalty interests for which reserve quantity information is unavailable.
    b. Reserves subject to long-term agreements with governments or authorities in which the entity participates in the operation or otherwise serves as producer.
    c. The entity's proportional interest in reserves of investees accounted for by the equity method.
    d. Subsequent events, important economic factors, or significant uncertainties affecting particular components of the reserve quantity information.
    e. Whether the entity's reserves are located entirely within its home country.
    f. Whether certain named governments restrict the disclosure of reserves or require that the reserve estimates include reserves other than proved.

3. The factors considered in determining the standardized measure of discounted future net cash flows to be reported.

The auditor should also do the following:

1. Inquire about whether the person who estimated the entity's reserve quantity information has appropriate qualifications (see Section 336, *Using the Work of a Specialist*).
2. Compare the entity's recent production with its reserve estimates for properties that have significant production or significant reserve quantities and inquire about disproportionate ratios.
3. Compare the entity's reserve quantity information with the corresponding information used for depletion and amortization, and make inquiries when differences exist.
4. Inquire about the calculation of the standardized measure of discounted future net cash flows. These inquiries might include matters such as the following:

a. The prices used to develop future cash inflows from estimated production of the proved reserves are based on prices received at the end of the entity's fiscal year and whether the calculation of future cash inflows appropriately reflects the terms of sales contracts and applicable governmental laws and regulations.
b. The entity's estimate of the nature and timing of future development of the proved reserves and the future rates of production are consistent with available development plans.
c. The entity's estimates of future development and production costs are based on year-end costs and assumed continuation of existing economic conditions.
d. Future income tax expenses have been computed using the appropriate year-end statutory tax rates, with consideration of future tax rates already legislated, after giving effect to the tax basis of the properties involved, permanent differences, and tax credits and allowances.
e. The future net cash flows have been appropriately discounted.
f. With respect to full cost companies, the estimated future development costs are consistent with the corresponding amounts used for depletion and amortization purposes.
g. With respect to the disclosure of changes in the standardized measure of discounted future net cash flows, the entity has computed and presented the sources of the changes in conformity with the requirements of FASB Accounting Standards Codification (ASC) 932-235.

5. Inquire about whether the methods and bases for estimating the entity's reserve information are documented and whether the information is current.

If the auditor believes that the information may not be presented within applicable guidelines, he or she should ordinarily make additional inquiries. However, the auditor may not be able to evaluate responses to the additional inquiries. In these circumstances, the auditor should report as follows from AU 9558.06:

> The oil and gas reserve information is not a required part of the basic financial statements, and we did not audit and do not express an opinion on such information. However, we have applied certain limited procedures prescribed by professional standards that raised doubts that we were unable to resolve regarding whether material modifications should be made to the information for it to conform with guidelines established by the Financial Accounting Standards Board. [*The auditor should consider including in the report the reason(s) why he or she was unable to resolve his/her doubts. For example, the auditor may wish to state that the information was estimated by a person lacking appropriate qualifications.*]

TECHNIQUES FOR APPLICATION

COORDINATION WITH OTHER AUDIT AREAS

The auditor should coordinate the application of procedures to supplementary information with procedures applied in other areas. For example, for an entity engaged in oil- and gas-producing activities, the entity might be required to pay state or federal taxes on oil and gas produced in particular geographical areas. In this circumstance, the auditor would want to coordinate work on tax expense and payables and segment disclosures with work on the required supplementary oil and gas information.

AU ILLUSTRATIONS

The following examples from AU 558 illustrate the separate explanatory paragraphs that might be added to the standard report in the indicated circumstances.

ILLUSTRATION 1. SUPPLEMENTARY INFORMATION IS INCLUDED AND PROCEDURES WERE PERFORMED

[*Identify the applicable financial reporting framework*] require that the [*identify the required supplementary information*] on page XX be presented to supplement the basic financial statements. Such information, although not a part of the basic financial statements, is required by [*identify the designated accounting standard setter*] who considers it to be an essential part of financial reporting for placing the basic financial statements in an appropriate operational, economic, or historical context. We have applied certain limited procedures to the required supplementary information in accordance with auditing standards generally accepted in the United States of America, which consisted of inquiries of management about the methods of preparing the information and comparing the information for consistency with management's responses to our inquiries, the basic financial statements, and other knowledge we obtained during our audit of the basic financial statements. We do not express an opinion or provide any assurance on the information because the limited procedures do not provide us with sufficient evidence to express an opinion or provide any assurance.

ILLUSTRATION 2. ALL REQUIRED SUPPLEMENTARY INFORMATION OMITTED

Management has omitted [*describe the missing required supplementary information*] that [*identify the applicable financial reporting framework*] require to be presented to supplement the basic financial statements. Such missing information, although not a part of the basic financial statements, is required by [*identify designated accounting standard setter*] who considers it to be an essential part of financial reporting for placing the basic financial statements in an appropriate operational, economic, or historical context. Our opinion on the basic financial statements is not affected by this missing information.

ILLUSTRATION 3. SOME REQUIRED SUPPLEMENTARY INFORMATION IS OMITTED AND SOME IS PRESENTED IN ACCORDANCE WITH THE PRESCRIBED GUIDELINES

[*Identify the applicable financial reporting framework*] require that [*identify the included supplementary information*] be presented to supplement the basic financial statements. Such information, although not a part of the basic financial statements, is required by [*identify designated accounting standard setter*], who considers it to be an essential part of financial reporting for placing the basic financial statements in an appropriate operational, economic, or historical context. We have applied certain limited procedures to the required supplementary information in accordance with auditing standards generally accepted in the United States of America, which consisted of inquiries of management about the methods of preparing the information and comparing the information for consistency with management's responses to our inquiries, the basic financial statements, and other knowledge we obtained during our audit of the basic financial statements. We do not express an opinion or provide any assurance on the information because the limited procedures do not provide us with evidence sufficient to express an opinion or provide any assurance.

Management has omitted [*describe the missing required supplementary information*] that [*identify the applicable financial reporting framework*] require to be presented to supplement the basic financial statements. Such missing information, although not a part of the basic financial statements, is required by [*identify designated accounting standard setter*] who considers it to be an essential part of financial reporting for placing the basic financial statements in an appropriate operation, economic, or historical context. Our opinion on the basic financial statements is not affected by this missing information.

> **ILLUSTRATION 4. MATERIAL DEPARTURES FROM PRESCRIBED GUIDELINES IDENTIFIED**

[*Identify the applicable financial reporting framework*] require that [*identify the supplementary information*] on page XX be presented to supplement the basic financial statements. Such information, although not a part of the basic financial statements, is required by [*identify designated accounting standard setter*] who considers it to be an essential part of financial reporting for placing the basic financial statements in an appropriate operational, economic, or historical context. We have applied certain limited procedures to the required supplementary information in accordance with auditing standards generally accepted in the United States of America, which consisted of inquiries of management about the methods of preparing the information and comparing the information for consistency with management's responses to our inquiries, the basic financial statements, and other knowledge we obtained during our audit of the basic financial statements. Although our opinion on the basic financial statements is not affected, the following material departures from the prescribed guidelines exist [*identify the required supplementary information and describe the material departures from the prescribed guidelines*]. We do not express an opinion or provide any assurance on the information.

> **ILLUSTRATION 5. SPECIFIED PROCEDURES NOT COMPLETED**

[*Identify the applicable financial reporting framework*] require that the [*identify the supplementary information*] on page XX be presented to supplement the basic financial statements. Such information, although not a part of the basic financial statements, is required by [*identify designated accounting standard setter*], who considers it to be an essential part of financial reporting for placing the basic financial statements in an appropriate operational, economic, or historical context. We were unable to apply certain limited procedures to the required supplementary information in accordance with auditing standards generally accepted in the United States of America because [*state the reasons*]. We do not express an opinion or provide any assurance on the information.

> **ILLUSTRATION 6. UNRESOLVED DOUBTS ABOUT WHETHER THE REQUIRED SUPPLEMENTARY INFORMATION IS IN ACCORDANCE WITH PRESCRIBED GUIDELINES**

[*Identify the applicable financial reporting framework*] require that the [*identify the supplementary information*] on page XX be presented to supplement the basic financial statements. Such information, although not a part of the basic financial statements, is required by [*identify designated accounting standard setter*] who considers it to be an essential part of financial reporting for placing the basic financial statements in an appropriate operational, economic, or historical context. We have applied certain limited procedures to the required supplementary information in accordance with auditing standards generally accepted in the United States of America, which consisted of inquiries of management about the methods of preparing the information and comparing the information for consistency with management's responses to our inquiries, the basic financial statements, and other knowledge we obtained during our audit of the basic financial statements. We do not express an opinion or provide any assurance on the information because the limited procedures do not provide us with sufficient evidence to express an opinion or provide any assurance. Although our opinion on the basic financial statements is not affected, the results of the limited procedures have raised doubts about whether material modifications should be made to the required supplementary information for it to be presented in accordance with guidelines established by [*identify designated accounting standard setter*].

AU-C 730 ILLUSTRATIONS

The following examples from AU-C 730 illustrate the separate explanatory paragraphs that might be added to the standard report in the indicated circumstances.

ILLUSTRATION 1. THE REQUIRED SUPPLEMENTARY INFORMATION IS INCLUDED, THE AUDITOR HAS APPLIED THE SPECIFIED PROCEDURES, AND NO MATERIAL DEPARTURES FROM PRESCRIBED GUIDELINES HAVE BEEN IDENTIFIED

[*Identify the applicable financial reporting framework (for example, accounting principles generally accepted in the United States of America)*] require that the [*identify the required supplementary information*] on page XX be presented to supplement the basic financial statements. Such information, although not a part of the basic financial statements, is required by [*identify designated accounting standards setter*], who considers it to be an essential part of financial reporting for placing the basic financial statements in an appropriate operational, economic, or historical context. We have applied certain limited procedures to the required supplementary information in accordance with auditing standards generally accepted in the United States of America, which consisted of inquiries of management about the methods of preparing the information and comparing the information for consistency with management's responses to our inquiries, the basic financial statements, and other knowledge we obtained during our audit of the basic financial statements. We do not express an opinion or provide any assurance on the information because the limited procedures do not provide us with sufficient evidence to express an opinion or provide any assurance.

ILLUSTRATION 2. ALL REQUIRED SUPPLEMENTARY INFORMATION OMITTED

Management has omitted [*describe the missing required supplementary information*] that [*identify the applicable financial reporting framework (for example, accounting principles generally accepted in the United States of America)*] require to be presented to supplement the basic financial statements. Such missing information, although not a part of the basic financial statements, is required by [*identify designated accounting standards setter*] who considers it to be an essential part of financial reporting for placing the basic financial statements in an appropriate operational, economic, or historical context. Our opinion on the basic financial statements is not affected by this missing information.

ILLUSTRATION 3. SOME REQUIRED SUPPLEMENTARY INFORMATION IS OMITTED AND SOME IS PRESENTED IN ACCORDANCE WITH THE PRESCRIBED GUIDELINES

[*Identify the applicable financial reporting framework (for example, accounting principles generally accepted in the United States of America)*] require that [*identify the included supplementary information*] be presented to supplement the basic financial statements. Such information, although not a part of the basic financial statements, is required by [*identify designated accounting standards setter*] who considers it to be an essential part of financial reporting for placing the basic financial statements in an appropriate operational, economic, or historical context. We have applied certain limited procedures to the required supplementary information in accordance with auditing standards generally accepted in the United States of America, which consisted of inquiries of management about the methods of preparing the information and comparing the information for consistency with management's responses to our inquiries, the basic financial statements, and other knowledge we obtained during our audit of the basic financial statements. We do not express an opinion or provide any assurance on the information because the limited procedures do not provide us with evidence sufficient to express an opinion or provide any assurance.

Management has omitted [*describe the missing required supplementary information*] that [*identify the applicable financial reporting framework*] require to be presented to supplement the basic financial statements. Such missing information, although not a part of the basic financial statements, is required by [*identify designated accounting standards setter*] who considers it to be an essential part of financial reporting for placing the basic financial statements in an appropriate operational, economic, or historical context. Our opinion on the basic financial statements is not affected by this missing information.

ILLUSTRATION 4. MATERIAL DEPARTURES FROM PRESCRIBED GUIDELINES IDENTIFIED

[*Identify the applicable financial reporting framework (for example, accounting principles generally accepted in the United States of America)*] require that the [*identify the supplementary information*] on page XX be presented to supplement the basic financial statements. Such information, although not a part of the basic financial statements, is required by [*identify designated accounting standards setter*], who considers it to be an essential part of financial reporting for placing the basic financial statements in an appropriate operational, economic, or historical context. We have applied certain limited procedures to the required supplementary information in accordance with auditing standards generally accepted in the United States of America, which consisted of inquiries of management about the methods of preparing the information and comparing the information for consistency with management's responses to our inquiries, the basic financial statements, and other knowledge we obtained during our audit of the basic financial statements.

Although our opinion on the basic financial statements is not affected, the following material departures from the prescribed guidelines exist [*identify the required supplementary information and describe the material departures from the prescribed guidelines*]. We do not express an opinion or provide any assurance on the information.

ILLUSTRATION 5. SPECIFIED PROCEDURES NOT COMPLETED

[*Identify the applicable financial reporting framework (for example, accounting principles generally accepted in the United States of America)*] require that the [*identify the supplementary information*] on page XX be presented to supplement the basic financial statements. Such information, although not a part of the basic financial statements, is required by [*identify designated accounting standards setter*] who considers it to be an essential part of financial reporting for placing the basic financial statements in an appropriate operational, economic, or historical context. We were unable to apply certain limited procedures to the required supplementary information in accordance with auditing standards generally accepted in the United States of America because [*state the reasons*]. We do not express an opinion or provide any assurance on the information.

ILLUSTRATION 6. UNRESOLVED DOUBTS ABOUT WHETHER THE REQUIRED SUPPLEMENTARY INFORMATION IS IN ACCORDANCE WITH PRESCRIBED GUIDELINES

[*Identify the applicable financial reporting framework (for example, accounting principles generally accepted in the United States of America)*] require that the [*identify the supplementary information*] on page XX be presented to supplement the basic financial statements. Such information, although not a part of the basic financial statements, is required by [*identify designated accounting standards setter*] who considers it to be an essential part of financial reporting for placing the basic financial statements in an appropriate operational, economic, or historical context. We have applied certain limited procedures to the required supplementary information in accordance with auditing standards generally accepted in the United States of America, which consisted of inquiries of management about the methods of preparing the information and comparing the information for consistency with management's responses to our inquiries, the basic financial statements, and other knowledge we obtained during our audit of the basic financial statements. We do not express an opinion or provide any assurance on the information because the limited procedures do not provide us with sufficient evidence to express an opinion or provide any assurance. Although our opinion on the basic financial statements is not affected, the results of the limited procedures have raised doubts about whether material modifications should be made to the required supplementary information for it to be presented in accordance with guidelines established by [*identify designated accounting standards setter*]. [*The auditor may consider including in the report the reason(s) he or she was unable to resolve his or her doubts.*]

AU 560 Subsequent Events[1]

AU-C 560 Subsequent Events and Subsequently Discovered Facts

AU EFFECTIVE DATE AND APPLICABILITY

Original Pronouncements	Statements on Auditing Standards (SASs) 1, 12, and 98.
Effective Date	These statements currently are effective.
Applicability	Audits of financial statements in accordance with generally accepted auditing standards (GAAS). (The accounting considerations apply whenever the accountant is reporting on financial statements. Thus, the accounting guidance also applies in compilation or review engagements.)

AU-C EFFECTIVE DATE AND SUMMARY OF CHANGES

SAS No. 122, *Codification of Auditing Standards and Procedures,* is effective for audits of financial statements with periods ending on or after December 15, 2012.

AU-C 560 supersedes AU 530; AU 560, *Subsequent Events*; AU 561, *Subsequent Discovery of Facts Existing at the Date of the Auditor's Report*; and paragraphs .51–.73 of AU 508.

AU-C 560 does not change extant requirements in any significant respect.

AU DEFINITIONS OF TERMS

Adjustment events. Events that provide additional evidence about conditions that existed at the date of the balance sheet and affect the estimates inherent in the process of preparing financial statements.

Date of the independent auditor's report. The date of completion of fieldwork.

---

[1] This section is affected by the Public Company Accounting Oversight Board's (PCAOB's) Standard, Conforming Amendments to PCAOB Interim Standards Resulting from the Adoption of PCAOB Auditing Standard No. 5, An Audit of Internal Control over Financial Reporting That Is Integrated with an Audit of Financial Statements.

Disclosure events. Events that provide evidence about conditions that did not exist at the date of the balance sheet being reported on but arose after that date. These events should not result in adjustment of the financial statements, but disclosure of them may be required to keep the financial statements from being misleading.

Subsequent events. Events or transactions that occur after the balance sheet date but before issuance of the financial statements that have a material effect on the financial statements and therefore require adjustment or disclosure in the statements.

Subsequent period. The period from the date of the balance sheet to the date of the auditor's report.

AU-C DEFINITIONS OF TERMS

Source: AU-C 560.07

Accounting estimate. An approximation of a monetary amount in the absence of a precise means of measurement. This term is used for an amount measured at fair value when there is estimation uncertainty, as well as for other amounts that require estimation. When this section addresses only accounting estimates involving measurement at fair value, the term *fair value accounting estimates* is used.

Auditor's point estimate or auditor's range. The amount or range of amounts, respectively, derived from audit evidence for use in evaluating the recorded or disclosed amount(s).

Estimation uncertainty. The susceptibility of an accounting estimate and related disclosures to an inherent lack of precision in its measurement.

Management bias. A lack of neutrality by management in the preparation and fair presentation of information.

Management's point estimate. The amount selected by management for recognition or disclosure in the financial statements as an accounting estimate.

Outcome of an accounting estimate. The actual monetary amount that results from the resolution of the underlying transaction(s), event(s), or condition(s) addressed by the accounting estimate.

OBJECTIVES AU SECTION 560

The date of the auditor's report is generally regarded as a cutoff point of significance for the auditor's responsibility for detection of important facts that arise after the date of the financial statements. Up through that date, the auditor should apply procedures specifically directed to keeping informed about events that have a material effect on the financial statements. After that date, the auditor cannot be expected to know of such events unless the information is brought to his or her attention.

This section deals with the procedures that should be applied specifically to search for material events in the subsequent period and explains how those events should be treated in the financial statements. The guidance on treatment of subsequent events in financial statements effectively establishes generally accepted accounting principles (GAAP) in this area. When the standard was issued, the section made the following changes in authoritative literature:

1. *Adjustment versus disclosure.* The distinction between events that require adjustment versus those that need only to be disclosed is pinned entirely on whether there is a condition existing at the balance sheet date that leads to the event. This has been

described as the *clean cutoff* approach. This means, for example, that whether a loss on receivables should be adjusted for or disclosed depends on the condition that caused the loss. If the loss resulted from a customer's major casualty that happened after the balance sheet date, then disclose (don't adjust). If the event was the culmination of a condition that existed at the balance sheet date, such as a customer's bankruptcy, then adjust.
2. *Nudge to adjust.* Because determining if a condition existed at the balance sheet date may not be easy, there is a nudge to adjust. Essentially, this means when in doubt, adjust.
3. *Extent of procedures.* The procedures specifically designed to search for subsequent events were expanded.
4. *Disclosure events.* Before issuance of the standard, the literature contained a third category of events: those that did not require adjustment or disclosure. This category was removed because it was not possible to give examples of events that might not under some circumstances be necessary to disclose to keep the financial statements from being misleading.

A subtle point about the accounting guidance is that it establishes a duty for management to identify and disclose subsequent events through the issuance date of the financial statements. The auditor's duty to detect, in contrast, cuts off earlier at the audit report date.

OBJECTIVES OF AU-C SECTION 560

AU-C Section 560.05 states that:

. . . the objectives of the auditor are to

    a. *obtain sufficient appropriate audit evidence about whether events occurring between the date of the financial statements and the date of the auditor's report that require adjustment of, or disclosure in, the financial statements are appropriately reflected in those financial statements in accordance with the applicable financial reporting framework and*

    b. *respond appropriately to facts that become known to the auditor after the date of the auditor's report that, had they been known to the auditor at that date, may have caused the auditor to revise the auditor's report.*

FUNDAMENTAL REQUIREMENTS

ACCOUNTING CONSIDERATIONS

The auditor should evaluate whether management has:

1. Adjusted the financial statements for any changes in estimates resulting from relevant events after the date of the statements but before issuance—*adjustment events.*

   NOTE: The section has a "nudge" toward adjustment. That is, there is encouragement to adjust for events that affect asset realization or settlement of estimated liabilities. The only exception is changes in quoted market price in securities, because the changes represent concurrent evaluation of new conditions rather than the culmination of existing conditions.

2. Disclosed events that occurred in the subsequent period that do not require adjustment but that require disclosure to keep the financial statements from being misleading—*disclosure events*.

> NOTE: *A substantial amount of judgment is required in evaluating these events, but they usually involve significant changes in the composition or valuation of assets or liabilities presented in the financial statements being reported on, such as the issuance of bonds or stock, purchase of a business, or loss of plant or inventories from catastrophes.*

AUDITING PROCEDURES

For the subsequent period, the auditor should apply the following procedures:

1. Compare latest interim financial statements with the financial statements being audited.
2. Ask officers and other executives responsible for financial and accounting matters whether:
   a. Interim financial statements are prepared on the same basis as annual financial statements
   b. During the subsequent period there were any:
      (1) Unusual adjustments
      (2) Significant changes in:
         (a) Capital stock
         (b) Long-term debt
         (c) Working capital
         (d) Status of items accounted for on the basis of tentative or inconclusive data
         (e) Existence of substantial contingent liabilities or commitments
3. Read minutes of meetings of stockholders, directors, and relevant committees. Ask about matters dealt with at meetings for which minutes are not available.
4. Ask client's legal counsel about litigation, claims, and assessments (see Section 337, *Inquiry of a Client's Lawyer Concerning Litigation, Claims, and Assessments*).
5. Get a representation letter from management (see Section 333, *Management Representations*) that includes information concerning subsequent events.
6. Ask additional questions or apply other procedures to dispose of any questions raised by the foregoing procedures.

INTERPRETATIONS

There are no interpretations for this section.

TECHNIQUES FOR APPLICATION

GENERAL

For subsequent events, the auditor is concerned about the following:

1. Types of events
2. Procedures for becoming aware of them
3. Their effect on the audit report

Types of Subsequent Events

Subsequent events may be classified as follows:

1. Require adjustment
2. Require disclosure
3. Change in number of shares outstanding

Require Adjustment

Ordinarily, the following subsequent events require adjustment of the current financial statements:

1. Customer bankruptcy arising from other than the customer's major casualty subsequent to the balance sheet date
2. Investee bankruptcy arising from other than the investee's major casualty subsequent to the balance sheet date
3. Resolution of an uncertainty concerning loss contingencies or asset realization

Require Disclosure

Ordinarily, the following subsequent events require disclosure in the current financial statements:

1. Issuing bonds or capital stock
2. Business combination
3. Loss of assets or decline in value of assets because of the following events occurring in the subsequent period:
   a. Expropriation
   b. Earthquake or similar event
   c. Customer or investee experiences major casualty such as fire

Events that require disclosure may be presented as follows:

1. Explanatory information in the notes to financial statements
2. *Pro forma* (as if) financial information in the notes to financial statements
3. *Pro forma* (as if) financial statements on the face of the historical statements

Ordinarily, subsequent events that require disclosure are explained in the notes to financial statements. Sometimes the effect of this type of event is so significant, however, that disclosure should be made by using *pro forma* financial information or by presenting *pro forma* financial statements. In those circumstances, the *pro forma* presentation may be marked "unaudited."

Change in Number of Shares

Effect should be given to subsequent events that change the number of shares outstanding, such as stock dividends, stock splits, and reverse stock splits. Generally, the number of shares is adjusted even if the event occurred after the balance sheet date.

Procedures

Specific procedures for becoming aware of subsequent events are in the checklist in the "AU Illustration" section. These procedures may be classified as inquiring, reviewing, and reading.

Inquiry

Management's responses to auditor inquiries about subsequent events should be included in the management representation letter (see Section 333).

In the letter to the client's lawyer (see Section 337), the auditor should make certain that he or she inquires about events that occurred up to the approximate date of the conclusion of the fieldwork. When the inquiry is sent, the auditor will estimate the date the fieldwork will end. If the response is received significantly before the audit report date, an updated response should be obtained.

Review

At the end of the fieldwork, the auditor should review the accounting records for unusual material transactions from the date of the balance sheet to the date of completion of the fieldwork. Records to be reviewed include the general ledger, the general journal, and other books of original entry.

The auditor should inquire about any subsequent unusual material transactions that come to his or her attention and determine their effect on the audited financial statements.

Read

The auditor should read subsequent client minutes and financial statements.

Minutes. The auditor should read minutes of meetings of stockholders, directors, and significant committees that occurred between the balance sheet date and the date of completion of the fieldwork. Items of concern include the following:

1. Issuance of debt or equity securities
2. Declaration of stock dividends, stock splits, and reverse stock splits
3. Debt modification
4. Refinancing of short-term debt with long-term debt
5. Business combinations
6. Disposal or discontinuance of a segment
7. Reduction in carrying value of assets
8. Adoption of pension or profit-sharing plan
9. Approval of long-term commitments

Unavailability of minutes. Minutes for all meetings may not have been prepared by the completion of the fieldwork. In these circumstances, the auditor should do the following:

1. Meet with the secretary of the entity or whoever is responsible for preparing the minutes
2. Review notes of the person who will prepare the minutes
3. Obtain a letter from the person responsible for preparing the minutes, confirming matters discussed and decisions made

Financial statements. The auditor should read the most recent interim financial statements of the entity. He or she should compare these statements with those of the corresponding prior period and the current audited statements. Explanations should be obtained for material fluctuations.

AUDITOR'S REPORT

When considering subsequent events and his or her report, the auditor is concerned with the following:

1. Dating the report
2. Dual dating the report
3. Reissuing the report

Dating the Auditor's Report

The report date signals the end of the auditor's responsibility for applying procedures specifically directed to obtaining knowledge of subsequent events. Section 530, *Dating of the Independent Auditor's Report*, states: "Generally, the date of completion of the fieldwork should be used as the date of the independent auditor's report." Because completion of fieldwork is not defined, this is a flexible standard that can be adapted to meet the variety of circumstances that occur in audit engagements.

The ordinary meaning of *fieldwork* is work outside the auditor's office and usually on the client's premises. Because completion of all important audit procedures usually coincides with completion of work at the client's office, use of this ordinary meaning is usually acceptable.

The audit report, of course, should not be dated before the auditor has obtained all the information essential for an opinion on the financial statements. Therefore, there should be no significant potential for material adjustments to the financial statements after the report date.

For a small, noncomplex business, the auditor's report can usually be dated at the date the staff leaves the client's office.

For a larger, more complex business, more coordination and care are needed in fixing the report date. A common practice is to schedule the report date to coincide with the closing conference with the client at which agreement is reached on the financial statements. This practice requires coordination of the subsequent events review procedures with this expected date, including the dating of representation letters.

The auditor wants to issue the report as soon after its date as is reasonably possible; however, sometimes this is not feasible. When the report is not issued promptly, the auditor should decide what procedures, if any, to apply to events that occurred between the report date and the issuance date. Many firms establish an arbitrary period such as two or three weeks by which a report should be issued. If its report is not issued during this period, the auditor will extend the subsequent events review to a date closer to issuance of the report.

The section states that the subsequent events review procedures should be performed at or *near* completion of fieldwork. Near, in this case, refers to a period slightly *before* completion of fieldwork. Fieldwork does not end until the subsequent events review is completed.

Sometimes, an event requiring financial statement adjustment or disclosure occurs after the date of the auditor's report but before its issuance. In these circumstances, the auditor should decide whether to update or to dual date the report. Because updating the report makes the auditor liable for reviewing for events occurring up to the new date, he or she ordinarily will dual date the report.

Dual Dating the Auditor's Report

To limit his or her liability and avoid extending his or her procedures, the auditor dual dates the report for a subsequent event that occurred after the report date but before the issuance of the report. Ordinarily, the specific event is described in a separate note to the financial statements. The auditor should apply appropriate auditing procedures to this event. For example, if the subsequent event was the issuance of debt or stock, the auditor would examine documents pertaining to the issuance and accounting records recording the event. The auditor also would consider confirming the event directly with the other party to the transaction.

When the auditor's report is dual dated, the date of the report is presented in a manner such as the following:

> February 10, 20X1, except with respect to the matters discussed in Note____ as to which the date is March 31, 20X1.

Reissuing Auditor's Report

Sometimes, financial statements are reissued. The auditor generally has no responsibility to apply procedures to search for events that occur after issuance of the financial statements. However, sometimes events that are significant to the financial statements, but that occurred after the financial statements and audit report were originally issued, come to the auditor's attention. Events that occurred between the issuance date and the reissuance date do not require adjustment of the financial statements, unless the adjustment meets the criteria for the correction of an error or the subsequent discovery of facts existing at the date of the auditor's report (see Section 561).

To prevent financial statements from being misleading, subsequent events between issuance date and reissuance date might have to be disclosed. This disclosure may be labeled "unaudited" and does not require a change of date or a dual dating of the auditor's report.

AU ILLUSTRATION

The following pages illustrate a subsequent events checklist.

ILLUSTRATION 1. SUBSEQUENT EVENTS CHECKLIST

_____   _____   _____
(Client)   (Prepared by)   (Date)

_____   _____   _____
(Period ended)   (Reviewed by)   (Date)

Instructions

This checklist is designed to assist in complying with the requirement that a review be made of transactions and events occurring between the date of financial statements being audited and the date of the auditor's report. The purpose of the review is to determine whether transactions or events occurred that require adjustment of the financial statements or disclosure in the notes to the financial statements. If this checklist is not used, the audit program should include appropriate procedures concerning subsequent events. This checklist may be modified to fit the needs of a specific audit.

Subsequent events are classified as follows:

1. Events that provide additional evidence about conditions that existed at the balance sheet date and affect estimates in the financial statements. The financial statements should be adjusted for changes in estimates resulting from the use of this evidence.

   > NOTE: Events affecting the realization of assets, such as receivables and inventories, or the settlement of estimated liabilities, ordinarily result in adjustment.

2. Events that provide evidence about conditions that did not exist at the balance sheet date but arose subsequent to that date. These events, except for stock dividends, stock splits, or reverse stock splits, do not result in adjustment of the financial statements. Some, however, may require disclosure to keep the financial statements from being misleading.

Ordinarily, the review of subsequent events is limited to transactions and events occurring between the date of the audited financial statements and the date of the issuance of financial statements. If there are circumstances in which a significant time lag exists between the date of the auditor's report and the date of its issuance, however, the subsequent events review may have to be extended.

This checklist includes procedures to be performed before the release of the financial statements. These procedures should be coordinated with other auditing procedures, such as cutoff tests, confirmation follow-up, review of subsequent cash collections, and so on. In some circumstances, this checklist might be supplemented by supporting audit documentation.

For all procedures listed below, the "Completed by" and "Date" columns should be completed. The "Inquiry of" and "W/P reference" columns should include the name of the client personnel queried or reference to supporting audit documentation. If a procedure is not applicable, "N/A" should be entered in the "Inquiry of" and "W/P reference" columns.

Procedure	Completed by	Date	Inquiry of	W/P reference
1. Read minutes of meetings of stockholders, board of directors, and other appropriate committees up to the date of completion of the fieldwork.				
2. Read the most recent interim financial statements prepared after the balance sheet date and compare them with the financial statements being reported on, budgets and forecasts, if available, and interim financial statements for the same period of the prior year.				
3. Review accounting records—general ledger, general journal, other books of original entry—for unusual material transactions from the balance sheet date to the date of completion of the fieldwork.				
4. Review reports of internal auditors prepared after the balance sheet date. If reports have not been prepared, inquire about the findings of the internal auditors.				
5. Inquire of appropriate executives about matters and events such as the following:				
a. The most recent interim financial statements				
(1) Accounting practices that differ from those in the financial statements being reported on				
(2) Components of operating results				
(3) Significant changes in working capital				
b. Property, plant, and equipment				
(1) Commitments for major additions or dispositions				
(2) New or modified leases				
(3) New or modified mortgages or other liens				
(4) Fire or other casualty losses				

Procedure	Completed by	Date	Inquiry of	W/P reference
c. Long-term debt and capital stock				
(1) New borrowings or modifications of existing debt				
(2) Early extinguishment of debt				
(3) Compliance with debt covenants				
(4) Stock conversions or conversions of debt to stock				
(5) Transactions involving equity securities, such as stock splits, stock options, and warrants				
(6) Declaration of dividends				
d. Personnel				
(1) Labor disputes				
(2) Adoption of new or amended employee benefit plans				
e. Contingencies				
(1) Status of contingencies existing at the balance sheet date				
(2) New contingencies				
(3) Notice of deficiencies from regulatory agencies				
f. Other				
(1) Significant sales, purchases, or other commitments				
(2) Unusual adjustments made subsequent to the balance sheet date				
(3) Negotiations or agreements involving business combinations or dispositions of corporate assets				
(4) Status of transactions with related parties entered into before or after the balance sheet date				
(5) New information about items in the financial statements being reported on that were accounted for on the basis of tentative or inconclusive data				
(6) Decisions that may affect carrying value or classification of assets or liabilities				
(7) Changes in lines of credit or compensating balances				
(8) Changes in financial policies				

Procedure	Completed by	Date	Inquiry of	W/P reference
6. Review letters received from entity lawyers in response to inquiries on litigation, claims, and assessments. If these letters are not dated close to the report date, consider whether it is necessary to obtain an updated letter.				
7. Review documents and financial statements provided to regulatory agencies, credit agencies, financial institutions, potential investors, and others subsequent to the balance sheet date.				
8. For documents prepared by the client that include audited financial statements and other information, read the other information.				
9. Review the management representation letter to determine that it includes matters pertaining to subsequent events.				

AU 561 Subsequent Discovery of Facts Existing at the Date of the Auditor's Report[1]

AU-C 560 Subsequent Events and Subsequently Discovered Facts

AU EFFECTIVE DATE AND APPLICABILITY

Original Pronouncement	Statement on Auditing Procedure (SAP) 41 (codified in Statement on Auditing Standards [SAS] 1) and SAS 98.
Effective Date	These statements currently are effective.
Applicability	The auditor's discovery of facts, after he or she has issued the report on the financial statements, that:

- Existed at the date of the report
- Were not known by the auditor at the date of the report
- Would have required the auditor to change the report had he or she been aware of them

NOTE: The section does not apply to matters identified in a subsequent events review that covers the period after the financial statements but before the original issuance date of the auditor's report (see Section 560, Subsequent Events*).*

The section applies only to audits; however, Statements on Standards for Accounting and Review Services (SSARSs) refer to it in situations in which the accountant becomes aware of facts existing at the date of the report after he or she issued a compilation or review report. The accountant might wish to consider the section in an analogous situation in a compilation or review engagement.

---

[1] This section is affected by the Public Company Accounting Oversight Board's (PCAOB's) Standard, Conforming Amendments to PCAOB Interim Standards Resulting from the Adoption of PCAOB Auditing Standard No. 5, An Audit of Internal Control over Financial Reporting That Is Integrated with an Audit of Financial Statements.

AU-C EFFECTIVE DATE AND SUMMARY OF CHANGES

SAS No. 122, *Codification of Auditing Standards and Procedures,* is effective for audits of financial statements with periods ending on or after December 15, 2012.

AU-C 560 supersedes AU 530; AU 560, *Subsequent Events*; AU 561, *Subsequent Discovery of Facts Existing at the Date of the Auditor's Report*; and paragraphs .51–.73 of AU 508.

AU-C 560 does not change extant requirements in any significant respect.

AU DEFINITIONS OF TERMS

This section contains no authoritative definitions.

AU-C DEFINITIONS OF TERMS

Source: AU-C 560.07

Accounting estimate. An approximation of a monetary amount in the absence of a precise means of measurement. This term is used for an amount measured at fair value when there is estimation uncertainty, as well as for other amounts that require estimation. When this section addresses only accounting estimates involving measurement at fair value, the term *fair value accounting estimates* is used.

Auditor's point estimate or auditor's range. The amount or range of amounts, respectively, derived from audit evidence for use in evaluating the recorded or disclosed amount(s).

Estimation uncertainty. The susceptibility of an accounting estimate and related disclosures to an inherent lack of precision in its measurement.

Management bias. A lack of neutrality by management in the preparation and fair presentation of information.

Management's point estimate. The amount selected by management for recognition or disclosure in the financial statements as an accounting estimate.

Outcome of an accounting estimate. The actual monetary amount that results from the resolution of the underlying transaction(s), event(s), or condition(s) addressed by the accounting estimate.

OBJECTIVES OF AU SECTION 561

Before the issuance of SAP 41, there was no authoritative guidance for the auditor if, after issuing the report on the financial statements, he or she became aware of facts that existed at the date of the report that would have required the auditor to change the report had he or she been aware of them. SAP 41 was a direct result of *Fischer v. Kletz*, commonly known as the *Yale Express* case.

In the case of *Yale Express*, a large CPA firm did not promptly disclose material errors in financial statements covered by its issued report that were subsequently discovered during a consulting services engagement. The court rejected the contention in the defendant's motion to dismiss the case that an auditor has no duty to those still relying on the report to disclose subsequently discovered errors in that report. The case was settled out of court, however, and the precise nature and extent of an auditor's duty to those relying on a previous report was unclear. SAP 41 was issued to delineate the nature and extent of the auditor's responsibility.

This section established the auditor's *continuing responsibility* for the validity of the report. It provides guidance on procedures the auditor should follow after the date of the report if he or she becomes aware of certain facts that may have existed when the report was issued.

This section is distinguishable from Section 560 on subsequent events. Under Section 560, the auditor has no responsibility to search for events subsequent to the date of the financial statements after the audit report has been issued. Under Section 561, an event subsequently comes to the auditor's attention that existed at the audit report date, and the auditor is required to apply procedures to investigate whether the event would have affected the audit report if known at that earlier date.

OBJECTIVE OF AU-C SECTION 560

AU-C Section 560.05 states that:

. . . the objective of the auditor is to obtain sufficient appropriate audit evidence about whether, in the context of the applicable financial reporting framework

    a. accounting estimates, including fair value accounting estimates, in the financial statements, whether recognized or disclosed, are reasonable and

    b. related disclosures in the financial statements are adequate.

FUNDAMENTAL REQUIREMENTS

CONSULTATION WITH ATTORNEY

The section states that the auditor is well-advised to consult with his or her attorney upon encountering circumstances to which this section applies.

NOTE: The auditing standard setters have always avoided making the failure to consult legal counsel a departure from professional standards because consultation is undertaken to protect the auditor.

DETERMINATION OF RELIABILITY OF INFORMATION

Whenever he or she becomes aware of information covered by this section, the auditor should determine its reliability and whether it existed at the date of the report. The auditor should discuss the matter with whatever level of management is appropriate, including the board of directors, and request cooperation to whatever extent necessary.

NOTE: Information about facts existing at the date of the auditor's report may come from many sources, such as:

1. *Tax engagements*
2. *Consulting engagements*
3. *Client executive or any other current or former employee of the client*
4. *Audit staff performing interim work*
5. *Unattributable rumors or an anonymous informant*

AUDITOR ACTION

The auditor should advise the client to disclose the newly discovered facts and their effect on the financial statements to persons known to be currently relying, or who are likely to rely, on the financial statements and the related auditor's report if:

1. The subsequently discovered information is reliable.
2. It existed at the date of the auditor's report.
3. The auditor's report would have been affected if all the information had been known to him or her at the date of the report and had not been reflected in the financial statements.
4. The auditor believes there are persons currently relying, or likely to rely, on the financial statements who would attach importance to the information.

The auditor should take whatever steps he or she believes necessary to satisfy himself or herself that the client has made the requested disclosures (see the section "Techniques for Application" for methods of disclosure).

CLIENT REFUSAL TO MAKE DISCLOSURES

If the client refuses to make the disclosures requested, the auditor should notify each member of the board of directors of the refusal and of the auditor's intention to take steps to prevent future reliance on the report.

NOTE: In this situation, if the auditor has not already done so, it is prudent to consult his or her attorney.

AUDITOR STEPS WHEN CLIENT REFUSES TO MAKE DISCLOSURES

Unless his or her attorney recommends otherwise, the auditor should take the following steps when the client fails to make the requested disclosures:

1. Notify client that the audit report must no longer be associated with the financial statements.
2. Notify regulatory agencies with jurisdiction over the client that the report should no longer be relied on.
3. Notify each person known specifically by the auditor to be relying on the financial statements that the report should no longer be relied on (see section on "Techniques for Application").

CONTENT OF AUDITOR DISCLOSURE

If the auditor determines that the information is reliable and the client refuses to make appropriate disclosures, the auditor should disclose:

1. The nature of the subsequently acquired information and its effect on the financial statements
2. What effect the subsequently acquired information would have had on the auditor's report had it been known at the date of the report and not reflected in the financial statements

NOTE: The disclosure should be precise and factual and should avoid comments concerning the conduct or motives of any person.

If the auditor takes the steps described in the prior section, "Auditor Steps When Client Refuses to Make Disclosures," and has not been able to determine the reliability of the information because the client refused to cooperate, he or she should disclose that:

1. Information has come to his or her attention that the client has not cooperated in trying to substantiate.
2. If the information is true, the auditor believes the report must no longer be relied on or associated with the client's financial statements.

NOTE: *These disclosures should be made only if the auditor believes that the financial statements may be misleading and that the report should not be relied on.*

INTERPRETATIONS

AUTHOR ASSOCIATION WITH SUBSEQUENTLY DISCOVERED INFORMATION WHEN THE AUDITOR HAS RESIGNED OR BEEN DISCHARGED (FEBRUARY 1989)

The investigation of whether subsequently discovered information is reliable and whether facts existed at the date of the original audit report should be performed even when the auditor has resigned or been discharged prior to undertaking or completing the investigation. In other words, Section 561 is equally applicable to a predecessor auditor and a continuing auditor.

TECHNIQUES FOR APPLICATION

PARTIES TO BE NOTIFIED

When the auditor has concluded that subsequently discovered information should be disclosed, some or all of the following might be notified:

1. Stockholders
2. Banks
3. Bond trustees
4. Major note holders, such as insurance companies
5. Major suppliers
6. Credit agencies
7. Securities and Exchange Commission (SEC)
8. Stock exchanges
9. Regulatory agencies
10. Other persons known to be currently relying or likely to rely on the financial statements and related auditor's report

Notification of parties other than the client is a serious step and should be undertaken only under the guidance of legal counsel. The requirement to notify applies only for persons actually known by the auditor to be relying and not to persons that the auditor might infer could be relying. However, whether to notify and whom to notify should be considered with the advice of legal counsel.

METHODS OF DISCLOSURE

The method of disclosing new information depends on the circumstances.

Revised Financial Statements and Auditor's Report

If the effect of the new information can be determined promptly, disclosure should consist of issuing, as soon as practicable, revised financial statements and auditor's report.

1. The reasons for the revision should be described in a note to financial statements and referred to in the auditor's report.
2. The opinion paragraph of the auditor's report accompanying revised financial statements would start as follows:

    In our opinion, the aforementioned financial statements, revised as described in Note X, present fairly . . .

3. The auditor's report accompanying the revised financial statements should contain two dates: the date of the original report and the date of the revision described in a separate note to the financial statements (see Section 530, *Dating of the Independent Auditor's Report*).

Current Financial Statements and Auditor's Report

When audited comparative financial statements and the related auditor's report for a subsequent period are about to be issued, disclosure of the revisions can be made in these reissued statements.

1. In these circumstances, the prior financial statements will be revised and the revision disclosed, but the auditor's report need not refer to the revision.
2. This method may be used only if disclosure of the new information is not seriously delayed.

Effect Not Promptly Determinable

Occasionally, the effect of subsequently discovered facts cannot be determined without prolonged investigation. In these circumstances, the issuance of revised financial statements and auditor's report would be delayed. If it appears that the new information will require revision of the financial statements and the report, the auditor should request that the client do the following:

1. Notify persons known to be relying, or who are likely to rely on, the financial statements and the related auditor's report that they should not be relied on.
2. Inform these persons that revised financial statements and auditor's report will be issued when the current investigation is completed.
3. Communicate with SEC, stock exchanges, and regulatory agencies.

AU 623 Special Reports

AU-C 806 Reporting on Compliance with Aspects of Contractual Agreements or Regulatory Requirements in Connection with Audited Financial Statements

AU-C 800 Special Considerations—Audits of Financial Statements Prepared in Accordance with Special-Purpose Frameworks

AU-C 805 Special Considerations—Audits of Single Financial Statements and Specific Elements, Accounts, or Items of a Financial Statement

AU EFFECTIVE DATE AND APPLICABILITY

Original Pronouncements Statements on Auditing Standards (SASs) 62 and 77, as revised to reflect the conforming changes necessary due to the issuance of SAS 87.

Effective Date These statements currently are effective.

Applicability Auditor's reports issued in connection with the following:

1. *Other comprehensive basis of accounting (OCBOA).* Audited financial statements prepared in accordance with a comprehensive basis of accounting other than generally accepted accounting principles (see the section "Definitions of Terms").
2. *Elements, accounts, or items.* Audited specified elements, accounts, or items of a financial statement.
3. *Compliance.* Compliance with aspects of contractual agreements or regulatory requirements related to audited financial statements.
4. *Special-purpose financial presentations.* Financial presentations prepared to comply with contractual agreements or regulatory provisions.
5. *Prescribed forms.* Financial information presented in prescribed forms or schedules that require a prescribed form of auditor's report.

Auditor's reports issued in connection with any of the above are special reports.

Not Applicable to Reports issued in connection with the following:

1. Reviews of interim financial statements
2. Financial forecasts, projections, or feasibility studies
3. Compliance with aspects of contractual agreements or regulatory requirements unrelated to financial statements

NOTE: When the auditor is engaged to perform an audit in accordance with Governmental Auditing Standards *(the "Yellow Book") issued by the Comptroller General of the United States or the Single Audit Act, he or she should follow guidance contained in Section 801,* Compliance Auditing Considerations in Audits of Governmental Entities and Recipients of Governmental Financial Assistance.

A review of specified elements, accounts, or items in accordance with Statements on Standards for Accounting and Review Services (SSARS) is not appropriate. However, the auditor may be engaged to make a review in accordance with attestation standards (see Section AT 101).

AU-C EFFECTIVE DATE AND SUMMARY OF CHANGES

SAS No. 122, *Codification of Auditing Standards and Procedures,* is effective for audits compliance issued in connection with audits of financial statements with periods ending on or after December 15, 2012.

The clarified SAS does not change the requirements of extant AU Section 623 in any significant respect.

AU DEFINITIONS OF TERMS

HISTORICAL FINANCIAL STATEMENTS

Generally accepted auditing standards (GAAS) are applicable whenever an auditor is engaged to audit and report on any historical financial statement.

Characteristics. A financial statement has the following characteristics:

1. It is a presentation of financial data, including accompanying notes.
2. It is derived from accounting records.
3. It is intended to communicate an entity's economic resources or obligations at a point in time or the changes in the economic resources or obligations for a period of time in accordance with generally accepted accounting principles (GAAP) or a comprehensive basis of accounting.

Examples of financial statements. For reporting purposes, the following types of financial presentations are financial statements:

1. Balance sheet
2. Statement of income or statement of operations
3. Statement of retained earnings
4. Statement of cash flows
5. Statement of changes in owners' equity
6. Statement of assets and liabilities that does not include owners' equity accounts
7. Statement of revenue and expenses
8. Summary of operations
9. Statement of operations by product lines
10. Statement of cash receipts and disbursements

Entities. A financial statement may be presented for any of the following:

1. A corporation
2. A consolidated group of corporations
3. A combined group of affiliated entities
4. A not-for-profit organization
5. A governmental unit
6. An estate or trust
7. A partnership
8. A proprietorship
9. A segment of any of the preceding
10. An individual

COMPREHENSIVE BASIS OF ACCOUNTING OTHER THAN GAAP

For purposes of this section, a comprehensive basis of accounting other than GAAP is a basis to which at least one of the following descriptions applies:

Regulatory. A basis of accounting used by the reporting entity in compliance with requirements or financial reporting provisions of a governmental regulatory agency with jurisdiction over the entity. Examples are the following:

1. Interstate Commerce Commission
2. Department of Housing and Urban Development
3. State insurance commissions

> NOTE: A special report cannot be used unless the statements are filed solely with the agency.

Tax. A basis of accounting that the reporting entity uses or expects to use in filing its income tax return for the period covered by the financial statements.

Cash. The cash receipts and disbursements basis of accounting and modifications of the basis that have substantial support. Modifications having substantial support include, for example:

1. Recording depreciation on long-lived assets
2. Accruing income taxes

Other. A definite set of criteria having substantial support that is applied to all material items appearing in the financial statements. An example of this type is financial statements prepared on the price-level basis of accounting.

> NOTE: Current-value financial statements that supplement historical-cost financial statements in a general-use presentation of real estate entities are not considered to be OCBOA financial statements. See the "Techniques for Application" section and AU Illustration 16 for additional information.

For this section to apply, the financial statements should conform to one of the four descriptions. Reporting on other kinds of financial statements is not necessarily prohibited; however, the guidance in this section is not applicable.

AU-C DEFINITIONS OF TERMS

AU-C 806 does not contain any definitions.

OBJECTIVES OF AU SECTION 623

ENGAGEMENTS THAT MAY BE ACCEPTED

An independent auditor expresses an opinion about whether the audited financial statements are presented fairly, in all material respects, in conformity with GAAP. GAAP requires financial statements to be prepared on the accrual basis. There are, however, organizations that believe that neither they nor the users of their financial statements need accrual-basis financial statements. Examples of these organizations are the following: (1) some not-for-profit entities, (2) certain nonpublic entities (e.g., service enterprises and small, closely held businesses), (3) regulated companies that must file financial statements based on accounting principles prescribed by a governmental regulatory agency, and (4) entities formed for special purposes, such as certain partnerships and joint ventures.

Sometimes an auditor is asked to express an opinion on parts (elements, accounts, or items) of a financial statement. Situations in which this may occur include audits of sales for purposes of computing royalties or additional rent. Unions sometimes require a special audit of the allocation of their expenses between those chargeable and those not chargeable to nonunion workers whom they represent in collective bargaining arrangements.

The objectives of this section are (1) to identify those engagements that the auditor may accept to audit and report on financial statements that are not prepared in conformity with GAAP without expressing a qualified or adverse opinion and (2) to identify those engagements that the auditor may accept to audit and report on parts of financial statements.

GAAS

The section establishes that whenever the auditor is engaged to audit and report on financial statements prepared in accordance with a comprehensive basis of accounting other than GAAP, the audit should be performed in accordance with GAAS.

For other audits described, the section indicates which of the standards apply.

AUDITOR'S REPORT

The section provides examples of reports that an auditor should issue under each type of engagement. It also provides guidance when the auditor's report contains wording prescribed by the regulatory body to whom the client's financial statements are submitted.

OBJECTIVES OF AU-C 623

AU-C 623 states that "the objective of the auditor is to report appropriately on an entity's compliance with aspects of contractual agreements or regulatory requirements, in connection with the audit of financial statements, when the auditor is requested to report on such matters."

FUNDAMENTAL REQUIREMENTS: FINANCIAL STATEMENTS PREPARED IN CONFORMITY WITH AN OCBOA

COMPONENTS OF AUDITOR'S STANDARD REPORT

When reporting on financial statements prepared in conformity with an OCBOA, the independent auditor's report should include the following:

1. A title that includes the word *independent*
2. A standard introductory paragraph
3. A standard scope paragraph, including an identification of the United States of America as the country of origin of the auditing standards used
4. A paragraph that
   a. Identifies the basis of presentation and refers to the note to the financial statements that describes that basis
   b. Indicates that the basis of presentation is a comprehensive basis of accounting other than GAAP
5. An opinion paragraph that presents the auditor's opinion as to whether the financial statements are presented fairly, in all material respects, in conformity with the basis of accounting described
6. The manual or printed signature of the auditing firm
7. The date

NOTE: *If the financial statements are prepared in conformity with the requirements or financial reporting provisions of a governmental regulatory agency, see the section on "Governmental Regulatory Agencies."*

(See Illustrations 1 and 2.)

Departures from Unqualified Opinions

The auditor may conclude that he or she cannot express an unqualified opinion on the financial statements in the following circumstances:

1. The financial statements are not presented fairly on the basis of accounting described.
2. There is a limitation on the scope of the audit.

In these circumstances, the auditor should do the following:

1. Include an explanatory paragraph before the opinion paragraph that discloses all substantive reasons for the modified opinion.
2. Include in the opinion paragraph appropriate modifying language and a reference to the explanatory paragraph.

Governmental Regulatory Agencies

Sometimes the auditor reports on financial statements prepared in conformity with the requirements on financial reporting of a governmental regulatory agency. (See Illustration 3.) In these circumstances, the auditor's report should include a paragraph after the opinion paragraph that restricts the use of the report solely to those within the entity and for filing with the regulatory agency. This paragraph is appropriate even though the auditor's report may be made a matter of public record by law or regulation.

Financial Statements Not in Conformity with OCBOA

If the financial statements do not meet the conditions for presentation in conformity with a comprehensive basis of accounting other than GAAP (see "AU Definitions of Terms"), the auditor should issue the standard auditor's report modified because of a GAAP departure (see Section 508, *Reports on Audited Financial Statements*).

Title of Financial Statements

Titles used for financial statements prepared in conformity with GAAP are not appropriate for financial statements prepared in conformity with a comprehensive basis of accounting other than GAAP. For example, cash-basis financial statements would be titled "Statement of Assets and Liabilities Arising from Cash Transactions" and "Statement of Revenue Collected and Expenses Paid."

If the auditor believes the financial statements are not titled appropriately, he or she should ask the client to change the titles and, failing that, disclose his or her reservations in an explanatory paragraph of the auditor's reports and issue a qualified opinion.

Financial Statement Disclosures

The notes to the financial statements prepared on an OCBOA should include a summary of significant accounting policies that describes the basis of presentation and indicates how that basis differs from GAAP. The effects of the differences do not have to be quantified.

Items that are similar to those in GAAP financial statements (for example, depreciation in modified cash-basis financial statements) require the same informative disclosures.

FUNDAMENTAL REQUIREMENTS: SPECIFIED ELEMENTS, ACCOUNTS, OR ITEMS OF A FINANCIAL STATEMENT

EXAMPLES AND OTHER SERVICES

An auditor may accept an engagement to express an opinion on one or more specified elements, accounts, or items of a financial statement, either as a separate engagement or in conjunction with the audit of the financial statements. The specified elements, accounts, or items may be presented in the auditor's report or in a document accompanying the report.

Examples of specified elements, accounts, or items of a financial statement on which an auditor may report include accounts receivable, investments, rentals, royalties, provision for income taxes, and total expenses. For specified elements, accounts, or items, the accountant may review the specified elements, accounts, or items in accordance with attestation standards (see Section AT 201).

GAAS

Nine of the ten GAAS are applicable to any engagement to express an opinion on one or more elements, accounts, or items of a financial statement. The first standard of reporting (GAAP conformity) is not applicable unless the specified elements, accounts, or items are intended to be presented in conformity with GAAP.

SCOPE OF AUDIT AND LEVEL OF MATERIALITY

In these types of engagements, the auditor expresses an opinion on *each* of the specified elements, accounts, or items encompassed by the auditor's report. The measurement of materiality, therefore, should be related to each individual element, account, or item reported on, and not to the aggregate of them or to the financial statements taken as a whole.

Because the amount considered material is usually smaller in an audit of this nature, the audit of the specified element, account, or item usually is more extensive than it is when the same information is being considered in conjunction with an audit of the financial statements taken as a whole.

Many financial statement elements, such as sales and receivables, inventory and payables, long-lived assets and depreciation, are interrelated. The auditor may therefore also apply audit procedures to elements, accounts, or items that are interrelated with those on which he or she has been engaged to express an opinion.

ADVERSE OPINION OR DISCLAIMER ON THE BASIC FINANCIAL STATEMENTS

An auditor may have expressed an adverse opinion or disclaimed an opinion on the basic financial statements. In these circumstances, the auditor still may report on one or more specified elements, accounts, or items of the basic financial statements if the following conditions exist:

1. The matters to be reported on and the scope of the audit were not intended to and did not include so many elements, accounts, or items that they compose a major portion of the basic financial statements.
2. The report on the elements, accounts, or items should be presented separately from the report on the financial statements of the entity.

Specified Element, Account, or Item Related to Net Income or Stockholders' Equity

The auditor should have audited the complete financial statements when expressing an opinion on a specified element, account, or item when that specified element, account, or item is, or is based upon, an entity's net income or stockholders' equity or their equivalent.

The Auditor's Report

The auditor's report on one or more specified elements, accounts, or items of a financial statement should include the following:

1. A title that includes the word *independent*
2. An introductory paragraph with statements that:
   a. The specified elements, accounts, or items identified in the report were audited.
      (1) If the audit was made in conjunction with the audit of the entity's financial statements, this should be stated, and the date of auditor's report on those financial statements should be indicated.
      (2) Any departure from the auditor's standard report on the entity's financial statements should be noted if considered relevant to the presentation of the specified element, account, or item.
   b. The specified elements, accounts, or items are the responsibility of the entity's management and the auditor's responsibility is to express an opinion on the specified elements, accounts, or items based on the audit.
3. A scope paragraph with statements that:
   a. The audit was conducted in accordance with auditing standards generally accepted in the United States of America.
   b. Those standards require that the auditor plan and perform the audit to obtain reasonable assurance about whether the specified elements, accounts, or items are free of material misstatement.
   c. An audit includes:
      (1) Examining, on a test basis, evidence supporting the amounts and disclosures in the presentation of the specified elements, accounts, or items.
      (2) Assessing the accounting principles used and significant estimates made by management.
      (3) Evaluating the overall presentation of the specified elements, accounts, or items.
   d. The auditor believes that the audit provides a reasonable basis for the opinion.
4. A paragraph with statements that:
   a. Describe the basis on which the specified elements, accounts, or items are presented and, if applicable, any agreements specifying the basis if the basis is not in conformity with GAAP. (If the presentation is prepared in conformity with GAAP, the paragraph should include an identification of the United States of America as the country of origin of those accounting principles.)
   b. Describe significant interpretations, if any, made by the entity's management relating to the provisions of a relevant agreement.

5. An opinion paragraph that states whether the specified elements, accounts, or items are fairly presented, in all material respects, in conformity with the basis of accounting described (or disclaims an opinion). If the auditor concludes that the specified elements, accounts, or items are not presented fairly on the basis of accounting described or if there has been a scope limitation, the auditor should:

    a. Disclose all the substantive reasons for his or her conclusion in an explanatory paragraph preceding the opinion paragraph of the report
    b. Modify the opinion and refer to the explanatory paragraph

6. A paragraph that restricts the use of the auditor's report to those within the entity and parties to a contract or agreement if the specified element, account, or item is prepared to comply with the requirements of a contract or agreement that results in a presentation not in conformity with GAAP or OCBOA.
7. The manual or printed signature of the auditing firm and the date of the report.

(See AU Illustrations 4 to 8.)

FUNDAMENTAL REQUIREMENTS: COMPLIANCE WITH CONTRACTUAL OR REGULATORY REQUIREMENTS RELATED TO AUDITED FINANCIAL STATEMENT

AGREEMENTS REQUIRING COMPLIANCE REPORTS

Bond indentures, loan and other agreements, or regulatory agencies may require compliance reports by independent auditors. For example, loan agreements may contain covenants for borrowers, such as payments into sinking funds, payments of interest, maintenance of current ratios, restriction of dividend payments, and use of proceeds of sales of property. Also, these agreements may require that the borrower provide annual financial statements that have been audited by an independent auditor.

If the auditor is testing compliance with laws and regulations in an audit in accordance with the *Government Auditing Standards* (the "Yellow Book") issued by the Comptroller General of the United States or a single audit act in accordance with an office of management budget circular, he or she should follow the guidance in Section 801, *Compliance Auditing Considerations in Audits of Governmental Entities and Recipients of Governmental Financial Assistance.*

REQUEST FOR ASSURANCE

In certain circumstances, lenders request from the independent auditor assurance that the borrower has complied with the covenants of the agreements relating to accounting or auditing matters. (The lender's request is made to the client, not the auditor.) The independent auditor usually satisfies this request by giving negative assurance concerning the applicable covenants. Such assurance may *not* be given if the auditor has not audited the financial statements related to the contractual agreements or regulatory requirements, if the auditor has issued an adverse opinion or disclaimer of opinion on those statements, or if the assurance extends to covenants addressing matters not subjected to auditing procedures.

The negative assurance given by the auditor may be provided in a separate report or in one or more paragraphs of the auditor's report accompanying the financial statements.

ASSURANCE GIVEN IN AUDITOR'S REPORT ON THE FINANCIAL STATEMENTS

The auditor may include his or her report on compliance with contractual agreements or regulatory provisions in the auditor's report on the financial statements. In this case, the auditor should include a paragraph, after the opinion paragraph, that provides the negative assurance relative to compliance with the applicable covenants of the agreement, insofar as they relate to accounting matters. The paragraph also should state that (1) the negative assurance is being given in connection with the audit of the financial statements and (2) the audit was not directed primarily toward obtaining knowledge regarding compliance.

The auditor's report should also include a paragraph that describes and states the source of any significant interpretations made by the entity's management and a paragraph that restricts its use to those within the entity and the parties to the contract or agreement or for filing with the regulatory agency, if appropriate.

SEPARATE AUDITOR'S REPORT

If an auditor's report on compliance with contractual agreements or regulatory provisions is a separate report, it should include the following:

1. A title that includes the word *independent*.
2. A paragraph stating that the financial statements were audited in accordance with auditing standards generally accepted in the United States of America and the date of the auditor's report on the financial statements. Any departure from the auditor's standard report on the financial statements should be disclosed.
3. A paragraph that:
    a. Refers to the specific covenants or paragraphs of the agreement
    b. Provides negative assurance relative to compliance with the applicable covenants of the agreement insofar as they relate to accounting matters
    c. Specifies that the negative assurance is being given in connection with the audit of the financial statements
    d. States that the audit was not directed primarily toward obtaining knowledge regarding compliance
4. A paragraph that describes and states the source of any significant interpretations made by the entity's management relating to provisions of the agreement.
5. A paragraph that restricts the use of the report to those within the entity and the parties to the contract or agreement or for filing with the regulatory agency, if appropriate.
6. The manual or printed signature of the auditing firm and the date of the report.

(See AU Illustrations 9 and 10.)

FUNDAMENTAL REQUIREMENTS: SPECIAL-PURPOSE FINANCIAL PRESENTATIONS TO COMPLY WITH CONTRACTUAL AGREEMENTS OR REGULATORY PROVISIONS

SPECIAL-PURPOSE FINANCIAL PRESENTATIONS

Sometimes an auditor is asked to report on special-purpose financial statements prepared to comply with a contractual agreement or regulatory provisions. Such presentations are generally intended for use of the parties to the agreement, regulatory bodies, or other specified parties. They include the following:

1. A financial presentation prepared in compliance with a contractual agreement or regulatory provision that is not a complete presentation of the entity's assets, liabilities, revenues, or expenses, but is otherwise prepared in conformity with GAAP or OCBOA (an incomplete presentation).
2. A financial presentation (a complete set of financial statements or a single financial statement) prepared on a basis of accounting prescribed in an agreement that is not a presentation in conformity with GAAP or OCBOA.

INCOMPLETE PRESENTATIONS

Situations That Would Involve Incomplete Presentations

The following situations involve incomplete presentations:

1. A governmental agency requires a schedule of gross income and certain expenses, exclusive of items such as interest, depreciation, and income taxes, of a entity's real estate operations.
2. A buy-sell agreement specifies a schedule of assets and liabilities measured in conformity with GAAP, but limited to certain designated assets and liabilities (for example, tangible assets and liabilities, exclusive of loans from stockholders).

These presentations should differ from complete financial statements only to the extent necessary to meet the special purposes for which they were prepared.

Disclosures

If these financial presentations contain items the same as, or similar to, those contained in a complete set of financial statements prepared in conformity with GAAP, similar informative disclosures should be made.

Title

The financial statements should be appropriately titled to avoid any implication that these incomplete presentations are intended to present financial position, results of operations, or cash flows.

Materiality

Although not complete financial statements, these financial presentations are considered to be financial statements for purposes of considering materiality. That is, the measurement of materiality for purposes of issuing an opinion should be related to the financial presentation taken as a whole.

Auditor's Report

When the auditor reports on financial statements prepared on a basis of accounting prescribed in a contractual agreement or regulatory provision that results in an incomplete presentation, but one that is otherwise in conformity with GAAP or OCBOA, the auditor's report should include the following:

1. A title that includes the word *independent*.
2. A standard introductory paragraph.

3. A standard scope paragraph, including an identification of the United States of America as the country of origin of the auditing standards used.
4. A paragraph that:
   a. Explains the intention of the presentation and refers to the note to the financial statements that describes the basis of presentation
   b. States that the presentation is not intended to be a complete presentation of the entity's assets, liabilities, revenues, and expenses if the basis of presentation is in conformity with GAAP or OCBOA
5. A paragraph that states the auditor's opinion related to the fair presentation, in all material respects, of the information the presentation is intended to present in conformity with GAAP or OCBOA. The paragraph should include an identification of the United States of America as the country of origin of those accounting principles if the presentation is prepared in conformity with GAAP. If the auditor decides that the information the presentation is intended to present is not presented fairly on the basis of accounting described or if there has been a scope limitation, the auditor should:
   a. Disclose all the substantive reasons for his or her conclusion in an explanatory paragraph preceding the opinion paragraph of the report
   b. Modify the opinion and refer to the explanatory paragraph
6. A paragraph that restricts the use of the auditor's report to the parties to the contract or agreement, to those with whom the entity is negotiating directly, or for filing with a regulatory agency.

NOTE: There should not be a restrictive paragraph when the report and related financial presentation are to be filed with a regulatory agency, such as the Securities and Exchange Commission (SEC), and are to be included in a document that is distributed to the general public, such as a prospectus.

7. The manual or printed signature of the auditing firm and the date of the report.

(See AU Illustrations 11 and 12.)

NON-GAAP OR NON-OCBOA PRESENTATIONS

Situations That Would Involve Non-GAAP or Non-OCBOA Presentations

The following situations involve special-purpose financial statements presented in conformity with a basis of accounting that departs from GAAP or OCBOA:

1. The borrower may be required by a loan agreement to prepare financial statements in which assets, such as inventory, are presented on a basis that does not conform with GAAP.
2. An acquisition agreement may require that the acquired entity's financial statements be prepared in conformity with GAAP, except for certain assets for which a valuation basis is stated in the agreement.

Another example would be when current-value financial statements supplement historical-cost financial statements in a general-use presentation of real estate entities.

Auditor's Report

When the auditor reports on financial statements described above, the auditor's report should include:

1. A title that includes the word independent.
2. A standard introductory paragraph.
3. A standard scope paragraph, including an identification of the United States of America as the country of origin of the auditing standards used.
4. A paragraph that:
   a. Explains the intent of the presentation and refers to the note to the financial statements that describes the basis of presentation.
   b. States that the presentation is not intended to be a GAAP presentation.
5. A paragraph that describes and provides the source of any significant interpretations made by the entity's management relating to provisions of a relevant agreement.
6. A paragraph that states the auditor's opinion related to the fair presentation, in all material respects, of the information the presentation is intended to present on the basis of accounting specified. If the auditor concludes that the information the presentation is intended to present is not presented fairly on the basis of accounting described or if there has been a limitation on the scope of the audit, the auditor should:
   a. Disclose all the substantive reasons for his or her conclusion in an explanatory paragraph preceding the opinion paragraph of the report.
   b. Modify the opinion and refer to the explanatory paragraph.
7. A paragraph that restricts the use of the report to those in the entity, to parties to the contract or agreement, to those with whom the entity is negotiating directly, or for filing with a regulatory agency.

   NOTE: When current-value financial statements of a real estate entity supplement the historical-cost financial statements and are not presented as a stand-alone presentation, it is not necessary to restrict the distribution of the auditor's report.

8. The manual or printed signature of the auditing firm and the date of the report.

(See AU Illustration 13.)

FUNDAMENTAL REQUIREMENTS: CIRCUMSTANCES REQUIRING EXPLANATORY LANGUAGE IN AN AUDITOR'S SPECIAL REPORT

CIRCUMSTANCES REQUIRING EXPLANATORY LANGUAGE

Circumstances that do not affect the auditor's unqualified opinion may nonetheless require that the auditor add explanatory language to the special report. These circumstances include the following:

1. Lack of consistency in accounting principles
2. Going concern uncertainties
3. Other auditors
4. Comparative financial presentations

Lack of Consistency in Accounting Principles

A change in accounting principles or in the method of their application for the financial statements or specified elements, accounts, or items of financial statements may cause a material lack of comparability. In these circumstances, the auditor should add an explanatory paragraph to the auditor's report. The explanatory paragraph should:

1. Follow the opinion paragraph
2. Describe the change
3. Refer to the note that discusses the change and the effect (see Section 508, *Reports on Audited Financial Statements*)

Change from GAAP to OCBOA. The auditor does not have to follow the above requirements if the financial statements or specified elements, accounts, or items were prepared in conformity with GAAP one year and OCBOA the following year. The auditor may, however, add an explanatory paragraph to the auditor's report to call attention to the difference in the bases of presentation.

GAAP and OCBOA financial statements. Sometimes, two sets of financial statements for the same year may be issued—one prepared in conformity with GAAP, the other in conformity with OCBOA. In these circumstances, the auditor may add an explanatory paragraph to each report stating that another set of financial statements prepared in conformity with another basis have been reported on and issued.

Change in the tax law. A change in the tax law is not considered to be a change in accounting principle for financial statements prepared in conformity with the tax basis of accounting. The auditor would not, therefore, need to add an explanatory paragraph to the auditor's report. However, disclosure of the tax law change may be necessary.

Going Concern Uncertainties

The auditor may have substantial doubt about the entity's ability to continue as a going concern for a period of time not to exceed one year beyond the date of the financial statements. In these circumstances, the auditor should add an explanatory paragraph after the opinion paragraph of the auditor's report if the going concern uncertainty is relevant to what the auditor is reporting on (see Section 341, *The Auditor's Consideration of an Entity's Ability to Continue as a Going Concern*).

Other Auditors

If the auditor decides to refer to the report of another auditor as a basis, in part, for his or her opinion, the auditor should disclose this in the introductory paragraph of the auditor's report and should refer to the other auditor's report in the opinion paragraph (see Section 508).

Comparative Financial Presentations

The auditor may issue an opinion on prior period financial statements or specified elements, accounts, or items that is different from the opinion he or she previously expressed on the same information. In these circumstances, the auditor should disclose all substantive reasons for the different opinion in a separate explanatory paragraph that precedes the opinion paragraph of the auditor's report.

FUNDAMENTAL REQUIREMENTS: FINANCIAL INFORMATION PRESENTED IN PRESCRIBED FORMS OR SCHEDULES

THE AUDITOR'S REPORT

Printed forms or schedules sometimes are designed or adopted by the agencies with which they are to be filed. These forms or schedules might prescribe wording of the auditor's report that is not acceptable to the auditor because it does not conform to the standards of reporting. When a printed auditor's report form contains an assertion that the independent auditor believes he or she is not justified in making, the auditor should either reword the form or attach a separate report.

AU INTERPRETATIONS

AUDITORS' SPECIAL REPORTS ON PROPERTY AND LIABILITY INSURANCE COMPANIES' LOSS RESERVES (ISSUED MAY 1981; REVISED FEBRUARY 1999; REVISED OCTOBER 2000; REVISED 2009)

State regulatory agencies may require property and liability insurance companies to file the statement of a qualified loss reserve specialist setting forth his or her opinion on the loss and loss adjustment expense reserves.

An independent auditor who has the competence may be a qualified loss reserve specialist. In these circumstances, the auditor who expresses an opinion on the loss and loss expense reserves should be guided by the provisions of the section pertaining to auditors' reports expressing an opinion on one or more specified elements, accounts, or items of a financial statement.

A report issued under these circumstances and the schedule of liabilities for losses and loss adjustment expenses that would accompany the report are illustrated in the interpretation. (See AU Illustration 14.)

REPORTS ON THE FINANCIAL STATEMENTS INCLUDED IN INTERNAL REVENUE FORM 990, "RETURN OF ORGANIZATIONS EXEMPT FROM INCOME TAX" (ISSUED DECEMBER 1991; REVISED FEBRUARY 1997; REVISED FEBRUARY 1999; REVISED OCTOBER 2000; REVISED JUNE 2009)

Form 990 may be used as a uniform annual report by charitable organizations in some states for reporting to both state and federal governments. Many states require an auditor's opinion on whether the financial statements included in Form 990 are presented fairly in conformity with GAAP. However, financial statements included in a Form 990 used by a charitable organization as a uniform annual report may contain certain material departures from the accounting principles in the Financial Accounting Standards Board (FASB) Accounting Standards Codification (ASC) 954 for *Health Care Organizations* and FASB ASC 958 for *Not-for-Profit Organizations*.

In most states, the report filed by the charitable organization is used to satisfy statutory requirements, but the regulators make the financial statements and the accompanying auditor's report a matter of public record. In some situations, there may be public distribution of the charitable organization's report.

Financial Statements in Conformity with GAAP

If the financial statements are in conformity with GAAP, the auditor can express an unqualified opinion.

Financial Statements Not in Conformity with GAAP

If the financial statements are not in conformity with GAAP, the auditor should consider the distribution of the report to determine whether it is appropriate to issue a special report on financial statements prepared on a basis prescribed by a regulatory agency solely for filing with that agency (see the "AU Illustrations" section). This type of reporting is appropriate if the report is intended solely for filing with regulatory agencies, even though the regulatory agencies might make the auditor's report a matter of public record by law or regulation. (See AU Illustration 15.)

If there is public distribution of the report of the charitable organization, and the financial statements included in it are not in conformity with GAAP, the auditor's report described in the preceding paragraph is not appropriate. In these circumstances, the auditor should issue a qualified or adverse opinion. Public distribution occurs when the report is sent unsolicited to contributors or others by the charitable organization.

REPORTING ON CURRENT-VALUE FINANCIAL STATEMENTS THAT SUPPLEMENT HISTORICAL-COST FINANCIAL STATEMENTS IN A GENERAL-USE PRESENTATION OF REAL ESTATE ENTITIES (ISSUED JULY 1990; REVISED FEBRUARY 1999; REVISED OCTOBER 2000)

The auditor may accept an engagement to report on current-value financial statements that supplement historical-cost financial statements in a general-use presentation of real estate entities only if the following two conditions are met:

1. The measurement and disclosure criteria used in preparing the current-value statements are reasonable.
2. Competent persons using the measurement and disclosure criteria would normally arrive at materially similar measurements or disclosures.

The auditor should consider whether disclosures relating to the current-value statements are adequate, including appropriate disclosure of the basis of presentation, nature of the reporting entity's properties, status of construction-in-process, valuation bases used for each classification of assets and liabilities, and sources of valuation. These disclosures should be made in the notes in a sufficiently clear and comprehensive manner that enables a knowledgeable reader to understand the current-value financial statements. A restriction on use of the auditor's report is not necessary because the presentation is only a supplement to historical financial statements rather than being a stand-alone presentation. (See AU Illustration 16.)

EVALUATION OF THE APPROPRIATENESS OF INFORMATIVE DISCLOSURES IN INSURANCE ENTERPRISES' FINANCIAL STATEMENTS PREPARED ON A STATUTORY BASIS (ISSUED DECEMBER 1991; REVISED FEBRUARY 1997. AMENDED DECEMBER 2001 BY SOP 01-5, *AMENDMENTS TO SPECIFIC AICPA PRONOUNCEMENTS FOR CHANGES RELATED TO THE NAIC CODIFICATION;* REVISED JANUARY 2005; REVISED NOVEMBER 2006)

When financial statements are presented on a statutory basis, the auditor should consider whether the financial statements and notes are informative of matters that may affect their use, understanding, and interpretation.

In the case of an insurance enterprise, most states are expected to adopt the updated *Accounting Practices and Procedures Manual,* revised by the National Association of Insurance Commissioners (NAIC). Since the revised Manual contains extensive disclosure requirements, the statutory basis of enterprises in states that have adopted the revised Manual will include informative disclosures appropriate for that basis of accounting. However, some states may not adopt the revised Manual or may adopt it with significant departures.

Disclosures in statutory-basis financial statements for items and transactions that are similarly accounted for under a statutory basis and under GAAP should be the same as, or similar to, the required GAAP disclosures unless the revised Manual specifically states the NAIC Codification rejected the GAAP disclosures. Any disclosures required by the revised Manual should also be included. If the state's required accounting for an item or transaction differs from the accounting in the revised Manual, but is in accordance with GAAP or superseded GAAP, the statutory basis financial statement disclosures for that item or transaction should be the applicable GAAP or superseded GAAP disclosures. Finally, if the accounting required by the state for an item or transaction differs from the accounting in the revised Manual, GAAP, or superseded GAAP, the auditor should be sure that sufficient relevant disclosures are made.

If state requirements have not been revised to reflect new GAAP disclosure requirements, sufficient relevant disclosures should be made.

REPORTING ON A SPECIAL-PURPOSE FINANCIAL STATEMENT THAT RESULTS IN AN INCOMPLETE PRESENTATION BUT IS OTHERWISE IN CONFORMITY WITH GAAP (ISSUED MAY 1995; REVISED FEBRUARY 1999)

An offering memorandum providing information as the basis for negotiating an offer to sell certain assets, or an entire business, or to simply raise funds does not constitute a contractual agreement. The auditor should follow the guidance for reporting GAAP departures in a standard audit report (Section 508) rather than the guidance for a special-purpose financial presentation as described in Section 623.

An agreement between a client and one or more third parties other than the auditor to prepare financial statements using a special-purpose presentation is a contractual agreement, and Section 623 applies. The report's use should be restricted to the entity, parties to the agreement, or parties negotiating the agreement directly with the entity.

EVALUATING THE ADEQUACY OF DISCLOSURE AND PRESENTATION IN FINANCIAL STATEMENTS PREPARED IN CONFORMITY WITH AN OTHER COMPREHENSIVE BASIS OF ACCOUNTING (ISSUED JANUARY 1998; REVISED JANUARY 2005; REVISED JUNE 2009)

Note disclosures in these types of OCBOA financial statements should contain disclosures similar to GAAP for financial statement items that are the same as, or similar to, those prepared in conformity with GAAP. However, in applying that general guideline, the following modifications may be made:

1. Brief and less detailed is fine.
2. Quantification is not necessary.
3. Communication of substance of the disclosure is enough.
4. Disclosures not relevant to the basis of accounting need not be considered.

Examples of these modifications are as follows:

- Disclosure of the basis of presentation may be limited to a brief identification of the basis and primary differences from GAAP. Quantification of the differences is not required.
- Disclosure of repayment terms of significant long-term borrowing communicates the substance of future principal reductions, and a schedule of payments for the next five years is not necessary.
- If the accounting basis does not adjust cost of securities to fair value, then fair value information is not relevant.
- Information on accounting changes, discontinued operations, and extraordinary items may be disclosed in a note without following the GAAP requirements for statement presentation and disclosing net-of-tax effects.
- Disclosure about use of estimates is not relevant in a presentation that has no estimates such as one based on cash receipts and disbursements.

AUDITOR REPORTS ON REGULATORY ACCOUNTING OR PRESENTATION WHEN THE REGULATED ENTITY DISTRIBUTES THE FINANCIAL STATEMENTS TO PARTIES OTHER THAN THE REGULATORY AGENCY EITHER VOLUNTARILY OR UPON SPECIFIC REQUEST (ISSUED JANUARY 2005)

When financial statements prepared for a regulated entity are to be used outside that entity, the auditor should modify the standard form of report because of departures from GAAP and then state in an additional paragraph an opinion on whether the financial statements are presented in conformity with the regulatory basis of accounting.

AU ILLUSTRATIONS

Illustrations 1–16 illustrate auditor's reports adapted from AU Section 623 and its interpretations.

ILLUSTRATION 1. FINANCIAL STATEMENTS PREPARED ON THE ENTITY'S INCOME TAX BASIS

To the Board of Directors
Main City, USA

Independent Auditor's Report

We have audited the accompanying statements of assets, liabilities, and capital-income tax basis of Widget Partnership as of December 31, 20X6, and 20X5, and the related statements of revenue and expenses-income tax basis and of changes in partners' capital accounts-income tax basis for the years then ended. These financial statements are the responsibility of the Partnership's management. Our responsibility is to express an opinion on these financial statements based on our audits.

We conducted our audits in accordance with auditing standards generally accepted in the United States of America. Those standards require that we plan and perform the audit to obtain reasonable assurance about whether the financial statements are free of material misstatement. An audit includes examining, on a test basis, evidence supporting the amounts and disclosures in the financial statements. An audit also includes assessing the accounting principles used and significant estimates made by management, as well as evaluating the overall financial statement presentation. We believe that our audits provide a reasonable basis for our opinion.

As described in Note A, these financial statements were prepared on the basis of accounting the Partnership uses for income tax purposes, which is a comprehensive basis of accounting other than generally accepted accounting principles.

In our opinion, the financial statements referred to above present fairly, in all material respects, the assets, liabilities, and capital of Widget Partnership as of December 31, 20X6 and 20X5, and its revenue and expenses and changes in partners' capital accounts for the years then ended, on the basis of accounting described in Note A.

Smith and Jones
February 15, 20X6

ILLUSTRATION 2. FINANCIAL STATEMENTS PREPARED ON THE CASH BASIS

To the Board of Directors
Main City, USA

Independent Auditor's Report

We have audited the accompanying statements of assets and liabilities arising from cash transactions of Widget Company as of December 31, 20X6 and 20X5, and the related statements of revenue collected and expenses paid for the years then ended. These financial statements are the responsibility of the Company's management. Our responsibility is to express an opinion on these financial statements based on our audits.

We conducted our audits in accordance with auditing standards generally accepted in the United States of America. Those standards require that we plan and perform the audit to obtain reasonable assurance about whether the financial statements are free of material misstatement. An audit includes examining, on a test basis, evidence supporting the amounts and disclosures in the financial statements. An audit also includes assessing the accounting principles used and significant estimates made by management, as well as evaluating the overall financial statement presentations. We believe that our audits provide a reasonable basis for our opinion.

As described in Note A, these financial statements were prepared on the basis of cash receipts and disbursements, which is a comprehensive basis of accounting other than generally accepted accounting principles.

In our opinion, the financial statements referred to above present fairly, in all material respects, the assets and liabilities arising from cash transactions of Widget Company as of December 31, 20X6 and 20X5, and its revenues collected and expenses paid during the years then ended, on the basis of accounting described in Note A.

Smith and Jones
February 15, 20X6

> **ILLUSTRATION 3. FINANCIAL STATEMENTS PREPARED ON A BASIS PRESCRIBED BY A REGULATORY AGENCY SOLELY FOR FILING WITH THAT AGENCY**[1]

To the Board of Directors
Main City, USA

Independent Auditor's Report

We have audited the accompanying statutory statements of admitted assets, liabilities, and surplus of Carmichael Insurance Company as of December 31, 20X6 and 20X5, and the related statutory statements of income and changes in surplus and cash flows for the years then ended. These financial statements are the responsibility of the Company's management. Our responsibility is to express an opinion on these financial statements based on our audits.

We conducted our audits in accordance with auditing standards generally accepted in the United States of America. Those standards require that we plan and perform the audit to obtain reasonable assurance about whether the financial statements are free of material misstatement. An audit includes examining, on a test basis, evidence supporting the amounts and disclosures in the financial statements. An audit also includes assessing the accounting principles used and significant estimates made by management, as well as evaluating the overall financial statement presentation. We believe that our audits provide a reasonable basis for our opinion.

As described more fully in Note A to the financial statements, these financial statements were prepared in conformity with the accounting practices prescribed or permitted by the Insurance Department of [*State*], which is a comprehensive basis of accounting other than generally accepted accounting principles.

In our opinion, the financial statements referred to above present fairly, in all material respects, the admitted assets, liabilities, and surplus of Carmichael Insurance Company as of [*at*] December 31, 20X6 and 20X5, and the results of its operations and its cash flows for the years then ended, on the basis of accounting described in Note A.

This report is intended solely for the information and use of the board of directors and the management of Carmichael Insurance Company and the New York State Insurance Department and is not intended to be, and should not be, used by anyone other than these specified parties.

Smith and Jones
February 15, 20X6

---

[1] *This report is presented in SOP 01-5,* Amendments to Specific AICPA Pronouncements for Changes Related to the NAIC Codification. *The amendments in SOP 01-5 are effective for audits of statutory financial statements for fiscal years ending on or after December 15, 2001. Retroactive application is not permitted.*

ILLUSTRATION 4. REPORT ON SPECIFIED ELEMENTS, ACCOUNTS, OR ITEMS RELATING TO ACCOUNTS RECEIVABLE

To the Board of Directors
Main City, USA

Independent Auditor's Report

We have audited the accompanying schedule of accounts receivable of Widget Company as of December 31, 20X6. This schedule is the responsibility of the Company's management. Our responsibility is to express an opinion on this schedule based on our audit.

We conducted our audit in accordance with auditing standards generally accepted in the United States of America. Those standards require that we plan and perform the audit to obtain reasonable assurance about whether the schedule of accounts receivable is free of material misstatement. An audit includes examining, on a test basis, evidence supporting the amounts and disclosures in the schedule of accounts receivable. An audit also includes assessing the accounting principles used and significant estimates made by management, as well as evaluating the overall schedule presentation. We believe that our audit provides a reasonable basis for our opinion.

In our opinion, the schedule of accounts receivable referred to above presents fairly, in all material respects, the accounts receivable of Widget Company as of December 31, 20X6, in conformity with accounting principles generally accepted in the United States of America.

Smith and Jones
February 15, 20X6

ILLUSTRATION 5. REPORT ON SPECIFIED ELEMENTS, ACCOUNTS, OR ITEMS RELATING TO AMOUNT OF SALES FOR THE PURPOSE OF COMPUTING RENTAL

To the Board of Directors
Main City, USA

Independent Auditor's Report

We have audited the accompanying schedule of gross sales [*as defined in the lease agreement dated March 4, 20X0, between Widget Company, as lessor, and Carmichael Stores Corporation, as lessee*] of ABC Stores Corporation at its Main Street Store, [*City*], [*State*], for the year ended December 31, 20X6. This schedule is the responsibility of Carmichael Stores Corporation's management. Our responsibility is to express an opinion on this schedule based on our audit.

We conducted our audit in accordance with auditing standards generally accepted in the United States of America. Those standards require that we plan and perform the audit to obtain reasonable assurance about whether the schedule of gross sales is free of material misstatement. An audit also includes examining, on a test basis, evidence supporting the amounts and disclosures in the schedule of gross sales. An audit also includes assessing the accounting principles used and significant estimates made by management, as well as evaluating the overall schedule presentation. We believe that our audit provides a reasonable basis for our opinion.

In our opinion, the schedule of gross sales referred to above presents fairly, in all material respects, the gross sales of ABC Stores Corporation at its Main Street store, Main City, USA, for the year ended December 31, 20X6, as defined in the lease agreement referred to in the first paragraph.

This report is intended solely for the information and use of the boards of directors and managements of ABC Stores Corporation and Widget Company and is not intended to be, and should not be, used by anyone other than these specified parties.

Smith and Jones
February 15, 20X6

ILLUSTRATION 6. REPORT ON SPECIFIED ELEMENTS, ACCOUNTS, OR ITEMS RELATING TO ROYALTIES WITH DISCLOSURE OF MANAGEMENT'S INTERPRETATION OF AGREEMENT

To the Board of Directors
Main City, USA

Independent Auditor's Report

We have audited the accompanying schedule of royalties applicable to engine production of the Q Division of Widget Corporation for the year ended December 31, 20X6, under the terms of a license agreement dated May 14, 20X0, between ABC Company and Widget Corporation. This schedule is the responsibility of Widget Corporation's management. Our responsibility is to express an opinion on this schedule based on our audit.

We conducted our audit in accordance with auditing standards generally accepted in the United States of America. Those standards require that we plan and perform the audit to obtain reasonable assurance about whether the schedule of royalties is free of material misstatement. An audit includes examining, on a test basis, evidence supporting the amounts and disclosures in the schedule. An audit also includes assessing the accounting principles used and significant estimates made by management, as well as evaluating the overall schedule presentation. We believe that our audit provides a reasonable basis for our opinion.

We have been informed that, under Widget Corporation's interpretation of the agreement referred to in the first paragraph, royalties were based on the number of engines produced after giving effect to a reduction for production retirements that were scrapped, but without a reduction for field returns that were scrapped, even though the field returns were replaced with new engines without charge to customers.

In our opinion, the schedule of royalties referred to above presents fairly, in all material respects, the number of engines produced by the Q Division of Widget Corporation during the year ended December 31, 20X6, and the amount of royalties applicable thereto, under the license agreement referred to above.

This report is intended solely for the information and use of the boards of directors and managements of Widget Corporation and ABC Company and is not intended to be, and should not be, used by anyone other than these specified parties.

Smith and Jones
February 15, 20X6

ILLUSTRATION 7. REPORT ON SPECIFIED ELEMENTS, ACCOUNTS, OR ITEMS RELATING TO A PROFIT PARTICIPATION WITH IDENTIFICATION OF RELEVANT AGREEMENTS

To the Board of Directors
Main City, USA

Independent Auditor's Report

We have audited, in accordance with auditing standards generally accepted in the United States of America, the financial statements of Basic Company for the year ended December 31, 20X5, and have issued our report thereon dated March 10, 20X6. We have also audited Basic Company's schedule of Jane Doe's profit participation for the year ended December 31, 20X5. This schedule is the responsibility of the Company's management. Our responsibility is to express an opinion on this schedule based on our audit.

We conducted our audit of the schedule in accordance with auditing standards generally accepted in the United States of America. Those standards require that we plan and perform the audit to obtain reasonable assurance about whether the schedule of profit participation is free of material misstatement. An audit includes examining, on a test basis, evidence supporting the amounts and disclosures in the schedule. An audit also includes assessing the accounting principles used and significant estimates made by management, as well as evaluating the overall schedule presentation. We believe that our audit provides a reasonable basis for our opinion.

We have been informed that the documents that govern the determination of Jane Doe's profit participation are (1) the employment agreement between Jane Doe and Basic Company dated February 1, 20X0, (2) the production and distribution agreement between Basic Company and Television Network Incorporated dated March 1, 20X0, and (3) the studio facilities agreement between Basic Company and QRZ Studios dated April 1, 20X0, as amended November 1, 20X0.

In our opinion, the schedule of profit participation referred to above presents fairly, in all material respects, Jane Doe's participation in the profits of Basic Company for the year ended December 31, 20X5, in accordance with the provisions of the agreements referred to above.

This report is intended solely for the information and use of the boards of directors and management of Basic Company and Jane Doe and is not intended to be, and should not be, used by anyone other than these specified parties.

Smith and Jones
February 15, 20X6

ILLUSTRATION 8. REPORT ON SPECIFIED ELEMENTS, ACCOUNTS, OR ITEMS RELATING TO FEDERAL AND STATE INCOME TAXES INCLUDED IN FINANCIAL STATEMENTS WITH REFERENCE TO AUDIT REPORT ON RELATED FINANCIAL STATEMENTS

To the Board of Directors
Main City, USA

Independent Auditor's Report

We have audited, in accordance with auditing standards generally accepted in the United States of America, the financial statements of Widget Company, Inc., for the year ended June 30, 20X5, and have issued our report thereon dated August 15, 20X5. We have also audited the current and deferred provision for the Company's federal and state income taxes for the year ended June 30, 20X5, included in those financial statements, and the related asset and liability tax accounts as of June 30, 20X5. This income tax information is the responsibility of the Company's management. Our responsibility is to express an opinion on it based on our audit.

We conducted our audit of the income tax information in accordance with auditing standards generally accepted in the United States of America. Those standards require that we plan and perform the audit to obtain reasonable assurance about whether the federal and state income tax accounts are free of material misstatement. An audit includes examining, on a test basis, evidence supporting the amounts and disclosures related to the federal and state income tax accounts. An audit also includes assessing the accounting principles used and significant estimates made by management, as well as evaluating the overall presentation of the federal and state income tax accounts. We believe that our audit provides a reasonable basis for our opinion.

In our opinion, the Company has paid or, in all material respects, made adequate provision in the financial statements referred to above for the payment of all federal and state income taxes and for related deferred income taxes that could be reasonably estimated at the time of our audit of the financial statements of Widget Company, Inc., for the year ended June 30, 20X5.

Smith and Jones
February 15, 20X6

ILLUSTRATION 9. REPORT ON COMPLIANCE WITH CONTRACTUAL PROVISIONS GIVEN IN A SEPARATE REPORT

To the Board of Directors
Main City, USA

Independent Auditor's Report

We have audited, in accordance with auditing standards generally accepted in the United States of America, the balance sheet of Widget Company as of December 31, 20X6, and the related statements of income, retained earnings, and cash flows for the year then ended, and have issued our report thereon dated February 16, 20X6.

In connection with our audit, nothing came to our attention that caused us to believe that the Company failed to comply with the terms, covenants, provisions, or conditions of Section XX to XX, inclusive, of the Indenture dated July 21, 20X0, with Basic Bank in so far as they relate to accounting matters. However, our audit was not directed primarily toward obtaining knowledge of such noncompliance.

This report is intended solely for the information and use of the boards of directors and management of Widget Company and Basic Bank and is not intended to be, and should not be, used by anyone other than these specified parties.

Smith and Jones
February 15, 20X6

ILLUSTRATION 10. REPORT ON COMPLIANCE WITH REGULATORY REQUIREMENTS GIVEN IN A SEPARATE REPORT WHEN THE AUDITOR'S REPORT ON THE FINANCIAL STATEMENTS INCLUDED AN EXPLANATORY PARAGRAPH BECAUSE OF A GOING CONCERN UNCERTAINTY

To the Board of Directors
Main City, USA

Independent Auditor's Report

We have audited, in accordance with auditing standards generally accepted in the United States of America, the balance sheet of Widget Company as of December 31, 20X6, and the related statements of income, retained earnings, and cash flows for the year then ended, and have issued our report thereon dated March 5, 20X6, which included an explanatory paragraph that described the substantial doubt about Widget Company's ability to continue as a going concern discussed in Note A of those statements.

In connection with our audit, nothing came to our attention that caused us to believe that the Company failed to comply with the accounting provisions in sections (1), (2), and (3) of the [*name of state regulatory agency*]. However, our audit was not directed primarily toward obtaining knowledge of such noncompliance.

This report is intended solely for the information and use of the board of directors and management of Widget Company and the NY Insurance Department and is not intended to be, and should not be, used by anyone other than these specified parties.

Smith and Jones
February 15, 20X6

ILLUSTRATION 11. REPORT ON A SCHEDULE OF GROSS INCOME AND CERTAIN EXPENSES TO MEET A REGULATORY REQUIREMENT AND TO BE INCLUDED IN A DOCUMENT DISTRIBUTED TO THE GENERAL PUBLIC[2]

To the Audit Committee, Board of Directors, and Shareholders
Main City, USA

Report of Independent Registered Public Accounting Firm

We have audited the accompanying Historical Summaries of Gross Income and Direct Operating Expenses of Basic Apartments, City, State (Historical Summaries), for each of the three years in the period ended December 31, 20X5. These Historical Summaries are the responsibility of the Apartments' management. Our responsibility is to express an opinion on the Historical Summaries based on our audits.

We conducted our audits in accordance with the standards of the Public Company Accounting Oversight Board (PCAOB; United States). This report is prepared to comply with the requirements of the SEC. Therefore, the authors have assumed that the auditor is preparing the report for an issuer client and has complied with the standards of the PCAOB. Those standards require that we plan and perform the audit to obtain reasonable assurance about whether the Historical Summaries are free of material misstatement. An audit includes examining, on a test basis, evidence supporting the amounts and disclosures in the Historical Summaries. An audit also includes assessing the accounting principles used and significant estimates made by management, as well as evaluating the overall presentation of the Historical Summaries. We believe that our audits provide a reasonable basis for our opinion.

The accompanying Historical Summaries were prepared for the purpose of complying with the rules and regulations of the Securities and Exchange Commission (for inclusion in the registration statement on Form S-11 of DEF Corporation) as described in Note A and are not intended to be a complete presentation of the Apartments' revenues and expenses.

In our opinion, the Historical Summaries referred to above present fairly, in all material respects, the gross income and direct operating expenses described in Note A of Basic Apartments for each of the three years in the period ended December 31, 20X5, in conformity with accounting principles generally accepted in the United States of America.

Smith and Jones
February 15, 20X6

ILLUSTRATION 12. REPORT ON STATEMENT OF ASSETS AND LIABILITIES TRANSFERRED TO COMPLY WITH A CONTRACTUAL AGREEMENT

To the Board of Directors
Main City, USA

Independent Auditor's Report

We have audited the accompanying statement of net assets sold of Widget Company as of June 8, 20X5. This statement of net assets sold is the responsibility of Widget Company's management. Our responsibility is to express an opinion on the statement of net assets sold based on our audit.

We conducted our audit in accordance with auditing standards generally accepted in the United States of America. Those standards require that we plan and perform the audit to obtain reasonable assurance about whether the statement of net assets sold is free of material misstate-

---

[2] *We assume that, since the historical summaries are prepared for the purpose of complying with the rules and regulations of the SEC, the client is most likely to be an issuer and the auditor would be following the standards of the Public Company Accounting Oversight Board (PCAOB).*

ment. An audit includes examining, on a test basis, evidence supporting the amounts and disclosures in the statement. An audit also includes assessing the accounting principles used and significant estimates made by management, as well as evaluating the overall presentation of the statement of net assets sold. We believe that our audit provides a reasonable basis for our opinion.

The accompanying statement was prepared to present the net assets of Widget Company sold to Basic Corporation pursuant to the purchase agreement described in Note X, and is not intended to be a complete presentation of Widget Company's assets and liabilities.

In our opinion, the accompanying statement of net assets sold presents fairly, in all material respects, the net assets of Widget Company as of June 8, 20X5, sold pursuant to the purchase agreement referred to in Note X, in conformity with accounting principles generally accepted in the United States of America.

This report is intended solely for the information and use of the boards of directors and managements of Widget Company and Basic Corporation and is not intended to be, and should not be, used by anyone other than these specified parties.

Smith and Jones
February 15, 20X6

> **ILLUSTRATION 13. REPORT ON FINANCIAL STATEMENTS PREPARED PURSUANT TO A LOAN AGREEMENT THAT RESULTS IN A PRESENTATION NOT IN CONFORMITY WITH GENERALLY ACCEPTED ACCOUNTING PRINCIPLES OR AN OTHER COMPREHENSIVE BASIS OF ACCOUNTING**

To the Board of Directors
Main City, USA

Independent Auditor's Report

We have audited the special-purpose statement of assets and liabilities of Widget Company as of December 31, 20X6 and 20X5, and the related special-purpose statements of revenues and expenses and of cash flows for the years then ended. These financial statements are the responsibility of the Company's management. Our responsibility is to express an opinion on these financial statements based on our audits.

We conducted our audits in accordance with auditing standards generally accepted in the United States of America. Those standards require that we plan and perform the audit to obtain reasonable assurance about whether the financial statements are free of material misstatement. An audit includes examining, on a test basis, evidence supporting the amounts and disclosures in the financial statements. An audit also includes assessing the accounting principles used and significant estimates made by management, as well as evaluating the overall financial statement presentation. We believe that our audits provide a reasonable basis for our opinion.

The accompanying special-purpose financial statements were prepared for the purpose of complying with Section 4 of a loan agreement between Basic Bank and the Company as discussed in Note X, and are not intended to be a presentation in conformity with generally accepted accounting principles.

In our opinion, the special-purpose financial statements referred to above present fairly, in all material respects, the assets and liabilities of Widget Company as of December 31, 20X6 and 20X5, and the revenues, expenses and cash flows for the years then ended, on the basis of accounting described in Note X.

This report is intended solely for the information and use of the boards of directors and managements of Widget Company and Basic Bank and is not intended to be, and should not be, used by anyone other than these specified parties.

Smith and Jones
February 15, 20X6

> **ILLUSTRATION 14. AUDITOR'S REPORT EXPRESSING AN OPINION ON AN INSURANCE COMPANY'S LOSS AND LOSS ADJUSTMENT EXPENSE RESERVES AND THE SCHEDULE THAT WOULD ACCOMPANY THE REPORT**

Board of Directors
X Insurance Company

We are members of the American Institute of Certified Public Accountants (AICPA) and are the independent public accountants of Basic Insurance Company. We acknowledge our responsibility under the AICPA's Code of Professional Conduct to undertake only those engagements which we can complete with professional competence.

We have audited the financial statements prepared in conformity with accounting principles generally accepted in the United States of America [*or prepared in conformity with accounting practices prescribed or permitted by the Insurance Department of the State of New York*] of Basic Insurance Company as of December 31, 20X5, and have issued our report thereon dated March 1, 20X6. In the course of our audit, we have audited the estimated liabilities for unpaid losses and unpaid loss adjustment expenses of Basic Insurance Company as of December 31, 20X5, as set forth in the accompanying schedule including consideration of the assumptions and methods relating to the estimation of such liabilities.

In our opinion, the accompanying schedule presents fairly, in all material respects, the estimated unpaid losses and unpaid loss adjustment expenses of Basic Insurance Company that could be reasonably estimated at December 31, 20X5, in conformity with accounting practices prescribed or permitted by the Insurance Department of the State of New York on a basis consistent with that of the preceding year.

This report is intended solely for the information and use of the board of directors and management of Basic Insurance Company and Insurance Department of the State of New York and is not intended to be, and should not be, used by anyone other than these specified parties.

Smith and Jones
February 15, 20X6

Basic Insurance Company
Schedule of Liabilities for Losses and Loss Adjustment Expenses
December 31, 20X5

Liability for losses	$xx,xxx,xxx
Liability for loss adjustment expenses	x,xxx,xxx
Total	$xx,xxx,xxx

Note 1—Basis of presentation

The above schedule has been prepared in conformity with accounting practices prescribed or permitted by the Insurance Department of the State of New York. [*Significant differences between statutory practices and generally accepted accounting principles for the calculation of the above amounts should be described, but the monetary effect of any such differences need not be stated.*]

Losses and loss adjustment expenses are provided for when incurred in accordance with the applicable requirements of the insurance laws [*and/or regulations*] of the State of New York. Such provisions include (1) individual case estimates for reported losses, (2) estimates received from other insurers with respect to reinsurance assumed, (3) estimates for unreported losses based on past experience modified for current trends, and (4) estimates of expenses for investigating and settling claims.

Note 2—Reinsurance

The Company reinsures certain portions of its liability insurance coverages to limit the amount of loss on individual claims and purchases catastrophe insurance to protect against aggregate single occurrence losses. Certain portions of property insurance are reinsured on a quota share basis.

The liability for losses and the liability for loss adjustment expense were reduced by $xxx,xxx and $xxx,xxx, respectively, for reinsurance ceded to other companies.

Contingent liability exists with respect to reinsurance which would become an actual liability in the event the reinsuring companies, or any of them, might be unable to meet their obligations to the Company under existing reinsurance agreements.

> **ILLUSTRATION 15. AUDITOR'S REPORT ON THE FINANCIAL STATEMENTS INCLUDED IN INTERNAL REVENUE SERVICE FORM 990, "RETURN OF ORGANIZATIONS EXEMPT FROM INCOME TAX"**

To the Board of Directors
Main City, USA

Independent Auditor's Report

We have audited the balance sheet (Part IV) of Basic Charity as of December 31, 20X5, and the related statement of revenue, expenses, and changes in net assets (Part I) and statement of functional expenses (Part II) for the year then ended included in the accompanying Internal Revenue Service Form 990. These financial statements are the responsibility of Basic Charity's management. Our responsibility is to express an opinion on these financial statements based on our audit.

We conducted our audit in accordance with auditing standards generally accepted in the United States of America. Those standards require that we plan and perform the audit to obtain reasonable assurance about whether the financial statements are free of material misstatement. An audit includes examining, on a test basis, evidence supporting the amounts and disclosures in the financial statements. An audit also includes assessing the accounting principles used and significant estimates made by management, as well as evaluating the overall financial statement presentation. We believe that our audit provides a reasonable basis for our opinion.

As described in Note X, these financial statements were prepared in conformity with accounting practices prescribed by the Internal Revenue Service and the Office of the State of New York, which is a comprehensive basis of accounting other than generally accepted accounting principles.

In our opinion, the financial statements referred to above present fairly, in all material respects, the assets, liabilities and fund balances of Basic Charity as of December 31, 20X5, and its revenue, expenses, and changes in fund balances for the year then ended on the basis of accounting described in Note X.

Our audit was made for the purpose of forming an opinion on the above financial statements taken as a whole. The accompanying information on pages 12–15 is presented for purposes of additional analysis and is not a required part of the above financial statements. Such information, except for that portion marked "unaudited," on which we express no opinion, has been subjected to the auditing procedures applied in the audit of the above financial statements; and, in our opinion, the information is fairly stated in all material respects in relation to the financial statements taken as a whole.

This report is intended solely for the information and use of the board of directors and management of Basic Charity, the Internal Revenue Service, and the Office of the State of New York and is not intended to be, and should not be, used by anyone other than these specified parties.

Smith and Jones
February 15, 20X6

ILLUSTRATION 16. AUDITOR'S REPORT ON CURRENT-VALUE FINANCIAL STATEMENTS THAT SUPPLEMENT HISTORICAL COST FINANCIAL STATEMENTS IN A GENERAL-USE PRESENTATION OF A REAL ESTATE ENTITY

To the Audit Committee and Board of Directors
Main City, USA

Independent Auditor's Report

We have audited the accompanying historical-cost balance sheet of Basic Company as of December 31, 20X3 and 20X6, and the related historical-cost statements of income, shareholders' equity, and cash flows for each of the three years in the period ended December 31, 20X3. We have also audited the supplemental current-value balance sheets of Basic Company as of December 31, 20X3 and 20X6, and the related supplemental current value statements of income and shareholders' equity for each of the three years in the period ended December 31, 20X3. These financial statements are the responsibility of the Company's management. Our responsibility is to express an opinion on these financial statements based on our audits.

We conducted our audits in accordance with auditing standards generally accepted in the United States of America. Those standards require that we plan and perform the audit to obtain reasonable assurance about whether the financial statements are free of material misstatement. An audit includes examining, on a test basis, evidence supporting the amounts and disclosures in the financial statements. An audit also includes assessing the accounting principles used and significant estimates made by management, as well as evaluating the overall financial statement presentation. We believe that our audits provide a reasonable basis for our opinion.

In our opinion, the historical-cost financial statements referred to above present fairly, in all material respects, the financial position of Basic Company as of December 31, 20X3 and 20X6, and the results of its operations and its cash flows for each of the three years in the period ended December 31, 20X3, in conformity with accounting principles generally accepted in the United States of America.

As described in Note 1, the supplemental current-value financial statements have been prepared by management to present relevant financial information that is not provided by the historical-cost financial statements, and are not intended to be a presentation in conformity with generally accepted accounting principles. In addition, the supplemental current-value financial statements do not purport to present the net realizable, liquidation, or market value of the Company as a whole. Furthermore, amounts ultimately realized by the Company from the disposal of properties may vary significantly from the current values presented.

In our opinion, the supplemental current-value financial statements referred to above present fairly, in all material respects, the information set forth in them on the basis of accounting described in Note 1.

Smith and Jones
February 15, 20X6

AU-C ILLUSTRATIONS

The following reports on compliance with aspects of contractual agreements or regulatory requirements in connection with audited financial statements are illustrated:

1. A Report on Compliance with Aspects of Contractual Agreements Provided in a Separate Report When No Instances of Noncompliance Are Identified
2. A Report on Compliance with Aspects of Contractual Agreements Provided in a Separate Report When Instances of Noncompliance Are Identified

3. A Report on Compliance with Aspects of Contractual Agreements Provided in a Separate Report When Instances of Noncompliance Are Identified and a Waiver Has Been Obtained
4. A Report on Compliance with Aspects of Contractual Agreements Provided in a Separate Report When Instances of Noncompliance Are Identified and the Auditor Has Disclaimed an Opinion on the Financial Statements
5. A Report on Compliance with Aspects of Contractual Agreements Given in a Combined Report, and No Instances of Noncompliance Were Identified

ILLUSTRATION 1. A REPORT ON COMPLIANCE WITH ASPECTS OF CONTRACTUAL AGREEMENTS PROVIDED IN A SEPARATE REPORT WHEN NO INSTANCES OF NONCOMPLIANCE ARE IDENTIFIED

Independent Auditor's Report

[*Appropriate Addressee*]

We have audited, in accordance with auditing standards generally accepted in the United States of America, the financial statements of XYZ Company, which comprise the balance sheet as of December 31, 20X2, and the related statements of income, changes in stockholders' equity, and cash flows for the year then ended, and the related notes to the financial statements, and have issued our report thereon dated February 16, 20X3.

In connection with our audit, nothing came to our attention that caused us to believe that XYZ Company failed to comply with the terms, covenants, provisions, or conditions of sections XX to YY, inclusive, of the Indenture dated July 21, 20X0, with ABC Bank, insofar as they relate to accounting matters. However, our audit was not directed primarily toward obtaining knowledge of such noncompliance. Accordingly, had we performed additional procedures, other matters may have come to our attention regarding the Company's noncompliance with the above-referenced terms, covenants, provisions, or conditions of the Indenture, insofar as they relate to accounting matters.

This report is intended solely for the information and use of the board of directors and management of XYZ Company and ABC Bank and is not intended to be and should not be used by anyone other than these specified parties.

[*Auditor's signature*]

[*Auditor's city and state*]

[*Date of the auditor's report*]

ILLUSTRATION 2. A REPORT ON COMPLIANCE WITH ASPECTS OF CONTRACTUAL AGREEMENTS PROVIDED IN A SEPARATE REPORT WHEN INSTANCES OF NONCOMPLIANCE ARE IDENTIFIED

Independent Auditor's Report

[*Appropriate Addressee*]

We have audited, in accordance with auditing standards generally accepted in the United States of America, the financial statements of XYZ Company, which comprise the balance sheet as of December 31, 20X2, and the related statements of income, changes in stockholders' equity, and cash flows for the year then ended, and the related notes to the financial statements, and have issued our report thereon dated March 5, 20X3.

In connection with our audit, we noted that XYZ Company failed to comply with the "Working Capital" provision of section XX of the Loan Agreement dated March 1, 20X2, with ABC Bank. Our audit was not directed primarily toward obtaining knowledge as to whether XYZ

Company failed to comply with the terms, covenants, provisions, or conditions of sections XX to YY, inclusive, of the Loan Agreement, insofar as they relate to accounting matters. Accordingly, had we performed additional procedures, other matters may have come to our attention regarding noncompliance with the above-referenced terms, covenants, provisions, or conditions of the Loan Agreement, insofar as they relate to accounting matters.

This report is intended solely for the information and use of the board of directors and management of XYZ Company and ABC Bank and is not intended to be and should not be used by anyone other than these specified parties.

[Auditor's signature]

[Auditor's city and state]

[Date of the auditor's report]

ILLUSTRATION 3. A REPORT ON COMPLIANCE WITH ASPECTS OF CONTRACTUAL AGREEMENTS PROVIDED IN A SEPARATE REPORT WHEN INSTANCES OF NONCOMPLIANCE ARE IDENTIFIED AND A WAIVER HAS BEEN OBTAINED

Independent Auditor's Report

[Appropriate Addressee]

We have audited, in accordance with auditing standards generally accepted in the United States of America, the financial statements of XYZ Company, which comprise the balance sheet as of December 31, 20X2, and the related statements of income, changes in stockholders' equity, and cash flows for the year then ended, and the related notes to the financial statements, and have issued our report thereon dated March 5, 20X3.

In connection with our audit, we noted that XYZ Company failed to comply with the "Working Capital" provision of section XX of the Loan Agreement dated March 1, 20X2, with ABC Bank. The Company has received a waiver dated February 5, 20X3, from ABC Bank. Our audit was not directed primarily toward obtaining knowledge as to whether XYZ Company failed to comply with the terms, covenants, provisions, or conditions of sections XX to YY, inclusive, of the Loan Agreement, insofar as they relate to accounting matters. Accordingly, had we performed additional procedures, other matters may have come to our attention regarding noncompliance with the above-referenced terms, covenants, provisions, or conditions of the Loan Agreement, insofar as they relate to accounting matters.

This report is intended solely for the information and use of the board of directors and management of XYZ Company and ABC Bank and is not intended to be and should not be used by anyone other than these specified parties.

[Auditor's signature]

[Auditor's city and state]

[Date of the auditor's report]

ILLUSTRATION 4. A REPORT ON COMPLIANCE WITH ASPECTS OF CONTRACTUAL AGREEMENTS PROVIDED IN A SEPARATE REPORT WHEN INSTANCES OF NONCOMPLIANCE ARE IDENTIFIED, AND THE AUDITOR HAS DISCLAIMED AN OPINION ON THE FINANCIAL STATEMENTS

Independent Auditor's Report

[Appropriate Addressee]

We were engaged to audit, in accordance with auditing standards generally accepted in the United States of America, the financial statements of XYZ Company, which comprise the balance sheet as of December 31, 20X2, and the related statements of income, changes in stockholders' equity, and cash flows for the year then ended, and the related notes to the financial statements, and have issued our report thereon dated March 5, 20X3. Our report disclaims an opinion on such financial statements because of [*describe the scope limitation or matter causing the disclaimer*].

In connection with our engagement, we noted that XYZ Company failed to comply with the "Working Capital" provision of section XX of the Loan Agreement dated March 1, 20X2, with ABC Bank. Our engagement was not directed primarily toward obtaining knowledge as to whether XYZ Company failed to comply with the terms, covenants, provisions, or conditions of sections XX to YY, inclusive, of the Loan Agreement, insofar as they relate to accounting matters. Accordingly, had we been able to complete the audit, other matters may have come to our attention regarding noncompliance with the above-referenced terms, covenants, provisions, or conditions of the Loan Agreement, insofar as they relate to accounting matters.

This report is intended solely for the information and use of the board of directors and management of XYZ Company and ABC Bank and is not intended to be and should not be used by anyone other than these specified parties.

[*Auditor's signature*]

[*Auditor's city and state*]

[*Date of the auditor's report*]

ILLUSTRATION 5. A REPORT ON COMPLIANCE WITH ASPECTS OF CONTRACTUAL AGREEMENTS PROVIDED IN A SEPARATE REPORT WHEN NO INSTANCES OF NONCOMPLIANCE ARE IDENTIFIED

Independent Auditor's Report

[*Appropriate Addressee*]

Report on the Financial Statements

We have audited the accompanying financial statements of ABC Company, which comprise the balance sheet as of December 31, 20X1, and the related statements of income, changes in stockholders' equity, and cash flows for the year then ended, and the related notes to the financial statements.

Management's Responsibility for the Financial Statements

Management is responsible for the preparation and fair presentation of these financial statements in accordance with accounting principles generally accepted in the United States of America; this includes the design, implementation, and maintenance of internal control relevant to the preparation and fair presentation of financial statements that are free from material misstatement, whether due to fraud or error.

Auditor's Responsibility

Our responsibility is to express an opinion on these financial statements based on our audit. We conducted our audit in accordance with auditing standards generally accepted in the United States of America. Those standards require that we plan and perform the audit to obtain reasonable assurance about whether the financial statements are free from material misstatement.

An audit involves performing procedures to obtain audit evidence about the amounts and disclosures in the financial statements. The procedures selected depend on the auditor's judgment, including the assessment of the risks of material misstatement of the financial statements, whether due to fraud or error. In making those risk assessments, the auditor considers internal control relevant to the entity's preparation and fair presentation of the financial statements in order to design audit procedures that are appropriate in the circumstances, but not for the purpose of expressing an opinion on the effectiveness of the entity's internal control.[fn 2] Accordingly, we express no such opinion. An audit also includes evaluating the appropriateness of accounting policies used and the reasonableness of significant accounting estimates made by management, as well as evaluating the overall presentation of the financial statements.

We believe that the audit evidence we have obtained is sufficient and appropriate to provide a basis for our audit option.

Opinion

In our opinion, the financial statements referred to above present fairly, in all material respects, the financial position of ABC Company as of December 31, 20X1, and the results of its operations and its cash flows for the year then ended in accordance with accounting principles generally accepted in the United States of America.

Other Matter

In connection with our audit, nothing came to our attention that caused us to believe that ABC Company failed to comply with the terms, covenants, provisions, or conditions of sections XX to YY, inclusive, of the Indenture dated July 21, 20X0 with XYZ Bank, insofar as they relate to accounting matters. However, our audit was not directed primarily toward obtaining knowledge of such noncompliance. Accordingly, had we performed additional procedures, other matters may have come to our attention regarding the Company's noncompliance with the above-referenced terms, covenants, provisions, or conditions of the Indenture, insofar as they relate to accounting matters.

Restricted Use Relating to the Other Matter

The communication related to compliance with the aforementioned Indenture described in the Other Matter paragraph is intended solely for the information and use of the boards of directors and management of ABC Company and XYZ Bank and is not intended to be and should not be used by anyone other than these specified parties.[fn 3]

Report on Other Legal and Regulatory Requirements

[*Form and content of this section of the auditor's report will vary depending on the nature of the auditor's other reporting responsibilities.*]

[*Auditor's signature*]

[*Auditor's city and state*]

[*Date of the auditor's report*]

[Illustration added, December 2011, to reflect conforming changes necessary due to the issuance of SAS No. 125.]

AU 625 Reports on the Application of Accounting Principles

AU-C 915 Reports on Application of Requirements of an Applicable Financial Reporting Framework

AU EFFECTIVE DATE AND APPLICABILITY

Original Pronouncement	Statements on Auditing Standards (SASs) 50 and 97.
Effective Date	These statements currently are effective.
Applicability	Reports providing advice on the application of accounting principles to specific transactions or providing advice on the type of opinion that may by rendered made as a part of a proposal or otherwise by an accountant other than the entity's continuing accountant. (See the following sections.)

AU-C EFFECTIVE DATE AND SUMMARY OF CHANGES

SAS No. 122, *Codification of Auditing Standards and Procedures,* is effective for audits of financial statements with periods ending on or after December 15, 2012.

AU-C 915 does not change extant requirements in any significant respect.

The term "financial reporting framework" replaces the term "generally accepted accounting principles," and "requirements of an applicable financial reporting framework" replaces "application of accounting principles."

APPLICABILITY

Section 625 applies to providing *written* advice

1. On the application of accounting principles to specified transactions (completed or proposed) involving facts and circumstances of a specific entity
2. On the type of opinion that may be rendered on a specific entity's financial statements

The section applies to these situations whether the advice is provided as part of a proposal to obtain a new client or as a separate engagement.

Section 625 applies to *oral* advice in the following circumstances:

1. The reporting accountant concludes the advice is intended to be used by a principal as an important factor in reaching a decision; and
2. The advice relates to the application of accounting principles to a specific transaction or the type of opinion that may be rendered on a specific entity's financial statements.

Section 625 does not apply to:

1. A *continuing* accountant engaged to report on the financial statements of a specific entity
2. An engagement to either assist in litigation involving accounting matters or provide expert testimony in litigation (i.e., litigation service engagements)
3. Advice provided to another accountant in public practice
4. Position papers on accounting principles or the type of opinion that may be rendered, including: newsletters, articles, speeches, lectures, or other public presentations; letters to standard-setting bodies

However, if position papers are intended to provide guidance on specific transactions or the type of opinion on a *specific* entity's financial statements, the section applies.

When facing a hypothetical transaction, a reporting accountant cannot know whether a continuing accountant has reached a different conclusion on applying accounting principles to the same transaction or how the specific entity previously accounted for similar transactions. Therefore, written reports on hypothetical transactions are prohibited.

AU DEFINITIONS OF TERMS

Continuing accountant. An accountant who has been engaged to report on the financial statements of a specific entity. An accountant engaged to perform services other than reporting on the entity's financial statements is not considered a continuing accountant.

Hypothetical transactions. Transactions that do not involve facts and circumstances of a specific entity.

Reporting accountant. An accountant other than the continuing accountant, engaged in the practice of public accounting as defined by American Institute of Certified Public Accountants (AICPA) Rules of Conduct, who prepares a written report or provides oral advice on the application of accounting principles to specified transactions involving facts and circumstances of a specific entity, or the type of opinion that may be rendered on a specific entity's financial statements.

Specific transactions. Completed or proposed specified transactions of a specific entity.

Written report. For the purposes of applying this section, a written report includes any written communication that expresses a conclusion on the appropriate accounting principles to be applied or the type of opinion that may be rendered on an entity's financial statements.

AU-C DEFINITIONS OF TERMS

Source: AU-C 915.08

For purposes of this section, the following terms have the meanings attributed as follows:

Continuing accountant. An accountant who has been engaged to report on the financial statements of a specific entity or entities of which the specific entity is a component.

Hypothetical transaction. A transaction or financial reporting issue that does not involve facts or circumstances of a specific entity.

Reporting accountant. An accountant, other than a continuing accountant, in the practice of public accounting, as described in ET Section 92, *Definitions*, who prepares a written report or provides oral advice on the application of the requirements of an applicable financial reporting framework to a specific transaction or on the type of report that may be issued on a specific entity's financial statements (a reporting accountant who is also engaged to provide accounting and reporting advice to a specific entity on a recurring basis is commonly referred to as an advisory accountant).

Specific transaction. A completed or proposed transaction or group of related transactions or a financial reporting issue involving facts and circumstances of a specific entity.

Written report. Any written communication that provides a conclusion on the appropriate application of the requirements of an applicable financial reporting framework to a specific transaction or on the type of report that may be issued on a specific entity's financial statements.

OBJECTIVES OF AU SECTION 625

In today's complex financial reporting environment, there is an increasing tendency for entities to consult with CPA firms other than their own auditors on accounting or financial reporting issues. This practice is sometimes called "opinion shopping"—a term that implies that the client will shop around until it finds an auditor who will agree with its position and then hire that auditor. A less pejorative term for the practice is obtaining a "second opinion." The implication of the term "second opinion" is that the motivation of the client arises from lack of clear-cut answers to accounting problems created by the fluid and constantly evolving environment of business today.

Section 625 addresses the concerns of financial statement users and regulators about opinion shopping. It would be inappropriate to prohibit second opinions because it would stifle the free exchange of ideas within the financial community and would restrict the ability of reporting entities and others to consider alternatives in determining appropriate financial reporting for new or emerging issues. Also, as a practical matter, the AICPA cannot afford to take action that might be viewed by the Federal Trade Commission as restricting competition.

Before providing advice to another CPA's client, a CPA should inform the entity of the need to consult with the other CPA and communicate with that CPA. The objective of this communication is primarily to determine whether the entity and its auditors have disagreed, and if so, whether the disagreement is about facts or about how relevant accounting principles should be applied.

SAS 50 permitted reports on hypothetical transactions, which were reports on the application of accounting principles not involving facts and circumstances of a particular principal. The SEC subsequently expressed concerns about the appropriate use of these reports and whether such reports were in the best interest of the public. In response to the SEC's concerns, the Auditing Standards Board issued SAS 97, *Amendment to Statement on Auditing Standards No. 50,* **Reports on the Application of Accounting Principles,** in June 2002. SAS 97 revised SAS 50 to prohibit written reports on hypothetical transactions.

OBJECTIVES OF AU-C SECTION 915

AU-C 915.07 states that:

> *. . . the objective of the reporting accountant, when engaged to issue a written report or provide oral advice on the application of the requirements of an applicable financial reporting framework to a specific transaction or on the type of report that may be issued on a specific entity's financial statements, is to address appropriately*
>
> a. *the acceptance of the engagement.*
> b. *the planning and performance of the engagement.*
> c. *reporting on the specific transaction or type of report.*

FUNDAMENTAL REQUIREMENTS

PERFORMANCE STANDARDS

1. The reporting accountant should:

    a. Exercise due professional care
    b. Be adequately trained and proficient
    c. Plan the engagement adequately and supervise the work of assistants, if any
    d. Accumulate sufficient information to provide a reasonable basis for the professional judgment described in the report

2. The reporting accountant should evaluate:

    a. The circumstances under which the written report or oral advice is requested
    b. The request's purpose
    c. The intended use of the written report or oral advice

3. The reporting accountant should:

    a. Understand the form and substance of the transaction(s)
    b. Review applicable generally accepted accounting principles (GAAP)
    c. If appropriate, consult with other professionals or experts
    d. If appropriate, perform research or other procedures to identify appropriate precedents or analogies

4. When evaluating accounting principles for a specific transaction or determining the type of opinion that may be issued on a specific entity's financial statements, the reporting accountant should:

    a. Consult with the entity's continuing accountant to determine all the available facts relevant to forming a professional judgment
    b. Obtain available facts that the continuing accountant may be able to provide that include:

(1) The transaction's form and substance
(2) How management has applied accounting principles to similar transactions
(3) Whether management disputes the accounting method the continuing accountant recommends
(4) Whether the continuing accountant has arrived at a different conclusion than the reporting accountant

c. In communicating with the continuing accountant, follow the guidance on communications between predecessor and successor auditors (Section 315).

REPORTING STANDARDS

A written report should be addressed to the requesting entity (for example, management or the board of directors of the entity) and should ordinarily:

1. Briefly describe the engagement
2. State that the engagement was performed in accordance with applicable AICPA standards
3. Identify the specific entity and describe the following:

   a. The transactions
   b. Relevant facts, circumstances, and assumptions
   c. Sources of information

4. Present a conclusion on the appropriate accounting principles (including an identification of the country of origin) to be applied or type of opinion that may be rendered.
5. If appropriate, describe the reasons for the conclusion.
6. If appropriate, state that the responsibility for proper accounting treatment rests with preparers of financial statements who should consult their continuing accountants.
7. State that any differences in the facts, circumstances, or assumptions presented might change the report.
8. Include a separate paragraph at the end of the report that:

   a. States that the report is intended solely for the information and use of the specified parties
   b. Identifies the parties
   c. States that the report is not intended to be, and should not be, used by nonspecified parties

INTERPRETATIONS

REQUIREMENT TO CONSULT WITH THE CONTINUING ACCOUNTANT (ISSUED JANUARY 2005)

An advisory accountant does not need to consult with the continuing accountant when the facts and circumstances of the engagement indicate that he or she is not being asked for a second opinion, and has obtained all relevant information to provide guidance to the client. This is especially the case for a recurring engagement, where the client is likely to be shopping for an opinion. If the advisory accountant does not consult with the continuing accountant, then consider documenting the reasons for not doing so.

TECHNIQUES FOR APPLICATION

The following practice problems that might arise are discussed:

1. Engagement acceptance
2. Applicability to proposals
3. Responding to intermediaries
4. Documentation

ENGAGEMENT ACCEPTANCE

A CPA firm should adopt policies and procedures concerning the acceptance and approval of engagements to furnish an opinion letter on the application of accounting principles or the type of opinion to be rendered on financial statements.

It is important to understand the purpose of the request, the nature of the issue on which advice is requested, and whether there is a disagreement between the client and its continuing accountant. Before Section 625 was issued, many CPAs would not accept such an engagement if the client would not permit contact with the continuing accountant. However, some firms made a distinction between completed and proposed transactions and did not insist on contact before providing advice on proposed transactions.

The rationale for not insisting on contact for proposed transactions was that future transactions could not affect current financial statements. Interpretation 201-3 of the Code of Professional Ethics, which was in effect at the time, referred to providing advice on matters in connection with the financial statements of another CPA's client. Section 625 now clearly requires contact with the other CPA in these circumstances because it applies to specific transactions, both completed and proposed.

APPLICABILITY TO PROPOSALS

For many practitioners, the most common situation in which Section 625 will apply is making a proposal for a new client. Not every proposal will be affected, but the requirements are applicable when a prospective client asks for the proposal to include the proposing firm's position on a specific accounting issue or the type of opinion that may be rendered on its financial statements in specific circumstances.

In all circumstances, before accepting an engagement, the successor auditor needs to communicate with the predecessor (Section 315, *Communications Between Predecessor and Successor Auditors*). However, when Section 625 applies, the communication should include more specific inquiries explicitly directed to disagreements about the subject on which a position is requested and should take place before the proposal is made rather than merely before acceptance of the audit engagement. In ordinary circumstances, communication does not take place until a predecessor has been terminated and does not take place during the proposal process (see Section 315). A request to include an opinion on accounting principles or type of audit opinion in a proposal changes the requirements.

Note that Section 625 focuses on accounting matters and the type of opinion that may be rendered. It does not broadly address auditing matters. This means that a proposal may discuss general matters of audit scope, such as overall approach, locations to be visited, and similar matters without creating a requirement to contact the continuing accountant before making the proposal.

Documentation

Section 625 does not impose any requirement to document the procedures used or information obtained to provide a basis for the professional judgment described in the report. However, the authors recommend the following documentation:

1. A description of the problem, including all relevant facts and circumstances. (Preferably this should be prepared by the client.)
2. If applicable, a summary of the discussions with the continuing accountant.
3. A description of the procedures followed to determine the accounting practices that would be appropriate in the circumstances, including citations to relevant authoritative literature.

If the engagement is terminated before a report is issued, documentation of the engagement to that point is generally desirable but not essential.

AU ILLUSTRATION

The following example of a report on the application of accounting principles to a specific transaction is from AU 625.11.

ILLUSTRATION 1. REPORT ON THE APPLICATION OF ACCOUNTING PRINCIPLES TO A SPECIFIC TRANSACTION

Introduction

We have been engaged to report on the appropriate application of accounting principles generally accepted in [*country of origin of such principles*] to the specific transaction described below. This report is being issued to Widget Company for assistance in evaluating accounting principles for the described specific transaction. Our engagement has been conducted in accordance with standards established by the American Institute of Certified Public Accountants.

Description of Transaction

The facts, circumstances, and assumptions relevant to the specific transaction as provided to us by the management of Widget Company are as follows:

[*Describe facts, circumstances, and assumptions or refer to attached description.*]

Appropriate Accounting Principles

[*Describe the advice on application of GAAP.*]

Concluding Comments

The ultimate responsibility for the decision on the appropriate application of accounting principles generally accepted in [country *of origin of such principles*] for an actual transaction rests with the preparers of financial statements, who should consult with their continuing accountants. Our judgment on the appropriate application of accounting principles generally accepted in [*country of origin of such principles*] for the described specific transaction is based solely on the facts provided to us as described in a prior section; should these facts and circumstances differ, our conclusion might change.

Restricted Use

This report is intended solely for the information and use of the board of directors and management of Widget Company and is not intended to be and should not be used by anyone other than these specified parties.

AU-C 915 ILLUSTRATION

ILLUSTRATION 1. ILLUSTRATIVE WRITTEN REPORT TO THE REQUESTING PARTY

The following is an illustration of the reporting accountant's written report to the requesting party (for example, management or those charged with governance) on the application of the requirements of accounting principles generally accepted in the United States of America to a specific transaction.

Introduction

We have been engaged to report on the appropriate application of the requirements of accounting principles generally accepted in the United States of America to the specific transaction described below. This report is being issued to ABC Company for assistance in evaluating accounting policies for the described specific transaction. Our engagement has been conducted in accordance with Statement on Auditing Standards No. 122, Section 915, *Reports on Application of Requirements of an Applicable Financial Reporting Framework*.

Description of Transaction

The facts, circumstances, and assumptions relevant to the specific transaction as provided to us by the management of ABC Company are as follows:

[*Text discussing the facts, circumstances, and assumptions relevant to the specific transaction*]

Appropriate Accounting Principles

[*Text discussing accounting principles generally accepted in the United States of America and how they apply to the described transaction*]

Concluding Comments

The ultimate responsibility for the decision on the appropriate application of the requirements of accounting principles generally accepted in the United States of America for an actual transaction rests with the preparers of financial statements, who should consult with their continuing accountant. Our conclusion on the appropriate application of the requirements of accounting principles generally accepted in the United States of America for the described specific transaction is based solely on the facts provided to us as previously described; should these facts and circumstances differ, our conclusion may change.

Restricted Use

This report is intended solely for the information and use of those charged with governance and management of ABC Company and is not intended to be and should not be used by anyone other than these specified parties.

AU 634 Letters for Underwriters and Certain Other Requesting Parties[1]

AU-C 920 Letters for Underwriters and Certain Other Requesting Parties

AU EFFECTIVE DATE AND APPLICABILITY

Original Pronouncements	Statements on Auditing Standards (SASs) 72, 76, and 86.
Effective Date	These statements currently are effective.
Applicability	Engagements to issue comfort letters for underwriters and certain other requesting parties in connection with financial statements and financial statement schedules contained in registration statements filed with the Securities and Exchange Commission (SEC) under the Securities Act of 1933 (the Act) and certain other securities offerings. (See "Applicability" section for additional discussion.)

AU-C EFFECTIVE DATE AND SUMMARY OF CHANGES

SAS No. 122, *Codification of Auditing Standards and Procedures,* is effective for comfort letters issued after December 15, 2012.

AU-C 920 does not change extant requirements in any significant way.

APPLICABILITY

In addition to issuing a comfort letter to an underwriter, accountants may also issue a comfort letter to a broker-dealer or other financial intermediary, acting as principal or agent in an offering or a placement of securities in connection with the following types of securities offerings:

---

[1] The illustrations in this section have been conformed to refer to standards of the PCAOB.

1. Foreign offerings, including Regulation S, Eurodollar, and other offshore offerings
2. Transactions exempt from the registration requirements of Section 5 of the Act, including those pursuant to Regulation A, Regulation D, and Rule 144A
3. Securities offerings issued or backed by governmental, municipal, banking, tax-exempt, or other entities that are exempt from registration under the Act

In those offerings, the accountant may issue a comfort letter only if the party provides a representation letter that represents that the party's review process is substantially consistent with the review process under the 1933 Act.

An accountant is also permitted to issue a comfort letter in connection with acquisition transactions in which there is an exchange of stock and comfort letters that are requested by the buyer or seller, or both, as long as a representation letter is provided that represents that the party's review process is substantially consistent with the review process under the 1933 Act.

A comfort letter may also be addressed to parties with a statutory due diligence defense under Section 11 of the Act, other than a named underwriter, when a law firm or attorney for the requesting party issues a written opinion to the accountants that states that the party has a due diligence defense under Section 11 of the Act. If the requesting party cannot provide a law firm's or attorney's written opinion to the accountant, the requesting party should provide a representation letter.

When one of the parties identified in the preceding paragraphs (other than an underwriter or other party with due diligence responsibilities) requests a comfort letter, but does not provide a representation letter, a special type of letter is permissible. (See Illustration 17.)

AU DEFINITIONS OF TERMS

Capsule financial information. Unaudited summarized interim information for periods subsequent to the periods covered by audited financial statements or unaudited condensed interim financial information. Capsule financial information (either in narrative or tabular form) often is provided for the most recent interim period and for the corresponding period of the prior year. It usually includes income statement items, often limited to sales and total and per share amounts for extraordinary items and net income.

Change period. The period that ends on the cutoff date (specified in the underwriting agreement) and which usually begins for balance sheet items immediately after the date of the latest balance sheet in the registration statement. For income statement items, the period usually begins immediately after the latest period for which those items are presented in the registration statement.

Closing date. The date on which the issuer or selling security holder delivers the securities to the underwriter in exchange for the proceeds of the offering.

Comfort letter. A letter issued by accountants to underwriters, or to other parties with a statutory due diligence defense under Section 11 of the Act, in connection with financial statements and financial statement schedules included (incorporated by reference) in registration statements filed with the SEC under the Act. Comfort letters are not required under the Act, and copies are not filed with the SEC. It is, however, a common condition of an underwriting agreement in connection with the offering for sale of securities registered with the SEC under the Act that the accountants are to furnish a comfort letter. Subjects covered in a comfort letter usually are limited to those specified in the underwriting agreement. Subjects that may be addressed in a comfort letter include:

1. The independence of the accountants
2. Compliance in form, in all material respects, of the audited financial statements and financial statement schedules included (incorporated by reference) in the registration statement with applicable accounting requirements of the Act and the related rules and regulation adopted by the SEC
3. Unaudited financial statements, condensed interim financial information, capsule financial information, pro forma financial information, financial forecasts, management's discussion and analysis (MD&A), and changes in selected financial statement items during a period subsequent to the date and period of the latest financial statements included (incorporated by reference) in the registration statement
4. Tables, statistics, and other financial information included (incorporated by reference) in the registration statement
5. Negative assurance about whether certain nonfinancial statement information included (incorporated by reference) in the registration statement complies as to form in all material respects with Regulation S-K

Cutoff date. A date specified in the underwriting agreement to which certain procedures described in the comfort letter are to relate (for example, a date five days before the date of the letter).

Effective date. The date on which the registration statement becomes effective. It is the date when the issuer's or selling security holder's securities may first be sold to the public.

Filing date. The date on which the registration statement is first filed with the SEC.

Negative assurance. A statement by accountants that, as a result of performing specified procedures, nothing came to their attention that caused them to believe that specified matters do not meet a specified standard (for example, that nothing came to their attention that caused them to believe that any material modifications should be made to the unaudited financial statements or unaudited condensed financial statements for them to be in conformity with generally accepted accounting principles [GAAP]).

Shelf registration statement. A registration statement in which the issuer registers a designated amount of securities for continuous or delayed offerings during an extended period. Ordinarily, the issuer does not have to prepare and file a new prospectus and registration statement for each sale.

Underwriter. Any person who has purchased from an issuer with a view to, or offers or sells for an issuer in connection with, the distribution of any security, or participates or has a direct or indirect participation in any such undertaking or participates or has a participation in the direct or indirect underwriting of any such undertaking. An underwriter does not include a person whose interest is limited to a commission from an underwriter or dealer not in excess of the usual and customary distributors' or sellers' commission (Section 2 of the Act).

Underwriting agreement. An agreement between issuers of securities or selling stockholders and the underwriter specifying terms and conditions of the offering and sale of securities. It usually contains provisions that affect the accountant including the provision that the accountant is to furnish a comfort letter.

AU-C DEFINITIONS OF TERMS

Source: AU-C 920.07

For purposes of this section, the following terms have the meanings attributed as follows:

Capsule financial information. Unaudited summarized interim financial information for periods subsequent to the periods covered by the audited financial statements or unaudited interim financial information included in the securities offering. Capsule financial information may be presented in narrative or tabular form and is often provided for the most recent interim period and for the corresponding period of the prior year.

Change period. The period ending on the cut-off date and ordinarily beginning, for balance sheet items, immediately after the date of the latest balance sheet in the securities offering and, for income statement items, immediately after the latest period for which such items are presented in the securities offering.

Closing date. The date on which the issuer of the securities or selling security holder delivers the securities to the underwriter in exchange for the proceeds of the offering.

Comfort letter. A letter issued by an auditor in accordance with this section to requesting parties in connection with an entity's financial statements included in a securities offering.

Comparison date and comparison period. The date as of which, and period for which, data at the cut-off date and data for the change period are to be compared.

Cut-off date. The date through which certain procedures described in the comfort letter are to relate.

Effective date. The date on which the securities offering becomes effective.

Entity. The party whose financial statements are the subject of the engagement.

Negative assurance. A statement that, based on the procedures performed, nothing has come to the auditor's attention that caused the auditor to believe that specified matters do not meet specified criteria (for example, that nothing came to the auditor's attention that caused the auditor to believe that any material modifications should be made to the unaudited interim financial information for it to be in accordance with GAAP).

Requesting party. One of the following specified parties requesting a comfort letter, which has negotiated an agreement with the entity:

- An underwriter
- Other parties that are conducting a review process that is, or will be, substantially consistent with the due diligence process performed when the securities offering is, or if the securities offering was, being registered pursuant to the 1933 Act, as follows:
  - A selling shareholder, sales agent, or other party with a statutory due diligence defense under Section 11 of the 1933 Act
  - A broker-dealer or other financial intermediary acting as principal or agent in a securities offering in connection with the following types of securities offerings:
    - Foreign offerings, including Regulation S, Eurodollar, and other offshore offerings
    - Transactions that are exempt from the registration requirements of Section 5 of the 1933 Act, including those pursuant to Regulation A, Regulation D, and Rule 144A
    - Offerings of securities issued or backed by governmental, municipal, banking, tax-exempt, or other entities that are exempt from registration under the 1933 Act
  - The buyer or seller in connection with acquisition transactions in which there is an exchange of stock

Securities offerings. One of the following types of securities offerings:

- Registration of securities with the SEC under the 1933 Act
- Foreign offerings, including Regulation S, Eurodollar, and other offshore offerings
- Transactions that are exempt from the registration requirements of Section 5 of the 1933 Act, including those pursuant to Regulation A, Regulation D, and Rule 144A
- Offerings of securities issued or backed by governmental, municipal, banking, tax-exempt, or other entities that are exempt from registration under the 1933 Act
- Acquisition transactions in which there is an exchange of stock

Underwriter. As defined in the 1933 Act:

> . . . *any person who has purchased from an issuer with a view to, or offers or sells for an issuer in connection with, the distribution of any security, or participates or has a direct or indirect participation in any such undertaking, or participates or has a participation in the direct or indirect underwriting of any such undertaking; but such term shall not include a person whose interest is limited to a commission from an underwriter or dealer not in excess of the usual and customary distributors' or sellers' commission. As used in this paragraph, the term "issuer" shall include, in addition to an issuer, any person directly or indirectly controlling or controlled by the issuer, or any person under direct or indirect common control with the issuer.*

Except when the context otherwise requires, the word *underwriter*, as used in this section, refers to the managing, or lead, underwriter, who typically negotiates the underwriting agreement or purchase agreement (hereafter referred to as the *underwriting agreement*) for a group of underwriters whose exact composition is not determined until shortly before a securities offering becomes effective.

OBJECTIVES OF AU SECTION 634

SAS 72 provides guidance to accountants for performing and reporting on the results of engagements to issue comfort letters for underwriters and certain other requesting parties. Those engagements are in connection with financial statements and financial statement schedules contained in registration statements filed with the SEC under the Act and certain other securities offerings.

SAS 72 addresses various matters, such as the following:

1. Whether it is proper for independent accountants, acting in their professional capacity, to comment in a comfort letter on specific matters, and, if so, the form the comment should take
2. Practical suggestions on which form of comfort letter is suitable in a given circumstance, procedural matters, the dating of letters, and what steps may be taken when information that may require special mention in a letter comes to the accountant's attention
3. Suggestions of ways of reducing or avoiding the uncertainties regarding the nature and extent of accountants' responsibilities in connection with a comfort letter

Providing comfort letters to underwriters is a service of accountants that developed after enactment of the Securities Act of 1933. Section 11 of the Act provides that underwriters, among others, could be liable if any part of a registration statement contained material omissions or misstatements. The Act also provides for an affirmative defense for underwriters if they can demonstrate that, after a reasonable investigation (called "due diligence"), the underwriter has reasonable grounds to believe that there were no material omissions or misstatements. In requesting a comfort letter, an underwriter is generally seeking assistance in performing a reasonable investigation of financial and accounting data in the registration statement that is not "expertized" (i.e., covered by a report of independent accountants, who consent to be named as experts, based on an audit in accordance with the standards of the Public Company Accounting Oversight Board [PCAOB]) as a defense against possible claims under Section 11 of the Act.

Ordinarily, underwriting agreements require comfort letters from the issuer's accountant to the underwriter. Comfort letters pertain primarily to financial data and information that have not been audited ("expertized"). What constitutes a reasonable investigation of unaudited data and information sufficient to satisfy the underwriter is not authoritatively established. Consequently, only the underwriter can determine what is sufficient for his or her purposes concerning procedures to be applied by the accountant.

The assistance the accountant can provide to the underwriter by way of the comfort letter is subject to limitations. Procedures short of an audit, such as those contemplated in a comfort letter, provide an accountant with a basis for expressing, at the most, negative assurance. Also, an accountant can properly comment only on matters to which the accountant's professional expertise is substantially relevant.

OBJECTIVES OF AU-C SECTION 920

AU-C 920.06 states that:

. . . the objectives of the auditor, when engaged to issue a letter to a requesting party in connection with an entity's financial statements included in a securities offering, are to

   a. address appropriately the acceptance of the engagement and the scope of services; and
   b. issue a letter with the appropriate form and content.

FUNDAMENTAL REQUIREMENTS: GENERAL

REPRESENTATION LETTER

According to AU 634.06, if the party requesting the comfort letter is a party other than a named underwriter with a due diligence defense under Section 11 of the Act, but is one of the types of parties described in the "Applicability" section, the accountant should obtain a representation letter that includes the following elements:

1. The letter should be addressed to the accountants.
2. The letter should contain the following:

   This review process, applied to the information relating to the issuer is (will be) substantially consistent with the due diligence review process that we would perform if this placement of securities (or issuance of securities in an acquisition transaction) were being registered pursuant to the Securities Act of 1933 (the Act). We are knowledgeable with respect to the due diligence review process that would be performed if this placement of securities were being registered pursuant to the Act.

3. The letter should be signed by the requesting party.

When the accountants receive the representation letter, they should refer in the comfort letter to the requesting party's representations (see Illustration 16 and Illustration 17 when requesting party has not provided the required representation letter).

REPORTS TO OTHER PARTIES

When a party other than those described in the "Applicability" section requests a report, the accountant should not provide a comfort letter or the letter in Illustration 17. Instead, the accountant should provide a report on agreed-upon procedures. (See Section 201.)

COMMUNICATIONS WITH UNDERWRITER

The accountant should suggest to the underwriter that they meet with the client to discuss the procedures to be followed related to the issuance of the comfort letter (procedures followed are described in the comfort letter; see Illustration 1). The underwriter should also provide the accountant with a draft of the underwriting agreement so that the accountant can indicate whether he or she will be able to furnish a letter in acceptable form.

DRAFT COMFORT LETTER

It is desirable for accountants to prepare a draft of the form of the comfort letter they expect to furnish as soon as they receive the draft of the underwriting agreement. The draft comfort letter should:

1. Deal, as completely as possible, with all matters to be covered in the final comfort letter
2. Use exactly the same terms as those to be used in the final comfort letter, with the understanding that the comments in the final letter cannot be determined until the underlying procedures have been performed
3. Be identified as a draft
4. Not contain statements or implications that the accountant is carrying out such procedures as he or she considers necessary

The following (from AU 634.16) is a suggested form of the legend that may be placed on the draft comfort letter for identification and explanation of its purposes and limitations:

This draft is furnished solely for the purpose of indicating the form of letter that we would expect to be able to furnish [*name of underwriter*] in response to their request, the matters to be covered in the letter, and the nature of the procedures that we would expect to carry out with respect to such matters. Based on our discussions with [*name of underwriter*], it is our understanding that the procedures outlined in this draft letter are those they wish us to follow.* Unless [*name of underwriter*] informs us otherwise, we shall assume that there are no additional procedures they wish us to follow The text of the letter itself will depend, of course, on the results of the procedures, which we would not expect to complete until shortly before the letter is given and in no event before the cutoff date indicated therein.

* *If the accountant has not met with the underwriter, this sentence should be as follows:*

In the absence of any discussions with [*name of underwriter*], we have set out in this draft letter those procedures referred to in the draft underwriting agreement (of which we have been furnished a copy) that we are willing to follow.

PRINCIPAL ACCOUNTANT

If more than one accountant is involved in the audit of the financial statements and the reports of those accountants appear in the registration statement, the principal accountant (the accountant reporting on the consolidated financial statements) should read the comfort letters of the other accountants who are reporting on significant components of the consolidated group. According to AU 634.18, the principal accountant should state in his or her comfort letter that (see Illustration 10):

1. Reading comfort letters of the other accountants was one of the procedures followed
2. The procedures performed by the principal accountant (other than reading the letters of the other accountants) related solely to companies audited by the principal accountant and to the consolidated financial statements

SHELF REGISTRATION

If the registrant has not chosen an underwriter by the effective date of a shelf registration statement, the accountant should not agree to furnish a comfort letter addressed to the client, legal counsel designated to represent the underwriting group, or a nonspecific addressee. The accountant may, however, agree to provide the client or legal counsel for the underwriting group with a draft comfort letter that describes the procedures performed by the accountant and the comments the accountant is willing to express based on those procedures. The following (from AU 634.19) is a suggested form of the legend that should be placed on the draft comfort letter to describe the letter's purpose and limitations:

> This draft describes the procedures that we have performed and represents a letter we would be prepared to sign as of the effective date of the registration statement if the managing underwriter had been chosen at that date and requested such a letter. Based on our discussions with [*name of client or legal counsel*], the procedures set forth are similar to those that experience indicates underwriters often request in such circumstances. The text of the final letter will depend, of course, on whether the managing underwriter who is selected requests that other procedures be performed to meet his or her needs and whether the managing underwriter requests that any of the procedures be updated to the date of issuance of the signed letter.

A signed comfort letter may be issued to the underwriter selected for the portion of the issue then being offered when the underwriting agreement for an offering is signed and on each closing date.

ISSUANCE OF LETTERS OR REPORTS UNDER OTHER STANDARDS

When issuing a comfort letter, the accountant may not issue any additional letters or reports under any other statements (SASs, Statements on Standards for Attestation Engagements [SSAEs], or Statements on Standards for Accounting and Review Services [SSARSs]) to the underwriter or other requesting parties in connection with the offering or placement of securities in which the accountant comments on items for which commenting is otherwise precluded by this section.

FUNDAMENTAL REQUIREMENTS: FORMAT AND CONTENTS OF COMFORT LETTERS

DATING OF COMFORT LETTER

The following apply to the date of the comfort letter:

1. The letter normally is dated on or shortly before the effective date. (In rare instances, requests have been made to date letters on or shortly before the filing date.)

2. Cut-off date. The letter should state that the inquiries and other procedures described in the letter did not extend from the cut-off date (specified in the underwriting agreement) to the date of the letter.
3. Subsequent letters.
   a. A subsequent letter may be dated on or before the closing date.
   b. The specified procedures and inquiries noted in the comfort letter should be completed as of the cut-off date for each letter.
   c. Comments contained in an earlier letter may be incorporated by reference in a subsequent letter (see Illustration 3); but a subsequent letter should address only information in the most recently amended registration statement.

Addressee

The following apply to determining the addressee of the comfort letter:

1. The letter should be addressed to the client and the intermediary (usually the underwriter) who negotiated the agreement with the client and with whom the accountants discussed the scope and sufficiency of the letter. (An example of an appropriate form of address is, "X Corporation and John Doe and Company, as Representative of Several Underwriters.")
2. The letter should not be addressed or given to any parties other than the client and the named underwriters, broker-dealer, financial intermediary, or buyer or seller.
3. A comfort letter for other accountants should be addressed in accordance with 1. above, and copies should be given to the principal accountant and his or her client.

Introductory Paragraph

The following apply to the introductory paragraph of the comfort letter:

1. It is good practice to include an introductory paragraph similar to the following (from AU 634.26):

   > We have audited the [*identify the financial statements and financial statement schedules*] included (incorporated by reference) in the registration statement (No. 33-00000) on Form ____ filed by the company under the Securities Act of 1933 (the Act); our reports with respect thereto are also included (incorporated by reference) in that registration statement. The registration statement, as amended as of _____, is herein referred to as the registration statement.

2. If the audit report on the financial statements included in the registration statement is not the standard report, for instance, if an explanatory paragraph has been added (see Illustration 9).
   a. Accountants should refer to that fact and discuss the content of the paragraph in the comfort letter.
   b. The accountants need not refer to or discuss explanatory paragraphs addressing the consistent application of accounting principles.
   c. If the SEC accepts a qualified opinion on historical financial statements, the accountants should refer to the qualification and discuss the subject matter in the comfort letter's opening paragraph.
3. The accountant should not repeat his or her opinion on the audited financial statements.

4. Negative assurance—Accountants should not give negative assurance concerning their audit report on the financial statements, nor should they give negative assurance concerning financial statements and financial statement schedules audited and reported on in the registration statement by other accountants.
5. Other reports issued by the accountants. The accountants may refer to their reports on:

   a. Condensed financial statements that are derived from audited financial statements (see Section 552, *Reporting on Condensed Financial Statements and Selected Financial Data*).
   b. Selected financial data (see Section 552).
   c. Interim financial information (see Section 722, *Interim Financial Information*).
   d. Pro forma financial information (see Section AT 401).
   e. A financial forecast (see Section AT 301).
   f. Management's discussion and analysis (see Section AT 701).

   If the above reports are not included (incorporated by reference) in the registration statement, they may be attached to the comfort letter. The accountant should not repeat the report in the comfort letter or otherwise imply that he or she is reporting as of the comfort letter date or that he or she is responsible for the sufficiency of the procedures for the underwriter's purposes.

6. The accountant should not:

   a. Attach to the comfort letter or refer to any restricted-use report except for a review report on MD&A
   b. Mention reports on internal control related matters (Section 325, *Communicating Internal Control Related Matters Identification in an Audit*).
   c. Mention restricted use reports on internal control (Section AT 501).
   d. Comment on unaudited interim financial information required by item 302(a) of Regulation S-K to which Section 722 applies, or required supplementary information to which Section 558 applies unless the underwriter asks the accountant to perform procedures in addition to those required by Sections 722 and 558. The accountant may then perform additional procedures and report the findings.

INDEPENDENCE

The following apply to statements on independence:

1. If, as is customary, the underwriting agreement in connection with an SEC filing requires a statement from the accountant concerning independence, the following wording from AU 634.31 is appropriate:

   > We are independent certified public accountants with respect to the XYZ Company, within the meaning of the Act and the applicable rules and regulations thereunder adopted by the SEC.

2. For a non-SEC filing, the following wording from AU 634.31 is appropriate:

   > We are independent certified public accountants with respect to XYZ Company, under Rule 101 of the American Institute of Certified Public Accountants (AICPA's) Code of Professional Conduct and its interpretations and rulings.

3. Accountants for previously nonaffiliated companies recently acquired by the registrant would make a statement similar to the following (from AU 634.32):

> As of [*date of the accountant's most recent report on the financial statements of his or her client*] and during the period covered by the financial statements on which we reported, we were independent certified public accountants with respect to [*name of client*] within the meaning of the Act and the applicable rules and regulations thereunder adopted by the SEC.

COMPLIANCE AS TO FORM WITH SEC REQUIREMENTS

The following apply to compliance with SEC requirements:

1. If the accountant is asked to express an opinion on whether the financial statements covered by his or her report comply as to form with pertinent accounting requirements adopted by the SEC, the following wording from AU 634.33 is appropriate:

   > In our opinion [*include the phrase "except as disclosed in the registration statement," if applicable*], the [*identify the financial statements and financial statement schedules*] audited by us and included (incorporated by reference) in the registration statement comply as to form in all material respects with the applicable accounting requirements of the Act and the related rules and regulations adopted by the SEC.

2. Material departures from pertinent rules and regulations adopted by the SEC should be disclosed in the comfort letter (see Illustration 11).
3. The accountant may provide positive assurance on compliance as to form with requirements under SEC rules and regulations only regarding those rules and regulations applicable to the form and content of financial statements and financial statement schedules that they have audited. When the financial statements or financial statement schedules have not been audited, the accountant may only provide negative assurance on compliance as to form.

FUNDAMENTAL REQUIREMENTS: COMMENTING IN A COMFORT LETTER ON INFORMATION OTHER THAN AUDITED FINANCIAL STATEMENTS

GENERAL

The following apply to (1) unaudited condensed interim financial information, (2) capsule financial information, (3) pro forma financial information, (4) financial forecasts, and (5) changes in capital stock, increases in long-term debt, and decreases in other specified financial statement items.

1. Agreed-upon procedures performed by the accountant should be stated in the comfort letter. If, however, the accountants have been requested to provide negative assurance on interim financial information or capsule financial information, the procedures involved in a Section 722 review need not be specified. The accountant should not make any statements or imply that he or she has applied procedures determined to be necessary or sufficient for the underwriter's purposes.
2. If the underwriter requests that the accountant apply procedures in addition to those specified in Section 722, the accountant may perform those procedures and should describe them in the comfort letter. The criteria specified by the underwriter should be included in the descriptions of procedures in the comfort letter.

3. The accountant should not use terms such as *general review*, *limited review*, *reconcile*, *check*, or *test* to describe the work done unless the procedures required by those terms are described in the comfort letter.
4. The accountant should not make a general statement that, as a result of carrying out procedures specified in the underwriting agreement and draft comfort letter, nothing else came to his or her attention that would be of interest to the underwriter.

Knowledge of Internal Control

If the accountant has not obtained knowledge of a client's internal control over financial reporting as it relates to the preparation of both annual and interim financial information, he or she should not comment in the comfort letter on (1) unaudited condensed interim financial information, (2) capsule financial information, (3) a financial forecast when historical financial statements provide a basis for one or more significant assumptions for the forecast, or (4) changes in capital stock, increases in long-term debt, and decreases in selected financial statement items.

Unaudited Condensed Interim Financial Information

The following apply to unaudited condensed interim financial information:

1. Accountants may comment in the form of negative assurance on this type of financial information only when they have conducted a review of the interim financial information in accordance with Section 722.
2. The comfort letter may state that the accountants have conducted review procedures in accordance with Section 722. If the letter states that the accountants issued a review report, the report should be attached unless the review report is included in the registration statement.
3. If the accountants have not conducted a review in accordance with Section 722, they may not comment in the form of negative assurance. In those circumstances, the accountants are limited to reporting procedures performed and findings obtained (see Illustration 15). The comfort letter should identify any unaudited condensed interim financial information and should state that the information has not been audited in accordance with the standards of the PCAOB and, therefore, no opinion is expressed concerning that information.

Capsule Financial Information

The following apply to capsule financial information:

1. Accountants may give negative assurance as to conformity with GAAP and may refer to whether the dollar amounts were determined on a basis substantially consistent with that of the corresponding amounts in the audited financial statements if (1) the capsule financial information meets the minimum disclosure requirements of Accounting Principles Board Opinion (APB) 28, *Interim Financial Reporting* (para 30), and (2) the accountants have reviewed the interim financial statements underlying the capsule financial information in accordance with Section 722.
2. If a review in accordance with Section 722 was performed, the accountants may give negative assurance as to whether the dollar amounts were determined on a basis substantially consistent with that of the corresponding amounts in the audited financial statements, even if the capsule financial information is more limited than the minimum disclosure required by paragraph 30 of APB Opinion 28 (see Illustration 12).

3. If a review has not been performed, the accountants are limited to reporting procedures performed and findings obtained.

Pro Forma Financial Information

The following apply to pro forma financial information:

1. Accountants should not comment on this type of information unless they have appropriate knowledge of the accounting and reporting practices of the entity.
2. Accountants should not give negative assurance on the application of pro forma adjustments to historical amounts, the compilation of pro forma financial information, or whether the pro forma financial information complies as to form in all material respects with the applicable requirements of Rule 11-02 of Regulation S-X unless they have (1) obtained the required knowledge described in 1. and (2) performed an audit of the annual financial statements or a review of interim financial statements of the entity to which the adjustments were applied.
3. For a business combination, the historical financial statements of each part of the combined entity on which the pro forma financial information is based should be audited or reviewed (see Illustration 4).
4. If the accountants have the required knowledge of internal control described earlier in "Knowledge of Internal Control," but have not met the requirements for giving negative assurance, they are limited to reporting procedures performed and findings obtained (see Illustration 15). In those circumstances, the accountants should comply with the guidance on reporting the results of agreed-upon procedures (see Section AT 201).

Financial Forecasts

The following apply to financial forecasts:

1. To perform agreed-upon procedures on a financial forecast and comment on it, accountants should obtain the knowledge described in "Knowledge of Internal Control" earlier and then perform the procedures prescribed in Section AT 301 for reporting on the compilation of a forecast.
2. The accountant's report on the forecast should be attached to the comfort letter.
3. If the forecast is included in the registration statement, the forecast should be accompanied by an indication that the accountants have not examined the forecast and, therefore, do not express an opinion on it.
4. Accountants may perform additional procedures on the forecast and report their findings in the comfort letter (see Illustrations 5 and 15).
5. Accountants are not permitted to provide negative assurance on the results of procedures performed. They may also not provide negative assurance with respect to compliance of the forecast with Rule 11-03 of Regulation S-X unless they have performed an examination of the forecast in accordance with Section AT 301.

Subsequent Changes

Comments on subsequent changes usually address:

1. Whether there have been any changes in capital stock, increases in long-term debt, or decreases in other specified financial statement items during the change period (see "Definitions of Terms")

2. Issues such as subsequent changes in the amounts of net current assets or stockholders' equity, net sales, total and per share amounts of income before extraordinary items, and net income.

Accountants generally will be asked to read minutes and make inquiries of company officials concerning the change period. The accountants should, therefore, base their comments solely on those limited procedures, and clearly state this in the comfort letter. (see AU Illustration 1, paragraph 6).

The following apply to other aspects of subsequent changes:

1. Accountants may provide negative assurance on subsequent changes in specific financial statement items up to 135 days from the end of the most recent audit or review period (see AU Illustration 1, paragraphs 5b and 6, and AU Illustration 13).
2. For periods 135 days or greater, accountants may not provide negative assurance but may only report procedures performed and findings obtained (see Illustration 15).
3. Changes in an accounting principle during the change period should be stated in the comfort letter.
4. Comments on subsequent changes are limited to those increases or decreases not disclosed in the registration statement.
5. The date and the period used to determine if subsequent changes occurred should be specified in both the draft and final comfort letters.

TABLES, STATISTICS, AND OTHER FINANCIAL INFORMATION

The following apply to tables, statistics, and other financial information:

1. Accountants may comment only on the following:

    a. Information expressed in dollars, or percentages derived from those dollars, obtained from accounting records that are subject to the entity's internal control.
    b. Information derived directly from the accounting records by analysis or computation.
    c. Quantitative information obtained from an accounting record if the information is subject to the same controls as the dollar amounts.

2. Accountants should not comment on matters such as the following, unless they are subjected to internal control over financial reporting (which is not ordinarily the case):

    a. Square footage of facilities
    b. Number of employees, except as related to a specific payroll period
    c. Backlog information

    In addition to the above, accountants should not comment on:

    d. Any matter or information subject to legal interpretation
    e. Segment information or the appropriateness of allocations made to derive segment information included in financial statements
    f. Tables, statistics, and other financial information relating to an unaudited period, unless they have:

(1) Audited the client's financial statements for a period including or immediately prior to the unaudited period or have completed an audit for a later period

(2) Otherwise obtained knowledge of the client's internal control over financial reporting

3. Procedures followed by the accountants with respect to this information should be described in both the draft and the final comfort letter. The letter should also contain a statement that the accountants are not furnishing any assurances with respect to the sufficiency of the procedures for the underwriter's intended purpose (see Illustration 7).

4. Regulation S-K requires the inclusion of certain financial information in registration statements. Accountants may comment and provide negative assurance about whether this information is in conformity with the disclosure requirements of Regulation S-K if the following conditions are met:

   a. The information is derived from the accounting records subject to the entity's internal control over financial reporting or has been derived directly from the accounting records by analysis or computation.
   b. The information is capable of evaluation against reasonable criteria established by the SEC.

   Regulation S-K disclosure requirements that meet those conditions are:

   a. Item 301, *Selected Financial Data*
   b. Item 302, *Supplementary Financial Information*
   c. Item 402, *Executive Compensation*
   d. Item 503(d), *Ratio of Earnings to Fixed Charges*

   Accountants should not comment in a comfort letter on compliance as to form of MD&A with SEC rules and regulations, but may examine or review MD&A in an attestation engagement (see Illustration 18 and Section AT 701).

5. Specific information commented on should be identified by referring to specific captions, tables, page numbers, paragraphs, or sentences. Descriptions of the procedures followed and the findings obtained may be stated individually for each item of specific information commented on.

6. Comments concerning tables, statistics, and other financial information included in the registration statement should include:

   a. A description of the procedures followed
   b. The findings, ordinarily expressed in terms of agreement between items compared
   c. Statements with respect to the acceptability of methods of allocation used in deriving the figures commented on:

      (1) Whether comments on allocation may be made depends on the extent to which they are made in, or can be derived directly by analysis or computation from, the client's accounting records.
      (2) Comments, if made, should make clear that the allocations are to a substantial extent arbitrary, that the allocation method used is not the only acceptable

one, and that other acceptable methods of allocation might produce significantly different results (see Illustrations 6, 7, and 8*)*.

FUNDAMENTAL REQUIREMENTS: OTHER MATTERS

CONCLUDING PARAGRAPH

It is desirable that the comfort letter conclude with a paragraph such as the following wording from AU 634.31:

> This letter is solely for the information of the addressees and to assist the underwriters in conducting and documenting their investigation of the affairs of the company in connection with the offering of the securities covered by the registration statement, and it is not to be used, circulated, quoted, or otherwise referred to within or without the underwriting group for any other purpose, including, but not limited to, the registration, purchase, or sale of securities, nor is it to be filed with or referred to in whole or in part in the registration statement or any other document, except that reference may be made to it in the underwriting agreement or in any list of closing documents pertaining to the offering of the securities covered by the registration statement.

DISCLOSURE OF SUBSEQUENTLY DISCOVERED MATTERS

Accountants may discover matters that should be included in the final comfort letter but that were not mentioned in the draft comfort letter. If these matters are not to be disclosed in the registration statement, the accountant should let the client know that they will be mentioned in the final comfort letter. Also, the accountant should suggest that the underwriter be informed immediately. It is advisable for the accountant to be present when these matters are discussed between the client and the underwriter.

INTERPRETATIONS

LETTERS TO DIRECTORS RELATING TO ANNUAL REPORTS ON FORM 10-K (ISSUED APRIL 1981; MODIFIED MAY 1981; REVISED JUNE 1993; REVISED JANUARY 2001)

Since annual reports to the SEC on Form 10-K must be signed by at least a majority of the board of directors, the directors might ask for assistance from the registrant's independent accountants. The accountant can report to the directors in accordance with the following guidelines:

- The auditor can express an opinion on whether the financial statements and schedules comply as to form with the accounting requirements of the 1934 Act.
- The auditor may affirm that the PCAOB standards require the auditor to read the information in addition to financial statements in the Form 10-K (see Section 550).
- The auditor may apply procedures requested by directors to tables, statistics, and other financial information. The guidance in Section 634 on comfort letters provides appropriate guidance in this area.
- The auditor may comment on whether information in Form 10-K is in conformity with disclosure requirements of Regulation S-K. The guidance in Section 634 provides appropriate general guidance in this area.

- The auditor may reaffirm independence in a manner similar to the guidance in Section 634.
- The auditor should clearly indicate to the directors that the auditor cannot make any representations as to whether any procedures performed at the request of the directors are sufficient for the directors' purposes.

COMMENTING IN A COMFORT LETTER ON QUANTITATIVE DISCLOSURES ABOUT MARKET RISK MADE IN ACCORDANCE WITH ITEM 305 OF REGULATION S-K (AUGUST 1998; REVISED JUNE 2009)

Regulation S-K, Item 305, *Quantitative and Qualitative Disclosures about Market Risk*, requires certain qualitative (descriptive) and quantitative disclosures with respect to the following, which are collectively referred to as "market-risk-sensitive instruments":

- Derivative and other financial instruments, generally as defined in the Master Glossary of the FASC Accounting Standards Codification (ASC).
- Derivative commodity instruments, such as commodity futures, forwards, and swaps that are permitted by contract or custom to be settled in cash.

These required disclosures:

- Generally include a combination of historical and fair value data and the hypothetical effects on such data of assumed changes in interest rates, foreign currency exchange rates, commodity prices, and other relevant market rates
- Should be disclosed outside the financial statements and related notes thereto

Assurance

An accountant may not provide either positive or negative assurance on conformity with Item 305 of Regulation S-K. Positive assurance is prohibited since Section 634 states that accountants may not give positive assurance on conformity of information with the disclosure requirements of Regulation S-K since this information is not in the form of financial statements and generally has not been audited by the accountants. Negative assurance is also not allowed, since much of the information provided by the registrant is not derived from accounting records subject to the entity's controls over financial reporting.

Comments on Qualitative Disclosures

Accountants may not comment in a comfort letter on the registrant's Item 305 qualitative disclosures since such information is not:

- Expressed in dollars or percentages obtained from dollar amounts
- Obtained from accounting records subject to the entity's controls over financial reporting.
- Derived from such accounting records by analysis or computation

Comments on Quantitative Disclosures

Item 305 requires quantitative disclosures that may be presented in the form of tabular presentation, sensitivity analysis, or value-at-risk disclosures. An accountant's ability to comment on such quantitative disclosures is largely dependent upon the degree to which the forward-looking information used to prepare these disclosures is linked to accounting records that are subject to the entity's controls over financial reporting. This link to the accounting records will vary with the three forms of presentation.

Tabular presentation. The tabular presentation includes the fair values of market-risk-sensitive instruments and contract terms to determine the future cash flows from these instruments that are categorized by expected maturity dates. This approach may require the use of yield curves and implied forward rates to determine expected maturity dates, as well as assumptions regarding prepayments and weighted-average interest rates.

The tabular presentation contains fewer assumptions and less complex mathematical calculations than the sensitivity analysis or value-at-risk disclosures. In addition, certain information, such as contractual terms in a tabular presentation, are derived from the accounting records. Therefore, the accountant may perform limited procedures related to tabular presentations to the extent that such information is derived from the accounting records.

When performing procedures related to tabular presentation disclosures, the accountant should:

- Consider whether the entity's documentation of its contractual positions in derivatives, commodities, and other financial instruments is subject to the controls over financial reporting
- Consider whether such documentation provides a complete record of the entity's market-risk-sensitive instruments

The accountant also should disclaim as to the reasonableness of the assumptions underlying the disclosures.

Sensitivity analysis. This term describes a general class of models that are designed to assess the risk of loss in market-risk-sensitive instruments, based on hypothetical changes in market rates or prices. Sensitivity analysis does not refer to one specific model and may include duration analysis or other "sensitivity" measures. The disclosures are dependent upon assumptions about theoretical future market conditions, and therefore, are not derived from the accounting records. Therefore, accountants should not agree to make any comments or perform any procedures related to these disclosures.

Value at risk. This term describes a general class of models that provide a probabilistic assessment of the risk of loss in market-risk-sensitive instruments over a selected period of time, with a selected likelihood of occurrences based upon selected confidence intervals. Value at risk disclosures are extremely aggregated and, in addition to the assumptions made for sensitivity analyses, may include additional assumptions regarding correlation between asset classes and future market volatilities.

As a result, these disclosures are not derived from the accounting records. Therefore, the accountant should not agree to make any comments or perform any procedures related to these disclosures.

Market Risk Category Disclosures

Registrants are required under Item 305 to stratify financial instruments according to market risk category (i.e., interest rate risk, foreign exchange risk, and equity price risk). If the instrument is at risk in more than one category, the instrument should be included in the disclosures for each applicable category. When reporting findings from agreed-upon procedures relating to market risk categories, the accountant should not provide any findings that the company's stratifications are complete or comply as to form with Item 305 requirements. The auditor should also issue a disclaimer regarding the company's determination of market risk categories.

Registrants are encouraged by Item 305 to provide quantitative and qualitative information about market risk in terms of, among other things, the magnitude of actual past market movements and estimates of possible near-term market movements. Accountants should not agree to perform any procedures related to such market data.

Understanding with the Underwriter/Need for Specialist

The accountant should establish a clear understanding with the underwriter regarding the limitations of the procedures to be performed related to market risk disclosures. Accountants should also consider whether to use a specialist in performing procedures related to these disclosures.

TECHNIQUES FOR APPLICATION

Accountants, in comfort letters, describe procedures applied and findings obtained by applying those procedures. Negative assurances may be provided in certain circumstances. The procedures applied are described in the comfort letters. Examples of comfort letters are presented in the following section.

AU ILLUSTRATIONS

The following illustrations of comfort letters are reprinted from SAS 72, SAS 86, and SSAE 8.

1. Typical Comfort Letter
2. Letter When a Short-Form Registration Statement Is Filed Incorporating Previously Filed Forms 10-K and 10-Q by Reference
3. Letter Reaffirming Comments in Illustration 1 (Typical Comfort Letter) as of a Later Date
4. Comments on Pro Forma Financial Information
5. Comments on a Financial Forecast
6. Comments on Tables, Statistics, and Other Financial Information: Complete Description of Procedures and Findings
7. Comments on Tables, Statistics, and Other Financial Information: Summarized Description of Procedures and Findings Regarding Tables, Statistics, and Other Financial Information
8. Comments on Tables, Statistics, and Other Financial Information: Description of Procedures and Findings, Regarding Tables, Statistics, and Other Financial Information—Attached Registration Statement (or Selected Pages) Identifies with Designated Symbols Items to Which Procedures Were Applied
9. Alternate Wording When Accountants' Report on Audited Financial Statements Contains an Explanatory Paragraph
10. Alternate Wording When More Than One Accountant Is Involved
11. Alternate Wording When the SEC Has Agreed to a Departure from Its Published Accounting Requirements
12. Alternate Wording When Recent Earnings Data Are Presented in Capsule Form
13. Alternate Wording When Accountants Are Aware of a Decrease in a Specified Financial Statement Item
14. Alternate Wording of the Letter for Companies That Are Permitted to Present Interim Earnings for a Twelve-Month Period

15. Alternate Wording When the Procedures That the Underwriter Has Requested the Accountant to Perform on Interim Financial Information Are Less Than an SAS 71 Review
16. A Typical Comfort Letter in a Non-1933 Act Offering, Including the Required Underwriter Representations
17. Letter to a Requesting Party That Has Not Provided the Normally Required Representation Letter
18. Comfort Letter That Includes Reference to Examination of Annual MD&A and Review of Interim MD&A

Shelf registration statements may have several closing dates and different underwriters. Descriptions of procedures and findings regarding interim financial statements, tables, statistics, or other financial information that is incorporated by reference from previous 1934 Act filings may have to be repeated in several comfort letters. To avoid restating these descriptions in each comfort letter, accountants may initially issue the comments in a format (such as an appendix) that can be referred to in, and attached to, subsequently issued comfort letters.

ILLUSTRATION 1. TYPICAL COMFORT LETTER

A typical comfort letter includes:

1. A statement regarding the independence of the accountants
2. An opinion regarding whether the audited financial statements and financial statement schedules included (incorporated by reference) in the registration statement comply as to form in all material respects with the applicable accounting requirements of the Act and related rules and regulations adopted by the SEC
3. Negative assurance on whether:

   a. The unaudited condensed interim financial information included (incorporated by reference) in the registration statement complies as to form in all material respects with the applicable accounting requirements of the Act and the related rules and regulations adopted by the SEC.

   b. Any material modifications should be made to the unaudited condensed consolidated financial statements included (incorporated by reference) in the registration statement for them to be in conformity with GAAP.

4. Negative assurance on whether, during a specified period following the date of the latest financial statements in the registration statement and prospectus, there has been any change in capital stock, increase in long-term debt, or any decrease in other specified financial statement items

Illustration 1 is a letter covering all these items. Letters that cover some of the items may be developed by omitting inapplicable portions of Illustration 1.

Illustration 1 assumes the following circumstances.[2] The prospectus (part I of the registration statement) includes audited consolidated balance sheets as of December 31, 20X5 and 20X4, and audited consolidated statements of income, retained earnings (stock-

---

[2] The example includes financial statements required by SEC regulations to be included in the filing. If additional financial information is covered by the comfort letter, appropriate modifications should be made.

holders' equity), and cash flows for each of the three years in the period ended December 31, 20X5. Part I also includes an unaudited condensed balance sheet as of March 31, 20X6, and unaudited condensed consolidated statements of income, retained earnings (stockholders' equity) and cash flows for the three-month periods ended March 31, 20X6 and 20X5, reviewed in accordance with Section 722 but not previously reported on by the accountants. Part II of the registration statement includes audited consolidated financial statement schedules for the three years ended December 31, 20X5. The cutoff date is June 23, 20X6, and the letter is dated June 28, 20X6. The effective date is June 28, 20X6.

Each of the comments in the letter is in response to a requirement of the underwriting agreement. For purposes of Illustration 1, the income statement items of the current interim period are to be compared with those of the corresponding period of the preceding year.

June 28, 20X6

[Addressee]

Dear Sirs:

We have audited the consolidated balance sheets of The Basic Company, Inc. (the company) and subsidiaries as of December 31, 20X5 and 20X4, and the consolidated statements of income, retained earnings (stockholders' equity), and cash flows for each of the three years in the period ended December 31, 20X5, and the related financial statements schedules all included in the registration statement (No. 33-00000) on Form S-1 filed by the company under the Securities Act of 1933 (the Act); our reports with respect thereto are also included in that registration statement. The registration statement, as amended on June 28, 20X6, is herein referred to as the registration statement.[3]

In connection with the registration statement:

1. We are independent certified public accountants with respect to the company within the meaning of the Act and the applicable rules and regulations thereunder adopted by the SEC.
2. In our opinion [*include the phrase "except as disclosed in the registration statement," if applicable*], the consolidated financial statements and financial statement schedules audited by us and included in the registration statement comply as to form in all material respects with the applicable accounting requirements of the Act and the related rules and regulations adopted by the SEC.
3. We have not audited any financial statements of the company as of any date or for any period subsequent to December 31, 20X5; although we have conducted an audit for the year ended December 31, 20X5, the purpose (and therefore the scope) of the audit was to enable us to express our opinion on the consolidated financial statements as of December 31, 20X5, and for the year then ended, but not on the financial statements for any interim period within that year. Therefore, we are unable to and do not express any opinion on the unaudited condensed consolidated balance sheet as of March 31, 20X6, and the unaudited condensed consolidated statements of income, retained earnings (stockholders' equity), and cash flows for the three-month periods ended March 31, 20X6 and 20X5, included in the registration statement, or on

---

[3] The example assumes that the accountants have not previously reported on the interim financial information. If the accountants have previously reported on the interim financial information, they may refer to that fact in the introductory paragraph of the comfort letter as follows:

> Also, we have reviewed the unaudited condensed consolidated financial statements as of March 31, 20X6 and 20X5, and for the three-month periods then ended, as indicated in our report dated May 15, 20X6, which is included (incorporated by reference) in the registration statement.

The report may be attached to the comfort letter. The accountants may agree to comment in the comfort letter on whether the interim financial information complies as to form in all material respects with the applicable accounting requirements of the published rules and regulations of the SEC.

the financial position, results of operations, or cash flows as of any date or for any period subsequent to December 31, 20X5.

4. For purposes of this letter we have read the 20X6 minutes of meetings of the stockholders, the board of directors, and [*include other appropriate committees, if any*] of the company and its subsidiaries as set forth in the minutes books at June 23, 20X6, officials of the company having advised us that the minutes of all such meetings[4] through the date were set forth herein; we have carried out other procedures from June 23, 20X6, as follows (our work did not extend to the period from June 24, 20X6, to June 28, 20X6, inclusive):

   a. With respect to the three-month periods ended March 31, 20X6 and 20X5, we have

   (1) Performed the procedures specified by the AICPA for a review of interim financial information as described in SAS 71, *Interim Financial Information*, on the unaudited condensed consolidated balance sheet as of March 31, 20X6, and unaudited condensed consolidated statements of income, retained earnings (stockholders' equity), and cash flows for the three-month periods ended March 31, 20X6 and 20X5, included in the registration statement.

   (2) Inquired of certain officials of the company who have responsibility to financial and accounting matters whether the unaudited condensed consolidated financial statements referred to in a(1) comply as to form in all material respects with the applicable accounting requirements of the Act and the related rules and regulations adopted by the SEC.

   b. With respect to the period from April 1, 20X6, to May 31, 20X6, we have

   (1) Read the unaudited consolidated financial statements[5] of the company and subsidiaries for April and May of both 20X5 and 20X6 furnished us by the company, officials of the company having advised us that no such financial statements as of any date or for any period subsequent to May 31, 20X6, were available.

   (2) Inquired of certain officials of the company who have responsibility for financial and accounting matters whether the unaudited consolidated financial statements referred to in b(1) are stated on a basis substantially consistent with that of the audited consolidated financial statements included in the registration statement.

The foregoing procedures do not constitute an audit conducted in accordance with the standards of the Public Company Accounting Oversight Board (United States). Also, they would not necessarily reveal matters of significance with respect to the comments in the following paragraph. Accordingly, we make no representations regarding the sufficiency of the foregoing procedures for your purposes.

5. Nothing came to our attention as a result of the foregoing procedures, however, that caused us[6] to believe that:

   a. (1) Any material modifications should be made to the unaudited condensed consolidated financial statements described in 4a(1), included in the registration statement, for them to be in conformity with generally accepted accounting principles.[7]

---

[4] *The accountants should discuss with the secretary those meetings for which minutes have not been approved. The letter should be modified to identify specifically the unapproved minutes of meetings that the accountants have discussed with the secretary.*

[5] *If the interim financial information is incomplete, a sentence similar to the following should be added:*

"*The financial information for April and May is incomplete in that it omits the statements of cash flows and other disclosures.*"

[6] *If there has been a change in accounting principle during the interim period, a reference to that change should be included herein.*

[7] *Section 722 does not require the accountants to modify the report on a review of interim financial information for a lack of consistency in the application of accounting principles, provided that the interim financial information appropriately discloses such matters.*

(2) The unaudited condensed and consolidated financial statements described in 4a(1) do not comply as to form in all material respects with the applicable accounting requirements of the Act and the related rules and regulations adopted by the SEC.

    b. (1) At May 31, 20X6, there was any change in the capital stock, increase in long-term debt, or decrease in consolidated net current assets or stockholders' equity of the consolidated companies as compared with amounts shown in the March 31, 20X6 unaudited condensed consolidated balance sheet included in the registration statement, or

(2) For the period from April 1, 20X6, to May 31, 20X6, there were any decreases, as compared to the corresponding period in the preceding year, in consolidated net sales or in the total or per share amounts of income before extraordinary items or of net income, except in all instances of changes, increases, or decreases that the registration statement discloses have occurred or may occur.

6. As mentioned in 4b, company officials have advised us that no consolidated financial statements as of any date or for any period subsequent to May 31, 20X6, are available; accordingly, the procedures carried out by us with respect to changes in financial statement items after May 31, 20X6, have, of necessity, been even more limited than those with respect to the periods referred to in 4. We have inquired of certain officials of the company who have responsibility for financial and accounting matters whether (1) at June 23, 20X6, there was any change in the capital stock, increase in long-term debt, or any decreases in consolidated net current assets or stockholders' equity of the consolidated companies as compared with amounts shown on the March 31, 20X6 unaudited condensed balance sheet included in the registration statement or (2) for the period from April 1, 20X6, to June 23, 20X6, there were any decreases, as compared with the corresponding period in the preceding year, in consolidated net sales or in the total or per share amounts of income before extraordinary items or of net income. On the basis of these inquiries and our reading of the minutes as described in item 4, nothing came to our attention that caused us to believe that there was any such change, increase, or decrease, except in all instances for changes, increases, or decreases that the registration statement discloses have occurred or may occur.

7. This letter is solely for the information of the addressees and to assist the underwriters in conducting and documenting their investigation of the affairs of the company in connection with the offering of the securities covered by the registration statements, and it is not to be used, circulated, quoted, or otherwise referred to within or without the underwriting group for any purpose, including but not limited to the registration, purchase, or sale of securities, nor is it to be filed with or referred to in whole or in part in the registration statement or any other document, except that reference may be made to it in the underwriting agreement or in any list of closing documents pertaining to the offering of the securities covered by the registration statement.

ILLUSTRATION 2. LETTER WHEN A SHORT-FORM REGISTRATION STATEMENT IS FILED INCORPORATING PREVIOUSLY FILED FORMS 10-K AND 10-Q BY REFERENCE

Illustration 2 is applicable when a registrant uses a short-form registration statement (Form S-2 or S-3) which, by reference, incorporates previously filed Forms 10-K and 10-Q. It assumes that the short-form registration statement and prospectus include the Form 10-K for the year ended December 31, 20X5, and Form 10-Q for the quarter ended March 31, 20X6, which have been incorporated by reference. In addition to the information presented below, the letter would also contain paragraphs 6 and 7 of the typical letter in Illustration 1. A Form S-2 registration statement will often both incorporate and include the registrant's financial statements. In such situations, the language in the following illustration should be appropriately modified to refer to such information as being both incorporated and included.

June 28, 20X6

[*Addressee*]

Dear Sirs:

We have audited the consolidated balance sheets of The Basic Company, Inc. (the company) and subsidiaries as of December 31, 20X5 and 20X4, and the consolidated statements of income, retained earnings (stockholders' equity), and cash flows for each of the three years in the period ended December 31, 20X5, and the related financial statement schedules, all included (incorporated by reference) in the company's annual report on Form 10-K for the year ended December 31, 20X5, and incorporated by reference in the registration statement (No. 33-00000) on Form S-3 filed by the company under the Securities Act of 1933 (the Act); our report with respect thereto is also incorporated by reference in that registration statement. The registration statement as amended on June 28, 20X6, is herein referred to as the registration statement.

In connection with the registration statement:

1. We are independent certified public accountants with respect to the company within the meaning of the Act and the applicable rules and regulations thereunder adopted by the SEC.
2. In our opinion, the consolidated financial statements and financial statement schedules audited by us and incorporated by reference in the registration statement comply as to form in all material respects with the applicable accounting requirements of the Act and the Securities Exchange Act of 1934 and the related rules and regulations adopted by the SEC.
3. We have not audited any financial statements of the company as of any date or for any period subsequent to December 31, 20X5; although we have conducted an audit for the year ended December 31, 20X5, the purpose (and therefore the scope) of the audit was to enable us to express our opinion on the consolidated financial statements as of December 31, 20X5, and for the year then ended, but not on the consolidated financial statements for any interim period within that year. Therefore, we are unable to and do not express any opinion on the unaudited condensed consolidated balance sheet as of March 31, 20X6, and the unaudited condensed consolidated statements of income, retained earnings (stockholders' equity), and cash flows for the three-month periods ended March 31, 20X6 and 20X5, included in the company's quarterly report on Form 10-Q for the quarter ended March 31, 20X6, incorporated by reference in the registration statement, or on the financial position, results of operations, or cash flows as of any date or for any period subsequent to December 31, 20X5.
4. For purposes of this letter, we have read the 20X6 minutes of meetings of the stockholders, the board of directors, and [*include other appropriate committees, if any*] of the company and its subsidiaries as set forth in the minutes books at June 23, 20X6, officials of the company having advised us that the minutes of all such meetings[8] through the date were set forth herein; we have carried out other procedures from June 23, 20X6, as follows (our work did not extend to the period from June 24, 20X6, to June 28, 20X6, inclusive):

   a. With respect to the three-month periods ended March 31, 20X6 and 20X5, we have:

      (1) Performed the procedures specified by AICPA for a review of interim financial information as described in SAS 71, *Interim Financial Information*, on the unaudited condensed consolidated financial statements for these periods, described in item 3, included in the company's quarterly report on Form 10-Q for the quarter ended March 31, 20X6, incorporated by reference in the registration statement.

      (2) Inquired of certain officials of the company who have responsibility for financial and accounting matters whether the unaudited condensed consolidated financial statements referred to in 4a(1) comply as to form in all material respects with the applicable accounting requirements of the Securities Exchange Act of 1934 as it applied to Form 10-Q and the related rules and regulations adopted by the SEC.

---

[8] *See footnote 4.*

b. With respect to the period from April 1, 20X6, to May 31, 20X6, we have:

   (1) Read the unaudited consolidated financial statements of the company and subsidiaries for April and May of both 20X5 and 20X6 furnished us by the company, officials of the company having advised us that no such financial statements as of any date or for any period subsequent to May 31, 20X6, were available.

   (2) Inquired of certain officials of the company who have responsibility for financial and accounting matters whether the unaudited consolidated financial statements referred to in item 4b(1) are stated on a basis substantially consistent with that of the audited consolidated financial statements incorporated by reference in the registration statement.

The foregoing procedures do not constitute an audit conducted in accordance with the standards of the Public Company Accounting Oversight Board (United States). Also, they would not necessarily reveal matters of significance with respect to the comments in the following paragraph. Accordingly, we make no representations about the sufficiency of the foregoing procedures for your purposes.

5. Nothing came to our attention as a result of the foregoing procedures, however, that caused us to believe that:

   a. (1) Any material modifications should be made to the unaudited condensed consolidated financial statements described in item 3, incorporated by reference in the registration statement, for them to be in conformity with GAAP.

   (2) The unaudited condensed and consolidated financial statements described in item 3 do not comply as to form in all material respects with the applicable accounting requirements of the Securities Exchange Act of 1934 as it applies to Form 10-Q and the related rules and regulations adopted by the SEC.

   b. (1) At May 31, 20X6, there was any change in the capital stock, increase in long-term debt, or decrease in consolidated net current assets or stockholders' equity of the consolidated companies as compared with amounts shown in the March 31, 20X6, unaudited condensed consolidated balance sheet incorporated by reference in the registration statement, or

   (2) For the period from April 1, 20X6, to May 31, 20X6, there were any decreases, as compared with the corresponding period in the preceding year, in consolidated net sales or in the total or per share amounts of income before extraordinary items or of net income, except in all instances of changes, increases, or decreases that the registration statement discloses have occurred or may occur.

ILLUSTRATION 3. LETTER REAFFIRMING COMMENTS IN ILLUSTRATION 1 AS OF A LATER DATE

If more than one comfort letter is requested, the later letter may, in appropriate situations, refer to information appearing in the earlier letter without repeating such information. Illustration 3 reaffirms and updates the information in Illustration 1.

July 25, 20X6

[*Addressee*]

Dear Sirs:

We refer to our letter of June 28, 20X6, relating to the registration statement (No. 33-00000) of The Basic Company, Inc. (the company). We reaffirm as of the date hereof (and as though made on the date hereof) all statements made in that letter except that, for the purposes of this letter

1. The registration statement to which this letter relates is as amended on July 13, 20X6 [*effective date*].

2. The reading of minutes described in paragraph 4 of that letter has been carried out through July 20, 20X6 [*the new cutoff date*].
3. The procedures and inquiries covered in paragraph 4 of that letter were carried out to July 20, 20X6 [*the new cutoff date*] (our work did not extend to the period from July 21, 20X6 to July 25, 20X6 [*date of letter*], inclusive).
4. The period covered in paragraph 4b of that letter is changed to the period from April 1, 20X6, to June 30, 20X6, officials of the company having advised us that no such financial statements as of any date or for any period subsequent to June 30, 20X6, were available.
5. The references to May 31, 20X6, in paragraph 5b of that letter are changed to June 30, 20X6.
6. The references to May 31, 20X6, and June 23, 20X6, in paragraph 6 of that letter are changed to June 30, 20X6, and July 20, 20X6, respectively.

This letter is solely for the information of the addressees and to assist the underwriters in conducting and documenting their investigation of the affairs of the company in connection with the offering of the securities covered by the registration statement, and it is not to be used, circulated, quoted, or otherwise referred to within the underwriting group for any other purpose, including but not limited to the registration, purchase, or sale of securities, nor is it to be filed with or referred to in whole or in part in the registration statements or any other document, except that reference may be made to it in the underwriting agreement or any list of closing documents pertaining to the offering of the securities covered by the registration statement.

ILLUSTRATION 4. COMMENTS ON PRO FORMA FINANCIAL INFORMATION

Illustration 4 is applicable when the accountants are asked to comment on (1) whether the pro forma financial information included in a registration statement complies as to form in all material respects with the applicable accounting requirements of Rule 11-02 of Regulation S-X, and (2) the application of pro forma adjustments to historical amounts in the compilation of the pro forma financial information. The material in this illustration is intended to be inserted between paragraphs 6 and 7 in Illustration 1. The accountants have audited the December 31, 20X5 financial statements and have conducted an SAS 71 [Section 722] review of the March 31, 20X6 interim financial information of the acquiring company. Other accountants conducted a review of the March 31, 20X6 interim financial information of XYZ Company, the company being acquired. The illustration assumes that the accountants have not previously reported on the pro forma financial information. If the accountants did previously report on the pro forma financial information, they may refer in the introductory paragraph of the comfort letter to the fact that they have issued a report, and the report may be attached to the comfort letter. In that circumstance, therefore, the procedures in 7b(1) and 7c ordinarily would not be performed, and the accountants should not separately comment on the application of pro forma adjustments to historical financial information, since that assurance is encompassed in the accountants' report on pro forma financial information. The accountants may, however, agree to comment on compliance as to form with the applicable accounting requirements of Rule 11-02 of Regulation S-X.

7. At your request we have
    a. Read the unaudited pro forma condensed consolidated balance sheet as of March 31, 20X6, and the unaudited pro forma condensed consolidated statements of income for the year ended December 31, 20X5, and the three-month period ended March 31, 20X6, included in the registration statement.
    b. Inquired of certain officials of the company and of XYZ Company (the company being acquired) who have responsibility for financial and accounting matters about:

(1) The basis for their determination of the pro forma adjustments, and
(2) Whether the unaudited pro forma condensed consolidated financial statements referred to in 7a comply as to form in all material respects with the applicable accounting requirements of Rule 11-02 of Regulation S-X.

c. Proved the arithmetic accuracy of the application of the pro forma adjustments to the historical amounts in the unaudited pro forma condensed consolidated financial statements.

The foregoing procedures are substantially less in scope than an examination, the objective of which is the expression of an opinion on management's assumptions, the pro forma adjustments, and the application of those adjustments to historical financial information. Accordingly, we do not express such an opinion. The foregoing procedures would not necessarily reveal matters of significance with respect to the comments in the following paragraph. Accordingly, we make no representation about the sufficiency of such procedures for your purposes.

8. Nothing came to our attention as a result of the procedures specified in paragraph 7, however, that caused us to believe that the unaudited pro forma condensed consolidated financial statements referred to in 7a included in the registration statement do not comply as to form in all material respects with the applicable accounting requirement of Rule 11-02 of Regulation S-X and that the pro forma adjustments have not been properly applied to the historical amounts in the compilation of those statements. Had we performed additional procedures or had we made an examination of the pro forma condensed consolidated financial statements, other matters might have come to our attention that would have been reported to you.

ILLUSTRATION 5. COMMENTS ON A FINANCIAL FORECAST

Illustration 5 is applicable when accountants are asked to comment on a financial forecast. The material in this illustration is intended to be inserted between paragraphs 6 and 7 in Illustration 1. The illustration assumes that the accountants have previously reported on the compilation of the financial forecast and that the report is attached to the letter (see Illustration 15).

7. At your request, we performed the following procedure with respect to the forecasted consolidated balance sheet and consolidated statements of income and cash flows as of December 31, 20X6, and for the year then ending. With respect to forecasted rental income, we compared the occupancy statistics about expected demand for rental of the housing units to statistics for existing comparable properties and found them to be the same.

8. Because the procedure described above does not constitute an examination of prospective financial statements in accordance with standards established by the Public Company Accounting Oversight Board (United States), we do not express an opinion on whether the prospective financial statements are presented in conformity with AICPA presentation guidelines or on whether the underlying assumptions provide a reasonable basis for the presentation. Had we performed additional procedures or had we made an examination of the forecast in accordance with standards established by the AICPA, matters might have come to our attention that would have been reported to you. Furthermore, there will usually be differences between the forecasted and actual results, because events and circumstances frequently do not occur as expected, and those differences may be material.

ILLUSTRATION 6. COMMENTS ON TABLES, STATISTICS, AND OTHER FINANCIAL INFORMATION—COMPLETE DESCRIPTION OF PROCEDURES AND FINDINGS

Illustration 6 is applicable when the accountants are asked to comment on tables, statistics, or other compilations of information appearing in a registration statement. Each of the comments is in response to a specific request. The paragraphs in Illustration 6 are intended to follow paragraph 6 in Illustration 1.

7. For purposes of this letter, we have also read the following, set forth in the registration statement on the indicated pages.[9]

Item	Page	Description
A	4	*Capitalization.* The amounts under the captions, "Amount Outstanding as of June 5, 20X6," and, "As Adjusted." The related notes, except the following in Note 2: "See 'Transactions with Interested Persons.' From the proceeds of this offering the company intends to prepay $900,000 on these notes, pro rata. See 'Use of Proceeds.'"
B	13	*History and Business—Sales and Marketing.* The table following the first paragraph.
C	22	*Executive Compensation—20X5 Compensation.*
D	33	*Selected Financial Data.*[10]

8. Our audit of the consolidated financial statements for the periods referred to in the introductory paragraph of this letter comprised audit tests and procedures deemed necessary for the purpose of expressing an opinion on such financial statements taken as a whole. For none of the periods referred to therein, or any other period, did we perform audit tests for the purpose of expressing an opinion on individual balances of accounts or summaries of selected transactions such as those enumerated above, and accordingly, we express no opinion thereon.

9. However, for purposes of this letter we have performed the following additional procedures, which were applied as indicated with respect to the items enumerated above.

Item in 7	Procedures and findings
A	We compared the amounts and numbers of shares listed under the caption "Amount Outstanding as of June 15, 20X6," with the balances in the appropriate accounts in the company's general ledger at May 31, 20X6 (the latest date for which postings had been made), and found them to be in agreement. We were informed by company officials who have responsibility for financial and accounting matters that there had been no changes in such amounts and numbers of shares between May 31, 20X6, and June 15, 20X6. We compared the amounts and numbers of shares listed under the caption "Amount Outstanding as of June 15, 20X6," adjusted for the issuance of the debentures to be offered by means of the registration statement and for the proposed use of a portion of the proceeds thereof to prepay portions of certain notes, as described under "Use of Proceeds," with the amounts and numbers of shares shown under the caption, "As Adjusted," and found such amounts and numbers of shares to be in agreement. (However, we make no comments regarding the reasonableness of the "Use of Proceeds," or whether such use will actually take place.) We compared the description of the securities and the information (except certain information in Note 2, referred to in 7) included in the notes to the table with the corresponding descriptions and information in the company's consolidated financial statements, including the notes thereto included in the registration statement, and found such descriptions and information to be in agreement.

---

[9] In some cases it may be considered desirable to combine in one paragraph the substance of paragraphs 7 and 9. This may be done by expanding the identification of items in paragraph 9 to provide the identification information contained in paragraph 7. In such cases, the introductory sentences in paragraphs 7 and 9 and the text of paragraph 8 might be combined as follows: "For purposes of this letter, we have also read the following information and have performed the additional procedures stated below with respect to such information. Our audit of the consolidated financial statements...."

[10] In some cases the company or the underwriter may request that the independent accountants report on "selected financial data" as described in Section 552, Reporting on Condensed Financial Statements and Selected Financial Data. When the accountants report on this data and the report is included in the registration statement, separate comments should not be included in the comfort letter.

Item in 7	*Procedures and findings*
B	We compared the amounts of military sales, commercial sales, and total sales shown in the registration statement with the balances in the appropriate accounts in the company's accounting records for the respective fiscal years and for the unaudited interim periods and found them to be in agreement. We proved the arithmetic accuracy of the percentages of such amounts of military sales and commercial sales to total sales for the respective fiscal years and for the unaudited interim periods. We compared such computed percentages with the corresponding percentages appearing in the registration statement and found them to be in agreement.
C	We compared the dollar amounts of compensation (salary, bonus, and other compensation) for each individual listed in the table "Annual Compensation," with the corresponding amounts shown by the individual employee earnings records for the year 20X5 and found them to be in agreement. We compared the dollar amount of aggregate executive officers' cash compensation on page 22 with the corresponding amount shown in an analysis prepared by the company and found the amounts to be in agreement. We traced every item over $10,000 on the analysis to the individual employee records for 20X5. We compared the dollar amounts shown under the heading of "Long-Term Compensation" on page 24 for each listed individual and the aggregate amounts for executive officers with corresponding amounts shown in an analysis prepared by the company and found such amounts to be in agreement.
	We compared the executive compensation information with the requirements of item 402 of Regulation S-K. We also inquired of certain officials of the company who have responsibility for financial and accounting matters whether the executive compensation information conforms in all material respects with the disclosure requirements of item 402 of Regulation S-K. Nothing came to our attention as a result of the foregoing procedures that caused us to believe that this information does not conform in all material respects with the disclosure requirements of item 402 Regulation S-K.
D	We compared the amounts of net sales, income from continuing operations, income from continuing operations per common share, and cash dividends declared per common share for the years ended December 31, 20X5, 20X4, and 20X3, with the respective amounts in the consolidated financial statements on pages 27 and 28 and the amounts for the years ended December 31, 20X2, and 20X1, with the respective amounts in the consolidated financial statements included in the company's annual reports to stockholders for 20X2 and 20X1 and found them to be in agreement.
	We compared the amounts of total assets, long-term obligations, and redeemable preferred stock at December 31, 20X5 and 20X4, with the respective amounts in the consolidated financial statements on pages 27 and 28 and the amounts at December 31, 20X3, 20X2, and 20X1, with the corresponding amounts in the consolidated financial statements included in the company's annual reports to stockholders for 20X3, 20X2, and 20X1 and found them to be in agreement.
	We compared the information under the heading, "Selected Financial Data" with the requirements of item 301 of Regulation S-K. We also inquired of certain officials of the company who have responsibility for financial and accounting matters whether this information conforms in all material respects with the disclosure requirements of item 301 of Regulation S-K. Nothing came to our attention as a result of the foregoing procedures that caused us to believe that this information does not conform in all material respects with the disclosure requirements of item 301 of Regulation S-K.

10. It should be understood that we make no representations regarding questions of legal interpretation or regarding the sufficiency for your purposes of the procedures enumerated in the preceding paragraph; also such procedures would not necessarily reveal any material misstatement of the amounts or percentages listed above. Further, we have addressed ourselves solely to the foregoing data as set forth in the registration statement and make no representa-

tions regarding the adequacy of disclosure or regarding whether any material facts have been omitted.

11. This letter is solely for the information of the addressees and to assist the underwriters in conducting and documenting their investigation of the affairs of the company in connection with the offering of the securities covered by the registration statement, and it is not to be used, circulated, quoted, or otherwise referred to within or without the underwriting group for any other purpose, including but not limited to the registration, purchase, or sale of securities, nor is it to be filed with or referred to in whole or in part in the registration statement or any other document, except that reference may be made to it in the underwriting agreement or in any list of closing documents pertaining to the offering of the securities covered by the registration statement.

> **ILLUSTRATION 7. COMMENTS ON TABLES, STATISTICS, AND OTHER FINANCIAL INFORMATION—SUMMARIZED DESCRIPTION OF PROCEDURES AND FINDINGS REGARDING TABLES, STATISTICS, AND OTHER FINANCIAL INFORMATION**

Illustration 7 illustrates, in paragraph 9a, a method of summarizing the description of procedures and findings regarding tables, statistics, and other financial information in order to avoid repetition in the comfort letter. The summarization of the descriptions is permitted. Each of the comments is in response to a specific request. The paragraphs in Illustration 7 are intended to follow paragraph 6 in Illustration 1.[11]

7. For purposes of this letter, we have also read the following, set forth in the registration statement on the indicated pages.

Item	Page	Description
A	4	*Capitalization.* The amounts under the captions, "Amount Outstanding as of June 5, 20X6," and, "As Adjusted." The related notes, except the following in Note 2: "See 'Transactions with Interested Persons.' From the proceeds of this offering the company intends to prepay $900,000 on these notes, pro rata. See 'Use of Proceeds.'"
B	13	*History and Business—Sales and Marketing.* The table following the first paragraph.
C	22	*Executive Compensation—20X5 Compensation.*
D	33	*Selected Financial Data.*

8. Our audit of the consolidated financial statements for the periods referred to in the introductory paragraph of this letter comprised audit tests and procedures deemed necessary for the purpose of expressing an opinion on such financial statements taken as a whole. For none of the periods referred to therein, or any other period, did we perform audit tests for the purpose of expressing an opinion on individual balances of accounts or summaries of selected transactions such as those enumerated above, and, accordingly, we express no opinion thereon.

9. However, for purposes of this letter and with respect to the items enumerated in item 7:

a. Except for item 7A, we have (1) compared the dollar amounts either with the amounts in the audited consolidated financial statements described in the introductory paragraph of this letter or, for prior years, included in the company's annual report to stockholders for the years 20X1, 20X2, and 20X3, or with amounts in the unaudited consolidated financial statements described in paragraph 3 to the extent such amounts are included in or can be derived from such statements and found them to be in agreement; (2) compared the

---

[11] *Other methods of summarizing the descriptions may also be appropriately used. For example, the letter may present a matrix listing the financial information and common procedures employed and indicating the procedures applied to specific items.*

amounts of military sales, commercial sales, and total sales and the dollar amounts of compensation for each listed individual with amounts in the company's accounting records and found them to be in agreement; (3) compared other dollar amounts with amounts shown in analyses prepared by the company and found them to be in agreement; and (4) proved the arithmetic accuracy of the percentages based on the data in the above-mentioned financial statements, accounting records, and analyses.

We compared the information in items 7C and 7D with the disclosure requirements of Regulation S-K. We also inquired of certain officials of the company who have responsibility for financial and accounting matters whether this information conforms in all material respects with the disclosure requirements of Regulation S-K. Nothing came to our attention as a result of the foregoing procedures that caused us to believe that this information does not conform in all material respects with the disclosure requirements of items 402 and 301, respectively, of Regulation S-K.

b. With respect to item 7A, we compared the amounts and numbers of shares listed under the caption "Amount Outstanding as of June 15, 20X6," with the balances in the appropriate accounts in the company's general ledger at May 31, 20X6 (the latest date for which postings had been made), and found them to be in agreement. We were informed by officials of the company who have responsibility for financial and accounting matters that there had been no changes in such amounts and numbers of shares between May 31, 20X6, and June 15, 20X6. We compared the amounts and numbers listed under the caption "Amount Outstanding as of June 15, 20X6," adjusted for the issuance of the debentures to be offered by means of the registration statement and for the proposed use of a portion of the proceeds thereof to prepay portions of certain notes, as described under "Use of Proceeds," with the amounts and numbers of shares shown under the caption, "As Adjusted," and found such amounts and numbers of shares to be in agreement. (However, we make no comments regarding the reasonableness of "Use of Proceeds," or whether such use will actually take place.) We compared the description of the securities and the information (except certain information in Note 2, referred to in item 7) included in the notes to the table with the corresponding descriptions and information in the company's consolidated financial statements, including the notes thereto, included in the registration statement and found such descriptions and information to be in agreement.

10. It should be understood that we make no representation regarding questions of legal interpretation or regarding the sufficiency for your purposes of the procedures enumerated in the preceding paragraph; also, such procedures would not necessarily reveal any material misstatement of the amounts or percentages listed above. Further, we have addressed ourselves solely to the foregoing data as set forth in the registration statement and make no representations regarding the adequacy of disclosure or regarding whether any material facts have been omitted.

11. This letter is solely for the information of the addressees and to assist the underwriters in conducting and documenting their investigation of the affairs of the company in connection with the offering of the securities covered by the registration statement, and it is not to be used, circulated, quoted, or otherwise referred to within or without the underwriting group for any other purpose, including but not limited to the registration, purchase, or sale of securities, nor is it to be filed with or referred to in whole or in part in the registration statement or any other document, except that reference may be made to it in the underwriting agreement or in any list of closing documents pertaining to the offering of the securities covered by the registration statement.

> **ILLUSTRATION 8. COMMENTS ON TABLES, STATISTICS, AND OTHER FINANCIAL INFORMATION: DESCRIPTIONS OF PROCEDURES AND FINDINGS REGARDING TABLES, STATISTICS, AND OTHER FINANCIAL INFORMATION—ATTACHED REGISTRATION STATEMENT (OR SELECTED PAGES) IDENTIFIES WITH DESIGNATED SYMBOLS ITEMS TO WHICH PROCEDURES WERE APPLIED**

This illustration illustrates an alternate format which could facilitate reporting when the accountant is requested to perform procedures on numerous statistics included in a registration statement. Each of the comments is in response to a specific request. The paragraph in Illustration 8 is intended to follow paragraph 6 in Illustration 1.

7. For purposes of this letter, we have also read the items identified by you on the attached copy of the registration statement (prospectus) and have performed the following procedures, which were applied as indicated with respect to the symbols explained below.

   ⓒ Compared the amount with the XYZ (Predecessor Company) financial statements for the period indicated and found them to be in agreement.

   ⓧ Compared the amount with the XYZ (Predecessor Company) financial statements for the period indicated contained in the registration statement and found them to be in agreement.

   ✓ Compared the amount with Basic Company's financial statements for the period indicated contained in the registration statement and found them to be in agreement.

   Ⓓ Compared with a schedule or report prepared by the Company and found them to be in agreement.

The letter would also contain paragraphs 8, 10, and 11 of the letter in Illustration 6. [*The following is an extract from a registration statement that illustrates how an accountant can document procedures performed on numerous statistics included in the registration statement.*]

The following summary is qualified in its entirety by the financial statements and detailed information appearing elsewhere in this Prospectus.

<u>The Company</u>

Basic Company (the Company) designs, constructs, sells, and finances single-family homes for the entry-level and move-up homebuyer. The Company and its predecessor have built and delivered more single-family homes in the metropolitan area than any other homebuilder for each of the last five years. The Company delivered 1,000 ⓒ homes in the year ending December 31, 20X5, and at December 31, 20X5, had 500 homes [12] under contract with an aggregate sales price of approximately $45,000,000. The Company's wholly owned mortgage banking subsidiary, which commenced operations in March 20X5, currently originates a substantial portion of the mortgages for homes sold by the Company.

The Company typically does not engage in land development without related home-building operations and limits speculative building. The Company purchases only that land which it is prepared to begin developing immediately for home production. A substantial portion of the Company's homes are under contract for sale before construction commences.

The DEF area has been among the top five markets in the country in housing starts for each of the last five years, with more than 90,000 single-family starts during that period. During the same period, the DEF metropolitan area has experienced increases in population, personal income, and employment at rates above the national average. The Company is a major competitive factor in three of the seven market areas, and is expanding significantly in a fourth area.

---

[12] *See paragraph .55 of SAS 72.*

The Offering

Common Stock Offered by the Company	750,000 Ⓓ shares of Common Stock—$.01 par value (the Common Stock) *
Common Stock to Be Outstanding	3,250,000 Ⓓ shares*
Use of Proceeds	To repay indebtedness incurred for the acquisition of the Company.
Proposed NASDAQ Symbol	BAS

* *Assumes no exercise of the Underwriters' overallotment option. See "Underwriting."*

Summary Financial Information
(In thousands, except per share data)

	XYZ (Predecessor Company) Year Ended December 31,				Basic Company Year Ended December 31,
Income Statement Data	20X1	20X2	20X3	20X4	20X5
Revenue from home sales	$106,603 ⊘	$88,977 ⊘	$140,110 ✗	$115,837 ✗	$131,032 ✓
Gross profit from sales	15,980 ⊘	21,138 ⊘	23,774 ✗	17,099 ✗	22,407 ✓
Income from home building net of tax	490 ⊘	3,473 ⊘	7,029 ✗	1,000 ✗	3,425 ✓
Earnings per share	--	--	--	--	$1.37 ✓

ILLUSTRATION 9. ALTERNATE WORDING WHEN ACCOUNTANTS' REPORT ON AUDITED FINANCIAL STATEMENTS CONTAINS AN EXPLANATORY PARAGRAPH

Illustration 9 is applicable when the accountants' report on the audited financial statements included in the registration statement contains an explanatory paragraph regarding a matter that would also affect the unaudited condensed interim financial statements included in the registration statement. The introductory paragraph of Illustration 1 would be revised as follows:

> Our reports with respect thereto (which contain an explanatory paragraph that describes a lawsuit to which the Company is a defendant, discussed in note 8 to the consolidated financial statements) are also included in the registration statement.

The matter described in the explanatory paragraph should also be evaluated to determine whether it also requires mention in the comments on the unaudited condensed consolidated interim financial information (paragraph 5b of Illustration 1). If it is concluded that mention of such a matter in the comments on unaudited condensed financial statements is appropriate, a sentence should be added at the end of paragraph 5b in Illustration 1.

> Reference should be made to the introductory paragraph of this letter which states that our audit report covering the consolidated financial statements as of and for the year ended December 31, 20X5, includes an explanatory paragraph that describes a lawsuit to which the company is a defendant, discussed in note 8 to the consolidated financial statements.

ILLUSTRATION 10. ALTERNATE WORDING WHEN MORE THAN ONE ACCOUNTANT IS INVOLVED

Illustration 10 applies when more than one accountant is involved in the audit of the financial statements of a business and the principal accountants have obtained a copy of the comfort letter of other accountants. Illustration 10 consists of an addition to paragraph 4c, a substitution for the applicable part of paragraph 5, and an addition to paragraph 6 of Illustration 1.

4c. We have read the letter dated _____ of [the other accountants] with regard to [the related company].
5. Nothing came to our attention as a result of the foregoing procedures (which, so far as [the related company] is concerned, consisted solely of reading the letter referred to in 4c) however, that caused us to believe that . . .
6. On the basis of these inquiries and our reading of the minutes and the letter dated _____ of [the other accountants] with regard to [the related company], as described in 4, nothing came to our attention that caused us to believe that there was any such change, increase, or decrease, except in all instances for changes, increases, or decreases that the registration statement discloses have occurred or may occur.

ILLUSTRATION 11. ALTERNATE WORDING WHEN THE SEC HAS AGREED TO A DEPARTURE FROM ITS PUBLISHED ACCOUNTING REQUIREMENTS

Illustration 11 is applicable when (1) there is a departure from the applicable accounting requirements of the Act and the related rules and regulations adopted by the SEC and (2) representatives of the SEC have agreed to the departure. Paragraph 2 of Illustration 1 would be revised to read as follows:

2. In our opinion [*include the phrase "except as disclosed in the registration statement," if applicable*], the consolidated financial statements and financial statement schedules audited by us and included (incorporated by reference) in the registration statement comply as to form in all material respects with the applicable accounting requirements of the Act and the related rules and regulations adopted by the SEC; however, as agreed to by representatives of the SEC, separate financial statements and financial statement schedules of Basic Company (an equity investee) as required by Rule 3-09 of Regulation S-X have been omitted.

ILLUSTRATION 12. ALTERNATE WORDING WHEN RECENT EARNINGS DATA ARE PRESENTED IN CAPSULE FORM

Illustration 12 is applicable when (1) the statement of income in the registration statement is supplemented by later information regarding sales and earnings (capsule financial information), (2) the accountants are asked to comment on that information, and (3) the accountants have conducted a review in accordance with Section 722 of the financial statements from which the capsule financial information is derived. The same facts exist as in Illustration 1, except for the following:

1. Sales, net income (no extraordinary items), and earnings per share for the six-month periods ended June 30, 20X6 and 20X5 (both unaudited), are included in capsule form more limited than that specified by APB Opinion 28 [AC Section 173.146].
2. No financial statements later than those for June 20X6 are available.
3. The letter is dated July 25, 20X6, and the cutoff date is July 20, 20X6.

Paragraphs 4, 5, and 6 of Illustration 1 should be revised to read as follows:

4. For purposes of this letter we have read the 20X6 minutes of the meetings of the stockholders, the board of directors, and [*include other appropriate committees, if any*] of the company and its subsidiaries as set forth in the minute books at July 20, 20X6, officials of the company having advised us that the minutes of all such meetings[13] through the date were set forth therein; we have carried out other procedures to July 20, 20X6, as follows (our work did not extend to the period from July 21, 20X6 to July 25, 20X6, inclusive):

---

[13] *See footnote 4.*

a. With respect to the three-month periods ended March 31, 20X6 and 20X5, we have:

   (1) Performed the procedures specified by the AICPA for a review of interim financial information as described in SAS 71, *Interim Financial Information*, on the unaudited condensed consolidated balance sheet as of March 31, 20X6, and unaudited condensed consolidated statements of income, retained earnings (stockholders' equity), and cash flows for the three-month periods ended March 31, 20X6 and 20X5, included in the registration statement.
   (2) Inquired of certain officials of the company who have responsibility for financial and accounting matters whether the unaudited condensed consolidated financial statements referred to in (1) comply as to form in all material respects with the applicable accounting requirements of the Act and the related rules and regulations adopted by the SEC.

b. With respect to the six-month periods ended June 30, 20X6 and 20X5, we have

   (1) Read the unaudited amounts for sales, net income, and earnings per share for the six-month periods ended June 30, 20X6 and 20X5, as set forth in paragraph [*identify location*].
   (2) Performed the procedures specified by the AICPA for a review of financial information as described in SAS 71, *Interim Financial Information*, on the unaudited condensed consolidated balance sheet as of June 30, 20X6, and the unaudited condensed consolidated statements of income, retained earnings (stockholders' equity), and cash flows for the six-month periods ended June 30, 20X6 and 20X5, from which the unaudited amounts referred to in b(1) are derived.
   (3) Inquired of certain officials of the company who have responsibility for financial and accounting matters whether the unaudited amounts referred to in (1) are stated on a basis substantially consistent with that of the corresponding amounts in the audited consolidated statements of income.

The foregoing procedures do not constitute an audit conducted in accordance with the standards of the Public Company Accounting Oversight Board (United States). Also, they would not necessarily reveal matters of significance with respect to the comments in the following paragraph. Accordingly, we make no representations regarding the sufficiency of the foregoing procedures for your purposes.

5. Nothing came to our attention as a result of the foregoing procedures, however, that caused us to believe that:

   a. (1) Any material modification should be made to the unaudited condensed consolidated financial statements described in 4a(1), included in the registration statement, for them to be in conformity with generally accepted accounting principles.
      (2) The unaudited condensed consolidated financial statements described in 4a(1) do not comply as to form in all material respects with the applicable accounting requirements of the Act and the related rules and regulations adopted by the SEC.

   b. (1) The unaudited amounts for sales, net income, and earnings per share for the six-month periods ended June 30, 20X6 and 20X5, referred to in 4b(1) do not agree with the amounts set forth in the unaudited consolidated financial statements for those same periods.
      (2) The unaudited amounts referred to in b(1) were not determined on a basis substantially consistent with that of the corresponding amounts in the audited consolidated statements of income.

   c. At June 30, 20X6, there was any change in the capital stock, increase in long-term debt, or decrease in consolidated net current assets or stockholders' equity of the consolidated companies as compared with amounts shown in the March 31, 20X6 unaudited condensed consolidated balance sheet included in the registration statement, except in all instances for changes, increases, or decreases that the registration statement discloses have occurred or may occur.

6. Company officials have advised us that no consolidated financial statements as of any date for any period subsequent to June 30, 20X6, are available; accordingly, the procedures carried out by us with respect to changes in financial statement items after June 30, 20X6, have been, of necessity, even more limited than those with respect to the periods referred to in 4. We have inquired of certain officials of the company who have responsibility for financial and accounting matters regarding whether (1) at July 20, 20X6, there was any change in the capital stock, increase in long-term debt, or any decreases on consolidated net current assets or stockholders' equity of the consolidated companies as compared with amounts shown on the March 31, 20X6 unaudited condensed consolidated balance sheet included in the registration statement; or (2) for the period from July 1, 20X6, to July 20, 20X6, there were any decreases, as compared with the corresponding period in the preceding year, in consolidated net sales or in the total or per share amounts before extraordinary items or of net income. On the basis of these inquiries and our reading of the minutes as described in item 4, nothing came to our attention that caused us to believe that there was any such change, increase, or decrease, except in all instances for changes, increases, or decreases that the registration statement discloses have occurred or may occur.

ILLUSTRATION 13. ALTERNATE WORDING WHEN ACCOUNTANTS ARE AWARE OF A DECREASE IN A SPECIFIED FINANCIAL STATEMENT ITEM

Illustration 13 covers a situation in which accountants are aware of a decrease in a financial statement item on which they are requested to comment. The same facts exist as in Illustration 1, except for the decrease covered in the following change in paragraph 5b.

5. b. (1) At May 31, 20X6, there was any change in the capital stock, increase in long-term debt or any decrease in consolidated stockholders' equity of the consolidated companies as compared with amounts shown in the March 31, 20X6 unaudited condensed consolidated balance sheet included in the registration statement, or

   (2) For the period from April 1, 20X6, to May 31, 20X6, there were any decreases, as compared with the corresponding period in the preceding year, in consolidated net sales or the total or per share amounts of income before extraordinary items or of net income, except in all instances for changes, increases, or decreases that the registration statement discloses have occurred or may occur and except that the unaudited consolidated balance sheet as of May 31, 20X6, which we were furnished by the company, showed a decrease from March 31, 20X6, in consolidated net current assets as follows (in thousands of dollars):

	Current assets	Current liabilities	Net current assets
March 31, 20X6	$4,251	$1,356	$2,895
May 31, 20X6	3,986	1,732	2,254

6. As mentioned in 4b, company officials have advised us that no consolidated financial statements as of any date or for any period subsequent to May 31, 20X6, are available; accordingly, the procedures carried out by us with respect to changes in financial statement items after May 31, 20X6, have been, of necessity, even more limited than those with respect to the periods referred to in 4. We have inquired of certain officials of the company who have responsibility for financial and accounting matters regarding whether (1) there was any change at June 23, 20X6, in the capital stock, increases in long-term debt, or any decreases in consolidated net current assets or stockholders' equity of the consolidated companies as compared with amounts shown on the March 31, 20X6 unaudited condensed consolidated balance sheet

included in the registration statement; or (2) for the period from April 1, 20X6, to June 23, 20X6, there were any decreases, as compared with the corresponding period in the preceding year, in consolidated net sales or in the total or per share amounts of income before extraordinary items of net income. On the basis of these inquiries and our reading of the minutes as described in 4, nothing came to our attention that caused us to believe that there was any such change, increase, or decrease, except in all instances of changes, increases, or decreases that the registration statement discloses have occurred or may occur and except as described in the following sentence. We have been informed by officials of the company that there continues to be a decrease in net current assets that is estimated to be approximately the same amount as set forth in 5b [*or whatever other disclosure fits the circumstances*].

ILLUSTRATION 14. ALTERNATE WORDING OF THE LETTER FOR COMPANIES THAT ARE PERMITTED TO PRESENT INTERIM EARNINGS DATA FOR A TWELVE-MONTH PERIOD

Certain types of companies are permitted to include earnings data for a twelve-month period to the date of the latest balance sheet furnished in lieu of earnings data for both the interim period between the end of the latest fiscal year and the date of the latest balance sheet and the corresponding period of the preceding fiscal year. The following would be substituted for the applicable part of paragraph 3 of Illustration 1.

3. . . .was to enable us to express our opinion on the financial statements as of December 31, 20X5, and for the year then ended, but not on the financial statements for any period included in part within that year. Therefore, we are unable to and do not express an opinion on the unaudited condensed consolidated balance sheet as of March 31, 20X6, and the related unaudited condensed consolidated statements of income, retained earnings (stockholders' equity), and cash flows for the twelve months then ended included in the registration statement. . .

ILLUSTRATION 15. ALTERNATE WORDING WHEN THE PROCEDURES THAT THE UNDERWRITER HAS REQUESTED THE ACCOUNTANT TO PERFORM ON INTERIM FINANCIAL INFORMATION ARE LESS THAN A SAS 71 REVIEW

The illustration assumes that the underwriter has asked the accountants to perform specified procedures on the interim financial information and report thereon in the comfort letter. The letter is dated June 28, 20X6; procedures were performed through June 23, 20X6, the cutoff date. Since an SAS 71 (Section 722) review was not performed on the interim financial information as of March 31, 20X6, and for the quarter then ended, the accountants are limited to reporting procedures performed and findings obtained on the interim financial information. In addition to the information presented below, the letter would also contain paragraph 7 of the typical comfort letter in Illustration 1.

June 28, 20X6

[*Addressee*]

Dear Sirs:

We have audited the consolidated balance sheets of The Basic Company, Inc. (the company) and subsidiaries as of December 31, 20X5 and 20X4, and the consolidated statements of income, retained earnings (stockholders' equity), and cash flows for each of the three years in the period ended December 31, 20X5, and the related financial statements schedules all included in the registration statement (No. 33-00000) on Form S-1 filed by the company under the Securities Act of 1933 (the Act); our reports with respect thereto are included in that registration statement. The registration statement as amended on June 28, 20X6, is herein referred to as the registration statement.

Also, we have compiled the forecasted balance sheet and consolidated statements of income, retained earnings (stockholders' equity), and cash flows as of December 31, 20X6, and for the year then ending, attached to the registration statement, as indicated in our report dated May 15, 20X6, which is attached.

In connection with the registration statement:

1. We are independent certified public accountants with respect to the company within the meaning of the Act and the applicable rules and regulations thereunder adopted by the SEC.
2. In our opinion [*include the phrase "except as disclosed in the registration statement," if applicable*], the consolidated financial statements and financial statement schedules audited by us and included in the registration statement comply as to form in all material respects with the applicable accounting requirements of the Act and the related rules and regulations adopted by the SEC.
3. We have not audited any financial statements of the company as of any date or for any period subsequent to December 31, 20X5; although we have conducted an audit for the year ended December 31, 20X5, the purpose (and therefore the scope) of the audit was to enable us to express our opinion on the consolidated financial statements as of December 31, 20X5, and for the year then ended, but not on the financial statements for any interim period within that year. Therefore, we are unable to and do not express any opinion on the unaudited condensed consolidated balance sheet as of March 31, 20X6, and the unaudited condensed consolidated statements of income, retained earnings (stockholders' equity), and cash flows for the three-month periods ended March 31, 20X6 and 20X5, included in the registration statement, or on the financial position, results of operations, or cash flows, as of any date or for any period subsequent to December 31, 20X5.
4. For purposes of this letter we have read the 20X6 minutes of meetings of the stockholders, the board of directors, and [*include other appropriate committees, if any*] of the company as set forth in the minute books at June 23, 20X6, officials of the company having advised us that the minutes of all such meetings[14] through that date were set forth herein; we have carried out other procedures to June 23, 20X6, as follows (our work did not extend to the period from June 24, 20X6, to June 28, 20X6, inclusive):

    a. With respect to the three-month periods ended March 31, 20X6 and 20X5, we have:

    (1) Read the unaudited condensed consolidated balance sheet as of March 31, 20X6, and unaudited condensed consolidated statements of income, retained earnings (stockholders' equity), and cash flows for the three-month periods ended March 31, 20X6 and 20X5, included in the registration statement, and agreed the amounts contained therein with the company's accounting records as of March 31, 20X6 and 20X5, and for the three-month periods then ended.

    (2) Inquired of certain officials of the company who have responsibility for financial and accounting matters whether the unaudited condensed consolidated financial statements referred to in 4a(1): (a) are in conformity with generally accepted accounting principles applied on a basis substantially consistent with that of the audited consolidated financial statements included in the registration statement, and (b) comply as to form in all material respects with the applicable accounting requirements of the Act and the related rules and regulations adopted by the SEC. Those officials stated that the unaudited condensed consolidated financial statements (a) are in conformity with generally accepted accounting principles applied on a basis substantially consistent with that of the audited financial statements, and (b) comply as to form in all material respects with the applicable accounting requirements of the Act and the related rules and regulations adopted by the SEC.

    b. With respect to the period from April 1, 20X6, to May 31, 20X6, we have:

---

[14] *See footnote 4.*

(1) Read the unaudited consolidated financial statements of the company for April and May of both 20X5 and 20X6 furnished us by the company, and agreed the amounts contained therein to the company's accounting records. Officials of the company have advised us that no such financial statements as of any date or for any period subsequent to May 31, 20X6, were available.

(2) Inquired of certain officials of the company who have responsibility for financial and accounting matters whether (a) the unaudited financial statements referred to in 4b(1) are stated on a basis substantially consistent with that of the audited consolidated financial statements included in the registration statement, (b) at May 31, 20X6, there was any change in the capital stock, increase in long-term debt or any decrease in consolidated net current assets or stockholders' equity of the consolidated companies as compared with amounts shown in the March 31, 20X6 unaudited condensed consolidated balance sheet included in the registration statement, and (c) for the period from April 1, 20X6, to May 31, 20X6, there were any decreases, as compared with the corresponding period in the preceding year, in consolidated net sales or in the total or per share amounts of income before extraordinary items or of net income.

Those officials stated that (a) the unaudited consolidated financial statements referred to in 4b(1) are stated on a basis substantially consistent with that of the audited consolidated financial statements included in the registration statement, (b) at May 31, 20X6, there was no change in the capital stock, no increase in long-term debt, and no decrease in net current assets or stockholders' equity of the consolidated companies as compared with amounts shown in the March 31, 20X6 unaudited condensed consolidated balance sheet included in the registration statements, and (c) there were no decreases for the period from April 1, 20X6, to May 31, 20X6, as compared with the corresponding period in the preceding year, in consolidated net sales or in the total or per share amounts of income before extraordinary items or of net income.

c. As mentioned in 4b(1), company officials have advised us that no financial statements as of any date or for any period subsequent to May 31, 20X6, are available; accordingly, the procedures carried out by us with respect to changes in financial statement items after May 31, 20X6, have, of necessity, been even more limited than those with respect to the periods referred to in 4a and 4b. We have inquired of certain officials of the company who have responsibility for financial and accounting matters whether (1) at June 23, 20X6, there was any change in the capital stock, increase in long-term debt or any decreases in consolidated net current assets or stockholders' equity of the consolidated companies as compared with amounts shown on the March 31, 20X6 unaudited condensed consolidated balance sheet included in the registration statement or (2) for the period from April 1, 20X6, to June 23, 20X6, there were any decreases, as compared with the corresponding period in the preceding year, in consolidated net sales or in the total or per share amounts of income before extraordinary items or of net income. Those officials stated that (1) at June 23, 20X6, there was no change in the capital stock, no increase in long-term debt and no decreases in consolidated net current assets or stockholders' equity of the consolidated companies as compared with amounts shown on the March 31, 20X6 unaudited condensed consolidated balance sheet, and (2) for the period from April 1, 20X6, to June 23, 20X6, there were no decreases as compared with the corresponding period in the preceding year, in consolidated net sales or in the total or per share amounts of income before extraordinary items or of net income.

The foregoing procedures do not constitute an audit conducted in accordance with the standards of the Public Company Accounting Oversight Board (United States). We make no representations regarding the sufficiency of the foregoing procedures for your purposes. Had we performed additional procedures or had we conducted an audit or a review, other matters might have come to our attention that would have been reported to you.

5. At your request we also performed the following procedures:

a. Read the unaudited pro forma condensed consolidated balance sheet as of March 31, 20X6, and the unaudited pro forma condensed consolidated statements of income for the year ended December 31, 20X5, and the three-month period ended March 31, 20X6, included in the registration statement.
b. Inquired of certain officials of the company and of XYZ Company (the company being acquired) who have responsibility for financial and accounting matters as to whether all significant assumptions regarding the business combination had been reflected in the pro forma adjustments and whether the unaudited pro forma condensed consolidated financial statements referred to in item 5a comply as to form in all material respects with the applicable accounting requirements of Rule 11-02 of Regulation S-X.

   Those officials referred to above stated, in response to our inquiries, that all significant assumptions regarding the business combination had been reflected in the pro forma adjustments and that the unaudited pro forma condensed consolidated financial statements referred to in 5a comply as to form in all material respects with the applicable accounting requirements of Rule 11-02 of Regulation S-X.
c. Compared the historical financial information for the company included on page 20 in the registration statement with historical financial information for the company on page 12 and found them to be in agreement.

   We also compared the financial information included on page 20 of the registration statement with the historical information for XYZ Company on page 13 and found them to be in agreement.
d. Proved the arithmetic accuracy of the application of the pro forma adjustments to the historical amounts in the unaudited pro forma condensed consolidated financial statements. The foregoing procedures are substantially less in scope than an examination, the objective of which is the expression of an opinion on management's assumptions, the pro forma adjustments, and the application of those adjustments to historical financial information. Accordingly, we do not express such an opinion. We make no representation about the sufficiency of the foregoing procedures for your purposes. Had we performed additional procedures or had we made an examination of the pro forma financial information, other matters might have come to our attention that would have been reported to you.

6. At your request, we performed the following procedures with respect to the forecasted consolidated balance sheet and consolidated statements of income and cash flows as of December 31, 20X6, and for the year then ending. With respect to forecasted rental income, we compared the occupancy statistics about expected demand for rental of the housing units to statistics for existing comparable properties and found them to be the same.

   Because the procedures described above do not constitute an examination of prospective financial statements in accordance with standards established by AICPA, we do not express an opinion on whether the prospective financial statements are presented in conformity with AICPA presentation guidelines or on whether the underlying assumptions provide a reasonable basis for the presentation. Furthermore there will usually be differences between the forecasted and actual results, because events and circumstances frequently do not occur as expected, and those differences may be material. We make no representations about the sufficiency of such procedures for your purposes. Had we performed additional procedures or had we made an examination of the forecast in accordance with standards established by the AICPA, matters might have come to our attention that would have been reported to you.

ILLUSTRATION 16. A TYPICAL COMFORT LETTER IN A NON-1933 ACT OFFERING, INCLUDING THE REQUIRED UNDERWRITER REPRESENTATIONS

Illustration 16 is applicable when a comfort letter is issued in a non-1933 Act offering. The underwriter has given the accountants a letter including the representations regarding their due diligence review process, and the comfort letter refers to those representations. In addition, the illustration assumes that the accountants were unable, or were not requested, to perform an SAS 71 (Section 722) review of a subsequent interim period, and therefore no negative assurance has been given.

November 30, 20X5

[*Addressee*]

Dear Sirs:

We have audited the balance sheets of Example City, Any State Utility System, as of June 30, 20X5 and 20X4, and the statements of revenues, expenses, and changes in retained earnings and cash flows for the years then ended, included in the Official Statement for $30,000,000 of Example City, Any State Utility System Revenue Bonds due November 30, 20X5. Our report with respect thereto is included in the Official Statement. This Official Statement, dated November 30, 20X5, is herein referred to as the Official Statement.

This letter is being furnished in reliance upon your representation to us that:

1. You are knowledgeable with respect to the due diligence review process that would be performed if this placement of securities were being registered pursuant to the Securities Act of 1933 (the Act).
2. In connection with the offering of revenue bonds, the review process you have performed is substantially consistent with the due diligence review process that you would have performed if this placement of securities were being registered pursuant to the Act.

In connection with the Official Statement:

1. We are independent certified public accountants with respect to Example City, Any State and its Utility System under Rule 101 of the AICPA's *Code of Professional Conduct*, and its interpretations and ruling.
2. We have not audited any financial statements of Example City, Any State Utility System as of any date or for any period subsequent to June 30, 20X5; although we have conducted an audit for the year ended June 30, 20X5, the purpose (and therefore the scope) of the audit was to enable us to express our opinion on the financial statements as of June 30, 20X5, and for the year then ended, but not on the financial statements for any interim period within that year. Therefore, we are unable to and do not express any opinion on the financial position, results of operations, or cash flows as of any date or for any period subsequent to June 30, 20X5, for the Example City, Any State Utility System.
3. For purposes of this letter we have read the 20X5 minutes of the meetings of the City Council of Example City, Any State, as set forth in the minutes books as of November 25, 20X5, the City Clerk of Example City having advised us that the minutes of all such meetings through that date were set forth therein.
4. With respect to the period subsequent to June 30, 20X5, we have carried out other procedures to November 25, 20X5, as follows (our work did not extend to the period from November 26, 20X5, to November 30, 20X5, inclusive):

    a. We have required of, and received assurance from, city officials who have responsibility for financial and accounting matters, that no financial statements as of any date or for any period subsequent to June 30, 20X5, are available.
    b. We have inquired of those officials regarding whether (1) at November 25, 20X5, there was any increase in long-term debt or any decrease in net current assets of Example City, Any State Utility System as compared with amounts shown on the June 30, 20X5 balance sheet, included in the Official Statement, or (2) for the period from July 1, 20X5, to November 25, 20X5, there were any decreases, as compared with the corresponding period in the preceding year, in total operating revenues, income from operations or net income. Those officials stated that (1) at November 25, 20X5, there was no increase in long-term debt and no decrease in net current assets of the Example City, Any State Utility System as compared with amounts shown in the June 30, 20X5 balance sheet; and (2) there were no

decreases for the period from July 1, 20X5, to November 25, 20X5, as compared with the corresponding period in the preceding year, in total operating revenues, income from operations, or net income, except in all instances for changes, increases, or decreases that the Official Statement discloses have occurred or may occur.

5. For accounting data pertaining to the years 20X3 through 20X5, inclusive, shown on page 11 of the Official Statement, we have (1) for data shown in the audited financial statements, compared such data with the audited financial statements of the Example City, Any State Utility System for 20X3 through 20X5 and found them to be in agreement; and (2) for data not directly shown in the audited financial statements, compared such data with the general ledger and accounting records of the Utility System from which such information was derived, and found them to be in agreement.

6. The procedures enumerated in the preceding paragraph do not constitute an audit conducted in accordance with the standards of the Public Company Accounting Oversight Board (United States). Accordingly, we make no representations regarding the sufficiency of the foregoing procedures for your purposes.

7. This letter is solely for the information of the addressees and to assist the underwriters in conducting and documenting their investigation of the affairs of the Example City, Any State Utility System in connection with the offering of securities covered by the Official Statement, and it is not to be used, circulated, quoted, or otherwise referred to for any purpose, including but not limited to the purchase or sale of securities, nor is it to be filed with or referred to in whole or in part in the Official Statement or any other document, except that reference may be made to it in the Purchase Contract or in any list of closing documents pertaining to the offering of securities covered by the Official Statement.

ILLUSTRATION 17. LETTER TO A REQUESTING PARTY THAT HAS NOT PROVIDED THE NORMALLY REQUIRED LETTER

Illustration 17 assumes that the procedures were performed at the request of a placement agent on information included in an offering circular in connection with a private placement of unsecured notes with two insurance companies. The letter is dated June 30, 20X6; procedures were performed through June 25, 20X6, the cut-off date.

June 30, 20X6

[*Addressee*]

Dear Sirs:

We have audited the consolidated balance sheets of XYZ Company, Inc. (the company) and subsidiaries as of December 31, 20X5 and 20X4, and the consolidated statements of income, retained earnings (stockholders' equity), and cash flows for each of the three years in the period ended December 31, 20X5, included in the offering circular for $40,000,000 of notes due June 30, 20X6. Our report with respect thereto is included in the offering circular. The offering circular dated June 30, 20X6, is herein referred to as the offering circular.

We are independent certified public accountants with respect to the company under Rule 101 of the AICPA's Code of Professional Conduct, and its interpretations and rulings.

We have not audited any financial statements of the company as of any date or for any period subsequent to December 31, 20X5; although we have conducted an audit for the year ended December 31, 20X5, the purpose (and, therefore, the scope) of the audit was to enable us to express our opinion on the consolidated financial statements as of December 31, 20X5, and for the year then ended, but not on the financial statements for any interim period within that year. Therefore, we are unable to and do not express any opinion on the unaudited condensed consolidated balance sheet as of March 31, 20X6, and the unaudited condensed consolidated statements of income, retained earnings (stockholders' equity), and cash flows for the three-month periods ended

March 31, 20X6 and 20X5, included in the offering circular, or on the financial position, results of operations, or cash flows as of any date or for any period subsequent to December 31, 20X5.

1. At your request, we have read the 20X6 minutes of meetings of the stockholders, the board of directors, and [*include other appropriate committees, if any*] of the company as set forth in the minutes books at June 25, 20X6, officials of the company having advised us that the minutes of all such meetings through that date were set forth therein; we have carried out other procedures to June 25, 20X6 (our work did not extend to the period from June 26, 20X6, to June 30, 20X6, inclusive) as follows:

   a. With respect to the three-month periods ended March 31, 20X6 and 20X5, we have:

      (1) Read the unaudited condensed consolidated balance sheet as of March 31, 20X6, and the unaudited condensed consolidated statements of income, retained earnings (stockholders' equity), and cash flows of the company for the three-month periods ended March 31, 20X6 and 20X5, included in the offering circular, and agreed the amounts contained therein with the company's accounting records as of March 31, 20X6 and 20X5, and for the three-month periods then ended.

      (2) Inquired of certain officials of the company who have responsibility for financial and accounting matters whether the unaudited condensed consolidated financial statements referred to in 1a(1) are in conformity with generally accepted accounting principles applied on a basis substantially consistent with that of the audited consolidated financial statements included in the offering circular. Those officials stated that the unaudited condensed consolidated financial statements are in conformity with generally accepted accounting principles applied on a basis substantially consistent with that of the audited consolidated financial statements.

   b. With respect to the period from April 1, 20X6, to May 31, 20X6, we have:

      (1) Read the unaudited condensed consolidated financial statements of the company for April and May of both 20X5 and 20X6 furnished to us by the company, and agreed the amounts therein with the company's accounting records. Officials of the company have advised us that no financial statements as of any date or for any period subsequent to May 31, 20X6, were available.

      (2) Inquired of certain officials of the company who have responsibility for financial and accounting matters whether (a) the unaudited condensed consolidated financial statements referred to in 1b(1) are stated on a basis substantially consistent with that of the audited consolidated financial statements included in the offering circular, (b) at May 31, 20X6, there was any change in the capital stock, increase in long-term debt, or any decrease in consolidated net current assets or stockholders' equity of the consolidated companies as compared with amounts shown in the March 31, 20X6, unaudited condensed balance sheet included in the offering circular, or (c) for the period from April 1, 20X6, to May 31, 20X6, there were any decreases, as compared with the corresponding period in the preceding year, in consolidated net sales or in the total or per share amounts of income before extraordinary items or of net income.

      Those officials stated that (a) the unaudited condensed consolidated financial statements referred to in 1b(2) are stated on a basis substantially consistent with that of the audited consolidated financial statements included in the offering circular, (b) at May 31, 20X6, there was no change in the capital stock, no increase in long-term debt, and no decrease in consolidated net current assets or stockholders' equity of the consolidated companies as compared with amounts shown in the March 31, 20X6 unaudited condensed consolidated balance sheet included in the offering circular, and (c) there were no decreases for the period from April 1, 20X6, to May 31, 20X6, as compared with the corresponding period in the preceding year, in consolidated net sales or in the total or per share amounts of income before extraordinary items or of net income.

c. As mentioned in 1b, company officials have advised us that no financial statements as of any date or for any period subsequent to May 31, 20X6, are available; accordingly, the procedures carried out by us with respect to changes in financial statement items after May 31, 20X6, have, of necessity, been even more limited than those with respect to the periods referred to in 1a and 1b. We have inquired of certain officials of the company who have responsibility for financial and accounting matters whether:

(1) At June 25, 20X6, there was any change in the capital stock, any increase in long-term debt, or any decreases in consolidated net current assets or stockholders' equity of the consolidated companies as compared with amounts shown on the March 31, 20X6 unaudited condensed consolidated balance sheet included in the offering circular or

(2) For the period from April 1, 20X6, to June 26, 20X6, there were any decreases, as compared with the corresponding period in the preceding year, in consolidated net sales or in the total or per share amounts of income before extraordinary items or of net income.

Those officials referred to above stated that (1) at June 25, 20X6, there was no change in the capital stock, no increase in long-term debt, and no decreases in consolidated net current assets or stockholders' equity of the consolidated companies as compared with amounts shown on the March 31, 20X6 unaudited condensed consolidated balance sheet, and (2) there were no decreases for the period from April 1, 20X6, to June 25, 20X6, as compared with the corresponding period in the preceding year, in consolidated net sales or in the total or per share amounts of income before extraordinary items or of net income.

2. At your request, we have read the following items in the offering circular on the indicated pages.

Item	Page	Description
A	13	*History and Business—Sales and Marketing.* The table following the first paragraph.
B	22	*Executive Compensation—20X5 Compensation.*
C	33	*Selected Financial Data.*

3. Our audits of the consolidated financial statements for the periods referred to in the introductory paragraph of this letter comprised audit tests and procedures deemed necessary for the purpose of expressing an opinion on such financial statements taken as a whole. For none of the periods referred to therein, nor for any other period, did we perform audit tests for the purpose of expressing an opinion on individual balances of accounts or summaries of selected transactions such as those enumerated above, and accordingly, we express no opinion thereon.

4. However, for purposes of this letter we have performed the following additional procedures, which were applied as indicated with respect to the items enumerated above.

Item in 2	Procedures and Findings
A	We compared the amounts of military sales, commercial sales, and total sales shown in the registration statement with the balances in the appropriate accounts in the company's accounting records for the respective fiscal years and for the unaudited interim periods and found them to be in agreement. We proved the arithmetic accuracy of the percentages of such amounts of military sales and commercial sales to total sales for the respective fiscal years and for the unaudited interim periods. We compared such computed percentages with the corresponding percentages appearing in the registration statement and found them to be in agreement.
B	We compared the dollar amounts of compensation (salary, bonus, and other compensation) for each individual listed in the table "Annual Compensation," with the corresponding amounts shown by the individual employee earnings records for the year 20X5 and found them to be in agreement. We compared

C We compared the amounts of net sales, income from continuing operations, income from continuing operations per common share, and cash dividends declared per common share for the years ended December 31, 20X5, 20X4, and 20X3, with the respective amounts in the consolidated financial statements on pages 27 and 28 and the amounts for the years ended December 31, 20X2 and 20X1, with the respective amounts in the consolidated financial statements included in the company's annual reports to stockholders for 20X2 and 20X1 and found them to be in agreement.

the dollar amounts shown under the heading of "Long-Term Compensation" on page 24 for each listed individual and the aggregate amounts for executive officers with corresponding amounts shown in an analysis prepared by the company and found such amounts to be in agreement.

We compared the amounts of total assets, long-term obligations, and redeemable preferred stock at December 31, 20X5 and 20X4, with the respective amounts in the consolidated financial statements on pages 27 and 28 and the amounts at December 31, 20X3, 20X2, and 20X1, with the corresponding amounts in the consolidated financial statements included in the company's annual reports to stockholders for 20X3, 20X2, and 20X1 and found them to be in agreement.

5. It should be understood that we have no responsibility for establishing (and did not establish) the scope and nature of the procedures enumerated in paragraphs 1 through 4 above; rather, the procedures enumerated therein are those the requesting party asked us to perform. Accordingly, we make no representations regarding questions of legal interpretation or regarding the sufficiency for your purposes of the procedures enumerated in the preceding paragraphs; also, such procedures would not necessarily reveal any material misstatement of the amounts or percentages listed above as set forth in the offering circular. Further, we have addressed ourselves solely to the foregoing data, and make no representations regarding the adequacy of disclosures or whether any material facts have been omitted. This letter relates only to the financial statement items specified above and does not extend to any financial statement of the company taken as a whole.
6. The foregoing procedures do not constitute an audit conducted in accordance with the standards of the Public Company Accounting Oversight Board (United States). Had we performed additional procedures or had we conducted an audit or a review of the company's March 31, April 30, or May 31, 20X6 and 20X5 condensed consolidated financial statements in accordance with standards established by the American Institute of Certified Public Accountants, other matters might have come to our attention that would have been reported to you.
7. These procedures should not be taken to supplant any additional inquiries or procedures that you would undertake in your consideration of the proposed offering.
8. This letter is solely for your information and to assist you in your inquiries in connection with the offering of the securities covered by the offering circular, and it is not to be used, circulated, quoted, or otherwise referred to for any other purpose, including but not limited to the registration, purchase, or sale of securities, nor is it to be filed with or referred to in whole or in part in the offering document or any other document, except that reference may be made to it in any list of closing documents pertaining to the offering of the securities covered by the offering document.
9. We have no responsibility to update this letter for events and circumstances occurring after June 25, 20X6.

ILLUSTRATION 18. COMFORT LETTER THAT INCLUDES REFERENCE TO EXAMINATION OF ANNUAL MD&A AND REVIEW OF INTERIM MD&A

Illustration 18 assumes the following circumstances. The prospectus (part I of the registration statement) includes audited consolidated balance sheets as of December 31, 20X5 and 20X4, and audited consolidated statements of income, retained earnings (stockholders' equity), and cash flows for each of the three years in the period ended December 31, 20X5. Part I also includes an unaudited condensed consolidated balance sheet as of March 31, 20X6, and unaudited condensed consolidated statements of income, retained earnings (stockholders' equity), and cash flows for the three-month periods ended March 31, 20X6 and 20X5. Part II of the registration statement includes audited consolidated financial statement schedules for the three years ended December 31, 20X5. The accountants have examined the company's Management's Discussion and Analysis (MD&A) for the year ended December 31, 20X5, in accordance with Statement on Standards for Attestation Engagements (SSAE) 8; the accountants have also performed reviews of the company's unaudited condensed consolidated financial statements, referred to above, in accordance with SAS 71, and the company's MD&A for the three-month period ended March 31, 20X6, in accordance with SSAE 8. The accountant's reports on the examination and review of MD&A have been previously issued, but not distributed publicly; none of these reports is included in the registration statement. The cutoff date is June 23, 20X6, and the letter is dated June 28, 20X6. The effective date is June 28, 20X6.

Each of the comments in the letter is in response to a requirement of the underwriting agreement. For purposes of Illustration 18, the income statement items of the current interim period are to be compared with those of the corresponding period of the preceding year.

June 28, 20X6

[Addressee]

Dear Sirs:

We have audited the consolidated balance sheets of The Basic Company, Inc. (the company) and subsidiaries as of December 31, 20X5 and 20X4, and the consolidated statements of income, retained earnings (stockholders' equity), and cash flows for each of the three years in the period ended December 31, 20X5, and the related financial statement schedules, all included in the registration statement (No. 33-00000) on Form S-1 filed by the company under the Securities Act of 1933 (the Act); our reports with respect thereto are also included in that registration statement. The registration statement, as amended on June 28, 20X6, is herein referred to as the registration statement. Also, we have examined the company's Management's Discussion and Analysis (MD&A) for the year ended December 31, 20X5, included in the registration statement, as indicated in our report dated March 28, 20X6; our report with respect thereto is attached. We have also reviewed the unaudited condensed consolidated financial statements as of March 31, 20X6 and 20X5, and for the three-month periods then ended, included in the registration statement, as indicated in our report dated May 15, 20X6, and have also reviewed the company's MD&A for the three-month period ended March 31, 20X6, included in the registration statement, as indicated in our report dated May 15, 20X6; our reports with respect thereto are attached.

In connection with the registration statement:

1. We are independent certified public accountants with respect to the company within the meaning of the Act and the applicable rules and regulations thereunder adopted by the SEC.
2. In our opinion [include the phrase "except as disclosed in the registration statement," if applicable] the consolidated financial statements and financial statement schedules audited by us and included in the registration statement comply as to form in all material respects with the applicable accounting requirements of the Act and the related rules and regulations adopted by the SEC.
3. We have not audited any financial statements of the company as of any date or for any period subsequent to December 31, 20X5; although we have conducted an audit for the year ended December 31, 20X5, the purpose (and therefore the scope) of the audit was to enable us to express our opinion on the consolidated financial statements as of December 31, 20X5, and for

the year then ended, but not on the financial statements for any interim period within that year. Therefore, we are unable to and do not express any opinion on the unaudited condensed consolidated balance sheet as of March 31, 20X6, and the unaudited condensed consolidated statements of income, retained earnings (stockholders' equity), and cash flows for the three-month periods ended March 31, 20X6 and 20X5, included in the registration statement, or on the financial position, results of operations, or cash flows as of any date or for any period subsequent to December 31, 20X5.

4. We have not examined any management's discussion and analysis of the company as of or for any period subsequent to December 31, 20X5; although we have made an examination of the company's MD&A for the year ended December 31, 20X5, included in the company's registration statement, the purpose (and therefore the scope) of the examination was to enable us to express our opinion on such MD&A, but not on the MD&A for any interim period within that year. Therefore, we are unable to and do not express any opinion on the MD&A for the three-month period ended March 31, 20X6, included in the registration statement, or for any period subsequent to March 31, 20X6.

5. For purposes of this letter we have read the 20X6 minutes of meetings of the stockholders, the board of directors, and [include other appropriate committees, if any] of the company and its subsidiaries as set forth in the minutes books at June 23, 20X6, officials of the company having advised us that the minutes of all such meetings through that date were set forth therein; we have carried out other procedures from June 23, 20X6, as follows (our work did not extend to the period from June 24, 20X6, to June 28, 20X6, inclusive):

   a. With respect to the three-month periods ended March 31, 20X6 and 20X5, we have inquired of certain officials of the company who have responsibility for financial and accounting matters whether the unaudited condensed consolidated balance sheet as of March 31, 20X6, and the unaudited condensed consolidated statements of income, retained earnings (stockholders' equity), and cash flows for the three-month periods ended March 31, 20X6 and 20X5, included in the registration statement, comply as to form in all material respects with the applicable accounting requirements of the Act and the related rules and regulations adopted by the SEC.

   b. With respect to the period from April 1, 20X6, to May 31, 20X6, we have:

   (1) Read the unaudited consolidated financial statements of the company and subsidiaries for April and May of both 20X5 and 20X6 furnished to us by the company, officials of the company having advised us that no such financial statements as of any date or for any period subsequent to May 31, 20X6, were available.

   (2) Inquired of certain officials of the company who have responsibility for financial and accounting matters whether the unaudited consolidated financial statements referred to in b(1) are stated on a basis substantially consistent with that of the audited consolidated financial statements included in the registration statement.

   The foregoing procedures do not constitute an audit of financial statements conducted in accordance with the standards of the Public Company Accounting Oversight Board (United States). Also, they would not necessarily reveal matters of significance with respect to the comments in the following paragraph. Accordingly, we make no representations regarding the sufficiency of the foregoing procedures for your purposes.

6. Nothing came to our attention as a result of the foregoing procedures, however, that caused us to believe that:

   a. The unaudited condensed consolidated financial statements described in 5a do not comply as to form in all material respects with the applicable accounting requirements of the Act and the related rules and regulations adopted by the SEC.

   b. (1) At May 31, 20X6, there was any change in the capital stock, increase in long-term debt, or decrease in consolidated net current assets or stockholders' equity of the consolidated companies as compared with amounts shown in the March 31, 20X6 unaudited condensed consolidated balance sheet included in the registration statement, or

(2) For the period from April 1, 20X6, to May 31, 20X6, there were any decreases, as compared with the corresponding period in the preceding year, in consolidated net sales or in the total or per share amounts of income before extraordinary items or of net income, except in all instances of changes, increases, or decreases that the registration statement discloses have occurred or may occur.

7. As mentioned in 5b, company officials have advised us that no consolidated financial statements as of any date or for any period subsequent to May 31, 20X6, are available; accordingly, the procedures carried out by us with respect to changes in financial statement items after May 31, 20X6, have, of necessity, been even more limited than those with respect to the periods referred to in 5. We have inquired of certain officials of the company who have responsibility for financial and accounting matters whether (1) at June 23, 20X6, there was any change in the capital stock, increase in long-term debt, or any decreases in consolidated net current assets or stockholders' equity of the consolidated companies as compared with amounts shown on the March 31, 20X6, unaudited condensed consolidated balance sheet included in the registration statement or (2) for the period from April 1, 20X6, to June 23, 20X6, there were any decreases, as compared with the corresponding period in the preceding year, in consolidated net sales or in the total or per share amounts of income before extraordinary items or of net income. On the basis of these inquiries and our reading of the minutes as described in item 5, nothing came to our attention that caused us to believe that there was any such change, increase, or decrease, except in all instances for changes, increases, or decreases that the registration statement discloses have occurred or may occur.

8. This letter is solely for the information of the addressees and to assist the underwriters in conducting and documenting their investigation of the affairs of the company in connection with the offering of the securities covered by the registration statement, and it is not to be used, circulated, quoted, or otherwise referred to within or without the underwriting group for any purpose, including but not limited to the registration, purchase, or sale of securities, nor is it to be filed with or referred to in whole or in part in the registration statement or any other document, except that reference may be made to it in the underwriting agreement or in any list of closing documents pertaining to the offering of the securities covered by the registration statement.

AU-C 920 ILLUSTRATIONS

The following illustrations of comfort letters are reprinted from AU-C 920.

1-A Typical Comfort Letter for a 1993 Act Offering
1-B Typical Comfort Letter for a Non-1933 Act Offering When the Required Representation Letter Has Been Obtained
2. Letter When a Short-Form Registration Statement Is Filed Incorporating Previously Filed Form 8-K by Reference
3. Letter Reaffirming Comments in Illustration 1 as of a Later Date
4. Comments on Pro Forma Financial Information
5. Comments on a Financial Forecast
6. Comments on Tables, Statistics, and Other Financial Information: Complete Description of Procedures and Findings
7. Comments on Tables, Statistics, and Other Financial Information: Summarized Description of Procedures and Findings Regarding Tables, Statistics, and Other Financial Information
8. Comments on Tables, Statistics, and Other Financial Information: Descriptions of Procedures and Findings Regarding Tables, Statistics, and Other Financial Infor-

mation—Attached Securities Offering (or Selected Pages) Identifies Items to Which Procedures Were Applied Through the Use of Designated Symbols
9. Alternate Wording When Auditor's Report on Audited Financial Statements Contains an Emphasis-of-Matter Paragraph
10. Alternate Wording When More Than One Auditor Is Involved
11. Alternate Wording When the SEC Has Agreed to a Departure from Its Accounting Requirements
12. Alternate Wording When Recent Earnings Data Are Presented in Capsule Form
13. Alternate Wording When Auditors Are Aware of a Decrease in a Specified Financial Statement Item
14. Alternate Wording of the Letter for Companies That Are Permitted to Present Interim Earnings Data for a 12-Month Period
15. Alternate Wording When the Procedures That the Requesting Party Has Requested the Auditor to Perform on Interim Financial Information Are Less Than a Review in Accordance with GAAS Applicable to Reviews of Interim Financial Information.
16. Letter to a Requesting Party That Has Not Provided the Legal Opinion or the Representation Letter Required by Paragraph .11
17. Intentionally Omitted (See Illustration 1-B).
18. Alternate Wording When Reference to Examination of Annual Management's Discussion and Analysis and Review of Interim Management's Discussion and Analysis Is Made

ILLUSTRATION 1-A. TYPICAL COMFORT LETTER FOR A 1933 ACT OFFERING

June 28, 20X6

[*Addressee*]

Dear Ladies and Gentlemen:

We have audited the consolidated financial statements of The Nonissuer Company, Inc. (the company) and subsidiaries, which comprise the consolidated balance sheets as of December 31, 20X5 and 20X4, and the related consolidated statements of income, changes in stockholders' equity, and cash flows for each of the years in the three-year period ended December 31, 20X5, and the related notes to the consolidated financial statements, all included in The Issuer Company's (the registrant) registration statement (no. 33-00000) on Form S-1 filed by the registrant under the Securities Act of 1933 (the Act); our report with respect thereto is also included in that registration statement. The registration statement, as amended on June 28, 20X6, is herein referred to as the registration statement.

In connection with the registration statement:

1. We are independent certified public accountants with respect to the company within the meaning of the 1933 Act and the applicable rules and regulations thereunder adopted by the SEC.
2. In our opinion [*include the phrase* "except as disclosed in the registration statement" *if applicable*], the consolidated financial statements audited by us and included in the registration statement comply as to form in all material respects with the applicable accounting requirements of the Act and the related rules and regulations adopted by the SEC.
3. We have not audited any financial statements of the company as of any date or for any period subsequent to December 31, 20X5; although we have conducted an audit for the year ended December 31, 20X5, the purpose (and, therefore, the scope) of the audit was to enable us to express our opinion on the consolidated financial statements as of December 31, 20X5, and for the year then ended, but not on the financial statements for any interim period within that year. Therefore, we are unable to and do not express any opinion on the unaudited condensed con-

solidated balance sheet as of March 31, 20X6, and the unaudited condensed consolidated statements of income, stockholders' equity, and cash flows for the three-month periods ended March 31, 20X6 and 20X5, included in the registration statement, or on the financial position, results of operations, or cash flows as of any date or for any period subsequent to December 31, 20X5.

4. For purposes of this letter we have read the 20X6 minutes of meetings of the stockholders, the board of directors, and [*include other appropriate committees, if any*] of the company and its subsidiaries as set forth in the minute books at June 23, 20X6, officials of the company having advised us that the minutes of all such meetings through that date were set forth therein and having discussed with us the unapproved minutes of meetings held on [*dates*]; we have carried out other procedures to June 23, 20X6, as follows (our work did not extend to the period from June 24, 20X6 to June 28, 20X6, inclusive):

a. With respect to the three-month periods ended March 31, 20X6 and 20X5, we have:

(1) Performed the procedures specified for a review in accordance with auditing standards generally accepted in the United States of America applicable to reviews of interim financial information on the unaudited condensed consolidated balance sheet as of March 31, 20X6, and the unaudited condensed consolidated statements of income, stockholders' equity, and cash flows for the three-month periods ended March 31, 20X6 and 20X5, included in the registration statement.

(2) Inquired of certain officials of the company who have responsibility for financial and accounting matters whether the unaudited condensed consolidated financial statements referred to in 4a(1) comply as to form in all material respects with the applicable accounting requirements of the Act and the related rules and regulations adopted by the SEC.

b. With respect to the period from April 1, 20X6 to May 31, 20X6, we have:

(1) Read the unaudited consolidated financial statements of the company and subsidiaries for April and May of both 20X5 and 20X6 furnished us by the company, officials of the company having advised us that no such financial statements as of any date or for any period subsequent to May 31, 20X6, were available. [*If applicable:* The financial information for April and May of both 20X5 and 20X6 is incomplete in that it omits the statements of cash flows and other disclosures.]

(2) Inquired of certain officials of the company who have responsibility for financial and accounting matters whether the unaudited consolidated financial statements referred to in 4b(1) are stated on a basis substantially consistent with that of the audited consolidated financial statements included in the registration statement.

The foregoing procedures do not constitute an audit conducted in accordance with generally accepted auditing standards. Also, they would not necessarily reveal matters of significance with respect to the comments in the following paragraph. Accordingly, we make no representations regarding the sufficiency of the foregoing procedures for your purposes.

5. Nothing came to our attention as a result of the foregoing procedures, however, that caused us to believe that:

a. (1) Any material modifications should be made to the unaudited condensed consolidated financial statements described in 4a(1), included in the registration statement, for them to be in conformity with generally accepted accounting principles.

(2) The unaudited condensed consolidated financial statements described in 4a(1) do not comply as to form in all material respects with the applicable accounting requirements of the Act and the related rules and regulations adopted by the SEC.

b. (1) At May 31, 20X6, there was any change in the capital stock, increase in long-term debt, or decrease in consolidated net current assets or stockholders' equity of the consolidated companies as compared with amounts shown in the March 31, 20X6 unaudited condensed consolidated balance sheet included in the registration statement, or

    (2) For the period from April 1, 20X6 to May 31, 20X6, there were any decreases, as compared to the corresponding period in the preceding year, in consolidated net sales or in income before extraordinary items or of net income, except in all instances for changes, increases, or decreases that the registration statement discloses have occurred or may occur.

6. As mentioned in 4b, company officials have advised us that no consolidated financial statements as of any date or for any period subsequent to May 31, 20X6 are available; accordingly, the procedures carried out by us with respect to changes in financial statement items after May 31, 20X6 have, of necessity, been even more limited than those with respect to the periods referred to in item 4. We have inquired of certain officials of the company who have responsibility for financial and accounting matters whether (a) at June 23, 20X6, there was any change in the capital stock, increase in long-term debt, or any decreases in consolidated net current assets or stockholders' equity of the consolidated companies as compared with amounts shown on the March 31, 20X6, unaudited condensed consolidated balance sheet included in the registration statement, or (b) for the period from April 1, 20X6 to June 23, 20X6, there were any decreases, as compared with the corresponding period in the preceding year, in consolidated net sales, or in income before extraordinary items or of net income. On the basis of these inquiries and our reading of the minutes as described in item 4, nothing came to our attention that caused us to believe that there was any such change, increase, or decrease, except in all instances for changes, increases, or decreases that the registration statement discloses have occurred or may occur.

7. This letter is solely for the information of the addressees and to assist the underwriters in conducting and documenting their investigation of the affairs of the company in connection with the offering of the securities covered by the registration statement, and it is not to be used, circulated, quoted, or otherwise referred to within or without the underwriting group for any other purpose, including but not limited to the registration, purchase, or sale of securities, nor is it to be filed with or referred to in whole or in part in the registration statement or any other document, except that reference may be made to it in the underwriting agreement or in any list of closing documents pertaining to the offering of the securities covered by the registration statement.

ILLUSTRATION 1-B. TYPICAL COMFORT LETTER FOR A NON-1933 ACT OFFERING WHEN THE REQUIRED REPRESENTATION LETTER HAS BEEN OBTAINED

This illustration is applicable when a comfort letter is issued in a non-1933 Act offering. It assumes the following:

- The offerer is not an SEC registrant.
- The requesting party has given the auditor a representation letter as required by paragraph .10 and described in paragraph .11.
- Interim financial information is included in the offering document, and the auditor has performed review procedures in accordance with GAAS applicable to reviews of interim financial information.
- The auditor did not perform an audit of the effectiveness of internal control over financial reporting in any period.
- There has not been a change in the application of a requirement of GAAP during the interim period. If there has been such a change, a reference to that change would be included in paragraph 4.

The cut-off date is June 23, 20X6, and the letter is dated June 28, 20X6.

Each of the comments in the letter is in response to a request from the requesting party. For purposes of this illustration, the income statement items of the current interim period are to be compared with those of the corresponding period of the preceding year.

June 28, 20X6

[Addressee]

Dear Ladies and Gentlemen:

We have audited the consolidated financial statements of The Nonissuer Company, Inc. (the company) and subsidiaries, which comprise the consolidated balance sheets as of December 31, 20X5 and 20X4, and the related consolidated statements of income, changes in stockholders' equity, and cash flows for each of the years in the three-year period ended December 31, 20X5, and the related notes to the consolidated financial statements, all included [*or incorporated by reference*] in the offering memorandum for $30,000,000 of Senior Debt due May 30, 20Z6. Our report with respect thereto is included in the offering memorandum. This offering memorandum, dated June 28, 20X6, is herein referred to as the Offering Memorandum.

This letter is being furnished in reliance upon your representation to us that:

a. You are knowledgeable with respect to the due diligence review process that would be performed if this placement of securities were being registered pursuant to the Securities Act of 1933 (the Act).
b. In connection with the offering of Senior Debt, the review process you have performed is substantially consistent with the due diligence review process that you would have performed if this placement of securities were being registered pursuant to the Act.

In connection with the Offering Memorandum:

1. We are independent certified public accountants with respect to the company under Rule 101 of the AICPA's Code of Professional Conduct and its interpretations and rulings.
2. We have not audited any financial statements of the company as of any date or for any period subsequent to December 31, 20X5; although we have conducted an audit for the year ended December 31, 20X5, the purpose (and, therefore, the scope) of the audit was to enable us to express our opinion on the consolidated financial statements as of December 31, 20X5, and for the year then ended, but not on the financial statements for any interim period within that year. Therefore, we are unable to and do not express any opinion on the unaudited condensed consolidated balance sheet as of March 31, 20X6, and the unaudited condensed consolidated statements of income, of cash flows, and of changes in stockholders' equity for the three-month periods ended March 31, 20X5 and 20X6, included in the Offering Memorandum, or on the financial position, results of operations, or cash flows as of any date or for any period subsequent to December 31, 20X5.
3. For purposes of this letter, we have read the 20X6 minutes of meetings of the stockholders, the board of directors, and [*include other appropriate committees, if any*] of the company and its subsidiaries as set forth in the minute books at June 23, 20X6, officials of the company having advised us that the minutes of all such meetings through that date were set forth therein and having discussed with us the unapproved minutes of meetings held on [*dates*]; we have carried out other procedures to June 23, 20X6, as follows (our work did not extend to the period from June 24, 20X6 to June 28, 20X6, inclusive):

    a. With respect to the three-month periods ended March 31, 20X6 and 20X5, we have:

       (1) Performed the procedures specified for a review in accordance with auditing standards generally accepted in the United States of America applicable to reviews of interim financial information on the unaudited condensed consolidated balance sheet as of March 31, 20X6, and unaudited condensed consolidated statements of income, stockholders' equity, and cash flows for the three-month periods ended March 31, 20X6 and 20X5, included in the Offering Memorandum.

b. With respect to the period from April 1, 20X6 to May 31, 20X6, we have:

   (1) Read the unaudited consolidated financial statements of the company and subsidiaries for April and May of both 20X5 and 20X6 furnished us by the company, officials of the company having advised us that no such financial statements as of any date or for any period subsequent to May 31, 20X6, were available. [*If applicable:* The financial information for April and May of both 20X5 and 20X6 is incomplete in that it omits the statement of cash flows and other disclosures.]

   (2) Inquired of certain officials of the company who have responsibility for financial and accounting matters whether the unaudited consolidated financial statements referred to in 3b(1) are stated on a basis substantially consistent with that of the audited consolidated financial statements included in the Offering Memorandum.

The foregoing procedures do not constitute an audit conducted in accordance with GAAS. Also, they would not necessarily reveal matters of significance with respect to the comments in the following paragraph. Accordingly, we make no representations regarding the sufficiency of the foregoing procedures for your purposes.

4. Nothing came to our attention as a result of the foregoing procedures, however, that caused us to believe that:

   (a) (i) Any material modifications should be made to the unaudited condensed consolidated financial statements described in 3a(1), included in the Offering Memorandum, for them to be in conformity with generally accepted accounting principles.

   (b) (i) At May 31, 20X6, there was any change in the capital stock, increase in long-term debt, or decrease in consolidated net current assets or stockholders' equity of the consolidated companies as compared with amounts shown in the March 31, 20X6 unaudited condensed consolidated balance sheet included in the Offering Memorandum, or

   (ii) For the period from April 1, 20X6 to May 31, 20X6, there were any decreases, as compared to the corresponding period in the preceding year, in consolidated net sales, or in income before extraordinary items or of net income, except in all instances for changes, increases, or decreases that the Offering Memorandum discloses have occurred or may occur.

5. As mentioned in item 3b, company officials have advised us that no consolidated financial statements as of any date or for any period subsequent to May 31, 20X6 are available; accordingly, the procedures carried out by us with respect to changes in financial statement items after May 31, 20X6, have, of necessity, been even more limited than those with respect to the periods referred to in item 3. We have inquired of certain officials of the company who have responsibility for financial and accounting matters whether (a) at June 23, 20X6, there was any change in the capital stock, increase in long-term debt, or any decreases in consolidated net current assets or stockholders' equity of the consolidated companies as compared with amounts shown on the March 31, 20X6 unaudited condensed consolidated balance sheet included in the Offering Memorandum, or (b) for the period from April 1, 20X6 to June 23, 20X6, there were any decreases, as compared with the corresponding period in the preceding year, in consolidated net sales or in income before extraordinary items or of net income. On the basis of these inquiries and our reading of the minutes as described in item 3, nothing came to our attention that caused us to believe that there was any such change, increase, or decrease, except in all instances for changes, increases, or decreases that the Offering Memorandum discloses have occurred or may occur.

6. This letter is solely for the information of the addressees and to assist the requesting party in conducting and documenting their investigation of the affairs of the company in connection with the offering of the securities covered by the Offering Memorandum, and it is not to be used, circulated, quoted, or otherwise referred to for any purpose, including but not limited to

the registration, purchase, or sale of securities, nor is it to be filed with or referred to in whole or in part in the Offering Memorandum or any other document, except that reference may be made to it in the Purchase Contract or in any list of closing documents pertaining to the offering of the securities covered by the Offering Memorandum.

> **ILLUSTRATION 2. LETTER WHEN A SHORT-FORM REGISTRATION STATEMENT IS FILED INCORPORATING PREVIOUSLY FILED FORM 8-K BY REFERENCE**

This illustration is an example of modifications to the letter that the auditor of a nonissuer may provide when a registrant has acquired the nonissuer, and the registrant uses a short-form registration statement (for example, Form S-3) that incorporates a previously filed Form 8-K that includes the nonpublic company's financial statements. The auditor was independent of the nonissuer but is not independent with respect to the registrant.

June 28, 20X6

[*Addressee*]

Dear Ladies and Gentlemen:

We have audited the consolidated financial statements of The Nonissuer Company, Inc. (the company) and subsidiaries, which comprise the consolidated balance sheets as of December 31, 20X5 and 20X4, and the related consolidated statements of income, changes in stockholders' equity, and cash flows for each of the years in the three-year period ended December 31, 20X5, and the related notes to the consolidated financial statements, all included in The Issuer Company's (the registrant) current report on Form 8-K dated May 15, 20X6, and incorporated by reference in the registration statement (no. 33-00000) on Form S-3 filed by the registrant under the Securities Act of 1933 (the Act); our report with respect thereto is also incorporated by reference in that registration statement. The registration statement, as amended on June 28, 20X6, is herein referred to as the registration statement.

In connection with the registration statement:

1. As of [*insert date of the auditor's most recent report on the financial statements of the entity*] and during the period covered by the financial statements on which we reported, we were independent certified public accountants with respect to the company under Rule 101 of the AICPA's Code of Professional Conduct and its interpretations and rulings.
2. In our opinion, the consolidated financial statements audited by us and incorporated by reference in the registration statement comply as to form in all material respects with the applicable accounting requirements of the Act and the Securities Exchange Act of 1934 and the related rules and regulations adopted by the SEC.
3. We have not audited any financial statements of the company as of any date or for any period subsequent to December 31, 20X5; although we have conducted an audit for the year ended December 31, 20X5, the purpose (and, therefore, the scope) of the audit was to enable us to express our opinion on the consolidated financial statements as of December 31, 20X5, and for the year then ended, but not on the consolidated financial statements for any interim period within that year. Therefore, we are unable to, and do not express any opinion on, the unaudited condensed consolidated balance sheet as of March 31, 20X6, and the unaudited condensed consolidated statements of income, stockholders' equity, and cash flows for the three-month periods ended March 31, 20X6 and 20X5, included in the registrant's current report on Form 8-K dated May 15, 20X6, incorporated by reference in the registration statement, or on the financial position, results of operations, or cash flows as of any date or for any period subsequent to December 31, 20X5.
4. For purposes of this letter, we have read the 20X6 minutes of the meetings of the stockholders, the board of directors, and [*include other appropriate committees, if any*] of the company and its subsidiaries as set forth in the minute books at June 23, 20X6, officials of the company having advised us that the minutes of all such meetings through that date were set forth therein, and having discussed with us the unapproved minutes of meetings held on [*dates*]; we

have carried out other procedures to June 23, 20X6, as follows (our work did not extend to the period from June 24, 20X6 to June 28, 20X6, inclusive):

With respect to the three-month periods ended March 31, 20X6 and 20X5, we have:

    a. Performed a review in accordance with auditing standards generally accepted in the United States of America applicable to reviews of interim financial information on the unaudited condensed consolidated balance sheet as of March 31, 20X6, and the unaudited condensed consolidated statements of income, stockholders' equity, and cash flows for the three-month periods ended March 31, 20X6 and 20X5, included in the registrant's current report on Form 8-K dated May 15, 20X6, incorporated by reference in the registration statement.

    b. Inquired of certain officials of the company who have responsibility for financial and accounting matters whether the unaudited condensed consolidated financial statements referred to in 4a comply as to form in all material respects with the applicable accounting requirements of the Securities Exchange Act of 1934 and the related rules and regulations adopted by the SEC.

    The foregoing procedures do not constitute an audit conducted in accordance with GAAS. Also, they would not necessarily reveal matters of significance with respect to the comments in the following paragraph. Accordingly, we make no representations about the sufficiency of the foregoing procedures for your purposes.

5. Nothing came to our attention as a result of the foregoing procedures, however, that caused us to believe that:

    a. Any material modifications should be made to the unaudited condensed consolidated financial statements described in 4a, incorporated by reference in the registration statement, for them to be in conformity with GAAP.

    b. The unaudited condensed consolidated financial statements described in 4a do not comply as to form in all material respects with the applicable accounting requirements of the Securities Exchange Act of 1934 and the related rules and regulations adopted by the SEC.

6. This letter is solely for the information of the addressees and to assist the underwriters in conducting and documenting their investigation of the affairs of the company in connection with the offering of the securities covered by the registration statement, and for use of the auditors of the registrant in furnishing their letter to the underwriters, and it is not to be used, circulated, quoted, or otherwise referred to within the underwriting group for any other purpose, including but not limited to the registration, purchase, or sale of securities, nor is it to be filed with or referred to, in whole or in part, in the registration statement or any other document, except that reference may be made to it in the underwriting agreement or any list of closing documents pertaining to the offering of the securities covered by the registration statement.

ILLUSTRATION 3. LETTER REAFFIRMING COMMENTS IN ILLUSTRATION 1-A AS OF A LATER DATE

If more than one comfort letter is requested, the later letter may, in appropriate situations, refer to information appearing in the earlier letter without repeating such information. This illustration reaffirms and updates the information in Illustration 1-A.

July 25, 20X6

[*Addressee*]

Dear Ladies and Gentlemen:

    We refer to our letter of June 28, 20X6, relating to the registration statement (no. 33-00000) of The Nonissuer Company, Inc. (the company). We reaffirm as of the date hereof (and as though made on the date hereof) all statements made in that letter except that, for the purposes of this letter:

a. The registration statement to which this letter relates is as amended on July 13, 20X6 [*effective date*].
b. The reading of minutes described in paragraph 4 of that letter has been carried out through July 20, 20X6 [*the new cut-off date*].
c. The procedures and inquiries covered in paragraph 4 of that letter were carried out to July 20, 20X6 [*the new cut-off date*] (our work did not extend to the period from July 21, 20X6 to July 25, 20X6 [*date of letter*], inclusive).
d. The period covered in paragraph 4*b* of that letter is changed to the period from April 1, 20X6 to June 30, 20X6, officials of the company having advised us that no such financial statements as of any date or for any period subsequent to June 30, 20X6, were available.
e. The references to May 31, 20X6 in paragraph 5*b* of that letter are changed to June 30, 20X6.
f. The references to May 31, 20X6 and June 23, 20X6 in paragraph 6 of that letter are changed to June 30, 20X6 and July 20, 20X6, respectively.

This letter is solely for the information of the addressees and to assist the underwriters in conducting and documenting their investigation of the affairs of the company in connection with the offering of the securities covered by the registration statement, and it is not to be used, circulated, quoted, or otherwise referred to within or without the underwriting group for any other purpose, including but not limited to the registration, purchase, or sale of securities, nor is it to be filed with or referred to, in whole or in part, in the registration statement or any other document, except that reference may be made to it in the underwriting agreement or any list of closing documents pertaining to the offering of the securities covered by the registration statement.

ILLUSTRATION 4. COMMENTS ON PRO FORMA FINANCIAL INFORMATION

Illustration 5 is applicable when the auditor is asked to provide negative assurance on (1) whether the pro forma financial information included in a registration statement complies as to form in all material respects with the applicable accounting requirements of Rule 11-02 of Regulation S-X, and (2) the application of pro forma adjustments to historical amounts in the compilation of the pro forma financial information (see paragraphs .52–.53). The material in this illustration is intended to be inserted between paragraphs 6 and 7 in Illustration 1-A. The illustration assumes that the auditor has not previously reported on the pro forma financial information. If the auditor did previously report on the pro forma financial information, they may refer in the introductory paragraph of the comfort letter to the fact that they have issued a report, and the report may be attached to the comfort letter (see paragraph .A32–.A33). Therefore, in that circumstance, the procedures in 6b(1) and 6c ordinarily would not be performed, and the auditor would not separately comment on the application of pro forma adjustments to historical financial information because that assurance is encompassed in the auditors' report on pro forma financial information. The auditor may, however, agree to comment on compliance as to form with the applicable accounting requirements of Rule 11-02 of Regulation S-X.

6. At your request, we have:
    a. Read the unaudited pro forma condensed consolidated balance sheet as of March 31, 20X6, and the unaudited pro forma condensed consolidated statements of income for the year ended December 31, 20X5, and the three-month period ended March 31, 20X6, included in the registration statement.
    b. Inquired of certain officials of the company who have responsibility for financial and accounting matters about:

(1) The basis for their determination of the pro forma adjustments and
(2) Whether the unaudited pro forma condensed consolidated financial statements referred to in 6a comply as to form in all material respects with the applicable accounting requirements of Rule 11-02 of Regulation S-X.

    c. Proved the arithmetic accuracy of the application of the pro forma adjustments to the historical amounts in the unaudited pro forma condensed consolidated financial statements.

The foregoing procedures are substantially less in scope than an examination, the objective of which is the expression of an opinion on management's assumptions, the pro forma adjustments, and the application of those adjustments to historical financial information. Accordingly, we do not express such an opinion. The foregoing procedures would not necessarily reveal matters of significance with respect to the comments in the following paragraph. Accordingly, we make no representation about the sufficiency of such procedures for your purposes.

7. Nothing came to our attention as a result of the procedures specified in item 6, however, that caused us to believe that the unaudited pro forma condensed consolidated financial statements referred to in 6a included in the registration statement have not been properly compiled on the pro forma bases described in the notes thereto. Had we performed additional procedures or had we made an examination of the pro forma condensed consolidated financial statements, other matters might have come to our attention that would have been reported to you.

ILLUSTRATION 5. COMMENTS ON A FINANCIAL FORECAST

Illustration 5 is applicable when an auditor is asked to comment on a financial forecast (see paragraph .54). The material in this illustration is intended to be inserted between paragraphs 6 and 7 in Illustration 1-A and 5 and 6 in Illustration 1-B. The illustration assumes that the auditor has previously reported on the compilation of the financial forecast and that the report is attached to the letter (see paragraph .A33 and Illustration 15).

7. At your request, we performed the following procedure with respect to the forecasted consolidated balance sheet and consolidated statements of income and cash flows as of December 31, 20X6, and for the year then ending. With respect to forecasted rental income, we compared the occupancy statistics about expected demand for rental of the housing units to statistics for existing comparable properties and found them to be the same.

8. Because the procedure described above does not constitute an examination of prospective financial statements in accordance with standards promulgated by the AICPA, we do not express an opinion on whether the prospective financial statements are presented in conformity with AICPA presentation guidelines or on whether the underlying assumptions provide a reasonable basis for the presentation. Had we performed additional procedures or had we made an examination of the forecast in accordance with standards promulgated by the AICPA, matters might have come to our attention that would have been reported to you. Furthermore, there will usually be differences between the forecasted and actual results because events and circumstances frequently do not occur as expected, and those differences may be material.

ILLUSTRATION 6. COMMENTS ON TABLES, STATISTICS, AND OTHER FINANCIAL INFORMATION: COMPLETE DESCRIPTION OF PROCEDURES AND FINDINGS

Illustration 6 is applicable when the auditor is asked to comment on tables, statistics, or other compilations of information appearing in a registration statement (paragraphs .65–.71). Each of the comments is in response to a specific request. The paragraphs in this illustration are intended to follow paragraph 6 in Illustration 1-A or paragraph 5 in Illustration 1-B.

In some cases, the auditor may wish to combine in one paragraph the substance of paragraphs 6 and 8, shown as follows. This may be done by expanding the identification of items in paragraph 8 to provide the identification information included in paragraph 6. In such cases, the introductory sentences in paragraphs 6 and 8 and the text of paragraph 7 might be combined as follows: "For purposes of this letter, we have also read the following information and have performed the additional procedures stated below with respect to such information. Our audit of the consolidated financial statements . . ."

6. For purposes of this letter, we have also read the following, set forth in the securities offering on the indicated pages.

Item	Page	Description
a	4	"Capitalization." The amounts under the captions "Amount Outstanding as of May 31, 20X6" and "As Adjusted." The related notes, except the following in Note 2: "See Transactions with Interested Persons." From the proceeds of this offering the company intends to prepay $900,000 on these notes, pro rata. See "Use of Proceeds."
b	13	"History and Business—Sales and Marketing." The table following the first paragraph.
c	33	"Selected Financial Data."

7. Our audit of the consolidated financial statements for the periods referred to in the introductory paragraph of this letter comprised audit tests and procedures deemed necessary for the purpose of expressing an opinion on such financial statements as a whole. For none of the periods referred to therein, or any other period, did we perform audit tests for the purpose of expressing an opinion on individual balances of accounts or summaries of selected transactions such as those enumerated above, and, accordingly, we express no opinion thereon.

8. However, for purposes of this letter, we have performed the following additional procedures, which were applied as indicated with respect to the items enumerated above.

Item in 6	Procedures and Findings
a	We compared the amounts and numbers of shares listed under the caption, "Amount Outstanding as of May 31, 20X6," with the balances in the appropriate accounts in the company's general ledger and found them to be in agreement. We compared the amounts and numbers of shares listed under the caption, "Amount Outstanding as of May 31, 20X6," adjusted for the issuance of the debentures to be offered by means of the securities offering and for the proposed use of a portion of the proceeds thereof to prepay portions of certain notes, as described under "Use of Proceeds," with the amounts and numbers of shares shown under the caption, "As Adjusted," and found such amounts and numbers of shares to be in agreement. (However, we make no comments regarding the reasonableness of the "Use of Proceeds" or whether such use will actually take place.)
b	We compared the amounts of military sales, commercial sales, and total sales shown in the securities offering with the balances in the appropriate accounts in the company's accounting records for the respective fiscal years and for the unaudited interim periods and found them to be in agreement. We proved the arithmetic accuracy of the percentages of such amounts of military sales and commercial sales to total sales for the respective fiscal years and for the unaudited interim periods. We compared such computed percentages with the corresponding percentages appearing in the registration statement and found them to be in agreement.

Item in 6	Procedures and Findings
c	We compared the amounts of net sales and income from continuing operations for the years ended December 31, 20X5, 20X4, and 20X3, with the respective amounts in the consolidated financial statements on pages 27 and 28 and the amounts for the years ended December 31, 20X2 and 20X1 with the respective amounts in the consolidated financial statements for 20X2 and 20X1 and found them to be in agreement.
	We compared the amounts of total assets, long-term obligations, and redeemable preferred stock at December 31, 20X5 and 20X4, with the respective amounts in the consolidated financial statements on pages 27 and 28 and the amounts at December 31, 20X3, 20X2, and 20X1, with the corresponding amounts in the consolidated financial statements for 20X3, 20X2, and 20X1 and found them to be in agreement.
	We compared the information included under the heading "Selected Financial Data" with the disclosure requirements of Item 301 of Regulation S-K. We also inquired of certain officials of the company who have responsibility for financial and accounting matters whether this information conforms in all material respects with the disclosure requirements of Item 301 of Regulation S-K. Nothing came to our attention as a result of the foregoing procedures that caused us to believe that this information does not conform in all material respects with the disclosure requirements of Item 301 of Regulation S-K.

9. It should be understood that we make no representations regarding questions of legal interpretation or regarding the sufficiency for your purposes of the procedures enumerated in the preceding paragraph; also, such procedures would not necessarily reveal any material misstatement of the amounts or percentages listed above. Further, we have addressed ourselves solely to the foregoing data as set forth in the registration statement and make no representations regarding the adequacy of disclosure or regarding whether any material facts have been omitted.

ILLUSTRATION 7. COMMENTS ON TABLES, STATISTICS, AND OTHER FINANCIAL INFORMATION: SUMMARIZED DESCRIPTION OF PROCEDURES AND FINDINGS REGARDING TABLES, STATISTICS, AND OTHER FINANCIAL INFORMATION

Illustration 9 illustrates, in paragraph 8a, a method of summarizing the descriptions of procedures and findings regarding tables, statistics, and other financial information in order to avoid repetition in the comfort letter. Each of the comments is in response to a specific request. The paragraphs in this illustration are intended to follow paragraph 6 in Illustration 1-A or paragraph 5 in Illustration 1-B.

Other methods of summarizing the descriptions may also be appropriately used. For example, the letter may present a matrix listing the financial information and common procedures employed and indicating the procedures applied to specific items.

6. For purposes of this letter, we have also read the following, set forth in the registration statement on the indicated pages.

Item	Page	Description
a	4	"Capitalization." The amounts under the captions "Amount Outstanding as of May 31, 20X6" and "As Adjusted." The related notes, except the following in Note 2: "See Transactions with Interested Persons." From the proceeds of this offering the company intends to prepay $900,000 on these notes, pro rata. See "Use of Proceeds."

Item	Page	Description
b	13	"History and Business—Sales and Marketing." The table following the first paragraph.
c	33	"Selected Financial Data."

7. Our audit of the consolidated financial statements for the periods referred to in the introductory paragraph of this letter comprised audit tests and procedures deemed necessary for the purpose of expressing an opinion on such financial statements as a whole. For none of the periods referred to therein, or any other period, did we perform audit tests for the purpose of expressing an opinion on individual balances of accounts or summaries of selected transactions, such as those enumerated above, and, accordingly, we express no opinion thereon.

8. However, for purposes of this letter and with respect to the items enumerated in 6 above:

   a. Except for item 6A, we have (1) compared the dollar amounts either with the amounts in the audited consolidated financial statements described in the introductory paragraph of this letter or, for prior years, included in the company's accounting records, or with amounts in the unaudited consolidated financial statements described in paragraph 3 to the extent such amounts are included in or can be derived from such statements and found them to be in agreement; (2) compared the amounts of military sales, commercial sales, and total sales with amounts in the company's accounting records and found them to be in agreement; (3) compared other dollar amounts with amounts shown in analyses prepared by the company and found them to be in agreement; and (4) proved the arithmetic accuracy of the percentages based on the data in the previously mentioned financial statements, accounting records, and analyses.

   We compared the information in item 6C with the disclosure requirements of Item 301 of Regulation S-K. We also inquired of certain officials of the company who have responsibility for financial and accounting matters whether this information conforms in all material respects with the disclosure requirements of Item 301 of Regulation S-K. Nothing came to our attention as a result of the foregoing procedures that caused us to believe that this information does not conform in all material respects with the disclosure requirements of Item 301 of Regulation S-K.

   b. With respect to item 6A, we compared the amounts and numbers of shares listed under the caption "Amount Outstanding as of May 31, 20X6" with the balances in the appropriate accounts in the company's general ledger at May 31, 20X6, and found them to be in agreement. We compared the amounts and numbers of shares listed under the caption "Amount Outstanding as of May 31, 20X6," adjusted for the issuance of the debentures to be offered by means of the securities offering and for the proposed use of a portion of the proceeds thereof to prepay portions of certain notes, as described under "Use of Proceeds," with the amounts and numbers of shares shown under the caption, "As Adjusted" and found such amounts and numbers of shares to be in agreement. (However, we make no comments regarding the reasonableness of "Use of Proceeds" or whether such use will actually take place.)

9. It should be understood that we make no representations regarding questions of legal interpretation or regarding the sufficiency for your purposes of the procedures enumerated in the preceding paragraph; also, such procedures would not necessarily reveal any material misstatement of the amounts or percentages listed above. Further, we have addressed ourselves solely to the foregoing data as set forth in the registration statement and make no representations regarding the adequacy of disclosure or regarding whether any material facts have been omitted.

> **ILLUSTRATION 8. COMMENTS ON TABLES, STATISTICS, AND OTHER FINANCIAL INFORMATION: DESCRIPTIONS OF PROCEDURES AND FINDINGS REGARDING TABLES, STATISTICS, AND OTHER FINANCIAL INFORMATION—ATTACHED SECURITIES OFFERING (OR SELECTED PAGES) IDENTIFIES ITEMS TO WHICH PROCEDURES WERE APPLIED THROUGH THE USE OF DESIGNATED SYMBOLS**

Illustration 8 illustrates an alternate format that could facilitate reporting when the auditor is requested to perform procedures on numerous statistics included in a securities offering. Each of the comments is in response to a specific request. The paragraph in Illustration 9 is intended to follow paragraph 6 in Illustration 1-A or paragraph 5 in Illustration 1-B.

7. For purposes of this letter, we have also read the items identified by you on the attached copy of the registration statement and have performed the following procedures, which were applied as indicated with respect to the symbols explained below:

    √   Compared the amount with ABC Company's financial statements for the period indicated included in the securities offering and found them to be in agreement.

8. Our audit of the consolidated financial statements for the periods referred to in the introductory paragraph of this letter comprised audit tests and procedures deemed necessary for the purpose of expressing an opinion on such financial statements as a whole. For none of the periods referred to therein, nor any other period, did we perform audit tests for the purpose of expressing an opinion on individual balances of accounts or summaries of selected transactions, such as those enumerated above, and, accordingly, we express no opinion thereon.

9. It should be understood that we make no representations regarding questions of legal interpretation or regarding the sufficiency for your purposes of the procedures enumerated in the preceding paragraph; also, such procedures would not necessarily reveal any material misstatement of the amounts or percentages listed above. Further, we have addressed ourselves solely to the foregoing data as set forth in the registration statement and make no representations regarding the adequacy of disclosure or regarding whether any material facts have been omitted.

[The following is an extract from a securities offering that illustrates how an auditor can document procedures performed on numerous statistics included in the securities offering.]

Summary Financial Information of ABC Company (in Thousands)

	ABC Company Year Ended December 31,		
Income statement data	*20X3*	*20X4*	*20X5*
Revenue from home sales	$104,110 √	$115,837 √	$131,032 √
Gross profit from sales	23,774 √	17,099 √	22,407 √
Income from home building net of tax	7,029 √	1,000 √	3,425 √

> **ILLUSTRATION 9. ALTERNATE WORDING WHEN AUDITOR'S REPORT ON AUDIT FINANCIAL STATEMENTS CONTAINS AN EMPHASIS-OF-MATTER PARAGRAPH**

Illustration 9 is applicable when the auditor's report on the audited financial statements included in the securities offering contains an emphasis-of-matter paragraph regarding a matter that would also affect the unaudited condensed consolidated interim financial statements included in the securities offering. The introductory paragraph would be revised as follows:

Our reports with respect thereto (which contain an emphasis-of-matter paragraph that describes a lawsuit to which the Company is a defendant, discussed in note 8 to the consolidated financial statements) are also included in the securities offering.

The matter described in the emphasis-of-matter paragraph would also be evaluated to determine whether it also requires mention in the comments on the unaudited condensed consolidated interim financial information (paragraph 5b of Illustration 1-A). If it is concluded that mention of such a matter in the comments on unaudited condensed consolidated financial statements is appropriate, a sentence would be added at the end of paragraph 5b in Illustration 1-A and paragraph 4b of Illustration 1-B:

> Reference should be made to the introductory paragraph of this letter, which states that our audit report covering the consolidated financial statements as of and for the year ended December 31, 20X5, includes an emphasis-of-matter paragraph that describes a lawsuit to which the company is a defendant, discussed in note 8 to the consolidated financial statements.

ILLUSTRATION 10. ALTERNATE WORDING WHEN MORE THAN ONE AUDITOR IS INVOLVED

Illustration 10 applies when more than one auditor is involved in the audit of the financial statements of a business, and the group engagement team has obtained a copy of the comfort letter of the component auditors (see paragraph .21). Illustration 10 consists of an addition to paragraph 4, a substitution for the applicable part of paragraph 5, and an addition to paragraph 6 of Illustration 1-A paragraphs 3, 4, and 5 of Illustration 1-B, respectively.

[4]c. We have read the letter dated _____ of [*the other auditors*] with regard to [*the related company*].
5. Nothing came to our attention as a result of the foregoing procedures (which, so far as [*the related company*] is concerned, consisted solely of reading the letter referred to in 4c), however, that caused us to believe that . . .
6. . . . On the basis of these inquiries and our reading of the minutes and the letter dated _____ of [*the other auditors*] with regard to [*the related company*], as described in 4, nothing came to our attention that caused us to believe that there was any such change, increase, or decrease, except in all instances for changes, increases, or decreases that the registration statement discloses have occurred or may occur.

ILLUSTRATION 11. ALTERNATE WORDING WHEN THE SEC HAS AGREED TO A DEPARTURE FROM ITS ACCOUNTING REQUIREMENTS

Illustration 11 is applicable when (1) there is a departure from the applicable accounting requirements of the 1933 Act and the related rules and regulations adopted by the SEC, and (2) representatives of the SEC have agreed to the departure. Paragraph 2 of Illustration 1-A would be revised to read as follows:

2. In our opinion [*include the phrase* except as disclosed in the registration statement *if applicable*], the consolidated financial statements and financial statement schedules audited by us and included (incorporated by reference) in the registration statement comply as to form in all material respects with the applicable accounting requirements of the Act and the related rules and regulations adopted by the SEC; however, as agreed to by representatives of the SEC, separate financial statements and financial statement schedules of ABC Company (an equity investee) as required by Rule 3-09 of Regulation S-X have been omitted.

> **ILLUSTRATION 12. ALTERNATE WORDING WHEN RECENT EARNINGS DATA ARE PRESENTED IN CAPSULE**

Illustration 12 is applicable when (1) the statement of income in the securities offering is supplemented by later information regarding sales and earnings (capsule financial information), (2) the auditor is asked to comment on that information (paragraphs .50–.51), and (3) the auditor has conducted a review in accordance with GAAS applicable to reviews of interim financial information of the financial statements from which the capsule financial information is derived. The same facts exist as in Illustration 1-A, except for the following:

- Sales and net income (no extraordinary items) share for the six-month periods ended June 30, 20X6 and 20X5 (both unaudited), are included in capsule form more limited than that specified by Financial Accounting Standards Board *Accounting Standards Codification* 270, *Interim Reporting*.
- No financial statements later than those for June 20X6 are available.
- The letter is dated July 25, 20X6, and the cut-off date is July 20, 20X6.

Paragraphs 4, 5, and 6 of Illustration 1-A would be revised to read as follows:

4. For purposes of this letter, we have read the 20X6 minutes of the meetings of the stockholders, the board of directors, and [*include other appropriate committees, if any*] of the company and its subsidiaries as set forth in the minute books at July 20, 20X6, officials of the company having advised us that the minutes of all such meetings through that date were set forth therein and discussed with us the unapproved minutes of meetings held on [*dates*]; we have carried out other procedures to July 20, 20X6, as follows (our work did not extend to the period from July 21, 20X6 to July 25, 20X6, inclusive):

    a. With respect to the three-month periods ended March 31, 20X6 and 20X5, we have:

    (1) Performed the procedures specified for a review in accordance with auditing standards generally accepted in the United States of America applicable to reviews of interim financial information, on the unaudited condensed consolidated balance sheet as of March 31, 20X6, and the unaudited condensed consolidated statements of income, stockholders' equity, and cash flows for the three-month periods ended March 31, 20X6 and 20X5, included in the registration statement.

    (2) Inquired of certain officials of the company who have responsibility for financial and accounting matters whether the unaudited condensed consolidated financial statements referred to in 4a(1) comply as to form in all material respects with the applicable accounting requirements of the Act and the related rules and regulations adopted by the SEC.

    b. With respect to the six-month periods ended June 30, 20X6 and 20X5, we have:

    (1) Read the unaudited amounts for sales, net income, and earnings per share for the six-month periods ended June 30, 20X6 and 20X5, as set forth in paragraph [*identify location*].

    (2) Performed the procedures specified for a review in accordance with auditing standards generally accepted in the United States of America, applicable to reviews of interim financial information, on the unaudited condensed consolidated balance sheet as of June 30, 20X6 and the unaudited condensed consolidated statements of income, stockholders' equity, and cash flows for the six-month periods ended June 30, 20X6 and 20X5, from which the unaudited amounts referred to in 4b(1) are derived.

    (3) Inquired of certain officials of the company who have responsibility for financial and accounting matters whether the unaudited amounts referred to in 4b(1) are stated on a

basis substantially consistent with that of the corresponding amounts in the audited consolidated statements of income.

The foregoing procedures do not constitute an audit conducted in accordance with generally accepted auditing standards. Also, they would not necessarily reveal matters of significance with respect to the comments in the following paragraph. Accordingly, we make no representations regarding the sufficiency of the foregoing procedures for your purposes.

5. Nothing came to our attention as a result of the foregoing procedures, however, that caused us to believe that:

   a. (1) Any material modifications should be made to the unaudited condensed consolidated financial statements described in 4a(1), included in the registration statement, for them to be in conformity with generally accepted accounting principles.

   (2) The unaudited condensed consolidated financial statements described in 4a(1) do not comply as to form in all material respects with the applicable accounting requirements of the Act and the related rules and regulations adopted by the SEC.

   b. (1) The unaudited amounts for sales and net income for the six-month periods ended June 30, 20X6 and 20X5, referred to in 4b(1) do not agree with the amounts set forth in the unaudited condensed consolidated financial statements for those same periods.

   (2) The unaudited amounts referred to in 4b(2) were not determined on a basis substantially consistent with that of the corresponding amounts in the audited consolidated statements of income.

   c. At June 30, 20X6, there was any change in the capital stock, increase in long-term debt, or any decreases in consolidated net current assets or stockholders' equity of the consolidated companies as compared with amounts shown in the March 31, 20X6, unaudited condensed consolidated balance sheet included in the registration statement, except in all instances for changes, increases, or decreases that the registration statement discloses have occurred or may occur.

6. Company officials have advised us that no consolidated financial statements as of any date or for any period subsequent to June 30, 20X6 are available; accordingly, the procedures carried out by us with respect to changes in financial statement items after June 30, 20X6 have, of necessity, been even more limited than those with respect to the periods referred to in item 4. We have inquired of certain officials of the company who have responsibility for financial and accounting matters whether (1) at July 20, 20X6, there was any change in the capital stock, increase in long-term debt, or any decreases in consolidated net current assets or stockholders' equity of the consolidated companies as compared with amounts shown on the March 31, 20X6, unaudited condensed consolidated balance sheet included in the registration statement; or (2) for the period from July 1, 20X6 to July 20, 20X6, there were any decreases, as compared with the corresponding period in the preceding year, in consolidated net sales, or in income before extraordinary items or of net income. On the basis of these inquiries and our reading of the minutes as described in item 4, nothing came to our attention that caused us to believe that there was any such change, increase, or decrease, except in all instances for changes, increases, or decreases that the registration statement discloses have occurred or may occur.

ILLUSTRATION 13. ALTERNATE WORDING WHEN AUDITORS ARE AWARE OF A DECREASE IN A SPECIFIED FINANCIAL STATEMENT ITEM

Illustration 13 covers a situation in which auditors are aware of a decrease in a financial statement item on which they are requested to comment (see paragraphs .58–.64). The same facts exist as in Illustration 1-A, except for the decrease covered in the following change in paragraph 5b.

5. b. (1) At May 31, 20X6, there was any change in the capital stock, increase in long-term debt, or any decrease in consolidated stockholders' equity of the consolidated companies as compared with amounts shown in the March 31, 20X6 unaudited condensed consolidated balance sheet included in the registration statement, or

(2) For the period from April 1, 20X6 to May 31, 20X6, there were any decreases, as compared with the corresponding period in the preceding year, in consolidated net sales, or income before extraordinary items or of net income, except in all instances for changes, increases, or decreases that the registration statement discloses have occurred or may occur and except that the unaudited consolidated balance sheet as of May 31, 20X6, which we were furnished by the company, showed a decrease from March 31, 20X6 in consolidated net current assets as follows (in thousands of dollars):

	Current Assets	Current Liabilities	Net Current Assets
March 31, 20X6	$4,251	$1,356	$2,895
May 31, 20X6	3,986	1,732	2,254

6. As mentioned in 4b, company officials have advised us that no consolidated financial statements as of any date or for any period subsequent to May 31, 20X6, are available; accordingly, the procedures carried out by us with respect to changes in financial statement items after May 31, 20X6, have, of necessity, been even more limited than those with respect to the periods referred to in item 4. We have inquired of certain officials of the company who have responsibility for financial and accounting matters whether (a) at June 23, 20X6, there was any change in the capital stock, increase in long-term debt, or any decreases in consolidated net current assets or stockholders' equity of the consolidated companies as compared with amounts shown on the March 31, 20X6, unaudited condensed consolidated balance sheet included in the registration statement; or (b) for the period from April 1, 20X6 to June 23, 20X6, there were any decreases, as compared with the corresponding period in the preceding year, in consolidated net sales or in income before extraordinary items or of net income. On the basis of these inquiries and our reading of the minutes as described in item 4, nothing came to our attention that caused us to believe that there was any such change, increase, or decrease, except in all instances for changes, increases, or decreases that the registration statement discloses have occurred or may occur and except as described in the following sentence: We have been informed by officials of the company that there continues to be a decrease in net current assets that is estimated to be approximately the same amount as set forth in 5b [*or whatever other disclosure fits the circumstances*].

ILLUSTRATION 14. ALTERNATE WORDING OF THE LETTER FOR COMPANIES THAT ARE PERMITTED TO PRESENT INTERIM EARNINGS DATA FOR A 12-MONTH PERIOD

Certain types of companies are permitted to include earnings data for a twelve-month period to the date of the latest balance sheet furnished in lieu of earnings data for both the interim period between the end of the latest fiscal year and the date of the latest balance sheet and the corresponding period of the preceding fiscal year. The following would be substituted for the applicable part of paragraph 3 of Illustration 1-A.

3. . . . was to enable us to express our opinion on the financial statements as of December 31, 20X5, and for the year then ended, but not on the financial statements for any period included in part within that year. Therefore, we are unable to, and do not express any opinion on, the unaudited condensed consolidated balance sheet as of March 31, 20X6, and the related unaudited condensed consolidated statements of income, stockholders' equity, and cash flows for the 12 months then ended included in the securities offering.

> **ILLUSTRATION 15. ALTERNATE WORDING WHEN THE PROCEDURES THAT THE REQUESTING PARTY HAS REQUESTED THE AUDITOR TO PERFORM ON INTERIM FINANCIAL INFORMATION ARE LESS THAN A REVIEW IN ACCORDANCE WITH GAAS APPLICABLE TO REVIEWS OF INTERIM FINANCIAL INFORMATION**

Illustration 15 assumes that the requesting party has asked the auditor to perform specified procedures on the interim financial information and report thereon in the comfort letter. The letter is dated June 28, 20X6; procedures were performed through June 23, 20X6, the cut-off date. Because a review in accordance with GAAS applicable to reviews of interim financial information was not performed on the interim financial information as of March 31, 20X6, and for the quarter then ended, the auditor is limited to reporting procedures performed and findings obtained on the interim financial information. The following would be substituted for paragraph 4a of Illustration 1-A. Illustration 15 assumes there has not been a change in the application of a requirement of GAAP during the interim period. If there has been such a change, a reference to that change would be included in subparagraph 4a(2), which follows.

4. For purposes of this letter, we have read the 20X6 minutes of meetings of the stockholders, the board of directors, and [*include other appropriate committees, if any*] of the company and its subsidiaries as set forth in the minute books at June 23, 20X6, officials of the company having advised us that the minutes of all such meetings through that date were set forth therein and having discussed with us the unapproved minutes of meetings held on [*dates*]; we have carried out other procedures to June 23, 20X6, as follows (our work did not extend to the period from June 24, 20X6 to June 28, 20X6, inclusive):

    a. With respect to the three-month periods ended March 31, 20X6 and 20X5, we have:

    (1) Read the unaudited condensed consolidated balance sheet as of March 31, 20X6, and the unaudited condensed consolidated statements of income, stockholders' equity, and cash flows for the three-month periods ended March 31, 20X6 and 20X5, included in the registration statement, and agreed the amounts included therein with the company's accounting records as of March 31, 20X6 and 20X5, and for the three-month periods then ended.

    (2) Inquired of certain officials of the company who have responsibility for financial and accounting matters whether the unaudited condensed consolidated financial statements referred to in a(1): (a) are in conformity with generally accepted accounting principles applied on a basis substantially consistent with that of the audited consolidated financial statements included in the registration statement, and (b) comply as to form, in all material respects, with the applicable accounting requirements of the Act and the related rules and regulations adopted by the SEC. Those officials stated that the unaudited condensed consolidated financial statements (a) are in conformity with generally accepted accounting principles applied on a basis substantially consistent with that of the audited consolidated financial statements, and (b) comply as to form, in all material respects, with the applicable accounting requirements of the Act and the related rules and regulations adopted by the SEC.

> **ILLUSTRATION 16. LETTER TO A REQUESTING PARTY THAT HAS NOT PROVIDED THE LEGAL OPINION OR THE REPRESENTATION LETTER REQUIRED BY PARAGRAPH 11**

Illustration 16 illustrates the letter to be provided in accordance with paragraph .11, in which the auditor does not provide negative assurance. This illustration assumes that these procedures are being performed at the request of the placement agent on information included in an offering circular in connection with a private placement of unsecured notes. The letter is dated June 30, 20X6; procedures were performed through June 25, 20X6, the cut-off date. The statements in paragraphs 4–8 of the example are illustrative of the statements required to be included by paragraph .12.

This illustration may also be used in connection with a filing under the 1933 Act when a party other than a named underwriter (for example, a selling shareholder) has not provided the auditor with the representation letter described in paragraph .11. In such a situation, this example may be modified to include the auditor's comments on independence and compliance as to form of the audited financial statements and financial statements schedules with the applicable accounting requirements of the 1933 Act and the related rules and regulations adopted by the SEC. Paragraph 1a(ii) may include an inquiry, and the response of company officials, on compliance as to form of the unaudited condensed interim financial statements.

June 30, 20X6

[*Addressee*]

Dear Ladies and Gentlemen:

We have audited the consolidated financial statements of The Nonissuer Company, Inc. (the company) and subsidiaries, which comprise the consolidated balance sheets as of December 31, 20X5 and 20X4, and the related consolidated statements of income, changes in stockholders' equity, and cash flows for each of the years in the three-year period ended December 31, 20X5, and the related notes to the consolidated financial statements, all included in the offering circular for $30,000,000 of notes due June 30, 20Z6. Our report with respect thereto is included in the offering circular. The offering circular dated June 30, 20X6, is herein referred to as the offering circular.

We are independent certified public accountants with respect to the company under Rule 101 of the AICPA's Code of Professional Conduct and its interpretations and rulings.

We have not audited any financial statements of the company as of any date or for any period subsequent to December 31, 20X5; although, we have conducted an audit for the year ended December 31, 20X5, the purpose (and, therefore, the scope) of the audit was to enable us to express our opinion on the consolidated financial statements as of December 31, 20X5, and for the year then ended, but not on the financial statements for any interim period within that year. Therefore, we are unable to, and do not express any opinion on, the unaudited condensed consolidated balance sheet as of March 31, 20X6, and the unaudited condensed consolidated statements of income, stockholders' equity, and cash flows for the three-month periods ended March 31, 20X6 and 20X5, included in the offering circular, or on the financial position, results of operations, or cash flows as of any date or for any period subsequent to December 31, 20X5.

1. At your request, we have read the 20X6 minutes of meetings of the stockholders, the board of directors, and [*include other appropriate committees, if any*] of the company as set forth in the minute books at June 25, 20X6, officials of the company having advised us that the minutes of all such meetings through that date were set forth therein and having discussed with us the unapproved minutes of meetings held on [*dates*]; we have carried out other procedures to June 25, 20X6, as follows (our work did not extend to the period from June 26, 20X6 to June 30, 20X6, inclusive):

    a. With respect to the three-month periods ended March 31, 20X6 and 20X5, we have:

      (1) Read the unaudited condensed consolidated balance sheet as of March 31, 20X6, and the unaudited condensed consolidated statements of income, stockholders' equity, and cash flows of the company for the three-month periods ended March 31, 20X6 and 20X5, included in the offering circular, and agreed the amounts included therein with the company's accounting records as of March 31, 20X6 and 20X5, and for the three-month periods then ended.

(2) Inquired of certain officials of the company who have responsibility for financial and accounting matters whether the unaudited condensed consolidated financial statements referred to in 1a(1) are in conformity with generally accepted accounting principles applied on a basis substantially consistent with that of the audited consolidated financial statements included in the offering circular. Those officials stated that the unaudited condensed consolidated financial statements are in conformity with generally accepted accounting principles applied on a basis substantially consistent with that of the audited consolidated financial statements.

b. With respect to the period from April 1, 20X6 to May 31, 20X6, we have:

(1) Read the unaudited condensed consolidated financial statements of the company for April and May of both 20X5 and 20X6, furnished us by the company, and agreed the amounts included therein with the company's accounting records. Officials of the company have advised us that no financial statements as of any date or for any period subsequent to May 31, 20X6 were available. [*if applicable:* The financial information for April and May of both 20X5 and 20X6 is incomplete in that it omits the statements of cash flows and other disclosures.]

(2) Inquired of certain officials of the company who have responsibility for financial and accounting matters whether (a) the unaudited condensed consolidated financial statements referred to in 1b(1) are stated on a basis substantially consistent with that of the audited consolidated financial statements included in the offering circular, (b) at May 31, 20X6, there was any change in the capital stock, increase in long-term debt, or any decrease in consolidated net current assets or stockholders' equity of the consolidated companies as compared with amounts shown in the March 31, 20X6, unaudited condensed consolidated balance sheet included in the offering circular, and (c) for the period from April 1, 20X6 to May 31, 20X6, there were any decreases, as compared with the corresponding period in the preceding year, in consolidated net sales, or in income before extraordinary items or of net income.

Those officials stated that (a) the unaudited condensed consolidated financial statements referred to in 1b(2) are stated on a basis substantially consistent with that of the audited consolidated financial statements included in the offering circular, (b) at May 31, 20X6, there was no change in the capital stock, no increase in long-term debt, and no decrease in consolidated net current assets or stockholders' equity of the consolidated companies as compared with amounts shown in the March 31, 20X6, unaudited condensed consolidated balance sheet included in the offering circular, and (c) there were no decreases for the period from April 1, 20X6 to May 31, 20X6, as compared with the corresponding period in the preceding year, in consolidated net sales, or in income before extraordinary items or of net income.

c. As mentioned in 1b, company officials have advised us that no financial statements as of any date or for any period subsequent to May 31, 20X6, are available; accordingly, the procedures carried out by us with respect to changes in financial statement items after May 31, 20X6, have, of necessity, been even more limited than those with respect to the periods referred to in 1a and 1b. We have inquired of certain officials of the company who have responsibility for financial and accounting matters whether (1) at June 25, 20X6, there was any change in the capital stock, increase in long-term debt, or any decreases in consolidated net current assets or stockholders' equity of the consolidated companies as compared with amounts shown on the March 31, 20X6, unaudited condensed consolidated balance sheet included in the offering circular or (2) for the period from April 1, 20X6 to June 25, 20X6, there were any decreases, as compared with the corresponding period in the preceding year, in consolidated net sales or in income before extraordinary items or of net income.

Those officials referred to above stated that (1) at June 25, 20X6, there was no change in the capital stock, no increase in long-term debt, and no decreases in consolidated net current assets or stockholders' equity of the consolidated companies as compared with amounts shown on the March 31, 20X6, unaudited condensed consolidated balance sheet, and (2) there were no decreases for the period from April 1, 20X6 to June 25, 20X6, as compared with the corresponding period in the preceding year, in consolidated net sales or in income before extraordinary items or of net income.

2. For purposes of this letter, we have also read the items identified by you on the attached copy of the offering circular and have performed the following procedures, which were applied as indicated with respect to the symbols explained below:

   ✓ Compared the amount with the company's financial statements for the period indicated and found them to be in agreement.

   ✕ Compared the amount with the company's financial statements for the period indicated included in the offering circular and found them to be in agreement.

   Ⓓ Compared with a schedule or report prepared by the company and found them to be in agreement.

3. Our audit of the consolidated financial statements for the periods referred to in the introductory paragraph of this letter comprised audit tests and procedures deemed necessary for the purpose of expressing an opinion on such financial statements as a whole. For none of the periods referred to therein, nor for any other period, did we perform audit tests for the purpose of expressing an opinion on individual balances of accounts or summaries of selected transactions, such as those enumerated above, and, accordingly, we express no opinion thereon.

4. It should be understood that we have no responsibility for establishing (and did not establish) the scope and nature of the procedures enumerated in paragraphs 1–3 above; rather, the procedures enumerated therein are those the requesting party asked us to perform. Accordingly, we make no representations regarding questions of legal interpretation or regarding the sufficiency for your purposes of the procedures enumerated in the preceding paragraphs; also, such procedures would not necessarily reveal any material misstatement of the amounts or percentages listed above as set forth in the offering circular. Further, we have addressed ourselves solely to the foregoing data and make no representations regarding the adequacy of disclosures or whether any material facts have been omitted. This letter relates only to the financial statement items specified above and does not extend to any financial statement of the company as a whole.

5. The foregoing procedures do not constitute an audit conducted in accordance with generally accepted auditing standards. Had we performed additional procedures or had we conducted an audit or a review of the company's March 31, April 30, or May 31, 20X6 and 20X5 condensed consolidated financial statements in accordance with generally accepted auditing standards, other matters might have come to our attention that would have been reported to you.

6. These procedures should not be taken to supplant any additional inquiries or procedures that you would undertake in your consideration of the proposed offering.

7. This letter is solely for your information and to assist you in your inquiries in connection with the offering of the securities covered by the offering circular, and it is not to be used, circulated, quoted, or otherwise referred to for any other purpose, including but not limited to the registration, purchase, or sale of securities, nor is it to be filed with or referred to, in whole or in part, in the offering circular or any other document, except that reference may be made to it in any list of closing documents pertaining to the offering of the securities covered by the offering document.

8. We have no responsibility to update this letter for events and circumstances occurring after June 25, 20X6.

ILLUSTRATION 17. INTENTIONALLY OMITTED.

Illustration 17 from the AU Standards was redrafted in the Clarity (AU-C) Standards and appears in this volume as Illustration 1-B.

> **ILLUSTRATION 18. ALTERNATE WORDING WHEN REFERENCE TO EXAMINATION OF ANNUAL MANAGEMENT'S DISCUSSION AND ANALYSIS AND REVIEW OF INTERIM MANAGEMENT'S DISCUSSION AND ANALYSIS IS MADE**

Illustration 18 applicable when the auditor is making reference to an examination of annual MD&A and a review of interim MD&A. The same facts exist as in Illustration 1-A, except for the following:

- The auditor has examined the company's Management's Discussion and Analysis (MD&A) for the year ended December 31, 20X5, in accordance with AT Section 701, *Management's Discussion and Analysis*.
- The auditor has also performed reviews of the company's unaudited condensed consolidated financial statements in accordance with generally accepted auditing standards applicable to reviews of interim financial information and the company's MD&A for the three-month period ended March 31, 20X6, in accordance with AT Section 701.
- The accountant's reports on the examination and review of MD&A have been previously issued, but not distributed publicly; none of these reports is included in the securities offering. In this example, the auditor has elected to attach the previously issued reports to the comfort letter (see paragraph .A33).

Appropriate modifications would be made to the opening paragraph of the comfort letter if the auditor has performed a review of the company's annual MD&A.

The following would be substituted for the first paragraph of Illustration 1-A.

> We have audited the consolidated financial statements of The Nonissuer Company, Inc. (the company) and subsidiaries, which comprise the consolidated balance sheets as of December 31, 20X5 and 20X4, and the related consolidated statements of income, changes in stockholders' equity, and cash flows for each of the years in the three-year period ended December 31, 20X5, the related notes to the consolidated financial statements, and the related financial statement schedules, all included in The Issuer Company's (the registrant) registration statement (no. 33-00000) on Form S-1 filed by the registrant under the Securities Act of 1933 (the Act); our reports with respect thereto are also included in that registration statement. The registration statement, as amended on June 28, 20X6, is herein referred to as the registration statement. Also, we have examined the company's Management's Discussion and Analysis (MD&A) for the year ended December 31, 20X5, included in the registration statement, as indicated in our report dated March 28, 20X6; our report with respect thereto is attached. We have also reviewed the unaudited condensed consolidated financial statements as of March 31, 20X6 and 20X5, and for the three-month periods then ended, included in the registration statement, as indicated in our report dated May 15, 20X6, and have also reviewed the company's MD&A for the three-month period ended March 31, 20X6, included in the registration statement, as indicated in our report dated May 15, 20X6; our reports with respect thereto are attached.

The following paragraph would be added after paragraph 3 of Illustration 1-A:

> 4. We have not examined any MD&A of the company as of or for any period subsequent to December 31, 20X5; although we have made an examination of the company's MD&A for the year ended December 31, 20X5, included in the registration statement, the purpose (and, therefore, the scope) of the examination was to enable us to express our opinion on such MD&A, but not on the MD&A for any interim period within that year. Therefore, we are unable to and do not express any opinion on the MD&A for the three-month period ended March 31, 20X6, included in the registration statement, or for any period subsequent to March 31, 20X6.

AU 711 Filings Under Federal Securities Statutes[1]

AU-C 925 Filings with the US Securities and Exchange Commission Under the Securities Act of 1933

AU EFFECTIVE DATE AND APPLICABILITY

Original Pronouncement	Statement on Auditing Standards (SAS) 37.
Effective Date	This statement currently is effective.
Applicability	Reports of independent accountants included in registration statements filed with the Securities and Exchange Commission (SEC) under the Securities Act of 1933.

AU-C EFFECTIVE DATE AND SUMMARY OF CHANGES

SAS No. 122, *Codification of Auditing Standards and Procedures,* is effective for audits of financial statements with periods ending on or after December 15, 2012.

AU-C 925 does not change extant requirements in any significant way.

AU DEFINITIONS OF TERMS

Effective date. The date after which securities registered with the SEC may be offered for sale to the public. Ordinarily, it is the date that the SEC completes its review of the registration statement.

---

[1] This section is affected by the Public Company Accounting Oversight Board's (PCAOB's) Standard, Conforming Amendments to PCAOB Interim Standards Resulting from the Adoption of PCAOB Auditing Standard No. 5, An Audit of Internal Control Over Financial Reporting That Is Integrated with an Audit of Financial Statements.

Prospectus. The major component of the registration statement. It also is distributed to prospective purchasers of the securities that will be offered for sale. It contains financial and other information of the issuer.

Registration statement. A statement required to be filed with the SEC by a company before its securities may be offered for sale to the public. Its primary purpose is to provide prospective investors with financial and other information concerning the company and the securities being offered for sale. Registration of an initial public offering of securities is governed by the Securities Act of 1933 and related regulations.

Shelf registration statement. A registration statement in which the issuer registers the amount of securities it reasonably expects to offer and sell within the next two years. Ordinarily, the issuer does not have to prepare and file a new prospectus and registration statement for each sale. A shelf registration statement can be updated after its original effective date by:

- Filing a posteffective amendment
- Incorporation by reference of subsequently filed material
- Addition of a supplemental prospectus (sometimes referred to as a "sticker")

AU-C DEFINITIONS OF TERMS

Source: AU-C 925.04

Auditor's consent. A statement signed and dated by the auditor that indicates that the auditor consents to the use of the auditor's report, and other references to the auditor, in a registration statement filed under the Securities Act of 1933.

Awareness letter. A letter signed and dated by the auditor to acknowledge the auditor's awareness that the auditor's review report on unaudited interim financial information is being used in a registration statement filed under the Securities Act of 1933. This letter is not considered to be part of the registration statement and is also commonly referred to as an *acknowledgment letter*.

Effective date of the registration statement. The date on which the registration statement filed under the Securities Act of 1933 becomes effective for purposes of evaluating the auditor's liability under Section 11 of the Securities Act of 1933.

OBJECTIVES OF AU SECTION 711

Section 11 of the Securities Act of 1933 imposes civil liability for material misstatements or omissions in registration statements on "every accountant . . . who has, with his consent, been named as having prepared or certified any part of the registration statement." Section 11 provides that the accountant will not incur this liability, however, if he or she sustains the burden of proof that as to the part of the registration statement purporting to be made on his or her authority as an expert, the accountant had, "after *reasonable investigation, reasonable ground* to believe and did believe, *at the time such part of the statement became effective*, that the statements therein were true." The courts have interpreted this statement to mean that *as of the effective date* of the registration statement the accountant must have *reasonable ground* for believing that statements expertized by him or her were, in fact, true. For example, if the effective date of a registration statement is May 10, 20X1, the auditor must have *reasonable ground* on that date for believing that the December 31, 20X0 financial statements were true and that there were no material omissions.

To sustain the burden of proof under Section 11 of the Securities Act of 1933 that he or she has made a *reasonable investigation*, the auditor must apply certain additional procedures. This section describes procedures the accounting profession believes the auditor should follow to fulfill his or her responsibility as an expert under the 1933 Act. The procedures relate to:

- The independent accountant's review report on interim financial information
- Subsequent events
- Reports of predecessor auditors

OBJECTIVES OF AU-C SECTION 711

AU-C Section 925.03 states that:

> . . . the objective of the auditor, in connection with audited financial statements of a nonissuer that are separately included or incorporated by reference in a registration statement filed under the Securities Act of 1933, is to perform specified procedures at or shortly before the effective date of the registration statement to sustain the burden of proof that the auditor has performed a reasonable investigation, as referred to in Section 11(b)(3)(B) of the Securities Act of 1933.

FUNDAMENTAL REQUIREMENTS

ACCOUNTANT'S RESPONSIBILITY

In a filing under the Securities Act of 1933, the prospectus frequently contains a statement that certain information is included in reliance on the reports of certain named experts. The accountant should read the section containing that statement and all other sections of the prospectus to make certain that the issuer of the securities is not attributing to the accountant greater responsibility than he or she intended. There should be no implication that the financial statements have been prepared by the accountant or that they are not the direct representations of management.

ACCOUNTANT'S REPORT: REVIEW OF INTERIM FINANCIAL INFORMATION

In Accounting Series Release (ASR) 274, the SEC ruled that an accountant's report on a review of unaudited interim financial information is not considered part of the registration statement prepared or certified by an accountant or a report prepared or certified by an accountant within the meaning of Section 11 of the Securities Act of 1933. The SEC requires a statement to this effect whenever the accountant's review report is presented or incorporated by reference in a registration statement. The accountant should read the registration statement to ensure that such a statement has been made.

SUBSEQUENT EVENTS PROCEDURES

Predecessor Auditor

An auditor who has not audited the financial statements for the most recent fiscal year, but whose reports on audits of prior years' financial statements are included in the registration statement, has a responsibility for material subsequent events from the date of the prior year financial statements through to the effective date. The predecessor auditor should:

1. Read relevant parts of the prospectus and the registration statement
2. Obtain a representation letter from the successor auditor regarding whether his or her audit revealed any matters that might materially affect the financial statements reported on by the predecessor or would require disclosure in the notes
3. Make inquiries and perform other procedures to satisfy himself or herself about the appropriateness of adjustments or disclosures affecting the financial statements covered by the reports (see Section 508, *Reports on Audited Financial Statements*)

NOTE: In addition to the three procedures above, the procedures in Section 508 under "Reissuance of Predecessor Auditor's Report" should be followed. Thus, the predecessor auditor should obtain a letter of representation from the management of the former client.

Current Auditor

The auditor should extend his or her procedures for subsequent events from the date of the audit report up to the effective date, or as close as possible to the effective date. Those procedures include the following:

1. Arrange with the client to be kept informed of the progress of the registration proceedings
2. Read the entire prospectus and other relevant parts of the registration statement
3. Inquire of and obtain written representations from officers and other executives responsible for financial and accounting matters about whether any events have occurred, other than those reflected or disclosed in the registration statement, that materially affect the audited financial statements in the registration statement or that should be disclosed to keep the financial statements from being misleading

In addition to the preceding procedures, the auditor should have applied the subsequent events procedures described in Section 560, *Subsequent Events,* up to the report date. They are as follows:

1. Compare latest interim financial statements to the statements being audited.
2. Ask officers and other executives responsible for financial and accounting matters whether:
    a. Interim statements are prepared on same basis as annual statements
    b. During the subsequent period there were any:

        (1) Unusual adjustments
        (2) Significant changes in:

            (a) Capital stock
            (b) Long-term debt
            (c) Working capital
            (d) Status of items accounted for on the basis of tentative or inconclusive data
            (e) Existence of substantial contingent liabilities or commitments

3. Read minutes of meetings of stockholders, directors, and relevant committees. Inquire about matters dealt with at meetings for which minutes are not available.

4. Ask client's legal counsel about litigation, claims, and assessments (see Section 337, *Inquiry of a Client's Lawyer Concerning Litigation, Claims and Assessments*).
5. Obtain written representations from management (see Section 333, *Management Representations*) concerning subsequent events.
6. Make additional inquiries or apply other procedures to the extent necessary to resolve issues raised in applying the foregoing procedures.

> NOTE: Normally, an auditor obtains supplementary representation letters from the client and the client's lawyer that update the original letters from the report date to the effective date.

RESPONSE TO SUBSEQUENT EVENTS AND SUBSEQUENTLY DISCOVERED FACTS: AUDITED FINANCIAL STATEMENTS

1. If, after the date of the report on audited financial statements, the auditor discovers subsequent events that require adjustment of or disclosure in the financial statements, he or she should follow the guidance in Section 560.
2. If, after the date of the report on audited financial statements, the auditor becomes aware that facts may have existed at the date of the report that might have affected the report had he or she then been aware of them, he or she should follow the guidance in Section 561, *Subsequent Discovery of Facts Existing at the Date of the Auditor's Report*.
3. In situations described in items 1 and 2, if the financial statements are adjusted or the required additional disclosure is made, the auditor should follow the guidance in Section 530, *Dating of the Independent Auditor's Report*, on dating the report.
4. In situations described in items 1 and 2, if the client refuses to adjust the financial statements or make the required additional disclosure, the auditor should apply the procedures described in Section 561. The auditor also should consider consulting with his or her lawyer about withholding consent to the use of the report on the audited financial statements in the registration statement.

RESPONSE TO SUBSEQUENT EVENTS AND SUBSEQUENTLY DISCOVERED FACTS: UNAUDITED FINANCIAL STATEMENTS OR UNAUDITED INTERIM FINANCIAL INFORMATION

If the accountant concludes that unaudited financial statements or unaudited interim financial information presented or incorporated by reference in a registration statement are not in conformity with generally accepted accounting principles (GAAP), he or she should insist that the statements or information be revised.

If the client refuses to make the revisions:

1. If he or she has reported on a review of the interim financial information and the subsequently discovered facts would have affected the report had they been known to him or her at the date of the report, the accountant should refer to Section 561.
2. If he or she has not reported on a review of the unaudited financial statements or interim financial information, the accountant should modify the report on the audited financial statements to describe the GAAP departure in the unaudited financial statements or interim financial information.
3. In situations described in items 1 or 2, the accountant should consider consulting with his or her lawyer about withholding consent to the use of the report on the audited financial statements in the registration statement.

NOTE: This is sometimes called the reach-out theory of auditor responsibility. Even though the auditor is not explicitly reporting on the unaudited data, if he or she is aware of a GAAP departure in unaudited statements, the report should be modified to add a separate paragraph disclosing the departure. The opinion on the audited financial statements would remain unqualified. Naturally, the auditor's objective is to persuade the client to correct the departure. Should the client fail to do so, the auditor has no alternative but to add a paragraph to the audit report that describes the departure.

INTERPRETATIONS

SUBSEQUENT EVENTS PROCEDURES FOR SHELF REGISTRATION STATEMENTS UPDATED AFTER THE ORIGINAL EFFECTIVE DATE (ISSUED MAY 1983)

This interpretation states that the accountant should perform the subsequent events procedures described in Section 711 (for predecessor auditor or current auditor, as appropriate) when:

1. A posteffective amendment is filed in accordance with the provisions of Item 512(a) of Regulation S-K.
2. A filing under the Securities and Exchange Act of 1934 that includes or amends audited financial statements is incorporated by reference into the shelf registration statement.

Posteffective Amendment

A posteffective amendment is considered to be a new registration statement. Therefore, whenever a posteffective amendment is filed, the accountant should perform the subsequent events procedures to a date as close as possible to the new effective date.

Incorporation by Reference

Each filing of a registrant's annual report (Form 10-K) and each filing of an employee benefit plan annual report (Form 11-K) that is incorporated by reference into a shelf registration statement is considered to be a new registration statement. Therefore, whenever a Form 10-K or Form 11-K is incorporated by reference into a shelf registration statement, the accountant should perform the subsequent events procedures to a date as close as possible to the date of the filing of the Form 10-K or Form 11-K. In these circumstances, the accountant should date his or her consent as of the date of completion of the subsequent events procedures.

Whenever other filings under the Securities and Exchange Act of 1934 (Form 10-Q, Form 8-K, etc.) include or amend audited financial statements and the filings are incorporated into a registration statement, the accountant who audited those statements must give a currently dated consent. Also, the accountant should perform subsequent events procedures to a date as close as possible to the date of incorporation.

Update by Sticker

When a shelf registration is updated by a supplemental prospectus (or sticker) the effective date is not changed. Thus, the accountant has no responsibility to update performance of subsequent event procedures.

Consenting to Be Named as an Expert in an Offering Document in Connection with Securities Offerings Other Than Those Registered Under the Securities Act of 1933 (Issued June 1992; Amended March 1995)

The auditor should not consent to be named, or referred to, as an expert in an offering document in connection with securities offerings other than those registered under the Securities Act of 1933. The term *expert* is typically undefined, other than in connection with the 1933 Act, and therefore the auditor's responsibility is not defined. The auditor's resultant responsibility would also be undefined.

If the term *expert* is defined under applicable state law, or in other instances in which the term and responsibilities are explicit, the accountant might agree to be named as an expert in an offering document.

Consenting to the Use of an Audit Report in an Offering Document in Securities Offerings Other Than One Registered Under the Securities Act of 1933 (Issued June 1992)

The auditor may consent to the use of an audit report in an offering document other than one registered under the 1933 Act by use of the following language:

> We agree to inclusion in this offering circular of our report dated [XX] on our audit of the financial statements of [name of entity].

TECHNIQUES FOR APPLICATION

GENERAL

SEC work is complex and highly specialized. The accountant who performs this work should be familiar with the following accounting-related pronouncements of the SEC:

1. Regulation S-X
2. Regulation S-K
3. Financial Reporting Releases (FRR)
4. Staff Accounting Bulletins (SAB)

REFERENCES

If he or she performs SEC work, the accountant might wish to use one or more of the following or similar references:

- Steven M. Bragg, *Running a Public Company: From IPO to SEC Reporting* (Hoboken, NJ: John Wiley & Sons, Inc.)
- Ted Trautmann and CCH staff, *2009 SEC Handbook: Rules and Forms for Financial Statements and Related Disclosure* (19th ed.) (Chicago, IL: Commerce Clearing House)

AU ILLUSTRATION

The wording of the following illustration would be considered a satisfactory description of the status of the accountant's review report that was included in a Form 10-Q filing that was later presented or incorporated by reference in a registration statement. The accountant should make certain that this wording from AU 711.09, or similar wording, appears in the prospectus.

ILLUSTRATION 1. REVIEW REPORT INCLUDED IN FORM 10-Q

Independent Public Accountants

The consolidated balance sheets as of December 31, 20X2 and 20X1, and the consolidated statements of income, retained earnings, and cash flows for each of the three years in the period ended December 31, 20X2, incorporated by reference in this prospectus, have been included herein in reliance on the report of Guy & Co., independent public accountants, given on the authority of that firm as experts in auditing and accounting.

With respect to the unaudited interim financial information for the periods ended March 31, 20X3 and 20X2, incorporated by reference in this prospectus, the independent public accountants have reported that they have applied limited procedures in accordance with professional standards for a review of such information. However, their separate report included in the company's quarterly report on Form 10-Q for the quarter ended March 31, 20X3, and incorporated by reference herein, states that they did not audit and they do not express an opinion on that interim financial information. Accordingly, the degree of reliance on their report on such information should be restricted in light of the limited nature of the review procedures applied. The accountants are not subject to the liability provisions of Section 11 of the Securities Act of 1933 for their report on the unaudited interim financial information because that report is not a "report" or a "part" of the registration statement prepared or certified by the accountants within the meaning of Sections 7 and 11 of the Act.

AU-C 925 ILLUSTRATION

ILLUSTRATION 1. ILLUSTRATIVE DISCLOSURES AND REPORTS

The following is an example of a typical "experts" section in a registration statement filed under the Securities Act of 1933:

Experts

The consolidated balance sheets of Company X as of December 31, 20X2 and 20X1, and the related consolidated statements of income and comprehensive income, changes in stockholders' equity, and cash flows for each of the three years in the period ended December 31, 20X2, included in this prospectus, have been so included in reliance on the report of ABC & Co, independent auditors, given on the authority of that firm as experts in auditing and accounting.

The following is an example of a disclosure for a registration statement filed under the Securities Act of 1933 that includes the auditor's review report on unaudited interim financial information when such disclosure is included in a separate section. This disclosure may also be included under a section titled "Experts":

Independent Auditors

With respect to the unaudited interim financial information of Company X for the three-month periods ended March 31, 20X3 and 20X2, included in this prospectus, ABC & Co. has reported that they have applied limited procedures in accordance with professional standards for a review of such information. However, their separate report dated May XX, 20X3, included herein, states that they did not audit and they do not express an opinion on that interim financial information. Accordingly, the degree of reliance on their report on such information should be restricted in light of the limited nature of the review procedures applied. ABC & Co. is not subject to the liability provisions of Section 11 of the Securities Act of 1933 for their report on the unaudited interim financial information because that report is not a "report" or a "part" of the registration statement prepared or certified by the accountants within the meaning of Sections 7 and 11 of the Act.

The following is an example of a typical description of the auditor's role when an issuer wishes to make reference to the auditor in an offering document prepared in connection with a securities offering that is not registered under the Securities Act of 1933:

Independent Auditors

The financial statements of Company X as of December 31, 20X2 and for the year then ended, included in this offering circular, have been audited by ABC & Co., independent auditors, as stated in their report appearing herein.

Although generally not necessary, the following is an example of language the auditor might use indicating that the auditor agrees to the inclusion of the auditor's report on the audited financial statements in offering materials prepared in connection with a securities offering that is not registered under the Securities Act of 1933:

We agree to the inclusion in the offering circular of our report, dated February 5, 20X3, on our audit of the financial statements of Company X.

AU 722 Interim Financial Information

AU-C 930 Interim Financial Information

AU EFFECTIVE DATE AND APPLICABILITY

Original Pronouncement	Statements on Auditing Standards (SASs) 100 and 116.
Effective Date	SAS 116 is effective for reviews of interim financial information for interim periods beginning after December 15, 2009. Earlier application is permitted.
Applicability	An accountant may conduct a review of interim financial information if:

1. The entity's latest annual financial statements have been audited by the accountant or a predecessor;
2. The accountant has been engaged to audit the entity's current year financial statements, or the accountant audited the entity's latest annual financial statements and expects to audit the current year financial statements;
3. The client prepares its interim financial information in accordance with the same financial reporting framework as that used to prepare the annual financial statements; and
4. If the interim financial information is condensed information, then

   a. The information conforms with a financial reporting framework such as International Accounting Standards (IAS) 34;
   b. It includes a note that the financial information does not represent complete financial statements and should be read in conjunction with the entity's latest annual audited financial statements; and
   c. The information accompanies the entity's latest audited annual financial statements.

NOTE: Although the section generally does not require a written report on a review, a review report should accompany interim financial information if the entity states in a written document that the interim information has been reviewed by an independent public accountant. The accountant may also issue a written report if there is a risk that users of the interim financial information may assume a higher level of assurance than that obtained by the accountant.

AU-C EFFECTIVE DATE AND SUMMARY OF CHANGES

SAS No. 122, *Codification of Auditing Standards and Procedures,* is effective for audits of financial statements with periods ending on or after December 15, 2012.

AU-C 722 does not change extant requirements in any significant way.

AU DEFINITIONS OF TERMS

Interim financial information or statement. Financial information or statements for less than a full year or for a twelve-month period ending on a date other than the entity's fiscal year-end. Interim financial information may be condensed or in the form of a complete set of financial statements. Additionally, the term applicable financial reporting framework means a set of criteria used to determine measurement, recognition, presentation, and disclosure of all material items appearing in the financial statements; for example, US generally accepted accounting principles (GAAP) or international financial reporting standards.

Likely misstatement. The accountant's best estimate of the total misstatement in the account balances or classes of transactions on which he or she has performed review procedures.

Specified regulatory agencies. For purposes of this section, specified regulatory agencies are the Securities and Exchange Commission (SEC) and the following agencies with which an entity files periodic reports pursuant to the Securities Exchange Act of 1934: Office of the Comptroller of the Currency, Federal Deposit Insurance Corporation, Federal Reserve System, and Office of Thrift Supervision.

AU-C DEFINITION OF TERM

Source: AU-C 930.06

Interim financial information. Financial information prepared and presented in accordance with an applicable financial reporting framework that comprises either a complete or condensed set of financial statements covering a period or periods less than one full year or covering a twelve-month period ending on a date other than the entity's fiscal year-end.

OBJECTIVES OF AU SECTION 722

The objective of a review of interim financial information is to provide the accountant with a basis for communicating whether he or she is aware of any material modifications that should be made to the information for it to conform to the applicable financial reporting framework. Review procedures consist primarily of inquiries, analytical procedures, and reading of certain documents and reports. A review is premised on the accountant's base of knowledge about the company's accounting and financial reporting practices and other aspects of its internal control. It is expected that this base of understanding will have been acquired by the accountant who audited the entity's financial statements for one or more annual periods. An accountant who has not audited annual financial statements can review interim financial information *if* he or she can acquire equivalent knowledge and understanding.

The service of review of interim information of a public entity is a product of the natural tension between government regulation and professional standard setting. Using its regulatory powers over financial reporting by public companies, the SEC pushed the American Institute of Certified Public Accountants' (AICPA's) auditing standard-setting group to develop a level of service for interim data somewhere in between an audit and the minimal responsibility for association with unaudited statements. Initially, when first considered in 1975, the idea of providing negative, or limited, assurance based on the limited scope of a review was very controversial.

In 1999, the Auditing Standards Board (ASB) amended SAS 71 (the predecessor SAS to SAS 100) by issuing SAS 90, *Audit Committee Communications*, to require that auditors of SEC clients determine that SAS 61 (see Section 380, *The Auditor's Communication with Those Charged with Governance*) matters identified in a review engagement be brought to the attention of the audit committee by management or the auditor.

In 2002, the ASB issued SAS 100, *Interim Financial Information*, which supersedes SAS 71. The ASB decided to issue this new standard to provide additional guidance on performing interim reviews, incorporate the requirements of the SEC for timely filings of interim financial information, and incorporate recommendations from the Public Company Accounting Oversight Board's (PCAOB's) Panel on Audit Effectiveness. The SAS also includes recommendations from the AICPA's Professional Issues Task Force that were included in PITF 2000-4, *Quarterly Review Procedures for Public Companies*.

Finally, the ASB issued SAS 116 in 2009; it removes the guidance for reviews of the interim financial statements of issuers, since that guidance is provided by the auditing standards of the PCAOB.

OBJECTIVE OF AU-C SECTION 930

AU-C 930.045 states that:

> . . . the objective of the auditor when performing an engagement to review interim financial information is to obtain a basis for reporting whether the auditor is aware of any material modifications that should be made to the interim financial information for it to be in accordance with the applicable financial reporting framework through performing limited procedures.

FUNDAMENTAL REQUIREMENTS: REVIEW PROCEDURES

STANDARDS

The three general standards of the generally accepted auditing standards (GAAS) apply to reviews. This section provides guidance on application of the fieldwork and reporting standards to reviews.

UNDERSTANDING WITH CLIENT

A clear written understanding should be established with the client regarding the services to be performed in an engagement to review interim financial information. If an understanding has not been established with the client, the accountant should not accept or perform the engagement.

The understanding is specifically required to include:

1. Objectives of the engagement
2. Responsibilities of management
3. Responsibilities of the accountant
4. Limitations of the engagement

The understanding should state whether the accountant will provide a written or oral report upon completion of the engagement.

Prior to accepting the engagement, the accountant should assess management's ability to acknowledge their responsibility to establish and maintain controls that are sufficient to provide a reasonable basis for the preparation of reliable interim financial information in accordance with the applicable financial reporting framework. The accountant should not accept the engagement if this is not the case.

NOTE: The best way to establish this understanding is to use an engagement letter (see "Techniques for Application").

KNOWLEDGE OF THE ENTITY'S BUSINESS AND INTERNAL CONTROL

The accountant should have knowledge of the entity's business and internal controls that is sufficient to:

- Identify types of potential material misstatements and the likelihood of such misstatements occurring.
- Determine the inquiries and analytical procedures to be performed. (The accountant should also use this knowledge to identify particular events, transactions, or assertions to determine where to direct inquiries or apply analytical procedures.)

Planning the Review

When planning the review, the accountant should perform procedures to update his or her knowledge of the entity's business and its internal control. This knowledge should be sufficient to aid in determining the inquiries to be made and the analytical procedures to be performed, and identify relevant events, transactions, or assertions to subject to inquiries or analytical procedures. The accountant should read:

- Prior year's audit documentation (The accountant should also consider whether results of audit procedures performed impact the current year's financial statements.)
- Documentation for prior interim period reviews of the current year
- Documentation of prior year's corresponding quarterly and year-to-date interim period reviews

NOTE: The accountant should specifically evaluate (1) corrected material misstatements; (2) issues identified in a summary of uncorrected misstatements (see Section 312); (3) identified risks of material misstatement due to fraud, including the risk of management override of controls; and (4) significant continuing financial accounting and reporting matters (e.g., significant deficiencies and material weaknesses).

- The most recent annual and comparable prior interim period financial information.

The accountant should ask management about:

- Changes in business activities of the entity
- The nature and extent of significant changes in internal control, including changes in policies, procedures, or personnel, occurring after the prior annual audit or review of interim financial information

The accountant should also consider the results of any audit procedures performed with respect to the current year's financial statements.

Initial Review of Interim Information

In an initial review of interim information, the accountant should perform procedures to enable him or her to obtain the understanding of the business and internal controls necessary to address the objectives of the review. In addition, the accountant should make inquiries of the predecessor accountant and, if permitted by the predecessor, review the predecessor's documentation for:

- The preceding annual audit, and
- Any prior interim periods in the current year reviewed by the predecessor

NOTE: *The accountant may also want to review the predecessor's documentation for reviews of prior year's interim periods.*
The accountant should specifically evaluate the nature of any (1) corrected material misstatements, (2) issues identified in any summary of uncorrected misstatements, (3) identified risks of material misstatement due to fraud, including the risk of management override of controls, (4) significant continuing financial accounting and reporting matters (e.g., significant deficiencies or material weaknesses).

The inquiries and procedures performed in the initial review and the conclusions reached are solely the responsibility of the successor accountant. The successor accountant should not make reference in his or her report to the predecessor's work as the basis for the successor's report. If the predecessor does not respond to inquiries or make documentation available for review, the accountant should perform alternative procedures to obtain the required knowledge.

If the accountant has not audited the most recent annual financial statements, the accountant should obtain sufficient knowledge of the entity's internal control as it relates to preparing interim financial information. Such knowledge includes relevant aspects of the control environment, the entity's risk assessment process, control activities, information and communication, and monitoring. The accountant should be aware that internal control over the preparation of interim information may differ from that over annual financial information because different accounting principles may be permitted for interim financial information by APB Opinion 28, *Interim Financial Reporting*.

NOTE: *The scope of the review may be restricted if the entity's internal control has deficiencies that are so significant that it is not practicable for the accountant to effectively perform necessary review procedures.*

REQUIRED REVIEW PROCEDURES

The following procedures should be tailored to the engagement based on the accountant's knowledge of the entity's business and internal control.

Analytical Procedures

The accountant should perform the following analytical procedures to identify and provide a basis for asking about the relationships and individual items that appear to be unusual and that may indicate a material misstatement in the interim financial information.

The accountant should compare:

- Quarterly interim financial information with comparable information for the immediately preceding interim period and the prior year's corresponding information. The accountant should factor in his or her knowledge of changes in the business or transactions.
- Recorded amounts or ratios developed from such amounts to the account's expectations.
- Disaggregated revenue data, such as comparing the current interim period's revenue reported by month and by operating segment with that of comparable prior periods.

The accountant should also consider plausible relationships among financial and relevant nonfinancial information. The accountant may want to consider information developed by the entity such as a director's information package.

AU Illustration 8 provides examples of analytical procedures.

The accountant should keep in mind that, although expectations from analytical procedures in a review are normally less precise than those of an audit, and the accountant is not required to corroborate management's responses with other evidence, the accountant should consider whether such responses are reasonable and consistent with other information from the review.

Inquiries and Other Procedures

The accountant should make the following inquiries of financial and accounting management:

- Has the interim financial information been prepared in conformity with the applicable financial reporting framework consistently applied?
- Are there any unusual or complex situations potentially affecting interim financial information? (See AU Illustration 9.)
- Have any significant transactions occurred or been recorded in the last several days of the interim period?
- Were uncorrected misstatements identified during the previous audit and interim review subsequently recorded? If so, when, and what were the final amounts of the adjustments?
- Were any issues identified while performing review procedures?
- Are there any subsequent events that could have a material effect on interim financial information?
- Does management know about any actual or suspected fraud involving management, employees who have significant roles in internal controls, or anyone else in a position to commit fraud that would materially affect the financial information?
- Does management know about any actual or suspected fraud alleged by anyone including employees, former employees, analysts, regulators, or short sellers?
- Are there any significant journal entries and other adjustments?
- Are there any communications from regulatory agencies?

- Are there any significant deficiencies, including material weaknesses, in internal control relating to the preparation of both annual and interim financial information?

The accountant should also read the following:

- Available minutes of meetings of stockholders, directors, and appropriate committees. The accountant should ask about issues discussed at meetings for which minutes are not available in order to identify issues that might affect interim financial information.
- The interim financial information to consider whether it conforms to the applicable financial reporting framework, based on the results of review procedures and other information that comes to the accountant's attention.
- Other information in documents containing the interim financial information, to consider whether the information or the manner of presentation is materially inconsistent with the interim financial information.

The accountant should also perform the following procedures:

- Obtain reports from other accountants engaged to perform a review of the interim financial information of significant components of the reporting entity, its subsidiaries, or its other investees. If reports have not been issued, make inquiries of those accountants.

NOTE: *The accountant may also find the guidance in Section 543,* Part of the Audit Performed by Other Independent Auditors, *helpful.*

- Obtain evidence that the interim financial information agrees or reconciles with the accounting records. The accountant should consider asking management about the reliability of the records to which the interim information is compared or reconciled.

INQUIRIES CONCERNING LITIGATION, CLAIMS, AND ASSESSMENTS

In a review, the accountant is ordinarily not required to send an inquiry letter to the entity's lawyer about litigation, claims, or assessments. However, it would be appropriate for the accountant to ask legal counsel about any specific matters that come to the accountant's attention that lead him or her to question whether there is a departure from the applicable financial reporting framework related to litigation, claims, or assessments.

INQUIRIES CONCERNING GOING CONCERN ISSUES

Although a review is not designed to identify conditions or events indicating substantial doubt about the entity's ability to continue as a going concern, such conditions may already exist, or the accountant may become aware of them while performing the review. In either case, the auditor should ask management about its plans for dealing with the adverse effects of conditions and events and consider whether these matters are adequately disclosed in the interim financial information.

EXTENSION OF INTERIM REVIEW PROCEDURES

During a review, an accountant may become aware of information that leads him or her to believe that the interim financial information may not be in conformity with the applicable financial reporting framework in all material respects. In this case, the accountant should make additional inquiries or perform other appropriate procedures to provide a basis for communicating whether he or she is aware of any material modifications that should be made to the interim information.

NOTE: For example, if an accountant questions whether a significant sales transaction is recorded in conformity with the applicable financial reporting framework, the accountant may perform procedures to resolve the question such as discussing the terms of the transaction with senior accounting and marketing personnel and/or reading the sales contract.

TIMING OF REVIEW PROCEDURES AND COORDINATION WITH THE AUDIT

Many review procedures can be performed before or at the same time that the entity is preparing interim financial information. Early performance of certain review procedures allows for early identification and consideration of significant accounting matters. Also, since the accountant performing the review is usually engaged to perform the year-end audit, the accountant may perform certain auditing procedures, such as reading the minutes of board of directors' meetings, concurrently with the interim review.

MANAGEMENT REPRESENTATION LETTER

The accountant should obtain written representations from management for all interim financial information presented and for all periods covered by the review. According to AU 722.24, specific representations should cover the following:

Interim Financial Information

1. Management's acknowledgment of its responsibility for the fair presentation of the interim financial information in conformity with the applicable financial reporting framework
2. Management's belief that the interim financial information has been prepared and presented in conformity with the applicable financial reporting framework applicable to interim financial information

Internal Control

3. Management's acknowledgment of its responsibility to establish and maintain controls that are sufficient to provide a reasonable basis for the preparation of reliable interim financial information in accordance with the applicable financial reporting framework
4. Disclosure of all significant deficiencies, including material weaknesses, in the design or operation of internal controls as it relates to the preparation of both annual and interim financial information
5. Acknowledgment of management's responsibility for the design and implementation of programs and controls to prevent and detect fraud
6. Knowledge of fraud or suspected fraud affecting the entity involving (a) management, (b) employees who have significant roles in internal control, or (c) others where fraud could have a material effect on the interim financial information
7. Knowledge of any allegations of fraud or suspected fraud affecting the entity received in communications from employees, former employees, analysts, regulators, short sellers, or others

Completeness of Information

8. Availability of all financial records and related data

9. Completeness and availability of all minutes of meetings of stockholders, directors, and committees of directors or summaries of actions of recent meetings for which minutes have not yet been prepared
10. Communications with regulatory agencies concerning noncompliance with or deficiencies in financial reporting practices
11. Absence of unrecorded transactions

Recognition, Measurement, and Disclosure

12. Management's belief that the effects of any unrecorded financial statement misstatements aggregated by the accountant during the current review engagement and pertaining to the interim period(s) in the current year are immaterial, both individually and in the aggregate, to the interim financial information as a whole (a summary of such items should be included in or attached to the letter)
13. Plans or intentions that may materially affect the carrying value or classification of assets or liabilities
14. Information concerning related-party transactions and amounts receivable from or payable to related parties
15. Guarantees, whether written or oral, under which the entity is contingently liable
16. Significant estimates and material concentrations known to management that are required to be disclosed in accordance with the AICPA's Statement of Position 94-6, *Disclosure of Certain Significant Risks and Uncertainties*
17. Violations or possible violations of laws or regulations whose effects should be considered for disclosure in the interim financial information or as a basis for recording a loss contingency
18. Unasserted claims or assessments that are probable of assertion and must be disclosed in accordance with Financial Accounting Standards Board (FASB) Statement of Financial Accounting Standards 5, *Accounting for Contingencies*
19. Other liabilities or gain or loss contingencies that are required to be accrued or disclosed by FASB Statement 5
20. Satisfactory title to all owned assets, liens or encumbrances on such assets, and assets pledged as collateral
21. Compliance with aspects of contractual agreements that may affect the interim financial information

Subsequent Events

22. Information concerning subsequent events

The representation letter should be tailored to include additional representations specific to the entity's business or industry. See the "Illustrations" section of this chapter for examples of representation letters.

EVALUATING THE RESULTS OF INTERIM REVIEW PROCEDURES

During a review, the accountant may become aware of likely misstatements and should accumulate such misstatements for further evaluation. The account should evaluate misstatements individually and in the aggregate to determine whether a material modification to the interim financial statements is necessary for it to conform to the applicable financial reporting framework. The accountant should use professional judgment in evaluating the materiality of uncorrected likely misstatements. When evaluating the materiality of uncorrected misstatements, the accountant should consider:

- The nature, cause, and amount of misstatements
- When the misstatement occurred (prior year or interim periods of the current year)
- Materiality judgments made in the prior or current year annual audit
- The potential effect of the misstatements on future interim or annual periods

When evaluating whether uncorrected likely misstatements, individually or in the aggregate, are material, the accountant should also consider:

- Whether it is appropriate to offset a misstatement of an estimated item with a misstatement of an item that can be precisely measured
- That accumulating immaterial misstatements in the balance sheet may contribute to material misstatements in the future

A review is incomplete, and a review report cannot be issued if the accountant is not able to:

- Perform procedures necessary for a review engagement
- Obtain required written representations from management

In this case, the accountant should communicate that information, following the guidance in "Fundamental Requirements: Communication with Management and Audit Committees."

DOCUMENTATION

The accountant should prepare documentation for the review engagement. The form and content of such documentation should be designed to meet the particular engagement's circumstances. The accountant should use professional judgment when evaluating the quantity, type, and content of the documentation. However, such documentation should:

1. Include any significant findings or issues, such as indications that the interim financial information is materially misstated
2. Include any actions taken to address these findings
3. Include the basis for final conclusions reached
4. Enable engagement team members with supervision and review responsibilities to understand the nature, timing, extent, and results of the review procedures performed
5. Identify the engagement team members who performed and reviewed the work
6. Identify the evidence obtained to support the conclusion that the interim financial information reviewed agreed or reconciled with accounting records

FUNDAMENTAL REQUIREMENTS: COMMUNICATION WITH AUDIT COMMITTEES

REQUIRED SAS 61 COMMUNICATIONS

The accountant should determine whether any of the matters described in Section 380, *The Auditor's Communication with Those Charged with Governance*, as they relate to interim financial information, have been identified. (Examples of such matters include the process used by management for determining particularly sensitive accounting estimates or changes in significant accounting policies affecting the interim financial information. SAS

100 states that the presentation to the audit committee should be similar to the presentation of uncorrected misstatements in the management representation letter.) If so, the accountant should communicate such matters to the audit committee or be satisfied, through discussions with the audit committee, that management has communicated these matters to the committee.

Since the objective of a review is significantly different from that of an audit, any discussion about the quality of an entity's accounting principles for interim financial information would generally be limited to the impact of significant events, transactions, and changes in accounting estimates considered by the accountant when conducting the review. Interim review procedures do not provide assurance that the accountant will become aware of all matters affecting the accountant's judgment that would be identified as a result of an audit.

REPORTABLE CONDITIONS

If the accountant becomes aware of matters relating to internal control over financial reporting that might be of interest to the audit committee, he or she should communicate those matters to the audit committee (see Section 325, *Communicating Internal Control Related Matters Identified in an Audit*).

FUNDAMENTAL REQUIREMENTS: COMMUNICATION WITH MANAGEMENT AND AUDIT COMMITTEES

COMMUNICATIONS TO MANAGEMENT

The accountant should communicate with management as soon as practicable, if he or she believes that material modification should be made to the interim financial information for it to conform with the applicable financial reporting framework, or that the entity issued the interim financial information before completion of the review, in those circumstances in which a review is required.

LACK OF APPROPRIATE MANAGEMENT RESPONSE

The accountant should inform the audit committee or others with equivalent authority and responsibility of these matters as soon as practicable if management does not respond appropriately to his or her communication within a reasonable period of time.

ORAL COMMUNICATION

If the accountant identifies issues that need to be communicated to those charged with governance, this information should at least be sent to the chair of the audit committee on a sufficiently timely basis to ensure that appropriate action can be taken. The accountant should document communications with the audit committee if that communication is oral.

LACK OF APPROPRIATE AUDIT COMMITTEE RESPONSE

The accountant should decide whether to resign from the engagement related to interim financial information and whether to remain as the auditor of the entity's financial statements if the audit committee does not respond appropriately to his or her communication within a reasonable period of time. The accountant may wish to consult with his or her attorney when making these decisions.

FRAUD OR ILLEGAL ACTS

If the accountant becomes aware of fraud, the accountant should communicate this to management. If the fraud involves senior management, or if it materially misstates the financial statements, then the accountant should communicate directly with the audit committees. (See Section 316, *Consideration of Fraud in a Financial Statement Audit*.)

If the accountant becomes aware of a possible illegal act, and the effect is not inconsequential, the accountant should assure himself or herself that the audit committee is informed.

SIGNIFICANT DEFICIENCIES OR MATERIAL WEAKNESSES

If the accountant becomes aware of significant deficiencies or material weaknesses in internal control relating to the preparation of annual and interim financial information, then this should be communicated to management and the audit committee.

FUNDAMENTAL REQUIREMENTS: ACCOUNTANT'S REPORT

DESCRIPTION OF INTERIM FINANCIAL INFORMATION

Each page of the interim financial information should be marked as "unaudited."

DATE OF REPORT AND ADDRESSEE

The report should be dated as of the date of completion of the review procedures.

NOTE: SAS 100 does not provide guidance on addressing the report. As discussed in Section 508, "Reports on Audited Financial Statements," under the Sarbanes–Oxley Act, the audit committee is responsible for appointment and oversight of the external auditor. Therefore, interim review reports, as well as year-end audit reports, should be addressed to the audit committee. It is acceptable to also address the report to the stockholders and boards of directors.

FORM OF ACCOUNTANT'S REVIEW REPORT

The accountant is not required to issue a report on a review of interim financial information; however, if the accountant does so, then according to AU 722.37 each page of the report should be clearly marked as unaudited, and the report should consist of the following:

1. A title that includes the word *independent*
2. Statements that:
   a. The interim financial information identified in the financial statements was reviewed.
   b. The financial information is the responsibility of the entity's management.
   c. The review of interim financial information was conducted in accordance with standards established by the AICPA.
3. A description of the procedures for a review of interim financial information
4. Statements that:
   a. A review of interim financial information is substantially less in scope than an audit conducted in accordance with auditing standards generally accepted in the United States, the objective of which is an expression of opinion regarding the fi-

nancial information taken as a whole, and accordingly, no such opinion is expressed.
b. Whether the accountant is aware of any material modifications that should be made to the accompanying financial information so that it conforms to the applicable financial reporting framework. (This should include an identification of the country of origin of the accounting principles used.)

5. The manual or printed signature of the accountant's firm
6. The date of the review report

REFERENCE TO REPORT OF ANOTHER ACCOUNTANT

When he or she reports on the review of interim financial information, the accountant may use and make reference to the review reports of other accountants (see "Illustrations").

MODIFICATION OF THE REVIEW REPORT

A departure from the applicable financial reporting framework that has a material effect on the interim financial information requires the accountant to modify the review report; this includes both inadequate disclosure and changes in accounting principle that are not in conformity with the applicable financial reporting framework. The modified report should describe the nature of the departure and, if practicable, should state the effects of the departure on the interim financial information (see "Illustrations").

If there is substantial doubt about the entity's ability to continue as a going concern or a lack of consistency in the application of accounting principles affecting the interim financial information, the accountant does not have to add an additional paragraph in the report, provided that the interim financial information discloses the issue.

If there is inadequate disclosure within the interim financial information, then the accountant should include the necessary information in the report (see "Illustrations").

If the auditor's report for the prior year-end indicated the existence of substantial doubt about the entity's ability to continue as a going concern, the supporting conditions continue to exist, and there is adequate disclosure of these conditions in the interim financial information, there is no need to modify the accountant's report. However, the accountant can emphasize the matter in the report (see "Illustrations").

Conversely, if the auditor's report for the prior year did *not* indicate the existence of substantial doubt about the entity's ability to continue as a going concern, but conditions now indicate such an issue, and there is adequate disclosure of the situation in the interim financial information, then the accountant is not required to issue a modified report. However, the accountant can emphasize the matter in the report (see "Illustrations").

CLIENT REPRESENTATION ABOUT ACCOUNTANT'S REVIEW

If a client states in a written communication containing the reviewed interim financial information that the accountant has reviewed the interim financial information, the accountant should advise the entity that his or her report must also be included.

If the client does not agree to include the report, the accountant should:

- Request that neither his or her name nor reference to him or her be associated with the interim financial information
- If the client does not comply, notify the client that the accountant does not permit either the use of his or her name or the reference

- Communicate the client's noncompliance with the request to those charged with governance
- Recommend that the client consult with legal counsel about applicable laws and regulations, if appropriate
- Consider other appropriate actions

NOTE: *In these circumstances, it is prudent for the accountant to consult with his or her lawyer.*

If the accountant cannot complete his or her review and the client has represented that the accountant has reviewed interim financial information in a document filed with a regulatory agency or issued to stockholders or third parties, the accountant cannot issue the report and must notify the appropriate level of management as soon as practicable, and also consider following the steps noted immediately prior to this paragraph.

FUNDAMENTAL REQUIREMENTS: INTERIM FINANCIAL INFORMATION ACCOMPANYING AUDITED FINANCIAL STATEMENTS

PRESENTATION OF INTERIM FINANCIAL INFORMATION

Interim financial information ordinarily is presented as supplementary information outside the audited financial statements. Each page of the interim financial information should be clearly marked "unaudited." If this information is presented in a note to the audited financial statements, it should be clearly marked "unaudited."

THE AUDITOR'S REPORT

Because interim financial information is not audited and is not required to be fairly stated in conformity with the applicable financial reporting framework, the auditor need not modify the audit report for the review of interim financial information accompanying audited financial statements. However, the auditor should modify his or her report in the following circumstances:

1. The interim financial information in a note to the financial statements is not marked as unaudited, in which case the auditor should disclaim an opinion on the interim financial information.
2. The interim financial information is not presented in conformity with the applicable financial reporting framework. The audit report does not need to be modified if the separate review report is presented with the information and addresses this issue.

INTERPRETATIONS

There are no interpretations for this section.

TECHNIQUES FOR APPLICATION

The following aspects of conducting a review of interim financial information are discussed below:

1. Engagement letter
2. Analytical procedures
3. Extent of procedures
4. Subsequent discovery of facts existing at the date of report
5. Other information
6. Successor auditors
7. Additional guidance

ENGAGEMENT LETTER

It is prudent for the accountant to confirm the nature and scope of his or her engagement in a letter to the client. The engagement letter includes the following matters:

1. The objective of the review is to provide the accountant with a basis for communicating whether he or she is aware of any material modifications that should be made to the interim financial information for it to conform to the applicable financial reporting framework.
2. The review includes obtaining sufficient knowledge of the entity's business and its internal control as it relates to the preparation of both annual and interim financial information to:
    a. Identify the types of potential material misstatements in the interim financial information and consider the likelihood of their occurrence.
    b. Select the inquiries and analytical procedures that will provide the accountant with a basis for communicating whether the accountant is aware of any material modifications that should be made to the interim financial information for it to conform to the applicable financial reporting framework.
3. The review engagement is limited in these areas:
    a. It does not provide a basis for expressing an opinion about whether the financial information is presented fairly, in all material respects, in conformity with the applicable financial reporting framework.
    b. It does not provide assurance that the accountant will become aware of all significant matters that would be identified in an audit.
    c. It does not provide assurance on internal control or to identify significant deficiencies and material weaknesses in internal control; however, the accountant is responsible for communicating to management and those charged with governance any significant deficiencies or material weaknesses in internal control that the accountant identified.
4. Management is responsible for:
    a. The interim financial information
    b. Establishing and maintaining effective internal control over financial reporting
    c. Compliance with laws and regulations
    d. Providing all financial records and related information to the accountant
    e. Providing a written representation letter to the accountant at the end of the engagement
    f. Adjusting the interim information to correct material misstatements

g. Affirming in the management representation letter that any uncorrected misstatements are immaterial, both individually and in the aggregate to the interim financial statements as a whole

5. The accountant is responsible for conducting the review in accordance with standards established by the AICPA. A review of interim financial information consists principally of performing analytical procedures and making inquiries of persons responsible for financial and accounting matters. It is substantially less in scope than an audit conducted in accordance with auditing standards generally accepted in the United States of America, the objective of which is the expression of an opinion regarding the financial information taken as a whole. Accordingly, the accountant will not express an opinion on the interim financial information.
6. The expected form of communication is a description of the expected form of the accountant's communication upon completion of the engagement, and a statement that if the entity states in any form of communication containing the interim financial information that the information has been reviewed by the accountant or makes other reference to the accountant's association, that the accountant's review report will be included in the document.

ANALYTICAL PROCEDURES

In applying analytical procedures, it is prudent for the accountant to develop a permanent file similar to the one illustrated in Section 329, *Analytical Procedures*. The file contains the following:

1. Comparative financial information:

    a. Current quarter and preceding quarters
    b. Current quarter and year-to-date and the same periods of preceding years
    c. Current quarter and year-to-date and budgets for similar periods

2. Analysis of relationships. Computation of relevant ratios (gross profit, net income, current, etc.) and comparison of these ratios with similar ratios of preceding years.
3. Sources of information for analytical procedures:

    a. Financial information for comparable prior periods giving consideration to known changes
    b. Anticipated results; for example, budgets or forecasts including extrapolations from interim or annual data
    c. Relationships among elements of financial information within the period
    d. Information regarding the industry in which the client operates; for example, gross margin data
    e. Relationships of financial information with relevant nonfinancial information; for example, the relationship of sales to interest rates in the housing industry

    NOTE: In applying analytical procedures, it is prudent for the accountant to follow the guidance of Section 329, Analytical Procedures.

4. Comparisons of disaggregated revenue data and other required procedures.

EXTENT OF PROCEDURES

The extent of procedures is influenced by significant changes in the client's accounting practices or in the nature or volume of its business activities. Examples of these changes are provided in AU Illustration 9.

NOTE: *Interim financial information requires more estimates than annual financial statements. The accountant, therefore, might wish to refer to the guidance of Section 342,* Auditing Accounting Estimates.

SUBSEQUENT DISCOVERY OF FACTS EXISTING AT THE DATE OF REPORT

If, subsequent to the date of the report, the accountant becomes aware of facts that existed at the date of the report that might have affected the report had he or she been aware of those facts, he or she is well-advised to refer to Section 561, *Subsequent Discovery of Facts Existing at the Date of the Auditor's Report*, for guidance.

OTHER INFORMATION

If interim financial information and the accountant's review report on such information appears in a document containing other information, the accountant might wish to refer to the guidance in Section 550, *Other Information in Documents Containing Audited Financial Statements*. For example, the SEC requires Form 10-Q to include a Management's Discussion and Analysis (MD&A) in addition to quarterly financial statements. The accountant might wish to read the MD&A and consider whether it is consistent with the accountant's knowledge obtained in reviewing the quarterly data.

SUCCESSOR AUDITORS

Successor auditors must complete inquiries of the predecessor auditor as required under Section 315, *Communications between Predecessor and Successor Auditors*, before accepting an engagement to perform an initial review of interim information.

ADDITONAL GUIDANCE

When performing reviews, the accountant may find that audit guidance for relevant sections is useful. Specifically, the accountant may wish to consider:

- Section 329, *Analytical Procedures*, when performing analytical procedures. The accountant should keep in mind that expectations developed during a review of interim information would ordinarily be less precise than those developed in an audit. In addition, the accountant is not required to corroborate management's answers with other evidence when performing a review, but should instead consider whether the response is reasonable and consistent with the results of other review procedures and the accountant's knowledge of the entity's business and its internal control.
- Section 380, *The Auditor's Communication with Those Charged with Governance*, when making communications to the audit committee.

AU ILLUSTRATIONS

The following illustrations are presented:

1. Accountant's Standard Review Report
2. Accountant's Standard Review Report on Comparative Interim Financial Information (Condensed Information Included)
3. Accountant's Review Report Referring to the Review Report of Another Accountant
4. Accountant's Review Report, Departure from GAAP
5. Accountant's Review Report, Inadequate Disclosure
6. Additional Going Concern Paragraph When:
    a. A Going Concern Paragraph Was Included in the Prior Year's Audit Report and the Conditions Continue to Exist
    b. A Going Concern Paragraph Was *Not* Included in the Prior Year's Audit Report and Conditions Exist That Cause Substantial Doubt
7. Management Representation Letters for a Review of Interim Financial Information
    a. Short Form
    b. Long Form
8. Analytical Procedures to Consider Performing When Conducting a Review
9. Unusual or Complex Situations to Consider in a Review.

Illustrations 1–9 are reproduced or adapted from Section 722, *Interim Financial Information*.

Following these illustrations are the exhibits and illustrations from AU-C 930.

ILLUSTRATION 1. ACCOUNTANT'S STANDARD REVIEW REPORT

Report of Independent Registered Public Accounting Firm

We have reviewed the accompanying [*describe the statements or information reviewed*] of DMG Company and consolidated subsidiaries as of September 30, 20X1, and for the three-month and nine-month periods then ended. This interim financial information is the responsibility of the company's management.

We conducted our review in accordance with the standards of the American Institute of Certified Public Accountants. A review of interim financial information consists principally of applying analytical procedures to financial data and making inquiries of persons responsible for financial and accounting matters. It is substantially less in scope than an audit conducted in accordance with auditing standards generally accepted in the United States, the objective of which is the expression of an opinion regarding the financial information taken as a whole. Accordingly, we do not express such an opinion.

Based on our review, we are not aware of any material modifications that should be made to the accompanying financial information for it to be in conformity with [*identify the applicable financial reporting framework; for example accounting principles generally accepted in the United States of America*]

[*Signature*]

[*Date*]

ILLUSTRATION 2. ACCOUNTANT'S STANDARD REVIEW REPORT ON COMPARATIVE INTERIM FINANCIAL INFORMATION (CONDENSED INFORMATION INCLUDED)

Report of Independent Registered Public Accounting Firm

We have reviewed the condensed consolidated balance sheet of DMG Company and subsidiaries as of March 31, 20X1, and the related condensed consolidated statements of income and cash flows for the three-month periods ended March 31, 20X1 and 20X0. This condensed financial information is the responsibility of the company's management.

We conducted our reviews in accordance with the standards of the American Institute of Certified Public Accountants. A review of interim financial information consists principally of applying analytical procedures and making inquiries of persons responsible for financial and accounting matters. It is substantially less in scope than an audit conducted in accordance with auditing standards generally accepted in the United States, the objective of which is the expression of an opinion regarding the financial information taken as a whole. Accordingly, we do not express such an opinion.

Based on our reviews, we are not aware of any material modifications that should be made to the condensed financial information referred to above for it to be in conformity with [*identify the applicable financial reporting framework; for example, accounting principles generally accepted in the United States of America*].

We have previously audited, in accordance with auditing standards generally accepted in the United States of America, the consolidated balance sheet of DMG Company and subsidiaries as of December 31, 20X0, and the related consolidated statements of income, retained earnings, and cash flows for the year then ended (not presented herein); and in our report dated February 15, 20X1, we expressed an unqualified opinion on those consolidated financial statements. In our opinion, the information set forth in the accompanying condensed consolidated balance sheet as of December 31, 20X0, is fairly stated, in all material respects, in relation to the consolidated balance sheet from which it has been derived.

[*Signature*]

[*Date*]

> **ILLUSTRATION 3. ACCOUNTANT'S REVIEW REPORT REFERRING TO THE REVIEW REPORT OF ANOTHER ACCOUNTANT**

Report of Independent Registered Public Accounting Firm

We have reviewed the accompanying [*describe the statements or information reviewed*] of DMG Company and consolidated subsidiaries as of September 30, 20X1, and for the three-month and nine-month periods then ended. This interim financial information is the responsibility of the company's management.

We were furnished with the report of other accountants on their review of the interim financial information of Basic Subsidiary, whose total assets as of September 30, 20X1, and whose revenues for the three-month and nine-month periods then ended, constituted 10%, 12%, and 15%, respectively, of the related consolidated totals.

We conducted our reviews in accordance with the standards established by the American Institute of Certified Public Accountants. A review of interim financial information consists principally of applying analytical procedures to financial data and making inquiries of persons responsible for financial and accounting matters. It is substantially less in scope than an audit conducted in accordance with auditing standards generally accepted in the United States, the objective of which is the expression of an opinion regarding the financial information taken as a whole. Accordingly, we do not express such an opinion.

Based on our review and the report of other accountants, we are not aware of any material modifications that should be made to the accompanying interim financial information for it to be in conformity with [*identify the applicable financial reporting framework; for example, accounting principles generally accepted in the United States of America*].

[*Signature*]

[*Date*]

ILLUSTRATION 4. ACCOUNTANT'S REVIEW REPORT, DEPARTURE FROM GAAP

[*Standard title, first and second paragraphs*]

Based on information furnished to us by management, we believe that the company has excluded from property and debt in the accompanying balance sheet certain lease obligations that we believe should be capitalized to conform with [identify the applicable financial reporting framework; for example, accounting principles generally accepted in the United States of America]. This information indicates that if these lease obligations were capitalized at September 30, 20X1, property would be increased by $_____, long-term debt by $_____, and net income and earnings per share would be increased [decreased] by $_____, $_____, $_____, and $_____, respectively, for the _____ and _____ periods then ended.

Based on our review, with the exception of the matter(s) described in the preceding paragraph(s), we are not aware of any material modifications that should be made to the accompanying interim financial statements [information] for them [it] to be in conformity with [identify the applicable financial reporting framework; for example, accounting principles generally accepted in the United States of America].

[*Signature*]

[*Date*]

ILLUSTRATION 5. ACCOUNTANT'S REVIEW REPORT, INADEQUATE DISCLOSURE

[*Standard title, first and second paragraphs*]

Management has informed us that the company is presently defending a claim regarding [*describe the nature of the loss contingency*], and that the extent of the company's liability, if any, and the effect on the accompanying information is not determinable at this time. The information fails to disclose these matters, which we believe are required to be disclosed in conformity with [*identify the applicable financial reporting framework; for example, accounting principles generally accepted in the United States of America*].

Based on our review, with the exception of the matter(s) described in the preceding paragraph(s), we are not aware of any material modifications that should be made to the accompanying interim financial information for it to be in conformity with [*identify the applicable financial reporting framework; for example, accounting principles generally accepted in the United States of America*].

[*Signature*]

[*Date*]

ILLUSTRATION 6A. ADDITIONAL GOING CONCERN PARAGRAPH WHEN A GOING CONCERN PARAGRAPH WAS INCLUDED IN PRIOR YEAR'S AUDIT REPORT AND THE CONDITIONS CONTINUE TO EXIST

Note 4 of the Company's audited financial statements as of December 31, 20X1, and for the year then ended discloses that the Company was unable to renew its line of credit or obtain alternative financing at December 31, 20X1. Our auditor's report on those financial statements includes an explanatory paragraph referring to the matters in Note 4 of those financial statements and indicating that these matters raised substantial doubt about the Company's ability to continue as a going concern. As indicated in Note 3 of the Company's unaudited interim financial information as of March 31, 20X2, and for the three months then ended, the Company was still unable to renew its line of credit or obtain alternative financing as of March 31, 20X2. The accompanying interim financial information does not include any adjustments that might result from the outcomes of this uncertainty.

> **ILLUSTRATION 6B. ADDITIONAL GOING CONCERN PARAGRAPH WHEN A GOING CONCERN PARAGRAPH WAS NOT INCLUDED IN PRIOR YEAR'S AUDIT REPORT AND THE CONDITIONS CONTINUE TO EXIST**

As indicated in Note 3, certain conditions indicate that the Company may be unable to continue as a going concern. The accompanying interim financial information does not include any adjustments that might result from the outcome of this uncertainty.

> **ILLUSTRATION 7A. MANAGEMENT REPRESENTATION LETTER FOR A REVIEW OF INTERIM FINANCIAL INFORMATION (SHORT FORM)**

NOTE: *This representation letter is used with the representation letter for the prior year audit. Management confirms the audit representations as they apply to the interim financial information, and makes any needed additional representations for the interim financial information.*

[*Date*]

To [*Independent Accountant*]

We are providing this letter in connection with your review of the [*identification of interim financial information*] of [*name of entity*] as of [*dates*] and for the [*periods*] for the purpose of determining whether any material modifications should be made to the [*consolidated*] interim financial information for it to conform with [*identify the applicable financial reporting framework (for example, accounting principles generally accepted in the United States of America), including, if appropriate, an indication as to the appropriate form and content of interim financial information (for example, Article 10 of SEC Regulation S-X)*]. We confirm that we are responsible for the fair presentation of the [*consolidated*] interim financial information in conformity with [*identify the applicable financial reporting framework; for example, accounting principles generally accepted in the United States of America*] and that we are responsible for establishing and maintaining controls that are sufficient to provide a reasonable basis for the preparation of reliable interim financial information in accordance with [*identify the applicable financial reporting framework; for example, accounting principles generally accepted in the United States of America*].

Certain representations in this letter are described as being limited to matters that are material. Items are considered material, regardless of size, if they involve an omission or misstatement of accounting information that, in light of surrounding circumstances, makes it probable that the judgment of a reasonable person relying on the information would be changed or influenced by the omission or misstatement.

We confirm, to the best of our knowledge and belief, [*as of (date of accountant's report or the completion of the review)*], the following representations made to you during your review:

1. The interim financial information referred to above has been prepared and presented in conformity with [*identify the applicable financial reporting framework; for example, generally accepted accounting principles*] applicable to interim financial information.
2. We have made available to you:

    a. All financial records and related data
    b. All minutes of the meetings of stockholders, directors, and committees of directors, or summaries of actions of recent meetings for which minutes have not yet been prepared; all significant board and committee actions are included in the summaries

3. We believe that the effects of any uncorrected financial statement misstatements aggregated by you during the current review engagement and pertaining to the interim period(s) in the current

year, as summarized in the accompanying schedule, are immaterial, both individually and in the aggregate, to the interim financial information taken as a whole.[1]
4. There are no significant deficiencies or material weaknesses in the design or operation of internal control as it relates to the preparation of both annual and interim financial information.
5. We acknowledge our responsibility for the design and implementations of programs and controls to prevent and detect fraud.
6. We have no knowledge of any fraud or suspected fraud affecting the company involving:

   a. Management;
   b. Employees who have significant roles in internal control; or
   c. Others where the fraud could have a material effect on the interim financial information

7. We have no knowledge of any allegations of fraud or suspected fraud affecting the company received in communications from employees, former employees, analysts, regulators, short sellers, or others.
8. We have reviewed our representation letter to you dated [*date of representation letter relating to most recent audit*] with respect to the audited financial statements for the year ended [*prior year-end date*]. We believe that representations A, B, and C, within that representation letter do not apply to the interim financial information referred to above. We now confirm those representations 1 through X, as they apply to the interim financial information referred to above, and incorporate them herein, with the following changes:

   [*Indicate any changes*]

9. [*Add any representations related to new accounting or auditing standards that are being implemented for the first time.*]

To the best of our knowledge and belief, no events have occurred subsequent to the balance sheet date and through the date of this letter that would require adjustment to or disclosure in the aforementioned interim financial information.

_____
[*Name of Chief Executive Officer and Title*]

_____
[*Name of Chief Financial Officer and Title*]

_____
[*Name of Chief Accounting Officer and Title*]

ILLUSTRATION 7B. MANAGEMENT REPRESENTATION LETTER FOR A REVIEW OF INTERIM FINANCIAL INFORMATION (LONG FORM)

NOTE: This representation letter is similar in detail to the management representation letter used for the audit of the financial statements of the prior year and thus need not refer to the written management representations received in the most recent audit.

[*Date*]

To [*Independent Accountant*]

We are providing this letter in connection with your review of the [*identification of interim financial information (statements)*] of [*name of entity*] as of [*dates*] and for the [*periods*] for the purpose of determining whether any material modifications should be made to the [*consolidated*] interim financial information for it to conform to [*identify the applicable financial reporting

---

[1] *If a summary of uncorrected misstatements is unnecessary because no uncorrected misstatements were identified, this representation should be eliminated.*

framework; *(for example, accounting principles generally accepted in the United States of America), including, if appropriate, an indication as to the appropriate form and content of interim financial information (for example, Article 10 of Regulation S-X)]*. We confirm that we are responsible for the fair presentation of the [*consolidated*] interim financial information in conformity with [*identify the applicable financial reporting framework; for example, accounting principles generally accepted in the United States of America*] and that we are responsible for establishing and maintaining controls that are sufficient to provide a reasonable basis for the preparation of reliable interim financial information in accordance with [*identify the applicable financial reporting framework; for example, generally accepted accounting principles*].

Certain representations in this letter are described as being limited to matters that are material. Items are considered material, regardless of size, if they involve an omission or misstatement of accounting information that, in light of surrounding circumstances, makes it probable that the judgment of a reasonable person relying on the information would be changed or influenced by the omission or misstatement.

We confirm, to the best of our knowledge and belief, [*as of (date of accountant's report or the completion of the review)*], the following representations made to you during your review:

1. The interim financial information referred to above has been prepared and presented in conformity with [*identify the applicable financial reporting framework; for example, generally accepted accounting principles*] applicable to interim financial information.
2. We have made available to you:
   a. All financial records and related data
   b. All minutes of the meetings of stockholders, directors, and committees of directors, or summaries of actions of recent meetings for which minutes have not yet been prepared; all significant board and committee actions are included in the summaries
3. There have been no communications from regulatory agencies concerning noncompliance with or deficiencies in financial reporting practices.
4. There are no material transactions that have not been properly recorded in the accounting records underlying the interim financial information.
5. We believe that the effects of any uncorrected financial statement misstatements aggregated by you during the current review engagement and pertaining to the interim period(s) in the current year, as summarized in the accompanying schedule, are immaterial, both individually and in the aggregate, to the interim financial information taken as a whole.[2]
6. There are no significant deficiencies or material weaknesses in the design or operation of internal controls as they relate to the preparation of both annual and interim financial information.
7. We acknowledge our responsibility for the design and implementation of programs and controls to prevent and detect fraud.
8. We have no knowledge of any fraud or suspected fraud affecting the company involving:
   a. Management;
   b. Employees who have significant roles in internal control; or
   c. Others where the fraud could have a material effect on the interim financial information.
9. We have no knowledge of any allegations of fraud or suspected fraud affecting the company in communications from employees, former employees, analysts, regulators, short sellers, or others.
10. The company has no plans or intentions that may materially affect the carrying value or classification of assets and liabilities.
11. The following have been properly recorded or disclosed in the interim financial information:

---

[2] *If a summary of uncorrected misstatements is unnecessary because no uncorrected misstatements were identified, this representation should be eliminated.*

a. Related-party transactions, including sales, purchases, loans, transfers, leasing arrangements, and guarantees, and amounts receivable from or payable to related parties
   b. Guarantees, whether written or oral, under which the company is contingently liable
   c. Significant estimates and material concentrations known to management that are required to be disclosed in accordance with the AICPA's Statement of Position 94-6, *Disclosure of Certain Significant Risks and Uncertainties*. [*Significant estimates are estimates at the balance sheet date that could change materially within the next year. Concentrations refer to volumes of business, revenues, available sources of supply, or markets or geographic areas for which events could occur that would significantly disrupt normal finances within the next year.*]

12. There are no:

   a. Violations or possible violations of laws or regulations whose effects should be considered for disclosure in the interim financial information or as a basis for recording a loss contingency.
   b. Unasserted claims or assessments that are probable of assertion and must be disclosed in accordance with Financial Account Standards Board (FASB) Statement No. 5, *Accounting for Contingencies*.
   c. Other liabilities or gain or loss contingencies that are required to be accrued or disclosed by FASB Statement No. 5.

13. The company has satisfactory title to all owned assets, and there are no liens or encumbrances on such assets; nor has any asset been pledged as collateral.
14. The company has complied with all aspects of contractual agreements that would have a material effect on the interim financial information in the event of noncompliance.
15. [*Add additional representations that are unique to the entity's business or industry. See Section 333, Management Represenations.*]
16. [*Add any representations related to new accounting or auditing standards that are being implemented for the first time.*]

To the best of our knowledge and belief, no events have occurred subsequent to the balance sheet date and through the date of this letter that would require adjustment to or disclosure in the aforementioned interim financial information.

_____
[*Name of Chief Executive Officer and Title*]

_____
[*Name of Chief Financial Officer and Title*]

_____
[*Name of Chief Accounting Officer and Title*]

ILLUSTRATION 8. ANALYTICAL PROCEDURES TO CONSIDER PERFORMING WHEN CONDUCTING A REVIEW

Examples of analytical procedures an accountant may consider performing in a review of interim financial information include (reproduced with permission from AU 722.54):

- Comparing current interim financial information with anticipated results, such as budgets or forecasts (for example, comparing tax balances and the relationship between the provision for income taxes and pretax income in the current interim financial information with correspond-

ing information in (1) budgets, using expected rates, and (2) financial information for prior periods).³
- Comparing current interim financial information with relevant nonfinancial information.
- Comparing ratios and indicators for the current interim period with expectations based on prior periods, for example, performing gross profit analysis by product line and operating segment using elements of the current interim financial information and comparing the results with corresponding information for prior periods. Examples of key ratios and indicators are the current ratio, receivable turnover or days' sales outstanding, inventory turnover, depreciation to average fixed assets, debt to equity, gross profit percentage, net income percentage, and plant operating rates.
- Comparing ratios and indicators for the current interim period with those of entities in the same industry.
- Comparing relationships among elements in the current interim financial information with corresponding relationships in the interim financial information of prior periods, for example, expense by type as a percentage of sales, assets by type as a percentage of total assets, and percentage of change in sales to percentage of change in receivables.
- Comparing disaggregated data. The following are examples of how data may be disaggregated.
  - By period, for example, financial statement items disaggregated into quarterly, monthly, or weekly amounts.
  - By product line or operating segment.
  - By location, for example, subsidiary, division, or branch.

Analytical procedures may include such statistical techniques as trend analysis or regression analysis and may be performed manually or with the use of computer-assisted techniques.

ILLUSTRATION 9. UNUSUAL OR COMPLEX SITUATIONS TO CONSIDER IN A REVIEW OF INTERIM FINANCIAL INFORMATION

The following are examples, reproduced with permission from AU 722.55, of situations about which the accountant would ordinarily inquire of management:

- Business combinations
- New or complex revenue recognition methods
- Impairment of assets
- Disposal of a segment of a business
- Use of derivative instruments and hedging activities
- Sales and transfers that may call into question the classification of investments in securities, including management's intent and ability with respect to the remaining securities classified as held to maturity
- Computation of earnings per share in a complex capital structure
- Adoption of new stock compensation plans or changes to existing plans
- Restructuring charges taken in the current and prior quarters
- Significant, unusual, or infrequently occurring transactions
- Changes in litigation or contingencies
- Changes in major contracts with customers or suppliers

---

³ *The accountant should exercise caution when comparing and evaluating current interim financial information with budgets, forecasts, or other anticipated results because of the inherent lack of precision in estimating the future and susceptibility of such information to manipulation and misstatement by management to reflect desire interim results.*

- Application of new accounting principles
- Changes in accounting principles or the methods of applying them
- Trends and developments affecting accounting estimates,[4] such as allowances for bad debts and excess or obsolete inventories, provisions for warranties and employee benefits, and realization of unearned income and deferred charges
- Compliance with debt covenants
- Changes in related parties or significant new related-party transactions
- Material off-balance-sheet transactions, special-purpose entities, and other equity investments
- Unique terms for debt or capital stock that could affect classification

AU-C 930 ILLUSTRATIONS

ILLUSTRATIVE MANAGEMENT REPRESENTATION LETTERS FOR A REVIEW OF INTERIM FINANCIAL INFORMATION

The following management representation letters, which relate to a review of interim financial information, are presented for illustrative purposes only:

1. Short Form Representation Letter for a Review of Interim Financial Information
2. Detailed Representation Letter for a Review of Interim Financial Information

It is assumed in these illustrations that the applicable financial reporting framework is accounting principles generally accepted in the United States of America, that no conditions or events exist that might be indicative of the entity's possible inability to continue as a going concern, and that no exceptions exist to the requested written representations. If circumstances differ from these assumptions, the representations would need to be modified to reflect the actual circumstances.

ILLUSTRATION 1. SHORT FORM REPRESENTATION LETTER FOR A REVIEW OF INTERIM FINANCIAL INFORMATION

This representation letter is to be used in conjunction with the representation letter for the audit of the financial statements of the prior year. Management confirms the representations made in the representation letter for the audit of the financial statements of the prior year end, as they apply to the interim financial information, and makes additional representations that may be needed for the interim financial information.

[*Date*]

To [*Independent Auditor*]:

This representation letter is provided in connection with your review of the [*consolidated*] balance sheet as of June 30, 20X1 and the related [*consolidated*] statements of income, changes in equity, and cash flows for the six-month period then ended of ABC Company for the purpose of reporting whether any material modifications should be made to the [*consolidated*] interim financial information for it to be in accordance with accounting principles generally accepted in the United States of America (U.S. GAAP) [*including, if appropriate, an indication as to the appropriate form and content of interim financial information (for example, Article 10 of SEC Regulation S-X)*].

---

[4] *The accountant may wish to refer to the guidance in AU 342,* Audited Accounting Estimates.

We confirm that [, *to the best of our knowledge and belief, having made such inquiries as we considered necessary for the purpose of appropriately informing ourselves*] [*as of (date of auditor's review report),*]:

Interim Financial Information

1. We have fulfilled our responsibilities, as set out in the terms of the engagement letter dated [*insert date*] for the preparation and fair presentation of interim financial information in accordance with US GAAP; in particular the interim financial information is presented in accordance therewith.
2. We acknowledge our responsibility for the design, implementation, and maintenance of internal control relevant to the preparation and fair presentation of interim financial information that is free from material misstatement, whether due to fraud or error.
3. The interim financial information has been adjusted or includes disclosures for all events subsequent to the date of the interim financial information for which US GAAP requires adjustment or disclosure.
4. The effects of uncorrected misstatements are immaterial, both individually and in the aggregate, to the interim financial information as a whole. A list of the uncorrected misstatements is attached to the representation letter.

[*Any other matters that the auditor may consider appropriate*]

Information Provided

5. We have provided you with:

    - Access to all information of which we are aware that is relevant to the preparation and fair presentation of the interim financial information such as records, documentation, and other matters;
    - Minutes of the meetings of stockholders, directors, and committees of directors, or summaries of actions of recent meetings for which minutes have not yet been prepared;
    - Additional information that you have requested from us for the purpose of the review; and
    - Unrestricted access to persons within the entity of whom you determined it necessary to make inquiries.

6. We have disclosed to you all significant deficiencies or material weaknesses in the design or operation of internal control of which we are aware, as it relates to the preparation and fair presentation of both annual and interim financial information.
7. We have disclosed to you the results of our assessment of the risk that the interim financial information may be materially misstated as a result of fraud.
8. We have [*no knowledge of any*] [*disclosed to you all information of which we are aware in relation to*] fraud or suspected fraud that affects the entity and involves:

    - Management;
    - Employees who have significant roles in internal control; or
    - Others when the fraud could have a material effect on the interim financial information.

9. We have [*no knowledge of any*] [*disclosed to you all information in relation to*] allegations of fraud, or suspected fraud, affecting the entity's interim financial information communicated by employees, former employees, analysts, regulators, or others.
10. We have disclosed to you the identity of the entity's related parties and all the related-party relationships and transactions of which we are aware.

[*Any other matters that the auditor may consider necessary*]

11. We have reviewed our representation letter to you dated [*date of representation letter relating to most recent audit*] with respect to the audited consolidated financial statements as of and for the year ended [*prior year-end date*]. We believe that representations [*references to applicable representations*] within that representation letter do not apply to the interim financial infor-

mation referred to above. We now confirm those representations [*references to applicable representations*], as they apply to the interim financial information referred to above, and incorporate them herein, with the following changes:

[*Indicate any changes.*]

12. [*Add any representations related to new accounting or auditing standards that are being implemented for the first time.*]

[*Name of Chief Executive Officer and Title*]

[*Name of Chief Financial Officer and Title*]

[*Name of Chief Accounting Officer and Title*]

> **ILLUSTRATION 2. DETAILED REPRESENTATION LETTER FOR A REVIEW OF INTERIM FINANCIAL INFORMATION**

This representation letter is similar in detail to the management representation letter used for the audit of the financial statements of the prior year and, thus, need not refer to the written management representations received in the most recent audit.

[*Date*]

To [*Independent Auditor*]:

This representation letter is provided in connection with your review of the [*consolidated*] balance sheet as of June 30, 20X1 and the related [*consolidated*] statements of income, changes in equity, and cash flows for the six-month period then ended of ABC Company for the purpose of reporting whether any material modifications should be made to the [*consolidated*] interim financial information for it to be in accordance with accounting principles generally accepted in the United States of America (US GAAP) [*including, if appropriate, an indication as to the appropriate form and content of interim financial information (for example, Article 10 of SEC Regulation S-X)*].

We confirm that [, *to the best of our knowledge and belief, having made such inquiries as we considered necessary for the purpose of appropriately informing ourselves*] [*as of (date of auditor's review report)*]:

Interim Financial Information

1. We have fulfilled our responsibilities, as set out in the terms of the engagement letter dated [*insert date*] for the preparation and fair presentation of the interim financial information in accordance with US GAAP; in particular the interim financial information is presented in accordance therewith.
2. We acknowledge our responsibility for the design, implementation, and maintenance of internal control relevant to the preparation and fair presentation of interim financial information that is free from material misstatement, whether due to fraud or error.
3. Significant assumptions used by us in making accounting estimates, including those measured at fair value, are reasonable.
4. Related-party relationships and transactions have been appropriately accounted for and disclosed in accordance with the requirements of US GAAP.
5. The interim financial information has been adjusted or includes disclosures for all events subsequent to the date of the interim financial information for which US GAAP requires adjustment or disclosure.

6. The effects of uncorrected misstatements are immaterial, both individually and in the aggregate, to the interim financial information as a whole. A list of the uncorrected misstatements is attached to the representation letter.

[*Any other matters that the auditor may consider appropriate*]

Information Provided

7. We have provided you with:

    - Access to all information of which we are aware that is relevant to the preparation and fair presentation of the interim financial information such as records, documentation, and other matters;
    - Minutes of the meetings of stockholders, directors, and committees of directors, or summaries of actions of recent meetings for which minutes have not yet been prepared;
    - Additional information that you have requested from us for the purpose of the review; and
    - Unrestricted access to persons within the entity of whom you determined it necessary to make inquiries.

8. All transactions have been recorded in the accounting records and are reflected in the interim financial information.
9. We have disclosed to you all significant deficiencies or material weaknesses in the design or operation of internal control of which we are aware, as it relates to the preparation and fair presentation of both annual and interim financial information.
10. We have disclosed to you the results of our assessment of the risk that the interim financial information may be materially misstated as a result of fraud.
11. We have [*no knowledge of any*][*disclosed to you all information of which we are aware in relation to*] fraud or suspected fraud that affects the entity and involves:

    - Management;
    - Employees who have significant roles in internal control; or
    - Others when the fraud could have a material effect on the interim financial information.

12. We have [*no knowledge of any*] [*disclosed to you all information in relation to*] allegations of fraud, or suspected fraud, affecting the entity's interim financial information communicated by employees, former employees, analysts, regulators, or others.
13. We have disclosed to you all known instances of noncompliance or suspected noncompliance with laws and regulations whose effects should be considered when preparing interim financial information.
14. There have been no communications from regulatory agencies concerning noncompliance with or deficiencies in financial reporting practices.
15. We have disclosed to you the identity of the entity's related parties and all the related-party relationships and transactions of which we are aware.

    [*Any other matters that the auditor may consider necessary*]

[*Name of Chief Executive Officer and Title*]

[*Name of Chief Financial Officer and Title*]

[*Name of Chief Accounting Officer and Title*]

ILLUSTRATIONS OF AUDITOR'S REVIEW REPORTS ON INTERIM FINANCIAL INFORMATION

1. A Review Report on Interim Financial Information
2. A Review Report on Condensed Comparative Interim Financial Information

3. A Review Report That Refers to a Component Auditor's Review Report on the Interim Financial Information of a Significant Component of a Reporting Entity
4. A Review Report on Comparative Interim Financial Information When the Prior Period Was Reviewed by Another Auditor

ILLUSTRATION 1. A REVIEW REPORT ON INTERIM FINANCIAL INFORMATION

Circumstances include the following:

- A review of interim financial information presented as a complete set of financial statements, including disclosures

Independent Auditor's Review Report

[*Appropriate Addressee*]

Report on the Financial Statements

We have reviewed the accompanying [describe the interim financial information or statements reviewed] of ABC Company and subsidiaries as of September 30, 20X1, and for the three-month and nine-month periods then ended.

Management's Responsibility

The Company's management is responsible for the preparation and fair presentation of the interim financial information in accordance with [identify the applicable financial reporting framework; for example, accounting principles generally accepted in the United States of America]; this responsibility includes the design, implementation, and maintenance of internal control sufficient to provide a reasonable basis for the preparation and fair presentation of interim financial information in accordance with the applicable financial reporting framework.

Auditor's Responsibility

Our responsibility is to conduct our review in accordance with auditing standards generally accepted in the United States of America applicable to reviews of interim financial information. A review of interim financial information consists principally of applying analytical procedures and making inquiries of persons responsible for financial and accounting matters. It is substantially less in scope than an audit conducted in accordance with auditing standards generally accepted in the United States of America, the objective of which is the expression of an opinion regarding the financial information. Accordingly, we do not express such an opinion.

Conclusion

Based on our review, we are not aware of any material modifications that should be made to the accompanying interim financial information for it to be in accordance with [identify the applicable financial reporting framework; for example, accounting principles generally accepted in the United States of America].

[*Auditor's signature*]

[*Auditor's city and state*]

[*Date of the auditor's report*]

> **ILLUSTRATION 2. A REVIEW REPORT ON CONDENSED COMPARATIVE INTERIM FINANCIAL INFORMATION**

The following is an example of a review report on a condensed balance sheet as of March 31, 20X1; the related condensed statements of income and cash flows for the three-month periods ended March 31, 20X1 and 20X0; and a condensed balance sheet derived from audited financial statements as of December 31, 20X0. If the auditor's report on the preceding year-end financial statements was other than unmodified or included an emphasis-of-matter paragraph because of a going concern matter or an inconsistency in the application of accounting principles, the last paragraph of the illustrative report would be appropriately modified.

Independent Auditor's Review Report

[*Appropriate Addressee*]

Report on the Financial Statements

We have reviewed the condensed consolidated financial statements of ABC Company and subsidiaries, which comprise the balance sheet as of March 31, 20X1, and the related condensed consolidated statements of income and cash flows for the three-month periods ended March 31, 20X1 and 20X0.

Management's Responsibility

The Company's management is responsible for the preparation and fair presentation of the condensed financial information in accordance with [*identify the applicable financial reporting framework; for example, accounting principles generally accepted in the United States of America*]; this responsibility includes the design, implementation, and maintenance of internal control sufficient to provide a reasonable basis for the preparation and fair presentation of interim financial information in accordance with the applicable financial reporting framework.

Auditor's Responsibility

Our responsibility is to conduct our reviews in accordance with auditing standards generally accepted in the United States of America applicable to reviews of interim financial information. A review of interim financial information consists principally of applying analytical procedures and making inquiries of persons responsible for financial and accounting matters. It is substantially less in scope than an audit conducted in accordance with auditing standards generally accepted in the United States of America, the objective of which is the expression of an opinion regarding the financial information. Accordingly, we do not express such an opinion.

Conclusion

Based on our reviews, we are not aware of any material modifications that should be made to the condensed financial information referred to above for it to be in accordance with [*identify the applicable financial reporting framework; for example, accounting principles generally accepted in the United States of America*].

Report on Condensed Balance Sheet as of [*Date*]

We have previously audited, in accordance with auditing standards generally accepted in the United States of America, the consolidated balance sheet as of December 31, 20X0, and the related consolidated statements of income, changes in stockholders' equity, and cash flows for the year then ended (not presented herein); and we expressed an unmodified audit opinion on those audited consolidated financial statements in our report dated February 15, 20X1. In our opinion, the accompanying condensed consolidated balance sheet of ABC Company and subsidiaries as of

December 31, 20X0, is consistent, in all material respects, with the audited consolidated financial statements from which it has been derived.

[*Auditor's signature*]

[*Auditor's city and state*]

[*Date of the auditor's report*]

> **ILLUSTRATION 3. A REVIEW REPORT THAT REFERS TO A COMPONENT AUDITOR'S REVIEW REPORT ON THE INTERIM FINANCIAL INFORMATION OF A SIGNIFICANT COMPONENT OF A REPORTING ENTITY**

Circumstances include the following:

- A review of interim financial information presented as a complete set of financial statements, including disclosures.
- The auditor is making reference to another auditor's review report on the interim financial information of a significant component of a reporting entity.

Independent Auditor's Review Report

[*Appropriate Addressee*]

Report on the Financial Statements

We have reviewed the accompanying [*describe the interim financial information or statements reviewed*] of ABC Company and subsidiaries as of September 30, 20X1, and for the three-month and nine-month periods then ended.

Management's Responsibility

The Company's management is responsible for the preparation and fair presentation of the interim financial information in accordance with [*identify the applicable financial reporting framework; for example, accounting principles generally accepted in the United States of America*]; this responsibility includes the design, implementation, and maintenance of internal control sufficient to provide a reasonable basis for the preparation and fair presentation of interim financial information in accordance with the applicable financial reporting framework.

Auditor's Responsibility

Our responsibility is to conduct our review in accordance with auditing standards generally accepted in the United States of America applicable to reviews of interim financial information. A review of interim financial information consists principally of applying analytical procedures and making inquiries of persons responsible for financial and accounting matters. It is substantially less in scope than an audit conducted in accordance with auditing standards generally accepted in the United States of America, the objective of which is the expression of an opinion regarding the financial information. Accordingly, we do not express such an opinion.

We were furnished with the report of other auditors on their review of the interim financial information of DEF subsidiary, whose total assets as of September 30, 20X1, and whose revenues for the three-month and nine-month periods then ended, constituted 15%, 20%, and 22%, respectively, of the related consolidated totals.

Conclusion

Based on our review and the review report of other auditors, we are not aware of any material modifications that should be made to the accompanying interim financial information for it to be in accordance with [*identify the applicable financial reporting framework; for example, accounting principles generally accepted in the United States of America*].

[*Auditor's signature*]

[*Auditor's city and state*]

[*Date of the auditor's report*]

> **ILLUSTRATION 4. A REVIEW REPORT ON COMPARATIVE INTERIM FINANCIAL INFORMATION WHEN THE PRIOR PERIOD WAS REVIEWED BY ANOTHER AUDITOR**

Circumstances include the following:

- A review of interim financial information presented as a complete set of financial statements, including disclosures as of March 31, 20X1, and for the three-month period then ended.
- Comparative information is presented for the balance sheet as of December 31, 20X0, and for the statements of income and cash flows for the comparable interim period.
- The December 31, 20X0, financial statements were audited, and the March 31, 20X0, interim financial information was reviewed, by another auditor.

Independent Auditor's Review Report

[*Appropriate Addressee*]

Report on the Financial Statements

We have reviewed the accompanying [*describe the interim financial information or statements reviewed*] of ABC Company and subsidiaries as of March 31, 20X1, and for the three-month period then ended. The consolidated statements of income and cash flows of ABC Company and subsidiaries for the three-month period ended March 31, 20X0, were reviewed by other auditors whose report dated June 1, 20X0, stated that based on their review, they were not aware of any material modifications that should be made to those statements in order for them to be in conformity with [*identify the applicable financial reporting framework; for example, accounting principles generally accepted in the United States of America*]. The consolidated balance sheet of the Company as of December 31, 20X0, and the related consolidated statements of income, changes in stockholders' equity, and cash flows for the year then ended (not presented herein), were audited by other auditors whose report dated March 15, 20X1, expressed an unmodified opinion on that statement.

Management's Responsibility

The Company's management is responsible for the preparation and fair presentation of the interim financial information in accordance with [*identify the applicable financial reporting framework; for example, accounting principles generally accepted in the United States of America*]; this responsibility includes the design, implementation, and maintenance of internal control sufficient to provide a reasonable basis for the preparation and fair presentation of interim financial information in accordance with the applicable financial reporting framework.

Auditor's Responsibility

Our responsibility is to conduct our review in accordance with auditing standards generally accepted in the United States of America applicable to reviews of interim financial information. A review of interim financial information consists principally of applying analytical procedures and making inquiries of persons responsible for financial and accounting matters. It is substantially less in scope than an audit conducted in accordance with auditing standards generally accepted in the United States of America, the objective of which is the expression of an opinion regarding the financial information. Accordingly, we do not express such an opinion.

Conclusion

Based on our review, we are not aware of any material modifications that should be made to the accompanying interim financial information as of and for the three months ended March 31, 20X1, for it to be in accordance with [*identify the applicable financial reporting framework; for example, accounting principles generally accepted in the United States of America*].

[*Auditor's signature*]

[*Auditor's city and state*]

[*Date of the auditor's report*]

ILLUSTRATIONS OF EXAMPLE MODIFICATIONS TO THE AUDITOR'S REVIEW REPORT DUE TO DEPARTURES FROM THE APPLICABLE FINANCIAL REPORTING FRAMEWORK

1. Modification Due to a Departure from the Applicable Financial Reporting Framework
2. Modification Due to Inadequate Disclosure
3. Emphasis-of-Matter Paragraph When a Going Concern Emphasis-of-Matter Paragraph Was Included in the Prior Year's Audit Report, and Conditions Giving Rise to the Emphasis-of-Matter Paragraph Continue to Exist
4. Emphasis-of-Matter Paragraph When a Going Concern Emphasis-of-Matter Paragraph Was Not Included in the Prior Year's Audit Report, and Conditions or Events Exist as of the Interim Reporting Date Covered by the Review That Might Be Indicative of the Entity's Possible Inability to Continue as a Going Concern

ILLUSTRATION 1. MODIFICATION DUE TO A DEPARTURE FROM THE APPLICABLE FINANCIAL REPORTING FRAMEWORK

The following is an example of a modification of the auditor's review report due to a departure from the applicable financial reporting framework:

[*Basis for Modification Paragraph*]

Based on information furnished to us by management, we believe that the Company has excluded from property and debt in the accompanying balance sheet certain lease obligations that we believe should be capitalized to be in accordance with [*identify the applicable financial reporting framework; for example, accounting principles generally accepted in the United States of America*]. This information indicates that if these lease obligations were capitalized at September 30, 20X1, property would be increased by $_____, long-term debt would be increased by $_____, and net income would be increased (decreased) by $_____ and $_____, respectively, for the three-month and nine-month periods then ended.

[*Conclusion*]

Based on our review, with the exception of the matter(s) described in the preceding paragraph(s), we are not aware of any material modifications that should be made to the accompanying interim financial information for it to be in accordance with [*identify the applicable financial reporting framework; for example, accounting principles generally accepted in the United States of America*].

ILLUSTRATION 2. MODIFICATION DUE TO INADEQUATE DISCLOSURE

The following is an example of a modification of the auditor's review report due to inadequate disclosure:

[*Basis for Modification Paragraph*]

Management has informed us that the Company is presently defending a claim regarding [*describe the nature of the loss contingency*] and that the extent of the Company's liability, if any, and the effect on the accompanying interim financial information is not determinable at this time. The interim financial information fails to disclose these matters, which we believe are required to be disclosed in accordance with [*identify the applicable financial reporting framework; for example, accounting principles generally accepted in the United States of America*].

[*Conclusion*]

Based on our review, with the exception of the matter(s) described in the preceding paragraph(s), we are not aware of any material modifications that should be made to the accompanying interim financial information for it to be in accordance with [*identify the applicable financial reporting framework; for example, accounting principles generally accepted in the United States of America*].

ILLUSTRATION 3. EMPHASIS-OF-MATTER PARAGRAPH WHEN A GOING CONCERN EMPHASIS-OF-MATTER PARAGRAPH WAS INCLUDED IN THE PRIOR YEAR'S AUDIT REPORT, AND CONDITIONS GIVING RISE TO THE EMPHASIS-OF-MATTER PARAGRAPH CONTINUE TO EXIST

The following is an example of an emphasis-of-matter paragraph when a going concern emphasis-of-matter paragraph was included in the prior year's audit report, and conditions giving rise to the emphasis-of-matter paragraph continue to exist:

[*Emphasis-of-Matter Paragraph*]

Note 4 of the Company's audited financial statements as of December 31, 20X1, and for the year then ended, discloses that the Company was unable to renew its line of credit or obtain alternative financing at December 31, 20X1. Our auditor's report on those financial statements includes an emphasis-of-matter paragraph referring to the matters in note 4 of those financial statements and indicating that these matters raised substantial doubt about the Company's ability to continue as a going concern. As indicated in note 3 of the Company's unaudited interim financial information as of March 31, 20X2, and for the three months then ended, the Company was still unable to renew its line of credit or obtain alternative financing as of March 31, 20X2. The accompanying interim financial information does not include any adjustments that might result from the outcome of this uncertainty.

ILLUSTRATION 4. EMPHASIS-OF-MATTER PARAGRAPH WHEN A GOING CONCERN EMPHASIS-OF-MATTER PARAGRAPH WAS NOT INCLUDED IN THE PRIOR YEAR'S AUDIT REPORT, AND CONDITIONS OR EVENTS EXIST AS OF THE INTERIM REPORTING DATE COVERED BY THE REVIEW THAT MIGHT BE INDICATIVE OF THE ENTITY'S POSSIBLE INABILITY TO CONTINUE AS A GOING CONCERN

The following is an example of an emphasis-of-matter paragraph when a going concern emphasis-of-matter paragraph was not included in the prior year's audit report, and conditions or events exist as of the interim reporting date covered by the review that might be indicative of the entity's possible inability to continue as a going concern:

[*Emphasis-of-Matter Paragraph*]

As indicated in note 3, certain conditions indicate that the Company may be unable to continue as a going concern. The accompanying interim financial information does not include any adjustments that might result from the outcome of this uncertainty.

AU 801 Compliance Auditing

AU-C 935 Compliance Audits

AU EFFECTIVE DATE AND APPLICABILITY

Original Pronouncements	Statement on Auditing Standards (SAS) 117.
Effective Date	This statement currently is effective.
Applicability	Engagements to perform a compliance audit in accordance with generally accepted auditing standards (GAAS), the standards for financial audits under governmental auditing standards, or a governmental audit requirement that requires an auditor to express an opinion on compliance. Not applicable when government audit requirements call for an examination under the Statements on Standards for Attestation Engagements (SSAEs) of an entity's internal controls over compliance.

AU-C EFFECTIVE DATE AND SUMMARY OF CHANGES

SAS No. 122, *Codification of Auditing Standards and Procedures,* is effective for audits of financial statements with periods ending on or after December 15, 2012.

To address practice issues, SAS No. 117, *Compliance Audits*, was one of the clarified standards issued before SAS No. 122. It was issued in December 2009 and is effective for compliance audits for fiscal periods ending on or after June 15, 2010.

SAS No. 117 was codified in AU 801 when issued, but was moved to AU-C 935 with the issuance of SAS No. 122. Some conforming changes were made in specific paragraphs and footnotes due to the issuance of SAS No. 122, but no substantive changes were made.

AU DEFINITIONS OF TERMS

Applicable risk of noncompliance. The risk that an auditor will express an inappropriate audit opinion on an entity's compliance when there is a case of material noncompliance.

Compliance audit. An audit of an entity's compliance with specific compliance requirements. These *compliance requirements* can include the laws, regulations, rules, and contract provisions applicable to government programs with which an entity is required to comply.

Detection risk of noncompliance. The risk that procedures performed by an auditor to reduce the risk of noncompliance will not detect material noncompliance, either individually or when aggregated with other cases of noncompliance.

Government program. The means by which a government entity achieves its objectives. Government programs relevant to this section include those in which the program provides an award to another entity, typically as a grant or contract.

Material noncompliance. If there is no definition of material noncompliance in a government audit requirement, material noncompliance is defined as the failure to follow compliance requirements or a violation of prohibitions included in applicable compliance requirements that result in material noncompliance, either individually or when aggregated.

Material weakness in internal control over compliance. A deficiency in internal control over compliance, such that there is a reasonable possibility that material noncompliance with a compliance requirement will not be prevented or detected and corrected on a timely basis. *Reasonably possible* is defined as the chance that a future event occurring is more than remote but less than likely. *Remote* is defined as the chance of a future event occurring is slight. *Probable* is defined as the chance that a future event occurring is likely.

Questioned costs. Those costs questioned by an auditor because of a possible violation of applicable compliance requirements, minimal supporting documentation, or the costs appearing unreasonable. *Likely questioned costs* are inferred by extrapolating from audit evidence obtained, while *known questioned costs* are those specifically identified by the auditor.

Significant deficiency in internal control over compliance. A deficiency in internal control over compliance that is less severe than a material weakness, yet which is important enough to merit attention by those in a position of governance.

AU-C 935 DEFINITIONS OF TERMS

Source: AU-C 935.11

Applicable compliance requirements. Compliance requirements that are subject to the compliance audit.

Audit findings. The matters that are required to be reported by the auditor in accordance with the governmental audit requirement.

Audit risk of noncompliance. The risk that the auditor expresses an inappropriate audit opinion on the entity's compliance when material noncompliance exists. Audit risk of noncompliance is a function of the risks of material noncompliance and detection risk of noncompliance.

Compliance audit. A program-specific audit or an organization-wide audit of an entity's compliance with applicable compliance requirements.

Compliance requirements. Laws, regulations, rules, and provisions of contracts or grant agreements applicable to government programs with which the entity is required to comply.

Deficiency in internal control over compliance. A deficiency in internal control over compliance exists when the design or operation of a control over compliance does not allow management or employees, in the normal course of performing their assigned functions, to prevent, or detect and correct, noncompliance on a timely basis. A deficiency in *design* exists when (1) a control necessary to meet the control objective is missing, or (2) an existing control is not properly designed so that, even if the control operates as designed, the control objective would not be met. A deficiency in *operation* exists when a properly designed control does not operate as designed or the person performing the control does not possess the necessary authority or competence to perform the control effectively.

Detection risk of noncompliance. The risk that the procedures performed by the auditor to reduce audit risk of noncompliance to an acceptably low level will not detect noncompliance that exists and that could be material, either individually or when aggregated with other instances of noncompliance.

Government Auditing Standards. Standards and guidance issued by the Comptroller General of the United States, U.S. Government Accountability Office for financial audits, attestation engagements, and performance audits. *Government Auditing Standards* also is known as generally accepted government auditing standards (GAGAS) or the "Yellow Book."

Government program. The means by which governmental entities achieve their objectives. For example, one of the objectives of the U.S. Department of Agriculture is to provide nutrition to individuals in need. Examples of government programs designed to achieve that objective are the Supplemental Nutrition Assistance Program and the National School Lunch Program. Government programs that are relevant to this section are those in which a grantor or pass-through entity provides an award to another entity, usually in the form of a grant, contract, or other agreement. Not all government programs provide cash assistance; sometimes noncash assistance is provided (for example, a loan guarantee, commodities, or property).

Governmental audit requirement. A government requirement established by law, regulation, rule, or provision of contracts or grant agreements requiring that an entity undergo an audit of its compliance with applicable compliance requirements related to one or more government programs that the entity administers.

Grantor. A government agency from which funding for the government program originates.

Known questioned costs. Questioned costs specifically identified by the auditor. Known questioned costs are a subset of likely questioned costs.

Likely questioned costs. The auditor's best estimate of total questioned costs, not just the known questioned costs. Likely questioned costs are developed by extrapolating from audit evidence obtained, for example, by projecting known questioned costs identified in an audit sample to the entire population from which the sample was drawn.

Material noncompliance. In the absence of a definition of material noncompliance in the governmental audit requirement, a failure to follow compliance requirements or a violation of prohibitions included in the applicable compliance requirements that results in noncompliance that is quantitatively or qualitatively material, either individually or when aggregated with other noncompliance, to the affected government program.

Material weakness in internal control over compliance. A deficiency, or combination of deficiencies, in internal control over compliance, such that there is a reasonable possibility that material noncompliance with a compliance requirement will not be prevented, or detected and corrected, on a timely basis. In this section, a reasonable possibility exists when the likelihood of the event is either reasonably possible or probable as defined as follows:

- **Reasonably possible.** The chance of the future event or events occurring is more than remote but less than likely.
- **Remote.** The chance of the future event or events occurring is slight.
- **Probable.** The future event or events are likely to occur.

Organization-wide audit. An audit of an entity's financial statements and an audit of its compliance with the applicable compliance requirements as they relate to one or more government programs that the entity administers.

Pass-through entity. An entity that receives an award from a grantor or other entity and distributes all or part of it to another entity to administer a government program.

Program-specific audit. An audit of an entity's compliance with applicable compliance requirements as they relate to one government program that the entity administers. The compliance audit portion of a program-specific audit is performed in conjunction with either an audit of the entity's or the program's financial statements.

Questioned costs. Costs that are questioned by the auditor because (1) of a violation or possible violation of the applicable compliance requirements, (2) the costs are not supported by adequate documentation, or (3) the incurred costs appear unreasonable and do not reflect the actions that a prudent person would take in the circumstances.

Risk of material noncompliance. The risk that material noncompliance exists prior to the audit. This consists of two components, described as follows:

- **Inherent risk of noncompliance.** The susceptibility of a compliance requirement to noncompliance that could be material, either individually or when aggregated with other instances of noncompliance, before consideration of any related controls over compliance.
- **Control risk of noncompliance.** The risk that noncompliance with a compliance requirement that could occur and that could be material, either individually or when aggregated with other instances of noncompliance, will not be prevented, or detected and corrected, on a timely basis by the entity's internal control over compliance.

Significant deficiency in internal control over compliance. A deficiency, or a combination of deficiencies, in internal control over compliance that is less severe than a material weakness in internal control over compliance, yet important enough to merit attention by those charged with governance.

OBJECTIVES OF AU SECTION 801

Governments frequently require entities to undergo an audit of their compliance with various requirements. The auditor's objectives in a compliance audit are to obtain sufficient audit evidence to form an opinion on whether an entity has complied in all material respects with the compliance requirements to a government entity, as well as to identify the audit and reporting requirements specified in governmental audit requirements that are in addition to GAAS and government auditing standards, and to perform procedures to address those additional requirements.

This section addresses the application of GAAS to a compliance audit, which is frequently performed in conjunction with a financial statements audit.

OBJECTIVES OF AU-C SECTION 935

AU-C 935 states that:

> ... the auditor's objectives in a compliance audit are to
>
> a. obtain sufficient appropriate audit evidence to form an opinion and report at the level specified in the governmental audit requirement on whether the entity complied in all material respects with the applicable compliance requirements; and

b. *identify audit and reporting requirements specified in the governmental audit requirement that are supplementary to GAAS and* Government Auditing Standards, *if any, and perform procedures to address those requirements.*

FUNDAMENTAL REQUIREMENTS

APPLICATION OF AU SECTIONS TO A COMPLIANCE AUDIT

The auditor should adapt all other AU Sections to the objectives of a compliance audit, with limited exceptions as noted in Appendix A of SAS 117.

THE COMPLIANCE AUDIT PROCESS FLOW

The auditor should follow these steps when conducting a compliance audit:

1. *Materiality.* Establish material levels and apply them to the compliance audit based on the governmental audit requirements.
2. *Identify programs.* Determine which government programs and compliance requirements to test.
3. *Perform procedures.* Perform risk assessment procedures to gain a sufficient understanding of the applicable compliance requirements and the entity's internal control over compliance. Also see if there are findings from previous audits, attestation engagements, or other monitoring that relate to the compliance audit. Additionally, gain an understanding of management's response to these findings that could have a material effect on the entity's compliance with applicable compliance requirements. Use this information to assess risk, as well as to determine the audit procedures for the compliance audit.
4. *Risk assessment.* Assess the risks of material noncompliance, whether due to fraud or error, for each applicable compliance requirement.
5. *Material noncompliance risk.* Assess the risk of material noncompliance, whether due to fraud or error, for each compliance requirement.
6. *Further audit procedures.* If there are risks of material noncompliance that are pervasive, then develop an overall response to these risks. The response should include further audit procedures, including tests of details, to obtain sufficient audit evidence. Tests of controls, analytical procedures, and risk assessment procedures are not sufficient. Test controls over compliance if there is an expectation of the operating effectiveness of controls over compliance, or substantive procedures alone do not provide sufficient evidence, or if these tests are mandated by a government audit requirement.

   NOTE: *Sample tests of details can include the areas of grant disbursements or expenditures, eligibility files, cost allocation plans, and periodic reports filed with grantor agencies.*

7. *Supplementary audit steps.* Determine if the government audit requirements include audit requirements that are in addition to GAAS and government auditing standards, and perform those procedures. If these requirements conflict with GAAS or government auditing standards, then use the GAAS or government auditing standards.
8. *Written representations.* Request from management written representations that align with the government audit requirement. Include the following items in the request:

a. Acknowledge management's responsibility for understanding and complying with the pertinent compliance requirements.
b. Acknowledge management's responsibility for a system of controls that provides reasonable assurance of administering government programs as per their compliance requirements.
c. State that management has identified and disclosed all of the programs related to the government audit requirement.
d. State that management has made available all contracts and related correspondence relevant to the programs subject to the government audit requirement.
e. State that management has disclosed all known noncompliance, or that there is no noncompliance.
f. State whether management believes the entity has complied with the compliance requirements.
g. State that management has made available all documentation related to compliance with the applicable compliance requirements.
h. Stating management's interpretation of compliance requirements that are subject to interpretation.
i. Stating that management has disclosed any grantor communications concerning possible noncompliance, through the date of the auditor's report.
j. Stating that management has disclosed the findings and related corrective actions taken for previous audits, attestation engagements, and monitoring related to the objectives of the compliance audit, through the date of the auditor's report.
k. Stating that management has disclosed all noncompliance with the compliance requirements subsequent to the period covered by the auditor's report, or states that there were no such cases.
l. Stating that management is responsible for taking corrective action on audit findings arising from the compliance audit.

9. *Subsequent events.* Perform audit procedures through the date of the auditor's report, to obtain evidence that subsequent events related to the entity's compliance have been identified.

NOTE: *If the auditor becomes aware of noncompliance in the period subsequent to the report date that is of such significance that report users would be misled without this information (such as the discovery of noncompliance of such size that the grantor halted funding), then the auditor should discuss the matter with management and those charged with governance, and explain the noncompliance in the report.*

10. *Evaluate evidence.* Evaluate the sufficiency and appropriateness of audit evidence. Then form an opinion on whether the entity materially complied with the compliance requirements. As part of this evaluation, review likely questioned costs, as well as known questioned costs.

NOTE: *When evaluating evidence, the auditor can consider the frequency of noncompliance identified during the audit, the nature of the noncompliance, the adequacy of the entity's system for monitoring compliance, the effect of noncompliance on the entity, and whether any identified noncompliance with the applicable compliance requirements resulted in likely questioned costs that are material.*

REPORTING REQUIREMENTS

There are three types of compliance reports, which are (1) the report on compliance only, (2) the combined report on compliance and internal control over compliance, and (3) the separate report on internal control over compliance. The contents of these reports follow.

Report on compliance only. If the auditor is only reporting on compliance, then the report must:

- Have a title containing the word "independent."
- Identify the government programs covered by the compliance audit.
- State the compliance requirements.
- State the period covered by the report.
- State that compliance with the compliance requirements is the responsibility of management.
- State that the auditor's responsibility is to express an opinion on the entity's compliance with the applicable compliance requirements, which is based on the compliance audit.
- State that the compliance audit was conducted in accordance with GAAS, the standards applicable to financial audits in government accounting standards, and the government audit requirements.
- State that the compliance audit included an examination of evidence about the entity's compliance with such requirements, as well as other procedures considered necessary by the auditor.
- State that the auditor believes the compliance audit provides a reasonable basis for an opinion.
- State that the compliance audit does not provide a legal determination of the entity's compliance.
- State an opinion, at the level required by the government audit requirement, regarding whether the entity materially complied with the compliance requirements.
- If there is an opinion modification due to noncompliance, describe the noncompliance.
- If there is noncompliance that does not result in an opinion modification, describe it.
- If the report is developed solely for specific parties, state that the report is intended solely for the use of the specified parties, and that it is not intended for use by any other parties.
- Include the signature of the auditor's firm.
- Include the date of the report.

Combined report on compliance and internal control over compliance. If the auditor combines the auditor's report on compliance with a report on internal control over compliance, then add the following items to the report just described for a report on compliance only:

- State that management is responsible for internal controls over compliance with the requirements of laws, regulations, rules, and contract provisions applicable to government programs.
- State that the auditor considered the entity's internal control over compliance with the applicable compliance requirements while planning and performing the audit, but only to determine procedures for expressing an opinion on compliance—not for expressing an opinion on the effectiveness of internal controls over compliance.

- State that the auditor is not expressing an opinion on internal control over compliance.
- State that the auditor's considerations were not designed to identify all deficiencies in internal control that might be significant deficiencies or material weaknesses in internal control over compliance.
- Define a "deficiency in internal control over compliance" and "material weakness in internal control over compliance."
- Describe identified material weaknesses in internal control over compliance.
- If there were significant deficiencies in internal controls over compliance, define "significant deficiency in internal control over compliance" and describe the deficiencies.
- If there were no material weaknesses in internal control over compliance, make a statement to that effect.

A combined report on compliance and internal control over compliance is noted later in the section "AU Illustration" at the end of this chapter.

Separate report on internal control over compliance. If the auditor is required by the government audit requirements to report on internal control over compliance, and the auditor elects to issue a separate report on this matter, then add the following items to the report just described for a combined report on compliance and internal control over compliance:

- A title containing the word "independent"
- A statement that the auditor audited the entity's compliance with the applicable compliance requirements for the named government program and specified time period, and refer to the auditor's report on compliance
- A statement that the compliance audit was conducted in accordance with GAAS, those government auditing standards applicable to financial audits, and the government audit requirement
- The signature of the auditor's firm
- The date of the report

The auditor should also report noncompliance in the manner specified by the government audit requirement. Further, if the auditor communicates significant deficiencies or material weaknesses in internal control over compliance, government auditing standards require the auditor to obtain a response from the responsible officials regarding their views on the findings, conclusions, and recommendations in the auditor's report, and to include a copy of any written response in the auditor's report.

The auditor should modify his or her opinion on compliance in accordance with Section 508, *Reports on Audited Financial Statements*, if the audit identifies material noncompliance, or a restriction on the compliance audit's scope.

NOTE: If there is no government audit requirement to report on internal control over compliance, the auditor should still report significant deficiencies and material weaknesses in internal control over compliance to both management and those charged with governance.

In addition to the reporting noted above, the auditor should report to those charged with governance the auditor's responsibilities as noted in GAAS, government auditing standards, and the government audit requirements. This report should also include an overview of the planned scope and timing of the compliance audit, as well as significant findings arising from it.

> NOTE: *If a government agency has provided a report format that requires the auditor to make a statement for which there is no basis, reword the report or attach a properly worded separate report.*

If the auditor reissues the report, include in it a note that the report replaces an earlier report, and explain why the report is replacing the prior report, as well as the changes from the prior report. Update the date of the reissued report if additional procedures were performed.

MANAGEMENT'S RESPONSIBILITIES

Management is responsible for an entity's compliance with compliance requirements. This responsibility includes:

- *Compliance*. Comply with the compliance requirements of government programs.
- *Controls*. Maintain a control system that gives reasonable assurance that the entity administers government programs that are in compliance with compliance requirements.
- *Monitoring*. Evaluate and monitor compliance with the compliance requirements.
- *Corrective action*. Take corrective action in the event of noncompliance.

DOCUMENTATION

The auditor should document all risk assessment procedures performed, as well as any responses to assessed risks of material noncompliance, any procedures performed to test compliance with the applicable compliance requirements, and the results of those procedures. Further, document materiality levels and the basis on which they were calculated.

INTERPRETATIONS

There are no interpretations for this section.

TECHNIQUES FOR APPLICATION

SOURCES OF INFORMATION REGARDING COMPLIANCE REQUIREMENTS

To gain an understanding of applicable compliance requirements, consult *The Compliance Supplement*, which is issued by the Office of Management and Budget. It contains the compliance requirements applicable to many federal government programs. It also includes a number of sample audit procedures that are applicable to compliance requirements. The grantor agency may also have issued a program-specific audit guide that similarly contains compliance requirements and suggested audit procedures.

SUGGESTED AUDIT PROCEDURES

If *The Compliance Supplement* or a program-specific audit guide are not available, the auditor may use the following procedures to obtain an understanding of the applicable compliance requirements:

1. Read the laws, regulations, rules, and contract provisions pertaining to the government program.
2. Make inquiries of management and other knowledgeable entity personnel.

3. Make inquiries of individuals outside the entity, such as government auditors, regulators, third-party specialists, and attorneys, regarding the laws and regulations applicable to entities within their jurisdictions.
4. Read the meeting minutes of the entity's governing body.
5. Read the audit documentation about applicable compliance requirements that were prepared during prior audits.
6. Discuss applicable compliance requirements with the auditors who performed prior audits.

MATERIAL NONCOMPLIANCE RISKS

The auditor may consider the following factors when assessing the risks of material noncompliance:

1. Complexity of the applicable compliance requirements
2. Susceptibility of the applicable compliance requirements to noncompliance
3. The time period during which the entity has been subjected to the applicable compliance requirements
4. Observations about how the entity has complied with the requirements in prior years
5. The potential effect on the entity of noncompliance with the requirements
6. The degree of judgment involved in adhering to the compliance requirements
7. The assessment of the risks of material misstatement in the financial statement audit

AU ILLUSTRATION

If an auditor's report contains a response from responsible officials concerning their views on the findings, conclusions, and recommendations included in the report, the auditor may include a paragraph, such as the following example, disclaiming an opinion on such information:

> ABC Company's written response to the significant deficiencies and material weaknesses in internal control over compliance identified in our compliance audit was not subjected to the auditing procedures applied in the compliance audit of ABC Company's compliance and, accordingly, we express no opinion on it.

The following is an example of a combined report on compliance with applicable requirements and internal control over compliance, containing an unqualified opinion on compliance with no material weaknesses or significant deficiencies in internal control over compliance identified.

ILLUSTRATION 1. COMBINED REPORT ON COMPLIANCE WITH APPLICABLE REQUIREMENTS AND INTERNAL CONTROL OVER COMPLIANCE

Compliance

We have audited ABC Company's compliance with the [*identify the applicable compliance requirements or refer to the document that describes the applicable compliance requirements*] applicable to ABC Company's [*identify the government program(s) audited or refer to a separate schedule that identifies the program(s)*] for the year ended June 30, 20X2. Compliance with the requirements referred to above is the responsibility of ABC Company's management. Our responsibility is to express an opinion on ABC Company's compliance based on our audit.

We conducted our audit of compliance in accordance with auditing standards generally accepted in the United States of America; the standards applicable to financial audits contained in Government Auditing Standards issued by the Comptroller General of the United States; and [*insert the name of the governmental audit requirement or program-specific audit guide*]. Those standards and [*insert the name of the governmental audit requirement or program-specific audit guide*] require that we plan and perform the audit to obtain reasonable assurance about whether noncompliance with the compliance requirements referred to above that could have a material effect on [*identify the government program(s) audited or refer to a separate schedule that identifies the program(s)*]. An audit includes examining, on a test basis, evidence about ABC Company's compliance with those requirements and performing such other procedures as we considered necessary in the circumstances. We believe that our audit provides a reasonable basis for our opinion. Our audit does not provide a legal determination of ABC Company's compliance with those requirements.

In our opinion, ABC Company complied, in all material respects, with the compliance requirements referred to above that are applicable to [*identify the government program(s) audited*] for the year ended June 30, 20X2.

Internal Control over Compliance

Management of ABC Company is responsible for establishing and maintaining effective internal control over compliance with the compliance requirements referred to above. In planning and performing our audit, we considered ABC Company's internal control over compliance to determine the auditing procedures for the purpose of expressing our opinion on compliance, but not for the purpose of expressing an opinion on the effectiveness of internal control over compliance. Accordingly, we do not express an opinion on the effectiveness of ABC Company's internal control over compliance.

A *deficiency in internal control over compliance* exists when the design or operation of a control does not allow management or employees, in the normal course of performing their assigned functions, to prevent, or detect and correct, noncompliance on a timely basis. A *material weakness* in internal control over compliance is a deficiency, or combination of deficiencies in internal control over compliance, such that there is a reasonable possibility that material noncompliance with the compliance requirement will not be prevented, or detected and corrected, on a timely basis.

Our consideration of internal control over compliance was for the limited purpose described in the first paragraph of this section and was not designed to identify all deficiencies in internal control that might be deficiencies, significant deficiencies, or material weaknesses in internal control over compliance. We did not identify any deficiencies in internal control over compliance that we consider to be material weaknesses, as defined above.

This report is intended solely for the information and use of management, [*identify the body or individuals charged with governance*], others within the entity, [*identify the legislative or regulatory body*], and [*identify the grantor agency(ies)*], and is not intended to be and should not be used by anyone other than these specified parties.

Jones and Smith
June 30, 20X2

AU 901 PUBLIC WAREHOUSES: CONTROLS AND AUDITING PROCEDURES FOR GOODS HELD

AU-C 501 AUDIT EVIDENCE—SPECIFIC CONSIDERATIONS FOR SELECTED ITEMS

AU EFFECTIVE DATE AND APPLICABILITY

Original Pronouncements	Statement on Auditing Procedure (SAP) 37 (codified in Statement on Accounting Standards [SAS] 1), SAS 43.
Effective Date	These statements currently are effective.
Applicability	Internal control of: 1. A warehouseman for goods in his or her custody 2. An owner of goods in the custody of a warehouseman Auditing procedures to be applied by: 1. An auditor of a warehouseman for goods in the custody of the warehouseman 2. An auditor of an owner of goods in the custody of a warehouseman

AU-C EFFECTIVE DATE AND SUMMARY OF CHANGES

SAS No. 122, *Codification of Auditing Standards and Procedures,* is effective for audits of financial statements with periods ending on or after December 15, 2012.

The clarified SAS rescinds AU 901.

AU DEFINITIONS OF TERMS

Commodity warehouse. A warehouse that stores certain bulk commodities, such as agricultural products and chemicals. Ordinarily this type of warehouse stores only one commodity.

Field warehouse. A warehouse that is established as part of a financing arrangement. It might be established on the premises of either:

1. The owner of the goods, or
2. A customer of the owner of the goods

A field warehouse is established so that the warehouseman may take and maintain custody of the goods. The warehouseman does the following:

1. Leases space on the premises of the owner or the customer of the owner
2. Ordinarily, temporarily employs personnel at the warehouse who are employees of the owner or the customer of the owner
3. Issues warehouse receipts to be used as collateral for a loan or other form of credit

General merchandise warehouse. A warehouse that stores merchandise not requiring special storage facilities, such as furniture, other household goods, and personal effects.

Negotiable warehouse receipt. A warehouse receipt that must be surrendered to the warehouseman before the release of the goods.

Nonnegotiable warehouse receipt. A warehouse receipt that need not be surrendered in order for goods to be released by the warehouseman. Goods may be released upon valid instructions to the warehouseman.

Refrigerated warehouse. A warehouse constructed and equipped to meet controlled-temperature and special-handling requirements. Ordinarily it stores perishable products and food.

Terminal warehouse. A warehouse that ordinarily furnishes storage only; however, it may provide other services, such as packaging and billing.

Warehouse. A facility operated by a warehouseman whose business is maintaining effective custody of goods for others.

Warehouse receipt. A document that represents goods stored in warehouse.

AU-C DEFINITIONS OF TERMS

Source: AU-C Section 501

There are no definitions in this section.

OBJECTIVES OF AU SECTION 901

In the early 1960s the Allied Crude Vegetable Oil Company case, or, as it is sometimes called, the DeAngelis fraud, shocked accountants and caused the American Institute of Certified Public Accountants (AICPA) Committee on Auditing Procedure (forerunner to the Auditing Standards Board) to reexamine the existing position that a confirmation from the warehouseman provided sufficient evidence on inventory held in a public warehouse. After all, the warehouseman is not a disinterested party and cannot necessarily be relied on to disclose shortcomings in his or her own performance.

The main change made by the committee was to indicate that if inventory were a significant portion of current assets or total assets, confirmation from the warehouseman would not be sufficient. More reliable evidence is necessary. The auditor may use judgment, however, in deciding how extensive his or her procedures need to be. One or more of several procedures, in addition to confirmation, might be appropriate depending on the circumstances.

OBJECTIVE OF AU-C SECTION 501

AU-C Section 501 states that

> ... the objective of the auditor is to obtain sufficient appropriate audit evidence regarding the
> a. valuation of investments in securities and derivative instruments;
> b. existence and condition of inventory;
> c. completeness of litigation, claims, and assessments involving the entity; and
> d. presentation and disclosure of segment information, in accordance with the applicable financial reporting framework.

FUNDAMENTAL REQUIREMENTS: CONTROLS FOR WAREHOUSEMAN

This section lists suggested controls for a warehouse. It emphasizes the segregation of duties in the performance of operating functions of the warehouse. Controls are classified as follows:

1. Receiving goods
2. Storing goods
3. Delivering goods
4. Warehouse receipts
5. Insurance
6. Additional controls for field warehouses

RECEIVING GOODS

1. Issue receipts for all goods admitted.
2. Have receiving clerks prepare reports for all goods received.
3. Compare quantities on receiving reports with quantities shown on bills of lading or other documents received from outside sources by an employee independent of receiving, storing, and delivering.
4. Inspect, count, weigh, measure, or grade goods received. Check machinery (or computers) used for these purposes periodically for accuracy.

STORING GOODS

1. When possible, store goods so that each lot is segregated and identified with its warehouse receipt. (This may not be possible with fungible goods.)
2. Be sure that warehouse records show the location of goods represented by each warehouse receipt.

3. Limit access to the storage area to employees whose duties require it.
4. Control custody of keys to the storage area.
5. Issue periodic statements to customers that identify the goods held and request that discrepancies be reported to a named employee who is not connected with receiving, storing, or delivering.
6. Physically count or test stored goods periodically and agree quantities to the records by an employee who is not connected with the storage function.
7. For perishable goods, establish a regular schedule for inspection of condition.
8. Regularly inspect protective devices, such as burglar alarms, fire alarms, sprinkler systems, and temperature and humidity controls.

DELIVERING GOODS

1. Issue instructions that goods may be released only on proper authorization. In the case of negotiable receipts, this includes surrender of the receipt.
2. Release goods only on written instructions from an authorized employee who does not have access to the goods.
3. Have shipping clerks or others independently check counts of goods to be released made by stock clerks and compare the two counts before the goods are released.

WAREHOUSE RECEIPTS

1. Use prenumbered warehouse receipts.
2. Establish procedures for accounting for all receipts used and for cancellation of negotiable receipts when goods have been delivered.
3. Safeguard unused receipts and assign their custody to a responsible employee who is not authorized to prepare or sign receipts.
4. Furnish receipts only to authorized persons and in a quantity limited to the number required for current use.
5. Be sure that the signer of receipts ascertains that the receipts are supported by receiving records.
6. Prepare and complete receipts in a manner designed to prevent alteration.
7. Be sure that only a limited number of responsible employees are authorized signers of receipts.

INSURANCE

1. Periodically review insurance coverage.

ADDITIONAL CONTROLS FOR FIELD WAREHOUSES

1. Only issue nonnegotiable warehouse receipts from field locations.
2. Furnish receipt forms to field locations by the central office in quantities limited to current requirements.
3. Other internal control procedures suggested for the central office are:

    a. Consider the business reputation and financial standing of the depositor.
    b. Prepare the field warehouse contract in accordance with the depositor's and lender's requirements.
    c. Determine that leased warehouse premises meet the physical requirements for segregation and effective custody of goods.

d. Obtain satisfaction about legal matters pertaining to the lease of the warehouse premises.
e. Investigate and bond employees at field locations.
f. Provide employees at field locations with written instructions.
g. Maintain inventory records that show quantity and stated value, where applicable, of goods represented by each outstanding warehouse receipt.
h. Examine the field warehouse. Inspect the facilities, observe compliance with prescribed procedures, perform physical counts or tests of goods in custody and reconciliation of quantities to records at both the central office and the field locations, account for all receipts furnished to the field locations, and confirm outstanding warehouse receipts with registered holders.

FUNDAMENTAL REQUIREMENTS: WAREHOUSEMAN'S AUDITOR

INTERNAL CONTROL POLICIES AND PROCEDURES

Understand controls relating to the accountability for, and the custody of, all goods placed in the warehouse. Perform tests of controls to evaluate their effectiveness.

ACCOUNTABILITY

The independent auditor of the warehouseman should perform the following procedures.

Goods Placed in Custody

Evaluate accountability for all goods placed in the warehouseman's custody by testing his or her records.

Outstanding Warehouse Receipts

Test the accountability of the warehouseman under recorded outstanding warehouse receipts. Procedures relating to accountability might include, on a test basis, the following:

1. Compare documentary evidence of goods received and delivered with warehouse receipts records.
2. Account for issued and unissued warehouse receipts by number.
3. Compare records of goods stored with billings for storage.

When necessary, confirm the serial numbers supplied with the printer of the warehouse receipts.

OBSERVATION

The auditor should observe physical counts of goods in custody and reconcile test counts with records of goods stored. In the case of a field warehouse where goods are stored at many scattered locations, the auditor may observe physical counts at certain selected locations.

CONFIRMATION

Directly communicate with holders of warehouse receipts to confirm accountability. Confirmation of negotiable receipts with holders may not be practicable because the holder's identity usually is not known to the warehouseman. Confirmation with the depositor to whom the outstanding receipt was originally issued, however, is evidence of accountability for certain designated goods. In some circumstances, the auditor may wish to request confirmations from former depositors who are not currently holders of record.

OTHER PROCEDURES CONSIDERED NECESSARY

The auditor might review:

1. Bonding arrangements
2. Financial statements of, and credit reports on, some depositors
3. Insurance coverage
4. Adequacy of reserves for losses for damage claims

FUNDAMENTAL REQUIREMENTS: OWNER OF GOODS

INVESTIGATION OF WAREHOUSEMAN BEFORE PLACING GOODS IN HIS OR HER CUSTODY

The auditor should:

1. Consider the business reputation and financial standing of the warehouseman
2. Inspect facilities
3. Review warehouseman's financial statements and the related auditor's reports
4. Make inquiries about:
   a. The warehouseman's controls and whether he or she holds goods for his or her own account
   b. The type and adequacy of the warehouseman's insurance
   c. Government or other licensing and bonding requirements and the nature, extent, and results of any inspection by government or other agencies

EVALUATION OF WAREHOUSEMAN'S PERFORMANCE

The auditor should do the following:

1. Review and update information developed from the previously described investigation.
2. Perform physical counts of goods at the warehouse, if practicable and reasonable.
3. Reconcile quantities shown on statements from warehouseman with owner's records.

OTHER PROCEDURES

1. Review the owner's insurance, if any, on goods at warehouse.

FUNDAMENTAL REQUIREMENTS: OWNER'S AUDITOR

AU Section 331.14 describes the procedures the owner's auditor should consider applying if inventories are held in a public warehouse. The auditor should get direct confirmation, in writing, from the warehouseman. If inventories at a warehouse are a significant proportion of current assets or total assets, the auditor should apply one or more of the following procedures:

1. Assess control risk related to the client's procedures for investigating the warehouseman and evaluating his or her performance.
2. Observe physical counts of goods at warehouse, if practicable.
3. If warehouse receipts have been pledged as collateral, confirm details of pledged receipts with lenders (see AU Section 330).
4. Do one of the following:

    a. Obtain auditor's report on the warehouse's controls relevant to custody of goods and pledging of receipts (see Section AU 324).
    b. Apply procedures at the warehouse to gain reasonable assurance that information received from the warehouse is reliable.

INTERPRETATIONS

There are no interpretations for this section.

AT 101 Attest Engagements

EFFECTIVE DATE AND APPLICABILITY

Original Pronouncements   Statement on Standards for Attestation Engagements (SSAE) 10, *Attestation Standards: Revision and Recodification,* as amended by SSAE 11, January 2002, and SSAE 12.

Effective Date   These statements currently are effective.

Applicability   Attest engagements, as defined below, are performed by a certified public accountant in the practice of public accounting (practitioner). See AT Section 301, *Financial Forecasts and Projections*, for additional guidance on applicability when engaged to provide an attest service on a financial forecast or projection.

NOTE: Practitioners performing agreed-upon procedures must follow the general, fieldwork, and reporting standards for attest engagements described in the section, but should refer to AT Section 201 for specific guidance on performing such engagements. When a practitioner accepts an attest engagement for a government body or agency and agrees to follow specified government standards, guides, procedures, statutes, rules, and regulations, the practitioner must follow those governmental requirements as well as the applicable attestation standards.

DEFINITIONS OF TERMS

Assertion. A declaration or set of related declarations about whether the subject matter is based on, or in conformity with, the selected criteria.

NOTE: A conclusion on the reliability of a written assertion may refer to that assertion or to the subject matter to which the assertion relates. However, if there are one or more material deviations from the criteria, the practitioner should modify the report and should ordinarily express his or her conclusion directly on the subject matter, not on management's assertion.

Attest engagement. An engagement in which a practitioner is engaged to issue or does issue an examination, a review, or an agreed-upon procedures report on subject matter, or an assertion about the subject matter, that is the responsibility of another party.

NOTE: Professional services that are not covered by this section include the following:

1. *Services performed under Statements on Auditing Standards (SASs).*
2. *Services performed under Statements on Standards for Accounting and Review Services (SSARSs).*
3. *Services performed under the Statement on Standards for Consulting Services (SSCSs) including litigation services.*

4. Engagements to advocate a client's position, such as representing the client when dealing with the Internal Revenue Service (IRS).
5. Engagements to prepare tax returns or provide tax advice.

Attestation risk. The risk that the practitioner may unknowingly fail to appropriately modify his or her attest report on an assertion that is materially misstated. It consists of the risk (inherent and control risk) that the assertion contains errors that could be material and the risk (detection risk) that the practitioner will not detect such errors.

Criteria. The standards or benchmarks used to measure and present the subject matter and against which the practitioner evaluates the subject matter.

Responsible party. The person or persons (either as individuals or representatives of the entity) responsible for the subject matter. If no such party exists due to the nature of the subject matter, then a party who has a reasonable basis for making a written assertion about the subject matter may provide such an assertion.

Subject matter. Examples of the subject matter of an attest engagement include:

- Historical or prospective performance or condition, such as prospective financial information, performance measurements, and backlog data
- Physical characteristics, such as a narrative description or square footage of facilities
- Historical events, such as the price of a market basket or goods on a certain date
- Analyses, such as breakeven analyses
- Systems and processes, such as internal control
- Behavior, such as corporate governance or compliance with laws and regulations

DEFINING PROFESSIONAL REQUIREMENTS IN STATEMENTS ON STANDARDS FOR ATTESTATION ENGAGEMENTS

SSAE 13 added AT Section 20 to the professional standards, which clarifies that the SSAEs use two categories of professional requirements to describe the degree of responsibility the standards impose on auditors.

- *Unconditional requirements.* The practitioner is required to comply with an unconditional requirement in all cases in which the circumstances exist to which the unconditional requirement applies. SSAEs use the words *must* or *is required* to indicate an unconditional requirement.
- *Presumptively mandatory requirements.* The practitioner also is required to comply with a presumptively mandatory requirement in all cases in which the circumstances exist to which the presumptively mandatory requirement applies; however, in rare circumstances, the practitioner may depart from a presumptively mandatory requirement provided the practitioner documents his or her justification for the departure and how the alternative procedures performed in the circumstances were sufficient to achieve the objectives of the presumptively mandatory requirement. SSAEs use the word *should* to indicate a presumptively mandatory requirement.

The term "should consider" means that the consideration of the procedure or action is presumptively required, whereas carrying out of the procedure or action is not.

AT Section 20 also clarifies that explanatory material, which is defined within SSAEs, is intended to explain the objective of the professional requirements, rather than imposing a professional requirement for practitioner to perform.

OBJECTIVES OF SECTION 101

At one time, attest services provided by CPAs were limited to expressing a positive opinion on historical financial statements on the basis of an audit made in accordance with generally accepted auditing standards (GAAS). However, CPAs are increasingly requested to provide assurance on representations other than historical financial statements and in forms other than the positive opinion. The main objective of adopting the attestation standards was to provide guidance and establish a broad framework for the variety of attest services demanded of CPAs.

There are eleven attestation standards and two levels of attest assurance that can be reported for general distribution, as follows:

1. Positive assurance in reports that express conclusions on the basis of an *examination*.
2. Moderate assurance in reports that express conclusions on the basis of a *review*.

The guidance on attest services also provides for reports based on agreed-upon procedures or agreed-upon criteria, as long as the use of the report is limited to the parties who agreed upon the procedures or criteria.

In 1999, the Auditing Standards Board issued SSAE 9, *Amendments to SSAE Nos. 1, 2, and 3*. SSAE 9:

- Provided the option of reporting directly on the subject matter of the assertion, while still permitting practitioners to report on management's assertion. (The practitioner would continue to be required to obtain management's assertion as a condition of engagement performance.)
- Eliminated the requirement for a separate presentation of management's assertion in certain cases where the assertion is included in the introductory paragraph of the practitioner's report. (This limited approach to direct reporting was modified by SSAE 10.)
- Conformed the reporting guidance to include reporting elements similar to those required in auditor reports on historical financial statements as contained in Section 508, *Reports on Audited Financial Statements*.
- Provided guidance on the relationship between SSAEs and the Statements on Quality Control Standards.

In 2001, the Auditing Standards Board issued SSAE 10, *Attestation Standards: Revision and Recodification*. SSAE 10 superseded SSAEs 1 through 9 and renumbered the AT sections in the American Institute of Certified Public Accountants' (AICPA's) *Codification*. The primary driver behind the issuance of SSAE 10 was not the need for substantive changes, but the need to make the guidance among attest services more consistent. The revisions to this section included:

- Changing the title of this section to Attest Engagements
- Changing the definition of an attest engagement
- Clarifying that the attestation standards may be applied to a broad range of subject matter
- Clarifying the relationship between the responsible party, the client (if different from the responsible party), and the practitioner

- Clarifying that the essential elements of criteria referred to in the third general standard are that the criteria must be suitable, available to users, and the subject matter must be capable of reasonably consistent measurement
- Providing guidance on restricting the use of the report when a practitioner performs and reports on engagements when written assertion cannot be obtained
- Permitting true direct reporting on the subject matter (There is no requirement to make reference to an assertion in the practitioner's report. The practitioner would also be permitted to report on the written assertion.)
- Expanding guidance on the circumstances in which the use of attest reports should be restricted to specified parties

Additional changes made by SSAE 10 are described in AT Sections 201 to 701.

In 2002, the Auditing Standards Board issued SSAE 11, *Attest Documentation*. SSAE 11 incorporates in the attestation standards the concepts and terminology in AU Section 339, *Audit Documentation*. In 2002, SSAE 12, *Amendment to Statement on Standards for Attestation Engagements No. 10, Attestation Standards: Revision and Recodification*, was issued. SSAE 12 clarifies that although an effective quality control system will assist in complying with attestation standards, deficiencies in or noncompliance with the quality control system does not, by itself, indicate that an engagement was not performed according to the appropriate standards.

FUNDAMENTAL REQUIREMENTS

A practitioner who is engaged to issue or does issue an examination, a review, or an agreed-upon procedures report on subject matter, or an assertion about the subject matter that is the responsibility of another party, should do so in accordance with the eleven attestation standards described later in this section.

Any professional engagement which results in an expression of assurance must be performed under the applicable AICPA standards. Reports issued in connection with other professional standards should be clearly distinguished from attest reports.

An identified responsible party is a prerequisite for an attest engagement. A practitioner may accept an examination, a review, or an agreed-upon procedures engagement on subject matter or a related assertion if one of the following is met:

- The client is responsible for the subject matter. If, due to the nature of the subject matter, a responsible party does not otherwise exist, then the client must have a reasonable basis for providing a written assertion about the subject matter.
- If the client is not responsible for the subject matter, then he or she must be able to provide the practitioner, or have a responsible third party provide the practitioner, with evidence of the third party's responsibility for the subject matter.

NOTE: *The practitioner should not take on the role of the responsible party in an attest engagement.*

The practitioner should obtain written acknowledgement or other evidence (e.g., reference to legislation, a regulation, or a contract) of the responsible party's responsibility for the subject matter.

The eleven attestation standards are a natural extension of, *but do not supersede*, the ten standards in GAAS. Further, they do not supersede existing standards in SASs and SSARSs. The practitioner who is engaged to perform an engagement subject to these existing standards should follow such standards and not look to the eleven attestation standards or the discussion of them in AT Section 101 for guidance.

ATTESTATION STANDARDS

The 11 standards are classified as follows:

General: 1 through 5.
Fieldwork: 6 and 7.
Reporting: 8 through 11.

1. *First general standard.* The engagement shall be performed by a practitioner who must have adequate technical training and proficiency to perform the attestation engagement. (AT 101.19)
2. *Second general standard.* The engagement shall be performed by a practitioner who must have adequate knowledge of the subject matter. (AT 101.21)
3. *Third general standard.* The practitioner must have reason to believe that the subject matter is capable of evaluation against reasonable criteria that are suitable and available to users. (AT 101.23)

    a. *Suitable* criteria must be

    (1) *Objective*—Free from bias.
    (2) *Measurable*—Permit reasonably consistent measurements (qualitative or quantitative) of subject matter. The practitioner should consider whether the criteria are sufficiently precise to permit people having competence in and using the same measurement criterion to be able to obtain materially similar measurements.
    (3) *Complete*—Relevant factors that would alter a conclusion about the subject matter are not omitted.
    (4) *Relevant*—Be relevant to the subject matter.

    Criteria issued by a body designated by Council under the AICPA's *Code of Professional Conduct*, or issued by regulatory agencies and other bodies composed of experts that follow due-process procedures, are considered suitable. Other criteria that lack authoritative support should be evaluated according to the characteristics described above. Regardless of who establishes the criteria, the responsible party or client is responsible for selecting the criteria. The client is responsible for determining whether the criteria are appropriate for its purpose.

    b. The criteria must be *available* to users in one or more of the following ways:

    (1) Publicly
    (2) Through inclusion in a clear manner in the presentation of the subject matter or the assertion, or in the practitioner's report
    (3) By being well understood by most users, although not formally available

    If the criteria are only available to specified parties, such as the terms of a contract or criteria issued by an industry association and available only to those in the industry, the practitioner's report should be restricted to parties that have access to the criteria.

4. *Fourth general standard.* The practitioner must maintain an independence in mental attitude in all matters relating to the engagement. (AT 101.35)
5. *Fifth general standard.* The practitioner must exercise due professional care in the planning and performance of the engagement and the preparation of the report. (AT 101.39)
6. *First standard of fieldwork.* The practitioner must adequately plan the work and must properly supervise any assistants. (AT 101.42) Factors to be considered in planning an attest engagement include the following (AT 101.45):
   a. The criteria to be used
   b. Preliminary judgments about attestation risk and materiality
   c. Nature of the subject matter or the items within the assertion that are likely to require revision or adjustment
   d. Conditions that may require extension or modification of attest procedures
   e. Nature of report (see reporting standards) to be issued
7. *Second standard of fieldwork.* The practitioner must obtain sufficient evidence to provide a reasonable basis for the conclusion that is expressed in the report. (AT 101.51)

NOTE: *The standard also covers engagements designed solely to meet the needs of specified users who have participated in establishing the nature and scope of the engagement (agreed-upon procedures or agreed-upon criteria).*

In establishing an appropriate combination of procedures to accumulate evidence and appropriately restrict attestation risk, the practitioner should consider the following:

a. Evidence obtained from sources outside an entity, such as through confirmation, provides greater assurance of an assertion's reliability than evidence secured solely from within the entity.
b. Information obtained from the attester's direct personal knowledge, such as through physical examination, observation, computation, operating tests, or inspection, is more persuasive than information obtained indirectly.
c. The more effective the controls over the subject matter, the more assurance they provide about the subject matter or the assertion.

In an attest engagement designed to provide a high level of assurance (an examination), the practitioner should select from *all* available procedures any combination that can limit attestation risk to an appropriately low level.

In an attest engagement designed to provide a moderate level of assurance (a review), the practitioner's procedures are ordinarily limited to inquiries and analytical procedures and do not include search and verification procedures, such as confirmation and physical examination.

NOTE: *In an attest engagement designed solely to meet the needs of specified parties who have participated in establishing the nature and scope of the engagement, the practitioner is required to perform only those procedures that have been designed or agreed to by the parties.*

If the practitioner cannot obtain a written assertion from the responsible party, the practitioner should consider the effects on his or her ability to obtain sufficient evidence to form a conclusion about the subject matter. If the practitioner's client is the responsible party, the practitioner should ordinarily conclude that a scope limitation exists. If the practitioner's client is not the responsible party, the practitioner may be able to conclude that he or she has sufficient evidence to form a conclusion about the subject matter.

8. *First standard of reporting.* The practitioner must identify the subject matter or the assertion being reported on and state the character of the engagement in the report. (AT 101.63) The statement of the character of the attest engagement includes:

   a. A description of the nature and scope of the work performed, and
   b. A reference to the professional standards governing the engagement (see the "Illustrations" section).

NOTE: When the assertion does not accompany the practitioner's report, the first paragraph of the report should also contain a statement of the assertion. This requirement would be met by using a hot link *within the practitioner's report to management's assertion.*

9. *Second standard of reporting.* The practitioner must state the practitioner's conclusion about the subject matter or the assertion in relation to the criteria against which the subject matter was evaluated in the report. However, if conditions exist that, individually or in combination, result in one or more material deviations from the criteria, the practitioner should modify the report and should ordinarily express his or her conclusion directly on the subject matter, not on the assertion. (AT 101.66)

10. *Third standard of reporting.* The practitioner must state all of the practitioner's significant reservations about the engagement, the subject matter, and, if applicable, the assertion related thereto in the report. (AT 101.71)

    Reservations about the engagement include unresolved problems that the practitioner had in complying with the attestation, other interpretative standards, or specified agreed-upon procedures.

    Reservations about the engagement also include scope limitations. Scope restrictions may require the practitioner:

    a. To qualify the assurance provided,
    b. To disclaim any assurance, or
    c. To withdraw from the examination or review engagement.

    Ordinarily, if the scope limit is pervasive or imposed by the client, a disclaimer of opinion or withdrawal is appropriate.

    In a review engagement, the review is incomplete and the practitioner should withdraw from the engagement when:

    - The practitioner is unable to perform the necessary inquiry and analytical procedures.
    - The client is the responsible party and does not provide a written assertion.

    Reservations about the subject matter or assertion refer to questions about whether the subject matter or assertion is fairly stated, in all material respects, based on established or stated criteria, including adequacy of disclosure. They can result in either qualified or adverse opinions.

Reservations also include questions about measurement, form, arrangement, content or underlying judgments and assumptions applicable to the subject matter or the assertion. Reservations may require modification of the practitioner's report.

11. *Fourth standard of reporting.* The practitioner must state in the report that the report is intended solely for the information and use of the specified parties under the following circumstances: (AT 101.78)

- When the criteria used to evaluate the subject matter are determined by the practitioner to be appropriate only for a limited number of parties who either participated in their establishment or can be presumed to have an adequate understanding of the criteria
- When the criteria used to evaluate the subject matter are available only to specified parties
- When reporting on subject matter and a written assertion has not been provided by the responsible party
- When the report is on an attestation engagement to apply agreed-upon procedures to the subject matter

A number of circumstances may affect the need to restrict a report, including

- The purpose of the report
- The criteria used in preparation of the subject matter
- The extent to which the procedures performed are known or understood
- The potential for the report to be misunderstood when taken out of context

Although a practitioner should consider informing the client that restricted-use reports are not intended for distribution to nonspecified parties, regardless of whether they are included in a document containing a separate general-use report, a practitioner is not responsible for controlling a client's distribution of restricted-use reports.

Restricted-use reports should contain:

a. A statement indicating that the report is intended solely for the information and use of the specified parties
b. An identification of the specified parties to whom use is restricted
c. A statement that the report is not intended to be and should not be used by anyone other than these specified parties

NOTE: *A practitioner may restrict the use of any report.*

If a practitioner issues a single combined report covering both subject matter or presentations that require restrictions and those that do not require restrictions, the use of a single combined report should be restricted to the specified parties.

If a separate restricted-use report is included in a document that contains a general-use report, this does not affect the intended use of either report (i.e., the restricted-use report remains restricted and the general-use report continues to be for general use).

Examination Reports

In an attest engagement designed to achieve a high level of assurance (an examination), the practitioner's conclusion should be expressed in the form of an opinion (see "Illustrations: Examination Reports").

The practitioner should clearly state, in his opinion, whether (1) the subject matter is based on (or in conformity with) the criteria, in all material respects, or (2) the assertion is presented (or fairly stated), in all material respects, based on the criteria. Reports may be qualified or modified because of the subject matter, the assertion, or the engagement. Reports also may emphasize certain matters relating to the engagement.

The form of the practitioner's report depends on whether the practitioner's opinion is on the subject matter or assertion. According to AT 101.85, the practitioner's examination report on subject matter should include the following:

- A title that includes the word *independent*
- An identification of the subject matter and the responsible party
- Statements that:

  - The subject matter is the responsibility of the responsible party.
  - The practitioner's responsibility is to express an opinion on the subject matter based on his or her examination.
  - The examination was conducted in accordance with attestation standards established by the AICPA, and accordingly, included procedures that the practitioner considered necessary in the circumstances.
  - The practitioner believes the examination provides a reasonable basis for his or her opinion.

- The practitioner's opinion on whether the subject matter is based on (or in conformity with) the criteria in all material respects
- A statement restricting the use of the report to specified parties when the criteria used to evaluate the subject matter are determined to be appropriate only for a limited number of parties who understand the criteria, or when such criteria are available only to the specified parties; the report should also be restricted when a written assertion has not been provided by the responsible party, and a statement to that effect should be included in the introductory paragraph
- The manual or printed signature of the practitioner's firm
- The date of the examination report

Under AT 101.86, the practitioner's examination report on an assertion should include the following:

- A title that includes the word *independent*
- An identification of the assertion and the responsible party (when the assertion does not accompany the practitioner's report, the first paragraph of the report should also contain a statement of the assertion)
- Statements that:

  - The assertion is the responsibility of the responsible party
  - The practitioner's responsibility is to express an opinion on the assertion based on his or her examination

- The examination was conducted in accordance with attestation standards established by the AICPA, and accordingly, included procedures that the practitioner considered necessary in the circumstances
- The practitioner believes the examination provides a reasonable basis for his or her opinion

* The practitioner's opinion on whether the assertion is presented (or fairly stated), in all material respects, based on the criteria
* A statement restricting the use of the report to specified parties when the criteria used to evaluate the subject matter are appropriate only for a limited number of parties who understand the criteria, or when such criteria are available only to the specified parties
* The manual or printed signature of the practitioner's firm
* The date of the examination report

The practitioner is not precluded from examining an assertion but opining directly on the subject matter.

Review Reports

In an attest engagement designed to achieve only a moderate level of assurance (a review), the practitioner's conclusion should be expressed in the form of negative assurance (see "Illustrations: Review Reports"). The practitioner should state whether any information came to his or her attention that indicated (1) the subject matter is not based on (or in conformity with) the criteria or (2) the assertion is not presented in all material respects based on established or stated criteria.

According to AT 101.89 the practitioner's review report on subject matter should include:

* A title that includes the word *independent*
* An identification of the subject matter and the responsible party
* Statements that:
  - The subject matter is the responsibility of the responsible party.
  - The review was conducted in accordance with attestation standards established by AICPA.
  - A review is substantially less in scope than an examination, the objective of which is an expression of opinion on the subject matter, and accordingly, no such opinion is expressed.
* A statement about whether the practitioner is aware of any material modifications that should be made to the subject matter in order for it to be based on (or in conformity with), in all material respects, the criteria, other than those modifications, if any, indicated in his or her report.
* A statement restricting the use of the report to specified parties when the criteria used to evaluate the subject matter are appropriate only for a limited number of parties who understand the criteria, or when such criteria are available only to the specified parties. The report should also be restricted when a written assertion has not been provided by the responsible party, and a statement to that effect should be included in the introductory paragraph.
* The manual or printed signature of the practitioner's firm.

- The date of the examination report.

Under AT 101.90 the practitioner's review report on an assertion should include the following:

- A title that includes the word *independent*
- An identification of the assertion and the responsible party (when the assertion does not accompany the practitioner's report, the first paragraph of the report should also contain a statement of the assertion)
- Statements that:
  - The assertion is the responsibility of the responsible party.
  - The review was conducted in accordance with attestation standards established by AICPA.
  - A review is substantially less in scope than an examination, the objective of which is an expression of opinion on the assertion, and accordingly, no such opinion is expressed.
- A statement about whether the practitioner is aware of any material modifications that should be made to the assertion in order for it to be presented (or fairly stated), in all material respects, based on (or in conformity with) the criteria, other than those modifications, if any, indicated in his or her report
- A statement restricting the use of the report to specified parties when the criteria used to evaluate the subject matter are appropriate only for a limited number of parties who understand the criteria, or when such criteria are available only to the specified parties
- The manual or printed signature of the practitioner's firm
- The date of the review report

RELATIONSHIP TO QUALITY CONTROL STANDARDS

Attestation and quality control standards are related, since attestation standards relate to the conduct of individual attest engagements and quality control standards relate to the firm's whole attest practice. The quality control policies and procedures that a firm adopts may affect both the conduct of individual attest engagements and the conduct of a firm's attest practice as a whole. Therefore, SSAE 10 requires firms to adopt a system of quality control in the conduct of their attest practice. However, deficiencies in or noncompliance with the quality control system does not, by itself, indicate that an engagement was not performed according to the appropriate standards.

ATTEST DOCUMENTATION

The practitioner should prepare and maintain documentation of the attest engagement. The form and content of the attest documentation will depend on the particular engagement's circumstances. The practitioner should use professional judgment in determining the quantity, type, and content of attest documentation.

Attest documentation is the principal record of the procedures applied, information obtained, and conclusions or findings reached by the practitioner. It serves to provide the primary support for the practitioner's report and assist in the conduct and supervision of the engagement. It should be sufficient to:

- Allow members of the engagement team with supervisory and review responsibilities to understand the nature, timing, extent, and results of attest procedures performed, and the information obtained, and
- Indicate which engagement team members performed and reviewed the work.

Attest documentation, which may be in paper or electronic form, includes work programs, analyses, memoranda, letters of confirmation and representation, abstracts or copies of the entity's documents, and schedules or commentaries prepared or obtained by the practitioner.

The practitioner owns the attest documentation, and some states recognize this right of ownership in their statutes. However, the practitioner has an ethical, and sometimes legal, obligation to maintain the confidentiality of the client or responsible party. The practitioner should adopt reasonable procedures to maintain the confidentiality of information contained in the attest documentation and to prevent unauthorized access to that documentation. The practitioner should also retain the attest documentation for a period sufficient to meet the needs of his or her practice, and to satisfy any pertinent legal or regulatory requirements for records retention. (The practitioner should be able to access electronic documentation throughout the retention period.)

Sometimes attest documentation may serve as a source of reference for the client, but such documentation should not be considered as part of, or a substitute for, the client's accounting records.

When performing an examination of prospective financial statements, attest documentation ordinarily should indicate that the practitioner considered the process by which the entity develops its prospective financial statements in determining the scope of the engagement.

NOTE: Although the requirement to maintain attest documentation is stated in SSAE 10, changes have been made by SSAE 11, which reflect the concepts and terms used in SAS 96.

ESTABLISHING AN UNDERSTANDING WITH THE CLIENT

According to AT 101.46, the practitioner should establish an understanding with the client on the services to be performed for each engagement that includes:

1. The objectives of the engagement
2. Management's responsibilities
3. Practitioner's responsibilities
4. Limitations of the engagement

The understanding should be documented, preferably through a written communication with the client. If the practitioner believes that an understanding has not been established, he or she should not accept the engagement.

REPRESENTATION LETTER

In an examination or review engagement, a practitioner should consider obtaining a representation letter from the responsible party. According to AU 101.60, examples of representations that may be included are:

- A statement acknowledging responsibility for the subject matter and the assertion (if applicable)
- A statement acknowledging responsibility for selecting the criteria (if applicable)

- A statement acknowledging responsibility for determining that such criteria are appropriate for its purposes, where the responsible party is the client
- The assertion about the subject matter based on the selected criteria
- A statement that all known matters contradicting the assertion and any communication from regulatory agencies affecting the subject matter or the assertion have been disclosed to the practitioner
- Availability of all records relevant to the subject matter
- A statement that any known events subsequent to the period (or point in time) of the subject matter being reported on that would have a material effect on the subject matter (or assertion, if applicable) have been disclosed to the practitioner

If the client is not the responsible party, the practitioner should consider obtaining a representation letter from the client. According to AU 101.61, examples of representations included in the letter are:

- A statement that any known material subsequent events have been disclosed
- A statement acknowledging the client's responsibility for selecting the criteria, if applicable
- A statement acknowledging the client's responsibility for determining that such criteria are appropriate

If the responsible party or client refuses to furnish necessary written representations in an examination engagement, the practitioner should consider the impact on the ability to issue a conclusion about the subject matter. If the representation is necessary to obtain sufficient evidence to issue a report, the responsible party or client's refusal may cause the practitioner to disclaim an opinion or withdraw. However, in other circumstances, a qualified opinion may be appropriate. The practitioner should also consider whether the refusal affects his or her ability to rely on other representations.

If the engagement is a review and a scope limitation exists, the practitioner should withdraw from the engagement.

NOTE: *Written representations are part of the evidential matter that the practitioner obtains.*

OTHER INFORMATION IN A CLIENT-PREPARED DOCUMENT CONTAINING THE PRACTITIONER'S ATTEST REPORT

A practitioner's report may appear in:

- Annual reports to holders of securities or beneficial interests
- Annual reports of organizations for charitable or philanthropic purposes
- Annual reports filed with regulatory authorities under the Securities Exchange Act of 1934
- Other documents to which the practitioner, at the client's request, devotes attention

In this case, the auditor should do the following:

1. Read the other information.

   NOTE: *This is the knowledgeable study of information by an auditor who has an understanding of the client's business, organization, and operating characteristics, as well as its financial characteristics.*

2. Consider whether the other information is materially inconsistent with information in the audited financial statements. This consideration includes the manner of presentation of both the other information and comparable information in the financial statements.
3. If there is a material inconsistency:
   a. Determine whether the financial statements, the report, or both require revision.

   > NOTE: This means the auditor should decide if the difference is caused by a misstatement in the financial statements.

   b. Request that the client revise the other information if it, rather than the financial statements, is misstated.
   c. If the other information is not revised, consider other actions such as:
      (1) Revising the report to include an explanatory paragraph describing the material inconsistency
      (2) Withholding the use of the report in the document
      (3) Withdrawing from the engagement
4. If the auditor's reading makes him or her aware of a material misstatement of fact, he or she should:
   a. Discuss the matter with the client.
   b. Consider that:
      (1) He or she may not have the expertise to assess the validity of the statement.
      (2) There may be no standards by which to assess its presentation.
      (3) There may be valid differences of judgment or opinion.

   > NOTE: This means that concluding there is a material misstatement is much more subjective than concluding there is a material inconsistency.

   c. Request that the client seek the advice of legal counsel on the matter.
   d. If the auditor concludes after discussion with the client that there is, in fact, a material misstatement of fact, he or she should consider steps such as:
      (1) Notifying the client in writing of his or her views
      (2) Consulting his or her own legal counsel on what other action is appropriate

SUBSEQUENT EVENTS

Subsequent events are events or transactions that occur after the point in time or period of time of the subject matter being tested but not before the date of the practitioner's report that have a material effect on the subject matter and therefore require adjustment or disclosure in the financial statements.

The two types of events that a practitioner must consider include:

1. Events that provide additional evidence about conditions that existed at the point in time or during the period of time of the subject matter being tested. The practitioner should use this information in considering whether the subject matter is presented in conformity with the criteria and may affect the presentation of the subject matter, the assertion, or the practitioner's report.

2. Events that provide evidence about conditions that arose after the point in time or period of time of the subject matter being tested that need to be disclosed to keep the subject matter from being misleading. This type of subsequent event will not normally affect the practitioner's report if the information is disclosed.

The practitioner is not responsible for to detecting subsequent events. However, the practitioner should ask the responsible party if they are aware of any subsequent events through the date of the practitioner's report that would have a material effect on the subject matter or assertion. If a representation letter is obtained, the letter should include a representation concerning subsequent events.

If the practitioner subsequently becomes aware of conditions that existed at the date of the practitioner's report that might have affected the report had the practitioner been aware of them, the practitioner should consider the guidance in Section 561, *Subsequent Discovery of Facts Existing at the Date of the Auditor's Report*.

COMPARISON OF ATTESTATION STANDARDS WITH GAAS

Following is a table that compares attestation standards with GAAS.

Attestation Standards	*GAAS*
General Standards	
1. The engagement shall be performed by a practitioner having adequate technical training and proficiency in the attest function.	1. The audit is to be performed by a person or persons having adequate technical training and proficiency as an auditor.
2. The engagement shall be performed by a practitioner having adequate knowledge of the subject matter.	
3. The practitioner shall perform the engagement only if he or she has reason to believe that the subject matter is capable of evaluation against criteria that are suitable and available to users.	
4. In all matters relating to the engagement, an independence in mental attitude shall be maintained by the practitioner.	2. In all matters relating to the assignment, an independence in mental attitude is to be maintained by the auditor or auditors.
5. Due professional care shall be exercised in the planning and performance of the engagement.	3. Due professional care is to be exercised in the performance of the audit and the preparation of the report.
Standards of Fieldwork	
1. The work shall be adequately planned and assistants, if any, shall be properly supervised.	1. The work is to be adequately planned and assistants, if any, are to be properly supervised.
	2. A sufficient understanding of internal control is to be obtained to plan the audit and to determine the nature, timing, and extent of tests to be performed.
2. Sufficient evidence shall be obtained to provide a reasonable basis for the conclusion that is expressed in the report.	3. Sufficient competent evidential matter is to be obtained through inspection, observation, inquiries, and confirmations to afford a reasonable basis for an opinion regarding the financial statements under audit.

Attestation Standards   GAAS

Standards of Reporting

Attestation Standards	GAAS
1. The report shall identify the subject matter or the assertion being reported on and state the character of the engagement.	
2. The report shall state the practitioner's conclusion about the subject matter or the assertion in relation to the criteria against which the subject matter was evaluated.	1. The report shall state whether the financial statements are presented in accordance with GAAP.
	2. The report shall identify those circumstances in which such principles have not been consistently observed in the current period in relation to the preceding period.
	3. Informative disclosures in the financial statements are to be regarded as reasonably adequate unless otherwise stated in the report.
3. The report shall state all of the practitioner's significant reservations about the engagement, the subject matter, and if applicable, the assertion related thereto.	4. The report shall either contain an expression of opinion regarding the financial statements taken as a whole, or an assertion to the effect that an opinion cannot be expressed. When an overall opinion cannot be expressed, the reasons therefore should be stated. In all cases where an auditor's name is associated with financial statements, the report should contain a clear-cut indication of the character of the auditor's work, if any, and the degree of responsibility he or she is taking.
4. The report shall state that the use of the report is restricted to specified parties under the following circumstances: • When the criteria used to evaluate the subject matter are determined by the practitioner to be appropriate only for a limited number of parties who either participated in their establishment or can be presumed to have an adequate understanding of the criteria. • When the criteria used to evaluate the subject matter are available only to specified parties. • When reporting on subject matter and a written assertion has not been provided by the responsible party. • When the report is on an attest engagement to apply agreed-upon procedures to the subject matter.	

INTERPRETATIONS

DEFENSE INDUSTRY QUESTIONNAIRE ON BUSINESS ETHICS AND CONDUCT (ISSUED AUGUST 1987; AMENDED FEBRUARY 1989; MODIFIED MAY 1989; REVISED JANUARY 2001; REVISED NOVEMBER 2006)

This interpretation provides detailed guidance to a practitioner engaged to examine or review a defense contractor's responses to a questionnaire related to principles of business ethics and conduct adopted by certain companies in the defense industry.

RESPONDING TO REQUESTS FOR REPORTS ON MATTERS RELATING TO SOLVENCY (ISSUED MAY 1988; AMENDED FEBRUARY 1993; REVISED JANUARY 2001; REVISED NOVEMBER 2006)

An accountant should not provide any form of assurance, through examination, review, or agreed-upon procedures, that an entity:

1. Is not insolvent at the time debt is incurred or would not be rendered insolvent thereby
2. Does not have unreasonably small capital
3. Has the ability to pay its debts as they mature

An accountant may provide a client with various professional services that might be useful to a client in connection with a financing, but the scope of services and form of report have to conform to the requirements of the relevant professional standards.

If an accountant reports on the results of applying agreed-upon procedures, in addition to the normal requirements, the report should make clear that no representations are provided on questions of legal interpretation and no assurance is provided concerning the borrower's solvency, adequacy of capital, or ability to pay its debts.

APPLICABILITY OF ATTESTATION STANDARDS TO LITIGATION SERVICES (JULY 1990; REVISED JANUARY 2001)

Attestation standards do not apply to litigation services unless the practitioner has been specifically engaged to express a written conclusion about the reliability of a written assertion that is the responsibility of another party and that conclusion and assertion are for the use of others who, under the rules of the proceedings, do not have an opportunity to analyze and challenge such work. The attestation standards would apply if the practitioner is specifically requested by a litigant to issue an attestation services report.

A practitioner is not prohibited from providing expert testimony on matters relating to solvency. The prohibition on providing written reports related to solvency does not apply in a legal forum in which the legal definition and interpretation of matters relating to solvency can be analyzed and challenged by the opposing party.

PROVIDING ACCESS TO, OR PHOTOCOPIES OF, WORKING PAPERS TO A REGULATOR (MAY 1996; REVISED JANUARY 2001; REVISED JANUARY 2002)

A regulator's request for access to or photocopies of working papers in an attestation engagement should be treated in the same manner as a request related to audit working papers (see Section 339).

ATTEST ENGAGEMENTS ON FINANCIAL INFORMATION INCLUDED IN XBRL INSTANCE DOCUMENTS (SEPTEMBER 2003)

NOTE: This interpretation was issued after the date that the PCAOB issued Release No. 2003-006, which recognized AICPA standards as interim transitional standards. Therefore, this guidance is not considered authoritative for practitioners with public company clients.

This interpretation provides guidance on the practitioner's considerations when he or she is engaged to examine and report on whether an Instance Document accurately reflects underlying financial information. (XBRL is the business reporting part of Extensible Markup

Language [XML], a freely licensable open technology standard, which makes it possible to store and transfer data. An entity's financial information is made available in XBRL in a machine-readable format called an "Instance Document," which can then be distributed electronically through e-mail, on a website, etc.)

The practitioner should first make sure that the subject matter is capable of evaluation against suitable and available criteria. Two criteria, XBRL taxonomies and XBRL International Technical Specifications, meet these criteria. Some entities may create their own taxonomies, which the practitioner must evaluate to determine if they are "suitable and available."

The interpretation offers examples of procedures that the practitioner should consider performing to obtain sufficient evidential matter to form an opinion, such as:

- Comparing the rendered (i.e., converted from machine language) Instance Document to the financial information
- Tracing and agreeing the Instance Document's tagged information to the financial information
- Testing that the financial information is tagged and included in the Instance Document
- Testing that tagging is consistent
- Testing that extension or custom taxonomy meets the XBRL International Technical Specification

When reporting on such an engagement, the practitioner should note whether the underlying financial information has been audited or reviewed. If so, reference to the audit or review should be made. If not, the practitioner should disclaim an opinion on the underlying financial information. If there is information in the Instance Document not covered by the practitioner's report, it should be clearly identified.

Examples of reports for these types of engagements are show in Examination Reports Illustrations 8 and 9.

REPORTING ON ATTESTATION ENGAGEMENTS PERFORMED IN ACCORDANCE WITH GOVERNMENT AUDITING STANDARDS (DECEMBER 2004; REVISED JANUARY 2008)

When an auditor performs an attestation engagement in accordance with generally accepted government auditing standards, the scope paragraph of the report should be modified to indicate that the work was "conducted in accordance with attestation standards established by the American Institute of Certified Public Accountants and the standards applicable to attestation engagements contained in *Government Auditing Standards* issued by the Comptroller General of the United States."

REPORTING ON THE DESIGN OF INTERNAL CONTROL (DECEMBER 2008)

The auditor cannot report on the suitability of the design of an entity's internal control, based on the risk assessment procedures performed to gain an understanding of the entity and its environment, since these procedures do not provide a sufficient basis of information to make such a report.

If the auditor is asked to sign a prescribed form developed by the party to whom the reports are to be submitted regarding the design of an entity's internal controls, the auditor should either revise the form or attach a separate report that conforms to the auditor's professional standards.

The auditor should not submit a report about an entity's ability to establish suitable internal controls.

INCLUDING A DESCRIPTION OF TESTS OF CONTROLS OR OTHER PROCEDURES, AND THE RESULTS THEREOF, IN AN EXAMINATION REPORT (JULY 2010)

The circumstances of a specific engagement are relevant to a practitioner's consideration of whether to include a description of tests of controls or other procedures performed, as well as the results of those tests, in the examination report. The practitioner should consider the following when determining whether to include this description:

- Whether there has been a request for this information
- Whether there is a business need for requesting it
- Whether report recipients have sufficient knowledge of the engagement to understand the description
- Whether including the description in the report will cause a misunderstanding of the opinion
- Whether tests of controls or other procedures by the practitioner directly relate to the engagement

Adding this description to the report may increase the need to restrict the use of the report to specific parties.

ILLUSTRATIONS: EXAMINATION REPORTS

These illustrations are adapted from SSAE 10.

ILLUSTRATION 1. STANDARD EXAMINATION REPORT ON SUBJECT MATTER FOR GENERAL USE

This report pertains to subject matter for which suitable criteria exist and are available to all users through inclusion in a clear manner in the presentation of the subject matter. A written assertion has been obtained from the responsible party.

Independent Accountant's Report

To the Board of Directors
Widget Company
Main City, USA

We have examined the accompanying schedule of investment returns of Widget Company for the year ended December 31, 20X1. Widget Company's management is responsible for the schedule of investment returns. Our responsibility is to express an opinion on this statement based on our examination.

Our examination was conducted in accordance with attestation standards established by the American Institute of Certified Public Accountants and, accordingly, included examining, on a test basis, evidence supporting Widget Company's schedule of investment returns and performing such other procedures as we considered necessary in the circumstances. We believe that our examination provides a reasonable basis for our opinion.

[Additional paragraph(s) may be added to emphasize certain matters relating to the attest engagement or the subject matter.]

In our opinion, the schedule referred to above presents, in all material respects, the investment returns of Widget Company for the year ended December 31, 20X1, based on the [XXX] criteria set forth in Note 1.

Smith and Jones
February 15, 20X2

> **ILLUSTRATION 2. STANDARD EXAMINATION REPORT ON AN ASSERTION FOR GENERAL USE**

This report pertains to subject matter for which suitable criteria exist and are available to all users through inclusion in a clear manner in the presentation of the subject matter. A written assertion has been obtained from the responsible party.

Independent Accountant's Report

To the Board of Directors
Widget Company
Main City, USA

We have examined management's assertion that the accompanying schedule of investment returns of Widget Company for the year ended December 31, 20X1, is presented in accordance with [XXX] criteria set forth in Note 1. Widget Company's management is responsible for the assertion. Our responsibility is to express an opinion on the assertion based on our examination.

Our examination was conducted in accordance with attestation standards established by the American Institute of Certified Public Accountants and, accordingly, included examining, on a test basis, evidence supporting management's assertions and performing such other procedures as we considered necessary in the circumstances. We believe that our examination provides a reasonable basis for our opinion.

[*Additional paragraph(s) may be added to emphasize certain matters relating to the attest engagement or the assertion.*]

In our opinion, management's assertion referred to above is fairly stated, in all material respects, based on the [XXX] criteria set forth in Note 1.

Smith and Jones
February 15, 20X2

> **ILLUSTRATION 3. EXAMINATION REPORT FOR GENERAL USE**

The introductory paragraph states the practitioner has examined management's assertion, but the practitioner opines directly on the subject matter. The report pertains to subject matter for which suitable criteria exist and are available to all users through inclusion in a clear manner in the presentation of the subject matter. A written assertion has been obtained from the responsible party.

Independent Accountant's Report

To the Board of Directors
Widget Company
Main City, USA

We have examined management's assertion that the accompanying schedule of investment returns of Widget Company for the year ended December 31, 20X1, is presented in accordance with the [XXX] criteria set forth in Note 1. Widget Company's management is responsible for the assertion. Our responsibility is to express an opinion on this statement based on our examination.

Our examination was conducted in accordance with attestation standards established by the American Institute of Certified Public Accountants and, accordingly, included examining, on a test basis, evidence supporting Widget Company's schedule of investment returns and performing such other procedures as we considered necessary in the circumstances. We believe that our examination provides a reasonable basis for our opinion.

[Additional paragraph(s) may be added to emphasize certain matters relating to the attest engagement or the assertion.]

In our opinion, the schedule referred to above presents, in all material respects, the investment returns of Widget Company for the year ended December 31, 20X1, based on the [XXX] criteria set forth in Note 1.

Smith and Jones
February 15, 20X2

ILLUSTRATION 4. EXAMINATION REPORT ON SUBJECT MATTER; USE OF REPORT RESTRICTED

In this example, use of the report is restricted because although suitable criteria exist, the criteria are available only to specified parties. A written assertion has been obtained from the responsible party.

Independent Accountant's Report

To the Board of Directors
Widget Company
Main City, USA

We have examined the accompanying schedule of investment returns of Widget Company for the year ended December 31, 20X1. Widget Company's management is responsible for the schedule of investment returns. Our responsibility is to express an opinion on this statement based on our examination.

Our examination was conducted in accordance with attestation standards established by the American Institute of Certified Public Accountants and, accordingly, included examining, on a test basis, evidence supporting Widget Company's schedule of investment returns and performing such other procedures as we considered necessary in the circumstances. We believe that our examination provides a reasonable basis for our opinion.

[Additional paragraph(s) may be added to emphasize certain matters relating to the attest engagement or the assertion.]

In our opinion, the schedule referred to above presents, in all material respects, the investment returns of Widget Company for the year ended December 31, 20X1, based on the criteria referred to in the investment management agreement between Widget Company and Basic Investment Managers, Ltd., dated November 15, 20X1.

This report is intended solely for the information and use of Widget Company and Basic Investment Managers, Ltd. and is not intended to be and should not be used by anyone other than these specified parties.

Smith and Jones
February 15, 20X2

ILLUSTRATION 5. EXAMINATION REPORT: QUALIFIED OPINION

In this example, the opinion is qualified because conditions exist that, individually or in combination, result in one or more material misstatements or deviations from the criteria. The report is for general use and pertains to subject matter for which suitable criteria exist and are available to all users through inclusion in a clear manner in the presentation of the subject matter. A written assertion has been obtained from the responsible party.

Independent Accountant's Report

To the Board of Directors
Widget Company
Main City, USA

We have examined the accompanying schedule of investment returns of Widget Company for the year ended December 31, 20X1. Widget Company's management is responsible for the schedule of investment returns. Our responsibility is to express an opinion based on our examination.

Our examination was conducted in accordance with attestation standards established by the American Institute of Certified Public Accountants and, accordingly, included examining, on a test basis, evidence supporting Widget Company's schedule of investment returns and performing such other procedures as we considered necessary in the circumstances. We believe that our examination provides a reasonable basis for our opinion.

Our examination disclosed the following [*describe condition(s) that, individually or in the aggregate, resulted in a material misstatement or deviation from the criteria*].

In our opinion, except for the material misstatement (or deviation from the criteria) described in the preceding paragraph, the schedule referred to above presents, in all material respects, the investment returns of Widget Company for the year ended December 31, 20X1, based on the [XXX] criteria set forth in Note 1.

Smith and Jones
February 15, 20X2

ILLUSTRATION 6. EXAMINATION REPORT: DISCLAIMER OF OPINION

This example illustrates a disclaimer of opinion because of a scope restriction. The report pertains to subject matter for which suitable criteria exist and are available to all users through inclusion in a clear manner in the presentation of the subject matter.

Independent Accountant's Report

To the Board of Directors
Widget Company
Main City, USA

We were engaged to examine the accompanying schedule of investment returns of Widget Company for the year ended December 31, 20X1. Widget Company's management is responsible for the schedule of investment returns.

Because of the restriction on the scope of our examination discussed in the preceding paragraph, the scope of our work was not sufficient to enable us to express, and we do not express, an opinion on whether the schedule referred to above presents, in all material respects, the investment returns of Widget Company for the year ended December 31, 20X1, based on the [XXX] criteria set forth in Note 1.

Smith and Jones
February 15, 20X2

NOTE: *The scope paragraph should be omitted, and paragraphs describing the scope restrictions should be included.*

ILLUSTRATION 7. EXAMINATION REPORT: SUBJECT MATTER IS THE RESPONSIBILITY OF A PARTY OTHER THAN THE CLIENT

In this example, the report is restricted as to use, since a written assertion has not been provided by the responsible party. The subject matter pertains to criteria that are suitable and are available to the client.

Independent Accountant's Report

To the Board of Directors
Widget Company
Main City, USA

We have examined the accompanying schedule of investment returns of Widget Company for the year ended December 31, 20X1. Widget Company's management is responsible for the schedule of investment returns. Widget management did not provide us a written assertion about their schedule of investment returns for the year ended December 31, 20X1. Our responsibility is to express an opinion based on our examination.

Our examination was conducted in accordance with attestation standards established by the American Institute of Certified Public Accountants and, accordingly, included examining, on a test basis, evidence supporting Widget Company's schedule of investment returns and performing such other procedures as we considered necessary in the circumstances. We believe that our examination provides a reasonable basis for our opinion.

[Additional paragraph(s) may be added to emphasize certain matters relating to the attest engagement or the subject matter.]

In our opinion, the schedule referred to above presents, in all material respects, the investment returns of Widget Company for the year ended December 31, 20X1, based on the [XXX] criteria set forth in Note 1.

This report is intended solely for the information and use of the management and the board of directors of Widget Company and is not intended to be and should not be used by anyone other than these specified parties.

Smith and Jones
February 15, 20X2

ILLUSTRATION 8. EXAMINATION REPORT ON SUBJECT MATTER FOR AN ENGAGEMENT ON FINANCIAL INFORMATION INCLUDED IN AN XBRL INSTANCE DOCUMENT

The following illustration, adapted from an interpretation of AT 101, assumes that the underlying financial information was audited by the practitioner.

Independent Accountant's Report

To the Board of Directors
Widget Company
Main City, USA

We have examined the accompanying XBRL Instance Document of Widget Company that reflects the data presented in the financial statements of Widget Company as of December 31, 20X1, and for the year then ended. Widget Company's management is responsible for the XBRL Instance Document. Our responsibility is to express an opinion based on our examination.

We have also audited, in accordance with auditing standards generally accepted in the United States of America, the financial statements of Widget Company as of December 31, 20X1, and for the year then ended, and in our report dated February 15, 20X2, we expressed an unqualified opinion on those financial statements. [*If the report is other than unqualified, disclose this and the reasons behind the modified opinion.*]

Our examination was conducted in accordance with attestation standards established by the American Institute of Certified Public Accountants and, accordingly, included examining, on a test basis, evidence supporting the XBRL Instance Document and performing such other procedures as we considered necessary in the circumstances. We believe that our examination provides a reasonable basis for our opinion.

In our opinion, the XBRL Instance Document of Widget Company referred to above accurately reflects, in all material respects, the data presented in the financial statements in conformity with the [*identify criteria*].

Smith and Jones
February 15, 20X2

ILLUSTRATION 9. EXAMINATION REPORT ON MANAGEMENT'S ASSERTIONS FOR AN ENGAGEMENT ON FINANCIAL INFORMATION INCLUDED IN AN XBRL INSTANCE DOCUMENT

The following illustration, adapted from an interpretation of AT 101, assumes that the underlying financial information was audited by the practitioner.

Independent Accountant's Report

To the Board of Directors
Widget Company
Main City, USA

We have examined management's assertion that the accompanying XBRL Instance Document accurately reflects the data presented in the financial statements of Widget Company as of December 31, 20X1 and for the year then ended in conformity with XBRL U.S. Consumer and Industrial Taxonomy and the XBRL International Technical Specifications 2.0. Widget Company's management is responsible for the assertion. Our responsibility is to express an opinion on the assertion based on our examination.

We have also audited, in accordance with auditing standards generally accepted in the United States of America, the financial statements of Widget Company as of December 31, 20X1, and for the year then ended; in our report dated February 15, 20X2, we expressed an unqualified opinion on those financial statements.

Our examination was conducted in accordance with attestation standards established by the American Institute of Certified Public Accountants and, accordingly, included examining, on a test basis, evidence supporting the XBRL Instance Document and performing such other procedures as we considered necessary in the circumstances. We believe that our examination provides a reasonable basis for our opinion.

In our opinion, management's assertion referred to above is fairly stated, in all material respects, in conformity with XBRL U.S. Consumer and Industrial Taxonomy and the XBRL International Technical Specifications 2.0.

Smith and Jones
February 15, 20X2

ILLUSTRATIONS: REVIEW REPORTS

These illustrations are adapted from SSAE 10.

ILLUSTRATION 1. STANDARD REVIEW REPORT ON SUBJECT MATTER FOR GENERAL USE

This report pertains to subject matter for which suitable criteria exist and are available to all users through inclusion in a clear manner in the presentation of the subject matter. A written assertion has been obtained from the responsible party.

Independent Accountant's Report

To the Board of Directors
Widget Company
Main City, USA

We have reviewed the accompanying schedule of investment returns of Widget Company for the year ended December 31, 20X1. Widget Company's management is responsible for the schedule of investment returns.

Our review was conducted in accordance with attestation standards established by the American Institute of Certified Public Accountants. A review is substantially less in scope than an examination, the objective of which is the expression of an opinion on Widget Company's schedule of investment returns. Accordingly, we do not express such an opinion.

[Additional paragraph(s) may be added to emphasize certain matters relating to the attest engagement or the subject matter.]

Based on our review, nothing came to our attention that caused us to believe that the schedule of investment returns of Widget Company for the year ended December 31, 20X1, is not presented, in all material respects, in conformity with the [XXX] criteria set forth in Note 1.

Smith and Jones
February 15, 20X2

ILLUSTRATION 2. REVIEW REPORT: SUBJECT MATTER IS THE RESPONSIBILITY OF A PARTY OTHER THAN THE CLIENT

This review report is restricted as to use since a written assertion has not been provided by the responsible party. The subject matter pertains to criteria that are suitable and are available to the client.

Independent Accountant's Report

To the Board of Directors
Widget Company
Main City, USA

We have reviewed the accompanying schedule of investment returns of Widget Company for the year ended December 31, 20X1. Widget Company's management is responsible for the schedule of investment returns. Widget Company's management did not provide us a written assertion about their schedule of investment returns for the year ended December 31, 20X1.

Our review was conducted in accordance with attestation standards established by the American Institute of Certified Public Accountants. A review is substantially less in scope than an examination, the objective of which is the expression of an opinion on Widget Company's schedule of investment returns. Accordingly, we do not express such an opinion.

[*Additional paragraph(s) may be added to emphasize certain matters relating to the attest engagement or the subject matter.*]

Based on our review, nothing came to our attention that caused us to believe that the schedule of investment returns of Widget Company for the year ended December 31, 20X1, is not presented, in all material respects, in conformity with the [XXX] criteria set forth in Note 1.

This report is intended solely for the information and use of the management and the board of directors of Widget Company and is not intended to be and should not be used by anyone other than these specified parties.

Smith and Jones
February 15, 20X2

ILLUSTRATION 3. REVIEW REPORT ON AN ASSERTION

Although suitable criteria exist for the subject matter, the report is restricted since the criteria are available only to specified parties. A written assertion has been obtained from the responsible party.

Independent Accountant's Report

To the Board of Directors
Widget Company
Main City, USA

We have reviewed management's assertion that the accompanying schedule of investment returns of Widget Company for the year ended December 31, 20X1, is presented in accordance with the [XXX] criteria referred to in Note 1. Widget Company's management is responsible for the assertion.

Our review was conducted in accordance with attestation standards established by the American Institute of Certified Public Accountants. A review is substantially less in scope than an examination, the objective of which is the expression of an opinion on management's opinion. Accordingly, we do not express such an opinion.

[*Additional paragraph(s) may be added to emphasize certain matters relating to the attest engagement or the assertion.*]

Based on our review, nothing came to our attention that caused us to believe that management's assertion referred to above is not fairly stated, in all material respects, based on the [XXX] criteria referred to in the investment management agreement between Widget Company and Basic Investment Managers, Ltd., dated November 15, 20X1.

This report is intended solely for the information and use of Widget Company and Basic Investment Managers, Ltd. and is not intended to be and should not be used by anyone other than these specified parties.

Smith and Jones
February 15, 20X2

AT 201 Agreed-Upon Procedures Engagements [1]

EFFECTIVE DATE AND APPLICABILITY

Original Pronouncement	Statement on Standards for Attestation Engagements (SSAE) 10, *Attestation Standards: Revision and Recodification,* as amended by SSAE 11.
Effective Date	These statements currently are effective.
Applicability	All agreed-upon procedures engagements, except the following:

1. Situations in which an accountant reports on specified compliance requirements based solely on an audit (see AU Section 623, *Special Reports*)
2. Engagements for which the objective is to report in accordance with AU Section 801, *Compliance Auditing Considerations in Audits of Governmental Entities and Recipients of Governmental Financial Assistance*
3. Circumstances covered by AU Section 324, *Service Organizations*, when the service auditor is requested to apply substantive procedures to user transactions or assets at the service organization and he or she makes specific reference in the service auditor's report to having carried out designated procedures
4. Engagements covered by AU Section 634, *Letters for Underwriters and Certain Other Requesting Parties*

When performing agreed-upon procedures on prospective information or compliance matters, the practitioner should refer to AT Section 301, *Forecasts and Projections*, and AT Section 601, *Compliance Attestation*.

---

[1] *Statement of Position (SOP) 01-3,* Performing Agreed-Upon Procedures Engagements That Address Internal Control over Derivative Transactions as Required by the New York State Insurance Law, *provides guidance to practitioners on performing an agreed-upon procedures engagement that enables insurance companies to meet the requirements of the New York Derivative Law (the Law) that amends Article 14 of the New York Insurance Law. The Law requires insurers who enter into derivative transactions to file with the State of New York Insurance Department (Department) a statement describing an independent CPA's assessment of the insurance company's internal control over derivative transactions. This assessment is considered part of the evaluation of internal control prescribed by section 307(b) of the New York State Insurance Law. An assessment is required regardless of whether the derivative transactions are material to the insurer's financial statements.*

DEFINITIONS OF TERMS

Agreed-upon procedures engagement. An agreed-upon procedures engagement is one in which a practitioner is engaged by a client to issue a report of findings based on specific procedures performed on subject matter. The client engages the practitioner to assist specified parties in evaluating subject matter or an assertion. The specified parties assume responsibility for the sufficiency of the agreed-upon procedures. In this type of engagement, the practitioner does not perform an examination or review and does not provide an opinion or negative assurance about the assertion. The practitioner's report is in the form of procedures and findings.

Assertion. An assertion is any declaration or set of declarations about whether the subject matter is based on, or in conformity with, the criteria selected.

OBJECTIVES OF AT SECTION 201

This section presents attestation standards and provides guidance to a practitioner concerning performance and reporting in all agreed-upon engagements, except those noted above in "Effective Date" and "Applicability." It was issued because of the diversity in practice in performing and reporting on agreed-upon procedures engagements.

In 2001 the Auditing Standards Board issued SSAE 10, *Attestation Standards: Revision and Recodification*. SSAE 10 superseded SSAEs 1 through 9 and renumbered the AT sections in the American Institute of Certified Public Accountants' (AICPA's) *Codification*. The revisions to this section include

- Eliminating the requirement for the practitioner to obtain a written assertion in an agreed-upon procedures engagement.
- Providing guidance on engagements to apply agreed-upon procedures to specified elements, accounts, or items of a financial statement previously covered by Statement on Auditing Standards (SAS) 75, *Engagements to Apply Agreed-Upon Procedures to Specified Elements, Accounts, or Items of a Financial Statement*. (SAS 75 was withdrawn as part of SAS 93, *Omnibus Statement on Auditing Standards—2000*).

In 2002, SSAE 11 amended this section to delete the guidance on working papers. Documentation requirements for attest engagements are now covered in AT Section 101, *Attest Engagements*.

FUNDAMENTAL REQUIREMENTS

STANDARDS

The practitioner should follow the general, fieldwork, and reporting standards for attestation engagements (see AT Section 101) in performing and reporting on agreed-upon procedures engagements as interpreted in this section.

SUBJECT MATTER

In an agreed-upon procedures engagement, the agreed-upon procedures are applied to the specific subject matter using the selected criteria. The subject matter may take many different forms and be at a point in time or covering a period of time. However, the subject matter and the criteria must meet the conditions in the third general standard (see AT Section 101). The criteria may be stated with the enumerated procedures or referred to in the practitioner's report.

ASSERTION

In general, a written assertion is not required in an agreed-upon procedures engagement, except when another attest standard specifically requires it (see AT Section 601). If, however, the practitioner asks that the responsible party provide an assertion, the assertion may be presented in writing in a representation letter or another written communication from the responsible party (such as a statement, narrative description, or schedule, appropriately identifying what is being presented and the point in time or period of time covered). The responsible party's refusal to furnish a written assertion is a scope limitation that requires the practitioner to withdraw from the engagement.

ACCEPTANCE OF ENGAGEMENT

The practitioner may perform an agreed-upon procedures attestation engagement if:

1. He or she establishes an understanding with the client about the services to be performed.
2. He or she has adequate knowledge of the subject matter to which the agreed-upon procedures are to be applied.
3. He or she is independent (ordinarily engagement team independence, not firmwide independence).
4. One of the following conditions is met:
    a. The client is responsible for the subject matter, or has a reasonable basis for providing a written assertion about the subject matter when a responsible party does not exist due to the nature of the subject matter.
    b. The client is not responsible for the subject matter but is able to provide the practitioner, or have a third party who is responsible for the subject matter provide the practitioner, with evidence of the third party's responsibility for the subject matter.
5. He or she and the specified parties agree upon the nature, timing, and extent of procedures performed or to be performed. Furthermore, the procedures agreed to should not be overly subjective and possibly open to varying interpretations. The practitioner should not report on the engagement if the specified users do not agree to the procedures.
6. The specified parties take responsibility for the sufficiency of the agreed-upon procedures for their purposes.
7. The specific subject matter to which the procedures are to be applied is subject to reasonably consistent measurement.
8. Criteria to be used in the determination of findings are agreed upon between the practitioner and the specified parties.
9. The procedures to be applied to the specific subject matter are expected to result in reasonably consistent findings using the criteria.

10. Evidence related to the specific subject matter to which the procedures are applied is expected to exist to provide a reasonable basis for expressing the findings in the practitioner's report.
11. If applicable, the practitioner and the specified parties agree to any materiality limits for reporting purposes.
12. The report is restricted to the specified parties.
13. For agreed-upon procedures engagements on prospective financial information, a summary of significant assumptions is included in the prospective financial statements (see AT Section 301).

INVOLVEMENT OF A SPECIALIST

The practitioner and the specified parties should explicitly agree to involving a specialist, if any, in assisting the practitioner in performing an agreed-upon procedures engagement. The practitioner should not agree to merely read the specialist's report solely to describe or repeat the specialist's findings in his or her report. The latter does not constitute assistance to the practitioner.

INVOLVEMENT OF INTERNAL AUDITORS OR OTHERS

Except as referred to in the prior section, the practitioner must perform the agreed-upon procedures included in his or her report. Internal auditors or others may prepare schedules and accumulate data or provide other information for the practitioner, but cannot perform agreed-upon procedures reported on by the practitioner.

ELEMENTS OF PRACTITIONER'S REPORT

According to AT 201.38, the practitioner's report on agreed-upon procedures should be in the form of procedures and findings. The report should contain the following elements:

1. A title that includes the word independent
2. Identification of the specified parties
3. Identification of the subject matter (or the written assertion related thereto) and the character of the engagement
4. Identification of the responsible party
5. A statement that the subject matter is the responsibility of the responsible party
6. A statement that the procedures performed were those agreed to by the specified parties identified in the report
7. A statement that the agreed-upon procedures engagement was conducted in accordance with attestation standards established by the AICPA
8. A statement that the sufficiency of the procedures is solely the responsibility of the specified parties, and a disclaimer of responsibility for the sufficiency of those procedures
9. A list of procedures performed (or reference thereto) and all related findings; negative assurance should not be given, and vague or ambiguous language in reporting findings should be avoided
10. If applicable, a description of any agreed-upon materiality limits
11. A statement that the practitioner was not engaged to, and did not, conduct an examination of the subject matter, the objective of which would be the expression of an opinion, a disclaimer of opinion on the assertion, and a statement that if the prac-

titioner had performed additional procedures, other matters might have come to his or her attention that would have been reported
12. A statement of restrictions on the use of the report because it is intended to be used solely by the specified parties
13. For an agreed-upon procedures engagement on prospective financial information, all items included in AT Section 301
14. If applicable, a description of the nature of the assistance provided by a specialist.
15. If applicable, and if the practitioner does not withdraw from the engagement, describe any restrictions (not agreed to) or reservations on the performance of the procedures
16. The manual or printed signature of the practitioner's firm
17. The date of the report

Other requirements are as follows:

1. If desired, explanatory language about matters such as disclosure of stipulated facts, assumptions, or interpretations; description of the conditions of records, controls, or data; explanation that the practitioner has no responsibilities to update the report; and explanation of sampling risk
2. If applicable, and if the practitioner does not withdraw from the engagement or change the engagement to another form of engagement, disclose in his or her report the inability to obtain representations from the responsible party (see the section "Representation Letter")
3. If, in connection with the application of agreed-upon procedures, matters come to the practitioner's attention by other means that significantly contradict the subject matter (or written assertions), include this matter in the report

DATING OF REPORT

The practitioner's report should be dated as of the date of completion of the agreed-upon procedures.

ADDING SPECIFIED PARTIES

The practitioner may be asked to consider adding another party as a specified party (a nonparticipant party) after the completion of the agreed-upon procedures engagement. If the practitioner agrees to add the nonparticipant party as a specified party, he or she should obtain affirmative acknowledgment from that party, normally in writing, agreeing to the procedures performed and agreeing to take responsibility for the sufficiency of those procedures.

If a nonparticipant party is added after the practitioner has issued his or her report, the practitioner may reissue the report or provide written acknowledgment that a party has been added. If the report is reissued, the report date should not be changed. If written acknowledgment is provided, the acknowledgment ordinarily should state that no procedures have been performed subsequent to the date of the report.

RESTRICTIONS ON THE PERFORMANCE OF PROCEDURES

The practitioner should attempt to have specified parties agree to any modification of the agreed-upon procedures when circumstances impose restrictions on the performance of those procedures. If an agreement cannot be obtained (for example, when the agreed-upon procedures are published by a regulatory agency that will not modify those procedures), the practitioner should either describe any restrictions in his or her report or withdraw from the engagement.

REPRESENTATION LETTER

Practitioners may find that a representation letter is useful in obtaining representations from the responsible party. Generally, a representation letter is not required for this type of engagement. However, a representation letter is required in an agreed-upon procedures engagement related to compliance with specified requirements (see AT Section 601). If the practitioner decides to request a representation letter from the responsible party and that party refuses to furnish one, the practitioner should do one of the following:

1. Disclose in the accountant's report the inability to obtain representations from the responsible party.
2. Withdraw from the engagement (required for an agreed-upon procedures engagement related to compliance with specified requirements).
3. Change to another form of engagement.

KNOWLEDGE OF OUTSIDE MATTERS

If matters come to the practitioner's attention by other means outside the agreed-upon procedures that significantly contradict the assertion referred to in the report, the practitioner should include the matter in the report.

CHANGE FROM ANOTHER ENGAGEMENT (ATTEST OR NONATTEST) TO AN AGREED-UPON PROCEDURES ENGAGEMENT

Before agreeing to change another type of engagement to an agreed-upon procedures engagement, the practitioner should consider the following:

1. Are there certain procedures performed as part of the other engagement that are not appropriate to include in an agreed-upon procedures engagement?
2. What are the reasons given for the request, especially any scope restrictions or restrictions on matters to be reported related to the other engagement?
3. What additional effort is required to complete the other engagement?
4. What is the reason for changing from a general-use to a restricted-use report?
5. Is it appropriate to accept a change in engagement if agreed-upon procedures are substantially complete (or effort to complete the procedures is relatively insignificant)?

INTERPRETATIONS

There are no interpretations for this section.

TECHNIQUES FOR APPLICATION

MEANING OF INDEPENDENCE

Independence requirements for an agreed-upon procedures engagement are less stringent than the independence requirements for other attest and audit engagements (refer to the Code of Professional Conduct, Interpretation 101.11, *Modified Application of Rule 101 for En-*

gagements Performed in Accordance with Statements on Standards for Attestation Engagements* [Revised February 2012, effective April 30, 2012].

ENGAGEMENT LETTER

The practitioner should establish a clear understanding regarding the terms of engagement, preferably in an engagement letter. Engagement letters should be addressed to the client, and, in some circumstances, to all specified parties. According to AT 201.10, the practitioner should consider including the following matters in the engagement letter:

1. Nature of the engagement
2. Identification of the subject matter (or the assertion related thereto), the responsible party, and the criteria to be used
3. Identification of specified parties
4. Specified parties' acknowledgment of their responsibility for the sufficiency of the procedures
5. Responsibilities of the practitioner
6. Reference to attestation standards established by AICPA
7. Agreement on procedures by enumerating, or referring to, the procedures
8. Disclaimers expected to be included in the practitioner's report
9. Use restrictions
10. Assistance to be provided to the practitioner
11. Involvement of a specialist, if applicable
12. Agreed-upon materiality limits, if applicable

COMMUNICATION WITH SPECIFIED PARTIES

Ordinarily, the practitioner should communicate directly with, and obtain affirmative acknowledgment from, each of the specified parties. This may be accomplished by:

1. Meeting with the specified parties
2. Distributing a draft of the anticipated report to the specified parties and obtaining their agreement
3. Distributing a copy of the engagement letter to the specified parties and obtaining their agreement

If the practitioner is unable to communicate directly with all of the specified parties, he or she should consider doing one or more of the following:

1. Comparing the procedures to be applied to written requirements of the specified parties
2. Discussing the procedures to be applied with appropriate representatives of the specified parties
3. Reviewing relevant contracts with, or correspondence from, the specified parties

PROCEDURES TO BE PERFORMED

The procedures agreed upon by the practitioner and the specified parties may be as limited or as extensive as the specified parties wish. Mere reading of an assertion or specified information, however, is not sufficient to permit a practitioner to report on the results of applying agreed-upon procedures.

Appropriate procedures might include:

1. Executing a sampling application after agreeing on relevant parameters
2. Inspecting specified documents
3. Confirming information with third parties
4. Comparing documents, schedules, or analyses with specified attributes
5. Performing specific procedures on work performed by others, including the work of internal auditors
6. Making mathematical computations

Examples of inappropriate procedures include evaluating the competency or objectivity of another party or interpreting documents outside the scope of the practitioner's professional expertise.

REPRESENTATION LETTER

Although, as a general rule, a representation letter is not required, it is advisable to obtain one. According to AT 201.38, examples of matters that might appear in a representation letter include:

1. A statement acknowledging responsibility for the subject matter or the assertion
2. A statement acknowledging responsibility for selecting the criteria and for determining that the criteria are appropriate
3. The assertion about the subject matter based on the criteria selected
4. A statement that all known matters contradicting the subject matter or the assertion and any communication from regulatory agencies affecting the subject matter or the assertion have been disclosed to the practitioner
5. Availability of all records relevant to the subject matter and the agreed-upon procedures
6. Other matters the practitioner deems appropriate

REPORT ON AGREED-UPON PROCEDURES IN A DOCUMENT CONTAINING FINANCIAL STATEMENTS

When the practitioner consents to the inclusion of his or her report on agreed-upon procedures in a document containing the entity's financial statements, he or she is associated with those financial statements. For a public entity, the practitioner should include his or her audit report (see AU Section 508, *Reports on Audited Financial Statements*), review report (see AU Section 722, *Interim Financial Information*), or unaudited disclaimer (see AU Section 504, *Association with Financial Statements*) in such document. For a private entity, the practitioner should include his or her audit report (see AU Section 508), review report (see AR Section 60-90), or compilation report (see AR Section 60-90) in such document. If the practitioner has not audited, reviewed, or compiled the private entity financial statements, the document should state that the practitioner has not audited, reviewed, or compiled the financial statements and assumes no responsibility for them. All combined reports (agreed-upon procedure and other reports) should be restricted to specified parties (see AT Section 101).

ILLUSTRATIONS

ILLUSTRATION 1. ACCOUNTANT'S STANDARD REPORT ON AN AGREED-UPON PROCEDURES ENGAGEMENT (FROM SSAE 10)

Independent Accountant's Report on Applying Agreed-Upon Procedures

To the Managements of Widget Inc. and Basic Fund:

We have performed the procedures enumerated below, which were agreed to by the audit committees and managements of Widget Inc., and Basic Fund, solely to assist you in evaluating the accompanying Statement of Investment Performance Statistics of Basic Fund (prepared in accordance with the criteria specified therein) for the year ended December 31, 20X1. Basic Fund's management is responsible for the statement of investment performance statistics. This agreed-upon procedures engagement was conducted in accordance with attestation standards established by the American Institute of Certified Public Accountants. The sufficiency of these procedures is solely the responsibility of the parties specified in the report. Consequently, we make no representation regarding the sufficiency of the procedures described below either for the purpose for which this report has been requested or for any other purpose.

The procedures and associated findings are as follows:

[Include paragraphs to enumerate procedures and findings.]

We were not engaged to, and did not conduct an examination, the objective of which would be the expression of an opinion on the accompanying Statement of Investment Performance Statistics of Basic Fund. Accordingly, we do not express such an opinion. Had we performed additional procedures, other matters might have come to our attention that would have been reported to you.

This report is intended solely for the information and use of the audit committees and managements of Widget Inc. and Basic Fund, and is not intended to be and should not be used by anyone other than these specified parties.

Smith and Jones
February 15, 20X2

NOTE: *The following are additional illustrations of reporting on applying agreed-upon procedures to elements, accounts, or items of a financial statement.*

ILLUSTRATION 2. REPORT IN CONNECTION WITH A PROPOSED ACQUISITION

Independent Accountant's Report on Applying Agreed-Upon Procedures

To the Board of Directors and Management of Widget Company:

We have performed the procedures enumerated below, which were agreed to by the Board of Directors and management of Widget Company, solely to assist you in connection with the proposed acquisition of Generic Company as of December 31, 20X1. Generic Company is responsible for its cash and accounts receivable records. This agreed-upon procedures engagement was conducted in accordance with attestation standards established by the American Institute of Certified Public Accountants. The sufficiency of these procedures is solely the responsibility of the parties specified in this report. Consequently, we make no representation regarding the sufficiency of the procedures described below either for the purpose for which this report has been requested or for any other purpose.

The procedures and the associated findings are as follows:

Cash

1. We obtained confirmation of the cash on deposit from the following banks, and we agreed the confirmed balance to the amount shown on the bank reconciliations maintained by Generic Company. We mathematically checked the bank reconciliations and compared the resultant cash balance per book to the respective general ledger account balances.

Bank	General ledger account balances as of December 31, 20X1
XY Bank	$ 2,500
AB Bank	4,200
Town Trust Company regular account	67,341
Town Trust Company payroll account	11,240
	$ 85,281

We found no exceptions as a result of the procedures.

Accounts Receivable

2. We added the individual customer account balances shown in an aged trial balance of accounts receivable (identified as Exhibit A) and compared the resultant total with the balance in the general ledger account.

   We found no difference.

3. We compared the individual customer account balances shown in the aged trial balance of accounts receivable (Exhibit A) as of December 31, 20X1 to the balances shown in the accounts receivable subsidiary ledger.

   We found no exceptions as a result of the comparisons.

4. We traced the aging (according to invoice dates) for fifty customer account balances shown in Exhibit A to the details of outstanding invoices in the accounts receivable subsidiary ledger. The balances selected for tracing were determined by starting at the eighth item and selecting every fifteenth item thereafter.

   We found no exceptions in the aging of the amounts of the fifty customer account balances selected. The sample size traced was 9.8% of the aggregate amount of the customer account balances.

5. We mailed confirmations directly to the customers representing the 150 largest customer account balances selected from the accounts receivable trial balance, and we received responses as indicated in the following paragraph and table. We also traced the items constituting the outstanding customer account balance to invoices and supporting shipping documents for customers from which there was no reply. As agreed, any individual differences in a customer account balance of less than $300 were to be considered minor, and no further procedures were performed.

   Of the 150 customer balances confirmed, we received responses from 140 customers; 10 customers did not reply. No exceptions were identified in 120 of the confirmations received. The differences disclosed in the remaining twenty confirmation replies were either minor in amount (as defined above) or were reconciled to the customer account balance without proposed adjustment thereto. A summary of the confirmation results according to the respective aging categories is as follows:

	Accounts receivable December 31, 20X1		
Aging categories	Customer account balances	Confirmations requested	Confirmations received
Current	$225,000	$ 115,000	$ 90,000
Past due:			
Less than one month	52,000	27,000	20,000
One to three months	36,000	20,000	9,000
Over three months	24,000	24,000	7,000
	$337,000	$186,000	$126,000

We were not engaged to and did not conduct an audit, the objective of which would be the expression of an opinion on cash and accounts receivable. Accordingly, we do not express such an opinion. Had we performed additional procedures, other matters might have come to our attention that would have been reported to you.

This report is intended solely for the information and use of the board of directors and management of Widget Company and is not intended to be and should not be used by anyone other than these specified parties.

Smith and Jones
February 15, 20X2

ILLUSTRATION 3. REPORT IN CONNECTION WITH CLAIMS OF CREDITORS

Independent Accountant's Report on Applying Agreed-Upon Procedures

To the Trustees of Widget Company:

We have performed the procedures described below, which were agreed to by the Trustees of Widget Company with respect to the claims of creditors, solely to assist you in determining the validity of claims of Widget Company as of May 31, 20X1 as set forth in the accompanying Schedule A. Widget Company is responsible for maintaining records of claims submitted by creditors of Widget Company. This agreed-upon procedures engagement was conducted in accordance with attestation standards established by the American Institute of Certified Public Accountants. The sufficiency of these procedures is solely the responsibility of the party specified in this report. Consequently, we make no representation regarding the sufficiency of the procedures described below either for the purpose for which this report has been requested or for any other purpose.

The procedures and associated findings are as follows:

1. Compare the total of the trial balance of accounts payable at May 31, 20X1 prepared by Widget Company, to the balance in the related general ledger account.

    The total of the accounts payable trial balance agreed with the balance in the related general ledger account.
2. Compare the amounts for claims received from creditors (as shown in claim documents provided by Widget Company) to the respective amounts shown in the trial balance of accounts payable. Using the data included in the claims documents and in Widget Company's accounts payable detail records, reconcile any differences found to the accounts payable trial balance.

    All differences noted are presented in column 3 of Schedule A. Except for those amounts shown in column 4 of Schedule A, all such differences were reconciled.
3. Obtain the documentation submitted by creditors in support of the amounts claimed and compare it to the following documentation in Widget Company's files: invoices, receiving reports, and other evidence of receipt of goods or services.

    No exceptions were found as a result of these comparisons.

We were not engaged to and did not conduct an audit, the objective of which would be the expression of an opinion on the claims of creditors set forth in the accompanying Schedule A. Accordingly, we do not express such an opinion. Had we performed additional procedures, other matters might have come to our attention that would have been reported to you.

This report is intended solely for the information and use of the Trustees of Widget Company and is not intended to be and should not be used by anyone other than this specified party.

Smith and Jones
February 15, 20X2

AT 301 Financial Forecasts and Projections

EFFECTIVE DATE AND APPLICABILITY

Original Pronouncement	Statement on Standards for Attestation Engagements (SSAE) 10, *Attestation Standards: Revision and Recodification*, as amended by SSAE 11 and 17.
Effective Date	These statements currently are effective.
Applicability	The Statement applies to engagements in which a practitioner either (1) submits, to his or her clients or others, prospective financial statements that he or she has assembled or assisted in assembling or (2) reports on prospective financial statements, and also believes under (1) or (2) that those financial statements are, or reasonably might be, expected to be used by a third party. (See the following information.)

APPLICABILITY

The practitioner should report when the practitioner *submits* to the client or others prospective financial statements the practitioner has assembled or assisted in assembling and also believes the prospective financial statements might be used by a third party.

This section also provides standards for a practitioner engaged to examine, compile, or apply agreed-upon procedures to partial presentations. (See the section "Definitions of Terms.")

There are also several circumstances in which the pronouncement does not apply, as explained in the following paragraphs.

The Statement does not apply to a financial analysis of a potential project where the practitioner obtains the information, makes the assumptions, and assembles the presentation. This type of analysis is not for general use; *however*, if the responsible party (see below) reviews and adopts the assumptions and presentation, or bases its assumption and presentation on the analysis, the Statement does apply.

The Statement does not apply to engagements involving prospective financial statements used solely in connection with litigation services if the practitioner's work is subject to analysis and challenge by all parties. This exception does not apply if:

1. The practitioner is specifically engaged to issue or does issue an examination, a compilation, or an agreed-upon procedures report on prospective financial statements.
2. The prospective financial statements are for use by third parties who, under the rules of the proceedings, do not have the opportunity for analysis and challenge by each party.

The Statement also does not apply to services involving the following:

1. Prospective financial statements restricted to internal use
2. Current year budgets presented with interim period historical financial statements

DEFINITIONS OF TERMS

For purposes of this section, the following definitions apply.

Assembly. Manual or computer processing of mathematical or other clerical functions related to the presentation of prospective financial statements.

Compilation of prospective financial statements. A professional service that involves:

1. Assembling prospective financial statements
2. Performing required procedures (see later sections), including reading the prospective financial statements and the accompanying summary of significant assumptions and accounting policies, and considering whether they appear to be presented in conformity with American Institute of Certified Public Accountants (AICPA) presentation guidelines (see AICPA *Guide for Prospective Financial Information*) and are not obviously inappropriate
3. Issuing a compilation report

A compilation does not provide assurance that the practitioner will become aware of significant matters that might be disclosed by more extensive procedures, such as those performed in an examination of prospective financial statements.

Entity. Any unit, *existing or to be formed*, for which financial statements could be prepared in accordance with generally accepted accounting principles or another comprehensive basis of accounting. It may be an individual, partnership, corporation, trust, estate, association, or governmental unit.

Examination of prospective financial statements. A professional service that involves:

1. Evaluating the preparation of the prospective financial statements
2. Evaluating the support underlying the assumptions
3. Evaluating the presentation of the financial statements for conformity with AICPA presentation guidelines (see AICPA *Guide for Prospective Financial Information*)
4. Issuing an examination report

An examination provides the practitioner with a basis for reporting on whether, in his or her opinion, the prospective financial statements are presented in conformity with AICPA guidelines and the assumptions provide a reasonable basis for the responsible party's forecast or projection given the hypothetical assumptions.

Financial forecast. Prospective financial statements that present, to the best of the responsible party's (see below) knowledge and belief, an entity's expected financial position (see following entry), results of operations, and cash flows. It is based on the responsible party's assumptions about the conditions it expects to exist and the course of action it expects to take. A financial forecast may be expressed in specific monetary amounts as a single point estimate of forecasted results or as a range.

Financial projection. Prospective financial statements that present, to the best of the responsible party's knowledge and belief, *given one or more hypothetical assumptions* (see entry in this section), an entity's expected financial position, results of operations, and cash flows. Ordinarily, it is prepared to answer the question, "What would happen if . . . ?" A financial projection may contain a range.

General use of prospective financial statements. Use of prospective financial statements by persons with whom the responsible party is not negotiating directly (e.g., prospective financial statements in an offering statement for an entity's debt or equity securities). Recipients of general-use prospective financial statements are unable to ask the responsible party directly about the presentation. *Only a financial forecast is appropriate for general use*.

Hypothetical assumption. An assumption used in a financial projection to present a condition or a course of action that may not occur but is consistent with the purpose of the projection.

Key factors. Significant matters on which an entity's future results are expected to depend. Key factors encompass matters that affect items such as sales, production, service, and financing activities. They are the foundation for prospective financial statements and are the bases for assumptions.

Limited use of prospective financial statements. Use of prospective financial statements by the responsible party alone or by the responsible party and *third parties with whom the responsible party is negotiating directly* (e.g., prospective financial statements used in loan negotiations, submission to a regulatory agency, or solely within the entity). *Financial forecasts and financial projections are appropriate for limited use.*

Partial presentation. A presentation of prospective financial information that excludes one or more of the items required for prospective financial statements (see "Fundamental Requirements: General"). Partial presentations are not ordinarily appropriate for general use and should be restricted for use by specified parties who will be negotiating directly with the responsible party.

Prospective financial statement. Financial forecasts or financial projections (see prior entry), *including* summaries of significant assumptions and accounting policies. Prospective financial statements may cover a period that has *partially* expired. The following are *not* prospective financial statements:

1. Statements for periods that have completely expired
2. Pro forma financial statements (see AT Section 401)
3. Partial presentations

Responsible party. Person or persons responsible for the assumptions underlying prospective financial statements. Ordinarily, the responsible party is management; however, it can be outsiders, such as a party considering acquiring the entity.

OBJECTIVES OF AT SECTION 301

For many years, practitioners have been requested to provide and have provided services relating to forecasts and projections. There was, however, little in the authoritative literature to guide the practitioner in these types of engagements for some time. In 1980, the AICPA issued a guide on reviews of financial forecasts, but many areas of practice were not covered by that guide. There was a need for more comprehensive guidance. This section provides that guidance.

The section does the following:

1. Defines a financial forecast and a financial projection, and related terms
2. Establishes procedures and reporting standards for prospective financial statements that require the following services:
   a. Compilation
   b. Examination
   c. Application of agreed-upon procedures

The service that was previously called a "review" was renamed an "examination," because that is the highest level of service available. Now there is no review service.

In January 2001, the Auditing Standards Board issued SSAE 10, *Attestation Standards: Revision and Recodification*. SSAE 10 superseded SSAEs 1 through 9 and renumbered the AT sections in the AICPA's codification. The revisions to this section include:

- Changing elements of the standard reports to conform to those elsewhere in the attestation standards
- Making the section applicable to partial presentations of prospective financial information
- Changing references to statements of changes in financial position to statement of cash flows

Additional guidance for practitioners' services relating to prospective financial statements is found in the AICPA *Guide for Prospective Financial Information*.

SSAE 11 amended this section to delete the guidance on working papers. Documentation requirements for attest engagements are now covered in Section 101, *Attest Engagements*.

FUNDAMENTAL REQUIREMENTS: GENERAL

A practitioner should perform one of the services described in this Statement—compilation, examination, or application of agreed-upon procedures—whenever he or she does the following:

1. Submits to the client or others prospective financial statements that he or she has assembled, or assisted in assembling, that are, or reasonably might be, expected to be used by others
2. Reports on prospective financial statements that are, or reasonably might be, expected to be used by others

A practitioner may *not* compile, examine, or apply agreed-upon procedures to prospective financial statements that omit the summary of significant assumptions.

A practitioner should *not* compile, examine, or apply agreed-upon procedures to a financial projection that excludes either an identification of hypothetical assumptions or a description of the limitations on the usefulness of the presentation.

A practitioner may *not* consent to the use of his or her name in conjunction with a financial projection if the projection is to be used by persons not negotiating directly (general use) with the responsible party *unless* the projection is used to supplement a forecast.

Prospective financial statements preferably should be in the format of the historical financial statements. According to AT 301, Appendix A, paragraph 1, at a minimum, however, the following must be presented:

1. Sales or gross revenues
2. Gross profit or cost of sales
3. Unusual or infrequently occurring items
4. Provision for income taxes
5. Discontinued operations or extraordinary items
6. Income from continuing operations
7. Net income
8. Basic and diluted earnings per share, if applicable
9. Significant changes in financial position (for examples, see AICPA *Guide for Prospective Financial Information*)
10. Summary of significant assumptions
11. Summary of significant accounting policies
12. A description of what the responsible party intends the prospective financial statements to present
13. A statement that the assumptions are based on the responsible party's judgment at the time the prospective information was prepared
14. A caveat that the prospective results may not be achieved

A presentation that omits any of items 1 through 9 is a partial presentation, which would not ordinarily be appropriate for general use. If an omitted applicable minimum item is derivable from the information presented, the presentation would not be deemed to be a partial presentation. A presentation that contains items 1 through 9 but omits 10 through 14 is *not* a partial presentation and is subject to the provisions of this section applicable to complete presentations.[1]

PARTIAL PRESENTATIONS

A practitioner who is engaged to or does compile, examine, or apply agreed-upon procedures to a partial presentation should follow the guidance in this section for complete presentations and make modifications necessary to reflect the nature of the presentation.

Procedures on a partial presentation may be affected by the nature of the information presented. When engaged to compile or examine a partial presentation, the practitioner should consider whether key factors affecting elements, accounts, or items that are interrelated with those in the partial presentation he or she has been engaged to examine or compile have been evaluated, including key factors that may not necessarily be obvious to the partial presentation. (An example of this might be productive capacity relative to a sales forecast.) The practitioner should also consider whether all significant assumptions have been disclosed. The scope of the examination or compilation of some partial presentations may need to be similar to that for the examination or compilation of a presentation of prospective financial statements.

---

[1] *Complete presentation guidelines for entities that choose to issue prospective financial statements are included in the AICPA Audit and Accounting Guide, Guide for Prospective Financial Information. The Guide also presents presentation guidelines for partial presentations.*

Because partial presentations are generally for limited use, reports on partial presentations of both forecasted and projected information should describe any limitations on the presentation's usefulness.

> NOTE: Chapter 23 of the AICPA *Guide for Prospective Financial Information* *explains how to apply the guidance for complete prospective financial statements to partial presentations.*

FUNDAMENTAL REQUIREMENTS: COMPILATION OF PROSPECTIVE FINANCIAL STATEMENTS

STANDARDS

The following standards apply to the compilation of prospective financial statements and the practitioner's report on these statements:

1. The person or persons performing the compilation should have adequate technical training and proficiency to compile prospective financial statements.
2. The practitioner should exercise due professional care in performing the compilation and preparing the report.
3. The work should be adequately planned, and assistants should be properly supervised.
4. The practitioner should perform the applicable compilation procedures.
5. The practitioner's report should conform to the guidance described in the following section.

> NOTE: Applicable compilation procedures should be performed (see Appendix B of this chapter).

PRACTITIONER'S REPORT

According to AT 301.18, the standard report on the compilation of prospective financial statements should include the following:

1. An identification of the prospective financial statements
2. A statement that the practitioner has compiled the prospective financial statements in accordance with attestation standards established by the AICPA
3. A statement that a compilation is limited in scope and does not enable the practitioner to express an opinion or any other form of assurance on the prospective financial statements or the assumptions
4. A warning that the prospective results may not be achieved
5. A statement that the practitioner assumes no responsibility to update the report for events and circumstances occurring after the date of the report
6. The manual or printed signature of the practitioner's firm
7. The date of the compilation report

Other requirements are as follows:

1. The date of the practitioner's report is the date of completion of the practitioner's compilation procedures.
2. If prospective financial statements contain a range, the practitioner's report should include a separate paragraph related to the circumstances.

3. For the compilation of a projection, the practitioner's report should include a statement describing the special purpose for which the projection was prepared, as well as a separate paragraph that restricts the use of the report to the specified parties.
4. A practitioner who is not independent may issue a compilation report. A separate paragraph of the report is as follows and may also include the reasons for independence impairment:

   We are not independent with respect to XYZ Company.

5. If prospective financial statements contain presentation deficiencies or omit disclosures other than those relating to significant assumptions, the practitioner's report should disclose the deficiency or omission.
6. If prospective financial statements are presented on a comprehensive basis of accounting other than generally accepted accounting principles (GAAP) and this is not disclosed, the practitioner's report should disclose the basis of presentation.

Examples of compilation reports on prospective financial statements are presented in Illustrations 1–3.

FUNDAMENTAL REQUIREMENTS: EXAMINATION OF PROSPECTIVE FINANCIAL STATEMENTS

STANDARDS

The practitioner should follow the general, fieldwork, and reporting standards for attestation engagements described in AT Section 101.

NOTE: Standards concerning technical training and proficiency and planning the examination engagement, as well as applicable examination procedures, are described in Appendix C of this chapter.

ACCOUNTANT'S REPORT

According to AT 301.33, the standard report on the examination of prospective financial statements should include the following:

1. A title that includes the word *independent*.
2. An introductory paragraph with statements that:

   a. Identify the prospective financial statements.
   b. Identify the responsible party.
   c. The prospective financial statements are the responsibility of the responsible party.
   d. The practitioner's responsibility is to express an opinion on the prospective financial statements based on his or her examination.

3. A scope paragraph with statements that:

   a. The examination was made in accordance with attestation standards established by the AICPA, and accordingly, included such procedures as the practitioner considered necessary in the circumstances.
   b. The practitioner believes that the examination provides a reasonable basis for his or her opinion.

4. An opinion paragraph that presents:
   a. The practitioner's opinion that the prospective financial statements are presented in conformity with AICPA presentation guidelines (see AICPA *Guide for Prospective Financial Statements*) and that the underlying assumptions provide a reasonable basis for the forecast. If a projection is presented, the practitioner's opinion should be that the underlying assumptions provide a reasonable basis for the projection given the hypothetical assumptions.
   b. A warning that the prospective results may not be achieved.
   c. A statement that the practitioner assumes no responsibility to update the report for events and circumstances occurring after the date of the report.
5. The manual or printed signature of the practitioner's firm
6. The date of the examination or report

Other requirements are as follows:

1. The date of the practitioner's report is the date of completion of the practitioner's examination procedures.
2. If prospective financial statements contain a range, the practitioner's report should include a separate paragraph that describes the responsible party's election to present a range and the assumptions involved.
3. For the examination of a projection, the practitioner's report should include a statement describing the special purpose for which the projection was prepared and a separate paragraph that restricts the report to the specified parties.

MODIFICATIONS OF PRACTITIONER'S OPINION

The practitioner should modify his or her opinion in the following circumstances.

1. If prospective financial statements depart from AICPA presentation guidelines, issue a qualified opinion or an adverse opinion.
2. If prospective financial statements fail to disclose significant assumptions, issue an adverse opinion.
3. If one or more of the significant assumptions do not provide a reasonable basis for the forecast, issue an adverse opinion.
4. If one or more of the significant assumptions do not provide a reasonable basis for the projection, given the hypothetical assumptions, issue an adverse opinion.
5. If there is a scope limitation, disclaim an opinion and describe the limitation.
6. If there is a departure from GAAP (e.g., failure to capitalize a capital lease), issue an adverse opinion.

Examples of modified reports on prospective financial statements are presented in "Illustrations."

Qualified Opinion

A practitioner's report with a qualified opinion should include a separate explanatory paragraph that states all substantive reasons for the qualification and describes the departure from AICPA presentation guidelines. The opinion should include the words "except" or "exception" and should refer to the separate explanatory paragraph.

NOTE: A qualified opinion cannot be issued for a measurement (GAAP) departure, unreasonable or omitted assumption, or scope limitation.

Adverse Opinion

A practitioner's report with an adverse opinion should include a separate explanatory paragraph that states all substantive reasons for the adverse opinion. The opinion should state that the presentation is not in conformity with AICPA presentation guidelines and should refer to the separate explanatory paragraph.

If the assumptions do not provide a reasonable basis for the financial statements, the opinion paragraph should make that statement.

If a significant assumption is not disclosed, the practitioner should describe the assumption in the report.

Disclaimer of Opinion

A practitioner's report with a disclaimer of opinion should include a separate explanatory paragraph that states how the examination did not comply with appropriate standards. The disclaimer of opinion paragraph should state that the scope of the examination was not sufficient to enable the practitioner to express an opinion on the prospective financial statements. The disclaimer of opinion should include a direct reference to the separate explanatory paragraph.

If there is a scope limitation and also material departures from presentation guidelines, the practitioner should describe the departures in the report.

MODIFICATION OF STANDARD EXAMINATION REPORT

There are circumstances under which the practitioner should modify the report without modifying the opinion included in the report. The circumstances and the modifications are explained in this section.

Emphasis of a Matter

The practitioner may present explanatory information or other informative material regarding the prospective financial statements in a separate paragraph of the report.

Part of Examination Made by Another Accountant

If more than one practitioner is involved in the examination, the guidance provided in Section 543, *Part of Audit Performed by Other Independent Auditors*, is generally applicable.

Comparative Historical Financial Information

Prospective financial statements may be included in a document that also contains audited, reviewed, or compiled historical financial statements and the practitioner's report on those financial statements. In addition, the historical financial statements in the document may also be summarized and presented comparatively with the prospective financial statements. In these circumstances, the concluding sentence of the last paragraph of the practitioner's report on the examination of the prospective financial statements is as follows:

> The historical financial statements for the year ended December 31, 20X1, (from which the historical data are derived) and our report thereon are set forth on pages xx–xx of this document.

Examination Is Part of Larger Engagement

If the practitioner's examination of prospective financial statements is part of a larger engagement (for example, a financial feasibility study or business acquisition study), the practitioner may expand the report on the examination of the prospective financial statements to describe the entire engagement.

Examples of reports on the examination of prospective financial statements are presented in "Illustrations."

FUNDAMENTAL REQUIREMENTS: APPLYING AGREED-UPON PROCEDURES TO PROSPECTIVE FINANCIAL STATEMENTS (SEE ALSO AT SECTION 201)

GENERAL

A practitioner may accept an engagement to apply agreed-upon procedures to prospective financial statements only when the following conditions are met:

1. Is the practitioner independent?
2. Do the specified parties and the practitioner agree upon the procedures to be performed by the practitioner, and do the specified parties take responsibility for the sufficiency of the procedures to be performed?
3. Is the use of the report restricted to the specified parties involved?
4. Do the prospective financial statements include a summary of significant assumptions?
5. Are the prospective financial statements to which the procedures are to be applied subject to reasonably consistent evaluation against criteria that are suitable and available to the specified parties?
6. Are the criteria to be used in the determination of findings agreed upon between the practitioner and the specified parties?
7. Are the procedures to be applied to the prospective financial statements expected to result in reasonably consistent findings using the criteria?
8. Is evidential matter expected to exist to provide a reasonable basis for expressing the findings in the practitioner's report?
9. Where applicable, do the practitioner and the specified parties agree on any materiality limits for reporting purposes?

The practitioner ordinarily should meet with the specified parties to discuss procedures to be followed. If the practitioner is not able to discuss the procedures directly with all specified parties who will receive the report, he or she should apply one of the following or similar procedures:

1. Discuss the procedures to be applied with appropriate representatives of the specified parties.
2. Review relevant correspondence from the specified parties.
3. Compare the procedures to written requirements of the specified parties.
4. Distribute a draft of the report or a copy of the client's engagement letter to the specified parties and obtain their agreement.

While the agreed-upon procedures generally may be as extensive or limited as the parties specify, mere reading of the prospective financial statements is not a procedure sufficient to permit a practitioner to report on the results of applying agreed-upon procedures to those statements.

PRACTITIONER'S REPORT

The practitioner's report on the results of applying agreed-upon procedures should include the elements as indicated in the example report presented in Illustration 11.

FUNDAMENTAL REQUIREMENTS: OTHER

PRACTITIONER-SUBMITTED DOCUMENT

If a practitioner-submitted document contains the practitioner's compilation, review, or audit report on historical financial statements and prospective financial statements, the practitioner should compile, examine, or apply agreed-upon procedures to the prospective financial statements and report accordingly. However, the practitioner does not have to compile, examine, or apply agreed-upon procedures to the prospective financial statements if (1) they are labeled "budget," (2) the budget is only for the current fiscal year, and (3) the budget is presented with current year interim financial statements. In these circumstances, the practitioner should report on the budget and indicate that he or she did not compile or examine it and disclaim an opinion or any other form of assurance.

The budgeted information may omit the summaries of significant assumptions and accounting polices required by the AICPA presentation guidelines as long as the omission is not undertaken with the intention of misleading a user of the budgeted information and is disclosed in the practitioner's report (see Illustration 12).

CLIENT-PREPARED DOCUMENT

If a client-prepared document contains the practitioner's compilation, review, or audit report on historical financial statements and prospective financial statements, the practitioner should not consent to the use of his or her name in the document unless one of the following conditions exist:

1. The practitioner (or another practitioner) has compiled, examined, or applied agreed-upon procedures to the prospective financial statements and the report of the practitioner accompanies them or is included in the document.
2. The prospective financial statements are accompanied by an indication by the responsible party or the practitioner that the practitioner has not compiled, examined, or applied agreed-upon procedures to the prospective financial statements and that the practitioner assumes no responsibility for them.

If the practitioner audited historical financial statements that accompany prospective financial statements that he or she did not compile, examine, or apply agreed-upon procedures to, he or she should refer to Section 550, *Other Information in Documents Containing Audited Financial Statements*, and determine if that pronouncement applies.

If a client-prepared document contains the practitioner's report on prospective financial statements and historical financial statements, the practitioner should not consent to the use of his or her name in the document unless one of the following conditions exists:

1. The practitioner (or another practitioner) has compiled, reviewed, or audited the historical financial statements and the report of the practitioner accompanies them or is included in the document.
2. The historical financial statements are accompanied by an indication by the responsible party or the practitioner that the practitioner has not compiled, reviewed, or audited the historical financial statements and that the practitioner assumes no responsibility for them.

Inconsistent Information

An entity may publish documents that contain information other than historical financial statements in addition to the compiled or examined prospective financial statements and the practitioner's report thereon. In these circumstances, the practitioner should read the other information and consider whether there are inconsistencies with the information appearing in the prospective financial statements.

If the practitioner examined prospective financial statements included in a document containing inconsistent information, the practitioner should consider whether the prospective financial statements, the practitioner's report, or both require revision. Depending on the conclusion reached, the practitioner should consider other actions, such as issuing an adverse opinion, disclaiming an opinion because of a scope limitation, withholding use of the practitioner's report in the document, or withdrawing from the engagement.

If the practitioner compiled the prospective financial statements included in the document containing inconsistent information, the practitioner should try to obtain additional or revised information. If the additional or revised information is not received, the practitioner should withhold use of the compilation report or withdraw from the compilation engagement.

Material Misstatement of Fact

If, in the document containing the compiled or examined prospective financial statements, the practitioner becomes aware of information he or she believes is a material misstatement of fact, he or she should discuss the matter with the responsible party. If the practitioner concludes that there is a valid basis for concern, he or she should suggest that the responsible party consult with a party whose advice might be useful, such as the entity's attorney.

If, after discussing the possible material misstatement of fact, the practitioner concludes that a material misstatement of fact exists, he or she should consider notifying the responsible party in writing and consulting his or her attorney.

INTERPRETATIONS

There are no interpretations for this section. The AICPA has issued the *Prospective Financial Information Guide,* which provides comprehensive guidance for engagements related to prospective financial statements.

ILLUSTRATIONS

The illustrations on the following pages are adapted from SSAE 10 (AT 300.19–.56).

NOTE: *These report forms are appropriate whether the presentation is based on GAAP or an other comprehensive basis of accounting (OCBOA). If the responsible party is other than management, the references to management in these reports should be changed to refer to the party who assumes responsibility for the assumptions.*

ILLUSTRATION 1. STANDARD REPORT: COMPILATION OF FORECAST (DOES NOT CONTAIN A RANGE)

To the Board of Directors of Widget Company
Main City, USA

Independent Accountant's Report

We have compiled the accompanying forecasted balance sheet, statements of income, retained earnings, and cash flows of Widget Company as of December 31, 20X1, and for the year then ending, in accordance with attestation standards established by the American Institute of Certified Public Accountants.[2]

A compilation is limited to presenting in the form of a forecast information that is the representation of management and does not include evaluation of the support for the assumptions underlying the forecast. We have not examined the forecast, and, accordingly, do not express an opinion or any other form of assurance on the accompanying statements or assumptions. Furthermore, there will usually be differences between the forecasted and actual results, because events and circumstances frequently do not occur as expected, and those differences may be material. We have no responsibility to update this report for events and circumstances occurring after the date of this report.

Smith and Jones
February 15, 20X2

ILLUSTRATION 2. STANDARD REPORT: COMPILATION OF PROJECTION (DOES NOT CONTAIN A RANGE)

To the Board of Directors of Widget Company
Main City, USA

Independent Accountant's Report

We have compiled the accompanying projected balance sheet, statements of income, retained earnings, and cash flows for Widget Company as of December 31, 20X1, and for the year then ending, in accordance with attestation standards established by the American Institute of Certified Public Accountants.[3] The accompanying projection and this report were prepared for the Anytown National Bank for the purpose of negotiating a loan to expand Widget Company's plant.

A compilation is limited to presenting in the form of a projection information that is the representation of management and does not include evaluation of the support for the assumptions underlying the projection. We have not examined the projection and, accordingly, do not express an

---

[2] When the presentation is summarized as discussed in "Fundamental Requirements: General," this sentence might read, "We have compiled the accompanying summarized forecast of Widget Company as of December 31, 20X1, and for the year then ended in accordance with attestation standards established by the American Institute of Certified Public Accountants."

[3] When the presentation is summarized as discussed in "Fundamental Requirements: General," this sentence might read, "We have compiled the accompanying summarized projection of Widget Company as of December 31, 20X1, and for the year then ended in accordance with attestation standards established by the American Institute of Certified Public Accountants."

opinion or any other form of assurance on the accompanying statements or assumptions. Furthermore, even if the loan is granted and the plant is expanded, there will usually be differences between the projected and actual results, because events and circumstances frequently do not occur as expected, and those differences may be material. We have no responsibility to update this report for events and circumstances occurring after the date of this report.

The accompanying projection and this report are intended solely for the information and use of Widget Company and Anytown National Bank and are not intended to be and should not be used by anyone other than these specified parties.

Smith and Jones
February 15, 20X2

ILLUSTRATION 3. STANDARD COMPILATION REPORT: SEPARATE PARAGRAPH—PROSPECTIVE FINANCIAL STATEMENTS CONTAIN A RANGE

As described in the summary of significant assumptions, management of Widget Company has elected to portray forecasted revenue at the amounts of $X,XXX and $Y,YYY, which is predicated upon occupancy rates of XX% and YY% of available apartments, rather than as a single point estimate. Accordingly, the accompanying forecast presents forecasted financial position, results of operations, and cash flows at such occupancy rates. However, there is no assurance that the actual results will fall within the range of occupancy rates presented.

Smith and Jones
February 15, 20X2

ILLUSTRATION 4. STANDARD REPORT: EXAMINATION OF FORECAST

To the Board of Directors of Widget Company
Main City, USA

Independent Accountant's Report

We have examined the accompanying forecasted balance sheet, statements of income, retained earnings, and cash flows of Widget Company as of December 31, 20X1, and for the year then ending.[4] Widget's management is responsible for the forecast. Our responsibility is to express an opinion on the forecast based on our examination.

Our examination was conducted in accordance with attestation standards established by the American Institute of Certified Public Accountants and, accordingly, included such procedures as we considered necessary to evaluate both the assumptions used by management and the preparation and presentation of the forecast. We believe that our examination provides a reasonable basis for our opinion.

In our opinion, the accompanying forecast is presented in conformity with guidelines for presentation of a forecast established by the American Institute of Certified Public Accountants, and the underlying assumptions provide a reasonable basis for management's forecast. However, there will usually be differences between the forecasted and actual results, because events and circumstances frequently do not occur as expected, and those differences may be material. We have no responsibility to update this report for events and circumstances occurring after the date of this report.

Smith and Jones
February 15, 20X2

---

[4] When the presentation is summarized as discussed in "Fundamental Requirements: General," this sentence might read, "We have examined the accompanying summarized forecast of Widget Company as of December 31, 20X1, and for the year then ending."

ILLUSTRATION 5. STANDARD REPORT: EXAMINATION OF PROJECTION

To the Board of Directors of Widget Company
Main City, USA

Independent Accountant's Report

We have examined the accompanying projected balance sheet, statements of income, retained earnings, and cash flows of Widget Company as of December 31, 20X1, and for the year then ending.[5] Widget's management is responsible for the projection, which was prepared for the purpose of obtaining a loan. Our responsibility is to express an opinion on the projection based on our examination.

Our examination was conducted in accordance with attestation standards for an examination of a projection established by the American Institute of Certified Public Accountants and, accordingly, included such procedures as we considered necessary to evaluate both the assumptions used by management and the preparation and presentation of the projection. We believe that our examination provides a reasonable basis for our opinion.

In our opinion, the accompanying projection is presented in conformity with guidelines for presentation of a projection established by the American Institute of Certified Public Accountants, and the underlying assumptions provide a reasonable basis for management's projection assuming the granting of the requested loan for the purpose of expanding Widget Company's plant as described in the summary of significant assumptions. However, even if the loan is granted and the plant is expanded, there will usually be differences between the projected and actual results, because events and circumstances frequently do not occur as expected, and those differences may be material. We have no responsibility to update this report for events and circumstances occurring after the date of this report.

The accompanying projection and this report are intended solely for the information and use of the board of directors and are not intended to be and should not be used by anyone other than these specified parties.

Smith and Jones
February 15, 20X2

ILLUSTRATION 6. STANDARD EXAMINATION REPORT: SEPARATE PARAGRAPH—PROSPECTIVE FINANCIAL STATEMENTS (FORECAST) CONTAIN A RANGE

As described in the summary of significant assumptions, management of Widget Company has elected to portray forecasted revenue at the amounts of $X,XXX and $Y,YYY, which is predicated upon occupancy rates of XX% and YY% of available apartments rather than as a single point estimate. Accordingly, the accompanying forecast presents forecasted financial position, results of operations, and cash flows at such occupancy rates. However, there is no assurance that the actual results will fall within the range of occupancy rates presented.

Smith and Jones
February 15, 20X2

---

[5] *When the presentation is summarized as discussed in "Fundamental Requirements: General," this sentence might read, "We have examined the accompanying summarized projection of Widget Company as of December 31, 20X1, and for the year then ending."*

ILLUSTRATION 7. EXAMINATION REPORT: QUALIFIED OPINION ON FORECAST

To the Board of Directors of Widget Company
Main City, USA

Independent Accountant's Report

We have examined the accompanying forecasted balance sheet, statements of income, retained earnings, and cash flows of Widget Company as of December 31, 20X1, and for the year then ending. Widget Company's management is responsible for the forecast. Our responsibility is to express an opinion on the forecast based on our examination.

Our examination was conducted in accordance with attestation standards established by the American Institute of Certified Public Accountants and, accordingly, included such procedures as we considered necessary to evaluate both the assumptions used by management and the preparation and presentation of the forecast. We believe that our examination provides a reasonable basis for our opinion.

The forecast does not disclose reasons for the significant variation in the relationship between income tax expense and pretax accounting income as required by generally accepted accounting principles.

In our opinion, except for the omission of the disclosure of the reasons for the significant variation in the relationship between income tax expense and pretax accounting income as discussed in the preceding paragraph, the accompanying forecast is presented in conformity with guidelines for presentation of a forecast established by the American Institute of Certified Public Accountants and the underlying assumptions provide a reasonable basis for management's forecast. However, there will usually be differences between the forecasted and actual results, because events and circumstances frequently do not occur as expected, and those differences may be material. We have no responsibility to update this report for events and circumstances occurring after the date of this report.

Smith and Jones
February 15, 20X2

ILLUSTRATION 8. EXAMINATION REPORT: ADVERSE OPINION ON FORECAST

To the Board of Directors of Widget Company
Main City, USA

Independent Accountant's Report

We have examined the accompanying forecasted balance sheet, statements of income, retained earnings, and cash flows of Widget Company as of December 31, 20X1, and for the year then ending. Widget Company's management is responsible for the forecast. Our responsibility is to express an opinion on the forecast based on our examination.

Our examination was conducted in accordance with attestation standards for an examination of a financial forecast established by the American Institute of Certified Public Accountants and, accordingly, included such procedures as we considered necessary to evaluate both the assumptions used by management and the preparation and presentation of the forecast. We believe that our examination provides a reasonable basis for our opinion.

As discussed under the caption "Sales" in the summary of significant forecast assumptions, the forecasted sales include, among other things, revenue from the Company's federal defense contracts continuing at the current level. The Company's present federal defense contracts will expire in March 20X2. No new contracts have been signed and no negotiations are under way for new federal defense contracts. Furthermore, the federal government has entered into contracts with another company to supply the items being manufactured under the Company's present contracts.

In our opinion, the accompanying forecast is not presented in conformity with guidelines for presentation of a financial forecast established by the American Institute of Certified Public Accountants because management's assumptions, as discussed in the preceding paragraph, do not provide a reasonable basis for management's forecast. We have no responsibility to update this report for events or circumstances occurring after the date of this report.

Smith and Jones
February 15, 20X2

ILLUSTRATION 9. EXAMINATION REPORT: DISCLAIMER OF OPINION ON FORECAST

To the Board of Directors of Widget Company
Main City, USA

Independent Accountant's Report

We were engaged to examine the accompanying forecasted balance sheet, statements of income, retained earnings, and cash flows of Widget Company as of December 31, 20X1, and for the year then ending. Widget Company's management is responsible for the forecast.

As discussed under the caption "Income From Investee" in the summary of significant forecast assumptions, the forecast includes income from an equity investee constituting 23% of forecasted net income, which is management's estimate of the Company's share of the investee's income to be accrued for 20X1. The investee has not prepared a forecast for the year ending December 31, 20X1, and we were therefore unable to obtain suitable support for this assumption.

Because, as described in the preceding paragraph, we are unable to evaluate management's assumption regarding income from an equity investee and other assumptions that depend thereon, the scope of our work was not sufficient to express, and we do not express, an opinion with respect to the presentation of or the assumptions underlying the accompanying forecast. We have no responsibility to update this report for events and circumstances occurring after the date of this report.

Smith and Jones
February 15, 20X2

ILLUSTRATION 10. EXPANSION OF PRACTITIONER'S REPORT ON OR FOR A FINANCIAL FEASIBILITY STUDY[6]

Independent Accountant's Report

The Board of Directors
Example Hospital
Maintown, Texas

We have prepared a financial feasibility study of Example Hospital's plans to expand and renovate its facilities. The study was undertaken to evaluate the ability of Example Hospital (the Hospital) to meet the Hospital's operating expenses, working capital needs, and other financial requirements, including the debt service requirements associated with the proposed $25,000,000 [*legal title of bonds*] issue, at an assumed average annual interest rate of 10.0% during the five years ending December 31, 20X5.

---

[6] *This form of report is also applicable to other entities such as hotels or stadiums. Although the illustrated report format and language should not be departed from in any significant way, the language used should be tailored to fit the circumstances that are unique to a particular engagement (e.g., the description of the proposed capital improvement program; the proposed financing of the program; the specific procedures applied by the practitioner; and any explanatory comments included in emphasis-of-matter paragraphs).*

The proposed capital improvements program (the Program) consists of a new two-level addition, which is to provide 50 additional medical-surgical beds, increasing the complement to 275 beds. In addition, various administrative support service areas in the present facilities are to be remodeled. The Hospital administration anticipates that construction is to begin June 30, 20X1, and to be completed by December 31, 20X2.

The estimated total cost of the Program is approximately $30,000,000. It is assumed that the $25,000,000 of revenue bonds that the Example Hospital Finance Authority proposes to issue would be the primary source of funds for the Program. The responsibility for payment of debt service on the bonds is solely that of the Hospital. Other necessary funds to finance the Program are assumed to be provided from the Hospital's funds, from a local fund drive, and from interest earned on funds held by the bond trustee during the construction period.

Our procedures included analysis of:

- Program history, objectives, timing, and financing
- The future demand for the Hospital's services, including consideration of:

  - Economic and demographic characteristics of the Hospital's defined service area
  - Locations, capacities, and competitive information pertaining to other existing and planned area hospitals
  - Physician support for the Hospital and its programs
  - Historical utilization levels

- Planning agency applications and approvals
- Construction and equipment costs, debt service requirements, and estimated financing costs
- Staffing patterns and other operating considerations
- Third-party reimbursement policy and history
- Revenue/expense/volume relationships

We also participated in gathering other information, assisted management in identifying and formulating its assumptions, and assembled the accompanying financial forecast based on those assumptions.

The accompanying financial forecast for the annual periods ending December 31, 20X1 through 20X5, is based on assumptions that were provided by or reviewed with and approved by management. The financial forecast includes:

- Balance sheets
- Statements of operations
- Statements of cash flows
- Statements of changes in net assets

We have examined the financial forecast. Example Hospital's management is responsible for the forecast. Our responsibility is to express an opinion on the forecast based on our examination. Our examination was conducted in accordance with attestation standards established by the American Institute of Certified Public Accountants (AICPA) and, accordingly, included such procedures as we considered necessary to evaluate both the assumptions used by management and the preparation and presentation of the forecast. We believe that our examination provides a reasonable basis for our opinion.

Legislation and regulations at all levels of government have affected and may continue to affect revenues and expenses of hospitals. The financial forecast is based on legislation and regulations currently in effect. If future legislation or regulations related to hospital operations are enacted, such legislation or regulation could have a material effect on future operations.

The interest rate, principal payments, Program costs, and other financing assumptions are described in the section entitled "Summary of Significant Forecast Assumptions and Rationale." If actual interest rates, principal payments, and funding requirements are different from those assumed, the amount of the bond issue and debt service requirements would need to be adjusted accordingly from those indicated in the forecast. If such interest rates, principal payments, and funding requirements are lower than those assumed, such adjustments would not adversely affect the forecast.

Our conclusions are presented below:

- In our opinion, the accompanying financial forecast is presented in conformity with guidelines for presentation of a financial forecast established by the AICPA.
- In our opinion, the underlying assumptions provide a reasonable basis for management's forecast. However, there will usually be differences between the forecasted and actual results, because events and circumstances frequently do not occur as expected, and those differences may be material.
- The accompanying financial forecast indicates that sufficient funds could be generated to meet the Hospital's operating expenses, working capital needs, and other financial requirements, including the debt service requirements associated with the proposed $25,000,000 bond issue, during the forecast periods. However, the achievement of any financial forecast is dependent on future events, the occurrence of which cannot be assured.

We have no responsibility to update this report for events and circumstances occurring after the date of this report.

Smith and Jones
February 15, 20X2

ILLUSTRATION 11. PRACTITIONER'S REPORT: APPLYING AGREED-UPON PROCEDURES TO A FORECAST

Independent Practitioner's Report on Applying Agreed-Upon Procedures

Board of Directors—Widget Corporation
Board of Directors—Basic Company

At your request, we have performed certain agreed-upon procedures, as enumerated below, with respect to the forecasted balance sheet and the related forecasted statements of income, retained earnings, and cash flows of Generic Company, a subsidiary of Basic Company, as of December 31, 20X1, and for the year then ending. These procedures, which were agreed to by the Boards of Directors of Widget Corporation and Basic Company, were performed solely to assist you in evaluating the forecast in connection with the proposed sale of Generic Company to Widget Corporation. [*Client*]'s management is responsible for the forecast.

This agreed-upon procedures engagement was conducted in accordance with attestation standards established by the American Institute of Certified Public Accountants (AICPA). The sufficiency of these procedures is solely the responsibility of the specified parties. Consequently, we make no representation regarding the sufficiency of the procedures described below either for the purpose for which this report has been requested or for any other purpose.

[*Include paragraphs to enumerate procedures and findings*]

We were not engaged to, and did not, conduct an examination, the objective of which would be the expression of an opinion on the accompanying prospective financial statements. Accordingly, we do not express an opinion on whether the prospective financial statements are presented in conformity with AICPA presentation guidelines or on whether the underlying assumptions provide a reasonable basis for the presentation. Had we performed additional procedures, other matters might have come to our attention that would have been reported to you. Furthermore, there will usually be differences between the forecasted and actual results, because events and circumstances frequently do not occur as expected, and those differences may be material. We have no responsibility to update this report for events and circumstances occurring after the date of this report.

This report is intended solely for the information and use of the Boards of Directors of Basic Company and Widget Corporation and is not intended to be and should not be used by anyone other than these specified parties.

Smith and Jones
February 15, 20X2

ILLUSTRATION 12. STANDARD PARAGRAPHS ADDED TO PRACTITIONER'S REPORT IN A PRACTITIONER-SUBMITTED DOCUMENT: BUDGETED FINANCIAL STATEMENTS—SUMMARIES OF SIGNIFICANT ASSUMPTIONS AND ACCOUNTING POLICIES OMITTED

The accompanying budgeted balance sheet, statements of income, retained earnings, and cash flows of Widget Company as of December 31, 20X1, and for the six months then ending, have not been compiled or examined by us, and, accordingly, we do not express an opinion or any other form of assurance on them.

Management has elected to omit the summaries of significant assumptions and accounting policies required under established guidelines for presentation of prospective financial statements. If the omitted summaries were included in the budgeted information, they might influence the user's conclusion about the company's budgeted information. Accordingly, this budgeted information is not designed for those who are not informed about such matters.

APPENDICES

The following appendices are reproduced with permission from SSAE 10. Appendix B is concerned with compilation of prospective financial statements, and Appendix C is concerned with examination of prospective financial statements. The appendices deal with the following:

1. Training and proficiency of the practitioners
2. Planning the engagement
3. Procedures to be applied

Appendix A from the Statement is included in "Fundamental Requirements: General" (list of fourteen minimum presentation requirements).

APPENDIX B: TRAINING AND PROFICIENCY, PLANNING AND PROCEDURES APPLICABLE TO COMPILATIONS

Training and Proficiency

1. The practitioner should be familiar with the guidelines for the preparation and presentation of prospective financial statements. The guidelines are contained in the AICPA *Guide for Prospective Financial Information*.
2. The practitioner should possess or obtain a level of knowledge of the industry and the accounting principles and practices of the industry in which the entity operates or will operate, that will enable him to compile prospective financial statements that are in appropriate form for an entity operating in that industry.

Planning the Compilation Engagement

3. To compile the prospective financial statements of an existing entity, the practitioner should obtain a general knowledge of the nature of the entity's business transactions and the key factors upon which its future financial results appear to depend. He or she should also obtain an understanding of the accounting principles and practices of the entity to determine if they are comparable to those used within the industry in which the entity operates.
4. To compile the prospective financial statements of a proposed entity, the practitioner should obtain knowledge of the proposed operations and the key factors upon which its future results appear to depend and that have affected the performance of entities in the same industry.

Compilation Procedures

5. In performing a compilation of prospective financial statements the practitioner should, where applicable:

    a. Establish an understanding with the client, preferably in writing, regarding the services to be performed. The understanding should include the objectives of the engagement, the client's responsibilities, the practitioner's responsibilities, and the limitations of the engagement. The practitioner should document the understanding, preferably through a written communication with the client. If the practitioner believes an understanding with the client has not been established, he or she should decline to accept or perform the engagement.
    b. Inquire about the accounting principles used in the preparation of the prospective financial statements.

        (1) For existing entities, compare the accounting principles used to those used in preparation of previous historical financial statements and inquire whether such principles are the same as those expected to be used in the historical financial statements covering the prospective period.
        (2) For entities to be formed or entities formed that have not commenced operations, compare specialized industry accounting principles used, if any, to those typically used in the industry. Inquire about whether the accounting principles used for the prospective financial statements are those that are expected to be used when, or if, the entity commences operations.

    c. Ask how the responsible party identifies the key factors and develops its assumptions.
    d. List, or obtain a list of, the responsible party's significant assumptions providing the basis for the prospective financial statements and consider whether there are any obvious omissions in light of the key factors upon which the prospective results of the entity appear to depend.
    e. Consider whether there appear to be any obvious internal inconsistencies in the assumptions.
    f. Perform, or test the mathematical accuracy of, the computations that translate the assumptions into prospective financial statements.
    g. Read the prospective financial statements, including the summary of significant assumptions, and consider whether

(1) The statements, including the disclosures of assumptions and accounting policies, appear to be not presented in conformity with the AICPA presentations guidelines for prospective financial statements.[7]

(2) The statements, including the summary of significant assumptions, appear to be not obviously inappropriate in relation to the practitioner's knowledge of the entity and its industry and, for a

    (a) *Financial forecast*, the expected conditions and course of action in the prospective period.

    (b) *Financial projection*, the purpose of the presentation.

h. If a significant part of the prospective period has expired, inquire about the results of operations or significant portions of the operations (such as sales volume), and significant changes in financial position, and consider their effect in relation to the prospective financial statements. If historical financial statements have been prepared for the expired portion of the period, the practitioner should read such statements and consider those results in relation to the prospective financial statements.

i. Confirm his or her understanding of the statements (including assumptions) by obtaining written representations from the responsible party. Because the amounts reflected in the statements are not supported by historical books and records but rather by assumptions, the practitioner should obtain representations in which the responsible party indicates its responsibility for the assumptions. The representations should be signed by the responsible party at the highest level of authority who the practitioner believes is responsible for and knowledgeable, directly or through others, about matters covered by the representations.

(1) For a *financial forecast*, the representations should include the responsible party's assertion that the financial forecast presents, to the best of the responsible party's knowledge and belief, the expected financial position, results of operations, and cash flows for the forecast period and that the forecast reflects the responsible party's judgment, based on present circumstances, of the expected conditions and its expected course of action. The representations should also include a statement that the forecast is presented in conformity with guidelines for presentation of a forecast established by the American Institute of Certified Public Accountants. The representations should also include a statement that the assumptions on which the forecast is based are reasonable. If the forecast contains a range, the representation should also include a statement that, to the best of the responsible party's knowledge and belief, the item or items subject to the assumption are expected to actually fall within the range and that the range was not selected in a biased or misleading manner.

(2) For a *financial projection*, the representations should include the responsible party's assertion that the financial projection presents, to the best of the responsible party's knowledge and belief, the expected financial position, results of operations, and cash flows for the projection period given the hypothetical assumptions, and that the projection reflects its judgment based on

---

[7] Presentation guidelines for entities that issue prospective financial statements are set forth and illustrated in the *AICPA Guide for Prospective Financial Information*.

present circumstances, of expected conditions, and its expected course of action given the occurrence of the hypothetical events. The representations should also

(a) Identify the hypothetical assumptions and describe the limitations on the usefulness of the presentation.
(b) State that the assumptions are appropriate.
(c) Indicate if the hypothetical assumptions are improbable.
(d) If the projection contains a range, include a statement that, to the best of the responsible party's knowledge and belief, given the hypothetical assumptions, the item or items subject to the assumption are expected to actually fall within the range and that the range was not selected in a biased or misleading manner.

The representations should also include a statement that the projection is presented in conformity with guidelines for presentation of a projection established by the AICPA.

j. Consider, after applying the above procedures, whether he has received representations or other information that appears to be obviously inappropriate, incomplete, or otherwise misleading and, if so, attempt to obtain additional or revised information. If he does not receive such information, the practitioner should ordinarily withdraw from the compilation engagement.[8] (Note that the omission of disclosures, other than those relating to significant assumptions, would not require the practitioner to withdraw; see "Fundamental Requirements.")

APPENDIX C: TRAINING AND PROFICIENCY, PLANNING AND PROCEDURES APPLICABLE TO EXAMINATIONS

Training and Proficiency

1. The practitioner should be familiar with the guidelines for the preparation and presentation of prospective financial statements. The guidelines are contained in the AICPA *Guide for Prospective Financial Information*.
2. The practitioner should possess or obtain a level of knowledge of the industry and the accounting principles and practices of the industry in which the entity operates or will operate that will enable him to examine prospective financial statements that are in appropriate form for an entity operating in that industry.

Planning an Examination Engagement

3. Planning the examination engagement involves developing an overall strategy for the expected scope and conduct of the engagement. To develop such a strategy, the practitioner needs to have sufficient knowledge to enable him to adequately understand the events, transactions, and practices that, in his judgment, may have a significant effect on the prospective financial statements.
4. Factors to be considered by the practitioners in planning the examination include

---

[8] The accountant need not withdraw from the engagement if the effect of such information on the prospective financial statements does not appear to be material.

a. The accounting principles to be used and the type of presentation.
   b. The anticipated level of attestation risk[9] related to the prospective financial statements.
   c. Preliminary judgments about materiality levels.
   d. Items within the prospective financial statements that are likely to require revision or adjustment.
   e. Conditions that may require extension or modification of the practitioner's examination procedures.
   f. Knowledge of the entity's business and its industry.
   g. The responsible party's experience in preparing prospective financial statements.
   h. The length of the period covered by the prospective financial statements.
   i. The process by which the responsible party develops its prospective financial statements.

5. The practitioner should obtain knowledge of the entity's business, accounting principles, and the key factors upon which its future financial results appear to depend. The practitioner should focus on such areas as

   a. The availability and cost of resources needed to operate. Principal items usually include raw materials, labor, short-term and long-term financing, and plant and equipment.
   b. The nature and condition of markets in which the entity sells its goods or services, including final consumer markets if the entity sells to intermediate markets.
   c. Factors specific to the industry, including competitive conditions, sensitivity to economic conditions, accounting policies, specific regulatory requirements, and technology.
   d. Patterns of past performance for the entity or comparable entities, including trends in revenue and costs, turnover of assets, uses and capacities of physical facilities, and management policies.

Examination Procedures

6. The practitioner should establish an understanding with the responsible party regarding the services to be performed. The understanding should include the objectives of the engagement, the responsible party's responsibilities, the practitioner's responsibilities, and the limitations of the engagement. The practitioner should document the understanding, preferably through a written communication with the responsible party. If the practitioner believes an understanding with the responsible party has not been established, he or she should decline to accept or perform the engagement. If the responsible party is different than the client, the practitioner should establish the understanding with both the client and the responsible party, and the understanding also should include the client's responsibilities.

---

[9] Attestation risk is the risk that the practitioner may unknowingly fail to appropriately modify his/her examination report on prospective financial statements that are materially misstated, that is, that are not presented in conformity with AICPA presentation guidelines or have assumptions that do not provide a reasonable basis for management's forecast, or management's projection given the hypothetical assumptions. It consists of (1) the risk (consisting of inherent risk and control risk) that the prospective financial statements contain errors that could be material and (2) the risk (detection risk) that the accountant will not detect such errors.

7. The practitioner's objective in an examination of prospective financial statements is to accumulate sufficient evidence to limit attestation risk to a level that is, in his or her professional judgment, appropriate for the level of assurance that may be imparted by his or her examination report. In a report on an examination of prospective financial statements, he or she provides assurance only about whether the prospective financial statements are presented in conformity with AICPA presentation guidelines and whether the assumptions provide a reasonable basis for management's forecast, or a reasonable basis for management's projection given the hypothetical assumptions. He or she does not provide assurance about the achievability of the prospective results because events and circumstances frequently do not occur as expected and achievement of the prospective results is dependent on the actions, plans, and assumptions of the responsible party.

8. In the examination of prospective financial statements, the practitioner should select from all available procedures—that is, procedures that assess inherent and control risk and restrict detection risk—any combination that can limit attestation risk to such an appropriate level. The extent to which examination procedures will be performed should be based on the practitioner's consideration of

   a. The nature and materiality of the information to the prospective financial statements taken as a whole.
   b. The likelihood of misstatements.
   c. Knowledge obtained during current and previous engagements.
   d. The responsible party's competence with respect to prospective financial statements.
   e. The extent to which the prospective financial statements are affected by the responsible party's judgment (i.e., its judgment in selecting the assumptions used to prepare the prospective financial statements).
   f. The adequacy of the responsible party's underlying data.

9. The practitioner should perform those procedures he considers necessary in the circumstances to report on whether the assumptions provide a reasonable basis for the

   a. *Financial forecast.* The practitioner can form an opinion that the assumptions provide a reasonable basis for the forecast if the responsible party represents that the presentation reflects, to the best of its knowledge and belief, its estimate of expected financial position, results of operations, and cash flows for the prospective period[10] and the practitioner concludes, based on his examination

      (1) That the responsible party has explicitly identified all factors expected to materially affect the operations of the entity during the prospective period and has developed appropriate assumptions with respect to such factors.[11]
      (2) That the assumptions are suitably supported.

---

[10] If the forecast contains a range, the representation should also include a statement that, to the best of the responsible party's knowledge and belief, the item or items subject to the assumption are expected to actually fall within the range and that the range was not selected in a biased or misleading manner.

[11] An attempt to list all assumptions is inherently not feasible. Frequently, basic assumptions that have enormous potential impact are considered to be implicit, such as conditions of peace and absence of natural disasters.

b. *Financial projection given the hypothetical assumptions.* The practitioner can form an opinion that the assumptions provide a reasonable basis for the financial projection, given the hypothetical assumptions, if the responsible party represents that the presentation reflects, to the best of its knowledge and belief, expected financial position, results of operations, and cash flows for the prospective period, given the hypothetical assumptions,[12] and the practitioner concludes, based on his examination

   (1) That the responsible party has explicitly identified all factors that would materially affect the operations of the entity during the prospective period if the hypothetical assumptions were to materialize and has developed appropriate assumptions with respect to such factors.
   (2) That the other assumptions are suitably supported given the hypothetical assumptions. However, as the number and significance of the hypothetical assumptions increase, the practitioner may not be able to satisfy himself about the presentation as a whole by obtaining support for the remaining assumptions.

10. The practitioner should evaluate the support for the assumptions.

    a. *Financial forecast.* The practitioner can conclude that assumptions are suitably supported if the preponderance of information supports each significant assumption.
    b. *Financial projection.* In evaluating support for assumptions other than hypothetical assumptions, the practitioner can conclude that they are suitably supported if the preponderance of information supports each significant assumption, given the hypothetical assumptions. The practitioner need not obtain support for the hypothetical assumptions, although he should consider whether they are consistent with the purpose of the presentation.

11. In evaluating the support for assumptions, the practitioner should consider

    a. Whether sufficient pertinent sources of information about the assumptions have been considered. Examples of external sources the practitioner might consider are government publications, industry publications, economic forecasts, existing or proposed legislation, and reports of changing technology. Examples of internal sources are budgets, labor agreements, patents, royalty agreements and records, sales backlog records, debt agreements, and actions of the board of directors involving entity plans.
    b. Whether the assumptions are consistent with the sources from which they are derived.
    c. Whether the assumptions are consistent with each other.
    d. Whether the historical financial information and other data used in developing the assumptions are sufficiently reliable for that purpose. Reliability can be assessed by inquiry and analytical or other procedures, some of which may have been

---

[12] If the projection contains a range, the representation should also include a statement that, to the best of the responsible party's knowledge and belief, given the hypothetical assumptions, the item or items subject to the assumption are expected to actually fall within the range and that range was not selected in a biased or misleading manner.

completed in past examinations or reviews of the historical financial statements. If historical financial statements have been prepared for an expired part of the prospective period, the practitioner should consider the historical data in relation to the prospective results for the same period, where applicable. If the prospective financial statements incorporate such historical financial results and that period is significant to the presentation, the practitioner should make a review of the historical information in conformity with the applicable standards for review.[13]

    e. Whether the historical financial information and other data used in developing the assumptions are comparable over the periods specified or whether the effects of any lack of comparability were considered in developing the assumptions.

    f. Whether the logical arguments, or theory, considered with the data supporting the assumptions are reasonable.

12. In evaluating the preparation and presentation of the prospective financial statements, the practitioner should perform procedures that will provide reasonable assurance that the

    a. Presentation reflects the identified assumptions.
    b. Computations made to translate the assumptions into prospective amounts are mathematically accurate.
    c. Assumptions are internally consistent.
    d. Accounting principles used in the

        (1) *Financial forecast* are consistent with the accounting principles expected to be used in the historical financial statements covering the prospective period and those used in the most recent historical financial statements, if any.

        (2) *Financial projection* are consistent with the accounting principles expected to be used in the prospective period and those used in the most recent historical financial statements, if any, or that they are consistent with the purpose of the presentation.[14]

    e. Presentation of the prospective financial statements follows the AICPA guidelines applicable for such statements.[15]
    f. Assumptions have been adequately disclosed based on AICPA presentation guidelines for prospective financial statements.

13. The practitioner should consider whether the prospective financial statements, including related disclosures, should be revised because of

    a. Mathematical errors.
    b. Unreasonable or internally inconsistent assumptions.
    c. Inappropriate or incomplete presentation.
    d. Inadequate disclosure.

---

[13] *If the entity is a public company, the accountant should perform the procedures in AU Section 722, Interim Financial Information. If the entity is nonpublic, the accountant should perform the procedures in SSARS 1,* Compilation and Review of Financial Statements (AR Section 60–90).

[14] *The accounting principles used in a financial projection need not be those expected to be used in the historical financial statements for the prospective period if use of different principles is consistent with the purpose of the presentation.*

[15] *Presentation guidelines for entities that issue prospective financial statements are set forth and illustrated in the* AICPA Guide for Prospective Financial Information.

14. The practitioner should obtain written representations from the responsible party acknowledging its responsibility for both the presentation and the underlying assumptions. The representations should be signed by the responsible party at the highest level of authority whom the practitioner believes is responsible for and knowledgeable, directly or through others in the organization, about the matters covered by the representations. Appendix B, paragraph 5i, describes the specific representations to be obtained for a financial forecast and a financial projection. See "Disclaimer of Opinion" under "Fundamental Requirements: Examination of Prospective Financial Statements" for guidance on the form of report to be rendered if the practitioner is not able to obtain the required representations.

AT 401 Reporting on Pro Forma Financial Information

EFFECTIVE DATE AND APPLICABILITY

Original Pronouncement	Statements on Standards for Attestation Engagements (SSAE) 10, *Attestation Standards: Revision and Recodification*.
Effective Date	This statement currently is effective.
Applicability	Reports on an examination or a review of pro forma financial information. When pro forma information is provided outside the financial statements and the accountant is not engaged to report on it, the guidance in Section 550, *Other Information in Documents Containing Audited Financial Statements*, applies.

DEFINITIONS OF TERMS

Pro forma financial information. Shows "what the significant effects on historical financial information *might have been* had a *consummated or proposed* transaction (or event) occurred at an earlier date." (Emphasis added.)

OBJECTIVES OF SECTION 401

A high rate of mergers and acquisitions in the late 1980s increased the need for guidance on pro forma financial information. The Auditing Standards Board issued an SSAE, *Reporting on Pro Forma Financial Information* (the Statement) in 1988. The attestation statement applies to the accountant's involvement with all presentations of pro forma financial information, including information required by Article 11 of Securities and Exchange Commission (SEC) Regulation S-X.

The statement explains the application of the general guidance for attestation engagements to engagements to report on pro forma information. The permitted levels of service that the accountant can provide related to pro forma information are a *review* or an *examination*.

The statement does not apply to the generally accepted accounting principles (GAAP) requirements in historical financial statements related to disclosure of a transaction consummated after the balance sheet date to achieve a more meaningful presentation, such as presentation of earnings per share revised for a subsequent stock split.

USE OF PRO FORMA INFORMATION

Pro forma information might be used to show the effects of a business combination, change in capitalization, disposition of a significant portion of a business, a change in form or status of a business (for example, from a division to a separate entity), or a proposed sale of securities and application of the proceeds.

In 2001, the Auditing Standards Board issued SSAE 10, *Attestation Standards: Revision and Recodification*. SSAE 10 superseded SSAEs 1 through 9 and renumbered the AT sections in the American Institute of Certified Public Accountants (AICPA) Codification.

FUNDAMENTAL REQUIREMENTS

CONDITIONS FOR REPORTING AND THE ACCOUNTANT'S OBJECTIVES

A practitioner may *examine* or *review* pro forma financial information if all three of the following conditions are achieved:

1. The document including the pro formas also includes complete historical financial statements (or incorporates them by reference) of the entity for the most recent year. If pro formas are for an interim period, historical interim information for that period is also presented (or incorporated by reference). If the circumstances are a business combination, the document includes historical data for significant constituent parts of the combined entity.
2. The historical financial statements on which the pro forma information is based have been audited or reviewed by a practitioner.

> NOTE: The level of assurance on the pro formas should be no greater than the level on the related historical statements. For a nonpublic entity, the review may be performed under AR Section 60–90.

3. The practitioner reporting on the pro forma information should have an appropriate level of knowledge of the entity's accounting and financial reporting practices.

> NOTE: Generally this knowledge will be the result of having audited or reviewed the historical statements. If the practitioner was not the auditor or reviewer of the historical statements, the practitioner "should consider whether, under the particular circumstances, he or she can acquire sufficient knowledge."

ENGAGEMENT OBJECTIVES

Examination

The objective of a practitioner's *examination* of pro forma information is to provide reasonable assurance that

1. Management's assumptions provide a reasonable basis for presenting the significant effects of the underlying transaction or event.
2. Pro forma adjustments give appropriate effect to the assumptions.
3. The pro forma column (historical information modified by adjustments) reflects the proper application of the adjustments.

Review

The objective of a practitioner's *review* of pro forma information is to provide negative assurance on the three aspects of the pro forma information listed in the preceding paragraph.

NOTE: "Negative assurance" indicates that no information came to the practitioner's attention that would cause him or her not to believe the three statements.

The objectives of an examination or review do not focus on the final pro forma column alone. The assurance is not that the pro forma column conforms with established criteria. The practitioner's objectives relate to the three separate aspects of a pro forma presentation:

- *Assumptions (reasonable)*
- *Adjustments (give effect to assumptions)*
- *Final column (application of adjustments is proper)*

PROCEDURES

The procedures for an examination or review include:

1. Obtaining an understanding of the underlying transaction or event
2. Obtaining a level of knowledge of each significant constituent part of the combined entity in a business combination
3. Discussing with management their assumptions about the effects of the transaction or event
4. Evaluating whether pro forma adjustments are included for all significant effects of the transaction or event
5. Obtaining sufficient evidence in support of such adjustments

NOTE: In considering the level of attestation risk the practitioner is willing to accept in a pro forma information engagement, the level of assurance on the underlying historical financial statements is a key factor. Accordingly, the procedures the practitioner should apply to the assumptions and pro forma adjustments are substantially the same for either an examination or a review engagement. The evidence needed is a matter of judgment and may vary with the level of service involved.

6. Evaluating whether the presentation of management's assumptions is sufficiently clear and comprehensive, and whether management's assumptions are consistent with each other and with the data used to develop them.
7. Determining whether computations of pro forma adjustments are mathematically correct and that the pro forma column reflects proper application of the adjustments.
8. Obtaining management's written representations on:
    a. Their responsibility for the assumptions
    b. Assertion that the assumptions provide a reasonable basis for presenting all of the significant effects directly attributable to the transaction or event
    c. Assertion that the related pro forma adjustments give appropriate effect to the assumptions
    d. Assertion that the pro forma column reflects the proper application of adjustments
    e. Their belief that significant effects of the transaction or event are appropriately disclosed
9. Reading the pro forma financial information and evaluating the appropriateness of the descriptions of:
    a. The underlying transaction or event,
    b. The pro forma adjustments, and
    c. The significant assumptions and significant uncertainties about those assumptions.

Also, evaluating whether the source of the historical information base is appropriately identified.

FORM OF REPORT ON PRO FORMA FINANCIAL INFORMATION

According to AT 401.12, a practitioner's examination report on pro forma financial information should include:

1. A title that includes the word *independent*
2. An identification of the pro forma financial information
3. A reference to the financial statements from which the historical financial information is derived and a statement as to whether such financial statements were audited (The report on pro forma financial information should refer to any modification in the practitioner's report on the historical financial information.)
4. An identification of the responsible party and a statement that the responsible party is responsible for the pro forma financial information
5. Statements that:
   a. The practitioner's responsibility is to express an opinion on the pro forma financial information based on his or her examination.
   b. The examination of the pro forma financial information was conducted in accordance with attestation standards established by the AICPA and, accordingly, included such procedures as the practitioner considered necessary in the circumstances.
   c. The practitioner believes that the examination provides a reasonable basis for his or her opinion.
6. A separate paragraph explaining the objective of pro forma financial information and its limitations
7. The practitioner's opinion as to whether management's assumptions provide a reasonable basis for presenting the significant effects directly attributable to the transaction (or event), whether the related pro forma adjustments give appropriate effect to those assumptions and whether the pro forma column reflects the proper application of those adjustments to the historical financial statements.
8. The manual or printed signature of the practitioner's firm.
9. The date of the examination report.

According to AT 401.13, a practitioner's review report on pro forma financial information should include the following:

1. A title that includes the word *independent*
2. An identification of the pro forma financial information
3. A reference to the financial statements from which the historical financial information is derived and a statement as to whether such financial statements were audited or reviewed (The report on pro forma financial information should refer to any modification in the practitioner's report on the historical financial information.)
4. An identification of the responsible party and a statement that the responsible party is responsible for the pro forma financial information
5. A statement that the review of the pro forma financial information was conducted in accordance with attestation standards established by the AICPA
6. A statement that a review is substantially less in scope than an examination, the objective of which is the expression of an opinion on the pro forma financial information and, accordingly, the practitioner does not express such an opinion

7. A separate paragraph explaining the objective of pro forma financial information and its limitations
8. The practitioner's conclusion as to whether any information came to the practitioner's attention to cause him or her to believe that management's assumptions do not provide a reasonable basis for presenting the significant effects directly attributable to the transaction (or event), or that the related pro forma adjustments do not give appropriate effect to those assumptions, or that the pro forma column does not reflect the proper application of those adjustments to the historical financial statements
9. The manual or printed signature of the firm
10. The date of the review report

The practitioner's report on the pro forma financial information:

- Should be dated as of the completion of the appropriate procedures
- May be added to the practitioner's report on historical financial information or may appear separately

If the reports are combined and the date of completion of procedures on the pro forma financial information is after the completion of fieldwork for the audit or review of the historical financial information, the combined report should be dual-dated, as shown in the following:

> February 15, 20X2, except for the paragraphs regarding pro forma financial information as to which the date is March 20, 20X2.

See "Illustrations" for example reports on examinations (Illustration 1) and reviews (Illustration 2) of pro forma information.

NOTE: A practitioner's report may combine a review of some pro forma information and an examination of other pro forma information (for example, an examination of annual pro formas with a review of quarterly pro forma information). An example of such a report is presented in Illustration 3.

Report Modifications

A practitioner should modify the report (qualify, adverse, or disclaim) or withdraw from the engagement for (1) restrictions on the scope of the engagement, or (2) reservations about the propriety of the assumptions or the conformity of the presentation with those assumptions, including inadequate disclosure of significant matters. Examples of modified reports appear as Illustrations 4 through 7.

NOTE: Uncertainty about whether the transaction/event will be consummated does not require a report modification.

INTERPRETATIONS

There are no interpretations for this section.

TECHNIQUES FOR APPLICATION

PRESENTATION OF PRO FORMA FINANCIAL INFORMATION

Pro forma financial information:

1. Should be labeled to distinguish it from historical financial information
2. Should describe the transaction or event that is presented as pro forma, the source of the historical information on which it is based, significant assumptions underlying the information, and any significant uncertainties
3. Should indicate that it should be read in conjunction with the related historical information
4. Should indicate that it is not necessarily indicative of results that would have been obtained if the transaction had taken place earlier

NOTE: *For presentation of pro forma information for a public company, the practitioner should also refer to Article 11 of Regulation S-X.*

NONAUDIT AND NONREVIEW CLIENTS

Can a practitioner who has not audited or reviewed the historical base financial statements have a sufficient level of knowledge of the entity's accounting and financial reporting practices to accept a pro forma review or examination engagement? The knowledge would have to be obtained to permit the practitioner to report on the pro forma information. A practitioner may be able to obtain this knowledge in some cases. For example, if the 20X1 pro forma information were based on historical financial statements audited by someone else, but the practitioner has audited the historical financial statements for 20X2, and as part of that audit, reviewed the workpapers of the predecessor auditors, the practitioner should have obtained an appropriate level of knowledge.

MOST RECENT YEAR HISTORICAL FINANCIAL STATEMENTS

There is a requirement that the historical financial statements for the most recent year be included in the document containing the pro forma financial information. If the historical financial statements for the most recent year are not yet available, can the practitioner accept the engagement to report on the pro formas? Yes. The Statement indicates that the historical financial statements for the preceding year should be included if financial statements for the most recent year are not available.

COMPILED HISTORICAL FINANCIAL STATEMENTS

An entity with audited financial statements acquires a small closely held business for which the practitioner has compiled the financial statements. Is it permissible for the practitioner to accept an engagement to report on pro forma financial information? No, not if the operating results of the closely held business are material to the combined entity. The historical base should be audited or reviewed. Compilation is not enough, but the practitioner can accept the engagement if he or she is able to perform a retroactive review or audit.

QUALIFIED REPORT ON HISTORICAL FINANCIAL STATEMENTS

The practitioner's report on pro forma financial information refers to the financial statements from which the historical financial information was derived, and states whether the financial statements were audited or reviewed. If the report on the historical financial statements was a qualified opinion or was otherwise modified, a reference to the modification should be included in the report on pro forma information.

ILLUSTRATIONS

The following are examples of reports on pro forma financial information (adapted from SSAE 10, AT 400 Appendices A–E).

ILLUSTRATION 1. REPORT ON EXAMINATION OF PRO FORMA FINANCIAL INFORMATION

To the Board of Directors of Widget Company
Main City, USA

Independent Accountant's Report

We have examined the pro forma adjustments reflecting the transaction [*or event*] described in Note 1 and the application of those adjustments to the historical amounts in [*the assembly of*] the accompanying pro forma condensed balance sheet of Widget Company as of December 31, 20X1, and the pro forma condensed statement of income for the year then ended. The historical condensed financial statements are derived from the historical financial statements of Widget Company, which were audited by us, and of Basic Company, which were audited by other accountants, appearing elsewhere herein [*or incorporated by reference*]. Such pro forma adjustments are based upon management's assumptions described in Note 2. Widget Company's management is responsible for the pro forma financial information. Our responsibility is to express an opinion on the pro forma financial information based on our examination.

Our examination was conducted in accordance with attestation standards established by the American Institute of Certified Public Accountants and, accordingly, included such procedures as we considered necessary in the circumstances. We believe that our examination provides a reasonable basis for our opinion.

The objective of this pro forma financial information is to show what the significant effects on the historical financial information might have been had the transaction [*or event*] occurred at an earlier date. However, the pro forma condensed financial statements are not necessarily indicative of the results of operations or related effects on financial position that would have been attained had the above-mentioned transaction [*or event*] actually occurred earlier.

In our opinion, management's assumptions provide a reasonable basis for presenting the significant effects directly attributable to the above-mentioned transaction [*or event*] described in Note 1, the related pro forma adjustments give appropriate effect to those assumptions, and the pro forma column reflects the proper application of those adjustments to the historical financial statement amounts in the pro forma condensed balance sheet as of December 31, 20X1, and the pro forma condensed statement of income for the year then ended.

Smith and Jones
February 15, 20X2

NOTE: Additional paragraph(s) may be added before the opinion paragraph to emphasize certain matters relating to the attest engagement or the subject matter.

> **ILLUSTRATION 2. REPORT ON REVIEW OF PRO FORMA FINANCIAL INFORMATION**

To the Board of Directors of Widget Company
Main City, USA

Independent Accountant's Report

We have reviewed the pro forma adjustments reflecting the transaction [*or event*] described in Note 1 and the application of those adjustments to the historical amounts in [*the assembly of*] the accompanying pro forma condensed balance sheet of Widget Company as of March 31, 20X2, and the pro forma condensed statement of income for the three months then ended. These historical condensed financial statements are derived from the historical unaudited financial statements of Widget Company, which were reviewed by us, and of Basic Company, which were reviewed by other accountants, appearing elsewhere herein [*or incorporated by reference*]. Such pro forma adjustments are based on management's assumptions as described in Note 2. Widget Company's management is responsible for the pro forma financial information.

Our review was conducted in accordance with attestation standards established by the American Institute of Certified Public Accountants. A review is substantially less in scope than an examination, the objective of which is the expression of an opinion on management's assumptions, the pro forma adjustments, and the application of those adjustments to historical financial information. Accordingly, we do not express such an opinion.

The objective of this pro forma financial information is to show what the significant effects on the historical financial information might have been had the transaction [*or event*] occurred at an earlier date. However, the pro forma condensed financial statements are not necessarily indicative of the results of operations or related effects on financial position that would have been attained had the above-mentioned transaction [*or event*] actually occurred earlier.

Based on our review, nothing came to our attention that caused us to believe that management's assumptions do not provide a reasonable basis for presenting the significant effects directly attributable to the above-mentioned transaction [*or event*] described in Note 1, that the related pro forma adjustments do not give appropriate effect to those assumptions, or that the pro forma column does not reflect the proper application of those adjustments to the historical financial statement amounts in the pro forma condensed balance sheet as of March 31, 20X2, and the pro forma condensed statement of income for the three months then ended.

Smith and Jones
February 15, 20X2

NOTE: Additional paragraph(s) may be added before the opinion paragraph to emphasize certain matters relating to the attest engagement or the subject matter.

> **ILLUSTRATION 3. REPORT ON EXAMINATION OF PRO FORMA FINANCIAL INFORMATION AT YEAR-END WITH A REVIEW OF PRO FORMA FINANCIAL INFORMATION FOR A SUBSEQUENT INTERIM DATE**

To the Board of Directors of Widget Company
Main City, USA

Independent Accountant's Report

We have examined the pro forma adjustments reflecting the transaction [*or event*] described in Note 1 and the application of those adjustments to the historical amounts in [*the assembly of*] the accompanying pro forma condensed balance sheet of Widget Company as of December 31, 20X1, and the pro forma condensed statement of income for the year then ended. The historical condensed financial statements are derived from the historical financial statements of Widget Company, which were audited by us, and of Basic Company, which were audited by other accountants, appearing elsewhere herein [*or incorporated by reference*]. Such pro forma adjustments are based upon management's assumptions described in Note 2. Widget Company's management is responsible for the pro forma financial information. Our responsibility is to express an opinion on the pro forma financial information based on our examination.

Our examination was conducted in accordance with attestation standards established by the American Institute of Certified Public Accountants and, accordingly, included such procedures as we considered necessary in the circumstances. We believe that our examination provides a reasonable basis for our opinion.

In addition, we have reviewed the related pro forma adjustments and the application of those adjustments to the historical amounts in [*the assembly of*] the accompanying pro forma condensed balance sheet of Widget Company as of March 31, 20X2, and the pro forma condensed statement of income for the three months then ended. The historical condensed financial statements are derived from the historical financial statements of Widget Company, which were reviewed by us, and Basic Company, which were reviewed by other accountants, appearing elsewhere herein [*or incorporated by reference*]. Such pro forma adjustments are based upon management's assumptions as described in Note 2. Our review was conducted in accordance with attestation standards established by the American Institute of Certified Public Accountants. A review is substantially less in scope than an examination, the objective of which is the expression of an opinion on management's assumptions, the pro forma adjustments, and the application of those adjustments to historical financial information. Accordingly, we do not express such an opinion on the pro forma adjustments or the application of such adjustments to the pro forma condensed balance sheet as of March 31, 20X2, and the pro forma condensed statement of income for the three months then ended.

The objective of this pro forma financial information is to show what the significant effects on the historical information might have been had the transaction [*or event*] occurred at an earlier date. However, the pro forma condensed financial statements are not necessarily indicative of the results of operations or related effects on financial position that would have been attained had the above-mentioned transaction [*or event*] actually occurred earlier.

In our opinion, management's assumptions provide a reasonable basis for presenting the significant effects directly attributable to the above-mentioned transaction [*or event*] described in Note 1, the related pro forma adjustments give appropriate effect to those assumptions, and the pro forma column reflects the proper application of those adjustments to the historical financial statement amounts in the pro forma condensed balance sheet as of December 31, 20X1, and the pro forma condensed statement of income for the year then ended.

Based on our review, nothing came to our attention that caused us to believe that management's assumptions do not provide a reasonable basis for representing the significant effects directly attributable to the above-mentioned transaction [*or event*] described in Note 1, that the related pro forma adjustments do not give appropriate effect to those assumptions, or that the pro forma column does not reflect the proper application of those adjustments to the historical financial statement amounts in the pro forma condensed balance sheet as of March 31, 20X2, and the pro forma condensed statement of income for the three months then ended.

Smith and Jones
February 15, 20X2

NOTE: *Additional paragraph(s) may be added before the opinion paragraph to emphasize certain matters relating to the attest engagement or the subject matter.*

> **ILLUSTRATION 4. REPORT ON EXAMINATION OF PRO FORMA FINANCIAL INFORMATION GIVING EFFECT TO A BUSINESS COMBINATION TO BE ACCOUNTED FOR AS A POOLING OF INTERESTS**

Independent Accountant's Report

We have examined the pro forma adjustments reflecting the proposed business combination to be accounted for as a pooling of interests described in Note 1 and the application of those adjustments to the historical amounts in the accompanying pro forma condensed balance sheet of X Company as of December 31, 20X1, and the pro forma condensed statements of income for each of three years in the period then ended. These historical condensed financial statements are derived from the historical financial statements of X Company, which were audited by us, and of Y Company, which were audited by other accountants, appearing elsewhere herein [*or incorporated by reference*]. Such pro forma adjustments are based upon management's assumptions described in Note 2. X Company's management is responsible for the pro forma financial information. Our responsibility is to express an opinion on the pro forma financial information based on our examination.

Our examination was conducted in accordance with attestation standards established by the American Institute of Certified Public Accountants and, accordingly, included such procedures as we considered necessary in the circumstances. We believe that our examination provides a reasonable basis for our opinion.

The objective of this pro forma financial information is to show what the significant effects on the historical financial information might have been had the transactions [*or event*] occurred at an earlier date.

[*Additional paragraph(s) may be added to emphasize certain matters relating to the attest engagement or the subject matter.*]

In our opinion, the accompanying condensed pro forma financial statements of X Company as of December 31, 20X1, and for each of the three years in the period then ended give appropriate effect to the pro forma adjustments necessary to reflect the proposed business combination on a pooling of interests basis as described in Note 1 and the pro forma column reflects the proper application of those adjustments to the historical financial statements.

[*Signature*]

[*Date*]

> **ILLUSTRATION 5. REPORT ON EXAMINATION OF PRO FORMA FINANCIAL INFORMATION—SCOPE LIMITATION QUALIFICATION**

To the Board of Directors of Widget Company
Main City, USA

Independent Accountant's Report

We have examined the pro forma adjustments reflecting the transaction [*or event*] described in Note 1 and the application of those adjustments to the historical amounts in [*the assembly of*] the accompanying pro forma condensed balance sheet of Widget Company as of December 31, 20X1, and the pro forma condensed statement of income for the year then ended. The historical condensed financial statements are derived from the historical financial statements of Widget Company, which were audited by us, and of Basic Company, which were audited by other accountants, appearing elsewhere herein [*or incorporated by reference*]. Such pro forma adjustments are based upon management's assumptions described in Note 2. Widget Company's management is responsible for the pro forma financial information. Our responsibility is to express an opinion on the pro forma financial information based on our examination.

Except as described below, our examination was conducted in accordance with attestation standards established by the American Institute of Certified Public Accountants and, accordingly, included such procedures as we considered necessary in the circumstances. We believe that our examination provides a reasonable basis for our opinion.

We are unable to perform the examination procedures we considered necessary with respect to assumptions relating to the proposed loan described as Adjustment E in Note 2.

The objective of this pro forma financial information is to show what the significant effects on the historical financial information might have been had the transaction [*or event*] occurred at an earlier date. However, the pro forma condensed financial statements are not necessarily indicative of the results of operations or related effects on financial position that would have been attained had the above-mentioned transaction [*or event*] actually occurred earlier.

In our opinion, except for the effects of such changes, if any, as might have been determined to be necessary had we been able to satisfy ourselves as to the assumptions relating to the proposed loan, management's assumptions provide a reasonable basis for presenting the significant effects directly attributable to the above-mentioned transaction [*or event*] described in Note 1, the related pro forma adjustments give appropriate effect to those assumptions, and the pro forma column reflects the proper application of those adjustments to the historical financial statement amounts in the pro forma condensed balance sheet as of December 31, 20X1, and the pro forma condensed statement of income for the year then ended.

Smith and Jones
February 15, 20X2

ILLUSTRATION 6. REPORT ON EXAMINATION OF PRO FORMA FINANCIAL INFORMATION—QUALIFICATION—PROPRIETY OF ASSUMPTIONS

To the Board of Directors of Widget Company
Main City, USA

Independent Accountant's Report

We have examined the pro forma adjustments reflecting the transaction [*or event*] described in Note 1 and the application of those adjustments to the historical amounts in [*the assembly of*] the accompanying pro forma condensed balance sheet of Widget Company as of December 31, 20X1, and the pro forma condensed statement of income for the year then ended. The historical condensed financial statements are derived from the historical financial statements of Widget Company, which were audited by us, and of Basic Company, which were audited by other accountants, appearing elsewhere herein [*or incorporated by reference*]. Such pro forma adjustments are based upon management's assumptions described in Note 2. Widget Company's management is responsible for the pro forma financial information. Our responsibility is to express an opinion on the pro forma financial information based on our examination.

Our examination was conducted in accordance with attestation standards established by the American Institute of Certified Public Accountants and, accordingly, included such procedures as we considered necessary in the circumstances. We believe that our examination provides a reasonable basis for our opinion.

The objective of this pro forma financial information is to show what the significant effects on the historical financial information might have been had the transaction [*or event*] occurred at an earlier date. However, the pro forma condensed financial statements are not necessarily indicative of the results of operations or related effects on financial position that would have been attained had the above-mentioned transaction [*or event*] actually occurred earlier.

As discussed in Note 2 to the pro forma financial statements, the pro forma adjustments reflect management's assumption that X Division of the acquired company will be sold. The net assets of this division are reflected at their historical carrying amount; generally accepted accounting principles require these net assets to be recorded at estimated net realizable value.

In our opinion, except for inappropriate valuation of net assets of X Division, management's assumptions described in Note 2 provide a reasonable basis for presenting the significant effects directly attributable to the above-mentioned transaction [*or event*] described in Note 1, the related pro forma adjustments give appropriate effect to those assumptions, and the pro forma column reflects the proper application of those adjustments to the historical financial statement amounts in the pro forma condensed balance sheet as of December 31, 20X1, and the pro forma condensed statement of income for the year then ended.

Smith and Jones
February 15, 20X2

ILLUSTRATION 7. DISCLAIMER OF OPINION ON PRO FORMA FINANCIAL INFORMATION—SCOPE LIMITATION

To the Board of Directors of Widget Company
Main City, USA

Independent Accountant's Report

We were engaged to examine the pro forma adjustments reflecting the transaction [*or event*] described in Note 1 and the application of those adjustments to the historical amounts in [*the assembly of*] the accompanying pro forma condensed balance sheet of Widget Company as of December 31, 20X1, and the pro forma condensed statement of income for the year then ended. The historical condensed financial statements are derived from the historical financial statements of Widget Company, which were audited by us, and of Basic Company, which were audited by other accountants, appearing elsewhere herein [*or incorporated by reference*]. Such pro forma adjustments are based upon management's assumptions described in Note 2. Widget Company's management is responsible for the pro forma financial information.

As discussed in Note 2 to the pro forma financial statements, the pro forma adjustments reflect management's assumptions that the elimination of duplicate facilities would have resulted in a 30% reduction in operating costs. Management could not supply us with sufficient evidence to support this assertion.

The objective of this pro forma financial information is to show what the significant effects on the historical financial information might have been had the transaction [*or event*] occurred at an earlier date. However, the pro forma condensed financial statements are not necessarily indicative of the results of operations or related effects on financial position that would have been attained had the above-mentioned transaction [*or event*] actually occurred earlier.

Since we were unable to evaluate management's assumptions regarding the reduction in operating costs and other assumptions related thereto, the scope of our work was not sufficient to express, and therefore, we do not express, an opinion on the pro forma adjustments, management's underlying assumptions regarding those adjustments, and the application of those adjustments to the historical financial statement amounts in the pro forma condensed financial statement amounts in the pro forma condensed balance sheet as of December 31, 20X1, and the pro forma condensed statement of income for the year then ended.

Smith and Jones
February 15, 20X2

AT 501 An Examination of an Entity's Internal Control Over Financial Reporting That Is Integrated with an Audit of Its Financial Statements

IMPORTANT NOTE: The guidance in this section applies to engagements for nonissuers. Auditors of issuers and public entities subject to Securities and Exchange Commission (SEC) rules should refer to the guidance in Public Company Accounting Oversight Board (PCAOB) 5, An Audit of Internal Control Over Financial Reporting That Is Integrated with an Audit of Financial Statements, *and should NOT follow the guidance in this section for the purpose of complying with Section 404 of the Sarbanes–Oxley Act.*

EFFECTIVE DATE AND APPLICABILITY

Original Pronouncements	Statements on Standards for Attestation Engagements (SSAE) 15, *An Examination of an Entity's Internal Control Over Financial Reporting That Is Integrated with an Audit of its Financial Statements*
Effective Date	This statement currently is effective.
Applicability	Applicable when an independent accountant is engaged to issue or does issue an examination report on the design and operating effectiveness of an entity's internal control over financial reporting that is integrated with an audit of financial statements.
	NOTE: A practitioner may also be engaged to examine the effectiveness of an entity's internal control over financial reporting as of a date other than the end of an entity's fiscal year. If so, the examination should still be integrated with the financial statement audit. *Review engagements are prohibited, but agreed-upon procedures engagements are not.*

This statement does not change the auditor's responsibility for considering or communicating internal control related matters in an audit. See Section 325, *Communicating Internal Control Related Matters Identified in an Audit.*

For reports on the processing of transactions at service organizations, Section 324, *Service Organizations*, continues to apply. For reports on the suitability of the design of internal controls or on controls over the effectiveness and efficiency of operations, AT Section 101, *Attest Engagements*, applies. For reports on controls over compliance with laws and regulations, AT Section 601, *Compliance Attestation*, applies.

DEFINITIONS OF TERMS

Control objective. The aim or purpose of specified controls. It normally addresses the risks that a control is designed to mitigate. For internal control, it addresses the risk that controls will not provide reasonable assurance that a misstatement or omission is either prevented, or detected and corrected on a timely basis.

Deficiency. A *deficiency* exists when the design or operation of a control does not allow management or employees to either prevent, or detect and correct misstatements on a timely basis. A *design deficiency* exists when either (1) a control needed to meet a control objective is missing; or (2) an existing control is incorrectly designed so that, even if the control operates as designed, the control objective would not be met. An *operation deficiency* exists when a properly designed control does not operate as designed, or when the person performing the control does not have the authority or competence to perform the control correctly.

Detective control. A control whose objective is to detect and correct errors or fraud that have already occurred, which could result in a misstatement of the financial statements.

Internal control over financial reporting. A process designed to provide reasonable assurance regarding the preparation of reliable financial statements in accordance with the applicable financial reporting framework. The controls should address the proper maintenance of records, transaction recordation, and prevention of unauthorized assets usage, resulting in the prevention of misstatements in the financial statements.

Management's assertion. Management's statement about the effectiveness of the entity's internal control, and which is included in management's report on internal control.

Material weakness. A deficiency in internal control resulting in a reasonable possibility that a material misstatement of the entity's financial statements will not be prevented, or detected and corrected.

Preventive control. A control having the objective of preventing errors or fraud that could result in a misstatement of the financial statements.

Relevant assertion. An assertion in the financial statements that has a reasonable possibility of containing a misstatement that would cause the financial statements to be materially misstated.

Significant account or disclosure. An account balance or disclosure that has a reasonable possibility that it could contain a misstatement, either individually or in aggregate with others, that has a material effect on the financial statements.

Significant deficiency. A deficiency or combination of deficiencies in internal control that is less severe than a material weakness, but is important enough to merit the attention of those charged with governance.

OBJECTIVES OF AT SECTION 501

The history of public reporting on internal control has been long and controversial. In the mid-1940s there was a debate about whether an auditor had a duty to modify the audit report to disclose serious deficiencies in accounting control. In the late 1960s, several large banks included accountants' reports on internal control in their annual reports. These reports were brief and stated, in effect, that the accountants had reviewed controls and believed that the control systems were effective.

There was disagreement about the desirability of this type of reporting. Some accountants believed that reports on internal control served no useful purpose unless the recipients were in a position to do something about internal control effectiveness.

In late 1971, Statement on Accounting Procedure (SAP) 49 was issued to put an effective halt to the small but growing practice of public reporting on internal control. It required two caveat paragraphs on the limitations of accounting control, and the only form of assurance permitted was negative assurance on the absence of material weaknesses. Critics of the accounting profession, most notably officials of the Securities and Exchange Commission (SEC), publicly derided the report as a triumph of technical precision over meaningful reporting and common sense.

There were no significant developments in the area until the illegal payments scandal broke in the mid-1970s. One outcome of the scandal was passage of the Foreign Corrupt Practices Act of 1977. The act adopted the accounting profession's definition of internal accounting control and required that all public companies have a system of internal accounting control sufficient to meet the objectives stated in the definition.

The SEC began what appeared to be a concerted drive to require independent accountants to report publicly on the internal accounting systems of public companies. Despite the momentum of the illegal payments scandal, the drive faltered because of unanticipated strong opposition from public companies and lack of support from large CPA firms. Ultimately, the SEC backtracked and withdrew its proposals. In response to the Foreign Corrupt Practices Act and related SEC proposals, however, the accounting profession had started several initiatives, and many of them had been virtually completed before the SEC's withdrawal.

In 1977, even before passage of the act was achieved, Statement on Auditing Standards (SAS) 20 had been issued. It imposed a responsibility on the auditor to communicate material weaknesses in accounting control to management.

In the mid-1980s, SAS 30 was issued. It provided a vehicle for an accountant to issue a positive opinion on accounting control. The unmodified opinion stated:

> In our opinion, the system of internal accounting control of XYZ Company and subsidiaries in effect at [date], taken as a whole, was sufficient to meet the objectives stated above insofar as those objectives pertain to the prevention or detection of errors or irregularities in amounts that would be material in relation to the consolidated financial statements.

However, this report was largely of academic interest only. Without the pressure of an SEC requirement, there was little incentive even for public companies to engage an independent accountant to express an opinion on an internal accounting control system. Small and privately owned companies never had any great interest in such reports. The report was a service that was all dressed up but had no place to go.

In the wake of the savings and loan crisis in the late 1980s, there was considerable regulatory and legislative activity to help reduce fraudulent financial reporting. A National Commission on Fraudulent Financial Reporting, known as the Treadway Commission, was created. The Commission's report, issued in 1987, included as one of its recommendations the requirement for a management report on internal control. Legislators and regulators agreed. The Federal Deposit Insurance Corporation (FDIC) Improvement Act of 1991 affecting financial institutions was passed, and the SEC issued another rule proposal, Report of Management's Responsibilities, proposing a requirement for public companies to provide such a management report publicly. However, a common definition of "internal control" was needed to make such management reporting consistent. A group called The Committee of Sponsoring Organizations of the Treadway Commission (COSO) developed a common definition to provide a standard for reporting. Their report, *Internal Control—Integrated Framework,* was issued in 1992.

SSAE 2 was issued by the American Institute of Certified Public Accountants (AICPA) in 1993. This Statement substantially changed the approach to reporting on control by requiring that management issue its report and the accountant provide an opinion on management's assertion. This parallels the audit process in which management issues the financial statements and the auditor provides an opinion on the statements. The report continued to include caveat paragraphs about the inherent limitation of internal control similar to those required by SAP 49 and SAS 30.

SSAE 6 was issued in 1995 to make the guidance compatible with the COSO definitions and criteria for internal control. Theoretically, management may use any reasonable criteria for effective internal control established by a recognized body. However, COSO is the only recognized body specifically identified in the SSAEs.

SSAE 9 was issued by the AICPA in 1999. This SSAE enabled the practitioner to report directly on a specified subject matter, such as internal control, rather than management's assertion. The practitioner continued to be required to obtain management's assertion in order to perform the engagement. SSAE 9 also eliminated the requirement for a separate presentation of management's assertion in certain cases where the assertion is included in the introductory paragraph of the practitioner's report.

In 2001, the Auditing Standards Board issued SSAE 10, *Attestation Standards: Revision and Recodification*. SSAE 10 superseded SSAEs 1 through 9 and renumbered the AT sections in the AICPA's *Codification*. The revisions to this section include clarifying that:

- The responsible party's refusal to provide a written assertion as part of an examination engagement should cause the practitioner to withdraw from the engagement. (An exception exists if an examination of internal control is required by law or regulation. In this case, the practitioner should disclaim an opinion unless he or she obtains evidential matter that warrants expressing an adverse opinion.)
- The responsible party's refusal to furnish the required representations constitutes a limitation on the scope of the engagement.
- If, in a multiple-party arrangement, the practitioner's client is not the responsible party, the practitioner has no responsibility to communicate reportable conditions to the responsible party. (However, the practitioner is not precluded from making that communication.)

SSAE 15, *An Examination of an Entity's Internal Control over Financial Reporting That Is Integrated with an Audit of Its Financial Statements*, was issued in 2008, and provides a broad array of detailed changes to and superseded SSAE 10.

FUNDAMENTAL REQUIREMENTS

The auditor's objective is to form an opinion on the effectiveness of an entity's internal control. An entity's internal control cannot be considered effective if a material weakness exists, so the auditor should plan an examination designed to obtain sufficient evidence to obtain reasonable assurance about whether material weaknesses exist as of the date of management's assertion regarding internal control. The auditor does not have to search for deficiencies that are less severe than a material weakness.

An engagement conducted in accordance with this section should comply with the general, fieldwork, and reporting standards in AT Section 101.

The Section (1) establishes conditions that should be met for an auditor to examine the effectiveness of an entity's internal control over financial reporting and (2) establishes the engagement performance and reporting requirements for the engagement.

Required Conditions for Engagement Acceptance

The following conditions should be present for the auditor to accept the engagement to examine the effectiveness of an entity's internal control. These are:

1. Management accepts responsibility for the effectiveness of the entity's internal control.
2. Management evaluates the effectiveness of the entity's internal control using suitable criteria.
3. Management supports its assertion about internal control effectiveness with sufficient evidence.
4. Management provides a report containing its assertion about the effectiveness of the entity's internal control.

If management refuses to provide a written assertion, the auditor should withdraw from the engagement. Withdrawal is *not* required if the engagement is required by law or regulation. In that case, the auditor should disclaim an opinion on internal control.

Evidence Supporting Management's Assertion

Management is responsible for documenting controls, which can be in the form of policy and procedure manuals, flowcharts, and decision tables. Management can also undertake ongoing monitoring activities to assess the effectiveness of internal controls, report deficiencies, and take corrective actions. Both documentation and ongoing monitoring activities form the foundation for management's assertion regarding internal control.

Integrating the Controls Examination with the Financial Statement Audit

The examination of internal control should be integrated with the audit, such that the objectives of both engagements can be achieved at the same time. To do so, the auditor should design tests of controls that obtain sufficient evidence to support the auditor's opinion on internal control, as well as the control risk assessment for the audit. The date of management's assertion should match the balance sheet date of the period covered by the financial statements.

Risk Assessment

The auditor should devote the most attention to those areas where a material weakness could exist in an entity's internal control. It is not necessary to test controls that would not present a reasonable possibility of material misstatement, even if those controls are deficient. The auditor must plan procedures based on the size and complexity of the organization, its business processes, and business units.

The auditor's planning should also include the results of the fraud risk assessment performed in the audit. The auditor should also evaluate whether the entity's controls adequately address the risk of misstatement due to fraud, and of management override of other controls. Examples of controls that can address these risks include:

- Controls over significant transactions, especially those resulting in late or unusual journal entries;
- Controls over journal entries made in the period-end closing process;
- Controls over related-party transactions;
- Controls related to significant estimates by management; and
- Controls that change management's willingness to inappropriately manage financial results.

Using the Work of Others

In the examination of internal controls, the auditor may use the work performed by internal auditors and other entity personnel, as well as third parties. The auditor's assessment of this work should include a review of the competence and objectivity of the individuals involved. *Competence* means the attainment and maintenance of a level of understanding, knowledge, and skills enabling a person to perform the tasks assigned to him or her, and *objectivity* means the ability to perform those tasks impartially and with intellectual honesty.

The extent to which the auditor uses the work of others depends on the risk associated with the control being tested. As the risk increases, the auditor should rely more on his or her own work.

PLANNING THE ENGAGEMENT

In planning the engagement, the auditor should consider factors such as the following:

1. Knowledge of the entity's internal control obtained during other professional engagements
2. Matters affecting the industry in which the entity operates, such as financial reporting practices, economic conditions, laws and regulations, and technological changes
3. Matters relating to the entity's business, including its organization, operating characteristics, capital structure, and distribution methods
4. The extent of recent changes, if any, in the entity, its operations, or its internal control
5. Preliminary judgments about materiality levels, inherent risk, and other factors relating to the determination of material weaknesses
6. Deficiencies previously communicated to management
7. Legal or regulatory issues of which the entity is aware
8. The type and extent of evidential matter pertaining to the effectiveness of the entity's internal control
9. Preliminary judgments about the effectiveness of internal control
10. Public information about the entity impacting the evaluation of misstatements and the effectiveness of internal control
11. Knowledge of the risks noted as part of the auditor's acceptance and retention evaluation
12. The level of complexity of the entity's operations

The auditor should use a top-down approach to selecting the controls to be tested. In sequence, this involves:

1. Starting at the financial statement level;
2. Utilizing the auditor's overall understanding of the risks to internal control;
3. Focusing on entity-level controls;
4. Moving down to significant accounts and disclosures, and their related assertions;
5. Focusing on accounts, disclosures, and assertions that present a reasonable possibility of material misstatement of the financial statements and disclosures;
6. Verifying the auditor's understanding of the risks in the entity's processes; and
7. Selecting controls for testing that sufficiently address the assessed risk of material misstatement.

Entity-Level Controls

The auditor should test those entity-level controls that will assist in reaching a conclusion about the entity's level of internal control. These controls include:

- Controls related to the control environment;
- Controls over management override;
- The entity's risk assessment process;
- Centralized processing and controls;
- Controls to monitor the results of operations;
- Controls to monitor other controls;
- Controls over the financial reporting process; and
- Programs and controls that address significant business control and risk management practices.

Control Environment

The auditor should evaluate the entity's control environment, since it has a significant impact on effective internal control. This evaluation should include an assessment of whether management's operating style and ethical values promote effective internal control, and whether those charged with governance understand and exercise oversight responsibility over financial reporting and internal control.

Financial Reporting Process

The auditor should evaluate the financial reporting process. This reporting process includes:

- Procedures to enter transaction totals in the general ledger
- Procedures that apply accounting policies
- Procedures related to journal entry creation
- Procedures for recording adjustments to the financial statements
- Procedures for preparing the financial statements

Evaluating this reporting process should include an assessment of the processes used to create financial statements, the level of management participation, the locations participating in the process, the types of journal entries used, and the extent of oversight of the process.

Significant Accounts and Disclosures

The auditor should identify significant accounts and disclosures, and their relevant assertions, which requires the evaluation of the quantitative and qualitative risk factors related to each financial statement line item and disclosure. Risk factors to consider in this analysis for each account and related disclosure are:

- Size and composition of the account
- Susceptibility to misstatements caused by errors or fraud
- Volume of transaction activity, as well as the complexity and homogeneity of each of these transactions
- Exposure to losses
- Possibility of significant contingent liabilities
- Existence of related-party transactions
- Changes from the prior period

When an entity has multiple locations or business units, the auditor should conduct this analysis based on the consolidated financial statements.

Sources of Misstatement

The auditor should obtain an understanding of the likely sources of potential misstatements by understanding the flow of transactions, identifying the process points where misstatements could arise, and identifying the controls used to address those potential misstatements. The auditor directly performs this analysis or supervises the work of others who do so. A good method for conducting this analysis is a walk-through of a transaction from its beginning until it appears in the financial statements. A walk-through can include such tasks as direct observation of processing steps, inspection of related documents, and recalculation.

Selection of Controls to Be Tested

The auditor should test those controls that are important to the auditor's conclusion about whether the entity's controls sufficiently address the assessed risk of material misstatement. It may not be necessary to test all controls related to a relevant assertion if more than one control addresses the assessed risk.

TESTING CONTROLS

The auditor should evaluate the design effectiveness of controls to determine if the controls, if prescribed as designed, can prevent, or detect and correct, misstatements in the financial statements. A test of operating effectiveness should include a determination of whether the control is operating as designed, and whether the person performing the control has the authority and competence to perform it effectively. This evaluation can include a walkthrough that incorporates a mix of inquiry, operational observation, and documentation inspection.

For each test of control, the evidence needed depends upon the risk associated with the control; this is the risk that the control might not be effective, and if not effective, that the risk of a material weaknesses exists. As a control's risk increases, so too should the level of evidence that the auditor obtains.

The auditor is not responsible for obtaining sufficient evidence to support an effectiveness opinion about each individual control, only about the entity's overall level of internal control.

A number of factors affect the risk associated with each control, including:

- The nature and materiality of the misstatements that a control is intended to prevent, or detect and correct;
- The inherent risk associated with the related accounts and assertions;
- The presence of changes in the volume or nature of transactions adversely affecting control design or operating effectiveness;
- Whether the account has a history of errors;
- The effectiveness of controls that monitor other controls;
- The nature and frequency of the control;
- The degree to which the control relies on the effectiveness of other controls;
- The competence of the personnel who perform the control, and whether there have been changes in these personnel;
- Whether the control is automated, or requires manual monitoring; and
- The complexity of the control.

In the event of a control deviation, the auditor should determine the effect of the deviation on his or her assessment of the risk associated with the control being tested. An individual control does not necessarily have to operate without any deviation to be considered effective.

Importance of Types of Tests of Controls

Some types of tests produce greater evidence of the effectiveness of controls than others. The following tests are presented in order of effectiveness from most to least effective:

1. Reperformance of a control
2. Recalculation
3. Inspection of relevant documentation
4. Observation
5. Inquiry

A test of documentation may be dependent upon whether the control results in documentary evidence of its operation.

Timing and Extent of Tests of Controls

Testing a control over a longer period of time, or testing close to the date of management's assertion provides additional evidence of control effectiveness. In general, the more extensively a control is tested, the greater the evidence obtained from that test.

Prior to the date of management's assertion, management may upgrade the entity's controls. If the auditor determines that the new controls achieve stated control objectives and have been in existence long enough to assess their design and operating effectiveness, then there is no need to test the design and operating effectiveness of the superseded controls. However, if the operating effectiveness of the superseded controls is important to the auditor's control risk assessment in the financial statement audit, then testing of the superseded controls is appropriate.

Interim Testing

Additional evidence needed to update the results of testing from an interim date to the entity's period-end depends on the specific controls tested and the sufficiency of the evidence obtained prior to the as-of date, as well as the length of the remaining period and the possibility of significant internal control changes subsequent to the interim testing.

Considerations for Subsequent Years' Testing

Information available in subsequent years' examinations might allow the auditor to assess risk as being lower than in the initial year of testing, which might lead to reduced testing in subsequent years.

The auditor should vary the nature, timing, and extent of controls testing in subsequent periods to introduce unpredictability into the testing. This may result in testing during different interim periods, changing the number and types of tests performed, or changing the combination of procedures used.

FORMING AN OPINION

The auditor should form an opinion on the effectiveness of internal control. The source of this opinion should be the auditor's own tests and reports issued by internal audit. After forming an opinion, the auditor should examine management's report to ensure that it contains the following items:

- A statement regarding management's responsibility for internal control
- A description of the subject matter of the examination
- An identification of the criteria against which internal control is measured (such as the COSO *Internal Control—Integrated Framework*)
- Management's assertion about the effectiveness of internal control
- A description of any material weaknesses
- The date as of which management makes its internal control assertion

If any of these items are missing or improperly presented, the auditor should request a revision. If this is not forthcoming, the auditor should include an explanatory paragraph in his or her report. If management provides no report, then the auditor should withdraw from the engagement. Sample opinions are noted later in *Illustrations*.

Management Representations and Responsibilities

The auditor should obtain written representations from management regarding the following items:

1. Acknowledgment of management's responsibility for the establishment and maintenance of internal control
2. A statement that management has performed an evaluation of the effectiveness of the entity's internal control, specifying the control criteria used
3. A statement that management did not use the auditor's procedures performed during the integrated audit as part of the basis for management's assertion
4. A statement of management's assertion about the effectiveness of the entity's internal control based on the control criteria as of a specified date
5. A statement that management has disclosed to the auditor all deficiencies in the design or operation of internal control, including separately disclosing all such deficiencies that it believes will be significant deficiencies or material weaknesses in internal control
6. A description of any fraud resulting in a material misstatement to the entity's financial statements and any other fraud that does not result in a material misstatement to the entity's financial statements, but which involves senior management, or other employees who have a significant role in the entity's internal control
7. A statement of whether the significant deficiencies and material weaknesses identified and communicated to management and those charged with governance during previous engagements have been resolved, and identifying any that have not
8. A statement whether there were, subsequent to the date being reported on, any changes in internal control or other factors that might significantly affect internal control, including any corrective actions taken by management with regard to significant deficiencies and material weaknesses

A sample management representation letter is included in Illustration 11. Section 333, *Management Representations*, provides guidance on the date as of which management should sign such a representation letter and which members of management should sign it.

Communication of Deficiencies and Material Weaknesses

If the auditor identifies significant deficiencies or material weaknesses, he or she should communicate them in writing to management and those charged with governance (even if the items were remediated during the audit). This communication should also include any such items that were previously communicated but not remediated. If the auditor concludes that the entity's oversight is ineffective, then the communication of these issues should also be extended to the board of directors. The communication should be made by the report release date. For a governmental entity, the communication should be made as soon as practicable, but no later than 60 days following the report release date.

The auditor should also communicate in writing all nonmaterial and nonsignificant deficiencies to management no later than 60 days following the report release date, and inform those charged with governance when the communication was made. The communication to management does not need to include an itemization of those nonmaterial and nonsignificant deficiencies that were included in previous written communications.

The auditor should *not* issue a report indicating that no nonmaterial or material weaknesses were identified during the integrated audit.

EVALUATING CONTROL DEFICIENCIES

The auditor must evaluate identified control deficiencies and determine whether these deficiencies, individually or in combination, are material weaknesses.

The significance of a control deficiency depends on the magnitude of a potential misstatement and whether there is a reasonable possibility that existing controls will fail to prevent, or detect and correct, a misstatement. Thus, the severity of a deficiency depends on the *potential for a misstatement, not on whether a misstatement actually has occurred.* Accordingly, the absence of identified misstatement does not provide evidence that identified control deficiencies are not significant deficiencies or material weaknesses.

The key factors affecting the magnitude of a misstatement include the financial statement amounts exposed to the deficiency, as well as the volume of activity exposed to the deficiency.

The possibility of a deficiency resulting in a misstatement is impacted by a number of risk factors, which include:

- The nature of the financial statement accounts, transactions, and disclosures involved
- The susceptibility of assets and liabilities to loss or fraud
- The subjectivity or complexity involved in determining the amounts involved
- The interaction of the control with other controls
- The interaction among deficiencies
- The possible future consequences of the deficiency

It is not necessary to quantify the probability of occurrence of a misstatement when evaluating deficiencies.

Multiple deficiencies affecting the same account, disclosure, or assertion increase the likelihood of material misstatement and may constitute a material weakness.

Compensating controls can reduce the effects of a deficiency, but they do not eliminate it. To have a mitigating effect, a compensation control should prevent, or detect and correct, a material misstatement.

Indicator of Material Weaknesses

There are certain key indicators of material weaknesses in internal control. They include

- Fraud by senior management, even if not material;
- Restatement of financial statements due to correct for material misstatements that were caused by error or fraud;

- Identification of material misstatements that would not have been detected and corrected by internal control; and
- Ineffective oversight of financial reporting and internal control.

REPORTING REQUIREMENTS

The auditor's examination report on the effectiveness of an entity's internal control over financial reporting should include the following:

1. A title that includes the word *independent*
2. A statement that management is responsible for maintaining effective internal control and for evaluating the effectiveness of internal control
3. An identification of management's assertion on internal control that accompanies the auditor's report, including a reference to management's report
4. A statement that the auditor's responsibility is to express an opinion on the entity's internal control (or on management's assertion) based on his or her examination
5. A statement that the examination was conducted in accordance with attestation standards established by AICPA
6. A statement that such standards require that the auditor plan and perform the examination to obtain reasonable assurance about whether effective internal control was maintained in all material respects
7. A statement that an examination includes obtaining an understanding of internal control, assessing the risk that a material weakness exists, testing and evaluating the design and operating effectiveness of internal control based on the assessed risk, and performing such other procedures as the auditor considers necessary in the circumstances
8. A statement that the auditor believes the examination provides a reasonable basis for his or her opinion
9. A definition of internal control (the auditor should use the same description of the entity's internal control as management uses in its report)
10. A statement that, because of inherent limitations, internal control may not prevent, or detect and correct, misstatements, and that projections of any evaluation of effectiveness to future periods are subject to the risk that controls may become inadequate because of changes in conditions, or that the degree of compliance with the policies or procedures may deteriorate
11. The auditor's opinion on whether the entity maintained, in all material respects, effective internal control as of the specified date, based on the control criteria; or the auditor's opinion on whether management's assertion about the effectiveness of the entity's internal control as of the specified date is fairly stated, in all material respects, based on the control criteria
12. The manual or printed signature of the auditor's firm
13. The date of the report

The auditor can issue either a combined report or separate reports on an entity's financial statements and internal control. If he or she chooses to issue separate reports, then the following paragraph should be added to the financial statements reports:

> We also examined [*or audited*] in accordance with attestation standards established by the American Institute of Certified Public Accountants, [*company names*]'s internal control over financial reporting as of December 31, 20X7, based on [*identify control criteria*] and our report

dated [*date of report, which should be the same as the date of the report on the financial statements*] expressed [*include nature of the opinion*].

Again, if separate reports are issued, the auditor should add the following paragraph to the report on internal control:

> We also have audited, in accordance with auditing standards generally accepted in the United States of America, the [*identify financial statement*] of [*company name*] and our report date [*date of report, which should be the same as the date of the report on internal control*] expressed [*include nature of opinion*].

When internal control is not effective, the auditor cannot express an opinion on management's assertion, and so should report directly on the effectiveness of internal control. The auditor's report should also include the following information:

- The definition of a material weakness (see the earlier section, "Definitions of Terms")
- A statement that one or more material weaknesses have been identified; the auditor need only refer to the material weaknesses described in management's report, as long as the referenced weaknesses are fairly presented.

If material weaknesses have not been included in management's report, then the auditor's report should state that one or more material weaknesses have been identified but not included in management's report, and also note each weakness and the actual and potential effect on the presentation of the entity's financial statements. In this situation, the auditor should communicate the missing information to those charged with governance, noting that the information was not included in management's report.

The auditor should date the report no earlier than the date when he or she has collected sufficient evidence to support an opinion. The dates of the audit and internal control reports should be the same.

Report modifications. The auditor should issue a modified report if:

- Management's report is either incomplete or improperly presented. If so, the auditor should include an explanatory paragraph in his or her report.
- There is a restriction on the engagement scope. If so, the auditor should either withdraw from the engagement or disclaim an opinion. If the latter, the auditor should state the reasons for the disclaimer; further, if the auditor concludes that a material weakness exists, the report should also include the definition of a material weakness, a description of those weaknesses identified, and their actual and potential impact on the entity's financial statements. The auditor should also communicate in writing that the examination of internal control cannot be completed.
- The auditor includes the report of another audit within his or her own report. If so, the auditor should review Section 543, *Part of Audit Performed by Other Independent Auditors,* for guidance on this decision.
- There is other information in management's report that is subject to the auditor's evaluation. If so, the auditor should disclaim an opinion on the additional information. Possible text for this purpose is "We do not express an opinion or any other form of assurance on [*describe additional information*]." If the additional information includes a material misstatement of fact, the auditor should communicate his or her views about the misstatement, in writing, to management and those charged with governance.

Examples of several of these reports are included in "Illustrations."

OTHER TOPICS

Subsequent Events

To determine the existence of changes to internal control in subsequent periods, the auditor should review subsequent control reports by internal audit, independent auditors, regulatory agencies, and information from other sources.

If the auditor becomes aware, before the audit report date, of a material weakness that existed as of the management assertion date, the auditor should issue an adverse opinion. If the auditor cannot determine the impact of the item on the entity's internal control as of the assertion date, the auditor should disclaim an opinion. If the material weakness arose between the assertion date and audit report date, then the auditor should include in his or her report a paragraph describing the event and its effects.

Multiple Location Entities

When the auditor is determining the entity locations where it should perform control tests, it is necessary to assess the risk of material misstatement associated with the entity location. It is reasonable to eliminate from testing those locations not presenting a reasonable possibility of material misstatement.

The scope of the controls examination should include any entities acquired on or prior to the date of management's assertion, as well as operations accounted for as discontinued operations.

If the entity has equity method investments, the examination scope does not include the investee's controls, but does include controls over the reporting of the entity's financial statements, its portion of the investee's income or loss, the investment balance, adjustments to the income or loss and investment balance, and related disclosures.

Use of Outsourced Services

If an entity outsources some or all of its information and communication systems, then the auditor should evaluate the controls of the service organization as part of the controls of the entity. This requires obtaining an understanding of the service organization's controls that are relevant to the entity's internal control, and of the entity's controls over the service organization.

The auditor must obtain evidence that these controls are operating effectively. This can be done with one or more of the following procedures:

- Obtain a service auditor's report on controls placed in operation and tests of operating effectiveness, or a report on the application of procedures that describes tests of controls. In the former case, the auditor should assess the time period covered, the scope of the examination and applications addressed, the manner in which tested controls relate to the entity's controls, the service auditor's opinion on the effectiveness of the controls, and the service auditor's reputation, competence, and independence. In the latter case, the auditor should evaluate whether the report provides sufficient appropriate evidence.
- Test the entity's controls over the activities of the service organization.
- Test the service organization's controls.

If there is a significant period of time between the service auditor's test of controls and the management assertion date, the auditor should conduct additional procedures. This should include an inquiry of management to see if management has identified any changes in the service organization's controls during the intervening period, as well as the auditor's own investigations. If so, the auditor should evaluate the effect of the changes on the effectiveness of the entity's internal control.

The auditor may elect to obtain additional evidence about the service organization's controls if there has been a significant amount of time between the dates of the service auditor's report and management's assertion, or if the activities of the service organization are significant to the entity. Other factors for the auditor to consider are the presence of errors in the service organization's transaction processing, and the significance of any changes made to the service organization's controls.

If the auditor decides to obtain additional evidence about the service organization's controls, possible options include:

- Evaluating the results of any procedures already performed by management
- Contacting the service organization directly for information, possibly including the performance of on-site procedures
- Requesting that a service auditor be engaged to supply the needed information

The auditor should not refer to the service auditor's report in his or her opinion on internal control.

Automated Controls

Automated controls are less likely to break down than those performed manually. Also, given no programming changes or access to those programs, the auditor can avoid duplicating tests of automated controls that were performed in the prior year (though this requires testing of program change controls).

Effect of Substantive Procedures on Controls Conclusion

The auditor should incorporate the results of substantive procedures performed in the audit of financial statements on the evaluation of internal control. This evaluation should include:

- Risk assessments related to fraud
- Findings regarding illegal acts and related-party transactions
- Indications of management bias related to accounting estimates and the selection of accounting principles
- Misstatements

However, the auditor cannot infer the effectiveness of a control from the above factors; that requires the direct testing of controls.

INTERPRETATIONS

REPORTING UNDER SECTION 112 OF THE FEDERAL DEPOSIT INSURANCE CORPORATION IMPROVEMENT ACT (ISSUED SEPTEMBER 2010)

To comply with the integrated audit requirement in AT Section 501, when an insured depository institution (IDI) uses the consolidated holding company's financial statements to satisfy the audited financial statements requirement, the auditor would be required to perform procedures necessary to obtain sufficient appropriate audit evidence to express an opinion on the financial statements and their internal control over financial reporting. When these financial statements are not prepared for external distribution, financial statements may consist of the financial information of the IDI in a reporting package or equivalent schedules and analyses that include the information needed for the preparation of the holding company's consolidated financial statements, including disclosures. Materiality is based on the financial information of the IDI, rather than the financial statements of the holding company. If the auditor cannot obtain sufficient audit evidence with respect to the financial information of the IDI, he or she is required to withdraw from the engagement or disclaim an opinion on the effectiveness of the IDI's internal control over financial reporting.

When an IDI does not prepare financial statements for external distribution, the auditor is still required to evaluate its period-end financial reporting process, which includes the IDI's procedures for preparing financial information for purposes of the consolidated holding company's financial statements.

The illustrative reports of Section 501 may be used to report on the effectiveness of the IDI's internal control over financial reporting. The requirement to add a paragraph to the internal control report that references the financial statement audit does not apply when the auditor does not issue a separate auditor's report on the IDI's financial statements.

ILLUSTRATIONS

The following are illustrations of opinions on internal control, communications of significant deficiencies and material weaknesses, and a management report. They are adapted from the SSAE 15 appendices (AT Section 501, Appendices A, B, and D).

ILLUSTRATION 1. UNQUALIFIED OPINION ON INTERNAL CONTROL

Independent Auditor's Report

We have examined XYZ Company's internal control over financial reporting as of December 31, 20XX, based on [*identify criteria*]. XYZ Company's management is responsible for maintaining effective internal control over financial reporting, and for its assertion of the effectiveness of internal control over financial reporting, included in the accompanying [*title of management's report*]. Our responsibility is to express an opinion on XYZ Company's internal control over financial reporting based on our examination.

We conducted our examination in accordance with attestation standards established by the American Institute of Certified Public Accountants. Those standards require that we plan and perform the examination to obtain reasonable assurance about whether effective internal control over financial reporting was maintained in all material respects. Our examination included obtaining an understanding of internal control over financial reporting, assessing the risk that a material weakness exists, and testing and evaluating the design and operating effectiveness of internal control based on the assessed risk. Our examination also included performing such other procedures as we considered necessary in the circumstances. We believe that our examination provides a reasonable basis for our opinion.

An entity's internal control over financial reporting is a process effected by those charged with governance, management, and other personnel, designed to provide reasonable assurance regarding the preparation of reliable financial statements in accordance with [*applicable financial reporting framework, such as accounting principles generally accepted in the United States of America*]. An entity's internal control over financial reporting includes those policies and procedures that (1) pertain to the maintenance of records that, in reasonable detail, accurately and fairly reflect the transactions and dispositions of the assets of the entity; (2) provide reasonable assurance that transactions are recorded as necessary to permit preparation of financial statements in accordance with [*applicable financial reporting framework, such as accounting principles generally accepted in the United States of America*], and that receipts and expenditures of the entity are being made only in accordance with authorizations of management and those charged with governance; and (3) provide reasonable assurance regarding prevention or timely detection of and correction of unauthorized acquisition, use, or disposition of the entity's assets that could have a material effect on the financial statements.

Because of its inherent limitations, internal control over financial reporting may not prevent, or detect and correct ,misstatements. Also, projections of any evaluation of effectiveness to future periods are subject to the risk that controls may become inadequate because of changes in conditions, or that the degree of compliance with the policies or procedures may deteriorate.

In our opinion, XYZ Company maintained, in all material respects, effective internal control over financial reporting as of December 31, 20XX, based on [identify criteria].

We also have audited, in accordance with auditing standards generally accepted in the United States of America, the [identify financial statements] of XYZ Company and our report dated [date of report, which should be the same as the date of the report on the examination of internal control] expressed [include nature of opinion].

[Signature]

[Date]

ILLUSTRATION 2. UNQUALIFIED OPINION ON MANAGEMENT'S ASSERTION

Independent Auditor's Report

We have examined management's assertion, included in the accompanying [title of management report], that XYZ Company maintained effective internal control over financial reporting as of December 31, 20XX, based on [identify criteria]. XYZ Company's management is responsible for maintaining effective internal control over financial reporting, and for its assertion of the effectiveness of internal control over financial reporting, included in the accompanying [title of management's report]. Our responsibility is to express an opinion on management's assertion based on our examination.

We conducted our examination in accordance with attestation standards established by the American Institute of Certified Public Accountants. Those standards require that we plan and perform the examination to obtain reasonable assurance about whether effective internal control over financial reporting was maintained in all material respects. Our examination included obtaining an understanding of internal control over financial reporting, assessing the risk that a material weakness exists, and testing and evaluating the design and operating effectiveness of internal control based on the assessed risk. Our examination also included performing such other procedures as we considered necessary in the circumstances. We believe that our examination provides a reasonable basis for our opinion.

An entity's internal control over financial reporting is a process effected by those charged with governance, management, and other personnel, designed to provide reasonable assurance regarding the preparation of reliable financial statements in accordance with [applicable financial reporting framework, such as accounting principles generally accepted in the United States of America]. An entity's internal control over financial reporting includes those policies and procedures that (1) pertain to the maintenance of records that, in reasonable detail, accurately and fairly reflect the transactions and dispositions of the assets of the entity; (2) provide reasonable assurance that transactions are recorded as necessary to permit preparation of financial statements in accordance with [applicable financial reporting framework, such as accounting principles generally accepted in the United States of America], and that receipts and expenditures of the entity are being made only in accordance with authorizations of management and those charged with governance; and (3) provide reasonable assurance regarding prevention or timely detection and correction of unauthorized acquisition, use, or disposition of the entity's assets that could have a material effect on the financial statements.

Because of its inherent limitations, internal control over financial reporting may not prevent, or detect and correct misstatements. Also, projections of any evaluation of effectiveness to future periods are subject to the risk that controls may become inadequate because of changes in conditions, or that the degree of compliance with the policies or procedures may deteriorate.

In our opinion, management's assertion that XYZ Company maintained effective internal control over financial reporting as of December 31, 20XX, is fairly stated, in all material respects, based on [*identify criteria*].

We also have audited, in accordance with auditing standards generally accepted in the United States of America, the [*identify financial statements*] of XYZ Company and our report dated [*date of report, which should be the same as the date of the report on the examination of internal control*] expressed [*include nature of opinion*].

[*Signature*]

[*Date*]

ILLUSTRATION 3. ADVERSE OPINION ON INTERNAL CONTROL

Independent Auditor's Report

We have examined XYZ Company's internal control over financial reporting as of December 31, 20XX, based on [*identify criteria*]. XYZ Company's management is responsible for maintaining effective internal control over financial reporting, and for its assertion of the effectiveness of internal control over financial reporting, included in the accompanying [*title of management's report*]. Our responsibility is to express an opinion on XYZ Company's internal control over financial reporting based on our examination.

We conducted our examination in accordance with attestation standards established by the American Institute of Certified Public Accountants. Those standards require that we plan and perform the examination to obtain reasonable assurance about whether effective internal control over financial reporting was maintained in all material respects. Our examination included obtaining an understanding of internal control over financial reporting, assessing the risk that a material weakness exists, and testing and evaluating the design and operating effectiveness of internal control based on the assessed risk. Our examination also included performing such other procedures as we considered necessary in the circumstances. We believe that our examination provides a reasonable basis for our opinion.

An entity's internal control over financial reporting is a process effected by those charged with governance, management, and other personnel, and designed to provide reasonable assurance regarding the preparation of reliable financial statements in accordance with [*applicable financial reporting framework, such as accounting principles generally accepted in the United States of America*]. An entity's internal control over financial reporting includes those policies and procedures that (1) pertain to the maintenance of records that, in reasonable detail, accurately and fairly reflect the transactions and dispositions of the assets of the entity; (2) provide reasonable assurance that transactions are recorded as necessary to permit preparation of financial statements in accordance with [*applicable financial reporting framework, such as accounting principles generally accepted in the United States of America*], and that receipts and expenditures of the entity are being made only in accordance with authorizations of management and those charged with governance; and (3) provide reasonable assurance regarding prevention, or timely detection and correction of unauthorized acquisition, use, or disposition of the entity's assets that could have a material effect on the financial statements.

Because of its inherent limitations, internal control over financial reporting may not prevent, or detect and correct, misstatements. Also, projections of any evaluation of effectiveness to future periods are subject to the risk that controls may become inadequate because of changes in conditions, or that the degree of compliance with the policies or procedures may deteriorate.

A material weakness is a deficiency, or a combination of deficiencies, in internal control over financial reporting, such that there is a reasonable possibility that a material misstatement of the entity's financial statements will not be prevented, or detected and corrected on a timely basis. The following material weakness has been identified and included in the accompanying [*title of management's report*].

[*Identify the material weakness described in management's report*]

In our opinion, because of the effect of the material weakness described above on the achievement of the objectives of the control criteria, XYZ Company has not maintained effective internal control over financial reporting as of December 31, 20XX, based on [*identify criteria*].

We also have audited, in accordance with auditing standards generally accepted in the United States of America, the [*identify financial statements*] of XYZ Company. We considered the material weakness identified above in determining the nature, timing, and extent of audit tests applied in our audit of the 20XX financial statements, and this report does not affect our report dated [*date of report, which should be the same as the date of the report on the examination of internal control*], which expressed [*include nature of opinion*].

[*Signature*]

[*Date*]

ILLUSTRATION 4. DISCLAIMER OF OPINION ON INTERNAL CONTROL

Independent Auditor's Report

We were engaged to examine XYZ Company's internal control over financial reporting as of December 31, 20XX, based on [*identify criteria*]. XYZ Company's management is responsible for maintaining effective internal control over financial reporting, and for its assertion of the effectiveness of internal control over financial reporting, included in the accompanying [*title of management's report*].

[*Paragraph that describes the substantive reasons for the scope limitation*] Accordingly, we were unable to perform auditing procedures necessary to form an opinion on XYZ Company's internal control over financial reporting as of December 31, 20XX.

An entity's internal control over financial reporting is a process effected by those charged with governance, management, and other personnel, designed to provide reasonable assurance regarding the preparation of reliable financial statements in accordance with [*applicable financial reporting framework, such as accounting principles generally accepted in the United States of America*]. An entity's internal control over financial reporting includes those policies and procedures that (1) pertain to the maintenance of records that, in reasonable detail, accurately, and fairly reflect the transactions and dispositions of the assets of the entity; (2) provide reasonable assurance that transactions are recorded as necessary to permit preparation of financial statements in accordance with [*applicable financial reporting framework, such as accounting principles generally accepted in the United States of America*], and that receipts and expenditures of the entity are being made only in accordance with authorizations of management and those charged with governance; and (3) provide reasonable assurance regarding prevention, or timely detection and correction of unauthorized acquisition, use, or disposition of the entity's assets that could have a material effect on the financial statements.

Because of its inherent limitations, internal control over financial reporting may not prevent, or detect and correct, misstatements. Also, projections of any evaluation of effectiveness to future periods are subject to the risk that controls may become inadequate because of changes in conditions, or that the degree of compliance with the policies or procedures may deteriorate.

A material weakness is a deficiency, or a combination of deficiencies, in internal control over financial reporting, such that there is a reasonable possibility that a material misstatement of the entity's financial statements will not be prevented, or detected and corrected, on a timely basis. If one or more material weaknesses exist, an entity's internal control over financial reporting cannot be considered effective. The following material weakness has been identified and included in the accompanying [*title of management's report*].

[*Identify the material weakness described in management's report and include a description of the material weakness, including its nature and its actual and potential effect on the presentation of the entity's financial statements issued during the existence of the material weakness.*]

Because of the limitation on the scope of our audit described in the second paragraph, the scope of our work was not sufficient to enable us to express, and we do not express, an opinion on the effectiveness of XYZ Company's internal control over financial reporting.

We have audited, in accordance with auditing standards generally accepted in the United States of America, the [*identify financial statements*] of XYZ Company and our report dated [*date of report*] expressed [*include nature of opinion*]. We considered the material weakness identified above in determining the nature, timing, and extent of audit tests applied in our audit of the 20XX financial statements, and this report does not affect such report on the financial statements.

[*Signature*]

[*Date*]

> **ILLUSTRATION 5. UNQUALIFIED OPINION ON INTERNAL CONTROL BASED, IN PART, ON THE REPORT OF ANOTHER AUDITOR**

Independent Auditor's Report

We have examined XYZ Company's internal control over financial reporting as of December 31, 20XX, based on [*identify criteria*]. XYZ Company's management is responsible for maintaining effective internal control over financial reporting, and for its assertion of the effectiveness of internal control over financial reporting, included in the accompanying [*title of management's report*]. Our responsibility is to express an opinion on XYZ Company's internal control over financial reporting based on our examination. We did not examine the effectiveness of internal control over financial reporting of ABC Company, a wholly owned subsidiary, whose financial statements reflect total assets and revenues constituting 20% and 30%, respectively, of the related consolidated financial statement amounts as of and for the year ended December 31, 20XX. The effectiveness of ABC Company's internal control over financial reporting was examined by other auditors whose report has been furnished to us, and our opinion, insofar as it relates to the effectiveness of ABC Company's internal control over financial reporting, is based solely on the report of the other auditors.

We conducted our examination in accordance with attestation standards established by the American Institute of Certified Public Accountants. Those standards require that we plan and perform the examination to obtain reasonable assurance about whether effective internal control over financial reporting was maintained in all material respects. Our examination included obtaining an understanding of internal control over financial reporting, assessing the risk that a material weakness exists, and testing and evaluating the design and operating effectiveness of internal control based on the assessed risk. Our examination also included performing such other procedures as we considered necessary in the circumstances. We believe that our examination and the report of the other auditors provide a reasonable basis for our opinion.

An entity's internal control over financial reporting is a process effected by those charged with governance, management, and other personnel, designed to provide reasonable assurance regarding the preparation of reliable financial statements in accordance with [*applicable financial reporting framework, such as accounting principles generally accepted in the United States of America*]. An entity's internal control over financial reporting includes those policies and procedures that (1) pertain to the maintenance of records that, in reasonable detail, accurately and fairly reflect the transactions and dispositions of the assets of the entity; (2) provide reasonable assurance that transactions are recorded as necessary to permit preparation of financial statements in accordance with [*applicable financial reporting framework, such as accounting principles generally accepted in the United States of America*], and that receipts and expenditures of the entity are being made only in accordance with authorizations of management and those charged with governance; and (3) provide reasonable assurance regarding prevention, or timely detection and correction of unauthorized acquisition, use, or disposition of the entity's assets that could have a material effect on the financial statements.

Because of its inherent limitations, internal control over financial reporting may not prevent, or detect and correct misstatements. Also, projections of any evaluation of effectiveness to future periods are subject to the risk that controls may become inadequate because of changes in conditions, or that the degree of compliance with the policies or procedures may deteriorate.

In our opinion, based on our examination and the report of the other auditors, XYZ Company maintained, in all material respects, effective internal control over financial reporting as of December 31, 20XX, based on [*identify criteria*].

We also have audited, in accordance with auditing standards generally accepted in the United States of America, the [*identify financial statements*] of XYZ Company and our report dated [*date of report, which should be the same as the date of the report on the examination of internal control*] expressed [*include nature of opinion*].

[*Signature*]

[*Date*]

ILLUSTRATION 6. COMBINED REPORT EXPRESSING AN UNQUALIFIED OPINION ON INTERNAL CONTROL AND ON THE FINANCIAL STATEMENTS

Independent Auditor's Report

We have audited the accompanying balance sheet of XYZ Company as of December 31, 20XX, and the related statements of income, retained earnings, and cash flows for the year then ended. We also have audited XYZ Company's internal control over financial reporting as of December 31, 20XX, based on [*identify criteria*]. XYZ Company's management is responsible for these financial statements, for maintaining effective internal control over financial reporting, and for its assertion of the effectiveness of internal control over financial reporting, included in the accompanying [*title of management's report*]. Our responsibility is to express an opinion on these financial statements and an opinion on XYZ Company's internal control over financial reporting based on our audits.

We conducted our audit of the financial statements in accordance with auditing standards generally accepted in the United States of America and our audit of internal control over financial reporting in accordance with attestation standards established by the American Institute of Certified Public Accountants. Those standards require that we plan and perform the audits to obtain reasonable assurance about whether the financial statements are free of material misstatement and whether effective internal control over financial reporting was maintained in all material respects. Our audit of the financial statements included examining, on a test basis, evidence supporting the amounts and disclosures in the financial statements, assessing the accounting principles used and significant estimates made by management, as well as evaluating the overall financial statement presentation. Our audit of internal control over financial reporting included obtaining an understanding of internal control over financial reporting, assessing the risk that a material weakness exists, and testing and evaluating the design and operating effectiveness of internal control based on the assessed risk. Our audits also included performing such other procedures as we considered necessary in the circumstances. We believe that our audits provide a reasonable basis for our opinions.

An entity's internal control over financial reporting is a process effected by those charged with governance, management, and other personnel, designed to provide reasonable assurance regarding the preparation of reliable financial statements in accordance with [*applicable financial reporting framework, such as accounting principles generally accepted in the United States of America*]. An entity's internal control over financial reporting includes those policies and procedures that (1) pertain to the maintenance of records that, in reasonable detail, accurately and fairly reflect the transactions and dispositions of the assets of the entity; (2) provide reasonable assurance that transactions are recorded as necessary to permit preparation of financial statements in accordance with [*applicable financial reporting framework, such as accounting principles generally accepted in the United States of America*], and that receipts and expenditures of the entity are being made only in accordance with authorizations of management and those charged with governance; and (3) provide reasonable assurance regarding prevention, or timely detection and correction, of unauthorized acquisition, use, or disposition of the entity's assets that could have a material effect on the financial statements.

Because of its inherent limitations, internal control over financial reporting may not prevent, or detect and correct, misstatements. Also, projections of any evaluation of effectiveness to future periods are subject to the risk that controls may become inadequate because of changes in conditions, or that the degree of compliance with the policies or procedures may deteriorate.

In our opinion, the financial statements referred to above present fairly, in all material respects, the financial position of XYZ Company as of December 31, 20XX, and the results of its operations and its cash flows for the year then ended in conformity with accounting principles generally accepted in the United States of America. Also in our opinion, XYZ Company maintained, in all material respects, effective internal control over financial reporting as of December 31, 20XX, based on [*identify criteria*].

[*Signature*]

[*Date*]

ILLUSTRATION 7. COMMUNICATION OF SIGNIFICANT DEFICIENCIES AND MATERIAL WEAKNESSES

In connection with our audit of XYZ Company's (the "Company") financial statements as of December 31, 20XX, and for the year then ended, and our audit of the Company's internal control over financial reporting as of December 31, 20XX ("integrated audit"), the standards established by the American Institute of Certified Public Accountants require that we advise you of the following internal control matters identified during our integrated audit.

Our responsibility is to plan and perform our integrated audit to obtain reasonable assurance about whether the financial statements are free of material misstatement, whether caused by error or fraud, and whether effective internal control over financial reporting was maintained in all material respects (that is, whether material weaknesses exist as of the date specified in management's assertion). The integrated audit is not designed to detect deficiencies that, individually or in combination, are less severe than a material weakness. However, we are responsible for communicating to management and those charged with governance significant deficiencies and material weaknesses identified during the integrated audit. We are also responsible for communicating to management deficiencies that are of a lesser magnitude than a significant deficiency, unless previously communicated, and inform those charged with governance when such a communication was made.

A deficiency in internal control over financial reporting exists when the design or operation of a control does not allow management or employees, in the normal course of performing their assigned functions, to prevent, or detect and correct misstatements on a timely basis. [*A material weakness is a deficiency, or a combination of deficiencies, in internal control over financial reporting, such that there is a reasonable possibility that a material misstatement of the Company's financial statements will not be prevented, or detected and corrected on a timely basis. We believe the following deficiencies constitute material weaknesses:*]

[*Describe the material weaknesses that were identified during the integrated audit. The auditor may separately identify those material weaknesses that exist as of the date of management's assertion by referring to the auditor's report.*]

[*A significant deficiency is a deficiency, or a combination of deficiencies, in internal control over financial reporting that is less severe than a material weakness, yet important enough to merit attention by those charged with governance. We consider the following deficiencies to be significant deficiencies:*]

[*Describe the significant deficiencies that were identified during the integrated audit.*]

This communication is intended solely for the information and use of management, [*identify the body or individuals charged with governance*], others within the organization, and [*identify any specified governmental authorities*] and is not intended to be and should not be used by anyone other than these specified parties.

ILLUSTRATION 8. MANAGEMENT REPORT

Management's Report on Internal Control Over Financial Reporting

XYZ Company's internal control over financial reporting is a process effected by those charged with governance, management, and other personnel, and designed to provide reasonable assurance regarding the preparation of reliable financial statements in accordance with [*applicable financial reporting framework, such as accounting principles generally accepted in the United States of America*]. An entity's internal control over financial reporting includes those policies and procedures that (1) pertain to the maintenance of records that, in reasonable detail, accurately and fairly reflect the transactions and dispositions of the assets of the entity; (2) provide reasonable assurance that transactions are recorded as necessary to permit preparation of financial statements in accordance with [*applicable financial reporting framework, such as accounting principles generally accepted in the United States of America*], and that receipts and expenditures of the entity are being made only in accordance with authorizations of management and those charged with governance; and (3) provide reasonable assurance regarding prevention, or timely detection and correction of unauthorized acquisition, use, or disposition of the entity's assets that could have a material effect on the financial statements.

Management is responsible for establishing and maintaining effective internal control over financial reporting. Management assessed the effectiveness of XYZ Company's internal control over financial reporting as of December 31, 20XX, based on the framework set forth by the Committee of Sponsoring Organizations of the Treadway Commission in *Internal Control—Integrated Framework*. Based on that assessment, management concluded that, as of December 31, 20XX, XYZ Company's internal control over financial reporting is effective based on the criteria established in *Internal Control—Integrated Framework*.

XYZ Company

[*Report signers, if applicable*]

[*Date*]

AT 601 Compliance Attestation

EFFECTIVE DATE AND APPLICABILITY

Original Pronouncements Statements on Standards for Attestation Engagements (SSAE) 10, *Attestation Standards: Revision and Recodification*.

Effective Date This statement currently is effective.

Applicability Applicable to agreed-upon procedures related to either of the following:

1. Compliance with requirements of specified laws, regulations, rules, contracts, or grants (specified requirements)
2. The effectiveness of internal control over compliance with specified requirements
3. Or both items 1 and 2

Also applicable to engagements to examine the entity's compliance with specified requirements or a written assertion thereon.

The Statement does not apply to the following:

1. Situations in which an auditor reports on specified compliance requirements based solely on an audit of financial statements (see AU Section 623, *Special Reports*).
2. Engagements for which the objective is to report in accordance with *Government Auditing Standards*, or the Single Audit Act, or Office of Management and Budget (OMB) circulars and releases (see AU Section 801, *Compliance Auditing Considerations in Audits of Governmental Entities and Recipients of Governmental Financial Assistance*).
3. Program-specific audits as addressed in Section 801 performed in accordance with federal audit guides issued prior to the effective date of this SSAE
4. Engagements covered by AU Section 634, *Letters for Underwriters and Certain Other Requesting Parties* (comfort letters)
5. The report that encompasses the internal control over compliance for a broker or dealer in securities as required by Rule 17a-5 of the Securities Exchange Act of 1934
6. Audits performed in accordance with generally accepted auditing standards (GAAS)

NOTE: An accountant is discouraged from accepting an engagement to examine the effectiveness of internal control over compliance or an assertion thereon because reasonable criteria for evaluation are typically not available. If such an engagement is accepted, the appropriate guidance is in AT 101 in American Institute of Certified Public Accountants (AICPA) publications (AT Section 101 herein). Additionally, AT 601 (AT Section 601 herein) may be helpful, but it is intended for reporting on internal control over financial reporting, not over compliance.

DEFINITIONS OF TERMS

Attestation risk.[1] The risk that the practitioner may unknowingly fail to modify appropriately his or her opinion. It is composed of inherent risk, control risk, and detection risk.

Control risk.[1] The risk that material noncompliance that could occur will not be prevented or detected on a timely basis by the entity's internal control.

Detection risk.[1] The risk that the practitioner's procedures will lead him or her to conclude that material noncompliance does not exist when, in fact, such noncompliance does exist.

Inherent risk.[1] The risk that material noncompliance with specified requirements could occur, assuming there are no related controls.

Internal control over compliance. The process by which management obtains reasonable assurance of compliance with specified requirements.

Specified requirements. A term that is used to refer to an entity's compliance with requirements of specified laws, regulations, rules, contracts, or grants.

OBJECTIVES OF AT SECTION 601

This SSAE provides guidance for engagements related to either (1) compliance with requirements of specified laws, regulations, rules, contracts, or grants (specified requirements) or (2) the effectiveness of internal control over compliance with specified requirements.

A practitioner may be engaged to perform agreed-upon procedures to assist users in evaluating management's written assertion about an entity's compliance with specified requirements, the effectiveness of internal control over compliance, or both. A practitioner also may be engaged to examine compliance with specified requirements or a written assertion thereon. For example, some electronic funds transfer associations or networks require their members who process transactions to complete a compliance exam.

In 2001, the Auditing Standards Board issued SSAE 10, *Attestation Standards: Revision and Recodification.* SSAE 10 superseded SSAEs 1 through 9 and renumbered the AT sections in the AICPA's *Codification.* The revisions to this section include clarifying that:

- The responsible party's refusal to furnish the required representations constitutes a limitation on the scope of the engagement.
- The responsible party's refusal to provide a written assertion as part of an examination engagement should cause the practitioner to withdraw from the engagement. (An exception exists if an examination of an entity's compliance with specified requirements is required by law or regulation. In this case, the practitioner should disclaim an opinion on compliance unless he or she obtains evidential matter that warrants expressing an adverse opinion.)
- If the engagement is to perform agreed-upon procedures and:
  - The client is the responsible party, that party's refusal to provide an assertion requires that the practitioner withdraw from the engagement.
  - The client is not the responsible party, the practitioner is not required to withdraw, but should consider the effects of the refusal on the engagement and report.

---

[1] *Terms that are related to risk in an examination engagement.*

FUNDAMENTAL REQUIREMENTS: GENERAL (APPLICABLE TO BOTH AGREED-UPON PROCEDURES AND EXAMINATION ENGAGEMENTS)

GENERAL

An engagement conducted in accordance with this section should comply with the general, fieldwork, and reporting standards in AT Section 101.

CRITERIA

The practitioner cannot accept an agreed-upon procedures or an examination engagement unless reasonable criteria have been established by a recognized body or are stated in or attached to the practitioner's report.

PROHIBITED ENGAGEMENTS

A practitioner should not accept an engagement to perform a review (see AT Section 101) about compliance with specified requirements or about the effectiveness of internal control over compliance or assertions thereon.

USING THE WORK OF A SPECIALIST

The practitioner should follow the guidance of AU Section 336, *Using the Work of a Specialist*, if he or she decides that a specialist is necessary for an engagement covered by this section.

MANAGEMENT'S REPRESENTATIONS

According to AT 601.68, for both an agreed-upon procedures engagement and an examination engagement, the practitioner should obtain the responsible party's written representations that:

1. Acknowledge the responsible party's responsibility for complying with the specified requirements
2. Acknowledge the responsible party's responsibility for establishing and maintaining effective internal control over compliance
3. State that the responsible party has performed an evaluation of (1) the entity's compliance with specified requirements, or (2) the entity's internal controls for ensuring compliance and detecting noncompliance with requirements, as applicable
4. State the responsible party's assertion about the entity's compliance with the specified requirements or about the effectiveness of the internal control over compliance, as applicable, based on the stated or established criteria
5. State that the responsible party has disclosed to the practitioner all known noncompliance
6. State that the responsible party has made available all documentation related to compliance with specified requirements
7. State the responsible party's interpretation of any compliance requirements that have varying interpretations
8. State that the responsible party has disclosed any communications from regulatory agencies, internal auditors, and other practitioners concerning possible noncompliance with the specified requirements, including communications received between the end of the period addressed in the written assertion and the date of the practitioner's report

9. State that the responsible party has disclosed any known noncompliance occurring subsequent to the period for which, or date as of which, the responsible party selects to make its assertion

AU Section 333, *Management Representations*, provides guidance on the dating and signatories of the representation letter.

The responsible party's refusal to furnish the required representations is a scope limitation. In an examination engagement, the practitioner ordinarily should disclaim an opinion or withdraw. However, based on the nature of the representations or circumstances, a qualified opinion may be appropriate.

In an agreed-upon procedures engagement in which the practitioner's client is the responsible party, the responsible party's refusal to provide written assertions is a scope limitation sufficient to cause the practitioner to withdraw. When the practitioner's client is not the responsible party, the practitioner:

- Is not required to withdraw, but should consider the effects of the responsible party's refusal on his or her report, as well as the ability to rely on other representations of the responsible party
- May also want to obtain written representations from the client (e.g., knowledge of any noncompliance)

OTHER INFORMATION IN A CLIENT-PREPARED DOCUMENT

The practitioner's report on either compliance with specified requirements or the effectiveness of internal control over compliance or written assertions thereon may be included in a client-prepared document that includes other information. In those circumstances, the practitioner should read the other information and follow the procedures discussed in Section 101.

FUNDAMENTAL REQUIREMENTS: AGREED-UPON PROCEDURES ENGAGEMENT

CONDITIONS FOR ACCEPTANCE

A practitioner may accept an agreed-upon procedures engagement related to an entity's compliance with specified requirements or the effectiveness of internal control over compliance, if the responsible party:

1. Accepts responsibility for the entity's compliance with specified requirements and the effectiveness of the entity's internal control over compliance
2. Evaluates the entity's compliance with specified requirements or the effectiveness of the entity's internal control over compliance

In addition, the conditions that apply to acceptance of all agreed-upon procedures engagements have to be met (see AT Section 201).

NOTE: A written management representation letter is required in agreed-upon procedure engagements relating to compliance matters.

The practitioner should obtain a written assertion about compliance with specified requirements or internal control over compliance from the responsible party. The written assertion may be provided in the representation letter or in a separate report accompanying the practitioner's report. If the client is the responsible party, that party's refusal to provide an assertion requires that the practitioner withdraw from the engagement. If the engagement is required by law or regulation withdrawal is *not* required. If the client is not the responsible party, the practitioner does not have to withdraw but should consider the effects of the refusal on the engagement and report.

UNDERSTANDING WITH SPECIFIED PARTIES

The specified parties should participate in establishing the procedures to be performed and take responsibility for the adequacy of those procedures. The practitioner should determine whether the specified parties understand the procedures to be performed by discussing the nature of management's assertion and the procedures with the specified parties (see "Techniques for Application").

UNDERSTANDING THE SPECIFIED COMPLIANCE REQUIREMENTS

The practitioner should obtain an understanding of the specified compliance requirements stated in management's assertion. To obtain this understanding, the practitioner should consider the following:

1. Laws, regulations, rules, contracts, and grants relevant to the specified compliance requirements.
2. Knowledge about the specified compliance requirements obtained from the following:
    a. Prior engagements and regulatory reports
    b. Discussions with appropriate individuals within the entity
    c. Discussions with appropriate individuals outside the entity, such as regulators or specialists

SCOPE RESTRICTIONS

The practitioner should attempt to obtain agreement from the specified parties for modification of the agreed-upon procedures if circumstances impose restrictions on the scope of those procedures. If an agreement for modification cannot be obtained, the practitioner should describe the restrictions in the attestation report or withdraw from the engagement.

SUBSEQUENT EVENTS

If the practitioner becomes aware of noncompliance related to management's assertion that occurs after the period addressed by that assertion but before the date of the report, he or she should consider including that information in the report. According to AT 601.24, the practitioner has no obligation to perform procedures to detect noncompliance in the subsequent period.

PRACTITIONER'S REPORT

The practitioner's report on agreed-upon procedures on an entity's compliance with specified requirements or about the effectiveness of an entity's internal control over compliance should be in the form of procedures and findings. The report should be dated as of the date of completion of the agreed-upon procedures. According to AT 601.24, the practitioner's report should contain the following elements:

1. A title that includes the word *independent*
2. Identification of the specified parties

3. Identification of the subject matter of the engagement (or management's assertion thereon), including the period or point in time addressed,[2] and a reference to the character of the engagement
4. An identification of the responsible party
5. A statement that the subject matter is the responsibility of responsible party
6. A statement that the procedures, which were agreed to by the specified parties identified in the report, were performed to assist the specified parties in evaluating the entity's compliance with the specified requirements or the effectiveness of its internal control over compliance
7. A statement that the agreed-upon procedures engagement was conducted in accordance with attestation standards established by the AICPA
8. A statement that the sufficiency of the procedures is solely the responsibility of the specified parties and a disclaimer of responsibility for the sufficiency of those procedures
9. A list of the procedures performed (or reference thereto) and related findings. The practitioner should not provide negative assurance
10. Where applicable, a description of any agreed-upon materiality limits
11. A statement that the practitioner was not engaged to and did not conduct an examination of the entity's compliance with specified requirements or about the effectiveness of an entity's internal control over compliance, a disclaimer of opinion thereon, and a statement that if the practitioner had performed additional procedures, other matters might have come to his or her attention that would have been reported
12. A statement restricting the use of the report to the specified parties (however, if the report is a matter of public record, the practitioner should include the following sentence: "However, this report is a matter of public record and its distribution is not limited.")
13. Where applicable, reservations or restrictions concerning procedures or findings
14. Where applicable, a description of the nature of the assistance provided by the specialist
15. The manual or printed signature of the practitioner's firm
16. The date of the report

FUNDAMENTAL REQUIREMENTS: EXAMINATION ENGAGEMENT

CONDITIONS FOR ENGAGEMENT PERFORMANCE

According to AT 601.10, a practitioner may accept an examination engagement related to an entity's compliance with specified requirements if the following conditions are met:

1. The responsible party accepts responsibility for the entity's compliance with specified requirements and the effectiveness of the entity's internal control over compliance.
2. The responsible party evaluates the entity's compliance with specified requirements.
3. Sufficient evidential matter exists or could be developed to support the responsible party's evaluation.

---

[2] Generally, management's assertion about compliance with specified requirements will address a period of time, whereas an assertion about internal control over compliance will address a point in time.

A practitioner may examine the effectiveness of the entity's internal control over compliance or an assertion thereon only if he or she has reason to believe that the subject matter is capable of reasonably consistent evaluation against criteria that are suitable and available to users. If such criteria exist for internal control over compliance, the practitioner should perform the engagement in accordance with AT Section 101. AT Section 501 may also be helpful on such an engagement.

The practitioner should obtain a written assertion about compliance with specified requirements or internal control over compliance from the responsible party. The written assertion may be provided in a representation letter to the practitioner or in a separate report accompanying the practitioner's report. The responsible party's written assertion may take various forms but should be specific enough that users having competence in and using the same or similar measurement and disclosure criteria ordinarily would be able to arrive at materially similar conclusions.

The responsible party's refusal to provide a written assertion as part of an examination engagement should cause the practitioner to withdraw from the engagement, regardless of whether the client is the responsible party. An exception exists if an examination of an entity's compliance with specified requirements is required by law or regulation. In this case, the practitioner should disclaim an opinion on compliance unless he or she obtains evidential matter that warrants expressing an adverse opinion. If the practitioner expresses an adverse opinion and the responsible party does not provide an assertion, the practitioner's report should be restricted.

EXTENT OF EVIDENCE

To express an opinion on an entity's compliance (or assertion related thereto), the practitioner should accumulate sufficient evidence about the entity's compliance with specified requirements and limit attestation risk to an appropriately low level.

ASSESSMENT OF INHERENT RISK

The practitioner should consider factors affecting inherent risk similar to the factors an auditor would consider when planning an audit of financial statements (see AU Section 316, *Consideration of Fraud in a Financial Statement Audit*). According to AT 601.33, in addition, the practitioner should consider the following factors:

1. The complexity of the specified compliance requirements
2. The length of time the entity has been subject to the specified compliance requirements
3. Prior experience with the entity's compliance
4. Potential impact of noncompliance

ASSESSMENT OF CONTROL RISK

The practitioner should assess control risk. To assess control risk for compliance with specified requirements and to plan the engagement, the practitioner should obtain an understanding of those parts of the internal control related to compliance.

ENGAGEMENT PROCEDURES

According to AT 601.39, in an examination of the entity's compliance with specified requirements, the practitioner should do the following:

1. Obtain an understanding of the specified compliance requirements
2. Plan the engagement

3. Consider relevant portions of the entity's internal control over compliance
4. Obtain sufficient evidence including testing compliance with specified requirements
5. Consider subsequent events
6. Form an opinion about whether the entity complied, in all material respects, with specified requirements (or whether the responsible party's assertion about such compliance is fairly stated in all material respects) based on the specified criteria

SUBSEQUENT EVENTS

The practitioner should consider information about subsequent events that comes to his or her attention between the end of the period addressed by the practitioner's report and prior to the issuance of the report.

The practitioner has no responsibility to detect noncompliance after the period being reported on but before the date of the report. However, if the practitioner becomes aware of this type of noncompliance, and its nature and significance may make management's assertion misleading, the practitioner should include in the report an explanatory paragraph describing the nature of the noncompliance.

PRACTITIONER'S REPORT

According to AT 601.55, the practitioner's report on an examination, which is ordinarily addressed to the entity, should include the following:

1. A title that includes the word *independent*
2. An identification of the specified compliance requirements, including the period covered, and of the responsible party[3]
3. A statement that compliance with the specified requirements is the responsibility of the entity's management
4. A statement that the practitioner's responsibility is to express an opinion on the entity's compliance with those requirements based on his or her examination
5. A statement that the examination was conducted in accordance with attestation standards established by the AICPA and, accordingly, included examining, on a test basis, evidence about the entity's compliance with those requirements and performing such other procedures as the practitioner considered necessary in the circumstances
6. A statement that the practitioner believes the examination provides a reasonable basis for his or her opinion
7. A statement that the examination does not provide a legal determination on the entity's compliance
8. The practitioner's opinion on whether the entity complied, in all material respects, with specified requirements based on the specified criteria
9. A statement restricting the use of the report to the specified parties when the criteria used to evaluate compliance:

    a. Are determined by the practitioner to be appropriate only for a limited number of parties who either participated in establishing the criteria or who can be assumed to have an adequate understanding of the criteria
    b. Are available only to specified parties

10. The manual or printed signature of the practitioner's firm
11. The date of the examination report

---

[3] A practitioner also may be engaged to report an entity's compliance with specified requirements as of a point in time. In this case, the reports in "Illustrations" should be adapted as appropriate.

The practitioner's report should be dated as of the date of completion of the examination procedures.

REPORT MODIFICATIONS

The practitioner should modify the standard report whenever any one of the following conditions exist:

1. There is material noncompliance with specified requirements (qualified or adverse opinion)
2. The scope of the engagement is restricted (qualified or disclaimer of opinion)
3. The practitioner refers to the report of another practitioner as the basis, in part, for the report (see Illustration 5 in AT Section 501)

INTERPRETATIONS

There are no interpretations for this section.

TECHNIQUES FOR APPLICATION

PLANNING THE ENGAGEMENT—GENERAL

For either an agreed-upon procedures engagement or an examination, the practitioner should properly plan the engagement. In planning the engagement, the practitioner should consider doing the following:

1. Discuss the purpose of the engagement with management
2. Read or obtain an understanding of relevant laws and documents
3. Obtain an engagement letter
4. Design a program of procedures to be applied

AGREED-UPON PROCEDURES ENGAGEMENT

In this type of engagement, the practitioner should try to meet with the specified parties or a representative of the specified parties to establish the procedures. If a meeting is not possible, the practitioner should do one of the following:

1. Compare the procedures to be applied to written requirements of the specified parties
2. Review relevant contracts with or correspondence from the specified parties
3. Distribute a draft of the anticipated report or a copy of a proposed engagement letter to the specified parties with a request for their comments
4. Discuss the procedures to be applied with appropriate representatives of the specified parties involved

The manner in which the procedures are established should be documented in the practitioner's workpapers.

At the conclusion of this type of engagement, the practitioner should obtain a management representation letter. If the management refuses, the practitioner should withdraw from the engagement.

PLANNING THE EXAMINATION ENGAGEMENT

The practitioner should consider the following when planning the engagement:

1. For an entity with multiple components, determine if it is necessary to examine all components for compliance. In making this determination, consider:

   a. To what degree do the specified compliance requirements apply at the component level?
   b. What are our judgments about materiality?
   c. How centralized are the records?
   d. How effective is the control environment, particularly management's direct control over the exercise of authority delegated to others and its ability to supervise activities at various locations effectively?
   e. What are the nature and extent of operations conducted at the various components?
   f. How similar are controls over compliance for different components?

2. Determine the need to use the work of a specialist (see AU Section 336, *Using the Work of a Specialist*).
3. Identify the existence of an internal audit function and the extent to which internal auditors are involved in monitoring compliance with specified requirements (see AU Section 322, *The Auditor's Consideration of the Internal Audit Function in an Audit of Financial Statements*).
4. Obtain an understanding of the parts of the internal control related to compliance with the specified requirements. This understanding may be obtained by:

   a. Inquiries
   b. Inspection of documents
   c. Observation of activities

5. Identify types of potential noncompliance.
6. Assess control risk. If the practitioner wishes to assess control risk below the maximum, he or she should perform tests of controls.

EXAMINATION PROCEDURES

The nature of procedures and the sufficiency of evidence are matters of practitioner judgment. Procedures to be considered include the following:

1. For engagements involving regulatory requirements:

   a. Review communication between regulatory agencies and the entity.
   b. Review examination reports of the regulatory agencies.
   c. If appropriate, make inquiries of regulatory agencies including inquiries about examinations in progress.
   d. Make inquiries of entity's outside and inside counsel responsible for such matters.

2. Identify subsequent events for the period from the reporting period to the date of the report that would provide evidence about compliance during the period under examination. Information concerning subsequent events would be obtained from the following sources:

   a. Relevant internal auditors' reports issued during the subsequent period.

b. Other practitioners' reports identifying noncompliance, issued during the subsequent period.
c. Regulatory agencies' reports on the entity's noncompliance, issued during the subsequent period.
d. Information about the entity's noncompliance, obtained through other professional engagements for that entity.

3. If the specified requirements relate to financial statement matters, compare the relevant parts of these statements with the specified requirements.
4. Obtain a management representation letter. If management refuses, the practitioner should consider issuing a qualified opinion or a disclaimer of opinion.

MATERIALITY

Materiality in an examination of compliance differs from materiality in an audit. In an examination, the practitioner should consider the

1. Nature of the compliance requirements, which may or may not be quantifiable in monetary terms
2. Nature and frequency of noncompliance, including sampling risks
3. Qualitative considerations, including user needs and expectations

ILLUSTRATIONS

The following illustrations are adapted from SSAE 10 (AT Section 601).

ILLUSTRATION 1. AGREED-UPON PROCEDURES REPORT IN WHICH THE PROCEDURES AND FINDINGS CONCERNING COMPLIANCE WITH SPECIFIED REQUIREMENTS ARE ENUMERATED[4]

To the Board of Directors of Widget Company
Main City, USA

Independent Accountant's Report on Applying Agreed-Upon Procedures

We have performed the procedures enumerated below, which were agreed to by [*list specified parties*], solely to assist the specified parties in evaluating Widget Company's compliance with [*list specified requirements*] during the year ended December 31, 20X1. Management is responsible for Widget Company's compliance with those requirements. This agreed-upon procedures engagement was performed in accordance with attestation standards established by the American Institute of Certified Public Accountants. The sufficiency of these procedures is solely the responsibility of the parties specified in this report. Consequently, we make no representation regarding the sufficiency of the procedures described below either for the purpose for which this report has been requested or for any other purpose.

[*Include paragraphs to enumerate procedures and findings.*]

We were not engaged to, and did not, perform an examination, the objective of which would be the expression of an opinion on compliance. Accordingly, we do not express such an opinion.

---

[4] *In some agreed-upon procedures engagements, the practitioner may issue one report on a combined management assertion about compliance with specified requirements and the effectiveness of internal control over compliance. The practitioner's combined report should address both specified requirements and internal control over compliance.*

Had we performed additional procedures, other matters might have come to our attention that would have been reported to you.

This report is intended solely for the information and use of [*list or refer to specified parties*] and is not intended to be and should not be used by anyone other than these specified parties.

Smith and Jones
February 15, 20X2

ILLUSTRATION 2. AGREED-UPON PROCEDURES REPORT IN WHICH THE PROCEDURES AND FINDINGS CONCERNING THE EFFECTIVENESS OF INTERNAL CONTROL OVER COMPLIANCE ARE ENUMERATED[5]

To the Board of Directors of Widget Company
Main City, USA

Independent Accountant's Report on Applying Agreed-Upon Procedures

We have performed the procedures enumerated below, which were agreed to by [*list specified parties of report*], solely to assist the specified parties in evaluating the effectiveness of Widget Company's internal control over compliance with [*list specified requirements*] as of December 31, 20X1. Management is responsible for Widget Company's internal control over compliance with those requirements. This agreed-upon procedures engagement was performed in accordance with attestation standards established by the American Institute of Certified Public Accountants. The sufficiency of these procedures is solely the responsibility of the parties specified in the report. Consequently, we make no representation regarding the sufficiency of the procedures described below either for the purpose for which this report has been requested or for any other purpose.

[*Include paragraphs to enumerate procedures and findings.*]

We were not engaged to, and did not, perform an examination, the objective of which would be the expression of an opinion on the effectiveness of internal control over compliance. Accordingly, we do not express such an opinion. Had we performed additional procedures, other matters might have come to our attention that would have been reported to you.

This report is intended solely for the information and use of [*list or refer to specified parties*] and is not intended to be and should not be used by anyone other than these specified parties.

Smith and Jones
February 15, 20X2

ILLUSTRATION 3. EXAMINATION REPORT EXPRESSING AN OPINION ON COMPLIANCE WITH SPECIFIED REQUIREMENTS

To the Board of Directors of Widget Company
Main City, USA

Independent Accountant's Report

We have examined Widget Company's compliance with [*list specified compliance requirements*] during the year ended December 31, 20X1. Management is responsible for Widget Company's compliance with those requirements. Our responsibility is to express an opinion on Widget Company's compliance based on our examination.

---

[5] In some agreed-upon procedures engagements, the practitioner may issue one report on a combined management assertion about compliance with specified requirements and the effectiveness of internal control over compliance. The practitioner's combined report should address both specified requirements and internal control over compliance.

Our examination was conducted in accordance with attestation standards established by the American Institute of Certified Public Accountants and, accordingly, included examining, on a test basis, evidence about Widget Company's compliance with those requirements and performing such other procedures as we considered necessary in the circumstances. We believe that our examination provides a reasonable basis for our opinion. Our examination does not provide a legal determination on Widget Company's compliance with specified requirements.

In our opinion, Widget Company complied in all material respects with the aforementioned requirements for the year ended December 31, 20X1.

Smith and Jones
February 15, 20X2

ILLUSTRATION 4. EXAMINATION REPORT WHEN EXPRESSING AN OPINION ON MANAGEMENT'S ASSERTION ABOUT COMPLIANCE WITH SPECIFIED REQUIREMENTS

To the Board of Directors of Widget Company
Main City, USA

Independent Accountant's Report

We have examined management's assertion, included in the accompanying [*title of management report*], that Widget Company complied with [*list specified compliance requirements*] during the year ended December 31, 20X1. Management is responsible for Widget Company's compliance with those requirements. Our responsibility is to express an opinion on management's assertion about Widget Company's compliance based on our examination.

Our examination was conducted in accordance with attestation standards established by the American Institute of Certified Public Accountants and, accordingly, included examining, on a test basis, evidence about Widget Company's compliance with those requirements and performing such other procedures as we considered necessary in the circumstances. We believe that our examination provides a reasonable basis for our opinion. Our examination does not provide a legal determination on Widget Company's compliance with specified requirements.

In our opinion, management's assertion that Widget Company complied with the aforementioned requirements during the year ended December 31, 20X1 is fairly stated, in all material respects.

Smith and Jones
February 15, 20X2

ILLUSTRATION 5. MODIFIED REPORT WHEN PRACTITIONER HAS IDENTIFIED MATERIAL NONCOMPLIANCE AND MANAGEMENT HAS APPROPRIATELY MODIFIED ITS ASSERTION

To the Board of Directors of Widget Company
Main City, USA

Independent Accountant's Report

We have examined Widget Company's compliance with [*list specified compliance requirements*] for the year ended December 31, 20X1. Management is responsible for compliance with those requirements. Our responsibility is to express an opinion on Widget Company's compliance based on our examination.

Our examination was conducted in accordance with attestation standards established by the American Institute of Certified Public Accountants and, accordingly, included examining, on a test basis, evidence about Widget Company's compliance with those requirements and performing such other procedures as we considered necessary in the circumstances. We believe that our examination provides a reasonable basis for our opinion. Our examination does not provide a legal determination on Widget Company's compliance with specified requirements.

Our examination disclosed the following material noncompliance with [*type of compliance requirement*] applicable to Widget Company during the year ended December 31, 20X1. [*Describe noncompliance.*]

In our opinion, except for the material noncompliance described in the third paragraph, Widget Company complied, in all material respects, with the aforementioned requirements for the year ended December 31, 20X1.

Smith and Jones
February 15, 20X2

ILLUSTRATION 6. ADVERSE REPORT WHEN PRACTITIONER HAS IDENTIFIED MATERIAL NONCOMPLIANCE AND MANAGEMENT HAS APPROPRIATELY MODIFIED ITS ASSERTION

To the Board of Directors of Widget Company
Main City, USA

Independent Accountant's Report

We have examined Widget Company's compliance with [*list of specified compliance requirements*] for the [*period*] ended [*date*]. Management is responsible for compliance with these requirements. Our responsibility is to express an opinion on Widget Company's compliance based on our examination.

Our examination was conducted in accordance with attestation standards established by the American Institute of Certified Public Accountants and, accordingly, included examining, on a test basis, evidence about Widget Company's compliance with those requirements and performing such other procedures as we considered necessary in the circumstances. We believe that our examination provides a reasonable basis for our opinion. Our examination does not provide a legal determination on Widget Company's compliance with specified requirements.

Our examination disclosed the following material noncompliance with [*type of compliance requirement*] applicable to Widget Company during the [*period*] ended [*date*]. [*Describe noncompliance*].

In our opinion, because of the effect of the noncompliance described in the third paragraph, Widget Company has not complied with the aforementioned requirements for the [*period*] ended [*date*].

Smith and Jones
February 15, 20X2

AT 701 Management's Discussion and Analysis (MD&A)—A Summary[1,2]

EFFECTIVE DATE AND APPLICABILITY

Original Pronouncement	Statements on Standards for Attestation Engagements (SSAE) 10, *Attestation Standards: Revision and Recodification.*
Effective Date	This statement currently is effective.
Applicability	When a practitioner is engaged by a public entity that prepares Management's Discussion and Analysis (MD&A) in accordance with the rules and regulations adopted by the Securities and Exchange Commission (SEC) (or a nonpublic entity following the same requirements) to either perform an examination or review of MD&A. A practitioner engaged to perform agreed-upon procedures on MD&A should follow the guidance in Section 201.

DEFINITION OF TERM

MD&A. Management's Discussion and Analysis of Financial Condition and Results of Operations adopted by the SEC and found in Item 303 of Regulation S-K, as interpreted by Financial Reporting Release (FRR) 36.

---

[1] The SSAE on examination or review of MD&A is essentially a detailed manual on how to perform examinations and reviews, and only the highlights are summarized here. A practitioner seeking to provide these services should refer to SSAE 10 and the SEC's rules and regulations on MD&A. Only the considerations for a public entity are covered here. The considerations for a nonpublic entity are very similar because only the SEC has, at this point, issued rules and regulations that provide guidance on the presentation of MD&A.

[2] Practitioners should be aware that, on April 15, 2002, the SEC issued "Commission Statement about Management's Discussion and Analysis of Financial Condition and Results of Operations." The release sets forth certain views of the SEC regarding disclosures that should be considered by registrants. Disclosure matters covered in the release are liquidity and capital resources, including off-balance-sheet arrangements; certain trading activities that include nonexchange traded contracts accounted for at fair value; and the effects of transactions with related and certain other parties. The release can be found on the SEC's website at www.sec.gov.

OBJECTIVES OF AT SECTION 701

The SEC adopted requirements for MD&A in 1974 to have management provide a narrative explanation of the financial statements. The idea was to allow the user to see the company's financial position and operating results through management's eyes.

Two levels of service are possible—an examination or a review. A review report is restricted as to use and is not intended to be filed with the SEC. An examination report is intended for general use, but at this stage, whether there will be a significant demand for this service is unknown. The SEC does not require a practitioner's report on MD&A—the narrative presentation is management's responsibility and not a part of the audited financial statements.

According to AT 701.05, the practitioner's objective in an examination of MD&A is to express an opinion on the presentation taken as a whole by reporting whether:

1. The presentation includes, in all material respects, the required elements of the rules and regulations adopted by the SEC.
2. The historical financial amounts included in the presentation have been accurately derived, in all material respects, from the entity's financial statements.
3. The underlying information, determinations, estimates and assumptions of the entity provide a reasonable basis for the disclosures contained in the presentation.

The objective of a review of MD&A is to provide negative assurance on these three items.

NOTE: "Negative assurance" indicates that no information came to the accountant's attention that would cause him or her not to believe the three statements.

An examination of MD&A would generally be expected to relate to the MD&A for annual periods, but a review might relate to the MD&A for annual or interim periods or some combination.

In an examination, the practitioner seeks to obtain reasonable assurance by accumulating sufficient evidence to support the disclosures and assumptions, thus limiting attestation risk to an appropriately low level. A review consists principally of applying analytical procedures and making inquiries and does not provide assurance that a practitioner would become aware of all significant matters that would be disclosed in an examination.

In 2001 the Auditing Standards Board issued SSAE 10, *Attestation Standards: Revision and Recodification*. SSAE 10 superseded SSAEs 1 through 9 and renumbered the AT sections in the American Institute of Certified Public Accountants' (AICPA's) *Codification*. SSAE 10 made only minor changes to this section, including modifying the reports in this section to conform to changes made by Statement on Auditing Standards (SAS) 93, *Omnibus Statement on Auditing Standards—2000*.

FUNDAMENTAL REQUIREMENTS: EXAMINATION

ACCEPTANCE

To accept an engagement to examine MD&A, the practitioner should audit the financial statements for at least the latest period to which the MD&A presentation relates and the financial statements for the other periods covered by the MD&A presentation should have been audited by the practitioner or a predecessor auditor.

PERFORMANCE

According to AT 701.41, the practitioner should do the following:

1. Obtain an understanding of the rules and regulations adopted by the SEC for MD&A and management's method of preparing MD&A.
2. Plan the engagement by developing an overall strategy considering factors such as matters affecting the entity's industry and similar knowledge obtained during the audit of financial statements.
3. Consider relevant portions of internal control applicable to the preparation of MD&A.
4. Obtain sufficient evidence, including testing completeness, by comparing the content of the MD&A to the information obtained in the audit of financial statements and considering whether the explanations in the MD&A are consistent with this information.
5. Consider the effect of events subsequent to the balance sheet date by extending subsequent events review procedures in the audit to the MD&A information.
6. Obtain written representations from management concerning its responsibility for MD&A, completeness of minutes, events subsequent to the balance sheet date, and other matters the practitioner considers relevant to the MD&A presentation.
7. Form an opinion about whether the MD&A presentation meets the objectives for an opinion on such a presentation.

REPORTING

The financial statements for the periods covered by the MD&A presentation and the related auditors' report should accompany the presentation or be incorporated by reference to information filed with a regulatory agency.

The report should include the elements as found in the example in Illustration 1.

FUNDAMENTAL REQUIREMENTS: REVIEW

ACCEPTANCE

A practitioner may accept an engagement to review an MD&A presentation for an annual period under the same circumstances as an examination.

To accept an engagement to review the MD&A presentation for an interim period, both of the following points should occur:

1. The practitioner should either:
   a. Review and report on the historical financial statements for the related comparative interim periods or
   b. Audit the interim financial statements
2. The practitioner or a predecessor auditor either has already or will examine the MD&A presentation for the most recent fiscal year.

PERFORMANCE

According to AT 701.76, the practitioner should do the following:

1. Obtain an understanding of the rules and regulations adopted by the SEC for MD&A and management's method of preparing MD&A.
2. Plan the engagement, considering factors such as matters affecting the industry, the types of information management reports to external analysts, and matters identified during the audit or review of historical financial statements.
3. Consider relevant portions of the entity's internal control applicable to the MD&A.
4. Apply analytical procedures and make inquiries of management and others.
5. Consider the effects of events subsequent to the balance sheet date.
6. Obtain written representations from management.
7. Form a conclusion as to whether any information came to the practitioner's attention that would cause him or her to believe the objectives related to the MD&A presentation were not achieved.

REPORTING

The financial statements for the periods covered by the MD&A presentation and the related auditors' or accountants' reports should accompany the presentation or be incorporated by reference to information filed with a regulatory agency.

The report should include the elements as found in the examples in Illustrations 2 and 3.

INTERPRETATIONS

There are no interpretations for this section.

ILLUSTRATIONS

The following reports are adapted from SSAE 10:[3]

1. An illustration of the wording of a standard examination report
2. A standard review report on an annual MD&A presentation
3. A standard review report on an MD&A presentation for an interim period

ILLUSTRATION 1. STANDARD EXAMINATION REPORT

Report of Independent Registered Public Accounting Firm

To the Audit Committee, Board of Directors, and Shareholders
Widget Company
Main City, USA

    We have examined Widget Company's Management's Discussion and Analysis taken as a whole, included [*incorporated by reference*] in the Company's [*insert description of registration statement or document*]. Management is responsible for the preparation of the Company's Management's Discussion and Analysis pursuant to the rules and regulations adopted by the Securities and Exchange Commission. Our responsibility is to express an opinion on the presentation based on our examination. We have audited, in accordance with the standards of the Public Company Accounting Oversight Board (United States), the financial statements of Widget Company as of

---

[3] If the entity is a nonissuer and complies with GAAS rather than the standards of the PCAOB, the references in the report to the PCAOB's standards should be changed to refer to "auditing standards generally accepted in the United States of America" and "attestation standards established by the American Institute of Certified Public Accountants."

December 31, 20X2 and 20X1, and for each of the years in the three-year period ended December 31, 20X2; in our report dated February 15, 20X3, we expressed an unqualified opinion on those financial statements.[4]

Our examination of Management's Discussion and Analysis was conducted in accordance with attestation standards established by the Public Company Accounting Oversight Board and, accordingly, included examining, on a test basis, evidence supporting the historical amounts and disclosures in the presentation. An examination also includes assessing the significant determinations made by management as to the relevancy of information to be included and the estimates and assumptions that affect reported information. We believe that our examination provides a reasonable basis for our opinion.

The preparation of Management's Discussion and Analysis requires management to interpret the criteria, make determinations as to the relevancy of information to be included, and make estimates and assumptions that affect reported information. Management's Discussion and Analysis includes information regarding the estimated future impact of transactions and events that have occurred or are expected to occur, expected sources of liquidity and capital resources, operating trends, commitments, and uncertainties. Actual results in the future may differ materially from management's present assessment of this information because events and circumstances frequently do not occur as expected.[5]

In our opinion, the Company's presentation of Management's Discussion and Analysis includes, in all material respects, the required elements of the rules and regulations adopted by the Securities and Exchange Commission; the historical financial amounts included therein have been accurately derived, in all material respects, from the Company's financial statements; and the underlying information, determinations, estimates, and assumptions of the Company provide a reasonable basis for the disclosures contained therein.

Smith and Jones
Honolulu, Hawaii
March 1, 20X3

---

[4] *If prior financial statements were audited by other auditors, this sentence would be replaced by the following:*

> *We have audited, in accordance with the standards of the Public Company Accounting Oversight Board (United States), the financial statements of Widget Company as of and for the year ended December 31, 20X2, and in our report dated Month XX, 20X3, we expressed an unqualified opinion on those financial statements. The financial statements of Widget Company as of December 31, 20X1, and for each of the years in the two-year period then ended were audited by other auditors, whose report dated Month XX, 20X2, expressed an unqualified opinion on those financial statements.*

If the practitioner's opinion on the financial statements is based on the report of other auditors, this sentence would be replaced by the following:

> *We have audited, in accordance with the standards of the Public Company Accounting Oversight Board (United States), the financial statements of Widget Company as of December 31, 20X2 and 20X1, and for each of the years in the three-year period ended December 31, 20X2, and in our report dated Month XX, 20X3, we expressed an unqualified opinion on those financial statements based on our audits and the report of other auditors.*

[5] *The following sentence should be added to the beginning of the explanatory paragraph if the entity is a nonpublic entity:*

> *Although Widget Company is not subject to the rules and regulations of the Securities and Exchange Commission, the accompanying Management's Discussion and Analysis is intended to be a presentation in accordance with the rules and regulations adopted by the Securities and Exchange Commission.*

ILLUSTRATION 2. STANDARD REVIEW REPORT ON AN ANNUAL MD&A PRESENTATION

Report of Independent Registered Public Accounting Firm

To the Board of Directors
Widget Company
Main City, USA

We have reviewed Widget Company's Management's Discussion and Analysis taken as a whole, included [*incorporated by reference*] in the Company's [*insert description of registration statement or document*]. Management is responsible for the preparation of the Company's Management's Discussion and Analysis pursuant to the rules and regulations adopted by the Securities and Exchange Commission. We have audited, in accordance with the standards of the Public Company Accounting Oversight Board (United States), the financial statements of Widget Company as of December 31, 20X2 and 20X1, and for each of the years in the three-year period ended December 31, 20X2, and in our report dated February 15, 20X3, we expressed an unqualified opinion on those financial statements.

We conducted our review of Management's Discussion and Analysis in accordance with attestation standards established by the Public Company Accounting Oversight Board. A review of Management's Discussion and Analysis consists principally of applying analytical procedures and making inquiries of persons responsible for financial, accounting, and operational matters. It is substantially less in scope than an examination, the objective of which is the expression of an opinion on the presentation. Accordingly, we do not express such an opinion.

The preparation of Management's Discussion and Analysis requires management to interpret the criteria, make determinations as to the relevancy of information to be included, and make estimates and assumptions that affect reported information. Management's Discussion and Analysis includes information regarding the estimated future impact of transactions and events that have occurred or are expected to occur, expected sources of liquidity and capital resources, operating trends, commitments, and uncertainties. Actual results in the future may differ materially from management's present assessment of this information because events and circumstances frequently do not occur as expected.[6]

Based on our review, nothing came to our attention that caused us to believe that the Company's presentation of Management's Discussion and Analysis does not include, in all material respects, the required elements of the rules and regulations adopted by the Securities and Exchange Commission; that the historical financial amounts included therein have not been accurately derived, in all material respects, from the Company's financial statements; or that the underlying information, determinations, estimates, and assumptions of the Company do not provide a reasonable basis for the disclosures contained therein.

This report is intended solely for the information and use of [*list or refer to the specified parties*] and is not intended to be, and should not be, used by anyone other than the specified parties.

Smith and Jones
March 1, 20X3

---

[6] *The following sentence should be added to the beginning of the explanatory paragraph if the entity is a nonpublic entity:*

> *Although Widget Company is not subject to the rules and regulations of the Securities and Exchange Commission, the accompanying Management's Discussion and Analysis is intended to be a presentation in accordance with the rules and regulations adopted by the Securities and Exchange Commission.*

ILLUSTRATION 3. STANDARD REVIEW REPORT ON AN INTERIM MD&A PRESENTATION

Report of Independent Registered Public Accounting Firm

To the Audit Committee, Board of Directors, and Shareholders
Widget Company
Main City, USA

We have reviewed Widget Company's Management's Discussion and Analysis taken as a whole, included in the Company's [*insert description of registration statement or document*]. Management is responsible for the preparation of the Company's Management's Discussion and Analysis pursuant to the rules and regulations adopted by the Securities and Exchange Commission. We have reviewed, in accordance with the standards of the Public Company Accounting Oversight Board, the interim financial information of Widget Company as of June 30, 20X3 and 20X2, and for the three-month and six-month periods then ended and have issued our report thereon dated July 15, 20X3.

We conducted our review of Management's Discussion and Analysis in accordance with attestation standards established by the Public Company Accounting Oversight Board. A review of Management's Discussion and Analysis consists principally of applying analytical procedures and making inquiries of persons responsible for financial, accounting, and operational matters. It is substantially less in scope than an examination, the objective of which is the expression of an opinion on the presentation. Accordingly, we do not express such an opinion.

The preparation of Management's Discussion and Analysis requires management to interpret the criteria, make determinations as to the relevancy of information to be included, and make estimates and assumptions that affect reported information. Management's Discussion and Analysis includes information regarding the estimated future impact of transactions and events that have occurred or are expected to occur, expected sources of liquidity and capital resources, operating trends, commitments, and uncertainties. Actual results in the future may differ materially from management's present assessment of this information because events and circumstances frequently do not occur as expected.[7]

Based on our review, nothing came to our attention that caused us to believe that the Company's presentation of Management's Discussion and Analysis does not include, in all material respects, the required elements of the rules and regulations adopted by the Securities and Exchange Commission; that the historical financial amounts included therein have not been accurately derived, in all material respects, from the Company's financial statements; or that the underlying information, determinations, estimates, and assumptions of the Company do not provide a reasonable basis for the disclosures contained therein.

This report is intended solely for the information and use of [*list or refer to the specified parties*] and is not intended to be, and should not be, used by anyone other than the specified parties.

Smith and Jones
March 1, 20X3

---

[7] *The following sentence should be added to the beginning of the explanatory paragraph if the entity is a nonpublic entity:*

> *Although Widget Company is not subject to the rules and regulations of the Securities and Exchange Commission, the accompanying Management's Discussion and Analysis is intended to be a presentation in accordance with the rules and regulations adopted by the Securities and Exchange Commission.*

AT 801 Reporting on Controls at a Service Organization

EFFECTIVE DATE AND APPLICABILITY

Original Pronouncement	Statements on Standards for Attestation Engagements (SSAE) 16, *Reporting on Controls at a Service Organization*.
Effective Date	This statement currently is effective.
Applicability	Examination engagements to report on controls at organizations that provide services to user entities when those controls are likely to be relevant to user entities' internal control over financial reporting.

DEFINITION OF TERMS

Carve-out method. A method for reviewing the services provided by a subservice organization, where management's definition identifies the nature of the services performed and excludes its control objectives and controls from the scope of the service auditor's engagement.

Complementary user entity controls. Controls that the management of a subservice entity assumes will be implemented by entities using the services of the subservice entity.

Control objectives. The purpose of specific controls.

Controls at a service organization. The policies and procedures used by a service organization that are likely to be relevant to the internal control over the financial reporting of user entities.

Controls at a subservice organization. The policies and procedures used by a subservice organization that are likely to be relevant to the internal control over the financial reporting of user entities.

Criteria. The standard against which the service auditor evaluates subject matter.

Inclusive method. A method of reviewing the services provided by a subservice organization, where management's definition of the organization's system includes a description of the services provided by the subservice organization and its control objectives and related controls.

Internal audit function. A service organization's internal auditors and others who perform activities similar to those performed by internal auditors.

Report on management's description of a service organization's system and the suitability of the design of controls. A report that includes management's description of a service organization's system, a written assertion about whether management's description fairly presents the system, and whether controls were suitably designed to achieve control objectives, as well as a service auditor's report expressing an opinion on the preceding items.

Report on management's description of a service organization's system and the suitability of the design and operating effectiveness of controls. A report that includes management's description of a service organization's system, a written assertion about whether management's description fairly presents the system, and whether controls were suitably designed to achieve control objectives, as well as a service auditor's report expressing an opinion on the preceding items and a description of the tests of controls and related results.

Service auditor. A practitioner who reports on the controls of a service organization.

Service organization. Either an organization or a segment of an organization that provides services to user entities; the services are likely to be relevant to the internal control over financial reporting of user entities.

Service organization's system. The policies and procedures used by the management of a service organization to provide user entities with the services addressed by a service auditor's report.

Subservice organization. A service organization that is used by another service organization to perform some services that it provides to user entities; these services are likely to be relevant to the internal controls over financial reporting of user entities.

Test of controls. A procedure to evaluate the operating effectiveness of controls in achieving the control objectives described in management's description of the system of a service organization.

User auditor. An auditor who audits and reports on the financial statements of an entity.

User entity. An entity that makes use of a service organization.

OBJECTIVES OF AT SECTION 801

According to AT 801.06, the objectives of the service auditor are to obtain reasonable assurance about whether, in all material respects, based on suitable criteria:

- Management's description of the service organization's system fairly presents the system that was designed and implemented throughout the specified period.
- The controls related to the control objectives stated in management's description of the service organization's system were suitably designed throughout the specified period.
- When included in the scope of the engagement, the controls operated effectively to provide reasonable assurance that the control objectives stated in management's description of the service organization's system were achieved throughout the specified period.

The service auditor also has the objective of reporting in accordance with his or her findings.

FUNDAMENTAL REQUIREMENTS

MANAGEMENT AND THOSE CHARGED WITH GOVERNANCE

The service auditor should determine the appropriate person within the management of the service organization or governance structure with whom to interact.

ACCEPTANCE AND CONTINUANCE

The service auditor should accept or continue an engagement to report on the controls of a service organization if:

1. The auditor has the competency and capability to perform the engagement.
2. The auditor's initial knowledge of the engagement indicates that the criteria used will be suitable, he or she will have access to appropriate evidence, and the scope of the engagement will not be so limited that it will be unlikely to be useful.
3. Management agrees to the terms of the engagement by its acceptance of responsibility for a description of the service organization's system and related assertion, having a reasonable basis for its assertion, selecting and stating the criteria to be used, specifying the control objectives, identifying risks that threaten achievement of the control objectives, providing the auditor with access to all information and people requested by the auditor, making written representations, and providing a written assertion that will be included in management's description of the service organization's system.

If management refuses to provide a written assertion, the service auditor should withdraw from the engagement. If there is a legal or regulatory restriction on withdrawing, then the service auditor should disclaim an opinion.

If management requests a scope change before the engagement is complete, the service auditor should be satisfied regarding the reason for the change before agreeing to it.

ASSESSING THE SUITABILITY OF THE CRITERIA

The service auditor should ascertain whether management has used suitable criteria

1. To prepare the description of the organization's system
2. To evaluate whether controls were designed to achieve control objectives
3. For a type 2 report, to evaluate whether controls operated effectively throughout the specified period to achieve control objectives

The service auditor should determine the following when assessing the suitability of criteria to evaluate whether management's description of a system is fairly presented:

1. Whether the description of the system presents how it was designed and implemented, including the following items (if applicable):
   a. The types of services provided
   b. The procedures by which services are provided
   c. The related accounting records
   d. How the system captures and addresses significant events and conditions
   e. The process by which reports and other information are prepared for user entities
   f. The control objectives and controls designed to achieve the objectives of the system
   g. Other aspects of the controls, risk assessment, and other systems that are relevant to the services provided
2. For a type 2 report, whether the system description includes relevant details of changes to the system during the period addressed by the description
3. Whether the description of the system does not omit or distort relevant information

When assessing the suitability of criteria, the service auditor should determine if the criteria address whether any risks threatening the control objectives have been identified, and if the identified controls would provide reasonable assurance that these risks would not keep the control objectives from being achieved. When making this assessment, the service auditor should verify whether the criteria include whether the controls were consistently applied throughout the period, including whether these controls were applied by those with appropriate competence and authority.

The service auditor should evaluate materiality for management's description of the organization's system, the suitability of the controls, and (for a type 2 report) the operating effectiveness of the controls needed to achieve the objectives stated in the description.

OBTAINING AN UNDERSTANDING OF THE SERVICE ORGANIZATION'S SYSTEM

The service auditor should acquire an understanding of the organization's system, including those controls included in the engagement scope.

OBTAINING EVIDENCE REGARDING MANAGEMENT'S DESCRIPTION OF THE SERVICE ORGANIZATION'S SYSTEM

The service auditor should read management's description of the organization's system and evaluate whether those elements of the description that are within the engagement scope are presented fairly. This assessment should address whether

1. The control objectives stated in the description are reasonable
2. The controls stated in the description were implemented
3. Any complementary user entity controls are adequately described
4. Any services performed by a subservice organization are adequately described, as well as whether the inclusive or carve-out methods were used

The service auditor should use inquiries and other procedures to determine whether the system has been implemented.

OBTAINING EVIDENCE REGARDING THE DESIGN OF CONTROLS

The service auditor should determine which controls are needed to achieve the control objectives for the system, and assess whether these controls were suitably designed by identifying those risks threatening control objectives and evaluating the linkage of the controls with those risks.

OBTAINING EVIDENCE REGARDING THE OPERATING EFFECTIVENESS OF CONTROLS

For a type 2 engagement, the service auditor tests those controls that he or she has determined are needed to achieve the control objectives of the system, as well as assess their effectiveness throughout the period. The service auditor should inquire about control changes implemented during the period covered by the service auditor's report. If the changes are significant, he or she should ascertain whether they are included in management's description of the system. If not, the service auditor should describe the changes in his or her report. If any superseded controls were relevant for meeting control objectives, the service auditor should test the controls prior to the change. If it is not possible to do so, the service auditor should determine the impact on his or her report.

When designing and testing controls, the service auditor should do the following:

1. Perform other procedures to procure evidence about how a control was applied, the consistency of application, and by whom or by what means it was applied

2. Determine whether the controls depend on other controls, and whether he or she should obtain evidence about the effectiveness of those other controls
3. Determine a method for selecting items to be tested to meet procedure objectives

To determine the extent of tests of controls and whether sampling can be used, the service auditor should consider the characteristics of the population of controls to be tested.

The service auditor should investigate any deviations identified, and ascertain the following:

1. Whether deviations are within the expected rate of deviation
2. Whether additional testing is needed to conclude whether the controls related to the objectives operated effectively in the specified period
3. Whether the testing provides a basis for concluding that a control did not operate effectively in the specified period

If the service auditor learns that any identified deviations were the result of intentional acts, he or she should assess the risk that management's description of the system is not fairly presented, that the controls are not suitably designed, and (in a type 2 engagement) that the controls are not operating effectively.

USING THE WORK OF THE INTERNAL AUDIT FUNCTION

If there is an internal audit function within the service organization, the service auditor should understand its responsibilities in order to determine whether it can be relevant to the engagement. This includes an evaluation of:

1. The technical competence and objectivity of the internal auditors
2. Whether they perform their work with due professional care
3. Whether there will be effective communication between the service auditor and the internal auditors

If the work of the internal auditor is likely to be adequate for the purposes of the engagement, the service auditor should evaluate the impact of internal audit work in terms of the work performed by the internal auditors, the significance of that work to the service auditor's conclusions, and the amount of subjectivity used by the internal auditors in their work.

To ascertain the adequacy of specific work done by the internal auditors for use by the service auditor, the service auditor should evaluate whether:

1. The work was done by auditors with adequate training and proficiency.
2. The work was properly supervised and documented.
3. There is sufficient evidence from which to draw conclusions.
4. Conclusions reached and reports written are appropriate in the circumstances.
5. Exceptions were properly resolved.

When the service auditor uses the work of the internal audit function, he or she should not reference that work in the opinion, since the service auditor has sole responsibility for the opinion. For a type 2 report, the service auditor should describe his or her use of the internal auditors in the report section that describes tests of controls and the results thereof.

WRITTEN REPRESENTATIONS

The service auditor should obtain from management the following written representations:

1. Reaffirmation of the assertion in management's description of the service organization's system.
2. That management has provided the service auditor with all relevant information and access.
3. That management has disclosed any situations where there:
   a. Are instances of legal or regulatory noncompliance or uncorrected errors
   b. Is knowledge of actual or suspected management or employee acts that may adversely affect the fairness of the description of the organization's system or the achievement of its control objectives
   c. Are any control design deficiencies
   d. Are instances where controls have not operated as described
   e. Are subsequent events that could have a significant effect on management's assertion

If there is a subservice organization providing services to a service organization, and management uses the inclusive method, then the service auditor should obtain written representations from the management of the subservice organization.

Written representations should be organized as a representation letter that is addressed to the service auditor, and the letter should be dated as of the same date as the service auditor's report.

If management does not provide written representations, the service auditor should discuss the matter with management, evaluate the effect of the refusal on his or her assessment of the integrity of management, and take such actions as disclaiming an opinion or withdrawing from the engagement.

OTHER INFORMATION

The service auditor should use other information to identify inconsistencies with or misstatements in management's description of the service organization's system. If there are inconsistencies or misstatements, the service auditor should discuss the matter with management. This may call for further appropriate action.

SUBSEQUENT EVENTS

The service auditor should inquire of management whether there have been any events during the period between management's description of the organization's system and the date of the auditor's report that could have a significant effect on management's assertion. The service auditor should disclose such items in his or her report.

The service auditor is not responsible for events subsequent to the date of his or her report.

DOCUMENTATION

The service auditor should prepare documentation that is sufficient to enable an experienced service auditor with no previous connection to the engagement to understand:

1. The nature, timing, and extent of any procedures used
2. The results of procedures performed and evidence obtained
3. Significant findings or issues, conclusions reached, and the judgments made in reaching those conclusions

The service auditor should record the following when documenting procedures performed:

1. The characteristics of items or matters being tested
2. Who performed the work and when he or she did so
3. Who reviewed the work and when he or she did so

If the service auditor used the internal audit staff, he or she should document the conclusions reached regarding the adequacy of the internal audit function and the procedures completed to do so.

The service auditor should document the discussion of significant findings or issues with management, as well as the names of the persons involved and the date of each discussion.

The service auditor should document how he or she addressed any inconsistency in the information examined and the final conclusion.

The service auditor should assemble all engagement documentation into an engagement file and complete the related administration no later than 60 days after the release date of the service auditor's report. The service auditor should not delete or discard documentation after assembling the final engagement file. If the service auditor must modify or add to the existing documentation after the file has been completed, he or she should document the reasons for the change, and when and by whom they were made and reviewed.

PREPARING THE SERVICE AUDITOR'S REPORT

The service auditor's type 2 report should contain the following information:

1. A title that includes the word *independent*
2. An addressee
3. Identification of the following items:

    a. Management's description of the service organization's system and the function performed by that system
    b. Any parts of management's description of the system that are not addressed by the service auditor's report
    c. Any information included in a document containing the service auditor's report that is not addressed by the report
    d. The criteria
    e. Any services performed by a subservice organization, and whether the carve-out or inclusive methods were used: If the carve-out method was employed, a statement that management's description of the organization's system does not include the control objectives and related controls located at subservice organizations, and that the service auditor's procedures do not address the subservice organization. If the inclusive method was employed, a statement that management's description of the organization's system includes the subservice organization's control objectives and related controls, and that the service auditor's procedures addressed the subservice organization.

4. If management's description of the organization's system notes the need for complementary user entity controls, a statement that the service auditor has not evaluated the suitability of the design or effectiveness of complementary user entity controls, and that the stated control objectives can only be achieved if complementary user entity controls are suitably designed and operate effectively (as well as the controls of the service organization)

5. A reference to the assertion by management, as well as a statement that management is responsible for:
   a. Preparing the description of the service organization's system and the assertion
   b. Providing the services covered by the description of the service organization's system
   c. Specifying the control objectives and stating them in the description of the system
   d. Identifying the risks that threaten the accomplishment of the control objectives.
   e. Selecting the criteria
   f. Designing, implementing, and documenting controls that are designed and operate effectively enough to achieve the objectives stated in the description of the organization's system
6. A statement that the service auditor's responsibility is to express an opinion on the fairness of the presentation of management's description of the system of the service organization, and on the suitability of the design and operating effectiveness stated in the description, based on the examination by the service auditor
7. A statement that the examination was conducted in accordance with the attestation standards established by the AICPA, and that those standards require the service auditor to plan and perform this examination in order to obtain reasonable assurance as to whether management's description of the organization's system is fairly presented and controls suitably designed and operated during the specified period in order to achieve related control objectives
8. A statement that an examination of management's description of the organization's system and the suitability of the design and effectiveness of the controls in achieving control objectives involves the performance of procedures to obtain evidence about the fairness of the presentation of the description and suitability of the design and effectiveness of the controls to achieve the related control objectives stated in the description
9. A statement that the examination included assessing the risks that management's description is not fairly presented and that the controls were not suitably designed or operated effectively to achieve the related control objectives
10. A statement that the examination included testing the effectiveness of the controls that the service auditor considered necessary to provide reasonable assurance that the related control objectives were achieved
11. A statement that an examination engagement of this type also includes the evaluation of the overall presentation of management's description of the service organization's system, as well as the suitability of the control objectives stated in the description
12. A statement that the service auditor believes that the examination provides a reasonable basis for his or her opinion
13. A statement about the inherent limitations of controls
14. The service auditor's opinion on whether, in all material respects, based on the criteria described in management's assertion:
    a. Management's description of the system fairly presents the system that was designed and implemented throughout the period.
    b. The controls related to the control objectives statement in management's description were suitably designed to provide reasonable assurance that the control objectives would be achieved if they operated effectively throughout the specified period.

c. The controls the service auditor tested operated effectively throughout the specified period.
d. The application of complementary user entity controls is necessary to achieve the control objectives stated in management's description, then make reference to this condition.

15. A reference to a description of the service auditor's tests of controls and the results, including:

    a. The identification of tested controls and the nature of the tests in enough detail to enable user auditors to determine the effects of such tests on their risk assessments
    b. The identification of any deviations in the operation of controls included in the description, the extent of the testing that identified the deviations, and the number and nature of deviations noted

16. A statement restricting the use of the service auditor's report to the management of the service organization, user entities of the service organization during the period covered by the report, and the independent auditors of those user entities
17. The date of the report
18. The name of the service auditor and the city and state where the auditor maintains the office that is responsible for the engagement

The service auditor's type 1 report should contain the following information:

1. A title that includes the word *independent*
2. An addressee
3. Identification of the following items:

    a. Management's description of the service organization's system and the function performed by that system
    b. Any parts of management's description of the system that are not addressed by the service auditor's report
    c. Any information included in a document containing the service auditor's report that is not addressed by the report
    d. The criteria
    e. Any services performed by a subservice organization, and whether the carve-out or inclusive methods were used: If the carve-out method was employed, a statement that management's description of the organization's system does not include the control objectives and related controls located at subservice organizations, and that the service auditor's procedures do not address the subservice organization. If the inclusive method was employed, a statement that management's description of the organization's system include the subservice organization's control objectives and related controls and that the service auditor's procedures addressed the subservice organization.

4. If management's description of the organization's system notes the need for complementary user entity controls, a statement that the service auditor has not evaluated the suitability of the design or effectiveness of complementary user entity controls, and that the stated control objectives can only be achieved if complementary user entity controls are suitably designed and operate effectively (as well as the controls of the service organization)

5. A reference to the assertion by management, as well as a statement that management is responsible for:
    a. Preparing the description of the service organization's system and the assertion
    b. Providing the services covered by the description of the service organization's system
    c. Specifying the control objectives and stating them in the description of the system
    d. Identifying the risks that threaten the accomplishment of the control objectives
    e. Selecting the criteria
    f. Designing, implementing, and documenting controls that are designed and operate effectively enough to achieve the objectives stated in the description of the organization's system
6. A statement that the service auditor's responsibility is to express an opinion on the fairness of the presentation of management's description of the system of the service organization, and on the suitability of the design and operating effectiveness stated in the description, based on the examination by the service auditor
7. A statement that the examination was conducted in accordance with the attestation standards established by the AICPA, and that those standards require the service auditor to plan and perform this examination in order to obtain reasonable assurance as to whether management's description of the organization's system is fairly presented and controls suitably designed and operated during the specified period in order to achieve related control objectives
8. A statement that the service auditor has not performed any procedures regarding the operating effectiveness of controls and, therefore, expresses no opinion about them
9. A statement that an examination of management's description of the organization's system and the suitability of the design and effectiveness of the controls in achieving control objectives involves the performance of procedures to obtain evidence about the fairness of the presentation of the description and suitability of the design and effectiveness of the controls to achieve the related control objectives stated in the description
10. A statement that the examination included assessing the risks that management's description is not fairly presented and that the controls were not suitbly designed or operated effectively to achieve the related control objectives
11. A statement that an examination engagement of this type also includes the evaluation of the overall presentation of management's description of the service organization's system, as well as the suitability of the control objectives stated in the description
12. A statement that the service auditor believes that the examination provides a reasonable basis for his or her opinion
13. A statement about the inherent limitations of controls
14. The service auditor's opinion on whether, in all material respects, based on the criteria described in management's assertion:
    a. Management's description of the system fairly presents the system that was designed and implemented as of the specified date.
    b. The controls related to the control objectives statement in management's description were suitably designed to provide reasonable assurance that the control objectives would be achieved if they operated effectively as of the specified date.
    c. The application of complementary user entity controls is necessary to achieve the control objectives stated in management's description, then make reference to this condition.

15. A statement restricting the use of the service auditor's report to the management of the service organization, user entities of the service organization as of the end of the period covered by the report, and the independent auditors of those user entities.
16. The date of the report.
17. The name of the service auditor and the city and state where the auditor maintains the office that is responsible for the engagement.

The service auditor should date the report no earlier than the date on which he or she obtained sufficient appropriate evidence to support the opinion.

The service auditor should modify his or her opinion, as well as modify the service auditor's report to clearly describe all of the reasons for a modification under the following circumstances:

1. Management's description of the system is not fairly presented.
2. The controls are not suitably designed to provide reasonable assurance that the control objectives would be achieved.
3. For a type 2 report, the controls do not operate effectively throughout the specified period to achieve the stated control objectives.
4. The service auditor is unable to obtain sufficient evidence.

If the service auditor plans to disclaim an opinion due to lack of evidence, and has concluded that some aspects of the description are not fairly presented, or some controls were not suitably designed to provide reasonable assurance regarding control objectives, or (for a type 2 report) some controls did not operate effectively throughout the specified period, then he or she should identify these findings in his or her report.

If the service auditor plans to disclaim an opinion, then he or she should not identify the procedures performed, nor describe characteristics of the engagement in the report.

OTHER COMMUNICATION RESPONSIBILITIES

If the service auditor is aware of incidents of legal or regulatory noncompliance, fraud, or uncorrected errors attributable to management or other personnel that are not trivial and which may affect user entities, then he or she should determine the effect of these incidents on the description of the organization's system, control objectives, and the service auditor's report. Further, the service auditor should take appropriate action if this information has not been communicated to affected user entities.

ILLUSTRATIONS

The following reports are adapted from SSAE 16.

1. An illustration of the wording of a Type 2 service auditor's report.
2. An illustration of the wording of a Type 1 service auditor's report.

> **ILLUSTRATION 1. TYPE 2 SERVICE AUDITOR'S REPORT**

Independent Service Auditor's Report on a Description of a Service Organization's System and the Suitability of the Design and Operating Effectiveness of Controls

To: XYZ Service Organization

Scope

We have examined XYZ Service Organization's description of its [*type or name of*] system for processing user entities' transactions [*or identification of the function performed by the system*] through the period [*date*] to [*date*] [*description*] and the suitability of the design and operating effectiveness of controls to achieve the related control objectives stated in the descriptions.

Service Organization's Responsibilities

On page XX of the description, XYZ Service Organization has provided an assertion about the fairness of the presentation of the description and suitability of the design and operating effectiveness of the controls to achieve the related control objectives stated in the description. XYZ Service Organization is responsible for preparing the description and the assertion, including the completeness, accuracy, and method of presentation of the description and the assertion, providing the services covered by the description, specifying the control objectives and stating them in the description, identifying the risks that threaten the achievement of the control objectives, selecting the criteria, and designing, implementing, and documenting controls to achieve the related control objectives stated in the description.

Service Auditor's Responsibilities

Our responsibility is to express an opinion on the fairness of the presentation of the description and on the suitability of the design and operating effectiveness of the controls to achieve the related control objectives stated in the description, based on our examination. We conducted our examination in accordance with attestation standards established by the American Institute of Certified Public Accountants. Those standards require that we plan and perform our examination to obtain reasonable assurance about whether, in all material respects, the description is fairly presented and the controls were suitably designed and operating effectively to achieve the related control objectives stated in the description throughout the period [*date*] to [*date*].

An examination of a description of a service organization's system and the suitability of the design and operating effectiveness of the service organization's controls to achieve the related control objectives stated in the description involves performing procedures to obtain evidence about the fairness of the presentation of the description and the suitability of the design and operating effectiveness of those controls to achieve the related control objectives stated in the description. Our procedures included assessing the risks that the description is not fairly presented and that the controls were not suitably designed or operating effectively to achieve the related control objectives stated in the description. Our procedures also included testing the operating effectiveness of those controls that we consider necessary to provide reasonable assurance that the related control objectives stated in the description were achieved. An examination engagement of this type also includes evaluating the overall presentation of the description and the suitability of the control objectives stated therein, and the suitability of the criteria specified by the service organization and described at page [*aa*]. We believe that the evidence we obtained is sufficient and appropriate to provide a reasonable basis for our opinion.

Inherent Limitations

Because of their nature, controls at a service organization may not prevent, or detect and correct, all errors or omissions in processing or reporting transactions [*or identification of the function performed by the system*]. Also, the projection to the future of any evaluation of the fairness of the presentation of the description, or conclusions about the suitability of the design or operating effectiveness of the controls to achieve the related control objectives is subject to the risk that controls at a service organization may become inadequate or fail.

Opinion

In our opinion, in all material respects, based on the criteria described in XYZ Service Organization's assertion on page [*aa*],

1. The description fairly presents the [*type or name of*] system that was designed and implemented throughout the period [*date*] to [*date*].
2. The controls related to the control objectives stated in the description were suitably designed to provide reasonable assurance that the control objectives would be achieved if the controls operated effectively throughout the period [*date*] to [*date*].
3. The controls tested, which were those necessary to provide reasonable assurance that the control objectives stated in the description were achieved, operated effectively throughout the period [*date*] to [*date*].

Descriptions of Tests of Controls

The specific controls tested and the nature, timing, and results of those tests are listed on pages [*yy–zz*].

Restricted Use

This report, including the description of tests of controls and results thereof on pages [*yy–zz*], is intended solely for the information and use of XYZ Service Organization, user entities of XYZ Service Organization's [*type or name of*] system during some or all of the period [*date*] to [*date*], and the independent auditors of such user entities, who have a sufficient understanding to consider it, along with other information including information about controls implemented by user entities themselves, when assessing the risks of material misstatements of user entities' financial statements. This report is not intended to be and should not be used by anyone other than these specified parties.

Smith and Jones
Honolulu, Hawaii
March 1, 20X3

Following is a modification of the scope paragraph in a type 2 service auditor's report if the description refers to the need for complementary user entity controls. (New language is shown in boldface italics):

We have examined XYZ Service Organization's description of its [*type or name of*] system for processing user entities' transactions [*or identification of the function performed by the system*] throughout the period [*date*] to [*date*] (description) and the suitability of the design and operating effectiveness of controls to achieve the related control objectives stated in the description. ***The description indicates that certain control objectives specified in the description can be achieved only if complementary user entity controls contemplated in the design of XYZ Service Organization's controls are suitably designed and operating effectively, along with related controls at the service organization. We have not evaluated the suitability of the design or operating effectiveness of such complementary user entity controls.***

Following is a modification of the applicable subparagraphs of the opinion paragraph of a type 2 service auditor's report if the application of complementary user entity controls is necessary to achieve the related control objectives stated in the description of the service organization's system (New language is shown in boldface italics):

2. The controls related to the control objectives stated in the description were suitably designed to provide reasonable assurance that those control objectives would be achieved if the controls operated effectively throughout the period [*date*] to [*date*] ***and user entities***

applied the complementary user entity controls contemplated in the design of XYZ Service Organization's controls throughout the period [date] to [date].

3. The controls tested, which **together with the complementary user entity controls referred to in the scope paragraph of this report, if operating effectively,** were those necessary to provide reasonable assurance that the control objectives stated in the description were achieved, operated effectively throughout the period [date] to [date].

Following is a modification of the paragraph that describes the responsibilities of management of the service organization for use in a type 2 service auditor's report when the control objectives have been specified by an outside party. (New language is shown in boldface italics):

On page XX of the description, XYZ Service Organization has provided an assertion about the fairness of the presentation of the description and suitability of the design and operating effectiveness of the controls to achieve the related control objectives stated in the description. XYZ Service Organization is responsible for preparing the description and for its assertion, including the completeness, accuracy, and method of presentation of the description and assertion, as well as for providing the services covered by the description, selecting the criteria, and designing, implementing, and documenting controls to achieve the related control objectives stated in the description. ***The control objectives have been specified by [name of party specifying the control objectives] and are stated on page [aa] of the description.***

ILLUSTRATION 2. TYPE 1 SERVICE AUDITOR'S REPORT

Independent Service Auditor's Report on a Description of a Service Organization's System and the Suitability of the Design of Controls

To: XYZ Service Organization

Scope

We have examined XYZ Service Organization's description of its [*type or name of*] system for processing user entities' transactions [*or identification of the function performed by the system*] as of [*date*], and the suitability of the design of controls to achieve the related control objectives stated in the descriptions.

Service Organization's Responsibilities

On page XX of the description, XYZ Service Organization has provided an assertion about the fairness of the presentation of the description and suitability of the design of the controls to achieve the related control objectives stated in the description. XYZ Service Organization is responsible for preparing the description and for its assertion, including the completeness, accuracy, and method of presentation of the description and the assertion, providing the services covered by the description, specifying the control objectives and stating them in the description, identifying the risks that threaten the achievement of the control objectives, selecting the criteria, and designing, implementing, and documenting controls to achieve the related control objectives stated in the description.

Service Auditor's Responsibilities

Our responsibility is to express an opinion on the fairness of the presentation of the description and on the suitability of the design of the controls to achieve the related control objectives stated in the description, based on our examination. We conducted our examination in accordance with attestation standards established by the American Institute of Certified Public Accountants. Those standards require that we plan and perform our examination to obtain reasonable assurance about whether, in all material respects, the description is fairly presented and the controls were suitably designed to achieve the related control objectives stated in the description as of [*date*].

An examination of a description of a service organization's system and the suitability of the design of the service organization's controls to achieve the related control objectives stated in the description involves performing procedures to obtain evidence about the fairness of the presentation of the description of the system and the suitability of the design of the controls to achieve the related control objectives stated in the description. Our procedures included assessing the risks that the description is not fairly presented and that the controls were not suitably designed to achieve the related control objectives stated in the description. Our procedures also included assessing the risks that the description is not fairly presented and that the controls were not suitably designed to achieve the related control objectives stated in the description. An examination engagement of this type also includes evaluating the overall presentation of the description and the suitability of the control objectives stated therein, and the suitability of the criteria specified by the service organization and described at page [*aa*].

We did not perform any procedures regarding the operating effectiveness of the controls stated in the description and, accordingly, do not express an opinion thereon.

We believe that the evidence we obtained is sufficient and appropriate to provide a reasonable basis for our opinion.

Inherent Limitations

Because of their nature, controls at a service organization may not prevent, or detect and correct, all errors or omissions in processing or reporting transactions [or identification of the function performed by the system]. The projection to the future of any evaluation of the fairness of the presentation of the description, or conclusions about the suitability of the design of the controls to achieve the related control objectives is subject to the risk that controls at a service organization may become inadequate or fail.

Opinion

In our opinion, in all material respects, based on the criteria described in XYZ Service Organization's assertion:

1. The description fairly presents the [*type or name of*] system that was designed and implemented as of [*date*], and
2. The controls related to the control objectives stated in the description were suitably designed to provide reasonable assurance that the control objectives would be achieved if the controls operated effectively as of [*date*].

Restricted Use

This report is intended solely for the information and use of XYZ Service Organization, user entities of XYZ Service Organization's [*type or name of*] system as of [*date*], and the independent auditors of such user entities, who have a sufficient understanding to consider it, along with other information including information about controls implemented by user entities themselves, when obtaining an understanding of user entities information and communication systems relevant to financial reporting. This report is not intended to be and should not be used by anyone other than these specified parties.

Smith and Jones
Honolulu, Hawaii
March 1, 20X3

Following is a modification of the scope paragraph in a type 1 report if the description of the service organization's system refers to the need for complementary user entity controls. (New language is shown in boldface italics.)

We have examined XYZ Service Organization's description of its [*type or name of*] system (description) made available to user entities of the system for processing their transactions [*or identification of the function performed by the system*] as of [*date*], and the suitability of the design of controls to achieve the related control objectives stated in the description. ***The description indi-***

cates that certain complementary user entity controls must be suitably designed and implemented at user entities for related controls at the service organization to be considered suitably designed to achieve the related control objectives. We have not evaluated the suitability of the design or operating effectiveness of such complementary user entity controls.

Following is a modification of the applicable subparagraph in the opinion paragraph of a type 1 report if the application of complementary user entity controls is necessary to achieve the related control objectives stated in management's description of the service organization's system (new language is shown in boldface italics):

2. The controls related to the control objectives stated in the description were suitably designed to provide reasonable assurance that those control objectives would be achieved if the controls operated effectively as of [*date*] ***and user entities applied the complementary user entity controls contemplated in the design of XYZ Service Organization's controls as of [date].***

Following is a modification of the paragraph that describes management of XYZ Service Organization's responsibilities to be used in a type 1 report when the control objectives have been specified by an outside party (new language is shown in boldface italics):

On page XX of the description, XYZ Service Organization has provided an assertion about the fairness of the presentation of the description and suitability of the design of the controls to achieve the related control objectives stated in the description. XYZ Service Organization is responsible for preparing the description and assertion, including the completeness, accuracy, and method of presentation of the description and assertion, providing the services covered by the description, selecting the criteria, and designing, implementing, and documenting controls to achieve the related control objectives stated in the description. ***The control objectives have been specified by [name of party specifying the control objectives] and are stated on page [aa] of the description.***

ILLUSTRATION 3. MODIFIED SERVICE AUDITOR'S REPORTS

The following examples of modified service auditor's reports are for guidance only and are not intended to be exhaustive or applicable to all situations. They are based on the illustrative reports above.

Example 1: Qualified Opinion for a Type 2 Report—The Description of the Service Organization's System Is Not Fairly Presented in All Material Respects

The following is an illustrative paragraph describing the basis for the qualified opinion. The paragraph would be inserted before the modified opinion paragraph. All other report paragraphs are unchanged.

Basis for Qualified Opinion

The accompanying description states on page [*mn*] that XYZ Service Organization uses operator identification numbers and passwords to prevent unauthorized access to the system. Based on inquiries of staff personnel and observation of activities, we have determined that operator identification numbers and passwords are employed in applications A and B but are not required to access the system in applications C and D.

Opinion

In our opinion, except for the matter described in the preceding paragraph, and based on the criteria described in XYZ Service Organization's assertion on page [*aa*], in all material respects . . .

Example 2: Qualified Opinion—The Controls Are Not Suitably Designed to Provide Reasonable Assurance That the Control Objectives Stated in the Description of the Service Organization's System Would Be Achieved if the Controls Operated Effectively

The following is an illustrative paragraph describing the basis for the qualified opinion. The paragraph would be inserted before the modified opinion paragraph. All other report paragraphs are unchanged.

Basis for Qualified Opinion

As discussed on page [*mn*] of the accompanying description, from time to time, XYZ Service Organization makes changes in application programs to correct deficiencies or to enhance capabilities. The procedures followed in determining whether to make changes, in designing the changes, and in implementing them do not include review and approval by authorized individuals who are independent from those involved in making the changes. There also are no specified requirements to test such changes or provide test results to an authorized reviewer prior to implementing the changes. As a result the controls are not suitably designed to achieve the control objective, "Controls provide reasonable assurance that changes to existing applications are authorized, tested, approved, properly implemented, and documented."

Opinion

In our opinion, except for the matter described in the preceding paragraph, and based on the criteria described in XYZ Service Organization's assertion on page [*aa*], in all material respects . . .

Example 3: Qualified Opinion for a Type 2 Report—The Controls Did Not Operate Effectively Throughout the Specified Period to Achieve the Control Objectives Stated in the Description of the Service Organization's System

The following is an illustrative paragraph describing the basis for the qualified opinion. The paragraph would be inserted before the modified opinion paragraph. All other report paragraphs are unchanged.

Basis for Qualified Opinion

XYZ Service Organization states in its description that it has automated controls in place to reconcile loan payments received with the various output reports. However, as noted on page [*mn*] of the description of tests of controls and results thereof, this control was not operating effectively throughout the period [*date*] to [*date*] due to a programming error. This resulted in the non-achievement of the control objective, "Controls provide reasonable assurance that loan payments received are properly recorded" throughout the period January 1, 20X1, to April 30, 20X1. XYZ Service Organization implemented a change to the program performing the calculation as of May 1, 20X1, and our tests indicate that it was operating effectively throughout the period May 1, 20X1, to December 31, 20X1.

Opinion

In our opinion, except for the matter described in the preceding paragraph, and based on the criteria described in XYZ Service Organization's assertion on page [*aa*], in all material respects . . .

Example 4: Qualified Opinion—The Service Auditor Is Unable to Obtain Sufficient Appropriate Evidence

The following is an illustrative paragraph describing the basis for the qualified opinion. The paragraph would be inserted before the modified opinion paragraph. All other report paragraphs are unchanged.

Basis for Qualified Opinion

XYZ Service Organization states in its description that it has automated controls in place to reconcile loan payments received with the output generated. However, electronic records of the performance of this reconciliation for the period from [*date*] to [*date*] were deleted as a result of a computer processing error and, therefore, we were unable to test the operation of this control for that period. Consequently, we were unable to determine whether the control objective, "Controls provide reasonable assurance that loan payments received are properly recorded" was achieved throughout the period [*date*] to [*date*].

Opinion

In our opinion, except for the matter described in the preceding paragraph, and based on the criteria described in XYZ Service Organization's assertion on page [*aa*], in all material respects . . .

ILLUSTRATION 4. REPORT PARAGRAPHS FOR SERVICE ORGANIZATIONS THAT USE A SUBSERVICE ORGANIZATION

Following are modifications of the illustrative type 2 report in Example 1 of Appendix A for use in engagements in which the service organization uses a subservice organization. (New language is shown in boldface italics; deleted language is shown by strikethrough.)

Example 1: Carve-Out Method

Scope

We have examined XYZ Service Organization's description of its system for processing user entities' transactions [*or identification of the function performed by the system*] throughout the period [*date*] to [*date*] (description) and the suitability of the design and operating effectiveness of controls to achieve the related control objectives stated in the description.

XYZ Service Organization uses a computer processing service organization for all of its computerized application processing. The description on pages [bb–cc] includes only the controls and related control objectives of XYZ Service Organization and excludes the control objectives and related controls of the computer processing service organization. Our examination did not extend to controls of the computer processing service organization.

All other report paragraphs are unchanged.

Example 2: Inclusive Method

Scope

We have examined XYZ Service Organization's ***and ABC Subservice Organization's*** description of its [***their***] [*type or name of*] system for processing user entities' transactions [*or identification of the function performed by the system*] throughout the period [*date*] to [*date*] (description) and the suitability of the design and operating effectiveness of ***XYZ Service Organization's and ABC Subservice Organization's*** controls to achieve the related control objectives stated in the description. ***ABC Subservice Organization is an independent service organization that provides computer processing services to XYZ Service Organization. XYZ Service Organization's description includes a description of ABC Subservice Organization's [type or name of] system used by XYZ Service Organization to process transactions for its user entities, as well as relevant control objectives and controls of ABC Subservice Organization.***

XYZ Service Organization's Responsibilities

On page XX of the description, XYZ Service Organization [***and ABC Subservice Organization***] has [***have***] provided an [***their***] assertion*s* about the fairness of the presentation of the description and suitability of the design and operating effectiveness of the controls to achieve the related control objectives stated in the description. XYZ Service Organization *and ABC Subservice Organization are* is responsible for preparing the description and assertions, including the completeness, accuracy, and method of presentation of the description and assertions, providing the services covered by the description, specifying the control objectives and stating them in the description, identifying the risks that threaten the achievement of the control objectives, selecting the criteria, and designing, implementing, and documenting controls to achieve the related control objectives stated in the description.

Inherent Limitations

Because of their nature, controls at a service organization *or subservice organization* may not prevent, or detect and correct, all errors or omissions in processing or reporting transactions. Also, the projection to the future of any evaluation of the fairness of the presentation of the description or any conclusions about the suitability of the design or operating effectiveness of the controls to achieve the related control objectives is subject to the risk that controls at a service organization *or subservice organization* may become ineffective or fail.

Opinion

In our opinion, in all material respects, based on the criteria specified in XYZ Service Organization*'s and ABC Subservice Organization's* assertions on page [*aa*]:

1. The description fairly presents *XYZ Service Organization's* the [*type or name of*] system *and ABC Subservice Organization's* [*type or name of*] *system used by XYZ Service Organization to process transactions for its user entities* [*or identification of the function performed by the service organization's system*] that [*were*] was designed and implemented throughout the period [*date*] to [*date*].
2. The controls related to the control objectives *of XYZ Service Organization and ABC Subservice Organization* stated in the description were suitably designed to provide reasonable assurance that the control objectives would be achieved if the controls operated effectively throughout the period [*date*] to [*date*].
3. The controls *of XYZ Service Organization and ABC Subservice Organization that* we tested, which were those necessary to provide reasonable assurance that the control objectives stated in the description were achieved, operated effectively throughout the period [*date*] to [*date*].

All other report paragraphs are unchanged.

ILLUSTRATION 5. ASSERTIONS BY MANAGEMENT OF A SERVICE ORGANIZATION

The assertion by management of the service organization may be included in management's description of the service organization's system or may be attached to the description. The following illustrative assertions are intended for assertions that are included in the description.

The following illustrative management assertions are for guidance only and are not intended to be exhaustive or applicable to all situations.

Example 1: Assertion by Management of a Service Organization for a Type 2 Report

XYZ Service Organization's Assertion

We have prepared the description of XYZ Service Organization's [*type or name of*] system (description) for user entities of the system during some or all of the period [*date*] to [*date*], and their user auditors who have a sufficient understanding to consider it, along with other information, including information about controls implemented by user entities of the system themselves, when assessing the risks of material misstatements of user entities' financial statements. We confirm, to the best of our knowledge and belief, that:

1. The description fairly presents the [*type or name of*] system made available to user entities of the system during some or all of the period [*date*] to [*date*] for processing their transactions [*or identification of the function performed by the system*]. The criteria we used in making this assertion were that the description:

   a. Presents how the system made available to user entities of the system was designed and implemented to process relevant transactions, including:

      (1) The classes of transactions processed
      (2) The procedures, within both automated and manual systems, by which those transactions are initiated, authorized, recorded, processed, corrected as necessary, and transferred to the reports presented to user entities of the system.
      (3) The related accounting records, supporting information, and specific accounts that are used to initiate, authorize, record, process, and report transactions; this includes the correction of incorrect information and how information is transferred to the reports presented to user entities of the system
      (4) How the system captures and addresses significant events and conditions, other than transactions
      (5) The process used to prepare reports or other information provided to user entities' of the system
      (6) Specified control objectives and controls designed to achieve those objectives
      (7) Other aspects of our control environment, risk assessment process, information and communication systems (including the related business processes), control activities, and monitoring controls that are relevant to processing and reporting transactions of user entities of the system

   b. Does not omit or distort information relevant to the scope of the [*type or name of*] system, while acknowledging that the description is prepared to meet the common needs of a broad range of user entities of the system and the independent auditors of those user entities, and may not, therefore, include every aspect of the [*type or name of*] system that each individual user entity of the system and its auditor may consider important in its own particular environment.

2. The description includes relevant details of changes to the service organization's system during the period covered by the description when the description covers a period of time.
3. The controls related to the control objectives stated in the description were suitably designed and operated effectively throughout the period [*date*] to [*date*] to achieve those control objectives. The criteria we used in making this assertion were that

   a. The risks that threaten the achievement of the control objectives stated in the description have been identified by the service organization;
   b. The controls identified in the description would, if operating as described, provide reasonable assurance that those risks would not prevent the control objectives stated in the description from being achieved; and
   c. The controls were consistently applied as designed, including whether manual controls were applied by individuals who have the appropriate competence and authority.

Example 2: Assertion by Management of a Service Organization for a Type 1 Report

XYZ Service Organization's Assertion

We have prepared the description of XYZ Service Organization's [*type or name of*] system (description) for user entities of the system as of [*date*], and their user auditors who have a sufficient understanding to consider it, along with other information including information about controls implemented by user entities themselves, when obtaining an understanding of user entities' information and communication systems relevant to financial reporting. We confirm, to the best of our knowledge and belief, that:

1. The description fairly presents the [*type or name of*] system made available to user entities of the system as of [*date*] for processing their transactions [*or identification of the function performed by the system*]. The criteria we used in making this assertion were that the description:

    a. Presents how the system made available to user entities of the system was designed and implemented to process relevant transactions, including:

        (1) The classes of transactions processed.
        (2) The procedures, within both automated and manual systems, by which those transactions are initiated, authorized, recorded, processed, corrected as necessary, and transferred to the reports presented to user entities of the system.
        (3) The related accounting records, supporting information, and specific accounts that are used to initiate, authorize, record, process, and report transactions; this includes the correction of incorrect information and how information is transferred to the reports provided to user entities of the system
        (4) How the system captures and addresses significant events and conditions, other than transactions
        (5) The process used to prepare reports or other information provided to user entities of the system
        (6) Specified control objectives and controls designed to achieve those objectives
        (7) Other aspects of our control environment, risk assessment process, information and communication systems (including the related business processes), control activities, and monitoring controls that are relevant to processing and reporting transactions of user entities of the system

    b. Does not omit or distort information relevant to the scope of the [*type or name of*] system, while acknowledging that the description is prepared to meet the common needs of a broad range of user entities of the system and the independent auditors of those user entities, and may not, therefore, include every aspect of the [*type or name of*] system that each individual user entity of the system and its auditor may consider important in its own particular environment

2. The controls related to the control objectives stated in the description were suitably designed as of [*date*] to achieve those control objectives. The criteria we used in making this assertion were that:

    a. The risks that threaten the achievement of the control objectives stated in the description have been identified by the service organization.
    b. The controls identified in the description would, if operating as described, provide reasonable assurance that those risks would not prevent the control objectives stated in the description from being achieved.

AR 60–90 Compilation and Review of Financial Statements

EFFECTIVE DATE AND APPLICABILITY

Original Pronouncement	Statements on Standards for Accounting and Review Services (SSARSs) 19, 20
Effective Date	These statements are currently effective.
Applicability	For the financial statement compilation engagements or reviews of financial statements.

RECENT DEVELOPMENTS

In February 2011, the Accounting and Review Services Committee (ARSC) issued SSARS No. 20, *Revised Applicability of Statements on Standards for Accounting and Review Services*. SSARS No. 20 excludes, from the applicability of SSARSs, engagements to review interim financial statements when:

- The accountant has audited the entity's latest annual financial statements,
- It is expected that the current year financial statements will be audited, and
- The appointment of another accountant to audit the current year financial statements is not effective prior to the beginning of the period covered by the review.

These engagements would be performed in accordance with Statement on Auditing Standards (SAS) No. 100, *Interim Financial Information*, as amended (American Institute of Certified Public Accountants [AICPA], *Professional Standards*, AU Section 722, clarified AU-C Section 930 effective December 15, 2012).

SSARS No. 20 is effective for reviews of financial statements for periods beginning after December 15, 2011, with early application permitted.

In October 2011, the ARSC issued the following interpretations:

- Interpretation No. 17, "Required Supplementary Information That Accompanies Compiled Financial Statements," of AR Section 80, *Compilation of Financial Statements*
- Interpretation No. 11, "Required Supplementary Information That Accompanies Reviewed Financial Statements," of AR Section 90

These interpretations provide guidance to accountants when:

- The compiled or reviewed financial statements are accompanied by supplementary analysis *and*

- That information is *required* by the Financial Accounting Standards Board (FASB), the Governmental Accounting Standards Board, the Federal Accounting Standards Advisory Board, or the International Accounting Standards Board.

The interpretations clarify that the accountant is not required to apply procedures to the required supplementary information that accompanies compiled or reviewed financial statements.

Interpretation No. 17 also clarifies that when required supplementary information is omitted from financial statements that omit substantially all disclosures required by US GAAP, the accountant may not combine the paragraph discussing the omission of substantially all disclosures with the paragraph referring to the omission of the required supplementary information.

The interpretations also provide illustrative paragraphs. These illustrations are presented in the section on interpretations in this chapter.

The interpretations are currently effective.

DEFINITIONS OF TERMS

Source: AR Section 60.04

Applicable financial reporting framework. The financial reporting framework adopted by management and, when appropriate, those charged with governance in the preparation of the financial statements, that is acceptable in view of the nature of the entity and the objective of the financial statements, or that is required by law or regulation.

Assurance engagement. An engagement in which an accountant issues a report designed to enhance the degree of confidence of third parties and management about the outcome of an evaluation or measurement of financial statements (subject matter) against an applicable financial reporting framework (criteria).

Attest engagement. An engagement that requires independence, as defined in AICPA's *Professional Standards*.

Financial reporting framework. A set of criteria that an entity uses to measure, recognize, present, and disclose the material items appearing in a set of financial statements.

Financial statements. A structured representation of historical financial information, including related notes, intended to communicate an entity's economic resources and obligations at a point in time or the changes therein for a period of time in accordance with a financial reporting framework. The related notes ordinarily comprise a summary of significant accounting policies and other explanatory information. The term *financial statements* ordinarily refers to a complete set of financial statements as determined by the requirements of the applicable financial reporting framework, but can also refer to a single financial statement or financial statements without notes.

Issuer. An issuer is defined in Section 3 of the Securities Exchange Act of 1934, securities of which are registered under Section 12 of the Act, or that is required to file reports under Section 15(d), or that files or has filed a registration statement that has not yet become effective under the Securities Act of 1993, and that it has not withdrawn.

Management. The persons charged with executive responsibility for the conduct of an entity's operations. For some entities, management includes some or all of those charged with governance (for example, executive members of a governance board or an owner-manager).

Nonissuer. All entities except for those defined as issuers.

Other comprehensive basis of accounting (OCBOA). A definite set of criteria, other than accounting principles generally accepted in the United States of America (US GAAP) or International Financial Reporting Standards (IFRSs), having substantial support underlying the preparation of financial statements prepared pursuant to that basis.

Examples of an OCBOA are as follows:

1. A basis of accounting that the reporting entity uses to comply with the requirements or financial reporting provisions of a governmental regulatory agency to whose jurisdiction the entity is subject (for example, a basis of accounting that insurance companies use pursuant to the rules of a state insurance commission).
2. A basis of accounting that the reporting entity uses or expects to use to file its income tax return for the period covered by the financial statements.
3. The cash basis of accounting and modifications of the cash basis having substantial support (for example, recording depreciation on fixed assets). Ordinarily, a modification would have substantial support if the method is equivalent to the accrual basis of accounting for that item and if the method is not illogical.

Review evidence. Information used by the accountant to provide a reasonable basis for obtaining limited assurance.

Submission of financial statements. Presenting to management financial statements that the accountant has prepared.

Third party. All persons except for members of management.

Those charged with governance. The person(s) with responsibility for overseeing the strategic direction of the entity and obligations related to the accountability of the entity. This includes overseeing the financial reporting process. Those charged with governance are specifically excluded from management, unless they perform management functions.

OBJECTIVES AND LIMITATIONS OF COMPILATION AND REVIEW ENGAGEMENTS

AR Section 60.05–.08 establishes a framework and provides guidance for the performance and reporting on compilation and review engagements.

A compilation is a service to assist management in presenting financial statements without obtaining or providing any assurance that there are no material modifications to be made to the financial statements for them to be in conformity with the applicable financial reporting framework. Although a compilation is not an assurance engagement, it is an attest engagement. A compilation differs significantly from a review or an audit of financial statements. A compilation does not contemplate performing inquiry, analytical procedures, or other procedures performed in a review. Additionally, a compilation does not contemplate obtaining an understanding of the entity's internal control; assessing fraud risk; testing accounting records by obtaining sufficient appropriate audit evidence through inspection, observation, confirmation, or the examination of source documents (for example, cancelled checks or bank images); or other procedures ordinarily performed in an audit. Therefore, a compilation does not provide a basis for obtaining or providing any assurance regarding the financial statements.

A review is a service in which the accountant obtains limited assurance that there are no material modifications to be made to the financial statements for them to be in conformity with the applicable financial reporting framework. In a review engagement, the accountant should accumulate review evidence to obtain a limited level of assurance. A review engagement is an assurance engagement as well as an attest engagement.

A review differs significantly from an audit of financial statements in which the auditor obtains a high level of assurance (expressed in the auditor's report as obtaining reasonable assurance) that the financial statements are free of material misstatement. A review does not contemplate obtaining an understanding of the entity's internal control; assessing fraud risk; testing accounting records by obtaining sufficient appropriate audit evidence through inspection, observation, confirmation, or the examination of source documents (for example, cancelled checks or bank images); or other procedures ordinarily performed in an audit. Accordingly, in a review, the accountant does not obtain assurance that he or she will become aware of all significant matters that would be disclosed in an audit. Therefore, a review is designed to obtain only limited assurance that there are no material modifications that should be made to the financial statements in order for the statements to be in conformity with the applicable financial reporting framework.

FUNDAMENTAL REQUIREMENTS

ELEMENTS OF A COMPILATION OR REVIEW ENGAGEMENT

Compilation and review engagements involve the following elements:

1. *Parties.* These engagements involve three parties, which are management, an accountant in the practice of public accounting, and the intended users of the financial statements. More specifically:

    a. *Management.* Management takes responsibility for the preparation and presentation of the financial statements in accordance with the applicable financial reporting framework (which they are responsible for identifying). The accountant cannot issue an unmodified compilation report or review report when management is unwilling to accept responsibility for the financial statements.

    b. *Accountant.* The accountant should possess a level of industry-specific accounting knowledge to compile or review financial statements that are appropriate for an entity operating in that industry. An accountant should not accept an engagement if his or her preliminary knowledge of the engagement indicates that ethical requirements for professional competence will not be met. However, the accountant can sometimes use the work of experts to satisfy this requirement. If so, the accountant should be satisfied that persons carrying out selected aspects of the engagement possess the required skills and knowledge, and that the accountant has adequate involvement in the engagement.

    c. *Intended users.* An intended user is one who understands the limitations of a compilation or review engagement and the resulting financial statements. An intended user may impose a requirement that additional procedures be performed.

    NOTE: *The accountant has no responsibility for identifying intended users.*

2. *Financial reporting framework.* Management is responsible for selecting the applicable financial reporting framework, as well as specific accounting policies when the framework contains multiple alternatives. The requirements of the selected framework determine the form and content of the financial statements.

3. *Financial statements.* The accountant may be engaged to compile or review either a complete set of financial statements or an individual financial statement, and for varying time periods.
4. *Evidence.* In a compilation engagement, the accountant has no responsibility to obtain evidence about the accuracy or completeness of the financial statements. In a review engagement, the accountant performs sufficient procedures to provide a limited assurance that there are no material modifications required for the financial statements to be in conformity with the applicable financial reporting framework. Professional judgment is needed to determine the specific nature, timing, and extent of these procedures.

> NOTE: *The nature, timing, and extent of procedures for gathering review evidence are limited relative to an audit.*

5. *Reports.* If an accountant performs a compilation, he or she must provide a written report or communication, or else withdraw from the engagement. If the accountant performs a review, he or she must issue a written review report, or else withdraw from the engagement.

MATERIALITY

Generally, misstatements and omissions are considered material if (individually or in aggregate) they could reasonably be expected to influence the economic decisions of users. The accountant's judgments about materiality are made in light of surrounding circumstances and are affected by the size or nature of a misstatement. Further, the accountant's judgments about materiality are based on a consideration of the information needs of users as a group (not individually). When making these judgments, it is reasonable for the accountant to assume that users have a reasonable knowledge of business and economic activities, understand that financial statements are prepared at certain levels of materiality, recognize the uncertainties in some forms of measurement, and make reasonable economic decisions on the basis of the information contained within financial statements.

These considerations may be dealt with in more detail in individual financial reporting frameworks.

COMPILATION OF FINANCIAL STATEMENTS

Establishing an Understanding

The accountant should both establish and document an understanding with management regarding compilation engagement services. Such written communications reduce the risk that management may inappropriately rely on the accountant to protect the entity against some types of risks, or expect the accountant to perform some tasks that are actually management's responsibility. The documentation should include the following:

- *Objective.* The objective is to assist management in presenting financial information in the form of financial statements.
- *Information source.* The accountant uses information that is the representation of management, and does not obtain any assurance that there are no material modifications that should be made.
- *Management responsibilities.* Management is responsible for the preparation and presentation of the financial statements in accordance with the applicable financial reporting framework.

- *Internal controls.* Management is responsible for internal controls relevant to the preparation and presentation of the financial statements.
- *Fraud.* Management is responsible for preventing and detecting fraud.
- *Legal compliance.* Management is responsible for complying with applicable laws and regulations.
- *Records availability.* Management is responsible for making financial and related records available to the accountant.
- *SSARS compliance.* The accountant is responsible for conducting the engagement in accordance with SSARS.
- *Differences from review or audit.* A compilation is different from a review or audit of financial statements, since it does not use inquiry, analytical procedures, or other procedures. A compilation also does not use an understanding of the entity's internal controls, or a fraud risk assessment, or the use of accounting record testing through inspection, observation, confirmation, or source document examinations. Thus, the accountant does not express an opinion or provide any assurance regarding the financial statements.
- *Reliance.* Do not rely on the engagement to disclose errors, fraud, or illegal acts.
- *Error reporting.* The accountant will inform management of any material errors, fraud, or illegal acts that come to the accountant's attention during the compilation work. The accountant does not need to report illegal acts that are clearly inconsequential.
- *Independence impairment.* The accountant will state the effect of any independence impairments on the compilation report.
- *Other.* If applicable, also note fees and billings, any limitations on the liability of the accountant or the client, conditions under which others may access compilation-related documents, and other services to be provided that relate to regulatory requirements. It may also be necessary to include the existence of any material departures from the applicable financial reporting framework, the omission of disclosures, and references to any supplementary information.

NOTE: If the compiled financial statements are not to be used by a third party, include in the engagement letter an acknowledgement by management that the statements are not to be used by a third party.

An example of an engagement letter for compilation services is shown later in the "Illustrations: Traditional Compilation Engagement" section.

Compilation Performance Requirements

The accountant should have knowledge of the following topics in order to perform a compilation engagement:

1. *Industry knowledge.* Have an understanding of the industry in which the client operates that is sufficient to compile financial statements that are appropriate for an entity in that industry. This does not prevent an accountant from accepting an engagement in an industry where the accountant has no previous experience, but does mean that the accountant should obtain the required level of knowledge.
2. *Client knowledge.* Have an understanding of the client's business and the accounting principles and practices used by it (including any differences in the client's business model from normal industry practices). This requires a general understanding of the

client's operating characteristics and the nature of its assets, liabilities, revenues, and expenses.
3. *Financials review.* Read the financial statements and consider whether they appear to be correct in form and free of obvious material errors.
4. *Other procedures.* If the accountant has made inquiries or performed other procedures, then ask management to consider the effects of these matters on the financial statements and respond with its findings to the accountant. If the accountant believes the financial statements may be materially misstated, obtain additional or revised information; if such information is not provided, then withdraw from the engagement.

Documentation in a Compilation Engagement

The accountant should prepare documentation for each compilation engagement in enough detail to provide a clear understanding of the work completed. The type of documentation depends on the circumstances of the engagement, but should at least include the engagement letter, significant findings and issues, and communications to management regarding fraud or illegal acts that came to the accountant's attention.

Reporting on the Financial Statements

If an accountant reports on compiled financial statements, they should be accompanied by a written report. This report should contain the following items:

- *Title.* The title indicates that it is the accountant's compilation report.
- *Addressee.* The report is addressed based on the circumstances of the engagement.
- *Introductory paragraph.* Identifies the entity whose financial statements have been compiled, notes that the statements have been compiled, identifies the financial statements that have been compiled, specifies the dates or period covered by them, and includes a statement that the accountant has not audited or reviewed the financial statements and therefore does not express an opinion or provide any assurance about whether the financial statements are in accordance with the applicable financial reporting framework.
- *Management's responsibility.* States that management is responsible for the preparation and fair presentation of the financial statements in accordance with the applicable financial reporting framework, as well as for internal controls relevant to the preparation and presentation of the financial statements.
- *Accountant's responsibility.* State that the accountant's responsibility is to conduct the compilation in accordance with SSARS, as well as a statement that the objective of a compilation is to assist management in presenting financial information in the form of financial statements without obtaining or providing assurance that there are no material modifications that should be made to the financial statements.
- *Accountant's signature.* The signature of the accounting firm or the accountant.
- *Report date.* The date of the compilation report.

Examples of compilation reports are shown later under "Illustrations: Traditional Compilation Engagement."

NOTE: *Each page of the financial statements that were compiled by the accountant should be labeled "See accountant's compilation report" or "See independent accountant's compilation report."*

> NOTE: If financial statements are prepared in accordance with an OCBOA, they are not appropriate in form unless the financial statements include a description of the OCBOA, including a summary of significant differences from generally accepted accounting principles (GAAP).

If an entity requests that the accountant compile financial statements that omit substantially all disclosures, the accountant may still compile the financial statements, provided that the omissions are not, to the accountant's knowledge, intended to be misleading to statement users. When issuing such financial statements, the accountant should include in the compilation report a paragraph stating that management has elected to omit substantially all disclosures, that the omitted disclosures might influence user conclusions about the company's financial results, and that the financial statements are not designed for those who are not informed about such matters.

> NOTE: If management only elects to include a few disclosures, they should be labeled "Selected Information—Substantially All Disclosures Required by [identify the applicable financial reporting framework] Are Not Included."

Reporting When the Accountant Is Not Independent

When the accountant is issuing a compilation report but is not independent of the entity for which the report is being compiled, modify the last paragraph of the accountant's report to indicate a lack of independence, such as "I am not independent with respect to ABC Company." It is acceptable to elaborate on this statement and describe why the accountant is not independent, such as pointing out that the accountant has a direct financial interest in the entity, or a family member is employed by the entity.

Reporting When Compiled Financial Statements Are Not to Be Used By a Third Party

If there is no expectation that compiled financial statements are to be used by a third party, the accountant does not have to issue a compilation report. However, the accountant should include a reference on each page of the financial statements that restricts their use, such as "Restricted for Management's Use Only."

If the accountant learns that the financial statements have been distributed to third parties, then discuss the matter with management to determine the best course of action, which may include the return of the financial statements. If the accountant requests the return of the financial statements and the client does not comply, then the accountant should notify the third parties that the financial statements were not intended for use by third parties.

Emphasizing a Matter

The accountant may elect to emphasize a matter disclosed in the financial statements. If so, include explanatory information in a separate paragraph of the accountant's report. Examples of items that might be emphasized are uncertainties, significant transactions with other parties, important subsequent events, and the comparability of the financial statements with those of a prior period.

> NOTE: An emphasis paragraph is never required.

Departures from the Applicable Financial Reporting Framework

If an accountant becomes aware of a departure from the applicable financial reporting framework during a compilation engagement that is material, and it is appropriate to modify the standard report, then disclose the departure in a separate paragraph, as well as the effects of the departure (if such effects have been determined). If the modification of the standard report does not adequately reveal the deficiency, the accountant should withdraw from the compilation engagement and provide no further services regarding those financial statements.

Restricting the Compilation Report

An accountant's report may be restricted to specific parties; this should be done when the subject matter of the report or the presentation being reported on is based on criteria in contracts or regulations that are not in conformity with an applicable financial reporting framework (since they are developed for the parties to the contract or regulatory agency responsible for the provisions).

If a report is restricted, the accountant should include a paragraph at the end of the report stating that the report is intended solely for the information and use of the specified parties.

If the accountant issues a combined report that addresses subjects requiring a use restriction and subject matter not requiring such a restriction, then the accountant should apply the use restriction to the entire report.

If a restricted-use report is included in a general-use report, then the restricted-use report is still restricted, and the general-use report is still available for general use.

If the accountant is asked to include additional parties in the distribution of a restricted-use report, and the engagement has already been completed, the accountant may agree to do so, based on such criteria as their identity, knowledge of disclosure criteria, and the intended use of the report. If so, the accountant should obtain acknowledgment from the other parties of their understanding of the nature of the engagement, disclosure criteria, and the related report. This may require reissuance of the report (though not with a new report date). If the accountant instead issues written acknowledgment that the new parties have been added as specified parties, then he or she should state that no procedures have been performed subsequent to the report date.

NOTE: The accountant is not responsible for controlling a client's distribution of restricted-use reports.

An Entity's Ability to Continue as a Going Concern

If the accountant learns that an uncertainty may exist about an entity's ability to continue as a going concern for a period not to exceed one year beyond the date of the compiled financial statements, then the accountant should request that management consider the possible effects of this uncertainty on the financial statements, including the need for a related disclosure of this condition. The accountant should then consider the reasonableness of management's response; if the response is unreasonable, the accountant should withdraw from the engagement and provide no further services relating to those financial statements.

It is acceptable to emphasize an uncertainty about an entity's ability to continue as a going concern.

Subsequent Events

The accountant may become aware of a material subsequent event either during the performance of compilation procedures or subsequent to the date of the compilation report but prior to its release. If so, request that management consider the effects of the event on the financial statements and related disclosures. If the subsequent event is not adequately accounted for in the financial statements or related disclosures, and management's response is not reasonable, then withdraw from the engagement and provide no further services relating to those financial statements.

If the subsequent event has a material impact on the financial statements, then consider including an explanatory paragraph in the compilation report.

Subsequent Discovery of Facts Existing at the Report Date

The accountant may become aware of facts subsequent to the report date that may have existed at that date, and which might have caused him or her to believe that information supplied by the entity was incomplete or incorrect. If so, determine whether the information is reliable and whether the facts existed as of the report date, discuss the matter with management, and request cooperation with the investigation. Obtain additional or revised information if the effect of the matter is such that the accountant's report or the financial statements would have been affected, and the accountant believes that persons using the financial statements would attach importance to the information.

If the accountant decides that further action should be taken to prevent further use of the financial statements or the accountant's report, then advise the client to disclose these facts and their impact to those persons using or likely to use the financial statements. This may call for the issuance of revised financial statements, or inclusion of the disclosure in the financial statements of the subsequent period (if their issuance is imminent), or notification that the existing financial statements should not be used and that revised statements will be issued shortly.

If the client refuses to make these disclosures, then notify appropriate personnel at the highest levels within the entity of the refusal and that the accountant will take immediate steps to prevent further use of the financial statements and accountant's report. Barring alternative recommendations by the accountant's attorney, the accountant should take these steps:

1. Notify the client that the accountant's report can no longer be associated with the financial statements.
2. Notify those regulatory agencies having jurisdiction over the client that they can no longer rely on the accountant's report.
3. Notify each known user of the financial statements that the financial statements and the accountant's report can no longer be used.

These notifications should include a description of the subsequently acquired information and its effect on the financial statements. The descriptions should be as factual as possible, and avoid any comments about the conduct or motives of any persons involved. Alternatively, if the client has not cooperated, it is acceptable not to describe the subsequently acquired information, but rather to indicate that the client has not cooperated in substantiating the information, and that, assuming the information is true, the accountant believes the compilation report can no longer be used or associated with the financial statements. It is not necessary to make this disclosure unless the accountant believes the financial statements are likely to be misleading.

Supplementary Information

If the compiled financial statements are accompanied by supplementary information, the accountant should indicate the degree of responsibility that he or she is taking for this information. If the accountant has compiled the supplementary information, then refer to the supplementary information in the accountant's report or issue a separate report for this information. If a separate report is issued for this purpose, state in it that the other information accompanying the financial statements is only presented for the purposes of additional analysis, and that the information has been compiled from information that is the representation of management, without audit or review, and that the accountant does not express an opinion or provide any assurance on the information. Also, see the "Interpretations" section of this chapter.

Communicating to Management and Others

When the accountant is made aware that fraud or illegal acts may have occurred, he or she should bring the issue to the attention of management, though it is not necessary to report illegal acts that are clearly inconsequential. If fraud or an illegal act involves senior management, then notification goes to a higher level within the entity. If fraud or an illegal act involves an owner of the entity, the accountant should consider resigning from the engagement. Further, whenever there is evidence of fraud or an illegal act, the accountant should consider consulting with legal counsel.

Communication of these matters can be oral or in writing. If oral, the accountant should document the conversation.

NOTE: There may be a duty to disclose fraud or illegal acts to outside parties to comply with legal and regulatory requirements, or in response to a subpoena, or to a successor accountant when the successor decides to communicate with the predecessor accountant.

Change in Engagement from Audit or Review to Compilation

An accountant may originally be engaged to audit or review an entity's financial statements, and then be requested, before the completion of the engagement, to change the engagement to a compilation. Before agreeing to this change, consider the following:

- The reason for the request, especially the implications of the scope restriction.
- The remaining incremental effort and cost required to complete the audit or review.

If the audit or review procedures are substantially complete or the completion cost is insignificant, the accountant should consider the propriety of accepting a change to a compilation engagement.

A change in circumstances impacting the entity's need for an audit or review, or a misunderstanding about the nature of the engagement, is a reasonable basis for requesting an engagement change to compilation services. If the accountant accepts the engagement change and issues a report, the report should not refer to the original engagement and audit or review procedures performed, or to the scope limitations resulting from the change.

NOTE: The accountant is normally precluded from issuing a compilation report if the client did not provide a signed representation letter as part of an audit or review, or if the accountant has been prohibited from corresponding with the entity's legal counsel as part of an audit.

REVIEW OF FINANCIAL STATEMENTS

The accountant is required to comply with the following provisions when he or she has been engaged to review financial statements, except for the review of interim financial statements if the following information is correct:

1. The entity's latest annual financial statements were audited by the accountant or a predecessor.

2. The accountant either has been engaged to audit the entity's current year financial statements or audited the entity's latest annual financial statements and, when it is expected that the current year financial statements will be audited, the appointment of another accountant to audit the current year financial statements is not effective prior to the beginning of the period covered by the review.
3. The entity prepares its interim financial information in accordance with the same financial reporting framework as that used to prepare the annual financial statements.

Where the latter situations apply, the accountant should perform reviews in accordance with Standard 100, *Interim Financial Information.*

Establishing an Understanding

An accountant should establish a written understanding with management for a review engagement. This document should include the following items:

- *Objective.* To obtain limited assurance that there are no material modifications to be made to the financial statements.
- *Management responsibilities.* Management is responsible for the preparation and fair presentation of the financial statements. Management is also responsible for internal controls relevant to the preparation and presentation of the financial statements, as well as for the prevention and detection of fraud. Further, management is responsible for ensuring that the entity complies with applicable laws and regulations. Management is also responsible for making all financial records available to the accountant, and will provide the accountant with a representation letter.
- *Accountant responsibilities.* The accountant is responsible for conducting the engagement in accordance with SSARSs issued by AICPA.
- *Review inclusions.* A review primarily involves applying analytical procedures to management's financial data and making inquiries of management. It is less in scope than an audit, which involves the expression of an opinion regarding the financial statements as a whole. A review does not involve gaining an understanding of an entity's internal control, nor of assessing fraud risk, testing accounting records, or the examination of source documents or other procedures performed in an audit. Thus, an accountant engaged in a review will not express an opinion regarding the financial statements as a whole.
- *Reliance regarding certain issues.* A review engagement cannot be relied upon to disclose errors, fraud, or illegal acts.
- *Material errors.* The accountant will inform management of any material errors or evidence of fraud or illegal acts, but need not report illegal acts that are clearly inconsequential.

A review engagement letter may include other matters, such as fees and billings, limitations on the liabilities of the parties, references to supplementary information, and additional services related to regulatory requirements.

A sample review engagement letter is shown later under "Illustrations: Review Engagements."

Review Performance Requirements

In a review, the accountant performs procedures to accumulate review evidence that provides a reasonable basis for obtaining limited assurance that no material modifications need be made to the financial statements in order for them to be in conformity with the applicable financial reporting framework. These procedures are tailored to the industry in which the client operates.

The accountant should have an understanding of the industry in which the client operates. He or she may accept a review engagement in an industry where the accountant has no previous experience, but then has a responsibility to obtain the required level of knowledge.

The accountant should also obtain sufficient knowledge about the client's business and accounting principles and practices to determine appropriate review procedures. This understanding should encompass the client's organization, operating characteristics, assets, liabilities, revenue, and expenses. The accountant should take note of unusual client accounting policies and procedures.

Designing and Performing Review Procedures

The accountant designs and performs analytical procedures, makes inquiries, and performs other procedures to accumulate review evidence for obtaining limited assurance that no material modifications are needed for financial statements to be in conformity with the applicable financial reporting framework. These procedures should be focused in those areas where there are increased risks of misstatements.

Analytical procedures involve comparisons of the accountant's expectations to recorded amounts or derived ratios. The accountant develops expectations for this comparison by identifying and using plausible relationships that are reasonably expected to exist based on the accountant's knowledge of the client's industry and of the client. Sources of information for developing this expectation include financial information for comparable prior periods, forecasted results, relationships among types of financial information, industry information, and relationships between financial and nonfinancial information (such as sales per employee).

If the accountant's analytical procedures identify fluctuations or relationships that are inconsistent with other information, or which differ significantly from expected amounts, the accountant should investigate these issues through management inquiries and other procedures. The accountant does not have to corroborate management's responses with other evidence.

When conducting review procedures, the accountant should consider performing these steps:

1. Make inquiries of knowledgeable management regarding:

    a. Whether the financial statements were prepared in conformity with the applicable financial reporting framework
    b. The accounting principles, practices, and procedures for summarizing and accumulating accounting transactions
    c. Unusual or complex situations that impact the financial statements
    d. Significant transactions occurring near the end of the reporting period
    e. The status of uncorrected misstatements that were identified during the previous engagement
    f. Questions that arose during other review procedures
    g. Material events subsequent to the date of the financial statements
    h. Fraud affecting the entity which could have a material effect on the financial statements
    i. Significant journal entries
    j. Communications from regulatory agencies

2. Make inquiries of those charged with governance regarding actions taken at stockholder meetings, and the board of directors and its committees.
3. Read the financial statements and consider whether they appear to conform with the applicable financial reporting framework.
4. Obtain reports from those accountants who have been engaged to audit or review the entity's financial statements.

NOTE: The accountant is not required to corroborate management's responses with other information, but should consider the reasonableness and consistency of management's responses in view of the results of other procedures, as well as the accountant's knowledge of the client's business and industry.

If the accountant becomes aware that some information is incorrect, incomplete, or unsatisfactory in some other way, he or she should request that management consider the effect of these matters on the financial statements. If the accountant believes the financial statements may be materially misstated, then perform additional procedures to obtain limited assurance that there are no material modifications required. If the accountant instead concludes that the financial statements are materially misstated, then consider whether modification of the standard report is sufficient for disclosing the issue, or whether he or she should withdraw from the review engagement and provide no further services regarding those financial statements.

Management must provide written representations for all financial statements and periods covered by the accountant's review report, as of the date of the accountant's review report. The letter should be addressed to the accountant and signed by those members of management who are responsible for and knowledgeable about the topics in the representation letter. Typically, the CEO and CFO sign the representation letter. The accountant should receive the signed letter from management before releasing the report.

The representation letter should at least include these items:

- Management acknowledges that it is responsible for the preparation and presentation of the financial statements in accordance with the applicable financial reporting framework.
- Management believes that the financial statements are fairly presented in accordance with the applicable financial reporting framework.
- Management acknowledges that it is responsible for the internal controls relevant to the preparation and presentation of the financial statements.
- Management acknowledges that it is responsible for preventing and detecting fraud.
- Management has (or does not have) knowledge of any fraud affecting the entity that involves management or others where fraud could have a material effect on the financial statements.
- Management responds fully and truthfully to all inquiries.
- The information provided is complete.
- Information is provided concerning subsequent events.

The representation letter is usually modified to include additional representations that are specific to its business or industry.

If the accountant does not issue the review report for a significant period of time after completing all review-related inquiries and procedures, he or she should consider obtaining an updated representation letter from the client. Further, if the client requests that the accountant reissue the review report on the financial statements of a prior period and those statements will be comparatively presented with the reviewed financial statements of a later period, this calls for an updated representation letter.

Several sample representation letters are noted later under "Illustrations: Review Engagement."

NOTE: If the current management team was not present during all periods being reported on, the accountant should still obtain written representations from them for all periods addressed by the review report.

Documentation in a Review Engagement

The accountant should provide sufficient documentation of a review engagement to clearly show the work performed, the review evidence obtained and its source, and the accountant's conclusions. It should include the following:

- *Engagement letter.* The signed engagement letter.
- *Procedures.* The analytical procedures performed, including the accountant's expectations, comparison results, and management's responses to the accountant's inquiries about inconsistent relationships or fluctuations from expected amounts. Also note any additional review procedures due to unexpected differences in initial results.
- *Significant matters.* The significant matters covered in the accountant's inquiry procedures and managements' responses.
- *Significant findings.* Any findings that the accountant considers to be significant.
- *Communications.* Any written or oral communications with management regarding fraud or illegal acts that came to the accountant's attention.
- *Representation letter.*

NOTE: An oral explanation is not sufficient support for an accountant's work, but it can be used to clarify information contained in the documentation.

Reporting on the Financial Statements

The accountant should accompany reviewed financial statements with a written report that includes the following information:

- *Title.* The report title indicates that it is the accountant's review report and includes the word *independent*, such as "Independent Accountant's Review Report."
- *Addressee.* The report is addressed as required under the terms of the engagement.
- *Introductory paragraph.* The introductory paragraph identifies the entity whose financial statements were reviewed, states that the financial statements were reviewed, identifies which statements were reviewed, specifies the date or period covered by the financial statements, states that a review primarily involves applying analytical procedures to management's financial data and making inquiries of management, and states that a review is substantially less in scope than an audit; the objective of an audit is to express an opinion regarding the financial statements as a whole, and that the accountant does not express such an opinion.
- *Management's responsibility.* States that management is responsible for the preparation and fair presentation of the financial statements in accordance with the applicable financial reporting framework, as well as for the internal controls relevant to the preparation and fair presentation of the financial statements.

- *Accountant's responsibility.* States that the accountant's responsibility is to conduct the review in accordance with SSARSs issued by AICPA. Also, states that those standards require the accountant to perform the procedures to obtain limited assurance that there are no material modifications that should be made to the financial statements. Further, states that the accountant believes that the results of his or her procedures provide a reasonable basis for his or her report.
- *Engagement results.* States that, based on his or her review, the accountant is not aware of any material modifications that should be made to the financial statements so that they will be in conformity with the applicable financial reporting framework, other than those modifications listed in the report.
- *Accountant's signature.* The signature of the accountant or accounting firm.
- *Report date.* The date of the review report.

In addition, include a reference on each page of the financial statements, such as "See Independent Accountant's Review Report."

It is acceptable to issue a review report on just one financial statement, such as a balance sheet, if the scope of the accountant's inquiries and procedures have not been restricted.

If a client prepares financial statements in accordance with an OCBOA, they are not appropriate in form unless the statements include a description of the OCBOA, a summary of significant accounting policies, and a summary of the primary differences from GAAP, as well as informative disclosures similar to those required by GAAP.

Several sample review reports are noted later under "Illustrations: Review Engagement."

NOTE: *If the accountant is unable to complete the procedures and inquiries needed for a review engagement, he or she should consider whether it is appropriate to issue a compilation report instead.*

Emphasizing a Matter

It is acceptable for an accountant to emphasize a matter in the review report, though it should be presented in a separate paragraph. Examples of such items are uncertainties, significant transactions with related parties, and important subsequent events. An emphasis paragraph is never required; it is added solely at the accountant's discretion.

Departures from the Applicable Financial Reporting Framework

If an accountant becomes aware of a departure from the applicable financial reporting framework that is material to the financial statements, the accountant should consider whether modification of the accompanying report is an adequate disclosure of the issue. If so, the issue can be disclosed in a separate paragraph of the report. The accountant does not have to determine the effects of this departure if management has not done so, as long as the accountant states in the report that he or she has not made such a determination.

If the accountant believes that modification of the standard report is not an adequate method for indicating the deficiency, the accountant should withdraw from the review engagement and provide no further services regarding those financial statements.

Restricting the Use of the Review Report

If an accountant's report is not restricted to specific parties, then it is for *general use*. The report is for *restricted use* if it is intended only for specific third parties. The accountant should designate the review report as being for restricted use when the report or presentation is based on disclosure criteria contained in a contractual agreement or regulatory provisions that are not in conformity with an applicable financial reporting framework. A restricted report should contain a separate paragraph at the end of the report that includes a statement indicating that the report is intended solely for the information and use of the specified parties, which identifies the parties to whom the report is restricted, and which states that the report is not intended to be and should not be used by anyone other than the specified parties.

If a review report contains subject matter or presentations that are for restricted use and other subject matter or presentations that are for combined use, then restrict the entire combined report to the parties specified in the restricted part of the report.

If the accountant is asked to consider adding other parties to the recipient list for a restricted report and this is subsequent to the completion of the engagement, the accountant may agree to do so, based on the consideration of such factors as identity of the other parties, their knowledge of the basis of the measurement or disclosure criteria, and the intended use of the report. If so, the accountant should obtain written acknowledgement from the parties of their understanding of the nature of the engagement, the measurement or disclosure criteria, and the related report.

If the other parties are added subsequent to the accountant's issuance of the review report, he or she may reissue the report or provide other written acknowledgement that the other parties have been added (and state that no procedures have been performed subsequent to the date of the report). If the accountant reissues the report, do not change the report date.

NOTE: The accountant is not responsible for controlling a client's distribution of restricted-use reports.

Going Concern Issues

During a review, it may come to the accountant's attention that there is uncertainty regarding an entity's ability to continue as a going concern for a reasonable period of time (not to exceed one year past the date of the financial statements). If so, the accountant should request that management consider the effects of the going concern uncertainty on the financial statements.

The accountant should consider the reasonableness of management's resulting response, including the adequacy of any related disclosures. If the accountant concludes that management's conclusions are unreasonable or the related disclosure of the situation is not adequate, he or she should consider whether modification of the review report is adequate to disclose the going concern issue. If so, the accountant should disclose the information in a separate paragraph of the report. If the accountant concludes that modification of the review report is not adequate, then he or she should withdraw from the review engagement and provide no further services regarding those financial statements.

NOTE: it is also acceptable to emphasize an uncertainty about a going concern issue, provided that the uncertainty is disclosed in the financial statements. An emphasis paragraph is added solely at the accountant's discretion.

Subsequent Events

The accountant may become aware of subsequent events that have a material effect on the reviewed financial statements. If so, request that management consider the effects on the financial statements. If the accountant concludes that the subsequent event is not adequately accounted for in the financial statements, he or she should determine whether modification of the standard review report would adequately disclose the information. If so, disclose the subsequent events in a separate paragraph of the report. If the accountant concludes that modification of the standard review report is not adequate, then withdraw from the review engagement and provide no further services regarding those financial statements.

The accountant may also emphasize a subsequent event in the review report simply as a point of emphasis; this is acceptable, provided that the matter is disclosed in the financial statements.

Subsequent Discovery of Facts Existing at the Report Date

Subsequent to the review report date, the accountant may become aware of facts that may have existed on the report date, which may have caused him or her to believe the information originally supplied by the entity was unsatisfactory.

After the date of the accountant's review report, the accountant has no obligation to perform other review procedures, unless new information comes to his or her attention. However, if such new information arises, the accountant should determine whether it is reliable and whether it existed at the report date. The accountant should request cooperation from management to investigate the new information. If the information would have affected the review report or the financial statements, and the accountant believes the persons using the financial statements would consider the information to be important, then perform additional procedures to obtain limited assurance that there are no material modifications to be made to the financial statements.

If the accountant concludes that the review report or financial statements should be blocked from further use, then advise the client to disclose the newly discovered information and their impact on the financial statements. There are three ways to handle this disclosure:

1. If the impact of the newly discovered information on the financial statements can be determined quickly, then issue revised financial statements and the review report, including reasons for the revision that are included in a note to the financial statements.
2. If financial statements for a subsequent period are about to be issued, then disclose the revision in those statements, rather than reissuing earlier statements.
3. If the impact of the newly discovered information cannot be determined quickly, then issuance of revised financial statements will likely be delayed; in this case, the client should notify those individuals known to be using or likely to use the financial statements. The notification should state that the financial statements should not be used, that revised statements will be issued, and that the accountant's review report will be issued as soon as practicable.

If the client refuses to make these disclosures, notify entity personnel at the highest levels of this refusal. State that, in the absence of disclosure by the client, the accountant will take steps to prevent further use of the financial statements and review report. These steps can include

- Client notification that the accountant's report can no longer be associated with the financial statements.
- Regulatory agency notification that the accountant's report should no longer be used.
- Individual user notification that the financial statements and the accountant's report should no longer be used.

Any disclosures made by the accountant to a third party should include a description of the nature of the subsequently obtained information and its effect on the financial statements. The accountant can indicate that the client has not cooperated with the accountant's attempt to substantiate the information, and that, if the information is true, the accountant believes the review report can no longer be used or associated with the financial statements. This disclosure should be as factual as possible, and avoid comments concerning the conduct or motives of any person.

NOTE: *Do not make this disclosure unless the accountant believes the financial statements to be misleading.*

Supplementary Information

If the financial statements are accompanied by supplementary information, the accountant should indicate the degree of responsibility that he or she is taking for it. The accountant includes an explanation of the supplementary information in either the review report or a separate report, which states that either:

- The supplementary data are presented only for purposes of additional analysis and have been subjected to the inquiry and analytical procedures applied in the review of the financial statements, and the accountant is not aware of any material modifications that should be made to it; or
- The supplementary data are presented only for purposes of additional analysis and have not been subjected to the inquiry and analytical procedures applied in the review of the financial statements, but were instead compiled from information that is the representation of management, without audit or review, and the accountant does not express an opinion or provide any assurance on the data.

Communication to Management and Others

If the accountant becomes aware during review procedures that fraud or illegal acts may have occurred, then bring the matter to the attention of management. If these acts involve senior management, then report the matter to those at a higher level within the entity, or those charged with governance. If these acts involve the owner of the business, then consider resigning from the engagement, and also consider consulting with legal counsel.

The communication may be oral or written; if oral, then document it.

It may be necessary to disclose the presence of fraud or illegal acts to outside parties in order to comply with legal and regulatory requirements, or to a successor accountant when the successor decides to initiate the communication, or in response to a subpoena.

NOTE: *The accountant does not need to bring illegal acts that are clearly inconsequential to the attention of management.*

Change in Engagement from Audit to Review

An accountant may be engaged to audit a client's financial statements, and then, before the completion of the audit, is requested to change the engagement to a review. Before agreeing to this change, the accountant should consider the reason for the client's request, and the additional audit effort and cost needed to complete the audit. If the audit procedures are substantially complete or additional costs are minimal, then consider the propriety of accepting a change in the engagement. Also, evaluate the possibility that information affected by the scope restriction may be incorrect, incomplete, or unsatisfactory.

NOTE: *When an accountant has been engaged to audit an entity's financial statements and has been prohibited from contacting the entity's legal counsel, the accountant is precluded from issuing a review report on the financial statements.*

A change in the entity's circumstances that affect its need for an audit, or a misunderstanding about the nature of an audit, are normally considered reasonable grounds for requesting a change in engagement.

If the accountant accepts the change to a review engagement and subsequently issues a review report, he or she should not refer to the original engagement, or any audit procedures performed, or scope limitations resulting from the changed engagement.

INTERPRETATIONS

Note: AR Section 80 covers compilation guidance and AR Section 90 covers guidance on reviews. The section on interpretations integrates related interpretations under AR Sections 9080 and 9090.

AR SECTION 9080 AND 9090 INTERPRETATION 1: REPORTING WHEN THERE ARE SIGNIFICANT DEPARTURES FROM GENERALLY ACCEPTED ACCOUNTING PRINCIPLES (ISSUED AUGUST 1981; REVISED NOVEMBER 2002; REVISED MAY 2004; REVISED JULY 2005)

The interpretation indicates that a statement in a compilation or review report that the financial statements are not in conformity with GAAP or OCBOA would be tantamount to expressing an adverse opinion on the financial statements taken as a whole; therefore, an accountant is precluded from making such a statement. Such an opinion can be expressed only in the context of an audit engagement. This interpretation does not preclude the accountant from emphasizing the limitation of the financial statements in a separate paragraph of the report. This separate paragraph is not, however, a substitute for disclosure of the specific GAAP or OCBOA departures or the effects of the departures.

AR SECTION 9080 AND 9090 INTERPRETATION 2: REPORTING ON TAX RETURNS (ISSUED NOVEMBER 1982; REVISED FEBRUARY 2008)

SSARS do not apply to tax returns. The interpretation exempts the accountant from compiling the financial information contained in a tax return, although the accountant may accept an engagement to compile or review such a presentation.

AR SECTION 9080 AND 9090 INTERPRETATION 3: ADDITIONAL PROCEDURES (ISSUED MARCH 1983; REVISED OCTOBER 2000; REVISED NOVEMBER 2002; REVISED MAY 2004)

The interpretation permits the accountant to perform additional procedures in a compilation or review engagement without requiring the accountant to change the engagement level. However, the accountant may consider including these additions in a written agreement with the client.

AR SECTION 9080 INTERPRETATION 4: DIFFERENTIATING A FINANCIAL STATEMENT PRESENTATION FROM A TRIAL BALANCE (ISSUED SEPTEMBER 1990; REVISED OCTOBER 2000; REVISED FEBRUARY 2008)

The interpretation identifies the attributes of a financial statement and those of a trial balance. It assists an accountant in determining whether a financial statement presentation is a financial statement, requiring compliance with the provisions of SSARS 1, or a trial balance that does not require compliance with the provisions of SSARS 1. It is useful to modify a presentation to eliminate features in the presentation that blur the distinction between a financial statement and a trial balance.

AR Section 9080 Interpretation 5 and AR Section 9090 Interpretation 4: Submitting Draft Financial Statements (September 1990; Revised October 2000)

Except in cases when the financial statements are not expected to be used by a third party (management-use-only financial statements), the interpretation prohibits an accountant from submitting draft financial statements without intending to submit those financial statements in final form accompanied by an appropriate compilation or review report. This interpretation requires that draft financial statements be so marked and suggests that an accountant document the reasons why he or she intended to submit, but never submitted final financial statements, should that situation occur.

AR Section 9080 Interpretation 6 and AR Section 9090 Interpretation 5: Reporting When Financial Statements Contain a Departure from Promulgated Accounting Principles That Prevents the Financial Statements From Being Misleading (Issued February 1991; Revised October 2000; Revised November 2002; Revised May 2004; Revised July 2005)

The interpretation addresses Rule 203, "Accounting Principles" of the AICPA *Code of Professional Conduct*, which prohibits a member from expressing an opinion that financial statements are presented in conformity with GAAP if the member is aware that the statements contain a departure from an authoritative pronouncement (such as a FASB Statement or Interpretation). If the statements contain a departure from an authoritative pronouncement, and the member can demonstrate that due to unusual circumstances compliance with the pronouncement would render the financial statements misleading, the member can comply with Rule 203 by describing in the report the departure; its approximate effects, if practicable; and the reasons why compliance with an authoritative pronouncement would result in misleading statements.

The interpretation indicates that if the circumstances contemplated by Rule 203 exist in a review engagement, the accountant's review opinion should be unmodified, but the accountant's review report should be modified to contain a separate paragraph, including the information required by Rule 203. The interpretation clarifies that Rule 203 does not apply to compilation engagements. If the circumstances contemplated by Rule 203 exist in a compilation engagement, an accountant should follow the guidance in paragraphs 56 through 58 of SSARS 1 for reporting on a compilation of financial statements with a GAAP departure.

AR Section 9080 Interpretation 7: Applicability of Statements on Standards for Accounting and Review Services to Litigation Services (Issued May 1991; Revised October 2000; Revised February 2008)

SSARS do not apply to financial statements submitted in litigation services that involve pending or potential proceedings before a court, regulatory body, or governmental authority (or the agent of any of these) such as a grand jury or an arbitrator (mediator) when the:

- Accountant is an expert witness or a "trier of fact" (or an agent for one).

- Accountant's work is subject to detailed analysis and challenge by each party to the dispute.
- Accountant is engaged by the attorney and protected by the attorney's work product privilege.

SSARS apply to litigation service engagements when the accountant submits unaudited financial statements when the proceedings do not allow recipients the opportunity to challenge the accountant's work, or when the accountant is specifically engaged to submit financial statements that are the representation of management.

AR SECTION 9080 INTERPRETATION 8: APPLICABILITY OF STATEMENT ON STANDARDS FOR ACCOUNTING AND REVIEW SERVICES WHEN PERFORMING CONTROLLERSHIP OR OTHER MANAGEMENT SERVICES (ISSUED JULY 2002)

An accountant who is:

- In the practice of public accounting,
- Providing an entity with controllership or other management services that involve the submission of financial statements, and
- *Not* a stockholder, partner, director, officer, or employee of the entity

must follow the performance and reporting requirements of SSARS 1, including any requirement to disclose the lack of independence. (If the financial statements are for management's use only, the accountant should follow the guidance as presented in "Fundamental Requirements.") A public accountant who provides such controllership services but is also a stockholder, partner, director, officer, or employee of the entity may either comply with SSARS 1's requirements or communicate the accountant's relationship to the entity, preferably in writing. An example of such a communication is as follows:

> The accompanying balance sheet of Company X as of December 31, 20XX, and the related statements of income and cash flows for the year then ended have been prepared by [*name of accountant*], CPA. I have prepared such financial statements in my capacity [*describe capacity, for example, as a director*] of Company X.

If an accountant is not engaged in the practice of public accounting, the issuance of a report under SSARS would be inappropriate. However, the accountant may communicate the accountant's relationship to the entity, using a communication similar to the above example.

Accountants may also wish to refer to Ruling 10, "Submission of Financial Statements by a Member in Public Practice," in the AICPA's *Code of Professional Conduct* for additional guidance.

AR SECTION 9080 INTERPRETATION 9: USE OF THE LABEL "SELECTED INFORMATION—SUBSTANTIALLY ALL DISCLOSURES REQUIRED BY GENERALLY ACCEPTED ACCOUNTING PRINCIPLES ARE NOT INCLUDED" (ISSUED DECEMBER 2002)

When more than a few required disclosures are included in the financial statements, the notes that are presented should not be labeled as "Selected Information—Substantially All Disclosures Required by Generally Accepted Accounting Principles Are Not Included." Instead, the omitted notes should be treated as GAAP departures.

AR Section 9080 Interpretation 10: Omission of the Display of Comprehensive Income in a Compilation (Issued September 2003; Revised May 2004; Revised July 2005; Revised June 2009)

If an element of comprehensive income exists, the display of comprehensive income is required by FASB Accounting Standards Codification (ASC) 220, *Comprehensive Income*, when a full set of financial statements is presented in conformity with GAAP. Such display can be omitted when the accountant issues a compilation report with substantially all disclosures omitted if the accountant identifies the omission in his or her report (or, for management-use-only engagements, the engagement letter). If the accountant performs a compilation and includes all disclosures other than the display of comprehensive income, that omission would be a GAAP departure.

Also, if an element of comprehensive income has not been calculated, this omission would also be a GAAP departure.

AR Section 9080 Interpretation 11 and AR Section 9090 Interpretation 6: Special-Purpose Financial Statements to Comply with Contractual Agreements or Regulatory Provisions (Issued December 2006)

When an accountant is compiling or reviewing financial statements that require a special basis of accounting, then the presentation should be in accordance with SSARS 1. If so, the report should include an explanation of what the financial statement is intended to present that this is not a complete presentation, and that the report is intended solely for the use of intended recipients. If the presentation is not in conformity with GAAP, then the explanation should also note the basis of presentation, that the presentation is not intended to be in conformity with GAAP, and significant interpretations made by management.

AR Section 9080 Interpretation 12 and AR Section 9090 Interpretation 7: Reporting on an Uncertainty, Including an Uncertainty about an Entity's Ability to Continue as a Going Concern (Issued February 2007; Revised February 2008; Revised June 2009)

Continuation of an entity as a going concern is assumed in financial reporting in the absence of significant information to the contrary. The accountant should follow the guidance in paragraphs 69 through 72 of Section 100 when considering an entity's ability to continue as a going concern as part of a compilation or review.

If an accountant becomes aware of a material uncertainty, this does not result in a modification to the standard report, provided that the financial statements appropriately disclose the issue.

AR Section 9080 Interpretation 13: Compilations of Financial Statements Prepared in Accordance with International Reporting Standards (Issued May 2008)

A report illustration of how an accountant would apply the reporting guidance in section 80 when reporting on financial statements presented in accordance with IFRSs is as follows:

Accountant's Compilation Report

[*Appropriate Salutation*]

I (*We*) have compiled the accompanying balance sheets of XYZ Company as of December 31, 20X2 and 20X1, and the related statements of income, retained earnings, and cash flows for the years then ended. I (*We*) have not audited or reviewed the accompanying financial statements and, accordingly, do not express an opinion or provide any assurance about whether the financial statements are in accordance with International Financial Reporting Standards as issued by the International Accounting Standards Board.

The management (*owners*) is (*are*) responsible for the preparation and fair presentation of the financial statements in accordance with International Financial Reporting Standards as issued by the International Accounting Standards Board and for designing, implementing, and maintaining internal control relevant to the preparation and fair presentation of the financial statements.

My (*Our*) responsibility is to conduct the compilation in accordance with the Statements on Standards for Accounting and Review Services issued by the American Institute of Certified Public Accountants. The objective of a compilation is to assist management in presenting financial information in the form of financial statements without undertaking to obtain or provide any assurance that there are no material modifications that should be made to the financial statements.

[*Signature of accounting firm or accountant, as appropriate*]

[*Date*]

When the accountant compiles financial statements that omit substantially all disclosures but are otherwise in conformity with IFRSs as issued by the International Accounting Standards Board (IASB), the accountant may wish to modify the third paragraph of the standard report as follows:

Management has elected to omit substantially all disclosures (and the statement of cash flows) required by International Financial Reporting Standards as issued by the International Accounting Standards Board. If the omitted disclosures and statement were included in the financial statements, they might influence the user's conclusions about the company's financial position, results of operations, and cash flows. Accordingly, these financial statements are not designed for those who are not informed about such matters.

Because IFRSs require an entity to disclose comparative information in respect of the previous comparative period for all amounts presented in the current year's financial statements, the failure to include such information in financial statements would be a departure from GAAP. An example of a paragraph that may be added to the accountant's compilation report is as follows:

Comparative information with respect to the year ended December 31, 20XX–1 has not been presented. International Financial Reporting Standards [or *IFRSs for SMEs*] as issued by the International Accounting Standards Board require an entity to disclose comparative information in respect of the previous comparative period for all amounts presented in the current year's financial statements.

When the accountant compiles financial statements that omit substantially all disclosures but are otherwise in conformity with IFRSs as issued by the IASB, the accountant may wish to modify the third paragraph of the standard report as follows:

Management has elected to omit substantially all disclosures (and the statement of cash flows and comparative financial information as of and for the year ended December 31, 20XX–1) required by International Financial Reporting Standards [or *IFRSs for SMEs*] as issued by the International Accounting Standards Board. If the omitted disclosures, statement, and comparative financial information were included in the financial statements, they might influence the user's conclusions about the company's financial position, results of operations, and cash flows. Accordingly, these financial statements are not designed for those who are not informed about such matters.

AR SECTION 9090 INTERPRETATION 8: REVIEWS OF FINANCIAL STATEMENTS PREPARED IN ACCORDANCE WITH INTERNATIONAL FINANCIAL REPORTING STANDARDS [ISSUE DATE: MAY 2008; REVISED: JUNE 2010; REVISED: AUGUST 2010; REVISED: DECEMBER 2010 (FORMERLY INTERPRETATION NO. 30 TO SECTION 100)]

A report illustration of how an accountant would apply the reporting guidance in AR Section 90 when reporting on financial statements presented in accordance with IFRSs is as follows:

Independent Accountant's Review Report

[*Appropriate Salutation*]

I (*We*) have reviewed the accompanying balance sheets of XYZ Company as of December 31, 20X2 and 20X1, and the related statements of income, retained earnings, and cash flows for the year then ended. A review includes primarily applying analytical procedures to management's (*owners'*) financial data and making inquiries of company management (*owners*). A review is substantially less in scope than an audit, the objective of which is the expression of an opinion regarding the financial statements as a whole. Accordingly, I (*we*) do not express such an opinion.

The management (*owners*) is (*are*) responsible for the preparation and fair presentation of the financial statements in accordance with International Financial Reporting Standards as issued by the International Accounting Standards Board and for designing, implementing, and maintaining internal control relevant to the preparation and fair presentation of the financial statements.

My (*Our*) responsibility is to conduct the reviews in accordance with Statements on Standards for Accounting and Review Services issued by the American Institute of Certified Public Accountants. Those standards require me (*us*) to perform procedures to obtain limited assurance that there are no material modifications that should be made to the financial statements. I (*We*) believe that the results of my (*our*) procedures provide a reasonable basis for our report.

Based on my (*our*) reviews, I am (*we are*) not aware of any material modifications that should be made to the accompanying financial statements in order for them to be in conformity with International Financial Reporting Standards as issued by the International Accounting Standards Board.

[*Signature of accounting firm or accountant, as appropriate*]

[*Date*]

Because IFRSs require an entity to disclose comparative information in respect of the previous comparative period for all amounts presented in the current year's financial statements, the failure to include such information in financial statements would be a departure from generally accepted accounting principles. An example of a paragraph that may be added to the accountant's review report is as follows:

Comparative information with respect to the year ended December 31, 20XX–1 has not been presented. International Financial Reporting Standards [or *IFRSs for SMEs*] as issued by the International Accounting Standards Board require an entity to disclose comparative information in respect of the previous comparative period for all amounts presented in the current year's financial statements.

AR Section 9090 Interpretation 10: Considerations Related to Reviews Performed in Accordance with International Standard on Review Engagements 2400, *Engagements to Review Financial Statements*, Issued by the International Audit and Assurance Standards Board [Issue Date: May 2008; Revised: June 2010; Revised: August 2010; Revised: December 2010 (Formerly Interpretation No. 30 to Section 100)]

An accountant performing a review of historical financial statements of a U.S. entity is required to follow the ARSC review standards. However, those standards do not prohibit an accountant from indicating that the review also was conducted in accordance with another set of review standards. In an engagement to review the historical financial statements in accordance with ISRE 2400, the accountant may perform the review in accordance with SSARSs as well as ISRE 2400. Such a review report may read as follows:

> I (*We*) have reviewed the accompanying balance sheets of XYZ Company as of December 31, 20X2 and 20X1, and the related statements of income, retained earnings, and cash flows for the years then ended. A review includes primarily applying analytical procedures to management (*owners'*) financial data and making inquiries of company management (*owners*). A review is substantially less in scope than an audit, the objective of which is the expression of an opinion regarding the financial statements as a whole. Accordingly, I (*we*) do not express such an opinion.
>
> The management (*owners*) is (*are*) responsible for the preparation and fair presentation of the financial statements in accordance with International Financial Reporting Standards as issued by the International Accounting Standards Board and for designing, implementing, and maintaining internal control relevant to the preparation and fair presentation of the financial statements.
>
> My (*Our*) responsibility is to conduct the reviews in accordance with Statements on Standards for Accounting and Review Services issued by the American Institute of Certified Public Accountants and in accordance with International Standard on Review Engagements (*ISRE 2400*) issued by the International Audit & Assurance Standards Board. Those standards require me (*us*) to perform procedures to obtain limited assurance that there are no material modifications that should be made to the financial statements. I (*We*) believe that the results of my (*our*) procedures provide a reasonable basis for our report.
>
> Based on my (*our*) reviews, I am (*we are*) not aware of any material modifications that should be made to the accompanying financial statements in order for them to be in conformity with International Financial Reporting Standards as issued by the International Accounting Standards Board.

If the report is for use only outside of the United States, the accountant is still required to apply SSARSs, except for requirements related to report form and content.

AR Section 9080 Interpretation 14: Compilations of Financial Statements Prepared in Accordance with a Financial Reporting Framework Generally Accepted in Another Country [Issue Date: May 2008; Revised: June 2010; Revised: August 2010; Revised: December 2010 (Formerly Interpretation No. 30 to Section 100)]

If the financial statements are intended for use only outside of the United States, the accountant may report using the standard form of US compilation report modified as appropriate to identify the applicable financial reporting framework, or alternatively, the accountant may report using the standard compilation report form and content of the other country. (See Interpretation No. 15 with respect to Considerations Related to Compilations Performed in

Accordance with International Standard on Related Services [ISRS] 4410, *Engagements to Compile Financial Statements*).

The standard compilation report used in another country, even when it appears similar to that used in the United States of America, may convey a different meaning and entail a different responsibility on the part of the accountant due to custom or culture. Issuing a standard compilation report of another country may require an understanding of local laws. When issuing the accountant's standard compilation report of another country, the accountant is required to obtain an understanding of applicable legal responsibilities, in addition to the compilation standards and accounting principles generally accepted in the other country, as indicated in paragraph .11 of Section 80. Therefore, depending on the nature and extent of the accountant's knowledge and experience, the accountant may wish to consult with persons having expertise in the reporting practices of the other country and associated legal responsibilities to obtain the understanding needed to issue that country's standard compilation report.

If the accountant's report is intended for use in the United States, the reporting requirements described in paragraphs .16–.19 of Section 80 would apply. Additionally, paragraph .31 of AR Section 80 states that a need for restriction on the use of the report may result from a number of circumstances, including, but not limited to, the purpose of the report and the potential for the report to be misunderstood when taken out of context in which it was intended to be used. Because of the nature of the basis of presentation of the financial statements there is a presumption that the report would be misunderstood or taken out of context in which it was intended to be used. In such instances, the accountant may use the following form of report:

Accountant's Compilation Report

[*Appropriate Salutation*]

I (*We*) have compiled the accompanying balance sheets of XYZ Company as of December 31, 20X2 and 20X1, and the related statements of income, retained earnings, and cash flows for the years then ended. I (*We*) have not audited or reviewed the accompanying financial statements and, accordingly, do not express an opinion or provide any assurance about whether the financial statements are in accordance with [*the financial reporting framework generally accepted in another country, including identification of the nationality of the framework*].

The management (*owners*) is (*are*) responsible for the preparation and fair presentation of the financial statements in accordance with [*the financial reporting framework generally accepted in another country, including identification of the nationality of the framework*] and for designing, implementing, and maintaining internal control relevant to the preparation and fair presentation of the financial statements.

My (*Our*) responsibility is to conduct the compilation in accordance with Statements on Standards for Accounting and Review Services issued by the American Institute of Certified Public Accountants. The objective of a compilation is to assist management in presenting financial information in the form of financial statements without undertaking to obtain or provide any assurance that there are no material modifications that should be made to the financial statements.

This report is intended solely for the information and the use of [*specified parties*] and is not intended to be and should not be used by anyone other than the specified parties.

[*Signature of accounting firm or accountant, as appropriate*]

[*Date*]

When the financial statements will be used both in and outside of the United States, nothing precludes the accountant from issuing two reports—a report to be used only outside of the United States and another report to be used in the United States.

AR Section 9080 Interpretation 15: Consideration Related to Compilations Performed in Accordance with International Standard on Related Services 4410, *Engagements to Compile Financial Statements*, of Section 80 [Issue Date: May 2008; Revised: June 2010; Revised: August 2010; Revised: December 2010 (Formerly Interpretation No. 30 to Section 100)]

The compilation standards issued by ARSC do not prohibit an accountant from indicating that the compilation also was conducted in accordance with another set of compilation standards. In an engagement to compile the historical financial statements in accordance with ISRS 4410, the accountant may perform the compilation in accordance with SSARSs as well as ISRS 4410. Such a compilation report may read as follows:

> I (*We*) have compiled the accompanying balance sheets of XYZ Company as of December 31, 20X2 and 20X1, and the related statements of income, retained earnings, and cash flows for the years then ended. I (*We*) have not audited or reviewed the accompanying financial statements and, accordingly, do not express an opinion or provide any assurance about whether the financial statements are in accordance with International Financial Reporting Standards as issued by the International Accounting Standards Board.
>
> The management (*owners*) is (*are*) responsible for the preparation and fair presentation of the financial statements in accordance with International Financial Reporting Standards as issued by the International Accounting Standards Board and for designing, implementing, and maintaining internal control relevant to the preparation and fair presentation of the financial statements.
>
> My (*Our*) responsibility is to conduct the compilation in accordance with Statements on Standards for Accounting and Review Services issued by the American Institute of Certified Public Accountants and in accordance with the International Standard on Related Services (ISRS 4410) issued by the International Audit & Assurance Standards Board applicable to compilation engagements. The objective of a compilation is to assist management in presenting financial information in the form of financial statements without undertaking to obtain or provide any assurance that there are no material modifications that should be made to the financial statements.

If the report is for use only outside of the United States, the accountant is still required to apply SSARSs, except for requirements related to report form and content.

AR Section 9090 Interpretation 9: Reviews of Financial Statements Prepared in Accordance with a Financial Reporting Framework Generally Accepted in Another Country [Issue Date: May 2008; Revised: June 2010; Revised: August 2010; Revised: December 2010 (Formerly Interpretation No. 30 to Section 100)]

If the financial statements are intended for use *only* outside of the United States, the accountant may report using the standard form of US review report modified as appropriate to identify the applicable financial reporting framework; or alternatively, the accountant may report using the standard review report form and content of the other country. (See Interpretation No. 10 with respect to Considerations Related to Reviews Performed in Accordance with International Standard on Review Engagements [ISRE] 2400, *Engagements to Review Financial Statements*).

The standard review report used in another country, even when it appears similar to that used in the United States of America, may convey a different meaning and entail a different responsibility on the part of the accountant due to custom or culture. Issuing a standard review report of another country may require an understanding of local laws. When issuing the accountant's standard review report of another country, the accountant is required to obtain an understanding of applicable legal responsibilities, in addition to the review standards and accounting principles generally accepted in the other country, as indicated in paragraph .13 of AR Section 90. Therefore, depending on the nature and extent of the accountant's knowledge and experience, the accountant may wish to consult with persons having expertise in the reporting practices of the other country and associated legal responsibilities to obtain the understanding needed to issue that country's standard review report.

If the accountant's report is intended for use in the United States of America, the reporting requirements described in paragraphs .27–.32 of Section 90 would apply. Additionally, paragraph .38 of Section 90 states that a need for restriction on the use of the report may result from a number of circumstances, including, but not limited to, the purpose of the report and the potential for the report to be misunderstood when taken out of context in which it was intended to be used. Because of the nature of the basis of presentation of the financial statements, there is a presumption that the report would be misunderstood or taken out of the context in which it was intended to be used. In such instances, the accountant may use the following form of report:

Independent Accountant's Review Report

[*Appropriate Salutation*]

I (*We*) have reviewed the accompanying balance sheets of XYZ Company as of December 31, 20X2 and 20X1, and the related statements of income, retained earnings, and cash flows for the year then ended. A review includes primarily applying analytical procedures to management's (*owners'*) financial data and making inquiries of company management (*owners*). A review is substantially less in scope than an audit, the objective of which is the expression of an opinion regarding the financial statements as a whole. Accordingly, I (*we*) do not express such an opinion.

The management (*owners*) is (*are*) responsible for the preparation and fair presentation of the financial statements in accordance with [*the financial reporting framework generally accepted in another country, including identification of the nationality of the framework*] and for designing, implementing, and maintaining internal control relevant to the preparation and fair presentation of the financial statements.

My (*Our*) responsibility is to conduct the reviews in accordance with Statements on Standards for Accounting and Review Services issued by the American Institute of Certified Public Accountants. Those standards require me (*us*) to perform procedures to obtain limited assurance that there are no material modifications that should be made to the financial statements. I (*We*) believe that the results of my (*our*) procedures provide a reasonable basis for our report.

Based on my (*our*) reviews, I am (*we are*) not aware of any material modifications that should be made to the accompanying financial statements in order for them to be in conformity with [*the financial reporting framework generally accepted in another country, including identification of the nationality of the framework*].

This report is intended solely for the information and the use of [*specified parties*] and is not intended to be and should not be used by anyone other than the specified parties.

[*Signature of accounting firm or accountant, as appropriate*]

[*Date*]

When the financial statements will be used both in and outside of the United States, nothing precludes the accountant from issuing two reports—a report to be used only outside of the United States and another report to be used in the United States.

AR Section 9080 Interpretation 16: Preparation of Financial Statements for Use by an Entity's Auditors (Issued December 2008).

When an entity engages an accountant to prepare unaudited financial statements, and then provides these statements to its outside auditors for the purposes of an annual audit, the outside auditors are not deemed to be using the financial statements.

AR Section 9080 Interpretation 17: Required Supplementary Information That Accompanies Compiled Financial Statements

(For information on this interpretation, see beginning section of this chapter on "Recent Developments." The illustrations from the Interpretations are included below)

The Required Supplementary Information Is Included and the Accountant Did Not Compile the Required Supplementary Information

[*Identify the applicable financial reporting framework (for example, accounting principles generally accepted in the United States of America)*] require that [*identify the required supplementary information*] on page XX be presented to supplement the basic financial statements. Such information, although not a part of the basic financial statements, is required by [*identify the designated accounting standard setter*] who considers it to be an essential part of financial reporting and for placing the basic financial statements in an appropriate operational, economic, or historical context. Such information was not audited, reviewed, or compiled by me (*us*) and, accordingly, I (*we*) do not express an opinion or provide any assurance on it.

The Required Supplementary Information Is Included, the Accountant Compiled the Required Supplemental Information and No Material Departures from the Prescribed Guidelines Regarding the Required Supplementary Information Have Been Identified

[*Identify the applicable financial reporting framework (for example, accounting principles generally accepted in the United States of America)*] require that [*identify the required supplementary information*] on page XX be presented to supplement the basic financial statements. Such information, although not a part of the basic financial statements, is required by [*identify the designated accounting standard setter*] who considers it to be an essential part of financial reporting and for placing the basic financial statements in an appropriate operational, economic, or historical context. Such information has been compiled by me (*us*) without audit or review and, accordingly, I (*we*) do not express an opinion or provide any assurance on it.

All Required Supplementary Information Omitted

Management has omitted [*describe the missing required supplementary information*] that [*identify the applicable financial reporting framework (for example, accounting principles generally accepted in the United States of America)*] require to be presented to supplement the basic financial statements. Such missing information, although not a part of the basic financial statements, is required by [*identify the designated accounting standard setter*] who considers it to be an essential part of financial reporting and for placing the basic financial statements in an appropriate operational, economic, or historical context.

Some Required Supplementary Information Is Omitted and Some Is Presented in Accordance with the Prescribed Guidelines Regarding the Required Supplementary Information

[*Identify the applicable financial reporting framework (for example, accounting principles generally accepted in the United States of America)*] require that [*identify the included supplementary information*] be presented to supplement the basic financial statements. Such information, although not a part of the basic financial statements, is required by [*identify designated accounting standard setter*], who considers it to be an essential part of financial reporting for placing the basic financial statements in an appropriate operational, economic, or historical context. Such information was not audited, reviewed, or compiled by me (us) and, accordingly, I (we) do not express an opinion or provide any assurance on it.

Management has omitted [*describe the missing required supplementary information*] that [*identify the applicable financial reporting framework*] require to be presented to supplement the basic financial statements. Such missing information, although not a part of the basic financial statements, is required by [*identify designated accounting standard setter*], who considers it to be an essential part of financial reporting for placing the basic financial statements in an appropriate operational, economic, or historical context.

Material Departures from the Prescribed Guidelines Regarding the Required Supplementary Information Were Identified While Compiling the Required Supplementary Information

[*Identify the applicable financial reporting framework (for example, accounting principles generally accepted in the United States of America)*] require that the [*identify the supplementary information*] on page XX be presented to supplement the basic financial statements. Such information, although not a part of the basic financial statements, is required by [*identify designated accounting standard setter*], who considers it to be an essential part of financial reporting for placing the basic financial statements in an appropriate operational, economic, or historical context. Such information was compiled by me (*us*) without audit or review and, accordingly, I (*we*) do not express an opinion or provide any assurance on it. However, during my (*our*) compilation, I (*we*) did become aware of the following material departures from the prescribed guidelines regarding the required supplementary information [*identify the required supplementary information and describe the material departures from the prescribed guidelines regarding the required supplementary information*].

AR Section 9090 Interpretation 11: Required Supplementary Information That Accompanies Reviewed Financial Statements [Issue Date: October 2011]

The interpretation states that "SSARS do not require the accountant to apply procedures to any information presented for supplementary analysis purposes, including required supplementary information."

However, the accountant may modify the accountant's review report by including a separate paragraph that:

- Refers to the required supplementary information and
- Explains the circumstances regarding its presentation.

Present that separate paragraph after the paragraph that reports the results of the engagement and may read as follows:

The Required Supplementary Information Is Included

[*Identify the applicable financial reporting framework (for example, accounting principles generally accepted in the United States of America)*] require that [*identify the required supplementary information*] on page XX be presented to supplement the basic financial statements. Such information, although not a part of the basic financial statements, is required by [*identify the designated accounting standard setter*], who considers it to be an essential part of financial reporting and for placing the basic financial statements in an appropriate operational, economic, or historical context. Such information was not audited, reviewed, or compiled by me (*us*) and, accordingly, I (*we*) do not express an opinion or provide any assurance on it.

All Required Supplementary Information Omitted

Management has omitted [*describe the missing required supplementary information*] that [*identify the applicable financial reporting framework (for example, accounting principles generally accepted in the United States of America)*] require to be presented to supplement the basic financial statements. Such missing information, although not a part of the basic financial statements, is required by [*identify the designated accounting standard setter*], who considers it to be an essential part of financial reporting and for placing the basic financial statements in an appropriate operational, economic, or historical context. The results of our review of the basic financial statements are not affected by this missing information.

Some Required Supplementary Information Is Omitted and Some Is Presented in Accordance with the Prescribed Guidelines Regarding the Required Supplementary Information

[*Identify the applicable financial reporting framework (for example, accounting principles generally accepted in the United States of America)*] require that [*identify the included supplementary information*] be presented to supplement the basic financial statements. Such information, although not a part of the basic financial statements, is required by [*identify designated accounting standard setter*], who considers it to be an essential part of financial reporting for placing the basic financial statements in an appropriate operational, economic, or historical context. Such information was not audited, reviewed, or compiled by me (*us*) and, accordingly, I (*we*) do not express an opinion or provide any assurance on it.

Management has omitted [*describe the missing required supplementary information*] that [*identify the applicable financial reporting framework*] require to be presented to supplement the basic financial statements. Such missing information, although not a part of the basic financial statements, is required by [*identify designated accounting standard setter*], who considers it to be an essential part of financial reporting for placing the basic financial statements in an appropriate operational, economic, or historical context. The results of our review of the basic financial statements are not affected by this missing information.

ILLUSTRATIONS: TRADITIONAL COMPILATION ENGAGEMENT

The following items are presented below, and are derived from SSARS 19:

TC-1.   Standard Engagement Letter for a Compilation
TC-2.   Engagement Letter for a Compilation Not Intended for Third Parties
TC-3.   Checklist for a Traditional Compilation Engagement
TC-4.   Standard Compilation Report
TC-5.   Standard Compilation Report Prepared on the Cash Basis of Accounting
TC-6.   Standard Compilation Report When the Accountant's Independence Has Been Impaired and the Accountant Does Not Determine the Reason for the Independence Impairment
TC-7.   Standard Compilation Report When the Accountant's Independence Has Been Impaired Due to the Accountant Having a Financial Interest in the Client and the Accountant Discloses the Reason for the Independence Impairment
TC-8.   Compilation Report with GAAP Departure

ILLUSTRATION TC-1. STANDARD ENGAGEMENT LETTER FOR A COMPILATION

[*Appropriate Salutation*]

This letter is to confirm our understanding of the terms and objectives of our engagement and the nature and limitations of the services we will provide.

We will perform the following services:

We will compile, from information you provide, the annual [*and interim, if applicable*] financial statements of ABC Company as of December 31, 20XZ, and issue an accountant's report thereon in accordance with Statements on Standards for Accounting and Review Services (SSARSs) issued by the American Institute of Certified Public Accountants (AICPA).

The objective of a compilation is to assist you in presenting financial information in the form of financial statements. We will utilize information that is your representation without undertaking to obtain or provide any assurance that there are no material modifications that should be made to the financial statements in order for the statements to be in conformity with [*the applicable financial reporting framework, (for example, accounting principles generally accepted in the United States of America)*].

You are responsible for:

1. The preparation and fair presentation of the financial statements in accordance with [*the applicable financial reporting framework (for example, accounting principles generally accepted in the United States of America)*]
2. Designing, implementing, and maintaining internal control relevant to the preparation and fair presentation of the financial statements
3. Preventing and detecting fraud
4. Identifying and ensuring that the entity complies with the laws and regulations applicable to its activities
5. Making all financial records and related information available to us

We are responsible for conducting the engagement in accordance with SSARSs issued by the AICPA.

A compilation differs significantly from a review or an audit of financial statements. A compilation does not contemplate performing inquiry, analytical procedures, or other procedures performed in a review. Additionally, a compilation does not contemplate obtaining an understanding of the entity's internal control; assessing fraud risk; testing accounting records by obtaining sufficient appropriate audit evidence through inspection, observation, confirmation, or the examination of source documents (for example, cancelled checks or bank images); or other procedures ordinarily performed in an audit. Accordingly, we will not express an opinion or provide any assurance regarding the financial statements being compiled.

Our engagement cannot be relied upon to disclose errors, fraud, or illegal acts. However, we will inform the appropriate level of management of any material errors, and of any evidence or information that comes to our attention during the performance of our compilation procedures that fraud may have occurred. In addition, we will report to you any evidence or information that comes to our attention during the performance of our compilation procedures regarding illegal acts that may have occurred, unless they are clearly inconsequential.

NOTE: *If, during the period covered by the engagement letter, the accountant's independence is or will be impaired, insert the following:*

We are not independent with respect to ABC Company. We will disclose that we are not independent in our compilation report.

If, for any reason, we are unable to complete the compilation of your financial statements, we will not issue a report on such statements as a result of this engagement.

Our fees for these services . . .

We will be pleased to discuss this letter with you at any time. If the foregoing is in accordance with your understanding, please sign the copy of this letter in the space provided and return it to us.

Sincerely yours,

_____

[*Signature of accountant*]

Acknowledged:
ABC Company

_____

President

_____

Date

ILLUSTRATION TC-2. ENGAGEMENT LETTER FOR A COMPILATION NOT INTENDED FOR THIRD-PARTY USE

[*Appropriate Salutation*]

This letter is to confirm our understanding of the terms and objectives of our engagement and the nature and limitations of the services we will provide.

We will perform the following services:

We will compile, from information you provide, the [*monthly, quarterly, or other frequency*] financial statements of ABC Company as of December 31, 20X1.

The objective of a compilation is to assist you in presenting financial information in the form of financial statements. We will use information that is your representation without undertaking to obtain or provide any assurance that there are no material modifications that should be made to the financial statements in order for the statements to be in conformity with [*the applicable financial reporting framework (for example, accounting principles generally accepted in the United States of America)*].

You are responsible for:

1. The preparation and fair presentation of the financial statements in accordance with [*the applicable financial reporting framework (for example, accounting principles generally accepted in the United States of America)*]
2. Designing, implementing, and maintaining internal control relevant to the preparation and fair presentation of the financial statements
3. Preventing and detecting fraud
4. Identifying and ensuring that the entity complies with the laws and regulations applicable to its activities
5. Making all financial records and related information available to us

We are responsible for conducting the engagement in accordance with SSARSs issued by the AICPA.

A compilation differs significantly from a review or an audit of financial statements. A compilation does not contemplate performing inquiry, analytical procedures, or other procedures performed in a review. Additionally, a compilation does not contemplate obtaining an understanding of the entity's internal control; assessing fraud risk; testing accounting records by obtaining sufficient appropriate audit evidence through inspection, observation, confirmation, or the examination of source documents (for example, cancelled checks or bank images); or other procedures ordinarily performed in an audit. Accordingly, we will not express an opinion or provide any assurance regarding the financial statements being compiled.

Our engagement cannot be relied upon to disclose errors, fraud, or illegal acts. However, we will inform the appropriate level of management of any material errors, and of any evidence or information that comes to our attention during the performance of our compilation procedures that fraud may have occurred. In addition, we will report to you any evidence or information that comes to our attention during the performance of our compilation procedures regarding illegal acts that may have occurred, unless they are clearly inconsequential.

The financial statements will not be accompanied by a report and are for management's use only and are not to be used by a third party.

NOTE: If, during the period covered by the engagement letter, the accountant's independence is or will be impaired, insert the following:

We are not independent with respect to ABC Company.

Our fees for these services . . .
We will be pleased to discuss this letter with you at any time.
If the foregoing is in accordance with your understanding, please sign the copy of this letter in the space provided and return it to us.

Sincerely yours,

_____

[*Signature of accountant*]

Acknowledged:
ABC Company

_____
President

_____
Date

ILLUSTRATION TC-3. CHECKLIST FOR A TRADITIONAL COMPILATION ENGAGEMENT

Step No.   *Action/Decision*

1. Obtain an understanding with the client, preferably in writing, about the engagement. (For a new client, determine if communication with the predecessor accountant is desirable.)
2. Acquire the necessary knowledge of the client industry's accounting principles and practices.
3. Acquire a general understanding of the nature of the client's business transactions, the form of the accounting records, the stated qualifications of the accounting personnel, the accounting basis used, and the form and content of the financial statements. (It is not necessary to make inquiries or perform other procedures; however, if the accountant becomes aware that information supplied by the entity is incorrect, incomplete, or unsatisfactory, the accountant should obtain additional or revised information.)
4. Read the financial statements and determine if they are appropriate in form and free from obvious material error.
5. Consider whether all disclosures required by GAAP are provided. If they are not, go to step 6. If they are, go to step 7.
6. If the client has engaged the accountant to prepare financial statements that omit all or substantially all of the disclosures required by GAAP, indicate this in a separate paragraph in the report. If most, but not all, disclosures are omitted, notes to the financial statements should be labeled "Selected Information—Substantially All Disclosures Required by Generally Accepted Accounting Principles Are Not Included."

7. Consider whether the financial statements contain departures from GAAP. If they do, go to step 8. If they do not, go to step 9.
8. Request the client to revise the financial statements. Failing that, consider modifying the report by adding a separate paragraph that describes the departure. If the effect of the departure has been determined by management or is known by the accountant, disclose the dollar effects in the report. (The report need not be modified for uncertainties, going concern matters, or inconsistencies if they are properly disclosed—see step 5.) Withdraw from the engagement if the departures are designed to mislead financial statement users.
9. Determine whether the firm is independent. If the firm is not, go to step 10. If the firm is, go to step 11.
10. If the firm is not independent, add a separate paragraph to the report stating "We are not independent with respect to XYZ Company."
11. Mark each page of the financial statements, including notes to the financial statements, "See Accountant's Compilation Report."
12. Sign and date (manual, stamped, electronic, or typed signature) the report using the date the compilation was completed.
13. Issue the financial statements and related compilation report.

NOTE: *This checklist is designed for a GAAP basis compilation. If the accounting basis is an OCBOA, questions should be added to address (1) disclosure of the basis of accounting and (2) appropriate titles for the financial statements.*

ILLUSTRATION TC-4. STANDARD COMPILATION REPORT

Accountants' Compilation Report

[*Appropriate Salutation*]

We have compiled the accompanying balance sheet of ABC Company as of December 31, 20XX, and the related statements of income, retained earnings, and cash flows for the year then ended. We have not audited or reviewed the accompanying financial statements and, accordingly, do not express an opinion or provide any assurance about whether the financial statements are in accordance with accounting principles generally accepted in the United States of America.

Management is responsible for the preparation and fair presentation of the financial statements in accordance with accounting principles generally accepted in the United States of America and for designing, implementing, and maintaining internal control relevant to the preparation and fair presentation of the financial statements.

Our responsibility is to conduct the compilation in accordance with Statements on Standards for Accounting and Review Services issued by the American Institute of Certified Public Accountants. The objective of a compilation is to assist management in presenting financial information in the form of financial statements without undertaking to obtain or provide any assurance that there are no material modifications that should be made to the financial statements.

[*Signature of accounting firm or accountant, as appropriate*]

[*Date*]

ILLUSTRATION TC-5. COMPILATION REPORT ON FINANCIAL REPORTS PREPARED IN ACCORDANCE WITH THE CASH BASIS OF ACCOUNTING

Accountant's Compilation Report

[*Appropriate Salutation*]

 I (*We*) have compiled the accompanying statement of assets and liabilities arising from cash transactions of XYZ Company as of December 31, 20XX, and the related statement of revenue collected and expenses paid for the year then ended. I (*We*) have not audited or reviewed the accompanying financial statements and, accordingly, do not express an opinion or provide any assurance about whether the financial statements are in accordance with the cash basis of accounting.

 The management (*owners*) is (*are*) responsible for the preparation and fair presentation of the financial statements in accordance with the cash basis of accounting and for designing, implementing, and maintaining internal control relevant to the preparation and fair presentation of the financial statements.

 My (*Our*) responsibility is to conduct the compilation in accordance with Statements on Standards for Accounting and Review Services issued by the American Institute of Certified Public Accountants. The objective of a compilation is to assist management in presenting financial information in the form of financial statements without undertaking to obtain or provide any assurance that there are no material modifications that should be made to the financial statements.

[*Signature of accounting firm or accountant, as appropriate*]

[*Date*]

The accountant may add the following paragraph after the conclusion paragraph when management has elected to omit substantially all disclosures, but the financial statements are otherwise in conformity with accounting principles generally accepted in the United States of America:

 Management has elected to omit substantially all of the disclosures required by accounting principles generally accepted in the United States of America. If the omitted disclosures were included in the financial statements, they might influence the user's conclusions about the company's financial position, results of operations, and cash flows. Accordingly, the financial statements are not designed for those who are not informed about such matters.

The accountant may add the following paragraph after the conclusion paragraph when management has elected to omit substantially all disclosures, but the financial statements are otherwise in conformity with the income tax basis of accounting:

 Management has elected to omit substantially all of the disclosures ordinarily included in financial statements prepared in accordance with the income tax basis of accounting. If the omitted disclosures were included in the financial statements, they might influence the user's conclusions about the company's assets, liabilities, equity, revenue, and expenses. Accordingly, the financial statements are not designed for those who are not informed about such matters.

> **ILLUSTRATION TC-6. ACCOUNTANT'S COMPILATION REPORT ON FINANCIAL STATEMENTS PREPARED IN ACCORDANCE WITH ACCOUNTING PRINCIPLES GENERALLY ACCEPTED IN THE UNITED STATES OF AMERICA WHEN THE ACCOUNTANT'S INDEPENDENCE HAS BEEN IMPAIRED, AND THE ACCOUNTANT DETERMINES TO NOT DISCLOSE THE REASON FOR THE INDEPENDENCE IMPAIRMENT**

Accountant's Compilation Report

[*Appropriate Salutation*]

I (*We*) have compiled the accompanying balance sheet of XYZ Company as of December 31, 20XX, and the related statements of income, retained earnings, and cash flows for the year then ended. I (*We*) have not audited or reviewed the accompanying financial statements and, accordingly, do not express an opinion or provide any assurance about whether the financial statements are in accordance with accounting principles generally accepted in the United States of America.

The management (*owners*) is (*are*) responsible for the preparation and fair presentation of the financial statements in accordance with accounting principles generally accepted in the United States of America and for designing, implementing, and maintaining internal control relevant to the preparation and fair presentation of the financial statements.

My (*Our*) responsibility is to conduct the compilation in accordance with Statements on Standards for Accounting and Review Services issued by the American Institute of Certified Public Accountants. The objective of a compilation is to assist management in presenting financial information in the form of financial statements without undertaking to obtain or provide any assurance that there are no material modifications that should be made to the financial statements.

I am (*we are*) not independent with respect to XYZ Company.

[*Signature of accounting firm or accountant, as appropriate*]

[*Date*]

> **ILLUSTRATION TC-7. COMPILATION REPORT WITH GAAP MEASUREMENT DEPARTURE WHERE THE ACCOUNTANT'S INDEPENDENCE HAS BEEN IMPAIRED DUE TO THE ACCOUNTANT HAVING A FINANCIAL INTEREST IN THE CLIENT AND THE ACCOUNTANT DETERMINES TO DISCLOSE THE REASON FOR THE INDEPENDENCE IMPAIRMENT**

Accountant's Compilation Report

[*Appropriate Salutation*]

I (*We*) have compiled the accompanying balance sheet of XYZ Company as of December 31, 20XX, and the related statements of income, retained earnings, and cash flows for the year then ended. I (*We*) have not audited or reviewed the accompanying financial statements and, accordingly, do not express an opinion or provide any assurance about whether the financial statements are in accordance with accounting principles generally accepted in the United States of America.

The management (*owners*) is (*are*) responsible for the preparation and fair presentation of the financial statements in accordance with accounting principles generally accepted in the United States of America and for designing, implementing, and maintaining internal control relevant to the preparation and fair presentation of the financial statements.

My (*Our*) responsibility is to conduct the compilation in accordance with Statements on Standards for Accounting and Review Services issued by the American Institute of Certified Public Accountants. The objective of a compilation is to assist management in presenting financial information in the form of financial statements without undertaking to obtain or provide any assurance that there are no material modifications that should be made to the financial statements.

I am (*we are*) not independent with respect to XYZ Company as during the year ended December 31, 20XX, I (*a member of the engagement team*) had a direct financial interest in XYZ Company.

[*Signature of accounting firm or accountant, as appropriate*]

[*Date*]

ILLUSTRATION TC-8. COMPILATION REPORT WITH GAAP MEASUREMENT DEPARTURE

Accountants' Compilation Report

[*Appropriate Salutation*]

We have compiled the accompanying balance sheet of ABC Company as of December 31, 20X2, and the related statements of income, retained earnings, and cash flows for the year then ended. We have not audited or reviewed the accompanying financial statements and, accordingly, do not express an opinion or provide any assurance about whether the financial statements are in accordance with accounting principles generally accepted in the United States of America.

Management is responsible for the preparation and fair presentation of the financial statements in accordance with accounting principles generally accepted in the United States of America and for designing, implementing, and maintaining internal control relevant to the preparation and fair presentation of the financial statements.

Our responsibility is to conduct the compilation in accordance with Statements on Standards for Accounting and Review Services issued by the American Institute of Certified Public Accountants. The objective of a compilation is to assist management in presenting financial information in the form of financial statements without undertaking to obtain or provide any assurance that there are no material modifications that should be made to the financial statements. During our compilation, we did become aware of a departure from accounting principles generally accepted in the United States of America that is described in the following paragraph.

As disclosed in Note X to the financial statements, generally accepted accounting principles require that land be stated at cost. Management has informed us that the company has stated its land at appraised value and that, if accounting principles generally accepted in the United States of America had been followed, the land account and stockholders' equity would have been decreased by $500,000.

[*Signature of accounting firm or accountant, as appropriate*]

[*Date*]

ILLUSTRATIONS: REVIEW ENGAGEMENT

The following items are presented below, and are derived from SSARS 19:

R-1. Review Engagement Letter
R-2. Checklist for a Review Engagement
R-3. Checklist for Change in Engagement from Audit/Review to Review/Compilation
R-4. Standard Review Report
R-5. Review Report on Financial Statements Prepared in Accordance with the Income Tax Basis of Accounting
R-6. Review Report with GAAP Departure
R-7. Illustrative Inquires for a Review
R-8. Suggested Analytical Procedures
R-9. Illustrative Representation Letter
R-10. Illustrative Updating Management Representative Letter

ILLUSTRATION R-1. REVIEW ENGAGEMENT LETTER

[*Appropriate Salutation*]

This letter is to confirm our understanding of the terms and objectives of our engagement and the nature and limitations of the services we will provide.

We will perform the following services:

We will review the financial statements of ABC Company as of December 31, 20X1, and issue an accountant's report thereon in accordance with Statements on Standards for Accounting and Review Services (SSARSs) issued by the American Institute of Certified Public Accountants (AICPA).

The objective of a review is to obtain limited assurance that there are no material modifications that should be made to the financial statements in order for the statements to be in accordance with [*the applicable financial reporting framework*].

You are responsible for:

1. The preparation and fair presentation of the financial statements in accordance with [*the applicable financial reporting framework*]
2. Designing, implementing, and maintaining internal control relevant to the preparation and fair presentation of the financial statements
3. Preventing and detecting fraud
4. Identifying and ensuring that the entity complies with the laws and regulations applicable to its activities
5. Making all financial records and related information available to us
6. Providing us, at the conclusion of the engagement, with a letter that confirms certain representations made during the review

We are responsible for conducting the engagement in accordance with SSARSs issued by the AICPA.

A review includes primarily applying analytical procedures to your financial data and making inquiries of company management. A review is substantially less in scope than an audit, the objective of which is the expression of an opinion regarding the financial statements as a whole. A review does not contemplate obtaining an understanding of the entity's internal control; assessing fraud risk; testing accounting records by obtaining sufficient appropriate audit evidence through inspection, observation, confirmation, or the examination of source documents (for example, canceled checks or bank images); or other procedures ordinarily performed in an audit. Accordingly, we will not express an opinion regarding the financial statements as a whole.

Our engagement cannot be relied upon to disclose errors, fraud, or illegal acts. However, we will inform the appropriate level of management of any material errors and of any evidence or information that comes to our attention during the performance of our review procedures that fraud may have occurred. In addition, we will report to you any evidence or information that comes to our attention during the performance of our review procedures regarding illegal acts that may have occurred, unless they are clearly inconsequential.

If, for any reason, we are unable to complete the review of your financial statements, we will not issue a report on such statements as a result of this engagement.

Our fees for these services . . .

We will be pleased to discuss this letter with you at any time. If the foregoing is in accordance with your understanding, please sign the copy of this letter in the space provided and return it to us.

Sincerely yours,

_____

[*Signature of accountant*]

Acknowledged:
ABC Company

_____

President

_____

Date

ILLUSTRATION R-2. CHECKLIST FOR A REVIEW ENGAGEMENT

Step No.	*Action/Decision*
1.	Obtain an understanding with the client, preferably in writing, regarding the engagement. (For a new client, determine if communication with the predecessor accountant is desirable.)
2.	Determine whether the firm is independent. If the firm is, go to step 3. If the firm is not, do not issue a review report. (However, it may be possible to issue a compilation report—see Illustration TC-3 "Checklist for a Traditional Compilation Engagement.")
3.	Acquire the necessary knowledge of the client industry's accounting principles and practices.
4.	Acquire an understanding of the client's business, including (a) a general understanding of the entity's organization, (b) its operating characteristics, and (c) the nature of its assets, liabilities, revenues, and expenses.
5.	Develop expectations for the planned analytical procedures, apply appropriate inquiry and analytical procedures to obtain a reasonable basis for expressing limited assurance that no material modifications should be made to the financial statements, and compare expectations to recorded amounts or ratios developed from recorded amounts.
6.	Read the financial statements to determine whether, based on the information presented, they appear to conform to the applicable financial reporting framework. Obtain reports of other accountants for subsidiaries, investees, etc., if any. Indicate division of responsibility if reference is made to other accountants.
7.	Perform additional procedures if information appears to be incorrect, incomplete, or otherwise unsatisfactory.
8.	Describe in the working papers matters covered in steps 5 and 7. Also, describe unusual matters that were considered and how they were resolved.
9.	Determine whether the inquiry and analytical procedures considered necessary to achieve limited assurance are incomplete or restricted in any way. If they are, go to step 10. If they are not, go to step 11.
10.	Consider whether a compilation report should be issued rather than a review report. (A review that is incomplete or restricted is not an adequate basis for issuing a review report.)
11.	Document the review engagement as required by SSARS.
12.	Consider whether the financial statements contain departures from the applicable financial reporting framework, including disclosure departures. If they do, go to step 13. If they do not, go to step 14.

13. Request that the client revise the financial statements. Failing that, consider modifying the review report by adding a separate paragraph or paragraphs. If the effect of the departure has been determined by management or is known by the accountant, disclose the dollar effects in the report. (However, the report need not be modified for uncertainties, going concern matters, or inconsistencies if they are properly disclosed.) Withdraw from the engagement if the departures are designed to mislead financial statement users.
14. Obtain a representation letter from the client.
15. Mark each page of the financial statements, including notes to the financial statements, "See Accountant's Review Report."
16. Sign and date (manual, stamped, electronic, or typed signature) the report using the date the inquiry and analytical procedures were completed.
17. Issue the financial statements and the related review report.

ILLUSTRATION R-3. CHECKLIST FOR CHANGE IN ENGAGEMENT FROM AUDIT/REVIEW TO REVIEW/COMPILATION

Step No.   *Action/Decision*

1. Consider (a) the reason given for the client's request, (b) the additional effort required to complete the engagement, and (c) the estimated additional cost to complete the engagement.
2. Determine whether the request for the change is caused by (a) a change in circumstances affecting the need for an audit or review, (b) a misunderstanding as to the nature of alternative services, or (c) restrictions caused by the client or by circumstances on the scope of the engagement. If (a) or (b)—which provide a reasonable basis for requesting a change—go to step 3. If (c), go to step 4.
3. Consider issuing an appropriate compilation or review report. Make no mention in the report of the original engagement, the procedures performed, or the scope limitations. Go to step 5.
4. Evaluate the possibility that the information affected by the scope restriction may be incorrect, incomplete, or otherwise unsatisfactory. If the client prohibited you from corresponding with the company's legal counsel or refused to sign a client representation letter, do not issue a review or compilation report.
5. If the audit or review is substantially complete or the cost to complete is insignificant, consider the propriety of accepting a changed engagement.
6. If an engagement letter has been obtained, revise the understanding with the client regarding the nature of the services to be rendered.

ILLUSTRATION R-4. STANDARD REVIEW REPORT

Accountants' Report

We have reviewed the accompanying balance sheet of ABC Company as of December 31, 20X1, and the related statements of income, retained earnings, and cash flows for the year then ended. A review includes primarily applying analytical procedures to management's financial data and making inquiries of company management. A review is substantially less in scope than an audit, the objective of which is the expression of an opinion regarding the financial statements as a whole. Accordingly, we do not express such an opinion.

Management is responsible for the preparation and fair presentation of the financial statements in accordance with accounting principles generally accepted in the United States of America and for designing, implementing, and maintaining internal control relevant to the preparation and fair presentation of the financial statements.

Our responsibility is to conduct the review in accordance with Statements on Standards for Accounting and Review Services issued by the American Institute of Certified Public Accountants. Those standards require us to perform procedures to obtain limited assurance that there are no material modifications that should be made to the financial statements. We believe that the results of our procedures provide a reasonable basis for our report.

Based on our review, we are not aware of any material modifications that should be made to the accompanying financial statements in order for them to be in conformity with accounting principles generally accepted in the United States of America.

Smith and Jones
February 15, 20X2

ILLUSTRATION R-5. STANDARD REVIEW REPORT PREPARED IN ACCORDANCE WITH THE INCOME TAX BASIS OF ACCOUNTING

Independent Accountant's Review Report

[*Appropriate Salutation*]

I (*We*) have reviewed the accompanying statement of assets, liabilities, and equity–income tax basis of XYZ Company as of December 31, 20XX, and the related statement of revenue and expenses–income tax basis for the year then ended. A review includes primarily applying analytical procedures to management's (*owners'*) financial data and making inquiries of company management (*owners*). A review is substantially less in scope than an audit, the objective of which is the expression of an opinion regarding the financial statements as a whole. Accordingly, I (*we*) do not express such an opinion.

The management (*owners*) is (*are*) responsible for the preparation and fair presentation of the financial statements in accordance with the income tax basis for accounting and for designing, implementing, and maintaining internal control relevant to the preparation and fair presentation of the financial statements.

My (*Our*) responsibility is to conduct the review in accordance with Statements on Standards for Accounting and Review Services issued by the American Institute of Certified Public Accountants. Those standards require me (*us*) to perform procedures to obtain limited assurance that there are no material modifications that should be made to the financial statements. I (*We*) believe that the results of my (*our*) procedures provides a reasonable basis for our report.

Based on my (*our*) review, I am (*we are*) not aware of any material modifications that should be made to the accompanying financial statements in order for them to be in conformity with the income tax basis of accounting, as described in note X.

[*Signature of accounting firm or accountant, as appropriate*]

[*Date*]

ILLUSTRATION R-6. REVIEW REPORT WITH GAAP MEASUREMENT DEPARTURE

Accountants' Report

We have reviewed the accompanying balance sheet of ABC Company as of December 31, 20X1, and the related statements of income, retained earnings, and cash flows for the year then ended. A review includes primarily applying analytical procedures to management's financial data and making inquiries of company management. A review is substantially less in scope than an audit, the objective of which is the expression of an opinion regarding the financial statements as a whole. Accordingly, we do not express such an opinion.

Management is responsible for the preparation and fair presentation of the financial statements in accordance with accounting principles generally accepted in the United States of America and for designing, implementing, and maintaining internal control relevant to the preparation and fair presentation of the financial statements.

Our responsibility is to conduct the review in accordance with Statements on Standards for Accounting and Review Services issued by the American Institute of Certified Public Accountants. Those standards require us to perform procedures to obtain limited assurance that there are no material modifications that should be made to the financial statements. We believe that the results of our procedures provide a reasonable basis for our report.

Based on our review, with the exception of the matters described in the following paragraphs, we are not aware of any material modifications that should be made to the accompanying financial statements in order for them to be in conformity with accounting principles generally accepted in the United States of America.

As disclosed in note X to the financial statements, accounting principles generally accepted in the United States of America require that inventory cost consist of material, labor, and overhead. Management has informed us that the inventory of finished goods and work in process is stated in the accompanying financial statements at material and labor cost only, and that the effects of this departure from accounting principles generally accepted in the United States of America on financial position, results of operations, and cash flows have not been determined.

Smith and Jones
February 15, 20X2

ILLUSTRATION R-7. ILLUSTRATIVE INQUIRIES FOR A REVIEW

1. General:
    a. Have there been any changes in the entity's business activities?
    b. Are there any unusual or complex situations that may have an effect on the financial statements (for example, business combinations, restructuring plans, or litigation)?
    c. What procedures are in place related to recording, classifying, and summarizing transactions and accumulating information related to financial statements disclosures?
    d. Have the financial statements been prepared in conformity with generally accepted accounting principles or, if appropriate, a comprehensive basis of accounting other than generally accepted accounting principles? Have there been any changes in accounting principles and methods of applying those principles?
    e. Have there been any instances of fraud or illegal acts within the entity?
    f. Have there been any allegations or suspicions that fraud or illegal acts might have occurred or might be occurring within the entity? If so, where and how?
    g. Are any entities other than the reporting entity commonly controlled by the owners? If so, has an evaluation been performed to determine whether those other entities should be consolidated into the financial statements of the reporting entity?
    h. Are there any entities other than the reporting entity in which the owners have significant investments (for example, variable interest entities)? If so, has an evaluation been performed to determine whether the reporting entity is the primary beneficiary related to the activities of these other entities?
    i. Have any significant transactions occurred or been recognized near the end of the reporting period?

2. Cash and cash equivalents:
    a. Is the entity's policy regarding the composition of cash and cash equivalents in accordance with Financial Accounting Standards Board Statement of Financial Accounting Standards 95, *Statement of Cash Flows* (paragraphs 7–10)? Has the policy been applied on a consistent basis?
    b. Are all cash and cash equivalents[1] accounts reconciled on a timely basis?
    c. Have old or unusual reconciling items between bank balances and book balances been reviewed and adjustments made where necessary?

---

[1] *Cash and cash equivalents include all cash and highly liquid investments that are both (a) readily convertible to cash, and (b) so near to maturity that they present insignificant risk of changes in value because of changes in interest rates, in accordance with paragraph 8 of Financial Accounting Standards Board Statement 95,* Statement of Cash Flows.

d. Has there been a proper cutoff of cash receipts and disbursements?
e. Has a reconciliation of intercompany transfers been prepared?
f. Have checks written but not mailed as of the financial statement date been properly reclassified into the liability section of the balance sheet?
g. Have material bank overdrafts been properly reclassified into the liability section of the balance sheet?
h. Are there compensating balances or other restrictions on the availability of cash and cash equivalents balances? If so, has consideration been given to reclassifying these amounts as noncurrent assets?
i. Have cash funds been counted and reconciled with control accounts?

3. Receivables:

   a. Has an adequate allowance for doubtful accounts been properly reflected in the financial statements?
   b. Have uncollectible receivables been written off through a charge against the allowance account or earnings?
   c. Has interest earned on receivables been properly reflected in the financial statements?
   d. Has there been a proper cutoff of sales transactions?
   e. Are there receivables from employees or other related parties? Have receivables from owners been evaluated to determine if they should be reflected in the equity section (rather than the asset section) of the balance sheet?
   f. Are any receivables pledged, discounted, or factored? Are recourse provisions properly reflected in the financial statements?
   g. Have receivables been properly classified between current and noncurrent?
   h. Have there been significant numbers of sales returns or credit memoranda issued subsequent to the balance sheet date?
   i. Is the accounts receivable subsidiary ledger reconciled to the general ledger account balance on a regular basis?

4. Inventory:

   a. Are physical inventory counts performed on a regular basis, including at the end of the reporting period? Are the count procedures adequate to ensure an appropriate count? If not, how have amounts related to inventories been determined for purposes of financial statement presentation? If so, what procedures were used to take the latest physical inventory and what date was that inventory taken?
   b. Have general ledger control accounts been adjusted to agree with the physical inventory count? If so, were the adjustments significant?
   c. If the physical inventory counts were taken at a date other than the balance sheet date, what procedures were used to determine changes in inventory between the date of physical inventory counts and the balance sheet date?
   d. Were consignments in or out considered in taking physical inventories?
   e. What is the basis of valuing inventory for purposes of financial statement presentation?
   f. Does inventory cost include material, labor, and overhead where applicable?
   g. Has inventory been reviewed for obsolescence or cost in excess of net realizable value? If so, how are these costs reflected in the financial statements?
   h. Have proper cutoffs of purchases, goods in transit, and returned goods been made?
   i. Are there any inventory encumbrances?
   j. Is scrap inventoried and controlled?

5. Prepaid expenses:

   a. What is the nature of the amounts included in prepaid expenses?
   b. How are these amounts being amortized?

6. Investments:
   a. What is the basis of accounting for investments reported in the financial statements (for example, securities, joint ventures, or closely held businesses)?
   b. Are derivative instruments properly measured and disclosed in the financial statements? If those derivatives are utilized in hedge transactions, have the documentation or assessment requirements related to hedge accounting been met?
   c. Are investments in marketable debt and equity securities properly classified as trading, available-for-sale, and held-to-maturity?
   d. How were fair values of the reported investments determined? Have unrealized gains and losses been properly reported in the financial statements?
   e. If the fair values of marketable debt and equity securities are less than cost, have the declines in value been evaluated to determine whether the declines are other-than-temporary?
   f. For any debt securities classified as held-to-maturity, does management have the positive ability and intent to hold the securities until they mature? If so, have those debt securities been properly measured?
   g. Have gains and losses related to disposal of investments been properly reflected in the financial statements?
   h. How was investment income determined? Is investment income properly reflected in the financial statements?
   i. Has appropriate consideration been given to the classification of investments between current and noncurrent?
   j. For investments made by the reporting entity, have consolidation, equity, or cost method accounting requirements been considered?
   k. Are any investments encumbered?

7. Property and equipment:
   a. Are property and equipment items properly stated at depreciated cost or other proper value?
   b. When was the last time a physical inventory of property and equipment was taken?
   c. Are all items reflected in property and equipment held for use? If not, have items that are held for sale been properly reclassified from property and equipment?
   d. Have gains or losses on disposal of property and equipment been properly reflected in the financial statements?
   e. What are the criteria for capitalization of property and equipment? Have the criteria been consistently and appropriately applied?
   f. Are repairs and maintenance costs properly reflected as an expense in the income statement?
   g. What depreciation methods and rates are utilized in the financial statements? Are these methods and rates appropriate and applied on a consistent basis?
   h. Are there any unrecorded additions, retirements, abandonments, sales, or trade-ins?
   i. Does the entity have any material lease agreements? If so, have those agreements been properly evaluated for financial statement presentation purposes?
   j. Are there any asset retirement obligations associated with tangible long-lived assets? If so, has the recorded amount of the related asset been increased because of the obligation, and is the liability properly reflected in the liability section of the balance sheet?
   k. Has the entity constructed any of its property and equipment items? If so, have all components of cost been reflected in measuring these items for purposes of financial statement presentation, including but not limited to capitalized interest?
   l. Has there been any significant impairment in value of property and equipment items? If so, has any impairment loss been properly reflected in the financial statements?
   m. Are any property and equipment items mortgaged or otherwise encumbered? If so, are these mortgages and encumbrances properly reflected in the financial statements?

8. Intangibles and other assets:
    a. What is the nature of the amounts included in other assets?
    b. Do these assets represent costs that will benefit future periods? What is the amortization policy related to these assets? Is this policy appropriate?
    c. Have other assets been properly classified between current and noncurrent?
    d. Are intangible assets with finite lives being appropriately amortized?
    e. Are the costs associated with computer software properly reflected as intangible assets (rather than property and equipment) in the financial statements?
    f. Are the costs associated with goodwill (and other intangible assets with indefinite lives) properly reflected as intangible assets in the financial statements? Has amortization ceased related to these assets?
    g. Has there been any significant impairment in value of these assets? If so, has any impairment loss been properly reflected in the financial statements?
    h. Are any of these assets mortgaged or otherwise encumbered?

9. Accounts and short-term notes payable and accrued liabilities:
    a. Have significant payables been reflected in the financial statements?
    b. Are loans from financial institutions and other short-term liabilities properly classified in the financial statements?
    c. Have significant accruals (for example, payroll, interest, provisions for pension and profit-sharing plans, or other postretirement benefit obligations) been properly reflected in the financial statements?
    d. Has a liability for employees' compensation for future absences been properly accrued and disclosed in the financial statements?
    e. Are any liabilities collateralized or subordinated? If so, are those liabilities disclosed in the financial statements?
    f. Are there any payables to employees and related parties?

10. Long-term liabilities:
    a. Are the terms and other provisions of long-term liability agreements properly disclosed in the financial statements?
    b. Have liabilities been properly classified between current and noncurrent?
    c. Has interest expense been properly accrued and reflected in the financial statements?
    d. Is the company in compliance with loan covenants and agreements? If not, is the noncompliance properly disclosed in the financial statements?
    e. Are any long-term liabilities collateralized or subordinated? If so, are these facts disclosed in the financial statements?
    f. Are there any obligations that, by their terms, are due on demand within one year from the balance sheet date? If so, have these obligations been properly reclassified into the current liability section of the balance sheet?

11. Income and other taxes:
    a. Do the financial statements reflect an appropriate provision for current and prior-year income taxes payable?
    b. Have any assessments or reassessments been received? Are there tax authority examinations in process?
    c. Are there any temporary differences between book and tax amounts? If so, have deferred taxes on these differences been properly reflected in the financial statements?
    d. Do the financial statements reflect an appropriate provision for taxes other than income taxes (for example, franchise, sales)?
    e. Have all required tax payments been made on a timely basis?

12. Other liabilities, contingencies, and commitments:
    a. What is the nature of the amounts included in other liabilities?
    b. Have other liabilities been properly classified between current and noncurrent?
    c. Are there any guarantees, whether written or verbal, whereby the entity must stand ready to perform or is contingently liable related to the guarantee? If so, are these guarantees properly reflected in the financial statements?
    d. Are there any contingent liabilities (for example, discounted notes, drafts, endorsements, warranties, litigation, and unsettled asserted claims)? Are there any potential unasserted claims? Are these contingent liabilities, claims, and assessments properly measured and disclosed in the financial statements?
    e. Are there any material contractual obligations for construction or purchase of property and equipment or any commitments or options to purchase or sell company securities? If so, are these facts clearly disclosed in the financial statements?
    f. Is the entity responsible for any environmental remediation liability? If so, is this liability properly measured and disclosed in the financial statements?
    g. Does the entity have any agreement to repurchase items that previously were sold? If so, have the repurchase agreements been taken into account in determining the appropriate measurements and disclosures in the financial statements?
    h. Does the entity have any sales commitments at prices expected to result in a loss at the consummation of the sale? If so, are these commitments properly reflected in the financial statements?
    i. Are there any violations, or possible violations, of laws or regulations the effects of which should be considered for financial statement accrual or disclosure?

13. Equity:
    a. What is the nature of any changes in equity accounts during each reporting period?
    b. What classes of stock (other ownership interests) have been authorized?
    c. What is the par or stated value of the various classes of stock (other ownership interests)?
    d. Do amounts of outstanding shares of stock (other ownership interests) agree with subsidiary record?
    e. Have pertinent rights and privileges of ownership interests been properly disclosed in the financial statements?
    f. Does the entity have any mandatorily redeemable ownership interests? If so, have these ownership interests been evaluated so that a proper determination has been made related to whether these ownership interests should be measured and reclassified to the liability section of the balance sheet? Are redemption features associated with ownership interests clearly disclosed in the financial statements?
    g. Have dividend (distribution) and liquidation preferences related to ownership interests been properly disclosed in the financial statements?
    h. Do disclosures related to ownership interests include any applicable call provisions (prices and dates), conversion provisions (prices and rates), unusual voting rights, significant terms of contracts to issue additional ownership interests, or any other unusual features associated with the ownership interests?
    i. Are syndication fees properly reflected in the financial statements as a reduction of equity (rather than an asset)?
    j. Have any stock options or other stock compensation awards been granted to employees or others? If so, are these options or awards properly measured and disclosed in the financial statements?
    k. Has the entity made any acquisitions of its own stock? If so, are the amounts associated with these reacquired shares properly reflected in the financial statements as a reduction in equity? Is the presentation in accordance with applicable state laws?

l. Are there any restrictions or appropriations on retained earnings or other capital accounts? If so, are these restrictions or appropriations properly reflected in the financial statements?

14. Revenue and expenses:

a. What is the entity's revenue recognition policy? Is the policy appropriate? Has the policy been consistently applied and appropriately disclosed?
b. Are revenues from sales of products and rendering of services recognized in the appropriate reporting period (that is, when the products have been delivered and when the services have been performed)?
c. Were any sales recorded under a "bill and hold" arrangement? If yes, have the criteria been met to record the transaction as a sale?
d. Are purchases and expenses recognized in the appropriate reporting period (that is, matched against revenue) and properly classified in the financial statements?
e. Do the financial statements include discontinued operations, items that might be considered extraordinary, or both? If so, are amounts associated with discontinued operations, extraordinary items, or both properly displayed in the income statement?
f. Does the entity have any gains or losses that would necessitate the display of comprehensive income (for example, gains/losses on available-for-sale securities or cash flow hedge derivatives)? If so, have these items been properly displayed within comprehensive income (rather than included in the determination of net income)?

15. Other:

a. Have events occurred subsequent to the balance sheet date that would require adjustment to, or disclosure in, the financial statements?
b. Have actions taken at stockholders, committees of directors, or comparable meetings that affect the financial statements been reflected in the financial statements?
c. Are significant estimates and material concentrations (for example, customers or suppliers) properly disclosed in the financial statements?
d. Are there plans or intentions that may materially affect the carrying amounts or classification of assets and liabilities reflected in the financial statements?
e. Have there been material transactions between or among related parties (for example, sales, purchases, loans, or leasing arrangements)? If so, are these transactions properly disclosed in the financial statements?
f. Are there uncertainties that could have a material impact on the financial statements? Is there any change in the status of previously disclosed material uncertainties? Are all uncertainties, including going concern matters that could have a material impact on the financial statements, properly disclosed in the financial statements?
g. Are barter or other nonmonetary transactions properly recorded and disclosed?

ILLUSTRATION R-8. SUGGESTED ANALYTICAL PROCEDURES

- Comparing financial statements with statements for comparable prior period(s).
- Comparing current financial information with anticipated results, such as budgets or forecasts (for example, comparing tax balances and the relationship between the provision for income taxes and pretax income in the current financial information with corresponding information in (1) budgets, using expected rates, and (2) financial information for prior periods).
- Comparing current financial information with relevant nonfinancial information.
- Comparing ratios and indicators for the current period with expectations based on prior periods; for example, performing gross profit analysis by product line and operating segment using elements of the current financial information and comparing the results with corresponding information for prior periods. Examples of key ratios and indicators are the current ratio, receivables turnover or days' sales outstanding, inventory turnover, de-

preciation to average fixed assets, debt to equity, gross profit percentage, net income percentage, and plant operating rates.
- Comparing ratios and indicators for the current period with those of entities in the same industry.
- Comparing relationships among elements in the current financial information with corresponding relationships in the financial information of prior periods; for example, expense by type as a percentage of sales, assets by type as a percentage of total assets, and percentage of change in sales to percentage of change in receivables.
- Analytical procedures may include such statistical techniques as trend analysis or regression analysis and may be performed manually or with the use of computer-assisted techniques.

ILLUSTRATION R-9. ILLUSTRATIVE REPRESENTATION LETTER[2]

[*Date*]

[*To the Accountant*]

We are providing this letter in connection with your review of the [*identification of financial statements*] of [*name of entity*] as of [*dates*] and for the [*periods of review*] for the purpose of obtaining limited assurance that there are no material modifications that should be made to the statements in order for them to be in conformity with [*the applicable financial reporting framework*]. We confirm that we are responsible for the fair presentation of the financial statements in accordance with [*the applicable financial reporting framework*] and the selection and application of the accounting policies.

Certain representations in this letter are described as being limited to matters that are material. Items are considered material, regardless of size, if they involve an omission or misstatement of accounting information that, in light of surrounding circumstances, makes it probable that the judgment of a reasonable person using the information would be changed or influenced by the omission or misstatement.[3]

We confirm, to the best of our knowledge and belief, [*as of* (*date of the accountant's review report*)], the following representations made to you during your review:

1. The financial statements referred to previously are fairly presented in accordance with [*the applicable financial reporting framework*].
2. We have made the following available to you:
   a. Financial records and related data
   b. Minutes of the meetings of stockholders, directors, and committees of directors, or summaries of actions of recent meetings for which minutes have not yet been prepared
3. No material transactions exist that have not been properly recorded in the accounting records underlying the financial statements.
4. We acknowledge our responsibility for the preparation and fair presentation of the financial statements in accordance with [*the applicable financial reporting framework*].
5. We acknowledge our responsibility for designing, implementing, and maintaining internal control relevant to the preparation and fair presentation of the financial statements.

---

[2] This representation letter is for illustrative purposes only. The accountant may decide, based on the circumstances of the review engagement or the industry in which the entity operates, that other matters should be specifically included in the letter or that some of the representations included in the illustrative letter are not necessary.

[3] The qualitative discussion of materiality used in this letter is adapted from Financial Accounting Standards Board Statement of Financial Accounting Concepts 2, *Qualitative Characteristics of Accounting Information.*

6. We acknowledge our responsibility to prevent and detect fraud.
7. We have no knowledge of any fraud or suspected fraud affecting the entity involving management or others where the fraud could have a material effect on the financial statements, including any communications received from employees, former employees, or others.
8. We have no plans or intentions that may materially affect the carrying amounts or classifications of assets and liabilities.
9. No material losses exist (such as from obsolete inventory or purchase or sales commitments) that have not been properly accrued or disclosed in the financial statements.
10. None of the following exist:

    a. Violations or possible violations of laws or regulations, whose effects should be considered for disclosure in the financial statements or as a basis for recording a loss contingency.
    b. Unasserted claims or assessments that our lawyer has advised us are probable of assertion that must be disclosed in accordance with Financial Accounting Standards Board (FASB) Accounting Standards Codification (ASC) 450, *Contingencies*.[4]
    c. Other material liabilities or gain or loss contingencies that are required to be accrued or disclosed by FASB ASC 450.

11. The company has satisfactory title to all owned assets, and no liens or encumbrances on such assets exist, nor has any asset been pledged as collateral, except as disclosed to you and reported in the financial statements.
12. We have complied with all aspects of contractual agreements that would have a material effect on the financial statements in the event of noncompliance.
13. The following have been properly recorded or disclosed in the financial statements:

    a. Related-party transactions, including sales, purchases, loans, transfers, leasing arrangements, and guarantees, and amounts receivable from or payable to related parties.
    b. Guarantees, whether written or oral, under which the company is contingently liable.
    c. Significant estimates and material concentrations known to management that are required to be disclosed in accordance with the FASB ASC 275, *Risks and Uncertainties*. (Significant estimates are estimates at the balance sheet date that could change materially with the next year. Concentrations refer to volumes of business, revenues, available sources of supply, or markets or geographic areas for which events could occur that would significantly disrupt normal finances within the next year.)

[*Add additional representations that are unique to the entity's business or industry. See below for additional illustrative representations.*]

14. We are in agreement with the adjusting journal entries you have recommended and they have been posted to the company's accounts (if applicable).
15. To the best of our knowledge and belief, no events have occurred subsequent to the balance sheet date and through the date of this letter that would require adjustment to or disclosure in the aforementioned financial statements.

---

[4] *If management has not consulted a lawyer regarding litigation, claims, and assessments, the representation might be worded as follows:*

We are not aware of any pending or threatened litigation, claims, or assessments or unasserted claims or assessments that are required to be accrued or disclosed in the financial statements in accordance with FASB ASC 450, Contingencies, *and we have not consulted a lawyer concerning litigation, claims, or assessments.*

16. We have responded fully and truthfully to all inquiries made to us by you during your review.

[*Name of Owner or Chief Executive Officer and Title*]

[*Name of Chief Financial Officer and Title, when applicable*]

The following additional representations may be appropriate in certain situations. This list of additional representations is not intended to be all-inclusive. In drafting a representation letter, the effects of other applicable pronouncements should be considered.

General

- *Effect of a new accounting principle is not known.* We have not completed the process of evaluating the impact that will result from adopting FASB ASC XXX, *Title*, as discussed in note X. The company is therefore unable to disclose the impact that adopting FASB ASC XXX will have on its financial position and the results of operations when such statement is adopted.
- *Change in accounting principles.* We believe that [*describe the newly adopted accounting principle*] is preferable to [*describe the former accounting principle*] because [*describe management's justification for the change in accounting principles*].
- *Financial circumstances are strained.* Note X to the financial statements discloses all of the matters of which we are aware that are relevant to the entity's ability to continue as a going concern, including significant conditions and events, and management's plans.
- *Asset impairment.* We have reviewed long-lived assets and certain identifiable intangibles to be held and used for impairment whenever events or changes in circumstances have indicated that the carrying amount of those assets might not be recoverable and have appropriately recorded the adjustment.
- *Variable interest in another entity.* Variable interest entities (VIEs) and potential VIEs and transactions with VIEs and potential VIEs have been properly recorded and disclosed in the financial statements in accordance with GAAP.

    We have considered both implicit and explicit variable interests in (a) determining whether potential VIEs should be considered VIEs, (b) calculating expected losses and residual returns, and (c) determining which party, if any, is the primary beneficiary.

    We have provided you with lists of all identified variable interests in (a) VIEs, (b) potential VIEs that we considered but judged not to be VIEs, and (c) entities that were afforded the scope exceptions of FASB ASC 810, *Consolidations*.

    We have advised you of all transactions with identified VIEs, potential VIEs, or entities afforded the scope exceptions of FASB ASC 810.

    We have made available all relevant information about financial interests and contractual arrangements with related parties, de facto agents, and other entities, including but not limited to, their governing documents, equity and debt instruments, contracts, leases, guarantee arrangements, and other financial contracts and arrangements.

    The information we provided about financial interests and contractual arrangements with related parties, de facto agents, and other entities includes information about all transactions, unwritten understandings, agreement modifications, and written and oral side agreements.

    Our computations of expected losses and expected residual returns of entities that are VIEs and potential VIEs are based on the best information available and include all reasonably possible outcomes.

    Regarding entities in which the company has variable interests (implicit and explicit), we have provided all information about events and changes in circumstances that could potentially cause reconsideration about whether the entities are VIEs or whether the company is the primary beneficiary or has a significant variable interest in the entity.

We have made and continue to make exhaustive efforts to obtain information about entities in which the company has an implicit or explicit interest, but that were excluded from complete analysis under FASB ASC 810 due to lack of essential information to determine one or more of the following:

- Whether the entity is a VIE
- Whether the company is the primary beneficiary
- The accounting required to consolidate the entity

- *Work of a specialist.* We agree with the findings of specialists in evaluating the [*describe assertion*] and have adequately considered the qualifications of the specialist in determining the amounts and disclosures used in the financial statements and underlying accounting records. We did not give or cause any instructions to be given to specialists with respect to the values or amounts derived in an attempt to bias their work, and we are not otherwise aware of any matters that have had an impact on the independence or objectivity of the specialists.

Assets

- *Cash restrictions.* Arrangements with financial institutions involving compensating balances or other arrangements involving restrictions on cash balances, lines of credit, or similar arrangements have been properly disclosed.
- *Held-to-maturity securities.* Debt securities that have been classified as held-to-maturity have been so classified due to the company's intent to hold such securities to maturity and the company's ability to do so. All other debt securities have been classified as available-for sale or trading.
- *Decline in value of securities.* We consider the decline in value of debt or equity securities classified as either available-for-sale or held-to-maturity to be temporary.
- *Fair value of financial instruments.* The methods and significant assumptions used to determine fair values of financial instruments are as follows: [*describe methods and significant assumptions used to determine fair values of financial instruments*]. The methods and significant assumptions used result in a measure of fair value appropriate for financial statement measurement and disclosure purposes.
- *Financial instrument risks.* The following information about financial statements with off-balance-sheet risk and financial instruments with concentrations of credit risk has been properly disclosed in the financial statements:

  1. The extent, nature, and terms of financial instruments with off-balance-sheet risk
  2. The amount of credit risk of financial instruments with off-balance-sheet risk and information about the collateral supporting such financial instruments
  3. Significant concentrations of credit risk arising from all financial instruments and information about the collateral supporting such financial instruments

- *Receivables at net realizable value.* Receivables reported in the financial statements represent valid claims against debtors for sales or other charges arising on or before the balance-sheet date and have been appropriately reduced to their estimated net realizable value.
- *Obsolete inventory.* Provisions have been made to reduce excess or obsolete inventories to their estimated net realizable value.
- *Equity accounting considerations.* [*For investments in common stock that are either nonmarketable or of which the entity has a 20% or greater ownership interest, select the appropriate representation from the following:*]

  - The equity method is used to account for the company's investment in the common stock of [*investee*] because the company has the ability to exercise significant influence over the investee's operating and financial policies.

- The cost method is used to account for the company's investment in the common stock of [*investee*] because the company does not have the ability to exercise significant influence over the investee's operating and financial policies.
- *Deferred charges*. We believe that all material expenditures that have been deferred to future periods will be recoverable.
- *Deferred tax assets*. The valuation allowance has been determined pursuant to the provisions of FASB ASC 740, *Income Taxes*, including the company's estimation of future taxable income, if necessary, and is adequate to reduce the total deferred tax asset to an amount that will more likely than not be realized. [*Complete with appropriate wording detailing how the entity determined the valuation allowance against the deferred tax asset.*]

or

A valuation allowance against deferred tax assets at the balance sheet date is not considered necessary because it is more likely than not that the deferred tax asset will be fully realized.

Liabilities

- *Short-term debt refinancing*. The company has excluded short-term obligations totaling $[*amount*] from current liabilities because it intends to refinance the obligations on a long-term basis. [*Complete with appropriate wording detailing how amounts will be refinanced as follows:*]
    - The company has issued a long-term obligation [*debt security*] after the date of the balance sheet but prior to the issuance of the financial statements for the purpose of refinancing the short-term obligations on a long-term basis.
    - The company has the ability to consummate the refinancing by using the financing agreement referred to in note X to the financial statements.
- *Tax-exempt bonds*. Tax-exempt bonds issued have retained their tax-exempt status.
- *Foreign subsidiary undistributed earnings reinvestment*. We intend to reinvest the undistributed earnings of [*name of foreign subsidiary*].
- *Environmental remediation liabilities*. Provision has been made for any material loss that is probable from environmental remediation liabilities associated with [*name of site*]. We believe that such estimate is reasonable based on available information and that the liabilities and related loss contingencies and the expected outcome of uncertainties have been adequately described in the company's financial statements.
- *Asset repurchases*. Agreements to repurchase assets previously sold have been properly disclosed.
- *Actuary usage*. We believe that the actuarial assumptions and methods used to measure pension liabilities and costs for financial accounting purposes are appropriate in the circumstances.
- *Multiemployer plan*. We are unable to determine the possibility of a withdrawal liability in a multiemployer benefit plan.

or

We have determined that there is the possibility of a withdrawal liability in a multiemployer plan in the amount of $ [*amount*].

- *Post-retirement benefits elimination.* We do not intend to compensate for the elimination of post-retirement benefits by granting an increase in pension benefits.

    or

    We plan to compensate for the elimination of post-retirement benefits by granting an increase in pension benefits in the amount of $ [*amount*].

- *Employee layoffs intended to be temporary.* Current employee layoffs are intended to be temporary.
- *Pension plan amendments.* We plan to continue to make frequent amendments to the pension or other post-retirement benefit plans, which may affect the amortization period of prior service cost.

    or

    We do not plan to make frequent amendments to the pension or other post-retirement benefit plans.

Equity

- *Stock options.* Capital stock repurchase options or agreements or capital stock reserved for options, warrants, conversions, or other requirements have been properly disclosed.

Income Statement

- *Sales commitment losses.* Provisions have been made for losses to be sustained in the fulfillment of or from the inability to fulfill any sales commitments.
- *Purchase commitment losses.* Provisions have been made for losses to be sustained as a result of purchase commitments for inventory quantities in excess of normal requirements or at prices in excess of prevailing market prices.
- *Undisclosed sales terms.* We have fully disclosed to you all sales terms, including all rights of return or price adjustments and all warranty provisions.

ILLUSTRATION R-10. ILLUSTRATIVE UPDATING MANAGEMENT REPRESENTATION LETTER

The following letter is presented for illustrative purposes only. It may be used in the circumstances described in paragraph .23. Management need not repeat all of the representations made in the previous representation letter.

If matters exist that should be disclosed to the accountant, they may be indicated by listing them following the representation. For example, if an event subsequent to the date of the accountant's review report is disclosed in the financial statements, the final paragraph could be modified as follows: "To the best of our knowledge and belief, except as discussed in note X to the financial statements, no events have occurred . . . "

[*Date*]

To [*Accountant*]

In connection with your review(s) of the [*identification of financial statements*] of [*name of entity*] as of [*dates*] and for the [*periods of review*] for the purpose of obtaining limited assurance that that there are no material modifications that should be made to the financial statements in order for the statements to be in conformity with [*the applicable financial reporting framework (for example, accounting principles generally accepted in the United States of America)*], you were previously provided with a representation letter under date of [*date of previous representation let-*

ter]. No information has come to our attention that would cause us to believe that any of those previous representations should be modified.

To the best of our knowledge and belief, no events have occurred subsequent to [*date of latest balance sheet reported on by the accountant or date of previous representation letter*] and through the date of this letter that would require adjustment to or disclosure in the aforementioned financial statements.

_____
[*Name of Owner or Chief Executive Officer and Title*]

_____
[*Name of Chief Financial Officer and Title, when applicable*]

AR 110 Compilation of Specified Elements, Accounts, or Items of a Financial Statement

EFFECTIVE DATE AND APPLICABILITY

Original Pronouncement	Statements on Standards for Accounting and Review Services (SSARSs) 13, 17
Effective Date	This statement currently is effective.
Applicability	When an accountant is engaged to compile or issue a compilation report on one or more specified elements, accounts, or items of a financial statement.

OBJECTIVES OF AR SECTION 110

This section established standards for performing a compilation of specified elements, accounts, or items of a financial statement, examples of which include schedules of rentals, royalties, profit participation, or provision for income taxes.

A compilation of specified elements, accounts, or items of a financial statement is limited to presenting financial information that is the representation of management without undertaking to express any assurance on that information.

FUNDAMENTAL REQUIREMENTS

GENERAL GUIDANCE

Reporting Obligation

An accountant may prepare or assist in the preparation of specified elements, accounts, or items of a financial statement and submitting such a preparation to management *without* the issuance of a compilation report, unless the accountant has been engaged to perform a compilation. However, in deciding whether to issue a compilation report, the accountant should consider how such a presentation of specified elements, accounts, or items of a financial statement will be used. If the accountant believes that he or she will be associated with the information, he or she should consider issuing a compilation report so a user will not infer a level of assurance that does not exist.

Understanding with the Client

The accountant should establish an understanding, preferably in writing, regarding the services to be performed. This understanding should include a description of the nature and limitations of the services to be performed and a description of the report.

Performance Requirements

Before completing a compilation of specified elements, accounts, or items of a financial statement, he or she must adhere to the compilation requirements, which require the accountant to possess a level of knowledge of the accounting principles and practices of the client's industry that will enable him or her to perform the compilation. The accountant should also understand:

1. The nature of the entity's business transactions
2. The form of its accounting records
3. The stated qualifications of its accounting personnel
4. The accounting basis of its financial statements
5. The form and content of the financial statements

The accountant should read the presentation of the specified elements, accounts, or items of a financial statement and consider whether the information appears to be in appropriate form and free of obvious material mistakes.

Reporting Requirements

The basis elements of a report on one or more specified elements, accounts, or items of a financial statement the basic reporting elements of the report are as follows:

1. A statement that the specified element(s), account(s), or item(s) identified in the report were compiled. If the compilation was performed in conjunction with a compilation of the company's financial statements, the paragraph should so state and indicate the date of the accountant's compilation report on those financial statements. Furthermore, any departure from the standard report on those statements should also be disclosed if considered relevant to the presentation of the specified element(s), account(s), or item(s).
2. A statement that the compilation was performed in accordance with SSARS issued by the American Institute of Certified Public Accountants (AICPA).
3. A description of the basis on which the specified element(s), account(s), or item(s) are presented if that basis is not generally accepted accounting principles (GAAP) and a statement that that basis of presentation is a comprehensive basis of accounting other than GAAP (OCBOA).
4. A statement that a compilation is limited to presenting financial information that is the representation of management (owners).
5. A statement that the specified element(s), account(s) or item(s) have not been audited or reviewed, and accordingly, the accountant does not express an opinion or any other form of assurance on it (them).

The report should be signed and dated the date of the completion of the compilation. Each page of the financial statements should include a reference such as "See Accountant's Compilation Report."

ILLUSTRATIONS

The following are example reports on specified elements, accounts, or items of a financial statement from AR Section 110.

ILLUSTRATION 1. REPORTING WHEN THE ACCOUNTANT IS NOT INDEPENDENT

When the accountant is issuing a report with respect to a compilation of specified element(s), account(s), or item(s) of a financial statement for an entity, with respect to which the accountant is not independent, the accountant's report should be modified. In making a judgment about whether he or she is independent, the accountant should be guided by the AICPA *Code of Professional Conduct*. The accountant should indicate his or her lack of independence in a final paragraph of the accountant's compilation report. An example of such a disclosure would be:

> I am (*We are*) not independent with respect to XYZ Company.

The accountant is not precluded from disclosing a description about the reason(s) that his or her independence is impaired. The following are examples of descriptions the accountant may use:

1. I am (*We are*) not independent with respect to XYZ Company as of and for the year ended December 31, 20XX, because I (*a member of the engagement team*) had a direct financial interest in XYZ Company.
2. I am (*We are*) not independent with respect to XYZ Company as of and for the year ended December 31, 20XX, because an individual of my immediate family (*an immediate family member of one of the members of the engagement team*) was employed by XYZ Company.
3. I am (*We are*) not independent with respect to XYZ Company as of and for the year ended December 31, 20XX, because I (*we*) performed certain accounting services (*the accountant may include a specific description of those services*) that impaired my (*our*) independence.

If the accountant elects to disclose a description about the reasons his or her independence is impaired, the accountant should ensure that all reasons are included in the description.

[Paragraph renumbered and revised, December 2010, to reflect conforming changes necessary due to the issuance of SSARS No. 19.]

ILLUSTRATION 2. ILLUSTRATIVE ENGAGEMENT LETTER FOR A COMPILATION OF SPECIFIED ELEMENTS, ACCOUNTS, OR ITEMS OF A FINANCIAL STATEMENT

[*Appropriate Salutation*]

This letter is to confirm our understanding of the terms and objectives of our engagement and the nature and limitations of the services we will provide.

We will perform the following services:

We will compile, from information you provide, [*identify specified element, account, or item of the financial statement, schedule of accounts receivable or schedule of depreciation—income tax basis*] of XYZ Company as of December 31, 20XX, and issue an accountant's report thereon in accordance with Statements on Standards for Accounting and Review Services (SSARS) issued by the American Institute of Certified Public Accountants (AICPA).

The objective of a compilation is to assist you in presenting financial information in the form of [*identify specified element, account, or item of the financial statement*]. We will utilize information that is your representation without undertaking to obtain or provide any assurance that there are no material modifications that should be made to the [*identify specified element, account, or item of the financial statement*] in order for [*identify specified element, account, or item of the financial statement*] to be in conformity with [*the applicable financial accounting framework (for example, accounting principles generally accepted in the United States of America)*].

You are responsible for:

1. The preparation and fair presentation of [*identify specified element, account, or item of the financial statement*] in accordance with [*the applicable financial reporting framework (for example, accounting principles generally accepted in the United States of America)*]
2. Designing, implementing, and maintaining internal control relevant to the preparation and fair presentation of [*identify specified element, account, or item of the financial statement*]
3. Preventing and detecting fraud
4. Identifying and ensuring that the entity complies with the laws and regulations applicable to its activities
5. Making all financial records and related information available to us

We are responsible for conducting the engagement in accordance with SSARSs issued by the AICPA.

A compilation differs significantly from a review or an audit of financial information. A compilation does not contemplate performing inquiry, analytical procedures, or other procedures performed in a review. Additionally, a compilation does not contemplate obtaining an understanding of the entity's internal control; assessing fraud risk; testing accounting records by obtaining sufficient appropriate audit evidence through inspection, observation, confirmation, the examination of source documents (for example, canceled checks or bank images); or other procedures ordinarily performed in an audit. Accordingly, we will not express an opinion or provide any assurance regarding the [*identify specified element, account, or item of the financial statement*] being compiled.

Our engagement cannot be relied upon to disclose errors, fraud, or illegal acts. However, we will inform the appropriate level of management of any material errors, and of any evidence or information that comes to our attention during the performance of our compilation procedures that fraud may have occurred. In addition, we will report to you any evidence or information that comes to our attention during the performance of our compilation procedures regarding illegal acts that may have occurred, unless they are clearly inconsequential.

If, during the period covered by the engagement letter, the accountant's independence is or will be impaired, insert the following:

We are not independent with respect to XYZ Company. We will disclose that we are not independent in our compilation report.

If, for any reason, we are unable to complete the compilation of your [*identify specified element, account, or item of the financial statement*], we will not issue a report on such schedule as a result of this engagement.

Our fees for these services . . .

We will be pleased to discuss this letter with you at any time.

If the foregoing is in accordance with your understanding, please sign the copy of this letter in the space provided and return it to us.

Sincerely yours,

_____
[*Signature of accountant*]

Acknowledged:
XYZ Company

_____
President

_____
Date

ILLUSTRATION 3. STANDARD COMPILATION REPORT ON A SCHEDULE OF ACCOUNTS RECEIVABLE PREPARED IN ACCORDANCE WITH ACCOUNTING PRINCIPLES GENERALLY ACCEPTED IN THE UNITED STATES OF AMERICA

Accountant's Compilation Report

[*Appropriate Salutation*]

I (*We*) have compiled the accompanying schedule of accounts receivable of XYZ Company as of December 31, 20XX. I (*We*) have not audited or reviewed the accompanying schedule of accounts receivable and, accordingly, do not express an opinion or provide any assurance about whether the schedule of accounts receivable is in accordance with accounting principles generally accepted in the United States of America.

The management (*owners*) is (*are*) responsible for the preparation and fair presentation of the schedule of accounts receivable in accordance with accounting principles generally accepted in the United States of America and for designing, implementing, and maintaining internal control relevant to the preparation and fair presentation of the schedule of accounts receivable.

My (*Our*) responsibility is to conduct the compilation in accordance with Statements on Standards for Accounting and Review Services issued by the American Institute of Certified Public Accountants. The objective of a compilation is to assist management in presenting financial information in the form of a schedule of accounts receivable without undertaking to obtain or provide any assurance that there are no material modifications that should be made to the schedule of accounts receivable.

[*Signature of accounting firm or accountant, as appropriate*]

[*Date*]

ILLUSTRATION 4. STANDARD COMPILATION REPORT ON A SCHEDULE OF DEPRECIATION PREPARED IN ACCORDANCE WITH THE BASIS OF ACCOUNTING THE ENTITY USES FOR FEDERAL INCOME TAX PURPOSES

Accountant's Compilation Report

[*Appropriate Salutation*]

I (*We*) have compiled the accompanying schedule of depreciation of XYZ Company as of December 31, 20XX. I (*We*) have not audited or reviewed the accompanying schedule of depreciation and, accordingly, do not express an opinion or provide any assurance about whether the schedule of depreciation is in accordance with the basis of accounting the Company uses for federal income tax purposes.

The management (*owners*) is (*are*) responsible for the preparation and fair presentation of the schedule of depreciation in accordance with the basis of accounting the Company uses for federal income tax purposes and for designing, implementing, and maintaining internal control relevant to the preparation and fair presentation of the schedule of depreciation.

My (*Our*) responsibility is to conduct the compilation in accordance with Statements on Standards for Accounting and Review Services issued by the American Institute of Certified Public Accountants. The objective of a compilation is to assist management in presenting financial information in the form of a schedule of depreciation without undertaking to obtain or provide any assurance that there are no material modifications that should be made to the schedule of depreciation.

[*Signature of accounting firm or accountant, as appropriate*]

[*Date*]

AR 120 Compilation of Pro Forma Financial Information

EFFECTIVE DATE AND APPLICABILITY

Original Pronouncement	Statements on Standards for Accounting and Review Services (SSARSs) 14, 17
Effective Date	This statement currently is effective.
Applicability	When an accountant is engaged to compile or issue a compilation report on pro forma financial information.

OBJECTIVES OF AR SECTION 120

This section established standards for performing a compilation of pro forma financial information. A compilation of pro forma financial information is limited to presenting financial information that is the representation of management without undertaking to express any assurance on that information.

Entities issue pro forma information to show what the significant effects on historical financial information might have been had a consummated or proposed transaction or event occurred at an earlier date—for example, a business combination or the disposal of a portion of the business.

FUNDAMENTAL REQUIREMENTS

GENERAL GUIDANCE

Reporting Obligation

An accountant may prepare or assist in the preparation of pro forma financial information and submitting such a preparation to management *without* the issuance of a compilation report, unless the accountant has been engaged to perform a compilation. However, in deciding whether to issue a compilation report, the accountant should consider how such a presentation of pro forma financial information will be used. If the accountant believes that he or she will be associated with the information, he or she should consider issuing a compilation report so a user will not infer a level of assurance that does not exist.

Additionally, the historical financial statements of the entity on which the pro forma information is based must have been compiled, reviewed, or audited and the related report should be included in the document containing the pro forma financial information.

Understanding with the Entity

The accountant should establish an understanding, preferably in writing, regarding the services to be performed. This understanding should include a description of the nature and limitations of the services to be performed and a description of the report.

Performance Requirements

Before completing a compilation of pro forma financial information, he or she must adhere to the compilation requirements contained in AR Section 100.07–.10, which require the accountant to possess a level of knowledge of the accounting principles and practices of the client's industry that will enable him or her to perform the compilation. The accountant should also understand:

1. The nature of the entity's business transactions
2. The form of its accounting records
3. The stated qualifications of its accounting personnel
4. The accounting basis of its financial statements
5. The form and content of the financial statements

The accountant should read the presentation of the pro forma financial information, including the summary of significant assumptions, and consider whether the information appears to be in appropriate form and free of obvious material mistakes.

Reporting Requirements

The basis elements of a report on one or more specified elements, accounts, or items of a financial statement are as follows:

1. An identification of the pro forma financial information
2. A statement that the compilation was performed in accordance with SSARSs issued by the American Institute of Certified Public Accountants (AICPA).
3. A reference to the financial statements from which the historical financial information is derived and a statement on whether such financial statements were compiled, reviewed, or audited. (The report on pro forma financial information should refer to any modifications in the accountant's or auditor's report on historical financial statements.)
4. A statement that the pro forma financial information was compiled. If the compilation was performed in conjunction with a compilation of the company's financial statements, the paragraph should so state and indicate the date of the accountant's compilation report on those financial statements. Furthermore, any departure from the standard report on those statements should also be disclosed if considered relevant to the presentation of the pro forma financial information.
5. A description of the basis on which the pro forma financial information is presented if that basis is not generally accepted accounting principles (GAAP) and a statement that that basis of presentation is a comprehensive basis of accounting other than GAAP.
6. A statement that a compilation is limited to presenting pro forma financial information that is the representation of management (owners).
7. A statement that the pro forma financial information has not been audited or reviewed and, accordingly, the accountant does not express an opinion or any other form of assurance on it.

8. A separate paragraph explaining the objective of pro forma financial information and its limitations.

The report should be signed and dated the date of the completion of the compilation. Each page of the financial statements should include a reference such as "See Accountant's Compilation Report."

ILLUSTRATIONS

ILLUSTRATION 1. ENGAGEMENT LETTER FOR A COMPILATION ON PRO FORMA FINANCIAL INFORMATION

The following is an example compilation report on pro forma financial information.

[*Appropriate Salutation*]

This letter is to confirm our understanding of the terms and objectives of our engagement and the nature and limitations of the services we will provide.

We will perform the following services:

We will compile, from information you provide, the pro forma financial information of XYZ Company as of December 31, 20XX, and issue an accountant's report thereon in accordance with Statements on Standards for Accounting and Review Services issued by the American Institute of Certified Public Accountants.

The objective of a compilation is to assist you in presenting financial information in the form of pro forma financial information. We will utilize information that is your representation without undertaking to obtain or provide any assurance that there are no material modifications that should be made to the pro forma financial information in order for the pro forma financial information to be in conformity with [*the applicable financial accounting framework (for example, accounting principles generally accepted in the United States of America*)].

You are responsible for:

1. The preparation and fair presentation of the pro forma financial information in accordance with [*the applicable financial reporting framework (for example, accounting principles generally accepted in the United States of America*)].
2. Designing, implementing, and maintaining internal control relevant to the preparation and fair presentation of the pro forma financial information.
3. Preventing and detecting fraud.
4. Identifying and ensuring that the entity complies with the laws and regulations applicable to its activities.
5. Making all financial records and related information available to us.

We are responsible for conducting the engagement in accordance with the Statements on Standards for Accounting and Review Services issued by the American Institute of Certified Public Accountants.

A compilation differs significantly from a review or an audit of financial information. A compilation does not contemplate performing inquiry, analytical procedures, or other procedures performed in a review. Additionally, a compilation does not contemplate obtaining an understanding of the entity's internal control; assessing fraud risk; testing accounting records by obtaining sufficient appropriate audit evidence through inspection, observation, confirmation, the examination of source documents (for example, canceled checks or bank images); or other procedures ordinarily performed in an audit. Accordingly, we will not express an opinion or provide any assurance regarding the pro forma financial information being compiled.

Our engagement cannot be relied upon to disclose errors, fraud, or illegal acts. However, we will inform the appropriate level of management of any material errors, and of any evidence or information that comes to our attention during the performance of our compilation procedures, that fraud may have occurred. In addition, we will report to you any evidence or information that comes to our attention during the performance of our compilation procedures regarding illegal acts that may have occurred, unless they are clearly inconsequential.

If, during the period covered by the engagement letter, the accountant's independence is or will be impaired, insert the following:

> We are not independent with respect to XYZ Company. We will disclose that we are not independent in our compilation report.
>
> If, for any reason, we are unable to complete the compilation of your pro forma financial information, we will not issue a report on such schedule as a result of this engagement.
>
> Our fees for these services . . .
>
> We will be pleased to discuss this letter with you at any time.
>
> If the foregoing is in accordance with your understanding, please sign the copy of this letter in the space provided and return it to us.

Sincerely yours,

_____
[Signature of accountant]

Acknowledged:
XYZ Company

_____
President

_____
Date

ILLUSTRATION 2. COMPILATION REPORT ON PRO FORMA FINANCIAL INFORMATION

Compilation report on pro forma financial information reflecting a business combination prepared in accordance with accounting principles generally accepted in the United States of America:

Accountant's Compilation Report

[*Appropriate Salutation*]

I (we) have compiled the accompanying pro forma financial information of XYZ Company as of December 31, 20XX, reflecting the business combination of the Company and ABC Company. The historical condensed financial statements are derived from the historical unaudited financial statements of XYZ Company, which were compiled by me (us), and of ABC Company, which were compiled by another (other) accountant(s). I (we) have not audited or reviewed the accompanying pro forma financial information and, accordingly, do not express an opinion or provide any assurance about whether the pro forma financial information is in accordance with accounting principles generally accepted in the United States of America.

The management (*owners*) is (*are*) responsible for the preparation and fair presentation of the pro forma financial information in accordance with accounting principles generally accepted in the United States of America and for designing, implementing, and maintaining internal control relevant to the preparation and fair presentation of the pro forma financial information.

My (*our*) responsibility is to conduct the compilation in accordance with Statements on Standards for Accounting and Review Services issued by the American Institute of Certified Public Accountants. The objective of a compilation is to assist management in presenting financial information in the form of pro forma financial information without undertaking to obtain or provide any assurance that there are no material modifications that should be made to the pro forma financial information.

The objective of this pro forma financial information is to show what the significant effects on the historical financial information might have been had the transaction (or event) occurred at an earlier date. However, the pro forma financial information is not necessarily indicative of the results of operations or related effects on financial position that would have been attained had the transaction (or event) actually occurred earlier.

Paragraph the accountant may add after the previous paragraph when management has elected to omit substantially all disclosures, but the pro forma financial information is otherwise in conformity with accounting principles generally accepted in the United States of America.

[*Signature of accounting firm or accountant, as appropriate*]

[*Date*]

AR 200 Reporting on Comparative Financial Statements

EFFECTIVE DATE AND APPLICABILITY

Original Pronouncement	Statements on Standards for Accounting and Review Services (SSARSs) 2, 3, 4, 5, and 7, as amended by SSARSs 11, 12, 15 and 17.
Effective Date	These statements currently are effective.
Applicability	When comparative financial statements of a nonpublic entity are presented and the current period has been compiled and reported on or reviewed in conformity with generally accepted accounting principles (GAAP) or other comprehensive basis of accounting (OCBOA).

> NOTE: *When current period financial statements of a nonissuer are audited and the prior period compiled or reviewed, the guidance in SASs applies.*
>
> *This section only applies to traditional compilations, not management-use-only compilations. The guidance in this section addresses reporting requirements, and a report ordinarily is not issued in a management-use-only compilation engagement.*

DEFINITIONS OF TERMS

Comparative financial statements. Financial statements of two or more periods presented in columnar form.

Continuing accountant. An accountant who has been engaged to audit, review, or compile and report on the financial statements of the current period and one or more consecutive periods immediately prior to the current period.

Reissued report. A report issued subsequent to the date of the original report that bears the same date as the original report. A reissued report may need to be revised for the effects of specific events; in these circumstances, the report should be dual-dated with the original date and a separate date that applies to the effects of such events.

Updated report. A report issued by a continuing accountant that takes into consideration information that he becomes aware of during his current engagement and that reexpresses his previous conclusions or, depending on the circumstances, expresses different conclusions on the financial statements of a prior period as of the date of his current report.

OBJECTIVES OF AR SECTION 200

This section established standards for reporting on comparative financial statements of a nonissuer when financial statements of the current period have been compiled and reported on or reviewed. SSARS 2 was issued to provide coverage for reporting on comparative financial statements in situations when the SASs do not apply.

SSARS 11 amended SSARS 2 to allow successor accountants to name predecessor accountants if the predecessor's practice was merged with, or acquired by, the successor accountant's practice.

FUNDAMENTAL REQUIREMENTS

GENERAL

When comparative financial statements of a nonissuer are presented, the accountant should issue a report covering each period presented.

If the accountant becomes aware that financial statements of other periods that have not been audited, reviewed, or compiled are presented in comparative form in a document containing financial statements that he or she has reported on and the accountant's name or report is used, the accountant should advise the client that the use of his or her name or report is not appropriate. The accountant may also wish to consult with an attorney.

The accountant should not report on comparative statements when statements for one or more of the periods, but not all, omit all or substantially all disclosures.

NOTE: Financial statements in columnar form with disclosures are comparative; financial statements that omit all or substantially all disclosures are comparative; but financial statements with disclosures are not comparative to financial statements without disclosures.

CONTINUING ACCOUNTANT'S STANDARD REPORT

A continuing accountant who performs the same or higher level of service on the current period financial statements should update his or her report on the prior period financial statements.

A continuing accountant who performs a lower level of service (20X2 compiled, 20X1 reviewed) should either:

1. Include a separate paragraph in the report describing the responsibility for the prior period financial statements, or
2. Reissue the report on the prior period financial statements

If option 1 from the previous list is selected, the description should include the original date of the report and should state that no review procedures were performed after that date.

If option 2 is selected, the report may be:

1. A combined compilation and reissued review report (the combined report should state that no review procedures were performed after the date of the review report)
2. Presented separately

The "Illustrations" section presents example reports on comparative financial statements for the continuing accountant when:

1. Each period is compiled.
2. Each period is reviewed.
3. The current period is reviewed and the prior period is compiled.

CONTINUING ACCOUNTANT'S CHANGED REFERENCE TO GAAP

The accountant should consider the effects on the prior period report of circumstances or events that came to his or her attention. When the accountant's report contains a changed reference to a GAAP departure, the report should include a separate paragraph indicating:

1. Date of previous report
2. Circumstances or events that caused the change
3. If applicable, that the prior period financial statements have been changed

The "Illustrations" section presents an example explanatory paragraph for a changed reference to GAAP.

PREDECESSOR'S COMPILATION OR REVIEW REPORT

A predecessor accountant is not required, but may reissue his or her report. If the predecessor's compilation or review report is not presented, the successor should either:

1. Make reference to the predecessor's report.
2. Perform a compilation, review, or audit of the prior period financial statements and report thereon.

If "reference to the predecessor's report" option is selected, the successor's reference should include:

1. A statement that the prior period financial statements were compiled or reviewed by another accountant (without identifying the predecessor by name; however, the successor may name the predecessor if the predecessor's practice was acquired by, or merged with, the successor's practice)
2. The date of prior accountant's report
3. A description of the disclaimer or limited assurance report
4. A description or quotation of any report modification or emphasis paragraphs

"Illustrations" contains examples of successor paragraphs when the predecessor reviewed or compiled the prior period financial statements.

If the predecessor report is to be reissued, before reissuing the predecessor should consider:

1. The current form and presentation of the prior period financial statements
2. Subsequent events that were not previously known
3. Changes in the financial statements that might require modifications to the report.

The predecessor should also:

1. Read the current period financial statements and the successor's report
2. Compare the prior period financial statements with the financial statements previously issued, and with the current period
3. Get a letter from the successor indicating whether he or she is aware of any matter that affects the prior period financial statements

If the predecessor becomes aware of any matter that affects the prior period financial statements, he or she should:

1. Make inquiries or perform analytical procedures similar to those that would have been applied to the information if it had been known at the report date

2. Perform other necessary procedures, such as discussing the matter with the successor or reviewing the successor's working papers

When reissuing the report, the predecessor should use the date of the previous report. However, if the financial statements are revised, the report should be dual-dated. Also, if the financial statements are revised, the predecessor should obtain a written statement from the former client describing the new information and its effect on the prior period financial statements.

If the predecessor is unable to complete the reissue procedures described above, he or she should not reissue the report and may wish to consult with an attorney.

CHANGED PRIOR PERIOD FINANCIAL STATEMENTS

Either the predecessor (as discussed above) or the successor should report on restated financial statements when the financial statements have been changed. If the successor reports on them, he or she should audit, review, or compile the financial statements and report accordingly. No references to the predecessor's report should be made in the successor's report.

REPORTING WHEN PRIOR PERIOD IS AUDITED

The accountant should issue a compilation or review report on the current period financial statements and either:

1. Reissue the audit report on the prior period or
2. Add a separate paragraph to the current period report that includes the following information:

   a. The financial statements of the prior period were audited
   b. The date of the audit report
   c. The type of opinion
   d. Substantive reasons for other than unqualified opinion
   e. No audit procedures performed after item b

"Illustrations" presents an example paragraph for the above situation.

REPORTING ON FINANCIAL STATEMENTS THAT PREVIOUSLY DID NOT OMIT ALL OR SUBSTANTIALLY ALL DISCLOSURES

The accountant may report on comparative financial statements that omit all or substantially all disclosures even if the prior period statements were originally compiled, reviewed, or audited (with disclosures) provided that his or her report includes an additional paragraph stating the nature of the previous service and the date of the previous report. "Illustrations" presents an example report (see also the "Interpretation" section later in this chapter).

CHANGE OF STATUS—ISSUER/NONISSUER

A previously issued compilation or review report should not be reissued or referred to in the current report if the entity is currently an issuer.

INTERPRETATION

REPORTING ON FINANCIAL STATEMENTS THAT PREVIOUSLY DID NOT OMIT SUBSTANTIALLY ALL DISCLOSURES (ISSUED NOVEMBER 1980; REVISED NOVEMBER 2002; REVISED MAY 2004; REVISED JULY 2005)

If the financial statements are compiled (disclosures omitted) from financial statements that previously did not omit disclosures, the accountant's reference to the previous reports should include a description or quotation of any report modification or emphasis matter. If the accountant had previously audited the financial statements, then the accountant should indicate the type of opinion expressed and the reasons for doing so.

TECHNIQUES FOR APPLICATION

CLIENT-PREPARED FINANCIAL STATEMENTS PRESENTED WITH COMPILED OR REVIEWED FINANCIAL STATEMENTS

Client-prepared financial statements of some periods that have not been audited, reviewed, or compiled should not be presented in columnar/comparative format. However, they may be presented on separate pages of a document (containing financial statements that the accountant has reported on) if they are accompanied by an indication by the client (1) that they have not been compiled, reviewed, or audited, and (2) that the accountant assumes no responsibility for them.

DECIDING REPORT OPTIONS UNDER SSARS 2

SSARS 2 is rather complex. The following summary decision aid helps simplify the report decision process in SSARS 2. The comparative statements are for years 20X1 and 20X2.

1. If 20X2 is audited, SASs apply.
2. If the entity's current status for 20X2 is a public company, SASs apply.
3. For continuing accountant:

    a. If 20X2 level of service is equal to or higher than 20X1, update report.
    b. If 20X2 is lower level of service, either refer to or reissue prior report.

4. For successor accountant:

    a. If predecessor does not reissue, refer to report of predecessor or perform audit, review, or compilation of 20X1.
    b. If financial statements are restated because of an error and predecessor doesn't report on restated financials, perform audit, review, or compilation of 20X2.

ILLUSTRATIONS

The following are reports on comparative financial statements from AR Section 200.

ILLUSTRATIVE COMPILATION REPORTS ON COMPARATIVE FINANCIAL STATEMENTS

ILLUSTRATION 1. COMPILATION REPORT ON COMPARATIVE FINANCIAL STATEMENTS WHEN A COMPILATION HAS BEEN PERFORMED FOR BOTH PERIODS

Accountant's Compilation Report

[*Appropriate Salutation*]

I (*We*) have compiled the accompanying balance sheets of XYZ Company as of December 31, 20X2 and 20X1, and the related statements of income, retained earnings, and cash flows for the years then ended. I (*We*) have not audited or reviewed the accompanying financial statements and, accordingly, do not express an opinion or provide any assurance about whether the financial statements are in accordance with accounting principles generally accepted in the United States of America.

The management (*owners*) is (*are*) responsible for the preparation and fair presentation of the financial statements in accordance with accounting principles generally accepted in the United States of America and for designing, implementing, and maintaining internal control relevant to the preparation and fair presentation of the financial statements.

My (*Our*) responsibility is to conduct the compilations in accordance with Statements on Standards for Accounting and Review Services issued by the American Institute of Certified Public Accountants. The objective of a compilation is to assist management in presenting financial information in the form of financial statements without undertaking to obtain or provide any assurance that there are no material modifications that should be made to the financial statements.

[*Signature of accounting firm or accountant, as appropriate*]

[*Date*]

ILLUSTRATION 2. COMPILATION REPORT WHEN THE FINANCIAL STATEMENTS OF THE CURRENT YEAR HAVE BEEN COMPILED AND THOSE OF THE PRIOR YEAR HAVE BEEN REVIEWED

Accountant's Compilation Report

[*Appropriate Salutation*]

I (*We*) have compiled the accompanying balance sheet of XYZ Company as of December 31, 20X2, and the related statements of income, retained earnings, and cash flows for the year then ended. I (*We*) have not audited or reviewed the 20X2 financial statements and, accordingly, do not express an opinion or provide any assurance about whether the financial statements are in accordance with accounting principles generally accepted in the United States of America.

The management (*owners*) is (*are*) responsible for the preparation and fair presentation of the financial statements in accordance with accounting principles generally accepted in the United States of America and for designing, implementing, and maintaining internal control relevant to the preparation and fair presentation of the financial statements.

My (*Our*) responsibility is to conduct the compilations in accordance with Statements on Standards for Accounting and Review Services issued by the American Institute of Certified Public Accountants. The objective of a compilation is to assist management in presenting financial information in the form of financial statements without undertaking to obtain or provide any assurance that there are no material modifications that should be made to the financial statements.

The accompanying 20X1 financial statements were previously reviewed by me (*us*) and I (*we*) stated that I was (*we were*) not aware of any material modifications that should be made to those financial statements in order for them to be in conformity with accounting principles generally accepted in the United States of America in my (*our*) report dated March 31, 20X2, but I (*we*) have not performed any procedures in connection with that review engagement since that date.

[*Signature of accounting firm or accountant, as appropriate*]

[*Date*]

> **ILLUSTRATION 3. COMPILATION REPORT ON COMPARATIVE FINANCIAL STATEMENTS WHEN THE ACCOUNTANT'S REPORT INCLUDES A CHANGED REFERENCE TO A DEPARTURE FROM ACCOUNTING PRINCIPLES GENERALLY ACCEPTED IN THE UNITED STATES OF AMERICA**

Accountant's Compilation Report

[*Appropriate Salutation*]

I (*We*) have compiled the accompanying balance sheets of XYZ Company as of December 31, 20X2 and 20X1, and the related statements of income, retained earnings, and cash flows for the years then ended. I (*We*) have not audited or reviewed the accompanying financial statements and, accordingly, do not express an opinion or provide any assurance about whether the financial statements are in accordance with accounting principles generally accepted in the United States of America.

The management (*owners*) is (*are*) responsible for the preparation and fair presentation of the financial statements in accordance with accounting principles generally accepted in the United States of America and for designing, implementing, and maintaining internal control relevant to the preparation and fair presentation of the financial statements.

My (*Our*) responsibility is to conduct the compilations in accordance with Statements on Standards for Accounting and Review Services issued by the American Institute of Certified Public Accountants. The objective of a compilation is to assist management in presenting financial information in the form of financial statements without undertaking to obtain or provide any assurance that there are no material modifications that should be made to the financial statements.

In my (*our*) report dated March 1, 20X2 with respect to the 20X1 financial statements, we referred to a departure from accounting principles generally accepted in the United States of America because the company carried its land at appraised values. As described in Note X, the Company has changed its method of accounting for land and restated its 20X1 financial statements to conform with accounting principles generally accepted in the United States of America.

[*Signature of accounting firm or accountant, as appropriate*]

[*Date*]

> **ILLUSTRATION 4. COMPILATION REPORT ON COMPARATIVE FINANCIAL STATEMENTS WHEN THE PRIOR PERIOD FINANCIAL STATEMENTS WERE COMPILED BY A PREDECESSOR ACCOUNTANT AND THE PREDECESSOR'S REPORT IS NOT PRESENTED**

Accountant's Compilation Report

[*Appropriate Salutation*]

I (*We*) have compiled the accompanying balance sheet of XYZ Company as of December 31, 20X2, and the related statements of income, retained earnings, and cash flows for the year then ended. I (*We*) have not audited or reviewed the accompanying financial statements and, accordingly, do not express an opinion or provide any assurance about whether the financial statements are in accordance with accounting principles generally accepted in the United States of America.

The financial statements of XYZ Company as of December 31, 20X1, were compiled by other accountants whose report dated February 1, 20X2 stated that they have not audited or reviewed the 20X1 financial statements and, accordingly, do not express an opinion or provide any assurance about whether the financial statements are in accordance with accounting principles generally accepted in the United States of America.

The management (*owners*) is (*are*) responsible for the preparation and fair presentation of the financial statements in accordance with accounting principles generally accepted in the United States of America and for designing, implementing, and maintaining internal control relevant to the preparation and fair presentation of the financial statements.

My (*our*) responsibility is to conduct the 20X2 compilations in accordance with Statements on Standards for Accounting and Review Services issued by the American Institute of Certified Public Accountants. The objective of a compilation is to assist management in presenting financial information in the form of financial statements without undertaking to obtain or provide any assurance that there are no material modifications that should be made to the financial statements.

[*Signature of accounting firm or accountant, as appropriate*]

[*Date*]

> **ILLUSTRATION 5. COMPILATION REPORT ON COMPARATIVE FINANCIAL STATEMENTS WHEN THE PREDECESSOR ACCOUNTANT'S REPORT IS NOT PRESENTED, AND THE SUCCESSOR ACCOUNTANT IS ENGAGED TO COMPILE THE RESTATEMENT ADJUSTMENT(S)**

Accountant's Compilation Report

[*Appropriate Salutation*]

I (*We*) have compiled the accompanying balance sheet of XYZ Company as of December 31, 20X2, and the related statements of income, retained earnings, and cash flows for the year then ended. I (*we*) have not audited or reviewed the accompanying financial statements and, accordingly, do not express an opinion or provide any assurance about whether the financial statements are in accordance with accounting principles generally accepted in the United States of America. The financial statements prior to adjustment of XYZ Company as of and for the year ended December 31, 20X1, were compiled by other accountants whose report dated February 1, 20X2, stated that they have not audited or reviewed the 20X1 financial statements and, accordingly, do not express an opinion or provide any assurance about whether the financial statements are in accordance with accounting principles generally accepted in the United States of America.

The management (*owners*) is (*are*) responsible for the preparation and fair presentation of the financial statements in accordance with accounting principles generally accepted in the United States of America and for designing, implementing, and maintaining internal control relevant to the preparation and fair presentation of the financial statements.

My (*Our*) responsibility is to conduct the compilations in accordance with Statements on Standards for Accounting and Review Services issued by the American Institute of Certified Public Accountants. The objective of a compilation is to assist management in presenting financial information in the form of financial statements without undertaking to obtain or provide any assurance that there are no material modifications that should be made to the financial statements.

I (*We*) also compiled the adjustments described in Note X that were applied to restate the 20X1 financial statements. I (*we*) have not audited or reviewed the adjustments described in Note X that were applied to restate the 20X1 financial statements and, accordingly, do not express an opinion or provide any assurance about whether the adjustments described in Note X that were applied to restate the 20X1 financial statements are in accordance with accounting principles generally accepted in the United States of America.

[*Signature of accounting firm or accountant, as appropriate*]

[*Date*]

ILLUSTRATION 6. COMPILATION REPORT ON COMPARATIVE FINANCIAL STATEMENTS WHEN THE PRIOR PERIOD FINANCIAL STATEMENTS WERE AUDITED

Accountant's Compilation Report

[*Appropriate Salutation*]

I (*We*) have compiled the accompanying balance sheet of XYZ Company as of December 31, 20X2, and the related statements of income, retained earnings, and cash flows for the year then ended. I (*We*) have not audited or reviewed the accompanying financial statements and, accordingly, do not express an opinion or provide any assurance about whether the financial statements are in accordance with accounting principles generally accepted in the United States of America.

The management (*owners*) is (*are*) responsible for the preparation and fair presentation of the financial statements in accordance with accounting principles generally accepted in the United States of America and for designing, implementing, and maintaining internal control relevant to the preparation and fair presentation of the financial statements.

My (*Our*) responsibility is to conduct the compilations in accordance with Statements on Standards for Accounting and Review Services issued by the American Institute of Certified Public Accountants. The objective of a compilation is to assist management in presenting financial information in the form of financial statements without undertaking to obtain or provide any assurance that there are no material modifications that should be made to the financial statements.

The 20X1 financial statements were audited by me (*us*) (*other accountants*) and I (*we*) (*they*) expressed an unqualified opinion on them in my (*our*) (*their*) report dated March 1, 20X2, but I (*we*) (*they*) have not performed any auditing procedures since that date.

[*Signature of accounting firm or accountant, as appropriate*]

[*Date*]

ILLUSTRATION 7. COMPILATION REPORT ON COMPARATIVE FINANCIAL STATEMENTS WHEN PRIOR PERIOD FINANCIAL STATEMENTS THAT OMIT SUBSTANTIALLY ALL DISCLOSURES HAVE BEEN COMPILED FROM PREVIOUSLY REVIEWED FINANCIAL STATEMENTS OF THE SAME PERIOD

Accountant's Compilation Report

[*Appropriate Salutation*]

I (*We*) have compiled the accompanying balance sheets of XYZ Company as of December 31, 20X2 and 20X1, and the related statements of income, retained earnings, and cash flows for the years then ended. I (*we*) have not audited or reviewed the accompanying financial statements and, accordingly, do not express an opinion or provide any assurance about whether the financial statements are in accordance with accounting principles generally accepted in the United States of America.

The management (*owners*) is (*are*) responsible for the preparation and fair presentation of the financial statements in accordance with accounting principles generally accepted in the United States of America and for designing, implementing, and maintaining internal control relevant to the preparation and fair presentation of the financial statements.

My (*Our*) responsibility is to conduct the compilations in accordance with Statements on Standards for Accounting and Review Services issued by the American Institute of Certified Public Accountants. The objective of a compilation is to assist management in presenting financial information in the form of financial statements without undertaking to obtain or provide any assurance that there are no material modifications that should be made to the financial statements.

Management has elected to omit substantially all of the disclosures required by accounting principles generally accepted in the United States of America. If the omitted disclosures were included in the financial statements, they might influence the user's conclusions about the company's financial position, results of operations, and cash flows. Accordingly, the financial statements are not designed for those who are not informed about such matters.

The 20X1 financial statements were compiled by me (*us*) from financial statements that did not omit substantially all of the disclosures required by accounting principles generally accepted in the United States of America and that I (*we*) previously reviewed as indicated in my (*our*) report dated March 1, 20X2.

[*Signature of accounting firm or accountant, as appropriate*]

[*Date*]

ILLUSTRATIVE REVIEW REPORTS ON COMPARATIVE FINANCIAL STATEMENTS

ILLUSTRATION 1. REVIEW REPORT ON COMPARATIVE FINANCIAL STATEMENTS WHEN A REVIEW HAS BEEN PERFORMED FOR BOTH PERIODS

Independent Accountant's Review Report

[*Appropriate Salutation*]

I (*We*) have reviewed the accompanying balance sheets of XYZ Company as of December 31, 20X2 and 20X1, and the related statements of income, retained earnings, and cash flows for the years then ended. A review includes primarily applying analytical procedures to management's (*owners'*) financial data and making inquiries of company management (*owners*). A review is substantially less in scope than an audit, the objective of which is the expression of an opinion regarding the financial statements as a whole. Accordingly, I (*we*) do not express such an opinion.

The management (*owners*) is (*are*) responsible for the preparation and fair presentation of the financial statements in accordance with accounting principles generally accepted in the United States of America and for designing, implementing, and maintaining internal control relevant to the preparation and fair presentation of the financial statements.

My (*Our*) responsibility is to conduct the reviews in accordance with Statements on Standards for Accounting and Review Services issued by the American Institute of Certified Public Accountants. Those standards require me (*us*) to perform procedures to obtain limited assurance that there are no material modifications that should be made to the financial statements. I (*We*) believe that the results of my (*our*) procedures provide a reasonable basis for our report.

Based on my (*our*) reviews, I am (*we are*) not aware of any material modifications that should be made to the accompanying financial statements in order for them to be in conformity with accounting principles generally accepted in the United States of America.

[*Signature of accounting firm or accountant, as appropriate*]

[*Date*]

ILLUSTRATION 2. REVIEW REPORT ON COMPARATIVE FINANCIAL STATEMENTS WHEN THE FINANCIAL STATEMENTS OF THE CURRENT PERIOD HAVE BEEN REVIEWED AND THOSE OF THE PRIOR PERIOD HAVE BEEN COMPILED

Independent Accountant's Review Report

[*Appropriate Salutation*]

I (*We*) have reviewed the accompanying balance sheet of XYZ Company as of December 31, 20X2, and the related statements of income, retained earnings, and cash flows for the year then ended. A review includes primarily applying analytical procedures to management's (*owners'*) financial data and making inquiries of company management (*owners*). A review is substantially less in scope than an audit, the objective of which is the expression of an opinion regarding the financial statements as a whole. Accordingly, I (*we*) do not express such an opinion.

The management (*owners*) is (*are*) responsible for the preparation and fair presentation of the financial statements in accordance with accounting principles generally accepted in the United States of America and for designing, implementing, and maintaining internal control relevant to the preparation and fair presentation of the financial statements.

My (*Our*) responsibility is to conduct the reviews in accordance with Statements on Standards for Accounting and Review Services issued by the American Institute of Certified Public Accountants. Those standards require me (*us*) to perform procedures to obtain limited assurance that there are no material modifications that should be made to the financial statements. I (*We*) believe that the results of my (*our*) procedures provide a reasonable basis for our report.

Based on my (*our*) reviews, I am (*we are*) not aware of any material modifications that should be made to the 20X2 financial statements in order for them to be in conformity with accounting principles generally accepted in the United States of America.

The accompanying 20X1 financial statements of XYZ Company were compiled by me (*us*). The objective of a compilation is to assist management in presenting financial information in the form of financial statements without undertaking to obtain or provide any assurance that there are no material modifications that should be made to the financial statements. Accordingly, I (*we*) do not express an opinion or provide any assurance about whether the financial statements are in accordance with accounting principles generally accepted in the United States of America.

[*Signature of accounting firm or accountant, as appropriate*]

[*Date*]

ILLUSTRATION 3. REVIEW REPORT ON COMPARATIVE FINANCIAL STATEMENTS WHEN THE ACCOUNTANT'S REPORT INCLUDES A CHANGED REFERENCE TO A DEPARTURE FROM ACCOUNTING PRINCIPLES GENERALLY ACCEPTED IN THE UNITED STATES OF AMERICA

Independent Accountant's Review Report

[*Appropriate Salutation*]

I (*We*) have reviewed the accompanying balance sheets of XYZ Company as of December 31, 20X2 and 20X1, and the related statements of income, retained earnings, and cash flows for the years then ended. A review includes primarily applying analytical procedures to management's (*owners'*) financial data and making inquiries of company management (*owners*). A review is substantially less in scope than an audit, the objective of which is the expression of an opinion regarding the financial statements as a whole. Accordingly, I (*we*) do not express such an opinion.

The management (*owners*) is (*are*) responsible for the preparation and fair presentation of the financial statements in accordance with accounting principles generally accepted in the United States of America and for designing, implementing, and maintaining internal control relevant to the preparation and fair presentation of the financial statements.

My (*Our*) responsibility is to conduct the reviews in accordance with Statements on Standards for Accounting and Review Services issued by the American Institute of Certified Public Accountants. Those standards require me (*us*) to perform procedures to obtain limited assurance that there are no material modifications that should be made to the financial statements. I (*We*) believe that the results of my (*our*) procedures provide a reasonable basis for our report.

In my (*our*) report dated March 1, 20X2, with respect to the 20X1 financial statements, we referred to a departure from accounting principles generally accepted in the United States of America because the company carried its land at appraised values. As described in Note X, the Company has changed its method of accounting for land and restated its 20X1 financial statements to conform with accounting principles generally accepted in the United States of America. Accordingly, my (*our*) present statement on the 20X1 financial statements, as presented herein, that I am (*we are*) not aware of any material modifications that should be made to the accompanying financial statements, is different from that expressed in our previous report.

Based on my (*our*) reviews, I am (*we are*) not aware of any material modifications that should be made to the accompanying financial statements in order for them to be in conformity with accounting principles generally accepted in the United States of America.

[*Signature of accounting firm or accountant, as appropriate*]

[*Date*]

> **ILLUSTRATION 4. REVIEW REPORT ON COMPARATIVE FINANCIAL STATEMENTS WHEN THE PRIOR PERIOD FINANCIAL STATEMENTS WERE REVIEWED BY A PREDECESSOR ACCOUNTANT, AND THE PREDECESSOR'S REPORT IS NOT PRESENTED**

Independent Accountant's Review Report

[*Appropriate Salutation*]

I (*We*) have reviewed the accompanying balance sheet of XYZ Company as of December 31, 20X2, and the related statements of income, retained earnings, and cash flows for the year then ended. A review includes primarily applying analytical procedures to management's (*owners'*) financial data and making inquiries of company management (*owners*). A review is substantially less in scope than an audit, the objective of which is the expression of an opinion regarding the financial statements as a whole. Accordingly, I (*we*) do not express such an opinion. The financial statements of XYZ Company as of December 31, 20X1, were reviewed by other accountants whose report dated February 1, 20X2, stated that based on their procedures, they are not aware of any material modifications that should be made to the financial statements in order for them to be in conformity with accounting principles generally accepted in the United States of America.

The management (*owners*) is (*are*) responsible for the preparation and fair presentation of the financial statements in accordance with accounting principles generally accepted in the United States of America and for designing, implementing, and maintaining internal control relevant to the preparation and fair presentation of the financial statements.

My (*Our*) responsibility is to conduct the review in accordance with Statements on Standards for Accounting and Review Services issued by the American Institute of Certified Public Accountants. Those standards require me (*us*) to perform procedures to obtain limited assurance that there are no material modifications that should be made to the financial statements. I (*We*) believe that the results of my (*our*) procedures provide a reasonable basis for our report.

Based on my (*our*) review, I am (*we are*) not aware of any material modifications that should be made to the 20X2 financial statements in order for them to be in conformity with accounting principles generally accepted in the United States of America.

[*Signature of accounting firm or accountant, as appropriate*]

[*Date*]

> **ILLUSTRATION 5. REVIEW REPORT ON COMPARATIVE FINANCIAL STATEMENTS WHEN THE PREDECESSOR ACCOUNTANT'S REPORT IS NOT PRESENTED, AND THE SUCCESSOR ACCOUNTANT IS ENGAGED TO REVIEW THE RESTATEMENT ADJUSTMENTS**

Independent Accountant's Review Report

[*Appropriate Salutation*]

I (*We*) have reviewed the accompanying balance sheet of XYZ Company as of December 31, 20X2, and the related statements of income, retained earnings, and cash flows for the year then ended. A review includes primarily applying analytical procedures to management's (*owners'*) financial data and making inquiries of company management (*owners*). A review is substantially less in scope than an audit, the objective of which is the expression of an opinion regarding the financial statements as a whole. Accordingly, I (*we*) do not express such an opinion. The financial statements of XYZ Company as of December 31, 20X1 prior to adjustment were reviewed by other accountants whose report dated February 1, 20X2, stated that based on their procedures, they are not aware of any material modifications that should be made to the financial statements in order for them to be in conformity with accounting principles generally accepted in the United States of America.

The management (*owners*) is (*are*) responsible for the preparation and fair presentation of the financial statements in accordance with accounting principles generally accepted in the United States of America and for designing, implementing, and maintaining internal control relevant to the preparation and fair presentation of the financial statements.

My (*Our*) responsibility is to conduct the review in accordance with Statements on Standards for Accounting and Review Services issued by the American Institute of Certified Public Accountants. Those standards require me (*us*) to perform procedures to obtain limited assurance that there are no material modifications that should be made to the financial statements. I (*We*) believe that the results of my (*our*) procedures provide a reasonable basis for our report.

Based on my (*our*) review, I am (*we are*) not aware of any material modifications that should be made to the 20X2 financial statements in order for them to be in conformity with accounting principles generally accepted in the United States of America.

I (*We*) also reviewed the adjustments described in Note X that were applied to restate the 20X1 financial statements. Based on my (*our*) review, I am (*we are*) not aware of any material modifications that should be made to the adjustments described in Note X that were applied to restate the 20X1 financial statements in order for them to be in conformity with accounting principles generally accepted in the United States of America.

[*Signature of accounting firm or accountant, as appropriate*]

[*Date*]

ILLUSTRATION 6. REVIEW REPORT ON COMPARATIVE FINANCIAL STATEMENTS WHEN THE PRIOR PERIOD FINANCIAL STATEMENTS WERE AUDITED

Independent Accountant's Review Report

[*Appropriate Salutation*]

I (*We*) have reviewed the accompanying balance sheet of XYZ Company as of December 31, 20X2, and the related statements of income, retained earnings, and cash flows for the year then ended. A review includes primarily applying analytical procedures to management's (*owners'*) financial data and making inquiries of company management (*owners*). A review is substantially less in scope than an audit, the objective of which is the expression of an opinion regarding the financial statements as a whole. Accordingly, I (*we*) do not express such an opinion.

The management (*owners*) is (*are*) responsible for the preparation and fair presentation of the financial statements in accordance with accounting principles generally accepted in the United States of America and for designing, implementing, and maintaining internal control relevant to the preparation and fair presentation of the financial statements.

My (*Our*) responsibility is to conduct the review in accordance with Statements on Standards for Accounting and Review Services issued by the American Institute of Certified Public Accountants. Those standards require me (*us*) to perform procedures to obtain limited assurance that there are no material modifications that should be made to the financial statements. I (*We*) believe that the results of my (*our*) procedures provide a reasonable basis for our report.

Based on my (*our*) review, I am (*we are*) not aware of any material modifications that should be made to the 20X2 financial statements in order for them to be in conformity with accounting principles generally accepted in the United States of America.

The 20X1 financial statements were audited by me (*us*) (*other accountants*) and I (*we*) (*they*) expressed an unqualified opinion on them in my (*our*) (*their*) report dated March 1, 20X2, but I (*we*) (*they*) have not performed any auditing procedures since that date.

[*Signature of accounting firm or accountant, as appropriate*]

[*Date*]

AR 300 Compilation Reports on Financial Statements Included in Certain Prescribed Forms

EFFECTIVE DATE AND APPLICABILITY

Original Pronouncement	Statements on Standards for Accounting and Review Services (SSARSs) 3, 5, 7, 15, and 17.
Effective Date	These statements currently are effective.
Applicability	The section provides for an alternative form of standard compilation report on financial statements in prescribed forms that call for departures from generally accepted accounting principles (GAAP) or other comprehensive basis of accounting (OCBOA) by either (1) specifying a measurement principle not in conformity with GAAP, or (2) failing to request the disclosures required by GAAP. The section does not apply to tax returns or to forms designed or adopted by the client. Also, the section does not apply to review engagements or to management-use-only financial statements that are provided to clients without issuing a compilation report.

DEFINITION OF TERM

Prescribed form. Any standard preprinted form designed or adopted by the body to which it is to be submitted—for example, forms used by banks, credit agencies, industry trade associations, or governmental and regulatory agencies.

OBJECTIVES OF AR SECTION 300

There is a presumption that the information required by a prescribed form is sufficient to satisfy the body that designed or adopted the form; thus, there is no need to call attention to departures required by the form.

FUNDAMENTAL REQUIREMENTS

GENERAL

The standards for performing a compilation as described in SSARS 1 (Section 3100) also apply to SSARS 3 engagements.

An accountant may issue either a compilation report as described in SSARS 1 or the alternative SSARS 3 report (see the section "Illustrations").

MEASUREMENT AND DISCLOSURE DEPARTURES

The SSARS 3 report does not require GAAP measurement or disclosure departures required by the prescribed form or the instructions to the form to be identified.

Departures from GAAP that are not permitted by the form or its requirements should be described in the SSARS 3 compilation report in accordance with SSARS 1.

PREPRINTED ACCOUNTANT'S REPORT

The accountant should not sign a preprinted prescribed report that does not meet the requirements of SSARS 1 or SSARS 3. Instead, the accountant should attach an acceptable report.

INTERPRETATIONS

OMISSION OF DISCLOSURES IN FINANCIAL STATEMENTS INCLUDED IN CERTAIN PRESCRIBED FORMS (ISSUED MAY 1982; REVISED FEBRUARY 2008)

An accountant who has reviewed financial statements of a nonissuer may issue a compilation report on financial statements for the same period in a prescribed form that calls for a departure from GAAP. When the difference between the previously reviewed financial statements and the financial statements included in the prescribed form is limited to the omission of disclosures not requested by the form, the accountant may wish to refer to the review report in the prescribed-form compilation report. If the measurement principles used in the compiled financial statements in the prescribed form cause the financial statements to be materially different from the previously reviewed financial statements, the accountant should not refer to the review engagement.

ILLUSTRATIONS

Illustrative Compilation Reports on Financial Statements Included in Certain Prescribed Forms

> **ILLUSTRATION 1. STANDARD COMPILATION REPORT WHEN THE COMPILED FINANCIAL STATEMENTS ARE INCLUDED IN A PRESCRIBED FORM THAT CALLS FOR A PRESENTATION DEPARTURE FROM ACCOUNTING PRINCIPLES GENERALLY ACCEPTED IN THE UNITED STATES OF AMERICA**

Accountant's Compilation Report

[*Appropriate Salutation*]

I (*We*) have compiled the (*identification of financial statements, including period covered and the name of entity*) included in the accompanying prescribed form. I (*We*) have not audited or reviewed the financial statements included in the accompanying prescribed form and, accordingly, do not express an opinion or provide any assurance about whether the financial statements are in accordance with accounting principles generally accepted in the United States of America.

The management (*owners*) is (*are*) responsible for the preparation and fair presentation of the financial statements included in the form prescribed by (*name of body*) in accordance with accounting principles generally accepted in the United States of America and for designing, implementing, and maintaining internal control relevant to the preparation and fair presentation of the financial statements.

My (*Our*) responsibility is to conduct the compilation in accordance with Statements on Standards for Accounting and Review Services issued by the American Institute of Certified Public Accountants. The objective of a compilation is to assist management in presenting financial information in the form of financial statements without undertaking to obtain or provide any assurance that there are no material modifications that should be made to the financial statements.

The financial statements included in the accompanying prescribed form are presented in accordance with the requirements of [*name of body*], and are not intended to be a presentation in accordance with accounting principles generally accepted in the United States of America.

This report is intended solely for the information and use of [*the specified parties*] and is not intended to be and should not be used by anyone other than these specified parties.

[*Signature of accounting firm or accountant, as appropriate*]

[*Date*]

> **ILLUSTRATION 2. COMPILATION REPORT WHEN THE COMPILED FINANCIAL STATEMENTS ARE PREPARED IN ACCORDANCE WITH A SPECIAL PURPOSE FRAMEWORK PRESCRIBED BY CONTRACT OR REGULATION AND THAT FRAMEWORK PRESCRIBES A FORMAT FOR THE FINANCIAL INFORMATION**

Accountant's Compilation Report

[*Appropriate Salutation*]

I (*We*) have compiled the [*identification of financial statements, including period covered and the name of entity*] included in the accompanying prescribed form. I (*We*) have not audited or reviewed the financial statements included in the accompanying prescribed form and, accordingly, do not express an opinion or provide any assurance about whether the financial statements are in accordance with the basis of accounting prescribed by [*describe contract or regulation*].

The management (*owners*) is (*are*) responsible for the preparation and fair presentation of the financial statements included in the form in accordance with the basis of accounting prescribed by [*describe contract or regulation*] and for designing, implementing, and maintaining internal control relevant to the preparation and fair presentation of the financial statements.

My (*Our*) responsibility is to conduct the compilation in accordance with Statements on Standards for Accounting and Review Services issued by the American Institute of Certified Public Accountants. The objective of a compilation is to assist management in presenting financial information in the form of financial statements without undertaking to obtain or provide any assurance that there are no material modifications that should be made to the financial statements.

The financial statements included in the accompanying prescribed form are presented in accordance with the requirements of [*describe contract or regulation*], and are not intended to be a complete presentation of [*name of entity's*] assets and liabilities.

This report is intended solely for the information and use of [*the specified parties*] and is not intended to be and should not be used by anyone other than these specified parties.

[*Signature of accounting firm or accountant, as appropriate*]

[*Date*]

AR 400 Communications between Predecessor and Successor Accountants

EFFECTIVE DATE AND APPLICABILITY

Original Pronouncement	Statements on Standards for Accounting and Review Services (SSARSs) 4, 7, 9, 15, and 17.
Effective Date	These statements currently are effective.
Applicability	Compilation and review engagements when a successor accountant decides (not mandatory) to communicate with the predecessor accountant about acceptance of an engagement. The successor accountant must request the client to communicate with the predecessor when the successor believes that the financial statements reported on by the predecessor are materially misstated.

DEFINITIONS OF TERMS

Predecessor accountant. An accountant who has reported on the most recent financial statements or was engaged to do so but did not complete the engagement and has resigned, declined to stand for reappointment, or been terminated.

Successor accountant. An accountant who has been invited to propose on a new engagement and is considering accepting the engagement or who has accepted an engagement to compile or review financial statements.

OBJECTIVES OF AR SECTION 400

This section discusses the circumstances when communications between predecessor and successor accountants may be desirable and the types of inquiries a successor may decide to make. The section was initially based on Statement on Auditing Standards (SAS) 7, *Communications between Predecessor and Successor Accountants* (superseded by SAS 84; see Section 315, *Communications between Predecessor and Successor Auditors*). However, unlike the auditor-to-auditor communications in SAS 84, communications are not required in a compilation or review engagement (with the exception noted when the financial statements are believed to be materially misleading).

FUNDAMENTAL REQUIREMENTS

GENERAL

A successor accountant may decide to communicate with a predecessor accountant when:

1. The information obtained about the prospective client is limited or requires special attention.
2. The change in accountants occurs substantially after the end of the accounting period for which financial statements are to be compiled or reviewed.
3. There have been frequent changes in accountants.

The successor accountant should (1) obtain the client's permission before communicating with the predecessor, and (2) ask the client to authorize the predecessor to respond fully to inquiries. The successor's inquiries may be either oral or written.

INQUIRIES ABOUT ENGAGEMENT ACCEPTANCE

Ordinarily, inquiries would include questions that might assist a successor in deciding whether to accept the engagement. Inquiries may cover:

1. Management's integrity
2. Disagreements about accounting principles or about the need to perform certain procedures
3. Management's cooperation in providing information
4. The predecessor's understanding of the reasons for the change in accountants

The predecessor should respond promptly and completely to the inquiries noted above. If the predecessor limits his or her response because of unusual circumstances, such as litigation, that should be disclosed. The successor should evaluate the reasons and implications of a limited response in deciding whether to accept the engagement.

ACCESS TO WORKING PAPERS

A successor may also wish, after the client obtains authorization from the predecessor, to review the predecessor's working papers. The predecessor and successor should agree on those working papers that are available and those that may be copied. Valid business reasons (e.g., unpaid fees) may cause the predecessor not to allow access to working papers.

MATERIALLY MISLEADING FINANCIAL STATEMENTS

If during the engagement, the successor accountant becomes aware of information that causes him or her to believe that the financial statements reported on by the predecessor may need to be revised, the successor should ask the client to communicate the matter to the predecessor. If the client refuses to do so or if the predecessor's response is inadequate, the successor should evaluate the implications for the engagement and consider whether to resign. The accountant may also wish to consult with legal counsel.

INTERPRETATION

REPORTS ON THE APPLICATION OF ACCOUNTING PRINCIPLES (ISSUED AUGUST 1987; REVISED NOVEMBER 2002)

An accountant who has been asked to provide written or oral advice on the application of accounting principles to a client whose financial statements are compiled or reviewed by another accountant is obligated to follow SAS 50, *Reports on the Application of Accounting Principles* (see Section 625, *Reports on the Application of Accounting Principles*).

TECHNIQUES FOR APPLICATION

APPLICABILITY OF SAS 84

SAS 84 does not apply to engagements governed by SSARS 4. Furthermore, no standards apply to situations where the prior years' financial statements were compiled or reviewed and the current year is to be audited, or vice versa. Footnote 3 of SAS 84 indicates that a successor *auditor* may find the guidance in Section 315 useful in communicating with the predecessor *accountant* who compiled or reviewed the prior financial statements. Similarly, a successor *accountant* may find the guidance in SSARS 4 useful in communicating with a predecessor *auditor*.

FACILITATING ACCESS TO WORKING PAPERS OF THE PREDECESSOR ACCOUNTANT

Before permitting access to the working papers, the predecessor accountant may wish to obtain a consent letter and an acknowledgement letter from the successor accountant. An example consent letter and an acknowledgement letter is presented in *Illustrations*.

ILLUSTRATION

ILLUSTRATION 1. ILLUSTRATIVE SUCCESSOR ACCOUNTANT ACKNOWLEDGMENT LETTER

Paragraph .08, footnote 7, states, "Before permitting access to the documentation, the predecessor accountant may wish to obtain a written communication from the successor accountant regarding the use of the documentation." The following letter is presented for illustrative purposes only and is not required by professional standards.

[*Date*]

[*Successor Accountant*]
[*Address*]

We have previously [*reviewed or compiled*] in accordance with Statements on Standards for Accounting and Review Services the December 31, 20X1, financial statements of ABC Enterprises (ABC). In connection with your [*review or compilation*] of ABC's 20X2 financial statements, you have requested access to our documentation prepared in connection with that engagement. ABC has authorized our firm to allow you to review that documentation.

Our [*review or compilation*], and the documentation prepared in connection therewith, of ABC's financial statements was not planned or conducted in contemplation of your [*review or compilation*]. Therefore, items of possible interest to you may not have been specifically addressed. Our use of professional judgment for the purpose of this engagement means that matters may have existed that would have been assessed differently by you. We make no representation about the sufficiency or appropriateness of the information in our documentation for your purposes.

We understand that the purpose of your review of our documentation is to obtain information about ABC and our 20X1 [*compilation or review*] procedures to assist you in planning your 20X2 [*compilation or review*] of the financial statements of ABC. For that purpose only, we will provide you access to our documentation that relate to that objective.

Upon request, we will provide copies of the documentation that provide factual information about ABC. You agree to subject any such copies, or information otherwise derived from our documentation, to your normal policy for retention of documentation and protection of confidential client information. Furthermore, in the event of a third-party request for access to your documentation prepared in connection with your [*reviews or compilations*] of ABC, you agree to obtain our permission before voluntarily allowing any such access to our documentation or information otherwise derived from our documentation, and to obtain on our behalf any releases that you obtain from such third party. You agree to advise us promptly and provide us a copy of any subpoena, summons, or other court order for access to your documentation that include copies of our documentation or information otherwise derived therefrom.

Please confirm your agreement with the foregoing by signing and dating a copy of this letter and returning it to us.

Very truly yours,

[*Predecessor Accountant*]

By: _____

Accepted:

[*Successor Accountant*]

By: _____ Date: _____

Even with the client's consent, access to the predecessor accountant's documentation may still be limited. Experience has shown that the predecessor accountant may be willing to grant broader access if given additional assurance concerning the use of the documentation. Accordingly, the successor accountant might consider agreeing to the following limitations on the review of the predecessor accountant's documentation in order to obtain broader access:

- The successor accountant will not comment, orally or in writing, to anyone as a result of the review about whether the predecessor accountant's engagement was performed in accordance with SSARS.
- The successor accountant will not provide expert testimony or litigation services or otherwise accept an engagement to comment on issues relating to the quality of the predecessor accountant's engagement.

The following paragraph illustrates the above:

Because your review of our documentation is undertaken solely for the purpose described above and may not entail a review of all our documentation, you agree that (1) the information obtained from the review will not be used by you for any other purpose, (2) you will not comment, orally or in writing, to anyone as a result of that review about whether our engagement was performed in accordance with Statements on Standards for Accounting and Review Services, (3) you will not provide expert testimony or litigation services or otherwise accept an engagement to comment on issues relating to the quality of our engagement.

AR 600 Reporting on Personal Financial Statements Included in Written Personal Financial Plans[1]

EFFECTIVE DATE AND APPLICABILITY

Original Pronouncement	Statement on Standards for Accounting and Review Services (SSARS) 6.
Effective Date	This statement currently is effective.
Applicability	An accountant may opt for an exemption from AR Section 80 for certain personal financial statements included in written personal financial plans. The section does not preclude an accountant from complying with AR Section 80. The section applies to personal financial statements whether the basis of accounting is generally accepted accounting principles (GAAP) or an other comprehensive basis of accounting (OCBOA).

DEFINITIONS OF TERMS

This section does not contain any definitions.

OBJECTIVES OF AR SECTION 600

Personal financial statements included in personal financial plans (1) frequently omit disclosures and (2) contain departures from GAAP (or OCBOA). If the purpose of those financial statements is solely to assist in developing the personal financial plan, SSARS 6 provides for an exemption from AR Section 80 and an alternative report that should be used if the exemption is followed.

---

[1] The accountant has the option of preparing management-use-only financial statements when preparing personal financial statements. However, in most cases, accountants will find it more useful to follow the guidance in this section.

FUNDAMENTAL REQUIREMENTS

EXEMPTION

According to AR 600.03, an accountant may submit a written personal financial plan containing unaudited personal financial statements to a client without following AR Section 80, if:

1. The accountant establishes an understanding, preferably in writing, with the client that the personal financial statements will:

    a. Be used solely to assist the client and his or her advisers to develop the client's personal goals and objectives
    b. Not be used for credit or any other purposes other than those in item a

2. Nothing comes to the accountant's attention during the engagement indicating anything other than items a and b

ALTERNATIVE REPORT REQUIRED

An accountant electing the SSARS 6 exemption should issue a report. The report should indicate that the financial statements:

1. Are designed solely to assist in developing the financial plan
2. May be incomplete or contain other GAAP departures
3. Should not be used to obtain credit or for any other purpose (exception for item 1)
4. Have not been audited, reviewed, or compiled; Illustration 1 presents an appropriate report

MARKING ON EACH PAGE

Each page of the personal financial statements should refer to the accountant's report.

INTERPRETATION

SUBMITTING A PERSONAL FINANCIAL PLAN TO A CLIENT'S ADVISERS (ISSUED MAY 1991)

The interpretation allows the accountant to submit a written personal financial plan, to be implemented by the client or his or her advisers, without complying with SSARS 1. Examples of implementation include an:

1. Insurance broker to identify specific products
2. Investment adviser to provide investment portfolio recommendations
3. Attorney to draft a will or trust agreement

ILLUSTRATION

The following is an illustrative report adapted from SSARS 6.

ILLUSTRATION 1. REPORT ON PERSONAL FINANCIAL STATEMENTS INCLUDED IN A PERSONAL FINANCIAL PLAN

Accountant's Report

The accompanying Statement of Financial Condition of X, as of December 31, 20XX, was prepared solely to help you develop your personal financial plan. Accordingly, it may be incomplete or contain other departures from accounting principles generally accepted in the United States of America and should not be used to obtain credit or for any purposes other than developing your financial plan. We have not audited, reviewed, or compiled the statement.

PCAOB 1 References in Auditors' Reports to the Standards of the Public Company Accounting Oversight Board

> *IMPORTANT NOTE:* The guidance in this section applies to the preparation and issuance of audit reports for all issuers as defined by the Sarbanes–Oxley Act.

EFFECTIVE DATE AND APPLICABILITY

Effective Date This standard currently is effective.

Applicability Auditors' reports on audits and other engagements relating to public companies and other issuers.

DEFINITIONS OF TERMS

Auditor. As used in the standard, the term refers to both public accounting firms registered with the Public Company Accounting Oversight Board (PCAOB) and associated persons.

FUNDAMENTAL REQUIREMENTS

When an engagement is performed in accordance with the standards of the PCAOB, and the auditor is required by the interim standards to refer in a report to generally accepted auditing standards, US generally accepted auditing standards (GAAP), auditing standards generally accepted in the United States of America, or standards established by the American Institute of Certified Public Accountants (AICPA), the auditor must instead refer to "the standards of the Public Company Accounting Oversight Board (United States)."

Auditors must also include the city and state from which the report is issued. (Non-US auditors are required to include the city and country.)

OTHER PCAOB GUIDANCE

In addition to the PCAOB standards and interpretations discussed in this volume, practitioners should be aware of the following guidance available on the PCAOB website.

STAFF AUDIT PRACTICE ALERTS

Staff Audit Practice Alerts highlight new, emerging, or otherwise noteworthy circumstances that may affect how auditors conduct audits under the existing requirements of PCAOB standards and relevant laws. The statements contained in Staff Audit Practice Alerts are not rules of the Board and do not reflect any Board determination or judgment about the conduct of any particular firm, auditor, or any other person:

- Alert No. 9: Assessing and Responding to Risk in the Current Economic Environment (Dec. 6, 2011)
- Alert No. 8: Audit Risks in Certain Emerging Markets (Oct. 3, 2011)
- Alert No. 7: Auditor Considerations of Litigation and Other Contingencies Arising from Mortgage and Other Loan Activities (Dec. 20, 2010)
- Alert No. 6: Auditor Considerations Regarding Using the Work of Other Auditors and Engaging Assistants from Outside the Firm (July 12, 2010)
- Alert No. 5: Auditor Considerations Regarding Significant Unusual Transactions (April 7, 2010)
- Alert No. 4: Auditor Considerations Regarding Fair Value Measurements, Disclosures, and Other-Than-Temporary Impairments (April 21, 2009)
- Alert No. 3: Audit Considerations in the Current Economic Environment (Dec. 5, 2008)
- Alert No. 2: Matters Related to Auditing Fair Value Measurements of Financial Instruments and the Use of Specialists (Dec. 10, 2007)
- Alert No. 1: Matters Related to Timing and Accounting for Option Grants (July 28, 2006)

STAFF QUESTIONS AND ANSWERS

Staff questions and answers set forth the staff's opinions on issues related to the implementation of the standards of the PCAOB. The PCAOB publishes questions and answers to help auditors implement, and the Board's staff administer, the Board's standards. The statements contained in the staff questions and answers are not rules of the Board, nor have they been approved by the Board.

- Auditing Standard No. 7, *Engagement Quality Review* (Feb. 19, 2010)
- References to Authoritative Accounting Guidance in PCAOB Standards (Sept. 2, 2009)
- Ethics and Independence Rules Concerning Independence, Tax Services, and Contingent Fees (April 3, 2007)
- Auditing the Fair Value of Share Options Granted to Employees (Oct.17, 2006)
- Adjustments to Prior-Period Financial Statements Audited by a Predecessor Auditor (June 9, 2006)
- Attest Engagements Regarding XBRL Financial Information Furnished under the XBRL Voluntary Financial Reporting Program on the EDGAR System (May 25, 2005)
- Audits of Financial Statements of Non-Issuers Performed Pursuant to the Standards of the Public Company Accounting Oversight Board (June 30, 2004)

OTHER STAFF GUIDANCE

Staff guidance sets forth the staff's views on issues related to the implementation of the standards of the PCAOB. The statements contained in staff guidance are not rules of the Board, nor have they been approved by the Board.

- Staff Views—An Audit of Internal Control Over Financial Reporting That Is Integrated with An Audit of Financial Statements: Guidance for Auditors of Smaller Public Companies (Jan. 23, 2009)
- Preliminary Staff Views—An Audit of Internal Control That Is Integrated with An Audit of Financial Statements: Guidance for Auditors of Smaller Public Companies (Oct. 17, 2007)
- Preliminary Staff Views—Comment letters

INTERPRETATION: *COMMISSION GUIDANCE REGARDING THE PUBLIC COMPANY ACCOUNTING OVERSIGHT BOARD'S AUDITING AND RELATED PROFESSIONAL PRACTICE STANDARD NO. 1*

The Securities and Exchange Commission (SEC) issued this interpretation to assist with the implementation of PCAOB 1. The interpretation states that references in SEC rules and staff guidance and in federal securities laws to generally accepted auditing standards (GAAS) or to specific standards under GAAS that relate to issuers are now understood to mean the PCAOB's standards and any applicable rules of the SEC.

The interpretation also states that when a report previously filed with the SEC is incorporated by reference, the report incorporated by reference would not need to include the reference to the PCAOB's standards.

The full text of the release can be found at www.sec.gov/rules/interp/33-8422.htm.

ILLUSTRATIONS

ILLUSTRATION 1. STANDARD REPORT

The following is an illustrative report on an audit of financial statements from PCAOB Standard 1:

Report of Independent Registered Public Accounting Firm

We have audited the accompanying balance sheets of X Company as of December 31, 20X3 and 20X2, and the related statements of operations, stockholders' equity, and cash flows for each of the three years in the period ended December 31, 20X3. These financial statements are the responsibility of the Company's management. Our responsibility is to express an opinion on these financial statements based on our audits.

We conducted our audits in accordance with the standards of the Public Company Accounting Oversight Board (United States). Those standards require that we plan and perform the audit to obtain reasonable assurance about whether the financial statements are free of material misstatement. An audit includes examining, on a test basis, evidence supporting the amounts and disclosures in the financial statements. An audit also includes assessing the accounting principles used and significant estimates made by management, as well as evaluating the overall financial statement presentation. We believe that our audits provide a reasonable basis for our opinion.

In our opinion, the financial statements referred to above present fairly, in all material respects, the financial position of the Company as of [*at*] December 31, 20X3 and 20X2, and the results of its operations and its cash flows for each of the three years in the period ended December 31, 20X3, in conformity with US generally accepted accounting principles.

[*Signature*]
[*City and State or Country*]
[*Date*]

ILLUSTRATION 2. INTERIM REPORT

The following is an illustrative report on a review of interim financial information from PCAOB Standard 1:

Report of Independent Registered Public Accounting Firm

We have reviewed the accompanying [*describe the interim financial information or statements reviewed*] of X Company as of September 30, 20X3 and 20X2, and for the three-month and nine-month periods then ended. This (*these*) interim financial information (*statements*) is (*are*) the responsibility of the Company's management.

We conducted our review in accordance with the standards of the Public Company Accounting Oversight Board (United States). A review of interim financial information consists principally of applying analytical procedures and making inquiries of persons responsible for financial and accounting matters. It is substantially less in scope than an audit conducted in accordance with the standards of the Public Company Accounting Oversight Board, the objective of which is the expression of an opinion regarding the financial statements taken as a whole. Accordingly, we do not express such an opinion.

Based on our review, we are not aware of any material modifications that should be made to the accompanying interim financial (statements) for it (them) to be in conformity with US generally accepted accounting principles.

[*Signature*]
[*City and State or Country*]
[*Date*]

PCAOB 3 Audit Documentation[1]

> *IMPORTANT NOTE: The guidance in this section applies to the preparation and issuance of audit reports for all issuers as defined by the Sarbanes–Oxley Act.*

EFFECTIVE DATE AND APPLICABILITY

Effective Date This standard currently is effective.

Applicability Engagements conducted pursuant to Public Company Accounting Oversight Board (PCAOB) standards, including an audit of financial statements, an audit of internal control over financial reporting, and a review of interim financial information.

DEFINITIONS OF TERMS

Audit documentation (also referred to as workpapers or working papers). The written record that serves as the basis for the auditor's conclusions that provide support for the auditor's representations, whether the representations are contained in the auditor's report or otherwise. Documentation includes records of the planning and performance of work, procedures performed, evidence obtained, and conclusions reached by the auditor. Such documentation may be in paper form, electronic form, or other media.

Examples of audit documentation include:

- Memoranda
- Confirmations
- Correspondence
- Schedules
- Audit programs
- Representation letters

Documentation completion date. The date the auditor should assemble a complete and final set of audit documentation for retention, which is not more than 45 days after the report release date.

Experienced auditor. An auditor who has a reasonable understanding of audit activities and has studied the entity's industry as well as the industry's relevant accounting and auditing issues.

Report release date. The date the auditor gives permission to use the auditor's report in connection with issuing the company's financial statements.

---

[1] *Practitioners should reference the additional guidance listed in the section* "Other PCAOB Guidance" *in this volume's chapter PCAOB 1.*

Significant findings or issues. Substantive matters that are important to the procedures performed, evidence obtained, or conclusions reached, and include but are not limited to:

- Significant matters and associated disclosures relating to selecting and applying accounting principles, and whether such accounting principles have been consistently applied (significant matters include, but are not limited to, accounting for complex or unusual transactions, accounting estimates, uncertainties, and related management assumptions)
- Results of auditing procedures that indicate a need for significant modification of planned auditing procedures, the existence of material misstatements, omissions in the financial statements, the existence of significant deficiencies, or material weaknesses in internal control over financial reporting
- Audit adjustments, which are corrections of a misstatement of the financial statement that was or should have been proposed by the auditor, whether or not recorded by management, that could, either individually or when aggregated with other misstatements, have a material effect on the company's financial statements
- Disagreements among members of the engagement team or with others consulted on the engagement about final conclusions reached on significant accounting or auditing matters
- Circumstances that cause significant difficulty in applying auditing procedures
- Significant changes in the assessed level of audit risk for particular audit areas and the auditor's response to those changes
- Any matters that could result in modification of the auditor's report

OBJECTIVES OF PCAOB STANDARD 3

Audit documentation:

- Facilitates the planning, performance, and supervision of the engagement
- Serves as the basis for the review of the quality of the work because it provides evidence supporting the auditor's conclusions
- Includes records of the planning and performance of the work, the procedures performed, the evidence obtained, and the conclusions reached

Audit documentation's importance also stems from the fact that it is reviewed by engagement team members and might be reviewed by others, such as:

- Auditors new to the engagement
- Supervisors on the engagement
- Engagement quality reviewers
- Successor auditors
- Internal and external inspection team
- Advisors to the audit committee or representatives of an acquiring party

FUNDAMENTAL REQUIREMENTS

BASIC REQUIREMENT

PCAOB Auditing Standard 3 sets forth the general documentation requirements that the auditor should prepare and retain for engagements governed by PCAOB standards; these engagements include financial statement audits, audits of internal control over financial reporting, and reviews of interim financial information.

The auditor must document, with respect to relevant financial statement assertions:

- Procedures performed
- Evidence obtained
- Conclusions reached

Audit documentation should:

- Have sufficient detail to provide a clear understanding of its purpose, source, and conclusions reached
- Be appropriately organized so that a clear link is provided to the significant findings or issues
- Demonstrate that the engagement complied with PCAOB standards
- Support the basis for the auditor's conclusions about every relevant financial statement assertion
- Show that the underlying accounting records agreed or reconciled with the financial statements

Audit documentation must clearly demonstrate that the work was actually performed.

NOTE: These requirements apply to all engagement participants as well as specialists, if the auditor uses the work of those specialists as evidential matter to evaluate relevant financial statement assertions.

The information in the documentation must be sufficient to allow an experienced auditor (see the section "Definitions of Terms"), with no previous connection to the engagement, to:

- Understand the nature, timing, extent and results of the procedures performed, evidence obtained and conclusions reached, and
- Determine the person who performed the work, the date of the work's completion, the reviewer of the work, and the date of the review

The auditor should consider the following when determining the appropriate nature and extent of documentation for a financial statement assertion:

- What is the nature of the auditing procedure?
- What is the risk of material misstatement associated with the assertion?
- To what extent is judgment required in performing the work and evaluating the results?
- What is the significance of the evidence obtained to the assertion being tested?
- What is the auditor's responsibility to document a conclusion not readily determinable from the documentation of the procedures performed and evidence obtained?

The auditor is also required to include in the audit documentation information that the auditor has identified related to significant findings or issues (see "Definitions of Terms") that is inconsistent with, or contradicts, the conclusions reached by the auditor. Such records include but are not limited to:

- Procedures performed in responding to such information

- Documentation of consultations on, or resolutions of, differences in professional judgment among members of the engagement team or between the engagement team and other parties consulted

DOCUMENTATION OF GENERAL CLIENT MATTERS

The auditor's documentation for certain matters, such as the auditor's independence, staff training and proficiency, and client acceptance and retention, may be in a central firm repository or in the office participating in the engagement. If documented in a central firm repository, the documentation should refer to the central depository. The auditor should document specific engagement matters in the pertinent engagement's audit documentation.

DOCUMENTATION OF SPECIFIC MATTERS

The auditor's documentation should include the following:

- The items inspected when performing auditing procedures that involve inspecting documents or confirmation (such as tests of details, tests of operating effectiveness of controls, and walk-throughs) should be identified.
- Abstracts or copies of significant contracts or agreements should be included when documenting audit procedures that involve inspecting such documentation.

PCAOB 3 provides the following examples of identification of the items inspected:

1. *Selecting a sample from a population of documents*. Documentation should include characteristics that identify the documents. Example: List the specific check numbers of items in a sample.
2. *Selecting all items over a specific dollar amount from a population*. Documentation only needs to describe the scope and identify the population. Example: All checks over $25,000 from the November disbursements journal.
3. *Selecting a systematic sample from a population of documents*. Documentation only needs to identify the source of the documents and indicate the starting point and the sampling interval. Example: Starting with invoice 320, every tenth sales invoice was selected from the sales journal from the period from October 1 to December 31 to provide a systematic sample of sales invoices.

THE ENGAGEMENT COMPLETION DOCUMENT

The auditor must document all significant findings or issues in an engagement completion document. The auditor is required to document:

- The significant findings or issues
- Actions taken to address them (including additional evidence obtained)
- The basis for conclusions reached in the engagement

The engagement completion document:

- May include either all information needed to understand the significant findings and issues, or cross-references to available supporting documentation
- Should, along with cross-referenced documentation, be as specific as necessary to allow a reviewer to thoroughly understand the significant findings and issues

- Should document significant findings or issues identified during the interim review of financial information, if the engagement completion document is for the annual audit

OMITTED PROCEDURES AND AUDIT DOCUMENTATION

After the documentation completion date, the auditor may become aware of audit procedures not performed, evidence not obtained, or appropriate conclusions not reached. This may be a result of lack of documentation or other factors. In this situation, the auditor must determine and then demonstrate that the sufficient procedures were performed and evidence obtained, and appropriate conclusions were reached. The auditor must accomplish this with persuasive other evidence.

NOTE: *Oral explanation is not by itself considered "persuasive other evidence," but it may be used to clarify written evidence.*

If the auditor both determines and can demonstrate that the procedures, evidence and conclusions are sufficient and appropriate, but the documentation for such is inadequate, the auditor should consider what additional appropriate documentation is needed. Additional documentation must indicate the date the information was added, the name of the preparer, and the reason for adding it.

If the auditor cannot determine or demonstrate that the procedures, evidence and conclusions are sufficient and appropriate, the auditor should comply with the provisions of AU Section 390, *Consideration of Omitted Procedures After the Report Date.*

RETENTION OF AND SUBSEQUENT CHANGES TO AUDIT DOCUMENTATION

Retention period. If an audit report is issued, retain audit documentation for seven years, starting with the report release date, unless a longer time period is required by law.

If a report is not issued, retain audit documentation for seven years from the date that fieldwork was substantially completed.

If the engagement is not completed, retain audit documentation for seven years from the date the engagement ceased.

Document completion. Before the report release date, all audit procedures must be completed (including clearing notes and supporting final conclusions) and sufficient evidence obtained to support the auditor's report. The auditor should assemble a complete and final set of audit documentation not more than forty-five days after the report release date.

If a report is not issued, the documentation completion date is not more than forty-five days after the date that fieldwork was substantially completed.

If the auditor could not complete the engagement, the documentation completion date should not be more than forty-five days after the date the engagement ceased.

Subsequent changes. The auditor may find it necessary to add to audit documentation after the report release date. However, *documentation must not be deleted or discarded after the documentation completion date.* Any documentation subsequently added must indicate the date it was added, the name of the preparer and the reason for adding it.

If the auditor is required to perform procedures after the report release date, the auditor must identify and document any additions necessitated by these procedures. An example is an auditor's required procedures up to the effective date of a registration statement, performed under AU Section 711, *Filings under Federal Securities Statutes.* Again, subsequently added documentation must have the date added, the name of the preparer, and the reason for adding it.

Responsibility for retention. The office of the firm that issues the audit report is responsible for making sure that all documentation needed to meet the requirements in PCAOB 3 is both prepared and retained.

Work of other auditors.[2] The office issuing the report must either retain or have access to audit documentation supporting the work performed by other auditors. That office also must obtain, review, and retain, before the report release date, the following documentation of the other auditor's work (including auditors associated with the firm's other offices, affiliated firms, or nonaffiliated firms):

- An engagement completion document that meets the requirements in PCAOB 3 and contains all cross-referenced supporting audit documentation
- A list of significant fraud risk factors, the auditor's response, and the results of the auditor's related procedures
- Sufficient information concerning any significant findings or issues that are not consistent with or contradict final conclusions
- Any findings that affect the consolidating or combining of accounts in the consolidated financial statements
- Sufficient information to allow the office issuing the report to agree or to reconcile the financial statement amounts audited by the other auditor to the information underlying the consolidated financial statements.
- A schedule of audit adjustments, including a description of the nature of each misstatement and its cause
- All significant deficiencies and material weaknesses in internal control over financial reporting, including a clear distinction between these two categories of items
- Management representation letters
- All matters to be communicated to the audit committee

NOTE: *The above requirements do not apply if the auditor decides to make reference in his or her report to the other auditor. Instead, the auditor should refer to AU Section 543,* Part of the Audit Performed by Other Independent Auditors.

OTHER DOCUMENTATION REQUIREMENTS

The auditor should also meet any other documentation requirements, such as the Securities and Exchange Commission's (SEC's) requirement to retain memoranda, correspondence, communications, (for example, electronic mail), other documents, and records (whether paper, electronic, or other media) that are created, sent, or received in connection with an engagement that contain conclusions, opinions, analyses, or data related to the engagement.

---

[2] *"Other auditors" includes auditors associated with other offices of the firm, affiliated firm, and non-affiliated firms.*

PCAOB 4 Reporting on Whether a Previously Reported Material Weakness Continues to Exist[1]

> *IMPORTANT NOTE:* The guidance in this section applies to the preparation and issuance of audit reports for all issuers as defined by the Sarbanes–Oxley Act.

EFFECTIVE DATE AND APPLICABILITY

Effective Date This standard currently is effective.

Applicability Engagements designed specifically to test for the continuing presence of previously reported material weaknesses.

DEFINITIONS OF TERMS

Control objective. Provides a specific target for the evaluation of the effectiveness of controls. When used in relation to controls over financial reporting, it states a criterion for evaluating whether an entity's control procedures provide reasonable assurance that a misstatement to or omission in that assertion is prevented or detected by controls on a timely basis.

Stated control objective. The specific control objective identified by management that, if achieved, would result in a material weakness no longer existing.

OBJECTIVES OF PCAOB STANDARD 4

Public Company Accounting Oversight Board (PCAOB) Auditing Standard 4 sets forth the general requirements for an auditor who is engaged to report on whether a previously reported material weakness in internal control over financial reporting continues to exist.

---

[1] *Practitioners should reference the additional guidance listed in the section "Other PCAOB Guidance" in this volume's chapter PCAOB 1.*

FUNDAMENTAL REQUIREMENTS

BASIC REQUIREMENT

An auditor may report on whether a previously reported material weakness continues to exist if the auditor has audited the company's financial statements and internal control over financial reporting in accordance with PCAOB Standard 5 either during the entity's most recent annual assessment or in the current year. This is a voluntary auditor engagement by the entity, since the PCAOB does not require an auditor to undertake an engagement specifically to report on whether a previously reported material weakness continues to exist.

The auditor's objective in this engagement is to obtain reasonable assurance about and report on the continued existence of a previously reported material weakness. This opinion relates only to the specific material weakness in question as of a specified date. Thus, the auditor is not expressing an opinion on the effectiveness of an entity's overall system of internal control over financial reporting.

To obtain a reasonable level of assurance, the auditor should obtain evidence about whether the specific controls designed for a stated control objective were designed correctly and operate effectively.

The auditor may *only* report on this topic if management agrees to the following five conditions:

1. It accepts responsibility for the effectiveness of internal control over financial reporting.
2. It evaluates the effectiveness of those controls that it believes address the material weakness, using the same control criteria that it used for its most recent annual assessment of internal control.
3. It asserts that the specific controls identified are effective in achieving its stated control objective.
4. It supports its assertion with sufficient evidence.
5. It presents a written report that will accompany the auditor's report.

The stated control objective provides a specific target against which to evaluate whether a material weakness continues to exist, so management and the auditor must be satisfied that the material weakness would no longer exist if the stated control objective were achieved. However, if management and the auditor cannot identify all of the stated control objectives affected by a material weakness, then the weakness is probably not suitable for this engagement; instead, it would be better to address the issue through the auditor's annual audit of internal control over financial reporting under PCAOB Standard 5.

FRAMEWORK FOR EVALUATION

Management and the auditor must use both the same control criteria used for the company's most recent annual assessment of internal control over financial reporting *and* the company's stated control objectives to evaluate whether a material weakness continues to exist.

NOTE: The performance and reporting requirements in this Standard are based on Internal Control—Integrated Framework, *which is published by the Committee of Sponsoring Organizations (COSO). The report provides a framework for management's annual assessment of internal control over financial reporting.*

When auditing internal control over financial reporting, the auditor should test the design effectiveness of controls by determining whether the company's controls, if they are operated as prescribed by those people possessing the authority and competence to perform the controls effectively, satisfy the company's control objectives and can effectively prevent or detect errors or fraud that could result in material misstatements in the financial statements.

PERFORMING THE ENGAGEMENT

In this engagement, the auditor must obtain sufficient competent evidence about the design and operating effectiveness of specific controls to obtain a reasonable assurance that the company's stated control objective is achieved. While doing so, the auditor must adhere to the engagement standards of the PCAOB, which involve:

1. Planning the engagement
2. Obtaining an understanding of internal control over financial reporting
3. Testing and evaluating whether a material weakness continues to exist
4. Forming an opinion on whether a previously reported material weakness continues to exist

The person performing the engagement must have adequate training and proficiency as an auditor. In matters related to the engagement, the auditor must maintain an independence in mental attitude, and exercise due professional care in performing the engagement and preparing the report. Further, the auditor must have a sufficient knowledge of the company and its internal control over financial reporting. An auditor who has audited the entity's internal control over financial reporting in accordance with PCAOB Standard 5 for the entity's most recent annual assessment should have sufficient knowledge in this area.

If the auditor is a successor auditor, then he or she must perform procedures to obtain a sufficient knowledge of the company's business and its internal control over financial reporting to achieve the objective of the engagement. These procedures include:

- Compliance with paragraphs 22–27 of PCAOB Standard 5 regarding obtaining an understanding of internal control over financial reporting. The more pervasive the effects of the material weakness, the more extensive the understanding of internal control over financial reporting should be. The entity-level controls noted in paragraphs 22–27 include controls related to the:

  - Control environment (i.e., management operating style, ethical values, and audit committee oversight)
  - Management override
  - Risk assessment process
  - Centralized processing
  - Monitoring of the results of operations
  - Monitoring of other controls
  - Period-end financial reporting process (i.e., procedures for transactions and journal entries, as well as record adjustments)

- Compliance with paragraphs 34–38 of PCAOB Standard 5 for those transactions directly affected by controls specifically identified by management as addressing the material weakness. The issues noted in paragraphs 34–38 include obtaining an un-

derstanding of the likely sources of misstatements, which can include process walkthroughs.
- Make inquiries of the predecessor auditor that address the basis for the predecessor auditor's determination that a material weakness existed in the entity's internal control over financial reporting and the predecessor auditor's awareness of any information relating to the entity's ability to successfully address the material weakness.

The successor auditor may not be able to obtain a sufficient basis for reporting on whether a previously reported material weakness continues to exist without performing a complete audit of internal control over financial reporting (as governed by PCAOB Standard 5).

EVALUATING WHETHER A MATERIAL WEAKNESS STILL EXISTS

If the auditor finds that management cannot support its assertion with sufficient evidence, then he or she cannot complete the engagement.

The auditor should determine if management is using an appropriate date for its assertion. This date is based on the following factors:

- It can be as of any date that gives management time to obtain sufficient evidence to support its assertion.
- It may need to be after the completion of a period-end financial reporting process, depending on the nature of the material weakness.
- It is more flexibly determined for those controls that operate on a nearly continuous basis.
- It can only be dated near a period-end for those controls that operate during the period-end financial reporting process.

The auditor should obtain sufficient evidence to support his or her opinion regarding the continued existence of the material weakness. To this end, all controls necessary to achieve the stated control objective should be identified and evaluated. The controls should include those that have been modified or newly implemented, and may include existing controls that were originally deemed effective during the most recent annual assessment of internal control over financial reporting.

The auditor should test the operating effectiveness of a specified control by determining whether the specified control operated as designed, and whether the person performing the control possesses the authority and qualifications to perform it effectively.

The duration of controls testing should be adequate to determine whether the controls are operating effectively as of the date of management's assertion. The duration of controls testing will extend with the level of risk, such that a daily transaction reconciliation can be tested quickly, while a control over management override may require considerably more time to test.

USING THE WORK OF OTHERS

The auditor should evaluate whether it is possible to use the work of others in the evaluation. Key factors in this determination are the competence and objectivity of the persons whose work the auditor plans to use, as well as the risk associated with the control. For high-risk controls, the auditor should be more inclined to perform his or her own work. Also, the auditor should perform any walkthroughs himself or herself because of the degree of judgment required in performing this work.

The work of others includes relevant work performed by internal auditors, company personnel (in addition to internal auditors), and third parties working under the direction of management or the audit committee that provide information about the effectiveness of internal control over financial reporting.

If the auditor decides to serve as the principal auditor and to use the work and reports of another auditor as a basis, in part, for his or her opinion, the principal auditor must not divide responsibility for the engagement with the other auditor. Thus, the principal auditor must not make reference to the other auditor in his or her report.

SCOPE LIMITATIONS

The auditor may only issue an opinion when there is no restriction on the scope of his or her work. If there is a scope limitation, then the auditor must either disclaim an opinion or withdraw from the engagement. A qualified opinion is not permitted.

The refusal of management to provide written representations is a scope limitation, and is discussed in the following section.

MANAGEMENT REPRESENTATIONS

The auditor should obtain the following written representations from management:

- Acknowledge its responsibility for establishing and maintaining effective internal control over financial reporting;
- State that it has evaluated the effectiveness of the specified controls, using the specified control criteria and management's stated control objective(s);
- State its assertion that the specified controls are effective in achieving the stated control objective(s) as of a specified date;
- State its assertion that the identified material weakness no longer exists as of the same specified date;
- State that it believes its assertions are supported by sufficient evidence;
- Describe any fraud resulting in a material misstatement to the company's financial statements, and any other fraud that does not result in a misstatement in the company's financial statements but involves senior management, management, or other employees who have a significant role in the company's internal control over financial reporting, and that has occurred or come to management's attention since the date of management's most recent annual assessment of internal control over financial reporting.
- State whether there were, subsequent to the report date, any changes in internal control over financial reporting or other factors that might significantly affect the stated control objective(s) or indicate that the identified controls were not operating effectively as of, or subsequent to, the date specified in management's assertion.

The written representations should be signed by those managers having overall responsibility for the company's internal control over financial reporting, and who are responsible for the matters covered by the representations. The most applicable managers would ordinarily be the chief executive officer and the chief financial officer.

If management does not supply written representations, this is a scope limitation. Scope limitations were discussed in the preceding "Scope Limitations" section.

If management refuses to provide written representations, the auditor should evaluate the effects of this refusal on his or her reliance on other management representations, including any representations obtained as part of the audit of the company's financial statements.

MANAGEMENT'S REPORT

Management must present a written report that will accompany the auditor's report. The management report should include the following items:

- A statement of management's responsibility for establishing and maintaining effective internal control over financial reporting for the company;
- A statement identifying the control criteria used by management to conduct the required annual assessment of the effectiveness of the company's internal control over financial reporting;
- An identification of the material weakness that was identified as part of management's annual assessment (which should be modified when only the auditor's report on management's annual assessment identified the material weakness);
- An identification of the control objective(s) addressed by the specified controls and a statement that the specified controls achieve the stated control objectives(s) as of a specified date; and
- A statement that the identified material weakness no longer exists as of the same specified date because the specified controls address the material weakness.

The auditor must evaluate management's report. In particular, the auditor should evaluate the following issues:

- Whether management has properly stated its responsibility for establishing and maintaining effective internal control over financial reporting;
- Whether the control criteria used by management to conduct the evaluation is suitable;
- Whether the material weakness, stated control objectives, and specified controls have been properly described; and
- Whether management's assertions, as of the date specified in management's report, are free of material misstatement.

If the auditor evaluates management's report and determines that it does not include the specified elements, the conditions for engagement performance have not been met.

THE AUDITOR'S REPORT

The auditor's report must include the following elements:

- A title that includes the word independent;
- A statement that the auditor has previously audited and reported on management's annual assessment of internal control over financial reporting as of a specified date based on the control criteria, as well as a statement that the auditor's report identified a material weakness;

NOTE: This statement should be modified when there is a successor auditor who has not yet opined on the effectiveness of internal control over overall financial reporting in accordance with PCAOB Standard 5. In this situation, the auditor's report should refer to the predecessor auditor's report on management's annual assessment and the predecessor auditor's identification of the material weakness.

- A description of the material weakness;

- An identification of management's assertion that the identified material weakness in internal control over financial reporting no longer exists;
- An identification of the management report that includes management's assertion, such as identifying the title of the report (if the report is titled);
- A statement that management is responsible for its assertion;
- An identification of the specific controls that management asserts address the material weakness;
- An identification of the company's stated control objective that is achieved by these controls;
- A statement that the auditor's responsibility is to express an opinion on whether the material weakness continues to exist as of the date of management's assertion based on his or her auditing procedures;
- A statement that the engagement was conducted in accordance with the standards of the PCAOB (United States);
- A statement that the standards of the PCAOB require that the auditor plan and perform the engagement to obtain reasonable assurance about whether a previously reported material weakness continues to exist at the company;
- A statement that the engagement includes examining evidence supporting management's assertion and performing such other procedures the auditor considered necessary in the circumstances, and that the auditor obtained an understanding of internal control over financial reporting as part of his or her previous audit of management's annual assessment of internal control over financial reporting and updated that understanding as it specifically relates to changes in internal control over financial reporting associated with the material weakness;

NOTE: *This statement should be modified when there is a successor auditor who has not yet opined on the effectiveness of internal control over overall financial reporting in accordance with PCAOB Standard 5. In this situation, the auditor's report should include a statement that the engagement includes obtaining an understanding of internal control over financial reporting, examining evidence supporting management's assertion, and performing such other procedures as the auditor considered necessary in the circumstances.*

- A statement that the auditor believes the auditing procedures provide a reasonable basis for his or her opinion;
- The auditor's opinion on whether the identified material weakness exists (or no longer exists) as of the date of management's assertion;
- A paragraph that includes the following statements:
  - That the auditor was not engaged to and did not conduct an audit of internal control over financial reporting as of the date of management's assertion, the objective of which would be the expression of an opinion on the effectiveness of internal control over financial reporting, and that the auditor does not express such an opinion, and
  - That the auditor has not applied auditing procedures sufficient to reach conclusions about the effectiveness of any controls of the company as of any date after the date of management's annual assessment of the company's internal control over financial reporting, other than the controls specifically identified in the auditor's report, and that the auditor does not express an opinion that any other

controls operated effectively after the date of management's annual assessment of the company's internal control over financial reporting.

> *NOTE: This statement should be modified when there is a successor auditor who has not yet opined on the effectiveness of internal control over overall financial reporting, to state that the auditor has not applied auditing procedures sufficient to reach conclusions about the effectiveness of any controls of the company other than the controls specifically identified in the auditor's report and that the auditor does not express an opinion that any other controls operated effectively.*

- A paragraph stating that, because of its inherent limitations, internal control over financial reporting may not prevent or detect misstatements and that projections of any evaluation of the effectiveness of specific controls or internal control over financial reporting overall to future periods are subject to the risk that controls may become inadequate because of changes in conditions, or that the degree of compliance with the policies or procedures may deteriorate;
- The manual or printed signature of the auditor's firm;
- The city and state (or city and country, in the case of non-US auditors) from which the auditor's report has been issued; and
- The date of the auditor's report.

The auditor should modify the standard report if any of the following conditions exist:

- Other material weaknesses that were reported previously by the company as part of its annual assessment of internal control are not addressed by the auditor's opinion.
- A significant subsequent event has occurred since the date being reported on.
- Management's report on whether a material weakness continues to exist includes additional information.

If the auditor reports on fewer than all of the entity's previously reported material weaknesses, the auditor should include language in the paragraph stating that the auditor was not engaged to perform an audit of internal control over financial reporting. When referring to his or her previously issued report on management's annual assessment, the auditor should either attach that report or include information about where it can be publicly obtained. Sample language follows:

> Our report on management's annual assessment of ABC Company's internal control over financial reporting, dated [*date of report*], [*attached or identify location of where the report is publicly available*] identified additional material weaknesses other than the one identified in this report. We are not reporting on those other material weaknesses and, accordingly, express no opinion regarding whether those material weaknesses continue to exist after [*date of management's annual assessment*].

If management's report includes additional information beyond that itemized previously in the Management's Report section, the auditor should disclaim an opinion on the additional information. Sample disclaimer language to include in the last paragraph of the report is:

> We do not express an opinion or any other form of assurance on management's statement referring to its plans to implement new controls by the end of the year.

If the auditor believes that management's additional information contains material misstatements, he or she should discuss the issue with management. If the auditor then believes that there is still a material misstatement, he or she should notify management and the audit committee, in writing, of the auditor's views concerning the information.

If the auditor determines that the previously reported material weakness continues to exist and the auditor reports on the results of the engagement, he or she must express an opinion that the material weakness exists as of the date specified by management.

If the auditor were engaged to report on whether two separate material weaknesses continue to exist and concluded that one no longer exists and one continues to exist, the auditor's report could include either of the following:

1. A report that contains two opinions: one on the material weakness that the auditor concluded no longer exists and one on the material weakness that the auditor concluded continues to exist; or
2. A report containing only a single opinion on the material weakness that the auditor concluded no longer exists if the company modifies its assertion to address only the material weakness that the auditor concluded no longer exists. In this case, the auditor must communicate, in writing, his or her conclusion that a material weakness continues to exist to the audit committee.

If the auditor does not issue a report, he or she must still communicate, in writing, his or her conclusion that the material weakness continues to exist to the audit committee. Also, if the auditor identifies a new material weakness during the engagement, this new circumstance must also be communicated in writing to the audit committee.

Several examples of the auditor's report are included in the "Illustrations" section.

REPORT DATE

Management's assertion that a material weakness no longer exists does not need to be made as of a period-end financial reporting date. Thus, the auditor's report related to this issue does not have to be associated with the issuance of the entity's financial statements; the report release date is the date when the auditor grants permission to use the auditor's report.

SUBSEQUENT EVENTS

A variety of factors may significantly affect the effectiveness of identified controls, or the achievement of the entity's stated control objective might occur subsequent to the date of management's assertion but before the date of the auditor's report. Therefore, the auditor should inquire of management whether there was any such change or factors. In addition, the auditor should examine, during this subsequent period, the following items:

- Internal audit reports relevant to the stated control objective or identified controls issued during the subsequent period;
- Independent auditor reports (if other than the auditor's) of significant deficiencies or material weaknesses relevant to the stated control objective or identified controls;
- Regulatory agency reports on the entity's internal control over financial reporting relevant to the stated control objective or identified controls; and
- Information about the effectiveness of the company's internal control over financial reporting relevant to the stated control objective or identified controls obtained as a result of other engagements.

If the auditor is unable to determine the effect of a subsequent event on the effectiveness of the identified controls or the achievement of the stated control objective, the auditor should disclaim an opinion.

IMPACT ON QUARTERLY DISCLOSURES

If the auditor concludes that a previously reported material weakness continues to exist, the auditor must consider that conclusion as part of his or her evaluation of management's quarterly disclosures about internal control over financial reporting, as discussed further in PCAOB Standard 5.

TECHNIQUES FOR APPLICATION

The following table includes examples of control objectives and the assertions related to them:

Control Objectives	Assertions
Recorded sales of product X initiated on the company's website are real	Existence or occurrence
Product X warranty losses that are probable and can be reasonably estimated are recorded as of the company's quarterly financial statement period-ends	Completeness
Interest rate swaps are recorded at fair value	Valuation or allocation
The company has legal title to recorded product X inventory in the company's Alabama warehouse	Rights and obligations
Pending litigation that is reasonably possible to result in a material loss is disclosed in the quarterly and annual financial statements	Presentation and disclosure

ILLUSTRATIONS

The following are illustrations of reports on whether a previously reported material weakness continues to exist. They are adapted from PCAOB Standard 4.

ILLUSTRATION 1. AUDITOR'S REPORT FOR A CONTINUING AUDITOR EXPRESSING AN OPINION THAT A PREVIOUSLY REPORTED MATERIAL WEAKNESS NO LONGER EXISTS

Report of Independent Registered Public Accounting Firm

We have previously audited and reported on management's annual assessment of ABC Company's internal control over financial reporting as of December 31, 20XX, based on [*identify control criteria, for example, "criteria established in* Internal Control—Integrated Framework *issued by the Committee of Sponsoring Organizations of the Treadway Commission (COSO)"*]. Our report, dated [*date of report*], identified the following material weakness in the company's internal control over financial reporting:

[*Describe material weakness*]

We have audited management's assertion, included in the accompanying [*title of management's report*], that the material weakness in internal control over financial reporting identified above no longer exists as of [*date of management's assertion*] because the following control(s) addresses the material weakness:

[*Describe controls(s)*]

Management has asserted that the control(*s*) identified above achieve(*s*) the following stated control objective, which is consistent with the criteria established in [*identify control criteria used for management's annual assessment of internal control over financial reporting*]: [*state control objective addressed*]. Management also has asserted that it has tested the control(*s*) identified above and concluded that the control(*s*) was (*were*) designed and operated effectively as of [*date of management's assertion*]. ABC Company's management is responsible for its assertion. Our responsibility is to express an opinion on whether the identified material weakness continues to exist as of [*date of management's assertion*] based on our auditing procedures.

Our engagement was conducted in accordance with the standards of the Public Company Accounting Oversight Board (United States). Those standards require that we plan and perform the engagement to obtain reasonable assurance about whether a previously reported material weakness continues to exist at the company. Our engagement included examining evidence supporting management's assertion and performing such other procedures as we considered necessary in the circumstances. We obtained an understanding of the company's internal control over financial reporting as part of our previous audit of management's annual assessment of ABC Company's internal control over financial reporting as of December 31, 20XX, and updated that understanding as it specifically relates to changes in internal control over financial reporting associated with the material weakness described above. We believe that our auditing procedures provide a reasonable basis for our opinion.

In our opinion, the material weakness described above no longer exists as of [*date of management's assertion*].

We were not engaged to and did not conduct an audit of internal control over financial reporting as of [*date of management's assertion*], the objective of which would be the expression of an opinion on the effectiveness of internal control over financial reporting. Accordingly, we do not express such an opinion. This means that we have not applied auditing procedures sufficient to reach conclusions about the effectiveness of any controls of the company as of any date after December 31, 20XX, other than the control(s) specifically identified in this report. Accordingly, we do not express an opinion that any other controls operated effectively after December 31, 20XX.

Because of its inherent limitations, internal control over financial reporting may not prevent or detect misstatements. Also, projections of any evaluation of the effectiveness of specific controls or internal control over financial reporting overall to future periods are subject to the risk that controls may become inadequate because of changes in conditions or that the degree of compliance with the policies or procedures may deteriorate.

[*Signature*]

[*City and State or Country*]

[*Date*]

ILLUSTRATION 2. AUDITOR'S REPORT FOR A SUCCESSOR AUDITOR EXPRESSING AN OPINION THAT A PREVIOUSLY REPORTED MATERIAL WEAKNESS NO LONGER EXISTS

Report of Independent Registered Public Accounting Firm

We were engaged to report on whether a previously reported material weakness continues to exist at ABC Company as of [*date of management's assertion*] and to audit management's next annual assessment of ABC Company's internal control over financial reporting. Another auditor previously audited and reported on management's annual assessment of ABC Company's internal control over financial reporting as of December 31, 20XX, based on [*identify control criteria, for example, "criteria established in* Internal Control—Integrated Framework *issued by the Committee of Sponsoring Organizations of the Treadway Commission (COSO)."*]. The other auditor's report, dated [*date of report*], identified the following material weakness in the company's internal control over financial reporting:

[*Describe material weakness*]

We have audited management's assertion, included in the accompanying [*title of management's report*], that the material weakness in internal control over financial reporting identified above no longer exists as of [*date of management's assertion*] because the following control(s) addresses the material weakness:

[*Describe control(s)*]

Management has asserted that the control(*s*) identified above achieve(*s*) the following stated control objective, which is consistent with the criteria established in [*identify control criteria used for management's annual assessment of internal control over financial reporting*]: [*state control objective addressed*]. Management also has asserted that it has tested the control(*s*) identified above and concluded that the control(*s*) was (*were*) designed and operated effectively as of [*date of management's assertion*]. ABC Company's management is responsible for its assertion. Our responsibility is to express an opinion on whether the identified material weakness continues to exist as of [*date of management's assertion*] based on our auditing procedures.

Our engagement was conducted in accordance with the standards of the Public Company Accounting Oversight Board (United States). Those standards require that we plan and perform the engagement to obtain reasonable assurance about whether a previously reported material weakness continues to exist at the company. Our engagement included obtaining an understanding of internal control over financial reporting, examining evidence supporting management's assertion, and performing such other procedures as we considered necessary in the circumstances. We believe that our auditing procedures provide a reasonable basis for our opinion.

In our opinion, the material weakness described above no longer exists as of [*date of management's assertion*].

We are not engaged to and did not conduct an audit of internal control over financial reporting as of [*date of management's assertion*], the objective of which would be the expression of an opinion on the effectiveness of internal control over financial reporting. Accordingly, we do not express such an opinion. This means that we have not applied auditing procedures sufficient to reach conclusions about the effectiveness of any controls of the company other than the control(s) specifically identified in this report. Accordingly, we do not express an opinion that any other controls operated effectively.

Because of its inherent limitations, internal control over financial reporting may not prevent or detect misstatements. Also, projections of any evaluation of the effectiveness of specific controls or internal control over financial reporting overall to future periods are subject to the risk that controls may become inadequate because of changes in conditions or that the degree of compliance with the policies or procedures may deteriorate.

[*Signature*]

[*City and State or County*]

[*Date*]

> **ILLUSTRATION 3. AUDITOR'S REPORT FOR A CONTINUING AUDITOR EXPRESSING AN OPINION ON ONLY ONE PREVIOUSLY REPORTED MATERIAL WEAKNESS WHEN ADDITIONAL MATERIAL WEAKNESSES PREVIOUSLY WERE REPORTED**

Report of Independent Registered Public Accounting Firm

We have previously audited and reported on management's annual assessment of ABC Company's internal control over financial reporting as of December 31, 20XX, based on [*identify control criteria, for example, "criteria established in* Internal Control—Integrated Framework *issued* by the Committee of Sponsoring Organizations of the Treadway Commission (COSO)."]. Our report, dated [*date of report*] identified the following material weakness in the company's internal control over financial reporting:

[*Describe material weakness*]

We have audited management's assertion, included in the accompanying [*title of management's report*], that the material weakness in internal control over financial reporting identified above no longer exists as of [*date of management's assertion*] because the following control(s) addresses the material weakness:

[*Describe control(s)*]

Management has asserted that the control(s) identified above achieve(s) the following stated control objective, which is consistent with the criteria established in [*identify control criteria used for management's annual assessment of internal control over financial reporting*]: [*state control objective addressed*]. Management also has asserted that it has tested the control(s) identified above and concluded that the control(s) was (*were*) designed and operated effectively as of [*date of management's assertion*]. ABC Company's management is responsible for its assertion. Our responsibility is to express an opinion on whether the identified material weakness continues to exist as of [*date of management's assertion*] based on our auditing procedures.

Our engagement was conducted in accordance with the standards of the Public Company Accounting Oversight Board (United States). Those standards require that we plan and perform the engagement to obtain reasonable assurance about whether a previously reported material weakness continues to exist at the company. Our engagement included examining evidence supporting management's assertion and performing such other procedures as we considered necessary in the circumstances. We obtained an understanding of the company's internal control over financial reporting as part of our previous audit of management's annual assessment of ABC Company's internal control over financial reporting as of December 31, 20XX, and updated that understanding as it specifically relates to changes in internal control over financial reporting associated with the material weakness described above. We believe that our auditing procedures provide a reasonable basis for our opinion.

In our opinion, the material weakness described above no longer exists as of [*date of management's assertion*].

We were not engaged to and did not conduct an audit of internal control over financial reporting as of [*date of management's assertion*], the objective of which would be the expression of an opinion on the effectiveness of internal control over financial reporting. Accordingly, we do not express such an opinion. This means that we have not applied auditing procedures sufficient to reach conclusions about the effectiveness of any controls of the company as of any date after December 31, 20XX, other than the control(s) specifically identified in this report. Accordingly, we do no express an opinion that any other controls operated effectively after December 31, 20XX. Our report on management's annual assessment of ABC Company's internal control over financial reporting, dated [*date of report*], [*attached or identify location of where the report is publicly available*] identified additional material weaknesses other than the one identified in this report. We are not reporting on those other material weaknesses and, accordingly, express no opinion regarding whether those material weaknesses continue to exist after [*date of management's annual assessment, e.g., December 31, 20XX*].

Because of its inherent limitations, internal control over financial reporting may not prevent or detect misstatements. Also, projections of any evaluation of the effectiveness of specific controls or internal control over financial reporting overall to future periods are subject to the risk that controls may become inadequate because of changes in conditions or that the degree of compliance with the policies and procedures may deteriorate.

[*Signature*]

[*City and State or Country*]

[*Date*]

PCAOB 5 An Audit of Internal Control Over Financial Reporting That Is Integrated with an Audit of Financial Statements[1]

> *IMPORTANT NOTE:* The guidance in this section applies to the preparation and issuance of audit reports for all issuers as defined by the Sarbanes–Oxley Act.

EFFECTIVE DATE AND APPLICABILITY

Effective Date This standard currently is effective.

Applicability Engagements to perform an audit of management's assessment of the effectiveness of internal control over financial reporting that is integrated with an audit of the financial statements.

DEFINITIONS OF TERMS

Competence. The attainment and maintenance of a level of understanding and knowledge that enables a person to perform ably the tasks assigned to him or her.

Control objective. Provides a specific target against which to evaluate the effectiveness of controls. It generally relates to a relevant assertion and states a criterion for evaluating whether the entity's control procedures provide reasonable assurance that a misstatement or omission in that assertion is prevented or detected by controls on a timely basis.

Deficiency in internal control over financial reporting. Exists when the design or operation of a control does not allow management or employees to prevent or detect misstatements on a timely basis.

Design deficiency. Exists when a control necessary to meet the control objective is missing, or an existing control is not properly designed so that, even if the control operates as designed, the control objective would not be met.

Detective controls. Controls having the objective of detecting errors or fraud that has already occurred that could result in a misstatement of the financial statements.

---

[1] *Practitioners should reference the additional guidance listed in the section "Other PCAOB Guidance" in this volume's chapter PCAOB 1.*

Material weakness. A deficiency, or a combination of deficiencies, in internal control over financial reporting, such that there is a reasonable possibility that a material misstatement of the entity's annual or interim financial statements will not be prevented or detected on a timely basis.

Objectivity. The ability to perform assigned tasks impartially and with intellectual honesty.

Operation deficiency. Exists when a properly designed control does not operate as designed, or when the person performing the control does not possess the necessary authority or competence to perform the control effectively.

Preventive controls. Controls having the objective of preventing errors or fraud that could result in a misstatement of the financial statements from occurring.

Relevant assertion. A financial statement assertion that has a reasonable possibility of containing a misstatement that would cause the financial statements to be materially misstated.

Senior management. The principal executive and financial officers signing the entity's certifications as required under Section 302 of the Act, as well as any other members of senior management who play a significant role in the entity's financial reporting process.

Significant account or disclosure. An account or disclosure for which there is a reasonable possibility of a misstatement that, individually or when aggregated with others, has a material effect on the financial statements.

Significant deficiency. A deficiency, or a combination of deficiencies, in internal control over financial reporting that is less severe than a material weakness, yet is important enough to merit attention by those responsible for oversight of the entity's financial reporting.

Walk-through. Following a transaction from origination through the entity's processes, including information systems, until it is reflected in the entity's financial records, using the same documents and information technology that the entity's personnel use. Walk-through procedures usually include a combination of inquiry, observation, inspection of relevant documentation, and reperformance of controls.

OBJECTIVES OF PCAOB STANDARD 5

Public Company Accounting Oversight Board (PCAOB) Auditing Standard 5 establishes the fieldwork and reporting standards applicable to an audit of internal control over financial reporting. Since a company's internal control cannot be considered effective if one or more material weaknesses exist, the auditor must plan and perform the audit to obtain evidence that is sufficient to obtain a reasonable assurance about whether material weaknesses exist as of the date specified in management's assessment.

In an integrated audit of internal control over financial reporting and the financial statements, the auditor should design his or her testing of controls to accomplish the objectives of both audits, which are to obtain:

- Sufficient evidence to support the auditor's opinion on internal control over financial reporting as of year-end; and
- Sufficient evidence to support the auditor's control risk assessments for purposes of the audit of financial statements.

> NOTE: If the auditor can support a low control risk assessment, he or she should be able to reduce the amount of audit work that otherwise would have been necessary to opine on the financial statements.

FUNDAMENTAL REQUIREMENTS

PLANNING THE AUDIT

When the auditor plans an audit of internal control over financial reporting, he or she should evaluate whether the following matters are important to the entity's financial statements and internal control and how they will affect audit procedures:

- Knowledge of the entity's internal control over financial reporting obtained during other engagements performed by the auditor;
- Matters affecting the industry in which the entity operates, such as financial reporting practices, economic conditions, laws and regulations, and technological changes;
- Matters relating to the entity's business, including its organization, operating characteristics, and capital structure;
- The extent of recent changes in the entity, its operations, or its internal control over financial reporting;
- The auditor's preliminary judgments about materiality, risk, and other factors relating to the determination of material weaknesses;
- Control deficiencies previously communicated to the audit committee or management;
- Legal or regulatory matters of which the entity is aware;
- The type and extent of available evidence related to the effectiveness of the entity's internal control over financial reporting;
- Preliminary judgments about the effectiveness of internal control over financial reporting;
- Public information about the entity relevant to the evaluation of the likelihood of material financial statement misstatements and the effectiveness of the entity's internal control over financial reporting;
- Knowledge about the risks related to the entity evaluated as part of the auditor's client acceptance and retention evaluation; and
- The relative complexity of the entity's operations.

If the auditor decides it is appropriate to serve as the principal auditor of the entity's financial statements, then that auditor also should be the principal auditor of the entity's internal control over financial reporting.

RISK ASSESSMENT

Risk assessment is the key underlying issue of this Standard. The auditor must consider risk when determining significant accounts and disclosures, relevant assertions, the selection of controls to be tested, and determining the evidence needed for a given control. The auditor should apply more effort in those areas where there is a higher degree of risk that a material weakness may exist. Conversely, it is not necessary to test controls that, even if deficient, would not present a reasonable possibility of material misstatement to the financial statements.

The complexity of an entity or business unit is of significant importance to the auditor in assessing risk and determining necessary procedures.

The auditor should incorporate a fraud risk assessment into the audit of internal control over financial reporting. This is an evaluation of whether the entity's controls sufficiently address identified risks of material misstatement due to fraud and controls intended to address the risk of management override of other controls. Examples of controls addressing these risks are:

- Controls over significant, unusual transactions, especially those resulting in late or unusual journal entries;
- Controls over journal entries and adjustments made in the period-end financial reporting process;
- Controls over related-party transactions;
- Controls related to significant management estimates; and
- Controls that mitigate incentives for, and pressures on, management to falsify or inappropriately manage financial results.

USING THE WORK OF OTHERS

For an audit of internal control, the auditor may use work performed by, or receive assistance from, internal auditors, company personnel other than internal auditors, and third parties working under the direction of management or the audit committee that provides evidence about the effectiveness of internal control over financial reporting. If the auditor is conducting an integrated audit of internal control over financial reporting as well as the financial statements, he or she may also use this work to obtain evidence supporting the assessment of control risk for purposes of the audit of the financial statements.

The higher the degree of competence and objectivity of the person the auditor plans to use, the greater use the auditor may make of the work. Competence and objectivity were defined earlier in "Definitions of Terms." To assess competence, the auditor should evaluate factors about the person's qualifications and ability to perform the work the auditor plans to use. To assess objectivity, the auditor should evaluate whether factors are present that either inhibit or promote a person's ability to perform with the necessary degree of objectivity the work the auditor plans to use. Internal auditors normally are expected to have greater competence and objectivity in performing the type of work that is useful to the auditor.

The auditor should not use the work of individuals who have either a low degree of objectivity or competence. Also, the auditor should be more inclined to perform his or her own work on a control as the risk associated with that control increases.

THE TOP-DOWN APPROACH FOR CONTROLS SELECTION

The auditor should use a top-down approach for the selection of controls in an audit of internal controls over financial reporting. This approach begins at the financial statement level and with the auditor's understanding of the overall risks to internal control over financial reporting. The auditor then focuses on entity-level controls, and then significant accounts and disclosures and their relevant assertions. By taking this approach, the auditor focuses on those accounts, disclosures, and assertions that present a reasonable possibility of material misstatement to the financial statements and related disclosures.

The auditor's evaluation of entity-level controls can result in changes to the testing that the auditor would otherwise have performed on other controls.

Entity-level controls include:

- Controls related to the control environment;
- Controls over management override (which are especially important in smaller entities where there is usually an increased involvement by senior managers in performing controls and in the period-end financial reporting process);
- The entity's risk assessment process;
- Centralized processing and controls, including shared service environments;
- Controls to monitor results of operations;
- Controls to monitor other controls, including activities of the internal audit function, the audit committee, and self-assessment programs;
- Controls over the period-end financial reporting process; and
- Policies that address significant business control and risk management practices.

Some entity-level controls, such as those impacting the control environment, have an indirect (though important) effect on the likelihood that a misstatement will be detected or prevented on a timely basis. Other entity-level controls monitor the effectiveness of other controls; as such, they may allow the auditor to reduce the testing of other controls. Other entity-level controls may operate at a level of precision that would adequately prevent or detect misstatements; if so, the auditor may not need to test additional controls related to that risk.

The auditor must evaluate the control environment at the entity. As part of this evaluation, the auditor should assess:

- Whether management's philosophy and operating style promote effective internal control over financial reporting;
- Whether sound integrity and ethical values, particularly of top management, are developed and understood; and
- Whether the board of directors or audit committee understands and exercises oversight responsibility over financial reporting and internal control.

The auditor must also evaluate the entity's period-end reporting process. The reporting process includes those procedures:

- Used to enter transaction totals into the general ledger;
- Related to the selection and application of accounting policies;
- Used to initiate, authorize, record, and process journal entries in the general ledger;
- Used to record recurring and nonrecurring adjustments to the annual and quarterly financial statements; and
- Used for preparing annual and quarterly financial statements and related disclosures.

NOTE: Since the annual period-end financial reporting process occurs after the "as of" date of management's assessment, those controls usually cannot be tested until after the "as of" date.

As part of evaluating the period-end financial reporting process, the auditor should assess the following:

- Inputs, procedures performed, and outputs of the processes the entity uses to produce its annual and quarterly financial statements;
- The extent of information technology involvement in the period-end financial reporting process;
- Who participates from management;
- The locations involved in the period-end financial reporting process;

- The types of adjusting and consolidating entries; and
- The nature and extent of the oversight of the process by management, the board of directors, and the audit committee.

NOTE: The auditor should obtain sufficient evidence of the effectiveness of those quarterly controls that are important for determining whether the entity's controls sufficiently address the assessed risk of misstatement; however, the auditor does not have to obtain sufficient evidence for each quarter individually.

Identification of Significant Accounts and Disclosures

The auditor should identify significant accounts and disclosures, as well as their relevant assertions. Financial statement assertions include existence or occurrence, completeness, valuation or allocation, rights and obligations, and presentation and disclosure.

To identify significant accounts and disclosures and their relevant assertions, the auditor should evaluate the qualitative and quantitative risk factors related to the financial statement line items and disclosures. Risk factors relevant to the identification of significant accounts and disclosures and their relevant assertions include:

- Size and composition of the account;
- Susceptibility to misstatement due to errors or fraud;
- Volume of activity, complexity, and homogeneity of the individual transactions processed through the account or reflected in the disclosure;
- Nature of the account or disclosure;
- Accounting and reporting complexities associated with the account or disclosure;
- Exposure to losses in the account;
- Possibility of significant contingent liabilities arising from the activities reflected in the account or disclosure;
- Existence of related-party transactions in the account; and
- Changes from the prior period in account or disclosure characteristics.

The auditor should also determine the likely sources of potential misstatements that would cause the financial statements to be materially misstated. The auditor might determine the likely sources of potential misstatements by asking what could go wrong within a given account or disclosure.

The risk factors that the auditor should evaluate in identifying significant accounts and disclosures and their relevant assertions are the same in the audit of internal control over financial reporting as in the audit of the financial statements; thus, significant accounts and disclosures and their relevant assertions are the same for both audits.

When an entity has multiple locations or business units, the auditor should identify significant accounts and disclosures and their relevant assertions based on the consolidated financial statements. See "Multiple Location Scoping Decisions" for more information.

Understanding Likely Sources of Misstatement

The auditor should pursue the following objectives in order to further understand the likely sources of potential misstatements:

- Understand the flow of transactions related to the relevant assertions, including how the transactions are initiated, authorized, processed, and recorded;

- Verify that the auditor has identified the points within the entity's processes at which a misstatement could arise that would be material (either individually or in combination with other misstatements);
- Identify the controls that management has implemented to address these potential misstatements; and
- Identify the controls that management has implemented over the prevention or timely detection of unauthorized acquisition, use, or disposition of the entity's assets that could result in a material misstatement of the financial statements.

As part of this evaluation, the auditor should also understand how information technology affects the entity's flow of transactions.

The auditor may find that a walk-through is the most effective way to understand likely sources of misstatement. In performing a walk-through, the auditor should question the entity's personnel about their understanding of what is required by the entity's procedures and controls. These questions, when combined with other walk-through procedures, allow the auditor to gain a sufficient understanding of the process, as well as be able to identify important points where a necessary control is either missing or not designed effectively.

Given the level of judgment required, the auditor should either directly perform the preceding procedures, or supervise the work of others who provide direct assistance to the auditor.

Selecting Controls for Testing

The auditor should test those controls that are important to the auditor's conclusion about whether the entity's controls sufficiently address the assessed risk of misstatement to each relevant assertion. It is not necessary to test all controls related to a relevant assertion, nor is it necessary to test redundant controls, unless redundancy is itself a control objective. The decision to select a control for testing depends on which controls, either individually or in combination, sufficiently address the assessed risk of misstatement to a given assertion.

TESTING CONTROLS

The auditor should test the *design effectiveness* of controls by determining whether the controls satisfy the entity's control objectives and can effectively prevent or detect errors or fraud that could result in material misstatements in the financial statements. Design effectiveness test procedures include a mix of personnel inquiry, operations observation, and relevant documentation inspection. Walk-throughs that include these procedures ordinarily are sufficient to evaluate design effectiveness.

The auditor should test the *operating effectiveness* of a control by determining whether the control is operating as designed and whether the person performing it possesses the authority and competence to perform the control effectively. If the entity uses a third party to provide assistance with some financial reporting functions, then the auditor may take into account the combined competence of company personnel and other parties that assist with functions related to financial reporting.

Relationship of Risk to the Evidence to Be Obtained

The evidence needed to persuade the auditor that a control is effective depends on the risk associated with the control. This is the risk that the control might not be effective, and if not effective, the risk that a material weakness would result. As this risk increases, the auditor should obtain additional evidence.

> NOTE: The auditor's objective is to express an opinion on the entity's overall internal control over financial reporting; he or she does not need to obtain sufficient evidence to support an opinion about the effectiveness of individual controls. Thus, the auditor can vary the evidence obtained regarding the effectiveness of individual controls selected for testing.

There are a number of factors influencing the risk associated with a control. These include:

- The nature and materiality of misstatements that the control is intended to prevent or detect;
- The inherent risk associated with the related account(s) and assertion(s);
- Whether there have been changes in the volume or nature of transactions that might adversely affect control design or operating effectiveness;
- Whether the account has a history of errors;
- The effectiveness of entity-level controls, especially controls that monitor other controls;
- The nature of the control and the frequency with which it operates;
- The degree to which the control relies on the effectiveness of other controls;
- The competence of the personnel who perform the control or monitor its performance and whether there have been changes in key personnel who perform the control or monitor its performance;
- Whether the control relies on performance by an individual or is automated (Note: an automated control is generally expected to be lower risk if information technology controls are effective); and

> NOTE: In areas in which off-the-shelf software is used, the auditor's testing of information technology controls might focus on the application controls built into the prepackaged software that management relies on to achieve its control objectives.

- The complexity of the control and the significance of the judgments that must be made in connection with its operation.

> NOTE: A conclusion that a control is not operating effectively can generally be supported by less evidence than is necessary to support a conclusion that a control is operating effectively.

When the auditor identifies deviations from the entity's controls, he or she should determine the effect of the deviations on the assessment of the risk associated with the control being tested and the associated evidence to be obtained, as well as on the operating effectiveness of the control. Given that effective internal control over financial reporting cannot provide absolute assurance of achieving the entity's control objectives, an individual control does not necessarily have to operate without any deviation to be considered effective.

When testing a control, the auditor will find that different combinations of the nature, timing, and extent of testing may provide sufficient evidence in relation to the risk associated with the control. The nature of the tests of effectiveness that will provide competent evidence depends considerably on the nature of the control to be tested.

Nature of Tests of Controls

Some tests produce greater evidence of control effectiveness than other tests. The following tests are presented in order of the most evidence provided to the least:

1. Reperformance of a control
2. Inspection of relevant documentation
3. Observation
4. Inquiry (which does not provide sufficient evidence to support a conclusion about control effectiveness)

Testing controls over a greater period of time provides more evidence of the effectiveness of controls than testing over a shorter period of time. Further, testing performed closer to the date of management's assessment provides more evidence than testing performed earlier in the year.

Using Results from the Audit of Financial Statements

The auditor should evaluate the effect of the findings of the substantive auditing procedures performed in the audit of financial statements on the effectiveness of internal control over financial reporting. This evaluation should include:

- The auditor's risk assessments in connection with the selection and application of substantive procedures, especially those related to fraud
- Findings with respect to illegal acts and related-party transactions
- Indications of management bias in making accounting estimates and in selecting accounting principles
- Misstatements detected by substantive procedures (the extent of such misstatements might alter the auditor's judgment about the effectiveness of controls)

Extent of Tests of Controls

The more extensively a control is tested, the greater the evidence obtained from that test.

Roll-Forward Procedures

When the auditor reports on the effectiveness of controls as of a specific date and obtains evidence about the operating effectiveness of controls at an interim date, he or she should determine what additional evidence concerning the operation of the controls for the remaining period is necessary. The additional evidence required depends on the following factors:

- The specific control tested prior to the as-of date, including the risks associated with the control and the nature of the control, and the results of those tests;
- The sufficiency of the evidence of effectiveness obtained at an interim date;
- The length of the remaining period; and
- The possibility that there have been any significant changes in internal control over financial reporting subsequent to the interim date.

NOTE: When the evaluation of these factors indicates a low risk that the controls are no longer effective during the roll-forward period, inquiry alone might be sufficient as a roll-forward procedure.

Special Considerations for Subsequent Years' Audits

In subsequent years' audits, the auditor should incorporate knowledge from past audits of the entity's controls into the decision-making process for determining the nature, timing, and extent of testing needed. After taking into account all risk factors, the auditor may be able to reduce testing in subsequent years.

The auditor should vary the nature, timing, and extent of controls testing from year to year, to introduce unpredictability into the testing and respond to changes in circumstances. Thus, the auditor could test controls during different interim periods, change the number and types of tests performed, or change the combination of procedures used.

EVALUATING IDENTIFIED DEFICIENCIES

The auditor must evaluate the severity of each control deficiency to determine whether the deficiencies, individually or together, are material weaknesses as of the date of management's assessment. However, in planning and performing the audit, the auditor is not required to search for deficiencies (either individually or in combination) that are less severe than a material weakness.

The severity of a deficiency depends on whether there is a reasonable possibility that the entity's controls will fail to prevent or detect a misstatement of an account balance or disclosure, and the magnitude of the potential misstatement resulting from the deficiency. The severity of a deficiency does not depend on whether a misstatement actually has occurred, but rather on whether there is a reasonable possibility that the entity's controls will fail to prevent or detect a misstatement.

Risk factors affect whether there is a reasonable possibility that a deficiency, or a combination of deficiencies, will result in a misstatement of an account balance or disclosure. The risk factors include

- The nature of the financial statement accounts, disclosures, and assertions involved;
- The susceptibility of the related asset or liability to loss or fraud;
- The subjectivity, complexity, or extent of judgment required to determine the amount involved;
- The interaction or relationship of the control with other controls, including whether they are interdependent or redundant;
- The interaction of the deficiencies; and
- The possible future consequences of the deficiency.

The valuation of whether a control deficiency presents a reasonable possibility of misstatement can be made without quantifying the probability of occurrence as a specific percentage or range.

Multiple control deficiencies that affect the same financial statement account balance or disclosure increase the likelihood of misstatement and may, in combination, constitute a material weakness, even though such deficiencies may individually be less severe. Thus, the auditor should determine whether individual control deficiencies that affect the same significant account or disclosure, relevant assertion, or component of internal control collectively result in a material weakness.

Factors affecting the magnitude of a misstatement that might result from a deficiency in controls include the financial statement amounts or total of transactions exposed to the deficiency, and the volume of activity in the account balance or class of transactions exposed to the deficiency that has either occurred in the current period or is expected in future periods.

When evaluating the magnitude of a potential misstatement, the maximum amount that an account balance or total of transactions can be overstated is generally the recorded amount, while understatements could be larger. Also, the probability of a small misstatement is greater than the probability of a large one.

The auditor should evaluate the effectiveness of compensating controls when determining whether a control deficiency or combination of deficiencies is a material weakness. To have a mitigating effect, the compensating control should operate at a level of precision that would prevent or detect a misstatement that could be material.

Indicators of Material Weakness

Indicators of material weakness in internal control over financial reporting include the following:

- Identification of fraud, whether or not material, on the part of senior management;
- Restatement of previously issued financial statements to reflect the correction of a material misstatement;
- Identification by the auditor of a material misstatement of financial statements in the current period in circumstances indicating that the misstatement would not have been detected by the entity's internal control over financial reporting; and
- Ineffective oversight of the entity's external financial reporting and internal control over financial reporting by the entity's audit committee.

When evaluating the severity of a deficiency or combination of deficiencies, the auditor should also determine the level of detail and degree of assurance that would satisfy prudent officials in the conduct of their own affairs that they have reasonable assurance that transactions are recorded as necessary to permit the preparation of financial statements in conformity with generally accepted accounting principles (GAAP). If the auditor determines that this is not the case, then he or she should treat the deficiency or combination of deficiencies as an indicator of a material weakness.

FORMING AN OPINION

The auditor should form an opinion on the effectiveness of the entity's internal control over financial reporting by evaluating evidence from all sources. This should include the auditor's controls tests, misstatements detected during the financial statement audit, any identified control deficiencies, and internal audit reports that address relevant controls.

The auditor should also evaluate the presentation of the elements that management is required to present in its annual report on internal control over financial reporting. If any elements of management's annual report are incomplete or improperly presented, the auditor should modify his or her report to include an explanatory paragraph describing the reasons for this determination.

The auditor may form an opinion only when there have been no scope restrictions on the auditor's work. If there is a scope limitation, the auditor must either disclaim an opinion or withdraw from the engagement. When disclaiming an opinion because of a scope limitation, the auditor should state that the scope of the audit was not sufficient to warrant the expression of an opinion and, in a separate paragraph, the reasons for the disclaimer; the auditor should not identify the procedures that were performed nor include the statements describing the characteristics of an audit of internal control over financial reporting.

OBTAINING WRITTEN REPRESENTATIONS

In an audit of internal control over financial reporting, the auditor should obtain written representations from management that:

- Acknowledges management's responsibility for establishing and maintaining effective internal control over financial reporting;

- States that management has performed an evaluation and made an assessment of the effectiveness of the entity's internal control over financial reporting and specifying the control criteria;
- States that management did not use the auditor's procedures performed during the audits of internal control over financial reporting or the financial statements as part of the basis for management's assessment of the effectiveness of internal control over financial reporting;
- States management's conclusion, as set forth in its assessment, about the effectiveness of the entity's internal control over financial reporting based on the control criteria as of a specified date;
- States that management has disclosed to the auditor all deficiencies in the design or operation of internal control over financial reporting identified as part of management's evaluation, including separately disclosing to the auditor all such deficiencies that it believes to be significant deficiencies or material weaknesses in internal control over financial reporting;
- Describes any fraud resulting in a material misstatement to the entity's financial statements and any other fraud that does not result in a material misstatement to the entity's financial statements but involves senior management or management or other employees who have a significant role in the entity's internal control over financial reporting;
- States whether control deficiencies identified and communicated to the audit committee during previous engagements have been resolved, and specifically identifying any that have not; and
- States whether there were, subsequent to the date being reported on, any changes in internal control over financial reporting or other factors that might significantly affect internal control over financial reporting, including any corrective actions taken by management with regard to significant deficiencies and material weaknesses.

If management does not provide written representations, this is a scope limitation on the audit. In this case, the auditor must either withdraw from the engagement or disclaim an opinion. In such a case, the auditor must also evaluate the effects of management's refusal on his or her ability to rely on other representations, including those obtained in the audit of the entity's financial statements.

COMMUNICATING MATTERS RELATED TO THE AUDIT

The auditor must issue written communications to management and the audit committee regarding all material weaknesses identified during the audit. This communication should be made prior to issuing the auditor's report on internal control over financial reporting. If the auditor concludes that the oversight by the entity's internal audit committee is ineffective, then he or she must communicate that conclusion in writing to the board of directors.

The auditor should consider whether there have been any deficiencies or combinations of deficiencies that have been identified during the audit that are significant deficiencies. If so, he or she must communicate these deficiencies, in writing, to the audit committee.

The auditor should also communicate to management, in writing, all deficiencies in internal control over financial reporting (i.e., those less-than-material weaknesses) identified during the audit and inform the audit committee when such a communication has been made. When formulating this communication to management, the auditor does not have to repeat information about deficiencies that have been communicated before.

The auditor should not issue a report stating that no deficiencies less severe than a material weakness were noted during the audit.

REPORTING ON INTERNAL CONTROL

The auditor's report on the audit of internal control over financial reporting must include the following components:

1. A title that includes the word *independent*
2. A statement that management is responsible for maintaining effective internal control over financial reporting and for assessing the effectiveness of internal control over financial reporting
3. An identification of management's report on internal control
4. A statement that the auditor's responsibility is to express an opinion on the entity's internal control over financial reporting based on his or her audit
5. A definition of internal control over financial reporting
6. A statement that the audit was conducted in accordance with the standards of the PCAOB (United States)
7. A statement that the standards of the PCAOB require that the auditor plan and perform the audit to obtain reasonable assurance about whether effective internal control over financial reporting was maintained in all material respects
8. A statement that an audit includes obtaining an understanding of internal control over financial reporting, assessing the risk that a material weakness exists, testing and evaluating the design and operating effectiveness of internal control based on the assessed risk, and performing such other procedures as the auditor considered necessary in the circumstances
9. A statement that the auditor believes the audit provides a reasonable basis for his or her opinion
10. A paragraph stating that, because of inherent limitations, internal control over financial reporting may not prevent or detect misstatements and that projections of any evaluation of effectiveness to future periods are subject to the risk that controls may become inadequate because of changes in conditions, or that the degree of compliance with the policies or procedures may deteriorate
11. The auditor's opinion on whether the entity maintained, in all material respects, effective internal control over financial reporting as of the specified date, based on the control criteria
12. The manual or printed signature of the auditor's firm
13. The city and state (or city and country, in the case of non-U.S. auditors) from which the auditor's report has been issued
14. The date of the audit report

The auditor may choose to issue a combined statement that contains an opinion on the financial statements and an opinion on internal control over financial reporting. It is also acceptable to issue separate reports on these topics.

Several examples of the auditor's report are included in the "Illustrations" section.

The Report Date

The auditor should date the audit report no earlier than the date on which the auditor has obtained sufficient competent evidence to support his or her opinion. Because the auditor cannot audit internal control over financial reporting without also auditing the financial statements, the reports should have the same date.

Material Weaknesses

If there are deficiencies (either individually or in combination) resulting in one or more material weaknesses, the auditor must express an adverse opinion on the entity's internal control over financial reporting.

When expressing an *adverse opinion* on internal control over financial reporting because of a material weakness, the auditor's report must include:

- The definition of a material weakness
- A statement that a material weakness has been identified and an identification of the material weakness that was described in management's assessment

If the material weakness was not included in management's assessment, then the auditor should modify his or her report to state that a material weakness has been identified but not included in management's assessment. Further, the report should include a description of the material weakness, which should provide the users of the audit report with specific information about the nature of the material weakness and its actual and potential effect on the presentation of the entity's financial statements issued during the existence of the weakness. In addition, the auditor should communicate to the audit committee in writing that the material weakness was not disclosed or identified as a material weakness in management's assessment.

If the material weakness was included in management's assessment but the auditor concludes that the disclosure of the material weakness is not fairly presented in all material respects, then the auditor's report should describe this conclusion as well as the information necessary to fairly describe the material weakness.

The auditor should determine the effect the adverse opinion has on his or her opinion on the financial statements. Further, the auditor should disclose whether his or her opinion on the financial statements was affected by the adverse opinion on internal control over financial reporting.

Report Modifications

The auditor should modify his or her report if any of the following conditions exist:

- Elements of management's annual report on internal control are incomplete or improperly presented.
- There is a restriction on the scope of the engagement.
- The auditor decides to refer to the report of other auditors as the basis, in part, for the auditor's own report.
- There is other information contained in management's annual report on internal control over financial reporting.
- Management's annual certification pursuant to Section 302 of the Sarbanes-Oxley Act is misstated.

If the auditor determines that elements of management's annual report on internal control over financial reporting are incomplete or improperly presented, the auditor should modify his or her report to include an explanatory paragraph describing the reasons for this determination.

When the auditor plans to *disclaim an opinion* and the limited procedures performed by the auditor cause the auditor to conclude that a material weakness exists, the auditor's report should include:

- The definition of a material weakness
- A description of any material weaknesses identified in the entity's internal control over financial reporting; this description should provide the users of the audit report with specific information about the nature of any material weakness and its actual and potential effect on the presentation of the entity's financial statements issued during the existence of the weakness

The auditor may issue a report disclaiming an opinion on internal control over financial reporting as soon as the auditor concludes that a scope limitation will prevent the auditor from obtaining the reasonable assurance necessary to express an opinion. The auditor is not required to perform any additional work prior to issuing a disclaimer, once the auditor concludes that he or she will not be able to obtain sufficient evidence to express an opinion.

Filings under Federal Securities Statutes

AU Section 711, *Filings under Federal Securities Statutes*, describes the auditor's responsibilities when the auditor's report is included in registration statements, proxy statements, or periodic reports filed under the federal securities statutes. The auditor should apply Section 711 with respect to the auditor's report on internal control over financial reporting included in such filings. In addition, the auditor should extend the direction in Section 711 to obtain written representations from officers and other executives responsible for financial and accounting matters about whether any events have occurred that have a material effect on the audited financial statements to matters that could have a material effect on internal control over financial reporting.

When the auditor intends to consent to the inclusion of his or her report on internal control over financial reporting in the securities filing, his or her consent should clearly indicate that both the audit report on financial statements and the audit report on internal control over financial reporting (or both opinions if a combined report is issued) are included in his or her consent.

Subsequent Events

There may be changes in internal control over financial reporting or other factors that significantly affect internal control over financial reporting, arising subsequent to the date as of which internal control over financial reporting is being audited, but before the date of the auditor's report. The auditor should make inquiries of management as to whether there were any such changes or factors, and obtain written management representations relating to such matters.

The auditor's inquiries during this subsequent period can include the following:

- Relevant internal audit reports issued during the subsequent period
- Independent auditor reports of deficiencies in internal control
- Regulatory agency reports on the entity's internal control over financial reporting
- Information about the effectiveness of the entity's internal control over financial reporting that is obtained through other engagements

If the auditor obtains knowledge about subsequent events that materially and adversely affect the effectiveness of the entity's internal control over financial reporting as of the date specified in the assessment, the auditor should issue an adverse opinion on internal control over financial reporting. If the auditor is unable to determine the effect of the subsequent event on the effectiveness of the entity's internal control over financial reporting, he or she should disclaim an opinion.

If a subsequent event has a material effect on the entity's internal control over financial reporting, then the auditor should include in his or her report an explanatory paragraph describing the event and its effects, or directing the reader's attention to the event and its effects as disclosed in management's report.

If, after issuance of the auditor's report, the auditor becomes aware of conditions that existed at the report date that might have affected the auditor's opinion, then follow the procedures noted in AU Section 561, *Subsequent Discovery of Facts Existing at the Date of the Auditor's Report.*

MULTIPLE LOCATION SCOPING DECISIONS

In determining the locations or business units at which to perform tests of controls, the auditor should assess the risk of material misstatement to the financial statements associated with the location or business unit, and correlate the amount of audit attention with the degree of audit risk. The auditor can eliminate from consideration those locations or business units that, individually or when aggregated with others, do not present a reasonable possibility of material misstatement to the entity's consolidated financial statements.

When determining the locations or business units at which to perform tests of controls, the auditor may take into account work performed by others on behalf of management. For example, this can involve the coordination of work with the entity's internal auditors.

The scope of the audit should include entities that are acquired on or before the date of management's assessment and operations that are accounted for as discontinued operations on the date of management's assessment.

For equity method investments, the scope of the audit should include controls over the reporting in accordance with GAAP, in the entity's financial statements, of the entity's portion of the investee's income or loss, the investment balance, adjustments to the income or loss and investment balance, and related disclosures. The audit ordinarily would not extend to the controls at the equity method investee.

If the Securities and Exchange Commission (SEC) allows management to exclude certain entities from its assessment of internal control over financial reporting, then the auditor may limit the audit in the same manner; this is not considered a scope limitation. However, the auditor should include in his or her report a disclosure similar to management's regarding the exclusion of the entity from the scope of both management's assessment and the auditor's audit of internal control over financial reporting. Further, the auditor should evaluate the reasonableness of management's conclusion that the situation meets the criteria of the SEC's allowed exclusion and the appropriateness of any required disclosure related to such a limitation.

USE OF SERVICE ORGANIZATIONS

AU Section 324, *Service Organizations*, applies to the audit of financial statements of an entity that obtains services from another organization that are part of the entity's information systems. The auditor may apply the relevant concepts described in Section 324 to the audit of internal control over financial reporting.

When a significant period of time has elapsed between the time period covered by the tests of controls in the service auditor's report and the date specified in management's assessment, additional procedures should be performed. The auditor should inquire of management to determine whether management has identified any changes in the service organization's controls subsequent to the period covered by the service auditor's report; these changes can include changes in the personnel at the service organization with whom management interacts, changes in reports or other data received from the service organization, changes in contracts or service level agreements with the service organization, or errors identified in the service organization's processing. The auditor should evaluate the effect of such changes in the effectiveness of the entity's internal control over financial reporting. The auditor should also evaluate whether the results of other procedures he or she performed indicate that there have been changes in the controls at the service organization.

The auditor should determine whether to obtain additional evidence about the operating effectiveness of controls at the service organization based (1) on the procedures performed by management or the auditor and the results of those procedures and (2) on an evaluation of the following risk factors:

- The elapsed time between the time period covered by the tests of controls in the service auditor's report and the date specified in management's assessment
- The significance of the activities of the service organization
- Whether errors have been identified in the service organization's processing
- The nature and significance of any changes in the service organization's controls identified by management or the auditor

If the auditor concludes that additional evidence about the operating effectiveness of controls at the service organization is required, his or her additional procedures might include:

- Evaluating procedures performed by management and the results of those procedures
- Contacting the service organization, through the user organization, to obtain specific information
- Requesting that a service auditor be engaged to perform procedures that will supply the necessary information
- Visiting the service organization and performing procedures

The auditor should not refer to the service auditor's report when expressing an opinion on internal control over financial reporting.

BENCHMARKING OF AUTOMATED CONTROLS

Automated application controls are usually not subject to breakdowns due to human failure, which allows the auditor to use a *benchmarking* strategy.

If controls over program changes, access to programs, and computer operations are effective and continue to be tested, and if the auditor verifies that the automated application control has not changed since he or she last tested the application control, then the auditor may conclude that the automated application control continues to be effective without repeating the prior year's tests of the operation of the automated application control.

To determine whether to use a benchmarking strategy, the auditor should assess a number of risk factors. As these factors indicate lower risk, the control being evaluated might be well-suited for benchmarking. However, as these factors indicate increased risk, the control being evaluated is less suited for benchmarking. The risk factors are:

- The extent to which the application control can be matched to a defined program within an application
- The extent to which the application is stable (i.e., there are few changes over time)

- The availability and reliability of a report of the compilation dates of the programs placed in production

Benchmarking automated application controls can be especially effective when it involves purchased off-the-shelf software, since the possibility of program changes is remote.

After a period of time, the baseline of the operation of an automated application control should be reestablished. To determine when to reestablish a baseline, the auditor should evaluate the following factors:

- The effectiveness of the information technology control environment, including controls over application and system software acquisition and maintenance, access controls and computer operations
- The auditor's understanding of the nature of changes, if any, on the specific programs that contain the controls
- The nature and timing of other related tests
- The consequences of errors associated with the application control that was benchmarked
- Whether the control is sensitive to other business factors that may have changed. For example, an automated control may have been designed with the assumption that only positive amounts will exist in a file. This control would no longer be effective if negative amounts were to be posted to the account

ILLUSTRATIONS

The following is an illustration of a combined report that expresses an unqualified opinion on financial statements and an unqualified opinion on internal control over financial reporting, as well as a format where the auditor issues a separate report on internal control over financial reporting. They are adapted from PCAOB Standard 5.

ILLUSTRATION 1. AUDITOR'S COMBINED REPORT FOR AN UNQUALIFIED OPINION ON FINANCIAL STATEMENTS AND AN UNQUALIFIED OPINION ON INTERNAL CONTROL OVER FINANCIAL REPORTING

Report of Independent Registered Public Accounting Firm

We have audited the accompanying balance sheets of ABC Company as of December 31, 20X8 and 20X7, and the related statements of income, stockholders' equity and comprehensive income, and cash flows for each of the years in the three-year period ended December 31, 20X8. We also have audited ABC Company's internal control over financial reporting as of December 31, 20X8, based on [*identify control criteria, for example, "criteria established in Internal Control—Integrated Framework issued by the Committee of Sponsoring Organizations of the Treadway Commission (COSO)"*]. ABC Company's management is responsible for these financial statements, for maintaining effective internal control over financial reporting, and for its assessment of the effectiveness of internal control over financial reporting, included in the accompanying [*title of management's report*]. Our responsibility is to express an opinion on these financial statements and an opinion on the company's internal control over financial reporting based on our audits.

We conducted our audits in accordance with the standards of the Public Company Accounting Oversight Board (United States). Those standards require that we plan and perform the audits to obtain reasonable assurance about whether the financial statements are free of material misstatement and whether effective internal control over financial reporting was maintained in all material respects. Our audits of the financial statements included examining, on a test basis, evidence supporting the amounts and disclosures in the financial statements, assessing the accounting principles used and significant estimates made by management, and evaluating the overall financial statement presentation. Our audit of internal control over financial reporting included obtaining an understanding of internal control over financial reporting, assessing the risk that a material weakness exists, and testing and evaluating the design and operating effectiveness of internal control based on the assessed risk. Our audits also included performing such other procedures as we considered necessary in the circumstances. We believe that our audits provide a reasonable basis for our opinions.

A company's internal control over financial reporting is a process designed to provide reasonable assurance regarding the reliability of financial reporting and the preparation of financial statements for external purposes in accordance with generally accepted accounting principles. A company's internal control over financial reporting includes those policies and procedures that (1) pertain to the maintenance of records that, in reasonable detail, accurately and fairly reflect the transactions and dispositions of the assets of the company; (2) provide reasonable assurance that transactions are recorded as necessary to permit preparation of financial statements in accordance with generally accepted accounting principles, and that receipts and expenditures of the company are being made only in accordance with authorizations of management and directors of the company; and (3) provide reasonable assurance regarding prevention or timely detection of unauthorized acquisition, use, or disposition of the company's assets that could have a material effect on the financial statements.

Because of its inherent limitations, internal control over financial reporting may not prevent or detect misstatements. Also, projections of any evaluation of effectiveness to future periods are subject to the risk that controls may become inadequate because of changes in conditions, or that the degree of compliance with the policies or procedures may deteriorate.

In our opinion, the financial statements referred to above present fairly, in all material respects, the financial position of ABC Company as of December 31, 20X8 and 20X7, and the results of its operations and its cash flows for each of the years in the three-year period ended December 31, 20X8, in conformity with accounting principles generally accepted in the United States of America. Also in our opinion, ABC Company maintained, in all material respects, effective internal control over financial reporting as of December 31, 20X8, based on [*identify control criteria, for example, "criteria established in* Internal Control—Integrated Framework *issued by the Committee of Sponsoring Organizations of the Treadway Commission (COSO)."*].

[*Signature*]

[*City and State or Country*]

[*Date*]

ILLUSTRATION 2. AUDITOR'S SEPARATE REPORT ON INTERNAL CONTROL OVER FINANCIAL REPORTING

If the auditor chooses to issue a separate report on internal control over financial reporting, he or she should add the following paragraph to the auditor's report on the financial statements:

We have also audited, in accordance with the standards of the Public Company Accounting Oversight Board (United States), ABC Company's internal control over financial reporting as of December 31, 20X8, based on [*identify control criteria*] and our report dated [*date of report, which should be the same as the date of the report on the financial statements*] expressed [*include nature of opinion*].

The auditor should add the following paragraph to the report on internal control over financial reporting:

> We also have audited, in accordance with the standards of the Public Company Accounting Oversight Board (United States), the [*identify financial statements*] of ABC Company and our report, dated [*date of report, which should be the same as the date of the report on the effectiveness of internal control over financial reporting*], which expressed [*include nature of opinion*].

PCAOB 6 Evaluating Consistency of Financial Statements[1]

> *IMPORTANT NOTE: The guidance in this section applies to the preparation and issuance of audit reports for all issuers as defined by the Sarbanes–Oxley Act.*

EFFECTIVE DATE AND APPLICABILITY

Effective Date This standard currently is effective.

Applicability Engagements conducted pursuant to Public Company Accounting Oversight Board (PCAOB) standards, including an audit of financial statements, an audit of internal control over financial reporting, and a review of interim financial information.

DEFINITIONS OF TERMS

Change in accounting principle. A change from one generally accepted accounting principle (GAAP) to another when there are at least two applicable GAAPs, or when the accounting principle formerly used by an entity is no longer generally accepted. A change in accounting principle also arises when there is a change in the method of *applying* an accounting principle.

NOTE: A correction of a misstatement occurs when an entity changes from an accounting principle that is not generally accepted to one that is generally accepted.

Change in reporting entity. A change resulting in financial statements that are now those of a different reporting entity.

Current period. The most recent year, or a period of less than one year, upon which the auditor is reporting.

OBJECTIVES OF PCAOB STANDARD 6

PCAOB Auditing Standard 6 sets forth the general requirements for evaluating the consistency of an entity's financial statements. The Standard's scope includes the evaluation of changes to an entity's previously issued financial statements, and the impact of this evaluation on the auditor's report.

---

[1] *Practitioners should reference the additional guidance listed in the section "Other PCAOB Guidance" in this volume's chapter PCAOB 1.*

FUNDAMENTAL REQUIREMENTS

BASIC REQUIREMENT

The auditor should identify whether the comparability of an entity's financial statements between periods has been materially affected by changes in accounting principles or material adjustments to financial statements that were issued for previous periods.

The auditor's evaluation of comparability only applies to those financial statements covered by the auditor's report. However, when the auditor's report only applies to the current period, the auditor should evaluate whether the current period financial statements are consistent with the statements for the immediately preceding period.

For example, ABC Company presents comparative financial statements covering three years, and changes auditors. For the new auditor's first year, the auditor evaluates consistency between the year on which he or she is reporting and the preceding year. In the new auditor's second year, the evaluation encompasses the two years on which he or she is reporting, and between those years and the earliest year presented.

When conducting a consistency evaluation, the auditor should take note of changes in accounting principle and adjustments to correct misstatements in previously issued financial statements, but only if these changes have a material effect on the financial statements.

CHANGES IN ACCOUNTING PRINCIPLE

The auditor's evaluation of a change in accounting principle should determine whether:

- A newly adopted accounting principle is a GAAP;
- The method of accounting for the effect of the change conforms to generally accepted accounting principles;
- The disclosures of the accounting change are adequate; and
- The entity has justified that the alternative accounting principle is preferable to the one it replaces.

If the auditor concludes that the preceding criteria have been met, then he or she should add an explanatory paragraph to the auditor's report, as noted in AU Section 508, *Reports on Audited Financial Statements*. If these criteria are *not* met, then the accounting change is a departure from GAAP and should also be addressed in accordance with AU Section 508.

NOTE: If an entity's financial statements contain an equity method investment, then the auditor should also evaluate the consistency of the financial statements of the investee. If the investee makes a change in accounting principle that is material to the investing company's financial statements, then the auditor should add an explanatory paragraph to the auditor's report, in accordance with Section 508.

If there is a change in *accounting estimate* effected by a change in accounting principle, the auditor should evaluate and report on this in the same manner as for other changes in accounting principle.

If there is a change in *reporting entity*, the auditor should include an explanatory paragraph in the auditor's report. However, if the change in reporting entity is caused by a transaction or event (such as the creation, cessation, or purchase or disposition of a subsidiary), then the auditor does not need to describe the change in his or her report.

CORRECTION OF A MATERIAL MISSTATEMENT

If an entity corrects a material misstatement in its previously issued financial statements, the auditor should recognize this in the auditor's report with an explanatory paragraph, in accordance with Section 508. If the entity has not provided sufficient disclosure of the misstatement, then the auditor should address the issue in accordance with AU Section 431, *Adequacy of Disclosure in Financial Statements*.

CHANGE IN CLASSIFICATION

An entity's change in classification in previously issued financial statements requires no recognition in the auditor's report, other than the previously noted corrections of material misstatements or changes in accounting principle. If a material change in classification is *also* a change in accounting principle or a correction of a material misstatement (such as shifting debt between the long-term and short-term classifications), then the auditor should address the issue in accordance with AU Section 508.

PCAOB 7 Engagement Quality Review[1]

EFFECTIVE DATE AND APPLICABILITY

Effective Date This standard currently is effective.

Applicability Audit engagements and engagements to review interim financial information conducted pursuant to Public Company Accounting Oversight Board (PCAOB) standards.

DEFINITIONS OF TERMS

Significant engagement deficiency. An audit condition that exists when an engagement team does not obtain sufficient evidence, it reached an inappropriate conclusion on the subject matter, the engagement report is not appropriate, or the firm is not independent of its client.

Significant risk. A risk of material misstatement that is important enough to require special audit consideration.

OBJECTIVES OF PCAOB STANDARD 7

PCAOB Auditing Standard 7 addresses the judgments made by an engagement team in forming an overall conclusion on an engagement quality review and in preparing the resulting report.

FUNDAMENTAL REQUIREMENTS

QUALIFICATIONS OF AN ENGAGEMENT QUALITY REVIEWER

An auditor engaged in an engagement quality review must possess the following characteristics:

- Be associated with a registered public accounting firm

  NOTE: The quality reviewer from the firm issuing the engagement report must be a partner or someone in an equivalent position. Anyone who was the engagement partner during either of the two audits preceding the audit that is subject to the quality review cannot be the engagement quality reviewer.

---

[1] Practitioners should reference the additional guidance listed in the section "Other PCAOB Guidance" in this volume's chapter PCAOB 1.

- Have competence, which is considered to be a sufficient level of knowledge to be the engagement partner on the engagement being reviewed.
- Have independence from the company being reviewed.
- Perform the engagement quality review with integrity.
- Have objectivity. To maintain objectivity, the engagement quality reviewer and those assisting the reviewer should not make decisions for the engagement team or assume any of its responsibilities. This means that the engagement partner is responsible for the engagement.
- Any assistants involved in the engagement should also be independent and conduct their work with integrity and objectivity.

NOTE: There should be provisions in a firm's policies and procedures that give the firm reasonable assurance that the reviewer has these characteristics.

ENGAGEMENT QUALITY REVIEW FOR AN AUDIT

The engagement quality review process requires an evaluation of the engagement team in the following areas:

- *Audit committee communications.* Evaluate whether appropriate matters were communicated, or are to be communicated, to the audit committee, management, and other parties.
- *Contentious matters.* Evaluate whether appropriate consultations have taken place on contentious or otherwise difficult matters.
- *Control deficiencies.* Evaluate significant judgments regarding the severity and disposition of identified control deficiencies.
- *Document inconsistencies.* Compare the financial statements to be filed with the Securities and Exchange Commission (SEC) with other information accompanying the financial statements, and evaluate whether appropriate actions were taken regarding any material inconsistencies with the financial statements, or material misstatements of fact.
- *Documentation.* Evaluate whether the engagement documentation indicates that the team responded appropriately to significant risks, and that it supports the engagement team's conclusions regarding the matters reviewed.
- *General reviews.* Review the financial statements, management's report on internal controls, and the related engagement report.
- *Independence.* Evaluation of the firm's independence in relation to the engagement.
- *Misstatements.* Evaluate significant judgments regarding the materiality and disposition of both corrected and uncorrected identified misstatements.
- *Risks.* Evaluate the engagement team's assessments of and responses to significant risks, including fraud risks.
- *Unresolved matters.* Review the engagement completion document and confirm that there are no significant unresolved matters.

NOTE: An analysis of significant judgments and related conclusions may require holding discussions with the engagement team and reviewing documentation.

The engagement quality reviewer should also evaluate the engagement team's assessment of and responses to other significant risks identified by the engagement quality reviewer through the procedures itemized in this standard.

In an audit, the audit firm can only grant permission to the client to use the engagement report *after* the engagement quality reviewer approves issuance of the report. The engagement quality reviewer should only approve the issuance if he or she is not aware of a significant engagement deficiency, following completion of the review steps required by this Standard.

ENGAGEMENT QUALITY REVIEW FOR A REVIEW OF INTERIM FINANCIAL INFORMATION

If a report concerning interim financial information is to be issued, the engagement quality reviewer should evaluate the engagement team in the following areas:

- *Audit committee communications.* Evaluate whether appropriate matters were communicated, or are to be communicated, to the audit committee, management, and other parties.
- *Business.* Evaluate the company's business, significant recent activities, and related financial reporting issues and risks.
- *Contentious matters.* Evaluate whether appropriate consultations have taken place on contentious or otherwise difficult matters.
- *Document inconsistencies.* Compare the interim financial information to be filed with the SEC with other information accompanying the financial information, and evaluate whether appropriate actions were taken regarding any material inconsistencies with the financial information, or material misstatements of fact.
- *Documentation.* Evaluate whether the engagement documentation indicates that the team responded appropriately to significant risks, and that it supports the engagement team's conclusions regarding the matters reviewed.
- *Fraud.* Evaluate the nature of identified risks of material misstatement caused by fraud.
- *Independence.* Evaluate the firm's independence in relation to the engagement.
- *Internal control changes.* Review interim financial information for all periods presented, and the engagement report, regarding changes in internal control over financial reporting.
- *Misstatements.* Evaluate the engagement team's judgments concerning the materiality and disposition of identified misstatements, as well as any material modifications that should be made to the disclosures concerning changes in internal controls over financial reporting.
- *Recent experience.* Review the firm's recent experience with the company and those risks connected to the firm's client acceptance and retention process.
- *Unresolved matters.* Review the engagement completion document and confirm that there are no significant unresolved matters.

NOTE: *An analysis of significant judgments and related conclusions may require holding discussions with the engagement team and reviewing documentation.*

In a review of interim financial information, the audit firm can only grant permission to the client to use the engagement report *after* the engagement quality reviewer approves issuance of the report. The engagement quality reviewer should only approve the issuance if he or she is not aware of a significant engagement deficiency, following completion of the review steps required by this Standard.

DOCUMENTATION ENGAGEMENT QUALITY REVIEW

The engagement quality reviewer should create documentation of a quality review that contains sufficient information to allow an experienced auditor who has no prior connection with the engagement to understand the reviewer's procedures to comply with the provisions of this Standard. Specifically, the documentation should identify the engagement quality reviewer and assistants, the documents reviewed, and the date when the engagement quality reviewer provided concurring approval or the reason(s) for not providing such approval.

NOTE: See PCAOB Standard 3, Audit Documentation, *for more information about the requirements to retain or subsequently alter audit documentation.*

PCAOB 8 Audit Risk[1]

EFFECTIVE DATE AND APPLICABILITY

Effective Date   This standard currently is effective.

Applicability   Audits of financial statements as part of an integrated audit or an audit of financial statements only.

DEFINITIONS OF TERMS

Audit risk. The risk that an auditor expresses an inappropriate opinion when the financial statements are materially misstated. It is a function of the risk of material misstatement and detection risk.

Control risk. The risk that a misstatement due to error or fraud that could occur in an assertion and that could be material, individually or in combination with other misstatements, will not be prevented or detected on a timely basis by internal controls. Thus, it is a function of the effectiveness of the design and operation of internal control.

Detection risk. The risk that the procedures performed by the auditor will not detect a misstatement that exists and that could be material, either individually or in combination with other misstatements.

Inherent risk. The susceptibility of an assertion to a misstatement, due to error or fraud, that could be material, individually or in combination with other misstatements, before consideration of any related controls.

OBJECTIVES OF PCAOB STANDARD 8

Public Company Accounting Oversight Board (PCAOB) Auditing Standard 8 sets the objective of conducting an audit of financial statements in a manner that reduces audit risk to an appropriately low level.

FUNDAMENTAL REQUIREMENTS

AUDIT RISK

To express an opinion on financial statements, an auditor must plan and perform an audit to obtain reasonable assurance about whether the financial statements are free of material misstatement due to error or fraud. The auditor obtains reasonable assurance by reducing

---

[1] *Practitioners should reference the additional guidance listed in the section "Other PCAOB Guidance" in this volume's chapter PCAOB 1.*

audit risk through the application of due professional care, which includes obtaining sufficient appropriate audit evidence.

NOTE: Use the requirements of the Securities and Exchange Commission (SEC) with respect to the accounting principles applicable to the company under audit.

RISK OF MATERIAL MISSTATEMENT

The auditor should assess the risk of material misstatement at the level of the financial statements and at the assertion level.

The risk of material misstatement at the level of the financial statements relate to the financial statements as a whole. This risk may be especially relevant due to fraud. As an example, the combination of an ineffective control environment, insufficient capital to continue operations, and a declining industry might create pressure on management to manipulate the financial statements, which therefore leads to a higher risk of material misstatement.

The risk of material misstatement at the assertion level is comprised of inherent risk and control risk. These risks are related to the company, its environment, and its internal controls. The auditor assesses these risks based on the evidence obtained. The assessment of inherent risk uses information obtained from performing risk assessment procedures, and by considering the characteristics of the accounts and disclosures in the financial statements. The assessment of control risk uses evidence obtained from tests of controls, if there is to be reliance on those controls to assess control risk at less than maximum, and from other sources.

DETECTION RISK

Detection risk is affected by the effectiveness of the substantive procedures and their application by the auditor. To determine the appropriate level of detection risk for a financial statement assertion, the auditor uses the assessed risk of material misstatement. The higher the risk of material misstatement, the lower the level of detection risk in order to reduce audit risk to a level considered appropriate.

An auditor reduces the level of detection risk through the nature, timing, and extent of the substantive procedures performed. As the appropriate level of detection risk declines, the evidence from substantive procedures that the auditor should obtain increases.

PCAOB 9 Audit Planning[1]

EFFECTIVE DATE AND APPLICABILITY

Effective Date This standard currently is effective.

Applicability All audit planning.

DEFINITIONS OF TERMS

Engagement Partner. The individual responsible for an audit engagement and its performance.

OBJECTIVES OF PCAOB STANDARD 9

Public Company Accounting Oversight Board (PCAOB) Auditing Standard 9 sets the objective of planning an audit so that it is conducted effectively.

FUNDAMENTAL REQUIREMENTS

RESPONSIBILITY OF THE ENGAGEMENT PARTNER

The audit partner is responsible for planning the audit. He or she may seek assistance from team members to fulfill this responsibility. Those individuals assisting the engagement partner with audit planning should also comply with those requirements of this standard pertaining to them.

PLANNING AN AUDIT

The auditor should properly plan the audit. This includes establishing the overall audit strategy and developing an audit plan. The plan should include risk assessment procedures and planned responses to the risks of material misstatement. This is not a discrete phase of the audit, but rather a continual and iterative process. It may begin with the completion of the previous audit and continue through the current audit.

PRELIMINARY ENGAGEMENT ACTIVITIES

The auditor should perform the following activities at the beginning of an audit:

---

[1] *Practitioners should reference the additional guidance listed in the section "Other PCAOB Guidance" in this volume's chapter PCAOB 1.*

- Perform procedures related to the continuance of the client relationship and the specific audit engagement.
- Ascertain compliance with independence and ethics requirements.

NOTE: Continually reevaluate compliance with the independence and ethics requirements as circumstances change.

- Establish an understanding with the client regarding the services to be performed.

PLANNING ACTIVITIES

The nature and extent of planning activities needed will depend on the size and complexity of the company, as well as the auditor's previous experience with the entity and any changes in circumstances occurring during the audit. When developing the audit strategy and plan, the auditor should evaluate whether the following issues impact the company's financial statements and internal control over financial reporting; if so, the auditor should determine how they will affect audit procedures. The issues are:

- Knowledge of the company's internal control over financial reporting obtained during other engagements.
- Industry issues, such as financial reporting practices, economic conditions, laws and regulations, and technological changes.
- Matters relating the company's business, such as its organization, operating characteristics, and capital structure.
- Recent changes in the company, its operations, or its internal control over financial reporting.
- Preliminary judgments about materiality, risk, and (in integrated audits) other factors relating to the determination of material weaknesses.
- Control deficiencies previously communicated either to the audit committee or management.
- Legal or regulatory matters of which the company has knowledge.
- The type and extent of evidence about the effectiveness of the company's internal control over financial reporting.
- Preliminary judgments about the effectiveness of internal control over financial reporting.
- Publicly available information about the company that is relevant to the likelihood of material financial misstatements, as well as the effectiveness of its internal control over financial reporting.
- Knowledge of risks pertaining to the company that were evaluated as part of the client acceptance and retention evaluation.
- The complexity of the company's operations.

NOTE: Factors that may indicate less complex operations include fewer business lines, less complex business processes and financial reporting systems, more centralized accounting functions, extensive involvement by senior management in day-to-day activities, and fewer levels of management (each having a wide span of control).

AUDIT STRATEGY

The auditor should establish an audit strategy that sets the scope, timing, and direction of the audit, as well as guide the development of the audit plan. When creating the strategy, the auditor should take the following into account:

- Reporting objectives of the engagement and the nature of communications as required by PCAOB standards.
- Significant factors in directing the activities of the engagement team.
- Results of preliminary engagement activities, as well as the auditor's evaluation of the planning activity issues noted earlier in this standard.
- Nature, timing, and extent of the resources needed to perform the engagement.

AUDIT PLAN

The auditor should develop and document an audit plan that includes a description of the planned nature, timing, and extent of risk assessment procedures, as well as of the tests of controls and substantive procedures. The plan should also describe other audit procedures required so that the engagement conforms with PCAOB standards.

MULTILOCATION ENGAGEMENTS

If the auditor is engaged in an audit of the financial statements of a company with operations in multiple locations or business units, he or she should ascertain the extent to which audit procedures should be performed at selected locations or business units in order to obtain sufficient appropriate evidence to obtain reasonable assurance as to whether the consolidated financial statements of the entity are free of material misstatement. This includes the determination of locations or business units at which to conduct audit procedures, as well as the timing, nature, and extent of the procedures to perform at those locations or business units.

The auditor should assess the risks of material misstatement to the consolidated financial statements that are associated with the location or business unit, and correlate the amount of audit attention assigned to the location or business unit with the degree of risk of material misstatement associated with it.

When assessing the risks of material misstatement associated with a particular location or business and related audit procedures, factors to consider include:

- The nature and amount of assets, liabilities, and transactions executed there, including significant transactions that are outside of the normal activities of the business, or that otherwise appear unusual in light of the auditor's understanding of the company and its environment
- The materiality of the location or business unit
- The risks associated with the location or business unit that present a reasonable possibility of material misstatement of the company's consolidated financial statements
- Whether these risks of material misstatement apply to other locations or business units such that, in combination, they present a reasonable possibility of material misstatement to the company's consolidated financial statements
- The degree of centralization of records or information processing
- The effectiveness of the control environment, especially in view of management's control over the exercise of authority delegated to others and its ability to effectively supervise activities at the location or business unit level

- The frequency, timing, and scope of monitoring activities by the company and others at the location or business unit

NOTE: When selecting the locations or business units at which to perform audit procedures, take into account relevant activities performed by internal audit, as described in AU Section 322, The Auditor's Consideration of the Internal Audit Function in an Audit of Financial Statements.

CHANGES DURING THE COURSE OF THE AUDIT

The auditor should modify the overall audit strategy and the audit plan as needed if circumstances change significantly during the course of the audit; this modification may be triggered by changes due to a revised assessment of the risks of material misstatement or the discovery of a previously unidentified risk of material misstatement.

PERSONS WITH SPECIALIZED SKILL OR KNOWLEDGE

The auditor should ascertain whether specialized skill or knowledge is needed to perform the appropriate risk assessments, plan or perform audit procedures, or evaluate audit risks. If such a person participates in the audit, the auditor should have sufficient knowledge of the subject matter to be addressed by the specialist to enable the auditor to communicate the objectives of that person's work, determine whether the specialist's procedures meet the audit objectives, and evaluate the results of the specialist's procedures as they relate to the timing, nature, and extent of other planned audit procedures and the effects on the auditor's report.

ADDITIONAL CONSIDERATIONS IN INITIAL AUDITS

Before starting an initial audit, the auditor should perform procedures regarding the acceptance of the client relationship and the specific audit engagement, as well as communicate with the predecessor auditor in situations where there has been a change of auditors in accordance with AU 315, *Communications Between Predecessor and Successor Auditors.*

For an initial audit, the auditor should determine the additional planning activities needed to establish an appropriate audit strategy and audit plan. This should include determining the audit procedures needed to obtain sufficient appropriate audit evidence regarding opening balances.

PCAOB 10 Supervision of the Audit Engagement[1]

EFFECTIVE DATE AND APPLICABILITY

Effective Date   This standard currently is effective.

Applicability   All audit engagements.

OBJECTIVES OF PCAOB STANDARD 10

Public Company Accounting Oversight Board (PCAOB) Auditing Standard 10 sets the objective for the auditor of supervising the audit engagement, which includes supervising the work of engagement team members so that the work is performed as directed and supports the conclusions reached.

FUNDAMENTAL REQUIREMENTS

RESPONSIBILITY OF THE ENGAGEMENT PARTNER FOR SUPERVISION

The audit partner is responsible for an audit engagement and its performance. Thus, the engagement partner is responsible for the proper supervision of the work of the engagement team members, and for compliance with PCAOB standards. This includes standards regarding using the work of specialists, other auditors, internal auditors, and others involved in testing controls.

The engagement partner may obtain assistance from the engagement team members in fulfilling the responsibilities stated by this standard. Those team members who assist the engagement partner with supervision of the work performed by other engagement team members should comply with the applicable requirements of this standard.

SUPERVISION OF ENGAGEMENT TEAM MEMBERS

The engagement partner and those other engagement team members who perform supervisory activities should do the following:

- Inform the engagement team members of their responsibilities, including the objectives, nature, timing, and extent of the procedures to be performed, as well as matters that could affect the procedures to be performed or the evaluation of the results of those procedures. These matters could include relevant aspects of the company, its

---

[1] *Practitioners should reference the additional guidance listed in the section "Other PCAOB Guidance" in this volume's chapter PCAOB 1.*

environment, and its internal control over financial reporting, and possible accounting and auditing issues.
- Direct the engagement team to bring significant accounting and auditing issues to the attention of the engagement partner or other team members performing supervisory activities, so they can evaluate the issues and ensure that appropriate actions are taken in accordance with PCAOB standards.
- Review the work of the engagement team members to determine whether the work was performed and documented, objectives were achieved, and the results of the work support the conclusions reached.

The engagement partner and those other engagement team members who perform supervisory activities should take the following issues into account when determining the extent of supervision needed:

- The nature of the company, which includes its size and complexity
- The nature of the assigned work for each team member, including the procedures to be performed, and the controls or accounts and disclosures to be tested
- The risks of material misstatement
- The knowledge, skill, and ability of each team member

NOTE: The extent of supervision of engagement team members should be commensurate with the risks of material misstatement.

PCAOB 11 Consideration of Materiality in Planning and Performing an Audit[1]

EFFECTIVE DATE AND APPLICABILITY

Effective Date This standard currently is effective.
Applicability All audit planning.

OBJECTIVES OF PCAOB STANDARD 11

Public Company Accounting Oversight Board (PCAOB) Auditing Standard 11 sets the objective of applying the concept of materiality appropriately in planning and performing audit procedures.

FUNDAMENTAL REQUIREMENTS

MATERIALITY IN THE CONTEXT OF AN AUDIT

The auditor should plan and perform audit procedures to detect misstatements that, individually or in combination with other misstatements, would result in material misstatement of the financial statements. This includes being alert while planning and performing audit procedures for misstatements that could be material due to quantitative or qualitative factors. It is ordinarily not practical to design audit procedures to detect misstatements that are material, based solely on qualitative factors.

For integrated audits, Auditing Standard 5, *An Audit of Internal Control over Financial Reporting that is Integrated with an Audit of Financial Statements,* states that the auditor should use the same materiality considerations in planning the audit of internal control over financial reporting that would be used in planning the audit of a company's annual financial statements.

ESTABLISHING A MATERIALITY LEVEL FOR THE FINANCIAL STATEMENTS AS A WHOLE

The auditor needs to establish a materiality level for the financial statements being audited that is appropriate for the circumstances. The auditor should consider the company's

---

[1] *Practitioners should reference the additional guidance listed in the section "Other PCAOB Guidance" in this volume's chapter PCAOB 1.*

earnings and other relevant factors. The materiality level should be expressed as a specific amount.

NOTE: If there are no financial statements available for the audit period, the auditor can establish an initial materiality level based on estimated or preliminary financial statement amounts.

ESTABLISHING MATERIALITY LEVELS FOR PARTICULAR ACCOUNTS OR DISCLOSURES

The auditor should evaluate whether there are certain accounts or disclosures for which there is a substantial likelihood that misstatements of lesser amounts than the materiality level established for the financial statements as a whole would influence the judgment of a reasonable investor. If this is the case, the auditor should establish separate materiality levels for those accounts or disclosures.

NOTE: A misstatement in a lesser amount could influence the judgment of a reasonable investor if there are qualitative factors, such as the conflicts of interest in related-party transactions.

DETERMINING TOLERABLE MISSTATEMENT

The auditor should determine the amount of tolerable misstatement in order to assess the risk of material misstatement, and for planning and performing audit procedures at the account or disclosure level. A tolerable misstatement should be at an amount that reduces to a low level the probability that the total of uncorrected and undetected misstatements would result in material misstatement of the financial statements. Thus, tolerable misstatement should be less than the materiality level for the financial statements as a whole and, if applicable, the materiality level for certain accounts or disclosures.

When determining the tolerable misstatement amount, the auditor should account for the nature, cause, and amount of misstatements accumulated in prior period audits of the financial statements.

CONSIDERATIONS FOR MULTILOCATION ENGAGEMENTS

If an auditor is auditing the consolidated financial statements of a company with multiple locations or business units, he or she should determine the tolerable misstatement for individual locations or business units at a level that reduces to an appropriately low level the probability that the total of uncorrected and undetected misstatements would result in material misstatement of the consolidated financial statements. Thus, tolerable misstatement at an individual location should be less than the materiality level for the financial statements as a whole.

CONSIDERATIONS AS THE AUDIT PROGRESSES

If there are changes in the circumstances, or if additional information comes to the auditor's attention that causes a substantial likelihood that misstatements of amounts could differ significantly from the materiality level that was established initially, the auditor should reevaluate the established materiality level and tolerable misstatement. Examples of such situations include:

- The materiality level and tolerable misstatement were established initially based on estimated or preliminary financial statement amounts that differ significantly from actual amounts.

- The events or changes occurring after the establishment of the materiality level and tolerable misstatement are likely to affect investors' perceptions about the company's financial position, results of operations, or cash flows.

NOTE: Examples of such events or changes in conditions include changes in the applicable financial reporting framework, and significant new contractual arrangements.

If the auditor's reevaluation results in a lower amount for the materiality level and tolerable misstatement than initially established, the auditor should reevaluate the effect of the lower amount on the risk assessment and audit procedures, and modify the nature, timing, and extent of audit procedures as required to obtain sufficient appropriate audit evidence.

NOTE: Reevaluating the materiality level and tolerable misstatement is also relevant to the auditor's evaluation of uncorrected misstatements, as described in Auditing Standard 14.

PCAOB 12 Identifying and Assessing Risks of Material Misstatement[1]

EFFECTIVE DATE AND APPLICABILITY

Effective Date   This standard currently is effective.
Applicability   All audit planning.

DEFINITIONS OF TERMS

Fraud risk factors. Events or conditions that indicate an incentive or pressure to perpetrate fraud, an opportunity to carry out fraud, or an attitude or rationalization that justifies the fraudulent action. Fraud risk factors do not necessarily indicate the existence of fraud. However, they are frequently present where fraud exists.

OBJECTIVES OF PCAOB STANDARD 12

Public Company Accounting Oversight Board (PCAOB) Auditing Standard 12 sets the objective of identifying and appropriately assessing the risk of material misstatement, thereby providing a basis for designing and implementing responses to that risk.

FUNDAMENTAL REQUIREMENTS

PERFORMING RISK ASSESSMENT PROCEDURES

The auditor should perform sufficient risk assessment procedures to provide a reasonable basis for identifying and assessing the risks of material misstatement due to error or fraud, and to design further audit procedures.

There are a variety of sources from which the risk of material misstatement can arise, including both internal and external factors. These factors can affect the judgments involved in the determination of accounting estimates, or create pressure to manipulate the financial statements in order to achieve financial goals. This standard addresses the following risk assessment procedures:

---

[1] *Practitioners should reference the additional guidance listed in the section "Other PCAOB Guidance" in this volume's chapter PCAOB 1.*

1. Obtaining an understanding of the company and its environment
2. Obtaining an understanding of internal control over financial reporting
3. Considering information from the client acceptance and retention evaluation, audit planning activities, past audits, and other engagements performed for the company
4. Performing analytical procedures
5. Conducting a discussion among engagement team members regarding the risks of material misstatement
6. Inquiring of the audit committee, management, and others within the company about the risks of material misstatement

In the case of an integrated audit, the risks of material misstatement of the financial statements are the same for both the audit of internal control over financial reporting and the audit of financial statements. Thus, the auditor's risk assessment procedures should apply to both the audit of internal control over financial reporting and the audit of financial statements.

OBTAINING AN UNDERSTANDING OF THE COMPANY AND ITS ENVIRONMENT

The auditor should obtain an understanding of the company and its environment that might reasonably be expected to have a significant effect on the risks of material misstatement. Obtaining this understanding includes:

- Relevant industry, regulatory, and other external factors
- The nature of the company
- The company's selection and application of accounting principles and disclosures
- The company's objectives and strategies and related business risks that might reasonably be expected to result in risks of material misstatement
- The company's measurement and analysis of its financial performance

The auditor should evaluate whether significant changes in the company from prior periods, including any changes in its internal control over financial reporting, affect the risks of material misstatement.

Industry, Regulatory, and Other External Factors

The auditor should obtain an understanding of the relevant industry, regulatory, and other external factors, including the competitive environment, technological developments, regulatory environment, legal and political environment, and general economic conditions.

Nature of the Company

The auditor should obtain an understanding of the nature of the company, which should include:

- Its organizational structure and management personnel
- The sources of funding for its operations and investment activities, including its capital structure, noncapital funding, and other debt instruments
- Its significant investments, including equity method investments, joint ventures, and variable interest entities
- Its operating characteristics, including its size and complexity

NOTE: *A company's size and complexity may affect the risks of misstatement and how it addresses those risks.*

- The sources of its earnings, including the relative profitability of key products and services.
- Key supplier and customer relationships.

NOTE: The auditor should consider the information gathered while obtaining an understanding of the nature of the company when determining the existence of related parties in accordance with AU 334, Related Parties.

The auditor should consider performing the following procedures:

- Read public information about the company relevant to the evaluation of the likelihood of material financial statement misstatements and, in an integrated audit, the effectiveness of the company's internal control over financial reporting (as may be found in press releases and analyst reports).
- Observe earnings calls and other meetings with investors or rating agencies.
- Obtain an understanding of senior compensation arrangements with senior management, including incentive compensation arrangements.
- Obtain information about trading activity and holdings in the company's securities by significant holders.

Selection and Application of Accounting Principles, Including Related Disclosures

The auditor should evaluate whether the company's selection and application of accounting principles are appropriate for its business and are consistent with the applicable financial reporting framework. The auditor should also identify and assess the risks of material misstatement related to omitted, incomplete, or inaccurate disclosures by developing expectations about the disclosures necessary for the company's financial statements to be presented fairly in conformity with the applicable financial reporting framework.

If the following matters are present, they are relevant to the auditor's understanding of the accounting principles that the company has selected:

- Significant changes in the company's accounting principles, financial reporting policies, disclosures, and the reasons for those changes
- The competencies of the company's financial reporting personnel in regard to selecting and applying significant or complex accounting principles
- Those accounts or disclosures where judgment is used in the application of significant accounting principles, especially those related to the determination of management's estimates and assumptions
- The impact of significant accounting principles in either controversial or emerging areas where there is a lack of authoritative guidance or consensus
- The methods used by the company to account for significant and unusual transactions
- The financial reporting standards, laws, and regulations that are new to the company

Company Objectives, Strategies, and Related Business Risks

The auditor obtains an understanding of a company's objectives, strategies, and related business risks in order to identify those business risks that could reasonably be expected to result in material misstatement of the company's financial statements.

NOTE: The auditor can identify some relevant business risks through other risk assessment procedures. These procedures can include obtaining an understanding of the nature of the company and by understanding the industry, as well as regulatory and other factors.

Following are examples of situations in which business risks may result in the material misstatement of a company's financial statements:

- Industry developments
- New products and services
- Use of information technology
- New accounting requirements
- Expansion of the business
- The effects of implementing a strategy, especially one that will involve new accounting requirements
- Current and prospective financing requirements
- Regulatory requirements

NOTE: Business risks can affect the risk of material misstatement at the financial statement level, as well as the level of particular accounts, disclosures, or assertions.

Company Performance Measures

The reason for obtaining an understanding of a company's performance measures is to identify any performance measures that affect the risks of material misstatement. The following are examples of performance measurements that may affect the risks of material misstatement:

- Measures used as the basis for contractual commitments or incentive compensation agreements.
- Measures used by such external parties as analysts and rating agencies to review a company's performance.
- Measures a company uses to monitor its operations that highlight unexpected results or trends that prompt management to investigate their cause and take corrective action.

NOTE: Of these examples, the first two can affect the risks of material misstatement by creating incentives for management to manipulate accounts or disclosures to achieve performance targets. The last example involves measurements that management might use to monitor risks affecting the financial statements.

Obtaining an Understanding of Internal Control over Financial Reporting

The auditor should have a sufficient understanding of each component of internal control over financial reporting to identify the types of potential misstatements, assess the factors that affect the risks of material misstatement, and design further audit procedures.

The timing, nature, and extent of the procedures used to obtain an understanding of internal control depend on:

- The size and complexity of the company
- The auditor's existing knowledge of the company's internal control over financial reporting

- The nature of the company's records
- The nature and extent of changes in systems and operations
- The nature of the company's documentation of its internal control over financial reporting

The auditor should obtain an understanding of the design of controls that are relevant to the audit, and determine whether the controls have been implemented. This step can include the inquiry of appropriate personnel, observation of the company's operations, and the inspection of relevant documentation. To determine if a control has been implemented, the auditor should determine whether the control exists, and whether the company is using it. This step can include inquiry of appropriate personnel, combined with the observation of the application of controls or the inspection of documentation.

Internal control over financial reporting consists of the following components:

- The control environment
- The company's risk assessment process
- Information and communication
- Control activities
- Monitoring of control

Management may use an internal control framework containing components that differ from the components just noted. In evaluating the design of controls and determining whether they have been implemented in an audit of financial statements, the auditor may use the framework used by management, or another suitable framework. For an integrated audit, Auditing Standard No. 5 states that the auditor should use the same control framework to perform the audit of internal control over financial reporting as management uses for its annual evaluation of the effectiveness of the company's internal control over financial reporting.

If the auditor uses a suitable internal control framework with components that differ from those just listed in this section, he or she should adapt the requirements in the following section to conform to the components in the framework used.

Control Environment

The auditor should obtain an understanding of the company's control environment, including the policies and actions of management, the board of directors, and the audit committee concerning the company's control environment. Obtaining this understanding includes assessing the following:

- Whether management's philosophy and operating style promote effective internal control over financial reporting
- Whether sound integrity and ethical values, especially of top management, are developed and understood
- Whether the board of directors or audit committee understands and exercises oversight responsibility over financial reporting and internal control

If the auditor identifies a control deficiency in the control environment of a company, he or she should evaluate the extent to which this deficiency is indicative of a fraud risk factor, as discussed later in this standard.

The Company's Risk Assessment Process

The auditor should obtain an understanding of management's process for identifying risks relevant to financial reporting objectives, assessing the likelihood and significant of misstatements resulting from those risks, and deciding about actions to address those risks. Obtaining an understanding of a company's risk assessment process includes obtaining an understanding of the risks of material misstatement that have been identified and assessed by management, as well as the actions taken to address those risks.

Information and Communication

The auditor should obtain an understanding of the information system of a company, including the related business processes that are relevant to financial reporting. This understanding should include the following:

- The classes of transactions in the company's operations that are significant to its financial statements
- The procedures by which those transactions are initiated, authorized, processed, recorded, and reported
- The related accounting records, supporting information, and specific accounts in the financial statements that are used to initiate, authorize, process, and record transactions
- How the information system captures events and conditions other than transactions that are significant to the financial statements
- The period-end financial reporting process

The auditor should also obtain an understanding of how information technology affects the company's flow of transactions. This is an integral part of the approach used to identify significant accounts and disclosures, and their relevant assertions, as well as the selection of controls to test.

A company's business processes are those activities designed to develop, purchase, produce, sell, and distribute a company's products or services, record information, and ensure compliance with laws and regulations relevant to the financial statements.

A company's period-end financial reporting process includes the following activities:

- Procedures used to log transaction totals into the general ledger
- Procedures for the selection and application of accounting principles
- Procedures to initiate, authorize, record, and process journal entries in the general ledger
- Procedures to record recurring and nonrecurring adjustments to the annual financial statements
- Procedures for preparing annual financial statements and related disclosures

The auditor should understand how the company communicates financial reporting roles and responsibilities and significant matters relating to financial reporting to company personnel and others, including communications between management, the audit committee, and the board of directors, as well as to such external parties as regulatory authorities and shareholders.

Control Activities

The auditor should gain an understanding of control activities that is sufficient to assess the factors that affect the risks of material misstatement, as well as to design further audit procedures. The auditor should use this knowledge of the presence or absence of control activities to determine the extent to which he or she should devote additional attention to understanding control activities to assess the factors affecting the risks of material misstatement, as well as to design further audit procedures.

> NOTE: In the audit of internal control over financial reporting, the auditor's understanding of control activities encompasses a broader range of accounts and disclosures than what is normally obtained in a financial statement audit.

Monitoring of Controls

The auditor should understand the major types of activities that a company uses to monitor the effectiveness of its internal control over financial reporting, as well as how the company initiates corrective actions related to its controls. This understanding includes understanding the source of the information used in the monitoring activities.

Performing Walk-throughs

The auditor may perform walk-throughs while obtaining an understanding of internal control over financial reporting. When performing a walk-through, the auditor tracks a transaction from its origination through the company's processes until it is reflected in the company's financial records, using the same documents and information technology that the company uses. This activity can include a combination of inquiries, observations, document inspections, and the reperformance of controls.

At the points in a process walk-through where important processes occur, the auditor should question company personnel about their understanding of what is required by the company's procedures and controls. These questions, combined with other walk-through procedures, improve the auditor's understanding of the process and enable him or her to identify important points at which a control is missing or not designed properly. These questions also allow the auditor to understand the different types of transactions handled by the process.

Relationship of Understanding of Internal Control to Tests of Controls

The auditor may obtain an understanding of internal control while performing tests of controls if he or she obtains sufficient appropriate evidence to achieve the objectives of both procedures. The auditor should take into account the evidence obtained from understanding internal control when assessing control risk and (in the audit of internal control over financial reporting) forming an opinion about the effectiveness of internal control over financial reporting.

The procedures performed by the auditor to understand certain components of internal control in accordance with Auditing Standard No. 5 (e.g., the control environment, the company's risk assessment process, information and communication, and monitoring of controls) may provide evidence that is relevant to the auditor's evaluation of entity-level controls. The auditor should take this evidence into account when determining the timing, nature, and extent of procedures necessary to support the auditor's conclusions about the effectiveness of entity-level controls in the audit of internal control over financial reporting.

Considering Information from the Client Acceptance and Retention Evaluation, Audit Planning Activities, Past Audits, and Other Engagements

The auditor should evaluate whether the information obtained from the client acceptance and retention evaluation process or audit planning activities is relevant to identifying risks of material misstatement. Such risks identified during those activities should be assessed as discussed later in the "Identifying and Assessing the Risks of Material Misstatement" section.

In subsequent years, the auditor should incorporate the knowledge obtained during past audits to update his or her process for identifying the risks of material misstatement, including when identifying significant ongoing matters that affect the risks of material misstatement or determining how changes in the company or its environment affect the risks of material misstatement.

If the auditor plans to limit the nature, timing, or extent of the risk assessment procedures by relying on such information from past audits, the auditor should evaluate whether the information from prior years remains relevant and reliable.

When the auditor has conducted a review of interim financial information as per AU 722, *Interim Financial Information*, he or she should evaluate whether information from the review is relevant to identifying the risks of material misstatement in the year-end audit.

The auditor should understand the nature of the services that have been performed for the company by the auditor or affiliates of the firm, and should take into account any relevant information obtained from those engagements to identify risks of material misstatement.

Performing Analytical Procedures

The analytical procedures that the auditor performs should be designed to enhance the auditor's understanding of the client's business and the significant transactions and events that occurred after the prior year-end, as well as to identify areas that might represent specific risks relevant to the audit, including the existence of unusual transactions and events, amounts, ratios, and trends.

When applying analytical procedures as risk assessment procedures, the auditor should perform analytical procedures for revenue with the objective of identifying unusual or unexpected relationships involving revenue accounts that might indicate a material misstatement, which includes material misstatement due to fraud. Further, when the auditor has performed a review of interim financial information in accordance with AU 722, he or she should take account of the analytical procedures used in that review when designing and applying analytical procedures as risk assessment procedures.

When performing an analytical procedure, the auditor should use his or her understanding of the company to create expectations about plausible relationships among the data to be used in the procedure. When the comparison of those expectations with relationships from recorded amounts results in unusual or unexpected results, the auditor should factor in those results in identifying the risks of material misstatement.

NOTE: Analytical procedures that are performed as risk assessment procedures often use data that is either preliminary or aggregated at a high level. Such procedures are not designed with the level of precision needed for substantive analytical procedures.

CONDUCTING A DISCUSSION AMONG ENGAGEMENT TEAM MEMBERS REGARDING RISKS OF MATERIAL MISSTATEMENT

Key members of the engagement team should discuss the company's selection and application of accounting principles and disclosure requirements, as well as the susceptibility of the company's financial statements to material misstatement due to error or fraud. Members of the key engagement team should include those who have significant engagement responsibilities; this includes the engagement partner. The engagement partner or other key engagement team members should communicate the important matters from the discussion to those engagement team members not involved in the discussion. This communication should continue throughout the audit, including when conditions change.

NOTE: If the engagement partner performs the entire audit, then this person, having personally planned the audit, is responsible for evaluating the susceptibility of the company's financial statements to material misstatement.

Discussion of the Potential for Material Misstatement Due to Fraud

When members of the key engagement team discuss the potential for material misstatement due to fraud, they should do so with a questioning mind, and should set aside any prior beliefs that management is honest and has integrity. This discussion should include the following:

- Brainstorming among the team members about how and where the company's financial statements might be susceptible to material misstatement due to fraud, how management could create and conceal fraudulent financial reporting, and how the assets of the company could be misappropriated. The discussion should include the susceptibility of the financial statements to material misstatement through related party transactions and how fraud might arise or be concealed by omitting or presenting incomplete or inaccurate disclosures.
- Consideration of the external and internal factors affecting the company that might create incentives or pressures for management and others to commit fraud, create the opportunity for fraud to be committed, and indicate a culture or environment that enables management to rationalize committing fraud.
- Consideration of the risk of management override.
- Consideration of the potential audit responses to the susceptibility of the company's financial statements to material misstatement due to fraud.

The auditor should point out the following matters to all members of the engagement team:

- They should maintain a questioning mind throughout the audit and exercise professional skepticism in gathering and evaluating evidence.
- They should be alert for information or other conditions that might affect the assessment of fraud risks.
- If there is an indication that a material misstatement due to fraud may have occurred, they should probe the issues, acquire additional evidence as necessary, and consult with other team members or others in the firm, including specialists.

Inquiring of the Audit Committee, Management, and Others within the Company about the Risks of Material Misstatement

The auditor should make inquiries of the audit committee or its equivalent, management, the internal audit function, and any others within the company who might be expected to have information important to the identification and assessment of risks of material misstatement. These inquiries should address fraud risks.

The auditor should employ his or her knowledge of the company and its environment, plus information from other risk assessment procedures, to determine the nature of the inquiries about risks of material misstatement.

Inquiries Regarding Fraud Risks

Inquiries by the auditor concerning fraud risks should include the following items:

1. Inquiries of management regarding:

    - Whether management has knowledge of alleged, suspected, or actual fraud affecting the company
    - Management's process for identifying and responding to fraud risks, including any identified fraud risks, or account balances or disclosures for which a fraud risk is likely to exist, as well as the nature, extent, and frequency of management's fraud risk assessment process
    - Controls established by the company to address identified fraud risks, or that otherwise help to prevent and detect fraud, as well as how management monitors these controls
    - If there are multiple locations, the nature and extent of monitoring operating locations or business segments, and whether there are specific operating locations or business segments for which a fraud risk is more likely to exist
    - How management communicates to employees (if at all) its views on business practices and ethical behavior
    - Whether management has received tips or complaints about its financial reporting, and management's response to those tips or complaints
    - Whether management has reported to the audit committee regarding how internal control serves to prevent and detect material misstatements due to fraud

2. Inquiries of the audit committee or the equivalent, or its chairperson regarding:

    - The committee's views about fraud risk in the company
    - Whether the committee has knowledge of any alleged, suspected, or actual fraud affecting the company
    - Whether the committee is aware of tips or complaints about the company's financial reporting and the committee's responses to those tips or complaints
    - How the committee exercises oversight of the company's assessment of fraud risks and the establishment of controls to address fraud risks

3. Inquiries of internal audit personnel (if there are any) regarding:

    - Their views about fraud risks in the company
    - Whether they have knowledge of any alleged, suspected, or actual fraud affecting the company

- Whether they have performed procedures to identify or detect fraud during the year, and whether management has responded in a satisfactory manner to the findings resulting from those procedures
- Whether they are aware of instances of management override of controls, as well as the nature and circumstances of such overrides

In addition to the inquiries just noted, the auditor should make inquiries of others within the company regarding their views about fraud risk, including any knowledge of alleged, suspected, or actual fraud. The auditor should identify others within the company to whom to make these inquiries, and determine the extent of the inquiries by considering whether others in the company may have additional information on this topic, or can corroborate fraud risks identified in discussions with management or the audit committee. These people may include:

- Employees with varying levels of authority within the company, including those with whom the auditor comes into contact during the audit
- Operating personnel not directly involved in the financial reporting process
- Employees involved in initiating, recording, or processing complex or unusual transactions
- In-house legal counsel

When evaluating responses to inquiries about fraud risks and determining when to corroborate their responses, the auditor should account for the fact that management is commonly in the best position to commit fraud. Further, the auditor should compile evidence to address inconsistencies in the responses to his or her inquiries.

IDENTIFYING AND ASSESSING THE RISKS OF MATERIAL MISSTATEMENT

The auditor should identify and assess the risks of material misstatement at both the financial statement level and the assertion level. In identifying these risks of misstatement, the auditor should:

- Identify risks of misstatement using information obtained from the performance of risk assessment procedures and consider the characteristics of the accounts and disclosures in the financial statements
- Evaluate whether the identified risks relate pervasively to the financial statements as a whole and may potentially affect many assertions
- Evaluate the types of potential misstatements that may result from the identified risks and the accounts, disclosures, and assertions that may be affected
- Assess the likelihood of misstatement and the magnitude of potential misstatement to assess the possibility that the risk could result in material misstatement of the financial statements
- Identify significant accounts and disclosures and their relevant assertions
- Determine whether any of the identified and assessed risks of material misstatement are significant risks

Identifying Significant Accounts and Disclosures and Their Relevant Assertions

To identify significant accounts and disclosures and relevant assertions, the auditor should evaluate the qualitative and quantitative risk factors related to the financial statement line items and disclosures. The risk factors relevant to the identification of significant accounts and disclosures and relevant assertions include:

- Size and composition of the account
- Susceptibility to misstatement due to error or fraud
- Volume of activity, complexity, and homogeneity of the transactions processed through the account or reflected in the disclosure
- Nature of the account or disclosure
- Accounting and reporting complexities associated with the account or disclosure
- Exposure to losses in the account
- Possibility of significant contingent liabilities arising from the activities reflected in the account or disclosure
- Existence of related party transactions in the account
- Changes from the prior period in account and disclosure characteristics

The auditor should also determine the likely sources of potential misstatements that could cause the financial statements to be materially misstated. The auditor may determine the likely sources of potential misstatements by asking "what could go wrong" within a significant account or disclosure.

The auditor should evaluate risk factors in the identification of significant accounts and disclosures and their relevant assertions that are the same in the audit of internal control over financial reporting as for the audit of the financial statements. Thus, significant accounts and disclosures and their relevant assertions are the same for both types of audits.

The components of a potential significant account or disclosure might be subject to significantly differing risks.

When a company has multiple locations or business units, the auditor should identify significant amounts and disclosures, as well as their relevant assertions based on the consolidated financial statements.

Factors Relevant to Identifying Fraud Risks

The auditor should evaluate whether the information gathered from the risk assessment procedures indicates that fraud risk factors are present, and should be taken into account in identifying and assessing fraud risks. The auditor may conclude that a fraud risk exists even when only one fraud condition exists (see the "Definitions of Terms" section).

The auditor's consideration of fraud risk factors should include an evaluation of how fraud could be perpetrated or concealed by presenting incomplete or inaccurate disclosures, or by omitting disclosures that are necessary for the financial statements to be presented fairly in conformity with the applicable financial reporting framework.

The auditor should presume that there is a fraud risk involving improper revenue recognition, and evaluate the types of revenue, related transactions, or assertions giving rise to these risks.

The auditor should include the risk of management override of controls in the identification of fraud risks.

NOTE: The controls over management override are important for effective internal control over financial reporting, and may be especially important at smaller companies due to the increased involvement of senior management in performing controls and the period-end financial reporting process. Consequently, the controls addressing the risk of management override may differ for a smaller company from those used in a larger company.

Factors Relevant to Identifying Significant Risks

The auditor must determine whether an identified risk is a significant risk from the perspective of a material misstatement, and so should evaluate whether the risk requires special consideration. Factors to evaluate in determining which risks are significant include:

- The effect of quantitative and qualitative risk factors on the likelihood and potential magnitude of misstatements
- Whether the risk is a fraud risk
- Whether the risk is related to recent significant economic, accounting, and other developments
- The complexity of the transactions
- Whether the risk involves significant transactions with related parties
- The degree of complexity or judgment in the recognition or measurement of financial information related to the risk
- Whether the risk involves significant transactions that are outside the normal course of business for the company or that appear to be unusual due to their timing, size, or nature

Further Consideration of Controls

When the auditor concludes that a significant risk exists, he or she should evaluate the design of the company's controls that are targeted at fraud risks and other significant risks to determine whether those controls have been implemented. Controls that address fraud risk include:

- Specific controls designed to mitigate specific risks of fraud
- Controls designed to prevent, deter, and detect fraud

Such controls include those addressing the risk of management override of other controls.

REVISION OF RISK ASSESSMENT

The auditor's assessment of the risks of material misstatement, including fraud risks, should continue throughout an audit. If evidence arises during the course of the audit that contradicts the audit evidence on which the auditor originally based a risk assessment, he or she should revise the assessment and modify planned audit procedures or perform additional ones in response to the revised risk assessments.

PCAOB 13 The Auditor's Responses to the Risks of Material Misstatement[1]

EFFECTIVE DATE AND APPLICABILITY

Effective Date   This standard currently is effective.
Applicability   All audit planning.

DEFINITIONS OF TERMS

Dual-purpose test. A substantive test of a transaction that is performed concurrently with a test of a control relevant to that transaction.

Professional skepticism. An attitude that includes a questioning mind and a critical assessment of the appropriateness and sufficiency of audit evidence.

OBJECTIVES OF PCAOB STANDARD 13

PCAOB Auditing Standard 13 sets the objective of addressing the risks of material misstatement through appropriate overall audit responses and audit procedures.

FUNDAMENTAL REQUIREMENTS

RESPONDING TO THE RISKS OF MATERIAL MISSTATEMENT

The auditor must design and implement audit responses addressing the risks of material misstatement that are identified and assessed in accordance with Auditing Standard 12, *Identifying and Assessing Risks of Material Misstatement.*

OVERALL RESPONSES

The auditor should design and implement overall responses to address the assessed risks of material misstatement with the following actions:

---

[1] *Practitioners should reference the additional guidance listed in the section "Other PCAOB Guidance" in this volume's chapter PCAOB 1.*

1. Ensure that the knowledge, skill, and ability of engagement team members with significant engagement responsibilities should be commensurate with the assessed risks of material misstatement.
2. Provide the extent of supervision appropriate for the circumstances, including the assessed risks of material misstatement.
3. Incorporate an element of unpredictability in the selection of auditing procedures to be performed from year to year. Examples of such unpredictability are procedures not normally performed based on their amount or risk assessment, varying the timing of audit procedures, selecting test items that are outside of customary selection parameters, performing audit procedures on an unannounced basis, and varying the location or the nature, timing, or extent of audit procedures at related locations or business units.
4. Evaluate whether the company's selection and application of significant accounting principles, especially those related to subjective measurements and complex transactions, are indicative of bias that could lead to material misstatement of the financial statements.

The auditor should determine whether it is necessary to make pervasive changes to the nature, timing, or extent of audit procedures in order to adequately address assessed risks of material misstatement. Examples of such changes are increasing the substantive testing of the valuation of significant accounts because of deteriorating market conditions, and obtaining more persuasive audit evidence from substantive procedures because of the identification of pervasive weaknesses in the control environment.

The auditor should exercise professional skepticism in gathering and evaluating audit evidence, particularly for fraud risks. Examples of the application of professional skepticism are modifying planned audit procedures to obtain more reliable evidence regarding assertions, obtaining evidence to corroborate management's explanations or representations, use of a specialist, or examining documentation from independent sources.

RESPONSES INVOLVING THE NATURE, TIMING, AND EXTENT OF AUDIT PROCEDURES

The auditor should design and perform audit procedures to address the assessed risks of material misstatement for each assertion of each significant amount and disclosure. In designing these procedures, the auditor should do the following:

- Obtain more persuasive audit evidence where there is a higher assessment of risk.
- Take into account the types of potential misstatements that could result from the identified risks, as well as the magnitude of potential misstatement.
- For an integrated audit, design the testing of controls to accomplish the objectives of both audits at once, which are to obtain sufficient evidence to support the control risk assessments for the audit of financial statements as well as to obtain sufficient evidence to support the opinion on internal control over financial reporting as of year-end.

Responses to Significant Risks

The auditor should perform substantive procedures for significant risks, including tests of details that are specifically responsive to the assessed risks.

NOTE: See Auditing Standard 12 for a discussion of the identification of significant risks.

Responses to Fraud Risks

The audit procedures used to address the assessed fraud risks depend upon the types of risks and the relevant assertions that might be affected. If the auditor identifies deficiencies in the controls that are intended to address assessed fraud risks, the auditor should take the deficiencies into account when designing a response to those risks.

NOTE: See Public Company Accounting Oversight Board (PCAOB) Auditing Standard No. 5 for requirements regarding addressing assessed fraud risks in the audit of internal control over financial reporting.

In the audit of financial statements, the auditor should perform substantive tests, including tests of details that are specifically responsive to the assessed fraud risks. The following are examples of ways to modify planned audit procedures to address assessed fraud risks:

1. Changing the nature of audit procedures to obtain evidence that is more reliable, or to obtain corroborating information
2. Changing the timing of audit procedures to be closer to the end of the period or to the date when fraudulent transactions are more likely to occur
3. Changing the extent of audit procedures to obtain more evidence

The auditor should perform audit procedures to specifically address the risk of management override of controls. They should include:

1. Examining journal entries and other adjustments for evidence of possible material misstatement due to fraud
2. Reviewing accounting estimates for biases that could result in material misstatement due to fraud
3. Evaluating the business rationale for significant unusual transactions

TESTING CONTROLS

Testing Controls in an Audit of Financial Statements

If the auditor plans to assess control risk at less than the maximum by relying on controls, and the timing, nature, and extent of the procedures are based on that lower assessment, then the auditor must obtain evidence that the controls selected for testing are designed effectively and operated effectively during the entire period when reliance is placed on the controls. The auditor is not required to assess control risk at less than the maximum level for all relevant assertions, and may choose not to do so.

The auditor must perform tests in the audit of financial statements for each relevant assertion for which substantive procedures by themselves cannot provide sufficient audit evidence, and when necessary to support the auditor's reliance on the accuracy and completeness of the financial information used in performing other audit procedures.

NOTE: When information supporting an assertion is electronically initiated, recorded, processed, or reported, the sufficiency and appropriateness of the audit evidence usually depends on the effectiveness of controls over their accuracy and completeness.

The evidence needed to support the auditor's control risk assessment depends on the degree of reliance the auditor plans to place on the effectiveness of a control. If the auditor places greater reliance on the effectiveness of the control, he or she should obtain more persuasive audit evidence. This is also the case for each relevant assertion for which the audit approach consists primarily of tests of controls, including situations where substantive procedures alone do not provide sufficient audit evidence.

Testing Design Effectiveness

The auditor should test the design effectiveness of any controls selected for testing by determining whether the controls, if they are operated as prescribed by persons possessing the necessary authority and competence to perform the control effectively, satisfy the company's control objectives and can effectively prevent or detect error or fraud that could result in material misstatements in the financial statements.

NOTE: A less complex or smaller company might achieve its control objectives in a different manner than a more complex or larger firm, since the less complex or smaller company may have fewer employees in the accounting department, which limits its ability to segregate duties. The result may be the use of alternative controls to achieve its control objectives. The auditor should examine whether these alternative controls are effective.

Procedures that an auditor can perform to test design effectiveness include a mix of inquiry of personnel, observation of company operations, and inspection of documentation. Walkthroughs including these procedures are usually sufficient for evaluating design effectiveness.

Testing Operating Effectiveness

The auditor should test the operating effectiveness of a control that has been selected for testing by determining whether the control is operating as designed, and whether the person performing the control possesses the authority and competence to perform the control effectively. Procedures that the auditor can perform to test operating effectiveness include a mix of inquiry of personnel, observation of company operations, inspection of documentation, and the reperformance of the control.

Obtaining Evidence from Tests of Controls

The evidence provided by the auditor's tests of the effectiveness of controls depends upon the mix of the nature, timing, and extent of the auditor's procedures. For an individual control, different combinations of these factors might provide sufficient evidence in relation to the degree of reliance in an audit of financial statements.

NOTE: The effectiveness of a control cannot be inferred from the absence of misstatements detected by substantive procedures.

Nature of Tests of Controls

The following tests that the auditor could perform are presented in the order of the evidence that they should produce, from least to most: inquiry, observation, inspection of documentation, and reperformance of a control. It is not sufficient to only use inquiry to support a conclusion about the effectiveness of a control.

The type of tests of controls to use depends on the nature of the control to be tested, as well as whether operation of the control results in documentary evidence of its operation.

Extent of Tests of Controls

More evidence is obtained from a test when it is more extensively tested. Issues that can affect the extent of testing in relation to the amount of reliance on a control include:

- The number of times the company performed the control
- The length of time that the auditor is relying on the effectiveness of the control.
- The expected rate of deviation from the control
- The relevance and reliability of the evidence to be obtained from the effectiveness of the control
- The extent to which audit evidence is obtained from other control tests related to the assertion
- The nature of the control, including whether it is a manual or automated control
- The effectiveness of information technology general controls

Timing of Tests of Controls

The auditor must obtain evidence that those controls selected for testing are designed and operated effectively through the entire period of reliance.

If the auditor obtains evidence about the operating effectiveness of controls through an interim date, he or she should determine what additional evidence is needed concerning the operation of the controls through the remainder of the period of reliance. This additional evidence depends on the following factors:

- The possibility of significant changes in internal control over financial reporting subsequent to the interim date
- The inherent risk associated with the related accounts or assertions
- The control tested prior to year-end, and the risk that it is no longer effective during the remaining period
- The planned amount of reliance on the control
- The sufficiency of evidence of the effectiveness obtained at the interim date
- The length of the remaining period since the interim date

When the auditor relies on controls that have been tested in past audits, and he or she plans to use evidence about the effectiveness of those controls that was collected in prior years, then they should take the following factors into account to determine the evidence needed during the current year audit:

- The nature and materiality of misstatements that the control was designed to prevent or detect
- The inherent risk associated with the related account or assertion
- The existence of any changes in the volume or nature of a transaction that might affect the control
- A history of errors at the account level
- The effectiveness of entity-level controls tested by the auditor, in particular those controls that monitor other controls
- The nature of controls and their frequency of operation
- The extent of reliance by a control on the effectiveness of other controls

- The competence of the personnel who perform the control or monitor it, as well as changes in key personnel who operate in this capacity
- Whether a control relies on manual or automated monitoring
- The complexity of the control and the significance of judgments made in connection with it
- The planned degree of reliance on a control
- The nature, timing, and extent of the procedures performed in past audits
- The results of the previous years' control testing
- Any changes in the control or the process with which it is associated
- For integrated audits, the effectiveness of any controls examined during the audit of internal control

Access Control Risk

The auditor should evaluate control risk for assertions by evaluating the evidence obtained from all sources, including the test of controls for the audit of internal control and the audit of financial statements, misstatements detected during the audit, and control deficiencies.

The auditor should assess control risk at the maximum level for relevant assertions when controls needed to address the assessed risk of material misstatement are missing or ineffective, or when there is no sufficient appropriate evidence to support a control risk assessment that is below the maximum level.

If the auditor detects deficiencies in the control on which he or she intends to rely, there should be an evaluation of the severity of the deficiencies and the effect on the control risk assessments. If the controls are ineffective, the auditor should:

- Test other controls related to the same assertion as the ineffective controls
- Revise the control risk assessment and modify the substantive procedures in light of the increased risk assessment

Testing Controls in an Audit of Internal Control

The objective of the tests of controls in an audit of internal control is to obtain evidence concerning the effectiveness of those controls used to support the auditor's opinion on a company's internal control over financial reporting.

SUBSTANTIVE CONTROLS

The auditor should perform substantive procedures for each assertion of each significant account and disclosure, irrespective of the assessed level of control risk. As the assessed risk of material misstatement increases, the auditor should obtain an increased amount of evidence from substantive procedures. This evidence depends on the nature, timing, and extent of the procedures. Different combinations of testing may be sufficient for the testing of an individual assertion.

Internal controls over financial reporting have limitations that can affect the evidence needed from substantive procedures. Thus, more evidence from substantive procedures is needed for assertions that are subject to management override or lapses in judgment.

Nature of Substantive Procedures

Substantive procedures usually provide persuasive evidence when they are designed and performed to obtain relevant and reliable evidence. The auditor should take into account the types of potential misstatements in the assertions that could arise from identified risks, which may help to determine the types and combinations of procedures needed to detect material misstatements in the assertions. The assertions must include the following audit procedures for the period-end financial reporting process:

- Reconcile the financial statements with the accounting records
- Examine material adjustments to the financial statements

Extent of Substantive Procedures

The extent of usage of a substantive audit procedure depends on the materiality of the account or disclosure, as well as the assessed risk of material misstatement, and the necessary degree of assurance from the procedure. Increasing the extent of an audit procedure may not adequately address an assessed risk of material misstatement unless any evidence obtained by doing so is reliable and relevant.

Timing of Substantive Procedures

The auditor can perform some substantive procedures at interim dates for early consideration of issues affecting the year-end financial statements. However, doing so without performing procedures at a later date increases the risk of a material misstatement within the year-end financial statements that would not be detected. This increases if there is a longer interval between the interim date and the year-end.

To determine whether to perform substantive procedures at an interim date, the auditor should consider the following:

1. The assessed risk of material misstatement, which includes the assessment of control risk, conditions or circumstances that may pressure management to misstate the financial statements, and the effects of changes in the company or its environment or controls over financial reporting during the remaining time period
2. The nature of substantive procedures
3. The nature of the account or disclosure, and the relevant assertion
4. The auditor's ability to perform procedures for the remaining time period

If the auditor performs substantive tests at an interim date, he or she should address the remaining period by performing substantive procedures, or such procedures in combination with tests of controls that create a reasonable basis for extending the audit conclusions for the period from the interim date to the period end. These procedures should compare information about the account balance at the interim date with comparable information at the end of the period to identify unusual amounts, and perform audit procedures for the remaining period.

If these actions result in evidence that contradicts the evidence on which the auditor based his or her original risk assessments, this may result in revising the related risk assessments and modifying the planned nature, timing, or extent of those substantive procedures covering the remaining time period.

Dual-Purpose Tests

When the auditor conducts a dual-purpose test, he or she should design the test to achieve the objectives of both the test of the control and of the substantive test. Also, the auditor should evaluate the results of the test when forming conclusions about both the assertion and the effectiveness of the control being tested.

PCAOB 14 Evaluating Audit Results[1]

EFFECTIVE DATE AND APPLICABILITY

Effective Date   This standard currently is effective.

Applicability   All audit planning.

OBJECTIVES OF PCAOB STANDARD 14

Public Company Accounting Oversight Board (PCAOB) Auditing Standard 14 sets the objective of evaluating the results of the audit to determine whether the evidence obtained is sufficient and appropriate to support the opinion to be expressed in the auditor's report.

FUNDAMENTAL REQUIREMENTS

EVALUATING THE RESULTS OF THE AUDIT OF FINANCIAL STATEMENTS

When forming an opinion about whether financial statements are presented fairly in all material respects, the auditor should consider all relevant audit evidence, whether or not it appears to corroborate or contradict the assertions in the financial statements. This evaluation should include:

1. The results of those analytical procedures performed in the review of the financial statements
2. Misstatements accumulated during the audit (especially uncorrected ones)
3. Qualitative aspects of the company's accounting practices
4. Conditions identified during the audit relating to the assessment of risk of material misstatement due to fraud
5. The presentation of the financial statements, including disclosures
6. The sufficiency and appropriateness of audit evidence obtained

Performing Analytical Procedures in the Overall Review

The auditor should read the financial statements and disclosures as part of an overall review and perform analytical procedures to evaluate his or her conclusions regarding significant accounts and disclosures, as well as to assist in forming an opinion on whether the financial statements are free of material misstatement. As part of this overall review, the auditor should evaluate the following:

---

[1] *Practitioners should reference the additional guidance listed in the section "Other PCAOB Guidance" in this volume's chapter PCAOB 1.*

1. Whether the evidence gathered in response to unusual or unexpected items previously identified is sufficient
2. Whether unusual or unexpected items indicate risks of material misstatement that were not previously identified

The nature and extent of these analytical procedures performed during the overall review may be comparable to those procedures performed as risk assessment procedures.

The auditor should perform analytical procedures related to revenue through the end of the reporting period.

The auditor should obtain corroboration of any management explanations about significant unusual or unexpected items; if management responses appear either implausible, inconsistent with other audit evidence, imprecise, or not at a level of detail to be useful, the auditor should initiate procedures to address the issue.

Accumulating and Evaluating Identified Misstatements

The auditor should accumulate misstatements identified during the audit, other than trivial items. The auditor can designate an amount below which misstatements are clearly trivial and so do not need to be accumulated. This amount should be set so that any misstatements below it would not be material to the financial statements, either individually or in combination with other misstatements.

This accumulation of misstatements should include a best estimate of the total misstatement in the accounts and disclosures that the auditor has tested, not just the amount of misstatements that have been specifically identified.

If the auditor concludes that the amount of an accounting estimate included in the financial statements is either unreasonable or not determined to be in conformity with the relevant requirements of an applicable financial framework, he or she should treat the difference between that estimate and a reasonable estimate as a misstatement.

The auditor should determine whether the overall audit strategy and audit plan should be modified under either of these circumstances:

1. The nature of the accumulated misstatements and the circumstances of their occurrence indicate that other misstatements may exist which, when combined with the accumulated misstatements, could be material.
2. The aggregate misstatements accumulated during the audit approach the level of materiality or those levels used in planning and performing the audit.

The auditor should communicate the amount of accumulated misstatements to management to provide them with an opportunity to correct the misstatements. If management has examined a misstatement and has made corrections, the auditor should evaluate management's work to determine whether the corrections were recorded properly.

The auditor should ascertain whether uncorrected misstatements are material. In making this evaluation, he or she should evaluate the misstatements in relation to the specific accounts and disclosures involved and to the financial statements as a whole, considering both qualitative and quantitative factors.

NOTE: *The interaction of quantitative and qualitative considerations in judgments concerning materiality can cause uncorrected misstatements of small amounts to have a material effect on the financial statements.*

The auditor's evaluation of uncorrected misstatements should include an evaluation of the effects of uncorrected misstatements detected in prior years, as well as misstatements detected in the current year that relate to prior years.

The auditor cannot assume that a case of error or fraud is an isolated event. Thus, he or she should evaluate the nature and effects of the individual misstatements that accumulated during the audit on the assessed risks of material misstatement. This evaluation is useful for determining whether risk assessments remain appropriate.

The auditor should evaluate whether identified misstatements are indicative of fraud, and how they affect his or her evaluation of materiality and related audit responses. If the auditor believes that a misstatement might be intentional, and the effect on the statements could be material (or cannot be determined), then the auditor should perform procedures to obtain additional audit evidence regarding whether fraud has occurred or is likely to have occurred, as well as the impact on the financial statements and the auditor's report.

When the auditor believes that a misstatement may be intentional, he or she should evaluate the implications on the integrity of management or employees, and the possible impact on other aspects of the audit. If the misstatement involved senior management, it may indicate a more pervasive problem, even if the amount of the misstatement is small. In this case, the auditor should reevaluate the assessment of fraud risk, as well as the effect of that assessment on the nature, timing, and extent of tests, as well as the assessment of the effectiveness of controls. The auditor should evaluate whether the situation indicates possible collusion involving employees, management, or external parties, and the effect of the collusion on the reliability of audit evidence obtained.

If the auditor becomes aware of an indication of fraud or another illegal act, the auditor should determine his or her responsibilities under AU Sections 316.79 to 316.82A, AU Section 317, and Section 10A of the Securities Exchange Act.

Evaluating the Qualitative Aspects of the Company's Accounting Practices

When reviewing whether a company's financial statements are free of material misstatement, the auditor should evaluate the qualitative aspects of the company's accounting practices, including any potential bias in management's judgments about the amounts and disclosures in the financial statements. The following are examples of management bias:

1. The selective correction of misstatements brought to their attention
2. The identification of offsetting entries
3. Bias in the selection and application of accounting principles
4. Bias in accounting estimates

If the auditor identifies that there is bias in management's judgments concerning the amounts and disclosures in the financial statements, he or she should evaluate whether the effect of that bias, when combined with the effect of uncorrected misstatements, could result in the material misstatement of the financial statements. This evaluation should also include whether the auditor's risk assessments (and especially the assessment of fraud risks) and the related audit responses are still appropriate.

The auditor should determine whether the difference between the estimates supported by audit evidence and those included in the financial statements indicate a possible bias by company management. If each of these estimates was individually reasonable, but the total effect in comparison to the estimates supported by audit evidence has the effect of altering the reported amount of profits, then the auditor should evaluate whether the circumstances indicate a potential bias by management in the estimates.

Bias can also arise from the cumulative effect of changes in multiple accounting estimates; if these estimates are grouped at one end of a range of reasonable estimates in the prior year and are grouped at the opposite end of the range in the current year, there should be an evaluation of whether management is using estimate alterations to achieve a desired outcome.

Evaluating Conditions Relating to the Assessment of Fraud Risks

When the auditor evaluates the results of the audit, he or she should evaluate whether the accumulated results of the auditing procedures and other observations affect the assessment of fraud risks made throughout the term of the audit, and whether procedures should be modified to respond to those risks. As part of this evaluation, the engagement partner should ascertain whether there has been appropriate communication with the team members throughout the audit concerning information about fraud risks.

Evaluating the Presentation of the Financial Statements, Including the Disclosures

The auditor must determine whether the financial statements are presented fairly, in all material respects, in conformity with the applicable financial reporting framework. As part of this determination, the auditor should evaluate whether the financial statements contain the information that is essential for a fair presentation of the financial statements in conformity with the applicable financial reporting framework. This evaluation includes consideration of the form, arrangement, and content of the financial statements, including terminology, the amount of detail included, the classification of items, and the stated bases of amounts. If this is not the case, the auditor should express a qualified or adverse opinion.

Evaluating the Sufficiency and Appropriateness of Audit Evidence

As part of the process of evaluating the results of an audit, the auditor must determine whether sufficient appropriate audit evidence was obtained to support his or her opinion on the financial statements. Factors relevant to this conclusion include:

1. The significance of uncorrected misstatements and the likelihood of their having a material effect, either alone or in combination, on the financial statements, as well as considering the possibility of further undetected misstatements
2. The results of audit procedures performed during the audit of financial statements, in addition to whether the evidence obtained supports or contradicts the assertions of management and whether these audit procedures identified specific cases of fraud
3. The auditor's risk assessments
4. The results of audit procedures performed during the audit of internal control over financial reporting, in the case of an integrated audit
5. The appropriateness of the audit evidence obtained

The auditor should perform additional procedures to obtain further audit evidence if he or she has not obtained sufficient appropriate audit evidence about an assertion or has substantial doubt about an assertion. If the auditor is unable to do so, then the auditor should express a qualified opinion or a disclaimer of opinion.

As part of this evaluation, the auditor should consider whether the assessments of the risks of material misstatement at the assertion level remain appropriate, and whether the audit procedures need to be modified or additional procedures performed due to any changes in the risk assessments.

EVALUATING THE RESULTS OF THE AUDIT OF INTERNAL CONTROL OVER FINANCIAL REPORTING

The auditor should form an opinion regarding the effectiveness of internal control over financial reporting by evaluating evidence obtained from all sources, including the auditor's controls tests, misstatements found during the financial statement audit, and any control deficiencies found.

PCAOB 15 Audit Evidence[1]

EFFECTIVE DATE AND APPLICABILITY

Effective Date   This standard currently is effective.

Applicability   All audit planning.

DEFINITIONS OF TERMS

Appropriateness. The measure of the quality of audit evidence.

Audit evidence. All of the information obtained from audit procedures and other sources that is used by the auditor to arrive at the conclusions on which his or her opinion is based. The evidence consists of information that supports and corroborates management's assertions regarding the financial statements or internal control over financial reporting, and information that contradicts these assertions.

Sufficiency. The measure of the quantity of audit evidence.

OBJECTIVES OF PCAOB STANDARD 15

PCAOB Auditing Standard 15 sets the objective of planning and performing the audit to obtain appropriate audit evidence that is sufficient to support the opinion expressed in the auditor's report.

FUNDAMENTAL REQUIREMENTS

SUFFICIENT APPROPRIATE AUDIT EVIDENCE

The auditor must plan and perform audit procedures to obtain sufficient audit evidence to provide a basis for his or her opinion. The quantity of audit evidence needed is affected by:

- The level of risk (quantity of evidence increases with the risk level)
- The quality of audit evidence (quantity of evidence decreases as the quality of evidence rises)

Audit evidence should be both relevant and reliable in providing support for the conclusions reached by the auditor.

---

[1] *Practitioners should reference the additional guidance listed in the section "Other PCAOB Guidance" in this volume's chapter PCAOB 1.*

Relevance and Reliability

The relevance of audit evidence depends upon the design and timing of the audit procedure used to test the assertion or control.

The reliability of evidence depends on the nature and source of the evidence, as well as the circumstances under which it was obtained. The following factors apply to the reliability of audit evidence:

- Evidence obtained from an independent, knowledgeable source is more reliable than evidence obtained from internal sources.
- Evidence obtained internally is more reliable when the controls over that information are effective.
- Evidence obtained directly is more reliable than evidence obtained indirectly.
- Evidence obtained from original documents is more reliable than evidence obtained from copies of documents.

The auditor does not have to be an expert in document authentication, but if it appears that a document may not be authentic or may have been modified, then the auditor should modify the audit procedures or perform additional ones to respond to the situation, as well as evaluate the effect on other aspects of the audit.

Using Information Produced by the Company

When using company-provided information as audit evidence, the auditor should evaluate whether it is sufficient and appropriate for the audit by engaging in procedures to test the accuracy of and completeness of the information, or the controls over accuracy and completeness, as well as evaluate whether the information is precise and detailed enough for the audit.

FINANCIAL STATEMENT ASSERTIONS

Management makes a variety of assertions when it represents that the financial statements are presented fairly in conformity with a financial reporting framework. These assertions can be grouped into the following categories:

- Assets or liabilities exist as of a given date, and recorded transactions occurred during a stated period.
- All transactions and accounts that should appear in the financial statements are included.
- The appropriate amounts of assets, liabilities, equity, revenue, and expenses have been included in the financial statements.
- The company holds the rights to its assets, and the liabilities are obligations of the company as of a given date.
- The various components of the financial statements are properly classified, described, and disclosed.

The auditor can use different assertions than those noted in this standard if they are sufficient to identify the types of potential misstatements, as well as to respond appropriately to risks of material misstatement in each significant account and disclosure that may contain misstatements that would result in the financial statements being materially misstated.

Audit Procedures for Obtaining Audit Evidence

Audit procedures are classified as risk assessment procedures and further audit procedures, which in the latter case are further subdivided into tests of controls and substantive procedures. The purpose of an audit procedure determines its classification.

Inspection

Inspection is the examination of records or documents in any format, which provides audit evidence of the effectiveness of the controls over their production.

Observation

Observation is looking at a process or procedure being performed by someone else. It can provide audit evidence about the performance of a process or procedure, but this evidence is limited to the time period when the observation takes place. It is also limited by how the act of observation may affect how the individuals being observed conduct the procedure.

Inquiry

Inquiry is seeking information from knowledgeable individuals both within and outside the company. This may range from written to oral inquiries. Inquiry does not constitute sufficient audit evidence to reduce audit risk to a low enough level for a relevant assertion, or to support a conclusion about the effectiveness of a control.

Confirmation

A response to a confirmation is a form of audit evidence that is obtained by the auditor from a third party.

Recalculation

Recalculation is the review of the mathematical accuracy of documents or records, and may be done either manually or electronically.

Reperformance

Reperformance is the independent execution of either procedures or controls that were originally done by company personnel.

Analytical Procedures

Analytical procedures involve the evaluation of financial information through an examination of plausible relationships among both financial and nonfinancial data. They also include the investigation of significant differences from expected amounts.

Selecting Items for Testing to Obtain Audit Evidence

The design of substantive tests for details and of controls includes the determination of the means of selecting items for testing from among the line items in an account or the instances of a control. The auditor should create a means for selecting items for testing to obtain evidence that, when combined with other evidence, is sufficient to meet the objective for an audit procedure. The methods available for selecting test items are to either select all items, select specific items, or to use audit sampling. The selection method depends on the nature of the audit procedure, the characteristics of the control or the account items being tested, and the evidence needed to meet the audit objective.

Selecting All Items

Selecting all items involves testing the entire population of line items in an account, or all of the occurrences of a control. This is an acceptable approach when the population is comprised of a small number of large value items, or when the audit procedure is responding to a significant risk and other selection methods do not provide sufficient appropriate evidence. This method is also acceptable when it can be automated and applied to the entire population.

Selecting Specific Items

Selecting specific items involves the testing of all items in a population that have certain characteristics. This may involve the selection of key items that are important to accomplishing an audit objective, or because they exhibit some other characteristics, such as having a history of errors. Specific item selection can also include the examination of items whose recorded values exceed a certain amount.

The auditor can also select specific items to obtain an understanding of specific issues, such as the nature of a transaction. If the auditor selects specific items, he or she cannot project the results of these procedures to the entire population, since it is not audit sampling.

Audit Sampling

Selecting items based on audit sampling involves the application of an audit procedure to less than 100% of the line items in an account balance or group of transactions, in order to evaluate a characteristic of the account balance or group.

INCONSISTENCY IN, OR DOUBTS ABOUT THE RELIABILITY OF, AUDIT EVIDENCE

If the auditor collects audit evidence from one source that is inconsistent with the evidence obtained from another source, or if he or she has doubts about the reliability of the information obtained, then the appropriate response is to perform those audit procedures necessary to resolve the matter, as well as to determine the effect of the issue on other aspects of the audit.

APPENDIX A:
ASB CLARITY PROJECT EXTANT AU SECTIONS MAPPED TO THE CLARIFIED AU-C SECTIONS

The following table maps the extant AU sections to the clarified AU-C sections. As a result of the ASB Clarity Project, all existing AU sections have been modified. In some cases, individual AU sections have been revised into individual clarified standards. In other cases, some AU sections have been grouped together and revised as one or more clarified standards. In addition, the ASB has revised the AU section number order established by SAS No. 1 to follow the ISA number order for all clarified AU sections for which there are comparable ISAs.

The following table also includes the type of change in the requirements from the ASB Clarity Project. The Project was not intended to create additional requirements; however, some revisions have resulted in substantive changes that require auditors to make adjustments in their practices as a result of the project. To assist auditors in the transition process, the AU-C sections have been organized into four types of changes, including the following:

- Substantive Changes
- Primarily Clarifying Changes
- Primarily Formatting Changes
- Standards Not Yet Issued in the Clarity Project

Substantive Changes

Substantive changes are considered likely to affect the firms' audit methodology and engagements because they contain substantive or other changes, defined as having one or both of the following characteristics:

- Change(s) to an audit methodology that may require effort to implement
- A number of small changes that, while not individually significant, may affect audit engagements

The auditor may need to address the changes in these AU-C sections early in the audit process. Some of the requirements may affect decisions to accept an engagement. Some will need to be communicated early in the planning process. The clarified standards are effective for periods ending on or after December 15, 2012, and may require the auditor to apply certain of the substantive changes as early as the planning stage for 2012 year-end audits. The auditor needs to review these AU-C sections to identify areas that apply to their practices.

Primarily Clarifying Changes

Primarily clarifying changes are intended to explicitly state what may have been implicit in the extant standards, which over time resulted in diversity in practice. Certain of these clarified standards address management responsibilities that may need to be communicated to clients early in the planning stage. Some of these requirements may already be performed in practice, although not explicitly required by the extant standards. Most notably, certain of the new requirements shift the timing of certain requirements from the reporting stage of an audit to the planning stage. The new requirements in this section may not have a substantial impact, but may result in adjustments to the timing and responsibilities of the auditor and their clients, and will need to be reviewed by the auditor to ensure that all requirements have been properly addressed.

Primarily Formatting Changes

Primarily formatting changes from the extant standards do not contain changes that expand the extant sections in any significant way and may not require adjustments to current practice.

Standard Not Yet Issued in the Clarity Project

Standard not yet issued in the Clarity Project is the final remaining section that is in exposure or has not yet been reworked.

Extant AU Sections Mapped to the Clarified AU-C Sections

	Extant AU Section	AU Section Superseded		New AU-C Section	Type of Change
110	Responsibilities and Functions of the Independent Auditor	All	200	Overall Objectives of the Independent Auditor and the Conduct of an Audit in Accordance with Generally Accepted Auditing Standards [1]	Primarily Formatting Changes
120	Defining Professional Requirements in Statements on Auditing Standards	All			
150	Generally Accepted Auditing Standards	All			
161	The Relationship of Generally Accepted Auditing Standards to Quality Control Standards	All	220	Quality Control for an Engagement Conducted in Accordance with Generally Accepted Auditing Standards	Primarily Clarifying Changes
201	Nature of the General Standards	All	200	Overall Objectives of the Independent Auditor and the Conduct of an Audit in Accordance with Generally Accepted Auditing Standards [1]	Primarily Formatting Changes
210	Training and Proficiency of the Independent Auditor	All			
220	Independence	All			
230	Due Professional Care in the Performance of Work	All			
311	Planning and Supervision	All except .08–.10	300	Planning an Audit	Primarily Formatting Changes
		.08–.10	210	Terms of Engagement	Primarily Clarifying Changes
312	Audit Risk and Materiality in Conducting an Audit	All	320	Materiality in Planning and Performing an Audit	Primarily Formatting Changes
			450	Evaluation of Misstatements Identified During the Audit	Primarily Formatting Changes

Extant AU Section		AU Section Superseded	New AU-C Section		Type of Change
314	Understanding the Entity and Its Environment and Assessing the Risks of Material Misstatement	All	315	Understanding the Entity and Its Environment and Assessing the Risks of Material Misstatement	Primarily Formatting Changes
315	Communications between Predecessor and Successor Auditors	All except .03–.10 and .14	510	Opening Balances—Initial Audit Engagements, Including Reaudit Engagements	Primarily Clarifying Changes
		.03–.10 and .14	210	Terms of Engagement	Primarily Clarifying Changes
316	Consideration of Fraud in a Financial Statement Audit	All	240	Consideration of Fraud in a Financial Statement Audit	Primarily Formatting Changes
317	Illegal Acts by Clients	All	250	Consideration of Laws and Regulations in an Audit of Financial Statements	Substantive Changes
318	Performing Audit Procedures in Response to Assessed Risks and Evaluating the Audit Evidence Obtained	All	330	Performing Audit Procedures in Response to Assessed Risks and Evaluating the Audit Evidence Obtained	Primarily Formatting Changes
322	The Auditor's Consideration of the Internal Audit Function in an Audit of Financial Statements	All	Planned to be Issued as AU-C 610	The Auditor's Consideration of the Internal Audit Function in an Audit of Financial Statements	Standard Not Yet Issued in the Clarity Project
324	Service Organizations	All	402	Audit Considerations Relating to an Entity Using a Service Organization	Primarily Clarifying Changes
325	Communicating Internal Control Related Matters Identified in an Audit	All	265	Communicating Internal Control Related Matters Identified in an Audit	Substantive Changes
326	Audit Evidence	All	500	Audit Evidence	Primarily Formatting Changes
328	Auditing Fair Value Measurements and Disclosures	All	540	Auditing Accounting Estimates, Including Fair Value Accounting Estimates and Related Disclosures [2]	Primarily Formatting Changes
329	Analytical Procedures	All	520	Analytical Procedures	Primarily Formatting Changes
330	The Confirmation Process	All	505	External Confirmations	Primarily Clarifying Changes

Extant AU Section		AU Section Superseded	New AU-C Section		Type of Change
331	Inventories	All	501	Audit Evidence—Specific Considerations for Selected Items [3]	Primarily Clarifying Changes
332	Auditing Derivative Instruments, Hedging Activities, and Investments in Securities	All	501	Audit Evidence—Specific Considerations for Selected Items [3]	Primarily Clarifying Changes
333	Management Representations	All	580	Written Representations	Primarily Formatting Changes
334	Related Parties	All	550	Related Parties	Substantive Changes
336	Using the Work of a Specialists	All	620	Using the Work of an Auditor's Specialist	Primarily Clarifying Changes
337	Inquiry of a Client's Lawyer Concerning Litigation, Claims, and Assessments	All	501	Audit Evidence—Specific Considerations for Selected Items [3]	Primarily Clarifying Changes
339	Audit Documentation	All	230	Audit Documentation	Primarily Formatting Changes
341	The Auditor's Consideration of an Entity's Ability to Continue as a Going Concern	All	570	The Auditor's Consideration of an Entity's Ability to Continue as a Going Concern	Primarily Formatting Changes
342	Auditing Accounting Estimates	All	540	Auditing Accounting Estimates, Including Fair Value Accounting Estimates and Related Disclosures [2]	Primarily Formatting Changes
350	Audit Sampling	All	530	Audit Sampling	Primarily Formatting Changes
380	The Auditor's Communication with Those Charged with Governance	All	260	The Auditor's Communication with Those Charged with Governance	Primarily Formatting Changes
390	Consideration of Omitted Procedures After the Report Date	All	585	Consideration of Omitted Procedures After the Report Release Date	Primarily Formatting Changes
410	Adherence to Generally Accepted Accounting Principles	All	700	Forming an Opinion and Reporting on Financial Statements [4]	Substantive Changes
420	Consistency of Application of Generally Accepted Accounting Principles	All	708	Consistency of Financial Statements	Primarily Clarifying Changes
431	Adequacy of Disclosure in Financial Statements	All	705	Modifications to the Opinion in the Independent Auditor's Report [5]	Primarily Formatting Changes

Appendix A: ASB Clarity Project

Extant AU Section		AU Section Superseded	New AU-C Section		Type of Change
504	Association with Financial Statements	All	N/A	Withdrawn	
508	Reports on Audited Financial Statements	.01–.11, .14–.15, .19–.32, .35–.52, .58–.70, .74–.76	700	Forming an Opinion and Reporting on Financial Statements [4]	Substantive Changes
			705	Modifications to the Opinion in the Independent Auditor's Report [5]	Primarily Formatting Changes
			706	Emphasis-of-Matter Paragraphs and Other-Matter Paragraphs in the Independent Auditor's Reports [6]	Substantive Changes
		.12–.13	600	Special Considerations—Audits of Group Financial Statements (Including the Work of Component Auditors)	Substantive Changes
		.16–.18, .53–.57	708	Consistency of Financial Statements	Primarily Clarifying Changes
		.33–.34	805	Special Considerations—Audits of Single Financial Statements and Specific Elements, Accounts, or Items of a Financial Statement	Primarily Clarifying Changes
		.71–.73	560	Subsequent Events and Subsequently Discovered Facts [7]	Primarily Formatting Changes
530	Dating of the Independent Auditor's Report	.01–.02	700	Forming an Opinion and Reporting on Financial Statements [4]	Substantive Changes
		.03–.08	560	Subsequent Events and Subsequently Discovered Facts [7]	Primarily Formatting Changes
532	Restricting the Use of an Auditor's Report	All	905	Alert That Restricts the Use of the Auditor's Written Communication	Primarily Clarifying Changes
534	Reporting on Financial Statements Prepared for Use in Other Countries	All	910	Financial Statements Prepared in Accordance with a Financial Reporting Framework Generally Accepted in Another Country	Primarily Clarifying Changes
543	Part of Audit Performed by Other Independent Auditors	All	600	Special Considerations—Audits of Group Financial Statements (Including the Work of Component Auditors)	Substantive Changes

Extant AU Section		AU Section Superseded	New AU-C Section		Type of Change
544	Lack of Conformity with Generally Accepted Accounting Principles	All	800	Special Considerations—Audits of Financial Statements Prepared in Accordance with Special Purpose Frameworks [8]	Primarily Clarifying Changes
550	Other Information in Documents Containing Audited Financial Statements	All	720	Other Information in Documents Containing Audited Financial Statements	Primarily Formatting Changes
551	Supplementary Information in Relation to the Financial Statements as a Whole	All	725	Supplementary Information in Relation to the Financial Statements as a Whole	Primarily Formatting Changes
552	Reporting on Condensed Financial Statements and Selected Financial Data	All	810	Engagements to Report on Summary Financial Statements	Primarily Clarifying Changes
558	Required Supplementary Information	All	730	Required Supplementary Information	Primarily Formatting Changes
560	Subsequent Events	All	560	Subsequent Events and Subsequently Discovered Facts [7]	Primarily Formatting Changes
561	Subsequent Discovery of Facts Existing at the Date of the Auditor's Report	All			
623	Special Reports	.19–.21	806	Reporting on Compliance with Aspects of Contractual Agreements or Regulatory Requirements in Connection with Audited Financial Statements	Primarily Formatting Changes
		.01–.10, .22–.34	800	Special Considerations—Audits of Financial Statements Prepared in Accordance with Special Purpose Frameworks [8]	Primarily Clarifying Changes
		.11–.18	805	Special Considerations—Audits of Single Financial Statements and Specific Elements, Accounts, or Items of a Financial Statement	Primarily Clarifying Changes
625	Reports on the Application of Accounting Principles	All	915	Reports on Application of Requirements of an Applicable Financial Reporting Framework	Primarily Formatting Changes
634	Letters for Underwriters and Certain Other Requesting Parties	All	920	Letters for Underwriters and Certain Other Requesting Parties	Primarily Formatting Changes

Extant AU Section		AU Section Superseded	New AU-C Section		Type of Change
711	Filings under Federal Securities Statutes	All	925	Filings with the US Securities and Exchange Commission under the Securities Act of 1933	Primarily Formatting Changes
722	Interim Financial Information	All	930	Interim Financial Information	Primarily Formatting Changes
801	Compliance Audits	All	935	Compliance Audits	Primarily Formatting Changes
901	Public Warehouses—Controls and Auditing Procedures for Goods Held	All	501	Audit Evidence—Specific Considerations for Selected Items [3]	Primarily Clarifying Changes

Legend:

[n]—Bracketed number indicates clarity standard that supersedes more than one extant AU section.

APPENDIX B:
CROSS-REFERENCES TO SASs, SSAEs, AND SSARSs

Statements on Auditing Standards (SASs)

No.	Date issued	Title	Guide section
1	Nov. 1972	Codification of Auditing Standards and Procedures	
2	Oct. 1974	(Superseded by SAS 58)	
3	Dec. 1974	(Superseded by SAS 48)	
4	Dec. 1974	(Superseded by SAS 25)	
5	July 1975	(Superseded by SAS 69)	
6	July 1975	(Superseded by SAS 45)	
7	Oct. 1975	(Superseded by SAS 84)	
8	Dec. 1975	Other Information in Documents Containing Audited Financial Statements	
9	Dec. 1975	(Superseded by SAS 65)	
10	Dec. 1975	(Superseded by SAS 24)	
11	Dec. 1975	(Superseded by SAS 73)	
12	Jan. 1976	Inquiry of a Client's Lawyer Concerning Litigation, Claims, and Assessments	337
13	May 1976	(Superseded by SAS 24)	
14	Dec. 1976	(Superseded by SAS 62)	
15	Dec. 1976	(Superseded by SAS 58)	
16	Jan. 1977	(Superseded by SAS 53)	
17	Jan. 1977	(Superseded by SAS 54)	
18	May 1977	(Withdrawn by Auditing Standards Board)	
19	June 1977	(Superseded by SAS 85)	
20	Aug. 1977	(Superseded by SAS 60)	
21	Dec. 1977	(Rescinded by Auditing Standards Board)	
22	Mar. 1978	(Superseded by SAS 108)	
23	Oct. 1978	(Superseded by SAS 56)	
24	Mar. 1979	(Superseded by SAS 36)	
25	Nov. 1979	The Relationship of Generally Accepted Auditing Standards to Quality Control Standards	
26	Nov. 1979	Association with Financial Statements	
27	Dec. 1979	(Superseded by SAS 52)	
28	June 1980	(Withdrawn by SAS 52)	
29	July 1980	Reporting on Information Accompanying the Basic Financial Statements in Auditor-Submitted Documents	
30	July 1980	(Superseded by SSAE 2)	
31	Aug. 1980	Evidential Matter	
32	Oct. 1980	Adequacy of Disclosure of Financial Statements	431
33	Oct. 1980	(Superseded by SAS 45)	
34	Mar. 1981	(Superseded by SAS 59)	
35	April 1981	(Superseded by SAS 75)	
36	April 1981	(Superseded by SAS 71)	
37	April 1981	Filings under Federal Securities Statutes	711
38	April 1981	(Superseded by SAS 49)	

No.	Date issued	Title	Guide section
39	June 1981	Audit Sampling	350
40	Feb. 1982	(Superseded by SAS 52)	
41	April 1982	(Superseded by SAS 96)	
42	Sept. 1982	Reporting on Condensed Financial Statements and Selected Financial Data	552
43	Aug. 1982	Omnibus Statement on Auditing Standards	
44	Dec. 1982	(Superseded by SAS 70)	
45	Aug. 1983	Omnibus Statement on Auditing Standards—1983	
46	Sept. 1983	Consideration of Omitted Procedures after the Report Date	390
47	Dec. 1983	Audit Risk and Materiality in Conducting an Audit	
48	July 1984	The Effects of Computer Processing on the Audit of Financial Statements	
49	Sept. 1984	(Superseded by SAS 72)	
50	July 1986	Reports on the Application of Accounting Principles	625
51	July 1986	Reporting on Financial Statements Prepared for Use in Other Countries	534
52	April 1988	Omnibus Statement on Auditing Standards—1987	551, 558
53	April 1988	(Superseded by SAS 82)	
54	April 1988	Illegal Acts by Clients	317
55	April 1988	Consideration of Internal Control in a Financial Statement Audit	
56	April 1988	Analytical Procedures	329
57	April 1988	Auditing Accounting Estimates	342
58	April 1988	Reports on Audited Financial Statements	508
59	April 1988	The Auditor's Consideration of an Entity's Ability to Continue as a Going Concern	341
60	April 1988	(Superseded by SAS 112)	
61	April 1988	(Superseded by SAS 114)	
62	April 1989	Special Reports	623
63	April 1989	(Superseded by SAS 68)	
64	Dec. 1990	Omnibus Statement on Auditing Standards—1990	
65	April 1991	The Auditor's Consideration of the Internal Audit Function in an Audit of Financial Statements	322
66	June 1991	(Superseded by SAS 71)	
67	Nov. 1991	The Confirmation Process	330
68	Dec. 1991	(Superseded by SAS 74)	
69	Jan. 1992	The Meaning of *Present Fairly in Conformity with Generally Accepted Accounting Principles*	
70	April 1992	Service Organizations	324
71	May 1992	(Superseded by SAS 100 for interim periods within fiscal years beginning after December 15, 2002)	
72	Feb. 1993	Letters for Underwriters and Certain Other Requesting Parties	634
73	July 1994	Using the Work of a Specialist	336
74	Feb. 1995	Compliance Auditing Considerations in Audits of Governmental Entities and Recipients of Governmental Financial Assistance	
75	Sept. 1995	(Withdrawn by SAS 93)	
76	Sept. 1995	Amendments to Statement on Auditing Standards 72, *Letters for Underwriters and Certain Other Requesting Parties*	

Appendix B: Cross-References to SASs, SSAEs, and SSARSs

No.	Date issued	Title	Guide section
77	Nov. 1995	Amendments to Statements on Auditing Standards 22, *Planning and Supervision;* 59, *The Auditor's Consideration of an Entity's Ability to Continue as a Going Concern;* and 62, *Special Reports*	
78	Dec. 1995	Consideration of Internal Control in a Financial Statement Audit: An Amendment to Statement on Auditing Standards 55	
79	Dec. 1995	Amendment to Statement on Auditing Standards 58, *Reports on Audited Financial Statements*	
80	Dec. 1996	Amendment to Statement on Auditing Standards 31, *Evidential Matter*	
81	Dec. 1996	(Superseded by SAS 92)	
82	Feb. 1997	(Superseded by SAS 99 for audits of financial statements for periods beginning on or after December 15, 2002)	
83	Oct. 1997	Establishing an Understanding with the Client	
84	Oct. 1997	Communications between Predecessor and Successor Auditors	315
85	Nov. 1997	Management Representations	333
86	Mar. 1998	Amendment to Statement on Auditing Standards 72, *Letters for Underwriters and Certain Other Requesting Parties*	
87	Sept. 1998	Restricting the Use of an Auditor's Report	532
88	Dec. 1999	Service Organizations and Reporting on Consistency	
89	Dec. 1999	Audit Adjustments	
90	Dec. 1999	Audit Committee Communications	
92	Sept. 2000	Auditing Derivative Instruments, Hedging Activities, and Investments in Securities	332
93	Oct. 2000	Omnibus Statement on Auditing Standards—2000	
94	May 2001	The Effect of Information Technology on the Auditor's Consideration of Internal Control in a Financial Statement Audit	
95	Dec. 2001	Generally Accepted Auditing Standards	150
96	Jan. 2002	Audit Documentation	
97	June 2002	Amendment to Statement on Auditing Standards 50, *Reports on the Application of Accounting Principles*	
98	Sept. 2002	Omnibus Statement on Auditing Standards—2002	
99	Oct. 2002	Consideration of Fraud in a Financial Statement Audit	316
100	Nov. 2002	Interim Financial Information	722
101	Jan. 2003	Auditing Fair Value Measurements and Disclosures	328
102	Dec. 2005	Defining Professional Requirements in Statements on Auditing Standards	120
103	Dec. 2005	Audit Documentation	339
104	Mar. 2006	Amendment to Statement on Auditing Standards 1	
105	Mar. 2006	Amendment to Statement on Auditing Standards 95	
106	Mar. 2006	Audit Evidence	326
107	Mar. 2006	Audit Risk and Materiality in Conducting an Audit	312
108	Mar. 2006	Planning and Supervision	311
109	Mar. 2006	Understanding the Entity and Its Environment and Assessing the Risks of Material Misstatement	318
110	Mar. 2006	Performing Procedures	327
111	Mar. 2006	Amendment to Statement on Auditing Standards 39, *Audit Sampling*	350

Appendix B: Cross-References to SASs, SSAEs, and SSARSs

No.	Date issued	Title	Guide section
112	May 2006	Superseded by SAS 115	
113	July 2006	Omnibus 2006	
114	Dec. 2006	The Auditor's Communication with Those Charged with Governance	380
115	Oct. 2008	Communicating Internal Control Related Matters Identified in an Audit	325
116	Feb. 2009	Interim Financial Information	722
117	Feb. 2010	Compliance Audits	801
118	Apr. 2010	Other Information in Documents Containing Audited Financial Statements	550
119	Apr. 2010	Supplementary Information in Relation to the Financial Statements as a Whole	551
120	Apr. 2010	Required Supplementary Information	558
121	Feb. 2011	Revised Applicability of Statement of Auditing Standard No. 100, *Interim Financial Information*	722
122	Oct. 2011	Codification of Auditing Standards and Procedures	Throughout
123	Oct. 2011	Omnibus Statement on Auditing Standards—2011	
124	Oct. 2011	Financial Statements Prepared in Accordance with a Financial Reporting Framework Generally Accepted in Another Country	534
125	Dec. 2011	Alert That Restricts the Use of the Auditor's Written Communication	532
126	July 2012	The Auditor's Consideration of an Entity's Ability to Continue as a Going Concern	341

Statements on Standards for Attestation Engagements (SSAEs)

No.	Date issued	Title	Guide section
1	Oct. 1985	Superseded by SSAE 10	
1	Mar. 1986	Superseded by SSAE 10	
1	Sept. 1988	Superseded by SSAE 10	
1	Dec. 1987	Superseded by SSAE 10	
2	May 1993	Superseded by SSAE 10	
3	Dec. 1993	Superseded by SSAE 10	
4	Sept. 1995	Superseded by SSAE 10	
5	Nov. 1995	Superseded by SSAE 10	
6	Dec. 1995	Superseded by SSAE 10	
7	Oct. 1997	Superseded by SSAE 10	
8	Mar. 1998	Superseded by SSAE 10	
9	Jan. 1999	Superseded by SSAE 10	
10	Jan. 2001	Attestation Standards: Revision and Recodification	AT 101, 201, 301, 401
11	Jan. 2002	Attest Documentation	
12	Sept. 2002	Amendment to SSAE 10, *Attestation Standards: Revision and Recodification*	
13	Dec. 2005	Defining Professional Requirements in Statements on Standards for Attestation Engagements	AT 20
14	Nov. 2006	SSAE Hierarchy	AT 50

No.	Date issued	Title	Guide section
15	Oct. 2008	An Examination of an Entity's Internal Control over Financial Reporting That Is Integrated with an Audit of Its Financial Statements	AT 501
16	Apr. 2010	Reporting on Controls at a Service Organization	AT 801
17	Dec. 2010	Reporting on Compiled Prospective Financial Statements When the Practitioner's Independence Is Impaired	AT 301

Statements on Standards for Accounting and Review Services (SSARSs)

No.	Date issued	Title	Guide section
1	Dec. 1978	Compilation and Review of Financial Statements	AR 100
2	Oct. 1979	Reporting on Comparative Financial Statements	AR 200
3	Dec. 1981	Compilation Reports on Financial Statements Included in Certain Prescribed Forms	AR 300
4	Dec. 1981	Communications between Predecessor and Successor Accountants	AR 400
5	July 1982	(Deleted by SSARS 7)	
6	Sept. 1986	Reporting on Personal Financial Statements Included in Written Personal Financial Plans	AR 3600
7	Nov. 1992	Omnibus Statement on Standards for Accounting and Review Services—1992	AR 100, 200, 300, 400
8	Oct. 2000	Amendment to Statement on Standards for Accounting and Review Services 1, *Compilation and Review of Financial Statements*	AR 100
9	Nov. 2002	Omnibus Statement on Standards for Accounting and Review Services—2002	AR 100, 400
10	May 2004	Performance of Review Engagements	AR 100
11	May 2004	Standards for Accounting and Review Services	AR 100, 200
12	July 2005	Omnibus Statement on Standards for Accounting and Review Services—2005	
13	July 2005	Compilations of Specified Elements, Accounts, or Items of a Financial Statement	
14	July 2005	Compilations of Pro Forma Financial Information	AR 120
15	July 2007	Elimination of Certain References to Statements on Auditing Standards and Incorporation of Appropriate Guidance into Statements on Standards for Accounting and Review Services	
16	Dec. 2007	Defining Professional Requirements in Statements on Standards for Accounting and Review Services	AR 20
17	Feb. 2008	Applicability of Statements on Standards for Accounting and Review Services	AR 100
18	Feb. 2009	Omnibus Statement on Standards for Accounting and Review Services—2008	
19	Dec. 2009	Compilation and Review Engagements	AR 100
20	Feb. 2011	Revised Applicability of Statements on Standards for Accounting and Review Services	AR 100

APPENDIX C:
LIST OF AICPA AUDIT AND ACCOUNTING GUIDES[1]

Along with auditing Interpretations of Statements on Auditing Standards (SASs), which are integrated in the appropriate sections, the auditing guidance in the following American Institute of Certified Public Accountants (AICPA) Audit and Accounting Guides and auditing Statements of Positions are recommendations on how to apply the SASs in specific circumstances and for entities in specialized industries that are issued under the authority of the Auditing Standards Board (ASB). Auditors who do not follow the guidance in an applicable interpretive publication should be prepared to explain how they complied with the relevant SAS requirements addressed by such guidance.

AICPA *Audit and Accounting Guides* summarize the practices applicable to specific industries and describe relevant matters, conditions, and procedures unique to these industries. In addition, general audit and accounting guides listed below may be of interest to CPAs performing audit and attest engagements. Guides are available from the AICPA:

Airlines
Analytical Procedures
Assessing and Responding to Audit Risk in a Financial Statement Audit
Audit Sampling
Auditing Derivative Instruments, Hedging Activities, and Investments in Securities
Auditing Revenue in Certain Industries
Brokers and Dealers in Securities
Casinos
Compilation and Review Engagements
Construction Contractors
Depository and Lending Institutions—Banks and Savings Institutions, Credit Unions, Finance Companies, and Mortgage Companies
Employee Benefit Plans
Entities with Oil and Gas Producing Activities
Government Auditing Standards and Circular A-133 Audits
Health Care Entities
Investment Companies
Life and Health Insurance Entities
Not-for-Profit Organizations
Property and Liability Insurance Companies
Prospective Financial Information
Service Organizations: Applying SSAE No. 16, Reporting on Controls at a Service Organization (SOC 1)
State and Local Governments

---

[1] *Accounting Statements of Position are not included in this listing.*

Statements of Position—Auditing and Attestation

Auditing and Attestation Statements of Position are issued to achieve one or more of several objectives: to revise, clarify, or supplement guidance in previously issued Audit and Accounting Guides; to describe and provide implementation guidance for specific types of audit and attestation engagements; or to provide guidance on specialized areas in audit and attestation engagements. The auditing and attestation guidance in a Statement of Position has the same authority as auditing and attestation guidance in an Audit and Accounting Guide.

Topic	*Title*
Claims Payment Reports	*Performing Agreed-Upon Procedures Engagements That Address Annual Claims Prompt Payment Reports as Required by the New Jersey Administrative Code*
Corporate Compliance	*Guidance to Practitioners in Conducting and Reporting on an Agreed-Upon Procedures Engagement to Assist Management in Evaluating the Effectiveness of Its Corporate Compliance Program*
Derivatives	*Performing Agreed-Upon Procedures Engagements That Address Internal Control over Derivative Transactions as Required by the New York State Insurance Law*
Greenhouse Gases	*Attest Engagements on Greenhouse Gas Emissions Information*
Health Care	*Auditing Health Care Third-Party Revenues and Related Receivables*
Insurance	*Auditing Insurance Entities' Loss Reserves*
	Auditing Property/Casualty Insurance Entities' Statutory Financial Statements Applying Certain Requirements of the NAIC Annual Statement Instructions
	Auditing the Statement of Social Insurance
Investment Companies	*Attestation Engagements That Address Specified Compliance Control Objectives and Related Controls at Entities That Provide Services to Investment Companies, Investment Advisers, or Other Service Providers*
Investments	*Reporting Pursuant to the Global Investment Performance Standards*
XBRL	*Performing Agreed-Upon Procedures Engagements That Address the Completeness, Accuracy, or Consistency of XBRL-Tagged Data*

To order the guides, call 888-777-7077 or go to www.aicpa.org.

APPENDIX D:
OTHER AUDITING PUBLICATIONS IN THE GAAS HIERARCHY

LIST OF AUDITING PRACTICE RELEASES, CURRENT AICPA RISK ALERTS, AICPA TECHNICAL PRACTICE AIDS, AND OTHER PUBLICATIONS

Auditing Practice Releases

Auditing Practice Releases (formerly titled *Auditing Procedures Studies*) provide practitioners with nonauthoritative practical assistance concerning auditing procedures. The releases available from the American Institute of Certified Public Accountants (AICPA) are listed below.

- *The Information Technology Age: Evidential Matter in the Electronic Environment* (1997)
- *Confirmation of Accounts Receivable* (1995)

Current AICPA Risk Alerts

- Communicating Internal Control Related Matters in an Audit
- Compilation and Review Developments
- Employee Benefit Plans Industry Developments
- Financial Institutions Industry Developments: Including Depository and Lending Institutions and Brokers and Dealers in Securities
- General Accounting and Auditing Developments
- Government Auditing Standards and Circular A-133 Developments
- Health Care Industry Developments
- Independence and Ethics Developments
- Insurance Industry Developments
- Investment Companies Industry Developments
- Not-for-Profit Entities Industry Developments
- Real Estate and Construction Industry Developments
- State and Local Governmental Developments
- Understanding the New Auditing Standards Related to Risk Assessment
- Understanding the Responsibilities of Auditors for Audits of Group Financial Statements

AICPA Technical Practice Aids, Accounting and Auditing Publications Technical Questions and Answers

- TIS Section 8000, *Audit Fieldwork*
- TIS Section 9000, *Auditor's Reports*

Other Publications

- *Accounting and Auditing for Related Parties and Related-Party Transactions Toolkit*
- *Alternative Investments—Audit Considerations* (available for download at www.aicpa.org/interestareas/frc/auditattest/fieldwork/pages/alternative_investments.aspx)
- *Auditing Recipients of Federal Awards: Practical Guidance for Applying OMB Circular A-133*
- *Audits of Futures Commission Merchants, Introducing Brokers, and Commodity Pools*
- *Fraud Detection in a GAAS Audit: SAS No. 99 Implementation Guide*
- *Applying OCBOA in State and Local Governmental Financial Statements*
- *Auditing Governmental Financial Statements: Programs and Other Practice Aids*
- *Auditing Multiemployer Plans*
- *SAS No. 70 Reports and Employee Benefit Plans*

INDEX

A

Acceptance and continuance of clients and engagements
Agreed-upon procedures attestation engagement, 843, 844, 920, 921
Comfort letters, 684
Communication with predecessor auditor, 82–84, 1047, 1048
Documentation, 1062
Fraud risk factors, 108
Group financial statement audits, 564
Information obtained from client acceptance, use of in understanding the entity, 55
Information obtained from client acceptance and evaluation process, relevance of in identifying risks of material misstatement, 1120, 1125
Initial audit engagements, 21, 1112
Internal control effectiveness engagement, 897
MD&A examination engagement, 932, 933
Opinion letters on application of accounting principles, 676
Quality control, 13, 80, 483
Service organizations, 941
Access control
IT general controls, 75
Risk, 1138
Access to documentation, 355, 359, 360, 362–364
Accountants
Communication between predecessor and successor, 1047–1050
Continuing accountant, 672, 673, 1029–1031
Predecessor accountant, 1031, 1032, 1047–1050
Principal accountant, 685, 686
Report, interim financial information, 770–772
Reporting accountant, definitions of, 672, 673
Successor accountant, 763

Accounting and Review Services Committee (ARSC)
Interpretation 11, "Required Supplementary Information That Accompanies Reviewed Financial Statements," 961, 962
Interpretation 17, "Required Supplementary Information That Accompanies Compiled Financial Statements," 961, 962
Statements on Standards for Accounting and Review Services. *See* **Statements on Standards for Accounting and Review Services (SSARS)**
Accounting change, 444, 475. *See also* **Consistency of Application of Generally Accepted Accounting Principles (AU 420)**
Accounting estimates
Auditing, 211, 212, 385–392
Changes in, 447
Communication with those charged with governance, 427
Defined (AU 342), 385, 386
Defined (AU-C 540), 212, 386
Defined (AU-C 560), 620, 632
Reviewing for biases that could result in fraud, 102
Accounting guides, App. C
Accounting information system, 57, 58
Accounting methods
Cost method, 556
Equity method, 270, 273, 274, 277, 550, 556, 906, 1094
Accounting policies
Communication with those charged with governance, 427
Management responsibility for, 7
Accounting practices, 1143, 1144
Accounting principles
Auditor's awareness of methods of application, 440

Auditor's judgments about quality of, 424, 426–428
Changes in, 446, 447, 1099–1101
Defined (AU 420), 444
Departure from, 472
Foreign countries, 540–544. *See also* **Reporting on Financial Statements Prepared for Use in Other Countries (AU 534)**
Reports on the application of, 671–678
Accounting Principles Board (APB)
APB Opinion 20, *Accounting Changes*, 444, 445
APB Opinion 28, 448
Accounting records, defined (AU-C 500), 206
Accounting Series Release (ASR) 274, 751
Accounting Standards Codification (ASC)
ASC 450, *Accounting for Contingencies,* 292, 337, 339, 340
ASC 815, *Accounting for Derivative Instruments and Hedging Activities,* 270, 271
ASC 850, *Related-Party Disclosures,* 311–314, 319
ASC 860, *Transfers and Servicing,* 328–331
ASC 932-235, *Extractive Activities – Oil and Gas Notes to Financial Statements,* 610–612
Accounts receivable
Compilation report, illustration, 1021
Confirmation of. *See* Confirmation Process (AU 330)
Defined (AU 330), 238
Adequacy of Disclosure in Financial Statements (AU 431), 451–453
Applicability, 451
AU-C 705, *Modifications to the Opinion in the*

Independent Auditor's Report, 451, 452
  Definitions, 451
  Disclosure checklists, use of, 453
  Effective date, 451
  Failure of client to disclose required information, 452, 453
  Fundamental requirements, 452, 453
  Material misstatements, 1101
  Objectives, 452
  Original pronouncement, 451
  Techniques for application, 453
Adherence to GAAP (AU 410)
  Applicability, 437
  AU-C 700, *Forming an Opinion and Reporting on Financial Statements,* 437–439
  Auditor's report and note to financial statements for Rule 203 departure, illustration, 441
  Definitions, 438
  Effective date, 437
  Fundamental requirements, 439, 440
  Interpretations, 440
  Objectives, 438
  Original pronouncements, 437
  Techniques for application, 440
Adjustment events, 619, 621
Administration of quality control system, 14
Adverse opinions, 465–467, 473–476, 484–486, 492, 509–511, 860, 861
Affiliate, defined (AU 334), 311
Agreed-Upon Procedures Engagements (AT 201)
  Acceptance of, 843, 844
  Applicability, 841
  Assertion, 842–845, 847, 848
  Attestation standards. *See* **Attest Engagements (AT 101)**
  Change to/from another engagement, 846
  Communications, 847
  Compliance attestation. *See* **Compliance Attestation (AT 601)**
  Definitions, 842

Effective date, 841
Engagement letter, 846, 847
Forecasts and projections, 841, 862. *See also* **Financial Forecasts and Projections (AT 301)**
Fundamental requirements, 842–846
Illustrations, 848–851
Independence, 843, 844, 846
Internal auditors or others, involvement of, 844
Objectives, 842
Original pronouncement, 841
Outside matters, knowledge of, 846
Procedures, 845, 847, 848
Prospective financial statements, 862
Reports, 844, 845, 848–851
Representation letter, 845, 846, 848
Specialists, involvement of, 844, 845, 847
Standards, 842
Subject matter, 842–845, 847, 848
Techniques for application, 846–848
AICPA (American Institute of Certified Public Accountants)
  Inquiries as to reputation and independence of other auditors, 555, 574
  Peer Review Program, 574
  Prospective Financial Information Guide, 854, 856, 857, 864, 872, 873, 875
  Understanding the Responsibilities of Auditors for Audits of Group Financial Statements – 2012, 561, 562
AICPA Accounting Guides, App. C
AICPA Audit Guides
  Auditing Derivative Instruments, Hedging Activities, and Investments in Securities, 270, 271
  List of, App. C
  Specialists, use of, 333
AICPA Code of Professional Conduct
  Applicability of, 540
  Attest engagements, 819
  Auditor independence, 10

Interpretation 101.11, *Modified Application of Rule 101 for Engagements Performed in Accordance with Statements on Standards for Attestation Engagements,* 846
Rule 202, Compliance with Standards, 9
Rule 203, 439–441, 472
AICPA PITF Practice Alerts. *See* **PITF Practice Alerts**
Alert That Restricts the Use of the Auditor's Written Communication (AU-C 905)
  Definitions, 532
  Effective date, 531
  Illustrations, 535–537
  Objectives, 533
  Sections related to the restricted use of auditor's written communication, 532, 535
  Summary of changes, 531, 532
Allied Crude Vegetable Oil Company case (DeAngelis fraud), 808
American Bar Association (ABA)
  Code of Professional Ethics, 348
  Statement of Policy (inquiries of lawyers), 338, 339
American Institute of Certified Public Accountants. *See* **AICPA (American Institute of Certified Public Accountants)**
Analytical procedures. *See also* **Analytical Procedures (AU 329); Analytical Procedures (AU-C 520)**
  Audit evidence, 1149
  Audit planning, 98, 110, 222, 223, 231, 232
  Defined (AU 329), 221
  Defined (AU-C 520), 222
  Results of audit of financial statements, evaluating, 1141, 1142
  Review engagements, 1009, 1010
  Risk assessment, 1126
  Types of, 225
Analytical Procedures (AU 329)
  Accounting estimates, 392
  Applicability, 221

AU-C 520, *Analytical Procedures,* 221–223
  Definitions, 221
  Documentation, 234
  Documentation requirements, 366
  Effective date, 221
  Fundamental requirements, 223, 224
  Illustrations, 234–236
  Interim financial information, review of, 774, 775
  Objectives, 222
  Original pronouncement, 221
  PITF Practice Alerts, 224, 225
  Techniques for application, 225–234
Analytical Procedures (AU-C 520)
  Definitions, 222
  Documentation requirements, 368
  Effective date, 221
  Objectives, 222, 223
Annual reports, 11, 481, 694, 754, 827, 894, 1089, 1092. *See also* **Form 10-K**
Applicable compliance requirements, defined (AU-C 935), 796
Applicable financial reporting framework
  Defined (AR 60-90), 962
  Defined (AU 558), 607
  Defined (AU-C 200), 2, 3
  Defined (AU-C 730), 608
Applicable risk of noncompliance, defined (AU 801), 795
Application controls, defined (AU 314), 50
Applied criteria, 594, 595, 597, 606
Appropriateness (of audit evidence)
  Defined (AU 326), 205
  Defined (AU-C 200), 3
  Defined (AU-C 500), 207
  Defined (PCAOB 15), 1147
  General guides (AU-C 500), 207
Arm's-length transaction, defined (AU-C 550), 312
ASC. *See* **Accounting Standards Codification (ASC)**
Assembly, defined (AT 301), 854

Assertion-level risk, 60
Assertion(s)
  Agreed-upon procedures engagements, 842–846
  Defined (AT 101), 815
  Defined (AU 326), 205, 206
  Defined (AU-C 315), 51
  Derivatives and securities, 271–285
  Procedures or evidential matter that may support specific assertions, source list, 152–159
  Use of, 208
Assessed level of control risk, defined (AU 314), 50
Assistants
  Defined (AU 311), 17
  Instructing, 21, 22
  Supervision of, 21, 22
Association with Financial Statements (AU 504)
  Applicability, 455
  AU-C 600, *Special Considerations – Audits of Group Financial Statements (Including the Work of Component Auditors)* (AU-C 600), 455
  Definitions, 455
  Effective date, 455
  Fundamental requirements, 456–460
  Illustrations, 461, 462
  Interpretations, 460
  Objectives, 456
  Original pronouncements, 455
  SEC filings, 461
  Tax return reporting, 460, 461
  Techniques for application, 460, 461
Assurance engagement, defined (AR 60-90), 962
Attest engagement(s). *See also* **Attest Engagements (AT 101)**
  Attest assurance levels, 817
  Attestation standards, 818–825, 829, 830
  Client, establishing an understanding with, 826
  Client-prepared document containing attest report, other information in, 827, 828
  Compliance attestation. *See* **Compliance Attestation (AT 601)**
  Defined (AR 60-90), 962

  Definitions, 815, 816
  Documentation, 825, 826
  Pro forma financial information. *See* **Pro forma financial information**
  Professional requirements, 816
  Quality control standards, 825
  Reports, 822, 823, 825, 827, 828, 833–840
  Representation letter, 826, 827
  Standards, 818–825, 829, 830
  Subsequent events, 828
Attest Engagements (AT 101)
  Applicability, 815
  Definitions, 815, 816
  Effective date, 815
  Examinations reports, illustrations of, 833–838
  Fundamental requirements, 818–828
  GAAS standards compared, 828–830
  Interpretations, 830–832
  Objectives, 817, 818
  Original pronouncements, 815
  Professional requirements in SSAEs, defining, 816
  Review reports, illustrations of, 838–840
Attestation risk
  Defined (AT 101), 816
  Defined (AT 601), 918
Attorney-client privilege, 339–341, 343, 345
Attorneys
  On board of directors, 347
  Consultation with on subsequent discovery of facts existing at date of auditor's report, 633, 635
  Inquiries of. *See* **Inquiry of a Client's Lawyer Concerning Litigation, Claims, and Assessments (AU 337)**
Attribute sampling, 401
Audit(s)
  Change to compilation engagement, 971, 1002
  Change to review engagement, 979, 1002
  Conduct of. *See* **Overall Objectives of the Independent Auditor and the Conduct of an Audit in Accordance with Generally**

Index

Accepted Auditing Standards (AU-C 200)
Defined (AU 508), 466
Engagement quality review (PCAOB 7), 1103–1106
Of financial statements, 161–172, 1141–1144
Internal control matters identified in. *See* **Communicating Internal Control Related Matters Identified in an Audit (AU 325)**
Of internal control over financial reporting, 1145. *See also* **Internal control over financial reporting**
Laws and regulations, consideration of in audit of financial statements. *See* **Consideration of Laws and Regulations in an Audit of Financial Statements (AU-C 250)**
Part of performed by other independent auditors. *See* **Part of Audit Performed by Other Independent Auditors (AU 543)**
Supervision of, 2, 21, 22, 1113, 1114
Audit committee
Communication with. *See* **Auditor's Communication with Those Charged with Governance (AU 380)**
Communication with regarding possible fraud, 104, 105
Fraud inquiries, 97
Inquiries about risks of material misstatement, 1127–1129
Internal auditors access to, 166
Oversight of management, 113
Audit Considerations Relating to an Entity Using a Service Organization (AU-C 402)
Definitions, 175, 176
Effective date, 173
Objectives, 177
Summary of changes, 173, 174
Audit differences, 41, 42
Audit Documentation (AU 339). *See also* **Documentation**
Applicability, 355

AU-C 230, *Audit Documentation,* 355, 356, 368
Client preparation of, 361
Deficiencies, 362
Effective date, 355
Fundamental requirements, 357–359
Illustrations, 362–367
Interpretations, 359, 360
Objectives, 356
Original pronouncement, 355
Preparation of, 360, 361
Quality of, 361, 362
SSAE 11, *Attest Documentation,* 815, 818
Standardization, 360
Techniques for application, 360–362
Audit Documentation (AU-C 230). *See also* **Documentation**
Audit documentation requirements in other AU-C sections, 368
Definitions, 355, 356
Effective date, 355
Objectives, 356
Audit Documentation (PCAOB 3). *See also* **Documentation**
Applicability, 1059
Definitions, 1059, 1060
Effective date, 1059
Fundamental requirements, 1060–1064
Objectives, 1060
Audit evidence
Appropriateness, 3, 207, 1147
AU-C 500, *Audit Evidence,* 205–208, 325
AU-C 620, *Using the Work of an Auditor's Specialist,* 325
AU 326, *Audit Evidence,* 205–210
Audit procedures for obtaining, 208, 209, 1149
Company-provided information, 1148
Defined (AU 326), 206
Defined (AU-C 200), 3
Defined (AU-C 500), 207
Defined (PCAOB 15), 1147
Documentation, 138
Evaluating, 103, 104, 138, 1144. *See also* **Performing Audit Procedures in Response to Assessed Risks and Evaluating the Audit**

Evidence Obtained (AU 318)
Evaluating analytical procedures as part of, 110
Evidential matter supporting specific assertions, examples of, 152–159
Fair value measurements and disclosures, 213, 216
Inconsistency in, or doubts about the reliability of, 1150
PCAOB 15, *Audit Evidence,* 1147–1150
Relevance and reliability, 1148, 1150
Selecting items for testing to obtain audit evidence, 1149, 1150
Specific considerations. *See* **Audit Evidence – Specific Considerations for Selected Items (AU-C 501)**
Sufficiency of, 3, 164, 207, 208, 1147
Audit Evidence (AU 326)
Applicability, 205
AU-C 500, *Audit Evidence,* 205–208
Definitions, 205, 206
Effective date, 205
Fundamental requirements, 208, 209
Interpretations, 209, 210
Objective, 207
Original pronouncements, 205
Audit Evidence (AU-C 500)
AU-C 620, *Using the Work of an Auditor's Specialist,* 325
Definitions, 206, 207
Effective date, 205
Objective, 207, 208
Summary of changes, 205
Audit Evidence (PCAOB 15)
Applicability, 1147
Definitions, 1147
Effective date, 1147
Fundamental requirements, 1147–1150
Objectives, 1147
Audit Evidence – Specific Considerations for Selected Items (AU-C 501)
Documentation requirements, 368
Effective date, 255, 269, 337, 807

Index

Objectives, 256, 271, 272, 339, 809
Summary of changes, 255, 269, 270, 337, 807
Audit file, defined (AU-C 230), 355
Audit findings, 35, 39–42, 796
Audit guides, 270, 271, 296, 326, 333, 803, 917, App. C
Audit objectives, defined (AU 326), 206
Audit of Internal Control Over Financial Reporting That Is Integrated with an Audit of Financial Statements (PCAOB 5)
  Applicability, 1079
  AU 342, *Auditing Accounting Estimates,* 385
  Automated controls, 1095, 1096
  Definitions, 1079, 1080
  Effective date, 1079
  Filings under federal securities statutes, 1093
  Fundamental requirements, 1081–1096
  Illustrations, 1096, 1097
  Materiality considerations, 1115
  Objectives, 1080
  Reports, 1090–1093, 1096, 1097
  Service organizations, use of, 1094, 1095
Audit plan, 20, 21, 24, 1111
Audit planning
  Analytical procedures, 98, 110, 222, 223, 231, 232
  AU-C 320, *Materiality in Planning and Performing an Audit,* 33, 35, 36, 368
  AU 311, *Planning and Supervision. See* **Planning and Supervision (AU 311)**
  Audit of internal control over financial reporting integrated with an audit of financial statements (PCAOB 5), 1081
  Audit risk and, 35, 36, 44–47. *See also* **Audit risk**
  Defined (AU 311), 18
  Materiality, consideration of (PCAOB 11), 1115–1117
  PCAOB 9, *Audit Planning,* 1109–1112
Audit Planning (PCAOB 9)
  Applicability, 1109
  Definitions, 1109
  Effective date, 1109
  Fundamental requirements, 1109–1112
  Objectives, 1109
Audit procedures
  Adjusting, 101
  Assertions about derivatives and securities, 272
  AU 318, *Performing Audit Procedures in Response to Assessed Risks. See* **Performing Audit Procedures in Response to Assessed Risks and Evaluating the Audit Evidence Obtained (AU 318)**
  Defined (AU 100-230), 2
  Designing nature, timing, and extent of further audit procedures, 133, 134, 140–142
  Fair value measurements and disclosures, 216
  Going concerns, 373
  Litigation, claims, and assessments (other than inquiry of lawyers), 340, 341
  Litigation, claims, and assessments, inquiry of client's lawyer, 341, 342. *See also* **Inquiry of a Client's Lawyer Concerning Litigation, Claims, and Assessments (AU 337)**
  For obtaining audit evidence, 208, 209, 1149
  Public warehouses, 807–813
  Related parties, 314–317, 319
  Risk of material misstatement, auditor's response to, 1134, 1135
  Subsequent events, 622
Audit program, defined (AU 311), 18
Audit results, evaluating (PCAOB 14), 1141–1145
Audit risk
  Account level, 38
  AU 312, *Audit Risk and Materiality in Conducting an Audit. See* **Audit Risk and Materiality in Conducting an Audit (AU 312)**
  Audit planning, 35, 36, 44–47. *See also* **Audit planning**
  Consideration of, techniques for, 44–47
  Defined (AU 312), 34
  Defined (AU 350), 393
  Defined (AU-C 200), 3
  Defined (PCAOB 8), 1107
  Financial statement level, 37, 38
  General requirements, 37
  Nature of, 36
  PCAOB 8, *Audit Risk,* 1107, 1108
Audit Risk (PCAOB 8)
  Applicability, 1107
  Audit risk, 1107, 1108
  Definitions, 1107
  Detection risk, 1108
  Effective date, 1107
  Fundamental requirements, 1107, 1108
  Objectives, 1107
  Risk of material misstatement, 1108
Audit Risk and Materiality in Conducting an Audit (AU 312)
  Applicability, 33
  AU-C 320, *Materiality in Planning and Performing an Audit,* 33, 35, 36
  AU-C 450, *Evaluation of Misstatements Identified During the Audit,* 33, 35–37
  Audit risk model (AR), 35, 38, 52
  Definitions, 34, 35
  Documentation requirements, 365
  Effective date, 33
  Fair value of derivatives and securities, 274
  Fundamental requirements, 37–41
  Objectives, 35
  Original pronouncement, 33
  PITF Practice Alerts, 41, 42
  Techniques for application, 42–48
Audit risk model (AR), 35, 38, 52, 132
Audit risk of noncompliance, defined (AU-C 935), 796
Audit sampling. *See also* **Audit Sampling (AU 350); Audit Sampling (AU-C 530)**

Defined (AU 350), 393, 395
Defined (AU-C 530), 394
PCAOB 15, *Audit Evidence,* 1150
Audit Sampling (AU 350)
Aggregation of misstatements, 397
Applicability, 393
AU-C 530, *Audit Sampling,* 393–396
Balance sheet and income statement sampling, 398
Confidence factors, 407, 408
Confidence limits, 409–416
Definitions, 393, 394
Documentation of procedures, 402, 403, 406
Dollar value sampling (probability proportional to size), 406, 408, 410–412, 415, 416
Effective date, 393
Fundamental requirements, 396–398
Interpretations, 398
Judgment sampling (nonstatistical sampling), 395–406
Nonsampling, 397–399
Nonstatistical sampling (judgment sampling), 395–406
Objectives, 395, 396
Original pronouncements, 393
Projection of misstatements, 397
Quantitative and qualitative aspects of sample results, 397, 398
References, 417
Sample selection, 396
Sample size, 397
Statistical audit sampling, 395, 398–400, 406–416
Statistical plan formula, 47
Stratification, 395, 396
Substantive tests, 394, 397, 399, 400, 402–411
Techniques for application: nonsampling, 398, 399
Techniques for application: nonstatistical audit sampling, 399–406
Techniques for application: statistical audit sampling, 406–416

Tests of controls, 394, 397–403, 406–408, 410
Unexamined sample items, 397
Audit Sampling (AU-C 530)
Definitions, 394, 395
Effective date, 393
Objectives, 396
Audit strategy, 20, 21, 24, 38, 39, 214, 1110, 1111. *See also* **Audit planning**
Audit team, discussion among, 55. *See also* **Engagement team**
Auditing Accounting Estimates (AU 342)
Accounting estimates, examples of, 386, 392
Applicability, 385
AU-C 540, *Auditing Accounting Estimates, Including Fair Value Accounting Estimates and Related Disclosures,* 211–213, 385–387
Circumstances that require accounting estimates, identifying, 390, 391
Definitions, 385, 386
Effective date, 385
Evaluating reasonableness, 386–389, 391, 392
Fair value estimates, 212
Fair value of derivatives and securities, 274
Fundamental requirements, 387, 388
Interpretations, 388, 389
Objectives, 386
Original pronouncement, 385
Subsequent events, 388, 392
Techniques for application, 389–392
Auditing Accounting Estimates, Including Fair Value Accounting Estimates, and Related Disclosures (AU-C 540)
AU-C 501, *Audit Evidence – Specific Considerations for Selected Items,* 269
Definitions, 212, 386
Documentation requirements, 368
Effective date, 211, 385
Objective, 213, 387
Summary of changes, 211, 385

Auditing Derivative Instruments, Hedging Activities, and Investments in Securities (AU 332)
Applicability, 269
AU-C 501, *Audit Evidence – Specific Considerations for Selected Items,* 255, 269–272, 337
Definitions, 270
Effective date, 269
Fundamental requirements, 272–278
Illustrations, 283–285
Interpretations, 278
Objectives, 271
Original pronouncement, 269
Substantive procedures, 273, 282–285
Techniques for application, 278–283
Auditing Fair Value Measurements and Disclosures (AU 328)
Applicability, 211
AU-C 540, *Auditing Accounting Estimates, Including Fair Value Accounting Estimates and Related Disclosures,* 211–213, 385–387
Definitions, 211, 212
Effective date, 211
Fundamental requirements, 213–216
Interpretations, 217
Objectives, 212
Original pronouncement, 211
Techniques for application, 217–220
Auditing Standards
ASB Clarity Project, extant AU sections mapped to AU-C sections, App. A
Defined (AU 100-230), 2
Fieldwork standards, 8
GAAS hierarchy, 8–10
General standards, 8
Reporting standards, 9
Auditor(s)
Change of, 21
Component auditors, work performed by. *See* **Special Considerations – Audits of Group Financial Statements (Including the**

Work of Component Auditors) (AU-C 600)
Defined (AU 311), 17
Defined (AU-C 200), 3
Defined (PCAOB 1), 1055
Other auditors, part of work performed by. *See* **Part of Audit Performed by Other Independent Auditors (AU 543)**
Overall objectives of. *See* **Overall Objectives of the Independent Auditor and the Conduct of an Audit in Accordance with Generally Accepted Auditing Standards (AU-C 200)**
Reports. *See* **Reports**
Responsibilities. *See* **Auditor's responsibilities**
Auditor's awareness, 440
Auditor's Communication with Those Charged with Governance (AU 380)
Applicability, 419
AU-C 260, *The Auditor's Communication with Those Charged with Governance,* 419–421
Communication process, 421, 422
Definitions, 420
Documentation requirements, 367
Effective date, 419
Fundamental requirements, 421–424
Interim financial information review, 768, 775
Judgments about quality of entity's accounting principles, 424, 426–428
Matters to be communicated, 422–424, 427, 428
Objectives, 420
Original pronouncement, 419
PITF Practice Alerts, 425, 426
Techniques for application, 427, 428
Auditor's Communication with Those Charged with Governance (AU-C 260)
Definitions, 420
Documentation requirements, 368
Effective date, 419
Objectives, 421

Summary of changes, 420
Auditor's consent, defined (AU-C 925), 750
Auditor's Consideration of an Entity's Ability to Continue as a Going Concern (AU 341)
Applicability, 369
AU-C 570, *The Auditor's Consideration of an Entity's Ability to Continue as a Going Concern,* 368–370
Audit procedures, 373
Auditor's report, 379, 380
Disclosures, 370–372, 379, 380
Documentation requirements, 367, 372
Effective date, 369
Financial statement effects, 379
Fundamental requirements, 371, 372
Going concern checklist, 380–383
Indications of problems, 374
Interpretations, 372, 373
Management forecasts, consideration of, 377, 378
Management's plans, consideration of, 374–377
Objectives, 370
Original pronouncements, 369
Techniques for application, 373–380
Auditor's Consideration of an Entity's Ability to Continue as a Going Concern (AU-C 570)
Definitions, 370
Documentation requirements, 368
Effective date, 369
Objectives, 370
Summary of changes, 369
Auditor's Consideration of the Internal Audit Function in an Audit of Financial Statements (AU 322)
Applicability, 161
AU-C status, 161
Checklist for using work of internal auditors, 169–171
Definitions, 161
Effective date, 1161
Flow chart, 172
Fundamental requirements, 163, 164
Objectives, 162, 163

Original pronouncement, 161
Techniques for application, 165–169
Auditor's opinion. *See* **Opinions**
Auditor's point estimate or auditor's range
Defined (AU-C 540), 212, 386
Defined (AU-C 560), 620, 632
Auditor's Responses to the Risks of Material Misstatement (PCAOB 13)
Applicability, 1133
Definitions, 1133
Effective date, 1133
Fundamental requirements, 1133–1139
Objectives, 1133
Auditor's responsibilities
Accounting estimates, 387
AU 100-230, 1–15
Compliance with GAAS and SAS, 12
Fundamental requirements, 7
Professional requirements, 7, 8
Summary of changes, 2
Understanding with client, 19, 23
Auditor's Responsibilities and Functions, Introduction to GAAS, and the General Standards (Including the Quality Control Standards) (AU 100-230)
Applicability, 2
AU-C 200, *Overall Objectives of the Independent Auditor and the Conduct of an Audit in Accordance with Generally Accepted Auditing Standards,* 2–6
AU-C 220, *Quality Control for an Engagement Conducted in Accordance with Generally Accepted Auditing Standards,* 2, 5–7, 17
Due professional care in performance of work, 11
Effective date, 1
Fundamental requirements, 7
GAAS hierarchy, 8–10
Independence, 10
Objectives, 6
Original pronouncements, 1
Professional requirements in SAS, 7, 8

Quality control standards, 10
Techniques for application, 11–14
Training and proficiency of independent auditor, 10
Auditor's specialist, defined (AU-C 620). See also Specialists
Auditor's standard report, defined (AU 508), 466
Automated controls, 907, 1095, 1096
Awareness letter, defined (AU-C 925), 750

B

Balance sheet
Audit sampling, 398
Date of, 619–621, 623, 624. See also **Subsequent events**
Bank trust departments, 173, 176. See also **Service Organizations (AU 324)**
Basic financial statements
Defined (AU 558), 607
Defined (AU-C 730), 608
Basis for auditor's opinion, 439
Blank form of confirmation request, defined (AU 330), 238
Block sampling, 400
Board of directors
Attorneys as members of, 347
Communication with. See **Auditor's Communication with Those Charged with Governance (AU 380)**
Broker-dealers, comfort letters to. See **Comfort letters**
Business risk
Defined (AU 312), 34
Defined (AU-C 315), 51
Entity and its environment, 56

C

Capsule financial information, 680–682, 689, 690
Carve-out method, defined (AT 801), 939
Cash flow, changes in presentation of, 447
Cash receipts and disbursements basis of accounting, 640
Change in accounting principle, defined (PCAOB 6), 1099
Change in classification, 1101
Change in engagement
From audit or review to compilation, 971, 1002
From audit to review, 979, 1002
Change in reporting entity, defined (PCAOB 6), 1099
Change of auditors, 82, 83, 483, 484, 554. See also **Communications Between Predecessor and Successor Auditors (AU 315)**
Change period
Defined (AU 634), 680
Defined (AU-C 920), 682
Changes during course of audit, 1112
Clean cutoff approach, 621
Client consent and acknowledgment letter (AU 315), 86
Client-prepared documents, 596–599, 920, 1033
Clients
Acceptance and continuance of. See **Acceptance and continuance of clients and engagements**
Accounting estimates, responsibility for, 389, 390
Attest engagements, 826
Attorney-client privilege, 339–341, 343, 345
Audit documentation, preparation by, 361
Continuing clients, obtaining business information from, 66, 67
Documents prepared by, 596–599, 920, 1033
Entity and its environment. See **Entities**
Failure of client to disclose required information, 452, 453
Illegal acts by. See **Illegal Acts by Clients (AU 317)**
Interim financial information, written understanding of engagement to review, 761, 762
New clients, understanding business of, 64–66
Refusal to disclose facts, 432, 634

Small nonpublic clients, auditor's relationship with, 292, 293
Specialist, engagement letter, 334, 335
Specialist, relationship to, 327, 332
Unaudited financial statements, naming of auditor in, 460
Understanding with, establishing, 19, 20, 23, 24
Without legal representation, 346
Closest reasonable estimate, 40
Closing date
Defined (AU 634), 680
Defined (AU-C 920), 682
Collateral, in fair value evaluations, 276
Comfort letters
Concluding paragraph, 694
Defined (AU 634), 680, 681
Defined (AU-C 920), 682
Draft form, 685
Format and contents of, 686–689
Illustrations of, 697–748
Information other than audited financial statements, commenting on, 89–693
Negative assurance, 684, 688–693, 695, 697, 698
Parties issued to, 679, 680
Representation letter, 684, 685
Standards, 686
Subsequently discovered matters, disclosure of, 694
Committee of Sponsoring Organizations of the Treadway Commission (COSO), 112, 113, 271, 895, 896
Commodity warehouse, defined (AU 901), 807
Common-size financial statements, 225, 229, 231, 232
Communicating Internal Control Related Matters Identified in an Audit (AU 325)
Applicability, 193
AU-C 265, *Communicating Internal Control Related Matters Identified in an Audit,* 193–195, 203, 204

Index

Communication indicating that no material weaknesses were identified, illustration, 202
Communication regarding significant deficiencies and material weaknesses, illustration, 201, 202
Definitions, 194
Effective date, 193
Fundamental requirements, 195–198
Interim financial information review, 769
Interpretations, 198
Objectives, 195
Original pronouncements, 193
Techniques for application, 199–201

Communicating Internal Control Related Matters Identified in an Audit (AU-C 265)
Communication indicating that no material weaknesses were identified, illustration, 204
Communication regarding significant deficiencies and material weaknesses, illustration, 203
Definitions, 194, 195
Documentation requirements, 368
Effective date, 193
Objectives, 195
Summary of changes, 193, 194

Communications
About possible fraud, 104, 105
Agreed-upon procedures engagement, 847
Compilation engagements, 971
Deficiencies and material weaknesses in internal controls, 902, 903
Electronic, 243
Fair value measurements, 216
Internal control related matters. See **Communicating Internal Control Related Matters Identified in an Audit (AU 325)**
Matters related to audit of internal control over financial reporting (PCAOB 5), 1090

Between predecessor and successor accountant, 1047–1050
Between predecessor and successor auditor, 79–91
Review engagements, 979
With those charged with governance. See **Auditor's Communication with Those Charged with Governance (AU 380)**
With underwriter, 685

Communications between Predecessor and Successor Accountants (AR 400)
Applicability, 1047
Definitions, 1047
Effective date, 1047
Fundamental requirements, 1048
Illustrations, 1049, 1050
Interpretations, 1049
Objectives, 1047
Original pronouncements, 1047
Techniques for application, 1049

Communications Between Predecessor and Successor Auditors (AU 315)
Applicability, 80
AU-C 210, *Terms of Engagement,* 79, 80
AU-C 510, *Opening Balances – Initial Audit Engagements, Including Reaudit Engagements,* 79–82, 88–91
Client consent and acknowledgment letter, illustration, 86
Definitions, 80
Effective date, 79
Fundamental requirements, 82–85
Initial audits, 1112
Interim financial information review, 775
Objectives, 81
Original pronouncement, 79
PITF Practice Alerts, 85
Prior to acceptance of engagement, 676
Reissuance of predecessor auditor's report, 477, 478, 484

Successor auditor acknowledgment letter, illustration, 87
Techniques for application, 85, 86

Comparative financial statements
Auditor's report, illustration, 499
Condensed financial statements, 598
Defined (AR 200), 1029
Defined (AU-C 700), 438, 467
Reports on, 476–478

Comparative information, defined (AU-C 700), 438, 467

Comparison date and comparison period, defined (AU-C 920), 682

Comparisons (analytical procedures), 221, 222, 224–227, 229–233

Competence, defined (PCAOB 5), 1079

Competence and objectivity of internal auditors, assessment of, 163, 164, 898

Compilation and Review of Financial Statements (AR 60-90)
Applicability, 961
Change from audit to compilation engagement, 971
Compilation engagement illustrations, 992–999
Compilation of financial statements, 965–971
Definitions, 962, 963
Effective date, 961
Elements of engagement, 964, 965
Fundamental requirements, 964–979
Interpretations, 980–992
Materiality, 965
Objectives and limitations of engagements, 963, 964
Original pronouncement, 961
Recent developments, 961, 962
Review engagement illustrations, 999–1016
Review of financial statements, 971–979

Compilation engagements

Communications between predecessor and successor accountants, 1047–1050
Financial statements. *See* **Compilation and Review of Financial Statements (AR 60-90)**
Pro forma financial information, 1023–1027
Prospective financial statements, 854
Reports on financial statements included in prescribed forms. *See* **Compilation Reports on Financial Statements Included in Certain Prescribed Forms (AR 300)**
Specified elements, accounts, or items of a financial statement, 1017–1021

Compilation of Pro Forma Financial Information (AR 120)
Applicability, 1023
Effective date, 1023
Fundamental requirements, 1023–1025
Illustrations, 1025–1027
Objectives, 1023
Original pronouncement, 1023
Reports, 1023, 1024, 1026, 1027

Compilation of Specified Elements, Accounts, or Items of a Financial Statement (AR 110)
Applicability, 1017
Effective date, 1017
Fundamental requirements, 1017, 1018
Illustrations, 1019–1021
Independence, 1019
Objectives, 1017
Original pronouncement, 1017
Reports, 1017, 1018, 1021

Compilation Reports on Financial Statements Included in Certain Prescribed Forms (AR 300)
Applicability, 1043
Effective date, 1043
Fundamental requirements, 1043, 1044
Illustrations, 1044, 1045
Interpretations, 1044
Objectives, 1043

Original pronouncement, 1043
Preprinted reports, 1044
Prescribed form, defined, 1043
Complementary user entity controls
Defined (AT 801), 939
Defined (AU-C 402), 175
Compliance Attestation (AT 601)
Applicability, 917
Definitions, 918
Effective date, 917
Fundamental requirements: agreed-upon procedures engagement, 920–922
Fundamental requirements: examination engagement, 922–925
Fundamental requirements: general (applicable to both agreed-upon procedures and examination engagements), 919, 920
Illustrations, 927–930
Materiality, 927
Objectives, 918
Original pronouncements, 917
Planning the engagement, 925, 926
Specialists, use of, 919
Techniques for application, 925–927
AT 201, *Agreed-Upon Procedures Engagements*, 841
Compliance audit
Defined (AU 801), 795
Defined (AU-C 935), 796
Compliance Auditing Considerations in Audits of Governmental Entities and Recipients of Governmental Financial Assistance (AU 801)
Applicability, 795
AU-C 935, *Compliance Audits*, 795–799
Combined report, illustration, 804, 805
The Compliance Supplement, 803
Definitions, 795–798
Documentation, 367, 803
Effective date, 795
Fundamental requirements, 799–803
Illustration, 804, 805

Management's responsibilities, 803
Material noncompliance, 795–799, 803, 804
Objectives, 798
Original pronouncements, 795
Procedures, 803, 804
Process flow, 799–801
Reporting requirements, 801–803
Techniques for application, 803, 804
Compliance Audits (AU-C 935)
Definitions, 796–798
Documentation requirements, 368
Effective date, 795
Objectives, 798, 799
Summary of changes, 795
Compliance requirements, defined (AU-C 935), 796
Component, defined (AU-C 600), 562
Component auditor, defined (AU-C 600), 562
Component management, defined (AU-C 600), 562
Component materiality, defined (AU-C 600), 562
Components of internal control, defined (AU 314), 50
Condensed financial statements
Defined (AU-C 700), 438, 467
Reporting on, 593–606
Confidence factors, 407, 408
Confidence limits, 409–416
Confidentiality of audit documentation, 355, 359
Confirmation Process (AU 330)
Applicability, 237
AU-C 505, *External Confirmations*, 237–240
Definitions, 238
Documentation requirements, 367
Effective date, 237
Evaluating results, 242
Fundamental requirements, 240–242
Illustrations, 249–254
Interpretations, 243
Objectives, 239
Original pronouncement, 237
PITF Practice Alerts, 243, 244
Steps, 244–247
Techniques for application, 244–248

Index

Confirmation request. *See also* **Confirmation Process (AU 330)**
  Control of, 241
  Designing, 240, 241
  Negative confirmation request, 238–241, 243, 244, 249, 250, 252
  Nondelivery of, 248
  Nonresponses, 239, 241–243, 247, 248
  Positive confirmation request, 238, 239, 242–244, 249–252
  Respondent, 241
  Timing of, 244
  Unexpected response, 248

Consideration of Fraud in a Financial Statement Audit (AU 316)
  Accounting estimates, 387
  Applicability, 93
  AU-C 240 Consideration of Fraud in a Financial Statement Audit, 93–95
  Definitions, 93, 94
  Documentation requirements, 365, 366
  Effective date, 93
  Fraud risk assessment, list of conditions that may change or support, 118
  Fraudulent entries or adjustments, worksheet for identifying, 117, 118
  Fundamental requirements, 95–105
  Interim financial information, 769
  Management override of internal control, example program for, 119–122
  Objectives, 94, 95
  Original pronouncement, 93
  PITF Practice Alerts, 106, 1007
  Risk factors – fraudulent financial reporting, illustration, 114–116
  Risk factors – misappropriation of assets, illustration, 116, 117
  Techniques for application, 107–114

Consideration of Fraud in a Financial Statement Audit (AU-C 240)
  Definitions, 94
  Documentation requirements, 368
  Effective date, 93
  Objectives, 95

Consideration of Internal Control in a Financial Statement Audit (AU 319), 162

Consideration of Laws and Regulations in an Audit of Financial Statements (AU-C 250)
  Definitions, 124
  Documentation requirements, 368
  Effective date, 123
  Inherent limitations of an audit, 123
  Objectives, 125
  Summary of changes, 123, 124

Consideration of Materiality in Planning and Performing an Audit (PCAOB 11)
  Applicability, 1115
  Effective date, 1115
  Fundamental requirements, 1115–1117
  Objectives, 1115

Consideration of Omitted Procedures After the Report Date (AU 390)
  Applicability, 429
  Applying the omitted procedures, illustration, 434, 435
  AU-C 585, *Consideration of Omitted Procedures After the Report Release Date*, 430, 431
  AU 561 distinguished, 431
  Definitions, 430
  Effective date, 429
  Fundamental requirements, 432
  Objectives, 430, 431
  Original pronouncement, 429
  Techniques for application, 433, 434

Consideration of Omitted Procedures After the Report Release Date (AU-C 585)
  Definitions, 430
  Effective date, 430
  Objectives, 431
  Summary of changes, 430

Consistency of Application of Generally Accepted Accounting Principles (AU 420)
  Applicability, 443
  AU-C 708, *Consistency of Financial Statements*, 443–445
  Definitions, 444
  Effective date, 443
  Fundamental requirements, 445–448
  Interpretations, 448, 449
  Objectives, 444, 445
  Original pronouncements, 443

Consistency of Financial Statements (AU-C 708)
  Definitions, 444
  Effective date, 443
  Objectives, 445
  Summary of changes, 443, 444

Continuing accountant
  Comparative financial statement reporting, 1030, 1031
  Defined (AR 200), 1029
  Defined (AU 625), 672
  Defined (AU-C 915), 673

Continuing auditor, defined (AU 508), 466

Control, defined (AU 334), 311

Control activities, 57, 1124

Control deficiency
  Defined (AU 325), 194
  Evaluation of, 199, 200
  Examples of circumstances that may be control deficiencies, significant deficiencies, or material weaknesses, 200, 201

Control deficiency – design, defined (AU 325), 194

Control deficiency – operation, defined (AU 325), 194

Control environment, 56, 899, 1123

Control objective
  Defined (AT 501), 894
  Defined (AT 801), 939
  Defined (PCAOB 4), 1065
  Defined (PCAOB 5), 1079

Control risk
  Audit planning, 42, 44–47
  Compliance with specified requirements, 918
  Defined (AU 312), 34
  Defined (AU 314), 50
  Defined (AU-C 200), 5
  Defined (PCAOB 8), 1107

Derivatives and securities, 271–273, 279–281, 284
Interim testing considerations, 139, 140
Risk of material misstatement, 34, 35, 37, 38
Controls at service organization. *See* **Reporting on Controls at a Service Organization (AT 801)**
Controls at subservice organization, defined (AT 801), 939
Controls placed in operation, defined (AU 314), 50
Corroborating information, defined (AU 326), 206
Cost method of accounting, 556
Criteria
Defined (AT 101), 816
Defined (AT 801), 939
Suitability of, assessing, 941, 942
Current period
Defined (AU-C 708), 444
Defined (PCAOB 6), 1099
Cut-off date, comfort letters, 681, 682, 687

D

Data processing service centers, 173, 176. *See also* **Service Organizations (AU 324)**
Date of auditor's report. *See also* **Dating of the Independent Auditor's Report (AU 530)**
Condensed financial statements, 598
Defined (AU 530), 526
Defined (AU-C 560), 526, 619
And subsequent events, 526–530, 620, 621, 625, 626
Date of financial statements, defined (AU-C 560), 526
Dating of the Independent Auditor's Report (AU 530)
Applicability, 525
AU-C 560, *Subsequent Events and Subsequently Discovered Facts*, 525–527, 619, 632
AU-C 700, *Forming an Opinion and Reporting on Financial Statements*, 437, 526

Completion of fieldwork, 526, 527, 529, 530
Definitions, 526
Dual dated report, 526–528, 530
Effective date, 525
Filing under Securities Act of 1933, 529
Fundamental requirements, 527–529
Objectives, 526, 527
Under ordinary conditions, 527–529
Original pronouncements, 525
Reissuance of report, 526–530, 625
Subsequent discovery of facts, 529
Subsequent events, 526–528, 530
Techniques for application, 529, 530
Unaudited note, 520
Defective controls, defined (PCAOB 5), 1079
Deficiency in internal control
Defined (AT 501), 894
Defined (AU-C 265), 194
Severity of, determining, 195, 196
Deficiency in internal control over compliance, defined (AU-C 935), 796, 797
Deficiency in internal control over financial reporting, defined (PCAOB 5), 1079
Depreciation, compilation report illustration, 1021
Derivatives and securities. *See also* **Auditing Derivative Instruments, Hedging Activities and Investments in Securities (AU 332)**
Assertions, 271–285
Control risk, 271–273, 279–281, 284
Fair value, 274–276
Inherent risk, 272, 273, 279, 280
Management's ability and intent, 277, 278
Presentation and disclosures, 276
Specialists, use of, 278, 279
Substantive procedures, 273, 282–285

Design deficiency, defined (PCAOB 5), 1079
Designated accounting standard setter
Defined (AU 558), 607
Defined (AU-C 730), 608
Detection risk
Audit planning, 44–47
Audit risk, 36, 38, 52, 61, 62, 132
Audits of financial statements, 1107, 1108
Defined (AT 601), 918
Defined (AU 312), 34
Defined (AU 314), 50
Defined (AU-C 200), 3
Defined (PCAOB 8), 1107
Nonsampling considerations, 46
Sampling considerations, 46, 47
Statistical sampling, 409
Detection risk of noncompliance
Defined (AU 801), 796
Defined (AU-C 935), 797
Detective control, defined (AT 501), 894
Disclaimer of opinion. *See* **Opinions**
Disclosure events, 620–622
Disclosures
Adequacy of. *See* **Adequacy of Disclosure in Financial Statements (AU 431)**
Auditor disclosure on subsequent discovery of facts existing at date of report, 634
Client's failure to disclose required information, 452, 453
Client's refusal to disclose facts, 432, 634
Communication with those charged with governance, 427
Fair value, 216
Going concern, 370–372, 379, 380
Inadequate, 474
Loss contingencies, 339, 340. *See also* **Inquiry of a Client's Lawyer Concerning Litigation, Claims, and Assessments (AU 337)**
Newly discovered facts, 432

Related parties, 311–314, 318, 319, 321
Subsequent events, 526–530, 620–623, 625, 626
Discovery sampling, 407
Documentation. *See also* **Audit Documentation (AU 339); Audit Documentation (AU-C 230)**
  Access to, 355, 359, 360, 362–364
  Attest engagements, 825, 826
  Audit evidence, 138
  Audit procedures, 138
  Audit sampling procedures, 402, 403, 406
  Audits conducted pursuant to PCAOB standards, 1059–1064
  Audits of group financial statements, 565
  Compilation engagements, 965–967
  Completion date, defined, 356, 1059
  Confidentiality, 355, 359
  Examples of audit documentation, 356
  Fraud considerations, 105
  Internal auditors, 166, 167
  Materiality, 41
  Misstatements, 41
  Ownership, 359
  Of predecessor auditor, 83
  Prepared by client (PBC), 361
  Quality review engagement, 1106
  Records retention, 355, 356, 359, 1063, 1064
  Reports on the application of accounting principles, 677
  Requirements of AU-C sections, 368
  Requirements of AU sections, 365–367
  Review of financial statements, 972, 975
  Review of in determining importance of omitted procedures, 433, 434
  Revisions, 359
  Risk assessment, 62
  Service organizations, 944, 945
  Significant findings, 358, 359
  Standardization, 360
  Sufficiency of, 357, 358

Dollar value sampling (probability proportional to size), 406, 408, 410–412, 415, 416
Dual-dated report, 526–528, 530, 625, 626
Dual-purpose sample, defined (AU 350), 393
Dual-purpose tests, 1133, 1139
Dual statements, defined (AU 534), 540
Due care, 11
Due diligence defense, comfort letters, 680, 682–684, 718–720

E

Early appointment of independent auditor, 17, 18, 23
Economic conditions, 62, 63
Effective date
  Defined (AU 634), 681
  Defined (AU 711), 749
  Defined (AU-C 920), 682
Effective date of registration statement, defined (AU-C 925), 750
Electronic communications, 243
Emphasis-of-matter paragraph
  Defined (AU-C 706), 467
  Explanatory language, 473
Emphasis-of-Matter Paragraphs and Other-Matter Paragraphs in the Independent Auditor's Report (AU-C 706), 465–469, 479, 518–523
  AU-C sections containing requirements for emphasis-of-matter paragraphs, 523
  AU-C sections containing requirements for other-matter paragraphs, 523
  AU superseded sections, 437
  Definitions, 467, 468
  Effective date, 465
  Illustrations, 518–523
  Objectives, 469
  Summary of changes, 465, 466
Engagement acceptance, 676, 897
Engagement letter
  Agreed-upon procedures engagement, 846, 847

  AU-C 210 illustration of, 30–32
  AU illustration of, 29, 30
  Compilation engagement, 992–995
  Compilation of pro forma financial information, 1024–1026
  Compilation of specified elements, accounts, or items of a financial statement, 1018–1020
  Management representation letter, 11
  Matters covered in, 23, 24
  Review engagements, 1000, 1001
  Review of financial statements, 972
  Review of interim financial information, 761, 762, 772–774
  Understanding with client, establishing, 19, 23, 24
Engagement partner
  Auditor distinguished, 3
  Defined (AU-C 220), 5
  Defined (PCAOB 9), 1109
  Responsibilities of, 1113, 1114
Engagement quality control review, defined (AU-C 220), 5
Engagement quality control reviewer, defined (AU-C 220), 5
Engagement Quality Review (PCAOB 7)
  Applicability, 1103
  Definitions, 1103
  Documentation, 1106
  Effective date, 1103
  Fundamental requirements, 1103–1106
Engagement team
  Defined (AU-C 220), 5
  Discussion about fraud (brainstorming), 96, 1127
  Discussion about risks of material misstatement, 1126, 1127
  Selection of, 28
  Supervision of, 1113, 1114
Engagements to Report on Summary Financial Statements (AU-C 810)
  Definitions, 595
  Effective date, 593

Illustrations, 602–606
Objectives, 597
Summary of changes, 593, 594
Entities
AU-C 315, *Understanding the Entity and Its Environment and Assessing the Risks of Material Misstatement,* 49, 50, 53, 205, 368
AU 314, *Understanding the Entity and Its Environment and Assessing the Risks of Material Misstatement,* 49–77
Change in reporting entity, 446
Defined (AT 301), 854
Defined (AU-C 920), 682
Entity consent and acknowledgment letter, illustration (AU-C 510), 89, 90
And its environment, obtaining understanding of, 53–56, 62–67, 1120–1125
Multiple location entities, 900, 906, 1093, 1094, 1111, 1116
Public entity, defined (AU 504), 455
Types of, 639
Equal-probability sampling, 411–416
Equity method of accounting, 270, 273, 274, 277, 550, 556, 906, 1094
Error, defined (AU 312), 34
Estimate uncertainty, defined (AU-C 540), 212
Estimates, changes in, 447
Estimation risk, statistical sampling, 409
Estimation uncertainty, defined, 386, 620, 632
Evaluating Audit Results (PCAOB 14)
Applicability, 1141
Effective date, 1141
Fundamental requirements, 1141–1145
Evaluating Consistency of Financial Statements (PCAOB 6)
Applicability, 1099
Definitions, 1099
Effective date, 1099
Fundamental requirements, 1100, 1101

Objectives, 1099
Evaluating reasonableness of accounting estimates, 386–389, 391, 392
Evaluation of effectiveness of control design, defined (AU 314), 50
Evaluation of Misstatements Identified During the Audit (AU-C 450)
Definitions, 35
Documentation requirements, 368
Effective date, 33
Objectives, 36, 37
Summary of changes, 33
Examination of an Entity's Internal Control Over Financial Reporting That is Integrated with an Audit of Its Financial Statements (AT 501). *See also* **Communicating Internal Control Related Matters Identified in an Audit (AU 325)**
Applicability, 893
Definitions, 894
Effective date, 893
Fundamental requirements, 896–904
Illustrations, 908–915
Interpretations, 907, 908
Material weakness, 894–900, 902–906, 910–912, 914
Objectives, 894–896
Original pronouncements, 893
Reporting requirements, 904–907
Significant deficiency, 894, 902–904, 914
Examination of prospective financial statements, defined (AT 301), 854
Exception, defined (AU-C 505), 239
Experienced auditor
Defined (AU-C 230), 356
Defined (PCAOB 3), 1059
Expert testimony, 486
Expertise, defined (AU-C 620), 326
Explanatory language added to auditor's standard report, defined (AU 508), 466
External Confirmations (AU-C 505)
Definitions, 239

Effective date, 237
Objectives, 240
Summary of changes, 237, 238

F

Fair presentation framework, 3, 438, 439
Fair value
Defined (AU 328), 211, 212
Derivatives and securities, 274–276
Measurements and disclosures. *See* **Auditing Fair Value Measurements and Disclosures (AU 328)**
Significant assumptions, 214–219
Specialists, use of, 214
FASB ASC. *See* **Accounting Standards Codification (ASC)**
Federal Deposit Insurance Corporation (FDIC) Improvement Act of 1991, 895, 907, 908
Field warehouse, defined (AU 901), 808
Filing date, defined (AU 634), 681
Filings Under Federal Securities Statutes (AU 711)
Applicability, 749
AU-C 925, *Filings with the US Securities and Exchange Commission Under the Securities Act of 1933,* 749–751, 756, 757
Audit documentation, 1063
Definitions, 749, 750
Effective date, 749
Fundamental requirements, 751–754
Interpretations, 754, 755
Objectives, 750, 751
Original pronouncement, 749
Report on internal control over financial reporting, 1093
Review report included in Form 10-Q, illustration, 756
Techniques for application, 755
Filings with the US Securities and Exchange Commission Under the Securities Act of 1933 (AU-C 925)
Definitions, 750
Effective date, 749

Illustration, 756, 757
Objectives, 751
Summary of changes, 749
Financial Accounting Standards Board (FASB)
Accounting Standards Codification. *See* **Accounting Standards Codification (ASC)**
Statements of Financial Accounting Standards (SFAS). *See* **Statements of Financial Accounting Standards (SFAS)**
Financial forecasts and projections
Comfort letters, 681, 688–691, 705
Comments on a financial forecast, illustration, 735
Financial Forecasts and Projections (AT 301)
AICPA *Prospective Financial Information Guide,* 854, 856, 864
Appendices, 872–880
Applicability, 853, 854
Client-prepared document, 863, 864
Compilation of prospective financial statements, 858, 859
Compilations – training and proficiency, planning, and procedures applicable to, 872–875
Definitions, 854–855
Effective date, 853
Examination of prospective financial statements, 859–861
Examinations – training and proficiency, planning, and procedures applicable to, 875–880
Fundamental requirements: applying agreed-upon procedures to prospective financial statements, 862
Fundamental requirements: compilation of prospective financial statements, 858, 859
Fundamental requirements: examination of prospective financial statements, 859–861

Fundamental requirements: general, 856, 857
Fundamental requirements: other, 863, 864
Illustrations, 864–872
Objectives, 855, 856
Original pronouncement, 853
Partial presentation, 857
Practitioner-submitted document, 863
Presentation, 856, 857
Prospective Financial Information Guide, 854, 856, 857, 864, 872, 873, 875
Reports, 858–860, 865–872
AT 201, *Agreed-Upon Procedures Engagements,* 841, 862
Financial reporting, internal control over. *See* **Internal control over financial reporting**
Financial reporting framework
Defined (AR 60-90), 962
Defined (AU 558), 609
Defined (AU-C 200), 2, 3
Defined (AU-C 730), 608
Departures from, 968, 976
Reports on application of requirements. *See* **Reports on Application of Requirements of an Applicable Financial Reporting Framework (AU-C 915)**
Financial Reporting Release (FRR)
FRR 36, 931
Financial statement-level risk, 60, 133
Financial statements
Adherence to GAAP. *See* **Adherence to GAAP (AU 410)**
Adjustment of and dating of report, 527, 528, 530
Assertions, 1148
Association with. *See* **Association with Financial Statements (AU 504)**
AU 322, *The Auditor's Consideration of the Internal Audit Function in an Audit of Financial Statements,* 161–172
Audits of, evaluating results, 1141–1144

Common-size, 225, 229, 231, 232
Comparative, 438, 458, 459, 476–478, 499, 598, 1029–1042
Compilation and review of, 961–1016
Compilation of specified elements, accounts, or items of, 1017–1021
Condensed, 438, 593–606
Consistency of. *See* **Consistency of Application of Generally Accepted Accounting Principles (AU 420); Consistency of Financial Statements (AU-C 708)**
Defined (AR 60-90), 962
Defined (AU-C 200), 3
Disclosures, 427, 458, 526–530. *See also* **Adequacy of Disclosure in Financial Statements (AU 431)**
Documents containing, other information in, 579–582
Evaluating consistency of (PCAOB 6), 1099–1101
Evaluation of, 47, 48
Examples of, 639
Fraud. *See* **Consideration of Fraud in a Financial Statement Audit (AU 316); Consideration of Fraud in a Financial Statement Audit (AU-C 240)**
Fraud risk factors, 114–116
General purpose, 438
Going concern doubts, effect of, 379
Group financial statements. *See* **Special Considerations – Audits of Group Financial Statements (Including the Work of Component Auditors) (AU-C 600)**
Historical, 639, 886, 887
Management responsibility for, 7
Materiality level, 117, 1115, 1116
Misstatement. *See* **Misstatement**
Not in conformity with GAAP, 457, 458

Notes to containing unaudited information, 474
Notes to disclosing existence of related parties, 321
Personal, 1051–1053
Prepared for use in other countries. *See* Reporting on Financial Statements Prepared for Use in Other Countries (AU 534)
In prescribed forms, 1043–1045
Presentation of, evaluating, 1144
Previously audited, audits of, 84
Pro forma financial information. *See* **Pro forma financial information**
Prospective. *See* **Financial forecasts and projections**
Reporting on. *See* **Forming an Opinion and Reporting on Financial Statements (AU-C 700)**
Reporting on Comparative Financial Statements (AR 200), 1029–1042
Reports on audited financial statements. *See* **Reports on Audited Financial Statements (AU 508)**
Restatement of prior period financial statement, 478
Revision of due to subsequent discovery of facts, 636
Revision of financial statements reported on by predecessor auditor, 85
Source list of procedures or evidential matter that may support specific assertions, 152–159
Summary financial statements, reporting on, 593–606
Supplementary information, 583–592, 607–617
Unaudited, 455–461
Financial Statements Prepared in Accordance with a Financial Reporting Framework Generally Accepted in Another Country (AU-C 910)
Effective date, 539
Illustrations, 545–548
Objectives, 541

Summary of changes, 539
Firm, defined (AU-C 220), 5
First year audits, 448
Fischer v. Kletz (*Yale Express* case), 632, 633
Flow-of-transaction tests (walk-throughs), 398, 399
Focus groups, 147–150
Forecasts and projections. *See* **Financial forecasts and projections**
Foreign auditing standards, 541. *See also* **Reporting on Financial Statements Prepared for Use in Other Countries (AU 534)**
Foreign Corrupt Practices Act of 1977, 895
Form 8-K, 111, 433, 754
Form 10-K, 49, 694, 701, 754
Form 10-Q, 701–703, 754–756, 775
Form 11-K, 754
Forming an Opinion and Reporting on Financial Statements (AU-C 700)
AU superseded sections, 437
Date of auditor's report, 526
Definitions, 438, 467
Effective date, 437, 465
Illustrations, 499–506
Objectives, 439, 468, 469
Summary of changes, 437, 438, 465, 466
Fraud. *See also* **Consideration of Fraud in a Financial Statement Audit (AU 316); Consideration of Fraud in a Financial Statement Audit (AU-C 240)**
Actions/communications required for discovered fraud, 110–112
Antifraud programs and controls, 112, 113
Audit differences, 42
Communication about possible fraud, 104, 105, 769
Defined (AU 312), 34
Defined (AU 316), 93
Defined (AU-C 240), 94
Description and characteristics of, 107, 108
Detection of illegal acts distinguished, 128
Engagement team discussion about, 96

Inventories, 256, 258
Material fraud, 7
Misappropriation of assets, 94, 99, 101, 107, 109, 110, 116, 117
Misstatements, 34–36
Professional skepticism, 94, 96, 100, 106
Fraud risk. *See also* **Risk of material misstatement**
Analytical procedures, use of for evaluating, 222, 225, 233
AU 312, *Audit Risk and Materiality in Conducting an Audit,* 35, 42, 44–46
Auditor's response to (PCAOB 13), 1134, 1135
Evaluating conditions relating to assessment of, 1144
Factors, 93, 94, 98, 108, 1119
Identifying, 99, 108–110
Inquiries regarding, 1127–1129
Obtaining information needed to identify, 96–99
Risk assessment, 897
Significant risk, 61
Fraud Task Force (2000), 95
Further audit procedures. *See also* **Performing Audit Procedures in Response to Assessed Risks and Evaluating the Audit Evidence Obtained (AU 318)**
Defined (AU 314), 51
Defined (AU 318), 131
Designing nature, timing, and extent of, 133, 134, 140–142

G

GAAS hierarchy. *See* **Hierarchy of GAAS**
General controls, defined (AU 314), 51
General merchandise warehouse, defined (AU 901), 808
General-purpose financial statements, defined (AU-C 700), 438, 467
General-purpose framework, defined (AU-C 700), 438, 467
General use of prospective financial statements, defined (AT 301), 855

General-use reports, defined (AU 532), 532
Generally accepted accounting principles (GAAP)
  Adherence to. *See* **Adherence to GAAP (AU 410)**
  Consistency of application. *See* **Consistency of Application of Generally Accepted Accounting Principles (AU 420)**
  Defined (AU 410), 438
  Departure from, qualified and adverse opinions, 474
  Departures from, regulated companies, 577
  Fair value measurements and disclosures, 213, 214, 216
  Lack of conformity with. *See* **Lack of Conformity with Generally Accepted Accounting Principles (AU 544)**
  Uncertainties and departures from, 475
Generally accepted auditing standards (GAAS)
  Attestation standards compared, 829, 830
  Conduct of audit in accordance with. *See* **Overall Objectives of the Independent Auditor and the Conduct of an Audit in Accordance with Generally Accepted Auditing Standards (AU-C 200)**
  GAAS hierarchy. *See* **Hierarchy of GAAS**
  Quality control. *See* **Quality Control for an Engagement Conducted in Accordance with Generally Accepted Auditing Standards (AU-C 220)**
Generally accepted government auditing standards (GAGAS), 797
Going concerns. *See also* **Auditor's Consideration of an Entity's Ability to Continue as a Going Concern (AU 341)**; **Auditor's Consideration of an Entity's Ability to Continue as a Going Concern (AU-C 570)**
  Compiled financial statements, 969

  Interim financial information, 775, 778, 792, 793
  Review of financial statements, 977
Governance, those charged with (responsibility for). *See* **Those charged with governance**
Government Auditing Standards, defined (AU-C 935), 797
Government program
  Defined (AU 801), 796
  Defined (AU-C 935), 797
Governmental audit requirement, defined (AU-C 935), 797
Governmental auditing standards. *See* **Compliance Auditing Considerations in Audits of Governmental Entities and Recipients of Governmental Financial Assistance (AU 801); Compliance Audits (AU-C 935)**
Grantor, defined (AU-C 935), 797
Group, defined (AU-C 600), 562
Group audit, defined (AU-C 600), 562
Group audit opinion, defined (AU-C 600), 562
Group engagement partner, defined (AU-C 600), 562
Group engagement team, defined (AU-C 600), 562
Group financial statements, defined (AU-C 600), 562
Group management, defined (AU-C 600), 562
Group-wide controls, defined (AU-C 600), 562

H

Haphazard sampling, 400
Hedging activities and hedge accounting. *See* **Auditing Derivative Instruments, Hedging Activities and Investments in Securities (AU 332)**
Hierarchy of GAAS
  About, 8
  Illustration, 15

  Tier 1: Auditing Standards, 8, 9, 12, 15
  Tier 2: Interpretive publications, 8, 9, 12, 15
  Tier 3: Other auditing publications, 8, 10, 12, 15, App. D
Historical financial information, defined (AU-C 200), 3, 4
Historical financial statements, 639, 886, 887
Hypothetical assumption, defined (AT 301), 855
Hypothetical transactions
  Defined (AU 625), 672
  Defined (AU-C 915), 673
Hypothetical transactions, reports on, 672–674

I

Identifying and Assessing Risks of Material Misstatement (PCAOB 12)
  Applicability, 1119
  Effective date, 1119
  Fundamental requirements, 1119–1131
  Objectives, 1119
Illegal acts
  By clients, 7. *See also* **Illegal Acts by Clients (AU 317)**
  Defined (AU 317), 124
  Informing audit committee about, 769
Illegal Acts by Clients (AU 317)
  Applicability, 123
  AU-C 250, *Consideration of Laws and Regulations in an Audit of Financial Statements,* 123–125
  Definitions, 124
  Documentation requirements, 366
  Effective date, 123
  Fundamental requirements, 125–127
  Management representations, 292
  No assurance, 123, 124
  Objectives, 124, 125
  Original pronouncement, 123
  Techniques for application, 128, 129
Immediate family, defined (AU 334), 311

Impairment losses, 276
Inclusive method, defined (AT 801), 939
Inconsistency
  Defined (AU 550), 579, 580
  Defined (AU-C 720), 580
Indemnification arrangements, 19, 20, 484
Independence
  Agreed-upon procedures engagement, 843, 844, 846
  Appointment of independent auditor, 17, 18, 22, 23
  Comfort letters, 688, 689
  Compilation of specified elements, accounts, or items of a financial statement, 1019
  Described, 10
  Of other auditors, 555
  Quality control, 14
  Specialists, 335
Independence Standards Board (ISB)
  Independence Standard 1, *Independence Discussions with Audit Committees,* 425, 426
  Interpretation 00-1, 426
  Interpretation 99-1, 271
Industry comparisons, 226
Industry considerations, 62, 63
Information technology (IT)
  Application controls, 144
  Defined (AU 314), 51
  Effect of on internal control, 69–71
  Specialists, use of, 20, 21
Inherent risk
  Audit planning, 42, 44–47
  Compliance with specified requirements, 918, 923
  Defined (AU 312), 34
  Defined (AU 314), 51
  Defined (AU-C 200), 5
  Defined (PCAOB 8), 1107
  Derivatives and securities, 272, 273, 279, 280
  Risk of material misstatement, 35, 37, 38
Initial audit. *See also* **Opening Balances – Initial Audit Engagements, Including Reaudit Engagements (AU-C 510)**
  Acceptance of clients and engagements. *See* **Acceptance and continuance of clients and engagements**
  Audit planning, 1112
  Defined (AU-C 510), 80
  First year audits, 448
Inquiries
  About risk of material misstatement, 1127–1129
  Of client's lawyer. *See* **Inquiry of a Client's Lawyer Concerning Litigation, Claims, and Assessments (AU 337)**
  For review engagement, 1004–1009
Inquiry of a Client's Lawyer Concerning Litigation, Claims, and Assessments (AU 337)
  Accounting considerations, 339
  Alternative form letter of inquiry, 349, 351, 352
  Applicability, 337
  Attorney-client privilege, 339–341, 343, 345
  AU-C 501, Audit Evidence – Specific Considerations for Selected Items, 255, 269, 337–339
  Audit procedures, 340–342
  Definitions, 338
  Effective date, 337
  Fundamental requirements, 339–342
  House or inside counsel, 348
  Insurance company representation, 348
  Interpretations, 343–345
  Lawyer's response, evaluation of, 342, 347
  Letters of inquiry, illustrations, 350, 351
  Management representation when entity has no attorney, 352–354
  Objectives, 338, 339
  Original pronouncement, 337
  Refusal of attorney to respond, 349
  Resignation of attorney, 349
  Scope limitations, 342, 343, 345–349
  Subsequent events, 622
  Techniques for application, 345–349
Integrity, 14
Interim financial information. *See also* **Interim Financial Information (AU 722)**
  Engagement quality review (PCAOB 7), 1103–1106
Interim Financial Information (AU 722)
  Accompanying audited financial statements, 772
  Accountant's report, 770–772
  Additional guidance, 772, 775
  Analytical procedures, 760, 762–764, 772–775, 782, 783
  Applicability, 759
  AU-C 930, Interim Financial Information, 760, 761, 783–793
  Audit, coordination with, 766
  Audit committee, communication with, 768–770
  Auditor's report, 772
  Definitions, 760
  Documentation, 367, 768
  Effective date, 759
  Engagement letter, 761, 762, 772–774
  Fraud or illegal acts discovered, 769
  Fundamental requirements: accountant's report, 770–772
  Fundamental requirements: communication with audit committees, 768, 769
  Fundamental requirements: communication with management and audit committees, 769, 770
  Fundamental requirements: interim financial information accompanying audited financial statements, 772
  Fundamental requirements: review procedures, 761–768
  Illustrations, 775–783
  Inquiries and other procedures, 760, 762–765, 773, 775
  Management, communication with, 769, 770
  Management representation letter, 766, 767
  Material weaknesses, 770
  Objectives, 760, 761
  Original pronouncement, 759
  Other information, 772, 775
  Procedures for review of, 760–768, 772–775, 782, 783

Index

Results of review, evaluating, 767, 768
Risk of material misstatement, 1126
Significant deficiencies, 770
Subsequent discovery of facts existing at date of report, 772, 774
Successor accountant, 763
Successor auditors, 772, 775
Techniques for application, 772–775

Interim Financial Information (AU-C 930)
Definitions, 760
Documentation requirements, 368
Effective date, 760
Illustrations, 783–793
Objectives, 761

Internal audit function. *See also* **Auditor's Consideration of the Internal Audit Function in an Audit of Financial Statements (AU 322)**
Defined (AT 801), 939
Defined (AU 322), 161
Flow chart for auditor's consideration of internal audit function in audit of financial statements, 172
Obtaining an understanding of, 165, 166
Use of work in reporting on controls at a service organization, 943

Internal auditors. *See also* **Auditor's Consideration of the Internal Audit Function in an Audit of Financial Statements (AU 322)**
Checklist for using work of, 169–171
Competence and objectivity, assessment of, 163, 164, 167, 168, 898
Coordination of work, 168, 169
Defined (AU 322), 161
Direct assistance to independent auditor, 164, 169
Effect of use of work, 165, 168
Effectiveness of work, evaluating and testing, 164, 169

Fraud inquiries, 97

Internal Control Issues in Derivatives Usage **(COSO), 271**

Internal control over compliance. *See* **Compliance Attestation (AT 601)**

Internal control over financial reporting
Audit of internal control integrated with audit of financial statements (PCAOB 5), 1079–1097
Audit results, evaluating, 1145
Automated controls, 1095, 1096
Commenting on in comfort letter, 690
Communication of matters identified in an audit. *See* **Communicating Internal Control Related Matters Identified in an Audit (AU 325)**
Control environment, 56, 899, 1123
COSO framework. *See* **Committee of Sponsoring Organizations of the Treadway Commission (COSO)**
Deficiencies, 894, 902–904, 914, 1087–1089
Defined (AT 501), 894
Defined (AU 314), 50
Defined (AU-C 315), 51
Design effectiveness, 1085
Design of, evaluating, 58–62, 67–69
Effect of IT on, 69–71
Entity-level controls, 899
Financial reporting process, 899
History of public reporting on, 894–896
Identified risks, assessment of, 99, 100
Internal auditor procedures, use of, 165
Management override of controls, 99, 101–102, 387, 897, 899
Management report, illustration, 915
Management responsibility for, 7, 902, 904

Management's assertion on effectiveness of, 894, 896, 897, 901, 902, 904–907
Management's report on, 901, 902, 904, 905, 915
Material weakness, 1079–1081, 1085, 1087–1092
Nonissuers. *See* **Examination of an Entity's Internal Control Over Financial Reporting That Is Integrated with an Audit of Its Financial Statements (AT 501)**
Obtaining understanding of, 54, 56–58, 1122, 1123
Operating effectiveness, 1085
Opinion on effectiveness of, 901–903
Opinions on, illustrations, 908–914
Public warehouses. *See* **Public Warehouses: Controls and Auditing Procedures for Goods Held (AU 901)**
Quarterly disclosures, 1073
Risk assessment, 897
Service organizations. *See* **Service Organizations (AU 324)**
Tests of controls, 59, 900, 901
Tests of internal control operating effectiveness, 142–147
Top-down approach for controls selection, 1082–1085

International Accounting Standards, 544

International Standards on Auditing (ISA)
ISA 240, *The Auditor's Responsibility to Consider Fraud and Error in an Audit of Financial Statements,* 95
ISA 320, *Materiality in Planning and Performing an Audit,* 33
ISA 450, *Evaluation of Misstatements Identified During the Audit,* 33
ISA 570, *Going Concern,* 369
ISA 600, *The Work of Related Auditors and Other Auditors in the Audit of Group Financial Statements,* 561

Interpretive publications

Defined (AU-C 200), 4
GAAS hierarchy, 8, 9
Inventories. *See also* **Inventories (AU 331); Public Warehouses: Controls and Auditing Procedures for Goods Held (AU 901)**
  Cost computation, 440
  Stated below cost, 461
Inventories (AU 331)
  Applicability, 255
  AU-C 501, *Audit Evidence – Specific Considerations for Selected Items,* 255, 256, 269
  AU 337, *Inquiry of a Client's Lawyer Concerning Litigation, Claims, and Assessments,* 337
  Beginning inventory, 257
  Confirmation of inventories in public warehouses, illustration, 268
  Confirmation of inventories on consignment, illustration, 267
  Definitions, 255
  Effective date, 255
  Fraud, 256, 258
  Fundamental requirements: observation, 256, 257
  Fundamental requirements: reporting, 257, 258
  Held by custodian other than public warehouse, 259
  Held in public warehouses, 257, 259, 260, 268
  Illustrations, 263–268
  Interpretations, 258
  Objectives, 256
  Observation checklist, 263–267
  Original pronouncements, 255
  Outside inventory-taking firms, 263, 479
  Perpetual records, 256, 258
  Physical count, 255–263
  PITF Practice Alert, 258
  Scope limitations, 257, 258
  Statistical sampling methods, 256, 257
  Steps in observation of, 259–261
  Techniques for application, 258–263
  Timing and extent of observation, 258, 259
Iron curtain approach, 48

Issuer(s). *See also* **Comfort letters; Underwriter(s)**
  Audit reports, references to PCAOB standards, 1055–1058
  Defined (AR 60-90), 962
  PCAOB standards, 1055–1150
  Securities law filings. *See* **Filings Under Federal Securities Statutes (AU 711); Filings with the US Securities and Exchange Commission Under the Securities Act of 1933 (AU-C 925)**

J

Journal entries and adjustments, 101, 102, 106, 107, 117, 118
Judgment sampling (nonstatistical sampling). *See* **Audit Sampling (AU 350)**

K

Key factors
  Defined (AT 301), 855
  Defined (AU 2301), 386
Key-item tests, 398, 399
Known misstatement, 34, 37, 39, 41, 44, 47, 48
Known questioned costs, defined (AU-C 935), 797

L

Lack of Conformity with Generally Accepted Accounting Principles (AU 544)
  Applicability, 575
  AU-C 800, *Special Considerations – Audits of Financial Statements Prepared in Accordance with Special-Purpose Frameworks,* 575–577
  Definitions, 576
  Effective date, 575
  Fundamental requirements, 577
  Objectives, 576
  Original pronouncements, 575
Land recorded at appraised values, 461
Laws and regulations, consideration of in audit of financial statements. *See* **Consideration of Laws and Regulations in an Audit of Financial Statements (AU-C 250)**
Lawyers. *See* **Attorneys**
Lawyers, inquiry of. *See* **Inquiry of a Client's Lawyer Concerning Litigation, Claims, and Assessments (AU 337)**
Letters for Underwriters and Certain Other Requesting Parties (AU 634)
  Applicability, 679, 680
  AU-C 920, *Letters for Underwriters and Certain Other Requesting Parties,* 679, 681–684, 726–748
  Definitions, 680, 681
  Effective date, 679
  Fundamental requirements: commenting in a comfort letter on information other than audited financial statements, 689–693
  Fundamental requirements: format and contents of comfort letters, 686–689
  Fundamental requirements: general, 684–686
  Fundamental requirements: other matters, 694
  Illustrations of comfort letters, 697–726
  Interpretations, 694–697
  Objectives, 683, 684
  Original pronouncements, 679
  Techniques for application, 697
Letters for Underwriters and Certain Other Requesting Parties (AU-C 920)
  Definitions, 681–683
  Effective date, 679
  Illustrations, 726–748
  Objectives, 684
Likely misstatement, 34, 37, 39–41, 47, 48, 760
Likely questioned costs, defined (AU-C 935), 797
Limited distribution in the United States, defined (AU 534), 540
Limited use of prospective financial statements, defined (AT 301), 855

Liquidation basis of accounting, 479, 498, 499
Litigation services, 486
Loss contingency, defined (AU 337), 338

M

Management
Ability and intent, assertions related to, 277, 278
Assertion on effectiveness of internal control, 894, 896, 897, 901, 902, 904–907
Audit planning discussions with, 21
Bias, 212, 386, 620, 632
Communication with regarding misstatements, 39
Communication with regarding possible fraud, 104, 105
Control environment, 899
Defined (AR 60-90), 962
Defined (AU 334), 312
Defined (AU 380), 420
Defined (AU-C 200), 4
Defined (AU-C 260), 420
Discussions with, 67
Fair value measurement, responsibility for, 217
Fair value measurement, written representations regarding, 216
Fraud inquiries, 97
Inquiries about risks of material misstatement, 1127–1129
Override of controls, 99, 101, 102, 387, 897, 899
Report on internal control over financial reporting, 901, 902, 904, 905, 915
Report on whether a previously reported material weakness continues to exist, 1070
Representation letter, 11, 498, 902, 974, 1010–1016
Representations. *See* **Management representations**
Response to auditor's communication of internal control related matters, 197, 198

Responsibilities, 4, 7, 11, 23, 107, 112, 113
Senior management defined (PCAOB 5), 1080
Management Discussion and Analysis (MD&A), 775, 931–937
Management representations
AU-C 580, *Written Representations,* 287–289, 303–310
AU 333, *Management Representations. See* **Management Representations (AU 333)**
Compliance, 919, 920
Internal control over financial reporting (PCAOB 5), 1089, 1090
Regarding internal control, 902
Reporting on whether a previously reported material weakness continues to exist, 1069
Service organizations, 943, 944
Management Representations (AU 333)
Additional representations, 288, 291, 296–302
Applicability, 287
AU-C 580, *Written Representations,* 287–289, 303–310
Dating of representation letter, 287, 291, 293, 294
Definitions, 287, 288
Documentation requirements, 367
Effective date, 287
Fundamental requirements, 289–292
Illustrations, 294–303
Internal control, 902
Interpretations, 292
Management representation letter, 287–296, 302–305, 309, 310
Objectives, 288, 289
Original pronouncement, 287
Related parties, 320
Scope limitations, 292
Signing of management representation letter, 291, 293, 294

Small nonpublic clients, auditor's relationship with, 292, 293
Subsequent events, 622
Techniques for application, 292–294
Updating letters, 292, 302, 303
Management's assertion, defined (AT 501), 894
Management's Discussion and Analysis (MD&A) – A Summary (AT 701)
Applicability, 931
Effective date, 931
Fundamental requirements: examination, 932, 933
Fundamental requirements: review, 933, 934
Illustrations, 934–937
MD&A defined, 931
Negative assurance, 932
Objectives, 932
Original pronouncement, 931
Reports, 932–937
Management's point estimate
Defined (AU-C 540), 212, 386
Defined (AU-C 560), 620, 632
Management's specialist
Defined (AU-C 500), 207
Defined (AU-C 620), 326
Material error, 7
Material fraud, 7
Material misstatement. *See also* **Misstatement**
Auditor responsibilities regarding, 7
Compilation and review engagements, 1047–1050
Correction of, 1100, 1101
Fraud. *See* **Consideration of Fraud in a Financial Statement Audit (AU 316)**
In prospective financial statements, 864
Risk of. *See* **Risk of material misstatement**
Material noncompliance
Defined (AU 801), 796
Defined (AU-C 935), 797
Material weakness. *See also* **Communicating Internal Control Related Matters Identified in an Audit (AU 325)**
Defined (AT 501), 894
Defined (AU 325), 194
Defined (AU-C 265), 195

Defined (PCAOB 5), 1079, 1080
Examples of circumstances that may be control deficiencies, significant deficiencies, or material weaknesses, 200, 201
Indicators of, 196
Interim financial information, 770
Internal control over financial reporting, 1079–1081, 1085, 1087–1092
Reporting on whether previously reported material weakness continues to exist, 1065–1077

Material weakness in internal control over compliance
Defined (AU 801), 796
Defined (AU-C 935), 797

Materiality
Account level, 38
Addressing in management representation letter, 294
AU-C 320, *Materiality in Planning and Performing an Audit,* 33, 35, 36, 368
AU 312, *Audit Risk and Materiality in Conducting an Audit,* 33–48
Bases for judgment, 43
Compilation and review engagements, 965
In compliance examinations, 927
Component materiality, 562, 564
Consideration of in planning and performing an audit (PCAOB 11), 1115–1117
Defined (AU 312), 34, 35
Financial statement level, 37, 38
General requirements, 37
Nature of, 36
Performance, 564
Planning materiality, 38, 39
Preliminary judgment about, 42–44
Rule of thumb, 43, 44

Materiality in Planning and Performing an Audit (AU-C 320)
Definitions, 35
Documentation requirements, 368

Effective date, 33
Objective, 36
Summary of changes, 33

MD&A. *See* **Management Discussion and Analysis (MD&A)**

Misappropriation of assets, 94, 99, 101, 107, 109, 110, 116, 117

Misstatement. *See also* **Material misstatement**
Accumulating and evaluating, 1142, 1143
Arising from fraudulent financial reporting, defined (AU 316), 94
Arising from misappropriation of assets, defined (AU 316), 94
Defined, 4, 35
Discovery of possible misstatements in financial statements reported on by a predecessor, 84
Error, 34–36
Of fact, 580
Financial statements as a whole, 41
Fraud, 34–36
Identified during audit, evaluation of. *See* **Evaluation of Misstatements Identified During the Audit (AU-C 450)**
Nature and causes of, 36, 37
Prior period, 38, 39, 48
Qualitative characteristics of, 40

Modification of reports, 468, 484, 485, 771, 905, 1092

Modifications to the Opinion in the Independent Auditor's Report (AU-C 705)
AU superseded sections, 437
AU 508, *Reports on Audited Financial Statements,* 465, 467, 469, 506–518
Definitions, 452, 467
Effective date, 451, 465
Illustrations, 506–518
Objectives, 452, 469
Summary of changes, 465, 466

Modified opinion. *See also* **Modifications to the Opinion in the Independent Auditor's Report (AU-C 705)**
Defined (AU-C 705), 452, 467

Prospective financial statements, 860, 861

Monitoring
Of controls, 1125
Defined (AU-C 220), 5, 6
Internal audit function, 165
Internal control, 58
Quality control, 14

Mortgage bankers, 173, 176. *See also* **Service organizations**

N

National economic data comparisons, 226

Negative assurance
Association with financial statements, 459
Comfort letters, 684, 688–693, 695, 697, 698
Defined (AU 634), 681
Defined (AU-C 920), 682
MD&A, 932

Negative confirmation request, 238–241, 243, 244, 249, 250, 252

Negative form of confirmation request, defined (AU 330), 238

Negotiable warehouse receipt, defined (AU 901), 808

Network, defined (AU-C 220), 6

Network firm, defined (AU-C 220), 6

Noncompliance, defined (AU-C 250), 124

Nonissuer(s)
Audit documentation. *See* **Audit Documentation (AU 339); Audit Documentation (AU-C 230)**
Comparative financial statements, reporting on. *See* **Reporting on Comparative Financial Statements (AR 200)**
Defined (AR 60-90), 962
Financial statements. *See* **Consistency of Financial Statements (AU-C 708); Special Considerations – Audits of Single Financial Statements and Specific Elements, Accounts, or Items of a Financial Statement (AU-C 600); Subsequent Events and**

Subsequently Discovered Facts (AU-C 560)
Internal control over financial reporting. *See* **Examination of an Entity's Internal Control Over Financial Reporting That Is Integrated with an Audit of Its Financial Statements (AT 501)**
Representations. *See* **Management Representations (AU 333)**; **Written Representations (AU-C 580)**
Nonnegotiable warehouse receipt, defined (AU 901), 808
Nonpublic entities
Client-prepared documents, 596–598
Omitted procedures, 433. *See also* **Consideration of Omitted Procedures After the Report Date (AU 390)**
Nonresponse, defined (AU-C 505), 239
Nonsampling risk
Defined (AU 350), 393
Defined (AU-C 530), 394
Nonstatistical sampling. *See* **Audit Sampling (AU 350)**
Notification of subsequent discovery of facts existing at date of auditor's report, 635, 636

O

Objectivity, 14, 1080
Observation
Control procedures, 152
Inventories, 255–257. *See also* **Inventories (AU 331)**
Oil and gas information, 610–612
OMB Circular A-133, *Audits of States, Local Governments, and Non-Profit Organizations,* 26
Omitted procedures. *See* **Consideration of Omitted Procedures After the Report Date (AU 390); Consideration of Omitted Procedures After the Report Date (AU-C 585)**
Opening Balances – Initial Audit Engagements, Including

Reaudit Engagements (AU-C 510)
Definitions, 80, 81
Effective date, 79
Entity Consent and Acknowledgment Letter, illustration, 89, 90
Objectives, 81, 82
Report with Disclaimer of Opinion on Results of Operations and Cash Flows and Unmodified Opinion on Financial Position, illustration, 88, 89
Successor auditor acknowledgment letter, illustration, 90, 91
Summary of changes, 79, 80
Operation deficiency, defined (PCAOB 5), 1080
Opinion shopping, 673
Opinions. *See also* **Adherence to GAAP (AU 410); Reports**
Adverse, 465–467, 473–476, 484–486, 492, 509–511
Basis for, 439, 465, 469–471
Disclaimer of, 88, 89, 456, 457, 459, 460, 465–467, 473, 474, 476, 484–486, 490, 491, 495, 496, 512–518, 861
On effectiveness of internal controls, 901–903
Forming. *See* **Forming an Opinion and Reporting on Financial Statements (AU-C 700)**
Modifications, 552, 860, 861. *See also* **Modifications to the Opinion in the Independent Auditor's Report (AU-C 705)**
On one of basic financial statements, 474
Qualified opinion, 465–467, 472–475, 484–486, 490–492, 495, 507–509, 511, 512, 515, 516, 521, 522
Scope limitations, 485, 486
On supplementary information, 585–592
Unqualified opinions, 466, 471–474, 479, 484, 485
Unqualified opinions, departures from, 473–476
Ordinary audit, objective of, 7
Organization charts, 166

Organization-wide audit, defined (AU-C 935), 798
Organizational culture, 112, 113
Other auditing publications
Defined (AU-C 200), 4
GAAS hierarchy, 8, 10
Other comprehensive basis of accounting (OCBOA)
Auditor's reports issued in connection with, 638, 639, 641, 642, 647, 648, 650
Cash basis, 576, 640
Change from GAAP to, 650
Client-prepared financial statements, 976
Defined (AR 60-90), 963
Regulated companies, 576, 577, 639
Representation letter requirement, 288
Restricted reports, 533
Tax basis, 576, 640
Unaudited financial statements, 456, 457
Other independent auditor, defined (AU 543), 550
Other Information in Documents Containing Audited Financial Statements (AU 550)
Applicability, 579
AU-C 720, *Other Information in Documents Containing Audited Financial Statements,* 579, 580, 582
Definitions, 579, 580
Effective date, 579
Explanatory paragraph to disclaim an opinion on other information, illustration, 582
Fundamental requirements, 581, 582
Interim financial information review, 775
Objectives, 580
Original pronouncement, 579
Other Information in Documents Containing Audited Financial Statements (AU-C 720)
Definitions, 580
Effective date, 579
Explanatory paragraph to disclaim an opinion on other information, illustration, 582
Objective, 580

Summary of changes, 579
Other-matter paragraph, defined (AU-C 706), 468
Outcome of an accounting estimate
  Defined (AU-C 540), 212, 386
  Defined (AU-C 560), 620, 632
Overall Objectives of the Independent Auditor and the Conduct of an Audit in Accordance with Generally Accepted Auditing Standards (AU-C 200)
  Audit risk, 33
  Effective date, 2
  Objectives, 6
  Professional skepticism, 50
  Summary of changes, 2
  Superseded AU sections, 2

P

Part of Audit Performed by Other Independent Auditors (AU 543)
  Applicability, 549
  AU-C 600, *Special Considerations – Audits of Group Financial Statements (Including the Work of Component Auditors),* 549
  Definitions, 550
  Effective date, 549
  Explanatory language, 471, 472
  Fundamental requirements, 550–552
  Group Audit standard, 561
  Illustrations, 556–559
  Interpretations, 552, 553
  Objectives, 550
  Original pronouncements, 549
  Techniques for application, 553–556
Partial presentation, defined (AT 301), 855
Partner, defined (AU-C 220), 6
Pass-through entity, defined (AU-C 935), 798
Performance materiality, defined (AU-C 320), 35
Performing Audit Procedures in Response to Assessed Risks and Evaluating the Audit Evidence Obtained (AU 318)
  Accounting estimates, 388
  Applicability, 131

AU-C 330, *Performing Audit Procedures in Response to Assessed Risks and Evaluating the Audit Evidence Obtained,* 131–133
Definitions, 131, 132
Documentation requirements, 366
Effective date, 131
Fundamental requirements, 133–138
Objectives, 132
Original pronouncement, 131
Source list of procedures or evidential matter, 153–159
Techniques for application, 139–152
Performing Audit Procedures in Response to Assessed Risks and Evaluating the Audit Evidence Obtained (AU-C 330)
  Definitions, 132
  Documentation requirements, 368
  Effective date, 131
  Objective, 133
  Summary of changes, 131
Personal financial statements included in written personal financial plans, 1051–1053
Personnel
  Defined (AU-C 220), 6
  Management, 13
Pervasive, defined (AU-C 705), 452, 467
PITF Practice Alerts
  About, 10
  00-2, *Guidance for Communication with Audit Committees Regarding Alternative Treatments of Financial Information within Generally Accepted Accounting Principles (Revised),* 426
  03-01, *Audit Confirmations,* 243, 244
  03-02, *Journal Entries and Other Adjustments,* 106, 107
  94-1, *Dealing with Audit Differences,* 41, 42
  94-2, *Consideration of Fraud in Audit Procedures Related to Inventory Observation,* 258

97-3, *Changes in Auditors and Related Topics,* 85, 483, 484
98-1, *The Auditor's Use of Analytical Procedures,* 224, 225
98-2, *Professional Skepticism and Related Topics,* 106
98-3, *Responding to the Risk of Improper Revenue Recognition,* 106
99-1, *Guidance for Independence Discussions with Audit Committees,* 425, 426
99-2, *How the Use of a Service Organization Affects Internal Control Considerations,* 181
2003-3, *Acceptance and Continuance of Clients and Engagements,* 483
2004-4, *Quarterly Review Procedures for Public Companies,* 761
Planning an Audit (AU-C 300)
  Appointment of independent auditor, 18
  Audit plan, 20
  Client, establishing an understanding with, 19, 20
  Communications with management and those charged with governance, 21
  Considerations in establishing the overall audit (appendix to AU-C 300), 26–28
  Documentation requirements, 368
  Effective date, 17
  Initial audit engagements, additional considerations, 21
  Objectives, 18
  Overall audit strategy, 20
  Preliminary engagement activities, 20
  Specialized skills needed, 20, 21
  Summary of changes, 17
  Supervision, 21, 22
Planning and Supervision (AU 311)
  Applicability, 17
  AU-C 210, *Terms of Engagement,* 17, 30–32
  AU-C 300, *Planning an Audit,* 17–22, 26–28, 368
  Communications required, 25

Definitions, 17, 18
Documentation requirements, 365
Effective date, 17
Engagement letter, illustration, 29, 30
Establishing an Understanding with the Client, 23
Fundamental requirements, 18–22
Interpretations, 22
Objectives, 18
Original pronouncements, 17
Planning, 18–21
Reporting objectives, 25
Scope of audit, 25, 26
Scope of audit engagement, 24, 25
Specialists, use of, 278, 279
Supervision, 21, 22
Techniques for application, 22–28
Timing of audit, 25
Population
Defined (AU 350), 393
Defined (AU-C 530), 394
Positive confirmation request, 238, 239, 242–244, 249–252
Positive form of confirmation request, defined (AU 330), 238
Practice Alerts
AICPA PITF Practice Alerts. *See* **PITF Practice Alerts**
PCAOB Staff Audit Practice Alerts, 1056
Practitioner-in-charge, defined (AU 100-230), 2
Predecessor accountant
Communications with successor accountant, 1047–1050
Comparative financial statement reporting, 1031, 1032
Defined (AR 400), 1047
Predecessor auditor. *See also* **Communications Between Predecessor and Successor Auditors (AU 315)**
Communication with, 676
Defined (AU 315), 80
Defined (AU-C 510), 81
Facts existing at date of report, subsequent discovery of, 635
Reissuance of report, 85, 86, 477, 478, 484
Report not presented, 478

Reports included in securities filings, 751, 752
Preliminary engagement activities, 20
Premise, defined (AU-C 200), 4
Prescribed forms, compilation reports on financial statements included in, 1043–1045
Prescribed guidelines, defined (AU-C 730), 608
Present ability to support previously expressed opinion, defined (AU 390), 430
Preventive control(s)
Defined (AT 501), 894
Defined (PCAOB 5), 1080
Principal accountant, comfort letters, 685, 686
Principal auditor, defined (AU 543), 550
Principal owners, defined (AU 334), 312
Prior period misstatements, 38, 39, 48
Prior periods
Analytical procedures permanent file, 231
Updating information from, 55
Private Securities Litigation Reform Act of 1995, 110
Pro forma financial information
Comfort letters, 681, 688, 689, 691, 704, 705, 734, 735
Compilation of, 1023–1027
Conditions for reporting, 882
Defined (AT 401), 881
Engagement objectives, 882, 883
Historical financial statements, 886, 887
Nonaudit and nonreview clients, 886
Presentation of, 886
Procedures for examination or review, 883, 884
Reporting on. *See* **Reporting on Pro Forma Financial Information (AT 401)**
Reports, 884, 885, 887–892
Use of, 881, 882
Probability-proportional-to-size sampling. *See* **Dollar value sampling**
Probable, defined (AU 337), 338

Professional disagreements, 431
Professional Issues Task Force Practice Alerts. *See* **PITF Practice Alerts**
Professional judgment, defined (AU-C 200), 4
Professional requirements
Presumptively mandatory, 8, 816
Unconditional, 7, 816
Professional skepticism
Accounting estimates, 387
Audit evidence, 133, 1127
Confirmation process, 240, 241
Consideration of fraud, 94, 96, 100, 106
Defined (AU 100-230), 2
Defined (AU-C 200), 4
Defined (PCAOB 13), 1133
Exercise of, 11
Inventory audits, 258
Professional standards, defined (AU-C 220), 6
Program-specific audit, defined (AU-C 935), 798
Prospective Financial Information Guide (AICPA), 854, 856, 857, 864, 872, 873, 875
Prospective financial statement, defined (AT 301), 855
Prospectus, defined (AU 711), 750
Public companies. *See also* **Public entities**
Financial statements, association with. *See* **Association with Financial Statements (AU 504)**
Omitted procedures, 433. *See also* **Consideration of Omitted Procedures After the Report Date (AU 390)**
PCAOB standards, 1055–1150
References to standards of PCAOB in auditors' reports, 1055–1058
Public Company Accounting Oversight Board (PCAOB)
Engagement standards, 1067
Panel on Audit Effectiveness, 761
Staff Audit Practice Alerts, 1056

Staff guidance, 1056, 1057
Staff Questions and Answers, 1056
Standards, 1055–1150
Public entities. *See also* **Public companies**
  Client-prepared documents, 460, 596, 598, 599
  Defined (AU 504), 455
Public warehouses
  Controls and auditing procedures, 807–813
  Inventories held in, 257, 259, 260, 268
Public Warehouses: Controls and Auditing Procedures for Goods Held (AU 901)
  Applicability, 807
  AU-C 501, *Audit Evidence – Specific Considerations for Selected Items,* 807–809
  Definitions, 807
  Effective date, 807
  Fundamental requirements: controls for warehouseman, 809, 810
  Fundamental requirements: owner of goods, 812
  Fundamental requirements: owner's auditor, 812
  Fundamental requirements: warehouseman's auditor, 811
  Objectives, 808
  Original pronouncements, 807

Q

Qualified opinion, 466, 473–475, 860
Quality Control for an Engagement Conducted in Accordance with Generally Accepted Auditing Standards (AU-C 220)
  Definitions, 5, 6
  Documentation requirements, 368
  Objectives, 7
  Summary of changes, 2, 17
Quality control standards
  Attest engagements, 825
  Audit firms, 10, 12–14
  Engagement quality control review, 5
  Engagement quality control reviewer, 5
  Establishing, 10, 12–14

Objectives of AU 100-230, 6, 7
Quality control system, 2, 5, 6, 10, 14
Quality reviews, 1103–1106
Questioned costs, defined, 796, 798

R

Random number sampling, 400
Ratio analysis, 222, 224–228, 231–233, 235
Reasonable assurance
  Defined (AU 100-230), 2
  Defined (AU-C 200), 5
  Due professional care, 11
Reasonable period of time, defined (AU-C 570), 370
Reasonableness testing, 225
Reasonably possible, defined (AU 337), 338
Reaudits. *See* **Opening Balances – Initial Audit Engagements, Including Reaudit Engagements (AU-C 510)**
Reconciliations, 151, 152
Records retention, 355, 356, 359
References in Auditors' Reports to the Standards of the Public Company Accounting Oversight Board (PCAOB 1)
  Applicability, 1055
  Auditor, defined, 1055
  Effective date, 1055
  Fundamental requirements, 1055
  Illustrations, 1057, 1058
  Interpretation, 1057
  Other PCAOB guidance, 1055–1057
Refrigerated warehouse, defined (AU 901), 808
Registration statement, defined (AU 711), 750
Regression analysis, 221, 225, 226, 230–232
Regulated companies, 575–577
Regulation S, 680
Regulation S-K, 471, 681, 688, 693–695, 755, 931
Regulation S-X, 754, 755, 881

Reissued reports, 85, 86, 477, 478, 484, 526–530, 625, 626, 1029
Related Parties (AU 334)
  Accounting considerations, 313, 314
  Applicability, 311
  AU-C 550, *Related Parties,* 311–313, 368
  Auditing procedures, 314–317, 319
  Auditor's report paragraph calling attention to existence of related parties, illustration, 320
  Checklist, 321–323
  Definitions, 311, 312
  Disclosures, 311–314, 318, 319, 321
  Effective date, 311
  Examining related-party transactions, 320
  Existence of related parties, determining, 319
  Fundamental requirements, 313–317
  Identifying related-party transactions, 319, 320
  Interpretations, 317, 318
  Management representation letter, 320
  Objectives, 312, 313
  Original pronouncement, 311
  Preliminary evaluation of risk, 318
  Techniques for application, 318–320
Related Parties (AU-C 550)
  Definitions, 312
  Documentation requirements, 368
  Effective date, 311
  Objectives, 313
  Summary of changes, 311
Related-party transactions, 61
Relevant assertion
  Defined (AT 501), 894
  Defined (AU-C 315), 51
  Defined (PCAOB 5), 1080
Relevant ethical requirements, defined (AU-C 220), 6
Remote (chance), defined (AU 337), 338
Report on management's description of a service organization's system and the suitability of the design and

operating effectiveness of controls
  Defined (AT 801), 940
  Defined (AU-C 402), 175
Report on management's description of a service organization's system and the suitability of the design controls, defined (AU-C 402), 175
Report on management's description of a service organization's system and the suitability of the design of controls, defined (AT 801), 939
Report release date
  Defined (AU 530), 526
  Defined (AU-C 230), 356
  Defined (PCAOB 3), 1059
Reporting accountant, defined, 672, 673
Reporting on Comparative Financial Statements (AR 200)
  Definitions, 1029
  Effective date, 1029
  Fundamental requirements, 1030–1032
  Illustrations, 1034–1042
  Interpretation, 1033
  Objectives, 1029, 1030
  Original pronouncement, 1029
  Techniques for application, 1033
Reporting on Compliance with Aspects of Contractual Agreements or Regulatory Requirements in Connection with Audited Financial Statements (AU-C 806)
  Effective date, 638
  Illustrations, 665–669
  Objectives, 641
Reporting on Condensed Financial Statements and Selected Financial Data (AU 552)
  Applicability, 593
  AU-C 810, *Engagements to Report on Summary Financial Statements,* 593–595, 597, 602–606
  Definitions, 595
  Effective date, 593
  Fundamental requirements, 597–599
  Illustrations, 600–602
  Objectives, 595–597
  Original pronouncements, 593
Reporting on Controls at a Service Organization (AT 801)
  Applicability, 939
  Definitions, 939, 940
  Effective date, 939
  Fundamental requirements, 940–949
  Illustrations, 949–959
  Objectives, 940
  Original pronouncement, 939
Reporting on Financial Statements Prepared for Use in Other Countries (AU 534)
  Applicability, 539
  AU-C 910, *Financial Statements Prepared in Accordance with a Financial Reporting Framework Generally Accepted in Another Country,* 539, 541, 545–548
  Definitions, 540
  Documentation requirements, 367
  Dual statements, 540, 543, 545
  Effective date, 539
  Fundamental requirements, 541–543
  Illustrations, 545
  Interpretations, 544
  Limited distribution in the U.S., 540, 542, 543
  Objectives, 540
  Original pronouncement, 539
  Techniques for application, 544
Reporting on Personal Financial Statements Included in Written Personal Financial Plans (AR 600)
  Applicability, 1051
  Effective date, 1051
  Fundamental requirements, 1052
  Interpretations, 1052
  Objectives, 1051
  Original pronouncement, 1051
  Report, illustration, 1053
Reporting on Pro Forma Financial Information (AT 401)
  Applicability, 881
  Definitions, 881
  Effective date, 881
  Fundamental requirements, 882–885
  Illustrations, 887–892
  Objectives, 881, 882
  Original pronouncement, 881
  Techniques for application, 886, 887
Reporting on Whether a Previously Reported Material Weakness Continues to Exist (PCAOB 4)
  Applicability, 1065
  Definitions, 1065
  Effective date, 1065
  Fundamental requirements, 1066–1073
  Illustrations, 1074–1077
  Objectives, 1065
  Techniques for application, 1074
Reports
  Accounting principles, reports on application of, 671–678
  Addressee, 470
  Agreed-upon procedures engagement, 844, 845, 848–851, 862
  On application of financial reporting framework, 368, 671, 673, 674, 678
  Attest engagements, 822, 823, 825, 827, 828, 833–838
  On audited financial statements. *See* **Reports on Audited Financial Statements (AU 508)**
  Audits of internal control over financial reporting integrated with audit of financial statements (PCAOB 5), 1090–1093, 1096, 1097
  Change of opinion, 477
  Compilation engagements, 996–999
  Compilation of pro forma financial information, 1023, 1024, 1026, 1027
  Compilation of specified elements, accounts, or items of a financial statement, 1017, 1018, 1021
  Compiled financial statements, 967–969
  Compliance attestation, 921, 922, 924, 925, 927–930

Compliance with contractual agreements or regulatory requirements, 638, 639, 641, 645–647, 660, 665–669
Continuing responsibility of auditor, 633
On controls placed in operation, 174, 182. *See also* **Service organizations**
Date of, 10–91, 526, 598, 1073. *See also* **Dating of the Independent Auditor's Report (AU 530)**
Elements, accounts, or items, 638, 640, 643–645, 650, 651, 657–659
Emphasis-of-matter paragraphs. *See* **Emphasis-of-Matter Paragraphs and Other-Matter Paragraphs in the Independent Auditor's Report (AU-C 706)**
Explanatory language, 471–473
On financial statements prepared for use in other countries. *See* **Reporting on Financial Statements Prepared for Use in Other Countries (AU 534)**
General use, 532, 533
Going concerns, 379, 380
On hypothetical transactions, 672–674
Illustrations (AU 508), 487–497
Illustrations (AU-C 700), 500–506
Illustrations (AU-C 705), 506–518
Illustrations (AU-C 706), 518–523
Interim financial information review, 770–772
Internal control over financial reporting (PCAOB 5), 1090–1093, 1096, 1097
Internal control over financial reporting, effectiveness of, 904, 905
On MD&A, 932–937
Modification, 468, 484, 485, 771, 905
Nonissuer comparative financial statements. *See* Reporting on Comparative Financial Statements (AR 200)
Other comprehensive basis of accounting (OCBOA), 638, 641, 642, 647, 648, 650
Other-matter paragraphs. *See* **Emphasis-of-Matter Paragraphs and Other-Matter Paragraphs in the Independent Auditor's Report (AU-C 706)**
PCAOB standards, 1055–1058
On personal financial statement included in written personal financial plan, 1051–1053
Prescribed forms or schedules, 638, 651
Pro forma financial information, 884, 885, 887–892
Reissuance of, 526–530, 625, 626
Reissuance of predecessor's report, 85, 86, 477, 478, 484
Reporting standards, 445, 446, 452, 542, 543
Restricting use of, 969, 976, 977. *See also* **Restricting the Use of an Auditor's Report (AU 532)**
Review engagements, 1002–1004
Review of financial statements, 975–977
Review reports, attestation engagements, 838–840
Revised due to subsequent discovery of facts, 636
In securities filings, 749–757
Service organization controls, 945–959
Special-purpose financial presentations, 638, 646–649, 653, 662
Special reports, 638–669
Standard examination reports, attestation engagements, 833–838
Standard report, components of, 469, 470
Subsequent discovery of facts existing at date of, 432
Unaudited financial statements, 455–461
Updated, 477
On whether previously reported material weakness continues to exist, 1065–1077
Reports on Application of Requirements of an Applicable Financial Reporting Framework (AU-C 915)
Definitions, 673
Documentation requirements, 368
Effective date, 671
Illustration, 678
Objectives, 674
Summary of changes, 671
Reports on Audited Financial Statements (AU 508)
Applicability, 464
Attestation reports, 817
AU-C 560, *Subsequent Events and Subsequently Discovered Facts,* 523, 619, 632
AU-C 700, *Forming an Opinion and Reporting on Financial Statements,* 437–439, 465, 467–469, 499–506, 523
AU-C 705, *Modifications to the Opinion in the Independent Auditor's Report,* 465, 467, 469, 506–518
AU-C 706, *Emphasis-of-Matter Paragraphs and Other-Matter Paragraphs in the Independent Auditor's Report,* 465–469, 479, 518–523
AU-C 708, *Consistency of Financial Statements,* 520, 523
AU 337, *Inquiry of a Client's Lawyer Concerning Litigation, Claims, and Assessments,* 342
Change in classification, 1101
Definitions, 466, 467
Documentation requirements, 367
Effective date, 464
Fundamental requirements: auditor's standard report, 469, 470
Fundamental requirements: departures from unqualified opinions, 473–476

Fundamental requirements: explanatory language added to auditor's standard report, 471–473
Fundamental requirements: reports on comparative financial statements, 476–478
Going concerns, 379, 380
Illustrations, 487–499
Interpretations, 479–483
Inventory scope limitations, 257, 258
Modification of standard report, 468, 484, 485
Objectives, 468
Original pronouncements, 464
PITF Practice Alerts, 483, 484
Scope limitations, 485, 486
Techniques for application, 484–486
Reports on controls placed in operation
Defined (AU 324), 174
Service auditors, 174, 183
Reports on controls placed in operation and tests of operating effectiveness
Defined (AU 324), 174
Service auditors, 182
User auditors, 182
Reports on the Application of Accounting Principles (AU 625)
Applicability, 671, 672
AU-C 915, *Reports on Application of Requirements of an Applicable Financial Reporting Framework,* 671, 673, 674, 678
Definitions, 672
Effective date, 671
Fundamental requirements, 674, 675
Illustration, 677, 678
Interpretations, 675
Objectives, 673, 674
Original pronouncement, 671
Techniques for application, 676, 677
Representation letter
Agreed-upon procedures engagements, 845, 846, 848
Attest engagements, 826, 827
For comfort letter engagements, 684
Defined (AU 333), 287, 288

Review engagements, 1010–1016
Representations of management. *See* **Management representations**
Requesting party, defined (AU-C 920), 682
Required Supplementary Information (AU 558)
Applicability, 607
AU-C 730, *Required Supplementary Information,* 607–609, 615–617
Definitions, 607, 608
Effective date, 607
Fundamental requirements, 609, 610
Illustrations, 613, 614
Interpretations, 610–612
Objectives, 608
Original pronouncement, 607
Techniques for application, 612
Required Supplementary Information (AU-C 730)
Definitions, 608
Effective date, 607
Illustrations, 615–617
Objectives, 608, 609
Summary of changes, 607
Responsible party
Defined (AT 101), 816
Defined (AT 301), 855
Restricted parties, 533
Restricted-use reports, defined (AU 532), 532
Restricting the Use of an Auditor's Report (AU 532)
Applicability, 531
AU-C 905, *Alert That Restricts the Use of the Auditor's Written Communication,* 531–533, 535–537
AU 325, *Communicating Internal Control Related Matters in an Audit,* 534
AU 380, *The Auditor's Communication with Those Charged with Governance,* 534
AU 623, *Special Reports,* 534
Definitions, 532
Effective date, 531
Fundamental requirements, 533, 534
Illustration, 534

Objectives, 532
Original pronouncement, 531
Techniques for application, 534
Retained earnings, 462
Revenue recognition, improper, 99, 106
Review engagements
Communications between predecessor and successor accountants, 1047–1050
Financial statements. *See* **Compilation and Review of Financial Statements (AR 60-90)**
Quality review (PCAOB 7), 1103–1106
Review evidence, defined (AR 60-90), 963
Review of financial statements. *See* **Compilation and Review of Financial Statements (AR 60-90)**
Review procedures, 973, 974
Risk assessment. *See also* **Performing Audit Procedures in Response to Assessed Risks and Evaluating the Audit Evidence Obtained (AU 318); Understanding the Entity and Its Environment and Assessing the Risks of Material Misstatement (AU 314)**
Assertions about derivatives and securities, 272
Audit of internal control over financial reporting integrated with an audit of financial statements (PCAOB 5), 1081, 1082
Audit risk model. *See* **Audit risk model (AR)**
Auditor response to risk of material misstatement due to fraud, 100–103
Fair value measurement and disclosures, 213, 214, 218, 219
Identified risks, 99, 100
Internal control, 897
Of material misstatement (PCAOB 12), 1119–1131
Procedures, 51, 54, 55
Risk-based, top-down approach to evaluating internal control, 67–69

Risk factors
  Deficiencies resulting in financial statement missstatement, 196
  Fraud, 108, 114–117
Risk of assessing control risk too high, defined (AU 350), 394
Risk of assessing control risk too low, defined (AU 350), 394
Risk of incorrect acceptance, defined (AU 350), 393
Risk of incorrect rejection, defined (AU 350), 393
Risk of material misstatement
  Assessing. *See* **Understanding the Entity and Its Environment and Assessing the Risks of Material Misstatement (AU 314)**
  Audit risk, 36, 52, 53, 132
  Auditor's response to (PCAOB 13), 1133–1139
  Defined (AU 312), 35
  Defined (AU-C 200), 5
  Fair value measurements, 213
  Identifying and assessing (PCAOB 12), 1119–1131
  Inquiries regarding, 1127–1129
  Risk of, 1108
Risk of material misstatement in financial statement assertions, defined (AU 314), 51
Risk of material noncompliance, defined (AU-C 935), 798
Rollover approach, 48

S

Sampling and nonsampling, 44, 46, 47, 145–147. *See also* **Audit Sampling (AU 350); Audit Sampling (AU-C 530)**
Sampling risk, defined, 394
Sampling unit, defined (AU-C 530), 395
Sarbanes-Oxley Act (SOX)
  Audit committee oversight of external auditor, 29, 426, 770
  Communication with audit committee, 426
  Independence requirements for auditors of public companies, 10
  Section 404, 67, 481
Scope of audit and scope limitations
  AU 311, *Planning and Supervision,* 24–26
  AU 333, *Management Representations,* 292
  Inventories, 257, 258
  Litigation, claims, and assessments, 342, 343, 345–349
  Multiple location entities, 1093, 1094
  Qualified and unqualified opinions, 473, 485, 486
  Reporting on whether a previously reported material weakness continues to exist, 1069
Scope restrictions, compliance attestation, 921
Second opinions, 673
Securities
  AU 332, Auditing Derivative Instruments, Hedging Activities, and Investments in Securities, 269–285
  Filings, reports included in, 749–757
Securities Act of 1933
  Comfort letters, 679, 680, 682–684, 687, 718–720
  Filings, reports included in, 349, 529, 749–757
  Liability of auditor under, 461
  Reasonable investigation requirement, 751
  Section 11 due diligence defense, 680, 682–684, 718–720
Securities and Exchange Commission (SEC)
  Compliance as to form with SEC requirements, opinion on, 689
  Filings with, reports included in, 749–757
  Financial Reporting Releases (FRR), 755
  Form 8-K, 111, 433, 754
  Form 10-K, 49, 694, 701, 754
  Form 10-Q, 701–703, 754–756, 775
  Form 11-K, 754
  Interpretive releases, level of authority, 440
  Principal auditor guidelines, 554
  References, 755
  Regulation S, 680
  Regulation S-K, 471, 681, 688, 693–695, 755, 931
  Regulation S-X, 754, 755, 881
  Selected financial data reporting requirements, 595
  Staff Accounting Bulletins (SAB), 755
Securities Exchange Act of 1934, 760
Securities offerings, defined (AU-C 920), 683
Selected financial data, 593–596, 599, 601, 602
Senior management, defined (PCAOB 5), 1080
Service auditor. *See also* **Service Organizations (AU 324)**
  Defined (AT 801), 940
  Defined (AU 324), 174
  Defined (AU-C 402), 175
  Fundamental requirements, 178, 179
  Report, modification of, 184, 185
  Reports, audit program for auditor's review of, 189–191
  Reports, illustrations of, 185–188
  Reports, types of, 178
  Reports of, considerations in using, 182, 183
  Techniques for application of AU 324, 183–185
Service organization, defined (AT 801), 940
Service organizations. *See also* **Service Organizations (AU 324)**
  Auditor's report on controls, 945–959
  Defined (AU 324), 174
  Defined (AU-C 402), 175
  Documentation, 944, 945
  Effect of on audit approach and procedures for derivatives and securities, 281–283
  Information systems for derivatives and securities, 278

Internal controls, 906
Management representations, 943, 944
Reporting on controls at. *See* **Reporting on Controls at a Service Organization (AT 801)**
Subsequent events, 944
Service Organizations (AU 324)
Applicability, 173
AU-C 402, *Audit Considerations Relating to an Entity Using a Service Organization,* 173, 175–177
Audit program for an auditor's review of a service auditor's report, illustration, 189–191
Controls placed in operation – inaccurate or incomplete description, service auditor's illustrative report, 186
Controls placed in operation – no exceptions, service auditor's illustrative report, 185, 186
Controls placed in operation – significant deficiencies in design or operation, service auditor's illustrative report, 186, 187
Controls placed in operation and tests of operating effectiveness – no exceptions, service auditor's illustrative report, 187, 188
Definitions, 174
Derivatives and securities, 281–283
Effective date, 173
Fundamental requirements for service auditors, 178, 179
Fundamental requirements for user auditors, 177, 178
Interpretations, 179–181
Objectives, 176
Original pronouncement, 173
PITF Practice Alerts, 181
Report on internal control over financial reporting (PCAOB 5), 1094, 1095
Service organization management representation letter, illustration, 188, 189
Techniques for application for service auditors, 183–185
Techniques for application for user auditors, 182, 183

Service organization's system, 176, 940, 942
Shared activities, 144, 145
Shelf registration, 681, 686, 698
Significant account or disclosure
Defined (AT 501), 894
Defined (PCAOB 5), 1080
Significant assumptions
Defined (AU 328), 212
Fair value measurements and disclosures, 214–219
Significant component, defined (AU-C 600), 563
Significant deficiency. *See also* **Communicating Internal Control Related Matters Identified in an Audit (AU 325)**
Defined (AT 501), 894
Defined (AU 325), 194
Defined (AU-C 265), 195
Defined (PCAOB 5), 1080
Examples of circumstances that may be control deficiencies, significant deficiencies, or material weaknesses, 200, 201
Interim financial information, 770
Significant deficiency in internal control over compliance
Defined (AU 801), 796
Defined (AU-C 935), 798
Significant engagement deficiency, defined (PCAOB 7), 1103
Significant findings, documentation of, 358, 359
Significant findings or issues, defined (PCAOB 3), 1059, 1060
Significant risk, 52, 57, 58, 60–62, 137, 1103
Special Considerations – Audits of Financial Statements Prepared in Accordance with Special-Purpose Frameworks (AU-C 800)
AU-C 550, *Related Parties,* 311
Definitions, 576
Effective date, 575
Objectives, 577
Summary of changes, 575

Special Considerations – Audits of Group Financial Statements (Including the Work of Component Auditors) (AU-C 600)
Applicability, 561
AU-C 501, *Audit Evidence – Specific Considerations for Selected Items,* 270
Definitions, 562, 563
Documentation requirements, 368, 565
Effective date, 549, 561
Fundamental requirements, 563–565
Illustrations, 565–574
Objectives, 563
Original pronouncements, 561
Summary of changes, 561, 562
Special Considerations – Audits of Single Financial Statements and Specific Elements, Accounts, or Items of a Financial Statement (AU-C 805), 637, 638
Special-purpose financial statements, defined (AU-C 800), 576
Special-purpose frameworks, audits prepared in accordance with. *See* **Special Considerations – Audits of Financial Statements Prepared in Accordance with Special-Purpose Frameworks (AU-C 800)**
Special-purpose frameworks, defined (AU-C 800), 576
Special Reports (AU 623)
Applicability, 638
AU-C 800. *See* **Special Considerations – Audits of Financial Statements Prepared in Accordance with Special-Purpose Frameworks (AU-C 800)**
AU-C 805. *See* **Special Considerations – Audits of Single Financial Statements and Specific Elements, Accounts, or Items of a Financial Statement (AU-C 805)**
AU-C 806, *Reporting on Compliance with Aspects of Contractual Agreements or Regulatory Requirements in*

Connection with Audited Financial Statements, 638, 641, 665–669
AU 336, *Using the Work of a Specialist,* 325
Compliance with contractual agreements or regulatory requirements, 638, 639, 641, 645–647, 660, 665–669
Definitions, 639, 640
Effective date, 638
Elements, accounts, or items, 638, 640, 643–645, 650, 651, 657–659
Fundamental requirements: circumstances requiring explanatory language in an auditor's special report, 649, 650
Fundamental requirements: compliance with contractual or regulatory requirements related to audited financial statement, 645, 646
Fundamental requirements: financial information presented in prescribed forms or schedules, 651
Fundamental requirements: financial statements prepared in conformity with an OCBOA, 641, 642
Fundamental requirements: special-purpose financial presentations to comply with contractual agreements or regulatory provisions, 646–649
Fundamental requirements: specified elements, accounts, or items of a financial statement, 643–645
Illustrations, 654–665
Interpretations, 651–654
Objectives, 640, 641
Original pronouncements, 638
Prescribed forms or schedules, 638, 651
Special-purpose financial presentations, 638, 646–649, 653, 662

Specialists. *See also* **Using the Work of a Specialist (AU 336); Using the Work of an Auditor's Specialist (AU-C 620)**
Agreed-upon procedures engagement, 844, 845, 847
Audit planning, 1112
Compliance attestation, 919
Defined (AU 336), 326
Defined (AU-C 620), 326
Derivatives and securities, 278, 279
Fair value measurement, 214
Use of, examples, 331

Specific transactions, 673
Specific transactions, defined, 672
Specified parties, 531–534
Specified regulatory agencies, defined (AU 722), 760
Specified requirements, defined (AT 601), 918
Staff, defined (AU-C 220), 6
Standards
Agreed-upon procedures engagement, 842
Attestation, 818–825, 829, 830
Auditing Standards, 2, 8–10
Consistency, 445, 446
Designated accounting standard setters, 607–610
Foreign auditing standards. *See* **Reporting on Financial Statements Prepared for Use in Other Countries (AU 534)**
GAAS, 829, 830
Of other countries, 541
PCAOB. *See* specific standards
PCAOB standards, references to in auditors' reports, 1055–1058
Performance, 674, 675
Prospective financial statements, compilation of and report on, 858
Prospective financial statements, examination of, 859
Reporting, 445, 446, 452, 542, 543, 675
Reviews, 761

Stated control objective, defined (PCAOB 4), 1065
Statement of cash flows, 474
Statements of Financial Accounting Concepts (CON)
CON 7, *Using Cash Flow Information and Present Value in Accounting Measurements,* 211, 212

Statements of Financial Accounting Standards (SFAS). *See also* **Accounting Standards Codification (ASC)**
SFAS 57, 311, 575
SFAS 71, *Accounting for the Effects of Certain Types of Regulation,* 576
SFAS 90, *Regulated Enterprises – Accounting for Abandonments and Disallowances of Plant Costs,* 576
SFAS 92, *Regulated Enterprises – Accounting for Phase-in Plans,* 576
SFAS 101, *Regulated Enterprises – Accounting for the Discontinuation of Application of FASB Statement,* 71, 576

Statements of Position (SOP)
SOP 01-3, *Performing Agreed-Upon Procedures Engagements That Address Internal Control Over Derivative Transactions as Required by the New York State Insurance Law,* 271
SOP 92-4, *Auditing Insurance Entities' Loss Reserves,* 333
Specialists, use of, 333

Statements on Accounting Procedures (SAP)
SAP 49, 896, SAP 49

Statements on Auditing Procedures (SAP)
SAP 33, 575
SAP 37, 807
SAP 41, 631, 633
SAP 43, 443
SAP 45, 549
SAP 53, 443
SAP 88, 443

Statements on Auditing Standards (SAS)
Cross-references, App. B
GAAS hierarchy, 8, 9
Interpretive publications, 9. *See also* **Interpretive publications**
Other auditing publications, use of, 10
Professional requirements, 7, 8

Index

SAS 1, 255, 437, 525, 549, 575, 619, 631, 807
SAS 7, *Communications between Predecessor and Successor Accountants,* 1047
SAS 19, *Client Representations,* 288
SAS 50, *Reports on the Application of Accounting Principles,* 671, 673
SAS 57, *Auditing Accounting Estimates,* 385, 427
SAS 75, *Engagements to Apply Agreed-Upon Procedures to Specified Elements, Accounts, or Items of a Financial Statement,* 842
SAS 82, *Consideration of Fraud in a Financial Statement Audit,* 95, 106
SAS 85, *Management Representations,* 287, 288, 464
SAS 89, *Audit Adjustments,* 287, 288
SAS 90, *Audit Committee Communications,* 426, 761
SAS 93, *Omnibus Statement on Auditing Standards – 2000,* 79, 464, 842, 932
SAS 97, *Amendment to Statement on Auditing Standards No. 50,* 671, 674
SAS 99, *Consideration of Fraud in a Financial Statement Audit,* 93, 95, 287, 289
SAS 100, *Interim Financial Information,* 761, 961
SAS 101, *Auditing Fair Value Measurements and Disclosures,* 211, 427
SAS 117, *Compliance Audits,* 795, 799
SAS 118, *Other Information in Documents Containing Audited Financial Statements,* 579
SAS 119, *Supplementary Information in Relation to the Financial Statements as a Whole,* 583
SAS 120, *Required Supplementary Information,* 607
SAS 122, *Codification of Auditing Standards and Procedures,* 2, 17, 33, 49, 79, 93, 123, 131, 173, 205, 211, 221, 255, 269, 287, 311, 325, 337, 355, 385, 393, 419, 430, 437, 443, 451, 455, 525, 539, 549, 561, 575, 579, 583, 593, 607, 619, 632, 638, 679, 749, 760, 761, 795, 807
SAS 125, *Alert That Restricts the Use of the Auditor's Written Communication,* 531
SAS 126, *The Auditor's Consideration of an Entity's Ability to Continue as a Going Concern,* 369
Statements on Quality Control Standards (SQCS)
SQCS 2, *System of Quality Control for a CPA Firm's Accounting and Auditing Practice,* 12, 21, 80, 430, 483
SQCS 4, *Amendment to System of Quality Control for a CPA Firm's Accounting and Auditing Practice,* 12
SQCS 5, *The Personnel Management Element of a Firm's System of Quality Control,* 13
SQCS 7, *A Firm's System of Quality Control,* 2
SQCS 8, *A Firm's System of Quality Control,* 2, 355
Statements on Standards for Accounting and Review Services (SSARS)
Cross-references, App. B
SSARS 1, *Compilation and Review of Financial Statements,* 456, 459, 1043, 1044
SSARS 2, 1029, 1030, 1033
SSARS 3, 1029, 1043, 1044
SSARS 4, 1029, 1047, 1049
SSARS 5, 1029, 1043
SSARS 6, 1051, 1052
SSARS 7, 1029, 1043, 1047
SSARS 9, 1047
SSARS 11, 1029
SSARS 13, 1017
SSARS 14, 1023
SSARS 15, 1043, 1047
SSARS 17, 1017, 1023, 1043, 1047
SSARS 19, 961
SSARS 20, *Revised Applicability of Statements on Standards for Accounting and Review Services,* 961
Statements on Standards for Attestation Engagements (SSAE)
Cross-references, App. C
SSAE 2, 896
SSAE 9, *Amendments to SSAE Nos. 1, 2, and 3,* 817, 896
SSAE 10, *Attestation Standards: Revision and Recodification,* 815, 817, 818, 825, 841, 842, 853, 856, 881, 882, 917, 918, 931, 932
SSAE 11, *Attest Documentation,* 815, 818, 841, 842, 855, 856
SSAE 12, *Amendment to Statement on Standards for Attestation Engagements No. 10,* 818
SSAE 13, 816
SSAE 15, *An Examination of an Entity's Internal Control Over Financial Reporting That Is Integrated with an Audit of its Financial Statements,* 893, 896
SSAE 16, *Reporting on Controls at a Service Organization,* 173, 939
SSAE 17, 853
Statistical sampling. *See* **Audit Sampling (AU 350)**
Statistical sampling, defined (AU-C 530), 395
Statistical sampling principles, 146. *See also* **Sampling and nonsampling**
Inventories, 256, 257
Stratification, defined (AU-C 530), 395
Subject matter, defined (AT 101), 816
Subservice organization, defined (AT 801), 940
Submission of financial statements, defined (AR 60-90), 963
Subsequent changes, comments on in comfort letters, 691, 692
Subsequent discovery of facts, 526, 529, 619–629
Compilation engagements, 970
Review engagements, 978

Subsequent discovery of facts existing at date of auditor's report, 432, 631–636
Subsequent Discovery of Facts Existing at the Date of the Auditor's Report (AU 561)
　Applicability, 631
　Attest engagements, 828
　AU-C 560, *Subsequent Events and Subsequently Discovered Facts,* 619, 632, 633
　AU 390 distinguished, 431
　AU 560, *Subsequent Events,* distinguished, 633
　Client refusal to disclose facts, 432, 634
　Effective date, 631
　Fundamental requirements, 633–635
　Interpretations, 635
　Interim financial information review, 774
　Objectives, 632, 633
　Original pronouncement, 631
　Report on internal control over financial reporting (PCAOB 5), 1093
　Techniques for application, 635, 636
Subsequent events, 619–629
　Changes to internal control, 906
　Compilation engagements, 969
　Compliance attestation, 921, 924
　And dating of report, 526–528, 530, 620, 621, 625, 626
　Defined (AU 324), 174
　Defined (AU 530), 526
　Defined (AU 560), 620
　Defined (AU-C 560), 526
　Disclosures, 620–623, 625, 626
　Internal control over financial reporting (PCAOB 5), 1093
　Reporting on whether a previously reported material weakness continues to exist, 1073
　Responsibility for, 179
　Review engagements, 977
　Securities filings, reports included in, 751–754
　Service organizations, 944
　Types of, 623
Subsequent Events (AU 560)
　Applicability, 619
　AU-C 560, *Subsequent Events and Subsequently Discovered Facts,* 619–621, 632
　AU 561, *Subsequent Discovery of Facts Existing at the Date of the Auditor's Report* distinguished, 633
　Checklist, illustration, 626–629
　Definitions, 619, 620
　Effective date, 619
　Fundamental requirements, 621, 622
　Objectives, 620, 621
　Original pronouncements, 619
　Techniques for application, 622–626
Subsequent Events and Subsequently Discovered Facts (AU-C 560)
　AU 508, Reports on Audited Financial Statements, 523, 525
　Definitions, 526, 620, 632
　Effective date, 525, 619, 632
　Extant AU sections, 525
　Objectives, 527, 621, 633
　Summary of changes, 525, 632
Subsequent period, defined (AU 560), 620
Subsequently discovered facts
　Comfort letters, 694
　Defined (AU-C 560), 526
　Securities filings, reports included in, 753, 754
Subservice organization, defined (AU-C 402), 176
Substantive procedures
　Controls, 1138, 1139
　Defined (AU 318), 131
　Defined (AU-C 330), 132
　Derivatives and securities, 273, 282–285
　Described, 137
　Effect of on evaluation of internal control, 907
　Extent of, 138
　Nature, timing, and extent of, 137, 138, 1138, 1139
　Nature of, 137
　Tests of by internal auditors, 165
　Timing of, 137, 138
Substantive tests, 223, 224, 232, 233
　Defined (AU 350), 394

Successor accountant
　Communication with predecessor, 1047–1050
　Defined (AR 400), 1047
Successor auditor. *See also* **Communications Between Predecessor and Successor Auditors (AU 315)**
　Acknowledgment letter, illustration (AU 315), 87
　Acknowledgment letter, illustration (AU-C 510), 90, 91
　Defined (AU 315), 80
　Facts existing at date of predecessor's report, subsequent discovery of, 635
Sufficiency
　Defined (AU 326), 206
　Defined (PCAOB 15), 1147
Sufficiency (of audit evidence), 3, 164
　Defined (AU-C 500), 207
　General guides (AU-C 500), 208
Suitably qualified external person, defined (AU-C 220), 6
Summary financial statements, reporting on, 593–606
Supervision
　Of an audit (AU 311), 2, 21, 22
　Of assistants, 21, 22
　Of audit engagement (PCAOB 10), 1113, 1114
　Defined (AU 311), 18
Supervision of the Audit Engagement (PCAOB 10)
　Applicability, 1113
　Effective date, 1113
　Fundamental requirements, 1113, 1114
　Objectives, 1113
Supplementary Information in Relation to Financial Statements as a Whole (AU-C 725). *See also* **Required Supplementary Information (AU-C 730)**
　Definitions, 584
　Effective date, 583
　Illustrations, 589–592
　Interpretations, 586
　Objective, 584
Supplementary Information in Relation to the Financial

Statements as a Whole (AU 551)
  Applicability, 583
  AU-C 725, *Supplementary Information in Relation to Financial Statements as a Whole,* 583, 584, 586, 589–592
  Definitions, 583, 584
  Effective date, 585
  Fundamental requirements, 584–586
  Illustrations, 587–589
  Objectives, 584
  Original pronouncements, 583
Systematic sampling, 400

T

Tables, statistics, and other financial information, comments on in comfort letters, 692, 693
Tax returns, 460, 461
Terminal warehouse, defined (AU 901), 808
Terms of Engagement (AU-C 210)
  AU 311, *Planning and Supervision,* 17
  Documentation requirements, 368
  Effective date, 79
  Engagement letter, illustration, 30–32
  Summary of changes, 79, 80
Tests of controls. *See also* **Performing Audit Procedures in Response to Assessed Risks and Evaluating the Audit Evidence Obtained (AU 318)**
  Access control risk, 1138
  Audits of financial statements, 1135, 1136
  Audits of internal control, 1138
  Audits of internal control integrated with audit of financial statements (PCAOB 5), 1085–1087
  Controls over financial reporting, 900, 901
  Defined (AT 801), 940
  Defined (AU 314), 51
  Defined (AU 318), 131
  Defined (AU-C 330), 132
  Derivatives and securities, 272, 273
  Design effectiveness, 900, 901, 1136
  Designing nature, timing, and extent of, 135–137
  Dual-purpose tests, 1133, 1139
  Evaluating test results, 152
  Evaluation of design distinguished, 59, 60
  Evidence from, 1136
  Extent of, 136, 137, 901, 1136, 1137
  Fair value measurements and disclosures, 214, 215, 218–220
  Interim testing, 139, 140, 901
  By internal auditors, 165
  Internal control operating effectiveness, 142–147
  Nature of, 1136
  Operating effectiveness, 1136
  Sample sizes, 145–147
  Selection of, 135, 900
  Timing, 136, 901, 1137, 1138
  Types of tests, 147–152, 901
  Understanding of internal control, 1125
  When used, 135
Tests of transactions, 150, 151
Third party, defined (AR 60-90), 963
Those charged with governance
  Communication with. *See* **Auditor's Communication with Those Charged with Governance (AU 380)**
  Defined (AR 60-90), 963
  Defined (AU 380), 420
  Defined (AU-C 200), 5
  Defined (AU-C 260), 420
Threatened legal proceeding, defined (AU 390), 430
Threatened litigation, defined (AU 337), 338
Tolerable misstatement, 39, 117, 394, 395, 1116
Tolerable rate, defined (AU 350), 394
Tolerable rate of deviation, defined (AU-C 530), 395
Top-down approach, internal control selection and evaluation, 67–69, 1082–1085
Training and proficiency
  Documentation of, 1062
  GAAS general standards, 8, 10, 829
  General attestation standards, 819, 829
  Independent auditor, 10
  Of internal auditors, 943
  Personnel, 13
  Prospective financial statements, 872–880
Treadway Commission, 895
Trend analysis, 222, 225, 226, 228, 229, 231, 232, 236

U

Unasserted claim or assessment, defined (AU 337), 338
Unaudited condensed interim financial information, 680–682, 688, 690
Unaudited financial statements, 456
Uncorrected misstatements, 35, 36, 39–44, 47, 48
Underlying accounting data, defined (AU 326), 206
Understanding the Entity and Its Environment and Assessing the Risks of Material Misstatement (AU 314)
  Applicability, 49
  AU-C 315, *Understanding the Entity and Its Environment and Assessing the Risks of Material Misstatement,* 49, 50, 53, 205, 368
  Audit risk model (AR), 52
  Documentation requirements, 365
  Effective date, 49
  Fundamental requirements, 53–62
  Objectives, 52, 53
  Original pronouncement, 49
  Risk assessment questionnaire, illustration, 72–77
  Techniques for application, 62–72
Understanding the Entity and Its Environment and Assessing the Risks of Material Misstatement (AU-C 315)
  Audit evidence, 205
  Definitions, 51, 52

Documentation requirements, 368
Effective date, 49
Objectives, 53
Summary of changes, 50
Understanding the Responsibilities of Auditors for Audits of Group Financial Statements – 2012 (AICPA), 561, 562
Underwriter(s)
Comfort letters. *See* **Comfort letters**
Communication with, 685
Defined (AU 634), 681
Defined (AU-C 920), 683
Underwriting agreement, defined (AU 634), 681
Undetected misstatement, 35, 40–44, 48
Unexamined items, defined (AU 350), 394
Unmodified opinion, defined (AU-C 700), 438, 467
Unqualified opinion, defined (AU 508), 466
Updated report
Defined (AR 200), 1029
Defined (AU 508), 467
US entity, defined (AU 534), 540
US-style report modified, defined (AU 534), 540
User auditor. *See also* **Service Organizations (AU 324)**
Defined (AT 801), 940
Defined (AU 324), 174
Defined (AU-C 402), 176
Fundamental requirements, 177, 178
Techniques for application of AU 324, 182, 183
User entity
Defined (AT 801), 940
Defined (AU-C 402), 176
User organization, defined (AU 324), 174
Using the Work of a Specialist (AU 336)

Accounting estimate assumptions, 391
Applicability, 325
AU-C 620, *Using the Work of an Auditor's Specialist,* 325–327
Audit guides or SOPs, need to reference, 333
Definitions, 326
Derivatives and securities, 279
Documentation, 332
Effective date, 325
Engagement letter from client to specialist, illustrative, 334, 335
Fundamental requirements, 327, 328
Interpretations, 328–331
Lawyer as specialist, 331, 332
Objectives, 326, 327
Original pronouncement, 325
Qualifications of specialist, 327
Specialist employed by CPA firm, 332, 333
Specialist's relationship to client, 327, 332
Statement of specialist's independence, illustrative, 335
Techniques for application, 331–333
Tests of data used by specialist, 333
Use of specialists, examples of, 331
Work of specialist, 327
Using the Work of an Auditor's Specialist (AU-C 620)
AU-C 500, Audit Evidence, 325
Definitions, 326
Effective date, 325
Objectives, 327
Summary of changes, 325, 326

V

Valuation
Derivatives and securities, 275
Model, 219

Variance analysis, 225, 226, 229

W

Walk-throughs (flow-of-transaction tests), 398, 399, 900, 1080, 1125
Warehouse, defined (AU 901), 808
Warehouse receipt, defined (AU 901), 808
Warehouses, public. *See* **Public warehouses**
Work of others
In audit of internal control over financial reporting integrated with an audit of financial statements (PCAOB 5), 1081, 1082
Use of in reporting on whether a previously reported material weakness continues to exist (PCAOB 4), 1068, 1069
Working papers, 355, 356, 842, 1048, 1049, 1059. *See also* **Documentation**
Written report, defined, 672, 673
Written Representations (AU-C 580)
Definitions, 288
Effective date, 287
Objectives, 289
Representation letter, illustrative, 303–305
Specific written representations, illustrative, 305–309
Updating management representation letter, illustrative, 309, 310

Y

Yale Express case (Fischer v. Kletz), **632, 633**
Yellow Book, 797